Early Connecticut Marriages

AS FOUND ON

ANCIENT CHURCH RECORDS
PRIOR TO 1800

Edited by Frederick W. Bailey

A REPRINT

With Additions, Corrections,

and Introduction by

Donald Lines Jacobus

And With Integrated Errata

Seven Books in One Volume

GENEALOGICAL PUBLISHING CO., INC.
BALTIMORE   1976

Originally Published
New Haven, 1896-1906

Reprinted
With Additions and Corrections
Genealogical Publishing Co., Inc.
Baltimore, 1968
Baltimore, 1976

Library of Congress Catalogue Card Number 68-18785
International Standard Book Number 0-8063-0007-8

Made in the United States of America

Early Connecticut Marriages

AS FOUND ON

ANCIENT CHURCH RECORDS

PRIOR TO 1800.

EDITED BY

FREDERIC W. BAILEY,

MEMBER AMERICAN HIST. ASSO., CONN. HIST. SO., NEW HAVEN COLONY HIST. SO.,
NEW YORK GEN. AND BIOG. SO., SONS OF THE AMERICAN REVOLUTION
(MASS.), MANAGER BUREAU OF AMERICAN ANCESTRY.

PUBLISHED BY THE

BUREAU OF AMERICAN ANCESTRY

FOR

Family   Researches

FREDERIC W. BAILEY, MGR.

P. O. BOX 587.   NEW HAVEN, CONN.

Introduction

In 1896 the Rev. Frederic W. Bailey of New Haven, Conn., began publishing a series called *Early Connecticut Marriages,* and this was continued through the next few years until seven volumes were in print. For more than half a century, these books have been helpful to many people with Connecticut ancestry. They are a great aid especially to compilers of family histories, who wish to locate every item pertaining to a specific surname. Sometimes the searcher finds the very marriage record he is seeking. If not, it is often of value to learn in what towns the desired surname appears.

Mr. Bailey rarely copied these records, mostly from church registers, personally. He wrote to the ministers or clerks of churches, and to people interested in genealogy, in the various towns, and requested copies of the marriage records. Some were copied for him gratis, for others a small charge was made. Some were copied by people of education or natural ability; a few were copied by careless or uninformed persons who obviously had trouble in reading the script (particularly the early script) in which the records were written. The late Albert C. Bates, for many years librarian of the Connecticut Historical Society, once told me that to his positive knowledge one of the church registers was copied for Mr. Bailey by a child!

Over the years I have had occasion to use these books a great deal, and have often found it profitable to do so. However, in view of the facts just stated, this small note of caution should be struck. While most of the records are reasonably accurate, those of three or four churches are replete with errors in reading names. I have entered marginal corrections in a few places where I have caught such errors, but doubtless there are others in records of churches I have never had occasion to consult.

Hence this word of advice. Of course a vast majority of the records in these volumes are correct. However, if the reader has the slightest reason to suspect that a name in which he is interested may have been misread, he should write to the State Library in Hartford and inquire. A large number of Connecticut church registers have now been deposited at the State Library, where gradually over the years skilled employees have been indexing them. Hence there is a very good chance that any doubtful entry can be verified or corrected upon request.

I am glad that this valuable series is now made available by the Genealogical Publishing Company to all who wish to acquire this useful genealogical tool.

THE INDEXES: NOTE WELL. Each volume is indexed separately, and by surname only. The indexes are alphabetical to this extent. All names beginning with the same letter are indexed together under the initial letter. Thus, Bradley and Beach will naturally be found under the letter B. However, the names are then placed in accordance with the first vowel in the name and not in strict alphabetical order. Hence, Bradley will appear considerably ahead of Beach, because the first vowel in Bradley is 'a' while the first letter in Beach is 'e.' Suppose the name sought to be Clement. Turn to the letter C and skip along through those in which the first vowel is 'a' such as Carrington and Crane until you reach names in which the first vowel is 'e' and read these through until you find Clement. When you reach C names in which the first vowel is 'o' such as Coburn, your index search, whether successful in locating the name Clement or not, is over.

DONALD LINES JACOBUS

Publisher's Preface

This work, as reprinted in a single volume with Additions and Corrections by Mr. Donald Lines Jacobus, forms the most complete collection extant of printed Connecticut church marriage records down to 1800. We have included in this reprint the indexes to Books 1 and 2 which were published separately as inserts and have integrated all printed errata into the text. We were also so fortunate as to have Mr. Jacobus write a new Introduction explaining how he, as a professional genealogist, has used these records over the years.

Compiled over a period of ten years and originally published by the Bureau of American Ancestry in seven separate books from 1896-1906, the work has since been very difficult to obtain in its entirety and, then, only at a substantial price. Our reprint, as part of our program to make basic genealogical reference books once again available as complete as possible and as economical as feasible, is offered to the researcher and librarian, as well as the general public, in the belief that this valuable series will be a useful tool.

Baltimore, 1968

EARLY CONNECTICUT MARRIAGES.

PREFACE.

The first settlers of Connecticut came from Massachusetts Bay and Plymouth Colonies and located at Windsor, Hartford and Wethersfield. All alike being devoted disciples of Christ, Gospel ministers came also, and at once Christian worship was established and parishes formed. The same condition of things prevailed among other settlers from the East who a little later located along the Connecticut shore. A church whose learned minister was to serve both in the capacity of instructor of youth and man's spiritual guide was the essential ambition of every permanent and promising settlement.

Since agriculture, both by necessity and choice, was in those trying times the only dependence of our sturdy ancestors, the possession of the necessary land with a little to spare became a common and prevailing impulse; while the occasional cessation of Indian warfares gave the ambitious sons and later arrivals the increased courage to locate for themselves farther and farther inland. And all naturally resulting in new parish organizations and later by division of the old or the opening of new territory, into other incorporated towns. In each and every case the church serving as that nucleus around which a township was formed.

We cannot do better than record here the dates of the organization of the earlier parishes: Windsor, 1630; Hartford, 1632; Wethersfield, 1635; Stamford, 1635; New Haven, 1639; Stratford, 1639; Old Saybrook, 1639; Milford, 1639; Fairfield, 1639; Guilford, 1643; Branford, 1644; New London, 1650.

Prior to the year 1659 there were in Connecticut eleven parish organizations. (And we have reference here to Congregational churches only, since they were the earliest and most prevalent everywhere). Before 1700 the eleven had increased to thirty-three. And by 1750 to 147, which number by the year 1800 had reached 200.

It is to this large but limited number that our attention has been directed. From among these copies of baptisms and marriages have been secured, out of which the following complete records of marriages have been taken.

We cannot speak in too high praise of that faithfulness to duty which seems as a rule to have possessed the early pastors who, amidst their studious cares, gave close attention to their parish records carefully to note both the marriages and baptisms among their own. Every parish seems to have possessed at some time these inherited treasures. At the same time have we reason to regret that lack of appreciation and careless indifference on the part of some responsible church official, whose possible neglect had been the cause of the total or partial loss of the interesting and valuable manuscripts alone telling the church's story of the first families' spiritual life. Over and over again has come to us the sad report that the early church records had been lost or burned or somehow destroyed, possibly carried away and never returned, no one seemingly enough interested to trace and restore them to their proper place. So that as from remote and inaccessible places there have come to us, one by one, copies of such records taken from old church books still extant through all the years, we feel a sense of gratitude not only that in all the many changes of time and circumstance some kind and watchful hand had given protection; but that by these alone were we still able to gain access to the inner life of some little flock of the Heaven-Bound that may even have embraced ancestors of our own name.

A good and sufficient reason exists therefore for this publication. Another and possibly still more appreciable reason lies in the additional aid which these records will afford an increasing number whose genealogical endeavors have been suddenly checked by an hopeless failure to secure much desired data. It is possible the very fact wanted is herein or may supply the long sought clue.

Our town records in a number of cases have been found to be imperfect, pages missing and mutilated, sometimes lost. The town clerks of Connecticut are not as a rule in sympathy with genealogical research, so that the satisfaction to be derived from them is at times extremely limited. With some very worthy exceptions, however, it is true that their interest in the preservation of ancient birth and marriage records amounts to a most ordinary willingness to allow the ancient books a place in the old and crowded safe by increased use to wear out slowly, feed a worm, or part piece by piece with a tattered leaf.

We are pleased to say, however, that somehow, whether altogether due to our colonial societies or otherwise, a gradual awakening is taking place, old towns themselves taking action till we trust that as in Massachusetts the State of Connecticut may yet make some enactment looking at last to a common reconstruction.

Now, with reference to the following marriages, permit us to say that all herein are from church books and are the complete records (so far as they exist) of those churches to 1800. It is probable that many of them may be found recorded on the town records, but it is true that herein is much the town records do not contain, which fact gives to the publication additional value.

It is to be noted, too, that the copy is exact, so far as the spelling is concerned. The arrangement is our own. Where a difficulty has been experienced with a name in copy two spellings are given, or a (?) used. The aim being to place before the reader just what the records contain.

We can but trust it may be of some little service to the many descendants of the old and patriotic Connecticut settlers scattered all over this great land.

FREDERIC W. BAILEY.

Bureau of American Ancestry,
NEW HAVEN, CONN., April 27, 1896.

CONTENTS.

RECORDS LOST.

The following is the list of Congregational Churches so far reporting the loss of their Baptism and Marriage records prior to 1800.

CHURCH.	COUNTY.	ORGANIZED.	REMARKS.
Westminster, of Canterbury,	Windham,	1770,	
Stamford,	Fairfield,	1635,	
Coventry,	Tolland,	1745,	none before 1818.
Hebron,	Tolland,	1716,	burned.
Ellington,	Tolland,	1736,	lost.
Sherman,	Fairfield,	1744,	burned.
~~New Fairfield,~~	~~Fairfield,~~	~~1742,~~	~~burned.~~
East Granby,	Hartford,	1737,	
Goshen,	Litchfield,	1740,	lost.
Watertown,	Litchfield,	1739,	lost.
Canton Center,	~~Tolland,~~ *Hartford*	1750,	before 1826, lost.
Meriden,	New Haven,	1729,	before 1848 taken away.
So. Manchester,	Hartford,	1779,	
North Guilford,	New Haven,	1725,	lost.
East Lyme,	New London,	1724,	lost.
Lyme,	New London,	1727,	lost.
West Haven,	New Haven,	1719,	before 1815, lost.

NEW HAVEN.

NEW HAVEN COUNTY.

The first Congregational Church in New Haven is as old as the town. April 13th, 1638, the first settlers having just landed, assembled for public worship. The organization of the church was completed in 1639, at which time the baptismal records begin.

The marriage records date only to 1758, and it is supposed that earlier records were lost in 1779, when the British troops visited the city.

NEW HAVEN FIRST CHURCH.

Stephen Howell & Elisabeth Miles,	Aug. 21, 1758
Peter Morris & Ann Cooke,	Jan. 28, 1759
Jabez Mix & Jemima Brown,	Feb. 12, 1759
Ezra Dorman & Mable Cooper,	May, 1759
James Rice & Mary Miles,	June 21, 1759
Hezekiah Tuttle & Martha Bradley,	Sept. 3, 1759
Benjamin Dorman & Mary Ball,	Sept. 20, 1759
Timothy Goodyear & Ruth Ives,	May 29, 1760
Richard Hood & Sarah Thompson,	Aug., 1760
Jeremiah Townsend, Jr., & Abigail Woodbridge,	
	Nov. 20, 1760
Samuel Toles & Hannah Thomas,	Nov. 20, 1760
Jacob Curtiss of Branford & Elisabeth Dickerman, N. H.,	
	Dec. 4, 1760
Dr. Eneas Munson & Susannah Howell,	Mch. 15, 1761
John Dolebear & Mable Gilbert,	May 8, 1761
John Kimberly & Lydia Wise,	May 21, 1761
Lemuel Humphreyvile & Molly Beecher,	July 30, 1761
Daniel Atwater, Jr., & Lois Mansfield,	Aug. 13, 1761
Philemon Potter & Phebe Mansfield,	Aug. 13, 1761
Thomas Green & Desire Sanford,	Sept. 30, 1761
Wm. Peck & Elisabeth Hall,	Oct. 1, 1761
John Hubbard, Esq., & Mrs. Mary Stevens,	Nov. 10, 1761
Joseph Sperry & Anna Humassen,	Nov. 11, 1761
Elijah Hotchkiss & Mehitable Hotchkiss,	Nov. 11, 1761
John Love & Abigail Andross,	Dec. 2, 1761
Isaac Bishop & Sarah Macumber,	Jan. 21, 1762

Charles Hotchkiss & Elisabeth Harriss,   Feb. 11, 1762
Richard Woodhull & Mrs. Rebecca Abigail Mix,

                          May 2, 1762
Adonijah (?) Sherman & Abigail Munson,   June 3, 1762
John Davies of Litchfield & Eunice Hotchkiss, Aug. 5, 1762
Solomon Pinto & Anna Green,   Oct. 4, 1762
Joseph Trowbridge & Elisabeth Bishop,   Oct. 20, 1762
Peter Bontecon & Susannah Thomas,   Nov. 14, 1762
Samuel Penfield of Branford & Esther Tuttle of
  N. H.,   Dec. 15, 1762
Nathaniel Spencer & Abigail English,   Dec. 30, 1762
David Ball & Hannah Johnson,   Feb. 21, 1763
Peter & Ann, free negroes,   Feb. 24, 1763
Jesse Alling & Sarah Atwater,   Apr. 27, 1763
Ben, a free negro, with Jenny, serv't to Mr. Isaac,

                        June 9, 1763
Gideon Parker of Wallingford & Elisabeth Thomas,
  N. H.,   Aug. 17, 1763
Isborn, a free negro, with Mindwell, widow to
  Jethro Lake,   Oct. 24, 1763
Ebenezer Downs & Sarah Sperry,   Nov. 28, 1763
Peley Sanford & Elisabeth Perkins,   Jan. 11, 1764
Stephen Peck & Luce Miles,   Jan. 26, 1764
Jeremiah Barrit & widow Jemima Mix,   Feb. 12, 1764
John Brown & Abigail Hitchcock, Springfield,

                        Mar. 1, 1764
Gad Smith & Elisabeth Bradley,   Mar. 1, 1764
Christopher Alling & Elisabeth Gilbert,   Apr. 19, 1764
Samuel Hitchcock & widow Mable Ives,   June 11, 1764
Edward Downee & Mary Reed,   Sept. 5, 1764
Daniel Merriman & Damariss Andross, Cheshire,

                        Oct. 3, 1764
John Gordon & Mary Sackett,   Oct. 3, 1764
Joseph Mix & Patience Sperry,   Oct. 15, 1764
Hezekiah Warner & Abiah Hitchcock,   Nov. 22, 1764
Stephen Tuttle, Jr. & Abigail Ball,   Dec. 6, 1764
Victor Baird & Nancy Abbott,   Dec. 6, 1764
James Bradley & Naomi Hotchkiss,   Dec. 13, 1764
Hezekiah Silliman & Emilia Hubbard,   Jan. 1, 1765

NEW HAVEN. 9

Hezekiah Riply & Dolly Brintnall, Jan. 9, 1765
John Willson & Anna Morrison, Jan. 31, 1765
Galliard Gregory of North Stratford & widow
  Mary Ives, N. H., Apr. 10, 1865
John Baldwin & Mercy Johnson, May 14, 1765
Timothy Jones, Jr., & Mary Trowbridge, June 20, 1765
Stephen Alling & Desire Bradley, July 4, 1765
Seth Coleman of Hadley & Sarah Beecher, Nov. 21, 1765
Jack & Cloe, negro serv't of Mr. A. Babcock, Nov. 14, 1765
Caleb Alling & Lois Dorman, Dec. 5, 1765
Yule, negro servant of Rev. Chauncey Whittebery
  & Rhoda Warnscrom, Dec. 19, 1765
Daniel Ford & Hannah Potter, Jan. 9, 1766
Cuff, serv't of heirs of Caleb Mix, dec. & Leah,
  serv't woman to Mr. Jared Ingersoll, Jan. 9, 1766
Joseph Howell & Hannah Hitchcock, Apr. 22, 1766
Jonathan Mansfield, Deacon, & widow Abigail Dor-
  man, May 13, 1766
Jonathan Fitch & Mrs. Elisabeth Mary Mix, May 15, 1765
John Watts & the widow Lois Woodhouse, July 13, 1766
Isaac Thomas & Sarah Andross, Sept. 15, 1766
Daniel Rexford & Martha Hitchcock, Oct. 9, 1766
Nathan Howell & Susannah Munson, Nov. 13, 1766
Francis Brown & Hannah Atwater, Jan. 9, 1767
Gilbert Greson & Anna Sperry, Feb. 18, 1767
Rutherford Trowbridge & Dorcas Hitchcock, July 9, 1767
Stephen Bradly & widow Hannah Lewis, July 19, 1767
Richard Cutler & Hannah Howell, July 29, 1767
Stephen Hotchkiss & Abigail Scot, Dec. 10, 1767
Samuel Humassen, Jr., & Mary Gills, Dec. 15, 1867
Stephen Tuttle, Jr., & Mable Brown, Feb. 22, 1768
Enoch Moulthrop & Mary Hotchkiss, Mch. 17, 1768
Belfast, negro serv't to Capt. Stephen Alling, &
  Ame Luke, dau. of Gad Luke, Mch. 20, 1768
John Smith of Hadley & Desire Cooper of N. H., Mch. 30, 1768
Jeremiah Pamely & Susannah Humasson, Apr. 14, 1768
Joseph Way of Woodbridge & Phila Bradley of
  N. H., Apr. 22, 1768

Yull, serv't of Rev. Chauncey Whittlesey, & Phillys,
    Mr. Whitney's serv't,   May 8, 1768
Isaac Jones & Elisabeth Trowbridge,   June 5, 1768
Benjamin English & Abigail Doolittle,   Nov. 17, 1768
Hezekiah Tuttle, Jr., & Dorothy Ball,   Nov. 30, 1768
Lemuel Benham & Mary Atwater,   Jan. 2, 1768
Thomas Smith & Elisabeth Tuttle,   Jan. 9, 1768
James Miles & Elisabeth Osborn,   Jan. 19, 1768
Jeremiah Townsend, Jr., & Sarah Sherman,   Jan. 19, 1768
Nehemiah Hotchkiss & Rebeckah Osborn,   Jan. 25, 1768
Peter Johnson & Cloe Tuttle,   Jan. 26, 1768
Oliver Bradley & Esther Ford,   April 4, 1768
Samuel Howell & Sybbel Star of Middletown,
          August 5, 1769
Caleb Mix & Peggy Perkins,   August 14, 1769
David Osborne & Mary Talmadge,   Oct. 12, 1769
Samuel Thomas & Sarah Ford,   Nov. 16, 1769
Caleb Trowbridge & Anna Sherman,   Nov. 29, 1769
Jonathan Ford & Phœbe Bassett,   Dec. 21, 1769
Amos Alling & Mabell Hitchcock,   Dec. 28, 1769
Thomas Trowbridge & Mary Macumber,   Dec. 28, 1769
Isaac Newton of Amity & Rebeccah Minott,   Jan. 10, 1770
Joseph Fenn of Waterbury & Esther Brown of N. H.,
          Feb. 26, 1770
John Clauss & Abigail Savi,   March 15, 1770
Lemuel Potter & Rachel Perkins,   April 19, 1770
Daniel Brown & Hannah English,   April 24, 1770
Christopher Alling & Abigail Gorham,   May 6, 1770
John Whiting, Esq., & Mrs. Sarah Trowbridge,
          May 24, 1770
Stephen Trowbridge, Jr., & Mary Bassett,   June 17, 1770
Benjamin Jillett & Margaret Munson,   July 5, 1770
Abel Stockwell & Lydia Gills,   July 9, 1770
John Smith & Frances Johnson,   August 23, 1770
Elijah Hills of Glassenbury & Hannah Munson
    of N. H.,   Oct. 2, 1770
Abraham Thompson, Jr., & Hannah Brown,   Nov. 8, 1770
—— Davis of Derby & Obedience Sperry of N. H.,
          Nov. 15, 1770

Thaddeus Beecher & Lois Bradley,	Nov. 15, 1770
Joseph Gilbert & Mercy Hitchcock,	Nov. 29, 1770
Pero Junior & Bett (negroes),	Nov. 29, 1770
Solomon Townsend & Anna Baldwin,	Dec. 25, 1770
Mr. Samuel Whittlesey & Mrs. Mary Hubbard,	Jan. 2, 1771
Stephen Bradley & Sarah Reed,	Jan. 2, 1771
Jonathan Perkins & Lydia Carrington of Amity,	
	Jan. 10, 1771
Dr. Leverett Hubbard & Esther Robinson,	Feb. 13, 1771
David Mix & Elisabeth Atwater,	March 7, 1771
Benjamin Osborn & Cloe Wheadon,	April 28, 1771
John Russell & Mary Ford of Bethany,	May 9, 1771
Alexander Moffat & Rachel Jillison,	May 13, 1771
Ely Beecher & Susanna Kimberly,	May 15, 1771
Capt. David Phips & Mary English,	June 13, 1771
Paul Noyes & Rebeccah Howell,	July 11, 1771
Isaac, servant to Mr. Douglas, & Esther, a mulatto	
woman,	July 18, 1771
Frederic Harding & Chloe Baldwin,	August 11, 1771
Leverett Stevens & Esther Macumber,	Oct. 24, 1771
Willard Brintnall & Sarah Atwater,	Oct. 27, 1771
Mr. Edward Carrington & Mrs. Susannah Whittlesey,	
	Nov. 4, 1771
Barnabus Mulford & Mabel Gorham,	Nov. 10, 1771
William Lyon & Lois Mansfield,	Jan. 13, 1772
Jonah Hotchkiss & Elisabeth Atwater,	March 18, 1772
Levi Ives & Lydia Augur,	April 22, 1772
Thomas Atwater & Margaret Macumber,	May 28, 1772
Ebenezer Johnson of Stratford & Sarah Stephen-	
son of N. H.	July 6, 1772
Joseph Eells & Susanna Brown,	July 28, 1772
Robert Matthews & Elisabeth Thomas,	August 30, 1772
Jacob Thompson & Esther Mansfield,	August 30, 1772
William McCrackin & Sally Miles,	Oct. 8, 1772
James Earl & Sybbill Bradley,	Oct. 28, 1772
Samuel Wilmot & Elisabeth Stores,	Nov. 8, 1772
Timothy White & Mercy Clark of Bethany,	Nov. 26, 1772
Nehemiah Higgins of Killingworth & Mary Groves	
of N. H.,	Dec. 14, 1772

Abraham Allen & Abigail Dorman, Dec. 16, 1772
Aaron Smith of New Fairfield & Lois Hotchkiss,

Dec. 29, 1772
Joseph Hull & Abiah Alling, March 17, 1773
Samuel Griswold & Luce Phips, March 21, 1773
Nando Cambridge Ruth Roberts (free negroes),

April 1, 1773
Samuel Gill & Abigail Atwater, June 27, 1773
Amos Hotchkiss & Rebeckah Gilbert, Sept. 12, 1773
Daniel Gilbert & Sarah Eaton, Sept. 15, 1773
John Scott & Mary Osborn, Nov. 16, 1773
Simeon Parmele & Katherine Gordon, Nov. 29, 1773
Tim & Chloe, negro servants of Esq. Darling, Jan. 4, 1774
Jedediah Cook & Hannah Miles, Jan. 19, 1774
Cato, negro serv't of Hezekiah Sabins, and Sabina,
      negro serv't of Dr. Munson, Jan. 20, 1774
Keirsted Mansfield & Mary Hitchcock, Feb. 2, 1774
Nathaniel Mix & Thankful Alling, Feb. 9, 1774
Timothy Chuck & Rebeccah Lines, Feb. 13, 1774
Jeremiah O'Brien & widow Rhoda Ford, March 15, 1774
Lemuel Benham & Margaret Green, April 14, 1774
Capt. Ezekial Hays & widow Abigail Brown, May 5, 1774
Daniel Jones of Wallingford & Joanna Chatterton,

May 25, 1774
Philosebins Treat of Milford & widow Sarah Alling,

May 26, 1774
Capt. Benjamin Brooks of Hartford & Rebecca
      Sherman of N. H., June 9, 1774
Elihu Hall & Sarah Trowbridge, July 26, 1774
Amos Potter & Sarah Warner, August 11, 1774
Stephen Gorham & Phebe Atwater, August 29, 1774
Ebenezer Alling & Molly Woolcot of Mt. Carmel,

Sept. 15, 1774
Richard Hunt & Sarah Burton, Sept. 19, 1774
Cotton Murray of Hartford & Martha Brown, Sept. 22, 1774
James Bradley & widow Esther Penfield, Sept. 25, 1774
James Gordon & Nancy Thompson, Oct. 17, 1774
Jonathan Alling & Hannah Bradley of Mt. Carmel,

Nov. 3, 1774

Elisha Mix & Mehitable Beecher,   Nov. 10, 1774
Isaac Gorham & Sarah Atwater,   Nov. 20, 1774
Joseph Cook & Abigail Peck,   Nov. 24, 1774
Benjamin Osborn & widow Elisabeth Bradley,
  Dec. 21, 1774
Charles Chauncey & Abigail Darling,   Feb. 2, 1775
Thomas Gilbert & widow Mehitable Sperry,   Feb. 23, 1775
Hanover Barney & Phœbe Wollcott,   March 12, 1775
John Hubbard & Anna Atwater,   April 4, 1775
Samuell Huggins & Sarah Miles,   April 11, 1775
Hezekiah Sperry & Martha Ives, Bethany,   May 22, 1775
Oliver Burr & Mary Hubbard,   June 14, 1775
Nathaniel Bishop & Elisabeth Tinker,   August 2, 1775
Reuben, a negro servant to Dr. Carrington and
  Rose, negro servant to Mr. Woodward,   August 3, 1775
Major Lines & Susanna Mansfield,   August 12, 1775
Edward Burke & Elisabeth Cook,   August 29, 1775
Reuben Curtiss of Newtown and Silene Allen of
  N. H.,   Oct. 4, 1775
John Peas & Eunice Atwater,   Dec. 18, 1775
Abel Humasson & Rachel Woodin, alias Hitchcock,
  Dec. 20, 1775
Joseph Hulse & Hannah Broughton,   Dec. 31, 1775
Thomas Mix & Rebecca Woodin,   Jan. 17, 1776
Abraham Gilbert & Abigail Cooper,   Jan. 18, 1776
Enos Bassett & Mehitable Goodyear,   March 14, 1776
Miles Gorham & Abigail Morriss,   March 20, 1776
Thomas Howell, Jr., & Sarah Hays,   March 28, 1776
Medad Atwater & Lowly Goodyear,   May 8, 1776
Nathan Oakes & Esther Peck,   May 15, 1776
Daniell Talmadge, Jr., & Thankfull Heaton,   June 12, 1776
Jacob Harrison of Branford & Mary McCleave,
  June 27, 1776
Ebenezer Huggins & Mary Dickerman,   July 29, 1776
Timothy Atwater & Susannah Macumber,
  August 27, 1776
Charles & Rhoda, negro servants of Samuel Thacher,
  Oct. 24, 1776
John Chandler & Sarah Whittelsey,   Oct. 31, 1776

John Trumble & Mrs. (or Miss) (?) Sarah Hubbard,
                                              Nov. 21, 1776
Eldad Atwater & Lydia Heaton,   Nov. 27, 1776
William Mansfield & Elisabeth Lyon,   Dec. 5, 1776
Abraham Johnson & Experience Barnes,   Dec. 29, 1776
Amos Gilbert & Dorcas Sherman,   Jan. 1, 1777
John Trowbridge & Thankfull Doolittle,   Feb. 13, 1777
John Lewis & Mrs. Mary Whittelsey,   March 9, 1777
Abel Fordham & Abigail Buter (free blacks),
                                              March 20, 1777
Joel Clarck & Lois Sperry,   May 1, 1777
Jonathan Ives, Mt. Carmel, & Sarah Bassett,   May 1, 1777
Pomp & Leah, free negroes,   June 12, 1777
Joshua Newell & Comfort Carrington,   Sept. 25, 1777
Chauncey Dickerman & Hannah Gills,   Nov. 26, 1777
John Miller & Lydia Trowbridge,   Nov. 26, 1777
Stephen Goodyear, Deacon, & Mary Peck, Mt. Carmel,
                                              Dec. 3, 1777
Daniell Trowbridge & Sibbyl Atwater,   Jan. 8, 1778
Nathan Howell & Anna Clarck,   Jan. 14, 1778
Joshua Atwater & Betty Goodyear,   Jan. 20, 1778
Joel Sperry, Amity, & Abigail Wheeler,   Jan. 22, 1778
William Miles & Polly Hitchcock,   April 12, 1778
Isaac Gilbert & Anna Mix,   May 31, 1778
Joseph Miles, Jr., & Mary Wise,   June 1, 1778
Joseph Bunnell & Hannah Butler,   June 8, 1778
Samuel Barney & Sarah Bassett,   Aug. 20, 1778
John Miles & Mary Bills,   Aug. 30, 1778
Medad Atwater & Rhoda Dickerman,   Sept. 10, 1778
Stephen Trowbridge & Margaret Hall,   Sept. 16, 1778
William Van Deursen & Martha Whittelsey, Sept. 30, 1778
Samuel Dunwell & Lois Atwater,   Oct. 9, 1778
Asa Trumbell & Mary Coes,   Nov. 8, 1778
Thomas Punderson & Hannah Booth,   Feb. 24, 1779
Henry Brown & Phebe Hitchcock,   March 7, 1779
Benjamin Warner & Anna Sperry,   April 6, 1779
Thomas Howell, Deacon, & Hannah Toles,   April 12, 1779
John Beecher & Mary Lyon,   May 27, 1779
Samuel Dwight & Mrs. Mary Todd,   June 10, 1779

John Cornish & widow Susanna Davis of Derby,
                                           Sept. 3, 1779
Bristol, negro servant of Silas Alling, & Abigail,
     negro servant of widow Perkins,   Oct. 28, 1779
Sterling Daniels & widow Charity Sperry,   Nov. 11, 1779
Seth Mattoon, Waterbury, & widow Sybbil Earl, N. H.,
                                           Nov. 17, 1779
Daniel Northrop & Rebecca Huggins,   Dec. 7, 1779
Jared Ingersoll & Mrs. Hannah Alling,   Jan. 9, 1780
Elias Forbes & Hannah Gorham,   Jan. 18, 1780
Edmund Sherman & Hannah Wise,   March 8, 1780
Philo Alling & Hannah Lines,   May 8, 1780
Stephen Dummer & Eunice Cook,   June 4, 1780
Stephen Atwater & Rebecca Gorham,   August 3, 1780
Richard Woodhull & Mrs. Susanna Cook,   August 22, 1780
Adnah Smith of Amity & Abiah Clark of Bethany,
                                           Oct. 19, 1780
David Bunce & Mary Hotchkiss,   Oct. 26, 1780
Uriah Rowland & Sarah Brintnall,   Oct. 26, 1780
James Dennison & Sarah Hotchkiss,   Nov. 16, 1780
Isaac Bishop & Lydia Kimberly,   Nov. 26, 1780
Hezekiah Gorham & Hannah Warner,   Dec. 7, 1780
Chillion Palmer, Litchfield, & Lois Beecher, New
     Haven,   Dec. 21, 1780
Eli Forbes & Rhoda Osborne,   Jan. 16, 1781
Titus Goodyear & Abigail Atwater,   Jan. 25, 1781
Joseph Cowdry, Stamford, & Patty Branston, N. H.,
                                           Feb. 15, 1781
Josiah Merriman & Lydia Simpson,   March 8, 1781
Timothy Potter, Jr., & Martha Turner,   March 14, 1781
Samuel Punderson & Eunice Gilbert,   May 1, 1781
Malone Downy & Lucy Barns,   May 15, 1781
Lieut. Nathan Beers & Mary Phelps,   May 26, 1781
Silas Baldwin & Abigail Brintnall,   June 14, 1781
Mathew Gilbert & Abiah Alling,   July 18, 1781
Dick & Leah, negroes,   August 2, 1781
Joshua Elderkin & Mary Brintnall,   Sept. 29, 1781
Sackett Gilbert & Sybbill Heaton,   Dec. 19, 1781
Jonathan Austin & Sarah Beecher,   Feb. 24, 1782

John Lord Thurston & Mary Honeywell,   March 6, 1782
William Brigdon & Esther Wise,   Oct. 13, 1782
Amos Bassett & Hannah Goodyear,   Oct. 24, 1782
Solomon Cook of New Marlborough & Elisabeth
    Peck,   Nov. 4, 1782
Daniel Crane & Sylvia Merriam of Meriden,   Nov. 12, 1782
James Bassett, Jr., & Odah Alling,   Dec. 31, 1782
David Atwater, Jr., & Rachel Hubbard,   Jan. 30, 1783
Joseph Hawley & Abigail Broughton,   Feb. 12, 1783
Henry Peck & Hannah Lewis,   Feb. 22, 1783
Ely Hotchkiss & Eunice Atwater,   Feb. 24, 1783
Caleb Davis & Merian Brackett,   April 5, 1783
Ebenezer Hitchcock, Jr., & Abigail Barns,   April 10, 1783
Thomas Johnston, N. Y., & Sybbil Hatch,   May 13, 1783
Samuel Russell Josselin & Almira Howell,   June 16, 1783
Enumis Sume, free negro, & Hagar, serv't of Mr.
    John Bragg, with his consent,   July 9, 1783
Samuel Russell & Mrs. Lucy Munson,   Sept. 21, 1783
Samuel Howell & Obedience Carrington,   Oct. 2, 1783
Solomon Townsend & Rachell Russell,   Oct. 19, 1783
James Gasdell & Hulda Carter,   Oct. 28, 1783
Rev. Jonathan Edwards & Mrs. Mary Sabins,   Dec. 18, 1783
Jeremiah Townsend, Jr., & Anna Atwater,   Jan. 4, 1784
Timothy Basset & Eunice Alling,   Jan. 8, 1784
Bristol & Jun, free negroes,   Jan. 22, 1784
Joseph Gorham & Elisabeth Alley,   Feb. 3, 1784
Samuel Covert & Hannah Goldsmith,   March 10, 1784
Reuben Lines & Rebecca Brown,   April 11, 1784
Amos Alling & Emillia Beecher,   April 12, 1784
Elijah Wolcott & Mary Beecher,   April 28, 1784
William Hartley & Catharine King,   May 14, 1784
Daniel Malone & Hannah Gordon,   May 27, 1784
John Bontecon & Lois Dunwell,   Aug. 7, 1784
Elias Gorham & Lydia Crane,   Aug. 22, 1784
James Cook & Martha Cowdrey,   Sept. 13, 1784
George Wheadon & Patience Branton,   Sept. 16, 1784
Ebenezer Mansfield & Polly Lewis,   Sept. 23, 1784
Ashbell Humasson of Harwinton & Phebe Bradley
    of N. H.,   Oct. 10, 1784

Nehemiah Hotchkiss & Hannah Johnson,   Nov. 3, 1784
William More & Elisabeth Howard,   Nov. 6, 1784
Charles Johnson, Derby, & Rhoda Sperry, Bethany,
   Nov. 25, 1784
Joseph Whiting & Mrs. Martha Lyman,   Nov. 27, 1784
William Fairchild & Elizabeth Miles,   Dec. 25, 1784
Daniel Woodin & Amy Coopor,   Jan. 3, 1785
Starcy Potter & Sarah Lines,   Jan. 24, 1785
Joel Gilbert, Jr., & Peggy Yeaman,   Feb. 27, 1785
Jared Atwater & Eunice Dickerman,   Sept. 7, 1785
John Webber & Nancy Chridenden,   Sept. 25, 1785
William Wise & Mary Tuttle,   Sept. 25, 1785
Cephas Ford, Northbury & Lois Clarck, N. H.,
   Sept. 27, 1785
John Arshel & Sarah Peckam,   Oct. 20, 1785
James Thompson & Elizabeth Crosly,   Oct. 27, 1785
Ebenezer Townsend & Mrs. Mother,   Nov. 20, 1785
Elisha Peck of Farminbury & Hulda Ford, N. H.,
   Nov. 24, 1785
Thomas Trowbridge & Sally Peck,   Dec. 27, 1785
David Dorman & Mable Dorman,   Jan. 1, 1786
Elnathan Tailor & Irena Thomas,   Jan. 4, 1786
Asa Blakeslie & Widow Anna Howell,   Feb. 5, 1786
David Humasson & Susanna Warren,   Feb. 8, 1786
Aner Adee & Abigail Potter,   Feb. 12, 1786
Elnathan Tyler, Northford, & Phebe Atwater, N. H.,
   March 8, 1786
Jonathan Finch, Northford, & Elisabeth Hotchkiss,
   N. H.,   March 19, 1786
Philip Klein & Mary Humasson,   March 23, 1786
Lyman Hotchkiss & Molly Bradly,   May 11, 1786
Thom, a negro man, & Dinah, a negro woman, May 11, 1786
Moses Hawkins Woodward & Sena Page,   May 26, 1786
William Bolin & Temperence Greenleaf,   May 28, 1786
David Peck & Anna Humphrivile,   July 3, 1786
Woodbridge Townsend & Sally Gorham,   Aug. 3, 1786
William Garvan & Dothesey Chridenton,   Aug. 6, 1786
John Anthony & Polly Yale,   Aug. 11, 1786
John Brown & Mary Hazzard,   Aug. 14, 1786

2

Samuel Whiting & Betsey Carrington,	Aug. 22, 1786
David Daggett & Mrs. Welthia Munson,	Sept. 10, 1786
David Gilbert, Jr., & Melissa Huggins,	Sept. 12, 1786
Markus Granby, a free negro, & Phillis, servant to	
Thaddeus Beecher,	Sept. 24, 1786
Simeon Cooper & Elizabeth Lewis,	Oct. 1, 1786
Benjamin Nichols of Berlin & Elizabeth Hitch-	
cock, N. H.,	Oct. 9, 1786
Eldad Atwater & Sally Lucas,	Oct. 15, 1786
Thomas Hasam & Rhoda Wise,	Oct. 29, 1786
William Cook & Sybbyl Parker,	Nov. 25, 1786
Col. John Strong, Torringford, & Anna Beecher,	
N. H.,	Nov. 28, 1786
Thomas Leek, Jr., & Rhoda Alling,	Jan. 1, 1787
Gad Peck & Asenath Osborn,	Feb. 6, 1787
John Cook & Anna Lyon,	May 26, 1787
James Sales & Jemima Patchen,	June 3, 1787
Huter Williams & Mary Beard,	June 3, 1787
Christopher Nicholas & Mary Thurston,	June 10, 1787
Benjamin Capron & Elisabeth Townsend,	June 14, 1787

Rev. Chauncey Whittelsey, pastor, died July 24, 1787.

Leut Hotchkiss & Sarah Ball (by Rev. James Dana),	
	Sept. 21, 1788
John Peck & Polly Lewis,	Oct. 26, 1788
Jeremiah Atwater & Elizabeth Daggett,	Feb. 3, 1789
Daniel Comstock & Mary Dana,	June 2, 1789
Capt. Asahel Hall of Wallingford & Widow Sarah	
Goldsmith of N. H.,	July 29, 1789
Edward Allen & Rachel Allen,	Sept. 1, 1789
Abraham Dummer & Lucy Hotchkiss,	Oct. 25, 1789
Stephen Hotchkiss & Widow Elizabeth Miles,	Nov. 15, 1789
Silas Pardee & Betsy Allen,	Nov. 18, 1789
Dr. Nathaniel Hubbard & Phebe McCleave,	Dec. 6, 1789
Nicholas Jebine & Mary Munson,	Jan. 23, 1790
Thomas Bonticon & Ruth Stores,	Feb. 13, 1790
Moses Brockett, North Haven, & Dorothy Allen,	
N. H.,	March 15, 1790
Medad Allen & Mary Allen,	July 14, 1790
William Hood & Elisabeth Bonticon,	July 31, 1790

Jotham Hitchcock & Lydia Thompson,	Oct. 4, 1790
Capt. Caleb Mix, Hamden, & Philena Potter,	Oct. 5, 1790
Abraham Tuttle, Jr., & widow Anna Thomas,	Nov. 10, 1790
Samuel Russel & Sarah Woodward,	Nov. 11, 1790
Capt. Ebenezer Peck & Rebecca Dickerman,	Nov. 20, 1790
Capt. Daniel Green & Hannah Howell,	Dec. 4, 1790
Cushing Smith & Desire Smith,	Dec. 23, 1790
Augustus Jocelin & Hannah Byinton,	Feb. 21, 1791
Chauncey Alling & Mehetable Thomas,	March 14, 1791
Thomas Kilby & Abigail Parmele,	April 17, 1791
Solomon Mudge & Sarah Kimberly,	April 23, 1791
Dyer White & Susanna Whittelsey,	March 18, 1791
Joseph Sperry & Sarah Beecher,	June 1, 1791
Joseph Lynde & Elisabeth Jones,	June 27, 1791
Samuel Barnes & Wealthy Trowbridge,	July 7, 1791
Benjamin Howel & Elisabeth Wilson,	July 10, 1791
Amos Wooden & Susanna Allen,	July 20, 1791
James Powers & Alma Herrick,	July 30, 1791
John Blakeslee of Middletown & Chloe Hotchkiss,	
Cheshire,	August 26, 1791
Isaac Cooper, Hamden, & Hannah Hitchcock, Hamden,	
	Sept. 2, 1791
Samuel Newel & Beulah Case,	Sept. 9, 1791
Thomas Bird & Nancy Stilwell,	Sept. 13, 1791
Thomas Philip Beardsley & Eunice Todd,	Oct. 19, 1791
Darius Higgins of N. H. & Hannah Nettleton of	
North Killingworth,	Nov. 9, 1791
Norman Griswold of Torringford & Susanna Munson of	
New Haven,	Feb. 8, 1792
William Lacy & Mary Parmele,	Feb. 22, 1792
Sherman Peet & Elizabeth Cutler,	March 3, 1792
Wickliff Cole of Southington & Martha Mix of N. H.,	
	March 22, 1792
Richard Wilson & Sally Smith,	March 29, 1792
Hendrick Dow of Ashford & Hannah Gilbert of N. H.,	
	April 4, 1792
William Howell & Anna Fairchild,	May 7, 1792
Adrian Forbes & Margaret Gilbert,	May 14, 1792
Samuel Haskell & Mary Fanning,	May 18, 1792

Joseph Hill & Mary Landcraft,	August 5, 1792
Daniel Truman & Amelia Thompson,	August 11, 1792
Jonathan Fenton & Rosalinda Lucas,	August 26, 1792
Luther Fitch & Lydia Beecher,	Sept. 28, 1792
Charles Whittlesey & Anna Cutler,	Oct. 9, 1792
Nathan Howel & Lucy Thomas,	Oct. 13, 1792
Cato Sauny & Phillis,	Oct. 19, 1792
Abraham Bradley, Jr., & Mary Ball,	Oct. 27, 1792
David Norrie & Lucy Brown,	Nov. 24, 1792
Joel Langdon & Polly Russell,	Nov. 29, 1792
Oliver Clark & Mary Thorp,	Dec. 15, 1792
John McDuel & Rachel Beecher,	Dec. 15, 1792
William Baldwin & Lois Johnson,	Jan. 1, 1793
Rutherford Trowbridge & widow Thankful Mix,	
	Jan. 1, 1793
Timothy Bradley & Lois Sperry,	Feb. 6, 1793
Jeremiah Atwater & Mary Cutler,	Feb. 14, 1793
Sylvanus Bills & Lydia Bradley,	Feb. 27, 1793
John Ball & Rebecca Johnson,	March 28, 1793
Amos Rogers & the widow Rebekah Gibbs,	March 31, 1793
Walter Brown & Mercy Beecher,	May 21, 1793
Michael Omenfetter & Hannah Stokes,	July 11, 1793
Cato & Phillis,	July 14, 1793
Col. Joseph Fay of Bennington, Vt., & Elizabeth	
Broome,	July 25, 1793
Benajah Wolcott & Elisabeth Bradley,	August 24, 1793
George Hepbun & Hannah Thompson,	July 28, 1793
Elnathan Smith of West Haven & Susanna	
Thomas of Woodbridge,	Sept. 19, 1793
Rev. Stephen Hawley & Mehetabel Hotchkiss,	Sept. 25, 1793
Leveret Mix & Sarah Ford,	Oct. 22, 1793
Benjamin Parmele & Thankful Higgin,	Nov. 7, 1793
John Hunt & Hannah Beers,	Nov. 12, 1793
Marcus Merriman & Susanna Bonticon,	Dec. 1, 1793
Newman Greenleaf & Mary Hull,	Dec. 14, 1793
Samuel Bishop, Jr., & Abigail Dingley,	Dec. 21, 1793
Samuel Helmes & widow Helmes,	Dec. 23, 1793
William Trowbridge & Eunice Merriman,	Jan. 8, 1794
Jeremiah Maccumber & Sarah Pardee,	Jan. 18, 1794

Justus Hotchkiss & Elizabeth Hotchkiss,   Feb. 15, 1794
Joseph Love & Martha Tuttle,   Feb. 23, 1794
Simeon Newton of Cheshire & Anna Johnson of
   N. H.,   March 19, 1794
William Mix & Elizabeth Plant,   March 23, 1794
Dr. Eneas Munson, Jr., of N. H. & Mary Shepard
   of Northampton,   May 3, 1794
Amaziah Lucas & Nancy Green,   May 4, 1794
Lemuel Cooper & Desire Woodin,   June 12, 1794
Thomas Trowbridge & Ruhanah Hall,   June 19, 1794
Jared Bellamy & Lucinda Kimberly,   July 30, 1794
Josiah Moulton & Rebecca Hughes,   August 14, 1794
Daniel Hommiston & Abigail Atwater,   Sept. 3, 1794
Amos Benedict & Polly Townsend,   Nov. 9, 1794
Benjamin Beecher & Wealthy Parmele,   Nov. 13, 1794
Parsons Stillman of Stamford & Esther Johnson
   of N. H.,   Nov. 22, 1794
Elisha Dickerman & Anna Scott,   Dec. 7, 1794
Asa Atwater of Hamden & Betsy Cotter of Hamden,
   Dec. 24, 1794
William Daggett & Mary Gorham,   Dec. 27, 1794
Timothy Plant & Chloe Dickerman,   Jan. 3, 1795
Pomp, servant to Capt. Elisha Forbes, & Cate,
   servant to Capt. Thomas Potter,   Jan. 27, 1795
Elihu Dorman & Anna Andrew,   Feb. 26, 1795
Joseph Talmadge & Isabella Everton,   March 29, 1795
Isaac Townsend, Jr., & Rhoda Atwater,   April 11, 1795
David Botsford of Milford & Mehitable Horton of N. H.,
   April 22, 1795
Samuel Vickere & Mary Elizabeth Smith,   May 4, 1795
Jabez Fitch & Esther Dummer,   May 16, 1795
Edward Granniss & Elizabeth Robinson,   May 16, 1795
Ephraim Brown & Sarah Alley,   June 13, 1795
Stephen Gilbert of Hamden & Elizabeth Fowler of N. H.,
   June 14, 1795
Benjamin English & Mary White,   June 18, 1795
Elijah Allen of West Haven & Rebecca Johnson
   of New Haven,   July 24, 1795
Joseph Sperry & Lucy Gilbert,   Sept. 11, 1795

James Ogden & Mary Harrison,   Oct. 13, 1795
Amos Townsend & Sarah Howe,   Oct. 15, 1795
Isaac Thomas, Jr., of Hamden & Elizabeth Ben-
    ham of Hamden,   Oct. 21, 1795
Abner Sperry of Hamden & Elizabeth Gilbert of
    Hamden,   Oct. 29, 1795
Joseph Banks & Polly Jones,   Nov. 15, 1795
Eldad Gilbert & Huldah White,   Nov. 21, 1795
William Hotchkiss & Mary Thompson,   Dec. 12, 1795
Ebenezer Warner, Jr., & Hannah Woodin,   Dec. 17, 1795
Eli C. Sherman of Hartford & Sarah Lyon of N. H.,
                                                Dec. 19, 1795
Herman Paine & Elizabeth Osborn,   Dec. 21, 1795
Sibley Pendexter of Biddeford & Hannah Hulse of
    New Haven,   Dec. 31, 1795
Jonathan Booth, Jr., of Hamden & Mable Mix of
    Hamden,   Jan. 5, 1796
Aaron Sperry of Cheshire & Lois Potter of Hamden,
                                                Jan. 7, 1796
James Prescott & Rebecca Atwater,   Feb. 6, 1796
John Miles & Sally Bills,   Feb. 6, 1796
Reuben Judd of Canaan & Esther Allen of Hamden,
                                                Feb. 16, 1796
Joseph Munson & Hannah Higgins,   Feb. 18, 1796
Josiah Mansfield & Anna Dickerman,   March 18, 1796
Daniel Brown & Polly Trowbridge,   March 23, 1796
William McCoy & Lois Bradley,   March 25, 1796
Daniel Woodin of Hamden & Keziah Jocelin of Hamden,
                                                March 29, 1796
Samuel Burrows & Esther Oaks.   April 5, 1796
Ezra Cooper of Hamden & Scena Mix of Hamden,
                                                April 13, 1796
Lent Bishop of North Haven & Lucinda Barnes of
    North Haven,   April 17, 1796
John Hunt & Elizabeth Atwater,   June 8, 1796
Stephen Lines & Elizabeth Gooley,   June 11, 1796
William Noyes, Jr., & Temperance Parmele,   June 25, 1796
Stephen Hitchcock of Hamden & Hannah Sugden
    of Hamden,   July 28, 1796

Ezekiel Chidsey & Lydia Gorham, July 30, 1796
Amasa Curtiss of Wallingford & Mehitable Hall of
  Wallingford, August 4, 1796
Ivah Curtiss of Wallingford & Hannah Ives of
  Wallingford, August 4, 1796
Silas Rice of Wallingford & Ruth Curtiss of Wal-
  lingford, August 4, 1796
John Butler of Wallingford & Ruth Parker of Wal-
  lingford, August 4, 1796
George Benham & Sarah Atwater, Sept. 4, 1796
David Moulthrop & Lydia Brown, Sept. 5, 1796
Capt. Abraham Bradley & widow Eunice Pease,
  Sept. 5, 1796
Leveret Stevens, Jr., & Nancy Thomas, Sept. 7, 1796
William Culver & Eunice Thomas, Sept. 13, 1796
Russel Osborne of Woodbridge & Polly Ball of
  New Haven, Sept. 18, 1796
David Covert & Mary Frisby, Sept. 22, 1796
William Harden & Martha Hulse, Sept. 22, 1796
Isaac Warner of Hamden & Demaris Woodin, in
  Hamden, Sept. 29, 1796
Caleb Alling, Jr., & Ruth Gorham, Sept. 29, 1796
Nehemiah Bradley & Anna Ford, Nov. 5, 1796
Merit Baldwin of N. H. & Patty Lefurger of Hamden,
  Nov. 8, 1796
Edward O'Brien & Polly Pierpont, Nov. 12, 1796
Conerad Wickwire & Elizabeth Moore, Dec. 5, 1796
Abijah Tuttle of North Haven & Mabel Shepard
  of North Haven, Jan. 8, 1797
Joseph Dalby of Jamaica & Melissa Trowbridge of
  New Haven, Jan. 17, 1797
Abijah Wolcott of Hamden & Wealthy Pamela
  Jones of N. H., Jan. 26, 1797
Joseph Foot of North Haven & Mary Bassett of
  Hamden, Feb. 16, 1797
William Jocelin & Lucretia Byinton, Feb. 16, 1797
Amos Warner of Hamden & Ruth Gilbert of Hamden,
  Feb. 21, 1797
John Ives, Jr., & Sarah Corey, Feb. 26, 1797

Joseph Mix, Jr., & Sarah Phipps,   March 11, 1797
Keirsted Mansfield, Jr., & Anna Thomson,   March 15, 1797
Amos Bradley of New Haven & Rebecca Wooden
      of Hamden,   March 18, 1797
Hervey Mulford & Nancy Bradley,   March 29, 1797
Justice Bradley & Sarah Hayes,   April 12, 1797
Charles Bostwick & Sarah Trowbridge,   June 1, 1797
David Beecher, Jr., & Prudence Samuel Chadburn,
                                                          June 10, 1797
Henry York & ——— Potter, widow of Joseph
      Skeath Potter,   June 17, 1797
Jared Thompson & Rebecca Tuttle,   August 12, 1797
Harry Sargeant & Mary Ball,   August 13, 1797
Henry Lynde & Elizabeth Ford,   August 26, 1797
Andrew Yates & Mary Austin,   Oct. 8, 1797
Wm. Mix & Lucy Benham,   Oct. 14, 1797
Peter Wilson & Phillis Warner,   Oct. 22, 1797
Josiah Stebbins & Laura Allen,   Oct. 29, 1797
Giles Doolittle & Emilia Thomas,   Nov. 12, 1797
William Venters & widow Esther McDuel,   Nov. 25, 1797
Daniel Brown & Sarah Mix,   Dec. 23, 1797
Elihu Munson & Silas Barney,   Jan. 17, 1798
Samuel Alley & Anna Tucker,   Jan. 21, 1798
Asahel Tuttle & Mary Connolley,   Feb. 15, 1798
Daniel Tallmadge & widow Rebecca Potter,   April 8, 1798
Robert Browne, Jr., & widow Eunice Howard,
                                                          July 28, 1798
Elias Allen & Elizabeth Parker,   August 26, 1798
John Scott, Jr., & Fanny Granniss,   Sept. 13, 1798
Joel Atwater & Sarah Townsend,   Sept. 29, 1798
Elisha Jones & Abigail Lewis,   Oct. 25, 1798
Jabez Dwight & Grace Trowbridge,   Nov. 3, 1798
Miles Sperry of Woodbridge & Betsy Bishop of
      New Haven,   Nov. 29, 1798
James Bronson & Rachel Hotchkiss,   Dec. 2, 1798
John H. Jacobs of Bertie Co., North Carolina, &
      Eunice Burritt of New Haven,   Dec. 18, 1798
William Mansfield, Jr., & Sally Oakes,   Feb. 25, 1799
Newport & Abigail,   May 9, 1799

Caleb Brintnall & Louisa Mix,   May 20, 1799
Joel Augur & Philomela Newel,   July 3, 1799
Jirah Isham of New London & Lucretia Hubbard
    of New Haven,   August 29, 1799
John Manser & Sarah Barney,   Sept. 2, 1799
William Thompson of East Haven & Polly Parm-
    ale of New Haven,   Sept. 25, 1799
——— Andrews of East Haven & Mehitable Pardy
    of East Haven,   Oct. 6, 1799
John Derrick & Sally Gillett,   Nov. 12, 1799
Isaac Wales & Lois Heaton,   Nov. 18, 1799
Seth P. Staples of Canterbury & Catharine Wales
    of New Haven,   Nov. 25, 1799
Bethel Tuttle & Hannah English,   Dec. 7, 1799

NEW HAVEN.

The first church in New Haven was formed in 1639. The second church (United) in 1742.
The third church (Yale College) in 1757. The following marriages are taken from the books
of the United Church, and are the earliest on record there.

NEW HAVEN SECOND CHURCH.

Timothy Atwater & Cloe Auger,   Feb. 3, 1773
Elijah Thompson & Mable Alling,   May 20, 1773
Jabez Brown & Rebecca Smith,   Nov. 18, 1773
Elijah Osborn & Phebe Tuttle,   Jan. 2, 1774
Amos Gilbert & Elizabeth Ann Alling,   April 14, 1774
Ashbel Beecher & Mary Thomas,   Nov. 4, 1774
Joseph Peck & Sarah Allcock,   Dec. 27, 1774
Asahel Todd & Phebe Phip,   Jan. 22, 1775
Persan Stilman & Elizabeth Allin,   Feb. 8, 1775
Joseph Thomas & Anne Hodge,   Feb. 9, 1775
Timothy Ohara & Eleanor Pattlebee (?),   Feb. 26, 1775
Dan Carrington & ——— Talmadge,   June 22, 1775
Abner Bristo & Eunice Dorchester,   August 1, 1775
Charles Sabens (?) & Jemima Barnard,   Nov. 14, 1775
Job Potter & Mary Bradley,   Nov. 16, 1775
Daniel Goff Phipps & Anny Townsend,   March 3, 1776

Timothy Johnson & Martha Humerston,   March 5, 1776
Henry Yorke & Susanna Chataton,   May 5, 1776
Samuel Denten & Eunice Humerston,   June 11, 1776
Samuel Gorham & Sarah Lines,   Dec. 8, 1776
David Molthrop & Hepzibath Hotchkiss,   Jan. 1, 1777
James Murray & Katharine Scovert (?),   May 28, 1777
John Troop & Susanna Bills,   May 30, 1777
Titus Smith & Martha Belding of West Haven,
                                             July 23, 1777
Stephen Mix & Esther Reed,   Nov. 19, 1777
William Osborn & Dorcas Peck,   Dec. 10, 1777
Medad Beecher & Eunice Johnsan (or Johnson),
                                             Dec. 14, 1777
Silas Hotchkiss & Esther Gilbert,   Dec. 17, 1777
David Warner & Sarah Wooden,   Dec. 30, 1777
Isaac Augur & Esther Dorman,   Jan. 1, 1778
Edmund Smith & Marian Malery,   Jan. 25, 1778
Samuel Mix & Martha Burret,   April 5, 1778
William Noyes & Rebecca Alling,   June 23, 1778
Hezekiah Augur & Lydia Atwater,   Oct. 28, 1778
Jabeth Turner & Rebecca Woolcott,   Oct. 29, 1778
Daniel Hubbard & Sarah Alling,   Nov. 26, 1778
Samuel White, Jr., & Sarah Barnes,   Dec. 28, 1778
Hezekiah Reed & Sarah Noyes,   Jan. 21, 1779
Jehial Arnold & Hanah Thompson,   May 6, 1779
William McNiel & Huldah Augur,   Sept. 25, 1779
James Howell & Rhoda Augur,   Oct. 31, 1779
Elihu Hotchkiss & Naomi Gilbert,   Dec. 14, 1779
John Stone & Mary Mansfield,   Jan. 25, 1780
John McCoy & Abigail Broughten,   Feb. 13, 1780
William Steward & Sarah McCone,   Feb. 17, 1780
Charles Fryers & Susanna Jonsen (?),   Feb. 23, 1780
John Peck & Louise Osborne,   March 12, 1780
Timothy Gilbert & Triphena Dummer,   March 15, 1780
Silas Graves & Mary Hubbard,   March 29, 1780
James Thompson & Lorinda Hotchkiss,   April 19, 1780
Zophar Atwater & Lucy Osborne,   April 27, 1780
Abijah Treet & Margaret Sperry (or Spany),   July 12, 1780
Josiah Burr & Mary Burr,   Sept. 7, 1780

Phineas Andrews & Hepbzibath Molthrop,	Nov. 14, 1780
Benjamin Grannis & Bathsheba Howel,	Sept. 29, 1780
James Gilbert & Sarah Cooper,	Oct. 5, 1780
Cebria Chaplin & Sarah Plimate (?),	April 22, 1781
John Gilbert & Mariam Phips,	July 30, 1781
Holbrook Atwater & Mehetable Alling,	August 2, 1781
Stephen Munson & Mary Goodyar,	August 16, 1781
Mark Levenworth & ——— ———,	Sept. 23, 1781
Thomas Bassel & Lydia Allcock,	Sept. 28, 1781
Joseph Dorman, Jr., & Patience Heaton,	Oct. 17, 1781
Isaac Munson & Elizabeth Phips,	Oct. 30, 1781
Mathew Gilbert & Phebe Dorman,	Jan. 2, 1782
Stephen Alling & Lidia Thompson,	Feb. 2, 1782
Elijah Hotchkiss & Rebecca Osbone,	March 3, 1782
John Dorman & Sybell Gilbert,	March 7, 1782
John Mason & Sarah Sears,	April 6, 1782
Ezra Lines & Lue Wheton,	June 4, 1782
Hathen Ramsdle & Sarah Danelson,	June 20, 1782 `
Soloman Meers of Hartford & Sally Daggett of New Haven,	June 22, 1782
Sturges Burr & Betsey Judson of New Town,	August 17, 1782
Daniel Hotchkiss & A—a Andrus,	August 20, 1782
Jared Thompson & Lydia Hotchkiss,	Sept. 26, 1782
Alexander Bradley & Lidia Bradley,	Nov. 28, 1782
Jared Bradley & Susanna Smith,	Dec. 8, 1782
Abner Scott of Waterbury & Alitheah Bradley of New Haven,	Feb. 5, 1783
Timothy Gorham & Mary White,	March 3, 1783
Roger Alling & Esther Smith,	Sept. 27, 1783
Harthan Ramsdell & Katherine Burn,	Jan. 1, 1784
Diman Bradley & Bule Turner,	Jan 14, 1784
Henry Daggett & Anne Ball,	July 7, 1784
Abner Tuttle & Elisabeth Mix,	June 5, 1783
John Thomas & Susanna Mahan,	June 17, 1783
James Dixon & Mary Smith,	July 31, 1783
Asa Potter & Phebe Mansfield,	Sept. 4, 1783
Thomas Kirkland & Cyble Sabens,	Sept. 20, 1783
John Manser & Elizabeth Wooden,	Oct. 16, 1783

James Peck & Sybyll Ford,   Oct. 30, 1783
John Lewis & Sarah Storer,   Oct. 30, 1783
John Waters & Rachel Redmon,   Nov. 3, 1783
John Johnson & Huldah Chittendon,   Dec. 21, 1783
Nathaniel Jocelin & Mrs. Sarah Bristol,   April 13, 1789
Ward Atwater & Aña Atwater,   1786
Benjamin Ally & Esther Bradley,   1786
Noah Barber & Temperence Wise,   1786
Nicholas Tuttle & Betsey Payne,   August 9, 1787
Christopher Fry & Betsey Humphrey,   Dec. 9, 1787
Moses Merriman & Lois Wantwood,   Nov., 1787
Thomas Goward & Lydia Thompson,   1787
Eber Sperry & Pamelia Page,   Dec. 17, 1787
John Gabriel & A. Ayres,   Jan. 3, 1788
Rev. David Higgins & Miss Eunice Gilbert,   Jan. 17, 1788
Soloman Phipps & Mrs. —— Dwight,   Feb. 3, 1788
Merit Carrington & Rebecca White,   Feb. 3, 1788
Prat Jones & Sarah Dickerman,   March 12, 1788
Lewis Hepburn & Huldah Hotchkiss,   April 4, 1788
John Knott & Esther Atwater Hotchkiss,   April 16, 1788
William Trowbridge & Lucy Peck,   July 27, 1788
Caleb Miller & Phebe Wooden,   August 3, 1788
Abraham Johnson & Mrs. —— Johnson,   Oct. 16, 1788
—— Barnett & —— Johnson,   Oct. 19, 1788
Charles Mothrop & Rachel Church,   Oct. 20, 1788
Noah Johnson & Sally Hill,   Oct. 20, 1788
Adrian Forbes & Esther Everton,   Nov. 3, 1788
James Law (or Lane) & Elizabeth Smith,   Nov. 23, 1788
Samuel Thomas & Lois Howel,   Nov. 23, 1788
Peter Gold & Laura Byington,   Dec. 18, 1788
Hezekiah Bradley & Lucy Hull,   Dec. 21, 1788
—— Pe—— & Azubah Atkins,   Dec. 25, 1788
Rossiter Griffin & Mrs. Hobby,   Jan. 5, 1789
Isaac Gorham & Eliza Brown,   March 10, 1789
John Tappin & Lydia Atwater,   March 14, 1789
Amos Hill & Miss Jerusha Towner,   Nov. 22, 1789
Kneeland Townsend & Miss Susanna Hampton (?),
     Thompson   Dec. 13, 1789
Alex. Booth & Miss Huldah Thompson,   Dec. 30, 1789

ASHFORD.

WINDHAM COUNTY.

Town named 1710. Congregational Church organized 1718. Marriage record begins

Jacob Fuller & Elizabeth Mackgoon,	April 1, 1719
Benjamin Read & Mary Wilson,	August 9, 1722
Samuel Sibley & Milla Squire,	March 23, 1769
John Smith & Merriam Denison,	June 29, 1769
William Hammond of Sturbridge & Zilvah Bugbee,	Oct. 25, 1769
John Southward & Levina Dana,	Feb. 20, 1770
John Lassell & Elizabeth Dana,	April 15, 1770
Jerub Preston & Sarah Hayward,	May 31, 1770
Jonas Keyes & Esther Bugbee,	August 6, 1770
Edward Bugbee & Thankful Curtis,	August 20, 1770
Phencos Jakis of Canaan & Hannah Lewis,	Dec. 10, 1770
Thomas Morey & Penelope Chapman,	Jan. 18, 1771
Samuel Whipple & Elizabeth Snow,	Jan. 29, 1771
Daniel Tenney & Priscilla Dana,	Feb. 14, 1771
Noah Payne & Zeruiah Humphrey,	March 5, 1771
James Snow & Anna Holmes,	Nov. 14, 1771
Thomas Stebbins & Sarah Tiffany,	Jan. 14, 1772
Amos Kendall & Zuruiah Chapman,	Jan. 29, 1772
David Chapman & Sarah Chubb,	March 4, 1772
John Hale & Mehitable Knowlton,	April 14, 1772
Ephraim Spaulding & Esther Snow,	May 20, 1772
Asa Eaton & Abigail Goodell,	Nov. 5, 1772
Benjamin Smith & Hannah Smith,	Nov. 12, 1772
Philip Holmes of Hardwick & Anna Powers of Greenwich,	Dec. 1, 1772
Joel Ward & Elizabeth Woodward,	Jan. 13, 1773
Cæsar, negro servant of Benjamin Sabin, & Dinah, negro servant girl of Benjamin Clark, married with the consent of masters as servants,	March 11, 1773
Jonathan Snow & Hannah Chubb,	March 30, 1773
Stephen Burgess & Susanna Abbott,	Sept. 15, 1773

3*

Tiras Preston & Esther Eaton,	Nov. 2, 1773
Stephen Hyemes & Hannah Watkins,	Nov. 11, 1773
Edward Fay & Sarah Torry,	Nov. 25, 1773
Samuel Snow, Jr., & Molly Wilson,	Nov. 25, 1773
Ebenezer Wales & Anna Babcock,	Dec. 26, 1773
James Keyes & Meriam Babcock,	Dec. 26, 1773
Joseph Woodward & Elizabeth Sumner,	Jan. 11, 1774
Hubbard Smith & Keziah Snow,	Oct. 4, 1774
Abel Simmons & Hannah Holmes,	Nov. 3, 1774
Nehemiah Howe & Mary Holt,	Jan. 2, 1775
Joseph Chidcy & Mary Barker,	Jan. 3, 1775
Jonathan Curtis & Mary Preston,	Jan. 12, 1775
Elisha Smith Wales & Mary Watkins,	March 7, 1775
Abner Loomis & Ruth Wilson,	June 11, 1775
William Tiffany & Molly Clark,	Nov. 16, 1775
Simeon Tiffany & Esther Clark,	Dec. 28, 1775
Clapp Sumner & Mehitable Lassell,	March 21, 1776
Ebenezer Smith, Jr., & Hannah Weston,	March 28, 1776
Jonathan Chaffee & Lucy Allen,	May 1, 1776
Nathan Stanton & Sarah Coggswell,	May 30, 1776
Daniel Lewis & Sarah Lyon,	Sept. 2, 1776
Benjamin Pitts & Freelove Whipple,	Sept. 19, 1776
Stephen Hayward & Lucy Brooks,	Dec. 4, 1776
John Johnson & Sarah Byles,	April 10, 1777
Aaron Cook & Mary Cummings,	May 21, 1777
Abel Simmons & Marcy Haven,	May 22, 1777
Nathaniel Hayward & Priscilla Chubb,	Nov., 1777
Samuel Bugbee & Thankful Snow,	Nov. 27, 1777
Adam Knox & Dorothy Chaffee,	Nov. 27, 1777
Samuel Eaton & Martha Tubbs,	Dec. 13, 1777
David Torry & Eunice Bicknell,	Feb. 5, 1778
Walter Himes & Abigail Scarborough,	March 4, 1778
Ebenezer Mason & Christian Fitts,	March 5, 1778
Thomas Southworth & Rachel Cummings,	March 23, 1778
John Warren & Abigail Eaton,	May 8, 1778
John Orcutt & Mary Hendee,	April 16, 1778
Joseph Palmer & Sarah Weld,	May 20, 1778
Rev. Elisha Hutchinson & Mrs. Jerusha Cadwell,	
	July 16, 1778
Benjamin Hanfield & Bridget Lewis,	Feb. 8, 1779

Ezra Snow & Levina Case,	May 20, 1779
William Price & Esther Palmer,	Nov. 3, 1779
Uriah Holt & Margaret Mason,	Nov. 11, 1779
Josiah Byles & Abigail Clark,	Nov. 18, 1779
Lemuel Clark & Elizabeth Bicknell,	Nov. 25, 1779
Nathaniel Bowdish & Betty Huntington,	Dec. 9, 1779
Josiah Eaton & Ann Knowlton,	April 24, 1780
Moses Horton & Silence Willison,	Dec. 3, 1780
Bilarky Snow & Molly Smith,	May 20, 1781
John Bicknell, Jr., & Anna Atwood,	August 30, 1781
James Bugbee & Hannah Morgan,	August 30, 1781
Stephen Eaton & Phanely Knowlton,	(?) Nov. 12, 1781
Benjamin Sumner & Ruth Palmer,	Sept. 22, 1789
Amasa Robinson & Harmony Chubb,	Nov. 24, 1789
Amos Goodale of Westminster, Vt., & Mehitable	
Hendee,	Feb. 17, 1790
Ezra Boutell & Cynthia Williams,	March 25, 1790
Benjamin Shaw of Benson, Vt., & Sybel Eaton,	
	March 25, 1790
Joseph Wilson & Landa Utley of Pomfret,	April 1, 1790
John Butler & Sally Brown,	Dec. 7, 1790
Michael Swinington of Pomfret & Lois Kendall,	
	Dec. 23, 1790
Andrew Work & Martha Phillips,	Feb. 17, 1791
Nehemiah Ripley of Windham & Amy Gould,	Feb. 24, 1791
Lovell Snow & Sarah Maynard of Pomfret,	April 7, 1791
Zuinglius Bullard & Sally Keyes,	August 28, 1791
Elijah Dean & Irene Sumner,	Sept. 22, 1791
———— Backus of Canterbury & Sally Tuft,	Oct. 20, 1791
Thomas Phinney & Anna Preston,	Nov. 7, 1791
Thomas Chaffee & Abigail Knowlton,	Nov. 21, 1791
Reuben Marcy, Jr., & Hannah Sumner,	Dec. 1, 1791
Samuel Clark of Hardwick, Mass., & Mehitable	
Ingersol,	Dec. 25, 1791
Smith Holt & Lydia Snow,	Jan. 26, 1792
Thomas Peck of Brookfield, Vt., & Priscilla Howard	
of Woodstock,	Feb. 8, 1792
Asa Phillips & Anna Work,	Feb. 9, 1792
Capt. Josiah Sabin of Pomfret & widow Sarah Work,	
	March 7, 1792

Samuel Bicknell & widow Mary Frink,   April 29, 1792
Willard Watkins & Tryphosa Burnham   August 26, 1792
John Bailey & Clarissa Snow,   August 30, 1792
Luther Gaylord & Sally Preston,   Sept. 27, 1792
Isaac Farnam & Mehitable Snow,   Oct. 15, 1792
Thomas Cheney & Polly Stowell,   Nov. 14, 1792
Ezra Smith & Roxana Kendall,   Nov. 22, 1792
Nathan Palmer & Polly Brown,   Nov. 27, 1792
Joshua Coggswell of Coventry & Thankful Eaton,
    Nov. 29, 1792
Bela Ormsby of Manchester, Vt., & Ruth Russ, Dec. 10, 1792
Gurdon Fletcher & Esther Clark Mansfield,   Dec. 13, 1792
Othniel Woodward & Zelinda Read,   Feb. 9, 1793
David Keyes & Sarah Sumner,   Feb. 9, 1793
John Frink & Roxana Bicknell,   Feb. 17, 1793
Stephen Carpenter of Killingly & Nancy Smith,
    March 25, 1793
Elijah Chapman & Esther Jennings,   March 25, 1793
Abial Abbee of Willington & Polly Chandler, March 3, 1793
Whitmore Shepherd of Pomfret & Lucy Parish, April 3, 1793
Elias Frink & Clarina Holt,   May 12, 1793
Benjamin Hutchins & Lois Babcock,   June 16, 1793
John Hendee & Annis Russ,   July 11, 1793
Erastus Root of Windsor & Mary Wright of Eling-
ton,   August 18, 1793
Lemuel Warren of Plainfield & Priscilla Spauld-
ing,   August 22, 1793
Richard Ware & Anna Russell,   August 22, 1793
Zera Preston & Hannah Smith,   April 20, 1794
John Stowell of Longmeadow & Polly Keyes,
    August 10, 1794
Henry Durkee of Hampton & Sally Russell, Sept. 25, 1794
Elisha Buck & Sarah Ryder,   Sept. 28, 1794
Paul Horton & Ruth Swinnington,   Oct. 12, 1794
John Fitch of Windsor, Vermont, & Phebe Work,
    Nov. 2, 1774
Jonathan Gould & Patience Dyer,   Jan. 1, 1795
Nathan Eastman & Miss Back of Hampton, April 30, 1795
Daniel Mecham of Stafford & widow Jerusha
    Boutell,   May 21, 1795

Billings Babcock & Zebia Winter,	May 21, 1795
Ezekiel Cotter & Hephzibah Smith,	June 18, 1795
Ephraim Brown & Sally Snow,	Sept. 20, 1795
George Steel of Hartford & Betsy Babcock,	Sept. 30, 1795
Asa Swift of Mansfield & Saloma Snow,	Nov. 5, 1795
Capt. Benjamin Hayward of Woodstock & Elizabeth Messinger,	Nov. 25, 1795
Eliphaz Parish & Jerusha Downing of Brooklyn,	Jan. 3, 1796
John Perry & Eunice Parish,	March 3, 1796
Benjamin Cresey of Pomfret & Anna Robinson,	March 9, 1796
James Cook of Franklin & Aphama Phelyn of Mansfield,	May 5, 1796
Capt. Roswell Burnham & Betsy Babcock,	May 22, 1796
Bela Bibbins of Windham & Elizabeth Farnam,	May 29, 1796
James Pearl & Polly Watkins,	Sept. 22, 1796
Benjamin Eastman & Sylva Jones or Janes,	Nov., 1796
Abner Boutell & Cynthia Lewis,	Dec. 22, 1796
Jonas Hannah of Burn, (?) N. Y., & Achsah Kowlton,	Jan. 17, 1797
Eliakim Williams of Tolland & Damaris Carey of Mansfield,	Feb. 1, 1797
Chester Storrs & Damaris Clark, both of Mansfield,	Feb. 2, 1797
Ebenezer Weeks of Stuborn, N. Y., & Olive Keyes,	Feb. 19, 1797
Jack Torry & Sylvia Clark, both negroes,	March 27, 1797
William Pierce of Woodstock & Betsy Brown,	March 28, 1797
Capt. Amos Snow of S. Brimfield & Eunice Burnham,	June 27, 1797
Alexander Coburn & Susanna Mason of Woodstock,	Oct. 26, 1797
Lemuel Brooks of Montpelier, Vt., & Rhoda Barber,	Jan. 15, 1798
Samuel Frizell of Cazonosia, N. Y., & Polly Tiffany,	Jan. 18, 1798
Lieut. Jacob Preston & Mrs. Mehitable Knowlton,	Jan. 25, 1798

Kinney (?) Hayward of Woodstock & Lucy Payne,
                                        April 4, 1798
Jesse Adams of Pomfret & Merriam Smith,   April 12, 1798
John Work & Hannah Payne,   May 9, 1798
Nathan Huntington & Ethalear Butler,   May 31, 1798
Daniel Read & Augustina Fenton of Mansfield, July 5, 1798
Dr. Samuel Willard of Stafford & Abigail Perkins,
                                        Aug. 16, 1798
Lovell Bass & Polly Russ, both of Mansfield, Aug. 21, 1798
Reuben Abbott & Polly Snow,   Nov. 8, 1798
Ephraim Deane of Woodstock & Percy Brown, Nov. 20, 1798
Seth Eastman & Betsy Lyon,   Nov. 29, 1798
John Ellis of Walpole, Mass., & Molly Richards,
                                        Nov. 29, 1798
Dyer Clark & Lucinda Holt,   Jan. 14, 1799
John Foote of Tolland & Betsy Carey of Mansfield,
                                        April 11, 1799
Jedediah Wentworth & Betsy Webb,   May 9, 1799
Dr.Vine Utley of Winchester & Rebecca Marcy, Aug., 1799
Samuel Whipple & Mary Chaffee,   Sept. 15, 1799
William Gillmore of Stafford & Rhoda Snow, Sept. 30, 1799

Second Congregational Church of Ashford was organized in Westford District, 1768.

BROOKLYN.

WINDHAM COUNTY.

Congregational Church and Society taken out of Canterbury, Pomfret and Mortlake, 1736.
Township formed 1752. Marriage record begun by Rev. Ephraim Avery, the first pastor.

Deliverance Woodward & Abigail Jewel of Wood-
  stock,   March 7, 1737
Nathaniel Aspinwell & Mary Darby,   Nov. 10, 1737
Ebenezer Pike & Abigail Adams,   Jan. 24, 1738
Abraham Hyde & Experience Adams,   Jan. 24, 1738
Joseph Adams, 2d, & Elizabeth Cary,   Feb. 23, 1738
Ebenezer Weeks & Anna Holland,   Sept. 5, 1738
Isaac Sabin & Elizabeth Holland,   Sept. 5, 1738

Joseph Sharp & Elizabeth Cady,	Nov. 9, 1738
Jonas Spaulding & Bridget Brown,	Nov. 16, 1738
David Kendal & Jane Adams,	Feb. 8, 1739
Moutserrat & Dinah (negro servants belonging to	
Dea. Williams),	Oct. 18, 1739
Zebulun Richards & Lydia Brown,	Nov. 8, 1739
Joseph Parks of Middletown & Amity Cady,	Jan. 16, 1740
Jabez Hide & Hannah Bacon,	Feb. 27, 1740
Robert Vine & Elizabeth Thatcher,	Dec. 8, 1740
Daniel Carr & Elizabeth Dunkin,	Jan. 27, 1741
Joseph Ross & Jane Sparks,	Feb. 25, 1741
James Pike & Hannah Hide,	May 25, 1741
Jacob Staples & Eunice Cady,	Oct. 29, 1741
Moses Smith & Mary Wheeler,	Nov. 5, 1741
Joseph Cady & Phebe Cady,	Dec. 3, 1741
Amariah Winchester & Hannah Cady,	Jan. 15, 1742
Samuel Wilson & Betsey Adams,	March 4, 1742
Joseph Adams, Jr., & Dorothy Hide,	April 12, 1742
Ebenezer Hide & Mercy Thatcher,	April 12, 1742
Joseph Gary & Alice Cary,	June 10, 1742
Daniel Tyler & Mehitabel Shurtleff,	Sep. 16, 1742
Nathan Cady & Rachel Cady,	Oct. 21, 1742
John Hutchins of Killingly & Sarah Bacon,	Nov. 2, 1742
Thomas Spaulding & Abigail Brown,	Nov. 4, 1742
Nathaniel Holmes & Desire Spicer,	Nov. 11, 1742
Jacob Smith, Jr., & Mary Hide,	Dec. 27, 1742
Abraham Paine & Rebekah Freeman,	March 8, 1743
John Farr & Eunice Adams,	June 13, 1744
Joseph Hubbard & Deborah Cleveland,	July 5, 1744
William Prince of Salem & Mary Holland,	Nov. 8, 1744
Moses Cady & Sybil Cleaveland,	Nov. 29, 1744
John Brett of Bridgewater & Alice Cady,	Jan. 14, 1745
Henry Bacon, Jr., & Persis Cleaveland,	Feb. 18, 1745
Simeon Cady & Ruth Harris,	Feb. 26, 1745
Elisha Lothrop of Norwich & Abigail Avery,	May 28, 1745
Jonathan Abbe of Willington & Rebekah Wedge,	
	Sept. 19, 1745
Adonijah Fasset & Anna Copeland,	Nov. 4, 1745
James Darbe, Jr., & Beulah Cutler,	Dec. 31, 1745
Benjamin Merriam & Sarah Smith,	April 15, 1746

Jabez Brown & Abigail Adams,	Sept. 3, 1746
Lieut. Henry Bacon & Elizabeth Chapman,	Sept. 17, 1746
Thomas Bowman & Sarah Blackmore,	Nov. 5, 1746
Jedidiah Downing & Abigail Cady,	Nov. 5, 1746
Benjamin Fassett, Jr., & Elizabeth Tucker,	Dec. 8, 1746
Abiel Cheney & Sarah Holland,	March 18, 1747
Benajah Rood of Norwich and Sarah Smith of Canterbury,	May 28, 1747
Ebenezer Fuller of Killingly & Mercy Cutler,	Dec. 21, 1747
William Wedge & Bridget Cleaveland,	March 3, 1748
Benjamin Bacon & Mary Eldridge,	April 21, 1748
Oliver Williams & Huldah Holland,	Sept. 25, 1748
Ezra Bowman & Mary Smith,	Nov. 3, 1748
Caleb Spaulding & Jerusha Cady,	Nov. 10, 1748
Jabez Holmes & Experience Cleaveland,	May 2, 1749
Ebenezer Preston & Hannah Smith,	Oct. 4, 1749
Seth Paine & Mabel Tyler,	Nov. 1, 1749
Eleazar Brown & Sarah Bacon,	Nov. 13, 1749
Daniel Robinson & Mary Smith,	Nov. 16, 1749
Samuel Ellis of Sturbridge & Abigail Smith,	May 15, 1750
John Litchfield & Lucy Cady,	July 17, 1750
William Cooper & Ruth Adams,	March 21, 1751
Joseph Chapman & Hannah Freeman,	May 16, 1751
John Holmes & Mary Freeman,	Sept. 12, 1751
Cornelius Whitney of Killingly & Zerviah Cleaveland,	Nov. 7, 1751
Eliashib Adams & Betty Phillips,	May 3, 1753
William Copeland & Sarah Smith,	May 3, 1753
Gideon Cady & Sarah Hutchins,	May 24, 1753
Abijah Cady & Lucy Adams,	June 7, 1753
Thomas Cotton, Jr., & Sarah Holbrook,	June 14, 1753
Josiah Chandler & Hannah Holbrook,	June 14, 1753
Capt. Zechariah Spaulding & Sarah Pike,	August 30, 1753
Samuel Sumner, Jr., & Dorothy Williams,	April 11, 1754
Abraham Stanton & Grace Wheeler,	May 1, 1754
Eleazar Darbe & Anna Doubledee,	August 22, 1754

MARRIED BY REV. JOSIAH WHITNEY.

Nehemiah Bacon & Ruth Adams, Dec. 29, 1756
Nathaniel Cogswell of Preston & Bridget Wedge,
                                        May 25, 1757
William Danielson of Killingly & Sarah Williams,
                                        Dec. 29, 1757
Lieut Benjamin Fassett & Eleanor Adams, Feb. 5, 1758
John Howard, Jr., & Mary Adams, March 1, 1758
Samuel Fowler of Douglas & Lois Cady, April, 1758
Jabez Allen & Mary Darbee, June 3, 1758
Stephen Burton of Preston & Hannah Pierce, Sept. 19, 1758
Elias Weld of Pomfret & Thankful Spaulding, Nov. 16, 1758
Abijah Goodale & Lucy Tyler, Feb. 1, 1759
Jonathan Ladd & Elizabeth Stiles, April 26, 1759
Moses Earle & Mary Stewart, May 8, 1759
Jonathan Raynsford & Hannah Hide, May 17, 1759
Darius Cady & Elizabeth Hull, April 24, 1760
Nathan Allin & Olive Cady, May 15, 1760
Aaron Goodale of Mansfield & Amy Tyler, Nov. 27, 1760
Samuel Fassett & Rebekah Fish, June 3, 1761
Joseph Harris & Lydia Cady, July 6, 1761
Jonathan Collar & Sarah Williams, July 21, 1761
Thomas Goodale & Betty Cady, Oct. 15, 1761
Barnabus Wood to Sibillah Darbee, Nov. 12, 1761
John Cotton & Abigail Williams, Dec. 3, 1761
Abner Adams & Abigail Hubbard, Dec. 3, 1761
James Alworth & Hannah Baker, March, 1762
Uriah Cady, Jr., & Joanna Hewit, April 8, 1762
Seth Dean of Plainfield & Mrs. Lydia Allyn, Sept. 30, 1762
Stephen Walker of Killingly & Lois Davison, Sept. 30, 1762
Daniel Cady & Mary Spaulding, Oct. 6, 1762
Dea. Daniel Davis of Killingly & Elizabeth Shurt-
    leff, Nov. 2, 1762
Thomas Smith & Elizabeth Wheeler, Dec. 16, 1762
Jesse Darbee & Lydia Meechem, May 2, 1763
Rev. Joseph Sumner of Shrewsbury & Mrs. Lucy
    Williams, May 12, 1763
William Underwood of Plainfield & Sarah Phillips,
                                        July 24, 1763

John Howard of Windham & Zerviah Hewit, Nov. 15, 1763
David Kendal & Hannah Kendal, both of Ashford,
          March 22, 1764
Timothy Adams & Susanna Adams,   May 3, 1764
Daniel Cloud & Mary Cleaveland,   May 13, 1764
Oliver Durkee of Windham & Mary Hide, June 21, 1764
John Winchester Dana & Hannah Putnam, Oct., 1764
Thomas Austin & Eleanor Adams,   Dec., 1764
James Eldridge & Sarah Ashcraft,   Feb. 20, 1765
Abel Cady & Elizabeth Russell,   Feb. 21, 1765
Increase Hewit & Elizabeth Tyler,   Feb. 28, 1765
Lieut. Joseph Cleveland & Abigail Miles, June 9, 1765
Samuel Williams & Mary Allen,   Sept. 5, 1765
Salter Searls & Alice Cady,   Oct. 24, 1765
Rufus Herrick & Prudence Cady,   Dec. 19, 1765
Nathaniel Coggswell, Jr., of Preston & Hannah Allen,
           Jan. 2, 1766
Benjamin Hide & Anna Eldridge,   Jan. 30, 1766
William Fassett & Zerviah Meechem,   Feb. 12, 1766
Asa Perkins & Abigail Cleveland,   Feb. 25, 1766
Zebulum Tyler & Betty Adams,   April 17, 1766
Stephen.Webb of Windham & Content Hewit, May 22, 1766
Joseph Abbott & Olive Pierce,   Sept. 7, 1766
Thomas Miles & Jerusha Hubbard,   Sept. 11, 1766
Benjamin Herrick & Amy Church,   Sept. 11, 1766
Phinehas Tyler & Lucy Hide,   Nov. 19, 1766
Thomas Adams & Mary Hubbard,   Dec. 1, 1766
David Kendall & Bridget Cady,   March 5, 1767
Charles Shanwan & Betty Sunsimun (Indians), July 20, 1767
Samson, negro man-servant of Daniel Tyler, & Lucy
  Church (Indian),   Sept. 24, 1767
Timothy Lovejoy & Mary Hide,   Oct. 25, 1767
Benjamin Fassett & Anna Fassett,   Dec. 17, 1767
Jonas Hubbard & Mary Brown,   Jan. 10, 1768
Peter Davison & Abigail Woodward, April 28, 1768
Pelatiah Lyon of Williamsboro to Sabra Cady, July 12, 1768
Isaac Row & Sarah Fassett,   July 28, 1768
James Phillips Putnam of —— & Molly Herrick,
          Sept. 19, 1768
Benoni Moon & Lois Warren,   May 4, 1769

Joseph Stanton & Mary Staples,	May 4, 1769
Jonathan Forster & Patience Cady,	June 22, 1769
Jesse Cleaveland & Annah Darbee,	Nov. 5, 1769
Samuel Ingals & Deborah Meechem,	Nov. 9, 1769
John Gilbert & Rachel Pierce,	Dec. 28, 1769
Jared Cook & Mary Brown,	Jan. 4, 1770
Jonathan Eddy & Mercy Cady,	Jan. 17, 1770
Amasa Pooler & Hannah Cady,	April 22, 1770
Abel Spaulding & Mehetabel Cady,	June 28, 1770
Isaac Adams & Prudence Jaquays,	July 8, 1770
Asahel Willard & Rachel Hubbard,	August 30, 1770
Nathan Day of Killingly & Hannah Hewit,	Sept. 20, 1770
Dilleno Pierce & Abigail Hammond,	Nov. 1, 1770
Joseph Staples & Eleanor Darbee,	Nov. 22, 1770
Noah Adams, Jr., & Elizabeth Fassett,	Nov. 22, 1770
Jedidiah Dana of Ashford & Lucy Holt,	Nov. 27, 1770
Thomas Dike of Killingly & Dorothy Davison,	Dec. 11, 1770
William Cushman, Jr., & Mary Weaver,	Dec. 27, 1770
Robert How of Killingly & Abigail Cushman,	Jan. 31, 1771
Daniel Tyler, Jr., & Mehitabel Putnam,	August 15, 1771
Samuel Grigs & Elizabeth Woodward,	Oct. 31, 1771
Ebenezer Story & Mehitabel Webb,	Nov. 15, 1771
Ephraim Adams & Deborah Adams,	Jan. 16, 1772
Thomas Goodale & Patience Carr,	Jan. 16, 1772
Eleazar Gilbert & Sarah Weeks,	April 23, 1772
Roger Eliot of Killingly & Betty Prince,	Nov. 12, 1772
Asa Hide of Woodstock & Lucy Winchester,	Dec. 23, 1772
Stephen Preston & Lois Hammond,	Jan. 4, 1773
Job Parkhurst of Plainfield & Abigail Holt,	Jan. 14, 1773
Dr. Joseph Baker & Deborah Avery,	March 4, 1773
William Ashcraft & Tamesia Cady,	June 24, 1773
Elijah Thayer & Anna Cady,	Dec. 30, 1773
John Ashcraft & Bridget Hubbard,	April 7, 1774
John Stevens & Thankful Allen,	May 5, 1774
William Osgood, Jr., & Mary Scarborough,	June 2, 1774
Samuel Danielson, Esq., & Mrs. Sarah Spaulding,	Oct. 26, 1774
Edward Goodale & Dorcas Sheperd,	Dec. 1, 1774
Peter Woodward & Mary Frost,	Dec. 22, 1774
Silas Chandler & Grace Fassett,	Dec. 29, 1774

Joseph Williams & Lucy Witter,	Jan. 11, 1775
Walter Bowman & Anna Litchfield,	Feb. 23, 1775
Simeon Gooodale & Martha Williams,	June 8, 1775
Philip Abbot & Anna Hewit,	July 6, 1775
Paul Davison & Sarah Hide,	Nov. 16, 1775
Pendar, a negro man-servant at Mr. Elihu Palmer's,	
& Mabel, an Indian woman,	Nov. 30, 1775
Samuel Haruden & Joanna Draper,	Feb. 15, 1776
Joseph Allen & Mary Spalding,	April 4, 1776
Charles Shawun & Hannah Babcock (Indians),	June 13, 1776
Peter Kendal & Betsy Wilson,	July 4, 1776
Samuel Williams, Jr., & Martha Phips,	July 23, 1776
Adonijah Fassett, Jr., & Anna Allen,	July 28, 1776
David Cady & Lois Fassett,	March 2, 1777
Gideon Cady & Biel Webber,	March 27, 1777
Samuel Adams & Betty Litchfield,	May 11, 1777
Joseph Hawkins of Coventry & Zerviah Howard,	
	August 7, 1777
Jonathan Fuller & Esther Cady,	August 28, 1777
Silas Palmer & Silence Fassett,	August 28, 1777
Alpheus Brown & Sarah Litchfield,	Oct. 16, 1777
Stephen Russ of Norwich & Thankful Spalding,	
	Nov. 20, 1777
Abel Staples & Cynthia Holt,	Dec. 3, 1777
Daniel Cushman & Molly Bowman,	Dec. 21, 1777
Ephraim Bacon & Sarah Cook,	Jan. 7, 1778
Elisha Avery & Eunice Putnam,	Feb. 5, 1778
William Barrett & Lucy Adams,	Feb. 26, 1778
Zebulun Cady & Zerviah Jaquays,	April 16, 1778
Sambo (negro) & Sarah Prime (mulatto),	April 30, 1778
Abijah Downing & Priscilla Hyde,	June 7, 1778
Willard Pike & Molly Spaulding,	July 21, 1778
(Shubael) Adams & Anna Winchester,	July 30, 1778
Joseph Downing & Abigail Williams,	Sept. 24, 1778
Stephen Hewit & Alice Shepherd,	Oct. 29, 1778
Benjamin Barden & Sarah Holland,	Nov. 12, 1778
Calvin Hubbard & Sarah Darbee,	Nov. 19, 1778
Rufus Darbee & Dority Morgan,	Nov. 26, 1778
Benjamin Wiggins & Anna Deane,	Dec. 16, 1778
Lemuel Storrs & Dinah Allen,	Dec. 17, 1778

Caleb Adams & Elizabeth Chapman,	Feb. 4, 1779
John Pike & Hannah Fassett,	Feb. 16, 1779
Joshua Barden & Elizabeth Holland,	March 11, 1779
Joshua Miles & Lucy Cady,	May 25, 1779
Abner Day & Mary Wilson,	Sept. 16, 1779
Lot Cook & Sarah Cleaveland,	Sept. 30, 1779
Samuel Whittaker & Mary Cloud,	Oct. 24, 1779
David Adams & Sarah Borden,	Dec. 9, 1779
Daniel Clark & Lydia Davison,	Jan. 30, 1780
Amasa Hide & Lucy Robinson,	Jan. 30, 1780
Samuel Turner & Elizabeth Fassett,	Feb. 15, 1780
Jesse Miles & Olive Adams,	Feb. 17, 1780
Nathaniel Rand & Phebe Adams,	Feb. 20, 1780
Joseph Scarborough & Deliverance Kingsbury,	Feb. 24, 1780
Jonathan Copeland & Esther Chapman,	March 9, 1780
Robert Languetty & Mary Darbee,	March 23, 1780
Nathaniel Goodspeed & Abigail Perkins,	May 26, 1780
Asa Williams & Hannah Shepherd,	June 1, 1780
Elisha Bowman & Elizabeth Kimball,	June 29, 1780
Ebenezer Hubbard & Molly Simons,	Oct. 12. 1780
Ezra Franklin & Mary Waters,	Nov. 21, 1780
Ignatius Wilson & Anna Allen,	Nov. 30, 1780
Zebadiah Plank & Olive Holmes,	Dec. 7, 1780
William Copeland & Anna Weeks,	Dec. 7, 1780
Timothy Prince, Jr., & Deidama Pierce,	Dec. 14, 1780
Capt. Joseph Cleveland & Olive Hubbard,	Jan. 11, 1781
Samuel Cleaveland & Molly Allen,	Jan. 11, 1781
Thomas Starkweather & Eunice Staples,	Jan. 11, 1781
Lemuel Fling & Ruth Cady,	April 17, 1781
Samuel Williams, 3rd, & Hannah Gardiner,	June 12, 1781
Isaac Cushman & Sarah Paine,	June 26, 1781
Dick Fortune & Lucy Grevous,	Aug. 19, 1781
Ambrose Deuro & Keziah Barker,	Aug. 30, 1781
Ebenezer Cady & Hannah Baker,	Oct. 1, 1781
James Rix Whitney & Polly Holland,	Oct. 31, 1781
Charles Brown & Azubah Goodale,	Dec. 12, 1781
Capt. James Tyler & Mehitabel Scarborough,	April 11, 1782
Amon Harris & Hopeful Pratt,	July 25, 1782
Eleazar Litchfield & Keziah Witter,	Nov. 28, 1782
Benjamin Allen & Sabra Cleaveland,	Dec. 4, 1782

Roger Starkweather & Lucy Holt,	Jan. 16, 1783
Jonah Witter & Eunice Cady,	Jan. 16, 1783
Ashael Cady & Ruth Lamphier,	March 13, 1783
Lemuel Grosvenor & Eunice Avery,	Sept. 7, 1783
Jacob Holt & Hannah Jefferds,	Oct. 1, 1783
Joel Day of Killingly & Sarah Wilson,	Oct. 16, 1783
Phinehas Downing & Anna Butt,	Nov. 20, 1783
Palmer Pierce & Eunice Kimball,	Nov. 20, 1783
Amasa Copeland & Mary White,	Feb. 26, 1874
Samuel Whittaker & Urana Wood,	June 6, 1784
John Wheeler & Almira Wethy,	Sept. 23, 1784
Abel Prince & Lucy Cady,	Nov. 25, 1784
Alpheus Darbee & Lucy Fassett,	Dec. 2, 1784
Richard Robinson & Huldah Bowman,	Dec. 23, 1784
Benjamin Holmes & Mary Cleaveland,	Dec. 23, 1784
Hazael Wethy & Sybil Smith,	Jan. 27, 1785
John Richmond & Rachel Cady,	Feb. 14, 1785
Benjamin Daily & Deborah James,	May 13, 1785
William Baker & Hannah Bowman,	July 7, 1785
Jonas Parks & Betsey Robbins,	Aug. 11, 1785
Shubael Brown & Nancy Dixon,	Dec. 15, 1785
James Ingalls & Sarah Williams,	Feb. 2, 1786
Leonard Herrick & Mary Lester,	June 25, 1786
Amaziah Weston & Mary Cady,	Sept. 22, 1786
Roswell Morgan & Cynthia Witter,	Nov. 22, 1786
Willard Adams & Experience Cady,	Nov. 23, 1786
Erastus Baker & Lois Whitney,	Nov. 4, 1787
Capt. William Smith & Esther York,	Nov. 15, 1787
Daniel Kimball of Hampton & Mirian Alworth,	Nov. 29, 1787
Ezekiel Eaton & Eleanor Staples,	Jan. 1, 1788
Richard Kimball & Susanna Holden,	Feb. 7, 1788
Isaac Hutchins of Killingly & Sarah Hubbard,	May 29, 1788
Joel Baker & Susanna Frost,	Oct. 1, 1788
Uriah Litchfield & Sally Witter,	Nov. 27, 1788
Ebenezer Allard & Lois Adams,	Dec, 25, 1788
Daniel Tiffany & Phebe Rand,	Jan. 26, 1789
Timothy Prince, Jr., & Prudence Denison,	Feb. 26, 1789
Charles Merrit & Mehitabel Hewit,	March 26, 1789
Josiah Fassett & Nabby Stephens,	April 17, 1789
Adin Cady & Deborah Garner,	May 25, 1789

Dr. John Brewster & Ruth Avery,	June 4, 1789
William Fillmore & Theda Cady,	June 7, 1789
Stephen Frost & Molly Coggswell,	June 21, 1789
Dr. John Noyes & Mary Ann Williams,	Nov. 19, 1789
Stoel Geer & Lucy Hibbard,	Nov. 25, 1789
Asa Collar & Abigail Adams,	Nov. 26, 1789
David Denison & Anna Paine,	Dec. 3, 1789
John Wilson & Chloe Dains,	Dec. 17, 1789
Robert Letwedge & Sarah Cady,	Dec. 31, 1789
Samuel Ward & Anna Adams,	April 11, 1790
John Parish & Elizabeth Whitney,	May 30, 1790
Peleg Heath & Abigail Kelly,	July 4, 1790
Benjamin Herrick & Sarah Pierce,	Dec. 30, 1790
Charles Davenport & Mabel Wilson,	March 3, 1791
William Alworth & Mary Frost,	March 17, 1791
Zaccheus Amy & Nancy Malbone (negroes),	March 31, 1791
William Fassett & Susanna Litchfield,	July 28, 1791
Benjamin Gilbert & Betsey Pierce,	Nov. 20, 1791
Ebenezer Cady & Mary Butt,	Dec. 1, 1791
Joseph Gelbert & Molly Cleaveland,	Dec. 4, 1791
William May & Sarah Paine,	Dec. 15, 1791
John Mosely Clement & Eunice Tyler,	Jan. 1, 1792
Joab Fassett & Lighty Herrick,	Jan. 5, 1792
William Spaulding & Amanda Cady,	Oct. 7, 1792
Davis Cleaveland & Lydia Cady,	Nov. 25, 1792
Capt. Elisha Lord & Lucy Danielson,	Dec. 6, 1792
Samuel Sumner & Polly Tyler,	Jan. 23, 1793
Esquire Weld & Sally Allen,	March 24, 1793
Daniel Hubbard & Lena Butt,	April 11, 1793
Aaron Adams & Huldah Cogswell,	April 21, 1793
Amos Whiting & Mary Hubbard,	June 16, 1793
Daniel Searls & Polly Herrick,	July 4, 1793
Joseph White & Charlotte Harris,	Oct. 13, 1793
Amos Cady & Lydia Babcock,	Feb. 10, 1794
Capt. Roger Woliot Williams & Polly Scarborough,	
	March 6, 1794
Jonathan James & Deborah Cady,	June 12, 1794
Samuel Chapman & Polly Searls,	Sept. 28, 1794
Timothy Parsons & Eunice Chapman,	Sept. 28, 1794
Peter Pike & Rachel Dorrance,	Oct. 15, 1794

Samuel Clark & Wealthy Cady,	Nov. 9, 1794
Barker Wells & Anna Herrick,	Nov. 23, 1794
Samuel Robbins & Ruth Collar,	Nov. 27, 1794
Trobad Marcy & Hannah Williams,	Feb. 5, 1795
Nathan Merrit & Elizabeth Wheat,	Dec. 24, 1795
James McClellan & Eunice Eldridge,	Feb. 25, 1796
Ebenezer Hayward & Deborah Stephens,	March 7, 1796
Daniel Litchfield & Olive Pierce,	Sept. 22, 1796
Benjamin Weaver & Betsey Butt,	Dec. 15, 1796
Dr. James Tyler & Eliza Williams,	Dec. 21, 1796
Gardiner Crafts & Salome Williams,	Feb. 1, 1797
Barzillai Reed & Elizabeth Spaulding,	April 9, 1797
Pascal Paoli Tyler & Betsey Baker,	Sept. 17, 1797
Thomas Hewit & Serepta Williams,	Jan. 18, 1798
John Davison & Elizabeth Williams,	March 12, 1798
Benjamin Lewis & Cynthia Merrit,	March 23, 1798
John Dresser & Delight Gilbert,	March 29, 1798
Stephen Backus & Eunice Whitney,	Sept. 2, 1798
Joseph Scarborough, Jr., & Deborah Thayer,	Oct. 30, 1798
Elias Sharp & Nabby Cady,	Nov. 4, 1798
Calvin Baylis & Sally Cogswell,	Nov. 4, 1798
Elisha Chapman & Tirzah Baker,	March 27, 1799
John Crane & Abigail Faulkner,	Oct. 24, 1799
Capt. Elisha Lord & Sophia Whitney,	Nov. 28, 1799
James Maxwell & Phebe Bowman,	Dec. 18, 1799

HADDAM.

MIDDLESEX COUNTY.

Town incorporated 1668. Congregational Church organized 1700, though public worship began 1668. No records have been preserved prior to 1756, when Rev. Eleazer May took charge.

David Smith & Martha Brooks,	July 27, 1756
Stephen Johnson of Middletown & Sarah Ellis of Haddam,	Sept. 4, 1756
Solomon Bates & widow Hannah Spicer,	Sept. 21, 1756
Jeremiah Ray of Haddam & "Mehitable Hough or Huff,"	Nov. 8, 1756

Eleazer Lewis & Abigail Tyler,	May 26, 1757
Elisha Cone & Martha Bates,	May 26, 1757
William Barnes of New Fairfield & Deborah Griswold of Haddam, *spicer*	Jan., 1758
Daniel Bates & Lucy ~~Squier~~,	Jan., 1758
Joseph Dickinson & Lydia Brooks,	July, 1760
William Marcum & Abigail Willey,	June, 1760
Francis Clark & Else Smith,	Oct., 1761
Jeremiah Hubbard & Mary Wells,	Feb. 25, 1762
Ezra Shailor & Jerusha Brainerd,	Nov. 11, 1762
Joshua Brooks & Elizabeth Brainerd,	Nov. 16, 1762
Joshua Strong of Middletown & Hope Smith of Haddam,	June, 1763
Peter Rich of Middletown & Penelope Bonfoye of Haddam,	June 30, 1763
Nehemiah Brainerd & Sarah Brainerd, both of Haddam,	Nov. 15, 1763
Jonathan Boardman & widow Sarah Smith,	Jan. 3, 1764
James Stephens & Lydia Hazelton,	Jan. 5, 1764
Isaack Williams & Mary Arnold,	June, 1764
Jabez Brainerd, Jr., & Deborah Brainerd,	Sept. 13, 1764
Samuel Lee of Guilford & Agnis Dickinson of Haddam,	Nov. 7, 1764
Ezra Tyler & Prudence Richardson,	Dec. 27, 1764
Samuel Shailor & Elizabeth Butler,	Jan. 3, 1765
David Smith & Hannah Brainerd,	Feb. 21, 1765
Oliver Welles & Ann Brainerd,	May 2, 1765
Otis Southworth of Saybrook & Nancy Ray of Haddam,	June, 1765
David Halloburt of Middletown & D. Arnold of Haddam,	Sept. 3, 1765
Gersham Thairs of Middletown & Susannah Hazelton of Haddam,	Sept., 1765
Charles Sears & Sarah Clark,	Nov. 2, 1765
Joshua Brooks & Hannah Smith,	Dec. 8, 1765
Ephraim Baley & Mary Kelley,	Feb. 6, 1766
Samuel Hurlburt of Middletown & Jerusha Higgins of Haddam,	Oct., 1766
Bryant Brown of Killingly & Mary Dunbar of Haddam,	Nov., 1766

Jacob Catling of Harwington & Dorothy Griswold of Haddam,	Dec., 1766
Stephen Venters & Mary Church,	May 30, 1767
Jonathan Huntington of East Haddam & Silence Selden of Haddam,	Sept. 17, 1767
Jonathan Brooks & Hope Baley,	Oct. 1, 1767
William Smith & Esther Brainerd,	Oct. 13, 1767
Bazaleel Shailor & Susannah Bailey,	Dec., 1767
David Clark & Abigail Hazelton,	Feb. 14, 1768
Abner Ives of Wallingford & Anne Ferguson of Haddam,	May 11, 1768
Solomon Wakely & Rebeckah Hazelton,	Sept. 1, 1768
John Brooks & Esther Brainerd, both of Haddam,	Oct. 6, 1768
Samuell Lord of Lyme & Elizabeth Bates of Haddam,	Dec., 1768
James Merwin & Martha Smith,	Jan. 1, 1769
Samuell Spencer & Anne Brooks,	Jan. 10, 1769
Abner Spencer & Deborah Clark,	March 18, 1769
Capt. Lemuel Hull of Killingworth & widow Sarah Porter of Haddam,	April 5, 1769
Evan Thomas & Ann Smith,	April 13, 1769
James Knowles & Martha Smith,	May 25, 1769
Stephen Clark & Martha Cone,	June 5, 1769
Aaron Hubbard & Demaris Wakely,	June 7, 1769
Theodore Ray & Abigail Higgins,	Nov., 1769
Samuel Scovil & Ruth Chapman,	Jan., 1770
Samuel Church of East Haddam & Sarah Higgins of Haddam,	April, 1770
John Smith & widow Susannah White,	July, 1770
Jephthah Brainerd & Anne Fisk,	Dec. 20, 1770
Abraham Spencer & Drusilla Brainerd,	March 15, 1771
James Arnold & Freelove Wellman,	May 30, 1771
William Kelley & Catherine Stillman,	June 3, 1771
Samuel Spencer & Abigail Porter, both of Haddam,	June 26, 1771
Reuben Brooks & Abigail Cone,	July 11, 1771
Osias Bidwell of Hartford & widow Esther Brooks of Haddam,	Sept. 4, 1771
Shailor Hubbard & Anne Wakeley,	Oct. 10, 1771

Thomas Hubbard, Jr., & Sarah Boardman,   Nov. 6, 1771
Joseph Selden, Jr., & Susannah Smith,   Nov. 12, 1771
Capt. Abraham Brooks & widow Eleanor Smith, Nov. 14, 1771
John Selden of Middle Haddam & Jerusha Clarke
     of Haddam,   May, 1772
John Mahans (?) of Hartford & Huldah Brainerd of
     Haddam,   Oct., 1772
Solomon Tyler of Branford & Dorcas Fisk of
     Haddam,   Nov. 9, 1772
Nathaniel Brainerd of Haddam & Ann Johnson of
     Middletown,   Feb. 10, 1773
Joseph Post of Saybrook & Bethia Higgins of
     Haddam,   Feb. 11, 1773
Necho, servant of Lieut. Arnold, & Tamur, my ser-
     vant,   Feb. 21, 1773
Sylvanus Hull of Durham & Phebe Smith of
     Haddam,   March, 1773
William Heskell & Martha Porter,   May, 1773
James Clark & Mary White,   May, 1773
Justus Augur & Rhoda Allen,   May, 1773
Daniel Brainerd & Susannah Clarke,   June, 1773
Asa Wakeley & Elisabeth Thomas, both of Had-
     dam,   August, 1773
Gideon Baley, Jr., & Lydia Spencer,   Sept. 6, 1773
——— Richardson of East Haddam & Sarah
     Towner of Haddam,   August, 1773
Jonathan Clarke & Ruth Clarke,   Oct., 1773
James Thomas & Jerusha Clarke,   Oct., 1773
Roger Thomas & Sarah Comstock,   Oct., 1773
Amos Baley of Haddam & Ruth Gibbs of Chat-
     ham,   Nov., 1773
Isaach Johnson of Middletown & Anne Towner of
     Haddam,   Dec. 9, 1773
Henry Rockwell of Middletown & Desire Cone of
     Haddam,   Dec. 14, 1773
Jonathan Chapman & Mary Smith,   Dec. 30, 1773
William Gladden & Ama Hotchkiss,   Dec. 31, 1773
Beniah Cone & Ann Thomas,   Jan. 4, 1774
Joshua Gates, Jr., of East Haddam & Eunice Fuller
     of Haddam,   Feb., 1774

Joseph Burr & Mary Knowles,	April, 1774
Joshua Smith & Abigail Knowles, both of Haddam,	April, 1774
William Brainerd & Lydia Smith,	May, 1774
Whitmore Crook & Phebe Clarke,	August, 1774
Abijah Fuller & Hannah Spencer,	August, 1774
Lewis Smith & Anne Hubbard,	Oct., 1774
Luther Boardman & Esther Smith,	Oct., 1774
Obadiah Dickinson & Susannah Knowles,	Oct., 1774
Stephen Tryon of Middletown & Prudence Baley of Haddam,	Nov. 17, 1774
Stephen Smith & Esther Church,	Nov. 17, 1774
David Hubbard & Hannah Clarke,	May 25, 1775
Abner Tibbels & Elisabeth Knowles,	July, 1775
Joshua Symons & Helen Stillman,	Nov. 16, 1775
Benjamin Pelton of Guilford & Hannah Snow of Haddam,	Dec. 9, 1775
Richard Bonfoye & widow Rebeckah Treadwell,	Dec. 21, 1775
Thomas Daniels of East Haddam & Lydia Kelsy,	Dec. 21, 1775
David Arnold & Jerusha Thomas,	Feb., 1776
Samuel Clark & Sussannah Thomas,	Feb., 1776
Jesse Brainerd & Mary Thomas,	May 23, 1776
Sylvenus Smith & Eunice Baley,	July, 1776
Porter Brooks & Elisabeth Clarke,	Sept., 1776
Henry Thomas & Jemima Baley,	Oct., 1776
John Brainerd & Hanah Hubbard,	Dec. 5, 1776
John Scovil & Elisabeth Spencer,	Jan. 2, 1777
Elias Cone & Ruth Crook,	March, 1777
Zachariah Brainerd & Dorothy Thomas,	May 6, 1777
David Clarke & Patience Kelley,	May, 1777
Josiah Brainerd & Abigail Lewis,	June 4, 1777
Arnold Hazelton & Mindwell Brainerd,	August, 1777
Cornelius Higgins, Jr., & Esther Kelsey,	Sept. 23, 1777
Stephen Spencer & Eunice Augur,	Oct. 16, 1777
John Smith, Jr., & Anne Clarke of Haddam,	Oct., 1777
Samuel Scovil & widow Mary Ventres,	Jan. 8, 1778
Nathan Chase of Yarmoth & Mary Treadwell of Haddam,	Jan., 1778
Joseph Crook & Esther Clarke,	Feb., 1778

Cesar Black & Peg (Negro), July, 1778
Doctor Eleazer Woodruff & widow Abigail Spencer,
                                        July 27, 1778
Daniel Chapman of East Haddam & Esther Shailor
    of Haddam, Nov. 18, 1778
Daniel Clark & widow Martha Ray, Dec., 1778
Cephas Selden & Martha Brainerd, Dec., 1778
Elias Spencer & Abigail Sexton, Dec. 30, 1778
Sylvenus Clarke & Dorothy Smith, May 6, 1779
Thomas Bailey & Ama Kelley, May 19, 1779
Joseph Taylor & Elisabeth Hotchkiss, June 1, 1779
Stephen Tibbels & Martha Burr, August, 1779
Reuben Buel of Killingworth & widow Anne
    Porter, Oct., 1779
John Parmely of Killingworth & Dorothy Scovil, Dec., 1779
Charles Williams of East Haddam & Susanah Shailor
    of Haddam, March 2, 1780
James Treadwell & Mary Spencer, April, 1780
Abraham Brooks & Abigail Clarke, May 4, 1780
Frederick Smith & Sarah Brainerd, July, 1780
Ebenezer Sage of Middletown & Diana Bailey, Sept., 1780
Eliphalet Clarke & Lydia Thomas, Oct. 1780
James Surtliff & Mehitable Clarke, Nov., 1780
William Clarke & Anne Johnson, Nov., 1780
David Thomas & Penelope Bonfoye, Dec., 1780
—— Johnson & Susannah Spencer, Jan., 1781
William Clarke & Christian Baley, March, 1781
Eliphalet Lester of Saybrook & Mary Smith of
    Haddam, May 1, 1781
Joseph Stillman of Weathersfield & Huldah Mahans
    of Haddam, Sept., 1781
Thomas Shailor, Jr., & widow Ann Brainerd, Nov., 1781
Seth Hand of Killingworth & Thankfull Ray of
    Haddam, Dec., 1781
John Hubbard of Middletown & Phebe Brainerd
    of Haddam, Jan., 1782
John Church & widow Dorothy Brainerd, March, 1782
William Brainerd & Susannah Tyler, March, 1782
John Dickinson & Dorothy Scovil, Nov., 1782
Hezekiah Whitmore & Elisabeth Brooks, July, 1782

William Bailey, Jr., & Ruth Thomas,   June, 1782
John Bailey & Mary Smith,   July, 1783
Aurunah Hubbard & Rebekeh Bates,   July, 1783
David Brooks of Middletown & Lucretia Sears of
    Haddam,   May, 1783
Josiah Carey of Middle Haddam & Lydia Clarke, Oct., 1783
Nathaniel Hazelton & Sarah Smith,   Nov., 1783
Reuben Cone & Marger Childs,   Dec., 1783
Abraham Spencer & Sarah Hubbard,   Dec., 1783
Jonathan Russel & Molly Ray,   Dec. 30, 1783
Calvin Hubbard & Sarah Knowles,   Jan., 1784
Edward Selden & my daughter Sibbil May,   Jan., 1784
John Willcox & Lois Augur,   Feb., 1784
Simon Hazelton & Jedidah Smith,   July, 1784
David Johnson of Middletown & Martha Pelton,   Aug., 1784
Calvin Brooks & Temperance Hubbard,   Aug., 1784
Walker Knowles & Elisabeth Wells,   Aug., 1784
Abraham Tyler, Jr., & Hannah Stephens,   Sept., 1784
Rev Mr. David Selden & *Cynthia* May,   1784
—— Brainard & Anner Burr,   1784
—— ——y & Martha Clarke,   1784
*Joh*n Ventrous & Hannah Ray,   1784
—— Johnson, Jr., & Phebe Burr,   1784
(Ste)phen Bailey, Jr., & Lydia *Freeman*   1784
——m Barnes of Middletown & —— —— of
    Haddam,   1785
*Noad*iah Cone & Elisabeth Clarke,   1785
Sylvester Child & Mary Cone,   1785
——than Fuller & my daughter Anne,   1785
Calvin Shailor & Sarah Clarke,   1785
James Smith & Elizabeth, *Ray (?)*   June, 1785
Abijah Bailey & widow Cone,   Nov., 1785
Joseph Arnold & widow Prudence Tyler,   Jan., 1786
Richard Knowles & Hepsibah Wells,   1786
Nathaniel Tyler, Jr., & widow [Hannah (Bushnell)]
    Towner,   1786
James Childs, Jr., & Prudence Brainerd,   April, 1786
William Nichols & Sarah Shailor,   1786
Richard Skinner & Martha Bailey,   June, 1786
Frederick Brainerd & Anne Brainerd,   Oct., 1786

Leaf of original record so torn that the dates between Sept.,
    1784, and June, 1785, are uncertain.

Adnah Clarke & Thankfull Bailey, Dec., 1786
Seymour Kelsey & Sarah Augur, Jan., 1787
Joseph Dickinson & Tammy Shailor, Feb., 1787
Levi Ray & Susanah Arnold, April, 1787
Amos Cook & Jane Bailey, 1787
Aaron ——— & Sarah Chapman of Haddam, April, 1787
James Pelton & ——— ——— of Haddam, May, 1787
Josiah Prior of (Middletown?) & Sussanah Smith of
    Haddam, Aug., 1787
James Smith & ——— Arnold, Nov., 1787
Humphry Treadwell & Hannah Thomas, Dec., 1787
Timothy Hubbard, Jr., & Miss ——— Thomas, Dec., 1787
Thomas Bailey & ——— Smith, Jan., 1788
——— Lane of Killingworth & Elisabeth Porter of
    Haddam, Jan., 1788
Robert Smith & Susannah Kelley, Jan., 1788
Benjamin Johnson & Else Smith, April, 1788
David Spencer & Damaris Brainerd, May, 1788
Cornelius Higgins, Esqr., & widow Mary Smith, Sept., 1788
James Tyler & Esther Dickinson, Dec., 1788
Aaron Thomas, Jr., & Martha Smith, Oct., 1789
Jonathan Hubbard & Sally Thomas, Nov., 1789
Curtis Smith & Arsenah Brainerd, Jan., 1789
Amasa Pettibone & Mary Augur, Jan. (?), 1789
James Bates & Mary Ventrees, 1789
James Spencer & Miss ——— Clarke, the ———
    of Stephen Clarke, 1789
Benjamin Stocking & Dimmis Shailor, August, 1789
My son John May & Dolly Arnold, Nov. 8, 1789
James Brooks & Caroline Smith, Dec., 1789
Joseph Augur & Samuel Tyler's daughter (Esther),
    Jan., 1790
Joseph Tyler, Jr., & Allira Smith, Jan., 1790
Nathan Tyler, Jr., & one of Ezra Shailor's daughters.
    (Her name was Esther), Feb., 1790
Capt. Edmond Porter & widow Mary Smith, Feb., 1790
James Brainerd & Edetha Hubbard, 1790
Ira Shailor & Anne Shailor, 1790
Joshua Knowles & Concurrence Porter, 1790
Gideon Brainerd, Jr., & Hepsibah Hubbard, 1790

Mr. Jesse Townsend of Andover & my daughter Anne,

Oct., 1790

Dan Dickinson & Pruda Augur,   1791

Shailor ——— & Miss ——— Ventres,   1792

Stephen Sears & *Phebe* Knowles,   Jan., 1793

William Wells & Prudence May,   Dec. 7, 1794

Huntington May & Clara Brainerd,   June 7, 1795

Eleazur Augur & Abigail Church,   April, 1795

David Rich & *Freelove* Brooks,   March, 1795

Mr. Williams of Middletown & Clara Shailor,   Sept., 1795

Russel Shailor & Anne Wells,   Sept., 1795

Shailor, son of Asa Shailor, & Miss Shailor, daugh-
    ter of Hez. Shailor,   1797

~~Robert Smith & Sarah Kelly,~~   ~~1797~~

Asher Smith & Betsey Bidwell,   1797

Ephraim Sawyer & Jabith Church,   1797

Stephen Dickinson & Susana Tyler,   1797

Heber Brainerd & Martha Tyler,   1796

Robert Smith & Sally Kelly,   *Feb.,* 1798

Jonathan Tyler & Rachael Porter,   March, 1798

David Smith & Jerusha Hubbard,   June, 1798

Joseph Clark & Ruae Shailor. (Ruea Shailor's hus-
    band was Warren Clark, son of Joseph),   Oct., 179–

Col. John Wells of Row & my daughter Elisabeth May,

Jan. 13, 1799

Simon Smith & Huldah Brainerd,   March, 1799

The Second parish in Haddam was organized at Haddam Neck, 1740.

NORTH STONINGTON,

NEW LONDON COUNTY.

Town was taken from Stonington in 1807. The Congregational Church was organized in 1727, being then the second church of Stonington. Records complete to 1781.

William Brand & Elizabeth Davis,	Sept. 6, 1733
David Tracy & Abigail Wallbridge,	Sept. 27, 1733
Jephthah Hewit & Mary York,	Jan. 31, 1734
Alexander Pattison & Mary Coats,	August 2, 1734
Theophilus Fitch & Grace Grant,	Oct. 2, 1734
Daniel Butler & Hannah Bennit,	Nov. 28, 1734
Capt. Christopher Avery & widow Esther Prentice,	Jan. 1, 1735
Elias Palmer & Mary Holmes,	Feb. 26, 1735
Henry Rowland & Irene Palmer,	March 27, 1735
Nathan Palmer & Phebe Billings,	April 21, 1735
Edmund Fanning & Hopestill Coats,	June 11, 1735
Ebenezer Brewster & Susanna Smith,	August 27, 1735
Nathaniel Holdridge & Lydia Holdridge,	Oct. 9, 1735
Joseph Hayward & Freelove Rhodes,	Oct. 27, 1735
Joseph Stanton & Anna Wheeler,	Nov. 6, 1735
Samuel Stockwell & Keziah Hewit,	Nov. 18, 1735
Clement Neff & Patience Brown,	Dec. 17, 1735
John Davison & Elizabeth Babcock,	Feb. 5, 1736
Joseph Hilliard & Freelove Minor,	Feb. 25, 1736
James Rennalls & Rebecca Burdick,	March 18, 1736
John Meeks & Mary Stevens,	August 25, 1736
Josias Hill, Jr., & Freelove Bennet,	Nov. 24, 1736
William Satterly & Mary Powers,	Dec. 1, 1736
Jonathan Shepherd & Love Palmer,	Dec. 23, 1736
Edward Hall & Joanna Chapman,	Jan. 12, 1737
Nathaniel Fellows & Hopestill Holdridge,	March 2, 1737
William Fanning & Anna Minor,	March 17, 1737
Simon Spaldin & Anna Billings,	June 1, 1737
Isaac Wheeler & Mary Wheeler,	June 2, 1737
Elias Babcock & Anna Plumbe,	Nov. 10, 1737
Thomas York, Jr., & Deborah Brown,	Nov. 10, 1737
Zebediah Andros & Elizabeth Swan,	Dec. 19, 1737
Samuel Mason & Mary Stanton,	Jan. 9, 1738

Ebenezer Worden & Burridel Butten,	Jan. 12, 1738
Thomas Holdridge & Mary Birch,	Jan. 24, 1738
Zecharia & Joanna (Indians),	Jan. 26, 1738
Allyne Breed & Anna Cole,	Feb. 1, 1738
Isaac Worden & Sarah Wilcocks,	May 3, 1738
Ichabod Palmeter & Thankfull Bennit,	May 18, 1738
Samuel Plumbe & Grace Babcock,	August 16, 1738
Aaron Cade & Anna Palmer,	Nov. 8, 1738
Ebenezer Cade & Prudence Palmer,	Nov. 8, 1738
Joseph Devell & Sarah Williams,	Dec. 13, 1738
Isaiah Babcock & Elizabeth Plumbe,	Dec. 25, 1738
Moses Start & Elizabeth Holdridge,	Dec. 27, 1738
William Lamphear & Abigail Butten,	Jan. 8, 1739
Jonathan Dye & Esther Lamphear,	Jan. 30, 1739
Joseph Eliot & Elizabeth Pendleton,	June 26, 1739
Nathaniel Williams & Amy Hewit,	July 3, 1739
George Hakes & Joanna Jones,	Nov. 14, 1739
William Chapman & Abigail Plumbe,	Jan. 31, 1740
Oliver Babcock & Anna Avery,	March 6, 1740
Thomas Partelow & Deborah Wells,	March 13, 1740
John Fanning & Abigail Minor,	April 14, 1740
Nathaniel Hewit & Rebecca Grant,	April 24, 1740
Richardson Avery & Sarah Plumbe,	Nov. 3, 1740
Thomas Holmes & Margarett Frink,	Nov. 12, 1740
Asa Swan & Marvin Holmes,	Nov. 19, 1740
William Stewart, Jr., & Elizabeth Stevens,	Dec. 4, 1740
Charles Minor & Mary Wheeler,	Dec. 9, 1740
Phinehas Stanton & Elizabeth Stanton,	Jan. 7, 1741
Timothy Savage & Dorothy Wilcocks,	March 19, 1741
Jedediah Rennals & Abigail Crandel,	June 17, 1741
Thomas Shaw, Jr., & Prudence Palmer,	Sept. 14, 1741
William Mannum & Hannah (Indians),	Sept. 23, 1741
Thomas Main, Jr., & Mary Pendleton,	Feb. 3, 1742
Jeremiah Main & Thankfull Brown,	April 27, 1742
John Chapman & widow Mary Boardman,	April 28, 1742
Benjamin Worden & Thankfull Edwards,	August 19, 1742
Hezekiah Coats & Freelove Frink,	Sept. 22, 1742
William Coats, Jr., & Austice Gray,	Sept. 28, 1742
Jonathan Brown of Westerly & Elizabeth Bur-roughs,	Sept. 30, 1742

Nathan Crarey & Dorothy Wheeler,	Nov. 2, 1742
Ben Adam Denisen & Anna Swan,	Nov. 3, 1742
Eleazer Brown of Westerly & Sarah Die,	Nov 10, 1742
Samuel Chapman & Mercy Eldridge,	Jan. 19, 1743
Jedediah Stevens & Mary Rothbone,	April 4, 1743
William Swan & Anne Smith,	April 14, 1743
John York & Ann Brown,	Sept. 13, 1743
Isaac Shepherd & Dorothy Prentice,	Nov. 23, 1743
Ephraim Smith & Lucy Stevens,	Jan. 3, 1744
David Tracy, Jr., & Unice Ellis,	April 18, 1744
John Noyes, Jr., & Marcy Breed,	May 30, 1744
Benjamin Blodgett & Mary Satterly,	July 3, 1744
Volentine Rothbone & Tabitha Brown,	August 1, 1744
James Patridge & Thankfull Stevens,	Dec. 24, 1744
Noah Grant & Hannah Minor,	Jan. 25, 1745
Jabez Duce (or Duee) & Hannah Brown,	March 21, 1745
Humphrey Avery, Jr., & Mary Baldwin,	June 19, 1745
Timothy Babcock & Lois Billings,	July 1, 1745
Jonathan Palmer & Prudence Holms,	Sept. 12, 1745
Simeon Benjamons & widow Anna Starkweather,	Jan. 22, 1746
James Thompson & Mary Dixon,	Feb. 19, 1746
Joseph Williams & Eunice Wheeler,	Feb. 20, 1746
Israel Standish & Content Ellis,	March 5, 1746
John Starkweather, Jr., & Jerusha Smith,	March 24, 1746
Joseph Page, Jr., & Mary Hewit,	May 1, 1746
William Herrick & Mercy Palmer,	May 15, 1746
Jonathan Dennison & Martha Williams,	June 5, 1746
Capt. Daniel Brown & widow Prudence Chesboro,	August 21, 1746
Joshua Stoddard & Rachel Pabodie,	Sept. 8, 1746
Rufus Hewitt & Abigail Frink,	Nov. 5, 1746
Bennajah Brumbley & Temperance Pollard,	Dec. 22, 1746
Nathaniel Worden & Anna Palmeter,	Jan. 8, 1747
John Butler & Mary Brown,	Feb. 11, 1747
Bill York & Ruth Main,	Feb. 18, 1747
Thomas Keeples & Jane Dixon,	March 25, 1747
John Gallup of Voluntown & Hannah Frink,	April 9, 1747
Caleb Rhodes & Elizabeth Starkweather,	Sept. 24, 1747
Daniel Andras & Temperance Holmes,	Oct. 7, 1747

Benjamin Garret & Irene (Indians),   Nov. 2, 1747
Garsham Palmer & Dorothy Brown,   Nov. 5, 1747
John Dennison & Martha Wheeler,   Jan. 13, 1748
Simon Fobes & Thankful Ellis,   March 24, 1748
Rogger Sterry & Abigail Holmes,   May 4, 1748
Thomas Dickinson & Mary Crandel of Westerly,
                                             May 20, 1748
Joshua Stanton & Hannah Randal,   Nov. 10, 1748
James Danielson of Lebanon & widow Irene Fish,
                                             Nov. 14, 1748
Robert Jemisen of Voluntown & Nancy Dixon, Nov. 24, 1748
John Jemisen & Dorothy Pendleton of Westerly, Dec. 20, 1748
Thomas Shaw & widow Sarah Miner,   Jan. 4, 1749
Joseph Safford of Preston & Martha Coates,   Jan. 11, 1749
Henry Jones & Unice Miner,   Jan. 19, 1749
Walter Warden & Anna Edwards,   Feb. 14, 1749
Elkanah Hewit, Jr., & Elizabeth Miner,   Oct. 11, 1749
John Richmond & Priscilla Palmer,   Dec. 28, 1749
John Randal, Jr., & Lucy Brown,   May 6, 1750
Uriah Hosmore of Norwich & Abigail Coates,
                                             August 30, 1750
Caleb Greene of Westerly & Lucy Grant of Stoning-
    ton,   Nov. 7, 1750
Benjamin Birch & Anna Udall,   Nov. 8, 1750
John Frink & Anna Pendleton,   Nov. 22, 1750
William Avery, Jr., & widow Abigail Williams, Dec. 13, 1750
Paul Wheeler & Lucy Swan,   May 1, 1751
Constant Searle & Hannah Miner,   May 16, 1751
George Babcock, Jr., & Meheteble Wheeler,   June 26, 1751
George Bentley, Jr., of Westerly & Amy Carter,
                                             June 27, 1751
Thomas Howse & widow Penelope Cadee of Hebron,
                                             June 27, 1751
Shepherd Wheeler & Hannah Hewit,   Oct. 18, 1751
Ichabod Pendleton & Esther Ayer,   Dec. 15, 1751
Jedediah Brown & Anna Holmes,   Dec. 19, 1751
Samuel Fish of Stonington & Hannah Palmer, Jan. 22, 1752
John Quiumps & Joanna Shawn (Indians),   Feb. 17, 1752
Jeremiah Wheeler & widow Anna Wheeler, March 11, 1752
William Stewart & Hannah Palmer,   April 29, 1752

Samuel Miner, Jr., & Abigail Miner, July 14, 1752
Thomas Robinson & widow Penelope Minick, July 21, 1752
John Palmeter of Westerly & Deborah Butten of
    Stonington, Nov. 9, 1752
Cæsar (mulatto) & widow Patience (Indian), Nov. 9, 1752
John Burdick & Sibbil Cheseborough, Nov. 23, 1752
Nathan Wilcocks & Tabitha Provier (?), Jan. 25, 1753
John Cavarley of Colchester & Mary Swan of Ston-
    ington, March 15, 1753
Samuel Brown & Sarah Randal, March 29, 1753
John Swan, Jr., & Mary Prentice, May 17, 1753
Tully ——— (negro) & Rose ——— (negro), June 29, 1753
George Hall of Charlestown & widow Jean Larkin
    of Westerly, Oct. 4, 1753
William Palmer, Jr., & Phebe Darrow, Nov. 8, 1753
David Miner & widow Bethiah Billings, Nov. 14, 1753
Simon Miner, Jr., & Anna Hewit, Nov. 15, 1753
Robert Swan & Abigail Randal, Jan. 31, 1754
Joshua Vose of Westerly & Grace Coates, Feb. 21, 1754
Eleazer Williams & Abigail Prentice, March 14, 1754
Solomon & Bathsheba (Indians), July 21, 1754
Abel Marsh of Lebanon & Dorothy Udale, Dec. 26, 1754
Thomas Larrison & Mary Wilcocks, Feb. 4, 1755
Henry Miner & Desire Brown, Feb. 20, 1755
Dr. Benjamin Blodgett & Abigail Swan, March 20, 1755
Joshua & Betty (Indians), April 13, 1755
Collins York & Eunice Grant, May 29, 1755
Capt. Joseph Hewit & widow Mehitabel Swan, June 4, 1755
Nathaniel Niles & Abigail Bentley, Sept. 21, 1755
Isaac Cammel (Cammet) (?) of Voluntown & Ann
    Dixon of Stonington, Dec. 11, 1755
Joseph Babcock, Jr., & Mary Bentley, Dec. 28, 1755
Charles Wheeler & Martha Williams, Feb. 26, 1756
William Robinson of Westerly & Avis Burdick of
    Stonington, March 18, 1756
Sylvester Walworth of Groton & Sarah Holmes of
    Stonington, April 8, 1756
Samuel Fitch & Priscilla Hillard, April 15, 1756
Joseph Page & Lucy Wheeler, May 9, 1756
Samuel Frink & Prudence Wilcocks, July 27, 1756

McK. Withee or Mr. S. Withee of Preston & Lydia
   Griffith of Stonington,   Nov. 17, 1756
John Cammel of Voluntown & Rebecca Philips,
                         Nov. 25, 1756
Stephen Maxson of Westerly & Martha Steward
   of Stonington,   Jan. 19, 1757
John Avery & Anna Miner,   Feb. 9, 1757
Thomas Miner & Desire Denison,   Feb. 10, 1757
Ichabod Brown, Jr., & Thankful Baldwin, March 17, 1757
Elias Palmer & Esther Randal,   April 28, 1757
Samuel Parker of Groton & Freelove Satterly of
   Stonington,   June 2, 1757
Joseph Moxley of Stonington & Elizabeth Smith
   of Groton,   June 2, 1757
Theophilus Fitch & Hannah Stevens,   Nov. 9, 1757
Dr. Charles Phelps & Hannah Denison, Nov. 10, 1757
Christopher Palmer, Jr., & Deborah Brown, Jan. 19, 1758
Elisha Denison & Keturah Miner,   Feb. 23, 1758
Elisha Satterley & Molly Geer,   March 9, 1758
Oliver Bentley & Hannah Wilcocks, March 16, 1758
Stephen Brown & Abigail Palmer,   Nov. 2, 1758
John Noyes of New Haven & Mary Fish, Nov. 16, 1758
Jesse Swan & Priscilla Hewit,   Nov. 19, 1758
Jesse Denison & Mary Denison,   Jan. 24, 1759
Simeon Miner, Jr., & Mary Owen of Groton, Feb. 1, 1759
Amos Frink & Mary Fitch,   Feb. 14, 1759
Samuel Prentice & Phebe Billings,   Feb. 15, 1759
Denison Palmer & Marvin Palmer,   July 10, 1759
Nathan McKoon of Hopkinton & Abigail Hall of
   Stonington,   Oct. 11, 1759
Christopher Gardner of South Kingston & Mercy
   Wheeler of Stonington,   Jan. 23, 1760
Sanford Billing & Lucy Geer,   Jan. 24, 1760
Dorus Champlin & Caroline Garrett (Indians), May 14, 1759
Peter ——— & Esther Tuggwiss (Indians), March 10, 1757
Joseph Peters & widow Patience Niles, May 4, 1758
Abel Lamphear of Westerly & Rebecca Dye of
   Stonington,   Feb. 6, 1760
David Palmer & Grace Plumbe,   April 24, 1760
Lemuel Darrow of Groton & Martha Palmer, July 17, 1760

Lieut. Jonathan Wells of Hopkinton & widow
    Rebecca Claggett,   Nov. 14, 1760
Joseph Frink & Content Hewit,   Dec. 16, 1760
William Walworth of Groton & Sarah Grant, Dec. 25, 1760
James Kinne, Jr., & Hannah Hewit,   Jan. 15, 1761
Remington Sears of Westerly & Esther Dise of
    Stonington,   Feb. 1, 1761
Dr. Jno. Bartlett of Lebanon & Lucretia Steward,
                          March 18, 1761
Isaac Miner & Lydia Pabodie,   May 7, 1761
William Gallop & Lucy Dennison,   July 2, 1761
Thomas Pabodie & Ruth Babcock,   August 6, 1761
Elijah Babcock & Sarah Brown,   Nov. 5, 1761
David McKoon of Hopkinton & Thankful Button
    of Stonington,   Nov. 26, 1761
Hubbart Burrows, Jr., & Priscilla Baldwin,   Dec. 24, 1761
Clement Miner, Jr., & Mary Wheeler,   Dec. 24, 1761
Ensign William Denison & Susanna Swan,   Feb. 25, 1762
Capt. Jno. Denison & widow Sarah Billing,   March 3, 1762
Rozzel Smith of Colchester & Abigail Holmes,
                          March 11, 1762
Reuben Hewit & Hannah Hakes,   May 6, 1762
Johnson Woyboy & Prudence Ball (Indians),   May 20, 1760
Nathan Abbot of Pomfret & Hephsibah Brown,
                         Nov. 24, 1762
Warner Fellows & Eunice Hall,   Nov. 25, 1762
Samuel Pabodie & Abigail Breed,   Nov. 17, 1762
Ephraim Wheeler & Lucy Lamb,   Dec. 2, 1762
Abel Garrington & Rebecca Keezer,   Dec. 9, 1762
Capt. Daniel Stanton of Charlestown & Prudence
    Treat of Preston,   Dec. 10, 1762
John Safford & Sarah Plumbe,   Dec. 23, 1762
Benjamin Douglass of New Haven & Rebecca
    Fish,   Jan. 24, 1763
Joseph Noyes & Prudence Denison,   Jan. 27, 1763
Richard Hakes & Mary Babcock,   Aug. 11, 1763
Ethel Palmer & Elizabeth Williams,   Dec. 22, 1763
Azariah Palmer & Mary Darrow,   Jan. 26, 1764
Thomas Swan & Amy Denison,   Feb. 2, 1764
Bennedick Ecclestone & Abigail Woodward,   Feb. 8, 1764

Samuel Jones & widow Mary Avery,   Feb. 9, 1764
Benjamin Grey of Groton & Temperance Baxter,
    April 5, 1764
John James & Esther Denison,   April 26, 1764
Edward Eells & Mercy Denison,   May 10, 1764
Nathan Brown & Lois Miner,   May 17, 1764
Nathan Babcock & Elizabeth Brown,   May 20, 1764
Daniel Brewster of Norwich & Eliz. Swan,   Oct. 4, 1764
Jno. Watson of South Kingston & Desire Wheeler,
    Oct. 17, 1764
Wm. Williams, Jr., & Eunice Prentice,   Oct. 25, 1764
Elisha Williams & widow Eunice Baldwin,   Nov. 1, 1764
Clark Reynolds of Hopkinton & Hannah Miner,
    Dec. 20, 1764
Daniel Prentice & Mary Billing,   Jan. 10, 1765
Charles Miner, Jr., & Eunice Holmes,   Jan 10, 1765
Thomas Wheeler & Lucy Prentice,   Jan. 17, 1765
Elijah Utley & Phebe Hillard,   Feb. 17, 1765
Samuel Fellows & Mary Udal,   March 7, 1765
Samuel Capron of Norwich & Eunice Miner,   May 2, 1765
Elias Lewis of Westerly & Prudence Hewit, August 25, 1765
Isaac Wheeler Stanton & Ruth Ayer,   Sept. 19, 1765
John Williams, 3d, & Keturah Randal,   Sept. 29, 1765
Nathan Randal, Jr., & Burridel Palmer,   Dec. 5, 1765
Christopher Brown & Margaret Holmes,   Dec. 25, 1765
Rufus Brown & Keziah Billings,   Dec. 26, 1765
Isaac Wheeler & Ruth Swan,   Dec. 31, 1765
Elijah Jones & Abigail Avery,   March 23, 1766
William Sisson & Mercy Noyes,   April 10, 1766
Moses Quiumps & Prudence Panheag (Indians),
    April 17, 1765
Jack Shaw & Sarah Togus (mulattos),   Dec. 25, 1765
Ephraim Fellows, Jr., & Rhoda Smith,   April 24, 1766
Robert Kinne & Abigail Brown,   May 6, 1766
Collings Brown & Hannah Pendleton,   Nov. 16, 1766
James Trowbridge & Francis Darrow,   Dec. 4, 1766
Phinehas Munsel & Eunice Frink,   Dec. 11, 1766
Benjamin Miner of New London & Ann Champlin,
    Dec. 24, 1766
Asa Brown & Deborah Grant,   Feb. 12, 1767

Benjamin Chester & Hannah Pabodie,	April 16, 1767
William Palmer & Mary Brown,	May 31, 1767
John Brown & Mary Holmes,	July 2, 1767
Christopher Edwards & Amy Hall,	Nov. 18, 1767
Capt. John Randal & Thankful Swan,	August 23, 1767
Joseph Holmes & Martha Wheeler,	Nov. 19, 1767
John Udall & Ann Stephens,	Jan. 17, 1768
Peleg Hart & Esther Shealy,	March 12, 1769
Elijah Hewit & Olive Hakes,	Dec. 3, 1769
Capt. Titus Hurlburt & widow Mercy Wheeler,	Feb. 17, 1770
Samuel Stanton & Abigail Ayer,	March 22, 1770
Alexander Stewart of Voluntown & Thankful Denison,	April 5, 1770
Isaiah Uncas (Mohegan Sachem) & Mary Sowop (Indian),	Nov. 30, 1769
John Coats & Elizabeth Stewart,	Nov. 29, 1770
Joseph Worden & Rachel Grant,	Dec. 6, 1770
Samuel Plumbe, Jr., & Grace Babcock,	Feb. 28, 1771
James Geer of Groton & Lucy Hewit,	March 31, 1771
Joseph Chapman & Prudence Lewis,	April 18, 1771
Noah Grant & Mary Palmer,	August 11, 1771
Oliver Udal & Austice Coats,	Nov. 10, 1771
Christopher Clark & Elizabeth Plumbe,	Dec. 18, 1771
Henry Hewit & Phebe Prentice,	Jan. 2, 1772
George Denison & Theody Brown,	Jan. 9, 1772
John Baldwin & Sarah Denison,	Jan. 23, 1772
Asher Brewster & Elizabeth Prentice,	Feb. 5, 1772
Hosea Wheeler & Bridget Grant,	Feb. 20, 1772
William Hewit & Sarah Coye,	March 1, 1772
James Pabodie & Phebe Gray,	March 8, 1772
Jabez Swan & Mehetabel Wheeler,	June 11, 1772
Oliver Wilcocks & Mary Stewart,	July 2, 1772
Isaiah Whipple & Eunice Hewit,	Nov. 26, 1772
Jedediah Holmes & Elizabeth Frink,	Dec. 10, 1772
Nehemiah Williams, 3d, & Mary Noyes,	April 11, 1773
Henry Stevens, 3d, of Canaan & Anna Babcock,	June 17, 1773
Dettrick Hewit & Elizabeth Searle,	July 11, 1773
Benjamin Diggins & Patience Hallet,	June 13, 1773
William Searle & Philene Frink,	Oct. 17, 1773

5

Isaac Denison & Eunice Williams,	Nov. 10, 1773
William Cheseborough, 2d, & Esther Williams,	Feb. 3, 1774
James Worden & Zeruiah Hewit,	Feb. 10, 1774
Paul Woodbridge of Groton & Sarah Ayer,	Feb. 16, 1774
George Palmer & Anne Denison,	April 17, 1774
Nathaniel Marsh of Plainfield & Grace Prentice,	
	June 1, 1774
William Stewart & Anner Coats,	Sept. 25, 1774
Joseph Plumbe & Deborah Miner,	Dec. 6, 1774
John Daboll of Groton & Sarah Miner,	Dec. 25, 1774
Edward Swan & Mehetebel Owen,	Feb. 16, 1775
Nathan Crary, Jr., of Groton & Keturah Ayer,	March 2, 1775
Amos Hewit & Anna Miner,	March 19, 1775
Isaac Brown & Esther Barrington,	March 30, 1775
Samuel Shaw & Zervia Herrick,	April 16, 1775
Joseph Randal of Voluntown & Sabre Hewit,	April 20, 1775
Col. Gold Silleck Silliman of Fairfield & widow	
Mary Noyes of New Haven,	May 24, 1775
John Randall, Jr., & Mary Swan,	Nov. 9, 1775
Joshua Prentice & widow Eliz. Stanton,	Jan. 14, 1776
Jedediah Leeds of Groton & Anna Hewit,	Feb. 25, 1776
Asa Palmer & Lois Stanton,	March 10, 1776
Elijah Barns of Preston & Lydia Hewit,	April 4, 1776
Doctor Benjamin Shearman of Swansy & Anna Swan,	
	March 16, 1776
Nathaniel Sunsamen & Sarah Sawass,	April 24, 1770
Ebenezer Williams & Prudence Fellows,	Sept. 5, 1776
Elijah Whipple & Rebecca Denison,	Jan. 16, 1777
Jedediah Brown, Jr., & Sarah Wheeler,	Feb. 2, 1777
Jeremiah Clark & Eliz. Dye,	April 6, 1777
Andrew Huntington of Norwich & Hannah Phelps,	
	May 1, 1777
Amos Denison & Hannah Williams,	July 3, 1777
Elijah Starr of Groton & Rebecca Hewit,	July 31, 1777
Joshua Smith of Groton & Lucy Wilcocks,	April 1, 1778
Randal Billing & Lucy Baldwin,	May 3, 1778
Rufus Brown & Lucy Hewit,	May 28, 1778
Dr. John Bartlett, Jr., & Lucy Treby,	July 2, 1778
John Richards of Norwich & Martha Prentice,	
	August 27, 1778

John Wheeler Geer & Sarah Denison, Sept. 3, 1778
James Miner & Esther Hillard, Nov. 29, 1778
George Williams of New London & Nancy Hewit,
Dec. 3, 1778
Rozzel Randal & Phebe Avery, March 4, 1779
James Morgan Groton & widow Lydia Miner, April 28, 1779
Christopher Eldridge & Sarah Satterly, June 24, 1779
George Hakes & widow Sarah Coy of Preston, Oct. 10, 1779
Samuel Prentice, Jr., & Lucretia Holmes, April 2, 1780
Nathaniel Church of Charlestown, R. I., & Dorcas
Austin, Dec. 2, 1780
Edward Nedson & widow Sarah Sunsamen (Indians),
Nov. 14, 1779
Jonathan Tindal & ——— Bazel (Indians), Feb. 3, 1780
Ephraim Miner & Thankfull Brown, March 1, 1781
Levi (negro) & Sinne Derrick, May 9, 1781
Stephen Kinne of Preston & Mary Crary, May 10, 1781

After Rev. Joseph Fish's death, May 16, 1781, sixteen days after performing the last marriage recorded, the church was practically without a pastor until 1800. The records are confused. No marriages recorded after 1781.

NORFOLK.

LITCHFIELD COUNTY.

Town incorporated 1758. Congregational Church formed 1760.

Dr. Ephraim ~~Guitea~~ *Guiteau* & Phebe Humphrey, Oct. 21, 1762
Daniel Richards & Anna Richards, June 2, 1763
Jonathan Bewel & Amyrilis Graves, June 13, 1763
Samuel Pettibone & Martha Phelps, Sept. 22, 1763
Samuel Howes & Mary Turner, Sept. 29, 1763
Phinehas Meeker & Sarah Brown, Feb. 29, 1764
William Walter, Jr., & Rolanda Rossiter, March 6, 1764
Eliphalet Marsh & Sarah Dickenson, April 26, 1764
Isaac Holt, Jr., & Mabel Dowd, May 8, 1764
Thomas Canfield & Lucy Burr, June 14, 1764
George Tobey & Abigail Knap, Jan. 17, 1766

Joseph Gaylord & Rachel Tibbals,	April 27, 1766
Oliver Burr & Sarah Canfield,	July 9, 1766
Steven Brown & Hephzibah Dowd,	June 8, 1767
John Phelps, Jr., & Desire Holt,	Nov. 18, 1767
Samuel Knap & Mercy Holt,	April 1, 1768
Moses Camp & Thankfull Gaylord,	April, 1768
Elijah Mason & Susanna Mills,	May, 1768
Jonathan Humphrey & Eunice Camp,	June, 1768
Alexander Knap & Mary Knap,	June, 1768
Abner Howe & Abigail Brooks,	August 11, 1768
Samuel Barber & Anna Knap,	August 25, 1768
Nathaniel Munger & Ruth Lee,	Feb. 9, 1769
Elijah Knap & Rachel Barden,	Oct., 1769
Ebenezer Norton & Content Dowd,	Dec. 24, 1769
Joel Sawyer & Abigail Barden,	May, 1769
Eleazar Orvis & Phebe Knap,	July 8, 1770
Sylvanus Norton & Eunice Tibballs,	Jan. 29, 1771
Benjamin Maltbie & Abigail Munger,	July 5, 1771
Ozias Bingham & Sarah Phelps,	July 18, 1771
Jonathan Holmes & Elizabeth Ketchum,	Dec., 1771
Thomas Day & Elizabeth Bunce,	Dec., 1771
Timothy Gaylord & Rosanna Humphrey,	May 6, 1772
Joseph Jones & Abigail Seward,	Sept. 3, 1772
Ruben Orvis & Ruth Picket,	Oct. 7, 1772
Jabez Remington & Penelope Mills,	April 27, 1773
Lemuel Cady & Eunice Dowd,	July 1, 1773
John Hubbel & Lucy Smith,	July 8, 1773
Joseph Seward, Jr., & Dorothy Case,	August 5, 1773
Asahel Humphrey & Prudence Merrills,	August 26, 1773
Valentine DeForrest & Sarah Bumps,	August 31, 1773
Caleb Aspinwall & Zerniah Cady,	Sept. 13, 1773
Peter Comstock & Sarah Walter,	Oct. 7, 1773
Daniel Burr & Betty Brown,	Oct. 7, 1773
Steven Walter & Hannah Mills,	Oct. 7, 1773
Joseph Case & Lydia Mills,	Oct. 7, 1773
Gains Trimmond & Elizabeth Day,	Nov. 25, 1773
John Treat & Esther Barber,	Oct. 27, 1774
Stephen Howe & Lois Barden,	Dec. 10, 1774
Eleazar Holt & Elizabeth Stone,	Feb. 16, 1775
Samuel Tibballs & Hannah Ives,	May 25, 1775

Joseph Mills & Abigail Cowles,   Oct. 18, 1775
Joseph Plumley & Deborah Field,   *New*   March, 1776
William Finch & Mary Huxley of ~~North~~ Marl-
  boro,   May 15, 1777
Elijah Bennet & Sarah Tuttle,   June 26, 1777
Daniel Heddy & Mary Shrove,   Sept. 18, 1777
David Howe & Phebe Cowls,   Oct. 8, 1777
Darius Phelps & Mary Akins,   Oct. 24, 1777
Eliakim Hamilton & Zilpah Brooks of North Marl-
  boro,   Nov. 6, 1777
Isaac Lane & Sabra Hurlbut of Canaan,   Jan. 1, 1778
Steven Walter & Mercy Mills,   Jan. 20, 1778
Cornelius Brown & Mary Loomis,   Jan. 22, 1778
Deacon Joseph Mills & Sarah Lewis,   March, 1778
Isaac Spaulding & Mercy Knap,   July 8, 1778
Gideon Lawrance & Lucy Holt,   August 13, 1778
Seth Crowfoot & Sarah Peck,   Oct. 15, 1778
Richard Lewis & Martha Curtis,   Nov. 5, 1778
David Beardsley & Lois Cowles,   Nov. 26, 1778
Aaron Burr & Martha Tobcy,   Dec. 17, 1778
Hemon Smith & Hannah Benham,   March, 1779
Francis Beech & Rachel Ives,   June, 1779
Miles Riggs & Abigail Mills,   June, 1779
Justus Miner & Mabel Plum,   Dec., 1779
Elijah Butolph & Deborah Plumly,   Feb., 1780
Lieut. William Walter & Beulah Sturtivant,   May, 1780
Zebinah Smith & Martha Benham,   August 1, 1780
John Adams & Abigail Forbes,   August 6, 1780
Noah Merrill & Hephzibah Pettibone,   August, 1780
Jedediah Phelps & Lidia Gaylord,   Sept., 1780
Joshua Hamilton & Mary Stewart,   Oct. 13, 1780
John Walter & Hannah Walter,   Oct. 23, 1780
Noah Cowles & Olle Mills,   Dec. 14, 1780
Luther Leason & Mary Knap,   Jan., 1781
Elisha Hawley & Margaret Orvis,   June 3, 1781
Steven Butler & Thankfull Bishop,   June 6, 1781
Amos Booth & Betthiah Beach,   June 27, 1781
Roswell Pettibone & Charlotte Laurance,   Nov. 6, 1781
Comfort Stalker & Sabra Beach,   Nov. 22, 1781
Ephraim Merrills & Esther Barden,   Dec. 7, 1781

Joel Grant & Zilpah Cowles,	Jan. 3, 1782
Simeon Pomeroy & Thede Miner,	March 28, 1782
John Beach & Sarah Burr,	June, 1782
Isaac Barber & Lois Benedict,	July 18, 1782
Calvin Pease & Sarah Ives,	Nov., 1782
Jehiel Hull & Lois Gaylord,	April 17, 1783
Nathaniel Pease & Jerusha Hall,	May 18, 1783
Samuel Orvis & Caroline Seward,	Sept. 10, 1783
Job Norton & Lois Case,	Dec., 1783
Ithiel Scott & Eunice Barber,	March, 1784
Constantine Mills & Philecta Way,	April 29, 1784
James Sturdivant & Rachel Brown,	Aug. 11, 1784
Aaron Simons & Mehitabel Simons of Colebrook,	
	Oct. 7, 1784
Samuel Olcott & Abigail Mills,	Oct. 7, 1784
Silas Seward & Charlotte Way,	Oct. 13, 1784
Allen Pease & Rachel Tibballs,	Oct. 25, 1784
N. Stanley Parmele & Rosannah Lucas,	Nov. 29, 1784
Ebenezer Barden & Mary Palmer,	Oct. 1, 1785
Chester Cady & Mary Sweet,	Nov. 24, 1785
Mathew Blakesley & Ruth Barber,	Dec. 29, 1785
Zadoc Seymour & Naomi Munger,	Jan. 19, 1786
Elizur Munger & Rhoda Gaylord,	Feb. 16, 1786
Seth Walter & Ruhamah Seward,	April 27, 1786
Samuel Hall & Lucy Parmele,	August, 1786
Joshua Moses & Elizabeth Balcam,	Oct., 1786
Jonathan Webster & Huldah Orvis,	Jan. 4, 1787
Lemuel Chase & Katherine Barden,	Jan. 10, 1787
Ebenezer Parde & Annie Munger,	May, 1787
Jacob McClean & Eleanor Thrall (?),	July 26, 1787
Amos Gaylord & Eunice Barber,	July 26, 1787
Ruben Field & Asenath Case,	Jan. 16, 1788
Charles Seward & Ruby Benedict,	Feb., 1788
Joel Phelps & Lorana Walter,	Feb., 1788
Ruben Palmer & Abigail Moses,	April, 1788
Hezekiah Butler & Hephzibah Burr,	July, 1788
Roger Orvis & Mirianne Roxana Seward,	July, 1788
Ira Cowles & Sarah Lane,	Oct. 1788
Steven Norton & Hannah Coy,	Nov., 1788
Samuel Cravath & Mamre Bishop,	April 9, 1789

Philemon Gaylord & Martha Curtis,	April, 1789
James Porter & Jerusha Lucas,	April, 1789
Abel Robert & Sally Loomis,	May, 1789
Hezekiah Goodwin & Semantha Beech,	July, 1789
Thaddeus Roys & Esther Abbot,	Sept. 6, 1789
Medad Curtis & Lucy Lawrence,	Oct. 12, 1789
Nathaniel Stevens, Jr., & Elizabeth Roys,	Nov. 19, 1789
Abraham Balcom & Abigail Barber,	Dec. 3, 1789
Grove Lawrance & Elizabeth Robbins,	Dec. 21, 1789
Heman Walter & Patience Butler,	Dec. 24, 1789
Francis Benedict & Jerusha Butler,	Dec. 24, 1789
Hezekiah Turner & Elizabeth Miner,	Dec. 31, 1789
Andrew Moor & Desia Mills,	Jan. 9, 1790
Noah Tibballs & Jemima Kellogg,	March 15, 1790
Augustus Cook & Sibel Beach of Goshen,	Sept., 1790
Aaron Root & Olive Stevens of Canaan,	Nov. 10, 1790
Adonijah Foot & Sabra Mott,	Nov. 12, 1790
Selah Holcomb & Sarah Wilcox,	Nov., 1790
Elijah Norton & Rebecca Sturdivant,	Nov., 1790
Isaac Balcom & Anna Burr,	Dec. 9, 1790
Steven Brown & Lois Nettleton,	Feb., 1791
Jonathan Brown & Rosanna Stevens,	March 16, 1791
David Collins & Lucy Bingham of Salisbury,	March 29, 1791
Noel Collins & Phebe Darby,	March, 1791
Asa Mills & Arathusa Phelps,	August, 1791
John W—— & Hephzibah Treat (?),	Nov., 1791
Asa Collins & Sibel Bishop,	Nov., 1791
George Norton & Jerusha Thrall,	Nov. 30, 1791
Abraham Camp & Mary Lee,	April 15, 1792
Seth Porter & Sarah Cowles,	June, 1792
John Oviatt & Hannah Sherman of Goshen,	Oct. 4, 1792
John Dowd & Corrance (Concurrance) Seward,	Nov. 16, 1792
Benjamin Bigelow & Eunice Akins,	Nov. 29, 1792
John Northrup & Elizabeth Stevens,	Jan. 22, 1793
Sterling Mills & Abigail Phelps,	Jan. 22, 1793
Bates Turner & Persis Humphrey,	Feb., 1793
Elijah Miner & Martha —— of Goshen,	Feb. 28, 1793
Theodore Bailey & Lorama Wilcox of Goshen,	Feb. 28, 1793
Theodore Dowd & Hannah Barber,	March 26, 1793
Samuel Pettibone & Paulina Smith,	March 25, 1793
Solomon Richards & Mary Woodruff	Oct. 12, 1792

Jonathan Humphrey & Rachel Dowd of Goshen, May 30, 1793
Eliphelet Mason & Betsy Leech,   June 13, 1793
Auren Roys & Elizabeth Knapp,   August, 1793
Ebenezer Cowles & Lucretia Wilcox,   Sept., 1793
William Bartlett & Rachel Ives of Bowman's Creek,
                                              Sept., 1793
Elijah Whitney & Rhoda Thrall,   Jan. 7, 1794
Benjamin Austin & Susanna Goodwin,   Feb. 2, 1794
Henry Calvin Akins & Rachel Murry,   May 9, 1794
David Knapp & Abigail Case,   June 14, 1794
Levi Sturdevant & Rebecca Norton,   Sept. 7, 1794
James Bailey & Thede Pomeroy,   Oct. 19, 1794
Isaac Turner & Martha Humphrey,   Nov. 19, 1794
Joseph Cowles & Lois Hungerford,   Nov. 20, 1794
Phinehas Meker & Sarah Burgiss,   Nov. 28, 1794
Chancy Hills (or Mills) & Lois Grant,   Jan., 1795
John Dolph & Catherine Chase,   March 1, 1795
Elijah Root & Elizabeth Barns,   March 26, 1795
Joseph Gaylord & Abigail Welch,   April 16, 1795
George Clark & Lydia Jackways,   April 23, 1795
James Norton & Mary Hull,   April 29, 1795
Benjamin Warren & Lucy Burr,   May 21, 1795
Abijah Northway & Olive Cowles,   May 30, 1795
Sylvanus Norton & Sarah Picket,   Dec. 21, 1795
John Roys & Polly Hinman,   Dec. 24, 1795
Martin Barber & Elizabeth Brown,   March 31, 1796
James Fellows & Phebe Leonard,   May 5, 1796
Mordicai Moorhouse & Mille Culver,   August 10, 1797
Gideon Curtis & Polly Roys,   Sept. 15, 1797
David Knapp & Sophia Knapp,   Dec. 28, 1797
David Dean & Phebe Root,   Jan. 18, 1798
Ezekiel Cravett & Roxania Bingham,   Feb. 22, 1798
Charles A. Dickinson & Abigail Jones,   March 23, 1798
Nathaniel Hoit & Lucretia Maltbie,   May 5, 1798
John Richard, Jr., & Polly Cobb of Canaan,   May 12, 1798
Simeon Johnson & Polly Roys,   June 2, 1798
Samuel Thomson & Esther Sheffield of Canaan,
    — of   June 19, 1798
————Pantindgefield & Polly Chapman,   Nov. 7, 1798
Simeon Coy & Ruhamah Cady,   Nov. 13, 1798

Abiram Mills & Esther Havis,	Nov. 29, 1798
Isaac Shepherd & Hannah Sturdivant,	Dec. 10, 1798
Simeon Maltbie & Martha Murry,	April 21, 1799
Wilson Phelps & Sally Gaylord,	May, 1799
David Knapp & ——— Knapp,	July, 1799
Elijah Benedict & Eunice Holt,	August, 1799
Lewis Rood & Anna M. Morehouse,	Oct., 1799
Capt. Mid'l Holcomb & Mabel Holt,	Nov., 1799
Benjamin Frisbie & Thankfull Gaylord,	Nov. 28, 1799
David Rockwell & Mary Lane,	Dec. 19, 1799
James Stone & Isabel Dewey of Canaan,	March 27, 1800
Levi Hamlin & Mary Barden,	August, 1800
Asahel Chapman & Polly Lane,	August 28, 1800
Jacob Cady & Katharine Spencer,	Sept. 4, 1800
Samuel Cowles, Jr., & Olive Phelps,	Oct., 1800
Noah Smith & Naomi Case,	Nov., 1800
Philo Pettibone & Sally Gaylord,	Nov. 19, 1800

MONTVILLE.

NEW LONDON COUNTY.

Town was taken from New London 1786. The first Congregational Church was organized in 1722 at Oakdale, being then in the North district of New London. The second church in 1832 at Mohegan. The following are the records of the Oakdale church and are all that exist:

not already published:

MARRIAGES BY REV. JAMES HILLHOUSE.

Sylvester Baldwin & Elizabeth Avery,	May 19, 1724
John Thompson & Mary Otis,	Nov. 5, 1724
John Denison & Patience Grazell,	Nov. 5, 1724
John Anderson & Margaret Dixon,	Nov. 9, 1724
Phinily Hallack & Margaret Young,	Jan. 12, 1725
Jonathan Church & Abigail Fairbanks,	Feb. 24, 1725
Edward Rogers & Sarah Gorton,	March 25, 1725
James Morgan & Susanna Rogers,	Oct. 27, 1725
Josiah Weeks & Levina Stebbens,	May 15, 1727
John Perkins & Lydia Malsworth,	May 27, 1727
Patrick McClellen & Dorothy Otis,	Nov. 25, 1727
Thomas Dixon & Mary Morgan,	Dec. 25, 1727

Elisha Mirick & Grace Rogers,	Nov. 14, 1727
John Way & Mary Holmes,	Nov. 21, 1727
James Fitch & Anna Denison,	Feb. 12, 1728
Nathaniel Comstock & Margaret Fox,	Feb. 12, 1728
Daniel Tuttle & Sarah Comstock,	April 4, 1728
Thomas Collit & Mary Rogers,	May 25, 1728
James Camp & Sarah Malsworth, or *Malzar*,	May 30, 1728
James Otis & Sarah Tudor,	June, 1728
John Brown & Dorothy Noyes,	July 4, 1728
John Mason, Jr., & Mary Copp,	Sept. 17, 1728
John Anderson & Susanna Morgan,	April 15, 1729
Samuel Fox, Jr., & Abigail Harris,	Nov. 12, 1730
Abraham Simons & Rebecca Chapman,	March, 1734
Joseph Atwell & Martha Comstock,	March 27, 1734
Rev. Joseph Lovett & Anna Holmes,	April, 1734
Jabez Lathrop & Delight Otis,	May 3, 1734
—— Phalan & Abigail Whitney,	August 21, 1734
Samuel Johnson & —— Atwell,	Dec. 15, 1734
Carey Latham & Dorothy McClelland,	Jan. 29, 1735
William Frink & Abigail ——,	April 3, 1735
Jonathan Harris & Rachel Otis,	August 4, 1735
John Bradford & Esther Sherwood,	Dec. 15, 1736
Alexander Johnson & Susanna Fox,	Dec. 21, 1738

REDDING.

FAIRFIELD COUNTY.

The town taken from Fairfield was organized 1767. The Congregational Church was formed in 1733 and the records beginning in 1734 are complete to 1780. They begin again in 1810. None exist of the intervening period.

MARRIAGES BY REV. NATHANIEL HUNN.

George Cornes (Corns) & Anne Hall,	Nov. 12, 1734
John Mallery & Elizabeth Adams,	April 10, 1735
James Bradley & Abigail Sanford,	Dec, 4, 1735
Peter Burr & Rebecca Wood,	May 7, 1736
Samuel Smith & Lidia Hull,	August 24, 1736
Peter Mallery & Joanna Hall,	Feb. 28, 1736-7

Daniel Burr & Abigail Sherwood, Dec. 22, 1737
Abraham Adams & Elizabeth Williams, May 9, 1740
Edmund Sherman & Rebecca Lee, July 2, 1740
Benjamin Tunrey (?) & Anne Lyon, Oct., 1740
Thomas Rowland & *Tinizeen Jacock* ~~Mason~~, Nov. 30, 1743
~~Matthew~~ *Thomas* Rowler (2) & ~~Deborah~~ *Sarah* Gray, Dec. 28, 1743
Ebenezer Mallery & Hannah Keys, Feb. 6, 1744
Daniel Meeker & Sarah Johnson, July 19, 1744
Lemuel Wood & Griswold Mallery, Oct. 29, 1744
David Meeker & Hannah Hill, Oct. 31, 1744
Benjamin Meeker & Catharine Burr, August 20, 1745
John Hoppin, Jr., (Milford, Ct.) & Mary Read, Sept. 4, 1745
Hezekiah Rowland & ~~Tamar~~ *Tamar* Treadwell, Dec. 24, 1745
William Trusdale & Deliverance ~~Jeason~~ *Jacock* (?), June 29, 1746
~Robert Meeker & Rebecca Morehouse, Sept. 19, 1746
Seth Wheeler & Ruth Knap, Oct. 27, 1746
John Read & Tabitha Hawley, Dec. 18, 1746
-Nehemiah Sanford & Elizabeth Morehouse, March 5, 1747
Samuel Wood & Mary Mallery, March 5, 1747
Samuel Coley & Mary Gray, Sept. 17, 1747
Nehemiah Smith & Rebecca Meeker, Oct. 8, 1747
Jonas Plat & Elizabeth Sanford, Oct. 17, 1747
Gurdon Marchant & Ellenor Chauncey, Dec. 9, 1747
Daniel Hall & Mary Betts, Nov. 1, 1748
Gershom Coley & Abigail Hull, Nov. 15, 1748
Daniel Mallery & Sarah Lee, Nov. 30, 1748
~ Gershom Morehouse & Anne Sanford, Jan. 18, 1749
William Burret & Elizabeth Burr, June 7, 1749

MARRIAGES BY REV. NATHANIEL BARTLETT.

Rev. N. Bartlett & Eunice Russel of Branford,
June 13, 1753
William Read & Sarah Hawley, Dec. 11, 1753
Benj. Hambleton & Hannah Bulkley, April 5, 1754
Daniel Coley & Sarah Sanford, April 16, 1754
Nathaniel Hall & Abigale Platt, May 28, 1754
Isaac Meeker & Eunice Coley, May 29, 1754
Thomas Gold & Anne Smith, Feb. 20, 1755
Daniel Dean & Mary Lee, June 29, 1755

Daniel Jackson & Abigale Sanford,	Oct. 2, 1755
Jehu Burr, Jr., & Sarah Griffin,	Nov. 22, 1755
Samuel Cable & Mary Platt,	Jan. 4, 1756
David Lion (Lyon) & Hannah Sanford,	Sept. 14, 1756
Paul Bartram & Mary Hawley,	————
Ebenezer Hull, Jr., & Ruth Betts,	————
John Bartram & Charity Bulkley,	————
Joseph Dikeman & Eunice Darling,	May 25, 1757
Eleazer Burrit & Elizabeth Platt,	————
William Murrow (?) & Eunice Dean,	Dec. 16, 1757
John Morgan & Joanna Banks,	Jan. 5, 1758
Daniel Sanford & Esther Hull,	April 18, 1758
Benjamin Davis & Eunice Nash,	May 21, 1758
Stephen Gray & Sarah Ferry,	Sept. 3, 1758
Michael Benedict & Bette Dikeman,	Nov. 5, 1758
Hezekiah Booth & Abigale Betts,	Dec. 13, 1758
Hezekiah Smith & Lydia Lee,	Jan. 11, 1759
Theophilus Hull & Martha Betts,	Jan. 25, 1759
Samuel Chegston (?) *Clugston* & Deborah Mallery,	Feb. 11, 1759
Elias Bates & Tabitha Read,	Feb. 25, 1759
Seth Sanford & Rebecca Burr,	April 25, 1759
John Gray & Ruamah Barlow,	August 7, 1759
Jonathan Couch & Eunice Griffin,	August 15, 1759
Alexander Briant & Elizabeth Burr,	Oct. 11, 1759
James Gray & Asena Taylor,	March 27, 1760
John Clugston & Eunice Mallery,	July 7, 1760
Joseph Stilson & Rebecca Wildman,	Oct. 29, 1760
Deacon Stephen Burr & Abigale Hall,	April 12, 1761
Reuben Squire & Elizabeth Bryant,	May 19, 1761
Joseph Lyon & Lois Sanford,	May 21, 1761
Isaac Rumsey & Abigale St. John,	May 25, 1761
Stephen Crofut & Adria Couch,	August 27, 1761
Richard Nichols & Abigale Gold,	Dec. 2, 1761
John Griffin & Katherine Johnson,	Dec. 23, 1761
Anthony Anghevine & Esther Burr,	Dec. 23, 1761
Timothy Sanford & Mary Sanford,	Feb. 14, 1762
David Bartram & Phœbe Morehouse,	April 30, 1762
Azael Patchin & Hannah Osborn,	May 10, 1762
Joseph Sanford & Hepzibah Griffith,	Nov. 2, 1762
David Jackson & Anna Sanford,	Nov. 18, 1762

Joseph Rumsey & Sarah Morehouse, Dec. 2, 1762
John Hawley & Abigail Sanford, Dec. 21, 1762
John Hull & Mollie Andrews, Feb. 3, 1763
George Gage & Sarah Adams, Sept. 7, 1763
Noah Hall & Sarah Banks, Nov. 13, 1763
John Byington & Sarah Gray, Nov. 16, 1763
Elnathan Lyon & Jain (Jane) Knap, Nov. 23, 1763
Elijah Birchard & Ruth Morehouse, Dec. 3, 1763
Samuel Olmstead & Sarah Bartram, Dec. 21, 1763
James Gray, Jr., & Mabel Phinney, Feb. 9, 1764
Jesse Banks & Mabel Wheeler, June 11, 1764
John June & Sarah Jenks, August 16, 1764
Hezekiah Batterson & Mary Sherwood, Sept. 24, 1764
Ephraim Deforest & Sarah Betts, Oct. 25, 1764
John Clugston & Charity Ginnins, Nov. 20, 1764
Zecheriah Summers & Martha Burr, Jan. 15, 1765
Samuel Rowley & Sarah Comes, Jan. 15, 1765
Eleazer Olmstead & Grace Pickett, Jan. 17, 1765
Hezekiah Whitlock & Anne Platt, July 11, 1765
Isaac Platt & Mary Pickett, Oct. 2, 1765
James Russica (?) & Sarah Rumsey, Feb. 19, 1766
William Hambleton & Martha Prince, June 3, 1766
Calvin Wheeler & Mary Thorps, June 3, 1766
Thomas Rockwell & Tabitha Sanford, June 26, 1766
Ephraim Jackson & Martha Hull, June 26, 1766
Joseph Griffin & Esther Hall, Sept. 18, 1766
David Turney & Sarah Gold, Nov. 7, 1766
Seth Banks & Sarah Platt, Nov. 20, 1766
Ezekiel Fairchild & Eunice Andrews, Jan. 8, 1767
Nehemiah Hull & Griswold Perry, Feb. 5, 1767
Hubbel Bennet & Rebecca Pickett, Feb. 17, 1767
Joseph Meeker & Mary Darling, March 12, 1767
Jacob Lyon & Hannah Wheeler, March 21, 1767
Elijah Burr & Rhoda Sanford, April 2, 1767
Elnathan Sturges & Ruth Hawley, April 22, 1767
Ezekiel Sanford & Sarah Sturges, April 23, 1767
James Prindle & Rhoda Mallery, June 27, 1767
Samuel Sanford, Jr., & Sarah Olmstead, July 23, 1767
Burgis Hall & Eunice Whitehead, ———
Abijah Fairchild & Huldah Burr, Nov. 5, 1767

Nathaniel Northrop & Esther Gold,	Nov. 10, 1767
Stephen Sanford & Abigail Ward,	Nov. 19, 1767
Joseph Banks & Ann Morehouse,	Nov. 29, 1767
Levi Selay & Anner Meeker,	Dec. 6, 1767
Stephen Meeker & Anne Lee,	March 25, 1768
Lieut. Peter Fairchild & Mary Lockwood,	March 27, 1768
John Parker & Sarah Sherwood,	August 22, 1768
Hezekiah Bulkley & Sarah Rumsey,	Sept. 20, 1768
Abel Morehouse & Beth Squire,	Nov. 8, 1768
Solomon Northrop & Sarah (Nap) Knap,	Nov. 9, 1768
John Darling Guire & Rebecca Hill,	Nov. 29, 1768
William Sloane & Mary Read,	March 4, 1769
Andrew Knap & Rebecca Monrow(e) *Munrow*,	April 7, 1769
Ephraim Robbins & Sarah Couch,	June 20, 1769
Henry Hopkins & Anna Burr,	July 26, 1769
Nathan Jackson & Elizabeth Osborn,	August 17, 1769
Silas Lee & Witelee Meeker,	August 23, 1769
Nehemiah Selay, Jr., & Sarah Dibble,	Sept. 26, 1769
Daniel Bartram & Ann Marchant,	Oct. 10, 1769
Samuel White & Huldah Sanford,	Oct. 28, 1769
James Morgan & *Mary* Osborn,	Jan. 22, 1770
Nathaniel Turill & Abigail Rumsey,	Jan. 23, 1770
Seth Meeker & Ellen Bixby,	March 27, 1770
Joseph Lyon & Sarah Bulkley,	Nov., 1770
Nathan Coley & Mabel Bixby,	Nov. 15, 1770
Ephraim Sanford & Tabitha Morehouse,	Nov. 15, 1770
Ezekiel Hawley, Jr., & Huldah Lyon,	Dec. 20, 1770
Daniel Fairchild & Sarah Lane,	Dec. 25, 1770
Seth Price & Mary Gold,	March 6, 1771
Justus Bates & Hannah Coley,	May 23, 1771
Ebenezer Coley & Rachel Sturges,	Nov. 12, 1771
Jonathan Bradley & Grace Johnson,	Dec. 8, 1772
Aaron Barlow & Rebecca Sanford,	Dec. 17, 1772
Lazarus Wheeler & Hannah Gorham,	Jan. 24, 1773
William Bradley & Mary Wescott,	Feb. 22, 1773
Elijah Burr & Eunice Hawley,	April 27, 1773
Elnathan Sturges & Martha Jackson,	April 28, 1773
Chauncey Marchant & Hannah Hambleton,	May 19, 1773
Samuel Platt & Abigail Hall,	Oct. 17, 1773
Henry Whinkler & Ruth Coley,	Nov. 10, 1773

Ezekiel Sanford & Abigail Starr,	Nov. 21, 1773
Daniel Read & Anne Hill,	Dec. 7, 1773
Stephen Andrus & Lois Osborn,	Dec. 27, 1773
Joseph Truesdale & Comfort Burr,	Jan. 11, 1774
David Jackson & Esther Ward,	Jan. 23, 1774
John Fairchild & Sarah Hull,	Jan. 27, 1774
Levi Dikeman & Rebecca Lines,	Feb. 9, 1774
Philip Burrit & Rachel Read,	March 1, 1774
John Pickett, Jr., & Mary Bates,	March 20, 1774
Augustus Sanford & Abigail Sturges,	August 18, 1774
Jonathan Persons & Elizabeth Thomas,	August 22, 1774
Isaac Hambleton & Eunice Platt,	August 28, 1774
Abijah Fairchild & Phœbe Smith,	Sept. 18, 1774
Robert Stow & Anne Darrow,	Jan. 26,. 1775
Seth Meeker & Millicent Davis,	March 14, 1775
Daniel Selay & Lydia Comstock,	March 28, 1775
Hezekiah Read & Anne Gorham,	May 14, 1775
Eli Nichols & Hannah Hull,	May 22, 1775
Enoch Betts & Mary Coley,	June 27, 1775
Thaddeus Benedict & Deborah Read,	July 12, 1775
Isaac Gregory & Sarah St. John,	Sept. 12, 1775
William Dunning & Sarah Osborn,	Oct. 9, 1775
Daniel Copley & Theoda Couch,	March 3, 1777
Jonathan Couch & Mabel Meeker,	Sept. 24, 1777
Samuel Mallery & Hannah Nichols,	Oct. 16, 1777
Samuel Ramong & Philena Bates,	Nov. 3, 1777
Benjamin Darling & Mary Chapman,	Nov. 6, 1777
Jeremiah Batterson & Bette Clugston,	Nov. 12, 1777
Abel Gold & Elizabeth Gold,	Dec. 18, 1777
Jesse Benedict & Mollie Ward,	Dec. 25, 1777
Daniel Collins Bartlett & Esther Read,	Jan. 7, 1778
Daniel Osborn & Jane Morehouse,	Jan. 28, 1778
Jabez Burr & Mary Bartram,	Feb. 12, 1778
Francis Andrews & Sabra Parsons,	March 5, 1778
Bille Morehouse & Ruth Guire,	March 11, 1778
Thomas Russice (?) & Phœbe Pickett,	March 28, 1778
Samuel Gold & Sarah Platt,	April 9, 1778
Enos Lee, Jr., & Ruth Bates,	April 22, 1778
Austin Baxter & Martha Darling,	May 29, 1778
James Gibbons, soldier in Putnam's division, and	
Ann Sullivan,	Feb. 7, 1779

John Lines (soldier) and Mary Hendrick,   March 18, 1779
Charles White & Amerillis Knap,   March 23, 1779
Daniel Evarts (soldier) & Mary Rowland,   March 30, 1779
Isaac Olmstead (soldier) & Mary Persons,   April 15, 1779
Jesse Belnap (soldier) & Eunice Hall,   April 28, 1779
William Little (soldier) & Phœbe Marchant,   May 7, 1779
Giles Gilbert (artificer in army) & Deborah Hall,
                                                 May 23, 1779
Joseph Jackson, Jr., & Mary Dimond, _Edmond_   Sept. 30, 1779
Russell Chapel (soldier) & Sarah Osborn,   Oct. 3, 1779
William Darrow (soldier) & Ruth Bartram,   March 9, 1780
John Dikeman & Sarah Meeker,   March 20, 1780

POMFRET.

WINDHAM COUNTY.

The town of Pomfret was named 1713. The first Congregational church was formed in 1715. The second church was formed in Abington District 1753. (From the Abington church records.)

MARRIED BY DAVID RIPLEY, PASTOR.

Nathaniell Rogers & Abiah Ingals,   March 19, 1753
Johnathan & Rebekah Lyon,   May 10, 1753
Pelatiah Smith & Mary Daniels,   Nov. 1, 1753
Daniel Holt & Keziah Rust,   Dec. 26, 1753
John Lyon, Jr., & Susannah Stowell,   May 16, 1754
James Grow & Anne Adams,   March 6, 1754
Daniel Winter & Mehitable Warner,   Dec. 5, 1754
John Sharp & Lucy Warren,   ———
Ebenezer Demon & Elizabeth Dana,   Jan. 5, 1755
Edward Coye & Ama Titus,   ———
John Fisk & May Ingalls,   Jan. 9, 1755
Zebediah Ingalls & Esther Goodell,   Feb. 20, 1755
Caleb May & Mehitabel Holbrook,   Feb. 26, 1755
Benjamin Sharp & Mary Craft,   March 5, 1755
Amos Grosvenor & Mary Hutchings,   May 1, 1755
Gershom Sharp & Hannah Dana,   June 5, 1755
Ebenezer Bullard & Judith Goodell,   July 8, 1755

Joseph Craft & Sarah Goodell,	Jan. 8, 1756
James Copling & Sarah Ingalls,	Feb. 26, 1756
Isaac Abbott & Mary Barker,	April 29, 1756
Jeremiah Utly & Elizabeth Kinney,	Nov. 18, 1756
Johnathan Allin & Martha Fisk,	———
Thomas Coe of Litchfield & Mary Keys,	Feb. 15, 1757
Nehemiah Dodge & Lois Pain,	Nov. 16, 1757
Thomas Pool & Sarah Warren,	Nov. 17, 1757
William Plank of Killingsley & Bathsheba Raymond,	Dec. 22, 1757
William Chaplain of Mansfield & Esther Holbrook,	June 30, 1758
Moses Rogers & Lois Holbrook,	Sept. 26, 1758
Matthias Smith of Lebanon & Comfort Carpenter,	Sept. 29, 1758
Simeon Case of Norwich & Mehitabel Allin,	March 13, 1759
Ezra Bullard of Dedham & Lois Goodell,	April 5, 1759
Nathan Dresser & Mrs. Orinda Carpenter,	April 19, 1759
Roger Kinney & Huldah Skinner,	Dec. 27, 1759
Johnathan Blanchard of Andover & Sarah Osgood,	March 17, 1760
Isaac Cady & Sarah Hendrick,	Oct. 1, 1760
Zechariah Goodell, Jr., & Hannah Cheney,	Oct. 6, 1760
Abiel Lyon & Mehetabel Osgood,	Nov. 27, 1760
Josiah Wheeler, Jr., & Eunice Holt,	Nov. 28, 1760
Daniel Trowbridge, Jr., & Phebe Pain,	Dec. 4, 1760
Ebenezer Allin & Mehetabel Dana,	Dec. 10, 1760
Joshua Raymond & Abigail Shaw,	Feb. 5, 1761
Joseph Phelps & Elizabeth Abbott,	Sept. 28, 1761
Nathaniel Coye & Bridgett Goodell,	Oct. 29, 1761
Elijah Sharp & Lois Hammond,	August 3, 1762
Samuel Brown & Sarah Bowmen,	August 26, 1762
Benjamin Webber & Abiah Fisk,	August 26, 1762
David Stoddard of Norwich & Elizabeth Reed,	Sept. 9, 1762
Thomas Baley of Groton & Rachel Dodge,	Oct. 2, 1762
Dan Davison & Martha Goodell,	Jan. 6, 1763
Elijah Dana & Mary Chandler,	July 7, 1763
Johnathan Coye of Munson & Deborah Barker,	July 12, 1763
William Sharp & Sarah Farrington,	Feb. 10, 1764
Daniel Stowell & Anne Bugbee,	April 12, 1764

George Martin of Windham & Derothy Brown of
    Leominster,   June 7, 1764
Moses Grosvenor & Dorcas Sharp,   Jan. 10, 1765
Daniel Goodell & Francis Craft,   Dec. 12, 1765
Stephen Griggs & Sarah Chandler,   Sept. 4, 1766
John Sessions & Allice Goodell,   Nov. 5, 1766
Asa Holt & Margaret Hammond,   Nov. 20, 1766
John Trowbridge & Anne Kinnee,   Nov. 27, 1766
Samuel Shaw of Brimfield & Susannah Shaw, Dec. 2, 1766
Thomas Grow, Jr., & Experience Goodell,   May 14, 1767
Hezekiah Cole, Jr., & Sarah Lyon,   July 9, 1767
Constantine Gilman of Walpole, New Hampshire,
    & Elizabeth Sharp,   Nov. 24, 1767
Amaziah Raymond & Joannah Cutler,   Nov. 26, 1767
Thomas Hutchins & Priscilla Dana,   July 21, 1768
Ephraim Holbrook & Esther Johnson,   Aug. 4, 1768
Samuel Farrington of Dedham & Ruth Warner, Oct. 6, 1768
Elisha Stowell & Jerusha Sabin,   Jan. 26, 1769
Dier Hastings of Norwich & Mary Ingalls,   June 3, 1769
Samuel Sessions & Abigail Ruggles,   Oct. 11, 1769
Jeremiah Bingham of Windham & Mehetabel Craft,
                                                 Oct. 12, 1769
Johnathan Case of Willington & Mehetabel Dana,
                                                 Nov. 22, 1769
Hezekiah Griggs & Mehetabel Adams,   Jan. 18, 1770
Joseph Griggs of Ashford & Penelope Goodell, Aug. 20, 1770
William Clark & Sarah Goodell,   Sept. 17, 1771
Benjamin Sharp Jr., & Ruth Foster,   Sept. 26, 1771
David Ingalls & Mary May,   March 1, 1772
Rheuben Goodell of Norwich & Abigail Sharp,
                                                 May 27, 1772
David Sharp & Cloe Holt,   Jan. 21, 1773
Whitman Jacobs of Athol & Rebekah Grow,   June 3, 1773
Nathan Kinnee & Deborah Knight,   June 17, 1773
Josiah Bullard of Kent & Olive Cutler,   July 12, 1773
William Trowbridge & Susannah Sessions,   Jan. 13, 1774
Jeduthan Trusdel & Abigail White,   Jan. 20, 1774.
Alexander Sessions & Sarah Grosvenor,   Feb. 29, 1774
Philip Pearl of Windham & Hannah Trowbridge,
                                                 Dec. 29, 1774

Amos Woodward & Elizabeth Winter, —— 13, 1775
Barnerd Case of Willington & Phebe Goodell, June 29, 1775
Amasa Sessions & Esther Grosvenor, Dec. 14, 1775
William Chandler of Woodstock & Mary Grosvenor,
Feb. 6, 1777
Ephraim Winter & Mary Brooks, April 17, 1777
Thomas Ingalls & Sarah Bowen, June 26, 1777

No further record till 1783.

MARRIED BY WALTER LYON, PASTOR.

Lemuel Stowel & Susannah Barrows, Jan. 23, 1783
Daniel Brown of Canterbury & Lydia Pratt, Jan. 26, 1783
Calvin Holbrook & Allice Ingalls, Feb. 13, 1783
Joseph Ashly of Windham & Rachel Allin, April 10, 1783
Samuel Kezar of Norwich & Elizabeth Griggs, May 27, 1783
Benjamin Dorr & Elisabeth Cotton, June 1, 1783
Icabod Griggs of Tolland & Mary Sharpe, June 3, 1783
Prescot Sawyer & Anna Stodard, Oct. 16, 1783
William Colston of Bellingham & Sarah Liscomb
Nov. 20, 1783
John Robinson & Esther Sharpe, Jan. 22, 1784
Caleb May of Woodstock & Sarah Sumner, Jan. 29, 1784
Joshua Grosvenor & Sarah Ingals, Feb. 10, 1784
John Blanchard of Windham & Anne Stowel,
March 25, 1784
Rowland Cotton & Kezia Holt, April 8, 1784
Thomas Grosvenor, 2d, & Alathea Grosvenor, June 3, 1784
Appleton Osgood & Abigail Welch of Windham,
Nov. 11, 1784
Chester Grosvenor & Polly Lyon, Dec. 16, 1784
Jared Warner & Polley Ripley, Dec. 28, 1784
Solomon Eldridge & Sarah Fiske, March 1, 1785
Samuel Craft, 2d, & Lucy Sumner, 2d, March 31, 1785
Joseph Ashley, Jr., of Windham & Elizabeth Rickard,
June 30, 1785
William Feild & Jerusha Goodell, April 5, 1787
Eleazar Baker & Hannah Trowbridge, both of Tol-
land, April 12, 1787
Abraham Ford of Hampton & Sarah Ingals, Jan. 22, 1788

Elijah Jaeson of Charleston, South Carolina, & Nancy
    Wheeler,   March 16, 1788
Hervey Holbrook of Hartland in Vermont & Dor-
    cas Cleveland,   March 31, 1788
Pelatiah Lyon of Plainfield & Hannah Lyon, Sept. 28, 1788
Benjamin Gould & Anne Fay,   Nov. 26, 1788
James Danielson of Killingly & Sarah Lord,   Dec. 2, 1788
John Fay & Polly Pierce,   Dec. 11, 1788
Pearly Dean of Ashford & Nabby Baxter,   Jan. 29, 1789
Peter Woodward of Canterbury & Ruth Whitney,
                           March 25, 1790
Asahel Elliot of Thomson & Jemima Edmands,
                           April 22, 1790
Aaron Stephens & Alethea Sharpe,   June 15, 1790
Calvin Stowel of Brooklin & Sarah Kinnee,   Oct. 21, 1790
Eleazer Williams of Killingly & Mary Ingals, Dec. 2, 1790
John Ellis of Ashford & Lois Griggs,   Dec. 9, 1790
Josiah Ingersol & Hannah Ingals,   Jan. 25, 1791
William Warner of Windham & Mary Trowbridge,
                          Feb. 23, 1791
Griggs Goffe of Bedford in N. Hampshire & Esther
    Griggs,   April 4, 1791
Nathaniel Coggswell of Brooklin & Freelove Wil-
    liams,   May 12, 1791
Rev. Asahel Huntington of Topsfield & Miss Ala-
    thea Lord,   June 5, 1791
Charles Bowing of Ashford & Polly Griggs,   Sept. 22, 1791
Elisha Dunham of Plimouth & Ruth Sharpe, Dec. 13, 1791
Ward Cotton & Nabby Grosvenor,   Jan. 31, 1792
John Keep of Whitestown & Frances Goodell,
                         Feb. 15, 1792
Darius Kinnee of Voluntown & Lydia Goodell,
                        March 29, 1792
Noah Carpenter of Mansfield & Charlotte Sharpe,
                        April 26, 1792
Nehemiah Cleaveland, Esqr., of Topsfield & Miss
    Speedy Lord,   July 1, 1792
Aaron Fay & Elizabeth Dennison,   Nov. 29, 1792
Elijah Phillips Cleveland of Brooklyn & Mary Kin-
    nee,   Nov. 30, 1792

Samuel Hartshorn of Ostego in the State of N.
    York & Sarah Trowbridge,   Feb. 5, 1793
Silvanus Eldridge of Springfield in the State of N.
    York & Allice Fiske,   Feb. 7, 1793
Stephen Hutchinson & Mary Fermin,   Feb. 14, 1793
Joshua Pratt of Brooklin & Theda Ingals,   Dec. 25, 1793
Josiah Morse of Canterbury & Rebecca Lyon, Jan. 1, 1794
Thomas Cleaveland & Anna Crafts,   Jan. 2, 1794
Squire Sessions & Lucy Sumner,   Jan. 21, 1794
David Griggs & Mary Cory of New London, May 25, 1794
Daniel Ingals & Bethiah Brown,   Nov. 2, 1794
Stephen Utley, Jr., & Elizabeth Chase,   Nov. 13, 1794
Aaron Wedge of Sturbridge & Lucy Bowing, Nov. 16, 1794
Appleton Osgood & Abilene Cleaveland,   Nov. 16, 1794
Clark Elliot & Lois Smith of Hampton,   Nov. 27, 1494
Joseph Baxter & Elizabeth Dresser,   Nov. 27, 1794
Nehemiah Lyon of Woodstock & Mehitabel Squire,
                       Dec. 18, 1794
Elijah Barber of Winsor & Polly Warner, Jan. 18, 1795
Elisha Williams of Spencertown & Lucia Grosvenor,
                       Feb. 5, 1795
Ebenezer Ruggles & Percy Goodell,   Feb. 15, 1795
John Morse & Sally Sharpe,   March 15, 1795
Eli Hartshorn of Franklin & Elizabeth Grosvenor,
                       June 10, 1795
Rufus Newel of Wardborough in the State of Ver-
    & Abigail Trowbridge,   Sept. 10, 1795
Edmund Badger of Ashford & Abigail Maynard,
                       Dec. 24, 1795
Joseph Weeks & Dilla Griggs of Ashford, Jan. 7, 1796
Matthew Campbell of Cherry Valley & Debby Put-
    nam,   Feb. 11, 1796
Oliver Goodell & Jerusha Truesdell,   April 10, 1796
Isaac Osgood & Jemima Bradbury Chandler, April 24, 1796
Ithiel Cargill & Lucy Grosvenor,   April 28, 1796
Joseph Burrows & Ruth Allen,   August, 1796
Epaphras Child of Woodstock & Sally Ingals, Sept. 18, 1796
Benjamin Champney of Southboro & Polly Sumner,
                       Nov. 9, 1796
Emery Willard of Brooklin & Vienna Stone, Dec. 11, 1796

Uriah Kingsley & Parnal Lathrop, Jan. 8, 1797
Amasa Storrs of Mansfield & Gratis Grosvenor, Jan. 10, 1797
Elijah Holt of Cherry Valley & Polley Adams,
Feb. 20, 1797
Elisha Chase & Lucy Sharpe, April 4, 1797
Amos Chaffee of Ashford & Harmony Crary, Oct. 1, 1797
Oliver Follet of Windham & Elizabeth Stowel,
March 29, 1798
John Dillebey & Phebe Beverly, both of Woodstock,
April 25, 1798
Theodore Atkinson Goffe of Bedford, New Hamp-
shire, & Anne Griggs, June 24, 1798
David Day of Killingly & Sarah Morse, Oct. 2, 1798
Elijah Holmes & Olive Ingals, Oct. 7, 1798
Augustus Boller of Ashford & Fanny Trowbridge,
Nov. 27, 1798
Keder Gallup & Phebe Darling of Woodstock,
Nov. 29, 1798
Abiezer Smith & Lucena Howard, Jan. 1, 1799
Siah Fuller of Woodstock & Mary Lord, April 22, 1799

EAST HADDAM.

MIDDLESEX COUNTY.

Was taken from Haddam and incorporated as a town 1734. The first Congregational Church was formed in East Haddam 1704. The second church in the district of Millington 1736. From the Millington Church records.

Daniel Brown of Lyme and Mary Townsend, Jan. 30, 1748
Aaron C. Usher & Rachel Church, Feb. 2, 1794
Hezekiah Usher & Lydia Baker, Nov. 3, 1757
Hezekiah Usher, Jr., & Alice Ransom, May 11, 1795
Asa Watson & Eunice Cone, Dec. 18, 1796
John Watson & widow Dorothy Gilbert, May 20, 1788
Joseph Way of Colchester & Hannah Spencer, Jan. 5, 1763
James Hamilton, 2d, of Colchester & Lois Wickwire,
Nov. 27, 1798
Timothy Freeman of Colchester & Mariam Wick-
wire, June 28, 1791

Andrew Carrier of Colchester & Phebe Wickwire,
Feb. 23, 1792
Samuel Wickwire & Jane Brown, June 24, 1761
Alfred Willey & Olive Cone, Oct. 29, 1789
Cyrus Willey of Hadlyme & Mary Ackley, Feb. 7, 1793
George Warren Willey & Deidemai Cowdry, May 11, 1788
Nathan Williams & Lois Lord, Oct. 1, 1799
Phillip Williams & Ruth Arnold, Feb. 24, 1761
Thomas Rauthburn of Lyme & Sarah Williams,
Dec. 23, 1790
Phineas Wright & Elizabeth Borden, Oct. 17, 1750
Samuel Fuller & Sarah Hall, June 30, 1749
Samuel Fuller, Jr., & Lois Andrews, Nov. 16, 1758
Timothy Fuller & Thankful Gray, Nov. 30, 1749
George Dudley Gates & Statira Cone, Nov. 10, 1793
Jacob Gates & Mary Steward, Oct. 13, 1763
Daniel Sterling of Lyme & Jedediah Gates, Nov. 14, 1792
Nathan Gates, 2d, & Polly Andrus, March 12, 1792
Nathaniel Gates & Lucy Gallup, Feb. 3, 1788
Samuel Gates & Rachel Willey, April 5, 1764
Thomas Gates & Rachel Smith, June 23, 1788
Pelatiah Bliss of Montville & Hannah Gilbert, Sept. 19, 1793
John Miller of Lyme & Lydia Gilbert, June 27, 1791
Benjamin Graves & Lucy Arnold, Nov. 24, 1790
Simeon Crosby of Hadlyme & Lidia Graves, August 10, 1749
Roswell Graves & Elisabeth Driggs, Nov. 15, 1763
Starling Graves & Anna Cone, Oct. 28, 1794
Joseph Lord of Lyme & Phebe Griffin, Nov. 25, 1794
John Harris of Plainfield & Irene Griffing, Dec. 27, 1753
Daniel Griggs, Jr., & Ruth Graves, Nov. 15, 1763
Charles Treadway of Colchester & widow Hannah
Hall, April 28, 1796
Sylvester Hall & Margaret Plumb, Jan. 10, 1798
John Harris & Statira Fuller, Feb. 7, 1790
Ezra Harvey & Grace Steward, Feb. 1, 1762
Russel Harvey & Rachel Hungerford, Dec. 24, 1789
Dyar Higgins & Phebe Mack, Nov. 17, 1791
Gilbert Holmes & Sally Brainard, July 12, 1791
Green Hungerford & Elizabeth Steward, Feb. 20, 1745-6
Nathaniel Hungerford, Jr., & Dolly Gates, Nov. 5, 1788

Thomas Hungerford & Rachel Cone,	Dec. 8, 1756
David Jewett & Sarah Selden of Lyme,	Nov. 3, 1757
Daniel Clark of Colchester & Hannah Jones,	Dec. 3, 1746
Thomas Cowdery & Mary Anderson,	Oct. 19, 1756
William Cowdery & Hannah Emmons,	Sept. 18, 1760
Increase Crosby & Rachel Graves,	Feb. 13, 1755
Elisha Done & Mary Atwell,	April 2, 1752
Amasa Dutton, Jr., & Mary Mather,	May 2, 1798
Ebenezer Dutton & Phebe Beebe,	April 26, 1753
Russell Dutton & Sally Chapman,	Oct. 14, 1788
James Ely of Lyme & Rizpah Beebe,	Jan. 15, 1792
Daniel Emmons & Mary Cone,	April 2, 1761
Ebenezer Emmons & Susanna Spencer,	April 4, 1754
Gilbert Emmons & Dolly Chapman, of first society of East Haddam,	Nov. 17, 1791
Samuel Emmons, Jr., & Sally Lord,	Oct. 6, 1793
Thomas Emmons & Huldah Cone,	May 21, 1752
Aaron Fox & Eunice Beebe,	July 8, 1792
Daniel Fox & Hannah Burr,	Oct. 15, 1747
Daniel Fox & Elisabeth Gates,	Nov. 12, 1761
Ebenezer Fox & Esther Purple,	Sept. 8, 1748
Sala Jones of Colchester & Elizabeth Fox,	Sept. 29, 1793
John Hewitt of Bozrah & Elizabeth Fox,	April 1, 1798
Ezekial Fox & Sarah Borden,	Sept. 22, 1765
Gershom Fox & Elisabeth Purple,	Oct. 30, 1760
Joseph Fox & Catherine Rogers,	April 3, 1755
Joseph Fox & Betsy Spencer, alias Garner,	April 3, 1796
Joshua Fox & Sarah Fox,	Jan. 24, 1760
Elisha Chapman of Collinsville & Mariam Fox,	April 28, 1791
Daniel Rogers of Lyme & Sarah Fox,	Dec. 7, 1790
William Fox & Annah Cone,	Nov. 29, 1759
Daniel Fuller & Mehetabel Cone,	May 5, 1756
Daniel Fuller & Eunice Andrews,	May 25, 1758
Elisha Fuller & Esther Hungerford,	May 5, 1748
John Fuller & Sarah Hamlin,	Feb. 10, 1746-7
Matthias Fuller & Mary Griswold,	June 27, 1754
James Sawyer & Anna Rogers,	Sept. 20, 1759
William Selby & Annah Sparrow,	Feb. 28, 1765
Abner Sewell & Elisabeth Harrison,	May 16, 1762

Medad Thornton & Rebecca Sewell,	Sept. 27, 1759
Abner Smith & Mehitable Emmons,	May 24, 1795
Ebenezer Smith & Rhoda Beebe,	March 23, 1763
Enoch Smith & widow Rachel Williams,	Oct. 13, 1794
Diodate Jones of Colchester & Polly Smith,	July 1, 1789
Hezekiah Goodrich & Anna Southmayd,	July 14, 1788
John Sparrow & Dolly Hungerford,	Feb. 2, 1792

Justin Worthington of Colchester & Sally Sparrow,
Nov. 27, 1794

Amasa Spencer & Rebeccah Beckwith of Hadlyme,
Oct. 24 (?), 1799

Asa Spencer & Deborah Patterson,	Sept. 12, 1763
Ely Spencer & Olive Huntley of Lyme,	Oct. 15, 1795

Rev. Ichabod Lord Skinner of Coventry & Hannah Spencer, Jr., Nov. 19, 1794

Hobart Spencer & Eunice Barns,	August 22, 1763
Jeremiah Spencer & Abigail Burr,	Jan. 7, 1747–8
William Mudge of Windham & Mary Spencer,	June 10, 1762
Nehemiah Spencer & Betsy Swan,	Feb. 14, 1793
Peter Spencer & Elizabeth Emmons,	Feb. 1, 1749–50
Ezekiel Crocker of Norwich & Sarah Spencer,	Dec. 19, 1759
Sylvester Spencer & Sally Beebe,	June 23, 1794

Moses Cleaveland of Windham & Tabitha Spencer,
May 31, 1759

Elijah Staples & Mary Grant,	Oct. 15, 1761
James Steward, Jr., & Rhoda Graves,	March 24, 1763
Nathan Steward & Martha Shaw,	March 11, 1760
William Steward & Mary McWilliams,	April 8, 1756
John Butler, Jr., & Alice Stockings,	Dec. 3, 1789
Hurlbut Swan & Hannah Estabrook, Jr.,	Sept. 16, 1794
Jabez Swan, Jr., & Huldah Olmsted, Jr.,	Oct. 24, 1799

Antipas Tisdell of Lebanon & Jerusha Huntley of
Lyme, Feb. 10, 1746–7

Jonathan Beebe, 2d, & Lydia Spencer,	July 30, 1761
John Niles of Colchester & Lydia Beebe,	March 17, 1789

David Bigelow of Colchester & Marsylvia Beebe,
Feb. 18, 1794

Samuel Beebe of New London & Mary Beebe,	Dec. 4, 1759
Thomas Williams of Colchester & Mary Beebe,	Nov. 7, 1793
Nathan Beebe & Ann Fuller,	June 25, 1761

Samuel Beebe & Margaret Steward,   Sept. 19, 1751
Silas Beebe & Elizabeth Emmons,   Jan. 16, 1752
Isaiah Armstrong& Deborah Bigelow,   May 15, 1794
Jared Brainerd & Sybil Bate,   April 19, 1763
John Parmele of Saybrook & Prudence Brainerd,
                                            Sept. 19, 1798
Abraham Doolittle of Middletown & Sarah Brockway,
                                            August 21, 1776
Daniel Bulkley of Colchester & Dorothy Olmsted,
                                            August 16, 1764
Phineas Sabin of Norwich & Abigail Burnam, April 22, 1756
David Burnham & widow Mary Beebe,   Oct. 29, 1795
Eddy Burnham & Mary Emmons,   June 29, 1788
Aaron Bigelow of Colchester & Lydia Burnham,
                                            Feb. 10, 1793
Richard Parker & Polly Burnham,   Dec. 4, 1794
Luther Wright of Wilbraham & Polly Calkins,
                                            August 21, 1791
Elisha Carrier & Mary Fuller,   Jan. 22, 1795
Daniel Jones of Hebron & Hannah Carrier,   March 22, 1763
Henry Wright of Wilbraham & Desire Caulkins,
                                            Nov. 22, 1792
Guy Chadwick & Mehitable Mather, both of Lyme,
                                            Dec. 24, 1793
Isaac Biggelow of Colchester & Mary Chamberlain,
                                            April 5, 1759
Joshua Chapen & Mary Brown,   March 8, 1753
Jabez Chapman & Anna Beebe,   April 2, 1752
Jonathan Chapman & Mary Steward,   Feb. 25, 1752
Daniel Peck of Norwich & Mary Chapman,   Oct. 7, 1765
Simeon Chapman & Sarah Barns,   May 21, 1760
George Huntley of Colchester & Betsy Church,
                                            Sept. 3, 1792
Ira Church& Dorthy Chauncey,   Oct. 10, 1763
John Church, Jr,, & Jane Park,   Jan. 21, 1762
Oliver Church & Elizabeth Cone,   Jan. 17, 1788
William Boothe of Colchester & Polly Church, May 15, 1794
Aaron Cleaveland & Eunice Spencer,   Sept. 4, 1755
Jesse Beckwith of Lyme & widow Phebe Comstock,
                                            March 28, 1791

David Bigelow of Springfield, N. Y., & Anna Cone,
              Jan. 27, 1796
Elihu Cone & Dorothy Smith,   Nov. 2, 1775
Asa Robinson of Hebron & Esther Cone,   May 15, 1760
George Cone, Jr., & Damaris Saxton,   Sept. 4, 1776
James Cone, Jr., & Mary Arnold,   Nov. 14, 1793
Jeremiah Cone & Ruth Spencer,   July 25, 1776
Dr. Jonah Cone & Polly Hall of 1st Society of E.
  Haddam,   Jan. 11, 1797
Joseph Cone, Jr., & Martha Spencer,   June 14, 1759
Joseph W. Cone & Mehitable Swan,   Nov. 7, 1796
Martin Cone & Rebecca Spencer,   June 5, 1764
Amos Jones of Colchester & Mary Cone,   Dec. 27, 1759
Phineas Newton of Windsor & widow Mary Cone,
            March 12, 1760
Woodward Marsh of Hadlyme & Mary Cone,   Jan. 7, 1788
David Warner of Saybrook & Mary Cone,   Sept. 10, 1799
Isaac Cone of East Haddam & widow Mary Cone,
            Dec. 17, 1795
Matthew Cone & Mary Barns,   June 24, 1760
Ensign Nathaniel Cone & Mary Graves,   Dec. 5, 1745
Nehemiah Cone & Jedida Andrews,   Jan. 17, 1764
Noadiah Cone & Lidya Cone,   May 1, 1755
Salmon Cone & Anna Anderson,   June 25, 1797
Samuel Cone, Jr., & Hannah Annable,   May 7, 1794
Solomon Cone & Mary Spencer,   May 30, 1776
Sylvanus Cone & Hannah Ackley,   Nov. 13, 1755
Sylvanus Cone, Jr., & Sarah Ackley,   June 26, 1760
John Jones & Thankful Cone,   Dec. 26, 1787
Calvin Freeman & widow Mary Judd,   June 26, 1788
Jacob Kendall & Prudence Beebe of Ashford.   Jan. 12, 1761
Thomas Knowlton & Abigail Ackley,   August 30, 1753
Diodate Lord & Polly Swan,   Oct. 22, 1799
John Lord of Westchester & Sarah Lord,   Jan. 21, 1747–8
Solomon Mack of Lyme & Lidya Gates,   Jan. 4, 1759
John Marsh & Mary Frink,   Nov. 27, 1788
Augusta Mather, Jr., & Polly Arnold,   March 30, 1797
Benjamin Griffin of Lyme & Clarissa Mather,   Dec. 20, 1798
William Rogers of Woodstock & Mehitable Mather,
  Jr.,   Sept. 21, 1797

Richard Rogers of Lyme & Lois Maynard,   Nov. 4, 1798
Jason Millard & Rachel Andrews,   May 17, 1750
John Miller & Annah Morgan, Jr.,   May 13, 1798
Turner Miner & Mary Spencer,   Sept. 18, 1788
Paul Moody of Newbury & Mary Jewett of Lyme,
                                              Oct. 25, 1762
Abijah Morgan, Jr., & Olive Church,   April 1, 1793
Daniel Starling of Lyme & Demas Morse,   Feb. 17, 1763
Burwell Newton of Danbury & Sybil Harvery of
      First Society, East Haddam,   Sept. 29, 1795
Phinehas, a servant of Capt. S. Olmsted, & Mary
      Button,   Oct. 11, 1759
Judah Lewis of Colchester & Polly Olmsted,   July 2, 1797
Aaron Cone Palmer & Arzubah Brainerd,   May 1, 1796
Levi Palmer, Jr., & Lydia Emmons,   Sept. 24, 1793
Timothy Patterson & Elisabeth Beebe,   March 13, 1760
Darius Peck of Lyme & Abigail Pratt,   Oct. 5, 1797
David Purple & Lucy S. Cone,   Sept. 13, 1753
Samuel Starkweather of Stonington & Sarah Purple,
                                              July 29, 1747
John Banning of Lyme & Deborah Reed,   June 2, 1757
Isaiah Rogers of Lyme & Mary Reeves,   Nov. 11, 1762
John Rogers & Sarah Borden,   June 1, 1758
Rev. Daniel Russell & Mrs. Catherine Chauncey,
                                              July 29, 1752
Amos Ackley & Rhoda Cone,   Dec. 5, 1793
Gideon Ackley & Deborah Rowley,   Oct. 27, 1763
Isaac Crocker Ackley & Lydia Plumb,   Feb. 25, 1795
Nathaniel Ackley (age 82) & widow Hannah Smith
      (age 75),   Dec. 20, 1792
Samuel Ackley & Jemima Barns,   March 1, 1764
Matthias Gates of Colchester & Thankful Ackley,
                                              May 13, 1756
Lemuel Fitch of Colchester & Rebecca Ames, Feb. 11, 1761
Isaiah Barnes Arnold & Azubah Williams,   June 9, 1794
Joseph Arnold, Jr., & Lucy Barns,   May 13, 1761
Joseph Arnold, 2d, & Stella Beebe   May 3, 1789
John Watson of Lebanon & Sarah Arnold,   Feb. 26, 1761
David Johnson of Colchester & Stella Arnold, April 29, 1799
Josiah Jewitt Baker & Betsy Chadwick,   Jan. 13, 1791

Samuel Banning & Lidya Scovill,   Sept. 13, 1764
William Banning & Lydia Church,   April 9, 1798
Isaiah Barns & Sarah Arnold,   Jan. 1, 1756
Barzillai Beckwith, Jr., & Livia Griffin,   Sept. 26, 1791
Allyn W. Griffin of Marietta & Betty Beckwith,
    March 26, 1797
Butler Beckwith & Hannah Cone.   Sept. 10, 1797
Jasper Beckwith & Candice Cone,   August 29, 1793
Nathan Beckwith & Betsey Spencer,   Oct. 26, 1797
Abner Beebe & Apphia Sparrow,   April 26, 1753
Amasa Beebe & Hannah Niles of Colchester,   Feb. 21, 1793
Ansel Beebe & Charlotte Arnold,   Jan. 18, 1791
Brockway Beebe & Phebe Dutton,   Feb. 10, 1757
John Loomys of Lebanon & Elisabeth Beebe,
    April 22, 1760
Gideon Beebe & Delina Rogers,   August 1, 1797
Benjamin Smith of East Windsor & Hannah Beebe,
    Dec. 10, 1790
Jepthah Beebe & Sally Ackley,   Feb. 21, 1796
Jonathan Beebe & widow Elizabeth Staples,   Oct. 11, 1759

SAYBROOK.

MIDDLESEX COUNTY.

A town settled in 1635 and covering an extensive territory which has since been divided into several townships. The Congregational church, formed in 1646, became the mother of several growing congregations within the limits of the original township. Two of these are now in the townships of Westbrook and Chester. The Second Church of Saybrook, formed in 1726, is now in Westbrook, a town incorporated in 1840. The Third Church, formed in 1742, is now in Chester, a town incorporated in 1836. The records of this old church have in the main been lost. The following alone remain of the marriages on Chester church records.

Phineas Parmlee of East Haddam & Prudence South-
    ward of Saybrook,   Nov. 25, 1759
Reuben Clark & Elizabeth Juba, both of Saybrook,
    Dec. 3, 1759
Edmund Shipman of Saybrook & Lois Willcocks
    of Killingworth,   May 22, 1760
John Carter, Jr., of Killingworth, & Sarah Water-
    house of Saybrook,   Nov. 27, 1760

John Holmes of East Haddam and Mary Canfield
    of Saybrook,   April 22, 1762
Samuel Waterhouse & Luce Warner,   Nov. 11, 1762
Jonathan Nicols & Joanna Webb,   Dec. 11, 1762
Jared Clark & Mehetable Demock,   Dec. 22, 1763
Eliphas Graves & Rebecka Webb,   Feb. 9, 1764
John Pittit & Rebecka Waterhouse,   Nov. 15, 1764
William Mitchel & Sarah Parmlee,   Dec. 13, 1764
David Baldwin & Parnel Clark,   Dec. 13, 1764
Gideon Southworth & Sarah Leet,   ————
Martin Southward & Anne Webb,   Jan. 3, 1773
Samual Parmlee & widow Mahetable Cooley,
                      March 23, 1773
Austin Waterhouse & Jerusha Buck,   June 14, 1773
John Harding of Middle Haddam & Thankfull
    Clark of Old Haddam,   Oct. 14, 1773
William Stanard of North Killingworth & widow
    Sarah Stoddard,   Nov. 11, 1773
James Webb & Elizabeth Douglas,   Dec. 9, 1773
Simeon Brooks & Lois Church,   March 3, 1774
Charles Pomeroy & Temperence Waterhouse,
                      March 17, 1774
Lewis Fairchild of Guilford and widow Mehetible
    Parmlee,   May 12, 1774
Joseph Clark of Haddam & Sarah Dudley, Oct. 13, 1774
John Mallery & Esther Webb,   Jan. 4, 1775
Zolotes Saunders of Lyme & Hannah Cramer of
    Saybrook,   March 8, 1775
Thomas Silliman & Lydia Warner,   Dec. 5, 1775
Isaiah Canfield & Anne Leet,   Jan. 3, 1776
William Ely of Haddam & Hannah Barker of Say-
    brook,   April 3, 1776
Paul Brooks & Dorothy Ray, both of Haddam, April 3, 1776
Noah Baldwin and Sarah Scott (but the latter
    Sarah Scott, lately from Long Island),   Dec. 5, 1776
Uriah Kelsey of North Killingworth & Elizabeth
    Buck of Saybrook,   July 10, 1777
David Dickinson & Lois Clark, both of Haddam,
                    August 21, 1777
Nathan Saunders & Esther Dunk,   Sept. 10, 1777

Samuel Norton of Farmington and Mary Bates of
    Saybrook,   Oct. 2, 1777
Simeon Church, Jr., & Theodora Beebe,   Dec. 30, 1778
Jonothan Warner of Saybrook & Hepzibah Ely of
    Hadlyme,   August 5, 1779
Isaiah Huntly of Marlborough & Elizabeth Church
    of Saybrook,   Sept. 5, 1779
James Titter of Pattepeauge & Hannah Spencer
    of Saybrook,   Sept. 16, 1779
Aaron Betts & Clarinda Ward, both of Richmond,
                                   Oct. 17, 1779
Henry Baldwin & Jane Shipman,   Nov. 1, 1779
Daniel Smith of Haddam & Jamesin Willard of Say-
    brook,   Nov. 18, 1779
Benjamin Webb & Anne Hannah Deangelish, Dec. 16, 1779
Abner Pratt of Pattepeauge & Lydia Cramer of
    Saybrook,   Dec. 7, 178c
Ebenezer Covil & Anne Shipman,   Dec. 7, 1780
Calven Cone of Hadlyme & Rebecca Leet of Say-
    brook,   Dec. 7, 1780
Gilbert Griswold of Walpole & Rebecca Nichols
    of Saybrook,   Oct. 26, 1786
Jedidiah Harris of Killingworth & Mary Leet of
    Saybrook,   Jan. 21, 1787
Gideon Leet & Lucinda Buckingham,   April 19, 1787
Samuel Church & Lydia Nichols,   Sept. 19, 1787
Elias Southworth & Judith De Angelis,   Oct. 4, 1787
Reynold Webb & Catherine Parmelee,   Nov. 15, 1787
Jonah Carter of Benlson (?) & Charlotte Mary De
    Angelis of Saybrook,   Dec. 24, 1787
Amos Randal of East Haddam & Jeniva Dudley of
    Saybrook,   Feb. 10, 1788
Daniel M. Callumb & Martha Baldwin of Saybrook,
                                 June 15, 1789
Capt. Zachariah Clarke & Anne Burhud of Saybrook,
                                July 2, 1789
Thomas Silliman, Esq., & Huldah Dunk of Saybrook,
                              Oct. 22, 1789
Dan. Parmelee of North Killingworth & Johanna
    Nicols of Saybrook,   June 3, 1790

Jonathan Talbert of Middletown & Deborah Lewis
 of Saybrook,   June 27, 1790
John Mitchel & Abigail Watrous,   Oct. 24, 1790
Richard Lord of Lyme & Anne Mitchel of Saybrook,
            Dec. 9, 1790
John Clark & Cloe Pratt of Pattepeauge, Feb. 6, 1791
Pascal De Angelis & Betsey Webb of Saybrook,
           March 8, 1791
Gideon Watrous & Fanny Franklin of Saybrook,
          March 31, 1791
Ambrose Kirtland of Saybrook & widow Mable
 Parmelee of Chester,   August 22, 1791
Daniel Spencer & Wealthy Warner, both of Say-
 brook,   Oct. 30, 1791
Joseph Clark of Chester & Anne Southworth of
 Pattepeauge,   Dec. 22, 1791
Aaron Gold of West Minster, Vermont, & Eliza-
 beth Clark of Saybrook,   Jan. 26, 1792
Eliak Sheel of Freehold, York State, & Abigail
 Shipman of Saybrook,   Jan. 29, 1792
Edward Shipman of Saybrook & Rosamond
 Southworth of Haddam,   Feb. 9, 1792
Daniel Ingram, widower, & widow Hannah Deni-
 zen, both of Saybrook,   Nov. 20, 1792
Midian Bradley of Guilford & Sarah Parmelee of
 Saybrook,   Feb. 25, 1793
Joel Canfield, widower, & widow Priscilla Mittar
 of Haddam,   April 9, 1793
Job Canfield of Durham & Esther Parmelee of
 Saybrook,   Oct. 24, 1793
Samuel Hough of Chester & Phebe Post of
 (Pechaug) Saybrook,   Oct. 31, 1793
Job Southworth & Ruth Shipman, Nov. 26, 1793
John Barker & Lucinda Gilbert, Feb. 21, 1794
Beta Norton of Guilford & Lydia Bushnel of Say-
 brook,   March 18, 1794
Nathan Post of Pechaug & Charity Lewis of Ches-
 ter,   Feb. 1, 1795
Ozias Pratt of Pettapaug & Elizabeth Barker of
 Chester,   May 10, 1795

Marsh Ely of Lyme & Sally Warner of Saybrook,
                                     Oct. 25, 1795
Noah Hodeley of Shinaug, York State, & Clara
    Buthly of Pettapouge,   Feb. 10, 1796
Ebenezer Denizen & Mehitable Denizen, both of
    Pettapouge,   Feb. 24, 1796
Giles Clark of Chester & Polly Southworth of
    Pettaprauge,   March 9, 1796
Asa Proctor of New London & Polly Clark of
    Chester,   April 19, 1796
Loranzo Smith & Minnie Post, both of Pettapeauge,
                                     May 3, 1796
Joseph Shipman & Jerusha Squire, both of Saybrook,
                                     July 17, 1796
Lazaous Milbar of East Haddam & Susannah
    Scovil of Haddam,   August 29, 1796
Israel Southworth & Hannah Watrous, both of
    Saybrook,   Oct. 13, 1796
Alexander Scranton of Guilford & Mercy Buthly
    of Saybrook,   Dec. 16, 1796
Levi Southworth of Saybrook & Polly Batess of
    Haddam,   Jan. 12, 1797
Elijah Hill of Granby & Betsey Sawyer of Say-
    brook,   April 3, 1797
Dyer Harris of Mordville & Temperence Watrous
    of Saybrook,   April 23, 1797
Cyrus Grimbs or Grayham of Hadlyme & Sally
    Bates of Haddam,   June 1, 1797
Daniel Barker & Hannah Shipman, both of Chester,
                                     June 1, 1797
Jesse Murray & Sally Ellis, both of Guilford, August 9, 1797
Jared Clark & Sarah Shipman, both of Chester, Oct. 2, 1797
John Warner & Mehitable Clark, both of Chester,
                                     Oct. 3, 1797
Samuel Webb & Temperence Smith, both of Chester,
                                     Nov. 15, 1797
Harman Dudley & widow Urania Havens, both of
    Saybrook,   Nov. 20, 1797
Dan Denizen & Sarah Bushnel, both of Saybrook,
                                     Dec. 14, 1797

7

Capt. Benjamin Holt of New London & Lucy
    Southworth of Saybrook,   Dec. 14, 1797
Joshua Bushnel & Anne Mercy Watrous, both of
    Saybrook,   Feb. 4, 1798
Samuel Mills of Chester & Rebecca Balden of
    Wethersfield,   Feb. 27, 1798
William Hough & Mary Barker, both of Chester,
                      March 22, 1798
William Buck & Mary Higley Mills,   March 27, 1798
Nathanael Clark & Mary Proctor, both of Saybrook,
                      June 24, 1798
William Jones of Berson & Bathshebah Clark of
    Saybrook,   August 6, 1798
William Gilbert of East Haddam & Rebecca Wat-
    rous of Saybrook,   Jan. 6, 1798
Benjamin Lord & Dorcas Tucker, both of Saybrook,
                      Feb. 3, 1799
Jabez Southworth & Sally Shipman, both of Ches-
    ter,   Feb. 8, 1799
Daniel Towner of Killingworth & widow Deborah
    Lyell of Chester,   Feb. 11, 1799
Noadiah Brainard of East Haddam & Lylvina
    Southworth of Haddam,   Feb. 11, 1799
Asa Southworth of Haddam & Lydia Brooks of
    Chester,   Feb. 11, 1799
Harris Watrous & Clarinda Sawyel of Saybrook,
                      Sept. 22, 1799
Benjamin Ray & Denise Dickinson, both of Haddam,
                      Oct. 6, 1799
Phinehas Warner & Lydia Clark, both of Chester,
                      Oct. 17, 1799
Josiah Watrous & Abigail Dickinson,   Nov. 7, 1799
Sam Post of East Haddam & Rebecca Pratt of
    Saybrook,   Nov. 21, 1799
David Spencer & Betsey Williams, both of Saybrook,
                      Dec. 24, 1799

WASHINGTON.

LITCHFIELD COUNTY.

Town incorporated 1779. The Congregational Church was formed in 1742, and the locality then called Judea.

Zechariah Hawley of Stratfield & Bethia Austin of Suffield,	April 27, 1749
Jonathan Rich of Kint & Abigail Macaboye of Bethlehem,	July 12, 1749
Charles Smith & Bersheba Bartholemy,	Jan. 31, 1750
Simon Burton of Sharon & Hannah Chapel of Kint,	March 19, 1750
Newton Smith & Rhoda Weeks,	May 10, 1750
John Guthrie & Patience Knap,	May 10, 1750
Lemuel Bartholemy & Mary Squires,	July 1, 1751
Henry Ingraham & Francis Nichols of Simsbury,	Oct. 28, 1751
Seth Castle & Tabitha Hurlburt,	Jan. 15, 1752
Ebenezer Andrews & Jemimah Hurd,	July 27, 1752
Benjamin Hurd & Anna Hopson,	Sept. 6, 1752
Enos Foot of Newtown & Mary Chappel of Kint,	Dec. 7, 1752
Jonathan Smith & Ann Hurd,	Oct. 3, 1753
Orias Wilcox of Middletown & Mabel Gould of Litchfield,	Oct. 31, 1753
Samuel Judson & Elizabeth Basker,	Nov. 12, 1753
Elijah Baker of Roxbury & Ruth Hurd of Judea,	Nov. 28, 1753
Amos Clark of Bethlehem & Neomi Weeks of Judea,	Nov. 20, 1753
Peleg Stone & Mindwell Baker,	June 10, 1754
Solomon Johnson of Southbury & Sarah Durkee of Litchfield,	March 15, 1754
Thomas Waugh of Litchfield & Roxana Watson of Bethlehem,	April 11, 1754
James Loggan & Rachel Weeks,	July 1, 1754
Joseph Lamb & Betsy Ingraham,	Oct. 28, 1754
James Calhoun & Mary Guthrie,	Dec. 31, 1754

Thomas Durkee & Abiah Smith,   March 5, 1755
Henry Fisher of New Preston & Eunice Palmer of
    New Preston,   April 29, 1755
Ezekiel Baker & Molly Chitenton,   Nov. 11, 1755
Ezra Gilbert of East Greenwich & Mary Hurlburt,
                                              Nov. 26, 1755
David Owen of New Preston & Isabel Macay of
    Judea,   Jan. 25, 1756
John Woodruff of Judea & Sarah Baker,   Feb. 3, 1756
Daniel Hurd of Roxbury & Anne Castle of Roxbury,
                                              March 8, 1756
Isaac Sanford & Jerusha Baker,   May 4, 1756
Eleiad Curtis of Bethlehem & Clotildre Weeks of
    Judea,   May 20, 1756
Abraham Kirby & Eunice Stenkweather of New
    Preston,   May 31, 1756
Daniel Orson of New Milford & Susanna Guthrie
    of Judea,   Nov. 15, 1756
Nathan Warner of Woodbury & Mary Durkee of
    Judea,   May 13, 1757
Abisha Moseley of Judea & Lois Dutton (money I
    refused becayse his Father was a Deacon),
                                              Dec. 14, 1757
Salmon Hurlburt & Anna Everett,   April 13, 1758
Samuel Loggan & Rachel Royce,   May 25, 1758
Judah Baldwin & Deborah Royce,   July 28, 1758
Lewis Munger of Bethlehem & Elizabeth Stone of
    Judea,   Feb. 23, 1759
Joseph Beman of East Greenwich & Catherine
    Durkee of Judea,   June 28, 1759
Gideon Hollister & Patience Hurd,   Dec. 6, 1759
Samuel Dutton & Joanna Root (at ye same time
    preached a sermon from Eph. 5:23),   Dec. 6, 1759
James Linn of Woodbury & Priscilla Weeks of Judea,
                                              March 11, 1760
Onesimus Titus & Huldah Curtis,   April 22, 1760
Jonathan Shepard of New Preston & Mehitable
    Barker of Juda,   April 29, 1760
David Durkee & Mary Warner of Woodbury, April 30, 1760
David Calhoun & Lois Chitenton,   May 1, 1760

Peruda Isbell of Litchfield & Mary Hurlburt of
    Judea, July 3, 1760

Samuel Clark & Anna Burnum, July 10, 1760

Paul Welch of New Milford & Rosanna Whitney of
    Judea, *Henmon (?)* Nov. 3, 1761

Joseph Hurlburt & Lucy ~~Henderson~~ of Woodbury,
    April 22, 1762

Ethan Allen & Mary Brownson of Roxbury, June 23, 1762

Luther Fowler of Westfield & Anna Woodend of
    Judea, Sept. 7, 1762

Elihu Smith & Anna Shaw, (?) Sept. 16, 1762

Ebenezer Clark & Hannah Tenney, Sept. 16, 1762

Thomas Parmele, Jr., & Elizabeth Roots, Sept. 16, 1762

Joel Titus & Mary Treat, Sept. 27, 1762

Daniel Baker & Jerusha Hurd of Roxbury, 1763

Ethan Stone & Elizabeth Macoy, Oct. 5, 1763

Alexander Hannah of Bethlehem & Mary Calhoun
    of Judea, Oct. 6, 1763

Ebenezer Fenn & Sarah Basset, Nov. 8, 1763

Jonathan Botchford of New Milford & Abigail Curtis
    of Judea, Feb. 23, 1764

Jonathan Griswold of Haddam & Elizabeth Weeks
    of Judea, March 15, 1764

John Davidson & Mary Macoy, August 2, 1764

Pelg Benit of Southbury & Rebekah Beers of New
    Preston, Sept. 10, 1764

John Hopson & Abiah Hassan, Oct. 30, 1764

Isaac Gillet of Lebanon & Susanna Durkee, Nov. 15, 1764

William Hooker of Bethlehem & Mary Moseley,
    Dec. 26, 1764

Benjamin Chitenton of Spensertown & Ann Baker,
    Jan., 1765

John Dutton & Martha Savage, April 22, 1765

Eleser Ingraham & Lodia Guthrie, August 6, 1765

Abner Mosely & Ann Clark, Sept. 18, 1765

Nathaniel Barnum of Danbury & Patience Hurlburt
    of Judea, Nov. 17, 1765

Jonathan Smith & Esther Bristol, Dec. 25, 1765

Asel Hurd & Rebecca Blakesley, Feb. 20, 1766

    No records of marriages until 1771.

Aaron Olds & Eunice Durkee,   April 22, 1771
Ephraim Baker & Elizabeth Easton,   May 6, 1771
Friend Bemon of New Preston & Mary Loggins of
    Judea,   May 9, 1771
John Baker & Elizabeth Masters,   May 16, 1771
James Hall & Belly Lamb,   June 5, 1771
Isaac Newton & Elizabeth Pitcher,   Oct. 10, 1771
Matthew Royce & Mary Potter,   Nov. 4, 1771
David Root & Abigail Parker,   Sept. 29, 1773
Samuel Slade & Sarah Durkee,   Nov. 23, 1773
Jeremiah Ingraham & Ruth Bell,   Feb. 16, 1774
Brinsmade Gibson & Phiebe Hicok,   March 31, 1774
Preston Hollister & Patience Mitchel,   May 3, 1774
Joseph Bassett & Lois Bailey,   July 6, 1775
Caleb Hitchcock of New Preston & Joanna Baker
    of Judea,   Jan. 4, 1776
Elijah Hicok & Hannah Keeler,   Jan. 24, 1776
Daniel Fenn & Anna Clark,   June 13, 1776
Isaac Armstrong & Deborah Roots,   Dec. 5, 1776
Daniel Sheldon & Charlotte Judson,   July 6, 1777
Timothy Goodsel & Sarah Pitcher,   Jan. 15, 1778
Andrew Hine & Kesiah Thorp,   Feb. 27, 1778
Ephraim Miner of New Preston & Elizabeth
    Goodsel,   Feb. 18, 1778
Samuel Carr of Woodbury & Olive Armstrong,
                                               Feb. 19, 1778
Isaac Goodsel of Wells in Vermont & Mary Gib-
    son,   Feb. 19, 1778
John Hurd & Lois Hurd,   March 5, 1778
Hall Curtis & Rhoda Titus,   May 4, 1778
Justus Dayton of Waterbury & Hannah Titus,   July 8, 1778
Philo Hodge & Ketunah Armstrong,   Sept. 12, 1778
Ephraim Baker & Mary Sperry of Bethlehem,
                                               Sept. 30, 1778
Michael Henanan of Roxbury & Sarah Curtus of
    Judea,   Oct. 28, 1778
Thomas Parmele & Bathsheba Thorp,   Nov. 23, 1778
Bartholomew Baker of Reden & Sarah Fenn,   Dec. 29, 1778
Luke Welch, continental soldier, & Abigail Tor-
    rence, both of Roxbury,   Feb. 17, 1779

William Slade & Rebeca Plumb, both of Wash-
    ington,   April 13, 1779
John Mallory of Roxbury & Elizabeth Goodsel,
                                    April 29, 1779
Reuben Hicok & Silence Easton,   April 28, 1779
Samuel Northrop & widow Sarah Dutton of Beth-
    lehem,   June 2, 1779
Seth Hastings & Eunice Parmele,   Nov. 10, 1779
Daniel Nathaniel Brinsmade & Abigail Farrand,
                                    Nov. 23, 1779
David Whittlesey & Abigail Judson,   Dec. 8, 1779
Samuel Woods & Molly Curtis,   Dec. 8, 1779
Samuel Carley & Rhoda Parmele,   Dec. 8, 1779
Thomas Hooker of Bethlehem & Ruth Parmele, Dec. 8, 1779
Isaac Parish & Mary Goodsel,   Feb. 20, 1780
Gideon Robbords of Waterbury & Jerusha Pitcher,
                                    March 8, 1780
William Fox of Hartlan alias Washington & De-
    borah Furrel or Funnel,   Oct. 26, 1780
Thomas Cole of Watertown & Susanna Pitcher, Nov. 18, 1780
Simeon Mitchel & Esther Farrand,   Nov. 16, 1780
Moses Hurd & Esther Hurd, both of Roxbury, Nov. 23, 1780
Reuben Parmele & Betty Thorp,   Dec. 7, 1780
Aaron Foot & widow Content Hurd,   Dec. 28, 1780
Elijah Hassan & Esther Hollister,   Jan. 25, 1781
David Kimberly & Anna Gunn,   June 4, 1781
Aaron Smith & Olive Hurd,   Jan. 2, 1782
Daniel Richards & Sarah Parker,   April 17, 1782
Ebenezer Williams of Sharon, Vt., & Martha Lewis
    of Washington,   April 23, 1782
Simeon Hicok & Ann Parmele,   May 22, 1782
Asa Baldwin & widow Lois Basset,   July 11, 1782
Samuel Durkee of Lynox & Rhoda Mott,   Nov. 25, 1782
Stephen Hutchinson of Hartford & Martah Bell,
                                    Jan. 21, 1783
John Sears & Prudence Hurd,   April 8, 1783
Thomas Hooker of Poultney, Vt., & Ruth Hicok,
                                    April 9, 1783
Ebenezer Salman of Roxbury & widow Hannah
    Gevens,   May 1, 1783

Peres Sturtevant & Freelove Crocker,   Nov. 13, 1783
Capt. David Judson & Elizabeth Davis,   Feb. 28, 1784
Reuben Carter of Canterbury & Elizabeth Newton,
                                      March 18, 1784
David Royce & widow Bathsheba Parmele,   May 11, 1784
Enos Baldwin & Sarah Tuttle,   May 13, 1784
John Herrick & Avis Newton,   May 17, 1784
Daniel Midkiff of Leabanon & Jedida Lasey, Sept. 9, 1784
Samuel Baker & Anne Hollister,   Nov. 29, 1784
David Walker & Eunice Woodruff,   Nov. 30, 1784
Samuel Waugh & Elizabeth Goodwin, both of
   Litchfield, South Farms,   Dec. 2, 1784
Elias Hinsdale & Thankful Farnam, both of Litch-
   field, South Farms,   Dec. 2, 1784
Abel Buel of Sharon, Vt., & Sibil Hine,   1785
Thomas Baley & Martha Hurd,   Feb. 13, 1785
James Stoddard of Woodbury & Mary Judson, Feb. 19, 1785
Daniel Sherman Brinsmade & Lydia Elliot of Kint,
                                       Feb. 24, 1785
Elijah Waler of Kent & widow Jerusha Baker, May 1, 1785
Thomas Thrueman Parmele & Mehitable Eston,
                                       June 22, 1785
John Stoddard of Woodbury & Phebe Northrop,
                                       Sept. 11, 1786
Ezekiel Newton, Jr., & Elizabeth Hurd,   Feb. 13, 1790
Jonathan Curtis & Thankful Hall,   Jan. 13, 1791
John Davidson & Charlote Marchant,   May 19, 1791
Charles Newton of Goshen & Charlotte Robinson
   of Litchfield,   August 28, 1791
Elijah Caray & Anna Hicok,   Nov. 27, 1796
Joseph Durkee & Fanny Camp,   Dec. 13, 1796
Amos Smith & Polly Loggan,   Dec. 14, 1796
Joseph Calhoun & Anna Clark,   Dec. 14, 1796
Gideon Foot & Susanna Parker,   March 14, 1797
John N. Gunn & Polly Ford,   Oct. 25, 1797
Nathan Dickinson & Prudence Drinkwater,   Feb. 11, 1798
—— Warner of Sandgate, Vt., & —— Coan of
   Woodbury,   1798
Benjamin Hine & Sally Humphreys,   April 19, 1798
John Woodruff & Polly Frisbee,   July 29, 1798

Alfred Treat of South Britain & Lydia Mallery of
  Roxbury,   Oct. 21, 1798
Samuel Ford, Jr., & Betsy Platt,   Oct. 28, 1798
Sherman P. Hollister & Sally Ford,   Nov. 29, 1798
George Fretts of Southbury & Hannah Burton, Jan. 30, 1799
Isaac Cowles & Sally Griswold,   Oct. 7, 1799
Jonathan Hicok & Elizabeth Taylor,   Oct. 8, 1799

MADISON.

NEW HAVEN COUNTY.

The town of Madison was incorporated in 1826, having originally been a part of Guilford. The First Congregational Church of Madison was organized in 1707. The Second Church, located at North Madison, was organized in 1757. The following are from the records of the North Madison Congregational Church, being complete from the beginning.

MARRIED AT NORTH MADISON BY REV. RICHARD ELY.

Timothy Munger & Mabel Stevens, both of Guil-
  ford,   Oct. 20, 1757
Phileman French & Mary Dudley, both of Guilford,
                                              Oct. 27, 1757
Ruben Bishop & Ann Wright, both of Guilford,
                                              March 9, 1758
David Dudley & Triphena Everts, both of Guilford,
                                              April 13, 1758
Aaron Stone & Lois Dudley, both of Guilford, Sept. 22, 1760
Stephen Johnson of Haddam & Elizabeth Pelton of
  Guilford,   April 30, 1761
Ephraim Willcocks of Middletown & Deidama
  French of Guilford,   August 24, 1761
Nathan Scranton & widow Mary Field of Guilford,
                                              Sept. 24, 1761
Simeon Saxton & Sarah Johnson of Guilford, Jan. 14, 1762
Nathaniel Stevens & Ruth Dudley,   Oct. 20, 1762
Shubael Shelley & widow Rue,   Jan. 31, 1764
Demetrius Crampton & Abigail Permale,   April 9, 1764
Samuel Field & Submit Willard,   August 1, 1764
Miles Munger & Sarah Munger,   Nov. 7, 1765
John Loggen & —— Royer   Nov. 15, 1753
Joseph Rundel & Experience Peck   May 5, 1756

Boswel
Roped...) Lane & Sarah Dudley,   August 25, 1766
Didymus French & Jerusha Stevens,   Dec. 25, 1766
Thomas Bishop of Guilford & Anna Frances of
    Killingworth,   Sept. 21, 1767
Isaac Stone & Parthena Dudley,   Nov. 4, 1767
Joaril (?) Field & Hannah Crampton,   Nov. 4, 1767
Moses Dowd & Lydia Foster,   Nov. 5, 1767
Timothy Field & Anna Dudley,   Nov. 25, 1767
Aaron Foster & Sarah Lee,   Dec. 10, 1767
Joseph Wheeler & Experience Willcocks,   Dec. 31, 1767
John Jones of Durham & Esther Crittenden of East
    Guilford,   Sept. 22, 1768
Zebulon Hail & Rachel Bishop,   Sept. 20, 1768
James Willcocks & Sarah Scranton,   Dec. 29, 1768
John Thomas Collins & Submit Field,   Nov. 23, 1769
Benjamin Norton & Azubah Munger,   Oct. 23, 1771
Ebenezer Bragg & Abigail Bishop,   Oct. 1, 1772
Ichabod Bartlett & Azubah Norton,   Oct. 21, 1772
Samuel Stannard of Killingworth & Lucy Pelton
    of Guilford,   Nov. 11, 1772
———— Holt of Westminster in Hampshire & Mary
    Dudley,   Dec., 1772
Eliel Crampton & Lydia Porter,   April 6, 1773
Nathaniel Bishop & Ruth Bartlet,   Sept. 29, 1773
Abraham Everts & Asenath Dudley,   Nov. 11, 1773
Joshua Field & Submit Collins,   March 30, 1774
Timothy Spencer & Rachel Solivan,   Oct. 27, 1774
Thomas Wheeler & Lucy Frisby,   Oct. 4, 1775
Francis Lewis of Haddam & Sarah Pelton of Guil-
    ford,   August 29, 1776
Ebenezer Wakely of Haddam & Ame Blatchley of
    Guilford,   Jan. 15, 1777
Levi Spinnage & Anna Blatchley,   Jan. 17, 1777
Luke Field & Patience Griswold,   March 17, 1777
John Harris & Lois Johnson,   Dec. 1, 1777
Heman Brainard & Deborah Hopson,   Feb. 4, 1778
Jonathan Willcox & Elizabeth Dudley, both of Kil-
    lingworth,   April 16, 1778
Moses Dow (Dowd) & Rebekah Griswold,   May, 1778
Phineas Pelton & Rebekah Johnson,   June, 1778

Zacheriah Field & Priscilla Crampton, June 3, 1779
John Dane (or Danes) & Suse Stephens, Nov. 26, 1779
Timothy Scranton & widow Anna Field, Dec. 15, 1779
Samuel Darling & Clarinda Ely, Dec. 22, 1779
David Seaward & Mabel Field, Dec. 14, 1780
Hezekiah Reynolds of Newport & Fanne Pane (?)
    (Pain) of Long Island, Oct. 31, 1781
Nathaniel Johnson & Esther Pains, Dec. 5, 1781
Benjamin Crampton, 2d, & Nabbe Scranton, Dec. 6, 1781
Nathan Crampton & Ada Seaward, July 15, 1782
Benjamin Crampton, 2d, & Anna Field, April 23, 1783
Henry Bibbins & Sarah Bears, both of Stratford,
    Sept. 23, 1783
Ruben Chittenden & Sarah Johnson, Oct., 1784
Jared Leet (?) & Elizabeth Scranton, Nov. 29, 1784
Josiah Munger & Hannah Munger, Dec. 9, 1785
Eben Munger & Clarissa (or Clorina) Bachus, July 11, 1791
Soloman Dowd (or Doud) & Abigail Thomson, both
    of East Guilford, August 15, 1791
Nathaniel Dudley of North Killingworth & Cloe
    Dowd of North Bristol, July 20, 1792
Thomas French & Eunice Wheeler, August 22, 1792
David Stone of North Guilford & Sarah Scranton
    of North Bristol, Nov. 14, 1793
———— Frances of Wallingford & Clarinda Hail of
    North Bristol, Nov. 14, 1793
Nathaniel Dudley of Killingworth & Hannah Dowd
    of Guilford, March 10, 1794
Lieut. David Dudley & widow Hannah Bishop,
    August 1, 1795
Joanib Field of East Guilford & Phebe Wellman of
    Killingworth, Sept. 7, 1795
Timothy Slone (?) (Stone) & Eunice Fowler, Dec. 22, 1796
Isaac Hall & Temperance Bebee, Dec. 25, 1796
Aaron Hubbard, Jr., & Thankful Stephens, Feb. 7, 1797
William Stone & Huldah Bristol, May 28, 1797
Amos Frisbe & Wealthy Hotchkiss, Summer, 1797
Rufus Hubbard of Haddam & Clarissa Norton of
    North Bristol, Oct. 2, 1797
Amos Tooley & Ruth Johnson, Nov. 9, 1797

Timothy Scranton & widow ~~Ruhmund (?)~~ *Richmond* (?)   Nov. 15, 1797
John Snow & Ana Johnson,   Dec. 7, 1797
~~Rayben~~ *Reuben* Blake & Cloe Atkins of Middletown, Dec. 19, 1797
Simeon Prat (or Rat), Jr., & Jemima Bulkley,

              Summer, 1797
James Field & Sarah Stephens,   Nov. 29, 1795
James Wright & a girl belonging in Durham, name
  forgotten,   Nov. 29, 1795
Phinehas Shelly & Hannah Collins,   Dec. 15, 1798

WOODSTOCK.

WINDHAM COUNTY.

The town of Woodstock was incorporated in 1690, being then attached to Massachusetts, and so continuing for some years after. The first Congregational Church of Woodstock dates from the settlement of the town and the marriage records of the church begin with its organization.

John Holmes & Hannah Newell,   April 9, 1690
Matho Davis & Margaret Corbin,   Feb. 27, 1690–91
Nathaniel Johnson of W. & Hannah Hadley of
  Branford,   Nov. ——
Joseph Frissell & Abigail Bartholomew,   Jan. 11, 1691–92
Jabez Corbin & Mary Morss,   ——
Ebenezar Morriss & Sarah Davis,   Sept. 1, 1692
John Chandler & Mary Ramond,   Nov. 10, 1692

A RETURN OF JOSIAH DWIGHT OF SUCH PERSONS AS WERE MARRIED
BY HIM IN WOODSTOCK.

James Corbin & Hannah Eastman,   April 7, 1697
John Morss & Hannah Williams,   May 10, 1697
William Coit & Sarah Chandler,   June 7, 1697
Peter Morss & Priscilla Carpenter,   Dec. 28, 1698
Peter Aspinwall & Elizabeth Leavens,   March 24, 1698–9
Edmund Chamberlain & Elizabeth Bartholomew,

             Nov. 21, 1699
James Leavens & Mary Chamberlain,   Nov. 21, 1699
Nathaniel Aspinwall & Abigail Bowen,   Nov. 11, 1698
William Lyon & Deborah Colburn,   Nov. 8, 1699
Samuel Warren & Mehitable Sabin,   Jan. 2, 1694–5

John Coit & Mehitable Chandler,	June 25, 1695
Benjamin Miller & Mary Johnson,	Sept. 18, 1695
John Scarbro & Mehitable Bugbee,	Oct. 17, 1695
John Bugbee & Abigail Corbit (?),	July 10, 1696
Benjamin Griggs & Patience ———,	June 18, 1701
Samuel Bugbee & Dorothy Carpenter,	Jan. 26, 1701–2
David Bishop & Rebecca Hubbard,	Feb. 4, 1701–2
Joseph Shaw of Stonington & Susannah Grosvenor of Mashamoquet,	March 26, 1702
Christopher Peake & Mary Stratton,	June 21, 1702
John Bartholomew & Elisabeth Morss,	June 28, 1702
John Goodall & Lydia Titus,	Nov. 10, 1702
Nathaniel Seshions of Pomfret & Hannah Corbin of Woodstock,	March 2, 1706–7
Samuel Hemingway & Hannah Morris,	Nov. 12, 1707
Jonathan Payson & Mary Cook,	Jan. 12, 1709–10
Samuel Gates & Mary Truesdale, both of Pomfret,	Feb. 12, 1709–10
John Goodell & Hannah Colburn,	Oct. 8, 1710
Benjamin Goodell & Hannah Gary, both of Pomfret,	May 22, 1711
Robert Mayson & Hannah Holmes,	Nov. 15, 1711
John Chamberlain & Esther Alcock,	Nov. 24, 1711
John May of W. & Elizabeth Child of Brookline, Mass.,	Dec. 18, 1711
Leicester Grosvenor & Mary Hubbard, both of Mashemoquet,	Jan. 16, 1711-12
Jessie Carpenter & Mary Bacon,	Feb. 27, 1711
Jeremiah Sabin & Abigail Davis, both of Pomfret,	May 8, 1712
Robert Buck of Killingly & Elizabeth Bacon of W.,	June 8, 1712
John Marcy & Experience Colburn,	Jan. 14, 1712-13
John March of Mendon & Abigail Eastman of W.,	Jan. 15, 1712-13
Samuel Carpenter of Pomfret & Hannah Johnson of W.,	Feb. 4, 1713
Ebenezer Eastman of W. & Sarar Pease of Haverhill,	June 3, 1713
Joseph Bartholomew & Elizabeth Sanger,	Nov. 12, 1713

Nathaniel Sanger & Ruth Cook,   Nov. 12, 1713
Daniel Peck of Rehoboth & Sarah Paine of Wood-
 stock,   April 15, 1714
Samuel Hemmingway & Margaret Johnson,   May 5, 1714
William Ward of Ashford & Rachel Humphrey,
 of W.,   August 5, 1714
Joseph Cady of Killingly & Elizabeth Hosmer
 of W.,   Sept. 14, 1714
William Lyon & Martha Morriss,   Jan. 6, 1714-15
Benjamin Franklin & Abigail Rice,   Feb. 14, 1714-15
Daniel Holt of Killingly & Lydia Preston of W.,
                                           Feb. 26, 1714-15
Edward Morriss & Bilthiah Peake,   Jan. 12, 1715
Nathaniel Sanger & Dorcas Peake,   Oct. 27, 1715
Joseph Wilson of Ashford & Marcy Parker of
 Woodstock,   April 3, 1716
John Johnson & Hannah Ainsworth,   May 2, 1716
John Franklin & Mary Earl,   August 31, 1716
John Chandler, Jr., & Hannah Gardner, married at
 Isle of Wight, Gardner's Island, L. I.,   Oct. 24, 1716
Davld Town & Mary Barton, both of Oxford, Mass.,
                                            Dec. 31, 1716
John Doodell & Hannah Coburn,   Oct. 19, 1717
Henry Elithorpe of Killingly & Mehitable Aspin-
 wall of Woodstock,   March 5, 1717-18
William Chapman of Mansfield & Abigail Lyon of
 Woodstock,   July 18, 1718
James Wetmore of New Haven & Anna Dwight of
 Woodstock,   Nov. 5, 1718
John Holmes & Mary Johnson,   Jan. 28, 1718-19
Nathan Keney (?) & Rebecca Chamberlin, both of
 Oxford, Mass.,   Feb. 23, 1718-19
Ichabod Peck of Rehoboth & Judith Paine,   Jan. 5, 1719
Isaiah Johnson & Abigail Peck,   April 28, 1720
Josiah Cummings & Mary Frissell,   May 15, 1721
John Child & Abigail Aspinwall,   Dec. 7, 1721
Ebnr. Holmes & Joanna Ainsworth,   July 1, 1719
Ephraim Town & Sarah Kenny, both of Oxford,
                                            Dec. 31, 1719
Henry Bowen & Margaret Davis of Pomfret,   May 10 1721

Joseph Peake & Mary Perrin,   March 1, 1721
Edward Ainsworth & Joanna Davis,   April 5, 1722
Samuel Bugbee & Mary Morrs,   June 26, 1722
James Marcy & Judith Ainsworth,   May 2, 1723
Manasseh Hosmer & Mary Carpenter,   May 30, 1723
Joshua Brown of Norwich & Mary Pettys of Wood-
   stock,   Sept. 23, 1723
Benjamin Roth & Eunice Lyon,   Dec. 12, 1723
Pennel Child & Dorothy Dwight,   April 9, 1724
Samuel Perrin & Dorothy Morriss,   June 14, 1724
Matturin Allard & Joanna Holmes,   July 13, 1724
Samuel Marcy of Woodstock & Mary Russell of
   Ashford,   Feb. 13, 1724-25
John Mors & Sarah Peake,   Feb. 7, 1725
Edward Bugbee & Katharine Peake,   Feb. 7, 1725
Joseph Bacon & Rebecca Carpenter, married in
   Boston,   May 15, 1725
Roger Cook of Killingly & Rebecca Scarbrough
   of Ky.,   March 15, 1726
Smith Johnson & Experience Parker,   Nov. 16, 1726
Clement Corbin & Harriet Morriss,   Nov. 7, 1726
Nathaniel Child of Killingly & Dorothy Johnson
   of Woodstock,   Dec. 3, 1726
John Frissell & Abigail Morriss,   Nov. 10, 1726
Joshua Chandler of Woodstock & Elizabeth Cutter
   of Medway, Mass.,   Feb. 16, 1726-7
Samuel Lilly & Mehitable Bacon,   March 23, 1726-7
Samuel Bugbee & Susannah Johnson,   May 16, 1727
Thomas Eaton of Tolland & Elizabeth Parker of
   Woodstock,   Nov. 31, 1727
Jabez Corbin & Mary Edmonds,   July 5, 1728
Joseph Griggs & Patience Parker,   Nov. 16, 1728
James Frissell & Elizabeth Chandler,   Feb. 13, 1728-9
Edward Johnson & Sarah Marcy,   Feb. 20, 1728-9
Ebenezer Robins & Experience Holmes, both of
   Walpole, Mass.,   Oct. 30, 1729
Thomas Child & Anna Morriss,   Nov. 24, 1729
Daniel Smith of Norwich & Sarah Deming of W.,
                                                     Feb. 4, 1729-30
Joseph Bacon, Jr., & Marcy Cutler,   Oct. 29, 1730

John Gary & Hannah Jackson,	May 13, 1731
Moses Lyon & Grace Child,	Oct. 10, 1731
Joseph Marcy of Woodstock & Mary Throop, in Bristol,	May 31, 1728
Samuel Morriss of Woodstock & Abigail Bragg, in Bristol,	Oct. 31, 1728
Ebenezer Lyon of Woodstock & Rebecca Throop,	Jan. 28, 1731-2

AN ACCOUNT OF THE PERSONS UNITED TOGETHER IN MAR-
RIAGE BY ME—AMOS THROOP.

Benjamin Morris & Hannah Hosmer,	Jan. 3, 1727–8
Caleb Lyon & Margaret Lyon,	Feb. 29, 1727–8
Jacob Child & Dorcas Ainsworth,	April 18, 1728
James Corbin & Susannah Bacon,	June 19, 1728
Jacob Lyon & Mehitable Bugbee,	June 20, 1728
Samuel Davis & Hannah Bacon,	August 6, 1728
Philip Newell & Mehitable Morris,	Dec. 3, 1728
Edward Johnson & Sarah Marcy,	Feb. 20, 1729
John Corbin & Martha Hosmer,	April 3, 1729
Jonathan Peake, Jr., & Metitable May,	May 20, 1729
Nathaniel Goun & Abigail Jackson,	April 30, 1730
Ephraim Hosmer & Dorcas Carpenter,	April 3, 1730
Ebnr. Chafee & Mary Scarborough,	April 22, 1730
Eliphalet Carpenter & Mary Bacon,	April 22, 1730
Joseph Bacon & Sarah Pike,	July 7, 1730
John Chafee & Mehitable Mascraft,	Dec. 17, 1730
Samuel Harmon & Eunis Bacon,	Dec. 31, 1730
Philip Corbin & Dorothy Barstow,	Jan. 13, 1731
Benjamin Corbin & Jemima Cutler,	April 19, 1731
John Gary & Hannah Jackson,	May 13, 1731
John Goodwell & Mary Bugbee,	May 25, 1731
Eleazar Sanger & Mary Jackson,	June 24, 1731
Amos Sexton & Elizabeth Morris,	Oct. 28, 1731
Philip Newel & Aannah Edmonds,	Nov. 29, 1731
John Carter & Susannah Bugbee,	Feb. 20, 1732
John Jennings & Elizabeth Ainsworth,	March 16, 1732
Josiah Comins & Mehitable Griggs,	May 30, 1732
William Marischal & Margaret Smith,	June 12, 1732

Ebenezar Roud & Anna Whitney,	Dec. 11, 1733
Edmund Chamberlin & Sarah Wright,	Jan. 17, 1734
Jesse Bugbee & Experience Peak,	March 14, 1734
Thomas Bacon, Jr., & Anna Johnson,	June 5, 1734
Anthony Morse & Mary Manning,	July 11, 1734
Nathan Orcott & Phebe Lillie,	July 31, 1734
Bemsle Petrs (?) & Hannah Wright,	Jan. 8, 1735
Ednezar Beben & Susannah Manning,	May 12, 1735
Japhet Utley of Windham & Anne Marcy of Woodstock,	Dec. 6, 1738

A CATALOGUE OF MARRIAGES PER ME, ABEL STILES, PASTOR, WOODSTOCK, CONN.

Pennel Bowen & Frances Throop,	Oct. 10 (30), 1737
Moses Lyon & ——— ———,	1737
James Bugby & ——— ———,	1737
Ebnezar Marcy & Mary Nicholson,	July 25, 1738
John Bartholomew & Hannah Abbot,	Jan 2, 1738-9
Caleb Grosvenor & Sarah Carpenter,	Nov. 30, 1739
Amor Morss & Mary Mascraft,	June 26, 1740
Elisha Cleveland & Esther Morss,	June 26, 1740
Eliezar Davenport & Elizabeth Smith,	evening after Thanksgiving, 1740
Timothy Hyde & Dorothy Bugbee,	Dec. 8, 1741
John Hinds & Judith Marcy,	Dec. 25, 1741
John Bishop & Sybill Holmes,	Jan. 7, 1742
Joshua May & Anna Bacon,	Jan. 20, 1742
Henry Child & Rebekah Bacon,	1742
David Craft & Mercy Brock,	——— 15, 1742
John Hutchins & Lucy Lyon,	Oct. 7, 1742
Nathaniel Mills & Sarah Holmes,	Oct. 21, 1742
John Sanger & Dorothy Peak,	Dec. 9, 1742
Richard Flynn & Sarah Manning,	Dec. 23, 1742
Philip Newel & Abigail Scarborough,	March, 1743
John Brock, Jr., & Sarah Southwick of Dudley,	Oct. 19, 1743
John Johnson & Grace Morris,	Oct. 31, 1743
Hezekiah Goff & Bethiah Morris,	Oct. 31, 1743
Nehemiah Underwood & Anna Marcy,	Feb. 1, 1743-4
Jesse Carpenter & Abigail Ainsworth,	April 16, 1744

8

Nathaniel Sanger, Jr., & Mary Roth,	May 10, 1744
John Newel & Susanna Child,	May 31, 1744
Nathaniel Warren & Althea Bugbee,	Nov. 7, 1744
John Camp & Eleanor Peck,	Nov. 23, 1744
Nathaniel Perrin & Phebe Holmes,	March 13, 1745
Samuel Monger & Abigail Barstow,	March 14, 1745
William Skinner & Thankful Mascraft,	Jan. 2, 1746
John Spaulding & Elizabeth Sanger,	Jan. 22, 1746
Job Rewel & Mary Child,	March 20, 1746
Silas Bowen & Dorothy Lyon,	April 17, 1746
Nathan Abbot & Anna Leach,	June 2, 1746
Daniel Ainsworth & Sarah Bugbee,	June 2, 1746
Isaac Skinner & Hannah Marcy,	June 19, 1746
Rev. Nehemiah Barker & Elizabeth Chandler,	Oct. 16, 1746

My negro servant & my negro servant Ann were
    joined in marriage by me, Abel Stiles, pastor,

Nov. 24, 1746

Daniel Child & Ruth Amedown,	1746
Jonathan Bugbee, Jr., & Eliza May,	Jan. 15, 1746–7
Ezra Perrin & Arma Perrin,	Feb. 19, 1747
Jebadiah Morss & Sarah Child,	1747
Joseph Monger & Jemima Lyon,	March 3, 1747

Capt. Thomas Buckminster & Mehitable Chandler,

May 21, 1747

Nathaniel Child & Jemima Bugbee,	May 28, 1747
Stephen May & Mary Child,	June 11, 1747
Pennel Bacon & Dorothy Wright,	August 3, 1747
Elijah Lyon & Sarah Monger,	Nov. 26, 1747
Stephen Harriman & Sarah Mascraft,	Feb. 25, 1748

Benjamin Bartholomew & Martha Carpenter,

March 17, 1748

Isaac Johnson, Jr., & Mary Durkee,	Nov. 1, 1748
Allenton Cushman & Deborah Lyon,	Nov. 28, 1748
Joseph Weld & Patience Child,	Dec. 8, 1748
Abijah Corbin & Abigail Wright,	April 20, 1749
Nehemiah Bugbee & Hannah Fox,	May 18, 1749

Sam & Leah, negro servants of David Wallis, were
    joined in marriage by me, Abel Stiles, pastor,

May 30, 1749

Joseph Scarborough & Esther Holmes,	June 29, 1749

Abijah Child & Abigail Johnson,	Oct. 3, 1749
John Frizell, Jr., & Sarah Roth,	Jan. 4, 1749–50
Elisha Child & Allice Manning,	Jan. 16, 1749–50
Moses Barrett & Abigail Harmon,	April 17, 1750
Jonathan Goold & Mary Corbin,	April 19, 1750
Thomas Jewett of Mansfield & Dorcas Wright of Woodstock,	April 26, 1750
John Lyon & Mary Evans,	July 26, 1750
Nahurn Green & Dorcas Sanger,	Nov. 7, 1750
Benjamin Chapin & Jemima Morris,	Jan. 3, 1751
Alexander Sessions & Huldah Perrin,	Jan. 28, 1751
Joseph Altton & Zerriah Lyon,	May 30, 1751
Benjamin Lyon & Mary May,	Jan. 2, 1752
Isaiah Chaffe & Betty Manning,	March 5, 1752
Nehemiah May, Jr., & Anna Lyon,	March, 1752
Uriah Johnson & Lucy Davenport,	May 21, 1752
Moses Child & Mary Payson,	June 26, 1752
Zebulon Baldwin & Hannah Lyon,	July 14, 1752
Ebenezar Haven & Abigail Child,	Oct. 5, 1752
Benjamin Lyon & Sarah May,	Jan. 25, 1753
John Ranson & Elizabeth Lyon,	Jan. 26, 1753
John Dyer & Anna Payson,	March 29, 1753
William Jones & Experience Bacon,	April 12, 1753
Thomas May & Lucy Child,	April 26, 1753
Ebenezer Eaton & Mary Humphray,	May 10, 1753
Asa Chaffe & Mary Howlet,	Sept. 5, 1753
Ebenezer Child, Jr., & Charity Bugbee,	May 9, 1754
Ezra May & Margaret Lyon,	June 13, 1754
John Bacon & Keziah Child,	June 20, 1754
Ephraim Manning & Mary Fox,	March 30, 1756
William Nelson, Jr., & Mary Carpenter,	May 13, 1756
Daniel Lyon, Jr., & Prudence May,	Nov. 23, 1756
Peter Child & Susanna Child,	Dec. 30, 1756
John Carpenter, Jr., & Mercy Morgan,	Feb. 9, 1757
Stephen Tucker & Lois Lyon,	March 31, 1757
Moses Johnson & Mercy Fox,	July 5, 1757
Henry Child & Dorothy Child,	July 6, 1757
Edward Bugbee & Mehitable Peake,	Jan. 25, 1758
Uriah Marcy & Urania Lyon,	May 23, 1758
Jonathan Smallige & Elizabeth Allard,	June 1, 1758

Ellkanah Stevens & Hannah Bartholomew,	July 13, 1758
Oliver Clark & Sarah Cogswell,	July 18, 1758
Jabez Corbin, Jr., & Sarah Abbott,	Dec. 27, 1758
Ezekiel Corbin & Dorcas Jewett,	Dec. 27, 1758
Ithamer Ammedown & Tabitha Green,	March 29, 1759
Ebenezer Holmes & Martha Howlet,	April 12, 1759
Peter Walker & Bethia Bugbee,	April 26, 1759
Hezekiah May & Elizabeth Carpenter,	April 26, 1759
Samuel Morris & Hannah Child,	May 3, 1759
Philip Newell, Jr., & Ruth Evans,	July 19, 1759
Smith Johnson & Sarah Gould,	Oct. 10, 1759
David Robbearts & Abigail Field,	Oct. 11, 1759
Amos Perrin & Anna Morse,	Dec. 6, 1759
Lemuel Peals or Peak & Joanna Ellingwood,	March 13, 1760
John Nellson & Mary Johnson,	May 8, 1760
Abijah Tucker & Lucy Lyon,	July 16, 1760
Samuel Chandler & Anna Paine,	July 17, 1760
Nathan Child & Dorcas Green,	Oct. 9, 1760
Joseph Ainsworth & Rebekah Allard,	Jan. 13, 1760
Benjamin Craft & Anna Richardson,	March 12, 1761
Joseph Narramore & Sarah Wright,	April 23, 1761
Ephraim Carpenter & Tabitha Chaffe,	May 14, 1761
Josiah Chandler & Lydia Richardson,	Nov. 18, 1762

Rev. Abiel Leonard, ordained Jan. 23, 1763.

John Chandler & Mary Chandler,	Oct. 20, 1763
Asa Child & Elizabeth Murray,	Nov. 17, 1763
Amos Paine & Priscilla Lyon,	Jan. 12, 1764
Nathan Grosvenor & Mary Holbrook,	May 10, 1764
Benjamin Freeman & Deborah Child,	June 13, 1764
Oliver Barrett & Hannah Chamberlin,	August 1, 1764
Hadlock Marcy & Alethea Stiles,	Oct. 29, 1764
James Bugbee, Jr., & Ann Morris,	Jan. 16, 1765
William Child & Mary Shafter,	May 28, 1765
Isaiah Lyon & Sybbil Ranny,	Oct. 24, 1765
Phineas Walker & Susanna Hide, the first marriage since my removal to North (now East) Woodstock, Abel Stiles,	Dec. 14, 1765
Benjamin Bacon & Eunice Sabin,	Feb. 6, 1766
Joshua Child & Dorothea Child,	Feb. 25, 1766

William Allard & Rebekah Davis,	April 26, 1766
Ralph Vinton & Phebe Holmes,	July 16, 1766
Parker Bacon & Mary Child,	April 9, 1767
Abiel Lyon & Elizabeth Hosmer,	June 4, 1767
Asahel Jewett & Hannah Wright,	Nov. 5, 1767
Nathaniel Blake & Abigail Child,	Nov. 19, 1767
Jonathan Bacon & Priscilla Child,	Feb. 9, 1768
Ebenezar Davidson & Patience Child,	April 21, 1768
Samuel Wright & Mary Coburn,	Oct. 27, 1768
Elijah Houghton & Rebekah Adams,	Nov. 17, 1768
Dr. Samuel Allen, Jr., of Warren, R. I., & Hannah	
Bowen,	Dec. 15, 1768
James Murray & Sarah Reynolds,	Jan. 26, 1769
Moses Corbin & Sarah Bacon,	Nov. 8, 1769
David Rawson & Sibyl Beals,	Nov. 23, 1769
Amasa Carpenter & Cynthia Child,	Jan. 11, 1770
Amasa Child & Anna Carpenter,	Feb. 1, 1770
John Hinds & Levina Brock,	March 22, 1770
Abel Morss & Sarah Holbrook,	June 7, 1770
Elisha Walker & Thankful Stone,	Nov. 15, 1770
Eliaklim May & Martha Lyon,	Dec. 27, 1770
John Lyon & Mrs. Miriam Frisket,	August 8, 1771
Ruben Ammedon & Olive Lyon,	August 8, 1771
Benjamin Brown & Dorothy Child,	Oct. 23, 1771
Asahel Clark & Dorothy Hide,	Nov. 12, 1771
Daniel Child & Anna Child,	Dec. 26, 1771
Ebenezer Davidson & Eunice Hebbard,	Feb. 20, 1772
Benjamin Stoddard & Esther Hide,	Feb. 27, 1772
Peley Corbin & Levina Lyon,	Jan. 14, 1773
Griffin Craft & Hannah May,	Jan. 21, 1773
Stephen Blackmar & Lydia White,	March 4, 1773
Jacob Ammedon & Joena Johnson,	June 10, 1773
Joseph Deming & Prudence Griffin,	Jan. 13, 1774
Samuel Chaffe, Jr., & Sarah Chaffe,	Nov. 17, 1774
Aaron Lyon & Elizabeth May,	Feb. 23, 1775
Nathaniel Child & Eleanor Fox,	Sept. 19, 1776
Lyman Lyon & Hannah Corbin,	Jan. 23, 1777
Alpha Child & Mary May,	March 27, 1777
Charles Child & Elizabeth May,	April 3, 1777
Samuel Corbin, Jr., & Mehitable Lyon,	April 8, 1777

Parker Bacon & Rachel Freeman,	April 24, 1777
Joshua Abel & Ruth Manning,	June 26, 1777
Abel White & Rebecca Solace,	Jan. 26, 1778
William Morris & Sarah Bowen,	Feb. 5, 1778
John May & Hannah Bugbee,	March 12, 1778
Zechariah Aldrich & Naomi Cook,	April 6, 1778
Ebenezer Holmes, Jr., & Marsalla Colburn,	April 7, 1778
Chester Chaffe & Caroline Walker,	April 23, 1778
Nehemiah Lyon & Betsey Bugbee,	——— 16, 1778
Davis Carpenter & Miriam Manning,	Dec. 24, 1778
Zephaniah Tucker & Huldah Holmes,	Feb. 4, 1779
Abel Child & Rebecca Allerd,	March 11, 1779
Elias Child & Dorothy Morss,	March 18, 1779
Parker Cummins & Joanna Ainsworth,	April 22, 1779
Ephraim Carryl & Lucy Clark,	April 29, 1779
Barnabus Evens, Jr., & Elizabeth Phillips,	May 9, 1779
John Bradford & Mary Dexter,	May 30, 1779

Rev. Eliphalet Lyman, ordained in South Parish, Sept. 2. 1779.

William Ranny & Abigail Bacon,	Sept. 26, 1779
Thomas Hunter & Elizabeth Newell,	March 19, 1780
Daniel Roberts & Asenath Tucker,	April 6, 1780
Benjamin Scott & Anna May,	May 2, 1780
Stephen Hide & Lois White,	May 25, 1780
Daniel Barret & Jemima Benson,	Nov. 16, 1780
Darius Bacon & Sarah Sheffield,	Dec. 21, 1780

EAST WINDSOR.

HARTFORD COUNTY.

The town of East Windsor was taken from Windsor and incorporated in 1768. The Congregational Church at East Windsor was organized in 1754. Old Windsor itself was settled as early as 1635, when the church there existed, going back to the year 1630 for its formaion.

David Bissell & Elizabeth Barkers,	Feb. 21, 1761
Thomas Foster & Martha Elmer,	Dec. 24, 1761
John Skinner & Sarah Renney of Hartford,	Nov. 21, 1762
Ebenezer Holman & Ruth Loomis,	Nov., 1763
Hezekiah Allyn & Abigail Bartlett of Stafford,	Dec. 13, 1768

Daniel Bissell & Lydia Munsel, Dec. 27, 1768
Oliver Barber of Windsor & Ann Root of Westfield,
Jan. 30, 1766
Abner Blodgett & Rachel Phelps of Enfield, March 23, 1768
Simeon Barber & Lois Allyn, Sept. 26, 1771
John Bliss & Betty White of Bolton, Jan. 15, 1766
Caleb Booth, Jr., & Anne Bartlett, May 1, 1775
Jacob Bottom & Prudence Hebard of Windham, Dec. 2, 1773
Jonathan Brown & Patience Kneeland, June 22, 1775
Smith Bailey & Jenipha Backus, Jan. 8, 1772
Nondeah Bissall & Sibbel Enos of Hartland, Vt.,
July 13, 1794
Noadiah Bissell & Betsey Shuttleworth of Dedham,
Mass., Jan. 29, 1797
Eliphalet Chapin & Mary Darling, Nov. 25, 1773
Aaron Chapin & Mary King, Sept. 15, 1777
Eliphalet Chapin & Anne Read of Canterbury,
June 18, 1778
David Carpenter & Martha Brunson, April 13, 1786
Nathaniel Drake & Anna Lodge of Colchester, Nov. 27, 1768
Silas Drake & Hannah West of Tolland, Nov. 12, 1771
David Davis & Lucy Parker, Jan. 1, 1777
Nathaniel Drake, Jr., & Hopefull Wolcott, April 4, 1774
Abner M. Ellsworth & Elcie Thomson, Dec. 31, 1797
Aaron Frost & Barnal Wood, April 12, 1773
Samuel Frost & Patience Hammond of Tolland,
Nov. 22, 1775
Aaron Frost & Margarett Hammond of Tolland,
August 13, 1777
Ashahel Green & Grace Grant, Oct. 1, 1778
Iabesh Green & Mary McCarty of Canterbury, Nov. 1, 1797
Ichabod Hatch & Hannah Munsell, Dec. 4, 1777
Ebenezer Holman & Rachel Wright, May 1, 1771
Charles Jincks & Martha Mowry of Smithfield, R. I.,
Jan. 22, 1797
Elisha Sadd or Ladd & Tabitha Strong, May 23, 1776
Jeremiah Lord, Jr., & Tryphena Pease of Enfield,
Feb. 5, 1777
Ephraim Ladd or Sadd & Lois Chapman of Bolton,
July 14, 1774

George Loomis & Anna Jepson of Hartford,   Nov. 20, 1788
Amasa Loomis & Priscilla Birge,   Feb. 1, 1783
Zaccheus Munsell & Hannah Drake of Windsor, May 4, 1768
Isaac Mason & Sarah Benton of Tolland,   June 28, 1770
Joel Nash & Sarah Boalk,   March 30, 1769
Samuel Osborn, Jr., & Hepsibath Scovel, both of
    Windsor,   Nov. 20, 1766
Moses Osborn & Mary Shaw,   August 27, 1794
Caleb Parsons & Lois Higgins of Chatham, Sept. 22, 1779
Jonathan Park or Pasks & Elizabeth Allin, April 29, 1784
Samuel Rockwell & Sarah Sheldon,   Feb. 16, 1775
Samuel Rogers & Sarah Skinner,   Nov. 24, 1785
James Rudd of Beckett, Mass., & Elizabeth Vining,
                                           June 8, 1788
Anthony Slafter & Experience Frost,   Jan. 4, 1769
Timothy Skinner & Hannah Treadway of Colchester,
                                          Sept. 21, 1774
Joseph Smith & Eunice Drake of Windsor,   Dec. 14, 1768
John Stiles & Jemima Allis of Bolton,   August 3, 1784
Jacob Strong & Elizabeth Loomis,   Nov. 1, 1787
Alexander Vining & Lovice Bease (?) of Enfield, Nov. 22, 1786
Alexander Vining & Olive Bease (?) of Enfield, Sept. 19, 1774
Jonathan Wood & Rachel Crow,   April 13, 1767
Robert Watson & Eunice Potwine (?),   Dec. 24, 1772
Ebenezer Watson & Sarah Watson,   Jan. 13, 1774
Bethuel Waldo & Ruth Wheler of Stafford, Dec. 23, 1775
Capt. Erastus Wolcott, Jr., & Chloe Bissell,   Dec. 27, 1783

INDEX.

Early Connecticut Marriages

AS FOUND ON

ANCIENT CHURCH RECORDS

PRIOR TO 1800.

SECOND BOOK.

EDITED BY

FREDERIC W. BAILEY,

MEMBER AMERICAN HIST. ASSO., CONN. HIST. SO., NEW HAVEN COLONY HIST. SO.,
NEW YORK GEN. AND BIOG. SO., SONS OF THE AMERICAN REVOLUTION
(MASS.), MANAGER BUREAU OF AMERICAN ANCESTRY.

PUBLISHED BY THE

BUREAU OF AMERICAN ANCESTRY
FOR
Family   Researches

FREDERIC W. BAILEY, MGR.
P. O. BOX 587.   NEW HAVEN, CONN.

EARLY CONNECTICUT MARRIAGES.

PREFACE.

Encouraged by the unexpected interest taken in our first book of
"Early Connecticut Marriages" which now seems to be fulfilling its
purpose; and desirous of assisting still further the efforts of persistent
seekers scattered all over our vast country who would know still more of
their early Connecticut ancestors, this second book is so soon issued;
being well assured that if original data is required this will prove to be
even more useful than the first.

While certain to be of service to many in supplying needful facts and
dates long sought for, it will necessarily prove disappointing to others,
who finding not just what they want, must still longer struggle with the
old and perplexing problems.

Realizing too truly how humble our effort is thus to bring to view
a portion of the valuable genealogical matter hidden away in obscure
quarters of the state, our own regret is that with what is even here dis-
closed absolute completeness in every detail cannot be secured. For
not only have the years left their destroying impress upon many a page,
but in other cases difficult indeed would it be to tell just what was there-
in written. If in this particular we seem to criticise the pastor's scrawling
hand, that in some cases was quite unique, we stand ready to defend him
against critics who in reading herein will see instead a spelling of names
seemingly unjustified. So far as our endeavor is concerned we have
followed closely the text. And in defense of the minister's apparent
mistakes here it might well be agreed that in those days there was no
standard for the spelling of surnames, however much the Holy Scrip-
tures may have guided all in the construction of Christian names.
Educated though he was, the art of printing, so limited in its employ-
ment then, had not touched a subject which, by the common use of the
printing press to-day, is fixed in every man's mind. On some of the old
town records a single page will bear the same surname spelled in several
different ways, merely from the want of a standard which even the owner
himself could not set. However, it is a matter deserving fuller treatment

historically by some able specialist who may settle forever some such questions as thus stand in the way to successful search. Our desire is to warn the reader not to allow any peculiar spelling of a name to throw him off the track, nor fail to give due weight to every name that in any degree could resemble that sought for. It has been observed that in a few extraordinary cases marked changes have occurred in some names to puzzle and bewilder the seeker; but in the large majority of instances it were well to follow the slight variations to their legitimate end.

For the benefit of those who do not quite understand how it is that our records all come from the Congregational church, a word may well be added to what has already been written in the Preface of the first book. Not alone is it because such records are found to be the oldest and the best, but it is well to remember that from the beginning of the settlement in 1635 to the year 1705, while there were, scattered here and there, a few Baptists, Episcopalians and Friends, no other organization of any kind existed. The whole territory was entirely theirs till, in 1705, a Baptist society was organized in Groton which stood alone of its kind for twenty years. In 1726 the second was formed at New London; and not till 1743 was the third, at North Stonington, to be found.

Up to this time there had been but little deviation from the tenets of Congregationalism, though with the organization of the Baptists in the East, the few isolated Episcopalians of the West, after persistent effort from the year 1706, had succeeded in organization at Fairfield in 1723 the first Connecticut Episcopal parish. Yet the year 1750 found the latter with but twenty-five struggling parishes against 147 Congregational located in all parts of the colony.

As to the Methodists their first society was organized at Stratford in 1789.

Should the success of this issue warrant a continuation of the work, it is to be hoped records of other organizations may be included, but it may be well here to state that Connecticut Churchmen themselves have had occasion to regret that their older parishes, from one reason and another, have preserved comparatively so few records of their early life and activity.

FREDERIC W. BAILEY.

NEW HAVEN, CONN., Oct. 1, 1896.

CONTENTS.

SECOND BOOK.

RECORDS LOST.

The following is a (revised) list of Congregational Churches so far reporting the loss of their records of Baptisms and Marriages prior to 1800.

CHURCH.	COUNTY.	ORGANIZED.	REMARKS.
Westminster, of Canterbury,	Windham,	1770,	
Stamford,	Fairfield,	1635,	
Coventry,	Tolland,	1745,	none before 1818.
Hebron,	Tolland,	1716,	burned.
Ellington,	Tolland,	1736,	lost.
Sherman,	Fairfield,	1744,	burned.
East Granby,	Hartford,	1737,	
Goshen,	Litchfield,	1740,	lost.
Watertown,	Litchfield,	1739,	lost.
Canton Center,	Hartford,	1750,	before 1826, lost.
Meriden,	New Haven,	1729,	before 1848, taken away.
So. Manchester,	Hartford,	1779,	
North Guilford,	New Haven,	1725,	lost.
East Lyme,	New London,	1724,	lost.
Lyme,	New London,	1727,	lost.
West Haven,	New Haven,	1719,	before 1815, lost.
Litchfield,	Litchfield,	1721,	before 1886, burned.
Tolland,	Tolland,	1723,	burned.
Bethany,	New Haven,	1763,	before 1823, lost.

NEW LONDON.

NEW LONDON COUNTY.

The first Congregational Church was organized at Gloucester, Mass., in 1642, removing from thence in 1650 to New London. Consequently we would here correct the mistake made in the Preface of the First Book "Early Connecticut Marriages" and number this as the 10th instead of the 13th Congregational Church organization of the state.

Record commencing March 31, 1691, containing the persons who were married by me. GURDON SALTONSTALL.

Ichabod Sayre, son of Francis Sayre of South-
ampton, on Nassau Island, was married to
Mary Hubbart of New London in Conn., March 31, 1697
Thomas Crocker & Mary Carpenter, daughter of
David, April 8, 1697
William Tubbs & Lydia Roach, Sept. 27, 1698
Jonathan Star & Elizabeth Morgan, Jan. 12, 1699
Daniel Young of Southold on Nassau Island &
Judith Frink of New London, Jan. 12, 1699
Peter Hachly & Elizabeth Baker (widow), Aug. 31, 1699
Daniel Comstock & Elizabeth Prentice, May 23, 1700
—— Osmar of Hartford & Ann Prentice, daugh-
ter of Capt. John Prentice of N. L., ——
John Backley of Weathersfield & Patience Prentiss,
daughter of Capt. John Prentiss of N. L., ——
—— Robins of Lyme & —— Carpenter, April, 1702
Jared Spencer of Saybrook & Sarah Douglas,
daughter of Deacon Douglas, Aug., 1702
Thomas Spencer of Saybrook and Ann Douglas,
daughter of Deacon Douglas, Sept. 3, 1702
John Young & Anne Wheeler, Nov. 26, 1702
Adam Pickett & Susanna Turner, Nov. 26, 1702
Ebenezer Griffin & widow Mary Hubbell, Feb. 10, 1703
John Keney & widow Naomi Rogers, Feb. 17, 1703
Richard Atwel & Elizabeth Baker, March 11, 1703
George Chappell & Mary Douglas, June 10, 1703
Thomas Douglas of N. L. & Ann Spencer *SPERRY* of New
Haven, Nov. 25, 1703

Thomas Jones & Mary Potter, Dec. 30, 1703
John Baker & Phebe Douglas, Jan. 17, 1704
John Mayhew & Sarah Latham, May 26, 1704
Henry Brooks & Eleph Chappell, May 30, 1704
Thomas Avery & Anne Shapley, July 12, 1704
John More of N. L. & Elizabeth Beckwith of
Lyme, Sept. 25, 1704
Thomas Prents & Mary Rogers, Jan. 31, 1705
Oliver Manwaring & —— Hough, March 14, 1705
Bartholomew Crossman & Elizabeth Rogers, April 17, 1705
Ebenezer Dart & Mary Golding, May 15, 1705
John Wickwire & Abigail Haughton, Dec. 27, 1705
Isaac Fox & Mary Jones, Feb. 28, 1706
John Stedman & Mary Beebe, July 29, 1706
Joseph Minor & Susanna Turner (widow), Aug. 22, 1706
Ebenezer Dible of Colchester & Annie Hatton,
Aug. 29, 1706
Jonathan Palmer of Stonington & Mercy Manwar-
ing, Dec. 1, 1706
William Holt & Phebe Tomlin, Dec. 25, 1706
John Holmes & Mary Willee, Feb. 11, 1707
Ebenezer Dennis & Sarah Hough, Feb. 10, 1707
William Crocker & Sarah Keney, May 22, 1707
Thomas Beebe & Anna Hobson, Dec. 17, 1707

Record commencing March 17, 1708-9, containing the persons who
were married by Eliphalet Adams.

Asa Harris & Elizabeth Stanton, March 17, 1709
Richard Goodrich & Hannah Bulkley, both of Glas-
tonbury, May 18, 1709
William Minard & Priscilla Strickland, Oct. 13, 1709
Eliphalet Adams & Lydia Pygan, Dec. 15, 1709
Samuel Beebe & Sarah Tubbs, May 29, 1710
John Fox, Jr., & Elizabeth Clark, Jan. 16, 1711
John Larabie of Windham & Mary Hatch, May 22, 1711
John Lester & Abigail Munsel, July 6, 1711
John Vibber of Groton & Joanna Williams, Aug. 9, 1711
Jonathan Ropp or Rapp of Norwich & Ann Avery,
Nov. 21, 1711
Thomas Williams & Sarah Rogers, Dec. 12, 1711

Thomas Pember & Hannah Turner, March 12, 1712
Thomas Grant & Patience Williams, March 15, 1712
John Pike & Hannah Spencer of Machamoodus, 1712
Thomas Daniell & Hannah Keeny, 1712
Robert Jachlin & Mary Wright (negroes), 1712
Joseph Minor & Grace Turner, 1713
Thomas Leach, Jr., & Mary Munsel, April 2, 1713
John Nobles & Mercy Williams, April 29, 1713
John Smith & Deliverence Munsel, June 8, 1713
James Rogers, Jr., & Freelove Holiboat, June 29, 1713
Samuel Williams & Bathshua Camp, July 17, 1713
John Emms & Paltiah Stebbins, July 20, 1713
Clement Stratford (a sailor) & Sarah Horton, July 30, 1713
Samuel Strickland & Elizabeth Williams, Aug. 6, 1713
William Rogers & Elizabeth Harris, Aug. 27, 1713
Robert Jarkin & Hagar ——— (negroes), Oct. 13, 1713
Samuel Daniels & Sarah Butler, Nov. 26, 1713
Joseph Tolman & Joanna Mayhew, Dec. 1, 1713
William Holt & Katharine Butler, Jan. 1, 1714
John Calkins & Frances Leach, Feb. 10, 1714
Solomon Coit & Elizabeth Short, Aug. 8, 1714
John Grey of Boston & Mary Christophers, Oct. 21, 1714
Samuel Mighil of Hartford & Mrs. Sarah Prentis,
Nov. 2, 1714
Ebenezer Way & Mary Harris, Nov. 9, 1714
Moses Fergo, Jr., & Elizabeth Camp, Dec. 1, 1714
Thomas Butler & Elizabeth Minor, Dec. 20, 1714
Stephen Beebe & Mary Leach, Nov. 16, 1715
Jonathan Dean of Plainfield & Sarah Douglas, Jan. 17, 1716
John Adams & Sarah Green, June 15, 1716
Jacob Ally & Elizabeth Beebe, June 26, 1716
Benjamin (Ingles) & Mary Stebbins July 5, 1716
David Huntly of Lyme & Mary Munsel, July 11, 1716
Thomas Bartlet & Elizabeth Plombe Oct. 9, 1716
Joshua Appleton & Jane Shapley, Feb. 5, 1717
Henry Dillamore & Joanna Edgecomb Feb. 14, 1717
Thomas Dart & Elizabeth Turner, May 8, 1717
William Minard & Lydia Woodworth, June 13, 1717
John Dodge & Elizabeth Stebbins, June 25, 1717
Roger Dart & Prudence Beckwith, July 24, 1717

Thomas Boole & Hopestill Chappel,	Sept. 12, 1717
Kinsley Comstock & Rachel Crocker,	Sept. 18, 1717
Archibald Campbel & Sarah Campbel,	Nov. 21, 1717
Nathan Howard of Endfield & Hannah Calkins,	
	Nov. 26, 1717
Samuel Beebe, Jr., of Long Island & Ann Lester,	
	Jan. 1, 1718
Jonathan Daniels & Mary Potts of Groton,	Jan. 1, 1718
John Keeney & Hannah Waller,	Feb. 5, 1718
Joseph Bayley of Groton & Mary Chapman,	Feb. 20, 1718
Joseph Church & Sevil Latham of Groton,	April 27, 1718
William Joyner & Elizabeth Eads,	July 15, 1718
Scipio (a mulatto) & Hannah (an Indian),	Aug. 29, 1718
John Hough & Hannah Denison,	Sept. 4, 1718
John Preston & Hannah Chapman,	Sept. 9, 1718
Benjamin Morgan & Sarah Giddens,	Oct. 27, 1718
George Chappel & Hannah Beckwith,	Nov. 5, 1718
Samuel Hough & Kezia Wood,	Feb. 26, 1719
Ebenezer Fox & Jane Stedman,	March 25, 1719
John Coit & Grace Christophers,	July 2, 1719
Timothy Lester & Abigail Willoughby,	Aug. 31, 1719
Robert Goller & Hannah Andross,	Sept. 8, 1719
Joshua Raymond & Elizabeth Christophers,	Sept. 8, 1719
John Campbel & Agnes Allen of Stonington,	Nov. 19, 1719
Samuel Edgecomb & Elizabeth Prentis,	Nov. 24, 1719
Thomas Boham & Sarah Sale,	Dec. 1, 1719
William Varcher & Patience Washburn,	Jan. 1, 1720
Richard Sutton of Charlestown & Mary Fosdyke,	Jan. 5, 1720
Gibson Harris & Phebe Denison,	Jan. 12, 1720
Daniel Lester & Sarah Brown of Colchester,	Feb. 2, 1720
Matthew Smith of Lyme & Sarah Rogers,	Feb. 25, 1720
William Brookfield & Katherine Rogers,	April 14, 1720
George Smith & Thankful Tomlinson,	June 5, 1720
William Davis & Abigail Hill,	June 9, 1720
Joseph Merrell of Kenelworth & Sarah Hallum,	
	June 23, 1720
Peter Wickwire & Patience Chapel,	Sept. 29, 1720
Ephraim Daton & Deliverance Willoughby,	Oct. 27, 1720
Samuel Gardner & Elizabeth Coyt,	Nov. 8, 1720
John Crank & Phebe Harris,	Nov. 29, 1720

Samuel Tinker & Elizabeth Harris, Nov. 30, 1720
Christopher Stebbins & Abigail Allen, Dec. 22, 1720
Josiah Rockwell & Ann Burchard of Norwich, Jan. 19, 1721
Joseph Minor of Lyme & Jemimah Cady, Jan. 19, 1721
Nathaniel Ray of Block Island & Ann Wilson, Feb. 8, 1721
Matthew Beckwith & Elishaba Reiner of Lyme,
Feb. 17, 1721
Jonathan Prentis & widow Mary Grey, Feb. 23, 1721
Joseph Calkins & Lucretia Turner, March 28, 1721
Jonathan Lattimore & Boradil Denison, April 6, 1721
Daniel Coyt & Lydia Christophers, May 9, 1721
Philip Want & Mary Comstock, May 25, 1721
James Hadgdel & Patience Ross, July 6, 1721
Edward Robinson & Mary Wilson, Nov. 8, 1721
James Beebe & Mary Beebe, Nov. 19, 1721
James Dixon & Janet Dixon, Nov. 30, 1721
Benjamin Beebe & Jane Plomley, Dec. 12, 1721
William Harris of Marblehead & Elizabeth Haines,
Jan. 3, 1722
Clement Minor & Abigail Turner, Jan. 9, 1722
Ebenezer Dart & Rebeckah More, Jan. 10, 1722
Thomas Manwaring & Esther Christophers, Feb. 14, 1722
Samuel Chapman & Dinah Hatch, March 8, 1722
William Steel & Ruth Bailey, March 14, 1722
David Minard & Rebeckah Richards, March 20, 1722
John Beckwith & Hannah Brooks, May 4, 1722
William Waterhouse & Hannah Lewis, July 3, 1722
Samuel Lynde of Saybrook & Mrs. Lucy Grey,
July 24, 1722
Peter Chapman & Ann Comstock, Aug. 15, 1722
Alexander Goff & Ann Rogers, Sept. 6, 1722
David Crocker & Hannah Beebe, Dec. 2, 1722
Thomas Hawkins & Mary Morgan, Jan. 17, 1723
Stephen Calkins of Norwich & Sarah Calkins, Jan. 22, 1723
John Ward of Salem & Elizabeth Chapman, Feb. 14, 1723
Jonathan Tinker & Elizabeth Manwaring, Feb. 27, 1723
John Lee of Lyme & Lydia Allen, March 14, 1723
James Rogers, Jr., & Mary Harris, March 21, 1723
James Rice & Mary Star, March 27, 1723
Jason Allen & Mary Atwell, April 2, 1723

Stephen Prentiss, Jr., & Phebe Crank,   May 1, 1723
John Thomas of Middletown & Mercy Willoughby,
                                               May 16, 1723
Ebenezer Pierce & Lydia Dart,   May 30, 1723
Samuel Lattimore & Elizabeth Hallum,   July 11, 1723
Nathaniel Hempstead & Mary Hallum,   July 18, 1723
Cornelius Roberts & Dorcas Jillet of Colchester,
                                               Aug. 20, 1723
Thomas Coit & Mary Prentiss,   Nov. 5, 1723
Thomas Skerrit & Johanna Chapman,   Nov. 14, 1723
John Munsel & Mary Lester,   Nov. 20, 1723
Jonathan Chester of Groton & Mary Rogers,   Jan. 2, 1724
Samuel Irwin & Isabel Macgonnel,   Jan. 14, 1724
William Whiting of Windham & Ann Raymond,
                                               March 5, 1724
Stephen Hurlbut & Mercy Plombe,   July 5, 1724
Robert Fergo & Sarah Camp,   July 22, 1724
Henry Miller of Lyme & Deliverance Page of
    Brainford or Braintree,   Sept. 21, 1724
Daniel Deshon & Ruth Christophers,   Oct. 7, 1724
Josiah Tucker & Abigail Williams of Groton,   Oct. 8, 1724
Jabesh Hough & Ann Denison,   Jan. 9, 1725
John Hamilton & Margaret Buchanan,   Jan. 12, 1725
John Procter of Boston & Lydia Richards,   Jan. 31, 1725
Jonathan Church of Colchester & Abigail Fairbanks,
                                               Feb. 26, 1725
Israel Richards & Mary Strickland,   March 25, 1725
John Dillen & Mary More,   April 2, 1725
Gershom Rogers & Sarah Wheeler of Groton,   April 8, 1725
Allen Mullins & Abigail Butler,   April 8, 1725
Gabriel Harris & Bathshua Rogers,   April 29, 1725
William Waterhouse & Sarah Crocker,   May 6, 1725
Jeremiah Richards & Mary Atwel,   May 27, 1725
James Campbel & Hannah Tailor,   June 3, 1725
John Griffin & Elizabeth Trueman,   June 8, 1725
William Beebe & Jerusha Rogers,   June 9, 1725
Thomas Prentiss & Elizabeth Palms,   June 13, 1725
Thomas Williams & Mary Driskil,   Sept. 16, 1725
John Hicks & Lydia Latham of Groton,   Sept. 20, 1725
Clement Leach & Elizabeth Culver,   Oct. 21, 1725

Samuel Chapman & Mary Stedman,   Oct. 22, 1725
Benjamin Williams of Narrhaganset & Sarah Bailey
    of Groton,   Nov. 10, 1725
John Richards & Ann Prentiss,   Dec. 16, 1725
Jeremiah Congden & Ann Chapel,   Dec. 16, 1725
Benjamin Kellum & Mary Stodder of Groton, Jan. 4, 1726
Richard Downer of Norwich & Mercy Horton, Jan. 13, 1726
Rev. James Hillhouse & Mrs. Mary Fitch,   Jan., 1726
Joshua Allen & Johanna Stodder of Groton,   1726
Jonathan Nash of Narhaganset & Jane Hallet of
    Groton,   March 7, 1726
Joseph Smith & Elizabeth Harris,   April 5, 1726
John Chapel, Jr., & Hannah Edgecomb,   April 28, 1726
John Dickson & Ann Lester,   May 3, 1726
Samuel Richards & Ann Hough,   May 9, 1726
Naboth Graves & Irene Prentiss,   May 13, 1726
Andrew Richards & Hephzibah Grant,   May 16, 1726
John Thomas of Rehoboth & Mercy Hurlbut, May 19, 1726
John Hazen of Norwich & Elizabeth Dart,   May 31, 1726
John Bradick of Long Island & Lucretia Christo-
    phers,   June 19, 1726
Samuel Atwel & Ruth Coy,   June 19, 1726
William Chapel & Elizabeth Atwell,   June 23, 1726
Peter Harris & Mary Trueman,   July 3, 1726
Ebenezer Beebe & Mary Miller of Lyme,   July 5, 1726
John Eams, Jr., & Ann Stebbins,   July 19, 1726
Benajah Leffingwell of Norwich & Johannah Chris-
    tophers,   Aug. 24, 1726
Stephen Gorton & Sarah Harris,   Aug. 31, 1726
Thomas Criddington of Guilford & Lydia Darrow,
    Sept. 4, 1726
Robert Chapman & Bathshua Fox,   Sept. 11, 1726
William Hatch & Susanna Baker,   Oct. 13, 1726
Witherel Denison & Lydia More,   Nov. 6, 1726
Robert Cox of Lebanon & Ruth Howard,   Nov. 9, 1726
Benjamin Lester & Hannah Lester,   Nov. 17, 1726
Michael Ewen of Boston & Lydia Richards,   Dec. 2, 1726
James Rogers & Grace Harris,   Dec. 8, 1726
Christopher Darrow, Jr., & Sarah Harris,   Dec. 22, 1726
Sam'l Davis of Groton & Sarah Gardiner,   Jan. 1, 1727

Jonathan Whipple & Elizabeth Dart,	Feb. 28, 1727
James Tilly & Ruth Fosdyke,	March 5, 1727
Trueman Powell & Elizabeth Carpenter of Coventry,	March 6, 1727
Abraham Avery & Jane Hill,	March 14, 1727
Ebenezer Darrow & Abbie Rogers,	April 17, 1727
Thomas Chapman & Ann Stedman,	July 6, 1727
John Bolles, Jr., & Lydia Star,	July 20, 1727
John Thomas & Sarah Talcot,	Aug. 14, 1727
Duncan Mackintosh & Jemima Daniels,	Aug. 24, 1727
Thomas Gladden & Mary Perry,	Aug. 30, 1727
Samuel Griffin & Ann Avery,	Nov. 16, 1727
Thomas Minor of Lyme & Martha Stebbins,	Nov. 21, 1727
Joseph Goddard of Boston & Hannah Richards,	Nov. 23, 1727
Thomas Turner & Patience Bolles,	Nov. 23, 1727
Israel Sawyer of Weathersfield & Lydia Beebe,	Dec. 7, 1727
Robert Stodder of Groton & Bathsheba Rogers,	Dec. 21, 1727
Samuel Leach & Ann Minor of Lyme,	Feb. 6, 1728
James Smith & Susanna Wyatt	Feb. 8, 1728
Ebenezer Gray of Lebanon & Mary Coit,	Feb. 20, 1728
Thomas Dill & Dorothy Gibbons,	March 13, 1728
Walter Boddington & Abigail Marsy,	April 6, 1728
Charles Hains & Lydia Tabor,	April 25, 1728
Isaac Lester & Thankful Willoughby,	June 17, 1728
Zachariah Whipple of Groton & Elizabeth Rogers,	June 27, 1728
Ezekiel Beebe & Hannah Rogers,	Nov. 13, 1728
Elisha Turner of Scituate & Ruhamah Arnold,	Dec. 19, 1728
Hezekiah Stodder & Margaret Harris of Groton,	Dec. 25, 1728
Joseph Huntley of Lyme & Ruth Williams,	Jan. 7, 1729
Jonathan Lester & Patience Tinker,	May 15, 1729
John Ford of Ireland & Ann Holloway,	May 26, 1729
Deacon James Morgan of Groton & Ann Roff,	June 24, 1729
Joseph Wanton of Rhode Island & Mrs. Mary Winthrop,	Aug. 21, 1729
Thomas Atwel & Sarah Strickland,	Oct. 20, 1729
Jabez Hamlin of Middletown & Mrs. Mary Christophers,	Nov. 19, 1729

Ebenezer Howard & Elizabeth Mayhew, Dec. 23, 1729
Henry Harris & Mary Fox, May 19, 1730
Hugh Woodberry of Beverley & Jane Green, May 21, 1730
Hugh Mosier of Long Island & Sarah Jones, May 28, 1730
Palmer Carew of Norwich & Hannah Hill, June 1, 1730
Roger Tyler of Brainford & Martha Harris, June 29, 1730
Joseph Southmaid of Middletown & Abiah Douglas,
July 14, 1730
Benjamin Shapley & Esther Rogers, Aug. 18, 1730
Samuel Jackson & Sarah Harris, Sept. 16, 1730
Nathaniel Shaw & Temperance Harris, Nov. 5, 1730
Ezekiel Chapman & Elizabeth Chapel, Nov. 23, 1730
John Booth & Mary Foot of Groton, Nov. 24, 1730
William Camp & Abigail Lester, Feb. 4, 1731
Daniel Collins & Alice Pell, Feb. 22, 1731
James Chapman & Mary Wyat, Feb. 25, 1731
William Douglas & Sarah Denison, March 4, 1731
Joseph Beebe & Elizabeth Fergo, April 26, 1731
John Perriman & Elizabeth Calkins, April 29, 1731
John Egerton of Norwich & Phebe Prentis, May 11, 1731
Silas Whipple & Susanna More, May 13, 1731
John Bishop & Rebeckah Whipple, May 20, 1731
Samuel Allen of Groton & Hannah Avery, May 27, 1731
Samuel Tarbox & Jemima Richards, May 27, 1731
John Thomas & Joanna Morris of Boston, June 8, 1731
Robert Lattimore & Mary Huntley of Lyme, June 17, 1731
Matthias Ryley & Sarah Benner, July 8, 1731
Jonathan Douglas & Lucy Christophers, Aug. 3, 1731
Robert Douglas & Sarah Edgcomb, Aug. 5, 1731
Daniel Hubbard & Mrs. Martha Coyt, Aug. 18, 1731
Clement Minor & Abigail Hempstead, Sept. 1, 1731
Ezekiel Daniels & Elizabeth Crocker, Oct. 27, 1731
Ezekiel Saxton of Enfield & Grace Calkins, Nov. 23, 1731
Nicholas Darrow & Mary Griffin, Dec. 9, 1731
Samuel Hobart & Sarah Dennis, Dec. 16, 1731
Daniel Comstock & Elizabeth Avery, Dec. 30, 1731
Joseph Waterhouse & Sarah Richards, Jan. 27, 1732
Christopher Chappel & Hannah Daniels, Feb. 7, 1732
Samuel Clark of Newport & Mary Dart, 1732
Stephen Potter & Lucy Hains, March 24, 1732

William Robbins of Lyme & Mary Ingles,   March 27, 1732
Samuel Brown of Salem & Mrs. Katharine Winthrop,
                                          March 30, 1732
William Chapel & Bethiah Dart,   April 14, 1732
Peter Lattimore & Hannah Picket,   April 23, 1732
Jonathan Hambleton & Anna Camp,   May 9, 1732
John Johnson & Hannah Chapel,   May 23, 1732
Benjamin Beckwith & Hannah Pember,   June 15, 1732
Jonathan Morgan & Grace Crocker,   June 22, 1732
Jonathan Wicks (a stranger) & Ann Rogers, Aug. 24, 1732
John Shackmaple & Elisabeth Christophers, Aug. 31, 1732
Richard Leach & Lucy Daniels,   Nov. 15, 1732
William Daniels of Boston & Anna Beebe,   Dec. 23, 1732
Samuel Mosset & Sarah Richards,   Jan. 22, 1733
Thomas Pember & Elizabeth Hackley,   Feb. 5, 1733
Peter Huntley & Sarah Robbins of Lyme,   Feb. 14, 1733
Jonathan Morgan & ——— Strickland,   Feb. 15, 1733
Nathaniel Saltonstall & Mrs. Lucretia Arnold,
                                          March 1, 1733
Samuel Green & Elizabeth Prentis,   March 11, 1733
Gurdan Saltonstall & Mrs. Rebeckah Winthrop,
                                          March 15, 1733
Joseph Trueman, Jr., & Mary Hempstead,   March 22, 1733
Cary Latham of Groton & Sarah Waterhouse,
                                          March 25, 1733
David Richards & Elisabeth Edgcomb,   April 3, 1733
Samuel Lee & Jane Trueman,   April 20, 1733
Noah Miller of Lyme & Mary Waller,   May 9, 1733
Ivory Lucas & Mary Coyt,   May 19, 1733
Titus Hurlbut & Lydia Buttolph,   Aug. 19, 1733
Culbert Bly (a stranger) & Johanna Atwell, Aug. 24, 1733
Abel Willee of Matchemoodas & Martha Minor, Oct. 25, 1733
Jonathan Gardiner & Mary Adams,   Nov. 13, 1733
Joseph Tabor & Mary Gladden,   Nov. 14, 1733
Richard Christophers & Mary Picket,   Dec. 10, 1733
John Rogers & Mary Tomkins (a stranger), Dec. 13, 1733
Ephriam Chapman & Elisabeth Morgan,   Dec. 25, 2733
Joseph Harris, Jr., & Phebe Holt,   Dec. 27, 1733
Thomas Sherret & May Fowler (strangers), Jan. 2, 1734
Joseph Daniels & Grace Edgcomb,   May 29, 1734

Henry Roland of Lyme & Mary Daniels, June 3, 1734
John Brown (a stranger) & Ruth Rogers, Aug. 8, 1734
Daniel Sexton of Enfield & Mary Douglas, Sept. 4, 1734
Joseph Beckwith of Lyme & Mary Pember, Oct. 3, 1734
John Dart & Ruth More, Oct. 10, 1734
William Swift of Lebanon & Elisabeth Wheeler,
Nov. 10, 1734
Daniel Mason of Stonington & Hannah Chapel,
Dec. 19, 1734
Lemuel Lanthur & Mary Chappel, Dec. 26, 1734
David Lester & Rachel Fox, Feb. 19, 1735
Caleb More & Esther Daniels, March 2, 1735
George Wright & Martha Webber (strangers), May 25, 1735
Soloman Hambleton & Zeruiah Wickwire, June 19, 1735
William Wheeler & Mary Hambleton, June 19, 1735
Samuel Beebe & Hannah Morgan, July 10, 1735
Nathaniel Holt & Mary Strickland, July 29, 1735
Joshua More, Jr., & Elisabeth Grant, July 31, 1735
John Morgan, Jr., & Grace Morgan, Oct. 16, 1735
Nathaniel Coyt & Margaret Douglas, Nov. 6, 1735
Daniel Star & Elisabeth Hempstead, Nov. 18, 1735
Samuel Brooks & Mary Calkins, Dec. 9, 1735
Japhet Mason of Stonington & Mary Chapel, Dec. 29, 1735
James Carrel (a stranger) & Rachel Richards, Jan. 5, 1736
Ichabod Wickwire & Deborah Fairbanks, March 19, 1736
John Calder & Hannah Curtice of Weathersfield,
March 30, 1736
Martin Clark of Weathersfield & Sarah Crocker,
April 21, 1736
William Holt & Sarah Way, May 12, 1736
Nathan Place & Sarah Lester, May 27, 1736
Thomas Pierpont of Roxborough & Mary Hempstead,
June 10, 1736
Jonathan Hambleton & Elisabeth Strickland, July 26, 1736
Isaac Ledyard & Elisabeth Christophers, Aug. 26, 1736
Wolstan Brockway of Lyme & Ann Brooks, Sept. 30, 1736
Daniel Ely of Lyme & Ruhamah Turner, Nov. 10, 1736
William Griffin & Margaret Osburn, Nov. 18, 1736
Anthony Whipple & Jane Chapel, Dec. 30, 1736
John Jonas of Boston & Abigail Rogers, March 8, 1737

James M. Star & Mercy Leach,   May 5, 1737
John Leeds of Groton & Mary Comstock,   June 16, 1737
Thomas Davis & Sarah Davis,   July 4, 1737
William Newport & Sarah Bill,   July 7, 1737
John Jerome & Hannah Turner,   July 27, 1737
William Minot of Lyme & Abigail Biggs of Saybrook,
                                                                    July 28, 1737
Stephen Hempstead & Sarah Holt,   Sept. 19, 1737
James Merrell (a stranger) & Katharine Rogers,
                                                                    Oct. 20, 1737
Amos Babcock & Anna Watkins of Ashford,   Oct. 25, 1737
Ebenezer Hill & Margaret Ingram of Lebanon, Oct. 28, 1737
Joseph Hurlbut & Elisabeth Buttolph,   Nov. 29, 1737
Samuel Rogers & Paltiah Eames,   Dec. 20, 1737
John Prentis & Sarah Christophers,   Dec. 28, 1737
Thomas Way & Sarah Savel,   Dec. 29, 1737
George Hill & Joanna Vibber,   Jan. 5, 1738
William Beckwith & Lucy Chappell,   Feb. 16, 1738
Nathaniel Etheridge & Jerusha Morgan,   March 9, 1738
John Gurley & Ruth Richards,   March 19, 1738
Matthew Polley of Norwich & Abigail Gilbert,
                                                                    April 17, 1738
James Comstock & ANN Allen, of Newport, April 17, 1738
Caleb Douglas & Mary More,   May 2, 1738
Daniel Rogers & Sarah Williams,   July 26, 1738
Nathaniel Williams & Love Richards,   Oct. 16, 1738
John Bulkley of Colchester & Mrs. Mary Gardiner,
                                                                    Oct., 1738
Daniel Whittemore & Jane Appleton,   Nov. 5, 1738
John Main of Stonington & Sarah Morgan,   Nov. 8, 1738
Stephen Beebe & Elisabeth Fergo,   Dec. 7, 1738
John Tinker & Elisabeth Daniels,   Dec. 19, 1738
Joseph Smith of Windsor & Eliza Bennet,   March 11, 1739
Joseph Lothrop & Elisabeth Dixwell,   April 22, 1739
William Hancock of Stonington & Ann Trueman,
                                                                    July 15, 1739
Charles Curtice of Weathersfield & Mary Shapley,
                                                                    Aug. 6, 1739
Daniel Lester & Elisabeth Darrow,   Sept. 27, 1739
Stephen Chappell & Elisabeth Tinker,   Nov. 13, 1739

Tom & Beck (two free negroes of New London), Dec. 23, 1739
Thomas Prentiss & Bethiah Chapel, Jan. 2, 1740
John Keeney, Jr., & Mary Tinker, Feb. 13, 1740
William Perkins & Mary Dart, March 26, 1740
John Chapman of Colchester & Bethiah Chapman,
April 10, 1740
Joseph Vincent of Amboy & Mary Tabor, Sept. 7, 1740
Charles Short & Johanna Talman, Sept. 14, 1740
John Lamphier & Sarah Mayhew, Oct. 2, 1740
Edward Palms & Lucretia Christophers, Oct. 18, 1740
Thomas Butler & Sarah Lewis, Oct. 30, 1740
Benjamin Truman & Mary Way, Nov. 9, 1740
Samuel Bill & Johanna Atwell, Nov. 27, 1740
David Gardiner & Elisabeth Gardiner, 1741
Moses Fergo & Johanna Beebe, May 21, 1741
Gilbert Foresith of Groton & Mary Bishop, June 4, 1741
Walter Harris & Elisabeth Smith, June 23, 1741
Joseph Calkins, Jr., & Judith Tinker, June 23, 1741
Charles Bulkley of Colchester & Ann Lattimore, Oct. 8, 1741
Jeremiah Whipple & Hannah Beebe, Oct. 8, 1741
Jedediah Chapel & Rachel Carril, Oct. 11, 1741
James Hutchins (a stranger) & Hannah Goddard,
Nov. 4, 1741
Daniel Truman & Deborah Dennis, Dec. 10, 1741
Richard Chapel & Jemima Comstock, Dec. 24, 1741
Samuel Strickland, Jr., & Sarah Chapel, Dec. 29, 1741
Simon Gager of Norwich & Sarah Manwaring, Feb. 25, 1742
Daniel Chapman of Norwich & Mary Brooks, Feb. 25, 1742
John Christophers & Jerusha Gardiner, March 7, 1742
Jonathan Chapel & Elisabeth Comstock, March 25, 1742
George Wade & Ann Lester, April 14, 1742
Simon Smith & Rebeckah More, April 22, 1742
John Wheeler & Elizabeth Hambleton, April 22, 1742
Abel Wright of Kent & Abigail Morgan, May 18, 1742
James Tilley & Hannah Savel, May 28, 1742
Stephen Douglas & Patience Atwell, June 9, 1742
Jonathan Cop of Stonington & Sarah Hobart, June 30, 1742
Isaac Fellow & Mary Want, Sept. 30, 1742
Samuel Maxon of Westerly & Ruth Rogers, Oct. 13, 1742
Ransford Avery & Annis Strickland, Dec. 22, 1742

Ezekiel Chapel & Hannah Atwell,	Jan. 12, 1743
Stephen Lee of Lyme & Mary Picket,	Jan. 25, 1743
John Fox of Millington & Jemima Rogers,	Feb. 24, 1743
John Daniels & Huldah Smith,	March 3, 1743
Nathan Howard & Lucy Minor,	March 17, 1743
John Preston & Hannah Harris,	June 23, 1743
Zebadiah Comstock & Bethiah Prentis,	July 11, 1743
Richard Coyt & Abigail Bradick,	Oct. 13, 1743
Benjamin Green & Margaret Strickland,	Oct. 30, 1743
Joshua Hempstead, Jr., & Lydia Birch,	Nov. 3, 1743
Andrew Waterhouse of Lyme & Dinah Westcot,	
	Dec. 22, 1743
James Gardiner of Boston & Mary Croswell,	Dec. 26, 1743
Ichabod Rogers & Mary Savel,	Feb. 23, 1744
Miles More of Lyme & Grace Rogers,	March 29, 1744
William Atwell & Phebe Amsbury,	March 29, 1744
Samuel Talman & Hannah Manwaring,	April 26, 1744
Jeremiah Miller & Margaret Winthrop,	May 16, 1744
Jethro Smith & Ann Williams,	May 17, 1744
Peter Strickland & Sarah Williams,	May 22, 1744
Pygan Adams & Ann Richards,	June 7, 1744
William Gold of Branford & Sarah Farr,	July 1, 1744
James Butler & Sarah Minard,	Aug. 20, 1744
Thomas Green of Boston & Martha Hubbard,	Sept. 6, 1744
Jesse Fox & Alithea Chapman,	Oct. 10, 1744
Samuel Pye & Lucy Uncas of Mohegan (Indians),	
	Oct. 23, 1744
Jonathan Dodge & Mercy Williams,	Nov. 7, 1744
Stephen Baker & Elisabeth Comstock,	Nov. 14, 1744
Thomas Waples of Hartford & Elisabeth Bramble,	
	Dec. 9, 1744
Abraham Slater (a stranger) & Mary Denison,	Dec. 9, 1744
James Harris & Johanna Star,	Dec. 11, 1744
Cæsar Mazzie & Dido Barzie (Indians),	Jan. 1, 1745
Elisha Stillman of Westerly & Hannah Rogers,	
	March 5, 1745
Joseph Davis & Lucretia Strickland,	June 13, 1745
Joseph Chapman & Mary Perkins,	June 20, 1745
Richard Smith of Lyme & Abigail Minor,	Aug. 1, 1745
Lemuel Rogers & Love Richards,	Oct. 6, 1745

Robert Horsmer of East Haddam & Mary Green,

Oct. 31, 1745

Robert Westcot & Esther Harris,	Nov. 28, 1745
James Douglas & Sarah Gee of Lyme,	Dec. 13, 1745
John Holt & Sarah Strickland,	Feb. 20, 1746
John Douglas & Esther Leach,	May 11, 1746
Elijah Knap (a stranger) & Mary Dart,	July 23, 1746
Elisha Bunce of Hartford & Mary Bramble,	Sept. 10, 1746

Robert Stephens (a stranger) & Elisabeth Perriman,

Dec. 16, 1746

David Minard & Sarah Eames,	March 30, 1746
Guy Richards & Elisabeth Harris,	Jan. 18, 1747
John Ashcraft & Mary Birch,	June 7, 1747
John Roberts & Elisabeth Clark,	July 12, 1747
Henry Dillamore & Miriam Graves,	Aug. 5, 1747
William Cardwell & Elisabeth Birch,	Sept. 4, 1747
William Stark of Norwich & Ann Appleton,	Nov. 5, 1747
George Richards, Jr., & Katherine Fosdyke,	Dec. 21, 1747
Nicholas Hallum & Elisabeth Lattimore,	Jan. 21, 1748
Andrew Minard & Phebe Minor,	Feb. 11, 1748

Nehemiah Rogers of Middletown & Mercy Ewen,

Feb. 25, 1748

Thomas Manwaring & Lydia Waterhouse,	April 14, 1748
Roger Dart & Keturah Beebe,	May 1, 1748
Pitman Collins of Guilford & Lydia Leach,	June 2, 1748
Thomas Robinson (a stranger) & Lydia Ewens,	Sept. 4, 1748
William Potter (a stranger) & Abigail Durfey,	Sept. 15, 1748
John Hawkins & Deborah Morgan,	Sept. 29, 1748
Nathaniel Star of Middletown & Ann Rice,	Oct. 13, 1748
Sterling Daniels & Elisabeth Chappel,	Oct. 23, 1748
John Monroe, Jr., & Elisabeth Howard,	Dec. 4, 1748
Amos Chapel & Phebe Daniels,	Dec. 20, 1748

John Custover (a Frenchman) & Lucretia Richards,

Dec. 21, 1748

Nicholas Bishop & Hannah Douglas,	Feb. 2, 1749
Daniel Eames & Elisabeth Whipple,	Feb. 21, 1749
William More & Grace Leach,	March 9, 1749

Thomas Marshall of Norwich & Ann Manwaring,

March 23, 1749

Deacon Timothy Green & Abigail Hill,	March 26, 1749

Ebenezer Waterman of Norwich & Elisabeth Com-
 stock,   June 27, 1749
James Grant & Mary Hull,   July 16, 1749
Timothy Winter & Elisabeth Weeks, Aug. 30, 1749
William Keeney & Lucretia Calkins, Nov. 14, 1749
Christopher Eldredge of Stonington & Mary
 Hempstead,   Nov. 29, 1749
Jedediah Smith of Lyme & Hannah Leach, Dec. 26, 1749
Thomas Skerrit & Hannah Goddard, Feb. 4, 1750
Nathaniel Chapman & Lydia Richards, Feb. 8, 1750
David Daniels & Anna Dart,   March 22, 1750
John Beebe & Lucretia Beebe,   March 23, 1750
Aaron Gun of Westfield & Jane Lee, April 3, 1750
Nathan Comstock & Mary Green,   April 26, 1750
John Griffin, Jr., & Mary Rogers, Aug. 22, 1750
Daniel Stow of Middletown & Hannah Plombe, Sept. 2, 1750
David Goodfaith & Mary Curtice,   Sept. 2, 1750
John Miller of Weathersfield & Lucy Star, Nov. 28, 1750
Bryan Palms & Sarah Way,   Nov. 29, 1750
Fairbanks Church & Jemima Angel, Feb. 21, 1751
Joseph Bailey of Nantucket & Elisabeth Smith,
           March 17, 1751
Ichabod Rogers & Ruth Shapley,   April 21, 1751
George Buttolph & Mary Collins,   April 25, 1751
Joseph Read of Norwich & Patience Rogers, June 20, 1751
Samuel Williams of Saybrook & Abigail Bishop,
           July 18, 1751
Benjamin Atwell & Mercy Fox,   Aug. 15, 1751
John Deshon & Sarah Starr,   Aug. 25, 1751
Christopher Strickland & Bethiah Stebbins, Nov. 7, 1751
Gideon Chapman of Colchester & Lucretia Chap-
 man,   Dec. 27, 1751
William Angel & Christian Church, Jan. 30, 1752
George Hondry (?) of Burlington & Ann Buttolph,
           March 29, 1752
Thurston Havens & Jerusha Polly, Aug. 2, 1752
Richard Jones & Hannah Lattimore, Nov. 9, 1752
Daniel Whittemore & Lydia Denison, Dec. 31, 1752
Samuel Coyt & Elisabeth Richards, Feb. 1, 1753
John Preston & Naomi Wager,   March 29, 1753

Nathan Lattimore & Jane Lee,   May, 1753
William Douglas, Jr., & Mary Lucas,   May 31, 1753
John Gun & Jane Lee,   June 24, 1753
Walliam Parker of Groton & Mary Truman, June 24, 1753
Thomas Davis (a stranger) & Katherine Stewart (?),
                                                              Aug. 30, 1753

MARRIAGES BY REV. MATHER BYLES.

David Allen & Sarah Shaw,   Nov. 20, 1757
Joseph Copp & Rachel Dennison,   Dec. 11, 1757
Samuel Strickland & Hannah Shipman of Lyme, Feb. 8, 1758
Edward Raymond & Sarah Douglas,   Feb. 14, 1758
George Worthylake & Rebecca Darrow,   Feb. 23, 1758
Joseph Chew & Grace Deshon,   March 12, 1758
Daniel Henry & Mary Potter,   March 19, 1758
Green Plombe & Margaret Lee,   March 22, 1758
Christopher Minor & Abigail Way,   May 28, 1758
David Mumford & Rebecca Saltonstall,   June 1, 1758
John Bolles & Miriam Dillamore,   June 25, 1758
Nathaniel Shaw & Lucretia Rogers,   July 20, 1758
Ephraim Browne & Mary Griffin,   Aug. 3, 1758
James Powers & Bathsheba Smith,   Sept. 10, 1758
John Chapman & Elizabeth Douglass,   Sept. 17, 1758
Michael Nathaen & Mary Leach,   Sept. 28, 1758
Benjamin Smith & Deborah Williams,   Oct. 9, 1758
Ebenezer Dart & Elizabeth Miner,   May 14, 1759
Samuel Bishop & Mary Mason,   May 24, 1759
Samuel Foster of Middletown & Ann Ward of New
    London,   May 27, 1759
Samuel Beldin & Sarah Coit,   June 17, 1759
Jabesh Maynard & Esther Bristow,   June 18, 1759
Henry Barter of Boston & Sarah Follet of New
    London,   July 11, 1759
Sylvanus Waterman of Middleton & Catherine
    Potter,   Sept. 11, 1759
Stutley Scranton & Dorcas Hull,   Sept. 13, 1759
Nathan Hinman & Elizabeth Christophers,   Oct. 23, 1759
Ebenezer Holt & Joanna Harris,   Nov. 4, 1759
Samuel Bill & Mercy Chapman,   Nov. 8, 1759
Nathaniel Coit & Love Rogers,   Nov. 18, 1759

Ebenezer Avery, Esq., of Groton & Rachel Dennison,
                                        Nov. 21, 1759
Thomas Hayes (a stranger) & Experience Oliver,
                                        Nov. 21, 1759
Samuel Talman & Bithiah Savel,   Nov. 22, 1759
Peter Ingles of Boston & Sarah Scranton,   Jan. 17, 1760
Christopher Leffingwell of Norwich & Elisabeth Har-
    ris,   Jan. 20, 1760
John Plombe & Elizabeth Kettle,   Feb. 13, 1760
George Shipman & Mary Chappel,   Feb. 20, 1760
Jacob Cheney & Jerusha Culver,   Feb. 24, 1760
John Williams & Rebecca Richards,   March 3, 1760
Clement Beebe & Sarah Rusk,   March 25, 1760
Luke Perkins, Esqr., of Groton & Kezia Green,
                                        April 15, 1760
Jabez Chappel & Mary Washburn of Lebanon, May 22, 1760
John Rogers & Abigail Salmon,   July 27, 1760
Job Dart & Mary Lamphire,   Sept. 4, 1760
Richard Law & Anna Prentis,   Sept. 21, 1760
Richard Harris & Mary Whittemore,   Nov. 2, 1760
Robert Waterhouse & Margaret Weeks,   Nov. 13, 1760
James Chapman & Hannah Acourt,   Nov. 16, 1760
William Crocker & Hannah Waterhouse,   Nov. 27, 1760
Henry Walton of Brimfield & Margaret Newport,
                                        Dec. 1, 1760
Joseph Chapel & Anna Chandley,   Dec. 9, 1760
Nathaniel Thorp of New Haven & Katherine Chap-
    man,   Dec. 14, 1760
Abner Brown & Eunice Lee,   Dec. 30, 1760
Samuel Thompson & Elisabeth Beebe,   Jan. 29, 1761
Robinson Mumford & Sarah Coit,   Feb. 1, 1761
John Manwaring of Lyme & Lydia Plombe, Feb. 4, 1761
Ephraim Leech & Hannah Kinyon,   Feb. 8, 1761
Elijah Hatch & Margaret Dart,   Feb. 12, 1761
David Allen & Esther Rogers,   Feb. 15, 1761
John Luchett & Sarah Larrabee,   Feb. 16, 1761
Peter Darrow & Eleanor Potter,   March 22, 1761
Edward Morgan & Zeruiah Shipman,   April 9, 1761
Samuel Lattimore & Elisabeth Prentis,   June 7, 1761
John Griffing of Lyme & Phœbe Tabor,   June 11, 1761

Jabez Manwaring & Mercy Minor,   June 25, 1761
Robert Lattimore & Lydia Bulkely,   June 25, 1761
Stephen Lee & Rebecca Smith,   June 28, 1761
Adam Shapley & Mary Harris,   Aug. 30, 1761
William Bishop & Elisabeth Brooks,   Sept. 6, 1761
William Champlin of Stonington & Jerusha Hany,
                                 Sept. 13, 1761
Isaac Belote & Abigail Hutchins,   Sept. 20, 1761
William Hoborn & Mary Brightman,   Oct. 25, 1761
Alexander Reche & Mary Ward,   Nov. 4, 1761
David Leech & Elisabeth Leech,   Nov. 5, 1761
William Dart & Mary Chapman,   Nov. 24, 1761
Enoch Bolles & Elisabeth Robinson,   Nov. 29, 1761
Isaac Tracy of Norwich and Elisabeth Rogers, Dec. 3, 1761
Thomas Douglas & Grace Richards,   Dec. 13, 1761
John Parsons & Mary Culver,   Dec. 27, 1761
Daniel Hurlburt & Naomi Tabor,   Jan. 21, 1762
William Cleveland & Mary Rothbon,   Feb. 21, 1762
John Smith & Mary Way,   Feb. 21, 1762
Jonathan Crocker & Jane Minor,   March 1, 1762
Peter Ingles & Lucy James,   March 18, 1762
James Jackson & Love Williams,   March 24, 1762
Richard Stanton & Lucretia Leech,   April 5, 1762
Thomas Johnson & Lydia Slaughter,   April 20, 1762
Zerubbabel Slater & Mary Billings,   June 8, 1762
Benjamin Oterbridge & Phillis Short (negroes), June 9, 1762
Benjamin Martin & Sarah Hawkins (negroes), June 9, 1762
William Hamilton & Patience Chappel,   July 5, 1762
Michael Darrow & Mary Macounlif,   July 15, 1762
Joseph Hurlbut & Mary Bolles,   July 15, 1762
Nathaniel Beebe & Grace Culver,   Oct. 17, 1762
Jabez Woodworth of Norwich & Martha Fox, Nov. 8, 1762
Adam Crisp & Esther Beebe,   Nov. 11, 1762
Daniel Holt & Mary Pierpont of Middleton, Dec. 16, 1762
Richard Cleveland & Bathsheba Brooks,   Dec. 26, 1762
Thomas Baron & Esther Rogers,   Dec. 30, 1762
Timothy Green & Rebecca Spooner,   Jan. 2, 1763
John Whipple & Deborah Smith,   March 14, 1763
Joseph Sheals & Hannah Marvin,   May 1, 1763
David Richards & Abigail Shapley,   May 30, 1763

3

Peter Tinker & Ruth Smith,	June 26, 1763
John George & Ann Beebe,	July 5, 1763
Daniel Gardiner of Norwich & Elisabeth Clark,	July 6, 1763
John Haly & Mary May,	July 12, 1763
Moses Fergo & Hannah Lamphire,	July 27, 1763
Henry Lattimore & Sarah Christophers,	Aug. 11, 1763
James Bulles (this may be a misspelling for Bolles) & Margaret Chappel,	Aug. 16, 1763
Moses Stork and Unice Mason,	Sept. 1, 1763
John Pyner & Anstis Powers,	Sept. 14, 1763
Ephraim Brown & Anna Beckwith of Lyme,	Sept. 15, 1763
James Penniman & Elisabeth Star,	Sept. 18, 1763
John Gardner & Jane Gun,	Oct. 23, 1763
Richard Deshon & Mary Harris,	Oct. 30, 1763
Boanerges Beebe & Elisabeth Cheney,	Oct. 31, 1763
John Ewets & Elisabeth Saltonstall,	Nov. 6, 1763
Harry Henry Crowder & Margaret Mason,	Nov. 17, 1763
Thaddeus Beebe & Susanna Douglass,	Nov. 29, 1763
William Coit & Sarah Prentis,	Dec. 18, 1763
Isaac Chapel & Lucy Whipple,	Dec. 27, 1763
Elijah Morgan & Lucy Morgan,	Dec. 29, 1763
Daniel Star & Lucy Douglass,	Jan. 5, 1764
Thomas Coit and Mary Gardiner,	Jan. 12, 1764
John Gorton & Mary Manwaring,	Feb. 2, 1764
Henry Noyes of East Hampton & Elisabeth Keeny,	Feb. 9, 1764
Thomas Walker & Sarah Carter,	Feb. 17, 1764
Stephen Fox & Jane Whipple,	April 12, 1764
Joseph Shantup & Hannah Ashpow (Indians),	April 18, 1764
John Freind of Philadelphia & Esther Leech,	May 13, 1764
John Lord of Lyme and Sarah Way,	July 1, 1764
Nathaniel Coit & Boradil Latimer,	July 5, 1764
Stephen Richards & Hannah Williams,	July 5, 1764
William Hubbard of Boston & Lydia Coit,	Aug. 28, 1764
Christopher Leffingwell of Norwich & Elisabeth Coit,	Aug. 28, 1764
John Preston & Zeruiah French,	Sept. 9, 1764
John Kelley of Norwich & Elisabeth Calkins,	Sept. 27, 1764
Thomas Hempsted & Mary Chapman,	Oct. 28, 1764
Daniel Edgerton of Norwich & Mary Douglass,	Nov. 8, 1764

John Fog & Mary Wacke, Nov. 8, 1764
Hugh Phidias & Hannah Eldridge, Nov. 22, 1764
John Dennis & Elisabeth Culver, Nov. 22, 1764
John-Clerk White of Dedham & Hannah Mentor,
    Nov. 25, 1764
Daniel Chappel & Esther Culver, Dec. 13, 1764
George Douglass & Elisabeth Lucas, Feb. 3, 1765
Daniel Lattimer & Sarah Douglass, Feb. 24, 1765
Jonathan Sachell & Eunice Swan, May 17, 1765
Silas Crocker & Martha Rogers, June 27, 1765
John Richards & Susanna Gray of Stonington, July 7, 1765
Richard Bevan of New York & Elizabeth Short,
    July 14, 1765
George Buttolphs Hurlbut & Mary Bulkley, Oct. 13, 1765
Anthony Whipple & Ame Beebe, Oct. 24, 1765
Samuel Udall of Stonington & Lydia Chapman, Nov. 14, 1765
Joseph Forbes of Hartford & Abigail Lucas, Nov. 16, 1765
John Crocker & Elisabeth Holt, Nov. 24, 1765
Richard Stroud & Elisabeth Billings, Nov. 25, 1765
Titus Hurlbut's Cæsar & Rebecca Hill (negroes),
    Dec. 1, 1765
Joan Baron & Mary Tinker, Dec. 5, 1765
Joseph Knox of Groton & Katherine Green, Feb. 6, 1766
John Foster of Liverpool & Lucy Leech, Feb. 12, 1766
John Sullivan & Elisabeth Chapman, Feb. 21, 1766
James Shearman & Elisabeth Morgan, Feb. 27, 1766
James Moor & Temperance Dayton, April 27, 1766
George Falkner & Katherine Ayer, June 8, 1766
Edward Culver & Esther Rotherage, June 8, 1766
Titus Whipple & Lucy Miner, June 12, 1766
Joseph Holt & Elisabeth Crocker, July 31, 1766
John Lester & Elisabeth Harris, Aug. 7, 1766
Edward Burk & Sarah Barter, Aug. 17, 1766
Thomas Durfey & Rebecca Manwaring, Oct. 23, 1766
Joseph Waterman & Bathsheba Powers, Nov. 2, 1766
John Daniels & Elisabeth Crocker, Nov. 7, 1766
Andrew Huntington of Norwich & Lucy Coit, Nov. 26, 1766
Jonathan Brooks & Mercy Bill, Dec. 2, 1766
Joshua Star & Mary Tilley, Dec. 14, 1766
Samuel Bolles & Margaret More, Dec. 18, 1766

John Prentis & Esther Richards,	Dec. 25, 1766
David Manwaring & Martha Saltonstall,	Jan. 15, 1767
Samuel Cheny & Rebecca Worthlake,	Jan. 15, 1767
James Darrow & Lucy Tinker,	Jan. 29, 1767
Allen Chadwick & Hannah Brooks,	Jan. 30, 1767
Lemuel More & Hannah Daniels,	April 2, 1767
Eliphalet Bulkley of Colchester & Ann Bulkley,	
	April 16, 1767
Jonathan Douglas & Ann Colfax,	April 30, 1767
James Chapman & Abigail Coit,	June 7, 1767
John Owen & Mary Douglass,	June 21, 1767
Edward Tinker & Mary Darrow,	June 25, 1767
Freeman Crocker & Lucy Tabor,	July 26, 1767
Japheth Mason & Patience Hempsted,	Aug. 2, 1767
Erastus Goddard & Ruth Latham of Groton,	Aug. 9, 1767
William Star & Hannah Talman,	Sept. 13, 1767
George Manwaring & Temperance Chappell,	Sept. 24, 1767
John Hempsted & Mary Bill,	Nov. 1, 1767
James Dennison & Esther Brown,	Nov. 18, 1767
Samuel Gardiner & Lydia Hurlbut,	Dec. 6, 1767
William Holt & Elisabeth Hempsted,	Jan. 21, 1768
Jeremiah Richards & Sarah Mossite,	Feb. 11, 1768
Moses Jeffrey & Lucy Otis,	March 12, 1768
John Champlin & Anne Adams, married by the Rev.	
David Jewitt,	May 5, 1769

RECORD OF MARRIAGES BY THE REV. EPHRAIM WOODBRIDGE.

James Watson & Hannah Cobb,	Oct. 12, 1769
James Reed & Lucy Chapman,	Nov. 7, 1769
Ephraim Woodbridge & Mary Shaw, married by	
Rev. David Jewitt,	Oct. 26, 1769
Patrick Robison & Margaret Church,	Nov. 14, 1769
Silas Dean of Wethersfield & Elizabeth Evets,	Nov. 16, 1769
Robert Douglas & Hannah Gardiner,	Nov. 19, 1769
Isaack Beckwith & Grace Edgcomb,	Nov. 20, 1769
Zechariah Brown & Millison Darrow,	Nov. 26, 1769
Benjamin Brown & Sarah Gorton,	Jan. 4, 1770
Thomas Strickland Prudence Chapil,	Jan. 11, 1770
Lemuel Clark & Susanna Miner,	Jan. 24, 1770
Avery Griswold of Withersfield & Lucy Lucas,	Jan. 24, 1770

Stephen Chappil & Sarah Darrow,	Feb. 10, 1770
Thomas Butler & Jemima Bebee,	March 24, 1770
Samuel Rose of Withersfield & Sarah Colfax,	April 15, 1770
John Leech & Mary Gray,	May 3, 1770
Peter Burker of Cape St. Nicola & Hannah Ames,	
	July 11, 1770
John Fiske Osgood of Boston & Lucy Tory,	Nov. 25, 1770
Elijah Peck of Lyme & Jane Miner,	Jan. 8, 1771
Amos Mason & Naomi Thomson,	Feb. 24, 1771
Jabez Winship of Norwich & Hannah Foresides,	
	Aug. 6, 1771
Thomas Lee & Constance Smith of Old England,	
	Aug. 12, 1771
Nathan Howard & Jane Miner,	Sept. 26, 1771
Joseph Fox & Elizabeth Coit,	Jan. 16, 1772
John S. Miller & Henrietta Saltonstall,	March, 1772
George Stilman of Saybrook & Catherine Roberts,	
	March, 1772
Reuben Clarke of Sturbridge & Lucy Darrow,	April 5, 1772
Robert Manwaring & Elizabeth Rogers,	Nov., 1772
William Rogers & Elizabeth Tinker,	Nov. 1, 1772
John Clarke & Elizabeth Worthylake,	Nov. 5, 1772
Joseph Collins and Doratha Springer,	Nov. 10, 1772
William Waistcoat & Esther Harris,	Dec., 1772
Ezekiel Rogers & Hannah Green,	Dec. 9, 1772
John Tinker & Desire Hilyard,	Dec. 21, 1772
James Reed & Hannah Chapman,	Dec. 25, 1772
Edward Richards & Sarah Bishop,	Jan. 25, 1773
Daniel Jennings & Anne Champlain,	Jan. 31, 1773
Richard Chapil & Grace Douglass,	Sept. 16, 1773
Hugh Smith & Elizabeth Daniels,	Sept. 22, 1773
James Holt & Elizabeth Corning,	Oct. 10, 1773
Thomas Leech & Lois Webb,	Oct. 14, 1773
Peter Rogers & Hannah Rogers,	Dec. 16, 1773
Benjamin Jerom & ——— Brown of Fishers Island,	
	Dec. 21, 1773
Simon Wolcott & Lucy Rogers,	Jan. 23, 1774
Samuel Graves of Stonington and Anne Hern,	
	March 4, 1774
Edward Wheler & Mary Tinker,	April 26, 1774

William Codney of Middletown and Catherine Holt,

	July 3, 1774
Samuel Mason & Elizabeth Rogers,	July 10, 1774
Jedediah Daniels & Elizabeth Williams,	Oct. 20, 1774
William Lane & Mary Trueman,	Oct. 30, 1774
James Davenport of Hartford & Welthy Mason,	Nov. 1, 1774
Joshua Plumb of Middletown & Mary Plumb,	Nov. 3, 1774
Josiah Lee of Middletown & Mary Christophers,	Nov. 6, 1774
William Weaver & Abigail Harris,	Nov. 10, 1774
Joseph Darrow of Stonington & Lydia Ward,	Nov. 20, 1774
Luke & Cloe (negroes),	Nov. 23, 1774
Dixwell Lothrop & Rebecca Rogers,	Dec. 4, 1774
Peter Clark & Sarah Fagins (Indians),	Dec. 11, 1774
Joseph Tinker & Marget Douglass,	Jan. 15, 1775
Nathan Spicer of Norwich & Sarah Clark,	Jan. 17, 1775
Zelemus Williams & Delight Williams,	Feb. 23, 1775
Peter & Sarah (negroes),	March 2, 1775
William Miner & Lucretia Wescoat	March 9, 1775
John Jeffrey & Margret Hancock,	April 6, 1775
Isaac Miner & Elizabeth Griffing,	May 11, 1775
Jonathan Latimer, Jr., & Elizabeth Chapell,	Aug. 3, 1775
Thomas Pool & Elizabeth Adams,	Oct. 27, 1775
Elisha Hide of Norwich & Ann Hallam,	Nov. 5, 1775
Nicholas Darrow & Sarah Rogers,	Nov. 12, 1775
Daniel Keeney & Rebecca Tinker,	Nov. 16, 1775
Ebenezar Bishop & Sarah Pierpoint,	May, 1776
David Bill & Temperance Harris.	May, 1776

MARRIAGES BY REV. HENRY CHANNING.

Joseph Fellows & Polly Ward,	June 10, 1787
Thomas Johnson of Richmond, Virginia, & Dolly Dunton,	July 15, 1787
Daniel Byrne & Bathsheba Rogers,	Aug. 13, 1787
Seaberry Fish of Nine Partners & Hannah Hall,	Sept. 9, 1787
Walter Budington of East Hartford & Bridget Champlin,	Nov. 29, 1787
Job Dart & Lydia Hadlock,	Dec. 2, 1787
John Crawford of Cornwall, England, & Olive Beckwith of Lyme,	Feb. 3, 1788

William Leverett of Middletown & Lucretia Hal-
lam,   Feb. 14, 1788
Josiah Hempstead of Hartford & Polly Hempstead,
                                                March 6, 1788
Stephen Waterhouse & Hannah Holt,   March 9, 1788
Jasper Harris & Elizabeth Shields,   March 26, 1788
Daniel Henshaw of Middletown & Sally E. Prentis,
                                                April 18, 1788
Joseph Sisson of Preston & Elizabeth Smith, April 27, 1788
Nicholas Henry Gilnor of Montville & Lydia
    Watson,   May 1, 1788
Alexander Richards & Mary Colfax,   May 15, 1788
James Edgerton of Norwich & Katherine Hinman,
                                                May 29, 1788
John Lathrop & Lucretia Rogers,   June 5, 1788
James Harker of Hardwich, New Jersey, & Eliza-
    beth Holdsworth,   July 10, 1788
Joseph Skinner & Jane Stark,   July 23, 1788
John Squire of Fairfield & Sophia Stroud,   Aug. 3, 1788
Abner Wakefield & Amelia Bliss,   Sept. 24, 1788
John Howard & Susanna Dart,   Sept. 30, 1788
Abel Procter of Westford, Mass., & Elizabeth Clark,
                                                Oct. 5, 1788
Joseph Owen & Sarah Kennedy,   Oct. 12, 1788
John Carter & Mary Hughes,   Jan. 15, 1789
Elijah Backus & Hannah Richards,   Feb. 3, 1789
Nicholas Loysel of Guilford & Ruth Harris, March 3, 1789
William Wheat & Mary Smith,   March 15, 1789
Abraham Bliss & Sarah Youngs,   April 29, 1789
James Cizane of Guadaloupe & Lydia Deshon,
                                                Sept. 10, 1789
David Pike & Elizabeth Pitman,   Sept. 20, 1789
Thomas Coit, Jr., & Mary Wanton Saltonstall, Nov. 29, 1789
John Coit & Lucy Smith,   Dec. 3, 1789
Samuel Allen of Montville and Mary Prentis, Dec. 6, 1789
Azariah Way & Grace Douglass,   Jan. 7, 1790
John Winand of Petersburg, Va., & Frances Rich-
    ards,   Jan. 28, 1790
Elias Perkins & Lucretia Shaw Woodbridge, March 14, 1790
George D. Avery & Mary Champlin,   April 1, 1790

Joseph Whalley of London, England, & Hannah Saltonstall,	April 8, 1790
Enoch Lord of Lyme & Esther Durpey,	June 3, 1790
Luther Gale & Lucretia Turner,	June 21, 1790
Joseph Young & Lydia Butler,	Aug. 8, 1790
Ezra Dodge & Elizabeth Hempstead,	Sept. 26, 1790
Richard Douglass & Abigail Starr,	Oct. 28, 1790
Gurdon Tracy & Lucy Starr,	Jan. 2, 1791
John Andrews Fullton & Mehitable Owen,	Jan. 9, 1791
William Potter of England & Margaret Laws,	Jan. 10, 1791
Picket Lattimer & Eunice Douglass,	Jan. 13, 1791
John McHoy & Susannah Smith,	Jan. 30, 1791
Giles Hempstead & Lucrétia Saltonstall,	Feb. 13, 1791
Jeduthun Cushman & Delight Rogers,	May 12, 1791
Samuel Strickland & Susanna Chapel,	June 23, 1791
Edward Danforth of Hartford & Jerusha Mossly,	Oct. 20, 1791
Samuel Chany, Jr., & Rebecca Stacey,	Oct. 23, 1791
Daniel G. Thacher & Eunice Starr,	Oct. 30, 1791
Joseph Griffing & Hannah Cheles,	Nov. 6, 1791
Edward Wicks & Anne George,	Nov. 13, 1791
Samuel Jennison of Middletown & Rebecca Douglass,	Nov. 20, 1891
Robert Nicholas of Barbadoes & Elca Pain,	Nov. 24, 1791
David Avery of Norwich & Abigail Goddard,	Dec. 8, 1791
Jacob Chany & Elizabeth Holmes,	Jan. 1, 1792
Walter McCall of Lebanon & Abigail Colfax,	Jan. 10, 1792
Peleg Church & Mary Leach of Montville,	Feb. 16, 1792
Jared Prentis & Mary Douglass,	Feb. 23, 1792
Amos Woodward & Elizabeth Bailey,	Feb. 26, 1792
Isaac Williams of Philadelphia & Sarah Henry,	March 4, 1792
John A. Lawrence & Sally Prentis,	March 11, 1792
John Bolles of Hartford & Betsy Avery,	April 1, 1792
Peter Christophers & Rebecca Saltonstall,	April 2, 1792
Dr. Charles Poulain & Nancy Spooner,	June 28, 1792
William Otis Southworth of Saybrook & Elizabeth Holt,	July 1, 1792
John Douglass & Mary Holmes,	August 13, 1792
Simeon Smith & Mary Avery of Groton,	Sept. 13, 1792

Howland Powers & Rebecca Clark,   Sept. 13, 1792
Jacob Cooper of West Springfield, Mass., & Rebecca
  Spooner,   Sept. 30, 1792
Samuel Booth Hempstead & Esther Prentis,   Oct. 29, 1792
Charles H. Sole & Dolly Prentice,   Nov. 11, 1792
John Penniman & Mary Starr,   Nov. 29, 1792
Etienne Riffaud of Rochelle & Angelique Louise
  Antoinette of Montfort La Maury, France,
  Dec. 26, 1792
Elisha Coit of Norwich & Rebecca Manwaring,
  Jan. 20, 1793
James Burtwell & Lucy Rogers,   Jan. 20, 1793
Henry Chesebrough of Whitestown & Elizabeth
  Hurlbut,   Feb. 3, 1793
James Grenlow of New Brunswick & Jerusha Wat-
  son,   Feb. 21, 1793
Joseph Caulkins & Polly Sistare,   April 4, 1793
Thompson Phillips of Middletown & Abigail Mum-
  ford,   April 22, 1793
Robert Byrne & Elizabeth Brown of Groton, April 22, 1793
Samuel Calkins of Norwich & Sarah Williams,
  April 29, 1793
Samuel Haynes & Rebecca Green,   May 3, 1793
Benjamin Butler of Norwich & Alice Meloney, May 12, 1793
Michael Melally & Esther Prentis,   July 20, 1793
Samuel Lee of Lyme & Esther Douglass,   July 25, 1793
Joel Watson & Nancy Meloney,   Aug. 1, 1793
Maynard Franklin of Groton & Rhoda Davis, Sept. 29, 1793
Dr. James Lee & Hephzibah Lord of Lyme,   Sept. 30, 1793
Oliver Raymond of Montville & Hannah Raymond,
  Oct. 3, 1793
George Way & Sarah Douglass,   Dec. 5, 1793
James Bulkley of Middletown & Caroline Hallam,
  Jan. 28, 1794
Samuel Holmes & Esther Cornell,   March 2, 1794
Samuel H. P. Lee & Elizabeth Sullivan,   March 30, 1794
John French of Derby & Mary Goddard,   April 8, 1794
Benjamin Hall & Phebe Daniels,   April 9, 1794
David Tinker & Elizabeth Hazard,   May 5, 1794
Jonathan Brooks, Jr., & Mary Deshon,   May 20, 1794

Elnathan Hatch of East Haddam & Anna Champlin,

June 8, 1794

John Pool & Esther Rogers,   July 27, 1794

Edward Merrill & Phebe Cornell,   Aug. 3, 1794

Joseph Smith of Lyme & Lucy Harris,   Aug. 28, 1794

John Brown of Newport, R. I., & Elizabeth Treby,

Sept. 7, 1794

Alexander Morgan & Sally Clay,   Sept. 21, 1794

Daniel Douglass & Lucy Douglas,   Oct. 2, 1794

Samuel Thompson & Hannah Hempsted,   Oct. 8, 1794

Lyman Law & Elizabeth Learned,   Oct. 12, 1794

Ebenezer Dunton & Hannah Jones,   Nov. 4, 1794

Shubael Preston of Ashford & Lucretia Miner, Nov. 9, 1794

Daniel Penniman of Hartford & Hannah R. Jepson,

Dec. 11, 1794

Levi Brown of Deerfield, N. H., & Deborah Sears,

Dec. 14, 1794

Henry Quilshy of New York and Phebe Martin,

Dec. 14, 1794

Richard Leach & Sarah Crocker,   Dec. 21, 1794

Joseph Sistare & Nancy Way,   Feb. 1, 1795

William Watson of Hartford & Sophia Purple, Feb. 12, 1795

William Penniman & Lucy Tracy,   March 15, 1795

Stephen Robbins of Fairfield & Anna Mathers,

March 17, 1795

Joel Loomis & Hannah Angell,   March 25, 1795

George Wake & Mehitabel Deshon,   April 4, 1795

Christopher Griffing & Susanna Deshon,   April 25, 1795

William Young of Stratford & Nabby Holt,   May 10, 1795

Lent Hamlin of Bristol & Elizabeth Davis of Groton,   May 14, 1795

Enoch Parsons of Middletown & Mary Sullivan,

May 19, 1795

David Pool & Hannah Brooks,   May 24, 1795

John Hiscox of New York & Sarah Youngs,   Sept. 8, 1795

John Ogden of Elizabeth Town & Avstis Baker,

Sept. 26, 1795

Robert Allyn & Rebecca Mumford,   Sept. 28, 1795

Richard Potter & Esther Chapman, married by
    Rev. Joseph Strong,   Dec. 6, 1795.

Benjamin Richards & Mary Coit, Dec. 20, 1795
Gurdon Furgo & Elizabeth George, Jan. 12, 1796
William Sam & Amey Christiana, Jan. 28, 1796
Richard Beebe & Elizabeth Holt, Jan. 31, 1796
William Holt, 3d, & Elizabeth Sistare, April 14, 1796
Ezra Chapman & Elizabeth Bailey, May 1, 1796
Simeon Beebe & Jerusha Maynard, May 15, 1796
Samuel Avery & Jerusha Arnold, June 26, 1796
James Springer & Rebecca Harris, July 3, 1796
Stephen Whittemore of Middletown & Elizabeth
    M. Chappel, July 14, 1796
Rev. William Patten of Newport & Hannah Hurlbut,
    Sept. 11, 1796
Daniel Starr & Hannah Way, Sept. 22, 1796
Isaac Tracy, Jr., & Elizabeth Huntington, Sept. 25, 1796
Coleby Chew & Frances Learned, Nov. 13, 1796
Nathan Waterhouse & Nancy Franklin, Nov. 26, 1796
Stephen Richards & Susanna Crocker, Nov. 27, 1796
Samuel Freeman of Norwich & Jerusha Culver,
    Dec. 2, 1796
Joshua H. Reeves & Sally Simmons, Dec. 21, 1796
Richard Chappell & Catherine Coit, Feb. 5, 1797
James McGibbon of New York & Nancy Newson,
    Feb. 9, 1797
Allen McLean of Hartford & Lucy Springer,
    Feb. 14, 1797
John Avery of Groton & Lucy Rogers, Feb. 26, 1797
Stephen Crocker & Lucy Brooks, March 3, 1797
John Hinson of Franklin & Lydia Manchester,
    April 6, 1797
Amos Leeds & Abigail Brooks, April 23, 1797
David Coit & Elizabeth Calkins, April 24, 1797
Henry Jepson & Hannah Holt, May 14, 1797
James Brooks & Margaret Halpin, July 9, 1797
Edward Steel of Jamaica & Lydia Smith, July 14, 1797
Lodwick Slator & Priscilla Anderson, July 16, 1797
David Johnson of Huntington & Nancy Rogers,
    July 16, 1797
Walter Hubbell of Windsor, North Carolina, &
    Anna Law, Sept. 4, 1797

James Beebe & Catherine Sheldon,	Oct. 6, 1797
Isaac Rogers & Sally Ishmael,	Oct. 15, 1797
William Leeds & Lucy Deshon,	Oct. 22, 1797
John C. Muinnichhausen & Esther Williams,	Oct. 31, 1797
John Turner of Stonington & Polly Newson,	Nov. 2, 1797
William Brown of Boston & Fanny Smith,	Nov. 15. 1797
John T. Duryee of New York & Nancy Mumford,	
	Dec. 18, 1797
Jeremiah Atwater of New Haven & Mary Saltonstall,	
	Dec. 19, 1797
Samuel Green & Sally F. Pool,	Jan. 4, 1798
John Daniels of Newport & Esther Crisp,	Jan. 7, 1798
Jonathan Rogers & Sarah Rogers,	Jan. 14, 1798
Alexander C. Wylly of Savannah, Georgia, & Martha	
Douglass,	March 5, 1798
Joseph Brown of England & Abigail Berry,	March 9, 1798
Joseph B. Manning & Sally Lampheer,	March 22, 1798
Isaac Thorpe & Catherine Jeffery,	March 25, 1798
Roswel S. Crandal Westerly & Abiah Culver,	April 19, 1798
Joshua Starr & Lucy Colfax,	April 19, 1798
William Ryon & Ann Boone,	Aug. 23, 1798
Samuel Cornel & Hannah Davis,	Sept. 23, 1798
Stephen J. Thacher of Stratford & Boadil Coit,	Oct. 31, 1798
Simon Wolcott & Charlotte Mumford,	Nov. 8, 1798
Charles Rockwell of Norwich & Sally Arnold,	Dec. 13, 1798
Hubbil Brooks & Lydia Clark,	Dec. 19, 1798
Barachiah Paine of Boston & Polly Lampheer,	Dec. 22, 1798
Isaac Sheffield of Stonington & Betsey Sizer,	Jan. 11, 1799
Samuel Treby & Polly Whittemore,	Jan. 13, 1799
Ebenezer Clark & Catherine Codner,	Feb. 3, 1799
William Potter & Lucretia Marshal,	Feb. 3, 1799
Oliver Barker of Norwich & Phebe Holt,	April 16, 1799
James Pitman & Sally Crocker,	May 5, 1799
John Dennis of Ipswich & Nancy Hull,	May 21, 1799
Samuel Sizer & Mary Treby,	May 23, 1799
Samuel Colt & Anna Hallett (at Geneva, in County	
of Ontario, State of New York),	July 2, 1799
Jude Prat of Saybrook & Rhoda Whittemore,	Aug. 28, 1799
William Hamilton & Elizabeth Dickinson,	Sept. 1, 1799
Douglass Woodworth of Bozrah & Sybil Harris,	Sept. 11, 1799

William B. Burgh of Maryland & Rebecca Stone,
Oct. 24, 1799
David G. Hubbard of New York & Lucy Manwar-
ing, Oct. 26, 1799
Samuel Pitman & Eunice Holt, Nov. 10, 1799
Daniel Eldredge & Betsey Sheffield, Nov. 21, 1799
David Hall & Elizabeth Harris, Nov. 28, 1799
Lyman Harrington of Montville & Polly Martin,
Dec. 1, 1799
George Packwood & Sarah Hinman, Dec. 1, 1799
Richard Tinker & Sally Harris, Dec. 14, 1799
Joseph Woodwell of E. Haddam & Rebecca Ryon,
Dec. 19, 1799
Nicholas Starr of Groton & Elizabeth Beebe, Jan. 1, 1800
Samuel Ames & Catherine Mathers, Jan. 9, 1800
John Morrison & Polly Stone of Preston, Feb. 17, 1800
Jack Almy & Cecilia Shaw, Feb. 22, 1800
Nathaniel Middleton of Groton & Polly Rogers,
March 27, 1800
Timothy Sparrow of Orleans, Mass., & Hannah
Douglass, April 14, 1800
Benjamin Spencer & Rebecca Bloyd, May 11, 1800
Nathaniel Saltonstall & Lucretia Lampheer, May 22, 1800
Joshua Hilburn & Lucy Holt, May 26, 1800
Daniel Helly of Ireland & Olive Smith of Lyme,
June 8, 1800
James Holt & Jerusha Calfrey, June 29, 1800
Jeremiah Thorpe & Mary Danzy, July 22, 1800
Ebenezer Dimon of Fairfield & Mary S. Hinman,
July 23, 1800
York Murfort & Violet Holmes, July 28, 1800
Abijah Beebe & Nancy Howard, Aug. 25, 1800
Walter Grace & Abigail Blackley, Aug. 31, 1800
Horace Steel of Hartford & Elizabeth Crocker, Sept. 21, 1800
Bliss Silsby of Norwich & Nancy Rogers, Sept. 21, 1800
George Frederick Harper of Halifax, N. S., &
Debbe Dupignac, Oct. 12, 1800
Zebadiah Rogers & Catherine Richards, Oct. 12, 1800
Morgan Brown of Philadelphia & Bridget Jeffery,
Oct. 26, 1800

Charles Beebe & Abigail Douglas,   Nov. 13, 1800
Samuel Beckwith of Lyme & Ame Slater,   Nov. 20, 1800
John Elwill of Pepperelborough & Sally Hancock,
                                            Nov. 21, 1800
John Rogers & Sarah Sears,   Nov. 23, 1800
Peter Richards & Ann Channing Huntington, Nov. 27, 1800
Joseph Dorr of Boston & Fanny Briggs,   Dec. 16, 1800

LEBANON.

NEW LONDON COUNTY.

The town of Lebanon was incorporated in October, 1700. The First Congregational Church was organized in 1700. The Second Church (Goshen) now in Bozrah, 1729. The Third Church (Exeter) at Leonard's Bridge, 1773. The following are the records of the First Church.

Benjamin Skinner & Elizabeth Dixon,   Nov. 3, 1712
Jacob Munsel & Sarah Calkin,   Dec. 30, 1713
Josiah Loomas & Esther ———,   Oct. 15, 1713
George Way & Lydia Sprague,   July 19, 1713
Jonathan Hutchinson & ——— ———,   Sept. 2, 1713
Nathaniel White & Anne ———,   Oct. 4, 1713
Jabez Warren & Mary ———,   1716
Samuel Raymant & Lydia Birchard,   Jan. 6, 1717
William Slade & Thankful Hutchinson,   July 12, 1718
Joshua Owen & Margaret Woodworth,   Nov. 5, 1718
Jonathan Cas—— & Bathsheba Williams,   Nov. 13, 1718
Nathaniel Fitch & Abigal Buttolph,   Nov. 25, 1718
Ephraim Loomas & Mary Tuttle,   Nov. 26, 1718
Ebenezer North & Mary Glover,   Jan. 15, 1718
Daniel Hide & Abigal Wattle,   March 3, 1718
Richard Man & Mary Colver,   1719
Jonathan Badcock & Mary Neybard,   1719
Gov. Thomas Mattoon & Jemima Abel,   1719
Daniel Birchard & Elizabeth Thomas,   about 1720–21
Amos Hullor & Priscilla Woodworth,   about 1720–21
Benjamin Woodworth & ——— ———,   about 1720–21

Ebenezer Williams & Mary Velch,	about 1720–21
James Holbrook & Sarah Bumsteed,	about 1720–21
William Sumner & Hannah Hum,	about 1720–21
Ebenezer Bruster & Elizabeth Dewolfe,	about 1720–21
Caleb Chappell & Elizabeth Hutchinson,	about 1720–21
John Gay & Lydia Colver,	about 1720–21
Benj. Bruster & Rebekah Blackman,	1722
John Wattlo & Judith Fitch,	1722
Jedidiah Strong & Elizabeth Webster,	1722
Samuel Huntington & Hannah Metcalfe,	1722
Joseph Marsh & Mercy Bill,	Sept. 25, 1722
Amos Woodworth & Elee Mathews,	Oct. 3, 1722
Daniel Denison & Mehitable Forster,	Nov. 7, 1722
George Woolcot & Mary Hartwell,	Nov. 7, 1722
Joseph Gay & Abigail Thorp,	Dec. 25, 1722
Elisha Blackman & Susanna ———,	Jan. 2, 1724
John Strong & Abijah Chappel,	Feb. 5, 1724
John Bruster & Mary Terry,	Feb. 6, 1724
Henry Bliss & Bethiah Spafford,	March 5, 1724
Joseph Strong & Elizabeth Strong,	May 12, 1724
John Ticknor & Mary Bayley,	May 14, 1724
Joseph Bayley & Abigail Ingram,	May 14, 1724
David Woodworth & Hannah Gay,	May 28, 1724
John Webster & Mary Dewey,	Aug. 20, 1724
John Forster & Hannah Thorp,	Aug. 26, 1724
Caleb Hide & Mary Blackman,	Sept. 17, 1724
Clodus Dillis (?) & Ruth Sprague,	Nov. 12, 1724
Hezekiah Loomas & Hepzibah Thatcher,	Nov. 18, 1724
Samuel Hide, Jun., & Priscilla Bradford,	Jan. 14, 1725
John Corbett & Experience Thomas,	April 27, 1725
Ebenezer Welsh & Lydia Dibble,	May 12, 1725
Stephen Powel & Elizabeth Blackman,	July 30, 1725
Stephen Lee & Mercy Bently,	May 20, 1725
Samuel Murdock & Submit Throope,	June 3, 1725
Nathanael Holbrook & Martha Right,	June 24, 1725
Eleazer Hutchinson & Jemima Right,	July 15, 1725
Pelatiah Webster & Jemima Crowfoot,	Dec. 14, 1725
Capt. Marsh & widow Webster,	Dec. 14, 1725
John Bill, Junior, & Hannah Swift,	March 30, 1726
John Sprague & Hepzibah Hartwell,	Sept. 7, 1726

Ebenezer Bill & Patience Ingram,	Sept. 8, 1726
Benjamin Pain & Mary Bruster,	Oct. 25, 1726
Joseph Dewey & Abigal Hill,	Oct. 31, 1726
Samuel Bruster & Tabitha Baldwin,	Nov. 30, 1726
John Dewey & Experience Woodward,	Nov. 30, 1726
John Gillit & Abigal Lee,	Dec. 30, 1726
James Tisdale & Mindwell Hutchinson,	Feb. 2, 1727
Josiah Cooke & Zebia Cushman,	March 9, 1727
Thomas Webster & Lydia Lyman,	Aug. 17, 1727
William Buel & Elizabeth Holbrook,	Sept. 15, 1727
Jerimiah Ingram & Hannah Norton,	Sept. 27, 1727
Jonathan Metcalfe & Lidia Hide,	Nov. 2, 1727
Samuel Gridley & Rebecca Chamberlin,	Dec. 12, 1727
Daniel Abel & Sarah Crane,	Dec. 25, 1727
Joshua Cole & Mary Murch,	Dec. 25, 1727
John Syms & Bathsheba Throope,	Jan. 8, 1730
Thomas Chapman & Mary Throope,	Feb. 26, 1730
Jabez Lyman & Martha Bliss,	Jan. 29, 1731
Peter Bruster & Mary Lee,	Feb. 18, 1731
James White & Abigal Lyman,	April 22, 1731
Ebenezer Johnson & Mary Johnson,	Nov. 1, 1731
Nehemiah Fitch & Elizabeth Vetch,	Nov. 1, 1731
Simeon Gray & Anna Hide,	Nov. 17, 1731
Peleg Sprague & Hannah Marsh,	Feb., 1732
Samuel Terry & Sarah Webster,	Feb., 1732
David Foster & Alethea Cogswell,	March 23, 1732
Gideon Hunt & Rebekah Ordoway,	June 7, 1732
Ebenezer Brown & Martha Loomas,	July 13, 1732
Robert Cogswell & Sarah Bayley,	Jan. 6, 1733
Daniel Rockwell & Margaret Loomas,	Feb. 20, 1733
Silas Owen & Elizabeth Hunt,	Feb. 14, 1733
Nathanael House & Abigal Bill,	March 1, 1733
James Fitch & Abiel Metcalfe,	Nov. 22, 1733
Abel Buel & Mehetable Dewey,	April 11, 1734
James Calkin & Abigal Huntington,	April 15, 1734
Silas Dean & Hannah Barker,	Nov. 21, 1734
John Morey & Jerusha Webster,	Nov. 28, 1734
Ebenezer Webster & Mehetable Thomas,	Dec. 5, 1734
Ebenezer Sprague & Elizabeth Thatcher,	Dec. 12, 1734
William Hunt & Sarah Lyman,	Dec. 19, 1734

Joshua Fuller & Experience Stedman,	Dec. 25, 1734
Benjamin Wright & Rachel Owen,	Jan. 9, 1735
Jonathan Clarke & Mercy Dewey,	Jan. 16, 1735
Thomas Woodward & Dorothy Pinio,	Feb. 13, 1735
Joseph Sluman & Hannah Trumbull,	Feb. 27, 1735
David Jacobs & Mary Owen,	Feb. 5, 1735
James Bettis & Hannah Wheeler,	Feb. 5, 1735
Joshua Allen & Abigal James,	-Feb. 12, 1735
Jonathan Janes & Irene Bradford,	March 18, 1735
Azariah Bliss & Mary Tilden,	April 29, 1735
David Lee & Mary Tilden, alias Pourl,	June 24, 1735
John Williams & Allis Metcalfe,	June 30, 1735
Simeon Hunt & Hannah Lyman,	July 29, 1735
Benjamin Owen & Margaret Taylor,	Oct. 14, 1735
Ignatius Barker & Mary Sprague,	Nov. 13, 1735
Andrew Liske & Elizabeth Bradford,	June 12, 1736
Jacob Phelps & Keziah Meacham,	July 14, 1736
Joshua Macgee & Elizabeth Bradford,	Sept. 27, 1736
John Hutchinson & Temperance Cogswel,	Nov. 10, 1736
Israel Loomas & Esther Hunt,	Dec. 15, 1736
Moses Hatch & Mary Bliss,	Jan. 1, 1738
Caleb Abel & Mary Clarke,	Jan. 7, 1738
John Morey & Abigal Loomas,	June 8, 1738
Isaiah Williams & Lucy Roberts,	July 12, 1738
Eleazer Bingham & Miriam Phelps,	July 13, 1738
Jeffy (a mulatto) & Mary George (an Indian),	July 14, 1738
Abraham Spafford & Hannah Chapman,	Nov. 1, 1738
Benjamin Chafie & Hannah Chapman,	Nov. 2, 1738
Joseph Clarke & Grace Thomas,	Feb. 15, 1739
Samuel Seabury & Ann Terry,	Feb. 22, 1739
Silas Newcomb & Submit Pinio,	March 1, 1739
Elijah Bingham & Theody Crane,	March 8, 1739
Joseph Sluman & Abigal Abel,	March 13, 1739
Joshua Barker & Mary Throope,	Nov. 8, 1739
Thomas Allen & Ruth Hunt,	Nov. 15, 1739
Asa Rood & Mary Calkin,	Jan. 24, 1740
Daniel Hunt & Hannah Burnham,	Feb. 15, 1740
Joseph Throope & Deborah Buel,	March 20, 1740
Phineas Wheeler & Mary Gillet,	April 30, 1740
Jonathan Owen & Patience Vallence,	May 11, 1740

Caleb Owen & Elizabeth Bruster,	June 22, 1740
Wade Clark & Martha Brown,	July 9, 1740
Elias Tupper & Jerusha Sprague,	Sept. 4, 1740
Josiah Heathe & Mercy Owen,	Oct. 2, 1740
David Millington & Mary Wright,	Nov. 5, ——
Paul Phelps & Jerusha Dewey,	Dec. 12, 1740
Timothy Loomas & Ann Taylor,	March 5, 1741
Joseph Hatch & Mary Clarke,	March 10, 1741
Ebenezer Hide & Elizabeth Graves,	June 3, 1741
Joseph Smith & Mary Webster,	June 4, 1741
Peter Pratt & Mary Metcalfe,	July 6, 1741
Aaron Gaylord & Mary Clarke,	July 7, 1741
John Williams & Margaret Metcalfe,	Aug. 24, 1741
William Whitely & Mehetable Fitch,	Sept. 30, 1741
Thomas Hovey & Abigal Phelps,	Oct. 22, 1741
Phinehas Clarke & Prisilla Cass,	Nov. 5, 1741
Joseph Lyman & Joanna Loomas,	Dec. 30, 1741
Rowland Swetland & Mary Rood,	Dec. 30, 1741
Benoni Wright & Elizabeth Smith,	Jan. 7, 1742
Jonathan Crane & Sarah Armstrong,	1742
Silas Phelps & Hannah Dewey,	Dec. 22, 1742
Bezaleel Hide & Mehetable Porter,	Jan. 13, 1743
Hector and Thora (servants Col. Trumbull),	Jan. 13, 1743
Constant Crandal & Hannah Bruster,	May 18, 1743
Matthew Polby(?) & Mary Root,	Aug. 1, 1743
Israel Loomas & Mary Holbrooke,	Sept. 27, 1743
Samuel Bushnel & Zerviah Lyman,	Oct. 5, 1743
Elijah Tisdale & Eunice Smith,	Nov. 6, 1743
Eliphalet Tracy & Sarah Manning,	Nov. 28, 1743
Samuel Lyman & Sarah Corbet,	Nov. 29, 1743
Ephraim Andrews & Elizabeth Loomas,	Dec. 1, 1743
Jonathan Hartshorn & Abigal Leonard,	Jan. 3, 1744
Job Pees & Eunice Phelps,	Feb. 24, 1744
Adonijah Fitch & Ann Gray,	April 22, 1744
Charles Bruster & Keziah Owens,	June 15, 1744
Robert Lane & Mary Thatcher,	July 4, 1744
Thomas Martin & Ann Clark,	Aug. 9, 1744
John Gray & Elizabeth Metcalfe,	Aug. 15, 1744
Jonathan Lee & Elizabeth Metcalfe,	Sept. 3, 1744
Rev. Richard Salter & Mrs. Mary Williams,	Sept. 11, 1744

Jonathan Cass & Eunice Porter,	Oct. 4, 1744
Gideon Hunt & Abigal Colver,	Oct. 16, 1744
Jonathan Lomas & Margaret Graves,	Oct. 28, 1744
Israel Jones & Jemima Clarke,	Nov. 29, 1744
James Badcock & Hannah Bayley,	May 2, 1745
James Cushman & Levina Downey,	May 8, 1745
Edmund Grandey & Rachel Lyman,	May 15, 1745
Adams Pierce & Judith Woodworth,	May 16, 1745
Moses Phelps & Sarah Meacham,	May 29, 1745
Lewis Terrill & Ann Badcock,	May 30, 1745
Benj. Badcock & Hannah Everat,	June 5, 1745
Moses Clark & Mary Ordoway,	June 6, 1745
Jacob Lyman & Mehitable Lyman,	June 26, 1745
Daniel Rudd & Mary Metcalfe,	July 1, 1745
Lemuel Cleaveland & Lydia Woodworth,	Nov. 5, 1745
John Gray & Lucy Baldwin,	Jan. 29, 1746
Oliver Collens & Sarah Hide,	June 22, 1746
Joseph Martin & Hannah Clarke,	Oct. 7, 1746
Elias Crowfoot & Mary Welsh,	Oct. 23, 1746
George Throope & Mehitable Bliss,	Nov. 5, 1746
Lemuel Taylor & Batsheba Dean,	Dec. 1, 1746
Prince Alden & Mary Fitch,	Dec. 18, 1746
Noah Jeans & Elizabeth Throope,	Jan. 12, 1747
Joseph Fowler & Sarah Metcalfe,	Feb. 3, 1747
Zaccheus Waldo & Tabitha Kingsbury,	Feb. 3, 1747
Daniel Bissell & Elizabeth Fitch,	Feb. 15, 1747
Israel Loomas & Mary Marsh,	April 8, 1747
Samuel Throope & Submit Clarke,	May 27, 1747
Israel Lothrop & Sarah Tuttle,	June 9, 1747
Elijah Owen & Patience Wright,	Oct. 22, 1747
Elee Swift & ———,	Oct. 22, 1747
Benjamin Hatch & Sarah Crane,	Oct. 26, 1747
William Finney & Abigal Black,	Nov. 2, 1747
Jethro Hatch & Martha Clarke,	Nov. 5, 1747
William Smith & Ann Cogswell,	Nov. 12, 1747
John Mirick & Deborah Williams,	Dec. 2, 1747
Thomas Bounie (?) & Susana Palmer,	Dec. 24, 1747
Abraham Loomas & Sarah Loomas,	Jan. 7, 1748
Daniel Kingsbury & Abigal Barstow,	Jan. 7, 1748
Dick (Caleb Prime's negro) & Ruth (David Richardson's negro),	Jan. 19, 1748

Ichabod Warner & Sarah Phelps,	Feb. 4, 1748
James Jetson & Sarah Webster,	April 14, 1748
John Tiffany & Mary Meacham,	April 28, 1748
John Johnson & Mary Bruster,	May 5, 1748
Isaiah Tiffany & Ann Lyman,	May 18, 1748
John Ordoway & Eunice Gillit,	May 19, 1748
Eleazer Wells & Ruth Waterman,	May 22, 1748
Abraham Hills & Jerusha Smith,	June 26, 1748
Nathan Richardson & Phebe Crocker,	Nov. 1, 1748
William Little & Sybil Metcalfe,	Nov. 10, 1748
Elisha Porter & Miridian Russ,	Dec. 1, 1748
Cuff & Phillis (Dr. Kingsbury's servants),	Dec. 1, 1748
Seth Alden & Lidia Alden,	March 9, 1749
Moses Spear & Submit Hastings,	March 9, 1749
John Johnson & Susanna Clark,	June 20, 1749
Jonathan Bill & Esther Owen,	Aug. 1, 1749
Silas Sprague & Hannah Beny,	Sept. 28, 1749
Elisha Doubleday & Hannah Bayley,	Oct. 2, 1749
Daniel Pumroy & Naomi Phelps,	Oct. 19, 1749
Elijah Lyman & Esther Clarke,	Dec. 14, 1749
Sam'll Hide & Ann Fitch,	Jan. 1, 1750
Jeremiah Silvy & Miriam Blyss,	Jan. 4, 1750
Timothy Clarke & Submit Williams,	Jan. 25, 1750
Nathan Bayley & Elizabeth Terry,	May 31, 1750
Isaac Davis & Lucy Storey,	Nov. 3, 1750
Amos Yeomans & Susanna Downer,	Nov. 21, 1750
Rev. John Porter & Mrs. Mary Huntington,	Jan. 3, 1751
Jedediah Strong & Hepzibah Webster,	Jan. 10, 1751
Jeremiah Hodges & Elizabeth Hodges,	March 11, 1751
John Bass & Mary Pain,	May 9, 1751
Nathan Bushnell & Hannah Clarke,	May 22, 1751
John Baldwin & Mary Binney,	June 12, 1751
Phineas Clarke & Hannah Collins,	June 20, 1751
Yetones Barstow & Esther Wood,	Aug. 6, 1751
Solomon Tisdale & Susanna Britton,	Aug. 18, 1751
Benjamin Smith & Abigal Sprague,	Sept. 19, 1751
Archibald Dixon & Eleanor Millar,	Oct. 1, 1751
Samuel Bayley & Hannah Lyman,	Oct. 31, 1751
Azel Fitch & Silence How,	Jan. 1, 1752
Ichabod Robinson & Lydia Brown,	Jan. 16, 1752

John Manning & Sarah Seabury,	Jan. 27, 1752
Benjamin Wesson & Elizabeth Bruster,	March 15, 1752
Amos Barrows & Mary Bayley,	May 21, 1752
Charles Collens & Ann Huntington,	June 18, 1752
Jonathan Marsh & Keziah Phelps,	Dec. 4, 1752
Pelatiah Marsh & Ann Marsh,	Dec. 28, 1752
Timothy Greene & Mrs. Rachel Dehane (?),	May 10, 1753
Judah Moro & Mary Swift,	May 24, 1753
Timothy Holbrook & Hannah White,	June 5, 1753
William Williams & Susannah Throope,	July 31, 1753
Jonathan Metcalfe & Beulah Dana,	Sept. 6, 1753
Jabez Metcalfe & Sybel Hide,	Dec. 11, 1753
Pinus Richards & Hannah ———,	Dec. 15, 1753
Elisha Harvey & Zerviah Huntington,	Dec. 26, 1753
Samuel Doggett & Anna Bushnell,	April 17, 1754
John Gray & Mercy Bayley,	May 23, 1754
Joseph Martin & Jerusha Webster,	June 25, 1754
Reuben Metcalfe & Elizabeth Marshe,	Sept. 16, 1754
Thomas Millar & Hannah Durkee,	Sept. 30, 1754
Samuel Terry & Susanna Taylor,	Oct. 16, 1754
Ebenezer Cheever & Ann Dewey,	Nov. 7, 1754
Samuel Hunt & Hannah Clarke,	Dec. 5, 1754
Walter Woodworth & Rachel French,	Jan. 9, 1755
John Phelps & Desire Dewey,	Jan. 16, 1755
Ebenezer Snow & Bridget Royce,	July 29, 1755
William Waterman & Rebekah Gladding,	Aug. 7, 1755
Beriah Southworth & Rebekah Williams,	Nov. 13, 1755
Jared Hincley & Ann Hide,	Nov. 20, 1755
Recompense Tiffany & Miriam French,	Feb. 5, 1756
James Metcalfe & Mehetable Hammond,	Feb. 16, 1756
Elijah Strong & Ruth Loomis,	March 18, 1756
Seth Pope & Martha Bacon,	May 20, 1756
Elisha Munsel & Dorothy Reddington,	May 26, 1756
Caleb Lyman & Mary Bettis,	June 2, 1756
Benjamin Woodworth & Katherine Shield,	June 18, 1756
Stephen Pain & Rebekah Bushnell,	Sept. 23, 1756
John Dewey & Rhoda Gillit,	Nov. 18, 1756
Elijah Jeans & Lucy Crocker,	Dec. 9, 1756
Nathaniel Holbrook & Eunice Holbrook,	Dec. 16, 1756
James Clarke & Ann Gray,	Jan. 20, 1757

Ezekiel Lyman & Elizabeth Bliss,	Feb. 10, 1757
Elijah Hide & Mary Clarke,	Feb. 24, 1757
Simon Gray & Mary White,	March 17, 1757
Daniel Deming & Sarah Tisdale,	March 30, 1757
Nathaniel Bliss & Eunice Fish,	April 7, 1757
Benjamin Owen & Lucy Wright,	Sept. 22, 1757
Jonathan Huntington & Sarah Huntington,	Oct. 27, 1757
William Huntington & Bethiah Throope,	Oct. 27, 1757
Eliab Hill & Naomi Woodworth,	Nov. 9, 1757
Rev. Eleazer May & Sibil Huntington,	Nov. 22, 1757
Benajah Strong & Mary Bacon,	April 13, 1758
David Strong & Deborah Terry,	April 27, 1758
Amos Robinson & Deborah Hide,	May 11, 1758
Abraham Fitch & Betty Bissell,	May 18, 1758
Stephen Harding Williams & Mercy Bill,	May 25, 1758
James Kesson & Margaret Dixon,	June 8, 1758
Joseph Wickwire & Martha Storey,	July 13, 1758
Joseph Bayley & Jerusha Webster,	Nov. 23, 1758
Benjamin Lyman & Sarah Foster,	Jan. 14, 1759
Maverick Johnson & Hannah Bruster,	Feb. 7, 1759
William Lyman & Mercy Wright,	Feb. 8, 1759
William Hall & Jerusha Martin,	Feb. 18, 1759
Joseph Doubleday & Elizabeth Phelps,	Feb. 18, 1759
Thomas Webster & Abigal Terry,	April 12, 1759
Capt. John Fillmore & Mary Roch,	Jan. 15, 1760
Dan Throope & Rachel Terry,	Jan. 31, 1760
Samuel Bruster & Experience Root,	May 12, 1760
Samuel Hatch & Naomi Phelps,	June 5, 1760
William Woodworth & Ann Syms,	Aug. 6, 1760
Ezekiel Simons & Esther Williams,	Oct. 9, 1760
John Wadsworth & Sarah Webster,	Nov. 4, 1760
James (a negro of Capt. Hide's) & Grace (a negro of Col. Trumble),	Nov. 14, 1760
William Murdock & Mary Paine,	Dec. 11, 1760
Elijah Dewey & Mary Dixon,	Dec 18, 1760
David Loomiss & Susanna Britton,	Dec. 23, 1760
Israel Gillit & Martha Throope,	Jan. 8, 1761
William Youngs & Lydia Swift,	Jan. 15, 1761
William Lyman & Mary Barker,	Feb. 12, 1761
Stephen Tilden & Judith Pierce,	May 20, 1761

Tony & Nill (two negroes),   Aug. 20, 1761
Zebulon Cass & Irene Fish,   Oct. 29, 1761
James Cooper & Lydia Sprague,   Nov. 16, 1761
Daniel Murry & Hannah Clew (?),   Nov. 26, 1761
Thomas Calkin & Abigal Vane,   Dec. 17, 1761
Shem Burbank & Ann Fitch,   Dec. 29, 1761
Sherry (a negro belonging to Eleazer Lord) &
    Phebe (a negro belonging to Elijah Mason),
                                                Jan. 28, 1762
Samuel & Flora (servants of Sim Grey and Col.
    Trumbull),   Feb. 18, 1762
Ebenezer Cass & Hannah Loomiss,   Feb. 18, 1762
William Bramble & Elizabeth Buel,   March 25, 1762
Daniel Hatch & Zerviah Phelps,   April 14, 1762
James Bayley & Lucy Gay,   May 26, 1762
Crisp & Lushe (negro servants of Mr. Fish and
    Col. Fowler),   July 29, 1762
Nathan Hovey & Jemima Phelps,   Nov. 11, 1762
Gideon Post & Ann Terry,   April 7, 1763
Jesse Heath & Hannah Johnson,   May 5, 1763
Charles Swift & Deborah Clark,   May 26, 1763
Abner Gardner & Esther Sprague,   June 2, 1763
Samuel Bayley & Abigal Gay,   June 23, 1763
Hezekiah Waters & Mary Bliss,   June 23, 1763
David Smalley & Mercy Clarke,   July 20, 1763
Moses Bliss & Abigail Metcalfe,   July 20, 1763
Consider Cushman & Submit Newcomb,   Oct. 27, 1763
Eleazer Robinson & Deborah Johnson,   Nov. 10, 1763
Allen Wightman & Rhoda Lothrop,   Feb. 9, 1764
John Thatcher & Abigal Swift,   May 31, 1764
Cephas (a mulatto) & Sarah (an Indian),   June 21, 1764
John Clauson & Sabrah Algar,   Sept. 6, 1764
Elisha Lyman & Eunice Lamphear,   Sept. 26, 1764
Josiah Hart & Abigal Sluman,   Oct. 16, 1764
Samuel Hall & Mary Pratt,   Nov. 15, 1764
Joshua Wills & Eunice Huntington,   Dec. 13, 1764
Peter Perkins & Hannah Webster,   April 18, 1765
Alexander Brink & Mary Wright,   April 25, 1765
Israel Loomiss, Jr., & Rebekah Bingham,   May 2, 1765
Joseph Abel & Lydia Tenny,   May 2, 1765

Josiah Arnold & Elizabeth Clarke,   July 11, 1765
Elias West & Mary Lothrop,   Oct. 31, 1765
Noah Smith & widow Ann Dewey,   Nov. 27, 1765
James Bettis, Jr., & Margaret Whitely,   Nov. 28, 1765
Isaac Bayley & Alethea Torrey,   Dec. 19, 1765
Thomas Bill & Anna Phelps,   Dec. 19, 1765
Jedidiah Huntington & Faith Trumble,   May 1, 1766
Moses Waters & Rachel Bliss,   May 8, 1766
Nathan Clarke & Abigal Abel,   May 22, 1766
Prince Tracy & Elizabeth Holbrook,   May 29, 1766
Daniel Taylor & Jerusha Terry,   June 26, 1766
William Ward & Mary Pierce,   Oct. 2, 1766
Dan Terry & Rachel Hutchinson,   Nov. 6, 1766
Abel Wright & Mary Lyman,   Nov. 26, 1766
Nathan Holt & Batsheba Williams,   Dec. 4, 1766
Benjamin Throope & Susanna Throop,   Dec. 11, 1766
Samuel Cockle & Elizabeth Hadlock,   Dec. 25, 1766
Israel Dewey & Jerusha Bayley,   Jan. 15, 1767
Samuel Robinson & Hannah Cass,   Feb. 26, 1767
Oliver Griswold & Experience Dewey,   April 9, 1767
Rev. Richard Salter & my daughter Nancy Williams,
                                                June 17, 1767
Josiah Wood & Ruth Thomson,   Nov. 9, 1767
Paul Phelps & Zervia Calkin,   Feb. 18, 1768
Silas Sprague & Abigal Hill,   April 14, 1768
Andrew Huntington & Ruth Hide,   April 17, 1768
Charles Hide & Mary Abel,   May 19, 1768
Josiah Rockwell & Lydia Marsh,   June 9, 1768
Timothy Goodwin & Lydia Ticknor,   June 30, 1768
John Salter & my daughter Christian Williams,
                                                Aug. 17, 1768
Solomon Calkin & Hannah Crandal,   Sept. 1, 1768
Isaiah Wright & Sarah Pain,   Oct. 2, 1768
Adonijah Crocker & Elizabeth Eells,   Oct. 6, 1768
David Gager & Mary Johnson,   Oct. 27, 1768
Daniel Tilden & Esther Mason,   Dec. 1, 1768
Elijah Bushnell & Eunice Pratt,   Feb. 12, 1769
Benajah Douglass & Mercy Bacon,   April 19, 1769
Samuel Gay & Elizabeth Bayley,   April 23, 1769
David Clarke & Jemima Hovey,   May 18, 1769

John Huntington & Lucy Metcalfe,	June 15, 1769
Jacob McKall & Lucy Rockwell,	Nov. 2, 1769
Robert Gambe & Mary Nichols,	Nov. 15, 1769
Zina Hide & Sarah Goodwin,	Nov. 30, 1769
Rev. Timothy Ston—& my daughter Eunice Williams,	
	Dec. 6, 1769
Nathaniel Williams & Lois Sacket,	Jan. 25, 1770
Comfort Bruster & Elizabeth Abel,	Feb. 15, 1770
Peleg Coming (?) & Molly Martin,	July 9, 1770
Josiah Huntington & Rhoda Loomiss,	Sept. 13, 1770
Daniel Terry & Christian Terry,	Oct. 10, 1770
Joseph Throope & Zerviah Bissel,	Nov. 8, 1770
Samuel Webster & Jerusha Smith,	Nov. 15, 1770
John Lyman & Lucy Phelps,	Nov. 15, 1770
John Wood & Sarah Goodwin,	Dec. 6, 1770
Caleb Abel, Jr., & Jerusha Lyman,	Dec. 6, 1770
James Noyes Barker & Zerviah Bushnell,	Dec. 19, 1770
My son William Williams & Mary Trumbull,	Feb. 14, 1771
Jabez Barrows & Abigal Hovey,	May 16, 1771
Abijah Badcock & Mercy Loomiss,	June 6, 1771
William Torry & Mary Gillit,	Aug. 22, 1771
Isaac Gillit & Ruth Demmon,	Sept. 11, 1771
John Terry & Mary Mason,	Sept. 19, 1771
Joshua Dewey & Mary Buel,	Sept. 25, 1772
David Wright & Hannah Bayley,	Sept. 26, 1771
Elisha Ticknor & Deborah Davis,	Jan. 2, 1772
Solomon Fenton & Sybil Snow,	Aug. 19, 1772
Rev. Joseph Lyman & Hannah Huntington,	Oct. 15, 1772
Benjamin Delano & Zerviah Clarke,	Oct. 22, 1772
David Clarke & Hannah Nichols,	Oct. 27, 1772
Ebenezer Cann (?) & Mary Bliss,	Dec. 1, 1772
Ephraim Terry & Anne Johnson,	Dec. 24, 1772
Ignatius Bayley & Hannah Badcock,	April 29, 1773
Sam'll Gross & Hannah Owen,	July 1, 1773
Rev. Stephen T—— & Mary Th——,	Sept. 23, 1773
John Loomiss & Elizabeth Fish,	Oct. 14, 1773
Andrew Richardson & Mercy Clauson,	Oct. 17, 1773
William Woodworth & Lydia Baldwin,	Oct. 28, 1773
William Warner & Mary Williams,	May 17, 1774
Daniel Bruster & Rosamond Richard ——,	June 2, 1774

Israel ——— & Allis Fuller,	Sept. 13, 1774
William Rogers & Ruth Hays,	Sept. 29, 1774
David Bruster & Lucretia Smith,	Feb. 2, 1775
Elijah Colman & Mercy Colman,	May 3, 1775
Benjamin Throope & Rachel Brown,	May 4, 1775
John Pain & Lydia Tisdale,	May 7, 1775
Eleazer Manning & Rhoda Loomis,	May 11, 1775

THOMPSON.

WINDHAM COUNTY.

Town incorporated 1785, having been previously a part of Killingly which dates back to 1708.

The Congregational Church of Thompson was organized in 1730, in what was then the North Society of Killingly and named "Thompson Parish" in honor of a non-resident English proprietor, Sir Robert Thompson, a distinguished nobleman, the first president of the "Society for the Propagation of the Gospel in Foreign Parts."

Rev. Marston Cabot, the first pastor, begins the marriage record in 1730, as follows:

John Burley & Miriam Fuller,	Oct. 8, 1730
Philemon Chandler of Pomfret & Lydia Eaton of Thompson,	Jan. 18, 1731
Jacob Bixby & Elisabeth Jewett,	Feb. 4, 1731
Joshua Cooper & Elisabeth Harrington of Lexington,	Feb. 26, 1731
Ebenezer Corbin of Keckamochaug (afterwards Dudley) & Martha Dresser,	April 15, 1731
Samuel Converse, Jun., & Sarah Atwell,	May 5, 1731
Deliverance Cleaveland of Canterbury & Kezia Eaton,	Jan. 20, 1732
Isaac Lee & Esther Green,	Aug. 15, 1731
David Poor & Samison Parmenter, both of Sudbury,	Nov. 16, 1731
Jacob Dresser & Elisabeth Martyn,	May 30, 1733
John Newman & Dorcas Jewett,	Oct. 31, 1733
Aaron Lyman of Northampton & Eunice Dwight,	Dec. 12, 1733
Thomas Goodale of Middletown & Mehitable Clough,	Feb. 14, 1734

Aaron Martyn & Sarah Newell,   May 10, 1734
Joseph Hascall & Catharine Green,   June 4, 1734
Jacob Goodell of Pomfret & Peggy Atwell,   July 31, 1734
Nathaniel Marsh & Mary Buffington,   Oct. 23, 1734
Nathaniel Stone & Hannah Marsh,   June 12, 1735
John Shapley & Abigail Johnson,   Nov. 10, 1735
Nehemiah Sabin, Jr., of Pomfret & Ruth Cooper,
                                                 Dec. 3, 1735
John Bixby & Jemima Green,   Dec. 4, 1735
Benjamin Mackintire of Providence & Keziah
    Munyan,   Jan. 14, 1736
Josiah Balch of Dudley & Patience Chamberlain,
                                                 Feb. 3, 1736
Zechariah Cutler & Hannah Barrett of Pomfret, Feb. 3, 1736
Joseph Leavens, Jun., & Alice Eaton,   Feb. 18, 1736
Nehemiah Cady of Mortlake & Lydia Clough, Jan. 13, 1737
Cyprian Morse & Zeruiah Cady,   April 27, 1737
Sampson Howe & Sarah Sabin,   Dec. 29, 1737
Ebenezer Coburn of Dudley & Phebe Shapley, Jan. 18, 1738
Israel Richards & Hannah White of Sutton,   May 18, 1738
Joseph Knight of Middletown & Mercy Dresser of
    Oxford,   May 30, 1738
Jonathan Wilson & Rebecca Russell,   May 31, 1738
Thomas Stevens of Oblong & Abigail Cooper, Oct. 17, 1738
Barsom Stone & Mehitable Wight,   Nov. 28, 1738
James Fuller & Abigail Rue,   Dec. 4, 1738
Edmund Hughes & Elisabeth Stevens,   March 27, 1739
Nathan Johnson & Mary Russel,   April 24, 1739
Capt. Nicholas Cook of Providence & Mrs. Han-
    nah Sabin,   Sept. 23, 1739
Israel Joslin, Jun., & Mary Brown,   Nov. 20, 1739
James Converse & Mary Leavens,   Jan. 8, 1740
Uriah Richardson of Dudley & Miriam Green, April 2, 1740
Noah Leavens & Mary Merrill,   Oct. 1, 1740
Thomas Buffington & Sarah Utter,   Oct. 5, 1740
John Burt & Eunice Russel,   Nov. 5, 1740
Ezra Hutchins & Abigail Leavens,   Dec. 10, 1740
Isaac Whitmore & Hannah Clark,   Dec. 10, 1740
Jesse Smith of ye Gore & Elisabeth Russel,   Jan. 24, 1741
Joseph Munyan & Sarah Joslyn,   March 11, 1741

Jonathan Knapp & Sarah Shapley,   April 21, 1741
James Dike of Dudley & Mary Narramore,   May 21, 1741
Ephraim Johnson & Sarah Basto,   May 27, 1741
Ebenezer Scott of Dudley & Mary Shapley,   Nov. 11, 1741
Levi Wight & Eliza Basto,   Dec. 1, 1741
Benajah Adams of Pomfret & Hannah Clough, Dec. 15, 1741
Samuel Larned & Rachel Green,   Dec. 29, 1741
Joseph Bachelder of Salem & Judith Rea,   April 6, 1742
Amos Green & Lydia Johnson,   April 21, 1742
Benjamin Grover & Mary Barret,   May 18, 1742
David Hibbert of Windham & Elisabeth Leavens,
                                                                            Sept. 15, 1742
Seth Johnson & Hanna Eaton,   Oct. 13, 1742
Samuel Cutler & Sarah Cutler,   Oct. 26, 1742
Timothy Green & Phebe Atwell,   Oct. 27, 1742
Jeremiah Baker of Dedham & Elisabeth Dwight,
                                                                            Nov. 22, 1742
Rev. Mr. Bass of Ashford & Mrs. Mary Danielson
    of Killingly (widow of Mr. James Danielson),
                                                                            Nov. 24, 1742
Comfort Starr & Abigail Cabot,   Jan. 19, 1743
——ory Upham & Mary Stone,   May 14, 1743
Samuel Fuller, Jun., & Sarah Fowle of Salem, May 17, 1743
Jonathan Converse & Zeruiah Hughes,   June 19, 1743
Nehemiah Clarke & Abigail Dupton,   March 7, 1744
—— ——rsh & Martha Coats,   March 18, 1734
—— —— of Sturbridge & Am— Converse, June 14, 1744
Dr. Robert Brooks of Haddam & Ruth Whitmore
    of Middletown,   Oct. 29, 1744
Henry Ellithorpe & Rebecca Ormsbee,   Dec. 4, 1744
William Whittemore of Plainfield & Mary Ellithorpe,
                                                                            Dec. 5, 1744
William Alton & Sarah Cummins,   Dec. 19, 1744
John Jeffery of Pomfret & Hannah Brown,   Dec. 23, 1744
Josiah Child & Sarah Green,   Feb. 6, 1745
Grindal Rawson of Mendon & Hannah Leavens,
                                                                            Feb. 26, 1745
Jotham Johnson & Lucy Johnson,   March 4, 1745
Ivory Upham, Jun., & Jerusha Stone,   Dec. 25, 1745
Abraham Cooper & Elisabeth Child,   Feb. 18, 1746

Capt. Thomas Amsden of Marlborough & Mrs.
    Hannah Morris,   July 16, 1746
Jonas Cady of Stafford & Mary Green,   Oct. 29, 1746
Joshua Fuller & Hannah Dyke,   Nov. 2, 1746
Joseph Pudney of Dudley & Mehitable Brown, June 6, 1747
William Richards & Kezia Pudney,   Nov. 2, 1747
Charles Sabin & Sybil Dwight,   Dec. 29, 1747
Gideon Joslyn & Sarah Merrill,   Jan. 12, 1748
Samuel Utter, Jun., & Susannah Curtis,   March 7, 1748
John Lee & Elisabeth Chaffee of Woodstock, March 29, 1748
Michael Adams & Sarah Abbe,   March 29, 1748
Nehemiah Merrill & Mercy Hallowel,   June 29, 1748
John Short of Gloucester & Zeruiah Utter, Sept. 27, 1748
Joseph Davis & Elisabeth Mansfield,   Oct. 26, 1749
Thomas Shapley & Joanna Utter,   Nov. 9, 1749
Capt. Nathaniel Brown & Mrs. Hannah Fowle, Dec. 14, 1749
John Ellithorpe & Elisabeth Marsh,   Dec. 26, 1749
Obadiah Merrill & Hannah Joslyn,   Dec. 28, 1749
Benjamin Joslyn & Esther Green,   Jan. 4, 1750
Amos Bixby & Elisabeth Sabin,   Jan. 18, 1750
John Plank & Lydia Jefferds,   Feb. 15, 1750
Ebenezer Chamberlain of Douglas & Abigail Marsh,
                         March 14, 1750
Seth Hibbert & Eunice Child,   March 19, 1750
John Parkhurst, Jun., of Pomfret & Martha Stone,
                          June 21, 1750
Jonathan Barrett & Sarah Hascall,   Nov. 1, 1750
John Barret & Lucy Hosmer,   Jan. 24, 1751
John Jacobs & Sarah Plank,   Jan. 24, 1751
Joseph Bucklin of Providence & Zeruiah Sabin,
                         Sept. 29, 1751
Joseph Newell of Lebanon & Abigail Bixby, Oct. 22, 1751
Abijah Bixby & Anne Corbin,   Jan. 23, 1752
William Mory and & Bathsheba Utter,   May 12, 1752
Nicholas Parker & Mary Converse,   May 28, 1752
Jesse Woodward of Leicester & Sarah Harr, Sept. 3, 1752
* (N. S.) Thomas Ormsbee & Hannah Carpenter of
    Pomfret,   Nov. 23, 1752
Benjamin Joslin & Abigail Barret,   Jan. 4, 1753

*(N. S.) New style.

Noah Barrows & Martha Bowen, April 26, 1753
Samuel Daley & Olive Bellows, June 27, 1753
James Holmes of Pomfret & Lois Dutton, Nov. 14, 1753
William Johnson & Sarah Daley, Nov. 29, 1753
Benjamin Cady & Jane Lipur, Dec. 17, 1753
Isaac Whitmore & Martha Child, Jan. 31, 1754
My daughter Mary to Capt. David Hosmer of Nor-
  wich, Feb. 17, 1754
Solomon Bixby & Abigail Ravel, April 7, 1754
Joseph Joslin & Mary Adams, April 18, 1754
Noah Merrill & Abigail Cooper, May 30, 1754
Jacob Converse & Anna White (or Wight), June 6, 1754
Samuel Barton & Ruth Sabin, Sept. 11, 1754
John Stone & Sarah Averil, Nov. 26, 1754
Archelaus Town & Sarah Brown of Pomfret, Dec. 10, 1754
Comfort Starr & Judith Cooper, Dec. 22, 1754
Paul Torrey & Hannah Jeffers, Dec. 26, 1754
Stephen Crosby & Hannah Caryll, Feb. 16, 1755
John Russel & Martha Green, Feb. 17, 1755
Nathan Bixby, Jun., & Mary Burrel, April 21, 1755
Reuben Merrill & Abigail Torrey, May 29, 1755
Ebenezer Price & Rebeca Caryl, June 29, 1755
Joseph Leavens, Esq., of Killingly and widow
  Hannah Larned, Dec. 17, 1755
Samuel Leavens of Killingly & Elisabeth Johnson,
  Jan. 9, 1756
Samuel Fuller of Stafford & Zillah Merrell, Jan. 15, 1756
Diah Johnson & Martha Converse, Feb. 15, 1756
Abraham Daley & Mary Nichols, Nov. 9, 1757
Samuel McClellan of Woodstock & Jemima Chan-
  dler of Thompson, Nov. 16, 1757
Jacob Bixby & Sarah Younglove, Jan. 2, 1758
Mr. Woodward of Canada Parish & widow Hughes
  of Thompson, Jan. 12, 1758
John Blois of Thompson & Hannah Allen of Pom-
  fret, March 9, 1758
John Utley of Canada & Amy Hughes of Thomp-
  son, April 13, 1758
Uriah Lee & Ruth Utter, April 13, 1758
Moses Knewland & Abigail Chamberlain, April 17, 1758

Jonathan Hascall & Tamer Morphat, June 8, 1758
Zebediah Marsh & Mary Coats, July 27, 1758
Benjamin Pierce of Canterbury & Sarah Mills,
 Aug. 31, 1758
Zebediah Sabin & Anna Dwight, Oct. 12, 1758
William Whittemore & Sarah Prince, Nov. 21, 1758
Joseph Davis & Deborah Wight, Nov. 31, 1758
Amos Carrol & Lucy Barret, Dec. 7, 1758
Richard Child & Abigail Green, Feb. 1, 1759
Robert Webster & Hannah Green, March 6, 1759
John Green & Abilene Guile, March 10, 1759
Noah Merrill & Sarah Lee, April 12, 1759
Eleazer Brown of Canterbury & Lydia Putnam
 of Thompson, June 21, 1759
Solomon Ormsby & Mary Prince, Sept. 4, 1759
Oliver Hulett & Elisabeth Seirls, both of Killingly,
 Nov. 15, 1759
Ephraim Ellingwood of Woodstock & Anna Blois
 of Killingly, Nov. 15, 1759
Joseph Loverain of Cumberland & Sarah Algiers
 of Killingly, April 6, 1760
Isaac Kendall of Ashford & Mary Brissat of Kil-
 lingly, July 3, 1760
Pain Converse & Mary Lee, Dec. 11, 1760
Stephen Lyon of Woodstock & Huldah Bugbee of
 Killingly, Jan. 7, 1761
John Corbin & Abigail Cabot, Feb. 9, 1761
Jonathan Russel, Jr., & Mary Brown, April 9, 1761
Lusher Gay & Judith Green, April 30, 1761
Simon Emerson of Douglas & Persis Davenport of
 Killingly, July 9, 1761
Robert Goddard of Sutton & Dorothy Child of Kil-
 lingly, Nov. 24, 1761
Samuel Bloss & Hannah Porter, Jan. 7, 1762
Samuel Phay & Bette Carrol, April 6, 1762
Nathaniel Daniels & Esther Lee, May 27, 1762
James Larned & Sybil Merrill, June 24, 1762
Thomas Converse & Mary Morse, July 22, 1762
Joseph Harris & Mary Clough, Aug. 25, 1762
William Wheelock & Mehitable Palmer, Sept. 29, 1762

David Jewett, Jr., & Elisabeth Hughes, Oct. 6, 1762
Isaac Whitmore & Mary Brooks, Nov. 18, 1762
Joseph Town & Abigail Thompson, Nov. 23, 1762
Jonathan Porter & Sarah Brown, Dec., 1762
Amos Green & Elisabeth Cooper, Jan. 3, 1763
William Mowrey & Susannah Jewett, Jan. 3, 1763
Uriah Hosmer of Norwich & Sybil Dwight, Aug. 4, 1763
Josiah Child & Sarah Adams, Sept. 1, 1763
Jonathan Lee & Mary Kilborn, Oct. 27, 1763
Comfort Starr & widow Sarah Knap, Nov. 3, 1763
Samuel Babbitt of Leicester & Bathshua Converse
 of Killingly, Nov. 15, 1763
Samuel Crosby of Vollingtown & Mary Haskell of
 Killingly, Nov. 17, 1763
Eliphalet Wight & Abigail Plummer, Nov. 25, 1763
David Prince & Eunice Porter, Dec. 20, 1763
John Plummer & Sarah Joslin, Dec. 22, 1763
Nathaniel Freeman & Triphosa Coller, Dec. 22, 1763
Seth Green & Hannah Winter, Jan. 3, 1764
Samuel Phay & Mary Kemball of Dudley, Jan. 18, 1764
Habbakuk Davison of Dudley & Elisabeth Merrill,
 Feb. 2, 1764
Joseph Green of Westborough & Abigail Converse
 of Killingly, Feb. 14, 1764
Diah Johnson & Susannah Converse, April 11, 1764
Nathaniel Ellithorpe & Jemima Younglove, June 14, 1764
James Farnum of Ashford & Jerusha Morse of Kil-
 lingly, Nov. 15, 1764
John Manly & Martha Marsh, Dec. 18, 1764
Daniel Barret & Huldah Elithorp, March 11, 1765
Abner Marsh & Hannah Plank, April 22, 1765
Lemuel Knap & Mary Marsh, Nov. 14, 1765
Elijah Corbin & Elisabeth Prince, Dec. 29, 1765
Joseph Jewet & Rachel Nichols, Jan. 30, 1766
Elijah Nichols & Martha Flint, Feb. 10, 1766
Peter Stockwell & Esther Atwell, April 3, 1766
John Tarbel & Huldah Lee, both of Sturbridge,
 April 30, 1766
John Russel of Ashford & Rebecca Wilson of Kil-
 lingly, May 1, 1766

Ephraim Russel & Mary Wilson,	June 5, 1766
John Grow & widow Phebe Cady,	Oct. 9, 1766
Thomas Holbrook & Abigail Adams,	Nov. 14, 1766
Robert Plank & Zerviah Brown Joslin,	Dec. 25, 1766
John Burril & Mary Eaton,	Jan. 12, 1767
Seth Smith of Stoughton & Hannah Manly of Killingly,	Jan. 22, 1767
Jonathan Flint & Hannah Brown,	June 4, 1767
James Hosmer & Lydia Green,	June 4, 1767
Eliakim Robinson of Dudley & Deborah Brown of Killingly,	July 13, 1767
Samuel Converse & Mereba Burrill,	Oct. 27, 1767
Henry Chaffee & Rachel Plank,	Dec. 17, 1767
Ebenezer Starr & Sarah Porter,	Dec. 21, 1767
Nathaniel Patten Russel & Susannah Carrol,	Jan. 21, 1768
William Stockwell of Douglas & Rhoda Knap of Killingly,	Feb. 23, 1768
Jonathan Bailey & Bette Nichols,	April 29, 1768
Thomas Joy & Priscilla Wilder,	Sept. 19, 1768
Mark Dodge & Susa Prince,	Nov. 17, 1768
Solomon Shumway of Oxford & Dolly Howard of Killingly,	Nov. 17, 1768
Thomas Town of Munson & Bette Town of Killingly,	Nov. 17, 1768
David Nichols & Lucy Elliott,	Dec. 1, 1768
Davis Flint & Esther Cooper,	Dec. 27, 1768
Jonathan Perrin & Sarah Mills,	Feb. 9, 1769
Josiah Hulet & Elisabeth Whittemore,	Feb. 16, 1769
Stephen Tucker & Anna Comins,	May 7, 1769
Ebenezer Burril & Ruth Peters of Douglas,	July 3, 1769
Israel Rich & Mary Joslin,	July 31, 1769
Matthew Walker & Milly Bowen,	Oct. 26, 1769
Samuel Palmer & Jemima Fairbanks,	Nov. 2, 1769
Joseph Munyan & Mary Marsh of Douglas,	Nov. 23, 1769
Jonah Carpenter of Pomfret & Zerviah Whitmore of Killingly,	Nov. 23, 1769
Ebenezer Kingsbury of Dedham and widow Mary Cabot of Killingly,	Nov. 29, 1769
Reuben Stone & Eunice Wight,	Nov. 30, 1769

Hezekiah Rhodes & Damaris Wilson,   Dec. 5, 1769
Joseph Haskal of Woodstock & Alice Fitch of Kil-
 lingly,   Dec. 14, 1769
John Stone & Jerusha Farrar,   Jan. 4, 1770
Jonathan Anderson of Chesterfield & Hannah
 Kies of Killingly,   Feb. 11, 1770
Jacob Wight & Mehetable Stone,   April 29, 1770
Clement Corbin, Jr., & Mary Philly Brown,   July 12, 1770
John Downing of Douglas & Mary Alger of Kil-
 lingly,   July 24, 1770
Benjamin Converse & Hannah Porter,   July 29, 1770
David Converse & Rachel Elliott,   July 29, 1770
Ebenezer Cooper & Eunice Elliot,   Aug. 30, 1770
Ebenezer Nichols & Sarah Brooks,   Aug. 30, 1770
Ebenezer Atwood & Abigail Younglove,   Sept. 13, 1770
Jonathan Wilson of Oxford & Anne Bowen of Kil-
 lingly,   Nov. 15, 1770
Peter Barret of Gloucester & Anne Cabot of Kil-
 lingly,   Dec. 13, 1770
William Jourdan & Comfort Palmer,   Dec. 20, 1770
Daniel Larned & Rebecca Wilkinson,   April 4, 1771
Jonathan Aldridge of Killingly & Olive Marsh of
 Douglas,   April 30, 1771
William Mitchel of Pomfret & Mary Alton of Kil-
 lingly,   May 23, 1771
Edward Houghton & Olive Russell,   May 30, 1771
John Holbrook & Susannah Cabot,   June 20, 1771
Jacob Atwood & Hannah Churchel,   July 14, 1771
Samuel Upham of Douglas & Margaret Place of
 Killingly,   Sept. 5, 1771
Comfort Eaton & Mehetable Whitmore,   Sept. 12, 1771
Hezekiah Smith of Gloucester & Margaret Cadren
 of Wrentham,   Oct. 31, 1771
Asa Nichols & Mary Cooper,   Nov. 3, 1771
Thomas Ormsby & widow Sarah Town,   Dec. 5, 1771
Samuel Prince of Pomfret & Mary Elliot of Kil-
 lingly,   Dec. 5, 1771
Nathaniel Upham & Rebecca Farrow,   Jan. 23, 1772
John Lawrence & Dorothy Adams,   March 12, 1772
James Manly & Hannah Marsh,   April 17, 1772

John Wakefield of Dudley & Lydia White of Kil-
lingly,   June 25, 1772
Israel Munyan & Alice Grover,   July 28, 1772
Samuel Adams & Rachel Burrill,   Nov. 5, 1772
Simon Howard & Hannah Walker,   Nov. 19, 1772
Robert Sharpe of Pomfret & Sarah Davis of Kil-
lingly,   Dec. 30, 1772
Jesse Larned & Elisabeth Leavens,   Jan 18, 1773
Ebenezer Starr & Mary Stewart of Dudley,
                                            Feb. 18, 1773
Jonathan Grow of Dudley & Mary Brown of Kil-
lingly,   March 18, 1773
Jeremiah Haskall & Hannah Nichols,   March 22, 1773
Moses Streeter of Douglas & Martha Alton of Kil-
lingly,   May 12, 1773
Joel Lee & Hannah Fay,   June 17, 1773
Benjamin Burrill & Bethia Aldridge, alias Cum-
mings,   Aug. 18, 1773
Jeremiah Wilke & Hannah White,   Oct. 7, 1773
Shem Tafft of Mendon & Deborah Keith of Kil-
lingly,   Nov. 18, 1773
Samuel Palmer of Dudley & Sarah Atwood of Kil-
lingly,   Jan. 26, 1774
John Converse & Kezia Nichols,   Jan. 27, 1774
Alpheus Converse & Rusha Elliot,   March 17, 1774
Justus Jewet of Dudley & Mary Robinson of Kil-
lingly,   March 24, 1774
Thaddeus Gilbert of Pomfret & Hannah Whitmore
of Killingly,   March 24, 1774
Sampson Howe & Hulda Davis,   March 31, 1774
Comfort Woodward & Lydia Carrol,   April 7, 1774
Thomas Ormsby & Sarah Hall,   July 13, 1774
Andrew Walker of Oxford & Sarah Carrol of Kil-
lingly,   Sept. 29, 1774
Moses Barret & Hannah Fuller,   Nov. 24, 1774
Matthew Walker & Abigail Nichols,   Dec. 1, 1774
Thomas Elliott of Killingly & Hannah Butman of
Sutton,   Dec. 7, 1774
Asa Alton & Priscilla Jefferds,   Dec. 21, 1774
Asa Converse & Ruth Lee,   Jan. 19, 1775

Barakiah Johnson of Gageborough & Lydia Green
   of Killingly,   Feb. 9, 1775
Calvin Skinner & Elinor Porter,   Feb. 12, 1775
Zadoc Spalding & Hannah Larned,   Feb. 16, 1775
Daniel Barrett & Marcy Manley,   April, 1775
David Alton, Jr., & Kezia Davis,   May 17, 1775
Jesse Brown & Experience Marcy Hughes,   June 29, 1775
Ebenezer Holmes of Woodstock & Elisabeth Barrett
   of Killingly,   Nov. 1, 1775
William Edmonds of Dudley & Lucy Fuller of Kil-
   lingly,   Nov. 22, 1775
Aaron Wilder & Abigail Younglove,   Nov. 22, 1775
Silas Tafft & Deborah Joslin,   Jan. 14, 1776
Levi Thompson & Mary Bixby,   Jan. 18, 1776
Edward Joslin & Elisabeth Alton,   Jan. 25, 1776
Charles Curtis of Dudley & Tabitha Upham of Kil-
   lingly,   Feb. 8, 1776
Robert Prince & Jemima Bixby,   March 14, 1776
Asa Short of Gloucester & Olive Burril of Dudley,
                                              Sept. 5, 1776
Jonathan Sheffield & Olive Bowen,   Oct. 3, 1776
Issachar Johnson of Shrewsbury & Dolly Barret of
   Killingly,   May 15, 1777
Samuel Wilson & Chloe Reynolds,   May 29, 1777
Isaac Lee & widow Sarah Adams,   Sept. 18, 1777
Daniel Davison of Pomfret & Catherine Davis of
   Killingly,   Nov. 20, 1777
David Brown of Ashford & Molly Watson of Kil-
   lingly,   Nov. 23, 1777
James Redway & Alethea Hicks,   Nov. 27, 1777
Moses Wilder & Molly Younglove,   Dec. 2, 1777
George Brown of Gloucester & Rachel Dike of Kil-
   lingly,   Dec. 9, 1777
David Hulet & Martha Whitmore,   Jan. 1, 1778
Levi Stone & widow Priscilla Alton,   Jan. 29, 1778
John Keith & Azubah Thayer,   April 23, 1778
Elisha Fuller & Sarah Call,   April 30, 1778
William Dwight & Sarah Elliott,   May 21, 1778
David Hooper of Uxbridge & Deborah Tafft of Kil-
   lingly,   June 4, 1778

Nathaniel Mills, Jr., & Rebekah Robinson,   Aug. 30, 1778
Joel Converse & Damaris Wilder,   Sept. 10, 1778
Perley Hughes & Esther Ormsby,   Nov. 19, 1778
Jeremiah Converse & Rhoda Converse,   Nov. 26, 1778
John Younglove & Thankful Cooper,   Dec. 18, 1778
Asa Corbin & Mary Harlow,   Dec. 31, 1778
Joseph Prince & Elizabeth Starr,   Feb. 4, 1779
Daniel Tafft of Mendon & Rhoda Ellis of Killingly,
                                               June 2, 1779
John Brown of Douglas & Mary Grow of Killingly,
                                               June 20, 1779
Jonathan Grow & widow Mary Harris,   July 1, 1779
John Elliot & Molly Nichols,   Aug. 1, 1779
Solomon Wolcott & Bette Chandler,   Aug. 13, 1779
Nathan Thayer & Abigail Green,   Nov. 3, 1779
John Carrol & Hannah Thayer,   Nov. 4, 1779
Joseph Adams & Hannah Cutler,   Nov. 11, 1779
James Keith & Esther Larned,   Dec. 9, 1779
John Cooper & Phebe Elliot,   Jan. 31, 1780
Matthew Watson & Isabel Thayer,   Feb. 3, 1780
John Gullen (a foreigner) & Deborah Cooper of Kil-
     ingly,   April 9, 1780
Moses Corbin & widow Elisabeth Corbin,   April 13, 1780
Ashahel Tafft of Uxbridge & Rachel Alton of Kil-
     lingly,   April 27, 1780
Samuel Carpenter & Dolly Alton,   April 27, 1780
Phinehas Copeland & Rachel Prince,   April 27, 1780
Hezekiah Bellows & Susannah Coats,   May 28, 1780
Elijah Carpenter of Ashford & Sarah Younglove of
     Killingly,   July 3, 1780
John Blackmore of Woodstock & Silence Child of
     Killingly,   July 7, 1780
David Rider of Chesterfield & Esther Joslin of Kil-
     lingly,   Aug. 24, 1780
―――― Joslin & Naomi Smith,   Sept. 21, 1780
Peter Sibley of Uxbridge & Mary Keith of Kil-
     lingly,   Nov. 23, 1780
Nathaniel Allen of Pomfret & widow Mary Ormsby
     of Killingly,   Nov. 28, 1780
Jesse Bixby & Sybil Johnson,   Dec. 7, 1780

Ebenezer Covel, Jr., & Sabra Child,   Dec. 21, 1780
David Hosmer & Elisabeth Cooper,   Jan. 18, 1781
John Trumbull of Leicester & Abigail Upham of
    Killingly,   Feb. 20, 1781
Abel Prince & Lucy Nichols,   March 8, 1781
Timothy Tomlin of Chesterfield & Susannah Web-
    ster of Killingly,   April 12, 1781
Jacob Foster of Dudley & Susannah Fairbanks of
    Killingly.   April 12, 1781
Aaron Foster of Dudley & Sarah Town of Killingly,
                                              April 12, 1781
Nathan Sly of Dudley & Elisabeth Mansfield of Kil-
    lingly,   Sept. 5, 1781
Jabez Whitmore & Hannah Larned,   Sept. 20, 1781
Uriah Hawkins of Scituate & Mary Keith of Kil-
    lingly,   Nov. 8, 1781
Peter Jacobs & Keziah Ellithorp,   Dec. 13, 1781
John Haskel of Dudley & widow Rachel Larned of
    Killingly,   Dec. 19, 1781
Elijah Crosby & Celia Bates,   Dec. 27, 1781
William Town & Lucy Prince,   Jan. 27, 1782
David White & Bette Crosby,   Jan. 31, 1782
Major Joseph Cady & Lucy Leavens,   April 10, 1782
William Russell & Sybil Crosby,   April 23, 1782
Melatiah Martin & Mary Stephens,   April 25, 1782
Samuel Holden Torrey & Judith Larned,   April 25, 1782
Joseph Russel & Mary Russel,   April 25, 1782
David Child & Ruth Brown,   Nov. 23, 1782
Cordial Storrs of Mansfield & Lettice Cummins of
    Killingly,   Nov. 23, 1782
Josiah Cummins & Esther Lyon,   Sept. 19, 1782
Barak Keith & Sybil Russel,   Dec. 5, 1782
Pearson Crosby & Hannah Bates,   Dec. 19, 1782
Pennel Child & Sarah Woodward,   1783
Elijah Bellows of Killingly & Ruth Stone of Oxford,
                                              Feb. 5, 1783
James Trumbull of Leicester & Judith Sheffield of
    Killingly,   Feb. 19, 1783
Jonathan Willard of Dudley & Mary Palmer of Kil-
    lingly,   March 26, 1783

Charles Brown & Hannah Palmer,	March 26, 1783
William Wilkinson & Chloe Learned,	April 10, 1783
William Gould of Marlborough, Mass., & Elisabeth	
Mills of Killingly,	May 7, 1783
Jacob Mashcraft of Woodstock & widow Hannah	
Crosby of Killingly,	May 8, 1783
Lowell Pulsifer of Douglas & Lucy Brown,	May 27, 1783
Russel Brown & Huldah Bates,	Aug. 20, 1783
Asa Winter & Lydia Child,	Oct. 8, 1783
Daniel Bixby & Sarah Town,	Oct. 30, 1783
Isaac Town & Anne Ormsby,	Nov. 20, 1783
Hobart Torrey & Rebecca Larned,	Nov. 27, 1783
Archelaus Town & Martha Johnson,	Dec. 25, 1783
Josiah Gary of Pomfret & Keziah Bundy of Kil-	
lingly,	Jan. 7, 1784
Nathan Bixby & widow Hannah Marsh,	Jan. 16, 1784
Joseph Town, 3d, & Anna Barret,	March 24, 1784
William Whittemore, 3d, & Charlotte Basto,	June 1, 1784
Solomon Wakefield of Dudley & Chloe Brown of	
Killingly,	July 1, 1784
James Tourtellotte & Molly Bixby,	Sept. 2, 1784
David Jewet & Hannah Elliot,	Nov. 28, 1784
Ebenezer Cooper & Ruth Porter,	Dec. 19, 1784
Benjamin Green & Tamer Moffat,	Dec. 23, 1784
Joel Converse & Elisabeth Bixby,	Jan. 20, 1785
Stephen Child & Zilpha Brooks,	Jan. 27, 1785
Asa Plank & Elisabeth Brooks,	Jan. 27, 1785
Jeremiah Harrington & Patience Grant,	March 3, 1785
Lemuel Barrows & Abigail Grant,	March 17, 1785
Rufus Brown & Olive Child,	March 24, 1785
Barnard Converse & Hannah Alton,	March 31, 1785
David Grow & Elisabeth Bixby,	April 21, 1785
Isaac Upham & Molly Robbins,	May 3, 1785
Chester Upham & Molly Upham,	May 31, 1785
Ebenezer Gay & Susannah Russel, alias Fuller,	
	Aug. 11, 1785
Peter Keith, Jr., & Esther Alton,	Nov. 10, 1785
Joseph Perrin & Sarah Barrows,	Feb. 11, 1786
Nathan Shaw of Palmer, in ye Bay State, & Esther	
Robinson of Thompson,	April 6, 1786

Samuel Ruggles of Hardwick & widow Susanna
    Johnson,   April 23, 1786
Samuel Carpenter & Sybil Alton,   May 3, 1786
Calvin Chase & Ruth Evarden,   May 31, 1786
William Copeland & widow Sarah Ormsby,   Dec. 19, 1786
Thadeus Larned & Abigail Russel,   Jan. 18, 1787
Isaac Upham & Mary Hall,   Feb. 11, 1787
John Read Watson & Ruth Keith,   March 15, 1787
Elias Converse & Sarah Barrows,   May 31, 1787
Jonathan Woodward of Williamstown, Mass., &
    Nabby Watson,   Aug. 16, 1787
Jotham Johnson & Hannah Crosby,   Oct. 4, 1787
Moses Bixby & Molly Green,   Jan. 3, 1788
Ephraim Houghton & Nabby Holbrook,   Jan. 17, 1788
James Hunter & Susannah Alton,   Jan. 24, 1788
Samuel Bixby & Esther Ellithorp,   Feb. 28, 1788
Josiah Brown of Killingly & Mary Joy,   Nov. 27, 1788
Asa Dresser & Matilda Keith,   Jan. 1, 1789
Allen Hancock & widow Lucy Corbin,   Jan. 6, 1789
Ebenezer Ormsby & Phebe Houghton,   Jan. 8, 1789
Hamlin Converse & Mary Green,   Jan. 8, 1789
Jesse Ormsby & Susannah Cummings,   April 7, 1789
Peter Stockwell & Lydia Fasset,   April 15, 1789
Amos Goodale & Susannah Holbrook,   Sept. 12, 1789
John Martin & Patience Bates,   Nov. 26, 1789
Bradley Green & Sally Moffat,   March 21, 1790
Silas Bundy & Lucy Mitchel,   May 3, 1790
Elijah Corbin & Orinda Child,   June 22, 1790
—— Atwood & Rebecca Prince,   Aug., 1790
Caleb Marsh of Walpole & Betsey Leavens, Dec. 19, 1790
John Cleveland & Polly Larned,   Jan. 6, 1791
Noah Green of Windsor & Bethiah Converse,
                                              Feb. 10, 1791
Charles Cady & Sarah Mills,   Feb. 12, 1791
Joseph Upham & Catharine Brown,   Feb. 24, 1791
Jonathan White & Mary Perry,   March 10, 1791
Joel Lee & widow Alice Lee,   July 7, 1791
John Robbins & Hannah Robbins,   July 25, 1791
Asa Jacobs & Sally Emerson,   Sept. 11, 1791
Nehemiah Upham & Polly Town,   Nov. 15, 1791

Amos Lawrence of Killingly & Rebecca Mason,
Nov. 17, 1791
Elisha Fuller & Chloe Barret, Jan. 17, 1792
John Upham of Union & Anna Richards, Feb. 7, 1792
William Dunkon & Molly Walker, April 3, 1792
Aaron Mason of Killingly & Molly Plank, April 19, 1792
Calvin Amedon & Martha Koulfer, Aug. 15, 1792
Alpheus Watkins of Ashford & Alice Fuller of
Woodstock, Aug. 23, 1792
David Graves of Killingly & Lydia Munyan,
Sept. 20, 1792
Stephen Crosby & Susanna Johnson, Nov. 29, 1792
Absalom Stockwell & Hepziba Upham, Dec. 5, 1792
Stephen Latham & Betsey Underwood, Jan. 3, 1793
David Town & Lucy Upham, Jan. 30, 1793
Joseph Everden & Sarah Haight, Feb. 19, 1793
Gaius Barret & Jerusha Lee, April 28, 1793
Rev. Royal Tyler of Andover and Lydia Watson,
June 10, 1793
Jasper Partridge of Guilford, Vt., and Jemima Bixby,
June 10, 1793
Thomas Elliot & Chloe Bates, June 10, 1793
Isaac Upham & Sarah Whittemore, Sept. 29, 1793
Aaron Mason & Esther Plank, both of Killingly,
Oct. 14, 1793
Richard Dresser of Charlton & Anna Converse, Oct. 17, 1793
Ephraim Green & Grata Wilson, Nov. 21, 1793
Barzillai Sawyer & Sarah Clough, March 2, 1794
Martin Spencer of Sturbridge & Hannah Child,
April 23, 1794
———— ———— of Ashford & Abigail Barret, Dec., 1794
Daniel H. Wickham & Mary Dresser, Dec. 31, 1794
Jonathan Nye of Oxford & Betsey Alton, Dec. 31, 1794
———— Hill of Dudley & Bella Whittemore, Feb. 17, 1795
Clark Bates of Dudley & Esther Alton, Feb. 19, 1795

PLAINFIELD.

WINDHAM COUNTY.

The town of Plainfield was incorporated in May, 1699. The First Congregational Church was organized in 1705.

The record of church marriages begins as follows :

John Fields of Providence & Lycia Warren,	April 5, 1748
Asa Kingsbury & Elisabeth Peirce,	Sept. 5, 1748
Andrew Hirrick of Preston & Abigal Hull,	Nov. 9, 1748
Ebenezer Robinson & Mary Bennet,	Nov. 14, 1749
William Antram of Providence & Sarah Dean,	
	April 11, 1750
John Crery, Jr., & Mary Raymond of Charlestown,	
	May 20, 1750
Barnabas Cady & Margaret Carpenter of Killingly,	
	Oct. 8, 1750
Micajah Adams & Elizabeth Dean,	Nov. 6, 1750
James Sancimon & Elizabeth Egin (?),	March 20, 1751
Ebenezer Cole & Elisabeth Wheeler,	April 23, 1751
Timothy Wheeler & Mary Shepard,	June 18, 1751
Daniel Dow & Elisabeth Marsh,	July 4, 1751
Joshua Whitney (aged 85) & Sarah Fellows (aged 84),	
	Dec. 11, 1751
Simon Shepard & Rachel Spalding,	Dec. 25, 1751
Robert Brownlee & Porsilla Marsh,	Jan. 15, 1752
Thomas Herd & Keziah Richison,	Oct. 30, 1752
Elijah Dyar & Elizabeth Williams,	Nov. 16, 1752
John Delop & Rachel Kingsbury,	Nov. 28, 1752
Samuel Warren & Abigale Spalding,	Feb. 8, 1753
James Longbottom & Mary Farnum,	March 20, 1753
David Stevens & Sarah Spalding,	July 18, 1753
David Spalding & Elizabeth Barrit,	Nov. 15, 1753
Jacob Kimbole of Preston & Esther Phillips,	Jan. 16, 1754
William Dean & Mary Pierce,	Jan. 24, 1754
Ezekel Spalding & Jane Mather,	March 26, 1754
William Young & Ruth Cole,	Dec. 27, 1754
Nathan Williams & Waitstill Davenport,	Aug. 26, 1755
Joseph Burge, Jr., & Mehitable Shepard,	March 15, 1756

David Shepard & Phebe Cady,	March 3, 1757
Ezekel Whitney & Elizabeth Knight,	March 7, 1757
Cyrus Marsh & Susannah Dow,	March 7, 1757
Joshua Delop & Elizabeth Canady,	March 28, 1757
Jonas Wheeler & Sarah Cole,	Oct. 12, 1757
William Turner & Catherine Boid,	Feb. 7, 1759
Nehemiah Pierce & Lydia Shepherd,	May 3, 1759
Lemuel Williams & Sarah Lawrence,	Nov. 1, 1759
Jonathan Woodman, Jr., & Delight Williams,	Dec. 5, 1759
Thomas Dixon & Lydia Parks,	Feb. 21, 1760
Robert Langeathy & Susanna Apply,	March 6, 1760
Robert Parks & Elizabeth Hall,	April 2, 1760
Asa Phillips & Mary Chesborrough,	Nov. 17, 1760
Ezra Whipple & Lydia Dow,	Jan. 1, 1761
Joseph Butler & Annie Harris,	Jan. 22, 1761
Simon Spalding & Ruth Shepherd,	April 15, 1761
Jesse Fox & Ruth Hall,	Nov. 20, 1777
General John Douglass & Susannah Friars,	Jan., 1778
Samuel Smith & Rachel Dean,	1778
Ezra Warren & Rebecca Dean,	1778
Silas Spalding & Eunice Bliss,	1778
Abel L. Bottom & Martha Whiting,	Nov. 3, 1778
Asa Shepard & Hannah Shepard,	Nov. 25, 1778
John Cleaveland & Polly Pierce,	Nov. 26, 1778
Lieut. Lemuel Cleft & Sarah Hall,	Dec. 6, 1778
Bithia Whipple & one Avery of Norwich,	Jan. 28, 1779
Asa Phillips, Jr., & Sara Warren,	Feb. 11, 1779
Capt. John McGreggor & Betsey Shepard,	Feb. 28, 1779
Squire How & Phebe Pierce,	April 8, 1779
Mr. Woodward of Windham & Abby Kinsly,	April 8, 1779
Joseph Rude & Martha Hazzard,	May, 1779
Philip Spalding, Jr., & Thankful Waterman,	June 24, 1779
Hazel Spalding & Alice Cole,	June 30, 1779
Capt. John Cady & Joanna Pemberton of Newport,	July 8, 1779
Rev. Mr. Jones of Weston & widow Elizabeth Coit,	Nov. 30, 1779
John Peirce, Jr., & widow Betty Peirce,	Dec. 9, 1779
Jonathan Hun & Betty Hall,	Dec. 31, 1779
Luther Smith & Ruth Harwood,	Jan. 6, 1780

Doctor Samuel Huntington & Bethia Daggett, 1780
William Johnson of Canterbury & widow Lodeme
    Fuller, Feb. 23, 1780
Abel Cleavland of East Greenwich, R. I., & Ruth
    Clark, Jan. 6, 1785
Knight Spalding of Sharon, Vt., & Olive Warren,
    Feb. 6, 1785
Jonathan Card of New York & Anna Andros, Feb. 16, 1785
Elisha Mattison of Smithfield & Betsey Satterly,
    April 19, 1785
Benjamin Prior & Tabitha Hutchins of Killingly,
    April 28, 1785
Ebenezer Witter of Preston & Zerniah Spalding,
    May 26, 1785
Joseph Jewet of Norwich & Sally Johnson of Pres-
    ton, Oct. 13, 1785
Thomas Cole of Voluntown & Lois Frink of Vol-
    untown, Nov. 3, 1785
George Dunworth & Lucretia Park, Nov. 27, 1785
Simeon Ingals of Pomfret & Eunice Wheeler of
    Pomfret, Jan. 10, 1786
Lemuel Warren & Mary Kinne, Jan. 26, 1786
Amos Jones & Hannah Johnson, Feb. 23, 1786
Samuel Frink of Voluntown & Margaret Gallop,
    March 16, 1786
Daniel Spalding & Mary Douglass of Voluntown,
    March 23, 1786
Lewis Davies of Preston & Thankful Peters, March 23, 1786
Nathaniel Pierce & Bathsheba Sheffield, April 20, 1786
Thomas Silvey of Pittsfield, Mass., & Ruth Philips,
    Oct. 1, 1786
William Tanner of Foster, R. I., & widow Sabrina
    Philips, Oct. 5, 1786
Capt. Abraham Shepard & Anna Lyon of Wood-
    stock, Nov. 23, 1786
Miles Merwin, Esq., of Brookline & Polly Per-
    kins, Nov. 26, 1786
Jack Babcock of South Kingston & Peggy Whitney, 1786
Thomas Dexter & Leah Philips, Sept. 13, 1787
Rosel Jones & Abigail Spalding, Dec. 20, 1787

Ebenezer Key of Killingly & Anna Harris,   Dec. 20, 1787
Jonathan Gallup & Elisabeth Dow,   Jan. 3, 1788
Elijah Fox & Mary Park,   Feb. 28, 1788
Rev. Joshua Spalding of Salem, Mass., & Susanna
    Douglass,   April 9, 1788
Joseph Shepard & Esther Pierce,   June 29, 1788
Thomas Wheler & Anna Johnson,   Jan. 1, 1789
John Hershel of ——— & Mary Dean,   March 15, 1789
Samuel Dow & Mary Philips,   May 19, 1789
Abel Smith of Voluntown & Magdalene Wheler,
    Sept. 20, 1789
Samuel Sterns & Rachel Shepard,   Nov. 26, 1789
Kuff Roberts & Genny Boston,   Nov. 26, 1789
Nathanael Whiting of Voluntown & Betsey Carey,
    Dec. 3, 1789
Stephen Peirce & Lucy Hall,   Dec. 20, 1789
Richard Starkweather & Merab (?) Corning,   Jan. 3, 1790
Squire Cady & Thankful Cutler,   April 18, 1790
Hezekiah Spalding & Mary Williams,   Aug. 24, 1790
Elisha Card of Voluntown & Hannah Yarrington,
    Aug. 29, 1790
Thomas Pierce & Bornadill Fox,   Sept. 26, 1790
Jael Starkweather of Mansfield & Abigail Spalding,
    Oct. 10, 1790
David Warren & Peggy Fowler,   Oct. 18, 1790
William Spalding of George Town, Mass. and Eu-
    nice Aply,   Oct. 24, 1790
Daniel Payne of Brooklyn & Mahitabel Lester, Dec. 2, 1790
Abel Herrick & Polly Partridge of Worthington,
    Mass.,   Jan. 2, 1791
Dr. Daniel Gordon & Priscilla Pierce,   Feb. 24, 1791
Capt. Stephen Hall & Tammy Herick,   March 6, 1791
Alpheus Hatch & Mahitabel Jones,   April 13, 1791
John Whiting of Voluntown & Parnell Spalding,
    April 14, 1791
Bradford Kinne of Royal Town, Vt., & Sally Park-
    hurst,   June 9, 1791
Elisha Branch & Rebekah Douglass,   Sept. 4, 1791
Simon Shepard & Elizabeth Moor of Canterbury,
    Sept. 15, 1791

Samuel Hall, Jr., & Zipporah Shepard,　　　　Sept. 25, 1791
Ezekiel Fox & Susanna Childs of Bristol, Mass.,
　　　　　　　　　　　　　　　　　　Oct. 10, 1791
Charles Sanders of Killingly & Nancy Hill,　Oct. 13, 1791
Waterman Shepard & Mary Shepard,　　　　Nov. 13, 1791
Timothy Parkhurst & Hannah Walker,　　　Nov. 24, 1791
Mr. Leonard of Shaftsbury, Vt., & Abigail Hall, Jan., 1792
Capt. William Cutler & Eunice Hall,　　　　Feb. 8, 1792
John Bowin of Coventry, R. I., & Sally Clark, March 15, 1792
Elias Fish of Norwich & Betsey Peters,　　April 19, 1792
Joshua Wolcot & Betsy Wheler,　　　　　　Oct. 14, 1792
Caleb Hill of Voluntown & Sally Wheeler,　Dec. 23, 1792
Caleb Clark & Abigail Philips,　　　　　　Jan. 10, 1793
Zadock Harries & Abigail Dean,　　　　　May 30, 1793
Levi Waters & Hannah Bottom,　　　　　Aug. 11, 1793
Stephen Thurston of Rowley, Mass., & Philomela
　　Paresh,　　　　　　　　　　　　June 13, 1794
William Swansborough & Rebekah Bottom,　June 26, 1794
Jeremiah Shepard & Ruth Webb,　　　　　Sept. 26, 1794
Thomas Dow & Anna Kinne,　　　　　　Dec. 11, 1794
T. Rodman Clark & Anna Brown,　　　　Jan. 11, 1795
Josias Lindon Arnold, Esq., of St. Johnsborough &
　　Susanna Perkins,　　　　　　　　Feb. 8, 1795
Nathan Cogswell of Washington, Vt., & Lydia
　　　　Woodward,　　　　　　　　March 1, 1795
Oliver Jones of ———, Vt., & Polly Whipple, March 3, 1795
John Richards of ——— & Meriam Jones,　March 4, 1795
John Wilber & Mehitabel Hatch,　　　　　April, 1795
Gurdon Buck of Preston & Rhod Buck,　　　　　1795
Dick Fortune & Dinah Thair,　　　　　　Nov. 19, 1795
Job Williams of Steuben, N. Y., & Olive Apley, Nov. 22, 1795
James Allen of Pomfret & Esther Otis of Pomfret,
　　　　　　　　　　　　　　　　Jan. 7, 1796
Zebulon Parkes & Patience Croswell,　　　Jan. 21, 1796
Sylvester Peirce & Eunice Shepard,　　　　　　1796
John Heric & Susanna Yarington,　　　　April 14, 1796
Stephen Parkhurst & Mary Starkweather,　April 21, 1796
Timothy Lester & Betsy Dunlap,　　　　May 8, 1796
George Middleton & Sally Eaton,　　　　June 12, 1796
John Lester & Polly Backus,　　　　　　　　　1796

Moses Branch & Rebecah Park,   1796
Capt. Stephen Clark & Anna Park,   1796
Zadock Hall & Sibbel Park,   1796
Jeremiah Starkweather of Boston & Bridget Kinne,
                                                            Jan. 12, 1797
John Tyler Rice of Foster, R. I., & Lucy Aply, Feb. 7, 1797
Ephraim Prentice of Preston & Mary Dow,   Feb. 9, 1797
Allen Gibbon of Coventry, R. I., & Esther Gallup,
                                                            Feb. 16, 1797
Mr. Freeman of St. Andrews, Vt., & Esther Park-
    hurst,   Feb. 19, 1797
Stephen Wheler & Sally Stringer,   Feb. 26, 1797
John Aply & Mercy Kenedy,   March 19, 1797
Simeon Harington & Nabby Hammitt,   March 26, 1797
Mr. Rowland of Windsor & Eunice Spalding,   1797
Capt. Benjamin Smith of Salem, Mass., & Abiah
    Douglass,   Sept. 17, 1797
Charles Clap Chander of Pomfret & Lydia Gray of
    Windham,   Sept. 24, 1797
James Burrill, Jr., Esq., of Providence, R. I., & Sally
    Arnold of St. Johnsborough, Vt.,   Oct. 8, 1797
Abraham Snow & Elisabeth Spalding,   Oct. 18, 1797
Stephen Johnson of Pomfret & Experience Wheeler,
                                                            Oct. 29, 1797
James Firman & Lucy Parkhurst,   Nov. 12, 1797
Ebenezer Gallup & Elisabeth Babcock,   Nov. 26, 1797
Thomas Rathbon of Hancock, Mass., & Sally Bab-
    cock,   Dec. 3, 1797
Simon Cutler & Betty Herick,   Dec. 17, 1797
Edward Corwin of Franklin & Olive Colegrove,
                                                            March 4, 1798
Charles Marsh, Esq., of Woodstock, Vt., & Susanna
    Arnold,   June 3, 1798
Samuel Carlile of Providence, R. I., & Elisabeth
    Gordon,   June 17, 1798
David Putnam & Betsey Perkins,   1798
John Dunlap & Betsey Lester,   Nov. 18, 1798
Jedadiah Rogers & Sally Jones,   Jan. 24, 1799
Thomas Dixon of Sterling & Ruth Shepard,
                                                            April 11, 1799

Benjamin Allen of North Kingston, R. I., & Mary
    Benedict,   May 6, 1799
Samuel Saterlee of Williamstown, Mass., & Eunice
    Peirce,   May 7, 1799
Joseph Lester & Lydia Angel,   May 19, 1799
Squire Cady & Abiah Spalding,   May 29, 1799
Sylvanus Cone of East Haddam & Katy Shepard,
                                 Jan. 1, 1800
Prentice Kinne of Manlius, N.Y., & Elisabeth Kinne,
                              Jan. 16, 1800
Elijah Gibs of Coventry, R. I., & Esther Colegrove,
                             Feb. 10, 1800
Anthony Crosby of Otsego, N. Y., & Roby Potter,
                            July 24, 1800
Newport Kinsman & Dorcas Boston,   Nov. 16, 1800
Silas Westcot, Esq., of Coventry, R. I., & Phebe
    Wheler,   Dec. 7, 1800
Nathan Burgess & Sally Gay,   Dec. 11, 1800

WEST HARTFORD.

HARTFORD COUNTY.

Town incorporated 1854, having been formerly a part of Hartford.
  The Congregational Church of West Hartford was organized in 1713, being then the third church of Hartford, (the other two—the first and second—having been organized in 1632 and 1670 respectively and records published).
  The marriage records of West Hartford begin :

Timothy Seymour & Rachel Allyn,   April 27, 1727
Daniel Seymour & Mabel ——— (Bigelow),   May 10, 1727
Ebenezer Smith & Zerviah ———,   June 15, 1727
Joseph Gillett & Anne ———,   Jan. 23, 1728
Styber Goodwin & Sarah ———,   June 27, 1728
Abiel Smith & Abigail ———,   Sept. 4, 1729
Ebenezer Judd & Hannah Richards,   Nov. 5, 1729
Nathan Messenger & Sarah ———,   Nov. 8, 1729
Daniel Olmstead & Mary Cadwell,   Jan. 27, 1730
Daniel Mills & Jerusha Steel,   Feb. 12, 1730
Ebenezer Merril & Mary Webster,   April 9, 1730

Noadiah Burr & Hannah ———,   Nov. 5, 1730
Abel Gillet & Abigail Ensign,   May 18, 1731
William Webster & Mary Watson,   June 3, 1731
John Welles & Jeannie Smith,   June 17, 1731
Jonathan Gillet & Mehitable ———,   July 15, 1731
Robert Webster & Susanna ———,   July 20, 1731
John Seymour & Hannah, daughter of David En-
    sign,   May 7, 1733
Nathaniel Pomroy & Susanna Seymour,   July 20, 1733
Caleb Merrill & Mercy Sedgwick,   Aug. 2, 1733
John Smith & Abigail ———,   Jan. 24, 1734
Samuel Nash & Margaret Merrill,   1734
Thomas Hosmer & Susanna Steel,   July 18, 1734
James Cadwell & Sarah (Merry),   July 25, 1734
Jonathan Center & Bethiah, daughter of Cornelius
    Merry,   Nov. 13, 1734
John Welles & Sarah Gaylord,   Dec. 23, 1735
Daniel Curtiss & Rebeckah ———,   Oct. 14, 1736
Ebenezer Buel & Dorothy ———,   Oct. 19, 1736
Thomas Bull & Martha ———,   Nov. 9, 1736
John Merry & Dinah Flower,   Oct. 16, 1736
John Fowler & Abigail ———,   July 6, 1737
Samuel Cadwell & Elishabc, daughter of Henry
    Brace,   July 15, 1737
John Ellery & Mary Austin, daughter of John, July 28, 1737
Thomas Phelps & Margaret Watson (?),   Nov. 23, 1737
Gideon Butler & Zerviah Ensign,   Nov. 24, 1737
John Welles & Hannah ———,   July 20, 1738
Abijah Bunce & Mary ———,   Oct. 18, 1738
Daniel Brown & Mary *SHEPARD*,   Nov., 1739
Samuel Steele & Elizabeth ———,   Dec. 20, 1739
Caleb Turner & Rachel Merry, daughter of Cornel-
    ius,   Dec. 20, 1739
Aaron Merril & Esther ———,   April 9, 1740
Benjamin Merril & Mary ———,   April 16, 1740
Benil Seymour & Thankful Merril,   April 23, 1740
William, son of Jonathan Sedgwick, & Elizabeth,
    daughter of Henry Brace,   May 18, 1740
Henry Brace, son of Henry, & Elisabeth Cadwell,
                                              July 15, 1740

6

Moses Merrill & Rachel ———,   Nov. 20, 1740
Jonathan Cadwell & Bethiah Butler, daughter of
    Joseph,   Dec. 11, 1740
Asa Hopkins & Abigail ———,   Oct. 1, 1741
Samuel Kellogg & Mary ———,   July 8, 1742
Eleazer Smith & Agnes Reynolds,   April 25, 1743
Elisha Seymour, son of John, & Abigail, daughter
    of Ebenezer Sedgwick,   July 5, 1743
Zachary Kelsey & Abigail ———,   Nov. 2, 1743
John Hubbard of Wintonbury & Hannah Cadwell,
    daughter of Thomas,   Sept., 1744
Zebulan Shephard & Elisabeth Blancher,   Feb. 9, 1745
Abraham Sedgwick & Ali Brace,   Sept. 19, 1745
Nathaniel Flower & Hulda Steele,   Sept. 30, 1745
Zebulan Merril & Susanna ———,   Feb. 6, 1746
Lamrock, son of Lamrock Flower, & Mehitable
    Goodwin, daughter of Isaac,   May 21, 1746
John Ensign & Mary Sedgwick, daughter of Eben-
    ezer,   May 6, 1746
Nathaniel Steele & Susanna Olmstead, daughter
    of Thomas,   Oct. 16, 1746
Benjamin Colt & Anne Whiting, daughter of John,
                                              Oct. 27, 1746
Alexander Porter & Rebekah ———,   July 16, 1747
Samuel Moodey & Anne Olmstead,   July 14, 1747
Reuben Flower & Susanna Steele,   ———
Elias Willard & Anne Stanley,   Aug. 25, 1748
Timothy Seymour & Lydia Kellogg,   Dec. 1, 1748
Noah, son of Daniel Webster, & Mercy, daughter
    of Eliphalet Steele,   Jan. 12, 1749
John Seymour, Jr., & Lydia Wadsworth,   June 19, 1749
Elijah Merrill & Rachel Welles,   Feb. 7, 1752
Allan Seymour & Elisabeth Smith,   Feb. 27, 1752
Jno. Strattan & Anne Reaves,   April 1, 1754
Elisha Ensign & Elizabeth Sedgwick, daughter of
    Ebenezer,   July 18, 1754
Theo Merrill & Martha Wood,   Oct. 8, 1755
Jno. Merrill of New Hartford & Irene Olmstead,
    daughter of Stephen,   Feb. 7, 1758
Elisha Welles of Farmington & Mindwell Wood, Feb. 26, 1758

Benjamin Hopkins, son of Thomas, & Rachel
    Steele, daughter of Eliphalet,   April 27, 1758
Jonathan Sedgwick & widow Anne Brace,   Aug. 6, 1758
Daniel Kellogg, son of Daniel, & Jerusha Kellogg,
     Oct. 20, 1758
Isaac Goodwin, son of Isaac, & Mercy Merrill, April 4, 1759
Amos Shepherd of Hartford & Mehitable Wood,
     May 8, 1759
Zenas Brace & Mary Skinner,   Dec. 13, 1759
Timothy Olmstead & Eunice Flower,   Dec. 23, 1759
Noah Woodruff of Farmington & Mary Cadwell of
    Hartford,   Jan. 3, 1760
Joseph Blancher of Hartford & Rosanna Merry,
     Dec. 26, 1760
Elisha Stilman of Wethersfield & Abigail Nast (?)
    (or Nash),   Jan. 22, 1761
William Sedgwick & widow Miriam Hopkins, May 14, 1761
William Stevens & Elizabeth Sedgwick,   July 9, 1761
Jonathan Gilbert & Lydia Olmstead,   July 19, 1761
Abraham Merril & Joanna Brace,   Dec. 31, 1761
Elisha Seymour & Rhoda Sedgwick,   June 13, 1762
Daniel Alling of Great Barrington & Esther Colton
    of Hartford,   July 15, 1762
Benjamin Gilbert & Anne Butler,   Aug. 21, 1762
Amos Stanley & Zerviah Gray,   Nov. 18, 1762
Ebenezer Crosby & Chloe Hooker,   July 15, 1763
Joab or (Joal) Griswold of Windsor & Elizabeth
    Collins,   Oct. 6, 1763
Ebenezer Welles & widow Elizabeth Seymour,
     Nov. 23, 1763
Zacheus Butler, son of Gideon, & widow Joanna
    Cadwell,   Dec. 18, 1763
Thomas Goodman, son of Thomas, & Sarah Sey-
    mour, daughter of Moses,   May 13, 1764
Isaac Cadwell, son of Abraham of New Hartford,
    & Elizabeth Brace of Hartford,   June 17, 1764
Jacob Bidwell & Sarah Belding, daughter of Tim-
    othy,   Dec. 31, 1764
Enos Kellogg of Sheffield & Abigaill, daughter of
    Elisha Seymour,   June 11, 1765

James Stanly, son of Augustus, & Esther Gridley,
    daughter of Timothy of Farmington, dec.,   July 28, 1765
Ephraim Kellogg, son of Silas of Sheffield, & Ruth
    Hosmer, daughter of Thomas,   Oct. 22, 1765
William Judd of Farmington & Elizabeth Mix,
    daughter of Ebenezer,   Dec. 8, 1765
Moses Gaylord & Susanna Welles,   Dec. 26, 1765
James Taylor & widow Elizabeth Stevens,   Jan. 23, 1766
John Martyn of Litchfield & Ducas Sedgwick,
    daughter of Stephen of Farmington,   March 20, 1766
Simeon More & Jemmia Welles, daughter of John
    of Farmington,   May 31, 1766
Joseph Cadwell, son of Samuel, & Thankful Sedg-
    wick, daughter of Abraham,   June 26, 1766
William Wheeler & Hulda, daughter of Nathaniel
    Flower,   Sept. 18, 1766
Alexander Catlin of Litchfield & Abigail Good-
    man, daughter of Timothy,   Feb. 26, 1766
Jeremiah, son of Jno. Tryon, & Lydia Bird,   Oct. 28, 1766
John Rowley, son of John of Windsor, & Mary Steele,
    daughter of Samuel,   Nov. 16, 1766
Samuel Merrill, son of Israel, & Nathl (?) Flower,
                                           Nov. 20, 1766
Henry Brace & widow Dinah Merry,   Dec. 1, 1766
John Whitman, son of John, & Anne Skinner,
    daughter of Timothy,   Dec. 6, 1766
Asabel Woodruff of Farmington & Rhode Brace,
    daughter of Henry,   Jan. 15, 1767
Cabel Croswell & Hannah Kellogg,   Feb. 26, 1767
Col. David Whitney of Canaan & widow Prudence
    Sedgwick of Hartford,   July 28, 1767
Gideon Butler, son of Gideon, & Abigail, daughter
    of Daniel Olmstead,   Aug. 23, 1767
Charles Seymour & Lucy Whitman, daughter of
    John,   Dec. 3, 1767
John Whitman & Hannah Wells,   Jan. 21, 1768
Ebenezer Sedgwick & Martha Steel, daughter of
    Samuel,   July 27, 1768
Seth Collens, son of Robert, & Lucy Sedgwick,
    daughter of William,   Aug. 25, 1768

Jonathan Sedgwick & widow Sarah Gillet,   Dec. 12, 1768
Thomas Hart Hooker of Farmington, son of Roger,
    & Sarah Whitman, daughter of John,·   Feb. 1, 1769
Baizy Welles, son of John of Farmington, & Ruth
    Gaylord of Hartford,   Feb. 1, 1769
Ithamar Colton of Symsbury & Lynde Wells of
    Farmington,   Feb. 19, 1769
Ichebod Forbes of Hartford & Mary Ann Merrill,
    daughter of Israel,   March 9, 1769
Ameziah Stanley & Mary, daughter of Francis
    Flower of Hartford,   March 26, 1769
Ebenezer Bibbins of Salisbury & Hulda Sedgwick
    of Farmington, daughter of Stephen,   June 1, 1769
John Kellogg Belding, son of John, & Mercy,
    daughter of Noah Webster,   Sept. 18, 1769
James Wadsworth, son of Elisha, & Mary Brace,
    daughter of Henry,   Oct. 15, 1772
Ebenezer Merry, son of John, & Sarah, daughter of
    John Whitney,   Nov. 5, 1772
Ebenezer Price & Lois Gray, daughter of Abiel
    Gray of Hartford,   Nov. 13, 1772
Stephen Hopkins & Sarah Olmsead, daughter of
    Daniel,   Feb. 14, 1773
John Chadwick of —— & Prudence Seymore,
    daughter of Elisha,   March 15, 1773
Ashbal Webster of Winterbury & Annie Kelsey,
    daughter of Zacheus Kelsey of Hartford, March 21, 1773
John Peirce of Litchfield & Mary Goodman of
    Hartford,   July, 1773
Fisher Gay of Farmington & Ruth Hooker,   Sept. 1, 1773
Stephen Sheperd & Abigail Butler,   Nov. 11, 1773
Nathan Benjamin of Sheffield & Hannah Wells,
    Dec. 23, 1773
Ebenezer Belding & Wealthy Sedgwick,   Jan. 2, 1774
Aaron Cadwell & Mary Hooker,   April 5, 1774
Abijah Colton & Mary Gaylor,   April 23, 1774
Hezekiah Cadwell & Sarah Flowers,   May 1, 1774
John Steele & Sarah Merrills,   May 5, 1774
Daniel Hosmer, son of Thomas, & Mary Belding,
    daughter of John,   June 5, 1774

William Hopkins & Mary Merrills,   July 13, 1774
Samuel Deming of Wethersfield & Bellisan Belding,
                                               Sept. 29, 1774
Samuel Sedgwick & Anne Steel,   Oct. 20, 1774
John North & Rhoda Merrill, both of Farmington,
                                               Jan. 19, 1775
Stephen Skinner & Ali Sedgwick,   May 25, 1775
George Wells of Farmington & Caroline Hooker,
                                               May 25, 1775
Caleb Turner & Parmelia Wadsworth,   Aug. 3, 1775
Elisha Austin of Sheffield & Johanna Cadwell of
      Hartford,   Jan. 26, 1776
———— Smith & Anna Sedgwick,   Feb. 1, 1776
Ebenezer Faxon & Elenor Whitman,   Feb. 9, 1776
Moses Steel & Nancy Whiting,   April 3, 1776
Gabriel Flowers & Jerusha Hosmer,   July 3, 1776
Joseph Hurlbert & Leandy Sedgwick,   July 31, 1776
Ashbel Shepherd of Hartford & Johanna Standly
      of Farmington,   Aug. 1, 1776
Gideon Merrells & Abigail Merrells,   Aug. 1, 1776
Joseph Colton & Hester Belding,   Aug. 11, 1776
Elijah Irish (?) & Rachel Seymour,   Nov. 15, 1776
Jonathan Skinner & Thankful Butler,   Jan. 30, 1777
Seneca Fuller of Sheffield & Eunice Wells,   July 17, 1777
Samuel Stanley, Jr., of Farmington & Abigail Waters,
                                               Oct. 6, 1777
Rev. Nathan Strong & Anna Smith,   Nov. 20, 1777
John Marsh & Meriam Segwick,   Nov. 27, 1777
Samuel Merrells & widow Sarah Steal,   Dec. 18, 1777
Isaac Flowers & Freelove Hopkins,   Jan. 1, 1778
Eleazer Fisher & Sally Bibbens,   Jan. 22, 1778
Phineas Kellogg of North Hartford & Oliver Phrager
      of Newington,   Jan. 22, 1778
Abraham Webster & Dolly Seymour,   Feb. 17, 1778
Rev. Warum Williams of Branford & Mrs. Mary
      Whiting,   March 5, 1778
Elijah Ensign & Lois Olmstead,   April 30, 1778
Gideon Hubbard of Middleton & Rachel Harsdale (?),
                                               June 25, 1778
Ebenezer Steal & Rachel Seymour,   July 1, 1778

Joel Lord & Jerusha Webster,	Nov. 12, 1778
Titus Merrell & Anna Belding,	Nov. 26, 1778
Thomas Olmstead & Rhoda Shepherd,	Dec. 10, 1778
Enos Kellogg & Kersiah Belding,	Dec. 17, 1778
Allen Steal & Anna Cadwell,	Jan. 14, 1779
Seth Collins & Sarah Hooker,	April 8, 1779
Samuel Woodbridge of Hartland & Elizabeth Goodman,	May 27, 1779
Norman Seymour & Catharine Seymour,	June 15, 1779
——— Gleson of Farmington & Abigail Alford,	June 20, 1779
Cimeon Merrells & Susanna Shepherd,	Sept. 3, 1779
Richard Huddlston of Rhode Island & Abigail Eggleston,	Sept 20, 1779
Enos Seymour & widow Belding,	Nov. 22, 1779
Gideon Webster & Sarah Cadwell,	Dec. 30, 1779
Lemuel Rowell of New Hampshire & Sarah Hooker,	1780
William Elsworth & Mary Whiting,	Feb. 25, 1780
Richard Heydon (?) & widow Hopkins,	March, 1780
——— Spalding (a Briton) & widow Abigail Smith,	April 9, 1780
George Greenwood of Farmington & Grace Brown,	Aug. 31, 1780
John Merry & widow Ruth Cadwell,	Oct. 14, 1780
Jonas Gibbs of Rutland & Hulda Merrells,	Nov. 3, 1780
——— Weston of Harwington & Sarah Steel,	Nov. 15, 1780
Thomas Merrells & Elizabeth Ensign,	Dec. 7, 1780
Simeon Belding & Abigail Wells,	Dec. 7, 1780
John White & a Wethersfield woman,	Jan. 3, 1781
Rositer Belding & Hester Merrells,	March 27, 1781
Mr. Morris of Alford & Sarah Wells of Farmington,	June 20, 1781
George Bidwell & Sarah Segwick,	Sept. 15, 1781
Mr. Stouten (?) of East Windsor & widow Elizabeth Gillett,	Sept. 28, 1781
Allen Seymour of Hartford & Mela Standly of Farmington,	Oct. 5, 1781
Asa Seymour of Granville & Abigail Demming,	Nov. 5, 1781
Jonathan Skinner & Jerusha Merrells,	Dec. 29, 1781
Moses & Amanda Steel,	Dec. 27, 1781

Nathan Flavis (?) Whiting & Ruth Hooker,   Jan. 13, 1782
Samuel Standly & Hannah Butler,   March 10, 1782
Gideon Demming of Farmington & Deborah Kellogg,
   May 15, 1782
Ebenezer Gibbs & Elisabeth Gillett,   July 23, 1782
David Currie of York state & Margaret Sebring,
   Aug. 25, 1782
William Whiting & Abigail Flowers,   Sept. 20, 1782
Simeon Hosmer & Lucretia Steal,   Oct., 1782
Joseph Brown & Anna Rogers,   Nov 28, 1782
Abner Curtis & widow Mary Whiting of Farming-
ton,   Nov. 28, 1782
John Standly & Anna Gibbs,   Jan. 12, 1783
Prentice Hosmer & Elizabeth Steal,   May 10, 1783
Dr. James Caswell (?) & Abigail L. Loyd (?),   May 23, 1783
Mr. Olcot & Mary Cadwell,   Aug. 25, 1783
Orid Burrall of Canaan & Lucy Wells,   Oct. 10, 1783
Mr. Wilson of Wintonbury & Hannah Cadwell, Oct. 26, 1783
Jesse Porter of Farmington & Sibel Steal,   Dec., 1783
Noadiah Stanly & Hannah King,   April 5, 1784
—— Beardsley & Mary Flower alias Hook,   —— 5, 1784
Elisha Whiting & Susanna Butler,   March 25, 1784
Joseph Whiting of Hartford & Abigail Goodwin of
Farmington,   April, 1784
Thomas Brace of Hartford & Aurelia Wells of
Farmington,   Aug. 14, 1784
Asher Segwick & Temperance Demming,   Nov. 3, 1784
Abel Butler & Mary Brace,   Nov. 15, 1784
William Segwick & Lucy Merrells,   Jan. 12, 1785
David Rowe of Farmington & Esther Gray,   1785
Horace Kellogg & Hannah Segwick,   Feb. 15, 1785
Jesse Shepherd & Amanda Wells, both of Farm-
ington,   April 15, 1785
George Larlum (?) & Ellenor Cadwell,   April 21, 1785
Ebenezer Oulds & Sarah Goodman,   May 5, 1785
Theodore Coles & Mary Gilbert,   Aug. 1, 1785
Stephen Segwick of Farmington & Ammi Brace,
   Sept. 3, 1785
Theron Demming & Leita Ensign,   Nov. 25, 1785
Benjamin Waters & Elizabeth Peirce,   Dec. 15, 1785

Frank (a negro man) & Milla (a molattoe girl),
  daughter of Rosana Merry, Dec., 1785
Simeon Merrells & Ruth, daughter of widow Web-
  ster, Feb. 25, 1786
Amos Burr of Farmington & Eunice Shepherd,
  March 24, 1786
Hezekiah Barret & Lydia Gilbert, May 31, 1786
Benjamin Fletcher & Esther Gilbert, May 31, 1786
Azariah Root of Sheffield & Cintha Ensign, Sept. 8, 1786
Mark F—ot & Ali Woodruff of Farmington, Oct. 1, 1786
Timothy Fisher (?) & Elizabeth Hooker, Oct. 16, 1786
Moses Fits & Dorotha Belden, Dec. 5, 1786
Charles Gilbert & Ruth Cadwell, Dec. 5, 1786
Levi Page & Susanna Kellogg, Feb., 1787
Ebenezer Owles (?) & Mehetabel King, March 25, 1787
Mr. Andrus of Wethersfield & Rhoda Seymour,
  April 16, 1787
Frederick Steele & Sabre Shepherd, April 19, 1787
Hezekiah Steele of Hartford & Lois Merrells of
  Farmington, June 8, 1787
Henry Wilson (?) Dwight of Stockbridge & Abigail
  Wells, June, 1787
Matthew Thompson of Suffield & Elizabeth Collins,
  Sept., 1787
Enoch Perkins, Esq., of Hartford & Nancy Pitkin
  of Farmington, Sept. 20, 1787
Joseph Waters & Susanna Vaugn, Sept. 27, 1787
Timothy Segwick & Lucy Segwick, Oct. 3, 1787
Stephen Segwick of Farmington & Hannah Olmsted,
  Nov. 15, 1787
Samson Heyes (?) of Ashford & Lucy Heyes, Nov. 15, 1787
Erastus King of Hartford & Mabel Wells of
  Farmington, Dec. 7, 1787
Mr. Garruyck of ye N.— city above Abanna & Mary
  Webster, Dec. 11, 1787
George Occott of Wethersfield & Clara Demming,
  Dec. 28, 1787
Alexander Standly & Nabby Standly, both of
  Farmington, Jan. 1, 1788
Elisha Allin & Rhoda Roberts of Wintonbury, Jan. 23, 1788

Zachariah Garywick (?) of Leasingburgh & Mar-
    garet Steele,   Feb. 11, 1788
Elisha Gilbert & Cloe Crosby,   May 27, 1788
Silas Curtiss of Farmington & Lucy Crosby,   July, 1788
Joseph Benjamin of Egremont & Susanna Gaylord,
                                         Oct. 12, 1788
Ezekiel Kellogg & Elizabeth Standly,   Oct. 12, 1788
Samuel Farnsworth of Washington, N. H., & Eliza
    beth Goodwin of Farmington,   Oct. 22, 1788
Elisha Gridly of Farmington & Sarah Goodman,
                                         Nov. 1, 1789
David Colvin of Coventry, R. I., & Rahael Wells of
    Farmington,   Nov. 1, 1789
William Love of Coventry, R. I., & Abi Brace, June 14, 1790
Joseph Cadwell, Jr., & Cloe Kellogg,   Oct., 1790
Roswell Francis & Anna Wadsworth,   Nov. 5, 1790
Solomon Allyn of Windsor & Rachel Tryon,   Feb. 3, 1791
Phinihas Ashman of Stockbridge & Alathea Wells,
                                         Feb. 8, 1791
Theodore Morgan & Esther Stocking of Chatham,
                                         July 26, 1791
Calvin Hyde of Lenox & Ammi Standly,   Sept. 5, 1791
Mr. Hubbard of Wintonbury & Wealthy Kellogg,
                                         Oct. 3, 1791
Isaac Talmadge & Olive Ensign,   Oct. 10, 1791
Samuel Pelton of Chatham & Joanna Merrells, Oct. 20, 1791
Morgan Goodwin, Jr., & Rowenea Wheeler,   Nov. 20, 1791
Roger Mills, Jr., & Miss Biddwell of Wintonbury,
                                         Nov. 24, 1791
Theron Seymour & Nabby Goodman,   Nov. 27, 1791
David Grant of Windsor & Rhoda Cadwell,   Jan. 12, 1792
Nathan Benjamin of Barrington & Ruth Seymour,
                                         Jan. 12, 1792
Elisha Strong of Bennington, Vt., & Silvia Gridly
    of Farmington,   Feb. 13, 1792
William Merrells & Rhobe Thornton,   Feb. 13, 1792
Manning Bibbens & Mary Standly,   Feb. 16, 1792
David Williams of E. Hartford & Rachel Bidwell,
                                         Feb. 28, 1792
Seth Pelton of Chatham & Abigail Brace,   March 9, 1792

Solomon Ensign, Jr., & Jerusha Merrells,   March 10, 1792
Gordon Whiting & Betsey Wells,   March 16, 1792
Leonard Braman & Amanda Segwick,   March 21, 1792
Larg (?) Brace & Lucinda Belden,   May 20, 1792
James Hicks & Thedee Kellogg,   May 22, 1792
Gad Segwick of Farmington & Lydia Standly,   July 3, 1792
Thomas Francis of Hartford & Priscila Cady of
   Tolland,   July 28, 1792
Selah Francis & Hannah Shepherd,   Sept. 29, 1792
Jared Bidwell & Miss Scott, both of Watertown,
   Nov. 14, 1792
Samuel Cadwell & Rhoda Cadwell,   Nov. 20, 1792
Gideon Hurlbut & Anna Gilbert,   Jan. 5, 1794
Joseph William Lawrence & Sibil Heath,   Jan. 25, 1794
Ebenezer Wells, Jr., & Rachel Francis,   Jan. 25, 1794
Seth Wilcox of Simsbury & Anna Hooker,   Feb. 10, 1794
Ozim Woodruff & Patty Scott, both of Farmington,
   April 13, 1794
Ozias Bidwell of Hartford & Elizabeth Hale of
   Chatham,   Sept. 7, 1794
Dr. Everitt of Winchester & Hannah Standly, Sept. 25, 1794
Amos Lawrence of Hartford & Waitstill Merrill
   of Farmington,   Dec. 11, 1794
Seth Goodwin & Gennit Crowell,   Jan. 12, 1795
Daniel Wilcox of Symsbury & Hephziba Pees of
   Glastonbury,   Jan. 12, 1795
Samuel Tolcott & Abigail Pantry Hooker,   Jan. 26, 1795
Rev. Asael Strong Norton of Whitestown, N. Y.,
   & Mary Clap Pitkins of Farmington,   Jan. 25, 1795
Rev. Timothy Langdon Danhug (?) of Danbury &
   Elizabeth Pitkins of Farmington,   Jan. 29, 1795
Samuel Scott of Farmington & Malinda Hurlburt,
   Feb. 12, 1795
Pelatiah Alford of Farmington & Amanda Cadwell,
   Feb. 22, 1795
Nehemiah Bailey of Grotton & Peggy Taylor, Feb. 22, 1795
John Belden, Jr., of Farmington & Asenah Darrow
   of Montville,   April 20, 1795
Joseph Booth of Enfield & Hannah Henery,   May 13, 1795
Mr. Turner & a daughter of Mr. Lawrence,   Oct. 26, 1795

Roswell Woodruff of Farmington & Hannah Benham, Nov. 3, 1795

Elisha Wells, Jr., & Eleanor King, both of Farmington, Nov. 12, 1795

Chauncy Segwick & Waitstill Heath, Dec. 20, 1795

Thomas Goodman, Jr., & Abigail Seymour, Dec. 24, 1795

Samuel Miller of Middletown & Lucy Standly, Jan. 17, 1796

Mr. Cowles & Bede Gridly, both of Farmington, Jan. 22, 1796

James Winchell of Union, N. Y., & Abigail Merrill, Feb. 20, 1796

Isaiah Gilbert & Cinthia Hosmer, March 17, 1796

Reuben Simmons of Simsbury & Susannah Whiting, May 1, 1796

Elijah Drake of Farmington & Lucy Stedman, June 3, 1796

John P. Whitman & Lucy Seymour, June 26, 1796

Benjamin White & Miriam Ensign, Aug. 1, 1796

William Goodwin & Abigail Croswell, Aug. 12, 1796

Elizer Loomis of Southwick & Sarah Shepherd, Oct. 23, 1796

Solomon Wells of East Windsor & Louisa Ensign, Oct. 29, 1796

Pollard Merrill & Susanna Brace, Oct. 29, 1796

Elisha Wells & Clara Olcott, Dec. 5, 1796

John Selden of Farmington & Hannah Hurlburt, Feb. 5, 1797

Stephen Woodbridge of Albany & Rachel Wells, Oct. 25, 1797

Jonathan Smith of Lanesborough & Elizabeth Hosmer, Dec. 25, 1797

Henry Brown of Stockbridge & Mary Wells, Dec. 28, 1797

James Whitman & Abigail Butler, Jan. 17, 1798

Martin Cadwell of Hartford & Diadema Hart of Farmington, April 9, 1798

Jeremiah Leming of Northampton & Amanda Kellogg, June 17, 1798

Mr. Plumb of Litchfield & Polly Mariah Cadwell, Sept. 1, 1798

Nathan Perkins, Jr., & Mabel Seymour, Sept. 7, 1798

Uriah Hanks of Mansfield & Sally Henny,   Nov. 27, 1798
—— Adams of Simsbury & Abigail Hurlburt,
                                          Nov. 29, 1798
Hezekiah Cadwell of Hartford & Mary Marvin of
    Simsbury,   Jan. 6, 1799
Asa Goodman, Jr., & Polly Henery,   Jan., 1799

EAST HARTFORD.

HARTFORD COUNTY.

The Congregational Church of East Hartford was organized in 1702. The town was incorporated in October, 1783, having been previously a part of Hartford. The church records have largely disappeared. The following are all of the early marriages.
Marriage records found among Rev. Dr. Williams' papers:

David Cadwell & Mindwell Judson,   Dec. 18, 1783
Theodore Treat & Mary Williams,   Dec. 18, 1783
James Morris & Martha Risley,   Dec. 18, 1783
Jason Miller & Hannah Chadwick,   Jan. 1, 1784
Jonathan Pratt & Betsey Merrow,   Jan. 30, 1784
Richard Goodwin & Ruth Roberts,   Feb. 6, 1784
Samuel Church & Dorothy Olmstead,   March 11, 1784
Lemuel Deming & Thankful Roberts,   April 1, 1784
Elijah Deming & Lucy Risley,   April 8, 1784
John Porter & Mary Williams,   May 20, 1784
Nehemiah Risley & Martha Bemont,   June 3, 1784
Ashbel Easton & Sarah Arnold,   Aug. 22, 1784
Samuel Roberts & Anne Pratt,   Sept. 16, 1784
Joseph Arnold & widow Sarah Smith,   Dec. 30, 1784
Stephen Roberts & Mary Burnham,   Jan. 6, 1785
John Church Hutchins & Eliza Williams,   Feb. 17, 1785
Philemon Stedman & Anne Crosby,   June 2, 1785
Peter Richie & Louisa Griswold,   July 21, 1785
Shubael Drake & Bathsheba Williams,   Dec. 8, 1785
Moses Ensign & Jennie Forbes,   Feb. 16, 1786
Ezra Brainard & Mabel Porter,   March 9, 1786
Shubael Griswold & Saffa Flagg,   May 25, 1786
Hezekiah Wilson & Mehetable Kendall,   June 27, 1786
Thomas Gulliver & Thankful Porter,   Sept. 21, 1786

Noah Risley & Mary Arnold,	Nov. 2, 1786
John Page & Jerusha Olmstead,	Nov. 9, 1786
Ashbel Olmstead, Jr., & Mary Forbes,	Nov. 16, 1786
Elisha Warren & Lucretia Brewer,	Dec. 28, 1786
Isaac (?) Jones & Anne Forbes,	Jan. 10, 1787
Aaron Colton & Eliza Olmstead,	April 5, 1787
Timothy Cowles & Eliza Olmstead,	April 26, 1787
Sergt. Timothy Cheeney & Martha White,	May 17, 1787
Elisha Roberts & Sally Risley,	June 7, 1787
George Pitkin & Mabel Olmstead,	July 5, 1787
Ebenezer Kellogg & Abigail Olmstead,	Jan. 22, 1789
Theodore ——— & Elizabeth Pitkin,	Jan. 29, 1789
Jonathan Thompson & Eunice Fitch,	April 24, 1789
Timothy Hills & Jerusha Stanley,	Aug. 13, 1789
Capt. Samuel Smith & widow Sarah Stanley,	Aug. 13, 1789
John Cotton & Eunice Warren,	April 4, 1790
Samuel Flagg & Polly Wyles,	Nov. 28, 1790
Shubael Griswold & Sarah Stanley,	Jan. 6, 1791
Capt. Moses Forbes & widow Mercy Wright,	1792
Samuel Pitkin & Sally Parsons,	July 25, 1792
Solomon Ensign & Elizabeth Chandler,	Oct. 11, 1792
John (?) Farrington & Ruth Deming,	Dec. 29, 1792
Enoch Kimball & Polly Kilbourn,	Dec. 1, 1793
George Hills & Anne Warren,	March 9, 1794
Daniel Roberts & Mabel Easton,	July 8, 1794
Elijah Fuller & Hannah Chandler,	Sept. 21, 1794
Solomon Warren & Kate Kennedy,	Oct. 12, 1794
Josiah White & Rebecca Hills,	Dec. 2, 1794
Benjamin Wicks & Nabby Roberts,	Oct. 21, 1795
Col. Jon. Wells & widow Mabel Hill,	Jan. 20, 1795
Jonah Williams & Phene (?) Forbes,	Jan. 26, 1795
Ozias Williams & Anne Smith,	Sept. 18, 1797
Ebenezer Hills & Elizabeth Kennedy,	Jan. 17, 1798

CROMWELL.

MIDDLESEX COUNTY.

The town of Cromwell was incorporated as late as 1851. The Congregational Church in Cromwell was organized in 1715, being then the second church of Middletown.

Records of the marriages performed by the Rev. Edward Eells, pastor of Congregational Church in Cromwell, from 1738 to 1776. Also marriages performed by Rev. Gershom Bulkley from 1776 to 1800:

Gideon Sage & Bushua White,	Oct. 10, 1738
Andrew Warner & Martha Willcock,	Oct. 19, 1738
Edmund Herrison & Anne Sage,	Dec. 14, 1738
Jonathan Sage & Hannah Gipson,	Feb. 14, 1738
Timothy Sage & Mary Warner,	May 23, 1739
Ebenezer Clark & Ann Warner,	Sept. 20, 1739
Nathaniel Eells & Martha Stow,	Oct. 29, 1739
Jonathan Riley & Martha White,	Nov. 15, 1739
John Johnson & Mercy Maker,	Nov. 19, 1739
Mark Hodgkees & Margaret Crowfoot,	Dec. 25, 1739
Elisha Willcock & Sarah Willcocks,	Nov. 20, 1740
Thomas Savage, Jr., & Martha Whitmore,	Jan. 1, 1740
Elisha Stocking & Margery Willcock,	Feb. 5, 1740
Stephen Johnson & Mary Sage,	March 5, 1741
Peter (servant to Samuel Ward) & Peg (servant to Samuel Frary),	April 2, 1741
John Warner & Rachel Burlison,	April 14, 1741
Moses Bush & Susannah Johnson, by Joseph White, Jr.,	May 14, 1741
Ruben Shaler & Abigail Stow,	Nov. 12, 1741
Francis Willcock, Jr., & Rachel Willcock,	Dec. 11, 1741
Benjamin Cornwell & widow Hannah Willcock,	Feb. 25, 1741
William Willcock & Rebeccah Willcock,	March 11, 1742
Josiah Willcock & Ann Butler,	May 27, 1742
John Brown & Mary Arnal,	Oct. 25, 1742
Ebenezer Ranny, Jr., & Margaret Ranny,	Nov. 25, 1742
Jeremiah Ranny & Martha Stow,	Dec. 30, 1742
Nathaniel Eells & Allis White,	Feb. 9, 1742
Jonathan Stow & Abiah Sage,	March 24, 1743
Ebenezer Savage & Rebecca Ranney,	April 14, 1743

Joseph Kirbey & Easter Willcock,	June 15, 1743
John Cole & Abigail Crowfoot,	Aug. 18, 1743
Daniel Burlison & Mary Burlison,	Sept. 20, 1744
Edward Shepard & Hepzibah Johnson,	Nov. 8, 1744
Daniel Warner & Lucy Stow,	Feb. 28, 1744
Elisha Williams & Mary Barlow,	Feb. 28, 1744
Solomon Sage & Hannah Kirbey,	April 25, 1745
George Ranney & Hannah Sage,	Jan. 23, 1745
Samuel Hall & Elizabeth Willcock,	Feb. 20, 1745
Joseph Cornwel & Mindwell Lane,	Feb. 20, 1745
Gideon Hale & Sarah Watts,	March 27, 1746
William Powel & Rebeckah White, by Justice White,	July 31, 1746
John Sage, 3d, & Ann Ranney, by Rev. Mr. Bartlett,	Aug. 7, 1746
Elijah Willcox & Sarah Churchil,	May 28, 1747
Daniel Bartlet & Lidea Sage,	June 19, 1747
Jonathan Stocking & Sarah Willcox,	Oct. 8, 1747
Timothy Cornwel & Martha Burr,	Dec. 2, 1747
Thomas Ranney, Jr., & Mary Little,	Feb. 25, 1747
John Bacon & Rhoda Gould,	March 1, 1748
John Gill & Ruth Johnson,	March 3, 1748
Lewis Samuel Sage & Deborah Ranney,	May 24, 1748
Fenner Ward & Martha Bacon,	June 27, 1748
Joseph Barns & Hannah Stow,	Oct. 6, 1748
Samuel Savage & Sarah Kirbey,	Oct. 18, 1748
Elijah Tuel & Lucy Lewis,	Jan. 17, 1748
Israel Willcox & Martha Barns,	April 4, 1749
Aaron White & Sarah Olmsteed, by Mr. Williams of Hartford,	April 6, 1749
Francis Whitmore & Rachel White,	July 13, 1749
Asa Belding & Mille Butler,	Oct. 12, 1749
Thomas Francis & Susannah Cornwell,	Feb. 12, 1749
Allen Sage & Abigail Willard,	May 3, 1750
James Olmsted & Mary White,	May 24, 1750
Hanover Snow & Martha Smith,	May 30, 1750
Nathaniel Chauncey & Mary Stocking (widow),	Jan. 10, 1750
Daniel Roberts & Ruth Clark,	Jan. 1, 1751
J or Z-naWillcox & Jemima Willcox,	Nov. 14, 1751
Joseph Star, Jr., & Tabatha Thayer,	Jan. 23, 1752

—— Roberts & —— Tryal   Dec. 18, 1751

_____ *Baion ? & ____ Adkins,*   *April 2, 1752*
John Cotton & Bathsheba Sage (widow),   June 3, 1752
Jacob Hall & Susannah White,   July 2, 1752
Moses Hale & Mary Edwards,   July 29, 1752
Daniel Kirbey & Lucrecia Porter,   Oct. 26, 1752
Willet Ranney & Mary Butler,   Nov. 30, 1752
Moses Willcox & Desire Ranney,   March 22, 1753
John Stevens & Sheba Slee,   April 19, 1753
Francio Whitomoro & Sibel White,   April 19, 1753
Henry Johnson & Abiah White,   July 10, 1753
Epraim Crofoot & widow Mary Williams,   July 26, 1753
Hugh White & Mary Clark,   Aug. 23, 1753
Samuel Frary & Abigail Sumner, *Edward*   Nov. 1, 1753
Samson & Cloe (negro servants to ~~Edwin~~ Eells),

                                                Nov. 7, 1753
Amos Johnson & Mary Kirbey,   Nov. 8, 1753
Henry Mitchel & _____ _____,   Nov. 15, 1753
Jabez Miller & Eunice Ward,   Jan. 17, 1754
Zacheus Bawn & Mercy Hubard,   Feb. 28, 1754
Nathaniel Hamlin & Lucrecia Ranney,   March 16, 1755
Nathaniel Bacon, Jr., & Ann Latemore,   March 20, 1755
George Butler & Anne Plumb,   April 10, 1755
Samuel Sage & Prudence Hurlbut,   April 10, 1755
Jonathan Savage & Elizabeth Ranney,   April 17, 1755
Elisha Savage & Thankful Johnson,   May 6, 1755
John Cornwell & Elizabeth Smith,   Aug. 27, 1755
Nathaniel Churchil, Jr., & Elizabeth Sage,   Sept. 25, 1755
Daniel Russel & Rebeckah Stow,   Oct. 15, 1755
Darius Weston & Lydia Bow,   Oct. 15, 1755
Aaron Hand & Sarah Willard,   Nov. 25, 1755
Thomas Kirby & Lucy Stocking,   Nov. 27, 1755
Stephen Scofel & Elizabeth Eggleston,   April 29, 1756
Robert Stephenson & Lois Ranney,   May 11, 1756
William Savage, 3d, & Martha Gipson,   May 20, 1756
Dr. Eliot Rawson & Mrs. Sarah Russel,   June 16, 1756
Charles Birn & Desire Johnson,   June 17, 1756
Elijah Johnson & Mary Hall,   July 19, 1756
Solomon Sage & Lois Willcox,   Sept. 14, 1756
Abraham Plumb & Ann White,   Nov. 17, 1756
Nathaniel Ranney & widow Thankful Willard,

                                                Nov. 25, 1756

Jehiel Williams & Ann Edwards,	Jan. 16, 1757
Thomas Goodwin & Abigail Stocking,	Oct. 28, 1757
John Dunkin & Thankful Lewis,	April 18, 1757
Amos Sawyer *Savage* & Sarah Montague,	June 2, 1757
Dr. Aaron Roberts & widow Hepzibah Shepard of Mass.,	July 21, 1757
Jonathan Steal & Bethiah Stow,	Aug. 8, 1757
Daniel Stocking & Bethiah Kirbey,	Sept. 21, 1757
Benjamin Bulkley & Susannah Kirbey,	Nov. 9, 1757
Elisha Stocking & Thankful Butler,	Feb. 4, 1758
William Marks & Easter Learning,	March 9, 1758
Joseph Ward & Lucy Butler,	March 16, 1758
Nathaniel Gilbert & widow Prudence Savage,	May 18, 1758
Josiah Savage & Sarah Stow,	July 13, 1758
John Robbens & Mary Savage,	Dec. 20, 1758
Peter Goodrich & Barsheba Miller,	Jan. 11, 1759
Fortunatus Tayter & Mary Whitemore *Savage*	April 12, 1759
Elijah Wright & Lucy Butler,	Jan. 31, 1760
Nathaniel Savage & Grace Stocking,	Jan. 31, 1760
Stephen Jankins & Marah Ranney,	March 20, 1760
John Scovel & Lucy Bradley,	Sept. 25, 1760
Elias White & Prudence Savage,	Nov. 13, 1760
Gideon Warner & Freelove Stow,	Nov. 13, 1760
Ebenezer Beckus & Mercy Edwards,	Nov. 25, 1760
Jacob White & Lucy Savage,	Nov. 25, 1760
William Southmaid & Elizabeth Green,	Nov. 27, 1760
Solomon Bill & Sarah Sizer,	Jan. 19, 1761
Theophilus Cande (?) & Rebekah Churchill,	May 28, 1761
John Gould & widow Prudence Gilbert,	July 5, 1761
Ashbel Burnham & Hannah Sage,	July 19, 1761
Simon Dewolf & Tabatha Booth,	Aug. 18, 1761
Ebenezer Roberts & Prissilla Hubberd,	Aug. 27, 1761
Stephen Van Overwork & Mary Warner,	Oct. 8, 1761
Joseph Brewer & Jane Derid,	Oct. 22, 1761
John Smith & Lucy Montigue,	Oct. 22, 1761
Solomon Stow & Ellis Abit,	Oct. 22, 1761
Giles Barns & Catharine Stow,	Nov. 11, 1761
James Masters & Mary Eaglestone,	Nov. 12, 1761
Samuel Guild & Abigail Doolittle,	Jan. 28, 1762
Rev. Benjamin Boardman & widow Ann Bowers,	Feb. 11, 1762

Comfort Butler & Sibel Ranney,	May 2, 1762
Joseph Akins & Mary Sage,	May 2, 1762
Edward Prouty & Elizabeth Warner,	Sept. 27, 1762
Churchil Edwards, Jr., & Lucy Eells,	Oct. 14, 1762
William Savage, 4th, & Linthol Eells,	Oct. 14, 1762
Dolphen Ely & Bathsheba Abro (negroes),	Oct. 28, 1762
Joseph Frary, Jr., & Elizabeth Kirbey,	Dec. 22, 1762
Gideon Hale & Mary White,	Dec. 23, 1762
Edward Eells, Jr., & Sarah Edwards,	Jan. 27, 1763
Jered Shepard & Abigail Edwards,	March 8, 1763
John Robenson & Mary Strickland,	March 10, 1763
John Stiley & Mary Rach,	July 11, 1763
Daniel Willcox, Jr., & Susannah Porter,	Sept. 22, 1763
David Bechley & Hepzibah Willcox,	Sept. 22, 1763
John Booth & Elizabeth Woodward,	Nov. 8, 1763
George Kilborn & Abigail Peirpoint,	Nov. 10, 1763
Samuel Markey & Abigail Gilbert,	Nov. 10, 1763
Josiah & Mary (negroes),	Jan. 11, 1764
Collin Roberts & Hannah Sears,	Feb. 9, 1764
Joseph Colhoone & widow Sibbel Whittemore,	March 20, 1764
John Bartlit & Margery Sage,	April 4, 1764
Josiah Roberts & Mary Fezey,	June 25, 1764
Ephraim Williams & Ruth Butler,	Oct. 5, 1764
Lot Benton & Katharine Lyman,	Oct. 12, 1764
Ruben Plumb & Mary Shepard,	Nov. 29, 1764
Dr. John Osborn & Ruth White,	Dec. 26, 1764
William Parmaly & widow Mary Johnson,	Dec. 27, 1764
Richard Hawley & Prudence White,	Feb. 6, 1765
William Strickland & Martha Savage,	Feb. 17, 1765
Eli Butler & Rachel Stocking,	Feb. 26, 1765
Samuel Treat & Lydea Stocking,	April 2, 1765
Thomas Ward, Jr., & Mary Johnson,	April 25, 1765
Jonathan Frary & Dorothy Stow,	May 26, 1765
Elijah Miller & Abijah Eells,	Sept. 22, 1765
Lott Pease & Sarah Miller,	Oct. 10, 1765
Aaron Evets & Sarah Stocking,	Oct. 15, 1765
Francis Cornwell & Eunice Tryal,	Oct. 28, 1765
Samuel Cooly & Experience Tubb,	Nov. 27, 1765
Stephen Savage & Triphena Riley,	March 14, 1765
Amos Wilkenson & Ruth Willcox,	March 14, 1765
Zebulon Stocking & Martha Edwards	*April 16, 1765*

John Gains & Submit Ranney,	Jan. 30, 1766
Thomas Selew & Patience White,	Feb. 9, 1766
Nathaniel Smith & Sarah Ranney,	April 21, 1766
David Blin & Deborah White,	May 13, 1766
Elisha Treat & Mary Willcox,	May 29, 1766
Joab Bowers & Jane Clark,	June 5, 1766
John Willcox & Eunice Newton,	Oct., 1766
Samuel Cooper & Martha Stow,	Oct., 1766
Joseph Smith & Margaret Gaylord,	Nov. 12, 1766
Elias Dickinson & Ruth Savage,	Dec. 25, 1766
Elixander Ross & Mary Bibbens,	Jan. 28, 1767
Nathaniel Alcot & Lydia Churchil,	Feb. 4, 1767
Nathaniel Hamlin & Abigail Moore,	March 5, 1767
Moses Buck & Lucy Warner,	April 21, 1767
Samuel Sizer & Abigail Mitchell,	April 30, 1767
John Collins & Sarah Gross,	June 9, 1767
Joseph Sharp & Elizabeth Thraker *sh (?)* (Dutch),	July 15, 1767
—— Wright & Martha Butler,	Nov. 4, 1767
Isaac Washborn & Bethiah Lathley,	Dec. 31, 1767
John Hart & Hepzibah Sage,	Jan. 28, 1768
Elisha Spencer & Rachel Ranney,	April 11, 1768
Samuel Stow & Naomi Olmsted,	April 28, 1768
Timothy Sage, Jr., & Abigail Riley,	May 5, 1768
Samuel Cady & widow Mary Bale,	May 12, 1768
Samuel Blake & widow Phœbe Antverd,	June 1, 1768
William Sizer & Abigail Willcox,	July 27, 1768
Daniel Antverd & Phœbe Hamlin,	Sept. 29, 1768
Job Talbut & Elizabeth Payton,	Oct. 10, 1768
Joseph Porter & Huldah Willcox,	Oct. 13, 1768
Aaron Robenson & Deborah Sage,	Nov. 3, 1768
Elisha Willcox & Abigail Ranney,	Dec. 1, 1768
Edward Shepard & Ann Sage,	Jan. 8, 1769
Archabell Steward & Elizabeth Wilson,	Jan. 19, 1769
Samuel Stocking & Elizabeth Scovel,	Feb. 2, 1769
Jonathan Kirby & Lucy Burgis,	March 1, 1769
Eliakim Ufford & Christian White,	April 23, 1769
—— Barns & —— Allen,	May 18, 1769
Josiah Brainard & Lois Barns,	May 18, 1769
David Robenson & Mary Sage,	April, 1769
Timothy Gipson & Hannah Sage,	Jan. 10, 1770
Edward Hamlin Jr. & Patience Hilton	*May 19, 1768*
Abraham Ranney & Meriam Treat	*Oct. 26, 1769*

John French & Abigail Sage,   March 28, 1770
Edward Eells, Jr., & widow Abigail Brandigee, April 26,1770
Nathaniel Gilbert, Jr., & Cloe Ranney,   April 29, 1770
Benjamin Ames & Mary Stephens,   May 3, 1770
David Hull & Esther Rockwell,   May 16, 1770
Lamberton Cooper & Elizabeth Brown,   May 27, 1770
Seth Higbe & Desire Dolittle,   Aug. 27, 1770
Giles Sage & Esther Hall,   Sept. 3, 1770
Thomas Darrel & Sarah Camp,   Oct. 15, 1770
Nathaniel Cornwell, Jr., & Mary Mildrum,   Nov. 1, 1770
Richard Hamlin & Mehitable Cook,   Nov. 4, 1770
Rev. James Eells & Mrs. Mary Johnson,   Nov. 7, 1770
Rev. Samuel Eells & Mrs. Hannah Butler,   Nov. 7, 1770
Bennet Eaglestone & Phœbe Alverd,   Nov. 17, 1770
Cornelius Cornwell & Elizabeth Bullvich,   Dec. 30, 1770
William Cotton & Katharine Bask,   April 18, 1771
Samuel Spencer & Martha Eells,   May 23, 1771
Nathan Pettis & Abigail Gilerease,   May 23, 1771
Isaiah Thompson & Lydea Norton,   May 30, 1771
Eliphelet Hubbard & Abigail Johnson,   May 30, 1771
Seth Goodrich & Eunice Wright,   June 6, 1771
Gideon Chridenden & Esther Cone,   June 6, 1771
John Bassel & Bethiah Gross,   Sept. 5, 1771
Daniel Wilcox, Jr. & Mercy Gypson,   Nov. 7, 1771
Daniel Kirbey & Margarit Cogswell,   Nov. 14, 1771
Samuel Willcox & Hannah Tharasker,   Nov. 28, 1771
Joseph Stow, Jr. & Lydia Hubbord,   April 2, 1772
Daniel Edwards & Jemima Hubbord,   April 2, 1772
Ruben Sage & Lucy Ranney,   Aug. 16, 1772
Jonathan Stow & Abigail Eells,   Aug. 20, 1772
Joseph Dreggs & Cloe Viets,   Aug. 26, 1772
Deacon Samuel Smith of Sanderfield & Thankful
    Sage,   Oct. 14, 1772
Nathaniel Savage & Mary Stow,   Oct. 25, 1772
Asher Riley & Rebecca Sage,   Oct. 25, 1772
Nathan Sage & Hulday Ranney,   Dec. 24, 1772
John Eells & Elizabeth Lord,   March 3, 1773
Zebulon Stow & Rositta Riley,   April 22, 1773
Oliver Cotton & Elizabeth Dolittle,   May 6, 1773
Jonathan Gaylord & Elisabeth Goodwin,   May 9, 1773

Josiah Willcox & ——— Treat,   Sept., 1773
Adner Cole & Rebeccah Boardman,   Oct. 19, 1773
——— Scovil & Hannah Frary,   Oct. 21, 1773
Hezekiah Baley & Hannah Banks,   Oct. 21, 1773
William Cole & Sarah Preston,   Nov. 25, 1773
Seth Willcox & Sarah Harriss,   May 25, 1774
Joseph Cone & Sarah Starr,   May 27, 1774
Edward Smith & Sarah Moore,   Aug. 25, 1774
Daniel Savage & Martha Norton,   Sept. 8, 1774
Hezekiah Sage & Mary Gipson,   Sept. 19, 1774
Thomas Johnson, Jr., & May Chauncey,   Nov. 3, 1774
John Clark & Sarah Wenthrop,   Nov. 10, 1774
John Swift & Abigail Sage,   Nov. 24, 1774
Edward Little & Rhoda Ranney,   Feb. 23, 1775
Nathaniel Chauncey & widow Susannah Gilbert,
                                            May 24, 1775
Samuel Peck & ——— Latamore,   Dec., 1775
Dr. Solomon Savage & Naomi Kirbey,   Dec., 1775
Enoch Sage & Sibel Sage,   Jan. 1, 1776
Timothy Cornal & Amy Sage,   Feb. 8, 1776
Nathaniel Eells & Hulday White,   Feb. 22, 1776
Rev. David Perry of Harrington & Jerusha Lord of
    Middletown,   Aug. 20, 1776

NAMES OF THOSE MARRIED BY GERSHOM BULKLEY SINCE JUNE
17, 1778.

Normond Morrison & Abigail Chauncey,   June 28, 1778
Joseph Ranney & Ruth White,   June 29, 1778
Isaac Willits & Submit Sage,   Aug. 16, 1778
Timothy White & Mehetable Smith,   Aug. 20, 1778
Ely Leavensworth & Sarah Eliot,   Dec. 23, 1778
Samuel Savage, Jr., & Mary Cornwell,   Dec. 27, 1778
John Sage & Elisabeth Burnham,   Dec. 29, 1778
William Bulkley & Mable Wilcox,   Feb. 25, 1779
Gideon Savage & Sarah White,   March 2, 1779
Elishama Brandigee & Lucy Weston,   March 10, 1779
Nathaniel Sage, Jr., & Lucretia Burt,   April 8, 1779
Jeremiah Goodrich & Prudence Gould,   April 29, 1779
Epaphras Sage & Elisabeth Wells Ranney,   Sept. 30, 1779
John Mildrum & Lucretia Kirbey,   Oct. 14, 1779

Casper Hamblin & Elizabeth Dewey,	Feb. 14, 1780
Samuel Sage & Elener Edwards,	May 11, 1780
James Johnson & Hephzibah Hubbard,	June 1, 1780
Joseph Shepherd & Sibbel Kirbey,	Dec. 7, 1780
Conshant Griswould & Rebeccah Boardman,	Dec. 27, 1780
Comfort Butler & Sarah Wells,	Dec. 31, 1780
Stephen Williams & Elisabeth Churchil,	Feb. 18, 1781
Elias Selden & Ruth Kirby,	May 23, 1781
Reuben Towner & Dorothy Smith,	June 7, 1781
Henry Doxy & Elisabeth Chilson,	Aug. 15, 1781
William Hamlin & Lucy Kirby,	Oct. 18, 1781
Timothy Hart & Abigail Brandigee,	Nov. 13, 1781
Simeon Savage & Mary Gaylord,	Nov. 14, 1781
Abijah Wright & Elisabeth Savage,	Dec. 9, 1781
Luther Savage & Jerusha Smith,	Dec. 13, 1781
Cheney Gaylord & Mary White,	May 16, 1782
Ozias Willcox & Mary Lusk,	May 30, 1782
John Cande & Mary Eells,	May 30, 1782
Charles Beard & Persis Brandigee,	Aug. 20, 1782
Benjamin Dowd & Mary Savage,	Nov. 21, 1782
Leverit Bishop & Sibble White,	Nov. 28, 1782
Richard Dowd & Rebeccah Savage,	Jan. 27, 1783
Samuel Grannis & Charity Johnson,	July 25, 1783
Jonathan Steal & Sary(?)Ann Savage,	Aug. 28, 1783
Daniel Robenson & Thankful Sage,	Sept. 25, 1783
Giles Sage & Anna Wright,	Oct. 9, 1783
Joseph Riley & Elisabeth Williams,	Dec. 25, 1783
Elisha Tryon & Mable White,	Feb. 2, 1784
Dr. Daniel Lad & Lydia Ann Eliot,	Feb. 4, 1784
Richard Treat & Hannah Sage,	June 3, 1784
Edward Coy & Flavia Gipson,	Aug. 4, 1784
Allen Gilbert & Lucy Ward (Newfield),	Aug. 24, 1784
Zacheus Stow & Rachel Roberts,	Sept. 6, 1784
Isaac Gridley & Elisabeth Smith,	Sept. 26, 1784
Abel Porter & Hannah Elliot,	Nov. 4, 1784
Hezekiah Ranney & widow Martha Stocking,	Nov. 4, 1784
Ebed Stocking & Olive Sage,	Nov. 11, 1784
Samuel Riley & Mary Savage,	Nov. 11, 1784
John Hamlin & Caroline Ranney,	Nov. 14, 1784
Eliphalt Willcox & Abigail Shepherd,	Nov. 18, 1784

Joel Burral & Martha Robinson about 1782

William White & Abigail Stow,   Feb. 5, 1785
Jacob Colban & Rositta Robinson,   Feb. 8, 1785
Simeon Sage & Olivet Cadnay (?),   March 25, 1785
Simeon Ranney & Mary Savage,   Aug. 21, 1785
Thomas Clark & Abigail Stocking,   Sept. 16, 1785
Elijah Atwood of East Haddam & Esther Whiting
    of Chatham, *of Ashford*   Sept. 18, 1785
Nathaniel Loomis *of Ashford* & Rebeckah White, Feb. 7, 1786
Gideon Butler & Betsey Sage,   March 3, 1786
Solomon Dunham, Jr., & Mary Kirby of Worthington,
                                                 May 4, 1786
David Edwards & Rosanna Hubbard,   Aug. 3, 1786
Simeon North & Lucy Savage,   Sept. 10, 1786
Naboth Lewis & Phœbe Roberts,   Nov. 2, 1786
Pelitiah Buck & Hannah Sage,   Nov. 2, 1786
John Pelton & Jerusha Sage,   Nov. 3, 1786
Ozias Deming *of Sandisfield* & Hannah Sage,   Jan. 31, 1787
John Williams & Jerusha Stow,   May 6, 1787
William Cornwell & Jane Cotton of Middletown,
                                                June 21, 1787
Benjamin Butler & Polly Treadway of Middletown,
                                                June 22, 1787
Lemuel Sage & Louise Savage,   Aug. 2, 1787
Samuel White & Anna Merrow,   Oct. 3, 1787
Nicholas Fox of East Hartford & Sarah Stocking,
                                                Oct. 14, 1787
Amos Treat & Rebeckah Stow of Westfield,   Dec. 26, 1787
Amos Savage & Louis Willcox,   Jan. 2, 1788
Solomon Sage *of Steeney* & Anna Williams,   Jan. 27, 1788
Richard Butler & Mary Sage,   Jan. 31, 1788
Hezekiah Warner & Lucy Stocking,   April 30, 1788
Reuben Eells & Hannah Brooks of Wethersfield,
                                                Sept. 7, 1788
Jacob Bliss & Rebeckah Goodrich,   Oct. 16, 1788
James Willcox & Joanna Gibson,   Nov. 10, 1788
Ephraim Goodrich & Deborah Thomas,   Dec. 4, 1788
George Butler & Mary Stephens,   Feb. 26, 1789
William Rowland *of Hartford* & Sarah Smith,   April 12, 1789
Elisha Hurlbut & Cloe Savage,   Sept. 28, 1789
Stephen Savage & Lucy Stow,   Nov. 1, 1789

Timothy Savage & Sarah Collins,	Nov. 26, 1789
Daniel Arnold & Louis Ranney,	Nov. 26, 1789
Abner Kirby & Anna Plumb,	Nov. 29, 1789
Samuel Stocking & Susannah Morrison,	March 16, 1790
Giles Savage & ~~Erby~~ *Olive* Smith,	March 14, 1790
Isaac Buck *Brush* & Sally Cheney, *of Chatam*	March 25, 1790
John White & Ruth Ranney,	March 31, 1790
Hezekiah Kirby & Lucretia Stocking,	May 2, 1790
William Ranney & Olive Hamblin,	June 20, 1799
Lewis S. Sage & Lucy Smith,	July 18, 1790
Eleazer Stocking & Dorothy *Howard*	Aug. 12, 1790
Capt. Thomas Goodwin & Lucy Harrison,	Oct. 24, 1790
Isaac Holister, *of Glastonbury* & Abigail Savage,	Nov. 11, 1790
Ashbell Butler & Sarah Williams,	April 5, 1791
Zebulon Penfield & Prudence Dixon of Chatham,	
	May 14, 1791
William Stocking & Anna Alcott, *of Hartford*	June 9, 1791
Abraham Benton & Sarah Kirby,	July 24. 1791
Samuel Tolcott of Bolton & Sarah Smith,	Sept. 8, 1791
John Smith & Lucy Ranney,	Oct. 10, 1791
Jehiel Williams, Jr., & Martha Spencer,	Nov. 10, 1791
Asa Sage & Sarah Ells,	Nov. 24, 1791
Asa ~~Stephon~~ *Shepard* & Martha Smith,	Jan. 12, 1792
Seth Willcox & Hannah Willcox,	Jan. 19, 1792
James Miller, Jr., & Lucy Butler,	March 8, 1792
Israel Kellsey, Jr., & Martha Stocking,	July 8, 1792
Reuben Kirby & Molle Butler,	Aug. 2, 1792
Capt, Zebulon Stow & Hannah Warner,	Oct. 24, 1792
Marshall Pelton & Betsey Sage,	Jan. 3, 1793
Robert Blair of Blanford & Polly Kellsey,	Jan. 17, 1793
Eben Dudly & Hannah Goodrich,	Feb. 28, 1793
Capt. William Sage & Abigail White,	March 21, 1793
Samuel Kirby & Abigail Sage,	April 21, 1793
Phenas Samuel Landow & Esther Savage,	May 8, 1793
James Porter & Margerey Stocking,	Sept. 4, 1793
Sylvester Savage & Mary Robbarts,	Oct. 10, 1793
J—— Goodsilb & Hannah Willcox,	Oct. 15, 1793
Elisha Stocking & Susannah Hamblin,	Dec. 15, 1793
Elijah Stocking, *of Chatham* & Molly Sage,	Jan. 2, 1794
Eleazer Savage & Percis Willcox,	Jan. 9, 1794

Moses Savage & Dorothy Bulkley,   Jan. 16, 1794
William Jones & Hannah Sage,   Jan. 23, 1794
Josiah Sage & Sarah Savage,   Feb. 17, 1794
Euclid Elliott of New London & Abigail Starr, May 11, 1794
Asahel Hough of Meriden & Abigail Bacon,   May 18, 1794
Samuel Eells & Anna Smith, *of Glastonbury*   July 20, 1794
Abner Smith, Jr., & Anna Brainard,   Aug. 24, 1794
Stephen Webster of Hartford & Prudence Butler,
                                                   Sept. 29, 1794
Wells Kellog & Polly Sage,   Nov. 12, 1794
Freeman Collins & Lucy White,   Nov. 27, 1794
Zebulon Stow, Jr., & Hannah Spencer,   Nov. 27, 1794
Siras Wilcox & Huldah Stocking,   March 29, 1795
Zebulon Kirby & Louisa Gibson,   May 3, 1795
Elizer White & Hannah Savage,   May 4, 1795
Moses Bulkley & Patty Arnold,   Aug. 23, 1795
Ebenezer Hunt, *of Bolton* & Mary Smith,   Oct. 15, 1795
Joseph White & Matty *Haskill or Hasgill*   Oct. 18, 1795
Levi Edwards, *of Stepney* & Rozitta Butler,   Oct. 26, 1795
William Stow & Esther Savage,   Nov. 5, 1795
Timothy Brigden & Naomi Savage,   Nov. 5, 1795
Jabez Brainard & Abigail Williams,   Nov. 15, 1795
Benjamin Willcox & Rachel Willcox,   April 6, 1796
William Stow & Margaret Gaylord,   June 12, 1796
David Edwards & Mary Wells,   Sept. 8, 1796
Daniel Southmaid & Patience Selew,   Dec. 1, 1796
Seth Belden & Sally Thomas,   Feb. 5, 1797
Samuel Latimer & Anna Stocking,   April 16, 1797
Enos Ingraham of Suffield & Olive Thomas,   Oct. 1, 1797
William Smith & Betsy Hosgill, *Haskell or Hasgill* Oct. 15, 1797
Jonathan Crittenden & Rebecca Blin,   April 8, 1798
Isaac Webber & Mary Goodrich,   June 26, 1798
Nathaniel Smith, Jr., & Hannah Barton,   Aug. 5, 1798
Jonathan Gaylord, Jr., & Polly Thomas,   Aug. 9, 1798
Robert Johnson & Lucy Wilcox,   Sept. 9, 1798
Phineas Davis & Sally Smith,   Sept. 16, 1798
Daniel Evets of Guilford & widow Mary Kirby, Jan. 22, 1799
Simon Hubbard & Cloe Williams,   Sept. 29, 1799
Seth Belden & Sarah Smith,   Feb. 2, 1800

BRANFORD.

NEW HAVEN COUNTY.

Branford was settled in 1644 under New Haven jurisdiction. The Congregational Church dates from the same year. The following are all the marriages recorded on the church book to 1800:

MARRIAGES BY REV. ABRAHAM PIERSON.

George Adams & widow Bradfield,	Sept. 5, 1651
Daniel Swaine & ~~Dorothy~~ *Dorcas* Rose	Jan. 26, 1653
John Lyman of Hartford & ~~Dorens~~ *Dorcas* Plum of Bran-	
ford,	Jan. 12, 1654
Francis Linsley & Susanna C*ULPEPPER*,	June 24, 1655
John Linsley & Sarah Pond,	July 2, 1656
Edward H~~istcrook~~ *HITCHCOCK* & Frances England,	May 20, 1656
Thomas Hopewell & Time ——, *(INDIANS)*	May 22, 1656
Thomas Linsley & Hannah Nettleton,	July 10, 1656
Samuel Ward & Maria Carter,	Jan. 1, 1658
John Robbins & Maria Abbott,	Nov. 4, 1659
John Whitehead & Martha Bradfield,	March 9, 1661
John Davenport & Abigail Pierson,	Nov. 27, 1662
Thomas Pierson & Maria Harrison,	Nov. 27, 1662
Jonathan Betts & Maria Ward,	Nov. 4, 1662
Michael B~~arnes~~ *PANER* & Elizabeth Butler,	Dec. 2, 1662
Samuel Pond & Mirriam Blatchley, *CHARLES*	Jan. 5, 1669
Jonathan Rose (?) & ~~Charley Ward~~ *DECIVERED*,	Jan. 5, 1669
John Robbins & Jane Tilleson,	June 23, 1670
Peter Tyler & Deborah Swaine,	Nov. 20, 1671
Noah Rogers & Elizabeth Taintor,	April 8, 1673
John Frisbie & Ruth Barnes,	Dec. 20, 1674
Samuel Bradfield & Sarah Graves,	June 27, 1677
John Nash & Elizabeth Howd,	Aug. 22, 1677

BY REV. SAMUEL RUSSELL.

Thomas Gutsill & Sarah Heminway,	June 4, 1684
John Butler & Hannah Potter,	Nov. 17, 1684
Peter Tyler, Sr., & Hannah Whitehead,	Dec. 25, 1688

William Luddington & Mary Whitehead,	June, 1690
Abraham Howd & Elizabeth Maltbie,	March 14, 1697
Samuel ~~Hannington~~ *HARRINGTON* & Hannah Barnes,	July 2?, 1698
John Collins & widow Dorcas Tainter,	March 6, 1699
Jonathan Barker & Mary Wardell,	June 13, 1700
John Barnes & Dorothy Stent,	Aug. 28, 1700
Daniel Maltbie & Esther Moss,	Oct. 27, 1702
John Rose of Branford & Hannah Williams of Kilenworth,	Dec. 9, 1702
John Harrison & Rebecca Truesdell,	Dec. 24, 1702
Edward Frisbie & Martha Pardee,	Dec. 30, 1702
Samuel Harrington & Hannah Rose,	Jan. 5, 1703
Ebenezer Frisbie & Hannah Page,	April 21, 1703
John Frisbie & Susanna *Henbury,*	April 21, 1703
Samuel Pond & Abigail Goodrich,	June 8, 1704
John Whitehead & Mehetible Bishop,	Aug. 9, 1704
Isaac Tyler & Abigail Pond,	Nov. 6, 1704
Benjamin Howd & Elizabeth Whitehead,	Oct. 1, 1705
Joseph Moss & Abigail Russell,	1716
John Baldwin & Joanna Goodrich,	1716
Jonathan Butler & Elizabeth Baldwin,	1717
Samuel Hoadley & Lydia Frisbie,	1720
Samuel Harrison & Hannah Hoadley,	1720
———— ———— & Ruth Rogers,	Nov. 28, 1720
William Goodrich & Dorcus Foot, *PALMER*	Nov. 30, 1720
Ephraim Parish & Bathsheba ~~Barnes,~~ *PALMER*	1729
Samuel Lewis & Mary Taintor,	1729
William Gould & Mary Whitehead,	Dec. 9, 1725
Micah ~~Barnes~~ *PALMER* & Jemima Farrington,	Dec. 25, 1725
Isaiah Butler & Martha Baldwin,	Dec. 28, 1725
~~Theoph~~ *STEPHEN* Barns & Martha *WHEADON* ,	Jan. 5, 1726
Daniel ~~Barnes~~ *PALMER* & Patience Foot,	Jan. 13, 1726
John Truesdale & Experience Maltby (?),	June 9, 1726
Jacob Johnson & Dorcas Linsley,	June 21, 1726
Moses Foote & Mary Byington,	June 27, 1726
Jonathan Harrison & Desire Farrington,	July 27, 1726
Jonas Richards & Mary ———,	Aug., 1726
Joseph Frizal & Lydia Rose,	Sept. 13, 1726
David Rose & Hannah *BARKER*	Nov. 23, 1726
J—— Russell & Jerusha ———,	Jan. 3, 1727

Caleb Parmerly & Jemima Harrison,	Jan., 1727
Benjamin Fenn—— & Mary Russell,	April 5, 1727
Timothy Pamerly & Desire ——,	May 3, 1727
John Williams & H—— —— of Wallingford,	May 11, 1727
John Read & Abigail Parmerly,	1727
Deacon Samuel Penfield & Bethia Rose, or Russell	1727
Benjamin Barns & Hannah Abbott,	Nov. 7, 1727
Ebenezer Johnson & Anna Barker,	Jan. 1, 1728
Joseph Elwell & Lydia Finch,	Jan., 1728
Benjamin Gailor & Jerusha Frisby,	Jan. 3, 1728
Joseph Harrison & Sarai Foot,	Jan. 8, 1729
Jonathan —— & Lydia Young,	Jan. 16, 1729
Benjamin Hand & —— Barnes Palmer	1729
Zachariah How & Mary Frisbie,	1729

BY REV. PHILEMON ROBBINS.

Noah Baldwin & Rebekah Frisbie,	March 21, 1733
Deacon Josiah Stevens & Mary Hoadley,	July 11, 1733
Nathaniel Palmer & Rebecca Tyler,	Sept. 11, 1733
David Parmelee & Patience Kirkum,	Nov. 28, 1733
Jonathan Byington & Hannah Mallery,	Dec. 5, 1733
Orchard (?) Guy & Mary Foot,	Dec. 5, 1733
Matthew Linsley & Rebecca Baldwin,	Jan. 2, 1734
Nathan Palmer & Rebecca Barker,	Jan. 10, 1734
Jacob Harrison & Sarah Wardell,	Jan. 24, 1734
Ichabod Foot & Hannah Harrison,	March 4, 1734
Joseph Frost & Mary Hoadley,	June 27, 1734
Peter Benedict of Ridgefield & Mary Parish,	Oct. 29, 1734
Ebenezer Linsley & Sarah Wilford,	Dec. 10, 1734
John Howd & Martha Hoadley,	Jan. 9, 1735
Admire Barker & Rebecca Kirkum,	Feb. 20, 1735
Samuel Page Jr. & Mary Rose,	Jan. 27, 1736
Jacob Carter & Elizabeth Coach,	March 9, 1736
Richard Darrow & Hannah Parish,	March 29, 1736
Moore & Modesty (negro servants of Mr. Foote),	
	May 31, 1736
Edward Carnody & Abigail Lodington,	July 19, 1736
Jack & Daphna (negro servants of Captain ——),	
	Aug. 20, 1736

Daniel Maltbie & Mary Harrison,   Sept. 16, 1736
John Blakiston & Rebecca Harrison,   Nov. 25, 1736
Josiah Pond & Abigail Harrison,   Dec. 9, 1736
Paul Cornwall & Mary Stroud,   Feb. 17, 1737
Isaac Tyler & Hannah Betts,   Feb. 24, 1737
John Barker & Sarah Russell,   March 16, 1737
Jacob Curtiss & Abigail Foote,   June 23, 1737
Josiah Foote & Susanna Frisbie,   June 23, 1737
Samuel Shelly & Sarah Hill,   Oct. 19, 1737
Joseph Tyler & Hannah Wardell,   Dec. 28, 1737
John Bray & Lydia Hoadley, *alias MARK*   April 28, 1737
Daniel Frisbie & Ruth Frisbie,   Jan. 24, 1738
Solomon Palmer & Mary Betts,   Feb. 9, 1738
James & Kate (negro servants of S. Foote),   ——
Benjamin Trull, i.e. *TRYON* & Lucy Wheadon,   April 25, 1738
Deacon John Peck & Martha Stent, *of Wallingford*   May 24, 1738
John Foot & Abigail Frisbie,   Aug. 16, 1738
Eleazur Stent & Sarah Coach,   Sept. 20, 1738
Timothy Johnson & Hannah Wheaden,   Nov. 30, 1738
Joseph Davin, Jr., of Litchfield & Elizabeth Bar-
    tholomew,   Dec. 14, 1738
Tom & Phillis (negro servants of Captain Sam),
                                                    Dec. 24, 1738
Joseph Hoadley & Abigail Bradfield,   Feb. 15, 1739
John Rose & Elizabeth Lodington,   March 15, 1739
Eliab & Peg (negro servants of John Blakiston), April, 1739
Demetrius Cook & Elizabeth Rogers,   April 26, 1739
Daniel Howd & Martha Maltbie,   May 9, 1739
Daniel Dunk & Sarah Tyler,   May 10, 1739
John Hall & Abigail Russell,   June 11, 1739
Deacon Samuel Todd & Esther Maltbie, *of New Haven* June 14, 1739
Stephen Foote & Hannah ~~Houd~~, *Howd,*   June 27, 1739
Elisha Frisbie & Rachel Levi,   July 5, 1739
Samuel Barnes & Mary Parmerly,   Aug. 2, 1739
Solomon Palmer & Abigail Curtiss,   Sept. 11, 1739
Abraham Page & Abigail Pond,   Nov. 22, 1739
William Hoadley, Jr., & Abigail Baldwin,   Dec. 20, 1739
Ezra Stone & Elizabeth Osborn, *both of Litchfield* March 18, 1740
Thomas Allen & Phebe Wardell,   April 10, 1740
John Robbins & Mary Tyler,   April 17, 1740

John Baldwin & Abigail Wardell,	April 20, 1740
Josiah Bartholomew & Lydia Harrington,	June 10, 1740
William Allen & Jemima Hoadley,	June 20, 1740
Rev. Thomas Clap & Madam Mary Saltonstall,	Nov. 9, 1740
John Swaine & Patience Page,	Aug. 27, 1741
Capt. Joseph Foot & Susanna Frisbie,	Sept. 8, 1741
Micah Palmer & Phebe Bartholomew,	March 5, 1741
John Fosdick & Hannah Hill,	Nov. 25, 1742
Benjamin Tyler & Elizabeth Page,	May 17, 1743
James Frisbie & Joanna Porter,	June 16, 1743
Daniel Lord & Elizabeth Palmer,	July 7, 1743
Jared Ingersoll & Hannah ~~Whitney~~ *Whiting*	Aug. 3, 1743
Samuel Maltbie & Abigail Wilford,	Oct. 13, 1743
Jonathan Towner & Mary Damons,	Nov. 10, 1743
John Rogers & Thankful Harrison,	Dec. 29, 1743
John Swaine, Jr., & Elizabeth Page,	March 22, 1744
John Tainter & Debora Monroe,	May 9, 1744
Yale Bishop & Sybel Gilbert, of *Wallingford*,	May 31, 1744
James Burgess & Sarah Dunks,	June 21, 1744
Abiel Page & Lydia Frizzle,	June 22, 1744
Oliver Thorp & Lydia Kirkum,	Sept. 11, 1744
Daniel Palmer & Hannah Frisbie,	Sept. 20, 1744
Jonathan Brown & Sarah Harrison,	Oct. 22, 1744
Rev. Thomas Canfield & Mary Russell,	Oct. 29, 1744
Daniel Russell & Rebecca Foster,	Nov. 15, 1744
Timothy Allen of East Haven and Sarah Palmerly,	Dec. 13, 1744
Timothy Plant & Lucy Parish,	Feb. 12, 1745
Joseph Wardell & Lois Frisbie,	May 30, 1745
Amos Morris & Lydia Camp of East Haven,	June 26, 1745
Ebenezer ~~Pierson~~ *Preston* & Martha Howd,	July 2, 1745
Nathaniel Frisbie & Abigail Harrison,	Oct. 25, 1745
Benjamin Barnes & Lydia Bray,	Oct. 28, 1745
Nathaniel Hoadley & Anna Scarrot,	Dec. 12, 1745
Amos Hitchcock *of New Haven* & Dorcas ——,	Jan. 9, 1746
Nathaniel Goodrich & Mary Pond,	Jan. 15, 1746
Samuel Maltbie, Jr., & Rebecca Foot,	Jan. 22, 1746
Benjamin Palmer & Patience ——,	Feb. 6, 1746
Samuel Baldwin & Hannah Hoadley,	April 15, 1746
Nathaniel Porter & Abigail Joselyn,	April 16, 1746

Gideon Goodrich & Abigail Barker,	June 19, 1746
Nathaniel Foot & Sarah Bears,	Jan. 5, 1747
Ebenezer Atwater & Mehitable Allen,	April 9, 1747
John Burgess & Hannah Tyler,	Aug. 17, 1747
Jonathan Harrison & Sarah Baldwin,	Aug. 20, 1747
Thomas Wheadon *of Sharon* & Mary Heath,	Sept. 8, 1747
John Sprague & Sarah Page,	Dec. 31, 1747
Stephen Wade & Abigail Hoadley,	Feb. 6, 1748
TimothyGoodrich & Sarah Foot,	March 24, 1748
David Leavit & Rebecca Camp *of East Haven*	April 27, 1748
Philip How & Elizabeth Pierre,	Sept. 7, 1748
Josiah Parish & Elizabeth Plant,	Sept. 21, 1748
Isaac Augers & Eunice Tyler,	Oct. 5, 1748
Samuel Tyler & Lydia Rose,	Jan. 5, 1749
Samuel Allen & Elizabeth Rose,	Jan. 23, 1749
Benjamin Bartholomew & Elizabeth Right,	Feb. 2, 1749
John ~~Morrise~~ *Monroe* & Sarah Hoadley,	Feb. 14, 1749
Charles Thomas *of Woodbury* & Mary Burgess,	Sept. 21, 1749
Jonathan Wheadon & Anna Cook,	Dec. 3, 1749
Zadoc Johnson & Hannah Penfield,	Feb. 1, 1750
Samuel Betts & Rachel Leete,	March 22, 1750
Isaac Pardy & Mary Leavit,	April 12, 1750
Jonathan Palmer & Mary Howd,	May 8, 1750
Abraham Hoadley & Abigail Blakiston,	Dec. 27, 1750
Samuel Palmer & Elizabeth Stint,	Jan. 3, 1751
John Whitney & Deborah Smith,	Jan. 17, 1751
Daniel Leek *of New Haven* & Rebecca Hitchcock, *Wallingford*	Jan. 25, 1751
Job Burkett & Martha Ebenwar——hed, *of n*	Feb. 2, 1751
Abraham Plant & Hannah Hoadley,	March, 1751
William Gould & Mary Maltbie,	Dec. 11, 1751
John Wilford & Elizabeth Harrison,	Feb. 6, 1752
Samuel Rose & Naomi Harrington,	April 15, 1752
Isaac Harrison & Hannah Johnson,	May 21, 1752
John Loyd & Mary Butler,	May 28, 1752
Daniel Rogers & Lydia Bartholomew,	June 18, 1752
Joseph Tyler & Jerusha Tyler,	June 18, 1752
Gideon Potter & Kerziah Leavit,	Aug. 27, 1752
Thomas Rogers & Rebecca Hobert,	Oct. 12, 1752
Joseph Brockway & Mary Gould,	Jan. 11, 1753
James Baldwin & Desire Palmerly,	May 23, 1753

Edward Russell & Sarah Maltbie,   May 30, 1753
John Tully, Esq., of Saybrook & Mary Russell, July 25, 1753
Levi Leete & Lydia Hodgkin,   Nov. 15, 1753
Nathaniel Johnson & Keturah Fos——,   Jan. 10, 1754
Samuel Howd and Amy Baldwin,   Feb. 14, 1754
Jonah Butler & Mary Wheaden,   Feb. 21, 1754
Daniel Olds & Ann Lodington,   Feb. 28, 1754
Samuel Allen & Ann Foot,   May 9, 1754
Amos Brower & Abigail Tyler,   Nov. 14, 1754
William Lucas & Triphena ——,   Jan. 16, 1755
George Dean & Abigail Wheaden,   Feb. 4, 1755
Samuel Bradfield & Dorcas Goodrich,   March 6, 1755
Moses Stork & Abigail Brown,   Sept. 4, 1755
Noah Rogers & Sarah Palmerly,   Oct. 23, 1755
Nathaniel Wheadon & Mary Morris,   Nov. 20, 1755
Abel Page & Sarah Towner,   Jan. 15, 1756
James Butler & Desire Harrison,   Jan. 22, 1756
Philemon Hall & Sarah Page,   May 6, 1756
Josiah Wheadon & —— ——,   June 24, 1756
Isaac Harrison & Rebecca Rogers,   Aug. 26, 1756
Ebenezer Hoadley & Martha Hoadley, *Haven* Sept. 27, 1756
Ebenezer Roberts & Elizabeth Jacobs, *of East* Dec. 15, 1756
Timothy Johnson & Mary Guy,   Feb. 10, 1757
Amos Page & Rebecca Burgess,   March 27, 1757
Isaac Hoadley & Elizabeth Blakistone,   March 31, 1757
Papillon Barker & Abigail Foot,   April 28, 1757
John Blakiston & Rebecca Baldwin,   May 19, 1757
Daniel Dudley of Woodbury & Elizabeth Goodrich
    of Branford,   Dec. 13, 1757
Jared Barker & Lucretia Palmer,   March 9, 1758
Culpepper Frisbie & Katherine Conklin,   July 13, 1758
Ebenezer Barker & Esther Russell,   Sept. 24, 1758
Richard Lucas & Sarah Dorson, *Darrow,*   Dec. 26, 1758
Charles Hazelton & Priscilla Smith,   Feb. 1, 1759
Moses Renters *Venters* of Wallingford & Mary Parish,
                                                 March 15, 1759
Thomas Allen & Mary Lloyd,   May 7, 1759
Caleb Chidsey & Mabel Moulthrop,   Sept. 3, 1759
Rev. Caleb Smith of Newark, N. J., & Rebecca
    Foote,   Oct. 17, 1759
8

Beriah Norton of Guilford & Rebecca Howd,   Feb. 24, 1760
Phineas Tyler & Abigail Harrison,   March 16, 1760
Samuel Holden ~~Tonny~~ *Terry* & Anna Gould,   April 3, 1760
Ephraim Parish & Jemima Palmer,   May 15, 1760
Samuel Huggens & Elizabeth Guy,   July 3, 1760
Ephraim Foote & Lucy Barker,   July 31, 1760
Stephen Rogers & Jerusha Hoadley,   Oct. 16, 1760
Stephen Smith & Sarah Damson (?),   Nov. 20, 1760
Edward Rogers & Lydia Frisbie,   Nov. 27, 1760
Ebenezer Linsley & Sybel Barker,   Dec. 17, 1760
Samuel Cooper & Mary (~~negroes~~) *Negus,*   Jan. 14, 1761
Daniel Palmer & Hannah Howd,   March 19, 1761
Elisha Frisbie & Martha Harrison,   April 14, 1761
Thomas Norton & Mercy Tyler,   May 29, 1761
Jacob Linsley & Mindwell Pond,   Aug. 18, 1761
Jonathan Foot & Lydia Baldwin,   Nov. 19, 1761
Isaac Linsley & Lydia Beach,   Dec. 23, 1761
Jonathan Goodsill & Hannah Tyler,   Jan. 13, 1762
Obediah Tyler & Hannah Barker,   Jan. 30, 1762
Joseph Smith & Lydia Harrison,   Feb. 24, 1762
Israel Frisbie & Hannah Johnson,   Dec. 15, 1762
Micah Palmer & Hannah Howd,   Dec. 30, 1762
Noah Baldwin & Abigail Frisbie,   Jan. 12, 1763
Edward Barker & Sarah Brown,   March 24, 1763
Abraham Plant & Tamar Frisbie,   May 5, 1763
William Gould & Mary Johnson,   May 5, 1763
Andrew Leete & Esther Blachly of North Guilford,
                                           May 12, 1763
Richard Towner & Bathsheba Goodrich,   June 2, 1763
John Frisbie & Eunice Burgess,   Sept. 22, 1763
Joseph Parmele & Sarah Howd,   Dec. 2, 1763
Timothy Frisbie & Mary Barker,   March 29, 1764
Peter Harrison & Mercy Frisbie,   April 5, 1764
Joseph Jones & Susanna Cornwall,   Sept. 19, 1764
Mulford Coan & Elizabeth Howd,   Sept. 20, 1764
Alexander Gordon & Lydia Linsley,   Nov. 5, 1764
Godkin Woodward & Anne Butler,   Nov. 8, 1764
John Hall & Hannah Frisbie,   Nov. 8, 1764
Rosewell Pond & Lydia Rogers,   Nov. 22, 1764
Daniel Dee & Lucy Plant,   Dec. 27, 1764

John Parker & Mary Allen,	March 17, 1765
Isaac Palmer & Rebecca Frisbie,	April 25, 1765
Thomas Russell & Bethiah Penfield,	May 9, 1765
Thomas Rose & Lucy Baldwin,	July, 1765
Timothy Way & Abigail Damson,	Oct. 3, 1765
John Gordon & Lydia Johnson,	Oct. 30, 1765
Ruben Tuttle of North Haven & Hannah Tyler,	Jan. 20, 1766
Stephen Potter & Sarah Linsley,	July 3, 1766
Abraham Linsley & Elizabeth Barker,	Nov. 18, 1766
John Blakiston & Sarah Huggins,	Nov. 26, 1766
Roger Tyler, Jr., & Martha Stent,	May 15, 1767
Thomas Wallston (?) & Mary Cook,	May 25, 1767
Josiah Howd & Hannah Leete,	June 18, 1767
William Stuart & Margaret Morris,	June 21, 1767
Roger Tyler & Mary Goodrich,	July 2, 1767
Nathan Frisbie & Sarah Harrison,	Aug. 13, 1767
Orchard Guy & Abigail Baldwin,	Aug. 20, 1767
Peter Baldwin & Anna Johnson,	Sept. 13, 1767
John Price & Abigail Barker,	Sept. 24, 1767
John Gonnell (?) & Hannah Barker,	Oct. 8, 1767
Jonathan Howd & Elizabeth Frisbie,	Oct. 26, 1767
Dick & Kate, servants of John Linsley,	Nov. 15, 1767
Ebenezer Palmer & Elizabeth Hoadley,	Feb. 2, 1768
Samuel Frisbie & Elizabeth Tyler,	March 23, 1768
James Hoadley & Lydia Hoadley,	March 31, 1768
William Brown & Rhoda Wheadon,	June 19, 1768
David Linsley & Lois Palmer,	Aug. 31, 1768
Amos Babcock, Esq., & Hannah Barker,	Jan. 5, 1769
Caleb Spencer & Johanna Stokes,	Jan. 17, 1769
Eleazur Stent, Jr., & Rhoda Ford,	June 21, 1769
Samuel Plant & Thankful Towner,	July 2, 1769
David Mallery & Mary Wardell,	Aug. 16, 1769
John Loire (Dutchman) & Abigail Stevens,	Sept. 5, 1769
Ebenezur Russell & Elizabeth Stork,	Sept. 13, 1769
Enoch Staples & Abigail Wilford,	Oct. 15, 1769
Robert Olds & Martha Linsley,	Nov. 6, 1769
Josiah Parish, Jr., & Thankful Plant,	Dec. 25, 1770
Simeon Linsley & Sarah Tyler,	Jan. 21, 1771
Abel Frisbie & Rebecca Hays,	June 7, 1771
Eli Rogers & Hannah Barker,	July 28, 1771

John Willman & Ruth Wheadon,	Jan. 31, 1772
Timothy Fowler & Sarah Guy,	Feb. 6, 1772
Josiah Fowler & Lucretia Maltbie,	Feb. 6, 1772
Matthias Butler & Hannah Palmer,	April 20, 1772
Pethes (?) Baldwin & Mary Foote,	June 8, 1772
Ebenezer Rogers & Lucy Beach,	Sept. 10, 1772
Farrington Harrison & Hannah Wilford,	Sept. 29, 1772
John Baldwin, Jr., & Althea Hobart,	Oct. 20, 1772
George Douglass Thomson & Irene Robbins,	Nov. 5, 1772
Solmon Wade & Mary Towner,	Nov. 27, 1772
Samuel Yates & Martha Butler,	Dec. 1, 1772
Daniel Olds & Sarah Russell,	Dec. 2, 1772
Rev. Peter Starr & Sarah Robbins,	Dec. 24, 1772
Isaac Palmer & Abigail Tyler,	Feb. 19, 1773
Abraham Rogers & Hannah Palmer,	March 12, 1773
John Clemons & Sarah Shelley,	April 15, 1773
Basil Munson & Mary Monroe,	May 4, 1773
Alpheus Johnson & Hannah Whitney,	June 16, 1773
Noah Tucker & Elizabeth How,	July 22, 1773
Nathaniel Parent of N. Y. & Mary Lanfear,	July 28, 1773
Bartholomew Goodrich & Hannah Baldwin, _of Yarmouth._	Sept. 22, 1773
Reuben Crosswell & Lois Wardell,	Nov. 14, 1773
Samuel Hoadley & Hannah Palmer, _of Stratford_	Feb. 16, 1774
Daniel Salmon & Hannah Beach, _of Guilford_	Feb. 16, 1774
Felix Norton & Hannah Harrison,	March 23, 1774
Samuel Russell & Sarah Monroe,	June 13, 1774
William Queen & Triphena Rose,	Jan. 12, 1775
Rev. John Keep & Hannah R. Robbins,	March 2, 1775
William Gould & Rebecca W. Robbins,	March 2, 1775
Samuel Goodsell & Abigail Goodrich,	March 23, 1775
Elias Hall & Ruhannah Barker,	April 4, 1775
Reuben Rice & Rebecca Harrison,	May, 1775
Timothy Rogers & Eunice Beach,	May 8, 1775
Samuel Baldwin & Lydia Lewis (?),	June 20, 1775
John Mallory & Mirriam Stokes,	June 20, 1775
Allen Smith & Elizabeth Rose,	Aug. 24, 1775
Peter Frisbie & Lydia Cook,	Nov. 16, 1775
Ebenezer Beach & Abigail Linsley,	Dec. 6, 1775
Levi Baldwin & Sarah Olds,	Dec. 31, 1775
Seth Morse & Desire Goodrich,	Jan. 4, 1776

Samuel Tyler & Rachel Bartholomew,	Jan. 11, 1776
Samuel Freelove & Hannah Tyler,	Jan. 24, 1776
Rosewell Chidsey & Hannah Landfear,	Feb. 1, 1776
William Frisbie & Rebecca Hoadley,	July 11, 1776
Zaccheus Baldwin & Sarah Bradfield,	Oct. 17, 1776
Benjamin Tyler & Sarah Baldwin,	Oct. 31, 1776
Nathaniel Wheadon & Hannah Foote,	Nov. 21, 1776
Mason Hobart & Hannah Harrison,	Nov. 28, 1776
Solomon Tomkins & Hannah Nails,	Dec. 13, 1776
John Whitney & Amy Howd,	Dec. 18, 1776
John Watrous & Temperance Landfear,	Jan. 15, 1777
Elisha Aldridge & Mary Wheadon,	Feb. 27 1777
Samuel Baldwin & Lois Page,	June 8, 1777
Oliver Landfear & Phebe Rogers,	June 29, 1777
Hooker Frisbie & Sarah Linsley,	Sept. 11, 1777
John Negus & Desire Harrison,	Jan. 20, 1778
Gideon Bartholomew & Welthean Sheldon,	Feb. 5, 1778
Asher Sheldon & Hannah Rogers,	March 25, 1778
George Friend & Mary Pasent (?),	May 11, 1778
Samuel Hoadley & Desire Wheadon,	June 14, 1778
Rev. Samuel Camp & Lucretia Barker,	Oct. 28, 1778
Obed Linsley & Lydia Beach,	Dec. 24, 1778
Lieut. Joseph Wilford & Mercy Barker,	Dec. 30, 1778
Timothy Goodrich & Hannah Rose,	Jan. 6, 1779
of Guilford	
Rufus Norton & Hannah Cook,	March 18, 1779
John Russell & Hannah Plant,	June 30, 1779
Joel Mulford & Betty Beach,	July 14, 1779
Russell Barker & Elizabeth Wilford,	Sept. 8, 1779
Elisha Reaye & Esther Butler,	Sept. 15, 1779
of Roxbury	
John Hunt, & Lydia Goodrich,	Nov. 23, 1779
of Salisbury	
William Baker & Phebe Wardell,	Jan. 3, 1780
Gideon Goodrich & Jerusha Tyler,	March 20, 1780
Ephraim Rogers & Martha Tyler,	March 22, 1780
Icobod Page & Mabel Gould,	July 26, 1780
Ralph Hoadley & Deborah Frisbie,	Oct. 17, 1780
William James & Louisa Prior,	Nov. 8, 1780
Elisha Forbes & Olive Page,	Nov. 15, 1780
Capt. James Barker & Lydia Monroe,	Nov. 22, 1780
Steward Gaylord & Thankful Rogers,	Dec. 7, 1780
Josiah Frisbie & Sarah Rogers,	April 12, 1781

BY REV. JASON ATWATER.

Benjamin Butler & Lydia Johnson,	April 4, 1784
Cambridge & Reah (negroes),	April 7, 1784
Capt. Edmon Rogers & Sally Barker,	April 11, 1784
Edmon Rogers, Jr., & Hester Wheadon,	April 22, 1784
Thomas Andrews & Abigail Stork,	July 14, 1784
Benj. Lines & Sally Brown,	July 26, 1784
Samuel Page & Mary Goodrich,	Aug. 26, 1784
Gamoliel Baldwin & Mary Sheldon,	Sept. 15, 1784
Richard Howland *Harland* & Hannah Rogers,	Sept. 16, 1784
Ebenezer Hoadley & Patience Palmer,	Oct. 12, 1784
John F. Harlow & Thankful Wheadon,	Oct. 20, 1784
Ephraim Page & Sally Judd,	Oct. 28, 1784
Jonathan Parish & Polly Russell,	Nov. 25, 1784
Aaron Griffin & Elizabeth Palmer,	Nov. 30, 1784
William Kirkum & Deborah Whitney,	Dec. 21, 1784
Silas Hoadley & Rachel Hoadley,	Jan. 6, 1785
James Gibs & Sarah Johnson,	Jan. 27, 1785
Philemon Tyler & Lucy Linsley,	April 27, 1785
Charles Joseph Dibboran & Molly Johnson,	Aug. 10, 1785
Daniel Howd & Johannah Burwell, *of North Haven or Bunnell*	Oct. 6, 1785
Joel Ives & Sarah Harrison,	Nov. 1, 1785
Josiah Tyler & Anna Goodrich,	Jan. 12, 1786
Washam (?) Williams & Rebecca Wilford,	Feb. 27, 1786
Elisha Scovil & Lydia Baldwin,	March 15, 1786
John & Gim (negroes),	April 2, 1786
George Ferald & Margaret Whitney,	April 10, 1786
Samuel Goodrich & Mary Johnson,	Sept. 16, 1786
Richard Eld & Esther Reave,	Nov. 19, 1786
John Tyler & Anna Rogers,	Nov. 20, 1786
Abraham Frisbie & Olive Butler,	Feb. 15, 1787
Charles Doolittle & Abigail Howd,	Feb. 18, 1787
Alexander Coventry & Elizabeth Butler,	March 11, 1787
Medad Stone & Mary Griffin,	March 25, 1787
John Harrison & Irene Wardell,	May 10, 1787
Charles Wellen & Polly Guy,	May 15, 1787
Edward Baldwin & Desire Hegans,	May 20, 1787
John Forney & Sarah Beach,	June 14, 1787
Ely Plant & Sarah Stent,	July 8, 1787

Timothy Blackstone & Margaret Goodrich,	Sept. 4, 1787
Daniel Brown & Lydia Rogers,	Sept. 5, 1787
Benjamin Hoadley & Hannah Frisbie,	Oct. 25, 1787
Abel Hoadley & Lucinda Bradley,	Nov. 8, 1787
John Hobart & Margaret White,	Nov. 11, 1787
Joel Page & Mabel Smith,	Nov. 13, 1787
Phineas Barker & Molly Easlick,	Dec. 16, 1787
Ezekiel Butler & Lydia Frisbie,	April 15, 1788
Nathaniel Frisbie & Anna Hamilton,	April 18, 1788
Jonathan Barker & Bethiah Norton,	May 13, 1788
John Higgins & Polly Gould,	May 20, 1788
Peter Grant & Peggy Stewart,	May 21, 1788
Lathrop Bradley & Abigail Frisbie,	Aug. 21, 1788
Timothy Parmele & Matty Norton,	Aug. 24, 1788
Stephen Maltbie & Abigail Williams,	Sept. 29, 1788
John Blackstone, Jr., & Rebecca Foot,	Nov. 7, 1788
Calvin Harrison & Abigail Linsley,	Nov. 25, 1788
Edmond *ward M* Morris & Hannah Parmelee,	Nov. 27, 1788
Stephen Cook & Esther Rogers,	March 8, 1789
John Hinman & Betsey Rogers,	June 12, 1789
Alexander Grant & Sylvia Gordon,	June 13, 1789
Samuel Penfield Russell & Margaret Parmelee,	
	June 13, 1789
Elihu Foot & Lucy Williams,	Nov. 11, 1789
Thomas Norton & Sarah Potter,	Nov. 16, 1789
William Huggins & Kate Hayson,	Dec. 15, 1789
Joseph Goodrich & Zoda Morris,	Dec. 31, 1789
Philemon Frisbie & Rhoda Butler,	Jan. 1, 1790
David Warren & Rachel Ingram,	Feb. 19, 1790
Edmond Hand & Hulda Hopson,	Feb. 20, 1790
Eliakim Ephraim Hall & Sarah Rogers,	March 3, 1790
Malichi Linsley & Rebekah Frisbie,	April 22, 1790
Daniel Ford & Anna Monroe,	June 6, 1790
Benjamin Plant & Abigail Palmer,	June 17, 1790
Jared Palmer & Desire Baldwin,	June 18, 1790
Orchard Gould & Polly Rogers,	Nov. 28, 1790
John Ford & Bathiah Russell,	Feb. 6, 1791
Jacob Molthrop & Elizabeth Goodrich,	March 30, 1791
Phineas Foot & Irene Hoadley,	April 28, 1791
John Guy & Roxanna Palmer,	May 6, 1791

Stuart Gaylord & Rebecca Hoadley,	May 9, 1791
Stephen Atwater & Rebecca Goram,	June 2, 1791
Elisha Linsley & Betsey Gordon,	Sept. 11, 1791
Jonathan Wardell & Matilda Hoadley,	Sept. 18, 1791
Samuel Bartlett & Cynthia Benton,	Oct. 4, 1791
Abraham Hoadley & Olive Price,	Oct. 10, 1791
Luke Teple & Orphana Towner,	Nov. 5, 1791
Daniel Cole & Elizabeth Frisbie,	Dec. 9, 1791
John Monroe & Anna Tuttle,	Jan. 22, 1792
Jacob Monroe & Sarah Benham,	March 1, 1792
Beverly Monroe & Abigail Rose,	June 14, 1792
Andrew Beach & Elizabeth Bradley,	June 14, 1792
Stephen F. Blackstone & Anna Wilford,	Jan. 23, 1793
Nathaniel Bailey & Ruth Hoadley,	Feb. 11, 1793
John Rogers & Mary Norton,	Feb. 20, 1793
John Barnes & Mary Lovewell,	Feb. 21, 1793
Jonathan Frisbie & Peggy Plant,	March 23, 1793
David Tyler & Abigail Brown,	May 25, 1793
Obadiah Walston & Huldah Cook,	May 29, 1793
William Monroe & Lucy Fowler,	Sept. 18, 1793
Rosewell Sheldon & Concurrance Brainard,	Dec. 28, 1793
Isaac Palmer & Tryphena Marquean,	Feb. 6, 1794

BY REV. LYNDE HUNTINGTON.

Aaron Morris & Elizabeth Norton,	Nov. 25, 1795
Jacob Page & Betsey Linsley,	Oct., 1796
Daniel Averill & Hannah Tyler,	Nov. 1, 1796
Jeremiah Morris & Polly Rogers,	Dec. 26, 1796
—— Hotchkiss & Sarah Whitney,	Jan. 1, 1797
Edmond Baldwin & Hannah Stent,	Jan. 7, 1797
Samuel Frisbie, Jr., & Irene Baldwin,	March 26, 1797
Linus Robinson & Rebecca Hobart,	May 22, 1797
Timothy Hubbard & Martha Rogers,	May 24, 1797
Samuel Linsley & Silence Stedman,	July 23, 1797
Joseph Linsley & Lorana Bradley,	Sept. 10, 1797
Benjamin Plant & Lois Frisbie,	Dec. 6, 1797
Timothy Bradley, Jr., & Irene Gorden,	Dec. 10, 1797
William Griffin & Mille Parish,	Jan. 23, 1798
Abraham Chidsey, Jr., & Abigail Beach,	June 20, 1798
Levi Bradley & Betsey Beach,	Nov. 28, 1798

Daniel Hubbs & Elizabeth Thyson (?),	Jan. 13, 1799
Abraham Coan & Patty Linsley,	Jan. 17, 1799
James Tinker & Rebekah Tyler,	Feb. 7, 1799
Amos G. Hull & Elizabeth Morris,	March 3, 1799
John Goodrich & Fanny Goodrich,	March 21, 1799
Elias Plant & Rebecca Trowbridge,	March 31, 1789
Solomon Freeman & Time Warner,	June 6, 1799
John Auger & Deborah Hoadley,	Dec. 19, 1799

SAYBROOK.

MIDDLESEX COUNTY.

A town settled in 1635, and covering an extensive territory, which has since been divided into several townships. The Congregational Church, formed in 1639, became the mother of several growing congregations within the limits of the original township. Two of these are now in the townships of Westbrook and Chester. The Second Church of Saybrook, formed in 1726, is now in Westbrook, a town incorporated in 1840. The Third Church of Saybrook, formed in 1742, is now in Chester, a town incorporated in 1836. The records of the Third Church, so far as they exist, were published in the First book, p. 89, "Early Connecticut Marriages." The following are the records of the Second or Westbrook Church:

A Catalogue of persons joined in Matrimony by WILLIAM WORTHINGTON, Pastor:

Ephraim Jones & Hannah Bates,	March 16, 1726-7
William Divall & Mercy Stannard,	Aug. 2, 1727
Samuel Jones & Sarah Spencer,	May 21, 1728
Mathew Lamb & Hannah Stannard,	Feb. 10, 1729-30
William Bushnell & Mary Bates,	March 4, 1729-30
John Chapman & Sarah Jones,	April 15, 1730
John Bailey & Hannah Tiffon,	Nov. 3, 1730
Michael Hill & Ann Spencer,	Dec. 15, 1730
John Waterhouse & Lydia Lay,	Feb. 3, 1730-31
David Blatchley & Temperance Spencer,	Oct. 5, 1731
Ichabod Chapman & Rachel Dibble,	June 22, 1732
Zebulon Dudley & Lucy Chapman,	Oct. 31, 1732
John Hunter & Deborah Jones,	March 14, 1732-3
John Wright & Phebe Large,	May 24, 1733
Jonathan Spencer & Content Platts,	May 24, 1733
William Parker & Mary Bushnell,	June 21, 1733
Ebenezer Platts & Dorothy Post,	Aug. 23, 1733

John Post & Lydia Bushnell,	Sept. 2, 1733
Charles Williams & Mary Denison,	Nov. 20, 1733
Joseph Post & Mary Post,	Nov. 30, 1733
Amos Stephens & Mary Stannard,	Dec. 1, 1734
Jared Willard & Kathrine Bates,	Dec. 12, 1734
Joseph Dayton & Temperance Jones,	Dec. 15, 1734
Benjamin Post & Mary Colt,	Dec. 2, 1734–5
James Clark & Sarah Post,	March 6, 1734–5
Thomas Morehouse & Prudence Wright,	April 18, 1735
Joseah Wright & Rhoda Dowde,	June 5, 1735
John Tammage & Deborah Maltbe,	Oct. 21, 1735
James Post & Mary Clark,	Nov. 26, 1735
Samuel Denison & Abagail Conklin,	Dec. 9, 1736
Nathaniel Chapman & Mercy Denison,	Feb. 17, 1737
James Jones & Sarah Willard,	March 31, 1737
Ebenezer Ingham & Elizabeth Stannard,	Aug. 18, 1737
Ezra Parmelee & Jamime Bushnell,	Feb. 22, 1737–8
Ephraim Spencer & Rebekah Spencer,	June 28, 1738
Jeremiah Nettleton & Deborah Kelcey,	July 20, 1738
Gamaliel Kelcy & Mary Gray,	Jan. 11, 1738–9
Job Buckley & Dorcass Conklin,	Feb. 21, 1738–9
Samuel Carter & Elizabeth Spencer,	March 15, 1738–9
John Jones & Mary Ingham,	March 22, 1738–9
Lemuel Stannard & Ruth Grenil,	March 22, 1738–9
Nehemiah Bushnell & Sarah Ingham,	Nov. 28, 1739
Jeremiah Lay & Prudence Belden,	March 20, 1739–40
Benjamin Morrill & Phebe Lay,	June 1, 1740
John Pike & Sarah Brooks,	Nov. 27, 1740
Deacon Andrew Lord & Huldah Lamb,	Aug. 6, 1741
Rev. William Hart & Mary Blague,	June 7, 1742

No marriages recorded after this date until the ordination of Rev. John Devotion, October 26, 1757.

Perybody Grenel & Charity Chapman,	March 8, 1758
Jedediah Griswold & Patience Bates,	April 19, 1758
Nathan Post, Jr., & Jemima Hurd,	May 3, 1758
Abraham Dowd & Phebe Kelsey (aged persons),	
	Sept. 7, 1758
Rowell Redfield & Mehitable Post,	Nov. 15, 1758
Ephraim Jones, Jr., & Keturah Post,	Dec. 21, 1758

Reuben Chapman & Sarah Lay,	Jan. 28, 1759
John Ely & Sarah Worthington,	July 12, 1759
Elijah Wilcocks & Mary Bushnell,	Aug. 23, 1759
David Post & Deborah Waid,	Dec. 12, 1759
Michael Hopkins & Mehitable Worthington,	Jan. 16, 1760
James Redfield & Sarah Grenell,	Jan. 24, 1760
Elnathan Chauncey & Elizabeth Gale,	Feb. 6, 1760
Thomas Spencer, Jr., & Phebe Grenell,	April 10, 1760
Stiles Stephens & Elizabeth Morehouse,	July 23, 1760
Ziba Loveland & Rebecca Greenell,	Aug. 27, 1760
George Wright & Anna Lay,	Oct. 1, 1760
Ezra Crane & Prudence Lay,	Nov. 27, 1760
Gideon Jones & Elizabeth Chapman,	Feb. 4, 1761
Phinehas Pierson & Betty Platts,	Feb. 5, 1761
Benjamin Carter & Phebe Spencer,	Feb. 24, 1761
John Denison & Mary Post,	Feb. 26, 1761
Nathan Whittlesey & Phebe Wright,	June 18, 1761
Benjamin Merrils & Rebecca Bushnel,	July 31, 1761
Jeremiah Kelsey & Margaret Morris,	Aug. 27, 1761
Elisha Lee & Abagail Murdock,	Oct. 4, 1761
Thomas Rumbell & Betty Carter,	Feb. 22, 1762
Ensign Gamaliel Kelsey & widow Mary Chapman,	
	March 25, 1762
Samuel Denison, Jr., & Temperance Post,	April 22, 1762
Henry L'Hommedieu & Jemima Spencer,	Sept. 8, 1762
William Marbell & Lydia Grenell,	Oct. 7, 1762
Abraham Towner & Sybil Bushnell,	Feb. 2, 1763
Daniel Lay & Mercy Chapman,	May 15, 1763
Andrew Tooley & Elizabeth Grenell,	June 2, 1763
Joshua Post & Anna Jones,	Aug. 11, 1763
Phinehas Chapman & Mary Hilliard,	Sept. 22, 1763
Job Kelsey & Sibil Lay,	Dec. 1, 1763
Samuel Spencer & Deborah Spencer,	Dec. 11, 1763
Adam Wilcocks & Esther Post,	Dec. 19, 1763
Ephraim Kelsey & Hannah Jones,	Dec. 28, 1763
William Chapman & Lydia Ingham,	Jan. 19, 1764
William Pratt & Abagail Bishop,	April 25, 1764
John Kelsey & Lucy Grenell,	April 26, 1764
John Hull & Phebe Lay,	Sept. 27, 1764
Elias Kelsey & Tamsen Jones,	Oct. 28, 1764

Caleb Chapman & Phebe Post,	Nov. 18, 1764
John Post & Cloe Chapman,	Nov. 22, 1764
Ephraim Jones & Mary Dowd,	Jan. 30, 1765
Joseph Post & Mary Denison,	March 21, 1765
Jacob Barney & Dothe Grenell,	Aug. 11, 1765
Abner Bushnell & Rachel Chapman,	Aug. 29, 1765
Daniel Grenell & Lois Loveland,	Nov. 14, 1765
Capt. Samuel Crane & widow Mary Lay,	Dec. 5, 1765
Robert Chapman & widow Hester Chapman,	April 22, 1766
William Post & Keziah Jones,	July 16, 1766
Christopher Clark & Peninnah Nott,	Oct. 30, 1766
Billy Willard & Phebe Post,	Nov. 19, 1766
Christopher Post & Sarah Chapman,	Jan. 1, 1767
Elijah Divall & Miriam Jones,	Jan. 19, 1767
William Clark & Jane Turner,	Aug. 27, 1767
Samuel Bushnell & Esther Kelsey,	Sept. 7, 1767
Titus Chapman & Elizabeth Kelsey,	Sept. 24, 1767
Isaac Pratt & Phebe Jones,	Oct. 15, 1767
James Lay & Abagail Bushnell,	Nov. 19, 1767
Stephen Webb & Lucy Spencer,	Nov. 19, 1767
Concklin Bukley & Sarah Spencer,	Jan. 7, 1768
Jonas Dibble & Mindwell Stannard,	March 10, 1768
Zebulon Jones & Beulah Grenell,	April 21, 1768
Robert Ely & Jerusha Lay,	April 28, 1768
Deacon Robert Lay & Elizabeth Denison,	June 24, 1768
Enoch Murdock & Mary Lay,	Nov. 9, 1768
Nathaniel Post & Ruth Spencer,	Dec. 21, 1768
Caleb Chapman & Elizabeth Bushnell,	Jan. 5, 1769
Jonathan Lay & Abagail Lay,	April 5, 1769
Ensign Caleb Spencer & widow Temperance Wright,	June 15, 1769
David Chapman & widow Sarah Bushnell,	Aug. 15, 1769
Joseph Spencer, Jr., & Elizabeth Clark,	Nov. 2, 1769
Aaron Ely & Sarah Denison,	Nov. 9, 1769
William Morgan & Miriam Murdock,	Nov. 23, 1769
Smith Ward & Temperance Grenell,	Nov. 23, 1769
Job Bukley & Jemima Utter,	Nov. 30, 1769
Benjamin Post & Deborah Chapman,	Jan. 2, 1770
Daniel Spencer & Temperance Dowd,	Jan. 17, 1770
Elisha Platts & Abagail Chapman,	Jan. 31, 1770

Samuel Crane & Mehitable Redfield (widow),   Feb. 21, 1770
Peter Pratt & Esther Wright,   March 1, 1770
Ebenezer Ingham & Sene Parmela,   April 12, 1770
Asa Lay & Sarah Woolcott,   April 18, 1770
Azariah Buel & Eleanor Post,   March, 1770
Elias Bushnell & Mehitable Post,   Oct. 18, 1770
Oliver Hull & Sarah Platts,   Nov. 15, 1770
Samuel Bailey & Molly Carter,   Nov. 15, 1770
Jonathan Greenell & Judith Waterhouse,   Jan. 7, 1771
Joseph Denison & Ann Lay,   May 5, 1771
Joseph Hand & Prudence Wright,   May 8, 1771
Bazaleel Hilliard & Mehitable Bushnell,   Jan. 1, 1772
Joseph Corby & Mabel Post,   Jan. 9, 1772
Jonathan Lay, Jr., & Anne Murdock,   Jan. 9, 1772
Abraham Murdock & Hannah Lay,   Feb. 5, 1772
Robert Lay & Desire Woolcott,   March 5, 1772
Francis Kelsey & Hannah Stannard,   July 30, 1772
William Bukley & Mary Chapman,   Sept. 3, 1772
Caleb Gardner & Mary Champen,   Oct. 15, 1772
John Pierce Dibble & Lucy Champen,   Nov. 30, 1772
Jeremiah Lay, Jr., & Statia Bushnell,   March 8, 1773
Jasper Greenell, Jr., & Mary Utter,   May 5, 1773
Hawes Higgins & Lucinda Bushnell,   Sept. 16, 1773
William Ingham & Jemima Bushnell,   Nov. 18, 1773
Joseph Lee, Jr., & Huldah Post,   April 7, 1774
William Dee, Jr., & Deborah Kirtland,   April 7, 1774
Phinehas Ely & Phebe Denison,   May 30, 1774
Lewis Jones & Frances Murdock,   Sept. 22, 1774
Nathan Bushnell & Rhoda Bushnell,   Oct. 20, 1774
Samuel Platts & Abigail Carter,   Oct. 31, 1774
Stephen Denison & Juliana Chapman,   Nov. 24, 1774
Benjamin Jones, Jr., & Molly Stannard,   Jan. 5, 1775
Asa Denison & Mindwell Jones,   March 9, 1775
Samuel Wright, Jr., & Hannah Spencer,   March 22, 1775
Elisha Willard & Ann Post,   May 8, 1775
Samuel Chapman & Martha Lee,   Nov. 2, 1775
Cornelius Post & widow Mary Greenell,   Dec. 25, 1775
Constant Bushnell & Temperance Kelsey,   Jan. 4, 1776
Jabez Arnold & Mary Wright,   Jan. 8, 1776
Stebbens Chapman & Sibil Kirtland,   March 7, 1776

Thomas Griffiths & Hannah Stannard,	May 21, 1776
Elijah Stannard, Jr., & Peggy Divall,	June 26, 1776
George Post & Flora Hill,	Jan. 16, 1777
Simeon Hoff & Lucy Wickham,	April 20, 1777
Augustus Jones & Mehitable Chapman,	Dec. 10, 1777
Seymour Belding & Priscella Jones,	Dec. 31, 1777
Elnathan Hurd, Jr., & Anna Ray,	Feb. 12, 1778
Daniel Lay, Jr., & widow Hannah Kelsey,	Jan. 14, 1779
Joseph Stannard & Phebe Denison,	March 1, 1779
Peter Stannard & Rebekah Chalker,	July 1, 1779
John Platts & Lucy Webb,	Oct. 12, 1779
Henry Hill & Mercy Denison,	Dec. 2, 1779
Jasper [Joseph] Stannard & Abagail Post,	March 9, 1780
Seth Smith & Hannah Murdock,	May 17, 1780
Jasper Spencer, Jr., & Lucy Post,	July 5, 1780
Jesse Wood & Mary Murdock,	July 27, 1780
Robert Sheffield & Temperance Doby,	Dec. 21, 1780
Elisha Platts & Lydia Spencer,	March 22, 1781
Benjamin Wright & Hester Chapman,	April 19, 1781
Daniel Willard & Sarah Silliman,	May 27, 1781
Stephen Atwater & Anna Clarke,	June 20, 1781
John Wright & Mercy Spencer,	July 19, 1781
Samuel Jones & Mercy Denison,	Oct. 4, 1781
Robert Ludlow & Elizabeth Concklin,	Oct. 7, 1781
Simeon Post & Mary Heck,	Oct. 25, 1781
George Havens & Lucretia Denison,	Nov. 22, 1781
Hezekiah Post & Saba Redfield,	Jan. 10, 1782
James Post & Tamar Jones,	Feb. 7, 1782
Oliver Clark & Hannah Post,	Oct. 29, 1782
James Post Redfield & Cloe Post,	Feb. 3, 1783
Gurdon Buel & Martha Whittlesey,	April 10, 1783
Col. Andrew Morehouse & Sarah Therril,	July 13, 1783
Ethiel Plaut & Hannah Denison,	Nov. 20, 1783
Abraham Waterhouse, Jr., & Abagail Leet,	May 2, 1784
Ezra Parmelee & Jemima Stannard,	Sept. 16, 1784
Thomas Dudley & Sarah Jones,	Oct. 3, 1784
William Murdock & Saba Denison,	Dec. 9, 1784
Nathaniel Ellis & Temperance Bushnell,	Jan. 27, 1785
Ezra Lay & Mehitable Kelsey,	March 31, 1785
Peter Spencer & Jerusha Post,	April 13, 1785

Samuel Beeman & Thankful Towner,	March 22, 1786
Simeon Lay & Hitty Denison,	May 24, 1786
Moses Chalker & Saba Chapman,	Aug. 3, 1786
William Eliott & Ethlinda Ely,	Sept. 27, 1786
Elias Stephens & Lucilla Chapman,	Jan. 24, 1787
Amos Stephens & Mary Leonard,	May 30, 1787
Joel Doane & Lydia Stannard,	June 24, 1787
Nathan Champin & Prudence Bushnell,	Aug. 5, 1787
David Post & Lucretia Post,	Jan., 1788
Ezra Post & Polly Stevens,	Jan. 31, 1788
Jedidiah Stone & Molly Post,	June 19, 1788
Hezekiah Post & Anne Gladden,	Feb. 26, 1789
Job Stannard & Sibbel Kelsey,	May 17, 1789
Bemont Clark, 2d, & Nabby Spencer,	May 21, 1789
Samuel Hull & Elizabeth Stephens,	June 21, 1789
Nathaniel Lay & Phebe Willard,	July 22, 1789
Doty Lord & Mary Chapman,	Feb. 22, 1790
Jedediah Post & Abagail Lay,	April 1, 1790
Lay Stannard & Mary Dee,	Dec. 20, 1790
James Stevens & Lucy Dibble,	July 7, 1791
George Stannard & Hannah Kelsey,	Nov. 29, 1791
Sawney of Lyme & Cashia of Saybrook,	Dec. 22, 1791
Amasa Ingham & Mary Chapman,	May 9, 1792
John Merrils & Ruth Dibble,	May 13, 1792
Uriah McGregory & Lucretia Ely,	Sept. 13, 1792
Billy Willard & Desire Denison,	Dec. 31, 1792
Gilbert Kirtland & Anne Chapman,	Dec. 2, 1793
Josiah Baldin & Martha Stannard,	Dec. 12, 1793
Reuben Bushnell, 2d, & Elizabeth Chapman,	April 10, 1794
Nathaniel Clarke & Hannah Chapman,	May 18, 1794
Eber Bushnell & Sarah Lay,	June 4, 1794
Samuel Spencer & Elizabeth Gladding,	Aug. 25, 1794
Benjamin Smith & Fanny Murdock,	Jan. 4, 1795
Jasper Stannard & Lydia Platts,	Jan. 26, 1795
John Douglass & Mary Spencer, 2d,	March 8, 1795
Joshua Post, 2d, & Molly Dee,	July 12, 1795
Edward Kelsey & Lucy Bushnell,	Aug. 3, 1795
Jeremiah Wright & Rachel Stannard,	Aug. 10, 1795
Theophilus Dudley & Kezia Kelsey,	Dec. 3, 1795
Darling Dudley & Artemesia Stannard,	Feb. 1, 1796

Jonas Dibble, 2d, & Naomi Dee,	Feb. 14, 1796
Daniel Carter & Thankful Post,	May 8, 1796
Edmund Field & Abagail Platts,	June 23, 1796
Nathan Kirtland & Rachel Towner,	Aug. 7, 1796
Aaron Chapman & Sylva Kelsey,	Oct. 13, 1796
Jonathan Bushnell & Betsey Lay,	Oct. 31, 1796
Lebbens Chapman & Jemima Greenell,	Feb. 7, 1797
John Hart Fowler & Phebe Lay,	July 1, 1797
Jacob Stannard & Rusha Kelsey,	Aug. 9, 1797
John Post, 2d, & Deuse Lay,	March 22, 1798
Oliver Hull, 2d, & Hannah Post,	Oct. 7, 1798
Thomas Hale & Lydia Murdock,	Nov. 18, 1798
Aden Post & Cloe Dee,	Feb. 10, 1799
Richard Doan & Anna Post,	Aug. 25, 1799
Samuel Wright & Rebina Post,	Aug. 28, 1799

CANTERBURY.

WINDHAM COUNTY.

The town of Canterbury was incorporated in October, 1703, having been taken from Plainfield. The Congregational Church dates from 1711. The marriage record begins :

Ebenezer Fitch, son of James, and Bridget Brown, daughter of Eben,	Sept. 18, 1712
Moses Hagget & Rebeca Adams, daughter of Richard, all of Norwich,	Oct. 16, 1712
Jonathan Cady, son of John, & Hannah ——,	Jan. 14, 1713
Daniel Cady, son of Daniel, & Hannah Winter of Killingly,	June 25, 1713
John Dyar of Windham & Abigail Fitch, daughter of Major James,	Oct. 22, 1713
Joseph Woodward, son of John, of Newton & Elizabeth Silsbey, daughter of Jonathan, of Windham,	June 24, 1714
John Felch, son of John, of Weston & widow Elizabeth Johnson,	Oct. 18, 1714
Samuel Rood & Mary Lambert, all of Norwich,	May 14, 1715

John Lungluff (Youngluff) of Killingly and
    Patience Winter,   July, 1715
Richard Smith & widow Mary Cleavland,   Jan. 30, 1716
Daniel Button & Anne Button,   Oct. 1, 1716
Matthias Button & Hannah Williams,   Oct. 1, 1716
John Ensworth, son of Tyxhal, & Elisabeth Cleav-
    land, daughter of Samuel,   April 21, 1717
Gideon Cobb & Margaret Cleavland,   Sept. 25, 1717
Moses Cleavland, son of Aaron, & Mary Johnson,
    daughter of Obadiah,   Oct. 21, 1717
Deliverance Brown, son of Deacon Ebenezer, &
    Mary or Abigail Waldo,   Oct. 28, 1717
John Fisk of Killingly and Mrs. Abigail Hobart,
    formerly of Newtown,   Nov. 26, 1717
Abraham Pain, son of Elisha, & Ruth Adams,
    daughter of John,   Dec. 19, 1717
Daniel Bissel & Jerusha Fitch, daughter of Major
    James, of Windsor,   March 18, 1718
Joseph Cleavland & Deborah ———,   May 19, 1718
William Darby & Elisabeth Spaulding, daughter of
    Ensign Edward,   June 9, 1718
David Adams, son of Henry, & Katherine Adams,
    daughter of Samuel,   June 17, 1718
Tryal Baker & widow Elisabeth Tippets,   Dec. 23, 1718
Henry Cleavland & Lucy Fitch, daughter of Major
    James,   March 19, 1719
Ensign Thomas Stephens & Mary Johnson, July 6, 1719
John Ensworth & Mary Cleavland,   Oct. 5, 1719
Samuel Cleavland & Sarah Buswell,   Dec. 10, 1719
Jonathan Walker & Mary Sampson,   Feb. 25, 1720
Benjamin Spaulding & Abigail Kight,   March 7, 1720
Gershom Mott & Anna Walton,   April 4, 1720
Ezra Cady & Joanna Leech,   April 18, 1720
Henry Bacon & Hannah Woodward,   Nov. 10, 1720
Elisha Payn & Mary Johnson,   Nov. 25, 1720
John Baldwin & Mary Adams,   Feb. 22, 1721
Isaac Cleaveland & Susannah Johnson (Mrs. Ste-
    vens, formerly Johnson),   Nov. 20, 1721
John Brown & Abigail Adams,   Nov. 30, 1721
Edward Cleavland, Sr., & Zerviah Church, Jan. 1, 1722

9

Robart Boswell & widow Mary Cleavland,	Jan. 22, 1722
Jabez Fitch & Lydia Gale,	May 29, 1722
Jonas Spaulding & Rachel Boswell,	July 5, 1722
Daniel Tyler & Jane Cady,	Dec. 31, 1722
Amos Kinsley & Ruth Adams,	June 12, 1723
David Adams & Dorcas Payn,	Aug. 27, 1723
Obadiah Johnson & Lydia, daughter of Mary Buswell,	Nov. 6, 1723
Uriah Cady & Hannah Boswell,	Jan. 2, 1724
Stephen Frost & Mary Adams,	Oct. 29, 1724
Samuel Cleavland & Mary Darbee,	Nov. 12, 1724
James Bradford & Susannah Adams,	Dec. 7, 1724
Joseph Cleavland & Sarah Ensworth,	March 31, 1725
Amos Woodward & Hannah Meecham,	May 6, 1725
John Youngluff & Jemima Price,	June 4, 1725
Joseph Cleavland & Mary Woodward,	June 26, 1725
Solomon Adams & Abigail Monroe,	April 28, 1726
Ebenezer Rood & Mary Green,	May 9, 1726
John Fish & Esther Johnson,	July 19, 1726
William Biggington & Esther Whitney,	Jan. 19, 1727
Jedidiah Smith & Biel Boswell,	Feb. 7, 1727
Nathaniel Flint & Mary Davis,	May 2, 1727
Nehemiah Ensworth & Abigail Davenport,	April 15, 1730
William Baker & Constance Pain,	April 27, 1730
Joseph Morse & Keziah Cleavland,	April 27, 1730
Ezekill Whitney & Sarah Parks,	July 22, 1730
Daniel Mason & Hannah Davis,	Oct. 27, 1730
John Proctor & Sarah Cleavland,	Dec. 9, 1731
Jonathan Stephens & Mary Tracy,	June 3, 1732
Stephen Baker & Hannah, daughter-in-law to John Bacon,	July 3, 1732
John Hopkins & Mary Rundils,	Oct. 9, 1732
Ephraim Davis & Hannah Steward,	March 20, 1733
David Ried & Hannah Rainsford,	March 22, 1733
Bennajah Deans & Mary Monrow,	March 23, 1733
Christopher Huntington & Elisabeth, daughter of Samuel Cleavland,	May 2, 1733
Nathaniel Robbins & Phebe Varnum,	Jan. 3, 1734
Jonathan Hides & Mary ———, formerly of Newtown,	Jan. 4, 1734

James Delop & Mercy Tippets,	Feb. 15, 1734
Samuell Wilson & Mary Davenport,	Nov. 25, 1734
Solomon Rainsford & Waitstil Adams,	July 17, 1735
Benjamin Throope & Sibil Dyar,	Nov. 27, 1735
William Witter & Zerviah Smith,	Jan. 1, 1736
Samuel Butt & Mary Adams,	Jan. 6, 1736
Joshua Payn & Constance Pain,	Jan. 6, 1737
Stephen Gates & Betty Monroe,	Jan. 6, 1737
John Felch & Mary Green,	March 7, 1737
Gideon Cobb & Abigail Dyar,	1739
William Fitch & Mary Pain,	1739
David Carver & Susannah ———,	1739
John Smith & Mehetabel Adams,	Feb. 26, 1739
Jonathan Carver & Abigail Robbins,	Oct. 20, 1746
Jeremiah Durkee & Abigail Adams,	——
John Ensworth & Hannah Butt,	——
John Backus & Jehannak Downing,	——
Paul Davenport, Jr., & Elisabeth Frost,	——
William Baker & Susannah Jones,	——
David Adams & Sarah Proctor,	——
Jabez Ensworth & Mehetabel Tracy,	Nov. 17, 1748
Jonathan Thompson & Hannah Dean,	Jan. 11, 1749
Joseph Dyar & Martha Darbe,	Feb. 1, 1749
Robert Green & Mary White,	April 26, 1749
Paul Harris & Mary Herrington,	Sept. 20, 1749
Benjamin Bacon & Deborah Adams,	Dec. 14, 1749
Thomas Tracy & Mary Hide,	Feb. 7, 1750
Joseph Eaton & Lucy Bacon,	March 1, 1750
Silas Cleavland & Elisabeth Hide,	May 10, 1750
Edward Murfee & Jane Long,	Aug. 13, 1750
Francis Simonds & Zipporah Cleavland,	Nov. 21, 1750
Simon Poney & Hannah Tobias,	Dec. 23, 1750
James Adams & Sarah Rich,	Feb. 5, 1751
Richard Raynsford & Zerviah Norwood,	1751
Samuel Woodward & Margaret Cleveland,	Feb. 13, 1751
Levi Adams & Margaret Perkins,	Dec. 26, 1751
Phinehas Adams & Lydia Fitch,	Dec. 31, 1751
Josiah Monroe & Mary Hyde,	April 16, 1752
Samuel Pellet & Hannah Underwood,	July, 1752
Samuel Standish & Abigail Backus,	Sept. 21, 1752

Ichabod Warner & Anne Rudd,	Oct., 1752
George Tocommowas & Hannah Tobias,	Jan. 5, 1753
Joel Dodge & Dorcas Smith,	Jan. 14, 1753
Elihu Adams & Jerusha Adams,	March 7, 1753
John Hide & Mary Thompson,	April 17, 1753
Joseph Safford & Lydia Ensworth,	April 25, 1753
Hezekiah Collier & Jennet Nevins,	1753
Bethuel Bond & Lydia Hide,	Sept. 20, 1753
John Herrick & Elisabeth Smith,	Sept. 27, 1753
John Fitch & Mercy Lothrop,	Nov. 7, 1753
Rev. David Rowland & Mrs. Mary Spalding,	Feb. 21, 1754
William Ensworth & Hannah Cogswell,	Feb. 21, 1754
Jabez Green, Jr., & Sarah Lambert,	May 1, 1754
Hopestil Cleavland & Patience Benjamin,	May 9, 1754
Joshua Phinney & Lucy Ensworth,	May 16, 1754
John Herrick & Sarah Smith,	June 6, 1754
William Bond & Sarah Woodward,	Sept. 25, 1754
James Hides & Miriam Woodward,	Dec. 3, 1754
Willard Stephens & Deborah Case,	Jan., 1755
Benjamin Brown & Hannah Benjamin,	Feb. 25, 1755
Peter Woodward & Alethea Armstrong,	Dec. 24, 1755
Samuel Adams, 3d, and Lydia Adams,	April 1, 1756
Eliphalet Farnam & Mary Adams,	Jan. 31, 1757
Samuel Conkling & Abigail Darbe,	May 15, 1757
Barnabas Lothrop & Sarah Davis,	July 7, 1757
Nathan Fish & Olive Ensworth,	Dec. 22, 1757
Lemuel Parrish & Zerviah Smith,	May 4, 1758
William Bingham & Mary Nevins,	Oct. 9, 1758
Jehiel Robbins & Mary Bennit,	Oct. 9, 1758
Josiah Dewey & Huldah Frost,	Jan. 3, 1759
Nathaniel Lothrop & Anna Fitch,	April 5, 1759
Peter Stevens, Jr., & Lois Glass,	1759
Ebenezer Brown & Susannah Bradford,	Jan. 8, 1760
Timothy Cleavland, Jr., & Esther Fish,	Jan. 30, 1760
Daniel Williams & Anna Bennet,	Feb. 18, 1760
James Matthews & Keziah Cady,	March 21, 1760
Stephen Harris & Mary Wentworth,	Feb. 24, 1761
Caleb Falkener & Esther Moss,	Feb. 27, 1761
Thomas Dimmock & Sibil Pain,	March 12, 1761
Asa Aspenwall & Anna Adams,	April 9, 1761

Hezekiah Capron & Charity Reed,	May 13, 1761
Asa Stephens & Sarah Adams,	Oct. 2, 1761
Doctor David Adams & Lucy Fitch,	Oct. 27, 1761
John Felch & Sarah Adams,	Nov. 5, 1761
Gideon Bingham & Abigail Baker,	Nov. 11, 1761
James Woodward & Abigail Harris,	Jan. 14, 1762
William Perkins & Dorcas Williams,	Feb. 11, 1762
John Sims & Mary Stevens,	April 11, 1762
Daniel Long Bottom & Sarah Dow,	June 3, 1762
Joseph Carter & Patience Pellet,	Oct. 3, 1762
Joseph Baldwin & Thankful Baldwin,	June 2, 1763
William Cady & Mercy Cady,	——
Josiah Wood & —— Hofford,	Sept., 1763
Samuel Ensworth & Sibil Tracy,	Nov. 17, 1763
Joseph King & Lucy Aspenwell,	Dec. 27, 1763
Abner Bacon & Abigail Ensworth,	Jan. 26, 1764
John Stark & Eunice Adams,	April 16, 1764
Matthias Button & Elisabeth Butt,	July 10, 1764
John Park, Jr., & Eunice Frost,	July 12, 1764
William Carew & Mary Bond,	Oct. 3, 1764
Elisha Herrington & Hannah Williams,	Oct. 11, 1764
Jonas Bond & Esther Wright,	Feb. 7, 1765
Henry Frost & Allice Butt,	Feb. 28, 1765
William Bacon & Jerusha Ensworth,	March 7, 1765
Asa Bacon & Edith Bradford,	May 16, 1765
Deacon Stephen Frost & widow Sarah Pike,	June 5, 1765
Samuel Felch & Mary Backus,	Aug. 25, 1765
Ira Kinnee & Miriam Goodale,	Nov. 12, 1765
Samuel Butt & Phœbe Brown,	Dec. 24, 1765
John Adams & Submit Butt,	Dec. 24, 1765
Peter Millar & Miriam Hide,	Oct. 1, 1766
Jacob Perkins, Jr., & Mary Fitch,	Oct. 10, 1766
Jonathan Hascal & Anna Lothrop,	Oct. 13, 1766
David Bacon & Elizabeth Ensworth,	Dec. 10, 1767
Ephraim Lyon & Eunice Leach,	Dec. 31, 1767
Elijah Williams & Abigail Adams,	Nov. 17, 1768
Ebenezer Bennet & Grace Ensworth,	Nov. 17, 1768
Ebenezer Butt & Prudence Glass,	Jan. 4, 1769
Eliashib Tracy & Zerviah Adams,	Feb. 19, 1769
David Hide & Sarah Adams,	Feb. 23, 1769

Shubael Cleavland & Eunice Luce,   March 30, 1769
Deacon Richard Hale & widow Abigail Adams,

                                                June 13, 1769
Reuben Carter & Sibil Smith,   June 29, 1769
Andrew Belcher & Abigail Burt,   Aug. 18, 1769
Samuel Adams & Eunice Cook,   Feb. 8, 1770
Robert Reynolds & Olive Smith,   March 13, 1770
Ebenezer Eaton & Lois Cobb,   April 15, 1770
John Herrick ye 3d, & Mary Butt,   March 27, 1771
Nathan Adams & Phœbe Ensworth,   April 3, 1771
James Delop & Susannah Frost,   April 24, 1771
Stephen Spalding & Sarah Brown,   Oct. 24, 1771

No more marriages are recorded until 1812.

MANSFIELD.

TOLLAND COUNTY.

Mansfield was incorporated May, 1702, having been previously a part of Windham. The First Congregational Church (Centre) was organized Oct. 18, 1710. The marriage record begins as follows:

Benjamin Upham & Ann Wood,   Oct. 8, 1744
Ebenezer Dunham, Jr., & Anis Atwood,   Feb. 21, 1744–5
Nathaniel Hall & Martha Storrs,   Nov. 7, 1745
Isaac Dexter & Esther Davis,   Dec. 15, 1745
Nathaniel Eli & Mary Esterbrook,   Dec. 15, 1745–6
Gideon Arnold & Eleanor Lewis,   Jan. 17, 1746
Skiff Freeman & Ann Sergeant,   July 5, 1746
Elijah Mackall & Mehitable Arnold,   Dec 15, 1746
Abner Hall & Mary Rust,   April 12, 1747
Mehumen Stebbens & Eliza Swift,   Nov. 5, 1747
Joseph Jacobs (ye 3d) & Bethiah Hodges,   June 6, 1747–8
Joseph Warwick & Sarah Howard,   Dec. 16, 1747–8
Jonathan Curtise, Jr., & Thankful Rudd,   Oct. 30, 1748
Hezekiah Crane & Tamson Eldrige,   June 8, 1749
Isaack Turner & Susannah Mayo,   Oct. 4, 1749
Edmond Hovey, Jr., & Mary Gilbert,   Dec. 8, 1749
Samuell Curtice & Susannah Bozworth,   Dec. 18, 1749

Thomas Davis & Martha Squire,	June 13, 1750
Joshua Palmer & Ruth Sargeant,	July 26, 1750
James Cummins & Rachell Swift,	Sept. 13, 1750
Isaack Hall & Abigail Swift,	Sept. 20, 1750
Elisha Williams & Abigail Gurley,	Sept. 20, 1750
John Spencer & Elenor Arnold,	Jan. 24, 1750–1
Samuel Sargeant & Hannah Baldwin,	April 26, 1751
Leonard Pike & Sarah Case,	Aug. 15, 1751
Obadiah Heth & Eunice Porter,	Dec. 17, 1751
Thomas Barrows, Jr., & Elizabeth Turner,	Jan. 9, 1752
Nehemiah Wood & Elizabeth Hovey,	March 5, 1752
Elisha Barrows & Hannah Mays,	Nov. 20, 1752
Experience Johnson & Elizabeth Sargeant,	Feb. 20, 1753
David Fuller & Desire Hopkins,	Dec. 20, 1753
Constant Southworth & Mary Porter,	Feb. 7, 1754
Samuell How & Eunice Conant,	Sept. 30, 1754
David Curtice & Mary Bozworth,	Nov. 29, 1754
Robert Snow & Sarah Chubb,	Dec. 26, 1754
Josiah Reed & Eunice Kingsberry,	Jan. 2, 1755
Josiah Southworth & Esther Porter,	April 2, 1755
Jonathan Davis & Rebekah Parker,	May 13, 1756
Perez Anderson & Ruth Wood,	July 14, 1756
Jonathan Wood & Lucy Drew,	Sept. 16, 1756
David Cary & Mary Webber,	Nov. 18, 1756
Ephraim Parker & Deborah Sargeant,	Feb. 3, 1757
Oliver Smith & Rachell Hodges,	March 8, 1757
Ephraim How & Sarah Gilbert,	Nov. 15, 1757
Nathaniel Linkon & Agnes Austin,	Dec. 21, 1757
Elias Birchard & Sarah Jacobs,	Jan. 25, 1758
Benjamin Bryant & Sarah Dean,	Feb. 22, 1758
Samuel Linkon & Mary Austin,	March 14, 1758
Richard Webber & Ruth Cammell,	March 28, 1758
William Hank & Hannah Sergeant,	May 4, 1758
Josiah Hall & Hannah Abbey,	March 29, 1759
Isaac Sergeant & Phebe Baldwin,	June 21, 1759
James Dana & Elizabeth Whitmore,	Nov. 27, 1759
Joseph Clarke, Esq., & Susannah Johnson,	Jan. 2, 1760
Joseph Davis, Jr., & widow Ruth Palmer,	Jan. 17, 1760
Benjamin Jacobs & Elizabeth Balkam,	Jan. 14, 1761
Nehemiah Gillett & Martha Storrs,	Jan. 22, 1761

Elijah Fenton & Lois Hovey,	June 3, 1761
Zachariah Parker, Jr., & widow Abigail Hall,	Aug. 21, 1761
Joseph Estabrook & Theode Porter,	May 20, 1762
Ebenezer Baldwin & Ruth Swift,	Nov. 12, 1762
John Hunt, Jr., and Mary Abbey,	March 24, 1763
Silas Hanks & Sarah Webber,	Oct. 6, 1763
Solomon Jacobs & Elizabeth Gillett,	Dec. 15, 1763
John Brown & Sybill Barrows,	Dec. 22, 1763
George Dorrance & Ellice Trumble,	March 15, 1764
Jonathan Bingham, Jr., & Elizabeth Warner,	April 12, 1764
Stephen Johnson & Sarah Arnold,	April 29, 1764
Jonathan Gurley, Jr., & Jerusha Bennett,	May 17, 1764
Thomas Hall & Susannah Dunham,	Sept. 20, 1764
Phineas Allen & widow Elizabeth Johnson,	Feb. 6, 1765
Joshua Woodworth & Elizabeth Willson,	May 15, 1765
John Turner & Mary Wright,	May 23, 1765
Nathaniel Cary, Jr., & Zerviah Storrs,	Dec. 5, 1765
Samuel Abbey & Temperance Linkon,	July, 1766
Zuriel Cammell & Lydia Barrows,	March 5, 1767
John Slaughter & Elizabeth Hovey,	March 26, 1767
Samuel Lane & Lucy Gilbert,	Oct. 15, 1767
Philip Turner & Deborah Baldwin,	Jan. 7, 1768
Nathaniel Hall, Jr., & Mehitable Storrs,	Feb. 18, 1768
Josiah Warner & Deborah Hall,	March 24, 1768
Azariah Freeman & Ann Wood,	March, 1768
Nathaniel Marsh & Rebekah Wright,	July 7, 1768
Pelatiah Holbrook & Mary Clarke,	Oct. 29, 1768
Jonathan Goodwin, Jr., & Anna Clarke,	Nov. 3, 1768
Benjamin Collins & Thankful Sergeant,	Dec. 22, 1768
John Russ, Jr., & Eunice Wood,	Jan. 12, 1769
Timothy Bugbee & Hannah Wood,	Jan. 12, 1769
Asa Moulton & Lydia Freeman,	Jan. 26, 1769
Abner Church & Sarah Linsey Coye,	March 16, 1769
William Lee & Mary Jacobs,	Nov. 7, 1769
Isaac Farewel & Mary Freeman,	Nov. 23, 1769
Joel Hall & Esther Dexter,	Nov. 23, 1769
Chysman Swift & Mary Laine,	Nov. 30, 1769
Joseph Upsham & Mary Fletcher,	March 29, 1770
Isaac Perkins & Tamison Chaplain,	July 5, 1770
Malachi Thomas & Mary Mackall,	Oct. 3, 1770

Thomas Swift, Jr., & Mehitable Barrows,	Oct. 31, 1770
Nathaniel Storrs & Ruth Hall,	Feb. 21, 1771
Nathan Hall & Deborah Swift,	May 8, 1771
Ephraim Cambell & Elizabeth Church,	June 5, 1771
Elnathan Bassett & Anna Southworth,	Oct. 30, 1771
William Farewell, Jr., & Phebe Crosby,	Oct. 30, 1771
Ephraim Perkins & Mary Chaplain,	Nov. 7, 1771
Daniel Dunham & Hannah Freeman,	Nov. 14, 1771
Cornelius Storrs & Mary Slap,	Jan. 22, 1772
Jonathan Blackman & Elizabeth Fletcher,	Jan. 30, 1772
James Royce, Jr., & Eunice Heth,	Feb. 14, 1772
Isaac Hall & Anna Palmer,	July 2, 1772
Nathaniel Storrs & Martha Barrows,	Oct. 29, 1772
Josiah Stowel & Mary Leavens,	Nov. 5, 1772
Jonathan Stoel & Anna Cummins,	Feb. 4, 1773
Benjamin Agard & Lydia Dana,	March 25, 1773
Ezra Bassett & Minervy Kee,	Oct. 4, 1773
Philip Turner & Sarah Barrows,	Jan. 6, 1774
Hezekiah Crain, Jr., & Rachell Hall,	April 14, 1774
Nathaniel Hunt, Jr., & Eunice Barrows,	May 11, 1774
Jesse Bowles & Sarah Nicholl,	May 11, 1774
Jonathan Fuller & Experience Hunt,	May 12, 1774
Timothy Fuller, Jr., & Delight Cary,	June 15, 1774
James Thomas & Hannah Mackall,	Oct. 5, 1774
Eliphalet Huntington & Eleanor Bugbee,	Dec. 14, 1774
Shephard Stearns & Olive Hall,	Jan. 12, 1775
Arad Simons & Bridget Arnold,	Feb. 15, 1775
Gideon Arnold & Mary Church,	March 15, 1775
Samuel Abbey & Miriam Hall,	April 11, 1775
John Howard & Dorcas Crain,	June 10, 1775
Anson Blackman & Mary Upsham,	Sept. 20, 1775
John Fenton & Lucy Warden,	Nov. 19, 1775
Skiff Freeman & Mary Aspinwall,	Jan. 10, 1776
Jacob Eaton & Abigail Hopkins,	Jan. 25, 1776
Jonathan Burgess & Mary Fuller Lord,	April 2, 1776
Benjamin Hanks and Ann Hall,	May 14, 1776
Isaac Palmer & Deborah Hovey,	Nov. 23, 1776
Eliphalet Dimmick & Ann Freeman,	Nov. 28, 1776
Jonas (?) Kinney & Mary Baker,	Feb. 13, 1777
Jonathan Hovey & Mary Storrs,	March 28, 1777

Amasa Church & Muctriphantheim Allen,	May 21, 1777
William Abbey & Abigail Hall,	June 4, 1777
Edy Trap & Miriam Sargeant,	March 16, 1778
Benjamin Nicholls, Jr., & Sybill Wood,	April 2, 1778
Benjamin Storrs & Olive Mackall,	Oct. 26, 1778
Phineas Gurley & Susannah Swift,	Nov. 10, 1778
Miner Grant & Eunice Swift,	Nov. 12, 1778
Billy Manning & Ruth Nichols,	Nov. 25, 1778
Gilbert Geary and Anna Dana,	Dec. 1, 1778
Elijah Yeomans & Lydia Simons,	Dec. 2, 1778
Zenas Hows & Eunice Hunt,	Dec. 16, 1778
Jesse Swift & Lydia Storrs,	Dec. 23, 1778
Asa Farewell & Kesiah Freeman,	March 23, 1780
Daniel Clark & Rebekah Davis,	May 18, 1780
Asa Southworth & Hannah Allen,	June 15, 1780
Micah Smith & Phebe Abbee,	Sept. 28, 1780
Elijah Baldwin & Asenath Allen,	Sept. 28, 1780
Constant Storrs & Lucinda How,	Oct. 3, 1780
Daniel Clark & Mehitable Slate,	Oct. 19, 1780
John Wood & Abigail Church,	Oct. 26, 1780
Andrew Hartstrom Jr., & Elizabeth Baldwin,	Nov. 28, 1780
Jonathan Nicholls, Jr., & Rebekah Swift,	Dec. 7, 1780
Experience Freeman & Jane Upham,	Jan. 2, 1781
Samuel Storrs & Persis How,	Jan. 23, 1781
Jonathan Bosworth & Mehitable Curtice,	Feb. 22, 1781
Elisha Barrows, Jr., & Mary Hall,	May 23, 1781
Jonathan Hibberd & Elizabeth Learned,	June 19, 1781
Varin Balch & Sarah Bosworth,	June 26, 1781
William Dodge & Lydia Nicholls,	July 11, 1781
Nathaniel Porter & Olive Stearns,	Sept. 20, 1781
Richard Hall & Allice Arnold,	Sept. 27, 1781
Rev. David Avery & Hannah Chaplain,	Oct. 10, 1781
Abner Huntington & Abigail Leavens,	Oct. 15, 1781
Azariah Baldman & Deborah Huntington,	Nov. 15, 1781
James Howard & Sarah Chaplain,	Dec. 4, 1781
Cyrus Lad & Amy Allen,	Dec. 5, 1781
Nathan Blodgett & Mary Balch,	May 8, 1782
John Martin & widow Mercy Harris,	Aug. 7, 1782
Aaron Hall & Zerviah Slate,	Nov. 27, 1782
John Martin, Jr., & Elizabeth Balcome,	Feb. 7, 1784

William Cummins & Rhody Barrows,   Feb. 14, 1784
Heman Storrs & Allice Cummins,   March 24, 1784
Isaac Bennett & Margaret Pain,   Sept. 2, 1784
John Balch, Jr., & Lucy Bowen,   April 7, 1785
John Butts & Elizabeth Huntington,   May 5, 1785

No further record exists till 1807.

NEWTOWN.

FAIRFIELD COUNTY.

Newtown was incorporated in October, 1711, the first settlers coming from Stratford and Milford. The Congregational Church was organized in 1715. The following records had been lost for twenty years, only recently coming to light.

Daniel Stephens of New Fairfield & Sarah Adams,
                                         Oct. 5, 1743
Rev. Benijah Cass of New Fairfield & Mrs. Ann
    Sherman,   Dec. 7, 1743
Joseph Summers of Stratford & Abel Booth, Jan. 11, 1743-4
Daniel Bears & Mabel Booth,   Dec. 27, 1744
Ephraim Bennit & Ann Baldwin,   June 19, 1745
Richard Fairman of Bedford & Jane Botsford,
                                        June 20, 1745
Daniel Foot & Sarah Mosger (?),   July, 1744
Daniel Sherman & Mary Northrop,   Aug. 21, 1745
Vincent Stilson & Abigall Peck,   Nov. 7, 1745
James Fairchild & Sarah Foot,   Feb. 26, 1745-6
Samuel Gillit, Jr., & Unice Clarck (?), April 23, 1746
George Foot of Stratford & Hannah Hurd, April 29, 1746
John Ferris & Mary Gillet,   Aug. 7, 1746
John Sherman & Hannah Clarck,   Jan. 17, 1746
Hezekiah Clark of Ammity & Mary Peck,   Jan. 20, 1746-7
Surrajah Blackman of Rifton & Bethiah Sherman,
                                        April 2, 1747
Samuel Strong of Woodbury & Uniss Booth, June 25, 1747
James Herd & Hester Booth,   Aug. 26, 1747
John Duning & Annah Kimberley,   Sept. 2, 1747
Samuel Bears & Abigall Blackman,   Oct. 14, 1747

Joshua Northrop & Mary Bennet,   Oct. 22, 1747
Jedidiah Hubbell & Elizabeth Northrop,   April 20, 1748
Ephraim Lake & Mary Bristol,   May 19, 1748
Josiah Burrit of Newtown & Mary Barlow of Dan-
    bury,   July 20, 1748
Nathanael Bears & Caroline French, both of North
    Stratford,   Aug. 30, 1748
John Smith of Derby & Christian Botford,   Oct. 13, 1748
George Smith & Annah Booth,   Nov. 24, 1748
Ebenezer Blackman & Mary Smith,   Nov. 24, 1748
Moses Peck & Elisabeth Baldwin,   Dec. 1, 1748
Amos Merchant & Uniss Sherman,   Dec. 8, 1748
Daniel Tuttle & Masoah Bristol,   May 18, 1749
Henry Peck & Mercy Wheeler,   Nov. 30, 1749
Richard Hubbell & Jedidah Scidmore,   Nov. 29, 1749
Abraham Bristol & Mehitabel Nichols,   Jan. 5, 1749–50
Daniel Crowfoot & Rachel Lyon,   March 28, 1750
Agur Judson of Stratford & Mehitabel Tousey, May 2, 1750
David Sherman & Abiar Wheeler,   June 6, 1750
Michael Duning & Abiar Kimberley,   July 19, 1750
Abraham Tonner of Danbury & Hannah Foot, Aug. 7, 1750
William ~~Burch or Purch (?)~~ *Birch* & Catharine Hubbell,
                                                             Sept. 27, 1750
Nathan Sherman & Abiar Adams,   Dec. 19, 1750
John Camp & Bethia Glover,   Feb. 7, 1750–1
Abraham Johnson of Newtown & Miriam Deet (?)
    of North Stratford,   June 6, 1751
Ebenezer Farchild & Sarah Kimberley,   Aug. 14, 1751
Joseph Blackman & Elizabeth Glover,   Oct. 7, 1751
Amos Turrel & Comfort Skidmore,   Nov. 7, 1751
Timothy Tredwell of Stratford & Phebe Foot, Dec. 4, 1751
Gideon Peck & Abiah Smith,   Jan. 29, 1752
Peter & Genny (servants of Matthew Curtiss), April 3, 1752
Josiah Hooker of Norwalk & Hannah Tousey, May 12, 1752
Thomas Benedick of Richfield & Jene Gunn,   May 27, 1752
Josiah Wheeler & Ann Sturge,   June 8, 1752
John Northrop & Lois Northrop,   July 30, 1752
Joseph Bristol, 3d, & Mary Nap,   Nov. 17, 1752
Isaack Bostick & Mary Kimberly,   Dec. 25, 1752
Daniel Baldwin & Jane Bennet,   Jan. 5, 1753

Caleb Mallery of Ripton & Ann Peck,   Feb. 28, 1753
Jared Baldwin & Damaras Booth,   Sept. 18, 1753
Elijah Smith of Derby & Charity Johnson,   Nov. 20, 1753
Joseph Smith & Jemimah Hubbel,   June 13, 1754
Abraham Northrop of Richfield & Mehetibel Gunn,
                                                     July 3, 1754
Rev. Elijah Gill of New Fairfield & Mrs. Dorcas
     Bennet,   Aug. 29, 1754
Jedidiah Wheeler & Phebe Burrit,   Nov. 18, 1754
George Turril & Sarah Sherman,   Dec. 4, 1754
John Griffen & Bulah Hubbel,   Dec. 18, 1754
Joseph Fairchild of North Stratford & Mary Bots-
     ford,   Dec. 25, 1754
Ephraim Sherman & Rhoda Chauncey,   Dec. 31, 1754
Jeriel French of North Stratford & Mary Foot, Jan. 8, 1755
Benjamin Hawley of Newbury & Anne Baldwin,
                                                     Jan. 14, 1755
Isaack Hanley or Hawley & Hannah Northrop,
     both of Newbury,   Jan. 16, 1755
Waite Northrop & Sarah Gunn, both of Newbury,
                                                     March 20, 1755
Benjamin Northrop & Sarah Prindle,   March 24, 1755
Jabez Baldwin & Mary Peck,   March 24, 1755
Joseph Wheeler & Keriah Botsford,   March 25, 1755
Abraham Botsford & Mary Chauncey,   April 1, 1755
Abraham Bennet & Hannah Peck,   April 24, 1755
John Febriene (?) & Anna Bears,   May 5, 1755
Obadiah Wheeler & Phebe Northrop,   Sept. 15, 1755
George Smith & Leucy (?) Botsford,   Oct. 13, 1755
John Tousey & Rebeckah Booth,   Oct. 14, 1755
Henry Peck & Ann Smith,   Dec. 23, 1755
Thomas Lake & Betty Jackson,   Dec. 25, 1755
John Febriene (?) & Rebeckah Sherman,   Feb. 25, 1756
Caleb Baldwin & Naomi Herd,   March 8, 1756
Job Northrop of Amity & Violet Peck,   April 8, 1756
John Sheperd, Jr., & Rhoda Wheeler,   Sept. 13, 1756
Lemuel Thomas & Mary Foot,   Sept. 15, 1756
John Hull & Sarah Hepburn,   Oct. 29, 1756
Collins Chapman of North Stratford & Mary
     Febrique (?),   Dec. 15, 1756

Amos Sanford & Mary Cluckstone,	Jan. 13, 1757
Ephraim Prindle & Mary Sherman,	Feb. 23, 1757
Ebennezar Peck & Sarah Booth,	March 15, 1757
Jeptha Hubbel & Experience Prindle,	May 30, 1757
Solloman Ferry of Danbury & Mrs. Christian Botsford (about 60 years old),	June 14, 1757
Silas Camp & Mary Sheperd,	July 6, 1757
Josiah Daton & Jemimah Griffin,	Sept. 21, 1757
Phineas Lee of Derby & Eve Sherman,	June 22, 1758
John Sturdesant (?) of Newbury & Mary Sanford,	July 5, 1758
William Gould of New Haven & Phebe Lyon,	Aug. 29, 1758
Samuel Prindle & Hannah Sanford,	Sept. 14, 1758
Josiah Plat & Sarah Sanford,	Nov. 13, 1758
James Fairchild & Sarah Johnson,	Dec. 7, 1758
Jamer Prindle & Anar Turner,	Jan. 2, 1759
Caleb Baldwin, Esq., & Jerusha Daton,	Feb. 8, 1759
Robert Summers & Annah Burret,	May 2, 1759
Gideon Baldwin & Ann Booth,	June 27, 1759
Jonathan Prindle & Damaris Peck,	July 12, 1759
Roger Turrel & Patience Foot,	July 12, 1759
Daniel Baldwin & Abigal Northrop,	Sept. 20, 1759
James Glover & Eunice Booth,	Nov. 15, 1759
Joseph Botsford & Else Northrop,	Jan. 1, 1760
James Lake of New Milford & Sarah Henry,	Jan. 23, 1760
Elijah Hull & Rebeckah Summers,	Jan. 31, 1760
Abraham Kimberly & Tamar Burret,	Feb. 14, 1760
Heth Peck, Jr., & Mary Schidmore,	March 27, 1760
Asael Cogswell of —— & Catharine Blackman,	May 8, 1760
Joseph Rockwell of Danbury & Phebe Northrop,	May 14, 1760
Benj. Stilson, Jr., & Martha Stilson,	May 14, 1760
Nathan Dickerson & Zilla Sherman,	May 20, 1760
Thomas Ford of Newtown & Bathsheba Nicols of North Stratford,	July 14, 1760
James Sanford & Agnes Devine,	Aug. 6, 1760
Samuel Camfield of Danbury & Mehetabel Stilson,	Sept. 9, 1760
John Fabraene & Elinor Plat,	Sept. 10, 1760

Nathaniel Peck & Mary Foot,	Oct. 16, 1760
Ezra Perry of Danbury & Ann Booth,	Oct. 20, 1760
Sillovant Hubbel & Ellen Wood,	Dec. 8, 1760
Enoch Person & Abigal Cluckstone,	Feb. 10, 1761
Elijah Foot & Unice Peck,	March 23, 1761
Lemuel Wheeler & Jerusha Summers,	April 9, 1761
Ezra Bryan & Sarah Peck,	May 21, 1761
Abel Prindle & Amerillys Tousey,	June 3, 1761
Daniel Peck & Hannah Johnson,	Dec., 1761
Moses Write & Hester Sanford,	Jan. 19, 1762
Benjamin Summers & Philana Shepard,	May 13, 1762
Rev. Benj. Duning of Marlborough & Mrs. Anna Botsford,	June 16, 1762
BENAJAH Dickason of Reading & Hannah Waring,	Nov., 1762
Timmothy Russel of Oxford & Mrs. Hannah Tousey,	Nov. 29, 1762
Simeon Shepard & Mary Hull,	Jan. 26, 1763
Othniel French of New Stratford & Jerusha Johnson,	Aug. 15, 1763
Joshua Hatch of New London & Phebe Botsford,	Oct. 16, 1763
Moses Chittenson or Chitterson & Cybel Cabot of New Stratford, AGNES	Dec. 13, 1763
John Summers & Aguin (?) Stilson,	Dec. 21, 1763
William Hall of Reading & Sarah Peck,	Jan. 10, 1764
Abel Botsford & Mary Bennet,	Jan. 19, 1764
Ezra Peck & Phebe Johnson,	March 7, 1764
Ralph Gregory of New Fairfield & Pamal Turrel,	May 30, 1764
Joseph Lake of Sharon & Sarah Warner,	July 11, 1764
Jabez Peck & Abi Sanford,	July 17, 1764
William Northrop & Elizabeth Northrop,	Aug. 7, 1764
John Johnson & Dolle Hurd,	Aug. 9, 1764
Gideon Northrop & Rhoda Northrop,	Nov. 15, 1764
Daniel Glover & Sarah Brian,	May 16, 1765
William Write & Thankful Bristol,	Aug. 1, 1765
Henry Peck & Hannah Levinsworth,	Aug. 6, 1765
Samuel Sanford & Abiah Duning,	Aug. 19, 1765
Zebulon Norton of Woodbury & Naomi Booth,	Nov. 7, 1765
Jeremiah Turner & Deborah Sterling,	Feb. 27, 1766

Francis Pierce & Dorcas Hibson,	April 28, 1766
Noah Parmeley, Jr., & Olive Prindle,	Oct. 26, 1766
Jabez Botsford & Mehetabel Bennet,	Nov. 20, 1766
Ebenezer Booth & Olive Sanford,	Nov. 20, 1766
John Judson & Patience Firman,	April 30, 1767
Eliakim Beardsley of New Stratford & Easter Sherman,	May 14, 1767
John Peck, Jr., & Millie Burrit,	Aug. 31, 1767
Icabod Fairman & Rebeckah Glover,	Nov. 17, 1767
Ebenezer Rusel White of Danbury & Hannah Judson,	Nov. 17, 1767
Benj. Duning of Newbury & Jemimah Booth,	Nov. 19 (?), 1767
Abel Baldwin & Rebeckah Shepard,	Dec. 3, 1767
Elihu Peck & Jane Stilson,	Dec. 24, 1767
Amos Burret & Sarah Seley,	Jan. 20, 1768
Ebenezer Smith & Easter Booth,	Jan. 27, 1768
Joel Basset & Rebeckah Burrel,	June 7, 1768
Ebenezer Grigory of Danbury & Phebe Booth,	July 12, 1768
Noah Parmeley, Jr., & Uniss Gillet,	July 14, 1768
Asher Peck & Sarah Judson,	Nov. 17, 1768
Jacob Stilson & Lensa (?) Busco,	Nov. 17, 1767
Ebenezer Castle of Roxbury & Uniss Northrop,	Nov. 17, 1768
Jared Botsford & Ann Sherman,	Dec. 15, 1768
James Shepard & Ruana Merrit,	Oct. 21, 1769
Thomas Wagstaff & Rebeckah Merrick,	March 5, 1769
Abel Judson & Ann Bennit,	March 16, 1769
Jonathan Beardsly & Huldah Faris (?),	June 22, 1769
Eli Mygot of Danbury & Phebe Judson,	July 6, 1769
Stephen Mix Mitchel of Weathersfield & Hannah Grant,	Aug. 2, 1769
Samuel Stephens of Stanford & Lois Sanford,	Aug. 14, 1769
John Hard & Mary Nettleton,	Sept. 6, 1769
John Bears & Sarah Starling,	Nov. 8, 1769
Henry Fairman & Ruth Judson,	Nov. 9, 1769
John Leavenworth of Woodbury & Abigal Peck,	Nov. 2, 1769
Nathan Norton & Susana Barnum,	Nov. 30, 1769
Zadock Henries & Thankful Allen (?),	April 12, 1770

Elnathan Schovil of Strarford (?) & Mary Sanford,
June 28, 1770

John Baldwin of Newtown & Judith Brace of Hartford, Aug. 30, 1770

Jabez Brace & Hannah Foot, March 23, 1771

Obadiah Gilbert & Bulah Babbott, both of New
Stratford, Aug. 22, 1771

Timothy Beardsley of Danbury & Mary Hubbell,
Sept. 19, 1771

Henry Fairman & Bethiah Bennet, Oct. 1, 1771

Gideon Botsford & Pulina (?) Fairman, Oct. 31, 1771

Richard Fairman, Jr., & Ana Botsford, Oct. 31, 1771

James Mitchel of Weathersfield & Mrs. Armanald (?)
Grat (?), Nov. 14, 1771

Matthew Peck & Mary Johnson, Dec., 1771

Noah Burr of New Stratford & Arthy (?) Hurd,
April 15, 1772

Thomas Bennet & Moth (?) Ford, Sept. 29, 1772

Cate & Dinah (colored servants of Moses Plat),
Jan. 4, 1773

Levi Moss of Litchfield & Martha Sherman, Jan. 14, 1773

Ephraim Bennet & Johanna Stilson, Jan. 28, 1773

Ammon Herd & Leuca Thomas, Feb. 24, 1773

Matthew Curtiss & Hannah Ford, March 25, 1773

Peter & Priscilla (colored servants of Capt. John
Glover), April 20, 1773

Elijah Hurd of New Stratford & Mabel Johnson,
May 26, 1773

Benj. Curtiss of Newtown & Bashsheba Ford (?) of
Stratford, June 17, 1773

Amos Gray of York Government, near Sharon, &
Uniss Lake, Aug. 10, 1773

Joseph Peck, Jr., & Mary Castle, Sept. 23, 1773

Samuel M——inne of Winchester & Lois Sherman,
Sept. 7, 1773

Benj. Duning & Mary Bristol, Oct. 13, 1773

Josiah Curtiss & Ann Ford, Jan. 27, 1774

Henry Wood & Leucy Botsford, March 9, 1774

James Raimant of Bedford & Mrs. Abigail Botsford,
June 23, 1774

Isaac Allebe of Long Island & Sarah Lesttin (?),
                                        Sept. 15, 1774
Clement Botsford & Mary Baldwin,   Nov. 15, 1774
Nathaniel Judson & Rhoda Hall,   June 6, 1775
Daniel Sherman & Jeremiah Crowfoot,   Sept. 23, 1775
Richard Fairman, Esq., & Mrs. Lydia Baldwin,
                                        Jan. 16, 1776
Eli Peck & Hannah Lacey (?),   May 8, 1776
Benj. Seeley of New Milford & Mary Judson, May 15, 1776
Nehemiah Birtch & Jane Bennet,   Aug. 29, 1776
Joseph Fairchild of Newtown & Amarillius Dibble
      of Danbury,   Oct. 27, 1799

INDEX.

HILTON, 98

PALMER, 8, 43, 55, 57, 58, 59, 62, 63, *100*, 101, 102, 103, 104, 105, 106, 107, 108, 110, 111, 112, 127, 129.* PAGE, 12, 81, 86, 100, 101, 102, 103, 104, 105, 109, 110 111, 112.* PARDEE, 100. PALMS, 12, 19, 22. PLAT, 134, 137. PLACE, 17, 58. PARENT, 108. PARKER, 23, 53, 107, 113, 127, 128. PLATTS. 113, 115, 116, 117, 118, 119, 120. PARSONS. 25, 35. 86. PAYNE, PAINE, PAIN, 32, 36, 40, 44, 45, 46, 48, 50, 69, 121, 122, 123, 124, 131. PATTEN, 35. PARMELA, 117. PRATT, 36, 42, 47, 48, 85, 115, 116, 117. PACKWOOD, 37. PARK, 68, 69, 71, 125 PARMENTER, 50. PASENT, 109. PLANK, 53, 56, 57, 63, 65. PARKHURST, 53, 69, 70, 71 PHAY, 55, 56. PLANT, 103, 104, 106, 107, 109, 110, 111, 112, 113, 118. PARTRIDGE, 65, 69. PARKES, PARKS. 67. 70, 122. PARISH, PARRISH, PARESH, 70, 100, 101, 103, 104, 105, 106, 107, 110, 112, 124.* PHRAGER, 78. PAYTON, 92. PARDY, 104. PLANK.* PRENTIS, PRENTICE, 7, 9, 10, 11, 12, 13, 15, 16, 18, 19, 20, 24, 26, 28, 31, 32, 33, 71 PRENTS, 8. PEMBER, 9, 16, 17. PRESTON, 10, 20, 22, 26, 34, 94,*123* PERRY, 14, 64, 94, 135. PELL, 15. PENNIMAN, 26, 33, 34. PERRIMAN, 15, 21. PERKINS, 19, 20, 24, 31, 47, 68, 70, 71, 81, 84, 123, 125, 128, 129. PECK, 29, 94, 102, 131, 132, 133, 134, 135, 136, 137, 138.* PETER, 30, 87, 132, 137. PEG, 87, 102. PHELPS, 41, 42, 43, 44, 45, 46, 47, 48, 49, 73. PEES, 42, 83. PETERS, 57, 68, 70. PHEBE, 47. PERKIN, 57. 63. PERSON, 135. PEMBERTON, 67. *PEASE*, 91. PELTON, 82, 96, 97. PETTIS, 93.* PENFIELD, 97, 101, 104, 107.* PELLET, 123, 125. PICKETT, 7, 16, 20. PIKE, 9, 31, 114, 125, 127. PEIRCE, PIERCE, 12, 43, 46, 48, 55, 66, 67, 68, 69, 70, 72, 77, 80, 104, 136. PIERPONT, PEIRPOINT, 17, 25, 30, 91. PHIDIAS, 27. PITMAN, 31, 36, 37. PHILLIPS, 33, 66, 67, 68, 69, 70. PINIO, 41. PRIME, 43. PHILLIS, 44, 102. PRICE, 54, 77, 107, 112, 122. PRINCE, 55, 56, 57, 58, 60 61, 62, 64. PRIOR, 68, 109. PITKINS,

81, 83, 86. PIERSON, 99. ~~103~~ 115. PHINNEY, 124. PRINDLE, 133, 134, 135, 136. PRISCILLA, 137. POTTER, 8, 15, 21, 23, 24, 32, 34, 36, 72, 99, 104, 107, 111. PLOMBE, 9, 12, 22, 23, 24. POTTS, 10. PLOMLEY, 11. PROCTER, 12, 31, 122, 123. POWELL, 14, 39. POLLEY, 18, 22. POWERS, 23 26, 27, 33. POOL, 30, 34, 36. POULAIN, 32. POURL, 41. PORTER, 42, 43, 44, 55, 56, 57, 58, 60, 63, 74, 80, 85, 89, 91, 92, 95, 97, 103, 127, 128, 130.* POLBY, 42. POPE, 45. POST, 47, 113, 114. 115, 116, 117, 118, 119, 120.* POND, 99, 100, 102, 103, 106.* POOR. 50. POWEL, 88. POMROY, 73. PROUTY, 91. PONEY, 123. PLUM, PLUMB, 30, 84, 89, 91, 97, 99.* PURPLE, 34. PUMROY, 44. PUDNEY, 53. PUTNAM, 55, 71. PLUMMER, 56. PULSIFER, 63. ~~PURCH.~~ ~~132.~~ PYGAN, 8. PYE, 20. PYNER, 26. *PAPILLON, 105, PAMER, 99.*

QUILSHY, 34. QUEEN, 108.

RAPP. 8 (see Ropp). RAYMANT, 38, 137. RAYMOND, 10, 12, 23, 33, 66. RAY, 11, 118.* RAWSON, 52, 89. RAVEL, 54. RATHBON, 71. RANNEY, RANNY, 87, 88, 89, 90, 91, 92, 93, 94, 95, 96, 97. RACH, 91. RAYNSFORD, RAINSFORD, 122, 123. REINER, 11. REED, READ, RIED. 22, 28, 29, 101, 122, 125, 127. RECHE, 25. REAVES, REEVES, 35. 74. REDDINGTON, 45. REA, 52. REYNOLDS, 60, 74, 126. REDWAY, 60. REAVE, 109, 110. ~~RENTENS,~~ ~~105.~~ REAH, 110. REDFIELD, 114, 115, 117, 118. RICHARDS, 11, 12, 13, 14, 15, 16, 17, 18, 20, 21, 22, 24, 25, 26, 27, 28, 29, 31, 35, 37, 38, 45, 51, 53, 65, 70, 72, 100.* RICE, 11, 21, 71, 108. RIFFAUD, 33. RIGHT. 39, 104. RICHISON, RICHARDSON, 43, 44, 49, 51, 66. RICH, 57, 123. RIDER, 61. RISLEY, 85, 86. RICHIE, 85. RILEY, 87, 91, 92, 93, 95. RICHMOND.* ROPP, 8. ROCH, 46. ROACH, 7. ROBBINS, ROBINS, ROBBENS, 7, 16, 34, 63, 64,

EARLY CONNECTICUT MARRIAGES

AS FOUND ON

ANCIENT CHURCH RECORDS

PRIOR TO 1800.

THIRD BOOK.

EDITED BY

FREDERIC W. BAILEY,

MEMBER AMERICAN HIST. ASSO., CONN. HIST. SO., NEW HAVEN COLONY HIST. SO.,
NEW YORK GEN. AND BIOG. SO., SONS OF THE AMERICAN REVOLUTION
(MASS.), MANAGER BUREAU OF AMERICAN ANCESTRY.

PUBLISHED BY THE

BUREAU OF AMERICAN ANCESTRY
FOR
Family   Researches

FREDERIC W. BAILEY, MGR.
P. O. BOX 587.   NEW HAVEN, CONN.

PREFACE.

A preface to this, the Third Book of "Early Connecticut Marriages," seems hardly necessary in view of the fact that so little is to be added to what has already been stated in our two previous issues. And yet a word must be said if only to express our sincere gratification that through sufficient patronage this unique genealogical enterprise should have been found popular enough to warrant the issue of a third book of the kind without financial loss.

However certain a gain all such productions always are to earnest seekers, we ourselves are not so sure but that its fate may yet be not unlike many another such—"a drug on the market;" still, with past encouragement and increasing interest the hope is augmented that as a natural consequence a fourth book may duly appear, leading to the ultimate completion of this most helpful work.

And the strength of this position rests upon these two indisputable facts.

The first is in the fact of the constantly increasing number devoted to the pursuit of a knowledge of their worthy American ancestors. To many it has been a sudden awakening and a surprise in view of the long-standing disparagement with which the subject was for years considered. Of course there have ever been scattered all over our land a few faithful ones, who, notwithstanding many insurmountable obstacles, diligently but quietly pursued these pressing inquiries. The desire was so born in them that no possible discouragement seemed in any way sufficient to destroy the determination of unearthing their past And, too, such knowledge came at times so slowly and in such driblets that but to veterans of genealogy life seemed all too short. Herein was their peculiar virtue revealed. But in these recent years, with the remarkable growth of our beloved country, the spirit of inquiry has gone more and more abroad, and the desire for this one particular kind of knowledge greatly increased, till on every hand there appears the wish to make up for those past deficiencies of both indifference and neglect by which so much had been irreparably lost.

To be sure, in some cases such knowledge is sought only under the spell of the momentary impulse, affording a little recreation and relief. Certain popular and patriotic movements have done a grand, good work in this direction if only in creating this slender interest to know both self and country better. So much be it said in praise. Patriotism has no better way of being enkindled, and manhood and womanhood, too, no more certain method of elevating itself than in these individual discoveries of our ancestors' virtues. For they did have virtues, too, of which we might well be proud. But it is our firm conviction that many of these new disciples will never be content to stop in the pursuit, once having shared in the delights which such knowledge always brings. They will in due time from a natural impulse, too, be found among those who ever seek to untangle themselves from the increasing masses that know no day but to day and no inspiration than that which is afforded by a commonplace everyday life.

Some learned writer has said that the three vital questions most concerning our race are briefly stated in these words: "Whence came I? What am I? Whither do I tend?" They all had a theological bearing as applying to the past, present and future condition of the human soul. And yet they do bear very decidedly upon life from its material aspects and are problems that with the unusual popularity of scientific knowledge, must interest multitudes of thoughtful people.

For years have we heard and known about those characteristic qualities of the various nationalities that go to make up our common manhood. Indeed a man's nationality goes far toward determining our opinion of him, and he mingles among us with this standard brand of a character stamped upon his name, no matter how much education in our American ideas may have altered his environment. Now this long-standing prejudice, if such it may be for the moment called, is in the light of scientific knowledge to-day recognized as a bald and an undeniable fact. A fact that is carried far into detail as applicable not only to foreign born, but to us natives of old time as well. All of us are in this way subject to a reduction into these primary elements or characteristics whose origin dates from some source other than ourselves. Of course man is more than an animal; but it is foolish to deny the fact of the animal in us even if not pleasant, refuse to recognize such traits as are inherited or to give them such attention as should serve to develop the better man. In the ideal state of the race science will have much to say about inherited tendencies, early training and marriage, too. Hence to know ourselves does involve the past and the distant past with all its hardships, its strifes, its successes, its heroic achievements of which we, ourselves, partake by an inheritance of blood. At some distant day genealogy will be part and parcel of every complete life.

The other fact to be remembered is the comparative ease with which one may pursue this fascinating subject. To be sure there will always be the unsolved problem, though by persistent effort it may be forced farther and farther away. But so far as determining who our immediate ancestors in America may be, the sources of information are much more numerous than once they were. Not, certainly, that the old records have in any way been increased, which is impossible, but they are being the better located and, as found, are now more tenderly cherished and protected for what they contain than they ever were before.

That indifference with which these old books were preserved is passing away and in its stead arises an interest, a pride and a spirit of helpfulness to make all such of service to seekers and inquirers. And let us say for the encouragement of our readers that so far as the old State of Connecticut is concerned, it is rich in much valuable matter sought for, but never probably to be seen in print or otherwise made public. But it is accessible enough at least to be of use, ultimately to throw its bright light upon many cases of despair.

As to the marriage records herein contained, we feel sure they will prove of great value as being of this nature; and should there among its pages be found a name or a date to gladden the tired eyes of some enthusiast such as we, may it be accepted as our contribution to this popular cause that can carry nothing but the purest patriotism in its steady trend.

FREDERIC W. BAILEY.

New Haven, Conn., June 15, 1898.

CONTENTS.

THIRD BOOK.

RECORDS LOST.

The following is a (revised) list of Congregational Churches so far reporting the loss of their records of Baptisms and Marriages prior to 1800.

CHURCH.	COUNTY.	ORGANIZED.	REMARKS.
Westminster, of Canterbury,	Windham,	1770,	none before 1824.
Stamford,	Fairfield	1635,	few before 1800.
Coventry,	Tolland,	1745,	none before 1818.
Hebron,	Tolland,	1716,	burned.
Ellington,	Tolland,	1736,	lost.
Sherman,	Fairfield,	1744,	burned.
East Granby,	Hartford,	1737,	
Goshen,	Litchfield,	1740,	lost.
Watertown,	Litchfield,	1739,	lost.
Canton Center,	Hartford,	1750,	before 1826, lost.
So. Manchester,	Hartford,	1779,	
North Guilford,	New Haven,	1725,	lost.
East Lyme,	New London,	1719,	lost.
Lyme (Hamburgh),	New London,	1727,	lost.
West Haven,	New Haven,	1719,	before 1815, lost.
Litchfield,	Litchfield,	1721,	before 1886, burned
Tolland,	Tolland,	1723,	burned.
Bethany,	New Haven,	1763,	before 1823, lost.
Andover,	Tolland,	1749,	B. and M. before 1818, burned at W. Springfield, Mass.
Glastonbury,	Hartford,	1693,	before 1797, lost.
Marlborough,	Hartford,	1749,	missing.
Harwinton,	Litchfield,	1738,	nothing before 1790
Ridgefield,	Fairfield,	1714,	nothing before 1800.
Plymouth,	Litchfield	1740,	no marriages before 1800.
Somers,	Tolland,	1727,	little before 1800.
Greenwich,	Fairfield,	1670,	nothing before 1787
Greenwich, (Stanwich),	Fairfield,	1735,	burned 1821.

WETHERSFIELD.

HARTFORD COUNTY.

Wethersfield was one of the three first settled towns of Connecticut. Sir Richard Saltonstall with his company settled at Watertown, Mass., but on account of the great number of immigrants from England, some of the people at Watertown left and settled Wethersfield.

Church organized 1635. Town settled 1635. Named 1637.

Elisha Borman & Hannah Dix (?),	Aug. 2, 1739
Thomas Hurlibut & ———,	Aug. 27, 1740
Jonathan Goodrich & widow Abigail ———,	Nov. 25, 1740
Nathaniel Coleman & Ruth Beadle,	Jan. 19, 1744
Joseph Biggeleo of Hartford & Mary Wells of Wethersfield,	March 12, 1745 (1744?)
Elisha Deming & Elizabeth Williams,	March 13, 1745
Samuel Robbins & Ester Wells,.	Feb. 25, 1745
Josiah Belding & Thankful Not,	Feb. 13, 1745-6
Timothy Belding & Abigail ———,	March, 1746
Israel Boardman & Rebecca Meekins,	Aug. 4, 1746
Oliver Atwood & Doraty Curtis,	Nov. 23, 1746
Josiah Francis & Millesset Stodderd,	——
Elisha Warren & Rhoda Andros of Newington,	May 9, 1747
Samuel Goodrich & Elizabeth Whiting,	June 10, 1747
Ebenezer Barnard & Thankful Nekels of Hartford,	July 17, 1747
Roger Hooker of Farmington & Anne Kellogg of Newington,	July 30, 1747
Hezekiah Wells & Mary Boardman,	Dec. 17, 1747
Daniel Foot of Wintonbury & Martha Stilman,	Jan. 14, 1747-8
Jannah Griswold of Harwinton & Martha Griswold,	——
Elijah Kent & Jemima Kellogg,	Oct. 25, 1748
——— Bushnel & Prudence Wells,	Oct. 25, 1748
Soloman Deming & Sarah Kirkum,	Oct. 27, 1748
Moses Deming & Martha Wells,	Nov. 10 (?), 1748
Ephraim Goodrich & Rebeckah (?) Goodrich,	Nov. 17, 1748
Joseph Webb & Mahitable Not,	Feb. 2, 1748-9

Rev. Samuel Lockwood of Andover & ——— May of
    Wethersfield,   April 24, 1749
James Curtis & Elizabeth Kilborn,   May 18, 1749
Charles Whiting & Honor Perrin—"Goodrich, not
    Perrin,"   May 18, 1749
Elisha Kilborn & Sarah Robbins,   June 8, 1749
Elisha Williams & Mehetabel Burnham,   Aug. 24, 1749
Jonathan Brooks & Hannah Clark,   Sept. 12, 1749
Richard Belding & Elizabeth Hurlbut,   ———
Stephen Kellogg & Elizabeth Russell,   ———
Rev. Mr. Joshua (?) Belding & Mrs. Anna Belding,
                               Nov. 30, ———
Eleazer Deming & Hannah Woodhouse,   Dec., ———
Josiah Robbins & Judah Wells,   Dec. 21, ———
Justus Hale & Martha Wright,   Feb. 28, 1749–50
Elisha Webster & Sarah Warner,   March 8, 1749
Nathaniel Belding & Lowis Deming,   March, 1750
Obadiah Dickinson & May Collins,
Samuel Wolcot & Lucy Wright,   March 29, 1750
David Morton of Hatfield & ——— Smith, May 3, 1750
Nathaniel Wright & Martha Goodrich,   May 13, 1750
David Webb & Mary Bulkley,   May 20, 1750
Josiah Griswold & Deborah Williams,   May 21, 1750
Ebenezer Balch & Sarah Belding,   June 28, 1750
John Bulkley & Honor Francis,   July 17, 1750
Ambrose Clark of Middletown & Mary (?) Kilborn,
                              Aug. 2, 1750
Joseph Francis & Sarah Buck,   Oct. 11, 1750
Ebenzer Young & Rebekah Flowers,   Nov. 8, 1750
Richard Montague & Olive Nott,   April 16, 1752´
Samuel Lattimer & Elizabeth Bunce,   Oct. 12, 1752
Nat. Coleman & Comfort Loveman,   Nov. 23, 1752
John White of Hartford & Honor Baxter, Dec. 7, 1752
Timothy Saxe of Middletown & Anne Montague,
                            Jan. 18, 1753
Charles Dix & Martha Baxter,   Jan. 25, 1753
James Wells & Prudence Wright,   Feb. 1, 1753
Josiah Biggelow of Hartford & Elizabeth Wells, 1753
Zechariah Bunce & Sarah Bowin,   June 13, 1753
Thomas Belding & Abigail Porter,   Aug. 1, 1753

Charles Boardman & Abigail Stilman,   Aug. 8, 1753
Samuel Lanselot & Hannah Belding,   Aug. 30, 1753
Reuben Belding of Hatfield & Elizabeth Pierce (?),
    Sept. 26, 1753
William Francis & Phebe Woodhouse,   Oct. 1, 1753
Thomas Norton of Farmington & Elizabeth ———,
    Oct. 5, 1753
Jonathan Porter & Honor Hurlbut,   Oct. 22, 1753
Geo. Kilborn & Rebeckah Belding,   Nov. 1, 1753
Elihú Phelps & Hannah Webb,   Nov. 18, 1753
Aaron Millor of Pantoosuck & Elizabeth Brewer,
    March 13, 1754
David Deming & Elizabeth Robbins,   March 21, 1754
Jonathan Boardman of Stepney & Martha Cole of
    Newington,   ——
Daniel Newcomb of Andover & Elizabeth May,   ——
David King of Number 4, (Sandisfield), Mass., &
    Eunice Boardman,   Aug. 22, 1754
Samuel Woodhouse & Thankful Blin,   Oct. 24, 1754
Solomon Williams & Lydie Francis,   Nov. 21, 1754
Israel Smith & Sarah Andross,   Dec. 30, 1754
James Ayrault & Abigail Kilborn,   Jan. 2, 1755
Samuel Sage of Middletown & ——— Hurlbut, April 10, 1755
David Goodrich & Hannah Boardman,   May 1, 1755
Andrew Tooley or Cooley & Mary Ashcraft, May 15, 1755
Capt. Joseph St. John of Norwalk & Mrs. Hannah
    Wright,   June 24, 1755
Samuel Butler & Abagail Adams,   June 24, 1755
Nathaniel Saltonstal of New London & Rebeckah
    Young,   Sept. 4, 1755
Elisha Robbins & Sarah Harris,   Sept. 8, 1755
John Wells & Rebeckah Butler,   Oct. 12, 1755
Stephen Munson of New Haven & Lucy Riley, Oct. 16, 1755
Hezekiah Hale & Abigail Hanmar,   Jan. 15, 1756
Aaron Belding & Mercy Belding,   ——
Timothy Cadwell of Westfield & Catharine Bulk-
    ley,   May 19, 1756
Gideon Wright & Elizabeth Buck,   July 8, 1756
Daniel Robbins, Jr., & Mary Robbins,   July 13, 1756
Cephas Smith & Sarah Bulkley,   Aug. 5, 1756

Ezekiel Fosdick & Annah W[elles (?),   Sept. 22, 1756
Thomas Wise of Middletown & ——— of Wethers-
    field,   Oct. 14, 1756
Hezekiah Robbins & Mehitabel (B ?),   Oct. 14, 1756
John Treat & Elizabeth C[anning,   Nov. 24, 1756
Abel Tryal of Middletown & Lament Risley, Jan. 12, 1757
David Welles & Sarah Woodhouse,   Jan. 13, 1757
John Buck & Sarah Hurl[but,   Feb. 10, 1757
Joshua Stoddard & Martha Deming,   March 13, 1757
Hezekiah Andrus of Farmington & Anne Stedman,   ——
Israel Markham & Penelope Bement,   June 23, 1757
Wilson Rowlison (Rowlandson) & Anne Bunce, July 6, 1757
Timothy Hurlbut & Sarah Clerk,   Oct. 5, 1757
Samuel Knowles of Hartford & Mary McCloud,
                                              Oct. 16, 1757
William Loveman & Abigail Adams,   Jan. 12, 1758
Silas Lomiss & Jerusha Treat,   Jan. 26, 1758
Samuel Buck & Hannah Wright,   March 22, 1758
William Killby & Dority Deming,   March 23, 1758
John Hanmar & Prudence Wright,   ——
Joseph Belding & Lowis Curtiss,   Sept. 21, 1758
Joshua Hempsted & Anne Buck,   Dec. 12, 1758
Joshua Robbins & ——— ———,   Dec. 21, 1758
Elizur Wright of Ca[naan & ——— Boardman, Jan. 11, 1759
Josiah Belding & Mehetabel Rob——,   Jan. 31, 1759
William Hurlbut & Catharine Deming,   March 21, 1759
Roger Robbins & Abigail Beadle,   June 19, 1759
Daniel Ayrault & Lucy Williams,   ——
Samuel Cotton & Mable Bibbud (?),   ——
Simeon Jud of Farmington & Damaris Frasier, Sept. 20, 1759
William Griswold & Elizabeth MacCloud,   Oct. 18, 1759
        (Capt. William Griswold married a London lady, S. W. A.)
Camp Addams & Mehetabel Baxter,   Dec. 13, 1759
John Calis & Elizabeth Ned (colored),   Jan. 3, 1760
Othniel Williams & Catharine Williams,   Feb. 21, 1760
Charles Bulkley & Mary Griswold,   March 10, 1760
Daniel Cone of East Haddam & Abigail Griswold, ——
David Welles & Lydie Williams,   ——
James Deming & Olive Bulkley,   ——
John Belding & Rebeckah Renals,   ——

Joseph Stilman & Sarah Wright,   ——
Thomas Nooson (Newson) & Sarah Dix,   ——
John Russel & Elizabeth Pettibon,   Sept. (?) 18, ——
Elizur Goodrich & Abigail Deming,   Sept. 25, 1760
Hosea Harris & Eunice ——,   Dec. 11, ——
Roger Riley & Comfort Loveland,   Feb. 12, 1761
Jonathan Brigden & Elizabeth Bordman,   March 2, 1761
Amos Fox & Susanna Dickinson,   March 12, 1761
Levi Bordman & Sarah Bordman,   April 23, 1761
William Smith, Esq., of New York & Mrs. Elizabeth
    Williams (widow Rector Elisha Williams ?),
                                           May 12, 1761
David Mitchel & Mary Wolcot,   June 11, 1761
Benjamin Henshaw (?) of Middletown & Hulda
    Sumner (?),   July 2, 1761
Chester Welles & Mabel Mitchel,   Oct. 29, 1761
Peleg Coleman & Rebeckah Dickinson,   Dec. 6, 1761
Joseph Moseley of Glassenbury & Hopeful Robbins,
                                          Dec. 10, 1761
Dr. Joseph Farnsworth & Honor Williams,   Jan. 7, 1762
Timothy Francis & Elizabeth Hanmer,   March 10, 1762
Roger Warner & Rhoda Butler of Stepney,   April 1, 1762
Samuel Buck & Elizabeth Blin,   April 22, 1762
Ebenezer Dickinson & (Lucy ? or Mabel),   July 12, 1762
Francis Hanmer, Jr., & Rhoda Boardman,   Sept. 13, 1762
William Warner & Eunice Warner,   Oct. 21, 1762
Abijah Tryon & Eunice Francis,   Nov. 3, 1762
Elizur Deming & Sarah Deming,   Dec. 16, 1762
Othniel Williams & Hannah Renels (Reynclds),
                                           Jan. 3, 1763
Samuel Andross of Wintonbury & Rebekah Tryon,
                                           April 7, 1763
Ezra Webb & Hannah Nott,   Aug. 30, 1763
Samuel Lancelot & Sarah Stilman,   Sept. 22, 1763
Silas Dean & Mehetibel Webb (she was the widow
    of Joseph Webb, Sr., and daughter of Capt.
    Gersham Nott and mother of Gen. Samuel B.
    Webb),   Nov. 8, 1763
Appleton Robbins & —— ——,   Nov. 17, 1763
Justus Riley & Martha Kilborn,   Jan. 19, 1764

Christopher Hurlbut & Mary Deming,	Jan. 19, 1764
John Benton & Mary Blin,	——
Thomas Kilby & Hannah Crane,	Aug. 23, 1764
John Francis & Rhoda Wright,	Sept. 20, 1764
Josiah Griswold, Jr., & Mercy Miller,	Oct. 7, 1764
Elisha Wright & Mary Buck,	Oct. 24, 1764
Jacob Riley & Abigail Williams of Stepney,	Dec. 12, 1764
Simeon Jennings & Elizabeth Kilby,	Dec. 13, 1764
William Rhodes & Rhoda Dix,	Dec. 19, 1764
Noadiah Hooker of Farmington & Rebeckah Gris-wold,	Jan. 2, 1765
George Kilborn & —— ——,	Nov. 10, 1763
Elizur Steel of Kensington & Mary Rhodes,	Jan. 17, 1765
Timothy Griswold & Hannah Tryon,	Jan. 17, 1765
Thomas Welles & Lucy Belding,	Jan. 20, 1765
John Stoughton & Ruth Belding,	Jan. 22, 1765
Peter Deming & Jerusha Welles,	Feb. 6, 1765
Joshua Rissly of East Hartford & Sarah (Mait-land ?),	Feb. 17, 1765
Robert Ames of Stepney & Sarah Moreton of Step-ney,	Feb. 20, 1765
David Riley & Lois Griswold,	March 28, 1765
Nathaniel Goodrich & Lucy Hanmer,	April 21, 1765
Daniel Cole & —— Rhodes,	April 25, 1765
Stephen Webster of Hartford & Anne McCloud,	May 9, 1765
Stephen Richardson of Stonington & Sarah Treat,	Aug. 20, 1765
Chester Welles & Hannah Belding,	Oct. 31, 1765
Simeon Belding & Martha Lockwood,	Nov. 3, 1765
Jonathan Bunce & Elizabeth Ranney (?),	Nov. 21, 1765
Stephen Mears (?) of Windsor & Lydia Welles,	Jan. 16, 1766
Benjamin Fisk of Middletown & Mary Deming,	Jan. 30, 1766
Samuel Pierce & Mary Willard,	Feb. 6, 1766
James Hanmer & Elizabeth Ayrault,	May 5, 1767
John Deming & Prudence Treat,	Aug. (?) 31, 1767
Jonathan Olmstead of Hartford & Sabra Stanley,	Oct. 25, 1767
Samuel Dun (?) or Deen (?) & Susannah Curtis,	Oct. 25, 1767

Joseph Butler & Abigail Boardman, Oct. 27, 1767
Josiah Hurlbut & Mabel Deming, Oct. 29, 1767
Timothy Elmer of Windsor & Mary Marsh, Nov. 19, 1767
Samuel Hanmar & Sarah Welles, Dec. 10, 1767
Jeremiah Standish & Hannah Wise, Dec. 22, 1767
Stephen Mears & Sarah Bradford, Dec. 23, 1767
Joseph Welles, Jr., & Jerusha Hurlbut, Dec. 24, 1767
Daniel Warner & Hannah Adams, Jan. 14, 1768
Joseph Marven & ———— ————, Jan. 28, 1768
William Miller of Glassenbury & Elizabeth Love-
land, Feb. 18, 1768
Thomas Brigden & Martha Bordman, March 24, 1768
Stephen Willard & Anne Harris, March 24, 1768
James Knowls & Prudence Benton, April 3, 1768
Toney (servant of Capt. Jonathan Belding) & Cloe,
April 6, 1768
Jonathan Smith & Thankful Wise, April 7, 1768
Simeon Hurlbut & May Furbs, Oct. 3, 1768
Edward Hopkins & Elizabeth Beadle, Aug. 17, 1768
Theodore Lee of New Britain & Olive Board[man,
Nov. 10, 1768
Ebenezer Wright & Grace Butler, Nov. 13, 1768
John Raynolds of Enfield & Mary Lockwood, Nov. 30, 1768
Israel Kellsey of Kensington & Mary Samborn,
Dec. 29, 1768
Roger Butler & Hannah Hanmar, 1769
Timothy Russell & Martha Deming, 1769
Leonard Boardman & Experience Pelton, ———
Pop Lewis & Nancy Steel (negroes), March 9, 1769
Jeremiah Markum of Middletown & Anna Deming,
April 20, 1769
Jonathan Welles & Elizabeth Deming, May 4, 1769
Simeon Griswold & Mary Anne Ayrault, May 4, 1769
Soloman Lomis of Colchester & ———— ————, ———
Samuel Riley, Jr., & Sarah Eggleston, May 21, 1769
Billy Welles & Cloe Butler, July 13, 1769
John Burgee (?) & Hannah Flowers, Oct. 17, 1769
Eliakim Fish & Sarah Lancelot, Oct. 18, 1769
Samuel Stilman & Millissent Riley, Oct. 19, 1769
Samuel Boardman & Anne Wright, Dec. 14, 1769

Jonathan Weaver & Hopewell Coleman,   Dec. 14, 1769
Ebenezer Deming, Jr., & Mabel Deming,   Jan. 5, 1769
Samuel Willcocks of Killingworth & Hopeful
 Williams of Stepney,   Jan. 19, 1769
Hezekiah Turner of Hartford & Azubah Hurlibut,

        Jan. 26, 1769
Samuel Cole & Jemima Clark,   Feb. 9, 1769
Mitchel Kingsman & Keturah Lattimer,   1770
John Goodrich & Mary Hale,   ——
James Butler & Hannah Wright,   April 8, 1770
Aaron Tryon & Sarah Lambfear,   May 17, 1770
Daniel Hale of East Hartford & Abigail Bunce, May 22, 1770
Abel Deming & Mary Benton,   Sept. 27, 1770
Daniel Marsh (?) of New Hartford & Jerusha Treat,

        Nov. 8, 1770
Christopher Warner & Elizabeth Adams,   Oct. 28, 1770
Thomas Harris, Jr., & —— Robbins,   Jan. 26, 1770
Ray Flint & Mary Kilby,   Feb. 3, 1774
William May & Martha Woolcott Treat,   April 28, 1774
Dennis Dogan & Mary Welles,   July 3, 1774
William Deming, Jr., & Elizabeth Griswold,   July 14, 1774
Benjamin Weston of Middletown & Mary Wood-
 house,   Aug. 30, 1774
Justus Riley & Mabel Buck,   Nov. 10, 1774
Joseph Webb & Abigail Chester,   Nov. 22, 1774
Elijah Andrews & Sarah Hurlbut,   Nov. 22, 1774
Elisha Welles & Lois Welles,   Nov. 24, 1774
John Adams & Mary Crane,   Dec. 6, 1774
William Butler of Wethersfield & Sarah Baldwin
 of Saybrook,   Dec. 12, 1774
Elisha Wolcott, Jr., & Mary Welles,   Jan. 19, 1775
Josiah Buck, Jr., & Hannah Deane,   Jan. 26, 1775
Daniel Woodruff of Farmington & Rebeckah Belden,

        Feb. 28, 1775
Samuel Dix, Jr., & Sarah Palmer,   May 15, 1775
Jonathan Thayer & Abigail Collins, both of Stepney,

        Aug. 2, 1775
Frederick Griswold & Mary Dickenson,   Sept. 11, 1775
Gurdon Wadsworth of Hartford & Mehetabel Wright,

        Oct. 17, 1775

Samuel Boardman & Naomi Butler, Dec. 7, 1775
Daniel Forbes & Lydia Hurlbut, Dec. 14, 1775
Josiah Welles & Rebekah Deming, Jan. 1, 1776
Luke Fortunc & Prudence Buck, Jan. 18, 1776
Timothy Harrison of Branford & Clorinda Fosdick,
March 14, 1776
David Beadle & Jerusha Hatch, April 24, 1776
Jonathan Belden Balch of Hartford & Hopey Hurl-
but, Dec. 8, 1776
Rev. John Eells of Glastenbury & Sarah Welles,
Dec. 24, 1776
Josiah Buck & Sarah Riley, Dec. 30, 1776
Josiah Curtis & Mabel Bulkley of Stepney, Jan. 2, 1777
Amasa Wade of Winchester & Anna Hale, Jan. 22, 1777
Joseph Dodge & Elizabeth Flowers, Jan. 23, 1777
Benjamin Bulkley & Elizabeth Brownell, Feb. 6, 1777
John Butler & Love Smith, Feb. 9, 1777
Parsons Greenwood & Sarah Latimer, Feb. 27, 1777
Jacob Williams & Elizabeth Butler, both of Stepney,
March 3, 1777
Elisha Brewster, Jr., of Middletown & Margaret
Curtiss, April 16, 1777
Simeon Dupee & Lucretia Griswold, April 26, 1777
William Sutton & Abigail Russell, Aug. 3, 1777
Dick (servant of Col. Chester) & Abigal Sampson
(negroes), Sept. 21, 1777
Thomas Parsons, Jr., of Farmington & Elizabeth Col-
lins of Stepney, Nov. 6, 1777
Solomon Williams & Eunice Robbins, Nov. 6, 1777
John Edwards & Lydia Collins of Stepney, Nov. 20, 1777
Noah Smith of Hadley & Abigail Robbins, Dec. 18, 1777
John Deming & Elizabeth Wells, Dec. 18, 1777
Nathan Baldwin of Stonington & Esther Deming,
Dec. 23, 1777
Joshua Howe of East Haven & Phebe Weaver, Jan. 12, 1778
Othniel Horsford & Sarah Willard of Stepney, Jan. 15, 1778
John Brown & Sarah McDoonam, Jan. 20, 1778
Silvanus Griswold of Windsor & Hannah Webb,
Jan. 22, 1778
John Bigelow of Hartford & Elizabeth Curtiss, Jan. 22, 1778

James Burnham & Martha Sandburne,   Jan. 29, 1778

Joseph Andruss of Chatham & Elizabeth Weaver,

               Feb. 16, 1778

Dr. Josiah Hart & Abigail Harris,   March 27, 1778

Simeon Deming & Mary Curtiss,   April 1, 1778

Josiah Coombs & Hannah Phelps,   April 21, 1778

Elisha Horsford of Farmington & Martha Cole of
 Newington,   April 8, 1778

John Knott & Sarah Robbins,   April 22, 1778

Elizur Goodrich & Abigail Grimes of Stepney, Aug. 13, 1778

Joseph Lewis & Esther Burnham,   Aug. 24, 1778

Joseph Waterberry of Stanford & Mary Adams,

               Aug. 27, 1778

William Warner of New Canaan & Rhoda Smith,

               Sept. 6, 1778

Rev. Gersham Bulkley of Middletown & Hopey Warner of Stepney,   Sept. 30, 1778

Daniel Deming & Judith Deming,   Oct. 1, 1778

Levi Robbins & Abigail Kilburn,   Nov. 12, 1778

Lewis Bettlehisar & Mary Adams,   Nov. 18, 1778

Joseph Barrell of Boston & Sarah Simpson, Nov. 18, 1778

Joseph Crane & Abigail Dix,   Dec. 3, 1778

Othniel Belden & Sarah Lindsy of Stepney, Dec. 24, 1778

Amos Porter of Tolland & Lucy Welles, Jan. 5, 1779

Epaphias Thompson of Saybrook & Peggy Horner,

               Jan. 11, 1779

John Lakeing & Rosannah Mcfee,   Jan. 14, 1779

William Morrison of N. Y. State & Hannah Ware,

               Jan. 16, 1779

Bernard Romans (a native of Holland) & Elizabeth Whiting,   Jan. 28, 1779

Josiah Wright, Jr., & Elizabeth Robbins, Feb. 9, 1779

Josiah Goodrich & Abigail Wright,   Feb. 25, 1779

John Woodhouse, Jr., & Sarah Buck, March 11, 1779

Amos Fox & Jerusha Kilby,   March 14, 1779

Reuben (negro servant of widow Griswold) &
 Lemon (negro servant of Daniel Griswold),

             March 23, 1779

Joshua Wells, ye 2nd, & Eunice Goffe, March 23, 1779

Stephen Skinner of Hartford & Polly Dorr, April 22, 1779

Thomas Alexander of Wrentham, Mass., & Jemima
   Cole,   April 26, 1779
Ebenezer Wells of Wethersfield & Margery Stock-
   ing of Middletown,   April 29, 1779
Aclee Riley & Lucretia Moreton of Stepney,   May 4, 1779
Silas Walton of Norwich & Elizabeth Deming, June 14, 1779
William Bunce & Elizabeth Lloyd,   July 4, 1779
David Dunham of Sheffield & Lucretia Adams, Aug. 5, 1779
Aaron Draper of Roxbury & Ruth Beadle,   Aug. 19, 1779
John Rose & Mary Warner,   Sept. 9, 1779
William Barnstable & Hannah Pelton,   Oct. 3, 1779
Theodore Hale & Sarah Forbes,   Oct. 20, 1779
Samuel Rockwell & Rebiner Collins,   1779
John Carter of Hartford & Sarah Miner,   Nov. 18, 1779
Samuel Churchill of Wallingford & Rebekah Wood-
   ruff,   Dec. 9, 1779
Jacob Hunt of N. Y. State & Catharine Hunt, Jan. 2, 1780
Thomas Warner of New Canaan & Hannah Treat,
                              Feb. 15, 1780
Asahel Thrasher & Phebe Culver,   March 8, 1780
James Hatch & Mehetabel Adams,   March 16, 1780
Asa Robbins & Hannah Coleman,   March 16, 1780
Benjamin Morcton & Lucy Edwards, both of Step-
   ney,   March 21, 1780
Elizur Wright, Jr., & Ruth Curtiss,   March 22, 1780
Ezra Selden, Esq., of Lyme & Hannah Meriam of
   Stepney,   April 13, 1780
Theodore Harrison of Saybrook & Cloe Wright,
                             April 17, 1780
John Marsh, Jr., & Pollicena Goodrich, both of
   Stepney,   July 20, 1780
Richard Price & Abigail Boardman, both of Stepney,
                             Aug. 24, 1780
Ezekiel Goodrich & Eunice Goodrich, both of Step-
   ney,   Oct. 4, 1780
Zebulon Robbins & Lucretia Goodrich, both of
   Stepney,   Oct. 19, 1780
Leonard Dix & Mary Goodrich,   Oct. 19, 1780
Joseph Adams & Mehetabel Barrett, both of
   Stepney,   Dec. 7, 1780

Levi Collins & Mehetabel Boardman, both of Step-
ney, Jan. 4, 1781
Francis Bulkley & Rhoda Griswold, Jan. 18, 1781
Nathaniel Stillman & Martha Hanmer, Jan. 18, 1781
Joseph Allyn Wright & Abigail Bostwick, Jan. 14, 1781
Roger Clarke & Eunice Latimer, Feb. 8, 1781
Joshua Cone & Mehetabel Blin, Feb. 20, 1781
Isaac Palmer & Hannah Flint, Feb. 22, 1781
Asahel Dudley of Middletown & Hannah Wood-
house, March 5, 1781
William Fosdick & Anna Robbins, March 8, 1781
Asa Francis of Hartford & Prudence Warner, March 8, 1781
William Clarke of Wethersfield & Eunice Weath-
erby or Weatherly of Glastenbury, March 13, 1781
Samuel Woodhouse, Jr., & Abigail Goodrich, March 14, 1781
Frederick Robbins & Mehetabel Wolcott, April 12, 1781
Jonathan Hobby of Boston & Sarah Walker, April 24, 1781
Moses Talcot & Elizabeth Griswold, May 8, 1781
William Barton of Farmington & Elizabeth Hopkins,
Aug. 19, 1781
John May & Abigail Boardman, Sept. 4, 1781
Ezekiel Porter Belden & Elizabeth Williams, Sept. 26, 1781
James Smith & Sarah Hanmer, Nov. 21, 1781
Nathanael Skinner of Hartford & Margaret Hunt,
Dec. 13, 1781
Joseph Stillman, Jr., & Rhoda Boardman, Dec. 17, 1781
Aaron Warner & Abigail Montague, Jan. 31, 1782
James Johnson of Middletown & Sarah Montague,
Feb. 28, 1782
Edward Bulkley & Prudence Welles, March 24, 1782
Benjamin Dix & Anna Beckley, March 28, 1782
Moses Griswold & Martha Dix, April 3, 1782
Joseph White of Middletown & Lucy Bulkley, April 4, 1782
David King & Mary Bulkley, April 28, 1782
Eli Welles of Wethersfield & Hannah Baldwin of
Saybrook, May 1, 1782
Moses Tryon & Eunice Treat, May 12, 1782
Solomon Latimer & Rebekah Crane, June 6, 1782
Josiah Robbins & Mary Wright, July 4, 1782
Seth Montague & Sybil Latimer, July 8, 1782

Abner Willcox of Killingworth & Lucy Ayrault,
July 22, 1782

John Barnum of Danbury & Catharine Kilby, Aug. 27, 1782
Frederick Fuller & Anne Barrett, Sept. 17, 1782
John Kilby & Mary Blair, Sept. 30, 1782
Thomas Coleman & Salome Kilby, Nov. 6, 1782
William Blin & Nancy Lucas, Nov. 7, 1782
Abigail Woodhouse & Jane James, Nov. 25, 1782
Thomas Havens & Lucinda Adams, Jan. 30, 1783
John Winn of Philadelphia & Rebecca Kilby, Feb. 17, 1783
Josiah Benton of Hartford & Prudence Welles,
March 9, 1783

Michael Couney of Waterbury & Mehetabel Wil-
liams, April 10, 1783
Japhet (negro of Capt. Thomas Welles) & Ann
(a mulatto), April 15, 1783
Norman Clap of Hartford & Huldah Wright, Aug. 3, 1783
Rosewell Grant & Fluvia Wolcott, both of East
Windsor, Aug. 20, 1783
Selah Barrett & Lucy Dickenson, Oct. 2, 1783
John Hudson & Elizabeth Latimer, Oct. 9, 1783
Daniel Deming & Olly Mark, Oct. 19, 1783
Josiah Deming & Susannah Seymour, Nov. 5, 1783
Joseph Flower, Jr., & Mehetabel Curtiss, Nov. 19, 1783
Thomas Stanley of Farmington & Anne Fords,
Nov. 27, 1783
Nathan Baldwin & Mary Deming, Dec. 7, 1783
George Colton of Springfield & Mary Welles, Dec. 11, 1783
Simeon Dupee & Jemima Goodrich, Dec. 21, 1783
Simeon Frasier of the New City, State of New York,
& Anne Loveland, Jan. 11, 1784
Jared Cone of Bolton & Elizabeth Welles, Jan. 15, 1784
Samuel Brace & Sibil Andruss, April 1, 1784
John Forbes & Mary Hatch, April 19, 1784
Elijah Wright & Penelope Welles, April 22, 1784
Elisha Welles & Sarah Robbins, April 26, 1784
Abijah Tryon & Charity Deming, May 6, 1784
Bezaleel Thrasher & Sarah Woodhouse, May 27, 1784
William Tryon & Anna Hurlbut, June 9, 1784
Nathan Cooke of Salisbury & Anna Grimes, July 8, 1784

Charles Kilburn of Sandisfield & Susannah Fos-
    dick,   Oct. 20, 1784
Elizur Wright of Canaan & Rhoda Hanmer,   Oct. 28, 1784
Hosea Goodrich of Wethersfield & Elizabeth
    Waterman of New London,   Nov. 8, 1784
William Warner, Jr., & Esther Boardman,   Nov. 11, 1784
Elisha Welles, 2nd, & Mary Griswold,   Dec. 16, 1784
Oswald Rockwell & Sarah Wetherel,   Dec. 16, 1784
John Warner, ye 2nd, & Abigail Hale,   Dec. 22, 1784
Allyn Stillman, 2nd, & Elizabeth Deming,   Dec. 23, 1784
Richard Bacon & Annar Fosdick,   Dec. 26, 1784
Levi Churchill & Hannah Belden,   Jan. 12, 1785
Isaac Dudley of Middletown & Anne Woodhouse,
                                            Jan. 19, 1785
Chester Marsh of Dalton & Hannah Burnham, Jan. 30, 1785
David Leonard of Richmond & Rhoda Tryon, Feb. 24, 1785
Samuel Harrington of Farmington & Hannah But-
    ler,   March 10, 1785
Moses Hatch & Abigail Loveland,   July 21, 1785
Thomas Wells, the 2nd, & Abigail Hart,   Aug. 18, 1785
Thomas Wells, the 3rd, & Mary Harris,   Sept. 22, 1785
Abel Lewis of Wethersfield & Joanna Bidwell of
    Glastenbury,   Oct. 27, 1785
Samuel Wm. Williams, Esq., & Emily Williams,
                                            Nov. 23, 1785
Rev. David Parsons of Amherst & Harriet Wil-
    liams,   Nov. 24, 1785
Cabel Hills of East Hartford & Martha Goodrich,
                                            Nov. 24, 1785
Joseph Goodrich & Rhoda Wolcott,   Dec. 1, 1785
Josiah Robbins & Anna Francis,   Jan. 12, 1786
George Hubbard of Berlin & Lydia Wright,   Jan. 18, 1786
Thomas Hollister of Berlin & Sarah Hurlbut, March 9, 1786
William Woodhouse & Mercy Dix,   April 13, 1786
John Standish & Eunice Tryon,   May 21, 1786
Samuel Barnard & Mehetabel Welles,   July 6, 1786
Elizur Deming & Martha Deming,   July 6, 1786
John Wolf & Susanna Fox,   Aug. 17, 1786
Moses Montague & Eunice Harris,   Aug. 23, 1786
Moses Clarke & Mary Hurlbut,   Aug. 28, 1786

Prince Storrs of Windsor & Hephzebah Belden, Sept. 2, 1786
Noah Stanley of Berlin & Experience Welles, Oct. 26, 1786
David Wright & Jerusha Dix,   Nov. 9, 1786
Samuel Blin & Anne Barrett,   Nov. 16, 1786
Jesse Churchill, Jr., & Hannah Boardman,   Nov. 22, 1786
Theodore Butler of Wethersfield & Nancy Baldwin
    of Saybrook,   Dec. 3, 1786
George Montague & Sarah Robbins,   Dec. 7, 1786
Joseph Treat of East Hartford & Martha Adams,
                                           Jan. 4, 1787
David Stillman & Prudence Hurlbut,   Jan. 11, 1787
Frederick Butler of Hartford & Mary Belden, Jan. 11, 1787
Gideon Noble, Jr., of Willington & Lucy Welles, Feb. 18, 1787
Seth Garnsey of Westfield & Mehetabel Jennings,
                                           April 1, 1787
Samuel Wells, 2nd, & Annar Griswold,   April 19, 1787
Noah Will & Hannah Sampson,   April 30, 1787
Robert Sline of Wethersfield & Martha Youngs of
    Hebron,   May 6, 1787
Leonard Dix of Wethersfield & Susannah Holister
    of East Haddam,   June 14, 1787
Ebenezer Webb & Hannah Wright,   July 22, 1787
Obadiah Smith & Lucy Wright,   July 26, 1787
Josiah Willard & Rhoda Welles,   Aug. 9, 1787
Elisha Robbins & Sarah Goodrich,   Aug. 19, 1787
Oliver Talcot of Glastenbury & Lois Balch,   Oct. 11, 1787
Daniel Holms & Eunice Boardman of Stepney, Oct. 17, 1787
Caleb Griswold & Lucy Francis,   Oct. 18, 1787
Ezekiel Sibley of Ashford & Mehetabel Hurlbut,
                                           Oct. 18, 1787
Elisha Williams & Sarah Newson,   Oct. 25, 1787
Joseph Sheldon, Jr., of Hartford & Mary May, Nov. 3, 1787
John Charles Dennis & Abigail Fox,   Nov. 15, 1787
William Rhodes, Jr., & Sarah Coleman,   Dec. 6, 1787
James Stantliff of Chatham & Meribah Welles, Dec. 6, 1787
Simeon Flower & Honor Montague,   Jan. 3, 1788
Simeon Goodrich & Hannah Welles,   Jan. 10, 1788
Capt. Simeon Huntington of Norwich & Patience
    Kenee,   Jan. 15, 1788
Daniel Woodhouse & Lucy Dix,   March 27, 1788

Samuel Wells, 3rd, & Eunice Hurlbut,	March 27, 1788
James Curtiss, Jr., & Sarah Fosdick,	April 6, 1788
William Griswold & Lucy Deming,	April 10, 1788
Jonathan Bunce, Jr., & Marelas Baldwin,	April 13, 1788
Samuel Riley & Elizabeth Howard,	April 22, 1788
Charles Treat & Hopey Robbins,	May 1, 1788
Robert Francis & Anne Francis,	May 8, 1788
Capt. Hezekiah Wells & Hannah Wells,	May 8, 1788
Isaac Buck of Farmington & Lydia Forbes,	July 16, 1788
Joshua Robbins, Jr., & Hannah Hart,	Aug. 17, 1788
Leonard Dix & Mary Forbes,	Sept. 4, 1788
John Putnam, from Gloucester, Great Britain, & Hannah Dillens,	Sept. 11, 1788
The Rev. John Lewis & Eunice Williams,	Oct. 5, 1788
George Benton & Hannah Dickenson,	Oct. 7, 1788
Peter Berry & Mabel Deming,	Oct. 9, 1788
Stephen Chester & Elizabeth Mitchell,	Nov. 5, 1788
Joshua Wells, Jr., & Judith Wells,	Nov. 13, 1788
Oliver Corey & Hannah Adams,	Nov. 27, 1788
George Boardman & Mary Hanmer,	Nov. 27, 1788
Samuel Buck of Wethersfield & Eunice Fox of Glastenbury,	Dec. 7, 1788
Samuel Talcot & Molly Hurlbut,	Dec. 25, 1788
John Benton & Thankful Kilby,	Dec. 28, 1788
Elisha Blin & Abigail Rhodes,	Jan. 8, 1789
Parsons Greenwood & Mary Wilson,	Jan. 14, 1789
Isaac Stevens & Sarah Wright,	Jan. 15, 1789
Isaac Johnson of Windsor & Lucy Hanmer,	Feb. 12, 1789
Elisha Stocking of Glastenbury & Abigail Rannay of Chatham,	March 15, 1789
David Bulkley & Elizabeth Flint,	May 6, 1789
Levi Wells & Sarah Deming,	May 21, 1789
Ezra Webb & Mary Barrett,	June 17, 1789
Benjamin Hunter of Glastenbury & Annah Palmer,	July 8, 1789
Simeon Wright & Lois Curtis,	Aug. 24, 1789
Ebenezer Wright & Mary Dix,	Aug. 26, 1789
Hezekiah Beardsly of Stratford & Mary Roach,	Sept. 6, 1789
Joseph McPherson of —— & Sarah Roberts of Westfield,	Oct. 7, 1789

Joseph Coombs & Elizabeth Rhodes,   Oct. 18, 1789
Cato Freeman of Chatham & Rebecca Modee, Nov. 12, 1789
Robert Robbins & Mary Wells,   Nov. 19, 1789
Nathan Beckwith of Hartford & Betsy Rich, Nov. 25, 1789
Wait Goodrich, Jr., of Glastenbury & Lucy Balch,
                        Dec. 17, 1789
Joseph Kellogg of Newington & Sarah Willard, Dec. 31, 1789
Timothy Stillman & Elizabeth Deming,   Jan. 3, 1790
James Gaines of Glastenbury & Lydia Loveland,
                        Jan. 7, 1790
Jacob Dix, Jr., & Sarah Hanmer,   Jan. 21, 1790
Gideon Wells & Emily Hart,   Feb. 28, 1790
Jonathan Huntington of Haddam & Mary May,
                     March 8, 1790
Daniel Webster of Hartford & Elizabeth Waterbury,
                    March 18, 1790
William Wolcott & Huldah Wells,   March 18, 1790
William Chadwick & Mehetabel Smith, March 25, 1790
Samuel Giles & Prudence Smith,   April 4, 1790
Simeon Hatch & Rebecca Kilborn,   April 4, 1790
Asahel Marks & Susannah Carter,   April 12, 1790
Alvin Montague & Anne Allen of Berlin, April 15, 1790
Daniel Graham of Suffield & Lydia Goodrich, May 10, 1790
Rev. Bezaleel Howard of Springfield & Prudence
  Williams,   May 12, 1790
William Kilby of Wethersfield & Rhoda Morgan
  of New London,   Aug. 15, 1790
James May of Wethersfield & Hannah Stillman of
  Saybrook,   Aug. 22, 1790
Richard Bunce & Olive Montague,   Sept. 12, 1790
Bille Wells, Jr., & Martha Wells,   Sept. 16, 1790
Joseph Pierce of Ellington & Mary Benton, Oct. 3, 1790
Jonathan Griswold & Huldah Francis,   Oct. 7, 1790
Amos Wheeler of Hartford & Lucy Baxter, Oct. 10, 1790
Ashbel Wright & Abigail Deming,   Oct. 25, 1790
John Harris & Martha Russell,   Nov. 21, 1790
Daniel Colton of Watertown & Ruth Rich of Mid-
  dletown,   Dec. 9, 1790
Asher (servant to Col. Chester) & Bridget (a negro),
                     Dec. 12, 1790

James Camp Adams & Sarah Barrett,   Dec. 23, 1790
Benjamin Newbury & Abigail Dickenson,   Dec. 23, 1790
Azel Backus of Norwich & Meliscent Deming,   Feb. 7, 1791
Samuel Hayford of Farmington & Thankful Adams,
                                                 March 22, 1791
Nehemiah Weston & Elizabeth Kilby,   April 3, 1791
Peter Rich & Phebe Clarke,   April 7, 1791
Eleazar Sweatland of East Hartford & Polly Han-
    mer,   April 12, 1791
Allyn Deming & Prudence Woodhouse,   May 28, 1791
Phineas Rowlandson & Mabel Berry,   Aug. 7, 1791
Ashbel Hills of East Hartford & Hannah Wright,
                                                 Aug. 18, 1791
Joshua Seely of Stratford & Martha Curtis,   Aug. 21, 1791
Ches. Rice & Anna Smith,   Nov. 20, 1791
Abijah Flagg of Hartford & Thankful Woodhouse,
                                                 Nov. 20, 1791
Roswell Hoskins of Winchester & Hannah Wells,
                                                 Dec. 1, 1791
Isaac Larkin of Charlestown, Mass., & Abigail
    Warner,   Dec. 15, 1791
Justus Griswold & Prudence Wells,   Dec. 29, 1791
Thomas Griswold & Lucretia Talcott, both of Glas-
    tenbury,   Jan. 25, 1792
Manna Wadsworth of Pittsfield & Anne Deming, Jan. 9. 1792
Elizur Wright & Hannah Wright,   Feb. 11, 1792
Asahel Deming & Lucy Moreton,   Feb. 14, 1792
George Goodrich & Esther Hatch,   March 19, 1792
Lemuel May & Huldah Deming,   June 17, 1792
Daniel Hale & Huldah Riley,   July 8, 1792
Daniel Warner, Jr., & Abigail Williams, both of
    Stepney,   July 14, 1792
Abraham Van Horn DeWitt of Milford & Martha
    Belding,   Aug. 22, 1792
Elias Williams & Christian Williams, both of Step-
    ney,   Oct. 1, 1792
Martyn Baker of New London & Mabel Weaver of
    East Hatford,   Oct. 4, 1792
Hervey Dickenson & Hannah Grimes, both of Step-
    ney,   Oct. 7, 1792

Stephen Stillwill of Ransle—— Ville, N. Y. State,
    & Lydia Tryon of Wethersfield,   Oct. 9, 1792
Moses Dix, Jr., & Ruth Crane,   Nov. 7, 1792
John Francis, Jr., & Huldah Bulkley,   Nov. 7, 1792
Silas Hurlbut & Sarah Kilby,   Nov. 16, 1792
James Francis & Pamela Wells,   Jan. 31, 1793
William Brattle, Jr., of Pittsfield & Hannah Wells,
                              Feb. 5, 1793
Thomas Curtiss & Elizabeth Woodhouse,   Feb. 7, 1793
Josiah Griswold & Abigail Harris,   Feb. 21, 1793
Selah Francis & Roxa Bulkley of Stepney,   Feb. 25, 1793
Nathaniel Sias of Durham, N. H., & Rebecca Ris-
    ley of East Hartford,   Feb. 28, 1793
John Hammond of Boston & Lucy Dillens,   March 30, 1793
Simeon Stillman & Rebekah Deming,   April 14, 1793
Simeon Francis & Mary Ann Adams,   May 26, 1793
Stephen Willard, Jr., & Martha Robbins,   June 20, 1793
Robert Robbins & Cynthia Wood,   June 22, 1793
Gideon Goodrich & Mary Deming, both of Stepney,
                              Aug. 15, 1793
John Woodbridge of East Hartford & Lydia Gris-
    wold,   Aug. 29, 1793
Jared Goodrich & Deborah Griswold, both of Step-
    ney,   Sept. 15, 1793
Samuel Montague & Polly Wolcott,   Sept. 19, 1793
Josiah Curtiss & Rebeckah Marsh, both of Stepney,
                              Oct. 3, 1793
Elijah Bostwick of New Canaan & Sarah Bulkley,
                              Oct. 11, 1793
Peter Deming & Mehetabel Stillman,   Nov. 10, 1793
John Underwood of Colebrook & Elizabeth Warner,
                              Dec. 8, 1793
Samuel Dorr & Abigail Bulkley,   Dec. 12, 1793
John Boardman & Abigail Goodrich,   Jan. 29, 1794
Timothy Horton, Jr., of West Springfield & Betsey
    Hanmer,   Feb. 2, 1794
Jonathan Stanley of East Hartford & Sarah Still-
    man,   Feb. 19, 1794
Ephraim Stoddard of Glastenbury & Jerusha Hurl-
    but,   March 18, 1794

George Barrett of Hartford & Rebekah Dix,   April 2, 1794
Frederick Riley & Rachel Williams,   April 23, 1794
James Treat & Sarah Talcott,   July 13, 1794
Jonathan Bull of Farmington & Mary Smith, Aug. 10, 1794
Benjamin Crane & Sally Lockwood,   Sept. 7, 1794
Joseph Deming & Honor Baxter,   Sept. 17, 1794
Uzziel Adams & Clarissa Lucas,   Sept. 14, 1795
Ebenezer Riley of Berlin & Anne Willard, Sept. 30, 1794
Richard Kane of Frankfort, Pa., & Fanny Scott of
    New Lebanon, N. Y.,   Oct. 11, 1794
Simeon Riley, Jr., & Eunice Wells,   Nov. 27, 1794
Levi Hatch & Mary Crane,   Dec. 7, 1794
John Montague & Persis Adams,   Feb. 18, 1795
Ebenezer Phelps of Windsor & Dolly Robbins, Feb. 19, 1795
James Hanmer & Abigail Wells,   Feb. 19, 1795
James Stillman of Wethersfield & Elizabeth Web-
    ster of East Hartford,   Feb. 26, 1795
Thomas Chester & Esther Margaret Bull, March 26, 1795
George Gardiner Flower & Rebekah Deming,
                        April 21, 1795
James Marsh of Hanover & Polly Wells,   May 14, 1795
Newport Tosa & Susanna Fortune (negroes), May 14, 1795
Solomon Wadsworth of East Hartford & Lucy Kilby,
                         July 1, 1795
Edward Bulkley & Dinah Bunce,   July 9, 1795
John Adams & Martha Curtiss,   Aug. 7, 1795
Bezaleel Latimer, Jr., & Nancy Riley,   Sept. 23, 1795
Justus Montague & Sarah Griswold,   Oct. 18, 1795
Norman Smith of Hartford & Mary Boardman, Nov. 23, 1795
Joseph Stevens & Mehetabel Hale, both of Glasten-
    bury,   Dec. 31, 1795
Joseph Winship of Hartford & Mehetabel Rhodes,
                         Jan. 5, 1796
Phineas Hurlbut of Hartford & Honor Goodridge,
                        Jan. 21, 1796
Amasa Adams & Caroline Dalibe,   Jan. 24, 1796
John Walbridge of Royalton, Vt., & Betsey Cal-
    lender,   Jan. 26, 1796
Aaron Warner & Rachel Curtiss,   Feb. 4, 1796
Elias Morgan of Hartford & Sarah Webb, March 6, 1796

Wilford Johnson & Anne Giffen, April 11, 1796
Asa Wright & Lucy Griswold, April 12, 1796
Charles Johnson & Cloe Frisby (negroes), May 1, 1796
Robert Robbins & Abigail Hanmer, June 1, 1796
Stephen Gaylord of Bristol & Anne Rhodes, July 19, 1796
Rev. Dr. James Dana of New Haven & Mrs. Abigail
  Bolden, Oct. 10, 1796
Henry Sheldon of Hartford & Anne May, Oct. 16, 1796
Josiah Hurlbut, Jr., & Prudence Curtiss, Oct. 23, 1796
Joseph Deming & Azubah Turner, Nov. 15, 1796
Phineas Beckwith of Lyme & Betsey Brown, Dec. 14, 1796
Levi Butler & Eunice Bulkley, Dec. 18, 1796
Benjamin Sleeper of Concord, N. H., & Clarissa
  Hurlbut, Dec. 31, 1796
Daniel Seymour, Jr., & Elizabeth Steel, both of
  Hartford, Jan. 2, 1797
Francis Bulkley & Elizabeth Fosdick, Jan. 5, 1797
Peleg Chapman of Chatham & Lucy Benjamin of
  East Hartford, Feb. 2, 1797
Josiah Francis, Jr., of Pittsfield & Sarah Boardman,
  Feb. 6, 1797
Warren Flower of West Springfield & Lois Belden,
  Feb. 6, 1797
Thomas Harris & Sarah Crane, Feb. 8, 1797
Abraham Crane, Jr., & Huldah Hanmer, Feb. 9, 1797
George Stillman & Martha Deming, March 22, 1797
James Wadsworth, Jr., of Hartford & Abigail May,
  April 9, 1797
John Loveland, Jr., & Rebekah Deming, April 12, 1797
William Savage of Middletown & Hannah Rhodes,
  April 19, 1797
Frederick Danielson of Lake Sago & Abigail Gay-
  lord of Danvil, Vt., May 3, 1797
Ephraim Willard & Lucy Griswold, May 11, 1797
Ebenezer Stillman & Rhoda Francis, May 16, 1797
Simeon Deming & Elizabeth Deming, May 21, 1797
Thomas Mygatt & Lucy Oakes, May 23, 1797
Samuel Rhodes & May Dix, June 27, 1797
Alexander Johnson, from the North of Scotland, &
  Lydia Hurlbut, July 20, 1797

William Hart & Sarah Waterhouse Wolcott,   Sept. 5, 1797
Perez Prentiss of Stonington & Rebekah Benton,
                                              Sept. 17, 1797
Daniel Griswold & Hetty Hanmer,   Sept. 25, 1797
Solomon Coombs & Molly Griswold,   Oct. 18, 1797
John Brewer of East Hartford & Hannah Curtiss,
                                               Oct. 22, 1797
James Fortune & Betsey Riley,   Nov. 5, 1797
Elisha Chamberlain of Pittsfield & Ruth Hurlbut,
                                               Nov. 12, 1797
Ichabod Woodruff of Milford & Sally Belden,
                                               Nov. 17, 1797
John Stillman Riley & Sarah Dix,   Nov. 15, 1797
Jonathan Walter Edwards of Hartford & Betsey
     Tryon,   Nov. 29, 1797
Daniel Galpin of Berlin & Mehetabel Dorr,   Dec. 7, 1797
Ithamar Churchill of Hubbardtown, Vt., & Sarah
     Bliss,   Dec. 12, 1797
Bezaleel Latimer & Rhoda May,   Dec. 17, 1797
Elizur Hurlbut & Mary Deming,   Jan. 3, 1798
Francis Hanmer, Jr., & Huldah Dickenson,   Jan. 11, 1798
Josiah Griswold & Charlotte Adams,   Jan. 14, 1798
Josiah Wright & Polly McClean,   Jan. 14, 1798
Cyrus Ranger of Sudbury, Vt., & Sarah Churchill,
                                               Jan. 18, 1798
Samuel Smith, Jr., of Glastenbury & Abigail Hale,
                                               Jan. 29, 1798
Rev. Samuel Mills of Chester & Rebekah Belden,
                                               Feb. 27, 1798
Samuel Hanmer, Jr., & Lucy Crane,   March 15, 1798
Nathanel Wolcott & Abigail Goodrich,   April 15, 1798
Hosea Bliss, Jr., & Mehetabel Wolcott,   April 15, 1798
Carey Leeds of Stamford & Anne Harris,   May 15, 1798
Simeon Hanmer & Mary Crane,   May 17, 1798
Elizah Crane, Jr., of Sandisfield & Honor Adams,
                                               May 20, 1798
Gershom Wolcott & Eunice Willard,   June 14, 1798
Joseph Curtiss & Abiah Seely,   June 17, 1798
Nathanel Dwight of Hartford & Rebecca Robbins,
                                              June 24, 1798

Benjamin Roberts of East Hartford & Sarah Dix,
July 26, 1798

Levi Goodridge & Clarissa Coombs, Oct. 7, 1798
Hezekiah Wells, Jr., & Hannah Wells, Oct. 18, 1798
Christopher Wells & Sarah Montague, widow of
    Justus, Nov. 28, 1798
Thomas Griswold & Mary Wolcott, Jan. 22, 1799
Calvin Dodge & Huldah Robbins, Feb. 26, 1799
Daniel Wells & Honor Francis, March 26, 1799
Jonathan Griswold & Melicent Francis, March 31, 1799
Samuel Crane & Dorothy Benton, April 9, 1799
Roger Wolcott & Mary Adams, April 11, 1799
Comfort Loveland & Prudence Buck, April 16, 1799
Daniel Francis & Mehetabel Goodrich, June 5, 1799
Charles Francis & Sarah Adams, June 16, 1799
Matthew Francis & Hannah Deming, July 7, 1799
Simeon Benton of Wethersfield & Anne Hubbard of
    Chatham, July 11, 1799
Utley Wakefield of Pomfret & Hannah Eells, July 17, 1799
James Goodrich & Betsey Bulkley, July 17, 1799
Timothy Russell, Jr., & Betsey Deming, July 17, 1799
John Hurlbut & Anne Wright, Aug. 25, 1799
Sampson Abraham & Dorcas Hopkins, Aug. 29, 1799
William Chamberlain Hatch of Colchester &
    Jerusha Deming, Sept. 16, 1799
Christopher Sheldon Stillwell of Hartford & Sarah
    Loveland, Oct. 10, 1799
Simeon Griswold & Joanna Riley, Oct. 27, 1799
Ezekiel Montague & Lucy Wells, Dec. 19, 1799

KILLINGWORTH.

MIDDLESEX COUNTY.

Killingworth was named in May, 1667. The First Church was organized in 1667 and is now located in Clinton. The Second Church, formed for the most part of members from the First Church, was organized January 18, 1738. The following marriages are taken from the records of the Second Church, now the only church in Killingworth proper. Rev. William Seward first pastor.

Daniel Allin & Phebe Ruttey,	March 29, 1739
Michael Griswold & Sarah Parmele,	July 3, 1740
Theophilus Redfield & Mary Buell,	Sept. 4, 1740
Daniel Clark & Margaret Chapman,	Oct. 9, 1740
Joseph Bradley & Prisilla Redfield,	Oct. 15, 1740
Ephraim Blin & Hannah Willcoks,	Oct. 30, 1740
Joseph Griswold & Rebecca Ruttey,	Dec. 4, 1740
Benjamin Kelsey & Ruth Willcoks,	April 29, 1741
Daniel Ruttey & Sarah Ruttey,	April 30, 1741
Jeremiah Buell & Mattariah Ward,	May 7, 1741
John Nott & Anna Parmele,	Dec. 21, 1741
Abraham Willcoks & Sarah Tooley,	April 15, 1742
John Williams & Elizabeth Turner,	Sept. 16, 1742
Ebenezer Stevens & Lucy Griswold,	Dec. 2, 1742
Ensign Nathaniel Hull & Hannah Farnom,	April 14, 1743
John Griswold & Elizabeth Hull,	Sept. 29, 1743
Samuel Nettleton & Bathsheba Clark,	Nov. 3, 1743
Samuel Pierson & Lydia Stevens,	Nov. 23, 1743
Josiah Hull, Jr., & Elizabeth Buell,	Dec. 1, 1743
John Wright, Jr., & Elizabeth Chittenden,	Dec. 26, 1743
Daniel Graves & Hannah Parmele,	Jan. 5, 1744
James Hill & Hannah Nettleton,	April 26, 1744
Benjamin Turner & Martha Davis,	Dec. 28, 1744
Nathan Griswould & Sarah Hull,	May 2, 1745
John Pierson & Sybil Parmele,	June 19, 1745
Jonah Kelsey & Martha Nettleton,	Sept. 9, 1745
Samuel Graves & Phebe Hull,	Jan. 14, 1746
Joseph Kelsey & Abigail Griswould,	Jan. 16, 1746
Nathaniel Kirtland & Rebecca Willcoks,	June 19, 1746
Nathaniel Kelsey & Martha Turner,	June 19, 1746

Josiah Chatfield & Hannah Nichols,	July 1, 1746
Asa Dowd & Experience Striker,	July 8, 1746
Giles Griswould and Mercy Chatfield,	Nov. 18, 1746
Ebenezer Griswould & Lydia Parmele,	Dec. 3, 1746
Solomon Davis, Jr., & Sybil Griswould,	Jan. 14, 1747
Jedidiah Bennit & Irena Ruttey,	March 27, 1747
Silas Willcoks & Sarah Stevens,	Aug. 27, 1747
Benjamin Richmond & Hannah Sackit,	Sept. 17, 1747
Daniel Baldwin & Mercy Eaton,	Dec. 2, 1747
Josiah Waterous & Damaris Leonard,	Dec. 3, 1747
Noah Isbel & Jerusha Ward,	Dec. 27, 1747
Samuel Brooks of New Haven and Mehetabel Ellis of Haddam,	June 23, 1748
Asael Ward & Esther Franklin,	Dec. 5, 1748
John Griswould & Mary Ward,	Jan. 19, 1749
Stephen Whitlesey & Elizabeth Hull,	March 9, 1749
Ebenezer Kelsey & Sarah Willcoks,	April 12, 1749
Jonathan Franklin, Jr., & Abigail Griswould,	Sept. 4, 1749
Isaac Turner & Mary Baldwin,	Sept. 14, 1749
Silvanus Kelsey & Elizabeth Stevens,	Nov. 10, 1749
Daniel Thorp & Sarah Brockit,	Nov. 13, 1749
Charles Stevens & Sarah Stevens,	May 24, 1750
Zebulum Parmele & Phebe Graves,	May 28, 1750
Ebenezer Page & Prudence Ruttey,	Sept. 27, 1750
Abraham Turner & Hannah Smith,	Jan. 24, 1751
Daniel Griswould & Lydia Hull,	April 26, 1751
Josiah Stevens & Phebe Kelsey,	June 20, 1751
Silvanus Meigs & Lydia Franklin,	Dec. 4, 1751
Nathan Buell & Thankful Griffin,	Dec. 4, 1751
Daniel Chittenden & Grace Waterous,	Dec. 9, 1751
David Blatchly and Luse Wright,	May 20, 1752
Samuel Davis & Elizabeth Hull,	Sept. 7, 1752
Joseph Kelsey, Jr., & Temperance Hand,	Sept. 16, 1752
Samuel Teall & Dina Chittenden,	Nov. 2, 1752
Daniel Wright & Lucey Stevens,	Nov. 9, 1752
Daniel Ruttey & Mary Hodgkin,	Jan. 3, 1753
Dan Kelsey & Jemima Turner,	Feb. 5, 1753
Sargnt. Benjamin Turner & widow Hannah Hull,	Feb. 11, 1753
Joseph Tooley & Anna Hollibert,	Oct. 29, 1753

Benjamin Turner, Jr., & Elizabeth Griffin,	Dec. 6, 1753
Isaac Kelsey, 2d, & Martha Willcoks,	Feb. 7, 1754
Joseph Farnom & Patience Roggers,	Feb. 14, 1754
John Sutlief & Lucy Hodgkin,	April 23, 1754
David Blatchley & Lydia Meigs,	May 2, 1754
Jeremiah Parmele & Temperance Blatchley,	May 2, 1754
Daniel Stevens & Naomi Chatfield,	May 15, 1754
Joseph Griswould & Lydia Farnom,	May 23, 1754
Deacon John Graves & Sarah Chapman,	June 18, 1754
Joseph Nettleton & Sarah Pike,	June 19, 1754
Elisha Crane & Elizabeth Stevens,	Sept. 26, 1754
Josiah Chatfield, Jr., & Rabina Griswould,	Oct. 17, 1754
Solomon Davis & Hannah Kelsey,	Nov. 14, 1754
Peter Hull & Ruth Kelsey,	Dec. 11, 1754
Samuel Stevens & Jane Kelsey,	Feb. 17, 1755
Joseph Farnom & Mindwell Willcoks,	Sept. 25, 1755
John Lane & Joanna Stevens,	Oct. 26, 1755
Hadon Davis & Elizabeth Griswould,	Jan. 12, 1756
Christopher Tooley & Curence Kelsey,	March 16, 1756
Ezekiel Hull & Sybil Hull,	March 30, 1756
Josiah Stevens & Ame Wetmore,	April 29, 1756
Elijah Willcoks & Sarah Willcoks,	Aug. 3, 1756
Robert Isbel & Lois Parmele,	Aug. 23, 1756
William Willcoks & Martha Stannard,	Sept. 2, 1756
Timothy Chittenden, Jr., & Abigail Ward,	Nov. 18, 1756
Abel Willcoks, Jr., & Mary Hull,	Nov. 25, 1756
Daniel Franklin & Hannah Arnold,	Dec. 7, 1756
Samuel Teal & Ann Field,	Jan. 13, 1757
Eliab Parmele & Rachel Smith,	Feb. 10, 1757
Abner Parmele & Lucy Buell,	March 20, 1757
Joseph Seldon & Jane Post,	June 6, 1757
Samuel Watcrous & Mary Houd,	Aug. 1, 1757
John Nichols & Lydia Griswould,	Aug. 18, 1757
Amos Kelsey & Mable Parmele,	Oct. 20, 1757
Benjamin Willcoks & Elizabeth Whittelsey,	Nov. 7, 1757
Josiah Redfield & Sarah Parmele,	Dec. 8, 1757
Michael Shipman & Sarah Franklin,	Feb. 2, 1758
Eliakim Steevens & Prudence Chittenden,	May 29, 1758
Samuel Steevens, 2d, & Catharine Wetmore,	Oct. 30, 1758
Aaron Kelsey & Lydia Nettleton,	Nov. 16, 1758

Benjamin Spencer & Abigail Francis,	Jan. 11, 1759
Abner Farnom & Elisabeth Willcocks,	Jan. 18, 1759
Silvanus Graves & Lydia Griswould,	March 12, 1759
Daniel Hand & Sibe Smith,	Oct. 28, 1759
Nathan Willcocks & Thankful Stone,	Jan. 14, 1760
Samuel Seward & Abigail Hull,	May 7, 1760
Peter Hull, Jr., & Esther Parmele,	June 16, 1760
Joel Hull & Mary Parmele,	Nov. 23, 1760
Jonathan Kelsey & Zerviah Steevens,	Dec. 18, 1760
Moses Hull & Rabina Chatfield,	Dec. 25, 1760
Caleb Baldwin & Jerusha Parmele,	April 16, 1761
Daniel Wright & Deborah Kelsey,	April 23, 1761
Samuel Evarts & Sarah Nettleton,	Aug. 19, 1761
Jeremiah Nettleton, 2d, & Love Buell,	Nov. 19, 1761
Reuben Steevens & Dina Parmele,	Dec. 10, 1761
Gideon Cirtland & Lydia Willcocks,	Dec. 17, 1761
Eliphalet Steevens & Susanah Blatchly,	Jan. 21, 1762
Benjamin Beach & Mercy Blatchly,	June 3, 1762
Daniel Parmele & Mary Nettleton,	Jan. 12, 1763
Samuel Burr & Jerusha Steevens,	March 28, 1763
Daniel Lane, 2d, & Mary Griswould,	July 14, 1763
Isai Nettleton & Jemima Nettleton,	Oct. 19, 1763
Simon Hough & Hannah Willcocks,	Oct. 27, 1763
Nathan Stevens & Mercy Parmele,	Nov. 17, 1763
Stephen Willcocks, 2d, & Sarah Hull,	Dec. 1, 1763
Jedidiah Lane & Phœbe Steevens,	June 11, 1764
Christopher Steevens & Naomi Steevens,	Sept. 27, 1764
Paul Dudley & Sarah Steevens,	Oct. 25, 1764
Daniel Field & Bathsheba Isbell,	Nov. 21, 1764
Nathan Hull & Cloe Hull,	Dec. 10, 1764
David Willcocks & Sarah Lane,	Dec. 13, 1764
Levi Redfield & Sybil Willcocks,	July 3, 1765
Edward Houd & Jerusha Steevens,	July 24, 1765
Samuel Roggers & Elisabeth Willcocks,	Aug. 22, 1765
William Nettleton & Thankful Buell,	Oct. 28, 1765
Simeon Willcocks & Lucretia Kelsey,	Dec. 18, 1765
Rosewell Parmele & Jerusha Kelsey,	Dec. 19, 1765
Eliakim Redfield & Priscilla Nettleton,	Jan. 1, 1766
Eliphalet Huntington & Mrs. Sarah Eliot,	April 24, 1766
Samuel Griffin & Mercy Nettleton,	May 15, 1766

Nehemiah Parmele & Sybil Parmele,	June 5, 1766
Daniel Clark & Anna Clark,	July 7, 1766
Samuel Gale & Elizabeth Gale,	Sept. 4, 1766
John Hull & Sarah Willcocks,	Dec. 28, 1766
George Redfield & Abigail Stone,	Jan. 8, 1767
Joshua Nettleton & Deborah Stone,	Feb. 4, 1767
Thomas Pratt & Ruth Willcocks,	Feb. 26, 1767
Curtis Kelsey & Submit Pierson,	April 30, 1767
Parker Steevens & Concurence Hull,	May 28, 1767
Abner Hull & Hannah Hill,	June 11, 1767
John Lewis & Hepzibah Willcocks,	Sept. 24, 1767
William Nettleton & Hannah Graves,	Oct. 22, 1767
Joseph Bradford & Anna Wellman,	Dec. 9, 1767
Josiah Pelton & Mary Griswould,	Dec. 10, 1767
Ozias Parmele & Lydia Pierson,	Dec. 24, 1767
Jonah Ruttey & Sarah Kelsey,	Dec. 30, 1767
Rosewell Steevens & Tryal Roggers,	Dec. 30, 1767
Samuel Hull & Lucy Willcocks,	Dec. 31, 1767
Dan Parmele & Mary Steevens,	Jan. 20, 1768
Rogger Rose & Abigail Spencer,	Jan. 22, 1768
Houghton Butler & Martha Smith,	Jan. 25, 1768
Joseph Lewis & Sarah Ruttey,	Jan. 27, 1768
Martin Lord & Concurence Seward,	Jan. 28, 1768
Philip Steevens & Sarah Kelsey,	March 31, 1768
James Hungerford & Sarah Steevens,	April 7, 1768
Nathan Graves & Mabel Willcocks,	April 7, 1768
Elisha Lane & Tryal Parmele,	Dec. 14, 1768
John Willcocks & Mary Kelsey,	Dec. 15, 1768
Samuel Parmele & Lois Hull,	Dec. 28, 1768
Daniel Glading & Dinah Willcocks,	Dec. 29, 1768
Joseph Bebee & Jerusha Ruttey,	Jan. 25, 1769
Ezra Parmele, 2d, & Sybil Hill,	May 1, 1769
Jesse Kelsey & Esther Hurd,	May 11, 1769
David Leach & Mary Griswould,	Aug. 30, 1769
Joseph Griswould, 3d, & Temperance Steevens,	
	Sept. 21, 1769
Jedediah Pierson & Patience Hasdel,	Oct. 25, 1769
Joel Graves & Mercy Hull,	Oct. 26, 1769
Samuel Higgins & Sarah Blatchley,	Nov. 9, 1769
Jedediah Buell & Esther Willcocks,	Nov. 29, 1769

Leveret Hubbard & Juliana Gale,	Dec. 21, 1769
Daniel Clark, Jr., & Catharine Cruttenden,	Jan. 18, 1770
Jacob Holt & Lucy Stone,	March 1, 1770
Samuel Griffin & Mercy Steevens,	March 15, 1770
William Stannard & Mindwell Buell,	Sept. 19, 1770
James Nettleton & Esther Griswould,	Oct. 4, 1770
Absalom Kelsey & Mercy Hill,	Oct. 11, 1770
Beriah Redfield & Dorothy Steevens,	Nov. 5, 1770
James Hull & Lydia Gray,	Jan. 24, 1771
Levi Rutty & Jerusha Griswould,	Feb. 28, 1771
Asael Parmele & Rhoda Norton,	May 13, 1771
William Seward, Jr., & Thankful Parmele,	Nov. 20, 1771
Israel Steevens & Sarah Kelsey,	Dec. 4, 1771
Martin Kelsey & Esther Chatfield,	Dec. 5, 1771
Jehiel Evarts, Jr., & Jerusha Nettleton,	Dec. 11, 1771
Joel Parmele & Elisabeth Whitelsey,	Dec. 12, 1771
Edmund Porter & Leah Willcocks,	Dec. 18, 1771
Ambros Kelsey & Jemima Griswould,	Dec. 19, 1771
Asa Stevens & Lois Kelsey,	April 22, 1772
Ishi Franklin & Martha Pierson,	Aug. 19, 1772
Oliver Parmele & Lucretia Smith,	Dec. 3, 1772
Didimus Doud & Mercy Griswould,	Oct. 8, 1772
Samuel Pierson, Jr., & Rebecca Parmele,	Jan. 7, 1773
Abel Nettleton & Lydia Kelsey,	Feb. 17, 1773
Samuel Griswould & Submit Turner,	March 4, 1773
Benjamin Teall & Catharine Willard,	Sept. 16, 1773
Cornelius Hull & Mary Norton,	Sept. 27, 1773
Peter Steevens & Patience Steevens,	Nov. 8, 1773
James Hull & Mary Seward,	Nov. 11, 1773
Rosewell Hull & Charity Chatfield,	Nov. 18, 1773
Jabez Carter & Deborah Jones,	Nov. 22, 1773
Paul Turner & Patience Bradley Cruttenden,	Nov. 25, 1773
Nehemiah Parmele, Jr., & Martha Turner,	Dec. 1, 1773
David Kelsey & Lydia Baily,	Dec. 2, 1773
Josiah Parmele, Jr., & Mary Buell,	Dec. 8, 1773
John Williams & Mary Dudley,	Dec. 9, 1773
Ezra Nettleton & Damaris Seward,	April 21, 1774
Nathan Bassit & Olive Clark,	May 12, 1774
Levi Davis & Martha Kelsey,	June 1, 1774
Nathan Kelsey & Huldah Ray,	June 8, 1774

James Davis & Hannah Norton,	June 16, 1774
Josiah Griswold & Jemima Parmele,	June 22, 1774
Samuel Franklin & Mabel Pierson,	July 6, 1774
Silvanus Redfield & Hannah Franklin,	July 13, 1774
Abner Post & Abigail Willcocks,	Aug. 3, 1774
Nathan Lee & Sybil Dudley,	Aug. 19, 1774
Silvanus Meigs & Sibe Parmele,	Oct. 27, 1774
Bezaleel Bristol & Mary Redfield,	Dec. 1, 1774
Joel Kelsey & Abigail Steevens,	Dec. 22, 1774
Noah Isbel & Sarah Redfield,	Jan. 2, 1775
Elihu Parmele & Deborah Lane,	Jan. 5, 1775
Moses Griswold & Lucetia Kelsey,	Feb. 2, 1775
Silas Willcocks & Sarah Griswould,	Feb. 9, 1775
Caleb Turner & Martha Redfield,	Feb. 9, 1775
Job Doud & Lydia Willcocks,	Feb. 27, 1775
Nathaniel Field & Tryal Stevens,	June 7, 1775
Hiel Parmele & Patience Farnom,	July 27, 1775
Levi Hull & Mary Clark,	Sept. 28, 1775
John Johnson & Hannah Steevens,	Jan. 3, 1776
John Ruttey & Tamar Willcocks,	Jan. 10, 1776
Stephen Spencer & Elisabeth Turner,	Jan. 18, 1776
Samuel Ruttey & Eunice Kelsey,	Feb. 8, 1776
Joseph Willcocks & Grace Willcocks,	March 5, 1776
Benjamin Post & Rabina Hull,	April 18, 1776
Elias Parmele & Thankful Hill,	Sept. 19, 1776
Nehemiah Parmele, 2nd, & Elisabeth Nettleton,	
	Sept. 30, 1776
William Nettleton & Zillah Parmele,	Dec. 3, 1776
Jeremiah Redfield & Rachel Pierson,	Feb. 13, 1777
Jonathan Murray & Abigail Hull,	Feb. 20, 1777
Bela Buell & Temperance Griswould,	Feb. 27, 1777
Cyrus Newton & Anna Willcocks,	June 4, 1777
Dan Chapman & Tamar Holmes,	June 9, 1777
Job Seward & Lois Farnom,	Sept. 4, 1777
Daniel Nettleton & Damaris Stevens,	Nov. 24, 1777
Josiah Buell & Hannah Peck,	Dec. 4, 1777
Simeon Redfield & Mercy Williams,	Dec. 11, 1777
Archibald Austin & Mehetabel Gale,	March 12, 1778
Constant Redfield & Amanda Buell,	April 9, 1778
Elijah Willcocks, Jr., & Mary French,	April 30, 1778

Ai Turner & Hannah Harris,	May 6, 1778
David Evarts & Sarah Hull,	May 20, 1778
Simeon Willcocks & Phebe Kelsey,	May 21, 1778
Uriah Willcocks & Hannah Wright,	June 11, 1778
Martin Redfield & Lydia Griffin,	Aug. 26, 1778
Zelotes Clark & Elisabeth Harris,	Sept. 1, 1778
Jonathan Burr & Lydia Baily,	Sopt. 17, 1778
Jonathan Williams & Mary Kelsey,	Oct. 15, 1778
Gardiner Isbell & Mary Graves,	Nov. 23, 1778
William Jones & Tryphena Atwell,	Dec. 10, 1778
Josiah Davis & Miriam Isbell,	Dec. 24, 1778
James Hill, Jr., & Elenor Hull,	Feb. 11, 1779
Nathaniel Barr & Jemima Steevens,	Feb. 17, 1779
Isaac Kelsey & Deborah Evarts,	Feb. 18, 1779
Achilles Mansfield & Mrs. Sarah Huntington,	
	March 10, 1779
Josiah Willcox & widow Jemima Kelsey,	April 8, 1779
Reuben Doud & Polley Griffin,	June 24, 1779
Abiathar Fowler & Sere French,	Aug. 19, 1779
Joel Norton & Ada Blatchley,	Sept. 15, 1779
Ebenezer Griswould & Phebe Chatfield,	Sept. 23, 1779
Nathan Willcox, Jr., & Rachel Bennit,	Nov. 18, 1779
Seth Redfield & Sarah Pierson,	Dec. 2, 1779
Noah Hill & Caroline Parmele,	Dec. 13, 1779
Ebenezer Davis & Ruth Kelsey,	Dec. 15, 1779
Daniel Blatchley & Rabina Steevens,	Jan. 27, 1780
Jabez Lane & Mary Isbell,	April 17, 1780
Eber Tibals & Sarah Willcox,	May 11, 1780
John Nettleton & Mattie Buell,	June 29, 1780
Josiah Nettleton & Hannah Shipman,	Sept. 25, 1780
Samuel Buell & Rachel Willcox,	Sept. 28, 1780
Aaron Norton & widow Eunice Rutty,	Nov. 23, 1780
Samuel Towner & Sylvia Stevens,	Nov. 30, 1780
Samuel Davis & Rabina Redfield,	Dec. 14, 1780
Zephaniah Bowers & Elisabeth Rutty,	Dec. 28, 1780
Nathaniel Griswould & Sarah Wells,	Jan. 11, 1781
Samuel Nettleton, 3rd, & Ame Kelsey,	Feb. 28, 1781
Thomas Willard & Lydia Graves,	March 22, 1781
Daniel Kelsey & Patience Franklin,	May 3, 1781
Samuel Hull & Freelove Kelsey,	June 20, 1781

Ichabod Ward & Lydia Towner,	June 21, 1781
Josiah Buell & Lois Clark,	Aug. 22, 1781
George Griswould & Artemisia Steevens,	Sept. 13, 1781
Joseph Nettleton, Jr., & Rachel Kelsey,	Sept. 20, 1781
Eliab Isbel & Deborah Stevens,	Oct. 7, 1781
Elihu Parmele & Phebe Crane,	Oct. 18, 1781
Samuel Crittenden & Margaret Clark,	Dec. 27, 1781
Lemuel Davis & Jemima Kelsey,	Feb. 7, 1782
Ebenezer Willcox & Mary Nettleton,	May 2, 1782
John Lane, 2nd, & Roxany Redfield,	Dec. 19, 1782
Bela Munger & Triphena Chittenden,	Jan. 15, 1783
Bani Parmele & Temperance Kelsey,	Jan. 22, 1783
Nathan Griswold & Jemima Pierson,	Jan. 30, 1783
Stephen Kelsey & Lois Griffin,	March 27, 1783
John Spencer (of the First Society) & Martha Will-cox,	Sept. 4, 1783
John Buel of Newport & Abigail Kelsey,	Oct. 9, 1783
Jeremiah Kelsey & Mary Buel,	Feb. 5, 1784
Lovewell Hurd & Margere Parmele,	Feb. 17, 1784
Jacob Hayden of Norwalk & Mary Rutty,	May 14, 1784
Jesse Jones & Mindwell Kelsey,	July 29, 1784
Zenos Griswold & Sarah Lane,	Dec., 1784
Stephen Butler & Phebe Graves,	Jan. 27, 1785
Josiah Graves & Jerusha Wilcox,	March 10, 1785
Moses Kelsey & Huldah Kelsey,	March 17, 1785
Eleazer Baldwin & Jane Redfield,	May 8, 1785
Eliakim Hull & Olive Richmont,	May 12, 1785
Phinehas Jones & Hannah Turner,	May 30, 1785
Hubbel Stevens, 2nd, & Elisabeth Clark,	1785
William Buel & Lucia Wilcox,	Aug. 4, 1785
Nicolas Gross & Eunice Stevens,	Nov. 10, 1785
Henry Davis & Azubah Griffin,	Dec. 22, 1785
Elisha Kelsey & Dinah Nettleton,	Dec. 29, 1785
Capt. Daniel Parmele & Dencey Pierson,	Jan. 12, 1786
Abel Wilcox, 2nd, & Bathsheba Clark,	Feb. 9, 1786
Aaron Parmele & Sally Stevens,	July 19, 1786
Israel Isbel & Miriam Parmele,	July 23, 1786
Benajah Dudley & Elisabeth Redfield,	Aug. 23, 1786
Benjamin Doolittle of Wallingford & Sarah French of North Bristol,	Sept. 20, 1786

Aaron Stone, 2nd, of North Bristol & Mindwell Farnom,	Oct., 1786
Joel Wilcox & Elisabeth Houd Coan,	Oct. 22, 1786
Thaddeus Wilson & Ollidine Field,	Oct. 29, 1786
Miles Dudley & Eunice Farnom,	Dec. 5, 1786
Salmon Crittenden & Lucy Griswold,	Dec. 25, 1786
William Snow & Lucretia Porter,	April 5, 1787
Josiah Chatfield & Susannah Hull,	April 26, 1787
Friend Thomas of Woodbury & Matilda Parmele,	June 26, 1787
Jabez Adkim of Middletown & Lydia Willard,	Sept. 20, 1787
Dudley Stone of Guilford & Rachel Lane,	Oct. 25, 1787
Samuel Denison of Saybrook & Ann Pratt,	Nov. 28, 1787
David Parmele & Polly Turner,	Dec. 5, 1787
Joel Curtis of Wallingford & Hannah Kelsey,	Dec. 17, 1787
Dan Platt of Saybrook & Katharine Lane,	Dec. 20, 1787
Reuben Bartlet of Guilford & Susannah Kelsey,	June 26, 1788
Edmund Crampton of Guilford & Nancy Kelsey,	July 2, 1788
Peter Wells Aldrich & Anna Butler,	July 20, 1788
John Hinkley & Mabel Kelsey,	Oct. 30, 1788
David Kelsey & Olive Parmele,	Dec. 11, 1788
Abner Graves & Polly Howd,	Jan. 4, 1789
Lemuel Kelsey & Abigail Chittenden,	Feb. 5, 1789
Josiah Nettleton & Drusilla Griswold,	Aug. 13, 1789
Rufus Crane & Tamor Brooker,	1789
Jonathan Wellman & Charity Hull,	Oct. 25, 1789
Samuel Pratt & Mary Wilcox,	Nov. 5, 1789
Arunah Lane & Submit Buel,	Dec. 10, 1789
Joseph Farnom, 2nd, & Betsey Kelsey,	Dec. 17, 1789
Nathan Parmele & Polly Stevens,	Dec. 24, 1789
Jonathan Chatfield & Dinah Chittenden,	Dec. 31, 1789
Didymus Johnson of Haddam & Ruhamah Stevens,	Jan. 7, 1790
Robert Isbel & Sarah Snow,	Feb. 15, 1790
Samuel Stevens, 2nd, & Azubah Whitmore,	Feb. 25, 1790
Moses Griswold & Huldah Evarts,	March 31, 1790

Nathaniel Davis & Electa Parmele,   Aug. 15, 1790
Silas Andrews of Norwich & Sylvina Field,   Feb. 18, 1790
(By Abraham Pierson, Justice of the Peace.)

Simeon Scranton of Guilford & Sibe Stevens, June 16, 1791
Joy Ward & Anna White,   Aug. 25, 1791
Nathan Hull & Adah Griswold,   Sept. 25, 1791
Abner Bishop of North Bristol & Thankful Buell,
  Oct. 20, 1791
Philo Mills & Sally Parmele,   Oct. 30, 1791
Ithamer Pelton & Mercy Griffin,   Nov. 11, 1791
John Ward of Guilford & Lucinda Clark,   Dec. 6, 1791
Reuben Stevens, 2nd, & Lydia Hull,   Dec. 11, 1701
Solomon Parmele & Hannah Houd,   Dec. 12, 1791
Nathan Buel & Hannah Turner,   Jan. 23, 1792
Joel Evarts & Lydia Kelsey,   Jan. 30, 1792
Noah Hodgkin & Merab Turner,   April 19, 1792
David Burr of Haddam & Joanna Lane,   May 3, 1792
Ambrose Crampton of Guilford & Mina Stone,
  Sept. 6, 1792
Samuel Lynn & Lucinda Crane,   Sept., 1792
—— Pratt of Saybrook & Lydia Graves,   Sept., 1792
Eliphas Nettleton & Lydia Nettleton,   June 21, 1792
(By Abraham Pierson, Justice of the Peace.)

Dan Stevens & Lois Buell,   Feb. 28, 1793
Charles Haynes of Haddan & Polly Stevens,   Feb., 1793
Asriel Hinkley & Azubah Chittenden,   Aug. 11, 1793
William Stevens & Anna Kelsey,   Sept. 5, 1793
Timothy Isbel & Esther Halsey,   Sept. 28, 1793
Isaiah Kelsey & Sally Wilcox,   Jan. 15, 1794
Levi Redfield & Wealthy Stevens,   March 9, 1794
Ebenezer Parmele & Cynthia Griswold,   April 9, 1794
Abraham Tooley & Anna Kelsey,   June 26, 1794
Benjamin Lynde of Saybrook & Diadema Parmele,
  Aug. 3, 1794
Jonathan Chittenden & Fanny Houd,   Oct. 4, 1794
Abel Nettleton & Sibel Davis,   Oct. 8, 1794
John Hull & Mabel Parmele,   Nov. 2, 1794
Lewis Clark & Tryal Lane,   Nov. 9, 1794
Nathan Howd & Miriam Clark,   Dec. 16, 1794
Dan Lane & Cynthia Lord,   Dec. 25, 1794

David Griswold & Thankful Redfield, Dec. 25, 1794
Phinehas Meigs of Guilford & Concurrence Lord,
Jan. 1, 1795
Nathan Evarts & Tamar Kelsey, Jan. 18, 1795
Samuel Dean of Cornwall & widow Lucinda Lynn,
March 12, 1795
Martin Blatchly of Guilford & Barbara Redfield,
June 25, 1795
Capt. John Joseph Ray of St. Domingo, West Indies,
& Mabel Stevens, July 19, 1795
Moses Doud of Guilford & Anna Nettleton, July 23, 1795
Eli Kelsey & Sarah Wilcox (of the First Society),
July 26, 1795
Alanson Parmele & Anna Jackson, Oct. 4, 1795
Billy Griswold & Lovice Parmele, Oct. 28, 1795
Roswell Hurd (First Society) & Mehitabel Tooley,
Nov. 8, 1795
Theodore Bates & Trial Redfield, Nov. 11, 1795
Phillip Lane & Rabina Nettleton, Nov. 30, 1795
Denison Pratt & Lois Hull, Dec. 2, 1795
Dr. Benjamin Hill & Jemima Standard, Dec. 6, 1795
Daniel Stevens & Rachel Hull, Dec. 17, 1795
Elias Stevens & Mercy Parmele, 1796
Worden Griffin & Rhoda Hull, Feb. 15, 1796
Orren Redfield & Rachel Graves, March 10, 1796
Joel Griswold & Sally Kelsey, Sept. 1, 1796
Eliakim Hull & Hannah Nettleton, Sept. 11, 1796
John Rossiter & Abigail Griswold, Sept. 21, 1796
Eliab Parmele & Lydia Pierson, Nov. 27, 1796
Leman Nettleton & Lydia Laboron, Dec. 18, 1796
Pardon Lane & Mary Snow, Jan. 1, 1797
John Blachley & Charity Kelsey, Jan. 23, 1797
Abel Nettleton, 2nd, & Barbara Parmele, Jan., 1797
Caleb Wilcox & Rabina Parmele, March 5, 1797
Linus Evarts & Rhoda Griswold, March 5, 1797
Benoni King of Suffield & Parmel Parmele, June 15, 1797
William Carter & Polly Wilcox of Killingworth
(First Society), June 22, 1797
John Chapman & Patty Howd, Oct. 30, 1797
Calvin Dudley & Millie Redfield, Nov. 9, 1797

Abraham Spencer of Haddam & Temperance Butler,

	Nov., 1797
Adin Parmele & Dorinda Hull,	Dec. 10, 1797
Nathan Pierson & Jane Towner,	Jan. 11, 1798
William Lord & Esther Parmele,	Jan. 25, 1798
Michael Rutty & Thankful Parmele,	Feb. 22, 1798
Jonathan Kelsey, 2nd, & Polly Parmele,	Feb. 22, 1798
Crippen Hurd of Haddam & widow Thankful Wilcox,	June 5, 1798
Calvin Gaylord & Rabina Kelsey,	Aug. 5, 1798
Jasper Griffin of Saybrook & Lydia Lane of Vermont,	Sept. 14, 1798
Samuel Griswold & Electa Hull,	Oct. 25, 1798
John Isbel & Irene Newel,	Nov. 1, 1798
Samuel Pratt & Martha Parmele,	Nov. 7, 1798
Francis Le Barron & Sabra Kelsey,	Nov. 11, 1798
Jeremiah Stevens & Jerusha Buel,	Dec. 2, 1798
James Davis, 2nd, & Joanna Willcox,	Dec. 12, 1798
Amos Hull & Lucretia Newel,	Nov. 11, 1798
Elisha Kelsey, 2nd, & Fanny Redfield,	Dec. 19, 1798
Ebenezer Stevens & Eleanor Hull,	Dec. 30, 1798
Bela Parmele & Temperance Isbel,	Jan. 6, 1799
Dan Carter & Polly Parmele,	Jan 16, 1799
Selah Hill & Sally Turner,	Feb. 6, 1799
Samuel Davis, 2nd, & Sally Kelsey,	April 25, 1799
Charles Norton & Polly Buel Kelsey,	Aug. 4, 1799
Pardon Stevens, 2nd, & Deborah Nettleton,	Sept. 4, 1799
Michael Chatfield & Assenah Hull,	Nov. 18, 1799
Michael Nettleton & Martha Ruttey,	Dec. 22, 1799
David Franklin & Molly Chittenden,	Dec. 23, 1799
Levi Davis & Molly Dudley,	Dec., 1799
James Hamilton, 2nd, & Jerusha Ruttey,	Dec. 30, 1799

SCOTLAND.

WINDHAM COUNTY.

Scotland was incorporated May, 1057, having been taken from Windham. The Congregational Church in Scotland is the Third Church of Windham and was organized October 22, 1735. Rev. Ebenezer Devotion was the first pastor, whose marriage record begins as follows:

Cornelius Waldo & Abigail Walden,	Feb. 3, 1735–6
Caleb Jewett & Rebekah Cook,	Feb. 3, 1735–6
Jacob Burnap & Abigail Clark,	Feb. 3, 1735–6
Daniel Cutler & Mary Woodward,	July 9, 1736
Benjamin Follet & Hannah Woodward,	Nov. 10, 1736
Seth Case & Sarah Griggs,	Nov. 11, 1736
William Case & Lucy Tracy,	Nov. 11, 1736
Zebulon Hebard & Hannah Bass,	March 30, 1737
Isaac Robinson & Deborah Hebard,	Dec. 22, 1737
Rev. Hezkiah Lord & Zerviah Backus,	June 2, 1738
John Devotion & Martha Lathrop,	July 27, 1738
(By Mr. Lord.)	
Isaac Lascl & Bertha Woodward,	Oct. 12, 1738
Ichabod Palmer & Pheebe Broughton,	Nov. 22, 1738
Samuel Hebard & Mary Kingsley,	Jan. 17, 1739
Samuel Palmer & Lidia Silsbey,	Jan. 18, 1739
James Brewster & Faith Ripley,	March 15, 1739
Seth Palmer & widow Mary Mosley,	Jan. 14, 1740
Benjamin Smith & Jerusha Tracey,	April 17, 1740
Jeremiah Bingham & widow Mary Luce,	Sept. 25, 1740
Benjamin Demming & Mercy Palmer,	Nov. 5, 1740
Daniel Ross & widow Warner,	Nov. 5, 1740
John Cary, Jr., & Rebekah Rudd,	Nov. 13, 1740
Ebenezer Palmer & Mary Webb,	March 11, 1741
Zebulon Rudd & Jerusha Brewster,	June 5, 1741
Rev. Stephen White & Mary Dyer,	Sept. 2, 1741
Ebenezer Wilkinson & Thankful Cutler,	Dec. 4, 1741
Josiah Manning & Mary Kingsley,	Dec. 4, 1741
Josiah Kingsley & Elizabeth Palmer,	Nov. 11, 1742
Benjamin Smith & Elizabeth Douty,	Nov. 11, 1742
Thomas Pardy & Weltheand Cook,	Nov. 24, 1743

Samuel Dean & Sarah Broughton,	Nov., 1743
Salmon Kingsley & Lidia Burges,	Jan. 24, 1744
Jonah Brewster & Joanna Waldo,	Jan. 25, 1744
William Croker & Hannah Baker,	March 15, 1744
Henry Silsbey & widow Bethia Lasell,	April 5, 1744
Elisha Hebard & Mary Palmer,	Aug. 15, 1744
John Baker & Mercy Cary,	Nov. 27, 1744
Jeremiah Ross & Anna Pain.	Oct. 31, 1744
Jeremiah Clemmons & Mary Moseley,	Sept. 5, 1745
Dr. John Allen & Jerusha Cook,	Sept. 12, 1745
John Boughton & I. D'ono Who,	Sept. 23, 1745
Joseph Manning & Pheebe Lillie,	Oct. 29, 1745
Zebulon Palmer & Lois Carpenter,	April 24, 1746
John Webb & Ann Devotion,	July 30, 1746
Josiah Manning & Mary Cook,	Oct. 13, 1746
Samuel Silsbey & Elizabeth Woodward,	Nov. 5, 1746
Josiah Smith & Elizabeth Robinson,	Nov. 13, 1746
Isiah Kingsley & Abigail Palmer,	Jan. 20, 1747
Jeduthan Rogers & Anne Farnam,	Oct. 21, 1747
John Johnson & Mary Robinson,	Oct. 29, 1747
Joseph Cary & Abigail Hebard,	Dec. 10, 1747
Timothy Hall & Rachel Morse,	March 10, 1748
Samuel Hebard & Mary Burnap,	Sept. 20, 1748
Samuel Bingham & Lidia Mudge,	Nov. 10, 1748
Zebulon Webb & Mehitabel Huntington,	Nov. 24, 1748
Jeremiah Ladd & Jerusha Seabin,	Nov. 27, 1748
Reubin Robinson & Esther Palmer,	Jan. 12, 1749
Experience Robinson & Zerviah Palmer,	Feb. 14, 1749
Nathaniel Kingsley & Sarah Walden,	March 16, 1749
William Parish & Doritha Kingsley,	May 11, 1749
Ebenezer Luce & Annah Robinson,	Oct. 26, 1749
Philemon Wood & widow Howard,	Nov. 1, 1749
Samuel Wood, A. B., & Lidia Ripley,	Jan. 11, 1750
Jacob Reed & widow Lidia Longbottom,	Jan 30, 1750
Jabez Kingsley & Irena Manning,	March 7, 1750
Samuel Murdock & Mary Wright,	March 15, 1750
Amos Woodward & Meribah Luce,	April 15, 1750
Elipalet Fairnum & Mary Rogers,	Oct. 11, 1750
Richard Kimbal & Abigail Huntington,	Nov. 7, 1750
John Parish & Hannah Herrington,	Oct. 7, 1750

Ebenezer Loomis & Hannah Snow,	Jan. 30, 1751
Napthali Webb & Mary Mudge,	Oct. 2, 1751
William Brewster & Esther Seabin,	Jan. 16, 1752
Walter Dimock & Mary Cammon,	Jan. 23, 1752
Simon Wood & Mary Silsbey,	March 5, 1752
Elijah Airs & Abigail Merril,	March 26, 1752
John Burgane & Mercy Stark,	July 13, 1752
James Bradford & widow Lear Cook,	Nov. 9, 1752
Nathaniel Harriman & widow Elizabeth Knight,	
	Feb. 14, 1752
Jacob Hide & Hannah Hazen,	July 5, 1753
Nathan Lillie & Sarah Kingsley,	Aug. 26, 1753
Samuel Kimbal & Ann Mudge,	April 18, 1754
Philemon Wood & widow Martha Davis,	Aug. 26, 1754
Jonah Palmer & Abiah Robinson,	Oct. 31, 1754
Elisha Avery & Sarrah Manning,	Nov. 13, 1754
David Yeomans & Abigail Hurlbutt,	Nov. 13, 1754
Jonathan Lillie & Hannah Tilden,	Dec. 12, 1754
Samuel Slader & Mehitabel Lewis,	Dec. 25, 1754
Amos Dodge & widow Sarah Smith,	Jan. 23, 1755
Daniel Rindge & Anne Robinson,	April 16, 1755
Joseph Ford & widow Sarah Greenslitt,	May 7, 1755
Samuel Morgan & Bethia Parish,	Oct. 2, 1755
Rhodolpha Fuller & Ann Robinson,	Oct. 9, 1755
—— White & widow Mahitable Crosbey,	Jan. 6, 1756
Eleazer Palmer, Jr., & Mary Bingham,	May 5, 1756
Seth Palmer & Allice Manning,	June 14, 1756
Abner Flynt & Patience Lasell,	July 1, 1756
Adonijah Kingsley & Bethiah Baker,	Sept. 23, 1756
Nathaniel Smith & Hannah Walden,	Oct. 21, 1756
Nathan Luce & Elizabeth Lasel,	Nov. 13, 1756
John Fuller & Hannah Kimball,	Nov. 15, 1756
Nathaniel Bingham & Martha Baker,	Jan. 2, 1757
Nathaniel Cary & Jerusha Downer,	Jan. 6, 1757
Jeremiah Kingsley & Hannah Lillie,	Jan. 9, 1757
William Ripley & Lydia Brewster,	Jan. 11, 1757
Joshua Lasell & Hannah Bingham,	Jan. 20, 1757
Benjamin Holden & Rebekkah Lillie,	Feb. 3, 1757
John Wood & Hannah Richardson,	Feb. 17, 1757
Capt. James Lasell & widow Jerusha Cary,	Jan. 19, 1758

John Kimball & Jerusha Meacham,	Feb. 9, 1758
Jonathan King & Abigail Manning,	July 9, 1758
Richard Ransom & widow Mary Luce,	Sept. 5, 1758
Benjamin Smith & Chloe Lasel,	Sept. 10, 1758
Moses Belcher & Esthe Rudd,	Nov. 8, 1758
Elisha Lord & Alithea Ripley,	Jan. 18, 1759
David Luce & Mehitable Dimik,	May 24, 1759
Jonah Smith & Alithea Cary,	Nov. 15, 1759
Nathan Hebard, Jr., & Mehitabel Crosby,	Sept. 27, 1759
John Warren & Elizabeth Burnap,	March 6, 1760
John Perkins, Jr., & widow Bethia Kingsley,	April 14, 1760
Ebenezer Fitch & Chloe Kingsley,	May 4, 1760
Ichabod Warner & Mary Lasell,	July 17, 1760
Jonathan Bingham, Jr., & Rachel Mudge,	Oct. 19, 1760
Joseph Meacham, Jr., & Lidia Dimik,	Nov. 27, 1760
Lemuel Church & Bethia Lasell,	Feb. 12, 1761
Samuel Huntington & Martha Devotion,	April 17, 1761
Soloman Pettingall & Zerviah Morgan,	April 17, 1761
James Luce, Jr., & Zillah Cary,	May 13, 1762
Christopher Banister & Abiah Manning,	Nov. 10, 1762
Eliphalet Huntington & Dinah Rudd,	Nov. 11, 1762
Joshua Wright, Jr., & Mary Smith,	Nov. 16, 1762
John Cleaveland & Elizabeth Downer,	Nov. 17, 1762
Eliphaz Kingsley & Triphena Palmer,	Nov. 24, 1762
Daniel Meacham & Disire Lewis,	Feb. 24, 1763
Aaron Reed & Sarah Bingham,	March 3, 1763
Abner Robinson & Mehitabel Palmer,	April 7, 1763
Jabez Tracey & Zippora Hebard,	May 26, 1763
Rev. John Ells & Sibil Huntington,	June 30, 1763
Edward Harris & Lidia White,	July 26, 1763
Samuel Adams & Phebe Pellet,	Nov. 3, 1763
Silas Lillie & Mehitabel Foster,	Nov. 10, 1763
Nathan Hebard & widow Irene Warner,	Dec. 4, 1763
John Goodale & Mary Warner,	Dec. 7, 1763
Samuel Baker, Jr., & Lydia Smith,	Dec. 8, 1763
Silas Bowen & widow Mehitabel Webb,	Jan. 11, 1764
Nathan Robinson & Jerusha Palmer,	Jan. 15, 1764
Joseph Ashley & Zerviah Lion,	April 26, 1764
Elisha Doubleday & Kersiah Phelps,	May 3, 1764
Ebenezer Devotion, Jr., & Eunice Huntington,	June 7, 1764

Rev. Joseph Huntington & Hannah Devotion, Nov. 7, 1764
Robert Lion & Allice Hall,   Nov. 13, 1764
Daniel Foster & Kersiah Sawyer,   April 1, 1765
Asa White & Mary Bingham,   May 8, 1765
Gamaliel Ripley & Elizabeth Hebard,   Dec. 15, 1765
Capt. Caleb Jewett & widow Faith Brewster, May 26, 1766
Jesse Sheperd & Sarah White,   Sept. 24, 1766
Samuel Bass & Hannah Woodward,   Oct. 2, 1766
—— Staples & Lidia Jennings,   Feb. 3, 1767
Capt. John Whiting & widow Mary Luce,   Aug. 6, 1767
Eliashib Adams & widow Mary Annable,   Aug. 20, 1767
Elisha Kingsley & Susanna Baker,   Nov. 4, 1767
Benjamin Peck & widow Mary Kingsley,   Nov. 11, 1767
Daniel Ellis & Sarah Robinson,   Jan. 17, 1768
Levi Johnson & Anna Manning,   Jan. 17, 1768
Josiah Lasel & Lidia Bingham,   Sept. 29, 1768
Amos Leonard & Jemima Wright,   Nov. 8, 1768
Phineas Cary & Mary Hurlbutt,   Feb. 26, 1769
Capt. Samuel Bingham & widow Ann Ripley, May 17, 1769
David Fisk & Sibil Jenning,   Oct. 25, 1769
Ensign Thomas Robinson & widow Abigail Dimick,
                                                            Feb. 8, 1770
Josiah Palmer & Pheebe Manning,   May 23, 1770
William Goodwin & Mary Manning,   May 16, 1771
Pennel Cheeny & Jerusha Manning,   June 20, 1771
William Cary & Irene Manning,   May 16, 1771

BY REV. JAMES COGSWELL.

John Fitch & Irene Warner,   March 5, 1772
Thimothy Allen & Mary Allen,   Oct. 6, 1772
Darius Peck & Hannah Warner,   Nov. 5, 1772
John Webb, Jr., & Zipporah Robinson,   Nov. 12, 1772
Dr. Abigense Waldo & Lydia Hurlbut,   Nov. 19, 1772
Capt. Thomas Fanning & widow Peobe Hurlbut,
                                                            Jan. 14, 1773
James Flynt, 3d, & Jerusha Lillie,   April 22, 1773
Crocker Jones & Lucy Utley,   Oct. 22, 1773
John Wentworth & Elizabeth Webb,   Nov. 25, 1773
John Knox & Sibil Burn ap,   Nov. 30, 1773
Jacob Bottom & Prudence Hebard,   Dec. 2, 1773

Joseph Hartshorn & Submit Tracy,	Feb. 14, 1774
Asa Bottom & Elizabeth Farnum,	April 7, 1774
John Young & Abigail Genings,	Sept. 22, 1774
Capt. Joseph Gennings & Tamizen Cady,	Nov. 8, 1774
William Robinson & Asenath Manning,	Nov. 10, 1774
Deen Manning & Lydia Peters,	March 2, 1775
William Cushman & Ruth Robinson,	May 4, 1775
Ephraim Smith & Elizabeth Bingham,	May 24, 1775
Jonathan Cary & Martha Hurlbut,	Sept. 21, 1775
Amaziah Grover & Dorcas West,	Nov. 16, 1775
Joel Phelps & Huldah Lillie,	Nov. 23, 1775
John Baker, Jr., & Elizabeth Manning,	Dec. 14, 1775
Walter Baker & Rebeckah Cary,	Dec. 21, 1775
Jonathan Kingsley & Zillah Luce,	Jan. 22, 1777
Aaron Cleaveland & Jemima Robinson,	June 13, 1777
Nathaniel Rudd & Martha Bingham,	June 26, 1777
Salmon Kingsley & Alethea Smith,	Aug. 20, 1777
John Burnham & Tryphena Robinson,	Oct. 23, 1777
Ebenezer Coburn & Sibil Robinson,	Nov. 20, 1777
Samuel Bingham, Jr., & Alethea Hebard,	Jan. 1, 1778
Thomas Liscomb & Elizabeth Lewis,	Jan. 7, 1778
Nathan Denison & widow Hannah Fuller,	March 15, 1778
James Burnap & Pheebe Baker,	May 14, 1778
James Rudd & Olive Manning,	May 27, 1778
Asher Robinson & Sarah West,	Sept. 3, 1778
Cifford Robinson & Lucy Morgan,	Oct. 22, 1778
Nathan Forbes & Patience Flynt,	Nov. 25, 1778
Dr. Joseph Baker & Lucy Devotion,	Jan. 10, 1779
Jedidiah Bingham & Elizabeth Webb,	April 30, 1779
Reuben Robinson, Jr., & Urania Kingsley,	Aug. 12, 1779
William Southwick & Sarah Butler,	Sept. 23, 1779
Jedidiah Leach & Pheebe Cossom,	Oct. 4, 1779
Elijah Baker & Olive Cossom,	Oct. 4, 1779
Dr. Luther Manning & Sarah Smith,	Oct. 12, 1779
Joshua Ripley & Deborah Bingham,	Nov. 25, 1779
Joshua Squire & Phoebe Hurlbut,	Nov. 25, 1779
Ebenezer Hebard & Eunice Kimbal,	Dec. 30, 1779
Roger Cary & Eunice Parrish,	Jan. 27, 1780
Jonathan Strong & widow Anna Spalding,	Feb. 17, 1780
Cornelius Coburn & Rachel Robinson,	April 5, 1780

Darius Liscomb & Olive Slader,	April 13, 1780
Daniel Burnham & Marth Smith,	April 20, 1780
Nathan Wales & Rosamond Robinson,	June 29, 1780
Timothy Allen & Mary Burnham,	Sept. 21, 1780
Abner Webb & Prudence Baker,	Nov. 2, 1780
Zopha Robinson & Charity Coburn,	Nov. 14, 1780
Capt. Thomas Adams & widow Mary Mudge,	Jan. 4, 1781
Joseph Jenning & Ruth Cartwright,	April 13, 1781
Uriah Bingham & Eunice Webb,	April 26, 1781
Elijah Lillie & Anna Smith,	June 7, 1781
Benjamin Rainsford & Jerusha Luce,	July 12, 1781
Joel Manning & Abigail Bundy,	Feb. 8, 1782
Veniah Palmer & Cynthia Fitch,	May 23, 1782
James Rudd & Alethea Manning,	Jan. 13, 1783
Jonah Lincoln & Lucy Webb,	May 1, 1783
David Hovey & Ann Robinson,	Aug. 28, 1783
Nathaniel Manning & Matilda Morgan,	Sept. 4, 1783
Marshal Palmer & Eunice Manning,	Oct. 9, 1783
Wardwell Green & Esther Robinson,	Oct. 30, 1783
David Rockwell & Mary Babcock,	Nov. 12, 1783
Alexander Bingham & Sally Larrabee,	Nov. 16, 1783
John Manning & Polly Perkins,	Feb. 18, 1784
Silas Stark & Deborah Cary,	April 8, 1784
Chester Lilly & Sally Tracy,	Nov. 11, 1784
Joseph Manning & Lydia Evereh,	Nov. 25, 1784
Charles Mudge & Lydia Lillie,	Nov. 25, 1784
Joseph Palmer & Hannah Fox,	Feb. 7, 1785
Asher Morgan & Cynthia Gager,	Feb. 24, 1785
Levi Green & Asenath Robinson,	June 9, 1785
David Fox & Alethea Robinson,	Oct. 27, 1785
Capt. David Dorance & Ann Hurlbut,	Feb. 2, 1786
Cyrus Tracy & Hannah Lillie,	March 15, 1786
John Burnap & Sarah Avery,	March 30, 1786
Darus Dewey & Rachel Bingham,	June 1, 1786
Capt. Joseph Hill & Naomi Bingham,	Dec. 14, 1786
Theodore King & Lydia Smith,	Dec. 25, 1786
Roswell Ripley & Lois Morgan,	Jan. 8, 1787
Nathan Fuller & Susannah Luce,	March 8, 1787
Winslow Page & Clarissa Kyes,	Sept. 25, 1787
Benjamin Kimbal & Ann Kimbal,	Nov. 1, 1787

John Woodward Dewey & Abigail Rudd,	Nov. 15, 1787
Joseph Loomis & Ruth Bingham,	Dec. 12, 1787
Zebadiah Tracy & Eunice Chaplin,	Jan. 10, 1788
Abner Follet & Mary Wood,	Jan. 7, 1788
Jonathan Hovey & Susannah Smith,	Feb. 7, 1788
Warner Hebard & Polly White,	April 2, 1789
Zacheus Spencer & Irene Robinson,	June 11, 1789
Elija Sabin & Abigail Luce,	June 26, 1789
Titus Darrow & Lucy Blackman,	Oct. 30, 1789
Asahel Kingsley & Elizabeth Luce,	Nov. 26, 1789
Gurdon Welch & Mary Manning,	Dec. 9, 1789
Eleazer Smith & Mehetibel Robinson,	Feb. 4, 1790
Aaron Flint & Mary Kimbal,	Sept. 2, 1790
Jacob Wilson & Desire Palmer,	Sept. 23, 1790
Stephen Jorden & Eunice Church,	Dec. 30, 1790
Nathan Lilly, Jr., & Lydia Robinson,	Jan. 7, 1791
David Hartshorn & Lemira Lilly,	Sept. 1, 1791
Eleazer Welch & Alethea Manning,	Jan. 20, 1792
William Cushman & Anna Rindge,	Jan. 31, 1792
Roger Smith & Alice Bingham,	April 29, 1792
Oliver Cary & Sarah Robinson,	May 4, 1792
Richard Martin & Dorcas Robinson,	Nov. 29, 1792
Barnabas Manning & Esther Belcher,	Dec. 20, 1792
Enock Meacham & Peggy Gyles,	April 11, 1793
Samuel Dorance & Lucy Rudd,	Oct. 28, 1793
Eliph Wood & Allice Flynt,	Nov. 10, 1793
Amasa Palmer & Clarissa Smith,	Jan. 30, 1794
Andrew Gager & Gerusha Smith,	March 25, 1794
Isaiah William & Lydia Webb,	April 6, 1794
Gurdon Lathrop & Betsey Rudd,	Jan. 7, 1795
John Manning & Irene Wood,	March 4, 1795
John Crosby & Polly Lasel,	April 1, 1795
Seth Palmer & Patience Forbes,	April 30, 1795
Elias Robinson & Amy Lure,	June 4, 1795
Jedidiah Smith & Sarah Martin,	Oct. 5, 1795
Joseph Bass & Lucy Gager,	Dec. 30, 1795
Asa Lord & Mary Rudd,	Jan. 28, 1796
Joseph Morse & Hannah White,	Feb. 11, 1796
Andrew Gager & Lois Webb,	April 3, 1796
Henry Francis, Esq., & Eliza Hebard,	Feb. 5, 1797

Rev. James Cogswell & widow Irene Hebard, May 5, 1797
(Married by Rev. Waterman of Windham.)
Ebenezer Waldo & Eunice Devotion,   Aug. 22, 1797
Sylvester Knight & Alice Luce,   Feb. 7, 1798
Ira Loomis & Rosamond Warner,   March 5, 1798
John Adams, Jr., & Elizabeth Ripley,   May 8, 1798
David Fuller & Lois Robinson,   March 15, 1799
Ichabod Warner & Hannah Collins,   April 2, 1799
Parker Morse & Abigail Cary,   Oct. 6, 1799
David Bradford Ripley & Polly Robinson,   Feb. 6, 1800

CHESHIRE.

NEW HAVEN COUNTY.

Cheshire was incorporated in May, 1780. Formerly a part of Wallingford. The Congregational Church in Cheshire was organized in December, 1724, though the first settlement there was in 1719. The following include all the church marriages before 1800.

Ephraim Tuttle & Hannah ———,   Jan. 16, 1734
Mathew Bellamy, Jr., & Rachel Clark,   Jan. 23, 1734
Abraham Barns & Mary Hotchkiss,   Feb. 27, 1734
Joseph Ives, Jr., & Mamre Munson,   June 13, 1734
Joseph Beach & Experience Beecher,   Oct. 31, 1734
Joseph Benham & Mary Bunnel,   July, 1735
Elnathan Andrews & Hannah Hitchcock,   May, 1740
Levinus Carrington & Lois Andrews,   May, 1740

MARRIAGES AT CHESHIRE CHURCH BY REV. JOHN FOOTE.

Isaac Martin & Lois Ives,   May 21, 1767
Bela Blakesly & Eunice Parker,   Aug. 6, 1767
Reuben Perkins & Thankful Smith,   Nov. 12, 1767
Benjamin Pritchet & Hannah Williams,   Dec. 24, 1767
Reuben Mathews & Ada Curtis,   April 15, 1768
Martin Curtiss & Eliada Mathews,   July 24, 1768
Samuel Merriam & Martha Smith,   July 24, 1768
Ralph Parker & Ruth Halley,   Oct. 6, 1768
John Upson & Lois Atwater,   Dec. 14, 1768
Uri Benham & Lois Doolittle,   Dec. 22, 1768
Ebenezer Lewis & Elizabeth Curtiss,   Jan. 8, 1769

Jonas Hills & Lydia Webb,	March 23, 1769
Capt. Hull & widow Humberstone,	April 26, 1769
Nathan Brownson & widow Lewis,	June 29, 1769
Daniel Hotchkiss, 3d, & Sarah Smith,	Aug. 26, 1769
Ephraim Smith & Susan Hotchkiss,	Sept. 28, 1769
Salma Culver & Sarah Merriam,	Nov. 6, 1769
John Ives & Lois Hotchkiss,	Jan. 3, 1770
Nathaniel Boardman & Eunice Moss,	May 24, 1770
Joseph Newton & Esther Sperry,	June 13, 1770
Joseph Hough & Elizabeth Atwater,	Nov. 8, 1770
Jotham Curtiss & Esther Hull,	Nov. 15, 1770
Jesse Welton & Sarah Tyler,	Dec. 13, 1770
Elisha Perkins & Lois Smith,	March 8, 1771
Judah Andrews & Dorcas Hine,	March 28, 1771
Benoni Plum & Esther Hitchcock,	June 6, 1771
William Law & Sarah Hotchkiss,	July 10, 1771
David Hitchcock & Lois Cook,	Aug. 7, 1771
Abel Woolcut & widow Elizabeth Bellamy,	Oct. 3, 1771
John Parker & Phebe Curtiss,	Nov. 7, 1771
Benjamin Bristol & Sibel Perkins,	Oct. 12, 1771
Isaac Beecher & Lois Benham,	Dec. 19, 1771
Ephraim Atwater & Abigail Row,	Dec. 25, 1771
David Hotchkiss & Abigail Merriam,	Dec 26, 1771
Joseph Benham & Elizabeth Bunnell,	Jan. 3, 1771
Enos Tyler & Lydia Hitchcock,	Jan. 30, 1771
Asa Brownson & Athieldred Parker,	Feb. 5, 1772
Thomas Gaylord & Hannah Ives,	Feb. 6, 1772
Stephen Brooks & Elizabeth Smith,	Feb. 13, 1772
Amos Atwater & Martha Cole,	April 30, 1772
Abel Forward & Ketura Collins,	Oct. 26, 1772
Nathan Andrews & Phebe Thompson,	Nov. 18, 1772
Timothy Atwater & Lucy Rice,	Dec. 8, 1772
Daniel Bradly & Esther Ives,	Dec. 10, 1772
Amos Bristol & Thankful Tuttle,	Dec. 17, 1772
Jothan Gaylord & Esther Hotchkiss,	Jan. 7, 1773
Samuel Warner & Abigail Mathews,	Feb. 10, 1773
Lucius Tuttle & Hannah Hull,	Feb. 10, 1773
Eli Brownson & Mehitabel Atwater,	March 4, 1773
Joel Peck & Martha Brooks,	March 25, 1773
Abner Hitchcock & Esther Hull,	May 19, 1773

Elisha Jones & Martha Hotchkiss,	Nov. 17, 1773
Joseph Doolittle & Sarah Hotchkiss,	Dec. 8, 1773
Ambrose Doolittle & Azubah Doud,	Jan. 6, 1774
Elish Sanford & Rhoda Johnson,	Feb. 1, 1774
Abner Bunnel & Sarah Atwater,	Feb. 10, 1774
Ebenezer Allen Brownson & Susanna Parker,	Feb. 17, 1774
Silas Clark & widow Curtiss,	March 3, 1774
Dummer or Immer Judd & Rhoda Atwater,	March 15, 1774
Peter Hall & Lydia Roe Humiston,	March 16, 1774
Samuel Huggins & May Collins,	March 23, 1774
Calvin Cole & Mariam Atwater,	April 14, 1774
Abijah Hull & Rachel Thompson,	April 20, 1774
Oben Doolittle & Rhoda Hitchcock,	April 20, 1774
Benjamin Hitchcock & Eunice Hotchkiss,	April 21, 1774
Reuben Bradly & Hannah Gaylord,	April 21, 1774
Benjamin Twist & Sarah Curtiss,	April 28, 1774
Wid. Jones & Lydia Hotchkiss,	April 28, 1774
Oben Clark & Hannah Thompson,	July 7, 1774
Thomas Hitchcock & Hannah Moss,	Aug. 3, 1774
Ichabod Tuttle & Sarah Hitchcock,	Nov. 26, 1775
Lemuel Moss & Anna Hall,	Dec. 22, 1774
Asa Blakesly & Lois Hull,	Jan. 19, 1775
Enos Tyler & Mary Hotchkiss,	Jan. 26, 1775
Moses Blakesly & Mary Smith,	Feb. 23, 1775
Jonathan Hall & Abigail Hall,	March 9, 1775
Isaac Brooks & Jemima Wright,	April 19, 1775
Bethel Smith & Deliverance Smith,	June 1, 1775
Jacob Lewis & Mary Martin,	June 22, 1775
Silas Bellamy & Lucy Hough,	Aug. 3, 1775
Bennet Rice & Abigail Hotchkiss,	Sept. 21, 1775
James Jones & Mable Hotchkiss,	Oct. 12, 1775
Noadiah Root & Marlo Hitchcock,	Oct. 24, 1775
George Dallas & Lois Rice,	Nov. 2, 1775
Reuben Bunnel & Eunice Roe,	Nov. 2, 1775
Roger Norton & Hannah Rice,	Dec. 7, 1775
Caleb Merriam & Sarah Rice,	Dec. 12, 1775
Amasa Hall & Dinah Ives,	Dec. 14, 1775
Joseph Hull & Damaris Hull,	Dec. 14, 1775
William Perkins & Ruth Hotchkiss,	Dec. 20, 1775
Oliver Bradly & Deborah Brooks,	Dec. 28, 1775

Asa Wilmot & Esther Curtiss,	Jan. 10, 1776
Samuel Rice & Hannah Beach,	Feb. 5, 1776
David Webb & Thankful Hotchkiss,	Feb. 15, 1776
Lemuel Hitchcock & Rozana Hotchkiss,	March 14, 1776
Simeon Grannis & Priscilla Brooks,	April 18, 1776
Lent Ives & Hannah Burr,	July 2, 1776
Zelous Blakesly & Sarah Paine,	July 2, 1776
Samuel Parker & Hannah Bunnel,	July 11, 1776
Nathaniel Barnes & Sarah Lewis,	July 24, 1776
John Griffin & Dinah Smith,	Nov. 21, 1776
Caleb Barnes & Lucy Merriman,	Dec. 5, 1776
Thomas Moss & Lucy Doolittle,	Jan. 16, 1777
Uriah Kimberly & May Squires,	Jan. 8, 1777
Enos Bunnel & Freelove Tuttle,	Jan. 20, 1777
Reuben Rice & Lois Doolittle,	Feb. 6, 1777
Joel Merriman & Lue Hitchcock,	Feb. 13, 1777
Stephen Rice & Sarah Atwater,	Feb. 27, 1777
Joseph Doolittle & Hannah Chatterton,	March 26, 1777
Heman Atwater & Patience Humiston,	April 3, 1777
Phineas Allen & Ruth Doge,	April 10, 1777
Timothy Ward & Hannah Moss,	May 1, 1777
Titus Munson & Mary Bradly,	June 12, 1777
Elias Hall & Sarah Hitchcock,	July 3, 1777
Giles Daily & Lydia Curtiss,	July 10, 1777
Samuel Bassett & Jerusha Hotchkiss,	Oct. 30, 1777
Gould Gift Norton & Martha Hull,	Nov. 20, 1777
Ezra Bristol & Elizabeth Hotchkiss,	Nov. 20, 1777
Justus Bellamy & Lydia Hall,	Dec. 3, 1777
Ichabod Merriman & Thankful Tuttle,	Dec. 10, 1777
Moses Mitchel & Patience Benham,	Dec. 11, 1777
Jonah Webb & Rhoda Kimbal,	Dec. 11, 1777
William Sanderson & Mary Grannis,	Dec. 15, 1777
Benjamin Yale & Abigail Parker,	Dec. 18, 1777
Joseph Hotchkiss & Ruth Doolittle,	Jan. 1, 1778
Thomas Gaylord & Lois Atwater,	Jan. 8, 1778
Jared Newton & Mary Bunnel,	Jan. 15, 1778
Erastus Lines & Sarah Doolittle,	Jan. 15, 1778.
John Hall & Hannah Atwater,	Jan. 22, 1778
Caleb Todd & Abigail Doolittle,	Jan. 22, 1778
Reuben Thorp & Damaris Hitchcock,	Feb. 26, 1778

Ebenezer Haward & Sarah Jones,	March 10, 1778
John Francis & Sarah Blakesly,	May 17, 1778
William Ives & Sarah Hotchkiss,	June 3, 1778
Capt. John Hall & Thankful Hotchkiss,	June 4, 1778
Thomas Wilson & Mary Woodhouse,	June 16, 1778
Titus Dawson & Sybel Denison,	Aug. 26, 1778
Jason Tyler & Rhoda Bellamy,	Nov. 5, 1778
Ira Dodge & Mary Curtiss,	
Samuel Perkins & Amy Beecher,	Nov. 26, 1778
Nathaniel Crittenden & Jerusha Lewis,	Jan. 6, 1779
Amasa Brooks & Hope Benham,	Jan. 20, 1779
Josiah Smith & Thankful Hitchcock,	Jan. 20, 1779
William Parker & Desire Bunnel,	Feb. 25, 1779
Amos Bristol & Ruth Parmele,	March 18, 1779
Timothy Jones & Lydia Ives,	April 8, 1779
Bela Hitchcock & Comfort Atwater,	June 2, 1779
Stephen Johnson & Ruth Smith,	June 9, 1779
Elihu Lawrence & Lucy Bellamy,	Aug. 5, 1779
Thomas Dutton & widow Parker,	Nov. 17, 1779
David Morgan & Abigail Row,	Oct., 1779
Robert Hotchkiss & Loly Hotchkiss,	Nov. 25, 1779
Joseph Morgan & Eunice Doolittle,	Nov. 25, 1779
Judah Palmer & Hannah Newell,	Dec. 13, 1779
Jedediah Hall & Abigail Atwater,	Feb. 17, 1780
Solomon Morris & Keziah Moss,	Feb. 24, 1780
Amos Bunnel & Catherine Meriam,	March 16, 1780
Stephen Atwater & Anna Moss,	March 23, 1780
Reuben Bristol & Em. Benham,	April 7, 1780
Allen Lewis & Esther Grannis,	May 11, 1780
Stephen B. Bradley & Mereb Atwater,	May 16, 1780
Enos Bunnel & Naomi Atwater,	June 1, 1780
Jonathan Hall, Jr., & Jerusha Gaylord,	July 18, 1780
Elam Smith & Catharine Hitchcock,	July 27, 1780
James Pardy & Sarah Pardy,	Aug. 10, 1780
James Wilmot & Sarah Hine,	Dec. 7, 1780
Isaac Doolittle & Desire Bellamy,	Dec. 7, 1780
Reuben Tyler & Merab Curtiss,	Dec. 28, 1780
Zenas Andrews & Elizabeth Hotchkiss,	March 19, 1781
Asahel Hotchkiss & Sarah William,	March 22, 1781
Elijah Peck & Sarah Bradley,	April 10, 1781

Lemuel Bradley & Eunice Durand,	April 12, 1781
Samuel Green & Hannah Rice,	May 8, 1781
William Kay & Olive Hitchcock,	May 14, 1781
Eben Hale & Merriam Bunnell,	May 16, 1781
Samuel Durand & Susannah Hitchcock,	June 7, 1781
Elisha Street & Jerusha Rice,	June 26, 1781
Andrew Hull & Elizabeth Ann Atwater,	April 21, 1781
Samuel Atwater & Patience Peck,	Dec. 6, 1781
Samuel Mix & Mary Hotchkiss,	Dec. 13, 1781
Samuel Talmadge & Phebe Hall,	Dec. 13, 1781
George Connolley & Sarah Barnes,	Jan. 1, 1782
Jonathan Hall & Ruth Atwater,	Feb. 14, 1782
Noah Hotchkiss & Abigail Hillhouse,	April 17, 1782
Caleb Lewis & Phebe Moss,	June 13, 1782
Merriman Cook & Loly Bradley,	Aug. 8, 1782
Isaac Basset & Desire Hotchkiss,	Sept. 16, 1782
Reuben William & Sarah Hotchkiss,	Sept. 19, 1782
Simeon Wheeler & Anna Sanford,	Sept. 19, 1782
Samuel Newton & Hannah Rice,	Nov. 5, 1782
Gideon Curtiss & Zerusiah Bristol,	Nov. 13, 1782
Elnathan Beach & Nabbie Atwater,	Dec. 21, 1782
Ebenezer Brooks & Hitta Smith,	Jan. 1, 1783
Selden Spencer & Mary Cook,	Jan. 1, 1783
Elihu Atwater & Ann Hudson,	Jan. 6, 1783
Asahel Tillotson & Mamie (?) Merriman,	Feb. 3, 1783
Samuel Tuttle & Martha Hall,	Feb. 16, 1783
Levi Hitchcock & Mary Andrews,	Feb. 24, 1783
David Curtiss & Huldah Andrews,	March 13, 1783
Josiah Talmadge, 2d, & Hannah Blaksley,	March 13, 1783
Eldad Porter & Abigail Hitchcock,	March 19, 1783
Elnathan Conner & Abigail Atwater,	March 20, 1783
Solomon Brooks & Thankful Gaylord,	June 12, 1783
Hezekiah Hine & Abigail Doolittle,	June 16, 1783
Lewis Hart & Celestia Hazard,	July 9, 1783
Isaac Doolittle & Susanna Barns,	July 24, 1783
Samuel Rice & Eunice Martin,	Aug. 19, 1783
Joel Barns & Elizabeth Williams,	Aug. 21, 1783
Joseph Atwater & Hannah Hitchcock,	Sept. 17, 1783
Caleb Parker & Dorothy Peck,	Nov. 1, 1783
David Rice & Martha Hull,	Dec. 11, 1783

Benjamin Hoppin & Esther Hitchcock,	Dec. 11, 1783
Elmore Russell & Asenah Hotchkiss,	Dec. 15, 1783
Amos Mix & Clarinda Barnes,	Jan. 4, 1784
Reuben Page & Lydia Goodrich,	Jan. 15, 1784
Hezekiah Hall & Susanna Lewis,	Jan. 27, 1784
Samuel Hotchkiss & Meriam Hotchkiss,	Feb. 12, 1784
Philologus Webster & Sarah Scott,	Feb. 12, 1784
Gould Crissey & Eunice Moss,	Feb. 12, 1784
Samuel Stone & Eunice Bassett,	March 8, 1784
Phineas Beers & Mary Cornwall,	May 5, 1784
Zenas Mitchell & Abigail Merriman,	June 9, 1784
John Gaylord & Phebe Brooks,	July 1, 1784
William Peck & Mary Heaton,	July 10, 1784
Guy Dodd & Hannah Heaton,	Oct. 4, 1784
William Austin & Mary Bellamy,	Oct. 6, 1784
Benjamin Holt & Abiah Hall,	Dec. 2, 1784
Gilbert Curtiss & Lucy Smith,	Dec. 8, 1784
Caleb Hitchcock & Adah Mallory,	Dec. 23, 1784
Aaron Hitchcock & Ruth Tuttle,	Jan. 13, 1785
George Cowles & Naomi Barns,	Jan. 27, 1785
Elisha Wilmot & Hannah Gladding,	Jan. 30, 1785
Benjamin Galpin & Sybel Talmage,	Jan. 13, 1785
Andrew Durand & Jerusha Lewis,	March 3, 1785
Laban Hall & Lucy Hotchkiss,	May 2, 1785
Lyman Atwater & Dorothy Hotchkiss,	May 2, 1785
Samuel Hull & Abigail Ann Doolittle,	May 26, 1785
Job Sperry & Azubah Hotchkiss,	June 30, 1785
Daniel Carrington & Catharine Humiston,	Sept. 15, 1785
Nathaniel Moss & Lucy Hall Beach,	Nov. 3, 1785
Amasa Clark & Lydia Judson,	Dec. 25, 1785
Merriman Hotchkiss & Esther Hull,	Dec. 30, 1785
Samuel Martin & Phebe Church,	Jan. 11, 1786
Oben Moss & Sarah Bunnel,	Jan. 22, 1786
Tristam Conner & Anna Hastings,	Jan. 25, 1786
Joel Brooks & Merriam Moss,	Jan. 26, 1786
John Peck & Merab Moss,	Feb. 22, 1786
Warren Benham & Jerusha Peck,	Feb. 23, 1786
Amos Andrews & Abigail Bristol,	March 29, 1786
Amos Atwater & Mary Moss,	April 19, 1786
Jesse Humiston & Lois Doolittle,	May 1, 1786

Edward Goodyear & Abigal Hull,	Oct. 8, 1786
Israel Dayton & Abiah Howd,	Oct. 22, 1786
Elam Smith & Elizabeth Dowd,	Dec. 17, 1786
Alexander McKergan & Elianor Scollay,	Dec. 31, 1786
Urial Lewis & Lucy Bunnel,	Jan. 18, 1787
Noah Dunin & Esther Merriman,	Feb. 12, 1787
Stephen Clark & MyrindaHitchcock,	Feb. 19, 1787
Bennet Humiston & Elizabeth Benham,	May 3, 1787
Jesse Turrel & Thankful Merriman,	May 3, 1787
Ephraim Hotchkiss & Sarah Talmage,	May 3, 1787
Titus Preston & Abigail Merriman,	Dec. 31, 1787
Samuel Cook & Sue Cook,	Jan. 10, 1788
Samuel Wales & Polly Bradley,	Jan. 17, 1788
Aaron Newton & Asenath Moss,	Jan. 24, 1788
Reuben Doolittle & Thankful Bunnel,	Jan. 31, 1788
David Hotchkiss & Abigail Atwater,	Feb. 27, 1788
Eben Bunnel & Loly Curtis,	July 2, 1788
Benjamin H. Hall & Lydia Hall,	July 3, 1788
Daniel Winchell & Sylvia Atwater,	Oct. 3, 1788
Roswell Bradly & Susanna Mathews,	Nov. 28, 1788
Ozias Yale & Hannah Hotchkiss,	Nov. 28, 1788
Joel Moss & Abigal Hotchkiss,	Dec. 4, 1788
Silas Doolittle & Clarina Hitchcock,	Dec. 18, 1788
Isaac Bowers Moss & Esther Moss,	Feb. 12, 1789
Eneas Moss & Sarah Moss,	Feb. 24, 1789
Nathan Baldwin & Eunice Hull,	July 20, 1789
Peter Moors & Lucy Naaman,	Oct. 7, 1789
Munson Merriam & Eunice Hotchkiss,	Oct. 26, 1789
Asa Hitchcock & Asenath Doolittle,	Dec. 3, 1789
Silas Gaylord & Hannah Hitchcock,	Dec. 23. 1789
Amos Rice & Kesiah Atwater,	Dec. 28, 1789
Rev. Aaron Hall & Hannah Hitchcock,	Jan. 20, 1790
Asa Peck & Elizabeth Hall,	Feb. 4, 1790
Samuel Doolittle & Hannah Doolittle,	Feb. 24, 1790
John Fields & Sarah Clark,	March 25, 1790
Samuel Bunnel & Mary Hitchcock,	June 10, 1790
Miles Curtiss & Molly Dunbar,	June 20, 1790
Thomas T. Cornwall & Lucinda Foot,	July 29, 1790
John Ford & Esther Cook,	Sept. 19, 1790
Esq. Reynolds & Patty Amelia Rice,	Oct. 13, 1790

John Smith & Hannel Bunnel,	Oct. 16, 1790
Luther E. Hall & Louisa Amelia Hull,	Oct. 17, 1790
Daniel Bradly & Eunice Beach,	Oct. 21, 1790
Lyman Hotchkiss & Olive Brown,	Oct. 28, 1790
Josephus Hotchkiss & Sarah Benham,	Nov. 11, 1790
Judah Root & Sarah Hough,	Dec. 8, 1790
Andrew Durand & Loly Andrews,	Dec. 22, 1790
Josiah Remington Graves & Lydia Hotchkiss,	
	Jan. 24, 1791
Levi Bristol & Martha Hotchkiss,	Nov. 21, 1791
Samuel Porter & Ann (Law ?) Hall,	Dec. 11, 1791
Jared Newton & Esther Parson,	Dec. 22, 1791
Ambrose Hotchkiss & Lucretia Baldwin,	Dec. 25, 1791
Thomas Brooks & Rebecca Merriam,	Jan. 5, 1792
Lyman Durand & Betsey Hall,	Jan. 23, 1792
Reuben Preston & Luse Hitchcock,	March 11, 1792
Samuel Clark & Eunice Hotchkiss,	March 12, 1792
Reuben Bradly & Roxana Thompson,	April 18, 1792
Gideon Walker & Lucy Tuttle,	Nov. 29, 1792
Joseph Ives & Sally Hitchcock,	Dec. 5, 1792
Abner Johnson & Patty Lewis,	Dec. 20, 1792
Joel Johnson & Mary Moss,	Dec. 24, 1792
Rufus Hotchkiss & Loly Doolittle,	Dec. 27, 1792
Theophilus Doolittle & Abiah Atwater,	Dec. 29, 1792
Oliver Parker & Abigail Lewis,	Jan. 2, 1793
William Stokes & Rebecca Parker,	Jan. 2, 1793
Samuel Hitchcock & Martha Ives,	Jan. 27, 1793
Thomas Tyler & Esther Parker,	March 4, 1793
Samuel Shepherd & Beede Grannis,	April 14, 1793
Asa Ashly Gaylord & Love Blakesley,	Sept. 14, 1793
David Hitchcock & Hannah Andrews,	Oct. 9, 1793
Enos Hitchcock & Sarah Stedman,	Oct. 29, 1793
Samuel Ufford Beach & Polly Tuttle,	Jan. 22, 1794
William Clark & Anna Newton,	Jan. 27, 1794
Jared Moss & Patience Hitchcock,	Feb. 2, 1794
James Scovil & Lydia Hall,	Feb. 13, 1794
Leman Judson & Lucy Doolittle,	March 23, 1794
Benjamin Dorchester & Abigail Sanderson,	March 27, 1794
Ephraim Preston & Mary Ann Hitchcock,	April 10, 1794
Asahel Hotchkiss & Phebe Merriam,	July 6, 1794

Jonah Hotchkiss & Chloe Bradley,	Oct. 6, 1794
Samuel Prestol & ——— Bristol,	1794
Joseph Hull & Abigail Hough,	Oct. 19, 1794
Rufus Beach & Anna Curtiss,	Oct. 19, 1794
Benjamin Bristol & Adah Benham,	Nov. 21, 1794
Lyman Hill & Hannah Hull,	Nov. 24, 1794
Salma Hotchkiss & Rebecca Hall,	Nov. 27, 1794
Moses Miles & Hannah Hall,	Dec. 18, 1794
J—— Hall Cook & Urana Hitchcock,	Jan. 12, 1795
Joel Hendrick & Esther Lewis,	Feb. 5, 1795
Abel Austin & Abigail Parker,	Feb. 5, 1795
Eliakim Hough & Sarah Lewis,	Feb. 12, 1795
Rufus Hall & Thankful Griswold,	Feb. 13, 1795
John Rice & Elizabeth Ward,	Feb. 15, 1795
Uri Benham & Amanda Dutton,	Feb. 19, 1795
John Basset & Abigail Hall,	Feb. 30, 1795
Amos Tibbal & Lucy Wright,	June 28, 1795
Titus Andrews & Merriam Lewis,	July 9, 1795
Joseph Hitchcock & Rachel Johnson Hall,	Sept. 14, 1795
Rev. Joel Bradley & Mary A. Beach,	1795
Reuben Page & Belinda Atwater,	Oct. 4, 1795
Amos Higby & Hannah Curtis,	Oct. 18, 1795
Rufus Johnson & Mary Beebe,	Dec. 14, 1795
Landa Bristol & Fanny Doolittle,	Dec. 23, 1795
Daniel Hughes & Sarah Atwater,	Dec. 24, 1795
James Todd & Lydia Fox,	Feb. 3, 1796
Nathaniel Beedle & Merab Hitchcock,	Feb. 7, 1796
Seth Hitchcock & Rosetta Bradley,	March 18, 1796
Merriman Hotchkiss & Betsey Durand,	March 27, 1796
Nathaniel Hitchcock & Merab Andrews,	April 24, 1796
John Bassett & Phebe Atwater,	May 1, 1796
Joseph Tyler & Rispha Clark,	Aug. 11, 1796
Roswell Smith & Lucy Ann Morton,	Sept. 5, 1796
Benoni Plum & Lydia Hotchkiss,	Oct. 12, 1796
Enoch Thomas & Mindwell Clark,	Oct. 23, 1796
Amasa Andrew & Roxy Dorchester,	Oct. 24, 1796
Abigail Beach & Jemima Cornwall,	Nov. 16, 1796
Ichabod Wright & Damaris Cook,	Nov. 17, 1796
Abigal Cornwall & Eunice Ives,	Nov. 17, 1796
Nathaniel Bunnell & Thankful Bristol,	Nov. 27, 1796

Amasa Hitchcock, Jr., & Abigail M. A. Foot,   Dec. 4, 1796
Roger Peck & Mary Atwater,   Dec. 19, 1796
Samuel Ives & Lucy Ann Atwater,   Jan. 5, 1797
Joseph Doolittle & Abigail Brian,   Feb. 16, 1797
Amos Atwater & Mehitable Brooks,   Feb. 19, 1797
Loveman Hills & Eunice Johnson,   Feb. 23, 1797
Titus Atwater & Eunice Hotchkiss,   March 12, 1797
Capt. Solomon Doolittle & Thankful Doolittle, April 5, 1797
Salmon Parker & Sybel Clark,   April 20, 1797
Joseph Hotchkiss & Nabby Bunnel,   May 10, 1797
Eliakim Hitchcock & Amy Andrews,   May 14, 1797
Roswell Pratt & Hannah Hull,   May 14, 1797
David Bunnel & Patience Smith,   May 24, 1797
Ephraim Hine & Silvia Curtis,   Aug. 7, 1797
Amasa Doolittle & Polly Hitchcock,   July 16, 1797
Jacob Chidsey & Abigail Ann Benham,   Sept. 10, 1797
Moses Benham & Esther Johnson,   Sept. 10, 1797
Samuel Benham & Betsey Ann Tuttle,   Oct. 19, 1797
Ebenezer Street & Rebecca Bradley,   Oct. 22, 1797
Appleton Lewis & Lois Hall,   Nov. 15, 1797
Thomas C. Osborn & Susanna Hotchkiss,   Jan. 7, 1798
David Scovil & Esther Gaylord,   Jan. 11, 1798
Rufus Merriam & Lucy Preston,   Jan. 14, 1798
John Brooks & Merab Blakesley,   Jan. 15, 1798
Benoni Bristol & Roxanna Gaylord,   Jan. 18, 1798
Ralph Doolittle & Rebecca Howe,   Feb. 4, 1798
John Cady & Abigail Baldwin,   Aug. 1, 1798
Levi Dickeman & Chloe Bradley,   Oct. 17, 1798
Asa Mandale & Eunice Hough,   Jan. 1, 1799
Bejamin Lewis & Abigail Hitchcock,   April 7, 1799
Lucius Hitchcock & Athelded Hall,   May 12, 1799
Gideon Rice & Mary Ann Sanderson,   July 28, 1799
Jesse Munson & Milla Dickerman,   July 29, 1799
John Rowes & Hannah Hall,   Oct. 14, 1799
David Stone & Sarah Hart,   Nov. 14, 1799
Eber Blakesley & Clarissa Brooks,   Nov. 25, 1799

WILTON.

FAIRFIELD COUNTY.

Wilton was incorporated in 1802, having been a part of the town of Norwalk. The Congregational Church of Wilton was organized June 20, 1726. The following are the marriages recorded on Society's records.

Isaac Amsdell & Sarah Belden,	Aug. 7, 1750
Thaddeus Abbott & Lydia Rockwell,	Sept. 27, 1755
Seth Abbott & Martha Bennet,	April 18, 1766
Enoch Abbott & Molly Betts,	March 19, 1778
Seth Abbott & Hannah Betts,	June 26, 1765
Benjamin Ayers of Bedford & Ruhamah Whelpsley,	Nov. 15, 1764
Peter Adams & Rebeccah Dunning,	Nov. 23, 1769
Thomas Acton (a soldier) & Abigail Everett of Canaan parish,	Oct. 6, 1799
Elias Betts & Abigail Berchard,	March 7, 1744-5
Benjamin Betts & Abigail Lockwood,	Sept. 16, 1762
Reuben Betts & Elen Olmstead,	March 25, 1778
Samuel Comstock Betts & Mary Taylor of Norwalk,	June 5, 1754
Daniel Betts & Abigail Patchen,	Dec. 3, 1754
James Betts of Middlesex & Mary Hubbell,	June 8, 1757
Thaddeus Betts & Deborah Mead,	May 3, 1764
Ebenezer Betts & Sally Gregory,	Dec. 6, 1795
Samuel Betts & Abigail Hubbell,	July 10, 1777
Ruben Betts & Eleanor Hawley,	March 26, 1778
Elias Betts & Abigail Burchard,	March 7, 1744-5
Matthew Betts of Norwalk & Mary St. John,	April 12, 1750
Samuel Betts & Sarah Raymond,	May 29, 1747-8
Isaiah Betts of Norwalk & Elizabeth Griffin,	Oct. 14, 1753
Azariah Betts & Susannah Church,	—— 20, 1799
David Betts & Mary Raymond,	Nov. 29, 1753
Joseph Birchard of Norwalk & Elizabeth Lambert,	June 29, 1710
James Birchard & widow Lockwood,	Dec. 10, 1761
Aaron Birchard & Abigail Hoyt,	Jan., 1799

Jesse Birchard & Ann Keeler, March 1, 1770
William Bell (a stranger) & Martha Abbott, Dec. 4, 1735
Daniel Burchard & Dorothy Stuart, Aug. 18, 1742–3
Isaiah Burchard & Sarah Betts, Aug. 27, 1745
John Burchard & Sarah Patchen, Feb. 4, 1745–6
James Burchard & Wait Gregory, Oct. 26–9, 1751
Eleazer Boughton of Canaan & Sarah Westcot,
Feb. 23, 1758

James Baker & Jane Griffin, July 7, 1754
James Baker & Mary Olmstead, Jan. 17, 1775
Seth Baker & Catharine DeForest, Aug. 10, 1777
Stephen Britto & Sarah Rockwell, Nov. 8, 1753
Nathaniel Benedict of Danbury & widow Hannah
Keeler, July 30, 1746
Thadeus Benedict & Ruth Lockwood of Norwalk,
Sept. 3, 1778

———— Benedic—— & Betty St. John, Dec. 31, 1795
Nathan Bates of Middlesex & Hannah Marione of
Norwalk, Nov. 8, 1750
Lieut. Daniel Belden & widow Mary Kimberly, Feb. 21, 1759
Abiel Beers of North Stratford & Jemima Abbott,
May 15, 1759

Jesse Bears & Ruth Bennet, Nov. 6, 1774
Gilead Bedient & Abigail Hurlbut, June 13, 1770
Jesse Bedient & Sarah Whitney, Nov. 25, 1772
Peter Buskpont (?) & Sarah Lockwood of Norwalk,
Sept. 21, 1799

Joseph Bardwell & Wait Raymond, April 20, 1762
Elias Bigsby & Grace Sterling, April 28, 1771
Samuel Baxter & Hannah Mead, Nov. 14, 1771
Capt. Caleb Baldwin & widow Betty Betts, Nov. 13, 1770
Ebenezer Bennett & Ruth Hurlbut, Jan. 25, 1776
James Benjamin & Hannah Keeler of Canaan,
Jan. 24, 1776

Josiah Canfield & Deborah Stuart, Sept. 20, 1757
Jabez Canfield & Mary Dikeman, June 14, 1746
Benaiah Strong Comstock & Abigail Westcott,
July 22, 1773
Nathan Comstock & Bethiah Strong, March or May, 1738–9
Aaron Comstock & Rebena Deforest, June 9, 1765

Samuel Comstock & Mercy Mead,	Dec. 26, 1765
Enos Comstock & Deborah Kellogg of Canaan,	Nov. 25, 1778
—— Comstock, son of Moses, & —— ——, daughter of Capt. Seymour,	——
Zebulon Crane & Sarah Belden,	March 27, 1742
Caleb Cole & Anne St. John,	Dec. 20, 1742
Jonathan Cole & widow Sarah Wood,	Nov. 15, 1749
Daniel Cole & Abigail Carpender,	June 10, 1759
Ezra Cole & Sabra Patchen,	Dec. 21, 1774
Thomas Cole & Mary Rockwill,	—— 29, 1778
John Cole of Wilton parish & Abigail Cable of Fairfield,	Feb. 21, 1748–9
—— Cable & —— Taylor of Wilton parish,	Sept. 15 (?), 1761
William Carpender & Phebe Olmsted,	Oct. 13, 1763
James Cooper (a soldier) & Sarah Green of Norwalk,	Jan. 28, 1779
Richard Dunning & Abigail Betts,	Aug. 8, 1733
John Dunning & Harriet Keeler,	Aug. 30, 1733
Mathew Dunning & Abigail Patchen,	Dec. 9, 1742
Michael Dunning & Hannah Green,	March 6, 1744–5
David Dunning & Hannah Mead,	Feb. 18, 1745–6
David Dunning, Jr., & Mary Sterling,	Oct. 2, 1775
Thadeus Dunning & Susannah Betts,	March 19, 1778
Hezekiah DeForest & Mary Sherwood,	March 21, 1747–8
Benjamin Dible of Stamford & Rebena Raymond,	Jan. 22, 1739–40
Benjamin Dible of Cornwal & Sarah Cole of Wilton,	Dec. 3, 1754
Lemuel DeForest & Phebe Keeler,	Dec. 26, 1751
David DeForest & Sarah Olmsted,	Aug. 5, 1754
Elihu DeForest & Rachel Lambert,	May 4, 1761
Nehemiah DeForest & Mary Lockwood,	Dec. 20, 1769
David DeForest, Jr., & Sabra Mead,	Jan. 13, ——
Samuel DeForest & Elanor Sterling,	Aug. 10, 1777
Uriah DeForest & Phebe Dunning,	Feb. 24, 1780
Jabez Darling & —— ——,	Dec., 1753
Ichabud Dolittle & Debrooh Birchard,	Nov. 18, 1756
Samuel Dean & Jehannah Stuart,	April, 1770

Nathaniel Darrow & Elizabeth Stuart, March 9, 1757
Rev. Moses Dikeman & Mrs. Hannah St. John, July 28, 1757
D. Dunkins of Grensfarms & Sarah Dolittle of
 Wilton, March 20, 1758
E—— D—— & S—— B——, Oct. 25, 1764
Ruben Disbrow & Ezebel Olmsted, June 24, 1796
Samuel Edmonson & Mary Bears, March 17, 1736
John Egleston (stranger) & Grace Bischard, Jan. 31, 1739–40
Eleakim Elmer & Lydia Trobridge, May 9, 1735–6
Jeremiah Ells & Mahitable Merwin of Canaan,
 April 30, 1778
—— Everet & widow —— Remington, April 28, 1746–7
Joseph Platt Fitch & Eunice Betts, Nov. 16, 1780
Dr. Fitch of Redding & Hannah Lockwood of
 Wilton, Oct. 4, 1764
Seymour Fitch & widow Sarah Raymond, Feb. 5, 1778
Stephen Fitch of Wilton & Hannah Betts of Nor-
 walk, Sept. 2, 1778
Samuel Fountain & Abigail Stuart, Jan. 20, 1746–7
Squire Fancer & Abigail Abbott, Oct. 12, 1796
Jonathan Fox & Margaret Cole, Sept. 18, 1765
Aaron Fox & Sally Dunning, Feb. 4, 1798
Ichobod French & Abigail Olmsted, Jan. 21, 1798
Solomen Ferry & Amer Betts, 1798
Ebenezer Green & Elizabeth Gilbert, March 24, 1747–8
Joseph Green & Sarah Beers, May 15, 1746
Nathaniel Griffin & Mable Noble, Aug. 5, 1746
Seth Griffin & Mary Westcoat, Jan. 2, 1758
Ebenezer Gray & Anne Lockwood of Grensfarms,
 Dec. 26, 1757
Samuel Gates & —— Olmsted, Nov. 19, 1758
Benjamin Grey & Elizabeth Waterbury, Nov. 25, 1779
Reuben Gregory & Hannah Dunning, Dec. 5, 1750
Denton Gregory & Elizabeth Sherwood, Jan. 18, 1753
Nathan Gregory & Sarah St. John, July 3, 1754
Joseph Gregory & Mary Morehouse, Nov. 8, 1756
Elijah Gregory & Ruhamah Gregory, Dec. 13, 1758
Jackin Gregory & Rebena Chard, Oct. 21, 1759
Daniel Gregory & Esther Hickox, May 17, 1763
Aaron Gregory & Betty Keeler,

Samuel Gregory & Martha Green,	May 23, 1775
Noah Gregory & Sarah Nash,	Jan. 25, 1776
Jehiel Gregory & Phebe Arnold,	March 13, 1776
Aaron Gregory & Bridget Belden,	Feb. 15, 1780
Elijah Gregory & —— Gregory of Norwalk,	—— 23, 1778
Gersham Gregory & Eunice Whitlock,	April 8, 1779
Ezra Gregory & Hannah Betts,	Nov. 20, 1751
Benjamin Gilbert & Sarah Higgins,	March, 1751
Nathan Gilbert & Sarah Betts,	April, 1770
David Grommand & Sarah Morehouse,	March 18, 1756
Nehemiah Grommand & Abigail Keeler,	May 18, 1744
Elias Gregory & Betty Raymond,	Dec. 29, 1777
Abraham Gregory & Dolly Lockwood,	Jan. 29, 1778
Ezra Gregory & Sarah Hubbell,	June 11, 1778
Moses Grumman & Dolly Birchard,	Oct. 22, 1797
John Grumman, Jr., & Elanor Tuttle,	—— 9, 1798
Jeremiah Grumman & Sabra Stuart,	March 4, 1772
Justus Gray & Mary Belden,	—— 4, 1799
William Gaylord & Elizabeth Davenport of Stamford,	Jan. 24, 1732-3
Daniel Holybert & Esther Belden,	Nov. 28, 1737
Ebenezer Holybert & widow Sarah Morehouse,	May 13, 1740
Stephen Holybert & Sarah Dolittle,	Jan. 5, 1746-7
Daniel Holybert & Naomi Stuart,	March 8, 1758
Elijah Holybert & Lydia Stuart,	June 12, 1764
John Holybert & Lydia Stuart,	Nov. 7, 1764
Daniel Holybert & —— ——, daughter of John Partrick,	March 21, 1764
Azor Holybert & Mary Mead,	July 13, 1766
Abraham Hurlbutt & Martha Morehouse,	Nov. 10, 1796
Lewis Hurlbutt & Molly Scribner,	Dec. 14, 1796
Joseph Hurlbutt & Sarah Lewis,	1772
John Hughstone & —— ——,	July 20, 1746-7
Elias Hawley & Ruth Lewis,	June 13, 1770
Ezekiel Hawley & Elenor Olmstead,	Jan. 4, 1775
Thomas Hawley & Kezie Scribner of Norwalk,	March 10, 1779
Nathan Hickox & Hannah Keeler,	Feb. 4, 1759
Benjamin Hickox & Rebecca Gregory,	March 31, 1762
Ebenezer Hickox & Minawell Scribner,	April 26, 1751

Ezra Hickox & Elizabeth Whelpley,	Dec. 29, 1756
Uriah Hickox & Hannah Keeler,	Dec. 22, 1763
Carter Hickox & Leah Taylor,	March 23, 1764
Aaron Hitchok of New Milford & Elizabeth Trowbridge of Wilton,	March 31, 1763
Ebenezer Hendrick & Mary Sturdevant,	April 30, 1751
Samuel Hustead & Phebe Hoit,	Oct. 31, 1771
Francis Hultenark & Naomi Stuart,	Nov. 20-5, 1776
Eliphalet Hull & Huldah Patchen,	Nov. 24, 1768
William Halloway of Fairfield & widow Hannah Smith of Wilton,	Jan. 24, 1758
Thaddeus Hubbell & Ruth Betts,	Dec. 26, 1753
Peter Hubbell & Sarah Stuart,	Jan. 11, 1764
Thaddeus Hubbell & widow Phebe Squire,	Nov. 24, 1747
Amos Hubbell & Eleanor Hubbell,	Dec. 18, 1776
Seth Hubbell & Elizabeth Guire,	Aug. 27, 1779
—— Hait of Canaan & —— Cole of Wilton,	Aug. 5, 1761
—— Hoit of Norwalk & Hannah Griffin,	
William Hait & Lydia Cofoot of Canaan,	Feb. 22, 1778
Joseph Hait & Phebe Benedict of Canaan,	Jan. 22, 1778
Ebenezer Hait & —— St. John of Canaan,	Nov. 25, 1778
Thomas Hoyt & Mercy Hoyt of Norwalk,	April 9, 1778
Stephen Hanford & Phebe Fitch,	Jan. 1, 1772
Matthew Hanford & Betsey Lyon of Norwalk,	March 11, 1779
David Hendrick & Anne Westcott,	Sept. 25, 1774
Andrew Hendricks & Elizabeth Gaylord,	—— 2, 1779
John Hanford & Mehitable Comstock,	Oct. 28, 1762
Samuel Jackson & Hannah Beddich or Didduck,	Dec. 10, 1741
Moses Johnson & Abigail Kellogg,	Oct. 21, ——
Joseph Judson of Stamford & Sarah Dunning of Wilton,	Oct. 5, 1740
Joseph Jellett & Phebe Nash,	July 31, 1796
Blackleach Jesup & Mary Kellogge,	Nov. 3, 1768
Shadrack Jean & Anne Olmstead,	May 16, 1776
Ephriam Ketchum & Mary Spencer,	April 2, 1746
Ebenezer Ketchum & Mary Sherwood,	Jan. 20, 1747-8
Thadeus Ketchum & Rachel Boughton,	Nov. 22, 1769
Ephram Kimberly & Mary Riggs,	April 5, 1769

Samuel Kellogg & Mrs. Sarah Hickox,	March 9, 1756
Fairchild Kellogge & widow —— Morehouse,	
	March 29, 1779
Asahel Kellogge & Anne Fancher of Canaan,	March 30, 1778
Elifalett Kellogge & Adah Benedict,	Dec. 12, 1771
John Keeler & Abigail Copsley,	May 16, 1754
Ralph Keeler & Betty Gregory,	Aug. 27, 1746
Samuel Keeler & Elizabeth Birchard,	July 4, 1739
Ebenezer Keeler & Jemima Gregory,	Oct. 5, 1742–3
Silas Keeler & Abigail Elmer,	April 4, 1746
Ralph Keeler & Elizi Gregory,	Aug. 27, 1746
John Keeler & Ruth St. John,	Nov. 14, 1749
John Keeler & Sarah Pardee,	May 6, 1751
Ezra Keeler & Mary Betts,	Nov 20, 1751
John Keeler & widow Finch,	Jan. 8, 1756
Ralph Keeler & Sarah Cooley,	March 15, 1757
James Keeler & Abagail Mead,	March 14, 1758
Timothy Keeler & Hannah Hickox,	April 15, 1758
Thaddeus Keeler & Rebena Keeler,	Dec. 22, 1763
Stephen Keeler & Sarah Burchard,	Nov. 5, 1765
Nathan Keeler & Marther Nash,	June 13, 1770
Stephen Keeler & Hannah Merven,	Jan. 12, 1773
Phenias Keeler & Rebeckah Mead,	July 9, 1775
Elijah Keeler & Naomi Gregory,	Jan. 20, 1778
—— Keeler & —— St. John, both of Canaan,	
	Oct. 28, 1799
—— Keeler & Esther Burchard,	Feb. 21, 1780
—— Keeler & Rebekah Nichols,	Feb. 22, 1780
John Keeler & Martha Olmsted,	Dec. 6, 1775
Peter Lockwood & Elizabeth Lambert,	Jan. 1, 1750–1
William Lockwood & Hannah Selleck,	Dec. 31, 1796
Nathaniel Lockwood & Eunice St. John,	Oct. 1, 1772
James Lockwood & Abigail DeForest,	Nov. 9, 1774
Samuel Lockwood & Sarah Bett,	Feb. 5, 1778
David Lockwood & widow Martha Trobridge,	——
James Lyon of Norwalk & widow E—— Canfield,	
	Dec. 22, 1757
David Lyon & Hannah Olmstead,	March 15, 1775
Pelatiah Lyon & Lydia Chard,	Jan. 25, 1776
Robert Livingstone & Mary Proctor,	June, 1769

Melatiah Lothrop & Anne Crofoot, July 11, 1771
Ichabod Lothrop & Susannah Green of Canaan, Nov. 25, 1778
Burrell Lobdell & Anne St. John, March 9, 1772
Matthew Mead & Phebe Whelply, Feb. 7, 1759
Samuel Mead & ——— Russica, 1798
Thaddeus Mead & Rebakoh Betts, July 27, 1748
Azor Mead & Susanah Fitch, Nov. 2, 1773
Theophilus Mead & Abigail Westcoot, Jan. 30, 1735-6
Jeremiah Mead & Joanna Scribner, Nov. 8, 1753
Thaddeus Mead & Rebena Betts, July 27, 1747-8
Jeremiah Mead & ——— Scribner, Nov. 8, 1753
Zacariah Mead & Betty Betts, Jan. 25, 1764
Jeremiah Mead, Jr., & Martha St. John, Dec. 20, 1775
Elias Mead & Elizabeth Gregory, Jan. 6, 1776
Jasper Mead & Elizabeth Benedict, April 8, 1779
Stephen Morehouse & Sarah St. John, Nov., 1733
Enos Morehouse & Sarah Patchen, Nov., 1774
Nathan Middlebrook & Ruth Whitlock, May 20, 1797
Michael Middlebrook & Martha Carpender, Sept. 11, 1765
Samuel Middlebrook & Polly Middlebrook, Nov. 17, 1769
Joseph Manrow & Elizabeth Stuart, Nov. 15, 1739
Nathan Manrow & Rebeckah Scribner, 1772 (?)
Joseph Marrow & Esther Fountain, Oct. 27, 1744
Robert Montgomery & Lyddia Morehouse, April 16, 1798
Jared Meeker & Mahitable Cole, May 3, 1770
John McKee & Isabel Hanford, April, 1772
Jonathan Nicols & Susannah Nicols, Oct. 20, 1799
Samuel Nichols & Millison Darrow, Oct. 15, 1750
Jonathan Nichols & Mary Chard, Oct. 21, 1751
Thaddeus Nichols & Experience Chard, June 14, 1754
Samuel Niccolls & Hannah Ressique, July 24, 1777
Nehemiah Niccolls & Sarah Jenkins, Nov. 15, 1770
James Niccolls & Abigail Hickox, June 6, 1774
Jediah Nash of Norwalk & Anne Person of Wilton,
Feb. 9, 1758
Ebenezer Nash of Wilton & Ruth Lockwood of Nor-
walk, Jan. 6, 1779
Eliakin Nash & Elizabeth Whitlock, June 13, 1770
Azariah Obedunt or Bedient & Phebe Holybert,
March 30, 1756

Isaac Osborn of Redding & Martha Higgins of
 Wilton,   Sept. 22, 1763
Isaac Osborn & Hannah Knap,   July 2, 1798
Joseph Oysburn of Salem & Mehitable Keeler of
 Wilton,   May 9, 1758
Ezra Ogden & Rachel Finch,   Nov. 6, 1797
James Small Olmsted & Dinah Steward,   April 8, 1779
Gardiner Olmsted & ——— Olmstead,   March 17, 1737-8
Richard Olmsted & Mary Keeler,   June 1, 1747-8
Silas Olmsted & Abigail Deforest,   March 5, 1753
James Olmsted & Mary Patchen,   April 8, 1754
James Olmsted & Sarah Trowbridge,   Sept. 18, 1754
Samuel Olmsted & Mary Keeler,   Nov. 12, 1795
Jasper Olmsted & Rachel St. John,   1797
Stephen Olmsted & Martha Scribner,   Nov. 2, 1797
David Olmsted & Gizel Bedient,   Jan., 1799
Stephen Olmsted & Sarah Fillow,   Jan. 18, 1770
Moses Olmsted & Patty Deforest,   Dec. 30, 1772
James Olmsted, 3rd, & Sarah Whitlock,   Feb. 8, 1775
Nathan Olmsted & Mary Middlebrook,   Dec. 14, 1775
——lon Pheleps & Hannah Whitman,   March 7, 1780
Daniel Patchen & Martha Hubble,   Aug. 9, 1749
Joseph Patchen & Hannah Collins,   March 22, 1749-50
Isaiah Patchen & Betty Stone,   Jan. 6, 1755
Asabel Patchen & Elizabeth Martin,   March 22, 1756
Jared Patchen & Nancy Nash,   Aug. 31, 1797
John Patchen & Desire Gregory,   Sept. 3, 1772
John Parketting & Susannah Abbott,   July 20, 1798
David Paddock of Phillipps & Marian Belden, Jan. 28, 1762
Joel Prindle & Sabra Kimberly,   May 22, 1757
Seth Raymond & Elizabeth Squire,   March 12, 1778
Clapp Raymond & Rebecca Betts,   Aug. 4, 1757
Clapp Raymond & Sally Dunning,   Feb. 1, 1787
Asahel Raymond & Mary Betts,   June 4, 1753
Clap Raymond & Rebena Betts,   Oct. 4, 1753
Ebenezer Raymond & Martha Henman,   Oct. 25, 1771
Jonathan Raymond & Molly Hawley,   Aug. 21, 1775
Benjamin Raymond & Abigail Cole,   Dec. 12, 1753
Asahel Raymond & Abigail Dunning,   Dec. 11, 1755
Seth Raymond & Phebe Mead,   Nov. 2, 1756

S—— R—— & S—— St. ——,   Feb. 24, 1761
John Rockwell & Sarah Whelpley,   Oct. 21 or 22, 1755
John Rockwell & Miriam Higgins,   Feb. 15, 1758
Joseph Rockwell & Mary Mead,   April 14, 1762
Jonah Rockwell & Mary Higgins,   Aug. 5, 1766
Silas Rockwell & —— Olmsted,   —— 14, 1799
John Rockwill & Esther Hulbert,   Nov. 22, 1769
Alexander Russeque of Ridgefield & Thankful
    Belden,   Feb. 16, 1737–8
John Roberson & Mary Laurance,   Jan. 24, 1763
Stephen Reed & Ellis Morris or Moril,   March 8, 1797
Ephriam Rumsey & Phebe Hurlbutt,   Jan. 4, 1775
Nathan Rumsey & Lois Hurlbert,   April 8, 1779
—— Rowley of Waterbury & widow —— Ray-
    mond of Norwalk,   Sept. 3, 1778
Joseph Riggs & Margaret Russeque,   Sept. 18, 1764
John Stewart & Hannah Taylor,   Jan. 25, 1776
James Stuard & Biah Burlace,   Jan. 21, 1762
Simeon Stuart & Abigail Smith,   Nov. 15, 1739
Thaddeus Stuart & Mary Whelply,   Oct. 21, 1755
James Stuart & Abiah Burlace,   Jan. 21, 1762
Samuel Stuart & Lydia Trowbridge,   June 19, 1765
Nathan Stuart & —— Lockwood,   Nov. 22, 1799
John Stuart & Sarah Hurlbutt,   Nov. 25, 1799
Lemuel Stewart of Sandwich & Rachel Landers of
    Wilton,   Dec. 8, 1750
Samuel Sherwood & Martha Ketchum,   April 3, 1759
Jonathan Sherwood & Elizabeth Gardiner,   March 20, 1766
Salmon Sherwood & Rachel Gilbert,   Dec., 1798
Ebenezer Sherwood & Sarah Raymond,   Nov. 3, 1773
Selah Squire & Hannah Abbott,   April 8, 1778
—— Squire & —— Dekeman,   Dec. 4, 1747–8
Thaddeus Squire & Margaret Sloan,   Dec. 26, 1753
John St. John & Eunice Hayes,   April 19, 1724
Matthew St. John & Mary Elmer,   —— 14, 1737
John St. John & Abigail Scribner,   Aug. 24, 1749
John St. John & widow Sarah Scribner,   Nov. 11, 1749
Thomas St. John & Eunice St. John,   Jan. 1, 1750–1
Stephen St. John & —— Fitch,   Dec. 9, 1757
Stephen St. John & Sarah Betts,   Jan. 1, 1797

Nehemiah St. John & ——— Achin,   March 7, 1780
Cornel Samuel St. John & widow Esther Wood,

                                            Jan. 10, 1776
James St. John & Molly St. John,   March 16, 1797
Phineas St. John & Sally Abbott,   Aug. 9, 1799
——— St. John & Mable Gregory,   Sept. 24, 1797
Abraham St. John & Anner Hoyt of Canaan, Sept. 23, 1799
David St. John & Elizabeth Waring,   Nov. 26, 1778
William Smith & Hannah Cole,   March 26, 1742–3
Amos Smith & Sarah Keeler,   June 26, 1797
Joel Smith of Redding & ——— Cole of Wilton,·

                                            Feb. 12, 1778
Daniel Smith of Norwalk & widow ——— Green
   of Canaan,   Oct. 13, 1778
Samuel Smith & Sarah Bletchley of Canaan,

                                   ——— 24 or 27, 1778
Samuel Smith & Esther Olmstead,   April 8, 1779
Elijah Sealy & Sally Buttery,   Aug. 27, 1799
——— Seymour & Sally Raymont,   Feb. 3, 1799
Job Stillwell & Esther Deforest,   June 15, 1756
——— Sturges & ——— Downs,   Oct. 8, 1753
Samuel Sturges of Greensfarm & Mary Hurlbutt,

                                     Nov. 30, 1796
Thaddeus Sturges & Molly Comstock,   Nov. 23, 1769
Simeon Spencer & Rachel St. John,   Feb. 22, 1743–4
Daniel Sterling & Thamasia Green,   July 16, 1765
Samuel Sterling & Elanor Westcoat,   May 1, 1746
William Sterling & Rebena Green,   June 4, 1754
William Starling, Jr., & Rhoda Hurlbutt,   April 8, 1779
James S—— & ——— ———,   Jan. 4, 1747–9
Samuel Scrivener of Norwalk & Mary Boulton of
   Canaan,   ——— 26, 1755
Levi Scribner & Ruth Bunts,   March 30, 1779
William Scot of Ridgefield & Abigail Belden,   Jan. 2, 1757
William Scot, Jr., & Susannah Stuart,   Jan. 20, 1778
Jonathan Stephens of Danbury & Mahitable Bedi-
   dit,   Nov. 23, 1778
James Trowbridge & Mary Belden,   April 19, 1798
James Trowbridge & Mary Dunning,   Nov. 27, 1752
Josiah Trowbridge & Martha Hickox,   March 9, 1763

David Tuttle of Canaan & Elizabeth Hickox of
    Wilton,   Oct. 24, 1754
Lieut. Noah Taylor & widow Elizabeth Marvin,
                                  Jan. 31, 1745-6
John Taylor & Rebecca Abbott,   May 7, 1746
Samuel Taylor & ―――― Kellogg, both of Mr. Dick-
    enson's parish,   Feb. 12, 1755
Seth Taylor & Martha Gaylord,   March 7, 1765
John Taylor & Mary Bears,   Feb., 1769
Samuel Turrel & Rachel Bennett,   July 30, 1797
Joseph Thomas & Phebe Gregory,   Nov. 9, 1749
Joseph Trusdale & Elizabeth Keeler,   Aug. 4, 1750
Deacon Thomas Talmage of Canaan & widow
    Sarah Weld of Wilton,   Aug. 21, 1758
James Trumbull & Phebe Clinton,   Jan., 1798
Lieut. Samuel Weed of Stamford & Sarah Dunning,
                                 Dec. 8, 1737
Jehiel Weed & ―――― Benedict of Canaan, ―― 2, 1779
Ephriam Wareing & Huldah Hickox of Canaan, Jan. 7, 1778
Nathaniel Westcoat & Sarah Trowbridge, Aug. 29, 1737
Jeremiah Westcoat & Martha Keeler,   April 27, 1763
Elijah Westcoat & Rachel Betts,   March 12, 1775
Jeremiah Westcoat & Hannah St. John,   Aug. 12, 1772
Samuel Westcoat & Irena Martin,   ―― 5, 1799
David Wood & widow Dorothy Rockwell, Feb. 27, 1743-4
Ezekeil Wood & Mary Collins,   April, 1752
Daniel Whitlock & Ruth Scribner,   Nov. 19, 1772
David Whitlock, Jr., & Ruth Betts,   March 3, 1773
Thaddeus Whitlock & Eunice Heaton,   April 24, 1776
Hezekiah Whitlock & Hannah Abbott,   April 8, 1778
Samuel Whelpley & Hannah Olmsted,   ―― 31, 1751
James Whelpley & Patty Gilbert,   June 13, 1770
Samuel Waterbury of Stamford & Hannah Stewart,
                               April 5, 1753
Ezra Waterbury & widow ―――― Finch,   Feb. 12, 1756
Stephen White of Stanwich & Margaret Belden of
    Wilton,   Oct. 18, 1759
Josiah Williams & Margery Patchen,   Dec. 14, 1756
John Williams & Sarah Williams,   Oct., 1769

CHATHAM.

MIDDLESEX COUNTY.

Chatham was incorporated in 1767. Formerly a part of Middletown. The First Congregational Church of Chatham was organized in 1721 and is now located in the town of Portland, which was set off from Chatham in 1841. The Second Congregational Church of Chatham was located at Middle Haddam and organized September 24, 1740. The Third Congregational Church of Chatham, organized November 30, 1748, is located at East Hampton. The following marriages are taken from the Second Church, Middle Haddam.

MARRIAGES BY REV. BENJAMIN BOWERS.

Jonathan Burr & Elizabeth Belden,	Oct. 30, 1740
Jeremiah Wright & Sarah Taylor,	Nov. 24, 1740
Thomas McCleve & Mary Burr,	July 9, 1741
John Spencer & Elisabeth Taylor,	Nov. 4, 1741
Jonathan Hinckly & Abigail Burr,	Nov. 26, 1741
Elisha Brewster & Lucy Yeomans,	Sept. 30, 1742
Nathan Brainerd & Sarah Gates,	Jan. 13, 1743
Robinson Williams & Elizabeth Hurd,	April 21, 1743
Francis Clark & Mary Lee,	May 20, 1743
Eleazer Bow & Mary Goff,	Nov. 10, 1743
Thomas Fuller & Elizabeth Arnold,	Nov. 10, 1743
Moses Wheeler & Susanna Arnold,	Feb. 2, 1744
Oziel Smith & widow Sarah Wright,	March 22, 1744
Ezra Andros & widow Keziah Macor,	June 21, 1744
James Brainerd, Jr., & Rebecca Hurd,	July 10, 1744
Heber Brainerd & Esther Brainerd,	Feb. 28, 1745
Jacob Hurd, Jr., & Thankful Hurlbert,	Feb. 28, 1745
Elisha Cornwell & Anna Johnson,	Feb. 28, 1745
John Taylor, Jr., & Mary Cobb,	May 16, 1745
Thomas Dart & Sarah Belden,	May 30, 1745
Ralph Smith & Mrs. Lydia Brown,	Aug. 13, 1745
Caleb Johnson & Mary Cook,	Sept. 19, 1745
Oliver Bosworth & Susanna Collins,	Sept. 26, 1745
John Hodgekin & widow Sarah Chubb,	Nov. 13, 1745
Daniel Smith & Elizabeth Rich,	Feb. 6, 1746
Moses West & Sarah Hopkins,	Feb. 13, 1746
Benjamin Strowbridge & Hope Snow,	March 31, 1746
Hezekiah Russ & Mehitable White,	April 23, 1746

Jonathan Lord & Ruth Rogers,	Nov. 20, 1746
Daniel Lucas & Elizabeth Foster,	Nov. 27, 1746
Thomas Akins & Hannah Brainerd,	Jan. 29, 1747
Zacheus Cook & Mary Hubbard,	May 14, 1747
Samuel Kilborn & Jerusha Shaler,	July 16, 1747
William Taylor & Susanna Freeman,	Sept. 24, 1747
William Markham & widow Deborah Patten,	——
Samuel Freeman & Eliza Knowles,	Feb. 4, 1748
Johnson Pelton & Kesiah Freeman,	March 3, 1748
Jabez Wood & Mary Alvord,	June 1, 1748
Jonathan Smith, Jr., & Anna Chipman,	July 7, 1748
John Markham & Desire Sears,	Nov. 3, 1748
Robert Pelton & Hannah Young,	Nov. 10, 1748
Joseph Selden & Silence Fuller,	Dec. 22, 1748
Hezekiah Whitmore & Mary Bigelow,	Aug. 17, 1749
Amos Rich & Mary Brown,	Sept. 25, 1749
William Green & Mercy Knowles,	Dec. 28, 1749
Abner Stocking & Ruth Higgins,	Feb. 8, 1750
Daniel Burton & Lydia Smith,	March 1, 1750
Othniel Brainerd & Lucy Swaddle,	May 10, 1750
Nathaniel Bozworth & Elizabeth Eddy,	June 14 or 4, 1750
Nathan Whiton & Phebe Spicer,	June 21, 1750
Nehemiah Lord & Deborah Willliams,	Sept. 18, 1750
—— Butler & Margaret Davis,	Oct. 11, 1750
John Eddy, Jr., & Elizabeth Brainerd,	Oct. 25, 1750
Amos Booge & Eunice Mayo,	Nov. 22, 1750
Gideon Hurlbut & Deborah Brainerd,	Feb. 14, 1751
William Taylor & widow Ruth Higgins,	Nov. 16, 1750
Isaac Mirick & Elizabeth Freeman,	July 25, 1751
—— Horton & widow —— Spicer,	Aug. 22, 1751
Thomas Hubbard, Jr., & Phebe Griffith,	Jan. 23, 1752
George Hubbard, Jr., & Mary Stocking,	Jan. 23, 1752
Israel Higgins, Jr., & Hannah Arnold,	Feb. 20, 1752
Daniel Brainerd, Jr., & Esther Brainerd,	April 9, 1752
Abijah Lee & Abiel Smith,	May 28, 1752
John Eddy & Mrs. Phebe Griffith,	July 23, 1752
Daniel Smith & widow Mary Rich,	Nov. 6, 1752
Jesse Higgins & Ruth Dart,	Nov. 16, 1752
—— Stevens & Elizabeth Taylor,	Feb. 1, 1753
Joseph Arnold & Huldah Hubbard,	Feb. 8, 1753

Israel Higgins, Jr., & Elizabeth Aken,	Feb. 15, 1753
John Sears & Elizabeth Freeman,	April 5, 1753
Samuel Goff & Hannah Tom,	April 12, 1753
John Stocking & Priscilla Mayo,	June 28, 1753
Jabez Fuller & Lois Hubberd,	Oct. 10, 1754
Richard Morgan, Jr., & Marcy Rich,	April 7, 1755
Thomas Wetmore & Rebekah Lewis,	May 22, 1755
Philip Goff, 3rd, & Desire Green,	May 22, 1755
David Wood & Marcy Butler,	Oct. 16, 1755
Isiaiah Swaddle & Susanna Warner,	Nov. 13, 1755
Hezekiah Sears & Deborah Spencer,	Dec. 25, 1755
Thomas Snow & Esther Taylor,	Jan. 29, 1756
Charles Williams & Elisabeth Hubbard,	March 11, 1756
Jeremiah Bradford & Rebecca Dart,	June 3, 1756
Eliphalet Smith & Rebecca Selden,	Nov. 11, 1756
Hezekiah Hills & Patience Taylor,	Nov. 16, 1756
Stephen Stiles & Rebecca Brown,	Dec. 2, 1756
Asa Kimball & Bethaih Morgan,	March 26, 1757
Ezra Smith & Bethiah Brown,	March 31, 1757
Reuben Cook & Bethiah Rich,	April 14, 1757
Andrew Carrier & Abigail Young,	May 4, 1757
Benjamin Fuller & Parthenia Hubbard,	May 19, 1757
Richard Mayo & Ruth Gibbs,	June 2, 1757
Sylvanus Higgins & Lucy Stocking,	July 21, 1757
David Higgins & Jane Higgins,	Oct. 6, 1757
Samuel Mack & Lydia Brainerd,	Feb. 23, 1758
Seth Doane & Mercy Parker,	Feb. 23, 1758
James Knowles & Lydia Higgins,	March 23, 1758
Lemuel Warren & Abigail Arnold,	May 31, 1758
David Burnet & Anna Roberts,	Aug. 3, 1758
Sylvanus Freeman & Leah Brainerd,	Oct. 30, 1758
Ebenezer Smith, Jr., & Abigail Brainerd,	Dec. 14, 1768
John Green & Rachel Higgins,	Nov. 23, 1758
Ozias Gibs & Rebecca Mayo,	Jan. 11, 1759
Josiah Brainerd, Jr., & Lois Hurlbut,	May 24, 1759
Elijah Smith & Mary Maker,	May 31, 1759
Joshua Griffin & Ruth Mayo,	July 19, 1759
Recompense Bailey & Dorothy Arnold,	Sept. 23, 1759
Dan Clark & Esther Swaddle,	Jan. 3, 1760
Jabez Arnold & Martha Freeman,	April 3, 1760

Jonathan Brainerd & Elizabeth Stocking,   May 1, 1760
Lemuel Smith & Lydia Stocking,   July 25, 1760
Benjamin Carrier & Sarah Goff,   Oct. 23, 1760
Thomas Bliss & Esther Eddy,   Nov. 6, 1760
Ebenezer Wilcox & Mary Eddy,   Nov. 17, 1760
Amos Lucas & Susannah Swaddle,   Dec. 3, 1760
Thomas Smith, Jr., & Mary Green,   Dec. 11, 1760
Jedediah Hubbard & Martha Stocking,   Dec. 18, 1760
Isaac Cotton & Elizabeth Sears, *née Knowles* Dec. 29, 1760
Josiah Strong & Mary Harris,   June 15, 1761

MARRIAGES BY REV. BENJAMIN BOARDMAN.

Thomas Stevenson & Hannah Taylor,   Jan. 14, 1762
Benjamin Smith & Mercy Maker,   Jan. 21, 1762
John Giddings & Mercy Harris,   May 27, 1762
Ezra Brainerd & Jerusha Smith,   Aug. 31, 1762
Jonathan Burr & Priscilla Freeman,   March 17, 1763
Maho Tupper of Lebanon & Elizabeth Tiffany,
    April 20, 1763
Jedediah Prior & Desire Cook,   June 9, 1763
Abijah Fuller & Martha Hale,   Sept. 7, 1763
Stephen Hosmer & Bathsheba Green,   Oct. 3, 1763
George Sexton & Elizabeth Bow,   Nov. 3, 1763
Samuel Taylor & Mary Smith,   Dec. 22, 1763
Abner Hubbard & Hannah Higgins,   Jan. 19, 1764
Elisha Shepard & Thankful Knowles,   May 15, 1764
Samuel Stocking & Jane Higgins,   Nov. 29, 1764
William Wright & Anna Hurlbut,   Dec. 18, 1764
Reuben Stocking & Sarah Hurlbut,   Sept. 19, 1765
David Brooks & Jemima Stocking,   Oct. 22, 1765
John Goff & Mary Rich,   Oct. 24, 1765
Asa Daniels & Elizabeth Fuller,   Oct. 24, 1765
Elias Hayden of Saybrook & Mary Selden,   Nov. 7, 1765
John Godfrey Houpt & Hannah Wheeler,   Jan. 23, 1766
John Haling & Barbara Roish (?), (Rich ?),   Feb. 7, 1766
Walley Adams of Falmouth & Rebekah Knowles,
    Feb. 13, 1766
Oliver Barber & Mercy Smith,   Feb. 27, 1766
Thomas Smith & Maria Wright,   March 20, 1766

David Smith & Lydia Knowles,   Oct. 1, 1766
Jabez Ranney & Penelope Bowers,   Jan. 15, 1767
David Bailey & Jemima Daniels,   July 9, 1767
David Caswell & Elisabeth Green,   Aug. 18, 1767
Joshua Cook, Jr., of Cohabit & Mary Cook of
    Chatham,   Nov. 5, 1767
Prosper Carey & Elisabeth Parker,   Nov. 19, 1767
Samuel Youngs of Haddam & Melatiah Fuller, Dec. 17, 1767
Nathan Brainerd, Jr., & Content Hannah Smith, Jan. 7, 1768
Josiah Cook, Jr., & Mary Ryder,   March 3, 1768
Jonathan Millard & Mary Akin,   March 24, 1768
Edward Cowel & Abigail Goff,   July 17, 1768
Heman Higgins & Eunice Sexton,   Dec. 15, 1768
Joseph Smith & Rachel Green,   Feb. 12, 1769
Israel Higgins & Ruth Smith,   March 9, 1769
John Smith of Hartford & Hannah Bidwell,   June 14, 1769
George Carey & Rachel Hurd,   Nov. 8, 1769
William Green of Middletown & Elizabeth Young,
                                                 Jan. 25, 1770
Daniel Kellogg, Jr., of Hebron & Rachel Taylor,
                                                 May 31, 1770
Warren Green, Jr., & Lucy Brainerd,   Nov. 1, 1770
John Parker & Eunice Doane of Eastham,   Dec. 24, 1770
Nathaniel Garnsey of Colchester & Damaris Alvord,
                                                 Jan. 24, 1771
Ephraim Cady of Pomfret & Hannah Wood,   Jan. 30, 1771
Sylvanus Parker & Jerusha Penfield,   Feb. 28, 1771
Jeremiah Harrington of Middletown & Mary
    Spencer,   Aug. 14, 1771
James Brainerd & Mercy Stocking,   Aug. 29, 1771
George Lucas of Middletown & Nancy Cary,   Oct. 31, 1771
Thomas Stocking & Elisabeth Hurd,   Oct. 31, 1771
Samuel Kilborn & Elisabeth Stillman,   Nov. 14, 1771
Samuel Pelton & Rachel Bosworth,   Dec. 23, 1771
Noadiah White, Jr., & Mercy Mayo,   Jan. 30, 1772
Jonathan Smith & Susanna Sexton,   Feb. 3, 1772
Amos Bates & Eunice Higgins,   July 28, 1772
George Lewis & Elizabeth Penfield,   Oct. 18, 1772
John Wright, Jr., & Ruth Higgins, Jr.,   May 5, 1773
Sylvanus Parker & Eunice Brainerd,   Sept. 2, 1773

Eleazer Treadwell & Hope Bailey,   Oct. 12, 1773
John Lucas & Anna Bow of Middletown,   Oct. 21, 1773
Samuel Butler of Wethersfield & Mary Hurlbut,
                                               Dec. 16, 1773
James Usher of Colchester & Sarah Brainerd,
                                               Jan. 20, 1774
Joseph Hurd & Mary Bowers,   Feb. 10, 1774
Zoeth Smith & Ruth Rowley of Colchester,
                                               March 10, 1774
Joseph Carey, Jr., & Rebecca Hurd,   July 1, 1774
Chauncey Bulkley & widow Sarah Doane,   Oct. 23, 1774
Eleazer Bates & Hannah Stocking,   Oct. 25, 1774
Ezekiel Wright & Phebe Smith,   1775
Jesse Higgins & Kesiah Stevens,   March 21, 1775
James Rich, Jr., & Margery Butler,   March 26, 1775
Joshua Merrick & Jane Stocking,   Nov. 27, 1775
George Pelton & Hannah Bow,   Dec. 13, 1775
Josiah Purple & Martha Cook,   Jan. 4, 1776
Zacheus Cook, Jr., & Mercy Goff,   Jan. 18, 1776
Ezekiel Goff & Hannah Hubbard,   Jan. 18, 1776
Benjamin Hunt of Long Island & Ruth Knowles,
                                               Jan. 16, 1777
Abner Stocking, Jr., & Lydia Bowers,   Feb. 20, 1777
George Talcott & Vienna Bradford,   March 16, 1777
Elias Jennings of Long Island & Dorothy Purple,
                                               April 6, 1777
Simon Brainerd, Jr., & Abigail Hurlbut,   April 18, 1777
Richard Giddings & Alice Smith,   April 15, 1777
Asaph Youngs & Abigail Brooks,   June 10, 1777
Lamberton Roberts & Elizabeth Smith,   Oct. 1, 1777
Aaron Wheeler & Dorothy Smith,   Oct. 30, 1777
Aaron Selden & Susanna Brainerd,   Nov. 6, 1777
Moses Wheeler, Jr., & Deborah Brainerd,   Nov. 13, 1777
Seymour Hurlbut & Deborah Cook,   Feb. 19, 1778
Nathaniel Spencer & Lydia Mack,   April 16, 1778
Elijah Johnson & Mary Hurd,   April 20, 1778
Lamberton Stocking & Mehitable Young,   April 21, 1779
Ezra Bigelow & Lois Horton,   May 6, 1779
Ashbel Arnold & Hannah Clark,   July 25, 1779
Luther Whittmore & Elizabeth Higgins,   Sept. 2, 1779

Caleb Parsons of Enfield & Lois Higgins,   Sept. 22, 1779
Jonathan Fisher & Hannah Bestor,   Oct. 29, 1779
Jonathan Doane & Phebe Horton,   Dec. 6, 1779
Benjamin Arnold & Margaret Bailey,   March 26, 1780
John Meacham of Enfield & Tabitha Daniels,
    May 4, 1780
Eldad Halcomb of Granville & Martha Brainerd,
    May 10, 1780
Abner Smith & Rebecca Gibbs,   Oct. 11, 1780
Joseph Berry & Olive Cook,   Oct. 12, 1780
Elias Smith & Eunice Arnold,   Oct. 12, 1780
Nathaniel Cook & Anniss Sears,   Dec. 7, 1780
William Exton & Sarah Rich,   Feb. 21, 1781
Cezar Beman & Sarah Gary,   March 8, 1781
Phineas Doan & Eunice Parker,   June 7, 1781
Jesse Brainerd & Hannah Cook,   June 28, 1781
Ezra Bigelow, Jr., & Rachel Wheeler,   Aug. 21, 1781
Oliver Emmons & Anna Brainerd,   Aug. 26, 1781
Nathan Eddy & Mercy Higgins,   Aug. 30, 1781
Thomas Parsons & Jemima Bailey,   Oct. 25, 1781
Elijah Smith & Anna Olmsted,   Jan. 3, 1782
Samuel Rich & widow Mary Goff,   Jan. 10, 1782
Josiah Goff & Anna Rowley,   Feb. 7, 1782
Philemon Ames of Weatherfield & Ruth Hurlbut,
    Feb. 19, 1782
Ralph Smith & Hannah Smith,   March 21, 1782
John Parmelee & Lucy Annabel,   March 28, 1782
Jeremiah Bradford, Jr., & Mary Smith,   May 19, 1782
Sylvanus Smith & Lydia Clark,   May 21, 1782
Jacob Hurd, Jr., & Abigail Carey,   Oct. 3, 1782
Paul Sears & Eleanor Smith,   Oct. 17, 1782
Jonathan Brainerd & Hope Strong,   Nov. 24, 1782
Jonathan Pelton & Elisabeth Doane,   Dec. 4, 1782
Reuben Chapman & Mary Doane,   Dec. 19, 1782
Timothy Doane & Mary Cary,   April 19, 1783
Robert Stuart & Dorcas Hurlbut,   April 24, 1783
Silas Beers & Thankful Hubbard,   June 26, 1783
Ebenezer Hills & Ruth Dewy,   Aug. 25, 1783
Thomas Shepard & Elisabeth Rider,   Aug. 28, 1783
Amos Shepard & Lament Goff,   Nov. 11, 1784

MARRIAGES BY REV. DAVID SELDEN.

Nathaniel Gates & Hannah Knowlton,	Nov., 1785
Isaac Williams & Mary Wheeler,	Feb. 16, 1786
Jonathan Brainerd & Jerusha Fielding,	Feb. 23, 1786
Nathaniel Cook & Olive Rowley,	March 2, 1786
Josiah Bidwell & Dimmis Giddings,	April 16, 1786
Edward Shepard & Susanna Miller,	June 1, 1786
Asaph Doan & Esther Strong,	Sept. 24, 1786
Jehiel Whitmore & Polly Higgins,	Nov. 26, 1786
Sylvanus Freeman & Huldah Goff,	Jan. 1, 1787
Timothy Higgins & Lucy Whitmore,	April 5, 1787
Elijah Clark & Mercy Doane,	April 15, 1787
Joel Brainerd & Eunice Brooks,	May 24, 1787
Robert Brainerd & Abigail Spencer,	May 24, 1787
Michael Creamer & Lydia Simmons,	June 28, 1787
Daniel Brainerd, Jr., & Hannah Cary,	July 28, 1787
Joseph B. Brooks & Eunice Johnson,	Aug. 7, 1787
Waitstill Cary & Prudence Hubbard,	Sept. 30, 1787
Samuel Northam & Hannah Arnold,	Nov. 18, 1787
Demas Strong & Polly Swift,	Feb. 24, 1788
Josiah Crittenden & Lydia Spencer,	Feb. 27, 1788
John Goodrich & Eunice Parmlee,	Feb. 28, 1788
Jabez Clark & Ruth Hinckley,	Feb. 28, 1788
Elihu Smith & Jemima Cook,	March 24, 1788
Jesse Hurd & Drusilla Dart,	April 24, 1788
Calvin Hubbard & Esther Ranny,	June 1, 1788
Israel Higgins, Jr., & Henrietta Bradford,	June 28, 1788
Nathaniel Doane & Prudence Smith,	July 20, 1788
Charles Smith & Polly Strong,	Sept. 11, 1788
Timothy Hubbard & Dolly Rowley,	Sept. 18, 1788
John Wright & Dolly Sears,	Nov. 24, 1788
———— Olds & Hannah Stevenson,	Dec. 3, 1788
Noadiah Taylor & Mercy Brainerd,	Dec. 18, 1788
Ebenezer Whitmore & Elisabeth Knowles,	Feb. 12, 1789
Samuel Stocking & Anne Belden,	April 7, 1789
Elisha Taylor & Lois Codus (?), Codrei (?),	April 7, 1789
James Higgins & Lydia Smith,	May 10, 1789
Daniel Morgan & Lydia Higgins,	June 7, 1789
Timothy Hale of Glastonbury & Ruth Smith,	July 1, 1789

Thomas Ackley & Olive Cook,	Oct. 22, 1789
John Cooper & Hannah Carey,	Nov. 19, 1789
Jedediah Hubbard, Jr., & Dolly Brainerd,	Nov. 26, 1789
York & Sylvia,	Nov. 29, 1789
John Kelly & Kate Bailey,	Nov. 30, 1789
Guernsey Goff & Asenath Brainerd,	Dec. 31, 1789
George Akins & Tamzen Higgins,	July 8, 1790
Jeremiah Stocking & Polly Wood,	Sept. 19, 1790
Caleb Pelton & Esther Crittenden,	Oct. 3, 1790
Jared Brainerd & Henrietta Smith,	Dec. 12, 1790
John W. Johnson & Jerusha Carey,	Dec. 29, 1790
Oliver Clark & Martha Strong,	Feb. 24, 1791
David Hurlbut & Hannah Fuller,	March 30, 1791
Ansel Brainerd & Hannah Dart,	Aug. 28, 1791
Samuel Smith & Ruth Cole,	Sept. 12, 1791
Daniel Hills & Cynthia Cook,	Sept. 18, 1791
Joel Bradford & Sally Stocking,	Sept. 22, 1791
Hendrick Cole & Phebe Griffith,	Oct. 2, 1791
Joel & Sylvia,	Oct. 20, 1791
Nathaniel Bailey & Rachel Sears,	Nov. 24, 1791
William Shepardson & Editha Cook,	Nov. 24, 1791
Abraham Andrews & Anne Higgins,	Jan. 4, 1792
Gillett Hinckley & Hannah Hall,	Jan. 19, 1792
Jacob Goff & Sally Taylor,	Jan. 24, 1792
Joshua Burnham & Polly Purple,	Jan. 26, 1792
Samuel Smith & Elisabeth Ackley,	Feb. 19, 1792
Benjamin Graham & Polly Crittenden,	Feb. 26, 1792
Ozias Griffith & Anne Chapman,	Feb. 26, 1792
David Arnold & Elisabeth Hubbard,	April 8, 1792
Benjamin Hall & Hannah Strong,	April 12, 1792
Mathew Haling & Silence Bailey,	May 24, 1792
Jesse Graham & Elisabeth Cook,	Aug. 16, 1792
Ebenezer Simmons & Nancy Carey,	Nov. 21, 1792
Joseph Hitchcock & Elisabeth Eddy,	Nov. 29, 1792
Joseph Dart & Sally Hurd,	Dec. 6, 1792
Orange Hurlbut & Arance Arnold,	Dec. 20, 1792
Samuel Young, Jr., & Mehitable Young,	Dec. 27, 1792
—— Ufford & —— Haselkause (?),	Jan. 31, 1793
Caleb Brainerd & Sally Snow,	March 27, 1793
Daniel Brooks, Jr., & Betsy Sexton,	March 27, 1793

Simon Smith & Ruth E. Mayo,	May 14, 1793
Ebenezer Washburn & Hannah Cady,	May 19, 1793
Edward Brine & Patience Cook,	June 3, 1793
John Brine & Lucy Goff,	July 28, 1793
David Bailey & Anne Tryon,	Aug. 15, 1793
Nathan Brainerd & Lydia Brooks,	Sept. 26, 1793
Remmick Knowles & Polly Taylor,	Sept. 29, 1793
Edward Bailey & Rebecca Smith,	Oct. 13, 1793
Chauncey Bulkley, Esq., & Mary Hurd,	Nov. 14, 1793
Stephen Stocking & Mehitable Swift,	Dec. 1, 1793
John Wilson & Sabrina Allibee,	Dec. 8, 1793
Amos Hubbard & Anne Smith,	Feb. 12, 1794
Morris McNary & Sarah Cooper,	May 7, 1794
Joseph Brooks & Grace Strong,	June 1, 1794
Thomas Spencer & Esther Sears,	Aug. 31, 1794
Samuel Sexton & Lucinda Rowley,	Dec. 25, 1794
Joseph Smith & Lucy Sears,	Jan. 15, 1795
Asa Brainerd & Abigail Fuller,	March 5, 1795
Lemuel Hedge & Sabra Higgins,	April 19, 1795
William Higgins & Abigail Strong,	May 31, 1795
Benjamin Bowers & Eunice Brainerd,	June 18, 1795
David Brainerd & Sarah Sears,	Oct. 25, 1795
Timothy Watkins & Sophia Hurd,	Nov. 15, 1795
Ichabod Lucas & Lydia Goff,	March 17, 1796
John Ufford & Mercy Taylor,	May 1, 1796
Samuel Smith & Polly Knowles,	May 12, 1796
Willard Sears & Betsy Strong,	May 22, 1796
Ichabod Pierce & Polly Goff,	May 26, 1796
Josiah Brainerd, Jr., & Clarissa Dart,	July 24, 1796
Jeremiah House & Ruth Purple,	Oct. 30, 1796
Elias Higgins & Statira Fuller,	March 1, 1797
Abijah Brainerd & Martha Arnold,	March 26, 1797
Francis Denoyer & Lucy Brooks,	May 7, 1797
Selden Smith & Hannah Shepard,	May 28, 1797
Roswell Sexton & Betsy Arnold,	Oct. 8, 1797
Joseph Shipman & Sarah Arnold,	Oct. 29, 1797
John Wier & Deborah Ackley,	Nov. 16, 1797
Asahel Brainerd & Lucretia Whitmore,	Jan. 4, 1798
Thomas Clark & Lura Sexton,	Jan. 22, 1798
Amasa Fielding & Polly Watrous,	Jan. 25, 1798

Samuel Dealing (?), Jr., & Elisabeth Ackley,	Feb. 4, 1798
Michael Deming & Martha Higgins,	Feb. 5, 1798
Amos Hubbard & Sabra Brainerd,	Feb. 20, 1798
John Tupper & Betsey Goff,	Feb. 22, 1798
Amasa Daniels, Jr., & Polly Shepard,	May, 15, 1798
Elias Young & Katy Wright,	May 16, 1798
Calvin Willey & Sally Brainerd,	Oct. 13, 1798
Jesse Higgins & Lucintha Smith,	Nov. 9, 1798
—— Holmes & —— Smith of Eastbury,	March 3, 1799
Aaron House & Martha Purple,	May 9, 1799
Solon Ramsdell & Vienna Stocking,	July 7, 1799
Ebenezer Thomas, Jr., & Azuba Brainerd,	July 25, 1799
Joseph Crouch & Betsey Fuller,	Oct. 27, 1799
Levi Caswell & Asenath Hubbard,	Nov. 17, 1799
Isaac Hinckley & Sally Shepard,	Dec. 12, 1799

RIDGEFIELD.

FAIRFIELD COUNTY.

The town of Ridgefield was incorporated October, 1709. The township was purchased of the Indians by a company of twenty-nine individuals from Norwalk and Milford, 1707-8. The First Congregational Church was organized in 1712 and is located at Ridgefield Center. The Second Congregational Church is at Ridgebury and was organized January 18, 1769. The following are the marriages from the Second Church records. Rev. Samuel Camp pastor from 1769 to 1804.

Peter Castle, Jr., of Danbury & Rebecca Osborn of Ridgefield,	March 6, 1769
Matthew Northrop & Hannah Abbott,	Sept. 14, 1769
Ezekiel Osborn & Sarah Bennet, Ridgebury parish,	Nov. 16, 1769
James Lockwood of Noble Town & Mary Street,	Nov. 18, 1769
Samuel Northrop & Prewe Riggs,	Nov. 29, 1769
Abraham Rockwell & Esther Riggs,	Nov. 29, 1769
Daniel Keeler & Abigail Isaacs,	March 22, 1770
Jonathan Taylor & Any Benedict,	April 26, 1770
Aaron Hull & Abigail Whitlock,	Oct. 8, 1770
Ephrim Smith of Philippi & widow Elizabeth Hamblin,	April 25, 1771

Benjamin Jones of Philip's Patent & Elisabeth
    Rockwell,   June 27, 1771
Thomas Conclin of Salisbury & Anna Keeler,
                             Aug. 14, 1771
Theophilus Taylor, Jr., of Danbury & Rachel North-
    rop,   Dec. 4, 1771
Jeremiah Burchard & Phebe Abbot,   Feb., 1772
Nehemiah Keeler & Eleanor Rockwell,   June 15, 1772
Nathaniel Northrop of Ridgefield & Chloe Baldwin
    of Danbury,   Nov. 5, 1772
Timothy Foster & Desire Sears,   Nov. 19, 1772
Samuel Baldwin of Danbury & Hannah Northrop,
                             Dec. 9, 1772
Caleb Parmer of Philippi & Tamar Stevens,   Dec., 1772
Jeremiah Keeler of Upper Salem & Lydia Keeler,
                         March 2, 1773
Daniel Tuttle & Naomi Stevens,   Aug. 10, 1773
Stephen Sherwood of ―――― & Ruth Benedict of
    Danbury, Ridgebury parish,   Aug. 11, 1773
Noah Starr & Sarah Keeler,   Aug. 11, 1773
Abijah Rockwell & Lydia Burchard,   Sept. 30, 1773
Ezekiel Hodge of the Nine Partners & Massah
    Foster,   Dec. 22, 1773
James Northrop, Jr., & Abiah Rockwell,   Jan. 26, 1774
Joseph Meeker of Redding & Hannah Street,   May 4, 1774
Bennajah Hoyt of Bethel & Abigail Starr,   July 7, 1774
Stephen Trusdale of the Little Nine Partners &
    Ruhama Keeler of Upper Salem,   Sept. 1, 1774
Benjamin Andrus, Jr., of Danbury & Sarah Starr,
                           Nov. 8, 1774
David Gates & Jerusha Whitney,   Dec. 22, 1774
John Wallace of Upper Salem & Esther Rockwell,
                          Jan. 3, 1775
Stephen Bennet, Jr., of Wilton, in Norwalk, & Mary
    Pulling,   Feb. 11, 1776
John Sherwood & Ann Rockwell,   April 17, 1776
Silvanus Sealy of Stanford, Canaan parish, &
    Esther Hyat,   July 2, 1776
Jachin Benedict of Bethel & widow Ann Starr,
                           Aug. 28, 1776

Thomas Hyat of Ridgefield First Society &
    Elizabeth Smith,   Sept. 11, 1776
Phineas Peck & Abigail Corban, both of Danbury,
                                          Oct. 13, 1776
Daniel Whitlock of Wilton, in Norwalk, & Esther
    Whitney,   Jan. 1, 1777
Silas Pierce of Philip's Patent & Mary Whitney,
                                          Feb. 27, 1777
Daniel Thomas & Eunice Foster,   Oct. 30, 1777
Arthur Forrester & Jemima Keeler,   Dec. 6, 1777
Timothy Weed & Sarah Silsbe,   Dec. 11, 1777
Elias Taylor of Danbury & Sarah Andrus,   Feb. 11, 1778
Jonathan Allebeen & Massah Bouton, both of
    Cortland's Manour,   Feb. 26, 1778
John Brown & Massah Bouton, both of Upper
    Salem,   Feb. 27, 1778
Ezekiel Bradley of Newburg & Martha Wood,
                                          April 23, 1778
Jabez Rockwell of Danbury & Phebe Bedient of
    Wilton, residing in Ridgebury,   Oct. 11, 1778
Thaddeus Searl of Bedford & Hannah Keeler, Dec. 18, 1778
Joseph Gray & Lydia Keeler,   April 1, 1779
Abram Pulling of Ridgebury & widow Susanna
    Wood of Ridgefield,   April 7, 1779
Noah Stone of Litchfield & Mary Gray,   May 25, 1779
Levi Shove of Danbury & Abigail Weed,   June 29, 1779
Leister Rooels of Kent & Phebe Scot,   1779
Stephen Northrop of Ridgebury & Elizabeth Hyat
    of Ridgefield,   Nov. 2, 1779
Nathan Benedict, Jr., of Danbury & Sarah Abbot,
                                          Nov. 25, 1779
Barak Nickerson of Ridgebury & Rebecca More-
    house of Dutches County,   Dec. 14, 1779
David Rockwell, Jr., & Sarah Nickerson,   Dec. 28, 1779
Abner Smith & Bettsy Kniffen, both of Upper Salem,
                                          Jan. 11, 1780
John Priest of Massachusetts State & Lucy Vick-
    ery,   Feb. 17, 1780
Gershom Jecocks & Abigail Smith, both of Upper
    Salem,   Feb. 22, 1780

Daniel Purdy of Cortlandt's Manour & Rebecca
    Rockwell of Upper Salem,   March 23, 1780
Zalmon Taylor & Hannah Benedict, both of Dan-
    bury, Ridgebury parish,   Oct. 26, 1780
Jonas Humans of Philip's Patent & Thankful
    Barber of Ridgebury,   Dec. 31, 1780
Muajah Wicks, a refugee from Long Island, & Phebe
    Barber of Ridgebury,   Jan. 30, 1781
Jonathan Conckling & Annis Smith of Upper Salem,
                  March 15, 1781
Patrick Magee of Pittsfield & Naomi Vickery, Aug. 5, 1781
Uriah Burchard & Eunice Taylor,   Oct. 16, 1781
David Rockwell, Jr., of Ridgebury parish &
    Susanna Wooden of Fredericksburgh,   Oct. 16, 1781
Jonah Foster, Jr., & Rebecca St. John,   No. 29, 1781
Gilbert Brush & Jenney Hunt, both of the State of
    New York,   Dec. 13, 1781
Phinehas Doolittle & Sarah Benedict,   March 7, 1782
Riah Nash & Esther Lynes , both of Ridgefield
    First Society,   August 15, 1782
James Scot, Jr., & Lucretia Olmsted, both of Ridge-
    field First Society,   Sept. 5, 1782
Josiah Rockwell of Ridgebury parish & Christiana
    Starr of Danbury, residing in Ridgebury, Sept. 9, 1782
Eleazar Taylor of Danbury & Hannah Starr, Nov. 7, 1782
Eleazar Curtiss of Kent & Eunice Starr,   Nov. 7, 1782
John Chapman of Salem & Chloe Keeler,   Nov. 27, 1782
James Abbot & Kate Weed,   March 26, 1783
Jacob Lobdell of Cortlandt's Mannour & Bettee
    Whitney,   Dec. 11, 1783
Abel Pulling & Sarah Whitlock,   Dec. 31, 1783
Lieut. Thaddeus Keeler & Ruth Kieler,   May 27, 1784
John Roods of Washington & Amy Smith,   July 8, 1784
Jonathan Andrus & Dorcas Stebbens,   July 18, 1784
Aaron Simmons & Polly Mitchel, both of Dutches
    County, N. Y.,   Nov. 3, 1784
Capt. Timothy Taylor & Elisabeth Cooke, both of
    Danbury,   Dec. 12, 1784
Peleg Arnold & Bettee Norris,   Jan. 9, 1785
Benjamin Fowler & Jane Forrester,   Feb. 10, 1785

Timothy Nixon Ran & Abigail Peck of Danbury,
                                        April 3, 1785
Samuel St. John & Chloe Weed,   April 6, 1785
Daniel Benedict of Danbury & Rhoda Benedict of
      Danbury and parish of Ridgebury,   April 7, 1785
Nathan Hawley of Redding & Betty Sears, April 14, 1785
Jonathan Dykeman & Hannah Street,   May 1, 1785
William Rockwell & Sarah Worden,   June 16, 1785
David Lambert Deforest, from Danbury, & Sarah
      Crosby of Fredericksburgh,   Sept. 15, 1785
John Howes & Anna Ball of Fredericksburgh,
                                    Sept. 15, 1785
Samuel Worden & Phebe Keeler,   Oct. 13, 1785
Thomas Bayly & Mary Lobdell, both of Upper
      Salem, State of New York,   Nov. 23, 1785
William Pulling & Jane Resen,   Nov. 24, 1785
—— Lacy & Lurana Wilson, both of North Strat-
      ford,   Nov. 24, 1785
Thomas Wildman of Danbury & Hannah Benedict
      of Danbury, Ridgebury parish,   Dec. 25, 1785
Capt. Peter Sanford of Redding & Abigail Keeler,
                                     Jan. 1, 1786
Christopher Leach of Bethel & Mary Lockwood
      of Danbury, Ridgebury parish,   May 8, 1786
George Loomis of Harwington & Deborah Steward
      of Wilton, resident in Ridgebury,   Sept. 21, 1786
Matthew Beal of Fredericksburgh & Phebe Keeler,
                                    Nov. 2, 1786
Phinehas Smith of Canaan Parish & Abiah Keeler,
                                    Nov. 2, 1786
Isaac Townsend of Fredericksburgh & Mary Sears,
                                   Nov. 23, 1786
Benjamin Lynes of Redding & Sarah Coley, Nov. 23, 1786
John Bryant of Lanesborough & Betsy Townsend,
                                  Dec. 27, 1786
John Reed of Salisbury & Sarah Wyat of Salem,
                                  Feb. 2, 1787
Nathan Comstolk & Rachel Keeler, both of ye
      State of New York,   Feb. 29, 1787
Eli Andrus of Danbury & Ruth Rockwell, Aug. 29, 1787

Isaac Rockwell, late of Ridgebury, & Phebe Hem-
    sted of Upper Salem,   Oct. 25, 1787

Nathan Whitney & Hannah Taylor of Danbury,
    both of Ridgebury parish,   Dec. 16, 1787

Thomas Bouton of Danbury & Rebekah Coley, Dec. 27, 1787

Timothy Keeler of Ridgefield & Urania Deforest
    of Danbury, both of Ridgebury parish,   Dec. 14, 1788

John Perry of Ridgefield, Ridgebury parish, &
    Elizabeth Corben of Danbury,   March 29, 1789

Stephen Brownson Benedict & Eunice Wildman,
    both of Danbury,   March 24, 1789

Joseph Rockwell of Ridgfield, Ridgebury, & Cloe
    Webb of Upper Salem, State of New York,
                             Oct. 22, 1789

Stephen Gates & Mary Abbot,   Nov. 22, 1789

John Weeks of Danbury & Abigail Street,   Feb. 3, 1790

Zadock St. John of Ballston & Hannah Wagstaff,
                             Feb. 11, 1790

John Norris & Rachel Northrop,   Oct. 20, 1790

Preserved Taylor of Redding & Susanna Keeler,
                             Nov. 10, 1790

Samuel Darling & Elisabeth Benedict,   Nov. 10, 1790

Runa Rockwell & Rachel Darling,   Nov. 11, 1790

Ezekiel Bradley & Abigail Pulling,   Jan. 30, 1791

Samuel Abiel Camp & Lemira Wilson,   May 26, 1791

Nathan Worden & Sarah Pulling,   June 12, 1791

Eliphalet Bennet & Hannah Mead,   June 16, 1791

Elias Thomas & Jane Forrester,   Feb. 13, 1794

Levi Taylor of Danbury & Rachel Gates,   Aug. 3, 1794

Matthew Northrop, Jr., & Hannah Kieler, Oct. 16, 1794

Lemuel Price & Rebecca Baldwin, both of Danbury,
    Ridgebury parish,   Nov. 27, 1794

John Munson Olmsted & Abigail Foster, Feb. 1, 1795

Eliphalet Brush, 2nd, of Ridgefield & Betty Burrit
    of Danbury, Ridgebury parish,   May 14, 1795

Joseph Allen of Fairfield & Phebe Seymour, Nov. 8, 1795

Platt Benedict & Sally D. Forest, both of Danbury,
    Ridgebury parish,   Nov. 12, 1795

Jacob Scofield of Poundridge & Hannah Finch,
                             Nov. 12, 1795

Orange Starr of Danbury & Hannah Northrop,
                                    Dec. 3, 1795
Hezekiah Raymond of Weston & Catharine Seymour,
                                    Feb. 15, 1796
Matthew Smith & Abigail Benedict,   Feb. 25, 1796
    (N. B.—This Abigail was from the State of New York.)
Israel Stone of Litchfield & Abigail Gates,   June 23, 1796
Thomas Benedict & Dorcas Nickerson,   Aug. 25, 1796
Caleb Rockwell & Olive Porter,   Oct. 30, 1796
Samuel Smith Baldwin of Danbury & Sarah Camp,
                                    Nov. 10, 1796
John Starr Benedict of Danbury & Patty Stebbens,
                                    Nov. 20, 1796
Ambross Millard of Milton & Betty Bennet,   Jan. 18, 1797
Abijah Hyat & Clarissa Hayes,   April 27, 1797
William Dan, 2nd, of Southeast & Ruth Keeler, May 25, 1797
Deacon ——— Bracket of Wolcott & Eunice Combs
    of Danbury,   June 20, 1797
Rufus Clark, resident of Hartford, & Sally Glover
    of Danbury,   Oct. 9, 1797
Elkanah Sherman & Lois H. King,   Oct. 12, 1797
Thomas Baxter, Jr., of North Salem, N. Y., & Sarah
    Wildman of Danbury,   Feb. 4, 1798
Daniel Andrus of Winchester & Sarah Platt, Sept. 10, 1798
Najah Wildman of Danbury & Rebecca DeForest
    of Danbury, Ridgebury Society,   Nov. 11, 1798
Noah Smith & Rachel St. John,   Nov. 12, 1798
Trowbridge Benedict of Danbury & Sarah Weed,
                                    Nov. 13, 1798
Timothy Weed, Jr., & Olive St. John,   Dec. 25, 1798
Martin Hays of Granby & Mary Camp, 2nd,   Dec. 25, 1798
Tyler Purdy of North Salem & Emila Northrop,
                                    March 21, 1799
Obil Rockwell & Betty Rockwell,   Nov. 27, 1799
William Gorham of Danbury & Polly Weed,   May 12, 1800
Seth Raymond of North Salem & Abigail Brush,
                                    Aug. 23, 1800

HEBRON.

TOLLAND COUNTY.

Hebron, incorporated May, 1708. The First Congregational Church in Hebron was organized in 1717. Early records burned. The Second Congregational Church, organized May, 1748, is located at Gilead. The following marriages are taken from the Gilead Church records.

Peter Swetland & Ann Bond,	June 11, 1752
Abner Waters & Lydia Root,	1752
Obadiah Dunham & Hannah Pinneo,	Dec. 6, 1752
John Tallcott & Abiah Phelps,	Dec. 22, 1752
Marten Townzen (send ?) & Rhoda Ingham,	Oct. 25, 1753
Samuel Abens (born ?) & Mary Ingham,	Sept. 7, 1753
James Calkins & Mary Man,	Sept. 26, 1754
Thomas Perrin & Eliseth Williams,	Oct. 2, 1754
Jabez Ellis & Mary Sawyer,	Nov. 14, 1754
Ebenezer Hall & Mary Wadsworth,	Nov. 14, 1754
Ebenezer Horton & Temperance Shipman,	Dec. 27, 1754
Abijah Rowle & Hannah Curtice,	Jan. 16, 1755
Simeon Porter & Sarah Kilburn,	March 13, 1755
William Shepherd & Rachel Hutchinson,	Oct. 16, 1755
Moses Hutchinson & Ruth Coox,	Jan. 1, 1756
Eliphelet House & Lucretia Howell,	Jan. 15, 1756
John Skinner & Elisath Merrel,	Jan. 22, 1756
Amasa Townzen & Phebe Ingham,	Jan. 29, 1756
Jonathan Adams & Hannah Yeamon,	March 11, 1756
John Mack & Eunice Fish,	April 22, 1756
Ebenezer Sumner & Persis Pease,	May 9, 1756
Gad Merril & Mary Skinner,	July 15, 1756
Elijah Horton & Sarah Coox,	March, 1757
Amos Hall & Martha Wilcox,	May, 1757
James Coox & Ann Polly,	Oct., 1757
Ephraim Youngs & Elizabeth Curtice,	Nov., 1757
Zadek Martindale & Sibil Shipman,	Feb., 1758
Asher Merrils & Delight Sawyer,	Jan., 1759
Gideon Waters & Lydia Polly,	April, 1759
Alexander Ingham & Catherine Noble,	May, 1759
Jonathan Booth & Tarza Noble,	1759

Nicholas Bond & Thankful Foot,	July, 1759
Capt. Benoni Trumbull & Phebe Post,	Jan., 1760
Samuel Gilbert, Jr., & Lydia Post,	May, 1760
Jazaniah Post & Elizabeth Bissell,	1760
Benjamin Swetland & Phebe Wilcox,	July, 1760
Ebenezer Dewey & Temperance Holdrige,	1760
Joshua Tillotson & Elizabeth Brooker,	Nov., 1760
Benjamin Trumbull & Martha Phelps,	Dec., 1760
Asaph Trumbull & Zilpah Phelps,	1760
John Ellis & Elizabeth Sawyer,	1760
Ichabod Phelps & Mary Trumbull,	Jan., 1761
Thomas Sumner & Rebeker Downer,	June, 1761
George Loveland & Anna Mallery,	July, 1761
John Merrel & Sarah Culver,	Sept. 1761
David Brown & Lydia Swetland,	Oct., 1761
Deacon Ebenezer Dewey & Christian Phelps,	Nov., 1761
John Peters, Jr., & Ann Barnett,	Nov., 1761
Benjamin Baldwin & Lydia Peters,	1761
Joseph Taylor & Elizabeth Sumner,	Jan., 1762
Abel Wilcox & Susanna Hall,	1762
Amos Hall & Betty Briant,	March, 1762
Thomas Post & Abitha Phelps,	June, 1762
Thomas Perrin & Martha Savery,	Sept., 1762
Elijah Owen & Deborah Holdridge,	Oct., 1762
Elijah Webster & Deborah Post,	Dec., 1762
Nathaniel Davis & Rachel Rollo,	April, 1763
Capt. Benoni Trumbull & Marget Warner,	1763
Jonathan Webster & Elizabeth Wilcox,	May, 1763
Ebenezer Skinner & Eunice Culver,	Sept., 1763
Henry White & Sarah Dewey,	Jan., 1764
Philip Judd & Mary Peters,	1764
James Row & Esther Mack,	1764
Joel Post & Sarah Bushnel,	Feb., 1764
John Foot & Ann Thomson,	March, 1764
Simeon Webster & Rebekah Brown,	Sept., 1764
Jonah Phelps & Sarah Mack,	Nov., 1764
Ebenezer Root & Deborah Buck,	1764
John Thomas & Lovina Brown,	1764
Eliphalet Youngs & Martha Burnham,	April, 1765
David Curtice & Judith Wright,	July, 1765

Elias Jagger & Mahetable Root,	Nov., 1765
Ashbel Phelps & Jerusha Perrin,	Jan., 1766
Isaac Riley & Hannah Youngs,	May, 1766
Jedediah Ward & Esther Post,	Aug., 1766
Jonathan Hutchinson & Elonor Post,	Sept., 1766
Timothy Stevens & Mary Wayers,	Dec., 1766
Ebenezer Kilborn & Sarah Bill,	Feb., 1767
Jesse Munson & Miriam Rowley,	April, 1767
Peter Robinson & Sarah Buck,	May, 1767
Elias Jagger & Sarah Perrin,	1767
Josiah Mack & Elizabeth Rowley,	July, 1767
Solomon Lothrop & Elizabeth Rollo,	Nov., 1767
Samuel Brown & Prudence Sawyer,	March, 1768
John Bissel & Susannah Youngs,	Nov., 1768
Nathaniel Darbe & Temperance Bond,	Nov., 1768
John Row, Jr., & Elizabeth Bill,	June, 1769
Zia Case & Asubah Phelps,	Sept., 1769
Charles Loomis, Jr., & Lucy Ford,	Oct., 1769
Benjamin Sawyer & Sarah Dewey,	Nov., 1769
Phineas Grover & Ruth Nicoles,	Nov., 1769
Samuel Covel & Anna Mack,	Jan., 1770
Edmund Wells & Welthia Goodrich,	Feb., 1770
William Rollo & Lucy Hall,	April, 1770
John Toon & Chloe Townsend,	April, 1770
James Post & Thankful Wells,	Dec., 1770
Jehiel Wilcox & Lydia Mack,	April, 1771
Thomas Loveland & Jerusha Loveland,	June, 1771
Ebenezer Wright & Jerusha Dunham,	Jan., 1772
Jacob Russel & Esther Dunham,	May, 1772
Enos Blossom & Mary Ellis,	June, 1772
Ezra Chapman & Mary Dewey,	June, 1772
John Hubbard & Thankful Rowlee,	Oct., 1772
Edward Grannis & Hannah Wells,	Nov., 1772
David Taylor & Resehannah Gilbert,	Dec., 1772
Ebenezer Bill & Rachel Root,	March, 1773
Julius Collins & Deborah Culver,	June, 1773
Solomon Perrin & Ann Cellogg (Kellogg ?),	June, 1773
Thomas Judd & Mary Rollo,	Aug., 1773
David Perry & Kezia Root,	Feb., 1774
Adam Negro & Cloe Cook,	March, 1774

David Mack & Mary Tallcott,	April, 1774
Asa Brown & Elizabeth Dunham,	May, 1774
Joshua Page & Margery Wells,	Sept., 1774
Thomas Champlin & Jemima Loveland,	Oct., 1774
William Wright & Comfort Post,	Oct., 1774
Abner Morley & Alice Townsend,	Oct., 1774
Joseph Davis & Dorithy Brown,	Nov., 1774
Nathaniel Davis & Sibil Mack,	Nov., 1774
Elihu Wells & Hannah Hutchinson,	Nov., 1774
Daniel Chapman & Lucy Talcott,	Jan., 1775
Nehemiah Porter & Abigail Strong,	March, 1775
Daniel Warner & Hannah Sumner,	Oct., 1775
Eleazer Wilcox & Mary Mack,	Nov., 1775
Larance Ralvlin & Thankful Hutchinson,	Jan., 1776
Jabez Ingraham & Naomi Root,	Jan., 1776
Daniel Wells & Hannah Lothrop,	Feb., 1776
Deacon Thomas Post & Elizabeth Culver,	Aug., 1776
Weltor Rollo & Mary Wells,	Sept., 1776
Daniel Brown & Anna Phelps,	Nov., 1776
John Finley, Jr., & Phebe Ford,	Jan., 1777
David Wright & Patience Bill,	Jan., 1777
Moses Goodrich & Mary Ford,	Feb., 1777
Adonijah White & Hannah Kingsbury,	June, 1777
Joseph Martain & Eleanor Shepard,	July, 1777
James Brown & Deborah Tarbox,	Dec., 1777
Gardner Gilbert & Anna Lothrop,	June, 1778
Alexander White & Azubah Townsend,	June, 1778
Oliver Cook & Elizabeth Sumner,	June, 1778
Joseph Peters & Sarah Wells,	Oct., 1778
Samuel Horton & Hannah Morris,	Oct., 1778
Erastus Ingham & Elizabeth Hutchinson,	Nov., 1778
Elijah Fox & Sabra Nettleton,	Jan., 1779
Ebenezer Carrier & Prudence Wells,	Feb., 1779
Ruel Bebe & Mercy Peters,	March, 1779
Joseph Hutchinson & Sibil Mack,	April, 1779
Elihu Marvin & Azubah Case,	July, 1779
Russel Wells & Sarah Carter,	Sept., 1779
Simeon Bliss & Anna Case,	Jan., 1780
Daniel Colburn & Roxelanie Phelps,	March, 1780
John Northum & Elizabeth White,	May, 1780

Thomas Rowlee & Eunice Cooper,	July, 1780
Col. Thomas Brown & Mary Lothrop,	Aug., 1780
Eleazer Phelps & Hannah Horton,	Sept., 1780
Ellis Luther & Sibil Post,	Oct., 1780
Abijah Rowlee & Elizabeth Culver,	1780
John Post & Mary Prat,	1780
Abial Bliss & Anna Brown,	1780
Zebulon Ishum & Rose Ellis,	Dec., 1780
Zachariah Perrin & Mary Tallcott,	Jan., 1781
Joseph Clark & Submit Dunham,	Feb., 1781
James McCullock & Hannah Rollo,	March, 1781
Peter Ripley & Lora Norton,	June, 1781
Seth King & Silence Lothrop,	Oct., 1781
John Strong & Lydia Sumner,	Nov., 1781
Joseph Tilden & Elizabeth Brown,	Jan., 1782
John Culver & Dinah Post,	Feb., 1782
Ezekiel Daniels & Elizabeth Perrin,	July, 1782
Henry Covel & Sarah Goodrich,	Sept., 1782
Samuel Peters & Hannah Trumbul,	1782
Thomas Wells & Clarissa Peters,	Oct., 1782
Ezekiel Brown & Martha Horton,	Nov., 1782
Eleazer Phelps & Deborah Mann,	1782
Samuel Abens & Dorothy Post,	Dec., 1782
Ralph Mack & Lydia Gilbert,	Feb., 1783
Job Hutchinson & Experience Mack,	May, 1783
Nehemiah Rosell & Mahetable Allen,	July, 1783
Samuel Marks & Content Dunham,	Oct., 1783
Daniel Tallcott & Lydia Ellis,	Jan., 1784
Thadeus Parker & Lydia Horton,	Feb., 1784
William Sumner & Jemima Tarbox,	June, 1784
Ebenezer Buck & Anna Tallcott,	Oct., 1784
Paul Pitkin & Abigail Lothrop,	1784
Eliakim Jones & Rebekah Webster,	Nov., 1784
Daniel Taylor & Ruhamah Ellis,	Dec., 1784
David Norton & Deborah Phelps,	Feb., 1785
Joseph Peters & Azubah Case,	April, 1785
Ruben Wells & Mary Trumbull,	May, 1785
Silas Perry & Thankful Norton,	1785
William Dart & Charlotte Perrin,	1785
William Peters & Lydia Phelps,	Sept., 1785

Jethro Norton & Sibil Sumner,	Dec., 1785
Micaiah Ingham & Eunice Mack,	Feb., 1786
Shipman Wells & Zilpah Trumbull,	April, 1786
Spencer Wood & Persis Buck,	1786
Capt. Ichabod Phelps & Hannah Post,	May, 1786
John Taylor & Elizabeth Wells,	1786
Henry Mack & Mahetable Hall,	Dec., 1786
Asa How & Eunice Buck,	Jan., 1787
John Waters & Mindwell Jones,	Feb., 1787
Roger Phelps & Anna Jones,	1787
Nathaniel Townsend & Mary Basset,	Sept., 1787
Samuel Kellogg & Elizabeth Septome Lathrop,	Nov., 1787
Joseph Rollo & Barbarry Allen,	Jan., 1788
Daniel Merrel & Heldah Ellis,	1788
David Buck & Abigail Palmeter,	1788
John Mann & Lydia Dutton,	Feb., 1788
Levi Loomis & Louisa Lothrop,	Dec., 1788
Chauncey Langdon & Lucynana Lathrop,	April 7, 1789
Joseph Wells & Abiah Dunham,	Sept. 29, 1789
Jabez Ellis, Jr., & Hannah Mack,	Dec., 1789
Daniel Hitchcock & Sarah Allen,	March, 1790
Jerred Burden & Silva Morgan (negroes),	March, 1790
George Hall & Azubah Trumbull,	Oct., 1790
Jacob Skinner & Phebe Palmerter,	Oct., 1790
Daniel Hutchinson & Mary Ellis,	March, 1791
Ichabod M. Warner & Mary Tallcott,	May, 1791
David Tillotson & Sarah Wells,	Nov., 1791
Col. Abial Pease & Mary Loomis,	Feb., 1792
Roswell Hubbard & Martha Jordan,	July, 1792
David Trumbull & Thankful Wells,	Aug., 1792
Simeon Dunham & Betty Hall,	Sept., 1792
Thomas Stevens & Lucy Perrin,	Feb., 1793
Charles Kellogg & Lydia Hosford,	Aug., 1793
Samuel Scott & Melicent Mack,	Oct., 1793
Charles Collins & Abelene Curtice,	Jan., 1794
Samuel Piper & Lucy Daniels,	Feb., 1794
Oliver Huntington & Abigail Tallcott,	May, 1794
Elijah L. Lathrop & Betty Hubbard,	May, 1794
Harvy Morrison & Prudence Dunham,	June, 1794
Reuben Sumner & Anna Perrin,	Nov., 1794

Israel Thompson & Sarah Foot,	Dec., 1794
Alvin Griswold & Anna Wass,	Dec., 1794
John Finley & Anna Morgan,	Jan., 1795
Mordica Ellis & Mary Hutchinson,	Feb., 1795
Amos Dean & Marilvah Ingham,	Nov., 1795
John Finley & Rhoda Morris,	Dec., 1795
John Rollo & Philomelia Trumbull,	Dec., 1795
Samuel Fielding & Lydia Hildreth,	Aug., 1796
Richard Crocker & Lucinda Kelley,	1796
Edward Root & Thankful Shadock,	Sept., 1796
Henry Sumner & Jerusha Perrin,	Oct., 1796
Daniel Loomer & Anna Hutchinson,	Nov., 1796
Nehemiah Seeley & Mabel Horton,	1796
Jonah Root, Jr., & Sally Root,	Dec., 1796
John Isham, 3rd, & Betsey Gilbert,	Jan., 1797

COLCHESTER.

NEW LONDON COUNTY.

Colchester was named October, 1699. The First Congregational Church was organized December 20, 1703. A Second Congregational Church of Colchester was organized at Westchester, December, 1729. The following marriages are recorded upon the books of the First Church, Rev. Ephraim Little, pastor.

Daniel *Pratt* Rolt (?) & Mary Swift,	1732
Joshua Douglas & Sarah, daughter of Ephraim Foot,	Feb. 22, 1733
Jonathan Silsbey & Abigail Randall,	April 26, 1733
Elijah Worthington & Mary Wells,	Oct. 4, 1733
Thomas Corlet & Grace Woadworth,	Oct. 10, 1733
Josiah Strong, Jr., & Hannah Fuller,	Nov. 1, 1733
Lewis Looridge (?) & Ann Fuller,	Dec. 31, 1733
Capt. James Newton & widow Mary Barnard,	Jan. 1, 1734
William Chamberlain, Jr., & Lydia Tradeway,	Jan. 3, 1734
Samuel Dodge of New London & Sarah Chapman,	Jan. 14, 1734
Isaac Biglow, Jr., & Abigail Skinner,	March 14, 1734
Jonathan Killborn, Jr., & Mary Skinner,	Oct. 20, 1734
Ephraim Wells & widow Elizabeth Kilborn,	Nov. 7, 1734

Rev. Judah Lewis & Mrs. Mercy Kellogg,	Dec. 24, 1734
Josiah Tradeway & Unis Foot,	May 13, 1735
James Ransom & Sarah Tradeway,	May 25, 1735
Knight Saxton & Elizabeth Skinner,	May 25, 1735
Amos Owen & Unis Waters,	July 3, 1735
John Haldridge & Abigail Tailor,	Aug. 27, 1735
Andrew Carrier, Jr., & Rebeckah Rockwell,	Oct. 27, 1735
Benejah Mackall & Hannah Otis,	Nov. 6, 1735
Richard Mentor & Elizabeth Roberts,	Dec. 11, 1735
Jonathan Kellog, Jr., & Mary Niles,	Jan. 1, 1736
Benjamin Owen & Sarah Gold,	Jan. 22, 1736
Samuel Roberts & Mercy Tradeway,	May 2, 1736
William Roberts, Jr., & Prudence Kellog,	May 6, 1736
David Johnson & Rebecka Foot,	Oct. 24, 1736
John Johnson, Jr., & Anstis Newton,	Jan. 6, 1737
Joseph Kneeland & widow Lydia Adams,	Feb. 23, 1737
Aaron Skinner & Unis Taintor,	Aug. 4, 1737
George Abbott & Ann Willey,	Aug. 24, 1737
Asa Bigelow & Dorothy Otis,	Dec. 13, 1737
John Kellog & Mary Newton,	April 2, 1738
Nathaniel Ackley & Sarah Saxton,	May 4, 1738
Moses Yeomans & Sarah Pratt,	Jan. 11, 1730
John Welles & widow Sarah Trumble,	June 29, 1738
Joseph Chamberlain & widow Hannah Gillet,	July 12, 1738
Deacon Samuel Lomis & widow Elizabeth Church,	
	Oct. 25, 1738
Timothy Merrills & Mary Kellogg,	Nov. 9, 1738
James Mun & Martha Smith,	Nov. 23, 1738
Josiah Foot, Jr., & Sarah Chamberlain,	Dec. 7, 1738
David Brown & Abigail Mills,	March 9, 1739
Bethuel Barnum & Elizabeth Willey,	April 15, 1739
James Sawyer & Hesadiah Bartlet,	April 30, 1739
John Welles, Jr., & Ann Kellog,	Oct. 15, 1739
Simeon Ackley & Ellis Fuller,	Nov. 8, 1739
Thomas Way & Sarah Welles,	Nov. 29, 1739
Elisha Smith & Elizabeth Brown,	Nov. 29, 1739
Jonathan Kilborn & widow Elizabeth Fuller,	Dec. 10, 1739
John Spencer & Mary Green,	Dec. 27, 1739
Rev. Joseph Lovett & Elinah Bugbee,	Feb. 6, 1740
Abner Kellog & Lydia ———,	June 26, 1740

Isaac —— & —— ——,	July 3, 1740
Aaron Kellogg & Mary Lewis,	July 10, 1740
Samuel Williams & Mary Roberts,	Aug. 21, 1740
Joseph Foot & widow Hannah Northum,	Sept. 2, 1740
Abraham Day & Irene Foot,	Nov. 20, 1740
James Mackall & Unis Bates,	Nov. 20, 1740
John Knox & Ann Waters,	Jan. 12, 1741
Joseph Kellogg & Sarah Clark,	Jan. 15, 1741
Thomas Carrier & Mary Peters,	Feb. 25, 1741
Peter Spenser & Hannah Brown,	June 4, 1741
James Glass & Rebeckah Roberts,	Dec. 13, 1741
Jonathan Rowlee & Abigail Green,	Feb. 4, 1742
Isaac Isom & Elizabeth Brown,	Feb. 16, 1742
Deacon John White & widow Mary Newton,	June 7, 1742
Isaac Neland & Content Rowlee,	Nov. 12, 1742
Epaphras Lord & Lucy Bulkley,	Nov. 25, 1742
John Ward & Mercy Chamberlain,	Dec. 8, 1742
David Randall & Temperance Price,	July, 1743
Daniel Burge & Elizabeth Knox,	Oct. 17, 1743
—ust— Hall of Lyme & Sarah Clark,	Nov., 1743
Ichabod Lord & Patience Bulkley,	Dec. 14, 1743
Nehemiah Daniels & Elizabeth Worthington,	Dec. 19, 1743
John Sweetland & widow Tradeway,	Jan. 19, 1744
Jonathan Daniels & his wife,	Feb., 1744
Simeon Welles & —— Churchill,	March 28, 1744
Adam Rogers & Anne Scovill,	May 22, 1744
John Chamberlain & Sarah Day,	June 7, 1744
Samuel Church & Phebe Fuller,	June 24, 1744
—— Whitney & Mary Adams,	Aug. 7, 1744
Dudley Wright & Dimis Lomis,	Aug., 1744
David Gardner & Jemima Gustin,	Oct. 1, 1744
Joseph Smith & Sarah Gillet,	Nov. 15, 1744
Joseph Barker & Elizabeth Foot,	Nov. 20, 1744
Joseph Thomas & Abigail Brown,	Jan. 25, 1745
John Robarts & Lois Waters,	Jan. 29, 1745
Edward Brown & Hannah Thomas,	Feb. 7, 1745
Nathan Sawyer & Desire Fuller,	May 23, 1745
—— Dorns (?) & Prudence Ellis,	May 23, 1745
Robin & Patience (Indians),	July 25, 1745
Charles Williams & Rachel Carrier,	Nov. 5, 1745

William Littel & Rachel Townsend,	Nov. 5, 1745
Joshua Wrathbone & Sarah Tenant,	Dec. 4, 1745
Dijah Fowler & Abigail Biglow,	Dec. 18, 1745
Cesar (negro) & Sarah (mulatto),	Dec. 25, 1745
Roger Clark & Hannah Biglow,	April 24, 1746
Elisha Wells & Mary Chamberlain,	May 15, 1746
Thomas Smith & Lydia Foot,	June 15, 1746
Noah Skinner & Sarah Biglow,	June 23, 1746
Samuel Hungerford & Mary Graves,	June 23, 1746
Bemur & Venice (servants to Daniel Morgan),	July 9, 1746
Mr. Joseph Lovett & Elinah Johnson,	Sept. 17, 1746
Thomas Gustin, Jr., & Hannah Griswold,	Dec. 11, 1746
Joseph Dailey, Jr., & Rebeckah Dewey,	Jan. 7, 1747
——der Clark & Elizabeth Williams,	1747
——— ——— & daughter of Abiel St——,	1747
Solomon & Floron (servants of John Smith),	April, 1747
Ichabod Bartlett & Desire Otis,	Oct. 29, 1748
Abel of Goshen & eldest daughter of Jonathan Northu,	March 9, 1748
Thomas Miller & Mary Fuller,	March 17, 1748
Abijah Hall & Margarett Dewey,	April 17, 1748
Nathaniel Kellog & widow Prissilla Williams,	May 29, 1748
Charles Kellog & Sarah Hitchcock,	April 24, 1748
Noah Pumroy & Irene Northum,	April 24, 1748
Nathan Scovell & Sarah Gates,	Sept. 8, 1748
Timothy Northum & Temperance Anabell,	Oct. 18, 1748
Benjamin Patridge & Elizabeth Morgan,	Oct. 27, 1748
Jeremiah Pardee & Ann Clark,	Oct. 27, 1748
Joseph Pitts & Ann Townsend,	Nov. 10, 1748
Thomas Gates & Randal Doughter (?),	Dec. 22, 1748
David Welles & May Taintor,	Jan. 19, 1749
Lemuel Stores & Hannah Gillet,	June 11, 1749
Amasa Jones & Elizabeth Chamberlain,	July 12, 1749
Hares (?) Graves & Irenee Chapman,	July 27, 1749
Jeremiah Foot & Ruhamah Northum,	Sept. 14, 1749
Jonas Wiles & Mary Foot,	Oct. 10, 1749
Beriah Lomis & Lydia Northum,	Oct. 19, 1749
John Dodge & Elizabeth Dodge,	Dec. 7, 1749
Joshua Smith & Elizabeth Pumroy,	Jan. 27, 1750

Jonathan Wrathbone & Irene Scovill,	Feb. 18, 1750
Ebenezer Hinkley & Mary Gillet,	April 5, 1750
Elihu Clark & Elizabeth Kellogg,	May 9, 1750
Peletiah Daniels & Abigail Daniels,	May 14, 1750
Joseph Tailor & Jemima Daniels,	May 21, 1750
Beriah Bacon & Elizabeth Dewey,	June 4, 1750
Israel Newton & Lois Tradoway,	June 7, 1750
Jonathan Stong & Mary Northum,	June 28, 1750
Jonathan Gillet & Tamar Day,	Oct. 18, 1750
Elijah Smith & Sibill Worthington,	Nov. 8, 1750
John Otis & Prudence Taintor,	Dec. 20, 1750
Jonathan Chapel & Lucy Tennant,	Dec. 26, 1750
Samuel Tubs & Ann Chapman,	Jan. 1, 1751
John Hinkley & Ruth Gillet,	April 4, 1751
Nathan Walbridge & Ame Start,	April 18, 1751
Richard Townsend & Nancy Stewart,	June 6, 1751
Elisha Biglow & Mary Kilborn,	May 23, 1751
Simeon Welles & Lydia Knight,	June 27, 1751
Daniel Welch & Lucy Spencer,	July 1, 1751
—— Harris & Margaret Downer,	Nov. 7, 1751
Benjamin Hodge & Lydia Welles,	Nov. 22, 1751
Noah Clark & Unis Quitafield (?),	Dec. 5, 1751
John Taintor & Esther Clark,	Dec. 12, 1751
Peleg Chamberlain & Jane Higgings,	Jan. 16, 1752
Joseph Dewey, Jr., & Esther Dodge,	Feb. 20, 1752
—— Daniels & daughter of Samuel Fuller, Jr.,	
	April 16, 1752
Stephen Kellog & Martha Welles,	April 24, 1752
Dr. John Watrous & Sarah Taintor,	April 30, 1752
Lemuel Clark & Mercy Brigges,	May 6, 1752
Ebenezer Kellogg & Abigail Rowly,	May 10, 1752
Isaac Williams & Lucy Fuller,	June 11, 1752
—— Swetland of Hebron & Sarah Nor——,	
	Aug. 27, 1752
Nathaniel Bartlett of Goshen & Mercy Otis,	Dec. 14, 1752
Jonathan Willard & widow Sarah Taintor,	Dec. 21, 1752
Jesse Jones & Silence Day,	Dec. 28, 1752
Josiah Blish (?) & daughter of ——,	March, 1753
Elisha Johnson & Elizabeth Hopson,	May 13, 1753
—— Woodworth & Abigail Thomas,	Dec. 6, 1753

Darius Brown & Sarah Bacon,   Dec. 6, 1753
—— Gun & Hannah Welles,   Jan. 24, 1754
John Bartlet & Jemima Downer,   Jan. 31, 1754
Israel Kellog & Abigail Northum,   Jan 31, 1754
Habk Foot & widow Mary Welles,   March 5, 1754
Benjamin Roberts & Sybill Colman,   March 14, 1754
John Baker & Rachel Scovill,   March 14, 1754
James Welles & Hannah Lomis,   March 28, 1754
Jonathan Northum, Jr., & Ann Mack Williams,
                                               April 11, 1754
Israel Newton & Jerusha Welles,   April 18, 1754
Benjamin Thompson & Mary Morris,   July 5, 1754
Thomas Smith of Hadley & Rhoda Worthington,
                                               Oct. 15, 1754
Adonijah Foot & Grace Day,   Oct. 24, 1754
Joel Jones & Margaret Day,   Oct. 24, 1754
Thomas Avery of Goshen & Lydia Brown,   Oct. 31, 1754
Asail Tailor & Berthiah Skinner,   Nov. 7, 1754
Stephen Barneby & Desire Chapell,   Dec. 5, 1754
Israel Dewey & Abigail Fuller,   Feb. 13, 1755
Tristram Brown & widow Thomas,   March 5, 1755
Daniel Pratt, Jr., & Abigail Biglow,   March 24, 1755
Jonathan Crocker & Rachel Skinner,   March 27, 1755
Jno. Adams & Sarah, daughter of Daniel Skinner,
                                               May 1, 1755
Rev. Ephraim Little & widow Abigail Bulkley,
                                               Nov. 5, 1755
Judah Welles & Unis Alcott,   Dec. 3, 1755
Asa Clark & Sarah Hopson,   Dec. 4, 1755
Samuel Bebee & Esther Skinner,   Jan. 27, 1756
Phineas Tailor & Mercy Welles,   Feb., 1756
Hosea Foot & Unis Chamberlain,   April 8, 1756
—— Scovill of Millington & Miriam Chamber-
    lain,   July 4, 1756
David Fuller & widow Williams,   Dec. 16, 1756
Daniel Isham & Katharine Foot,   July 14, 1756
Robert Cariyg (?) & Hannah Welles,   Jan. 2, 1757
Job Whitcomb & Ann Skinner,   March 10, 1757
Aaron Gillet & Ann Pratt,   March 31, 1757
Nehemiah Gillet & Lydia Gillet,   Sept. 13, 1757

Nathaniel Clark & Elizabeth Jones,	Oct. 25, 1757
Daniel Morgan & Mary Welles,	Dec. 12, 1757
Henry Bliss & widow Lydia Hopson,	Dec. 18, 1757
Kullick Elis & Sarah Foot,	Jan. 15, 1758
Jonathan Birdge of Hebron & Rachel Strong,	Feb. 23, 1758
Elisha Hubbard & Unis Johnson,	May 4, 1758
John Fuller & Loademia Newton,	May 31, 1758
Caleb Geer & Ann Hitchcock,	Aug. 31, 1758
Daniel Skinner, Jr., & Tabitha Worthington,	Nov. 9, 1758
John Taintor & Sarah Bulkley,	Nov. 23, 1758
Josiah Lyman & Sarah Worthington,	Jan. 9, 1759
John Bulkley & Judith Worthington,	——
John Hopson & Mary Worthington,	——
Levi Welles & Jerusha Clark,	——
—— Biglow & Elizabeth Otis,	——
Elijah Thomas & Margery Williams,	Nov. 15, 1759
Asa Treadway & Mabel Roberts,	Dec. 27, 1759
Judah Wells & Ann, daughter of Isaac Biglow,	Jan. 31, 1760
Wm. Booth & Hannah Chamberlin,	Jan. 31, 1760
—— Craw of Windsor & Thankful Beebee,	Feb. 28, 1760
John Post of Hebron & Kate Northum,	May 8, 1760
Rufus Roberts & Abigail Daily,	Sept. 22, 1760
Alpheus Hills & Hannah Brown,	Oct. 5, 1760
—— Bancroft of Windsor & Jerusha Foot,	Dec. 17, 1760
Jonathan Harris & daughter of Samuel Tosier (?),	Jan. 1, 1761
Amos Thomas & widow Lydia Kellogg,	March 19, 1761
Benjamin Start & Sarah Denison,	April 28, 1761
Jonathan Robins & Dorothy Biglow,	March 19, 1761
Asa Harris & Faith Mackall,	July 23, 1761
—— Beebee of Millington & Mary Biglow,	Sept. 9, 1761
Samuel Mather, Jr., & Ellis Ransom,	Oct. 1, 1761
Elias Ransom & Sarah Biglow,	Nov. 19, 1761
Ezrah Waterman & Lydia Kilborn,	Nov. 19, 1761
Daniel Morgan & Irene Wrathbone,	Nov. 18, 1761
Orlando Root & Mary Worthington,	Nov. 24, 1761
Joseph Chamberlain & Abia Wells,	(Summer), 1761
Joseph Tailor & Sybill Northum,	Dec. 3, 1761
James Treadway & widow Temperance Smith,	Dec. 10, 1761
Judah Lewis & —— Brainard,	Feb. 4, 1762

Stephen Otis & Lucy Chandler,	Feb. 9, 1762
Noah Saxton & Ame Worthington,	April 8, 1762
Jonathan Crittenden & Bethya Chapman,	May 5, 1762
Joseph Kellogg & Jean Fuller,	May 6, 1762
Ezekiel Huntington & Rachel Mariner,	June 21, 1762
Elijah Metcalf & Molle Hopson,	Sept. 23, 1762
John Skinner & Ann Day,	Sept. 30, 1762
Isaac Day & widow Dorothy Biglow,	Oct. 12, 1762
Timothy Biglow & Rhoda Williams,	Dec. 2, 1762
Noah Day & Abigail Cahoon,	Feb. 10, 1763
Ephraim Scovel & Sarah Saxton,	March 15, 1763
Hezekiah Holdridge & Unis Northum,	April 20, 1763
William Metson & Unis Skinner,	June 9, 1763
John Hastings & Content Little,	Nov. 29, 1763
Joseph Bulkley & Mercy Chamberlain,	Feb. 15, 1764
Eliphalet Welles & Mary Skinner,	March 29, 1764
Aaron Skinner & Mehitable Worthington,	April 12, 1764
—— Anderson & Rebekah Glass (?),	July 19, 1764
John Johnson & Ann Smith,	Sept. 6, 1764
—— Wood of Somers & Hannah Kellogg,	Dec. 5, 1764
Ruben Arnold & Hannah Skinner,	Dec. 13, 1764
Joseph Isham & Sarah Bulkley,	Jan. 17, 1765
Elnathan Rowlee & widow Unis Brown,	Feb. 21, 1765
Ephraim Lewis & Lois Ransom,	Aug. 15, 1765
David Smith & —— —— daughter of Nathan Start (?)	Oct. 31, 1765
Asa Tiler & Anstis Johnson,	Jan. 1, 1766
Abraham Dewey & Cloe Brown,	May 20, 1766
Aaron Kellogg & Rhoda Jones,	July 3, 1766
Stephen Beckwith & Lydia Daniels,	July 24, 1766
Charles Taintor & Mary Wells,	Aug. 20, 1766
Asaiel Willey & Abigail Skinner,	Nov. 13, 1766
Elijah Skinner & Mercy Pr——,	Nov. 20, 1766
David Otis & Millee Day,	Nov. 30, 1766
Charles Williams & Bethia Treadway,	Dec., 1766
Josiah Brown & Lucy Skinner,	Jan. 8, 1767
Richard Skinner & Lucretia Otis,	Jan. 15, 1767
Isaiah Mun & Abia Tiffeny,	Jan. 18, 1767
Soloman Wolcoot & Abigail Hastings,	Feb. 11, 1767
Martin Wells & Lurena Pomroy,	Oct. 15, 1767

Jacob Townsend & Lydia Little,	Nov. 11, 1767
Epraim Rowlee & Pegge Lilie,	Nov. 8, 1767
Jonathan Deming & Ellis Skinner,	Dec. 31, 1767
Samuel Hills & Thankful Rowley,	March 3, 1768
John Williams & Dimis Chamberlain,	March 3, 1768
Elijah Hills & Grace Marriner,	March 3, 1768
Richard Harris Huntloy & Rachel Little,	March 17, 1768
Daniel Caswell & Irena Strong,	March 31, 1768
Noah Foot & Ester Kellogg,	April 18, 1768
James Treadway & Olive Smith,	April 21, 1768
Prince Brewster & Elithea Foot,	April 25, 1768
Isaac Foot & Millee Kellog,	May 24, 1768
Jedediah Bill & Annis Gillet,	May 25, 1768
Samuel Emons & Mercy Kellog,	May 26, 1768
Silas Kellog & Sarah Cook,	June 21, 1768
Aaron Baxter & Mercy Menter,	Oct. 6, 1768
Charles Wing & Phebee Waters,	Nov. 3, 1768
Jesse Stebings & Bulah Mun,	Dec. 6, 1768
John Barnes & Martha Foot,	Dec. 8, 1768
—— —— & Dorothy Day,	——
Nathaniel Kellogg & Hannah Hastings,	Jan 12, 1769
Benjamin Chamberlain & Lucretia Little,	Jan. 12, 1769
Noah Bulkley & Ann Wright,	Feb. 2, 1769
Israel Holdridge & Bettee Northum,	Feb. 14, 1769
David Phelps & Dimis Pratt,	March 16, 1769
James Ackley & Mary Ford,	May 18, 1769
Elisha Lord & Unis Bulkley,	May 25, 1769
Nathaniel Emmons & widow —— Fuller,	June 14, 1769
Nathaniel Johnson & Ann Chester,	Oct. 10, 1769
Reuben Clark & Lucy Johnson,	Oct. 12, 1769
Samuel Williams & Ann Northum,	Nov. 24, 1769
Joseph Ackley & Hannah Archer,	Dec. 11, 1769
John Worthington & Abigail Wright,	Jan. 4, 1770
Nathan Tiffeny & Mary Kellogg,	April 12, 1770
Asa Marriner & Mary Welch,	April 17, 1770
Frederick Smith & Elizabeth Margery Williams,	May 3, 1770
William Worthington & Sarah Wells,	July 5, 1770
Richard Holdridge & Elizabeth Brown,	Aug. 23, 1770
Elijah Ackley & Ellis Fuller,	Nov. 6, 1770
Abner Rockwell & Sarah Kellogg,	Dec. 5, 1770

8

Simon Cone & Hannah Clark,	Dec. 30, 1770
Asa Swan & Ann Bulk——,	May 29, 1771
Israel Hollister & Sarah Skinner,	May 29, 1771
Ezekiel Kellogg & Elishaba Wells,	May 30, 1771
Daniel Coleman & Elisabeth Little,	Sept. 12, 1771
Elias Worthington & Ann Morgan,	Oct. 24, 1771
Charles Bulkley & Bettee Taintor,	Oct. 27, 1771
Joseph Moor & Abigail Ames,	Nov. 26, 1771
David Bulkley & Hannah Beckwith,	Dec. 18, 1771
Daniel Menter & Submit Waters,	Dec. 23, 1771
Jeremiah Rogers & Lucy Start,	Jan. 1, 1772
Nathan Goodspeed & Mary Kellogg,	Jan. 2, 1772
Roger Bulkley & Jerusha Root,	May 28, 1772
—————— Robinson & Ann Watrous,	June 18, 1772
Ebenezer Done & Sarah Daniels,	June 18, 1772
Joseph Kneeland & Ruth Pratt,	Nov. 5, 1772
Daniel Worthington & Lois Foot,	Nov. 10, 1772
Daniel Day & Elizabeth Chamberlain,	Dec. 10, 1772
Daniel Strong of Coventry & Sarah Taintor,	Dec. 24, 1772
Avery Heath & Hannah Brooks,	Feb. 14, 1773
Aaron Dewey & Johannah Strong,	March 11, 1773
Joshua Hall & Hannah Coverley,	April 8, 1773
Anderson Martin & Elizabeth Scovel,	April 29, 1773
John Breed & Lucy Bulkley,	May 13, 1773
Edmund Clark & Mallee Morgan,	May 19, 1773
Azariah Wright & Mercy Treadway,	July 29, 1773
Elisha Biglow & Thankful Beebee,	Aug. 5, 1773
John Talcot & Lydia Welles,	Sept. 6, 1773
Daniel Day & Martha Isham,	Sept. 10, 1773
Amasa Daniels & Hannah Clark,	Sept. 25, 1773
Lemuel Dickinson & Molle Little,	Nov. 27, 1773
Cary Leeds & Jerusha Scovil,	March 17, 1774
Deacon Israel Wells & Mary Worthington,	March 23, 1774
Elijah Dodge & Hulda Tiffeny,	May 15, 1774
Joseph Isham & Esther Taintor,	May 18, 1774
Cripin Archer & Jemima Rogers,	Sept. 12, 1774
—————— Skinner of Windsor & Hannah Treadway,	
	Sept. 21, 1774
Aphalet (?) Simmons & Silence Clark,	Oct. 6, 1774
Eleazer Dewey & Rhoda Daniels,	Oct. 11, 1774

Zenas Coleman & —— Carrier,   Oct. 20, 1774
John Fox & Mehetabel Welch,   Feb. 15, 1778
Robbin & Su——,   March 2, 1778
Jonathan Gillet & Zilpha Pratt,   March 19, 1778
Noah Skinner & Ann Gillet,   May 14, 1778
Jabez Fuller, Jr., & Abigail Kellog,   Aug. 25, 1778
Justin Little & Violate Clark,   July 23, 1782
Nathan Baxter & Anna Dodge,   Oct. 14, 1782
Rev. David Huntington & Elizabeth Foot,   Nov. 5, 1778
Nathaniel Otis & Mary Foot,   Nov. 5, 1778
Martin Kellogg & Hannah Otis,   Nov. 5, 1778
Israel Foot, Jr., & Sarah Otis,   Nov. 5, 1778
Rev. Emerson Foster of Killingly & Margaret Foot,
                                            Nov. 11, 1778
Charles Foot, Jr., & Sarah Day,   Dec. 17, 1778
Joseph Johnson & Jerusha Foot,   Feb. 25, 1779
Samuel Northum & Sarah Day,   April 8, 1779
Asail Strong & Rhoda Tiffany,   April 15, 1779
Stephen Foot & Esther Clark,   April 29, 1779
Frederick W—ck & Lydia Mosier,   May 24, 1779
John Caverley & Caroline Newton,   May 26, 1779
Joshua Morgan & Wealthy Palmer,   June 3, 1779
Daniel Morgan & Grace Billings,   June 10, 1779
Ebenezer Kellog & Ann Ransom,   June 12, 1779
Daniel Pratt & Margaret Ransom,   Aug. 19, 1779
Noah Pumroy & Rhoda Welles,   Jan. 12, 1780
Darius Clark & Bette Dewet (?),   Jan. 26, 1780
Zadock Ford & Unis Bridges,   Jan. 27, 1780
—— Townsend & Miriam Newton,   May 18, 1780
—— Churchel & Elizabeth Hurlbut,   July 2, 1780
Daniel Hosford & Hannah Day,   Nov. 9, 1780
Hezekiah Kilborn & Elizabeth Bliss (?),   Nov. 16, 1780
Rev. Lemuel Parsons & Faith Little,   Dec. 13, 1780
Abner Chapman & Molle Biglow,   March 29, 1781
Elias Palmer & Molle Caverly,   March 29, 1781
Peter Harris & Bettee Rockwell,   May 24, 1781
Alpheus Low (?) & Abigail Kellock,   March 12, 1781
—— Swift of Kent & Thedosia Hosford,   April 7, 1781
—— —— & Lydia Northum,   April 7, 1781
John Otis & Louisa Pomroy,   Sept. 29, 1782

Jonathan Daniels & —— Chapman of Glassenbury,
                                       Oct. 28, 1782
William Thompson & Mary Daniels,   Nov. 12, 1782
Elisha (?) Porter & Molle Gillet,   Nov. 28, 1782
Moses Fuller & Susannah Tailor,   Dec. 19, 1782
Isaiah Brown & Abigail Pratt,   May 13, 1783
Jno. Watson & Lydia Wright,   June 10, 1783
Isaac Tubs & Zilpha Ann Thomas,   May 24, 1775
Israel Kellog & Hannah Ingram,   June 1, 1775
David Wilis (?) & Jemima Randal,   June 22, 1775
Russell Kellogg & Esther Bridges,   Feb. 20, 1776
John White & Sarah Parish,   April 18, 1776
John Carrier & Lydia Ingram,   June 13, 1776
Ebenezer Carter & Unis Kellogg,   Jan. 16, 1777
Joseph Foot & Bettee Foot,   April 3, 1777
Joseph Packwood (?) & Dimis Wright,   July 20, 1777
Daniel Wattles & Ann Otis,   Oct. 19, 1777
Daniel Kellogg & Elisabeth Wells,   Jan. 14, 1778
Asail Ransom & Sophia Little,   Jan. 15, 1778
Ephraim Little, Jr., & widow Ann Bulkley, Jan. 29, 1778

NEW MILFORD.

LITCHFIELD COUNTY.

Incorporated in October, 1712. The Congregational Church was organized November 2, 1716. Rev. Daniel Boardman, first pastor; Rev. Nathaniel Taylor, 1748; Rev. Stanley Griswold, 1790. The following are all the marriages recorded.

Ebenezer Bostwick & Rebeccah Bonnel,   April, 1717
Enoch Buck & Mary Beebe,   May, 1717
John Welsh & Deborah Ferriss,   Aug. 27, 1719
Nathan Terrill & Ruth Buck,   June 8, 1721
Titus Hinman of Woodbury & Sarah Noble,   June 8, 1721
Ebinezer Washbourn & Patience Miles,   June, 1721
Theophilus Baldwin & Jerusha Beecher,   July 5, 1722
William Warriner & Sarah Bostwick,   Nov. 5, 1724
Ezekiel Buck & Lydia Brownson,   Dec. 15, 1724
Thomas Brownson & Sarah Hichcock,   Nov., 1726

Samuel Hichcock & Rebeccah Brownson,	Oct. 11, 1726
Jonathan Hichcock & Mary Brownson,	Oct. 11, 1726
Zephaniah Hoose of New Fairfield & —— ——,	
	May 21, 1728
Jonathan Hichcock & Meream Mallery,	Oct. 16 (?), 1728
Matthew Benedict & Mable Noble,	May 21, 1729
Joseph Buck & Ann Goold,	June 5, 1729
Jonathan Peirce & Rachell Buck,	Sept. 11, 1729
Jonathan Hoose & widow Terrill,	Sept. (?), 1729
John Prindle & Martha Prime,	Feb. 5, 1730
Samuel Hichcock & Deborah Mallery,	April 23, 1730
Moses Buck & Eunice Miles,	Sept. 29, 1730
Nathan Tallcott & Hannah Ferriss,	Dec. 4, 1730
Job Goold & Sarah Prindle,	June 17, 1731
James Lewis & Zeruiah Peninton, both of New Fairfield,	Nov. 24, 1731
Nathaniel Hollister of New Fairfield & Mary Buck,	Dec. 29, 1731
Benjamin Benedict of Ridgefield & Hannah Bostwick,	Jan. 18, 1732
Isaac Deforest & Elizabeth Noble,	Aug. 17, 1732
Joseph Miles & Deborah Welch,	Sept. 25, 1732
Jacob Brownson & Abigall Jones,	Nov. 30, 1732
Jonathan Buck & Betty Bostwick,	Jan. 9, 1733
John Noble & Sarah Slaughter of Ridgefield,	March 23, 1733
Zerubbable Cantfield & Mary Bostwick,	July 26, 1733
Japhet Collins & Abigall Bostwick,	March 28, 1734
David Camp & Sarah Terrill,	June 26, 1735
Joseph Selye & Thankfull Weller,	Aug. 4, 1735
Ephraim Hubill & Johanah Gaylord,	Dec. 25, 1735
David Cantfield & Mary Baldwin,	Jan. 20, 1736
Jonathan Botsford & Elizabeth Camp,	Feb. 5, 1736
John Hichcock & Sarah Barnum,	May 27, 1736
Elkana Bobit & Obediance Prindle,	Jan. 20, 1737
John Hull & Abigall Gillet,	Nov. 1, 1737
Thomas Evans & Martha Shed, both of Oblong,	July 4, 1738
Nathan Barnum of Danbury & Hannah Bonnel,	Aug. 10, 1738
Benjamin Hoose & Ruth Brownson,	Aug. 22, 1738

Samuel Baldwin & Grace Buck,	Oct. 31, 1739
William Ostrandress of Duchess County & Comfort Buck,	Jan. 2, 1740
Matthew Hawley & Hannah Buck,	Dec. 3, 1740
Samuel Smith of Ridgefield & Ruth Gaylord,	Dec. 24, 1740
Henry Garlick & Mary Williams,	Jan. 18, 1741
Nathan Gunn & Hannah Weltch,	May 10, 1741
Amos Collins & Prudence Noble,	May 10, 1741
John Pierce of ye Oblong & Rebeccah ———,	June 1, 1741
James Terrill & Abigall Buck,	June 22, 1741
Benaja Bostwick & Hannah Fisk,	Oct. 22, 1741
Peter Scott of Rinebach & Thankfull Buck,	Feb. 2, 1742
Jonathan Lomm of Derby & Lydia Brownson,	March 2, 1742
Gideon Halebut of Shepauge & Emlen Garlick,	June 23, 1742
Dr. Riverus Carrinton & Penelope Bordman,	July 7, 1742
Jacob Warner of Deerfield & Ann Fowler,	July 29, 1742
Ensign William Gaylord & Mercy Bostwick,	Oct. 14, 1742
John Way (?) of Sharon & Dorcas Brownson,	Dec. 27, 1742
Thomas Andrews of Danbury & Ann Prime,	Jan. 17, 1743
Alexander Nelson & Dorcas Cash (?), both of Oblong,	Jan. 27, 1743
David Noble & Mary Gaylord,	Nov. 8, 1743
Samuel Wright of Kent & Phebe Morgan of New Fairfield,	Nov. 24, 1743
John Comstock & Deborah Welch,	Dec. 14, 1743
Ebenezer Buck & Thankfull Baldwin,	Feb. 29, 1744
Daniel Beaman of Kent & Lydia Cogswell,	Oct. 6, 1748
Theophilus Baldwin & Mary Noble,	Nov. 2, 1748
Matthew Sullivan & Frances Caulford (?),	Nov. 10, 1748
Ebenezer Lacy & Freelove Canfield,	Dec. 15, 1748
James Buck & Elizabeth Sherman,	Feb. 14, 1749
Daniel Cole or Sole & Hannah Pickett,	Feb., 1749
Samuel Platt & Anne Welch,	Aug. 17, 1749
John Treat & Phebe Hawley,	Nov. 23, 1749
Daniel Hurd of Roxbury & Experience Smith of New Fairfield,	Dec., 1749
Asael Noble & Catern Peet,	Jan. 3, 1750
Benjamin Ruggles & Sarah Selah (?) (possibly Klap),	Jan., 1750

Daniel Washburn & Patience Washburn,	Feb., 1750
Moses Knap of New Fairfield & Sarah Warner,	May 29, 1750
James Benedict of Danbury & Mercy Noble,	Sept. 17, 1750
James Bradshaw & Rachel Bostwick,	Sept. 19, 1750
William Spooner of Kent & Rachel Noble,	Nov. 8, 1750
John Griswold & Phebe Collins,	Nov. 29, 1750
William Barnum & Susanah Barlow, both of Danbury,	Jan. 30, 1751
Samuel Comstock & Elizabeth Baldwin,	Feb. 7, 1751
Joseph Heartwell & Rebekah Sherman,	May 24, 1751
John Murry & Martha Howard,	May 30, 1751
Butler Peat & Sarah Martin of Bethlem,	Aug. 27, 1751
Emerson Cogswell & Mary Miles,	Aug. 29, 1751
Israel Baldwin & Hannah Gunn,	Oct. 9, 1751
Oliver Warner & Lowis Ruggles,	Oct. 16, 1751
Thomas Brunson & Betty Bauldwin,	Oct. 24, 1751
Joshua Stevens of Danbury & Hannah Waller,	Nov. 13, 1751
Joseph Atwell & Martha Squire of Shippaug,	1752
John Gray & Hannah Noble,	1752
Charles Ferry of Redding & Mary Henry,	Oct. 18, 1752
Reed Garlick & Mary Stone,	Dec. 7, 1752
Simon Baldwin & Mercy Brownson,	Dec. 20, 1752
Abel Camp & Abigail Gold,	Dec. 20, 1752
John Lake of Newtown & Rhody Warner,	Jan. 10, 1753
Jonathan Clark & Eunice Bostwick,	Jan. 18, 1753
Ithiel Stone & Martha Baldwin,	June 6, 1753
Joseph Northrop & Rachel Hine,	June 7, 1753
William Hurd & Rebeka Weller,	Nov. 1, 1753
David Judson of Judea & Abigail Canfield,	Nov. 21, 1753
Amos Northrop of Newtown & Mary Murry,	Feb. 7, 1754
James Bradshaw & Lydia Moss,	Feb. 14, 1754
William Hooker of Bethlem & Rachel Waller,	March 13, 1754
Isaac Bostwick & Prudence Warner,	Nov. 27, 1754
Ebenezer Durand & Hannah White, both of Darby,	Dec. 17, 1754
Oliver Canfield & Tabatha Robburds,	March 6, 1755
Rev. Daniel Farrand of Canaan & Jerusha Bordman,	Oct. 20, 1755

James Murry & Patience Hawley,   Nov. 5, 1755
Benajah Stone & Mary Canfield,   Nov. 19, 1755
Sherman Bordman & Sarah Bostwick,   Dec. 3, 1755
Nathaniel Benton of Litchfield & Abigail Gillet,

                                           Dec. 17, 1755
Hezekiah Brownson of Torrington & Abigail Drink-
   water,   April 19, 1756
Dr. John Carrington & Susana Noble,   June 16, 1756
Benjamin Gaylord & Ruth Sherman,   Sept. 28, 1756
Ezra Steward & Sarah Brownson,   Nov., 1756
James Blackman of Newtown & Ester Hitchcock,

                                           Dec. 22, 1756
Gideon Botsford of Newtown & Meriam Hitchcock,

                                           Jan. 13, 1757
Joseph Ferriss & Joanna Gaylord,   Jan. 19, 1757
William Gaylord Hubbell of New Fairfield & Anner
   Stilson,   March 3, 1757
Ephraim Buck & Sarah Camp,   July, 1757
Jonathan Hitchcock & Christian Wanzer or Warner,

                                           Nov. 16, 1757
John Phillips & Anne Burden,   Nov. 18, 1757
Robert Hawkins & Rachel Baldwin,   Jan. 3, 1758
Rev. Judah Champion of Litchfield & Elizabeth
   Welch,   Jan. 4, 1758
Ebenezer Leonard & Meriam Stevens,   Jan. 5, 1758
Lemuel Warner & Sarah Gaylord,   Feb. 15, 1758
Grover Buel of Ninepartners & Jerusha Buck,   Feb. 15, 1758
Joseph Lines & Phebe Baldwin,   Sept. 12, 1758
Thomas Porter of Waterbury & Mehetabel Hine,

                                           Dec. 12, 1758
Rev. Mr. Goold & Mrs. Mary Sedgwick, both of
   Cornwall,   Nov. 23, 1758
         (On a public Thanksgiving Day.)

Elias Kenny of New Preston & Lowis Stone, Jan. 23, 1759
Jeremiah Canfield & Mary Everton,   March 7, 1759
Abner Seely & Hannah Thayre,   March 22, 1759
Rev. Mr. Bordwell & Mrs. Jane Mills, both of Kent,

                                           Sept. 6, 1759
Nathaniel Taylor, Jr., & Hannah Gillit,   March 5, 1760
Benjamin Stone & Anne Fobes,   May 8, 1760

Eleazer Beecher, Jr., & Ellice Britton,   Dec. 24, 1760
Elnathan Botchford & Lucy Stone,   Jan., 1761
Israel Baldwin & Elizabeth Warner,   Feb., 1761
Domini Duglas & Mary Warner,   May, 1761
Zechariah Sanford & Rachel Goold,   May 28, 1761
Caleb Nichols of Newbury & Deborah Hitchcock,
    Sept. 23, 1761
Enos Northrop & Anne Drake, both of Newbury,
    March 4, 1762
John Hall & Eunice Jackson,   April 20, 1762
Benjamin Buckingham & Anne Botchford,   June 30, 1762
John Cogswell & Sarah Ferriss,   Dec. 1, 1762
Theophilus Baldwin & Eunice Noble,   Dec. 30, 1762
Isaac Deforest & Rachel Bostwick,   Jan. 11, 1763
Reynolds Marvin of Litchfield & Mrs. Ruth Weltch,
    Feb. 23, 1763
James McKien of Guilford & Prudence Brownson,
    Feb. 24, 1763
John Warner & Hannah Westover,   July 6, 1763
Elizur Warner & Mary Welch,   Oct. 26, 1763
Timothy Moses of Simsbury & Anne Warner, Dec. 15, 1763
Aaron Gaylord, Jr., & Irene Brigs,   Feb. 13, 1764
Enos Camp, Jr., & Sarah Botchford,   July, 1764
Nathaniel Smith & Hannah Thayre,   Sept. 28, 1764
Isaac Baldwin & Hannah Davis,   Sept. 28, 1764
Rev. David Brownson of Oxford & Anne Camp, June, 1765
John Brownson & Mabel Hine,   Aug. 29, 1765
Steven Chittenden & Lucy Beardslee,   Sept. 26, 1765
Nathaniel Boen & Hannah Hitchcock,   Nov. 14, 1765

Nathaniel Boen, a transient person, after living in New Milford nine or ten months, was married as above, with consent of ye woman's parents and friends; when about a month or six weeks after marriage it was made to appear from Attleborough in Boston government that he was a married man, had a wife and six or seven children upon which he was apprehended and sent by authority from constable to constable back to ye place from whence he came.

Deacon Joseph Fuller of Kent & Zeruiah Noble, Jan. 8, 1766
Zechariah Ferriss & Phebe Gaylord,   March 13, 1766
Ketchell Bell of Cornwall & Abigail Waller, April 30, 1766
Israel Hows of East Greenwich & Anna Noble, May 7, 1766

David Fabrique & Deborah Wooster of Oxford,

	May 14, 1766
Asael Baldwin & Esther Baldwin,	Aug. 13, 1766
Asael Hitchcock & Hannah Collins,	Dec. 15, 1766

Rev. Whitman Welch of Williamstown & Mrs. Ruth

Gaylord,	Feb. 2, 1767
Josiah Lacy of Newtown & Judith Betts,	April 29, 1767
Angus Nickelson & Sarah Plat,	May 11, 1767
Riverius Stilson & Anna Baldwin,	Aug. 6, 1767
Benjamin Phippene, Jr., & Hannah Weller,	Sept. 23, 1767
Elihu Northrop & Keziah Seeley,	Oct. 15, 1767
John Peet, Jr., & Phebe Wakelee,	Jan. 26, 1768
Noble Hine & Patience Hubbil,	Feb. 2, 1768
Samuel Prindle & Hannah Hamlin,	June 8, 1768
Jonathan Downs & Mabel Bostwick,	July 21, 1768
Enoch Buck & Sarah Wildman,	Aug. 29, 1768
Amasa Moss & Ruth Clark,	Nov. 3, 1768
Peter Peck & Sarah Terrill,	Dec. 7, 1768

Deliverance Wakelee of New Preston & Susanna

Roburds,	Dec. 8, 1768
Asa Warner & Eunice Camp,	Dec. 29, 1768
John Brown & Rachel Stevens,	Jan. 5, 1769
William Dunwell & Hannah Buck,	March 23, 1769
Isaac Bennit & Catherine Daton,	May 4, 1769
John Plat, Jr., & Mary Himes,	Dec. 7, 1769
Uri Jackson & Sarah Burchard,	April, 1770

Abner Benedict of Salem & Mrs. Lowis Northrop,

	Oct. 31, 1770
Gideon Treat & Lucretia Washburn,	Nov. 13, 1770
Andrew Summers & Ruth Beach,	Nov. 15, 1770
Nathan Stilson & Elizabeth Stevens,	Jan. 29, 1771
Icabod Bostwick & Lucy Warner,	Feb. 26, 1771
Ebenezer Gaylord & Catharine Chittenden,	April 3, 1771
David Murwin, Jr., & Tamarin Comstock,	July 15, 1771
Abel Gun & Martha Trion,	July 18, 1771
Edward Edwards & Margaret Oviat,	Oct. 10, 1771
Ebenezer Peck of Kent & Susannah Forbes,	Nov. 21, 1771
Ezra Noble & Eunice Bostwick,	June 24, 1772

Abraham Castle of Roxbury & Joanna Wildman,

| | June 25, 177 |

David Canfield, Jr., & Sarah Gray,   Aug. 5, 1772
William Trobridge of Norwalk & Heppy Weller,
  Aug. 8, 1772
Abel Weller & Polly Wright,   Sept. 3, 1772
James Phippeny of Ripton & Rosanah Brownson,
  Sept. 16, 1772
Thomas Hayes & Anna Carrington,   Dec. 2, 1772
John Draper of Dover & Lidea (?) Stuart,   Dec. 9, 1772
Nathan Camp & Esther Bostwick,   Dec. 10, 1772
Clement Hubbel & Sarah Murwin, both of New-
  bury,   Jan. 25, 1773
Gilbert Gregory of North Stratford & Sarah Hamlin,
  Feb. 17, 1773
Almon Perry & Patience Washburn,   April 1, 1773
David Summers & Sarah Treat,   April 29, 1773
Ephraim Plat & Hopewell Hamblin,   1773
Levi Lovwell of Sharon & Mary Bradshaw,   Sept. 14, 1773
Reuben Stone & Deborah Comstock,   Sept. 21, 1773
Daniel Hitchcock & Comfort Pourter (?),   Nov. 3, 1773
Samuel Waller & Sarah Chapman (?),   Nov. 23, 1773
Abel Buckingham & Hannah Botchford,   Dec. 28, 1773
Isaac Terrill & Sarah Prince or Prime,   Jan. 25, 1774
Samuel Ferriss & Abigail Brownson,   Jan. 26, 1774
Lemuel Canfield & Sarah Burton,   Feb. 9, 1774
Deacon Trobridge of New Fairfield & widow
  Mojen (?),   1774
Nathan Gaylord & Ruth Heartwell,   1774
Nathaniel Taylor, 3d, & Anne Northrop,   Aug. 31, 1774
Andrew Clark & Sarah Trion,   Dec. 7, 1774
Abraham Peet & Hannah Roburds,   March 16, 1775
Ben Starr Mygatt & Triphena Warner,   April 5, 1775
Sherman Noble & Sarah Davis,   May 3, 1775
Robert Burton & Hannah Matthews of Judea, June 20, 1775
Samuel Buck & Hannah Fairchild,   Aug. 31, 1775
Richard Hubbel of Ripton & Mercy Bennit,   Aug. 31, 1775
Riverius Camp & Hulda Clark,   Oct. 10, 1775
Samuel Garlick & Hannah Woods,   Dec., 1775
Darius Olmsted & Mary or Mercy Hill,   Jan. 4, 1776
Ebenezer Baldwin, Jr., & Abiah Chapman,   April 18, 1776
Elihu Gregory & Hulda Osborn,   April 25, 1776

Abijah Bennit & Abigail Stone,   Jan. 23, 1777
Aaron Hawley of Stratfield & Sarah Picket,   July 16, 1777
Moses Camp & Anah Sherwood,   Sept. 1, 1777
Nathaniel Brown & Mary Were (?), both of Kent,

                                                  Sept. 4, 1777
Major Daniel Buck of New Canaan &Olive Stevens,

                                                  Sept. 21, 1777
John Murwin & Mrs. Ruth Welch,   Dec. 30, 1777
Daniel Everit & Eurania Taylor,   Jan. 1, 1778
Nathanael Durke, Jr., & Lucy Bostwick,   Feb. 22, 1778
Peter Gaylord & Sarah Heartwell,   Feb. 22, 1778
John Warner & Eunice Waller,   May 20, 1778
Stephen Powel of the Nine Partners & Polly Burge,

                                                  May 24, 1778
John Plat & Sarah Buck,   June, 1778
Asa Prime & Phebe Rusuke,   June 25, 1778
Joel Buck & Hulda Bostwick,   July 2, 1778
Timothy Cole & Sarah Buckly,   Jan. 11, 1779
Sergeant Prime Doan & Jean Smith,   Feb., 1779
Hezekiah Treadwell of Stratfield & Abiah Stilson,

                                                  March 17, 1779
Enos Camp, Jr., & Eunice Bostwick,   April 12, 1779
John Bostwick & Patience Hubbell, both of Newbury,

                                                  May 26, 1779
Jonah Todd, Jr., & Lucy Fisher,   June 2, 1779
Ebenezar Seelye of Litchfield & Mabel Todd, June 2, 1779
Nathan Baldwin of New Canaan & Olive Burrit,   June, 1779
Isaac Nichols & Sarah Stevens,   June 15, 1779
Abner Gun & Susanah Noble,   July 1, 1779
Samuel Andrus of Kent & Annis Murry,   July 2, 1779
Paul Welch, Jr., & Abigail Crane,   Aug. 19, 1779
Ralph Keeler of Newbury & Hannah Treat,   Dec. 9, 1779
Matthew Wildman, Jr., & Polly Reed,   Dec., 1779
Thomas Wells & Anne Northrup,   Jan. 11, 1780
Oliver Trobridge & Anna Noble,   1780
Thaddeus Cole & Phebe Oviatt,   June 2, 1780
David Beech & Annah Smith,   June 7, 1780
David Beebe of Bethel & Sarah Beech,   June 8, 1780
Cornelius Hamlin & Esther Oviatt,   1780
Reuben Bostwick, Jr., & Polly Allen,   Oct. 18, 1780

Robert Beech & Sarah Washburn,	Nov. 16, 1780
William Foot & Mabel Wilkisson,	Dec. 18, 1780
Nicholas S. Masters & Hannah Starr,	Jan. 28, 1781
John Canfield & Phebe Treat,	March 6, 1781
Josiah Bearse & Freelove Canfield,	1781
William Gillett & Anna Garlick,	1781
John Stevens & Phebe Warner,	May 13, 1781
Stephen Collins & Dolle Olmsted,	June 13, 1781
Charles Hurstfield & Lidia Nichols of New Fairfield,	
	July 9, 1781
John Baile & Elma Birch,	July 11, 1781
Theophilus Comstock & Lucindy Comstock,	Oct., 1781
Perez Partridge & Hannah Boen,	Nov. 26, 1781
Isaac Clark & Jane Baldwin,	Dec. 6, 1781
Stephen Couch & Pollipheme Carington,	Dec. 16, 1781
Joseph Clark & Cloe Comstock,	Jan. 20, 1782
Lieut. Augustine Taylor & Hulda Canfield,	May 5, 1782
Joseph Olmstead of Ridgefield & Susanna Oviatt,	
	July 4, 1782
Joel Smith & Patience Bearse,	July 11, 1782
Lieut. Daniel Camp & Lorania Chittenden,	Aug. 13, 1782
Benjamin Stone, Jr., & Sarah Hartwell,	Sept. 30, 1782
Jonathan Mygatt & Patience Noble,	Dec. 5, 1782
Isaac Brownson & Joannah Beardslee,	Dec. 5, 1782
Solomon Hill & Ame Stone,	Jan. 16, 1783
Moses Wanzer of New Fairfield & Sarah Hill,	Jan. 16, 1783
Elijah Hoyt & Polly Canfield,	March 18, 1783
Ralph Smith & Anne Treat,	March 18, 1783
David Merwin & Molly Durkee,	May 29, 1783
Thomas Northrup of New Fairfield & Clarry Cone,	
	Oct. 29, 1783
John Reseque & Anne Camp,	Nov. 20, 1783
Daniel Noble Bennit of New Fairfield & Anna Phippene,	Nov. 27, 1783
Moss Leavenworth & Sarah Benedict,	Dec. 4, 1783
Elisha Booth & Elizabeth Clark,	Dec. 23, 1783
William Lamfer of Woodbury & Jean Smith,	Dec. 23, 1783
Wolcot Burnham of Cornwell & Hannah Shove Sturdevant,	Jan. 22, 1784
John Baldwin & Susanna Bristol,	March 7, 1784

Truman Stilson & —— Lum,   May 10, 1784
Charles McDonald & Mary Sanford,   May 12, 1784
Daniel Sherwood of Stratford & —— Hill,   May 13, 1784
Epinetus Gun & Sarah Botchford Camp,   May 20, 1784
Nehemiah Phippen & Hannah Taylor of Woodbury,

                                                 July 29, 1784
Chauncey Lowrey & Aurelia Booth,   Aug. 22, 1784
Philo Camp & Abigail Prince or Prime,   Nov., 1784
William Hitchcock & Rachel Ketchum,   Nov. 25, 1784
Achilles Comstock & Sarah Botsford,   Dec. 16, 1784
Stephen Morehouse & Huldah Peet,   Feb. 3, 1785
John Morehouse & Mabel Ferriss,   March 21, 1785
Benedict Davis & Hannah Merwin,   March 21, 1785
Eli Tood & Mercy Merwin,   March 21, 1785
Israel Baldwin, Jr., & Levina Todd,   July 18, 1785
Ire Hitchcock & Hannah Hotchkiss,   Sept. 29, 1785
Daniel Clark, Jr., & Anne Canfield,   Nov. 27, 1785
Jeremiah Canfield & widow Abigail Oviatt,   Nov. 30, 1785
James Bell & Clarre Phippene,   Dec. 6, 1785
Israel Luther of Newtown & Sarah Marks,   Jan. 17, 1786
Jonathan Chase, State of New York, & Sarah Buck,

                                                 Jan. 24, 1786
Ire Penoch of Woodbury & Polly Trobridge,   Jan. 26, 1786
Nehemiah Sanford, Jr., & Hannah Beach,   April 6, 1786
Jeremiah Holms of Bedford & Diadama Taylor,

                                                 April 6, 1786
Nicholas S. Masters & Tamar Taylor,   May 9, 1786
William Taylor & Abigail Starr of Danbury,   Dec. 3, 1786
Benjamin Mead & Abigail Woster,   March 4, 1787
Ebenezer Hurd of Ripton & Mary Bostwick,   July 22, 1787
Caleb Beach & Clarre Treat,   1787
Philip Corban & Mercy Wilkisson,   Oct., 1787
Nehemiah Plat & Eunice Anne Plat,   Dec. 11, 1787
Reuben Lum & Vashti Sherman,   Dec. 26, 1787
Jehiel Smith & Parthena Hill,   Jan. 17, 1788
Lemuel Benedict of Danbury & Annis Hitchcock,

                                                 Jan. 30, 1788
Philander Vaughn & Polly Roe,   April 27, 1788
Botchford Buckingham & Rebekah Heartwell,

                                                 May 14, 1788

Benjamin Picket, Jr., of New Fairfield & Mary
    Bristol,   June 5, 1788

James Miller of Fishkill & Abigail Duning, June 24, 1788

Samuel Gregory of Kent & Mehetabel Buck,   July 9, 1788

Tibbels Baldwin of Brookfield & Salle Booth of
    Southbury,   Sept. 25, 1788

Daniel Garlick & Thala Beecher,   Nov. 5, 1788

George Milligan & Catherine Taylor,   Nov. 9, 1788

Reuben Mills Booth & Anne Eunice Northrup,
                               Nov. 25, 1788

Joseph Heartwell, Jr., & Rachel Stone,   Jan. 15, 1789

Gershom Morehouse of Fairfield & Hannah Smith,
                               Jan. 29, 1789

Jared Terril & Hannah Buck,   Feb. 22, 1789

Samuel Couch & Hannah Ferriss,   March 19, 1789

Seely Richmond & Mehitabel Blakeslee of Roxbury,
                               Aug. 12, 1789

—— Guthery of Washington & Phebe Stone,
                               Aug. 27, 1789

Nathanael Porter & Prudence Mead,   Jan. 3, 1790

David Cole & Mary Fox of Heartland,   Jan. 11, 1790

Nathan Sherwood & Lucy Hollister,   July 8, 1790

Archibald Gilmore & Charlotte Pegnam, July 15, 1790

Jarius Green & widow Mary Stilson,   July 25, 1790

David Sanford & Ame Heartwell,   Aug. 3, 1790

Daniel Lampson of New Preston & Molly Peat, Oct. 21, 1790

Daniel Morgan & Rhody Stone,   Oct. 27, 1790

James Prout & Cloe Jordan,   Nov. 14, 1790

Beecher Fisher & Elenor Peat,   Jan. 5, 1791

Austine Bostwick & Mary Sturdevent,   Jan. 13, 1791

Chene Clark of Canaan & Aner Duning of Brookfield,
                               Jan. 19, 1791

Oliver Canfield, Jr., & Sarah Bradley,   Jan. 27, 1791

Jonathan Hawley & Phebe Betts,   July 17, 1791

Lemuel Morehouse of Brookfield & Mehetable
    Treadwell,   Sept. 1, 1791

Capt. Nathan Botchford & Eunice Porter, Sept. 22, 1791

Samuel Stevens & Abiah Beers,   Sept. 28, 1791

James Brush of New Fairfield & Amarilis Hollister,
                              Sept. 28, 1791

Eliphalet Gilbert & Bette Bishop,	Nov. 23, 1791
Isaac Wilkinson & Tamar Smith,	Dec. 18, 1791
Reuben Sherwood & Keziah Hill,	Dec. 22, 1791
Wells Stone & Polle Wetmore,	Dec. 29, 1791
Bushnell Downs & Hannah Clark,	April 25, 1792
John Buck, Jr., & ——— ———,	Aug. 29, 1792
Abraham Peet & Polle Glassford,	Oct., 1792
Angus Ferriss & Lutilda Ruggles,	Nov. 21, 1792
Samuel Frisby & Nancy St. John, both of Sharon,	
	April 28, 1793
Jasper Bennit & Lydia Wheton,	Aug. 28, 1793
Stephen Crane & Hannah Baldwin,	Sept. 5, 1793
Ira Cannon of Lee, Mass., & Olive Bears,	Oct. 10, 1793
Czar Stevens of Lee, Mass., & Abigail Bears,	Oct. 10, 1793
Oliver Ruggles & Phebe More of Salisbury,	Oct. 22, 1793
Abraham Duning & Lidia Strong, both of Warren,	
	Nov. 14, 1793
Salmon Buck & Urania Beacher,	March 5, 1794
Samuel Lockwood & Eunice Weller,	March 19, 1794
Samuel Benedict & Thankful Knap, both of Norfolk,	
	May 5, 1794
Faithfull Smith & Elizabeth Browning,	May 7, 1794
Elnathan Peet & Anne Beach,	Sept. 16, 1794
Cirus Warner & Polle Weller,	Oct. 30, 1794
Joseph B. Tomlinson & Susanah Mead,	Nov. 2, 1794
Silas Bennit & Anne Dudley,	Feb. 19, 1795
Calvin Cohoon & Hulda Ferry, both of Washington,	
	March 22, 1795
Jedediah Strong of Warren & Jerusha Morgan,	April 7, 1795
Nathan Howard of the Jersies & Annie Canfield,	
	Oct. 27, 1795
David Lancaster & Rille Hill,	Jan. 8, 1796
Nathan Pearce, Jr., & Rachel St. John of South Britain,	
	Jan. 24, 1796
Samuel Knap & Phebe McMahan,	Feb. 14, 1796
John Warner Merwin & Esther Gaylord,	Feb. 18, 1796
Benjamin Rumsey of Roxbury & Sarah Warner,	
	March 22, 1796
——— Harrison & Annie Sperry, in Washington,	
	May 15, 1796

Marvin Warner of South Britain & Clarissa Pun-
    derson of Roxbury,   May 26, 1796
Andrew Minor & Rachel Wildman,   Dec. 28, 1796
Bildad Hine & Lowis Bostwick,   Jan. 18, 1797
Elisha Perry & ——— Wilkisson,   Feb. 2, 1797
Rev. Ebenezer Porter & Mrs. Lucy Merwin, both
    of Washington,   May 14, 1797
Jehiel Hawley Summer & Tabathy Betts, Jan. 24, 1798

(End of record on first book.)

In the year 1790, January 20, Rev. Stanley Griswold was ordained as colleague pastor with Rev. Nathaniel Taylor. He commenced his record of marriages performed by him as follows: "From 20th of January, 1790, to 16th of September, 1791, they are recorded without dates according to my best recollection. From thence I intend to be accurate."

John Dickinson & Tryphena Willson.
David Beard & ——— Comstock.
Austin Brunson & ——— Stilson.
Sol. N. Sanford & ——— Lockwood.
Heth Camp & ——— Frisbie.
Valentine Lovely & Abigail I. Weller.
Perry Lovely & Phebe Turril.
Nathan Leavenworth & Anne Buckingham.
Friend Northrop & Mabel Hine.
Daniel Smith & Polly Blanchard,   1790–91
Joseph Peck & Lorana Bennett,   1790–91
Jeremiah Canfield & Polly Bennett,   1790–91
——— Wood & ——— Hurlbutt,   1790–91
Isaac Crane & ——— Vaughn,   1790–91
Asa Morgan & Polly Hitchcock,   Sept. 16, 1791
Jonathan Bostwick, Jr., & Abigail Trowbridge,
                        Sept. 22, 1791
Rufus Clark & Tamar Oviatt,   Oct. 18, 1791
Daniel Lines & Hannah Todd,   Nov. 20, 1791
Joel Canfield & Ruth Chittenden,   Jan. 12, 1792
Enos Beach & Esther Hurlbutt,   Feb. 2, 1792
Jonathan Burrall & Esther Boardman, Feb. 5, 1792
John Ruggles & Affa Warner,   Sept., 1792
Joab Picket & Mabel Platt,   Sept. 26, 1792
Samuel Sommers & Marilla Downs, Oct. 24, 1792

9

Curtis Warner & Eunice Hull,	Nov. 4, 1792
Daniel Picket & Sara Cole,	Nov. 24, 1792
James Lockwood & Susannah Swift,	Nov. 29, 1792
Matthew Bronson & Mary Richmond,	Dec. 27, 1792
Elnathan Sanford & Patience Northrop,	Dec. 30, 1792
Abel Hall & Molly Fisher,	Jan. 3, 1793
David Hull & Sally Hitchcock,	March 24, 1793
Ebenezer Peet & Deborah Beecher,	March 27, 1793
Gideon Wilkinson & Emilia Bostwick,	May 28, 1793
—— Canfield & —— West,	July, 1793
Garry Decker & Mary Crane,	Sept. 22, 1793
Clark Blackney & Thalia War—— (?),	Oct. 10, 1793
David Sommers & Anne Durke,	Nov. 6, 1793
Orange Warner, Jr., & Lucy Sanford,	Nov. 10, 1793
Lanadar Prindle & Hannah Bostwick,	Nov. 17, 1793
Jedidiah Merchant & Hepsibah Be—— (?),	Nov. 18, 1793
James Leech & Anna Hollister,	Dec. 1, 1793
David Smith & Rana Edwards,	Jan. 26, 1794
Ezbon Bostwick & Lois Warner,	Feb. 12, 1794
John Stilson, Jr., & Rachel Bostwick,	April 29, 1794
David Malery & Dinah Punderson,	May 20, 1794
Doct—— Benton & Rebecca Bostwick,	June 24, 1794
Joseph Hartwell & Polly Mead,	Aug. 26, 1794
Castle Warner & Annie Trowbridge,	Aug. 31, 1794
John Smith & Ophelia Edwards,	Sept. 1, 1794
Micah Pool & Sarah Ketchum,	Sept. 28, 1794
Fowler Merwin Platt & Catas —— (?),	Oct. 6, 1794
Nathan Betts & Polly Treat,	Nov. 20, 1794
John Hawley Treat & Sally Rains—— (?),	Nov. 25, 1794
Daniel Bristol & Deborah Hitchcock,	Jan. 29, 1795
Joseph Conner & Tryphena Flagg (colored),	Feb. 8, 1795
Erastus Bostwick & Sally Welch,	Feb. 10, 1795
Edmund Baldwin & Susanna Stone,	March 10, 1795
Isaac Johnson & Polly Bostwick,	March 26, 1795
John Lane & Lutra Bostwick,	April 14, 1795
Jethro Tabor & Betsey Newton (colored),	Oct. 12, 1795
William Nickerson & Jane Beecher,	Oct. 28, 1795
Wakefield Noble & Rachel Starr,	Nov. 8, 1795
Ansel Cole & Sally Bishop,	Jan. 3, 1796
Cyrus Bostwick & Tabby Sanford,	Jan. 4, 1796

Isaac Downs & Prudence Polly Sperry,	Jan. 4, 1796
Peter Middleton & Mary Wattin (colored),	Feb. 25, 1796
Daniel Weller & Mary Blakeslee,	June 16, 1796
Samuel Clark & Patty Richmond,	July 17, 1796
Caleb Hill & Sybil Hubbell (colored),	Aug. 8, 1796
Capt. Francis Terrill & —— ——,	Nov. 1, 1796
Benjamin Lake & Mabel Smith,	Nov. 13, 1796
Aden Stevens & Annie Warner,	1796
Eli Perry & Hopy Knowles,	1796
Samuel Dibble & Sarah Downs,	1796
David Northrop & Ruamah Rogers,	1796
Israel White & Jedidah Jackson,	1796
Samuel Gregory & widow Barns,	Jan. 4, 1797
Elijah Stone & Anna Northrop,	1797
Daniel Bass & Hannah Chase,	1797
Isaac Briggs & Abigail Warner,	1797
David Fenn & Prudence Hurlbut,	Feb. 6, 1797
Nathaniel Stone & Polly Trowbridge,	March 9, 1797
Asher Canfield & Thalia Ruggles,	1797
Stephen Chittenden, Jr., & Laura Canfield,	May 13, 1797
Samuel Summers & Hannah Wooster,	1797
Eli Starr & Susannah Higgins,	1797
Joel Baldwin & Mable Sanford,	June 18, 1797
Jonathan Brown & Judith Betts,	Sept. 6, 1797
Stiles Curtis & Betsey Hitchcock,	1797
Thomas Davis & Abigail Phippene,	Nov. 29, 1797
Ezra Botsford & Mable Warner,	Feb. 14, 1798
Silas Gregory & Betsey Hoyt,	March 8, 1798
Gerardus Booth & Sally Clark,	April 7, 1798
Samuel Wakeley of Oxford & Anthy Turrill,	Nov. 10, 1798
Gilbert Ferriss & Olive Griswold,	March 3, 1799
Leman Stone & Anna Camp,	1799
Wanzer Marsh & Sally Bulkley,	1799
David Bennett & Polly Botsford,	May 5, 1799
Richard Barlow & Sally Wheaton,	Sept. 29, 1799
Samuel Gregory & Deborah Gilbert,	Oct. 12, 1799
Nathanael Taylor, 3d, & Thalia Stilson,	Oct. 20, 1799
Elihu Marsh & Urania Stilson,	Nov. 25, 1799
Samuel Hawkins & Hannah Ruggles,	Nov. 28, 1799
Elijah Peet & Polly Straight,	Dec. 12, 1799

VOLUNTOWN.

NEW LONDON COUNTY.

Voluntown named May, 1708. This township was granted by the Court of Connecticut to the volunteers who served in the Narragansett war. The Congregational Church was organized (first as a Presbyterian Church), October 15, 1723. Rev. Samuel Dorrance, pastor, 1723–1770. The following are the marriages.

Francis Dean & Esther Dean,	Oct. 20, 1729
Robert Dixon & Elizabeth Houston,	Jan. 29, 1730
Mathew Rea & Margaret Niven,	March 19, 1730
Benjamin Parke & Mary Church,	Dec. 29, 1730
John Kasson & Mary Dorrance,	Oct. 14, 1731
Peter Miller & Isabella Locker,	Dec. 28, 1731
John Gordon & Jennet Carr,	March 30, 1732
Jonathan Rhodes & Martha Stanbury,	June 5, 1732
Alexander Stewart & Jennet Rogers,	Nov., 1732
James Parke & Jane McDowell,	Nov., 1732
David Hopkin & Esther Wilson,	Aug. 27, 1734
Philip Ellsworth & Elizabeth Gordon,	Dec., 1734
John Montgomery & Mary Gordon,	April, 1735
Benjamin Gallup & Theody Parke,	May 22, 1735
Joseph Parke & Sarah Jamison,	May 27, 1735
Samuel Gordon & Elizabeth Carr,	Nov. 20, 1735
Thomas Stewart & Anne Rogers,	Jan. 29, 1736
Daniel Miller & Jennet McCurdy,	1736
Richard Keigwin & —— Downing,	Aug., 1736
Robert Thompson & Mary Taylor,	Dec. 16, 1736
Robert Campbell & Mary Trumbull,	Jan., 1737
James Wilson & Martha Hopkin,	Feb. 10, 1737
Thomas Kasson & Alice Gibson,	Jan. 7, 1741
William McNeil & Jane Henry,	1741
William Kinne & Hannah Gallup,	April, 1741
Samuel Torrance & Jemima Parke,	July, 1741
John Loudon & Agnes Campbell,	June, 1741
John Dixon & Jennet Kennedy,	Aug. 7, 1741
Gain Miller & Mary Hunter,	1741
Samuel Dorrance & Nancy Alexander,	
Moses Barnet & Mrs. Safford,	Nov. 11, 1742

John Wylie & Sarah Campbell,	1742
Robert Hunter & Jean Wylie,	——
John Rhodes & Dorothy Gallup,	1744
Mr. Billings & Ruth Lawrence,	——
Archibald Kasson & Jane Dixon,	June 15, 1744
William Jackson & Jennet Dixon,	Dec. 26, 1744
James Trumbull & J—— Kennedy,	——
Samuel Kasson & Eleanor Dixon,	Jan. 22, 1745
Thomas Converse & Esther Wilson,	April 10, 1746
Robert Orr & Mary Martin,	Aug. 11, 1746
John Hineman & Elizabeth Parke,	May 12, 1747
Obadiah Rhodes & Mary Stanbury,	June 4, 1747
Benjamin Cady & Mary Nichols,	Jan. 12, 1748
Samuel Dorrance & Margaret Trumbull,	Oct., 1748
George Gordon & Jenet Gibson,	Dec., 1748
James Campbell & Dinah McMain,	May, 1749
Abijah Cady & Alice Miles,	June, 1749
Mr. Strowbridge & Jane Gordon,	Oct., 1749
Barnet Dixon & Mary Bellow,	Feb., 1750
Mr. Cole & Mary Young,	Dec., 1749
Mingo Gallup & Sarah Babcock,	Feb. 28, 1750
James Sweet & Mary Nichols,	March 1, 1750
Matthew Patrick & Isabella Stranahan,	April 20, 1750
Abner Ames & Rachel Mansfield,	Oct. 14, 1755
John Dixon, Jr., & Jane Gordon,	Jan. 5, 1758
George Dorrance & Mary Wilson,	Jan. 25, 1758
Robert Dixon & Sarusana Dorrance,	Jan. 26, 1758
John Dorrance & Nancy Dixon,	1759
Daniel Gordon & Jennet Hineman,	——
Joseph Alexander & Sarah Dorrance,	——
Robert Patrick & Mary Phillips,	——
Amariah Parke & Hannah Mansfield,	1759 (?)
David Kennedy & Mary Campbell,	
John Phillips & Sarah Dixon,	——

(Congregational Church organized June 30, 1779.)

Benjamin Gallup of Plainfield & Martha Gallup of Voluntown,	Dec. 6, 1781
William Green of Warrick, R. I., & Susannah Dorrance of Voluntown,	Jan. 14, 1782

Robert Dixon of Groton & Sarah Wylie,   Jan. 15, 1782

Stephen Spaulding of Plainfield & Sarah Keigwin,

       May 23, 1782

Jonas Brown of Stonington & Lucy Fish,   June 13, 1782

John Curtis of Canterbury & Nancy Dorrance, July 4, 1782

Manassah Bliss of Pomfret & Lydia Griffith, Dec. 19, 1782

Nathaniel Gallup & Rachel Smith, both of Voluntown,   Jan. 30, 1783

John Cole of Partridgefield & Eunice Cole of Voluntown,   June 19, 1783

Daniel Wylie & Elizabeth Gardner,   Oct. 9, 1783

Stephen Allen of West Greenwich, R. I., & Sarah Rhodes,   Feb. 12, 1784

William Wilkinson & Lydia Cady,   March 11, 1784

John Green & Mehitabel Tuckerman,   March 18, 1784

Jared Lillie of Windham & Susanna Tuckerman,

       March 18, 1784

Joseph Huston & Elizabeth Campbell,   April 1, 1784

Anthony Rhodes & Rehebiah Budlong,   April 15, 1784

John Cogswell of Preston & Hannah Gallup, May 13, 1784

John Briggs & Mary Hall of Plainfield,   May 27, 1784

Amos Lawrence of Providence, R. I., & Phebe Babcock,   Dec. 5, 1784

Obed Spaulding of Killingly & Margaret Eames,

       Dec. 30, 1784

James Knox & Nancy Morse,   Jan. 20, 1785

William Bennet & Sarah Knox,   Jan. 20, 1785

John Larkham & Desire Morgan,   Feb. 6, 1785

Philemon Eaton of Ashford & Sarah Frink,   Feb. 10, 1785

Hugh Kennedy of Cliftonpark & Sarah Thornton,

       Feb. 24, 1785

Benadam Gallup & Elizabeth Dorrance,   March 31, 1785

Edward Hammond & Phebe Whiting,   Aug. 4, 1785

Lazarus Cory of Coventry & Mary Montgomery,

       Dec. 1, 1785

H. Ledlie Dunlap of Plainfield & Cynthia Campbell,   Dec. 22, 1785

Edward Merriss of Exeter, R. I., & Mary Sheffield,

       Jan. 8, 1786

Nathan Gallup & Zeruiah Gallup,   Jan. 19, 1786

Increase Blair of Worcester & Huldah Campbell,
Feb. 9, 1786
Andrew Colegrove & Martha Larkin, Feb. 19, 1786
William Bardsley & Elizabeth Lathrop, March 23, 1786
John Stanton of Stonington & Elizabeth Fish,
April 13, 1786
Reuben Thayer of Thompson & Hannah Hord,
April 20, 1786
Archibald Campbell & Molly Wylie, May 4, 1786
Capt. Benjamin Horton of Barrington & Aleanor
Green, June 4, 1786
Nathaniel Gallup, Jr., & Kesiah Kinne, Sept. 7, 1786
Benjamin Brewster of Windham & Susanna Green,
Sept. 28, 1786
Capt. John Stewart & Susanna Briggs, Oct. 5, 1786
Nehemiah Hill & Mercy Knight, Oct. 12, 1786
Jonathan King & Margaret Knox, Oct. 19, 1786
Elisha Tucker & Elizabeth Keigwin, Oct. 29, 1786
Burden Potter of Johnston & Deborah Avery, Nov. 23, 1786
Patrick Campbell & Martha Babcock, Dec. 7, 1786
Levi Kinne of Plainfield & Hannah Gallup, Jan. 7, 1787
Vose Palmer of Plainfield & Celinda Stewart, Jan. 12, 1787
Robert Harris of Preston & Lucretia Kennedy,
Feb. 15, 1787
Rufus Mulkin of Preston & Hannah Partelow,
March 14, 1787
Asahel Partelow & Mary Kennedy, March 15, 1787
Nathan Dow & Agnes Gordon, Sept. 16, 1787
Henry Dow of Plainfield & Rebecca Dow, Dec. 6, 1787
John Huston & Jennet Douglass, Feb. 14, 1788
William Douglass & Ruth Wilkinson, March 13, 1788
James Douglass & Sarah Rouse, March 16, 1788
Joseph Campbell, Jr., & Anna Whipple of Plain-
field, March 30, 1788
Isaac Gallup, Jr., & Mary Dean, April 24, 1788
James Alexander & Mary Babcock, May 8, 1788
Joseph Tillinghast of West Greenwich & Sarah
Gorton, Sept. 14, 1788
George Warren & Mary Moreland (transient per-
sons), Sept. 21, 1788

Benjamin Clark of Plainfield & Bridget Palmer, Oct. 2, 1788
Seth L. Cutler, said to be of Mansfield, & Sabrana
    Jencks of Ellington,   Nov. 27, 1788
Nehemiah Potter & Phebe Babcock, both of Plain-
    field,   Nov. 27, 1788
Elijah Gates of Preston & Anna Palmer,   Dec. 4, 1788
Ephraim Keigwin of Preston & Eunice Kennedy,
                                                 Jan. 1, 1789
John Smith of Saratoga & Lydia Sheffield,   Feb. 24, 1789
Benjamin Colgrove & Sarah Larkam,   March 1, 1789
Preserved Pierce & Dorcas Pierce,   March 1, 1789
Jesse Matteson of West Greenwich & Hannah Dow,
                                                 March 26, 1789
James Gibson, Jr., of Coventry & Elizabeth Thomp-
    son,   April 9, 1789
Josiah Montgomery & Ruth Bennet,   April 10, 1789
Squire Hide & Hannah Montgomery,   April 22, 1789
Peter Burlingame & Elizabeth Montgomery, April 23, 1789
Thomas Dixson & Phebe Smith,   May 3, 1789
Elisha Whipple of Plainfield & Lydia Hutchinson,
                                                 May 3, 1789
Col. Nathaniel Brown of Foster, R. I., & Mrs. Mary
    Rhodes,   May 30, 1789
William Stone & Mercy Bailey,   July 16, 1789
Moses Campbell, Jr., & Phebe Stewart,   Sept. 10, 1789
Levi Phillips of Preston & Abigail Kinne,   Nov. 19, 1789
William Green Rhodes & Rebekah Kennedy,   Dec. 6, 1789
Samuel Douglass, Jr., & Catharine Hall,   Dec. 24, 1789
James Campbell of Kinderhook & Elisabeth Wylie,
                                                 Jan. 14, 1790
Stephen Stacy & Sarah Williams,   Feb. 4, 1790
Alexander Dorrance of Hampton & Rebekah Dix-
    son,   March 18, 1790
Job Bly & Olive Rathbun of West Greenwich, R. I.,
                                                 April 8, 1790
Roswell Palmer & Sarah Campbell,   April 8, 1790
Jesse Wheaton & Elisabeth Dixson,   May 5, 1790
Abraham Allis of West Greenwich & Polly Bowdish,
                                                 Aug. 2, 1790
William Gallup, Jr., & Almy Gallup,   Sept. 2, 1790

Benjamin Morse & Phebe Hall,	Sept. 2, 1790
Hansom Perkins & Huldah Montgomery,	Sept. 19, 1790
Levi Cole & Hannah Kinne,	Nov. 25, 1790
Allen Campbell & Mary Gordon,	Feb. 24, 1791
Joseph Douglass & Mary Campbell,	Aug. 11, 1791
Nicholas Rhodes & Sarah Adams,	Aug. 21, 1791
William Barber of Mason, N. H., & Mary Campbell,	
	Sept. 11, 1791
James Knight of Plainfield & Polly Herd,	Sept. 25, 1791
Ambrose Coats of Stonington & Lucy Partelow,	
	Oct. 2, 1791
Robert Gordon & Nancy Dixon,	Oct. 20, 1791
Douglass Woodworth of Norwich & Charlotte Dor-rance,	Oct. 20, 1791
John Dixson, Jr., & Mary Matteson,	Oct. 30, 1791
William Dixson & Mary Kinyon,	Dec. 1, 1791
Amos Wells of Charlton & Mary Campbell,	Dec. 8, 1791
Ayer Phillips, Jr., of Plainfield & Anna Keigwin,	
	Dec. 22, 1791
Adam Kasson, Jr., of Coventry, R. I., & Margaret Gallup,	Dec. 29, 1791
Moses Little of Patridgefield & Anna Stoyell,	Feb. 2, 1792
John Adams & Jerusha Cooper, both of Killingly,	
	Feb. 16, 1792
Colonel Vaughn & Anna Matteson, both of Volun-town,	Feb. 16, 1792
Job Pope of Plainfield & Sarah Denison,	Feb. 23, 1792
Peter Parker of West Greenwich, R. I., & Mary Bly,	
	March 4, 1792
Alexander Campbell, Jr., & Salome Frink,	March 29, 1792
Stephen Stacy & Lucy Avery,	April 19, 1792
Archibald Gordon & Ann Mercy Green,	May 6, 1792
Moses Gibson of Coventry, R. I., & Esther Mont-gomery,	June 7, 1792
Daniel Phillips of Plainfield & Olive Keigwin,	
	Aug. 16, 1792
Alexander Campbell & Polly Frink,	Sept, 3, 1792
Elisha Brown & Thankful Colgrove,	Oct. 11, 1792
Thomas Gordon & Elisabeth Stewart,	Dec. 23, 1792
Oliver Perkins, Jr., & Anna Kennedy,	Dec. 24, 1792

Charles Campbell & Phebe Gorton,   Dec. 24, 1792
William Popple & Rachel Frink,   March 24, 1793
David Lawrence & Morven Wilkinson,   April 21, 1793
Samuel Boardman of Preston & Nancy Wylie,
                                             Aug. 22, 1793
James Dorrance of Foster, R. I., & Mehitabel Green,
                                             Oct. 14, 1793
Joseph Hill & Sarah Budlong,   Dec. 29, 1793
Robert Douglass & Jane Hall,   Feb. 6, 1794
Douglass Park of Plainfield & Olive Douglass,
                                             April 24, 1794
Stephen Colgrove & Elisabeth Partelow,   June 12, 1794
Jareph Kasson of Granby & Margaret Wylie of
    Sterling,   Oct 9, 1794

   (The town of Sterling was set from Voluntown about the time of
above date.)

Thomas Burlingame & Sarah Montgomery, both of
    Sterling,   Oct. 16, 1794
Jeremiah Kinne of Plainfield & Martha Dow of
    Sterling,   Oct. 30, 1794
Ebenezer Dow, Jr., of Sterling & Anna Stewart of
    Voluntown,   Nov. 30, 1794
Gideon Waters of Glastenbury & Thankful Wells
    of Voluntown,   Dec. 25, 1794
Asa Brown of Stonington & Lucy Dow of Sterling,
                                             Jan. 15, 1795
George Alexander Taylor of Plainfield & Hannah
    Matteson of Sterling,   Feb. 19, 1795
Zachariah Frink, Jr., of Voluntown & Mary Frink
    of Sterling,   Oct. 22, 1795
Porter Thayer & Rosanna Hall,   Dec. 24, 1795
Mumford Kinyon of Charlestown, R. I., & Hannah
    Wage of Voluntown,   Jan. 12, 1796
Soloman Place of Coventry, R. I., & Martha Heard
    of Sterling,   Feb. 7, 1796
Joseph Gallup & Hannah Smith, both of Sterling,
                                             April 7, 1796
Lot Larkham & Elizabeth Kennedy, both of Volun-
    town,   April 28, 1796

William Almy & Mary Olney, both of Sterling,
Sept. 15, 1796

Jedediah Bailey of Groton & Mercy Stone of Sterling, Oct. 30, 1796

Alexander Dorrance of Foster & Elisabeth Frink
of Voluntown, Nov. 10, 1796

Russel Stevens & Margaret Frink, both of Voluntown, Nov. 17, 1796

Elias Keigwin & Rebekah Rhodes, both of Voluntown, Jan. 3, 1797

John Park & Barbara Wylie, both of Voluntown,
Jan. 12, 1797

Dorrance Knox & Nancy Bennet of Sterling, Jan. 30, 1797

Lieut. Nicholas Keigwin & Mary Gordon, both of
Voluntown, Feb. 2, 1797

Joseph Mot & Mary Vaughn, both of Voluntown, Feb. 2, 1797

Nathan Rice of Coventry, R. I., & Sarah Hoxsie of
Voluntown, Feb. 2, 1797

John McNeil of Sterling & Polly Dixon of Voluntown, Sept. 10, 1797

Samuel Herrick of Plainfield & Betsey Dewyer of
Sterling, March 25, 1798

Lieut. William Briggs of Voluntown & Hannah
Stephens of Sterling, May 3, 1798

George Babcock of Pittsfield & Sarah Briggs of
Voluntown, June 21, 1798

Warden Johnson of Coventry, R. I., & Phebe Knox
of Sterling, June 28, 1798

Ebenezer Sweet of Greenwich & Elizabeth Avery
of Sterling, Nov. 25, 1798

Capt. Thomas Gordon & Sarah Susanna Dixon,
both of Sterling, Dec. 2, 1798

Thomas Cole of Fairfield, N. Y., & Sally Brown of
Sterling, Jan. 24, 1799

Samuel Millet of New York & Rachael Douglass
of Sterling, Feb. 7, 1799

Daniel Dow & Susanna Douglass, both of Sterling,
March 28, 1799

John Kinyon, Jr., & Susanna Thurston, both of
Sterling, April 14, 1799

Archibald Gordon of Sterling & Mrs. Sally Wylie
    of Voluntown,   June 23, 1799
Jonathan Bitgood & Hannah Stanton, both of
    Voluntown,   July 4, 1799
Samuel Robbins, 3d, & Phebe Wage, both of Vol-
    untown,   July 16, 1799
Hezekiah Brown & Elisabeth Cole, both of Ster-
    ling,   July 21, 1799
Caleb Perkins of Sterling & Sally Alexander of
    Voluntown,   July 25, 1799
Allen Shurden of West Greenwich, R. I., & Dorcas
    Button of Sterling,   Dec. 15, 1799
James Potter & Olive Wilson, both of Sterling,
                                                     Feb. 10, 1800

LYME.

NEW LONDON COUNTY.

Lyme was named May, 1667. Local records show that Lyme was set off from Saybrook by a committee in 1665. The First Congregational Church was organized in 1693. It is located in South Lyme. The Second Congregational Church of Lyme was organized at East Lyme in 1719. This church has lost its early records. The Third Church of Lyme, organized in 1727, in Hamburgh, has also lost its early records. The following are the marriages upon the records of the First Church.

Thomas West & Elizabeth Lewis,   April 22, 1731
John Bennet & Mary Moss,   Sept. 2, 1731
Benjamin Beckwith & Patience Eden,   Oct. 21, 1731
        (By Mr. G. Beckwith.)

Jasper Peck & Sarah Clark,   Nov. 25, 1731
William Clark & Hannah Peck,   Nov. 30, 1731
Rev. Jonathan Parsons & Phebe Griswold, Dec. 14, 1731
      (By Rev. George Griswold.)

Abithai Bingham of Windham & Mary Tubbs, Dec. 28, 1731
Philip Beckwith & Abigail Harvey,   Feb. 17, 1732
Soloman Gee & Deborah Huntley,   March 29, 1732
Reynold Beckwith & Martha Marvin,   April 4, 1732
Matthew Marvin & Mary Beckwith,   April 20, 1732
Benjamin Huntly & Lydia Beckwith,   April 28, 1732

Joseph Alger & Mary Huntly,	April 28, 1732
John Robbins & Ruth Alger,	Nov. 2, 1732
John Noyes & Mary Hudson,	Dec. 14, 1732
Elisha Wright of New London & Elizabeth Lester,	
	April 3, 1733
Richard Waite & Elizabeth Marvin,	Nov. 8, 1733
Jonathan Reid & Elizabeth Smith,	March 14, 1734
John Sears & Elizabeth Watrous,	June 13, 1734
Samuel Court & Abigail Marven,	Nov. 7, 1734
Joseph Harvard *Houd* of Branford & Elizabeth Pinnuck,	
	Dec. 10, 1734
Isaac Dunham of Hebron & Elizabeth Watrous, Feb. 9, 1735	
Joseph Lay & Mercy Deming,	Feb. 6, 1735
Thomas Baker & widow Hannah Huntley,	March 6, 1735
Jonathan Beebe of New London & Hannah Lewis,	
	March 18, 1735
John Petty & Martha Cogsel,	April 24, 1735
Robert Ames of New London & Deborah Brock-	
way,	May 15, 1735
Samuel Lord & Catharine Ransom,	June 26, 1735
Nathaniel Clark, Jr., & Lydia Peck,	July 10, 1735
Joseph Tubbs & Luce Robbins,	Jan. 14, 1736
Timothy Mather & Sarah Lay,	Feb. 12, 1736
William Ely & widow Mary Noyes,	Feb. 19, 1736
John Peck & Catharine Lay,	March 4, 1736
Robert Miller & Martha Wade,	April 29, 1736
Rev. George Griswold & Elizabeth Lee,	July 20, 1736
Simon Tubbs & Sarah Wait,	Dec. 7, 1736
John Lay, 3d, & Hannah Lee,	Jan. 27, 1737
John Hazen & Deborah Peck,	March 10, 1737
James Marvin & Ruth Mather,	May 25, 1737
Thomas Taylor of Maryland & Esther Robbins, Oct. 6, 1737	
Uriah Roland & Lydia Lee,	Oct. 14, 1737
Jesse Minor of New London & Jane Watrous,	Nov. 3, 1737
Nathaniel Beckwith & Jane Brockway,	Oct. 26, 1738
Nathan Grisbie of Branford & Elizabeth Wade, Dec. 12, 1738	
John Adget & Abigail Graves,	Jan. 18, 1739
Robert Lay & Lydia Tinker,	Feb. 1, 1739
Samuel Beckwith of Norwich & Miriam Marvin, Feb. 1, 1739	
Elisha Marvin & Catharine Mather,	May 17, 1739

Daniel Ayre & Esther Champion,	April 17, 1740
Benjamin Hyde & Abigail Lee,	May 1, 1740
Benoni Hillard & Martha Lord,	July 6, 1740
Ezra Lee & Rebekah Southworth,	Oct. 9, 1740
Benaiah Bushnal of Norwich & Hannah Griswold,	
	Nov. 5, 1740
Ensign Isaac Watrous & widow Mary Lee,	Dec. 23, 1740
Samuel Waller & Elizabeth Brockway,	Nov. 5, 1740
John Anderson & Elizabeth Minor,	Feb. 12, 1741
Eleazar Clarke of Lyme & Sarah Clarke of Nantucket,	Oct. 10, 1741
Eleazar Mather & Ann Watrous,	Nov. 5, 1741
Jonathan Smith & Jane Lewis,	Nov. 10, 1741
Gershom Gardner & Susannah Smith,	Dec. 10, 1741
Amos Tinker & Hannah Minor,	June 6, 1742
George Dorr & Sarah Marvin,	March 16, 1742
John Scovill & Sarah Alger,	Nov. 3, 1742
Benjamin Marvin & Deborah Mather,	Nov. 11, 1742
David Huntley & Mary Tinker,	Dec. 2, 1742
Stephen Beckwith & Jerusha Watrous,	Dec. 16, 1742
David Peck & Abigail Southworth,	June 16, 1743
Benjamin Niles & Lure Sill,	June 30, 1743
Stephen Champion & Abigail Broos (?),	July 11, 1743
Joseph Waite & Margaret Beckwith,	Aug. 10, 1743
Nathaniel Peck & Lure Mather,	May 24, 1744
Andrew Sill & Phebe Mather,	June 19, 1744
Stephen Lee, Jr , & Mehetable Marvin,	Sept. 25, 1744
Elijah Lothrop of Norwich & Susannah Lord,	Jan. 23, 1745
Simon Dewolf & Lucy Calkin,	Jan. 31, 1745
John Mather & Mercy Higgins,	June 13, 1745

MARRIAGES BY REV. STEPHEN JOHNSON.

John Carter of Killingworth & Juda DeWolfe,	—— 18, 1746
Alpheus Tubbs & Phebe DeWolfe,	1747
John Beckwith & Patience Waters,	April 25, 1747
Ezekiel Minor & Margaret Weight,	June 11, 1747
Mr. Smith of Groton & Elizabeth Denison,	June 30, 1747
John Colt & Mary Lord,	July 16, 1747
William Dawry & Mary ——,	Oct. 14, 1747

John Abbot & Sarah Baker,   Dec. 20, 1747
Joseph Sill & Ruth Matson,   Dec. 31, 1747
Frank Ayers & Ruth Matson,   Jan. 14, 1748
Mr. Huntington of Norwich & Hannah Watrous,
                                         Feb. 22, 1748
Phinehas Watrous & Rhoda Smith,   March 3, 1748
Enoch Lord & Hepsibah Marvin,   March 31, 1748
Moses Noyes & ———— Sheldon,   June 2, 1748
Joseph Wade & Esther Chadwick,   June 2, 1748
Samuel Z. Ely & Templias (?) Mather,   July 6, 1748
———— Aciley of Moodus & Bridget Champion, Nov. 23, 1748
Jeremiah Brown & Lydia Smith,   April 3, 1749
Jeremiah Minor & Elizabeth Minor,   Nov. 28, 1749
John Atwell of New London & Ruth Holton, Dec. 12, 1749
Benjamin Tinker & Elizabeth Chadwick,   Dec. 13, 1749
Jabez Sill & Elizabeth Noyes,   Dec. 26, 1749
Josiah Smith, Jr., & Abigail Tinker,   April 16, 1750
Phil—— ———— of Plainfield & Parnel Champion,
                                         April 20, 1750
Noah Beebe & Ede Waller,   May 2, 1750
Mr. Frisley of Branford & Mary ————,   June 13, 1750
Mr. Tully of Saybrook & Elizabeth ————, July 26, 1750
———— ———— of Norwich & Hepsibah ————, Sept. 11, 1750
———— Hill & widow ———— ————,   Oct. 16, 1750
———— Hillhouse of New London & Sarah Griswold,
                                         Nov. 1, 1750
———— Rice of Waterbury & widow Lord,   July 2, 1751
Joshua Harvey & Joanna Sill,   Nov. 17, 1751
———— Carier of Colchester & Elizabeth Robbins,
                                         Nov. 21, 1751
Henry Champion & Sarah Peck,   Dec. 19, 1751
Azariah Mather of Saybrook & Hannah Tucker,
                                         Dec. 26, 1751
J. McCurdy & Anna Lord,   Jan. 16, 1752
John Hacket & Joanna DeWolfe,   Feb. 27, 1752
Stephen Jerome & Mary Graves,   April 2, 1752
Ezra Champion & Mary Bronson,   Oct. 24, 1752
———— Richards of Norwich & Lucy Griswold, Jan. 9, 1753
———— Burnham & Thankful Higgins,   Nov. 5, 1753
Jabez DeWolfe & Eunice Caulkins,   Nov. 15, 1753

Timothy Tiffany & Elizabeth Lord,   Dec. 20, 1753
Doctor Tracy of Norwich & Elizabeth Dorr, April 16, 1754
—— Smith of East Society & —— Smith of
    First Society,   Dec. 5, 1754
Ebenezer Staples & Charity Leonard,   Jan. 30, 1755
Joseph Reynolds of Norwich & Mrs. Phebe Lee,
                                           March 11, 1755
Isaac Watrous & Mrs. Phebe Watrous,   July 17, 1755
Adonijah Marvin & Diodama Miller,   Aug. 20, 1755
Marshfield Parsons & Lois Wait,   Oct. 9, 1755
William Noyes & Eunice Marvin,   April 5, 1756
Seth Tinker & Elizabeth ——,   June 21, 1756
William Kent & Mehetable Lee,   June 21, 1756
Joseph Peck of Norwich & Mrs. Stephen Brockway,
                                           Oct. 12, 1756
Ebenezer Rogers & Elizabeth Mather,   Nov. 18, 1756
Israel Rowley & Lydia Clark,   Dec. 2, 1756
Ensign Josiah Mather & Mrs. Joanna Matson, Dec. 7, 1756
Nathan Jewett & Mrs. Deborah Griswold,   Dec. 9, 1756
Abel More & widow Eunice Hill,   Jan. 6, 1757
Capt. Richard Wait & Rebecca Higgins,   Jan. 13, 1757
Abner Lord & Temperance Coult,   Feb. 28, 1757
Thomas Lee & Mrs. Mehetabel Peck,   July 14, 1757
Levi Bartholomew of Saybrook & Hannah Mack,
                                           Oct. 11, 1757
Jonathan Brockway & Phebe Smith,   Oct. 20, 1757
Phinehas Beckwith & Phebe Wait,   Nov. 24, 1757
William Lay & Phebe Sill,   Dec. 15, 1757
Ezra B—— of Norwich & Mercy Lay,   Jan. 10, 1758
Joseph Chadwick & Parthenia Turps (?),   April 13, 1758
Henry Dalens of Long Island & Ruth Marvin, July 3, 1758
Timothy Tucker of Saybrook & Eunice Wade, Nov. 23, 1758
Stephen Otis & Lois Edgerton,   Feb. 5, 1759
John Bordon & Elizabeth Wait,   Feb. 8, 1759
—— —— & widow Mary Frisby,   April 12, 1759
Ezekiel Huntley & Naomi Tiffany,   Nov. 5, 1759
Jehiel Beriel (?) of Killingworth & Mrs. Abigail
    Peck,   Nov. 21, 1759
Hymas Reed & Margaret Brockway,   Dec. 9, 1759
Jonathan Rogers & Lydia Watrous,   Dec. 30, 1759

John Sears & Judah Peck,   Jan. 24, 1760
John Lay, 4th, & Anna Sill,   Feb. 28, 1760
Jared Elliot of Killingworth & Mrs. Elizabeth Lord,
                                                  April 17, 1760
William Brockway & Susannah Tinker,   Nov. 10, 1760
Lemuel Rogers & Mrs. Hannah Miller,   Dec. 10, 1760
John Alger, Jr., & Elizabeth Wade,   Dec. 25, 1760
Ephraim Brockway, Jr., & Esther Corkins,   Dec. 30, 1760
John Alger & Lucy DeWolf,   Jan. 15, 1761
Ezra Miller & Sarah Mather,   Feb. 19, 1761
Joseph Smith & Mary Matson,   Feb. 26, 1761
William Mordock of Saybrook & Jerusha Lay,
                                                  March 19, 1761
Samuel Watrous & Zeriuah Beckwith,   June 7, 1761
Zachariah Marvin, Jr., & Anna Lee,   July 23, 1761
Waterous Clark & Taphena Lord,   Aug. 13, 1761
Nathaniel Haven, Jr., & Esther Graves,   Aug. 24, 1761
Capt. Timothy Mather & Elizabeth Matson,   Oct. 29, 1761
Lieut. Richard Hays & Dinah Waterouse,   Dec. 24, 1761
Benjamin Hudson, Jr., & Bridget Brockway,   Dec. 29, 1761
Enoch Reed & Phebe Peck,   Jan. 7, 1762
Isaac Terrel of Waterbury & Sarah Smith,   Feb. 25, 1762
George Griffin of East Haddam & Eve Dorr,   March 9, 1762
Simion Bumpus & Experience Gladding,   March 29, 1762
Samuel Griswold & Mary Marvin,   April 13, 1762
Samuel Loudon of New York & Lydia Griswold,
                                                  April 26, 1762
Edward DeWolf & Hannah Huntley,   Oct. 5, 1762
Daniel Chadwick & Hannah Anderson,   Jan. 19, 1763
Benjamin Mather & Abigail Worthington of Col-
   chester,   March 14, 1763
John Snow & Hepzibah Hall,   March 31, 1763
Thomas Rathbone & Mary Wait,   May 5, 1763
——— Beebe of Saybrook & Mary Miller,   Oct. 6, 1763
Rev. Sylvanus Griswold of Springfield & Eliza-
   beth Marvin,   Nov. 17, 1763
Evy Roland & Caroline Chadwick,   Dec. 1, 1763
Ebenezer West of New London & Eunice Griswold,
                                                  Feb. 2, 1764
David Hamel (?) & Esther Hillyards,   March 22, 1764

10

Daniel Lord & Elizabeth Lord,   April 12, 1764
Capt. Barnaby Tuthill of Lyme & Abiah Towne of
    Saybrook,   May 31, 1764
William Roland & Eunice Tinker,   Aug., 1764
John Hayes & Azubah Roland,   Sept. 20, 1764
Uriah Hyde & Mehetable Marvin,   Oct. 9, 1764
Jehoida Mather & Eunice Miller,   Dec., 1764
Benjamin Lathrop of Norwich & Huldah Lord,
                                              Jan. 8, 1765
Elijah Ely & Catharine Lee,   Feb. 14, 1765
Elisha Wade of Lyme & Mary Jones of Saybrook,
                                             April 11, 1765
Joseph Sill & Azubah DeWolf,   April 23, 1765
Peter Lay & Hepzibah Peck,   June 13, 1765
Ezra Marvin & Susanna Peck,   Jan. 17, 1766
William Miller & Urania Brockway,   Aug. 26, 1766
William Marshfield Parsons & Abigail Marvin,
                                             Nov. 20, 1766
Timothy Mather, Jr., & Martha DeWolf,   Dec. 18, 1766
Ira Buel of Litchfield & Prudence Deming,   Jan. 29, 1767
Isaiah Rogers & Elizabeth Sill,   Jan. 15, 1767
Noah Miller & Wealthy Brockway,   March 3, 1767
Jonathan Royce & Sarah Marvin,   March 19, 1767
Nathaniel Willard & Sibil Jones, both of Saybrook,
                                             June 16, 1767
Daniel Hall & Mahitable Peck,   Aug. 13, 1767
Noah Miller & widow Sarah Smith,   Aug. 27, 1767
Silvanus Smith & Elizabeth Wait,   Oct. 1, 1767
Benjamin Marvin, Jr., & Phebe Roland,   Oct. 29, 1767
Reuben Chadwick & Martha Miller,   Dec. 11, 1767
George Miller & Fanny Chadwick,   Dec. 30, 1767
John Wade, Jr., & Hannah Huntley,   March 31, 1768
William Mather & Rhoda Marvin,   May 1, 1768
James Ely & Catharine Hays,   June 30, 1768
—— Carter of Marlborough & Huldah Marvin,
                                              Nov. 3, 1768
Edward Havens & Patience Beebe,   Dec. 15, 1768
Samuel Hill & Ede Bailey,   Jan. 2, 1769
Christopher Ely & Ede Marvin,   April 13, 1769
Ezra Hall & Sarah Gillette,   April 20, 1769

Ephraim Hubbell of New Fairfield & Sarah Sill,
                                    Sept. 14, 1769
Charles Church Chandler of Woodstock & Marian
    Griswold,   Sept. 28, 1769
Abel Hall & Caroline Brockway,   Oct. 13, 1769
Martin Tinker & Mary Peck,   Nov. 2, 1769
Thomas Lee & widow Tillerly (?) Terril,   Jan. 22, 1770
William Livingston & Rachel Brockway,   March 12, 1770
Jared Buckingham of Saybrook & Lucy Mather,
                                    May 3, 1770
Lee Lay & Louisa Griswold,   Jan. 1, 1771
Mather Peck & Esther Coult,   April 25, 1771
Roswell Clark & Parnel Peck,   May 9, 1771
George Wade & widow Lydia DeWolf,   Oct. 3, 1771
Elias Mather & Lucinda Lee,   Oct. 17, 1771
Ezra Lay & Deborah Mather,   Nov. 14, 1771
William Smith & Mary More,   Jan. 8, 1772
Barnaby Herrick of North Kingston & Abigail
    Brown,   March 22, 1772
Josiah Beebe of Millington & Ruth Dowly (?),
                                    April 14, 1772
Martin Miner & Elizabeth Davis,   June 11, 1772
Dr. Hezekiah Brainerd of Haddam & Elizabeth
    Johnson,   Nov. 5, 1772
John Griswold & Sarah Johnson,   Nov. 5, 1772
Allen McKnight & Esther Comstock,   Nov. 5, 1772
John Wait & Rebecca Mather,   Nov. 19, 1772
Samuel Ingraham, Jr., & Abigail Clark,   Nov. 26, 1772
Richard Lay & Mercy Mather,   April 18, 1773
Amasa Ransom of Colchester & Nabby Mather, May 6, 1773
John Coult & Abigail Matson,   May 11, 1773
Andrew Sill, Jr., & Eleanor Dorr,   June, 1773
Silvanus Higgins & Elizabeth Clark,   July 15, 1773
Jared Cone & Mary Brockway of Millington, Aug. 10, 1773
John Ayres & Clarisia Lay,   Nov. 4, 1773
Francis Ingram & Lucretia Tinker,   Nov. 24, 1773
Silas Tinker & Lois Wade,   Dec. 14, 1773
Timothy Tiffany & Parthena Coult,   Jan., 1774
Capt. Levi Riley of Wethersfield & Mehetable Bailey,
                                    Jan. 23, 1774

Edward Roland & Catharine Weed,	Jan. 27, 1774
Edward Dorr & Judith Champion,	Jan. 26, 1774
Reynold Gillet & Martha Marvin,	June 9, 1774
Stephen Johnson & Anna Lord,	Sept. 1, 1774
Silas Leonard & Mary Hacket,	Sept. 1, 1774
Isaac Perkins & Lois Beebe,	Oct. 25, 1774
John Peck, Jr., & Elizabeth Smith,	Nov. 3, 1774
Samuel Selden, Jr., & Sarah Marvin,	Nov. 24, 1774
David Conkling of Long Island & Parnel Perkins of Norwich,	May 17, 1775
John Anderson, Jr., & Lydia Clark,	May 25, 1775
Silvanus Clark & Eunice Anderson,	May 28, 1775
Dan Chadwick & Hannah Huntley,	May 28, 1775
Latham Smith & Lois Miller,	March 3, 1776
Gershom Waterous, Jr., & Mehetable Ransom,	April 11, 1776
John Daniels & Lucretia Waterouse,	April 21, 1776
Stephen DeWolf & Sarah Greenfield,	May 16, 1776
Robert Denison & ―― Wade,	Feb. 16, 1777
David Pratt of Saybrook & Eunice ――,	March 23, 1777
Benjamin Higgins & Jane Peck,	Nov. 26, 1777
Capt. Gates of Colchester & widow Judith Sears,	Nov. 26, 1777
Dr. Caulkins & widow More,	Jan. 1, 1778
Robert Saunders & Sarah Armstrong,	Jan. 7, 1778
Amos Smith & Lucinda Miller,	March 12, 1778
Greenfield Alger & Lucy Wade,	March 26, 1778
Constant Baker of Millington & ―― Brockway,	March 26, 1778
Mr. Green of Middletown & widow Smith,	April 8, 1778
Nathaniel Rogers of Lebanon & Susanna Marvin,	April 23, 1778
Gurdon Clark & Ruth Sill,	July 16, 1778
Clemens Fostick of New London & Eunice Way,	Oct. 20, 1778
John Scovel & Esther Manchester, both of Tivertown,	Jan. 22, 1779
Josiah Smith, Jr., & Parthena Rowland,	Feb. 17, 1779
John Parsons & Joanna Mather,	Feb. 25, 1779
William Wallace & Esther DeWolf,	April 8, 1779
Ensign Zachariah Marvin & Hannah Lay,	April 15, 1779

Silvanus Clark & Elisabeth Kent, Aug. 1, 1779
William Peck & Judith Marvin, Aug. 5, 1779
Mr. Chubbs of Glastonberry & Sally Tinker, Nov. 24, 1779
Dan Lee & Lurania Champlin, Nov. 25, 1779
Nathaniel Rogers, Jr., of Lebanon & Abigail Lay,
Dec. 9, 1779
Matthew Peck & Polly King, Dec. 9, 1779
Silas Sill & Hannah Lynde Griswold, Dec. 9, 1779
Elisha Brockway & Abigail Hall, Dec. 16, 1779
William Champlin & Polly Mather, Jan. 13, 1780
Roswell Beckwith & Lydia Dow, Jan. 13, 1780
Nathan Tinker & Mehetable Beckwith, Feb. 17, 1780
William Higgins & Fanny Bailey, Feb. 24, 1780
Thomas Doolittle of Middletown & Elisabeth Beck-
with, March 16, 1780
Moses Marvin & Zilpah Gillette, March 20, 1780
Richard Chadwick & Mehetable Terry, April 6, 1780
Uriah Sandford of Saybrook & Lois Huntley, May 11, 1780
Mr. Fosdwick of Wethersfield & Prudence Bailey,
June 12, 1780
Rev. Richard Roswell Elliot of Watertown, in Massa-
chusetts Bay, & Catherine Johnson, Oct. 5, 1780
Christopher Higgins & Hepzibah Read, Oct. 12, 1780
George Chadwick, Jr., & Wealthy Brown, Dec. 7, 1780
Joseph Peck & Sally Miller, Dec. 21, 1780
Reuben Champion & Esther Chadwick, Dec. 28, 1780
Obadiah Jones of Saybrook & Elisabeth Miller,
May 17, 1781
Samuel Beckwith & Polly Greenfield, June 21, 1781
Alexander Stewart of Philadelphia & Betsy McCurdy,
Sept. 16, 1781
Silas Champlin & Betsy Lay, Oct. 18, 1781
Samuel DeWolf & Susanna Keney, Jan. 17, 1782
Samuel Sanford of Saybrook & Deborah Matson,
Feb. 21, 1782
John Lewis & Lucinda Read, March 7, 1782
John Daniels & Eunice Beckwith, March 13, 1782
Peter Tinker & Ann Johnson, April 4, 1782
Joseph Hyde & Esther Tinker, April 18, 1782
Stephen Mather & Elisabeth Peck, Sept. 5, 1782

Nathaniel Rogers of Colchester & Sarah Tubbs,
                                    Sept. 23, 1782
Mr. Burnham of Hartford & Molly Lewis,   Sept. 23, 1782
Abraham Pratt of Saybrook & Mehetable Marvin,
                                    Sept. 26, 1782
Stephen DeWolf & Theodosia Anderson,   Dec. 1, 1782
Tory Maswel of Westerly & Betty Champlin, Dec. 11, 1782
John Miner & Phœbe Robbins,   Dec. 12, 1782
John Weaks of New London & Charlotte Richards,
                                    Dec. 26, 1782
Richard Peck & Elisabeth Mather,   March 13, 1783
John Nicholas Gennin & Anna Furmensee,   Sept. 4, 1783
Lieut. John Sill & widow Lucy Peck,   Sept. 22, 1783
David Howell of Long Island & Ruhamah Sill,
                                    Oct. 30, 1783
Capt. Elisha Champion & Phebe Miller,   Nov. 27, 1783
Benjamin Greenman of Stephenton & Lydia Brown,
                                    Dec. 9, 1783
Ezra Ingraham & Betsy Robbins,   Jan. 15, 1784
Elisha Robbins & widow Lydia Cooley,   Jan. 15, 1784
Zenas Huntley & Elisabeth Peck,   Feb. 14, 1784
Joseph Miller & Dolly Chadwick,   Feb. 19, 1784
Abel Rogers & Hannah Rogers,   Feb. 19, 1784
Ezra Chadwick & Sally Lay,   May 11, 1784
Thomas Marvin & Sarah Lay,   May 23, 1784
Lebbeus Peck & Lydia Lee,   June 17, 1784
Joseph Noyes & Jane Lord,   July 26, 1784
Lieut. Elkanah Higgins of East Haddam & Sarah
    Dorr   Aug. 4, 1784
Elijah Beckwith & Sarah Miller,   Aug. 22, 1784
Joseph Read & Phebe Read,   Aug. 23, 1784
Lynde Champion & Hepsibah Chadwick,   Jan. 18, 1785
John Mather & widow Esther Robbins,   Feb. 20, 1785
John Brown & Eunice Robbins,   Feb. 24, 1785
Richard Rogers & Elisabeth Kenny,   March 22, 1785
Silvanus Mather & Caroline Chadwick,   May 12, 1785
William Noyes, Jr., & Sally Banks of Newark, N. J.,
                                    Oct. 2, 1785
Eliphalet Wheeler of Norwalk & Jane L. Robbins,
                                    March 12, 1786

Elisha Hart of Saybrook & Gennet McCurdy, June 12, 1786
Remick Wait & Susanna Matson,   June 29, 1786
Stephen Tucker, Jr., & Lavinia Wade,   July 11, 1786
Richard McCurdy & Ursula W. Griswold,   Sept. 10, 1794
Nathaniel Mather & Eunice DeWolf,   Feb. 19, 1795
Jonathan Douglass of New London & Nabby Lay,
                                             May 31, 1795
Ezra Robbins & Hannah Chadwick,   June 25, 1795
John Prentice & Miss Frink of New London,   Nov. 1, 1795
Nehemiah Clark & Elisabeth Wood,   Nov. 5, 1795
Ezra Mather & Phebe Wade,   Nov. 8, 1795
Caleb Dart & Anna Tinker,   Jan. 13, 1796
John Mack & Betsy Miner,   Feb. 1, 1796
Daniel P. Lee & Polly Miller, both of New London,
                                             Feb. 14, 1796
Woolcott Lord & Polly Wilkinson,   Feb. 21, 1796
John J. Cornell of New London & ——— Smith,
                                             March 20, 1796
Daniel Robbins & Susanna Lay,   March 26, 1796
Andrew Watrous & Sally Mather,   March 27, 1796
Elias Hutson & Lucinda Miller,   June 25, 1796
William Coult & Nancy Denison,   Oct. 2, 1796
Timothy Tucker of Saybrook & Naomi Daniels,
                                             Oct. 28, 1796
Edward Havens, Jr., & Nancy Wood,   Dec. 11, 1796
John Van DeHourage & Huldah Rogers,   Jan. 8, 1797
Clark Peck of Bloomfield, N. Y., & Caroline Hall,
                                             Jan. 18, 1797
Francis Havens of Shelter Island & Martha Jane
   Lay,   April 16, 1797
Matthew Roland & Sally DeWolf,   April 23, 1797
Josiah Burnham, Jr., & Lucy Smith,   Aug. 1, 1797
Ichabod Smith, Jr., & Nabby Marvin,   Oct. 29, 1797
David Lay & Lucy Ingraham,   Feb. 8, 1798
Jesse Roland & Sally Greenfield,   Feb. 11, 1798
Daniel Havens & Phebe Galway of Stonington,
                                             March 4, 1798
Samuel Buckingham of Saybrook & Joanna Matson,
                                             March 8, 1798
Seth Lee & Anna Hill,   March 22, 1798

Richard Sparrow of Harrison County, Va., & Eunice
    Smith,   May 13, 1798
Daniel Jacobs & Polly Chadwick,   June 14, 1798
Levi Hathaway & Polly Clark,   Oct. 18, 1798
James Gillet & Elisabeth Peck,   Nov. 29, 1798
Charles Strong of Colchester & Abigail Derby,
                                             Nov. 29, 1798
Phineas Watrous & Hannah Chadwick,   Dec. 25, 1798
Stephen DeWolf & Abigail Beckwith,   Jan. 3, 1799
Thomas Smith of New York & Azubah Wade,   Jan. 30, 1799
Joseph Peck & Anna Reed,   Feb. 7, 1799
Joseph Chadwick & Phebe Peck,   June 13, 1799
Rufus Huntley & Polly Lay,   Dec. 22, 1799

NEW HARTFORD.

LITCHFIELD COUNTY.

New Hartford incorporated in October, 1738. The First Congregational Church was organized in 1738. Rev. Jonathan Marsh, pastor 1739-1794. The following are all the marriages.

Daniel Church & Eunice R——y (?),   Dec. 1, 1743
Asa Hill & Elizabeth Richards,   March, 1744-5
Jonathan Marsh, Jr., & Theodia Kellogg (?), April 4, 1745
Abraham Kellogg & Sarah Marsh,   June 17, 1747
Joseph Marsh & Elizabeth Marsh,   ——
Uriah Seymour & Elizabeth Andrus,   ——
Justus Acdman (?) & Ann Merrell,   April 27, 1756
Seth Smith & Deliverance Cadwell,   Feb. 17, 1757
John Miller & Hannah Merrill,   Feb. 17, 1757
Moses Marsh & Sarah Merrill,   May, 1757
—— Parks & Sibil Douglass,   Nov., 1757
John Marsh & Lucina Seymour,   Feb. 2, 1758
—— Smith & Mehatibel Goodwin,   Feb. 2, 1758
Roger Olmstead & Eunice Marsh,   Feb. 9, 1758
Samuel Merrell & Mary Merrell,   March, 1758
Jonathan Goodwin & Esther Benham,   May 10, 1758
John Wallin & Hannah Merrell,   June 1, 1758

Oliver Collar & Mary Wallin,   Oct. 30, 1758
Otis Ensign & Ruth Wallin,   Dec. 8, 1758
Samuel Nio—— (Indian) & Patience ——,   Feb. 8, 1759
Ashbel Kellogg & Sarah Loomis,   April 5, 1759
Zebulon Seymour, Jr., & Ann Marsh,   Sept. 25, 1759
Ashbel Andrus & Hannah Seymour,   Dec. 30, 1759
Thomas Ollcott, Jr., & —— Humphrey of Symes-
  bury,   Dec. 18, 1760
Ichabod Merrell & Mary Merrell,   March 15, 1761
William Charles Hulitt & Mary Ann Keith,   Nov. 29, 1761
Joseph Merrell, 2d, & Mary Merrell,   March 2, 1762
Jonathan Merrell, Jr., & Hannah Douglass,   June 10, 1762
Samuel Cravatt & Phebe Austin,   Oct., 1762
Cyprian Watson & Dorothy Binton,   Oct. 17, 1762
Joseph Bacon & Mary Douglass,   Nov. or Dec., 1762
Joseph Phelps & Sarah Cadwell,   Feb 1, 1763
Dudley Case & Susanna Merrell,   April 29, 1763
Eliezer Goodwin, Jr., & Mehetibel Cadwell,   1763
James Benham & Huldah Kellogg,   1763
Joseph King & ——isha Marsh,   Sept. 21, 1763
George Merrell & Sarah Case,   April 25, 1763
Nehemiah Andrus & Phebe Byham (?),   Oct. 30, 1765
Elias Merrell & Lydia Andrus,   Jan., 1766
Ashbell Kellogg & Lydia Steel,   July 17, 1766
Hezekiah Seymour & Ruth Kellogg,   Sept. 11, 1766
Israel Loomis (?) & Anna Merrell,   ——
Solomon Woodruff & Hannah Goodwin,   Nov. 20, 1766
Elijah Seymour & Asenath Hurlburt,   Jan., 1767
Edward Bliss & Susanna Shepard,   May 28, 1767
John Gilbert & Theodosia Marsh,   Aug. 9, 1767
Samuel Ensign & Mary Ives,   Sept. 4, 1767
Eli Andrus & Abigail Merrell,   Nov. 2, 1767
Joseph Merrell, Jr., & Lydia Flower,   May 29, 1768
John Nicholson of Sheffield & Sarah Steel,   July 21, 1768
Timothy Wells & Meriam Douglass,   Oct. 6, 1768
Matthew Gillet, Jr., & Lois Douglass,   ——
James Peck (?) & Huldah Steel,   Nov. 10, 1768
Ebenezer Moodey & Zerviah Seymour,   Nov. 17, 1768
Nathaniel Foot of Colchester & Jerusha Cadwell,
                                                                          March 24, 1769

Nathaniel Doud of Sandisfield & Bulah Merrell,

          July 13, 1769

Rev. Ebenezer Davenport of Greenwich & Mrs.

 Lois Marsh of New Hartford,   Nov. 30, 1769

Joseph Smith of Weathersfield & Elizabeth Merrell,

           Jan. 17, 1770

  (A line in pencil, " Was Josiah Smith of Winsted.")

Elijah Seymour & Abigail Chapin,   March 1, 1770

John Ives of Wallingford & Sarah Henderson (?),

          May 29, 1770

Jonathan Amo—— (?) & Hannah Loomis, —— 28, 1770

Alisha or Abijah Rice (?) & Elizabeth Watson, Jan., 1771

Zebulon Robbins of Canaan & Lois Steel, July 16, 1771

Solomon Woodruff & Thodosia Merrell,   1771

Tim —— (?) & Mrs. Gillet,   1771

Jonathan Marsh (Nuftus fuit Cum) & Elisabetha

 Sheldon of Hartfordia, pr. D. Whitman. She

 died May 20, 1749, aged 30 years, Feb. 26, 1740–1

Jonathan Marsh (Nuptus fuit Cum) & Mariana

 Keith of Hartfordia, pr. D. Dorr, May 27, 1751

Zebulon Seymour, Jr., & Ann Marsh, my daughter,

         Sept. 25, 1759

William Charles Hulett (?) & Mary Ann Keith,

 Mrs. Marsh 2d daughter,   Nov. 29, 1761

Joseph King of Middletown & Jerusha Marsh, my

 daughter,   Sept. 31, 1765

Isaac Marsh & Lucy Smith,   Sept. 8, 1775

Abner Beech of Goshen & Mary Marsh, my daugh-

 ter,   June 27, 1775

Caleb Watson & Hannah Marsh,   Nov. 15, 1779

Jerijah (?) Merrell & Elizabeth Marsh, Aug. 10, 1780

Luke Cooley & Margret Marsh,   Sept. 12, 1786

John Collins & Fanny or Ireney (?) Marsh, Feb. 25, 1788

Elias Benham & —— ——,   1771

—— Ives & Rhoda Merrell,   ——

Timothy Steel & Abigail Church, Dec. 28, 1772

Abraham Kellogg, Jr., & Sarah Seymour, Feb. 5, 1772

Theodore Gilbert, Jr., & Hannah Chapin, July 25, 1772

David Seymour & Martha Chapin, Aug. 29, 1772

Ambrose Humphry & Rebecca Chubb,	Sept. 24, 1772
Elijah Flower & Cloe Marsh,	Oct. 1, 1772
Zebulon Shepard & Ruth Hurlbert,	Dec. 23, 1773
Bildad Merrell & Damarus Mix,	Jan. 16, 1774
Joseph Gilbert & Miriam Hopkins,	March 21, 1774
Ezekiel Markham & Phebe (?) Balcom (?),	July, 1774
Stephen Merrell & Ann Flower,	Oct., 1774
Oliver Bronson (?) of Dothan & Sarah Merrell,	J—, 1775
Abraham Webster of Hartford & Rachel Marsh (?),	
	Jan., 1775
James Richards, Jr., of Lenox & Sarah W——,	Feb. 2, 1775
Nathaniel Ives, Jr., & Susanna Henderson,	April 13, 1775
John Spencer, Jr., & Jerusha Henderson,	June 1, 1775
Abner Beach of Goshen & Mary Marsh, my daughter,	June 27, 1775
Nathan Webster & Mary Andrus,	Aug., 1775
Timothy Barns & Elizabeth Goodwin,	Oct. 12, 1775
Isaac Loomis & Rachel Merrell,	Nov. 2, 1775
Asher Bull & Hannah Hopkins,	May 23, 1776
Isaac Spencer & Anna Tyler,	July 18, 1776
David Butler & Mary Kellogg,	Nov. 28, 1776
Stephen Pitkin (?) & Jemima Tyler,	Jan. 9, 1777
Elijah Seymour & Mary Marsh,	July 3, 1777
Benoni Jones & Lucy Hudson of Barkhamsted,	July 24, 1777
George Humphry of Symsbury & Eliz. Pe—bou (?),	
	Aug. 7, 1777
Josiah Russel & Margaret Smith,	Sept. 4, 1777
Isaac Steel & Dorothy Pitkin,	Sept. 11, 1777
Benjamin Bartholomew & Mary Spencer,	Nov. 17, 1777
Eliphalet Ensign, Jr., & Esther Dickinson,	Nov. 20, 1777
——eriah Seymour, Jr., & Dorcas Ensign,	Nov. 20, 1777
Seth Steel & Hannah Keener (?),	Nov. 20, 1777
Cyprian (?) Kellogg & Mary Merrell,	Dec. 10, 1777
Jesse Steel & Mehetable Segur,	Dec. 10, 1777
William Richards & Mary Shepard,	April 23, 1778
James Henderson & Mary Cook (?),	——
Roger Sheldon & Eliz. Marsh,	May 7, 1778
Abraham Pettibone, Jr., & Amelia Smith,	May 21, 1778
Nathan Munro of Canaan & Mehitable Seymour,	
	Aug. 16, 1778

Riverius Newell & Sarah Peck of Harwinton,   Nov. 9, 1778
Isaac Cornwell & Candace Smith,   Dec. 3, 1778
Doctor Eldad Merrell & Hannah Ames,   Dec. 17, 1778
John (J.) Parks of Farmington & Sarah Walton, Jan. 12, 1778
Samuel Cole of Norfolk & Elizabeth Marsh (?), April 7, 1779
Moses Bran (?) of Hartford & Martha B—ow,   —— 8, 1779
Seth Spencer & Jerusha Pettibone,   May 20, 1779
Jesse Hyatt & Sabra Chapin,   June 10, 1779
Thomas Paine & Elizabeth Paine,   Oct. 10, 1779
Matthias Hulbert & Experience Kellogg,   ——
Caleb Watson & Hannah Marsh,   Nov. 15, 1779
Stephen Knowlton & Diadema Chubb,   Feb. 3, 1780
Samuel Johnson of Harwinton & Obedience Barns,
                                               April 20, 1780
Jonathan Marsh, Jr., & Damarus ——tkin,   —— 29, 1780
Frederick Webster Kellogg & Margaret Moor,   —— 4, 1780
Ebenezer Newile of Richmont & Nancy Flower, —— 24, 1780
Jesse Goodwin, Jr., & Nabby Mix,   —— 7, 1780
Joseph Smith of Ashford & Sarah —aylord,   —— 13, 1780
Phinehas Cadwell & Eleanor Heydon,   Dec. 21, 1780
William Barret & Susanna Spencer,   Jan. 3, 1781
Elisha Kelsey (?) & Martha ——,   May 1, 1781
Moses Douglass & Han— (?) Spencer,   June 28, 1781
Rhoderick Hopkins & Mary M—— (?),   Oct. 4, 1781
David Covil (?) & Sarah Marsh,   Oct. 25, 1781
George Flower & Roxelinda Crow,   Feb. 5, 1782
Josiah Gaylord & Mary Ann Kellogg,   May 2, 1782
Eldest son of John Foot of Symsbury & Lois Mills,
                                               July 4, 1782
Solomon Woodruff & Ruth Ensign,   Aug. 8, 1782
Ezekiel Lewis & —— Andrus,   Sept. 3, 1782
James Hill & Rachel Millar,   Oct. 17, 1782
Jesse Gilbert & Lucy Chapman,   June 25, 1783
Joseph Scovil (?) of Cornwall & Lomhamah (?)
     Chapin,   July 5, 1782
Jonathan Porter of East Hartford & Hannah Fit-
     kin (?),   July 10, 1783
Caleb Watson & Cloe Merrell,   Dec. 25, 1783
Ezra Yale of Farmington & Lydia Merrell,   Jan. 22, 1784
—— Churchill of Newington & Ruth Merrell, Feb. 4, 1784

Amos Tyler & Esther Kellogg,	May 27, 1784
Jonas Safford of Poultney & Joanna Merrell,	Aug. 1, 1784
Charles Day of Hartford, East Side, & Sarah Merrell,	Oct. 20, 1784
James Spencer & Thankful Potter,	Nov. 14, 1784
Noah Seymour & Miriam Kellogg,	Dec., 1784
Shubael Crow & Huldah Adams,	March 25, 1785
William Thrall & Joana Kellogg,	May 5, 1785
Chauncey Seymour & Isabel Sedwick,	June 2, 1785
Amos Marsh & Lydia Benham,	July 21, 1785
James Benham & Sally Sedwick,	Oct. 14, 1785
Ephraim Tucker & widow Esther Roberts,	Dec. 12, 1785
Amos Rust & Allbray Spencer,	Nov. 24, 1785
———— ———— of Wallingford & Ruth Ives,	Nov. 24, 1785
Thomas Cook & Hannah Catlin, both of Harwinton,	Feb. 18, 1786
Moses Kellogg & Mabel Merrell,	Jan. 19, 1786
Gamaliel Hemstead & Esther Goodwin,	Feb. 9, 1786
Luke Cooley of Somers & Margaret Marsh,	Sept. 12, 1786
———— Fox & Eleanor Wallin,	Dec. 13, 1786
Preserved Crisie of Winchester & Rah (?) Kellogg,	Jan. 11, 1787
William Henshaw of Wells & Rus (?) Brace (?),	Jan. 11, 1787
William Heydon & Elizabeth Webster, at Harwinton,	Jan. 31, 1787
Amos Parker of Colebrook & Lois Ives,	Feb. 8, 1787
John Collar & Sophia Hills,	Aug. 26, 1787
Elisha Lewis & Rhoda Tyler,	Sept. 27, 1787
Robert Coe or Cox & Tryphena Tyler,	Oct. 15, 1787
Eliezer Goodwin & Hannah Merrell,	Jan. 24, 1788
Truman Kellogg & Hannah Merrell,	Feb. 3, 1788
Levi Neal & Abigail Andrus,	Feb. 7, 1788
John Collins of Enfield & Fanny Marsh,	Feb. 25, 1788
Jonathan Heydon & Livinia Ensign,	Feb. 28, 1788

(NOTE—Married 173 in New Hartford ye last, Feb. 28, 1788.)

Noah Merrell & Zulima (?) Flowers,	April 20, 1788
William Cook & Theodosia Gilbert,	1788
Tyrus Goodwin & Polly Canary,	Aug. 14, 1788
Ashbel Marsh & Abigail Ward of Barkhamsted,	Nov. 27, 1788

Eli Seymour of Hartford & Amy Marsh,	Nov. 27, 1788
Phinehas Chapin & Sarah Mix,	Dec. 7, 1788
David Risley & Cynthia Gillet,	Jan. 8, 1789
Roswell Marsh & Anna Crow,	Jan. 18, 1789
Nathan Gurney & Polly Seymour,	Feb. 12, 1789
Thomas Mather & Hannah Woodruff,	June 14, 1789
Elijah Covey of Bristol & Sarah Burdick,	Sept. 16, 1789
Jerijah (?) Merrell & Tryphena Merrell,	Sept. 20, 1789
Josiah Shepard & Esther Gilbert,	Sept. 21, 1789
Solomon Williams of Groton & Lucy Barns,	Sept. 27, 1789

(NOTE—Married 187 before Jan. 1, 1790.)

Timothy Pitkin & Sybil Cowles,	May 27, 1790
Ashbel Kellogg & Martha Bacon Ward,	June 3, 1790
Israel Barns & Lucy Gillet,	June 24, 1790
Abraham Filley of Winchester & Lucretia Merrell,	
	July 29, 1790
Francis West of Stephentown, N. Y., & Abigail Burdick,	
	Dec. 30, 1790
Nathaniel Betts of Sandisfield & Candace Ives,	
	Jan. 27, 1791
Rufus Northway (?) & Cynthia Marsh,	Feb. 13, 1791
Constantine S——h & Artenath (?) Seymour,	——17, 1791
Nathaniel Parks of Bristol & I——na Walling (her legal residence unknown),	May 17, 1791
Eliphalet Bill of Farmington & Lois Hubbard of Granville,	July 4, 1791
Benjamin Henshaw, Jr., & El—— (?) Wheeler of Hartford,	Aug. 18, 1791
John Marsh, Jr., & Anna Cale (?) of Middletown,	
	Aug. 18, 1791
Sebe Mather & Susanna Wells,	Sept. 7, 1791
Elijah Kellogg & Deborah Ward,	Oct. 2, 1791
Nehemiah Andrus, Jr., & Zerviah Gillet,	Oct. 3, 1791
Birzavith Hopkins of Berlin & Phebe Fain or Fair (?),	
	Feb. 16, 1791
Arnold Humphry of Symsbury & Amelia Spencer,	
	May 3, 1792
Samuel Douglass & Theodosia Spencer,	May 3, 1792
Michael Merrell & Tryphena Merrell,	May 3, 1792

George Hopkins & Rachel Russel,   July 26, 1792
Isaac Steel & Lavinia Goodwin,   Oct. 28, 1792
William Calloway of Sandisfield, Mass., & Sally Col-
     lar,   Dec. 27, 1792
Sylvester Seymour & Lucretia Gillet,   Feb. 25, 1793
Samuel Kelly & Polly Ward,   March 6, 1793
Billy Seymour of Hartford & Hannah Goodwin,
                                               Aug. 19, 1793
Isaac Williams & widow Hale,   Sept. 19, 1793
Denny or Denison Andrus & Huldah Andrus, Oct. 13, 1793
Fredan Wright of Winchester & Jerusha Sheldon,
                                               Oct. 31, 1793
James Landon of Warren & Elizabeth Frisbe, Dec. 1, 1793
Noah Holcom of Canaan & Elizabeth Cadwell,
                                               Jan. 26, 1794
Mr. Peck of Bristol, Esq., & Mindwell Chubb, May 21, 1794
John Buck of Bristol & Polly Wilcocks,   June 13, 1794

FAIRFIELD—WESTPORT.

FAIRFIELD COUNTY.

Fairfield was settled in 1639. Named 1645. Of the several Congregational churches in old Fairfield, the one located at Green's Farms (in Westport) was organized in 1715. The following are the marriages recorded. Rev. David Chapman, pastor from 1715 to 1741. Rev. Daniel Buckingham, 1742 to 1766.

Phinehas Chapman & Sarah Cetchum,   Sept. 22, 1742
Richard Elwood & Rachel Davis,   Feb. 21, 1742–3
Joshua Disbrow & Mary Gray,   June 7, 1743
Humphrey Ogden & Hannah Bennet,   Nov. 22, 1743
David Hendrick & Mary Fountain,   Nov. 22, 1743
Mr. Stephen Wakeman & Sarah Jesup,   Jan. 11, 1743–4
Ebenezer Mead & Mary Frost,   Aug. 1, 1744
Harry & Elizabeth (servants of George Cable), Nov. 21, 1744
Jeremiah Sturges, Jr., & Rebeccah Lyon,   Feb. 14, 1744–5
David Crissy & Eunice Frost,   March 26, 1745
Gershum Lyon & Mary Buckley,   April 25, 1745
John Morehouse & Mary Jesup,   May 16, 1745

Ephraim Beers & Mary Fanten,	Dec. 24, 1745
Nathan Bennet & Hannah Sturges,	June 17, 1746
Moses Bennet & Eunice Hurlburt,	June 17, 1746
Peter Blackman & Abigail Beers,	Oct. 14, 1746
Eleazer Godfrey & Rachel Bennet,	Jan. 21, 1746–7
Shubael Gorham & Rebecca Hurlburt,	Jan. 21, 1746–7
Jeremiah Sherwood & Abigail Sturges,	Feb. 3, 1746–7
Joseph Couch & Hannah Sherwood,	May 7, 1747
Stephen Lyon & Grace Webb,	July 21, 1747
Ebenezer Stebins & Ann Davis,	Jan. 13, 1747–8
David Adams & Sarah Squire,	Nov. 2, 1748
Ichbod Gorham & Sarah Barlow,	Feb. 2, 1748–9
Nathan Guire & Elizabeth Darling,	March 1, 1748–9
Ebenezer Squire & Eunice Morehouse,	April 21, 1749
Joseph Betts & Abigail Whitney,	Nov. 29, 1749
Moses Saintjohn of Norwalk & Mary Couch of Fairfield,	Dec. 19, 1749
Abel Sherwood & Hannah Fountain,	Jan. 1, 1749–50
Nathan Johnson & Sarah Nicols,	Jan. 11, 1749–50
Nathan Beers & Ann Burr,	Jan. 16, 1749–50
David Sherwood & Eunice Cable,	Jan. 16, 1749–50
Christopher Sturges, Jr., of Stamford & Hannah Davis of Fairfield,	Jan. 18, 1749–50
Benjamin Steward of Norwalk & Eleanor Sherwood of Fairfield,	Feb. 7, 1749–50
Mingo (negro servant of Joseph Wakeman) & Nany (negro servant of Stephen Wakeman),	Feb., 1749–50
Thomas Couch & Elizabeth Jesup,	Feb. 25, 1749–50
Joseph Cetchum of Norwalk & Elizabeth Hurlburt of Fairfield,	March 8, 1749–50
Michael Morehouse & Elizabeth Mills,	Aug. 23, 1750
Samuel Turny & Mary Baker,	Nov. 5, 1750
David Barlow & Esther Sturges,	Nov. 29, 1750
Isaiah Cole of Rhode Island & Eleanor Nicols of Fairfield,	Jan. 30, 1750–51
Jack (negro servant of Deacon Hide) & Cate (negro servant of Nathaniel Adams),	April, 1751
Isaac Oysterbanks & Sarah Jecox,	June 20, 1751
Ebenezer Munrow & Mary Dunkin,	Jan. 1, 1751–52

John Hazard & Mary Wakeman,	April 9, 1752
Isaac Gorham & Ann Wakeman,	July 26, 1752
Elnathan Hanford, Jr., of Norwalk & Anna Cable	
of Fairfield,	Sept. 15, 1752
Joseph Smith & Esther Lyon of Greenfield,	
	(N. S.), Oct. 3, 1752
Gershom Whitehead & Martha Buckley,	Nov. 1, 1752
Jabez Gorham & Mary Couch,	Nov. 27, 1752
Oliver Taylor of Danbury & Jane Williams,	Nov. 29, 1752
Benjamin Dean & Mary Squire,	Dec. 6, 1752
Obediah Platt & Eunice Bradley,	Dec. 19, 1752
Simon Couch, Jr., & Rebeccah Nash,	Dec. 27, 1752
John Davis & Elizabeth Meker,	Jan. 3, 1753
John Dikeman & Mary Coley,	Jan. 3, 1753
Jabez Gray & Betty Jecox,	Jan. 17, 1753
Samson (negro of Sarah Jesup) & Betty (negro of	
John Andrews),	Jan. 23, 1753
Joseph Elwood & Eleanor Dibble,	Feb. 20, 1753
Seth Down & Hannah Price (?),	May 9, 1753
Nehemiah Beers & Eunice Fantain,	June 28, 1753
Joseph Hide & Betty Sherwood,	Aug. 1, 1753
John Hendricks, Jr., & Eunice Bradley,	Nov. 13, 1753
James Pickett of Norwalk & Margaret Hurlburt,	
	Dec. 13, 1753
Jabez Cable & Mary Denbo (?),	Feb. 24, 1754
John Fantain & Eunice Lyon,	Feb. 28, 1754
Jonathan Nash & Sarah Andrews,	March 14, 1754
Thomas Bennet, Jr., & Mary Couch,	April 1, 1754
James Batison, Jr., & Rachel Oysterbanks,	May 16, 1754
Cuffe (negro of Nathaniel Adams) & Betty (negro	
of Deacon John Hide),	July 4, 1754
Gershom Sturgis & Mary Morehouse,	July 30, 1754
John Gorham & Abigail Wakeman,	Oct. 2, 1754
Jabez Lockwood & Sarah Bennet,	Oct. 17, 1754
Jabez Disbrow & Mabel Jecox,	Nov. 3, 1754
Seth Murwin & Ann Sherwood,	Feb. 13, 1755
Daniel Morehouse & Sarah Sturgis,	April 17, 1755
Oliver Whittock & Mary Hull,	June 5, 1755
Jonathan Mallery of Reading & Elizabeth Bennet,	
	Sept. 22, 1755

James Davis of Greenfield & widow Sarah Hase,

         Oct. 12, 1755

Hezekiah Bradley & Abigail Sherwood, Jan. 1, 1756
Jonathan Taylor of Norwalk & Lois Coley, Jan. 14, 1756
Samuel Couch, Jr., & Rachel Allen,   Feb. 23, 1756
James Beers, Jr., & Hannah Burr,   March 18, 1756
John Cable & Ann Laberrie of Stratford, May 3, 1756
John Gilbert & Lydia Murwin,   June 17, 1756
Gideon Morehouse & Eunice Sturgis, Sept. 13, 1756
James Morehouse of Stratfield & Levina Morehouse,

         Oct. 2, 1756

Daniel Nicols & Mary Allen,   Oct., 1756
Eli Taylor of Norwalk & Eunice Hull, Nov. 9, 1756
John Crosman of Dartmouth & Ann Allen, Dec. 15, 1756
Samuel Allen & Eunice Nicols,   Jan. 17, 1757
John Fillow of Norwalk & Sarah Sherwood, March 10, 1757
Rowland Hughs of Virginia & Sarah Hendrick,

        March 17, 1757

Benjamin Frost & Mary Foot,   April 11, 1757
Reuben Bradley & Elizabeth Nash,   April 13, 1757
David Adams, Jr., & Adrai (?) Couch, Nov. 10, 1757
Gamaliel Taylor of Norwalk & Abigail Cable, Nov. 27, 1757
John Andrews, Jr., & Temperance Cable, March 28, 1758
William Hawley & Lydia Nash,   July 12, 1758
John Hurlburt & Sarah Godfrey,   Feb. 7, 1759
Thaddeus Gray & Susannah Carly,   Feb. 28, 1759
Joseph Pacthin & Martha Nott,   July 15, 1759
Samuel Hendrick & Mary Rumsey,   Aug. 30, 1759
Mr. Daniel Sherwood & Abigail Andrews, Jan. 27, 1760
Ebenezer Allen & Tabitha Philips,   April 27, 1760
David Buckley & Deborah Couch,   May 11, 1760
Eliphalet Sturges & Mary Osborn,   Oct. 23, 1760
David Ramond & Sarah Fountain,   Nov. 24, 1760
York & Parry (negroes of Capt. Thomas Nash),

         Feb. 10, 1761

John Sherwood & Mary Gorham,   March 24, 1761
Jedidiah Hull & Mary Chapman,   April 2, 1761
Jacob Hait of Salem & Sarah Sturges, April 16, 1761
Asaph Chelson of Middletown & Lucretia Han-
 ford of Fairfield,   Jan. 17, 1762

Solomon Gray & Ann Disbrow,   Feb. 18, 1762
March (negro servant of Simon Couch) & Mageret
    (negro servant of widow Mary Morehouse), Feb. 25, 1762
Silvanus Fransher of Stanford & Hannah Gray,
                                                April 28, 1762
Joseph Wakeman, Jr., & Rebeccah Adams,   July 28, 1762
Isaac Bulkley & Deborah Couch,   Nov. 18, 1762
James Rogers of Norwalk & Eleanor Wakeman,
                                                March 30, 1762
John Davis & Olive Jecox,   Jan. 5, 1763
Stephen Wakeman & Mary Adams,   Feb. 3, 1763
Gabrel Higgins of Bedford & Sarah Gray,   March 2, 1763
Eben Lewis & Betty Godfrey,   March 3, 1763
Samuel Gray & Joanna Stone of Providence,   June 19, 1763
Ebenezer Coley of Northfield & Abigail Morehouse,
                                                Aug. 11, 1763
Peter Perry & Sarah Bradley,   Nov. 6, 1763
Joseph Gorham, Jr., & Mary Gray,   Nov. 16, 1763
Daniel Meker & Abigail Gorham,   Nov. 17, 1763
Joseph Bennet & Sarah Lyon,   Dec. 21, 1763
Nathan Godfrey & Sarah Nash,   Jan. 24, 1764
David Morehouse & Thankful Couch,   Jan. 25, 1764
Ebenezer Allen, Jr., & Sarah Allen,   Feb. 16, 1764
Stephen Gyer & Rebeccah Burr,   Feb. 21, 1764
William Batison & Grissel Jacox,   April 16, 1764
Ebenezer Jesup & Eleanor Andrews,   May 6, 1764
Parrot (negro servant of Nathaniel Adams) &
    Tamon (negro servant of Joseph Disbrow), June 10, 1764
Cornelius Straten of Long Island & Abigail Hull,
                                                Aug. 15, 1764
William Peck & Sarah Cable,   Nov. 15, 1764
Benjamin Whitear & Sarah Bulkley,   Nov. 15, 1764
Neda (negro servant of Thomas Couch) & Dorcas
    (negro servant of Jeremiah Sherwood),   Nov. 21, 1764
Daniel Frasor & Eunice Oysterbank,   Dec. 11, 1764
Joseph Osborn & Mary Couch,   Jan. 23, 1765
Samuel Taylor of Norwalk & Mary Sturges,   Feb. 7, 1765
Moses Nicols & Mary Jecox,   March 14, 1765
Ebenezer Baker & Mable Lockwood,   Aug. 8, 1765
Nathan Perry & Eben. Smith,   Sept. 19, 1765

MARRIAGES BY HEZEKIAH RIPLEY.

Gersham Lockwood & Martha Allen,	Feb. 22, 1767
Moses Gray & Sarah Disbrow,	March 19, 1767
Ebenezer Redfield & Martha Burr,	March 26, 1767
David King of Greens Farms & Elizabeth Fitch of Norwalk,	April 9, 1767
Isaac Osterbanks & Abigail Cahoon,	May 27, 1767
Stephen Bradley & Abigail Adams,	June 25, 1767
Josiah Webb & Elizabeth Sherwood,	Aug. 26, 1767
Samuel Nash of Norwalk & Eunice Bennet,	Oct. 28, 1767
Elisha Hibbard & Elizabeth Osborn,	Nov. 5, 1767
George Cable & Easter Handford,	Feb. 28, 1768
Daniel Sherwood & Charity Whitehead,	March 3, 1768
Stephen Scribner of Norwalk & Deborah Allen,	March 22, 1768
Joseph Disbrow, Jr., & Phebee Hendrick or W.,	April 10, 1768
John Allen & Martha Lyon,	April 12, 1768
Stephen Godfrey, Jr., & Abigail Mills,	April 21, 1768
Grummon Morehouse & Hulda Elwood,	May 29, 1768
Capt. David Banks & widow Sarah Wakeman,	June 2, 1768
Samuel Smith & Abigail Bennit,	Aug. 28, 1768
Rev. Hezekiah Gold of Cornwall & Elizabeth Wakeman of Greensfarms,	Oct. 11, 1768
John Elwood & Ann Batterson,	Nov. 23, 1768
William Tharp & Patt Disbrow,	Nov. 23, 1768
Andrew Buckley of Greenfield & Abigail Darrows of Fairfield,	Feb. 15, 1769
Joshua Baker & Abigail Sturges,	March 15, 1769
Daniel Bur & Abigail Buckley,	April 20, 1769
Ansil Trube & Isabel Beers of Fairfield,	Dec. 17, 1769
Stephen Marvin of Norwalk & Lois Disbrow,	Jan. 21, 1770
Joseph Holister of Glosonbury & Anne Handford,	March 8, 1770
Titus (servant of Col. Smedly) & Lydia (servant of Mr. Gideon Wakeman),	April 12, 1770
Avery Baker & Hannah Bowrn,	June 10, 1770
Augustus Pulling & Esther Perry,	July 27, 1770
William Ward Hill & Grace Hull,	Aug. 26, 1770

Jonathan Stratten & Mary Godfrey,	Aug. 30, 1770
Moses Bradley & Molly Chapman,	Sept. 2, 1770
John Scribner of Norwalk & Lidia Lion,	Sept. 6, 1770
Benjamin Banks & Sarry Wakeman,	Oct. 11, 1770
Tolent Burr & Midwell Banks,	Nov. 15, 1770
Simon Andrews & Elizabeth Handford,	May 16, 1771
Gershom Gilbert & Rachel Buckingham,	June 13, 1771
Jabez Gorham & Mary Oysterbanks,	Sept. 19, 1771
Joseph Elwood & Naomi Batterson,	Oct. 3, 1771
Ebenezer Buckingham & Esther Bradley,	Dec. 23, 1771
Daniel Perry of Reading & Elizabeth Gorham,	
	Feb. 19, 1772
Moses Sherwood & Mary Chapman,	Feb. 20, 1772
Thomas Couch & Sarah Nash,	April 2, 1772
Gideon Bebee & Rebeccah Gray,	April 23, 1772
Joseph Johnson & Rhuana Patchen,	Aug. 24, 1772
Joseph Handford & Abigail Bradley,	Sept. 20, 1772
Jonathan Beers of Norfield & Olive Cahoon,	Sept. 20, 1772
Hezekiah Banks & Sarah Couch,	Oct. 14, 1772
John Beer & Martha Godfrey,	Oct. 18, 1772
Daniel Rowland & Esther Beers,	Oct. 21, 1772
Stephen Lockwood of Norwalk & Rebecca Alen,	
	Oct. 22, 1772
Moses Allen & Ann Hendrick,	Nov. 2, 1772
Tom (a servant of John Hide) & Till (a servant of Eben. Ogden),	Nov. 5, 1772
Titus (servant of Ensign Stephen Wakeman) & James (servant of widow Jane Sherwood),	Jan. 7, 1773
Benjamin Couch & Naomi Couch,	Jan. 10, 1773
Ceasar (servant of Thomas Nash) & Dina (servant of Nathaniel Adams),	Jan. 14, 1773
Moss Kent of Dutchess County, N. Y., & widow Mary Hazard,	March 15, 1773
Gersham Bulkley & Elizabeth Chapman,	June 3, 1773
John Disbrow & Jemima Wir,	July 29, 1773
Justus Disbrow & Elizabeth Sherwood,	Sept. 30, 1773
John Philips & Molly Bennet,	Oct. 15, 1773
Ezekel Canfield & Anne Jecox,	Oct. 20, 1773
Thaddeus Morehouse of Wilton & widow Abigail Bennet,	Oct. 24, 1773

Justus Bradley & Mable Bradley,   Nov. 9, 1773
Captain Gideon Hurlbut & widow Hannah Couch,
                                                   Nov. 21, 1773
Joseph Morehouse & Mary Buckley,   Dec. 19, 1773
Tom (servant of Dr. Eben. Jesup) & Rose (servant
     of Nathan Adams),   Jan. 21, 1774
Rev. Robert Ross of Stratfield & Eulalia Bartram,
                                                   March 25, 1774
Joseph Mills & Amelia Osterbanks,   May 11, 1774
Dr. Ebenezer Jesups & Abigail Squire,   April 25, 1774
Icahob Canfield & Mary Batterson,   Aug. 18, 1774
Ned (servant of John Hide) & Dinah (servant of
     Abraham Andrews),   Oct. 19, 1774
Daniel Seymour of Norwalk & Phebe Allen,   Jan. 15, 1775
Hezekiah Buckley & Abigail Blackman,   Feb. 23, 1775
Walter Carson & Sarah Squire,   March 12, 1775
Thaddeus Whittock & Grace Bur,   April 2, 1775
David Gennings & Eunice Bur,   April 6, 1775
John Bur & Mary Sturges,   July 9, 1775
Nathaniel Adams, Jr., & Salome Hide,   Dec. 31, 1775
Simon Couch, Jr., & Elenor Nash,   Jan. 7, 1776
John Fanton of North Fairfield & Anne Burr,   Jan. 18, 1776
Elias Bonnet or Bennet & Abigail Crossman,   Feb. 25, 1776
Moses Betts of Wilton & Anne Sturgis,   March 7, 1776
John Hide & Abigail Gennings,   April 7, 1776
Cato & Vine (servants of Mr. Kent),   June 6, 1776
Jabez Raymond of Norwalk & widow Abigail More-
     house,   Aug. 24, 1776
Andrew Bennet & Elizabeth Couch,   Dec. 15, 1776
Queph (negro servant of Jer. Sherwood) & Rose
     (negro servant of Lieut. Jed. Hull),   Dec. 19, 1776
Daniel Mills of Norwalk & Abigail Roberts,   Dec. 20, 1776
Zebulon Williams of Long Island & Abigail
     Par—sick (?),   June 22, 1777
Jesse Jecox & Deborah Hendrick,   Aug. 3, 1777
Russel Disbrow & Eunice Godfrey,   Aug. 17, 1777
Thomas Elwood & Susanna Barlow,   Oct. 16, 1777
Jonathan Lewis & Elizabeth Burr,   Nov. 16, 1777
Judson Sturges & Abigail Squire,   Dec. 7, 1777
Joshua Osterbanks & Sarah Sturges,   Jan. 11, 1778

Isaac Godfrey of Northfield & Abigail Couch, Feb. 8, 1778
Stephen G. Thatcher & Anna Platt of Norwalk,
March 5, 1778
Daniel Andrews of Norfield & Betsey Hide, May 27, 1778
Rev. Hezekiah Gold of Cornwall & widow Abigail
Sherwood, Sept. 24, 1778
Daniel Bennet & Mary Munroe, Oct. 7, 1778
Caleb Disbrow, Jr., & Rhoda Morehouse, Oct. 8, 1778
Samuel Wood & Rebeccah Lion, Nov. 19, 1778
Denny Chapman, Jr., & Mable Godfrey, Nov. 26, 1778
Elias Disbrow & Susanna Green, Jan. 17, 1779
James Hurlbut & Nancy Pearsall, March 3, 1779
Lieut. James Chapman & Abigail Sherwood, March 5, 1779
Joseph Batterson, Jr., & Fanny (?) Hendricks, ——
John S. Perscall (?) & Polly Handford, April 29, 1779
Isaac Disbrow & Elizabeth Gray, May 16, 1779
George Batterson, Jr., & Mary Ceiley (?), May 23, 1779
Jesse Morehouse & Hannah Mills, June 16, 1779
Gilbert Fairchild of Norwalk & Hannah Bennet,
June 24, 1779
Joshua Couch & Patty Patchen, July 15, 1779
Joseph Green, Jr., of Norfield & Rachel Couch, July 21, 1779
Christopher Godfrey of Norfield & Sarah Ogden,
Sept. 12, 1779
Ensign Ebr. Morehouse & widow Temperance
Andrews, Sept. 22, 1779
—— Triglish (?) & Hannah Couch, Sept. 23, 1779
Syman Couch & Abigail Chapman, Nov. 25, 1779
Lovel Chapman & Ellenor Buckley, Dec. 30, 1779
Gideon Hurlburt & widow Hannah Lion, Feb. 22, 1780
George Moyar (?) & Asenath Allen, Feb. 24, 1780
John Osborn & Jerusha Buckley, March 16, 1780
Nathan Ogden of Norfield & Hannah Goodsell,
April 13, 1780
Thomas Scribner of Norwalk & Elizabeth Webb,
May 3, 1780
Zopher Brush & Sarah Bennet, May 4, 1780
Joseph Guyer of Reading & Polly Burcham of Nor-
walk. May 24, 1780
Stephen Godfrey & Eunice Davis, May 29, 1780

Seth Meeker, Jr., & Abigail Beers,   June 8, 1780
Lemuel Raymond of Norwalk & widow Mary Sat-
    erly,   Oct. 5, 1780
Noah T. Handford & Hannah Morehouse,   Nov. 12, 1780
Nehemiah Couch & widow Abigail Baker,   Nov. 19, 1780
Talent Banks & Eunice Chapman,   Jan. 4, 1781
Isaac Elwood & Elizabeth Batterson,   March 7, 1781
Richard West of Long Island & Anna Hamlet (?) of
    Norwalk,   March 7, 1781
Silas Gregory of Norwalk & Sarah Bennet, March 14, 1781
Daniel Platt of Long Island & Mary Betts of Nor-
    walk,   April 15, 1781
Elisha Lincoln & Rhuama Crosman,   April 18, 1781
Joseph Meeker & Sally Hilton of Norfield, April 19, 1781
Moses Oysterbanks & Sarah Bennet,   May 6, 1781
Tan & Sarah (servants of Simon Couch),   June 7, 1781
Justus Whittock or Whitlock & Abigail Meeker,
                                               July 29, 1781
Richard Fry & Sarah Spears,   Sept. 24, 1781
George Smith of Smithtown, L. I., & Lucy Beers of
    Stratford,   Oct. 4, 1781
Ebenezer Redfield & widow Sarah Sturges,   Nov. 4, 1781
Abraham Perry of New Hampshire & Mary Downs,
                                              Nov. 29, 1781
Jonathan Banks & Mary Wakeman,   Dec. 20, 1781
Gideon Couch & Elenor Wakeman,   Dec. 26, 1781
Samuel King & Sarah Munroe,   Jan. 27, 1782
William Benedict & Nancy Fitch of Norwalk, Feb. 20, 1782
Thomas Squire of Norfield & Naomi Bennet, Feb. 7, 1782
Samuel Brotherton & Patience Batterson,   Feb. 21, 1782
John Couch & Rhoda Bennet,   Feb. 27, 1782
Rev. John Avery & Anne Hazard,   April 3, 1782
Joseph Haise (?) & Sarah Bradley,   April 23, 1782
Aaron Sturges & ———— Morehouse of Norwalk,
                                              June 27, 1782
Daniel Brotherton & Rachel Batterson,   Sept. 5, 1782
Zachariah Hawkins of Long Island & Esther Hill,
                                             Sept. 26, 1782
Samuel Gorham & Phebe Buffet,   Nov. 21, 1782
Thomas Perry & ———— Bradley,   1782

William Raymond & Mary Sherwood, Feb. 9, 1783
Samuel Morehouse & Mary Bradley, Feb. 23, 1783
Gad Alderman of Simsbery & Hoppy (?) Buckley,
            May 1, 1783
Philo Fairchild of Newtown & Lois Beers of Nor-
 field,   June 12, 1783
Thaddeus Bradley & Elen Beers of Norfield, ——
Daniel Plat & Polly Nash of Norwalk, June 29, 1783
Thomas Taylor of Norwalk & Mary Morehouse, July 20, 1783
Ezekiel Bennet of Newtown & Sarah Perry, July 23, 1783
William Chub of Ashford & Rachel Downs, Sept. 4, 1783
Asa Sherwood & Molly Philips, Sept. 14, 1783
John Andrews & Lidia Gorham, Oct. 9, 1783
William Bully & Isabel Raymont, Oct. 16, 1783
Jabez Man (?) & Ruhamah Osterbanks, ——
Asa Squire & —— Wakeman, Oct. 23, 1783
Stephen Adams & Abigail Gorham, Nov. 13, 1783
Aaron Jennings & Eunice Taylor, Nov. 16, 1783
John Bennet & Grissel Chapman, Dec. 4, 1783
Gideon Wakeman, Jr., & Clorina (?) Stratton, Dec. 8, 1783
William Riside (?) & Elizabeth Obriant, Dec. 9, 1783
Joseph Bradley & Rachel Burr, Jan. 18, 1784
Samuel Downs & Elizabeth Sturges, Feb. 2, 1784
Aaron Adams & Rhoda Handford of Norwalk, March 4, 1784
Peter Adams of Norwalk & Melesent Hurlbutt,
           March 17, 1784
Daniel Darrow & Hannah Downs, March 31, 1784
Hez. Rumsey & Aletheia Wood, March 31, 1784
Seth Wakeman & Mary Stratten, April 4, 1784
Moses Sherwood & Mary Couch, May 5, 1784
Cesar & Allice (servants of Cornet Moses Sher-
 wood),   June 14, 1784
Jabez Bennet & Abigail Bennet, June 27, 1784
Banks Morehouse of Norfield & Jane Sturges, Aug. 5, 1784
John Lockwood & Eunice Smith of Norfield, Oct. 24, 1784
Peter (servant of Deacon Thomas Nash) & Lid
 (servant of Eben. Jesup, Esq.), Nov. 10, 1784
Peter Thorp & Annie Fauntain of Norfield, Dec. 16, 1784
Hayns Bennet & Keziah Right, Dec. 23, 1784
Daniel Chapman & Deborah Meeker, Jan. 3, 1785

Noah Beers & Elizabeth Lewis (?),   March 10, 1785
William Allen & Rebecca Green,   March 24, 1785
Edmond Weatherhead (?) & Comfort Patchin, May 5, 1785
Deacon Thomas Nash & Mary Nicols of New York,
                           June 9, 1785
Reuben Lockwood & Elizabeth Raymond, Sept. 29, 1784
Abraham Morehouse & Mary Taylor,   Oct. 5, 1785
Alexander Smith Platt of North Fairfield & Anne
    Wakeman,   Oct. 6, 1785
William Dunkum of Stratfield & Sarah Sturges,
                         Nov. 20, 1785
David Canfield of Wilton & Abigail Godfrey, Nov. 23, 1785
John Thorp of Norfield & Ruth Sturges,   Dec. 8, 1785
Nathan Elwood & Abigail Smith,   Dec. 29, 1785
Jesup Darling of Clovericks (?) & Lidia Morehouse
    of Norwalk,   Jan 13, 1786
Joseph Wakeman & Rachel Hide,   Jan. 25, 1786
Jabez Plat of Norwalk & Gillen Bennet,   Feb. 5, 1786
Ozaias Merwin (?) of Norwalk & Mary Bennet, Feb. 23, 1786
Isaac Beers & Rhuama Fountain of Norfield, April 16, 1786
Thomas Davies & Abigail Wakeman,   April 20, 1786
George Hanford & Elizabeth Wright,   April 30, 1786
Ebenezer McRow, Jr., & Ruth Bennet,   May 28, 1786
Samuel Sherwood & Priscilla Burr,   Aug. 13, 1786
Thomas Cable, Jr., & Charlotte Guyer,   Sept. 6, 1786
Peter Bets & Bathsheba Wright of Norwalk, Oct. 15, 1786
John Batterson & Sarah Alling,   Oct. 26, 1786
Adam Edson & Mercy Hazard,   Dec. 3, 1786
John Patterson & Molly Raymong,   Dec. 20, 1786
Stephen Morehouse & Eben Morehouse of Norwalk,
                         Dec. 31, 1786
Henry (servant of John Bets of Norwalk) & Gin
    (servant of Samuel Pearsall),   Jan. 2, 1787
Samuel Green & Timizin Batterson,   March 15, 1787
Daniel Sherwood & Catharine Burr,   March 21, 1787
Harry Cussl (?) & Idda ——— of Norwalk, Aug. 22, 1787
Elnathan Smith & Mary Thorp,   Nov. 17, 1787
Edmund Tuttle of Norwalk & Salome Phillips, Nov. 18, 1787
Abraham Elwood of Saratoga & Sarah Johnson,
                         Nov. 29, 1787

Robert William Toles or Ides of Norwalk & Rhoda
    Bennet,   Dec. 19, 1787
Daniel Lockwood & Elizabeth Tuttel of Norwalk,
                                  Feb. 24, 1788
David Raymong, Jr., & Abigail Sherwood,   March 1, 1788
Eliphalet Thorp & Esther Jenning,   April 27, 1788
Charles Willson of Norwalk & Olive Allen,   May 15, 1788
Gershom Allen & Ann Crosman,   May 18, 1788
Samuel Cable & Charity Nash,   July 13, 1788
Trowbridge Crosman & Eunice Bradley of Nor-
    walk,   Aug. 10, 1788
Ralf Sherwood & Abigail Gorham,   Aug. 21, 1788
John William Rowe (?) & Anne Batterson,   ———
Thomas Bennet, Jr., & Sarah Stratten,   Aug. 24, 1788
John Mills of Weston & Eunice Ross (?),   Sept. 16, 1788
Eliphalet Allen & Abigail McRowe,   Sept. 21, 1788
Eli Mills & Anne Meeker,   Sept. 29, 1788
Edward & Florio (servants of John Hide), Oct. 16, 1788
John Barns & Molly Baker,   Oct. 17, 1788
Samuel Persall, Jr., & Rachel Wakeman,   Oct. 19, 1788
Thomas Nash, Jr., & Grau (?) Cable,   Nov. 16, 1788
Jonathan Godfrey & Esther Whitehead,   Nov. 30, 1788
Jonathan Poor & Susanna Handford,   Dec. 18, 1788
John Roberson & Sarah Thorp,   Dec. 21, 1788
Stephen Allen & Waighty Thorp,   Dec. 31, 1788
Morehouse Cooley of Weston & Abigail Ogden, Feb. 17, 1789
Meeker Murwin & Sarah Hull,   Feb. 21, 1789
Nathan Prise of Weston & Hulda Downs, Feb. 22, 1789
Thomas Lockwood of Norwalk & Lidia Bennet,
                              March 8, 1789
Jabez Disbrow, Jr., & Esther Godfrey,   March 19, 1789
John Taylor of Norwalk & Esther Bennet, March 22, 1789
John Finch, Jr., of Norwalk & Hulda Ogden, April 18, 1789
Stephen Wakeman, Jr., & Sarah Whitehead, June 29, 1789
William Little & Martha Loveman of Stratfield,
                              Oct. 3, 1789
William Buckley & Sarah Redfield,   Oct. 25, 1789
Samuel Gregory of Norwalk & Rhoda Ogden, Nov. 27, 1789
Abiel Babit of New Stratfield & Abigail Sturges,
                              Dec. 25, 1789

John Ogden & Comfort Couch,	May 6, 1790
John Cooley & Eunice Morehouse,	May 13, 1790
Solomon Morehouse & Elenor Meeker,	June 27, 1790
Ebenezer Godfrey & widow Mary Taylor,	July 25, 1790
Jason Disbrow & Anna Gray,	Aug. 26, 1790
Timothy Parsons of Reading & Hannah Hurlbutt,	
	Oct. 31, 1790
Adam Oysterbanks & Abigail Morehouse,	Nov. 21, 1790
Joseph Hide, Jr., & Arite Jesup,	Dec. 16, 1790
Burr Thorp & Rebecckah Nash,	Jan. 16, 1791
Stephen Morehouse & Esther Taylor of Norwalk,	
	Jan. 20, 1791
Daniel Morehouse of Norfield & widow Eunice Morehouse,	Jan. 27, 1791
Tim (servant to Jo. Bennet) & Lill (servant to Asahel Disbrow),	Feb. 17, 1791
Daniel Rayment & Hannah Sturges,	March 3, 1791
Jonathan Burr & Sarah Redfield,	May 8, 1791
Lockwood McRowe & Mary Batterson,	May 8, 1791
Joshua Jennings, Jr., & Sarah Morehouse,	June 5, 1791
Joseph Gorham of Greenfield & Abigail Gorham of Norwalk,	July 3, 1791
Holsey Patrick & Phebe Lockwood of Norwalk,	Sept. 8, 1791
Amos (servant of widow Abigail Osborn) & Sall (servant of William Pike, Mill River),	Oct. 2, 1791
Burr Gennings & Mercy Morehouse,	Dec. 7, 1791
David Beers & Molly Ogden,	Jan. 18, 1792
Dr. Ebenezer Jesup & Anna Winekoop,	Jan. 22, 1792
Joshua Disbrow & widow Deborah Jeacocks,	Feb. 2, 1792
Abraham Gregory of Norwalk & Damaris Disbrow,	
	April 18, 1792
Elijah Gray of Norfield & Rhoda Disbrow,	May 6, 1792
Libbeus Sword & Ruhamah Batterson,	May 30, 1792
Peter Jennings & Sarah Wakeman,	July 1, 1792
John Wilson of Norwalk & Elizabeth Shute,	Aug. 26, 1792
Jeremiah Osborn & Abigail Osborn,	Nov. 6, 1792
Thaddeus Burr Guyer & Mary or Mercy Disbrow,	
	Dec. 16, 1792
Michael Cooly & Eunice Hide,	Jan. 13, 1793
David Bennet & Charity Disbrow,	—

James Culy & Betty Smith,	March 28, 1793
Justus Plat & Hannah Smith,	May 5, 1793
Ebenezer Baker & Rebeckah Batterson,	Aug. 1, 1793
Amos (servant of Deacon Benedict of Norwalk) & Luse (a free woman who lives with Moses Clos) (?),	—
Samuel Olmsted of Norwalk & Betsy Disbrow,	Aug. 9, 1793
Joseph Allen & Molly Nichols,	Aug. 18, 1793
Elizur Wood & Eleanor Jesup,	Sept. 19, 1793
Abraham Sherwood & Abigail Burr,	Oct. 20, 1793
Hezekiah Augustus Ripley & Hannah Marsey (?) of Windham,	Nov. 3, 1793
Josiah Barlow Gorham & Abigail Stratton,	Nov. 16, 1793
Taylor Hurlbutt & Betty Bennett,	Dec. 5, 1793
Seymour Taylor & Mercy Bennet,	Dec. 11, 1793
Lewis Cable & Sally Bryon,	Dec. 17, 1793
Amos Gray & Mary Burr,	Dec. 22, 1793
Lockwood Baker & Betty Raymond,	March 12, 1794
Hezekiah Nichols & Abigail Burr,	May 19, 1794
Ebenezer Smith of Norwalk & Rachel Winton Disbrough,	Aug. 20, 1794
Eben. Squire Disbrow & Clary Bulkley,	Sept. 3, 1794
Joseph Young & Rhoda Oysterbanks,	Nov. 16, 1794
Ned & Priscilla (negroes),	Jan. 1, 1795
John Sherwood, Jr., of Reading & Abigail Sherwood,	Feb. 1, 1795
William Forbs & Salome Baker,	March 26, 1795
Stephen B. Handford & Esther Burr,	May 7, 1795
Stephen Godfrey & Salome Elwood,	July 9, 1795
Christopher H. Star of Middletown & Betsey Taylor of Norwalk,	Sept. 3, 1795
Selek (?) Batterson & Molly Batterson,	Dec. 13, 1795
Seymour Lockwood & Mary Godfrey,	Dec. 14, 1795
Joseph Whitehead & Grace Gennings,	Dec. 20, 1795
Eli Bradley & Elenor Sherwood,	Dec. 24, 1795
Daniel Meeker & Elizabeth Downs,	Dec. 31, 1795
William B. Smith & Eunice Stratton,	Feb. 11, 1796
Silas Burr & Charity Banks,	March 6, 1796
Hezekiah Sherwood & Eleanor Ogden,	March 16, 1796

Benjamin Merchant of Reading & Sarah Bradley,
                                        April 28, 1796
Moses Jorrard of Long Island & Elizabeth Can-
    field,   June 8, 1796
Moses Taylor & Abigail Morehouse,   June 23, 1796
Banks Wakeman & Elenor Jinnings,   Nov. 20, 1796
David Sherwood & Abigail Meeker,   Nov. 27, 1796
David Jennings & Abigail Meeker,   Dec. 25, 1796
Seaborn Folliot (?) of Norwalk & widow Sarah
    Forbs,   Jan. 5, 1797
Stephen Patrick of Norwalk & Kezia Bennet,   ——
Zalmon Burr & Abigail Hide,   Jan. 15, 1797
David Allen & Hannah Sherwood,   Jan. 24, 1797
Abijah Hurd & Grissel Wynkoop,   March 21, 1797
Daniel Disbrow & Elizabeth Bulkley Morehouse,
                                        April 27, 1797
Bradley Bulkley & Molly Burr,   July 13, 1797
Joseph Baker & Sarah Jesup,   July 27, 1797
William Nichols & Eunice McRow,   Aug. 13, 1797
John Merchant of Reading & Eunice Bradley, Aug. 20, 1797
Jonathan Ogden & Rebecckah Adams,   Aug. 27, 1797
John P. Austin of New Haven & Susan Rogers,
                                        Sept. 10, 1797
Thaddeus Folliot of Ridgfield & Olive Bradley, Oct. 8, 1797
Lyman Hull & Amelia Bulkly,   Oct. 22, 1797
Joseph Squire of Weston & Data Batterson,   ——
Samuel Russicue (?) of South Easttown & Freelove
    Disbrow,   Nov. 2, 1797
Hezekiah Cooly & Anna Burr,   Nov. 5, 1797
Henry Munrow & Lyzett ——,   ——
Lyman Banks & Charity Sherwood,   Jan. 7, 1798
Oliver Middlebrook & Mary Bradley,   Jan. 14, 1798
Hezekiah Wakeman & Mary Godfrey,   Feb. 18, 1798
Jesse Bradley of Weston & Abigail Buckley, Feb. 28, 1798
John Hull & Betsy Price,   April 1, 1798
Abraham Gregory, Jr., of Norwalk & Polly Allen,
    2d,   April 10, 1798
Joseph Allen & Patty Thorp,   April 15, 1798
William Johnson Nash of Norwalk & Polly Allen,
                                        May 8, 1798

Thómas Hart Tayler of New York & Nancy Fitch
   of Norwalk,   May 9, 1798
John Goodsell, Jr., & Rachel Meeker,   May 17, 1798
Uriah Beers of Weston & Chariarm (?) Goodsell,   ——
Jesup Tayler & Sarah Coley,   May 31, 1798
Joseph Dury (?) of Stonington & Elizabeth Sturges,
                            Sept. 16, 1798
Benjamin Whitehead & Mary Nutermoch (?), Nov. 22, 1798
Aaron Thorp of Weston & Betsy Hull,   Nov. 26, 1798
Isaac Bennett & Lidia Wood,   Dec. 20, 1798
Ezra Burr, Jr., & Abigail Burr,   Dec. 23, 1798
John Disbrow, Jr., & Prisilla Mallery,   Jan. 17, 1799
Jesse Gennings & Sarah Morehouse,   Jan. 27, 1799
Hezekiah Hull & Sarah Goodsell,   Feb. 28, 1799
Stephen Gorham & Rhoda Cable of New York,
                         March 20, 1799
Aaron Burr & Hulda Morehouse,   April 3, 1799
Jabez Comstock of Wilton & Amelia Ogilvie, June 16, 1799
James Bennett & Mary Burr,   July 4, 1799
Shubail Gorham of Weston & widow Abigail Ray-
   mont,   Sept. 8, 1799
Phineas Curtiss of Farmington & Phebe Toby of
   Norwalk,   Sept. 29, 1799
Stephen Bradley & Betty Downs,   Oct. 6, 1799
Isaac Sears of South Easttown & Priscilla Bennett,
                         Nov. 26, 1799

INDEX.

13

EARLY CONNECTICUT MARRIAGES

AS FOUND ON

ANCIENT CHURCH RECORDS

PRIOR TO 1800.

FOURTH BOOK.

EDITED BY

FREDERIC W. BAILEY,

OFFICIAL COPYIST PAROCHIAL ARCHIVES, DIOCESE OF CONNECTICUT; EDITOR "EARLY MASSA-
CHUSETTS MARRIAGES;" DESIGNER BAILEY'S PHOTO-ANCESTRAL RECORD, "THE RECORD
OF MY ANCESTRY;" MEMBER AMERICAN HISTORICAL ASSOCIATION; NEW ENGLAND
GENEALOGICAL AND BIOGRAPHICAL SOCIETY; CONNECTICUT HISTORICAL
SOCIETY; NEW HAVEN COLONY HISTORICAL SOCIETY; SONS
OF THE AMERICAN REVOLUTION (MASSACHUSETTS).

PUBLISHED BY THE

BUREAU OF AMERICAN ANCESTRY
FOR
Family Researches

FREDERIC W. BAILEY, MGR.
P. O. BOX 587.   NEW HAVEN, CONN.

PREFACE.

EARLY CONNECTICUT MARRIAGES.

FOURTH BOOK.

It is exceedingly gratifying to be able through kindly patronage to present herewith the Fourth Book of "Early Connecticut Marriages"—a title which by this time has become quite familiar to a few at least in all parts of the country who have been permitted thereby to link themselves with Connecticut's early colonial life.

Even if not without some prospect of a financial loss, still the satisfaction that comes from being the means of saving a portion of our old and valuable records from the too common fate is at least part payment for the sacrifice involved.

Then, too, it may be said that had not old Benoni Bailey of Danbury, born 1697, settled on Connecticut soil, leaving for the colony a goodly line of descendants, though no information of his ancestry, our unswerving interest in Connecticut records might not have been so apparent. And yet one with any degree of love for American antiquity could hardly live in this venerable State, with its intensely sober history and a thought of the multitudinous fruitage scattered everywhere, and at the same time be a constant witness to the decaying condition in which the old records exist, without making some feeble attempt to save.

The facts upon which this statement is based are not far to seek. Indeed, a faint idea of our serious losses and dangers may be gathered from the list of "Records Lost" to be found herein. It has reference alone to the old church records, which, though in private hands, have not been most wisely cared for. And when it is understood how in many cases our organized townships have been the outgrowth of such churches, it may be seen that the loss of the church records means everything. And as for town records themselves, it is not the actual loss at present that we have to lament, even if in several cases fire has destroyed them. From our constant experience among them during the last six years, during which time it has been our privilege to examine the records of almost every old town in the State, it may be truthfully and candidly said that lest some definite action on their behalf is quickly taken by State authorities, this very conservative old commonwealth is likely to lose a goodly number of the most precious archives within its territory. And that, too, not necessarily by fire, but simply in the fact, which any one can appreciate, that even the best paper and the best binding an hundred and fifty and two hundred years old, subject to the hard usage they have had and still have, must wear out. This, we are free to say, is a pertinent fact too frequently met with among the records of our old towns. And is made more real when we understand that towns themselves in numbers of cases have done nothing and are doing less to preserve other than to continue to furnish meager safe room. In an atmosphere of utter indifference and neglect, with old books fast decaying and with no attempt made to secure copies, every descendant of Connecticut ancestry has good reason to be alarmed and as well to protest.

To be sure there are praiseworthy exceptions to this broad state-ment—cases where towns themselves are alive to the seriousness of the situation, and where town clerks, too, taking oft the initiative, have deeply interested themselves in the protection and preservation of the books in their care. Such towns as Hartford, Norwich, Norwalk, Stamford and other cities, where perhaps the ready means and public demands have opened the way. Also in some of the smaller towns, where the influence of some interested party or town clerk has prevailed, as at Plainfield, Preston, Guilford, Windsor, Woodbury, Ridgefield, East Haddam, New Hartford, Saybrook. But in others, where there has been neither the personal interest nor the means, such as Lyme, Colchester, Willington, Farmington, Stratford, Simsbury, Haddam, Sharon, Greenwich, Stonington, Wallingford, Salisbury, Enfield, Windham, Union, Lebanon, Fairfield, Canterbury, Newtown, there may be seen ancient records which should either have been carefully transcribed long ago, or else placed in good repair. As it is here in these towns may be found valuable historical records rapidly passing beyond recall.

With considerable satisfaction we read in the annual message of His Excellency, Governor Lounsbury, a reference to this subject. Upon his suggestion the Assembly, just before adjournment, was pleased to take action and to provide for the appointment of a Commission of Public Records that should in due time make report. And yet it seems as if two years were a long period under the circumstances to await a report which is, after an examination, merely to recommend the best methods of preserving the old archives. Surely the subject so very familiar to our town representatives might have found some ready expedient to effectually check at once all further danger of loss or damage in this direction.

The prevailing system of record keeping, which has never been changed since first the colony was organized, and which provides that each town retain its land records under the care of the town clerk, who also is recorder, might for public safety and convenience have been improved upon long ago. As it is we to-day, who are reading and thinking of expansion and progress everywhere, have the opportunity of seeing herein an indication of the old conservatism that exists among us. It may do very well for a city or large centralized village, having the means and permanent quarters to retain possession of all land records within the township, but when it comes to searching for a town clerk afar from the railroad centers, who, perhaps, suddenly and unexpectedly coming into public office by some sudden change of political power, has, for his own personal convenience and economy, carried the old books away to his own inaccessible home, the incongruity of the thing impresses the mind amazingly.

It will be found, too, that the towns themselves have no uniform way of protecting their records. The question of expense being a vital one, and the office of town clerk—with little remuneration—not largely sought for, the problem becomes one of expediency. And so we find three different methods in vogue. The town records may be found in private houses at Pomfret, Ashford, Mansfield, Lyme, Lisbon, Lebanon, Union, Somers, Killingworth, Woodbridge, Wilton, Easton, East Windsor, Thompson (in part), Wethersfield, Harwinton, Hebron, a safe being provided. In other towns the country store has been the most convenient repository for the public safe, as at Preston, Canterbury, Killingly, Colchester, East Haddam, Avon, Granby, Cornwell, Kent, Willington. A bank vault is used at Norfolk and Canaan; while in the majority of cases a building is provided for the town clerk's use, though it is not the case everywhere that the safe is at all adequate for the protection of all papers deserving of it.

It may be remarked in passing how many early records have never been provided with indexes of the Grantors, though quite as essential as that of the Grantees to be found.

To the stranger searching among us, our probate system, perhaps, possesses the most unintelligible complications. He finds the probate offices scattered about the State, as if choses in some lottery scheme, and so ordered that they cover varying degrees of territory. The early history of our old towns may offer a solution to this question, as we see how with the dissection of original towns into new townships the probate still remained intact till public convenience made necessary a larger extension of districts. The whole system is for our day rather antiquated and sadly inconvenient, but in so ignoring township lines it did establish a fortunate precedent that might well have been followed in the case of the town records themselves. As to the probate records, it can hardly be said that they are in any more satisfactory condition than the town, though less in number. The early probate at Fairfield, New Haven, Sharon, Stafford, Colchester, Plainfield, are sadly deficient with indexes especially wanting, while in the latter case an old safe is provided and located in a country store. Such old books as can be are crowded into it, but, strange to say, the door cannot be locked nor yet closed securely. And these records date back to 1747. And this, notwithstanding that the town of Plainfield possesses a capacious vault in which its own thoroughly indexed records are safely kept.

In addition to the above, the State possesses valuable court records reaching back into the early colonial days, and located at Hartford, Norwich, Bridgeport and elsewhere, but which are seldom consulted for lack of any index whatever. Windham, New Haven and Litchfield County records have more or less perfect indexes, but the old historic county books are almost sealed to the casual searcher. It is in these we find proof how that the "Scarlet Letter" was a penalty not unknown to this colony in its earlier days, that robbery was punished by a brand upon the forehead, while other facts equally interesting are hidden from view.

Let us hope we are on the eve of a new departure in this particular. That the enterprising spirit shown in our neighboring State, the evidence of whose good work all can see, may ultimately reach us; and that along with good roads and good schools and good public buildings, liberal appropriations may be made for preserving all the records of the early lives of our people and of those impressive facts upon which all present and future greatness rests.

FREDERIC W. BAILEY.

New Haven, Conn., Oct. 1, 1899.

CONTENTS.

FOURTH BOOK.

RECORDS LOST.

The following is a (revised) list of Congregational Churches so far reporting the loss of their records of Baptisms and Marriages prior to 1800.

CHURCH.	COUNTY.	ORGANIZED.	REMARKS.
Westminster, of Canterbury	Windham,	1770,	none before 1824.
Stamford,	Fairfield,	1635,	few before 1800.
Coventry,	Tolland,	1745,	none before 1818.
Hebron,	Tolland,	1716,	burned.
Ellington,	Tolland,	1736,	lost.
Sherman,	Fairfield,	1744,	burned.
East Granby,	Hartford,	1737,	
Goshen,	Litchfield,	1740,	lost.
Watertown,	Litchfield,	1739,	lost.
Canton Center,	Hartford,	1750,	before 1826, lost.
So. Manchester,	Hartford,	1779,	
North Guilford,	New Haven,	1725,	lost.
East Lyme,	New London,	1719,	lost.
Lyme (Hamburgh),	New London,	1727,	lost.
West Haven,	New Haven,	1719,	before 1815, lost.
Litchfield,	Litchfield,	1721,	before 1886, burned.
Tolland,	Tolland,	1723,	burned.
Bethany,	New Haven,	1763,	before 1823, lost.
Andover,	Tolland,	1749,	B. and M. before 1818, burned at W. Springfield, Mass.
Glastonbury,	Hartford,	1693,	before 1797, lost.
Marlborough,	Hartford,	1749,	missing.
Harwinton,	Litchfield,	1738,	nothing before 1790
Ridgefield,	Fairfield,	1714,	nothing before 1800.
Plymouth,	Litchfield,	1740,	no marriages before 1800.
Somers,	Tolland,	1727,	little before 1800.
Greenwich,	Fairfield,	1670,	nothing before 1787.
Greenwich, (Stanwich),	Fairfield,	1735,	burned 1821.
Torringford,	Litchfield,	1764,	burned, nothing before 1837.
East Haddam, (Hadlyme),	Middlesex,	1745,	no marriages before 1800, baptisms begin 1745.
Monroe,	Fairfield,	1764,	no marriages before 1821, baptisms begin 1776.
Bristol,	Hartford,	1747,	no marriages before 1792, baptisms begin 1800.

FARMINGTON — BERLIN.

HARTFORD COUNTY.

The town of Berlin was organized in May, 1785, having been a part of Farmington, Wethersfield and Middletown, The Church in Kensington was originally the Second Church of Farmington. It was organized December 10, 1712. From this church the New Britain Church was organized in 1758, and the Worthington Church in 1775. The following cover the Kensington Church records. Rev. Samuel Clark pastor from 1756 to 1775.

Nathaniel Cole & Anna Way,	Oct. 14, 1756
William Hubbard & Elizabeth Root,	Dec. 8, 1756
Matthew Cole & Rhoda Smith,	Dec. 9, 1756
Nathaniel Winchel, Jr., & Lucy Strong,	Dec. 15, 1756
Jedediah North & Sarah Wilcox,	Jan. 27, 1757
John Goodrich of Kensington & Hannah Dewy of New Britain,	April 17, 1757
Robert Booth & Ruth Kilborn, both of New Britain,	May 9, 1757
David Mather of New Britain & Hannah Dunham of Kensington,	June 2, 1757
Elias Beckly & Lois Parsons,	Aug. 4, 1757
Benjamin Bulkly of Wethersfield & Susannah Kirby of Middletown,	Nov. 3, 1757
Jonathan Nott & Sarah Hubbard,	Dec. 15, 1757
Benjamin Smith & Elizabeth Prout, both of New Britain,	Jan. 19, 1758
Jacob Andrys of Kensington & Eunice Emons of Litchfield,	Feb. 2, 1758
Solomon Dunham of Kensington & Elizabeth Ives of Wallingford,	March 2, 1758
Zacheriah Hart & Abigail Beckley,	March 23, 1758
David Atkins of Middletown & Elisabeth Hinsdale of Kensington,	April 28, 1758
John Beckley & Ruth Hubbard,	June 11, 1758
Ephraim Holister & Ann Beckley,	Aug. 3, 1758
Nathaniel Hart & Martha Norton,	Nov. 23, 1758
Samuel Porter of East Hartford & Elizabeth Hubbard of Kensington,	Feb. 1, 1759
Samuel Galpen of Kensington & Mary Smally of New Britain,	May 8, 1759

Austin Migate & Lament Blinn,	May 24, 1759
Charles Brownson & Martha Barret,	May 30, 1759
Judah Hart of New Britain & Sarah North,	Sept. 27, 1759
Caleb Galpen & Eunice Lee,	Jan. 17, 1760
Ashbil Hooker & Susannah Lankton,	Jan. 31, 1760
Joseph Deming, Jr., & Bathsheba Sage,	April 17, 1760
Thomas Gilbert & Mary North,	April 24, 1760
Samuel Thatcher of Lebanon & Ruth Burnham of Kensington,	Aug. 14, 1760
Noah Cowles of Kensington & Ann Powel of Middletown,	Aug. 14, 1760
Jonathan Pitkin of Hartford East & Lucy Steel of Kensington,	Sept. 11, 1760
Stephen Mix of Wallingford & Ann Porter,	Sept. 17, 1760
Moses Dickenson & Lydia Cole,	Nov. 11, 1760
Silas Brownson & Ann Winchel,	Nov. 27, 1760
John Allen of Windsor & Ruth Burnham,	Dec. 18. 1760
Asahel Cowles of Kensington & Rachel Bell of Southington,	Feb. 5, 1761
Benjamin Beckley & Eunice Williams,	April 23, 1761
Selah Hubbard & Esther Gilbert,	May 28, 1761
Elnathan Hubbard & Sibbil Hubbard,	July 5, 1761
Gideon Judd of Kensington & Silance Welton of Farmington,	July 22, 1761
William Baston & Abigail Sage,	Aug. 13, 1761
Ozias Brownson & Abigail Peck,	Oct. 22, 1761
David Webster of Weathersfield & Servia Allis,	Oct. 29, 1761
Jonathan Lankton & Elisabeth Edwards,	Dec. 17, 1761
Joseph Hopkins & Ann Smith,	March 18, 1762
Jessy Cole & Sally Smith,	April 15, 1762
Giles Hamlin & Eunice Kingsman, both of Middletown,	May 21, 1762
John Root & Ann Steel,	May 26, 1762
Ebenezer Gilbert & Mary Butrick,	May 27, 1762
Samuel Plumb of Middletown & Lucy Hinsdale,	Jan., 1763
Ozias Gilbert & Mary Yale,	May 5, 1763
Timothy Brownson, Jr., of Kensington & Abigail Brownson of Southington,	Dec. 1, 1763
Selah Hart of Kensington & Ruth Cole of Blew Hills,	Dec. 22, 1763

Elisha Cole & Rebekah Beckwith,   Dec. 29, 1763
Thomas Hart, Deacon, aged 84, & Elisabeth Norton,
    aged 79,   Jan. 11, 1764
Ebenezer Elton & Rhoda Hurlburt,   Feb. 7, 1764
Moses Dickenson & Susannah Hooker,   March 8, 1764
Samuel Landress & Sarah Williams, both of Weath-
    ersfield,   July 11, 1764
Alexander Rhodes & Mercy Steel, both of Weath-
    ersfield,   Sept. , 1764
Gideon Williams of Sheffield & Patience Graham of
    New Britton,   Sept. 26, 1764
William Barber of Briton & Abigail Cole,   Nov. 8, 1764
Elisha Marsh of Litchfield & Honour Beckley, Nov. 29, 1764
Abijah Hubbard & Axa Beckley,   Dec. 20, 1764
Joseph Richards, Jr., & Mary Kelsey, both of Weath-
    ersfield,   Jan. 26, 1765
Caleb Hopkins & Mehetible Scovel,   Feb. 21, 1765
Samuel Johnston & Ann Hopkins,   March 13, 1765
Daniel French & Eunice Hubbard,   May 20, 1765
Asa Brownson & Mary Winchel,   Aug. 22, 1765
Charles Dix of Weathersfield & Sarah Hooker, March 6, 1766
John Wells & Mary Mitchel, both of Weathersfield,
                                            March 13, 1766
Isaac Lankton & Thankful Smith, both of New
    Briton,   May 1, 1766
Raphael Halbert & Sarah Hubbard,   Nov. 17, 1766
Zacheriah Hart & Sarah Parsons,   June, 1766
Joseph Spalding & Hulda Hubbard,   Nov. 19, 1766
Oliver Hart & Mary Scovel,   Dec. 17, 1766
Aseriah Glading & Ann Hudson,   Dec. 18, 1766.
Jonathan Gilbert, Jr., & Hannah Collins,   Jan. 1, 1767
David Williams & Mindwell Sage,   Feb. 19, 1767
Josiah Halbert of Farmington & Sarah Butrick,
    alias Fullar,   March 9, 1767
Benjamin Hall, Jr., of Wallingford & Hannah
    Burnham,   April 16, 1767
Jesse Brownson & Abigail Allen,   May 7, 1767
Asa Kelsey & Content Parsons,   May 21, 1767
Abner Fullar & Mary Hilyard Crowfoot, both of
    Weathersfield,   July 16, 1767

1½

Elijah Hooker of Kensington & Susannah Say-
　　mour of Weathersfield,　　　　　　Aug. 26, 1767
John Goo(d)rich & Ruth Gilbert,　　　Sept. 10, 1767
Asa Deming & Hepzibah Edwards,　　Sept. 24, 1767
Joseph Peck of Kensington & Sarah Bristol of
　　Southington,　　　　　　　　　　Dec. 17, 1767
Robert Bassett & Elisabeth Lankton,　Jan. 14, 1768
Amos Clark & Lois Winchel,　　　　　Feb. 25, 1768
John Lusk & Abigail Brownson,　　　April 14, 1768
Thomas Gridly & Mary Hooker,　　　　　　——
Abraham Gridly & Theda Hosington,　　July 7, 1768
James Elton of Waterbury & Naomy Halbert, Nov. 17, 1768
Ozias Andrus of Southington & Ann Knott, Dec. 28, 1768
John Heyfords & Elisabeth Riley,　　　April 6, 1769
Samuel Parsons, Jr., of Durham & Abigail Galpen
　　(widow),　　　　　　　　　　　June 12, 1769
Barnabas Dunham & Martha Cowles,　June 15, 1769
Abel Heart & Mary Galpen,　　　　　Sept. 13, 1769
Gorsham Graham & Ester Pattison,　　Oct. 10, 1769
Samuel Stow Salvage of Middletown & Mary Cole,
　　　　　　　　　　　　　　　　Nov. 29, 1769
Gideon Hills & Ester Kirtis,　　　　　Dec. 7, 1769
Benjamin Rose & Mary Patison,　　　　Feb. 1, 1770
Hezekiah Judd & Mary Standly,　　　　　　——
Ebenezer Heart, Jr., & Lydia Benton,　April 5, 1770
Samuel Bartholomew of Pauge & Martha Heart,
　　　　　　　　　　　　　　　April 25, 1770
Samuel Williams of Weathersfield & Ruth Cole of
　　Farmington,　　　　　　　　　　April 26, 1770
Charles Ede of Glasenbury & Hannah Kelsey, Oct. 25, 1770
James Porter & Lucy Burnham,　　　　　　——
John Bell of Southington & Lydia Collens,　Jan. 16, 1771
Stephen Wilcox & Mary Kelsey,　　　Jan. 31, 1771
Daniel Gilbert & Thankful Dickenson,　Aug. 8, 1771
Bononi Hodgkiss of Chesher & Hannah Norton,
　　　　　　　　　　　　　　　　Sept. 5, 1771
Theodore Beckly & Lucy Kirby,　　　Dec. 25, 1771
Stephen Cole & Lucy Deming,　　　　Dec. 26, 1771
Benjamin Heart of Briton & Mary Fullar of Weth-
　　ersfield,　　　　　　　　　　　Aug. 19, 1772

Eldad Brownson of Worthington & Esther Mildrum
    of Rocky Hill,   Nov. 5, 1772
Oliver Atwood of Woodbury & Anne Wells,   Dec. 8, 1772
John Rily of North Hampton & Huldah Porter of
    Worthington,   April 1, 1773
David Sage of Middletown & Mary Rosseter of
    Farmington,   May 14, 1773
Calvin Halbert of Kensington & Mary Beckly of
    Worthington,   July 29, 1773
Jedediah Foster & Rachel Hollister,   April 21, 1774
Jonathan Benton & Olive Peck, both of Worthing-
    ton,   May 5, 1774
Joseph Stocking & Olive Cole,   Aug. 18, 1774
Elijah Lóveland & Anne Deming, both of Worth-
    ington,   Dec. 22, 1774
William Barns of Claremont & Eunice Andrus of
    Worthington,   Jan. 25, 1775
Luther Stocking & Sarah Goodrich,   July 17, 1775
Roger Rily & Sarah Deming, both of Worthington,
                                Oct. 19, 1775

A LIST OF MARRIAGES FROM THE 21ST DAY OF APRIL, 1779.

Abijah Porter & Hannah Deming, both of Worth-
    ington,   1779
Joel Root of Kensington & Ruth Messenger of
    Southington,   Jan., 1779
Joel Barlow & Ruth Baldwin, both of New Haven,
                            Dec. 26, 1779
Asa Goodrich & Lydia Bronson,
Abel Gridley & Rhoda Hills,   Jan. 27, 1780
Elnathan Norton of Worthington & Sibyll Goodrich,
                          Feb. 28, 1780
Levi Hart & (Philathea) Allen, both of Southington,
                          May 3, 1780
Jonathan Root, Jr., & Eunice Judd, both of South-
    ington,   July 6, 1780
Elizur Andrus & Mercy Cole,   July 27, 1780·
Ephraim Doolittle & Lydia Gridley,   Dec. 7, 1780
Oliver Gridley & Martha Goodrich,   Dec. 21, 1780
Daniel Smith & Sabra Winchell,   Dec. 27, 1780

Mark Mildren & Huldah Winchel,	Jan. 14, 1781
Capt. Matthew Cole & Mary Norton,	June 13, 1781
Seth Goodrich & Rachel Cowles,	Sept. 2, 1781
Seth Standly & Anne Hooker,	Nov., 1781
James Tryon & Lois Cole,	Dec. 26, 1781
Josh Doolittle of Middletown & Azubah Allen,	Dec. 27, 1781
John Stanley & Anne Bronson,	Jan. 7, 1782
Matthew Hart, Jr., & Urania Hooker,	Jan. 11, 1782
Abraham Jaggar & Rhoda Winchel,	March 14, 1782
John House of Glastenbury & Esther Hooker,	July 31, 1782
Reuben Peck of Southington & Sarah Gridley,	Aug., 1782
Levi Norton of Clarimount & Mercy Payne,	——
Joshua Root of Canaan & Lydia Root,	Oct., 1782
Ozias Cowles & Lucy Gridley,	Oct. 29, 1782
Samuel Goodrich, Jr., & Mary Strong,	Aug., 1783
Abel Aspenwell & Sibil Lewis,	——
Elijah Stanley & Elizabeth Peck,	Nov. 19, 1783
George Jones & Thankful Bronson,	Nov. 20, 1783
John Treat of Westfield & Betsey Lankton,	Nov. 27, 1783
Joseph Wells, Jr., & Ruthy Allen,	Dec. 31, 1783
Thomas Pattison of Stockbridge & Prudence Williams,	March 25, 1784
Salmon Cowles & Eunice Strong,	March 25, 1784
John Deming of Canaan & Hannah Johnson of Worthington,	Oct. 28, 1784
Samuel Lee of Worthington & Sybil Stanley,	Nov. 17, 1784
Oren Lee & Charlotte Heart, both of Worthington,	Dec. 2, 1784
Benjamin Gilbert & Mary Hamlin, both of Middletown,	Dec. 16, 1784
Edmond Meriam of Meriden & Huldah Peck,	Dec. 23, 1784
David Cowles & Eunice Payne,	April 21, 1785
John Williams & Allis Baily,	May 15, 1785
Moses Deming, Jr., of Worthington & Sally Norton,	June 16, 1785
Jonathan Sage of Westfield & Mary Bronson,	Aug. 11, 1785
Simeon Saxton of Guilford & Rhoda Belden,	Nov. 24, 1785
Oliver Stanley & Kezia Judd,	Dec. 25, 1785
Allen Pryor of Windsor & Polly Wells,	Jan. 24, 1786
Jabez Cowles & Betsey Scovil,	March 12, 1786

Selah Stanley & Rhoda Goodrich, April 3, 1786
Solomon Winchell, Jr., & —— Doolittle, June 15, 1786
Gideon Hart & Lyntha Langton, June 25, 1786
Ezekiel Root, Jr., of Farmington & Sintha Cole,
March 19, 1787
Solomon Evarts of New Durham & Betsey Cole, April, 1787
Amos Hosford of Worthington & Jerusha Clark,
April 26, 1787
Joseph Foard of New Durham & Mitty Scott, May 2, 1787
Salmon Goodrich & Abi Hart, both of Worthington,
May 3, 1787
Edward Pattison of Worthington & Charlotte Holis-
ter of New Britain, May 30, 1787
Nathaniel Thomson of Farmington & Sarah Root,
June 14, 1787
Rev. William Robinson of Southington & Anne Mills
of Simsbury, Aug. 13, 1787
Abel Barnes of Meriden & Charlotte Winchel, Aug. 15, 1787
Rev. Nathaniel Gaylord of Hartland & Persis Steb-
bins, Oct., 1787
Amos Newel & —— Root, both of Southington, Dec. 4, 1787
Isaac Upson of Waterbury & Sylvia Lewis of
Southington, Jan. 10, 1788
Rev. John Willard of Wallingford & Huldah
Lankton, Jan. 17, 1788
William Pattison & Wealthy Lawrance, ——
Salmon Hart & Ruthe Norton, Jan. 13, 1788
Bela Strong & Sarah Hart, Feb., 1788
Elisha Woodruff of Southington & Abigail Galpen,
March 5, 1788
Elijah Stanly & Sabra Smith, Nov. 27, 1788
Benjamin Cowles of Meriden & Lavina Peck, ——
Joseph Finch of Southington & Sarah Peck, ——
Zebedee Beckley of Worthington & Elizibeth Bel-
den, Feb. 8, 1789
Christopher Meriman of Meriden & Polly Bron-
son, Nov. 26, 1789
Roger Winchel & Martha Shaw, Dec. 30, 1789
John Gilbert of Worthington & Olive Welton, Dec. 31, 1789
James Percival, Jr., & Betsey Hart, Jan., 1790

Matthew Peck & Huldah Rice, April 22, 1790
Selah Cowles of Kensington & Lucy Smith of
 Worthington, Aug., 1790
John Hooker & Abigail Goodrich, Sept. 5, 1790
Asahel Hart of Worthington & Abigail Cowles,
Sept. 23, 1790
Joshua Parsons of Farmington & Abigail Moor, Oct., 1790
George Atkins of Middletown & Betsey Hart, Dec. 23, 1790
Submit Bailey & Phebe Rugg, April, 1791
Joseph Alcox of Farmingbury & Selina Cowles, ——
Israel Williams of Hartland & Martha Stanley, Oct. 31, 1791
Amos Gridley, Jr., & Drusilla Barrit, Nov. 16, 1791
Leman Gaylord of Bristol & Rhodaa Drigs, Dec. 12, 1791
Jesse Dickinson & Chloe Allen, April 12, 1792
Stephen Kelsey of Worthington & Hannah Hart,
Aug. 12, 1792
Apollos Dean & Sally Cowles, Dec. 31, 1792
Timothy Tryon & Roxa Smith, April, 1793
William Gaylord Cobley of Harwington & Phebe
 Tryon, Nov. 6, 1793
Asa Hopkins of Hartford & Abigail Burnham of
 Wethersfield, Oct. 16, 1793
Ozias Cowles & Sally Belden, Jan. 1, 1794
Gideon Judd, Jr., & Zitty Belden, Jan. 29, 1794
Samuel Lee & Sally Burnet, Oct. 30, 1794
Frenus Hulbert of Kensington & Lucy Hart of
 Southington, Nov. 6, 1794
Samuel Peck, Jr., of Kensington & Polly Upson
 of Meriden, Nov. 27, 1794
John Dunham of Kensington & Lucy Tryon of
 Worthington, ——
Aaron Parsons & Dorcas Bronson, Jan. 15, 1795
Linus Saxton of Guilford & Thankful Cole, May 4, 1795
David Wright of New Britain & Abigail Wadsworth, ——
Cyprian Hart & Lucy Hooker, Dec. 24, 1795
Elijah Hooker, Jr., & Polly Judd, April 21, 1796
Elijah Atkins & Sarah Williams, Sept. 4, 1796
Samuel Pardy of Southington & Lucretia Peck, ——
Joel Camp & Rebeckah Nichols, Jan., 1797
Moses Cook of Chatham & Dorithy Percival, Jan., 1797

Leonard Goodrich of New Durham & Susannah
    Dickinson,   ——
Ashbel Dickinson & Lucy Peck,   May 7, 1797
Submit Hart & Clarissa Hopkins,   May 9, 1797
James Jones of Cheshire & Polly Stanly,   Aug. 2, 1797
Darius Minor & —— Butler, both of Meriden, Aug. 2, 1797
Thomas Blake & Sally Smith,   Aug. 10, 1797
—— —— of Buckland & Polly Smith,   Sept., 1797
Asa Andrus of Farmington & Hannah Burnet, ——
John Edward Blake & Lydia Gridley,   Oct. 25, 1797
Reuben Dunham & Betsey Norton,   Dec. 14, 1797
Amos Upson of Southington & Dorcas Alford, April, 1798
Russel Cole & Susannah Hooker,   May 7, 1798
Gideon Norton & Lydia Cole,   ——
Roswel Hinsdale of Harwington & Sibil Winchel, Aug., 1798
David White, Esq., of Chatham & Polly Prior, Sept. 15, 1798
Sylvanus Dunham of Southington & Theodotia
    Peck,   Nov. 5, 1798
Isaac Smith, Jr., of Southington & Huldah Atwood,
                        Nov. 11, 1798
Levi Hough & Lois Meriman, both of Meriden, Dec. 24, 1798
Martin Bronson & Asphia Bronson,   Dec. 30, 1798
Saxa Hooker & Clarissa Stocking,   Jan. 23, 1799
Ira Graham & Asenath Peck,   May 14, 1799
Joseph Hulet & Mary Hopkins,   Aug. 22, 1799
Ozias Gilbert & Polly Wright, both of Worthing-
    ton,   Oct. 20, 1799
Seth Beckley & Huldah Richinson, both of Worth-
    ington,   Oct. 27, 1799
Bridgman Brown & Roxa Hart, both of Worthing-
    ton,   Oct. 31, 1799
Oliver Hart, Jr., & Sally Bronson,   Nov. 25, 1799
Dean or Dan Johnson & Lois Sage, both of
    Worthington,   Oct., 1799
Gideon Williams & Eunice Cowles,   Nov. 28, 1799
Joseph Peck, Jr., of Kensington & Lucy Pardy of
    Southington,   ——
Titus Bronson, Jr., & Mary Dickinson of Southing-
    ton,   Dec. 30, 1799
George McKee of East Hartford & Esther Spencer
    of East Haddam,   Jan. 27, 1800

FARMINGTON—AVON.

HARTFORD COUNTY.

The Northington Church in Farmington was organized November 20, 1751. It is now located in Avon (West), a town organized from Farmington in 1830. Rev. Ebenezer Booge pastor, 1751 to 1767. Following are the Northington Church records.

Rev. Ebenezer Booge & Damaris Cook of Walling-
ford,   Dec. 19, 1750
Elijah Hollister of Glastonbury & Mehetable Judd,
                                                  Oct. 12, 1752
Thomas Andrews & Lydia Woodford,   Jan. 18, 1753
Elnathan Gridly & Sarah Pratt,   Feb. 27, 1753
Noah Hart & Sarah Miller,   June 7, 1753
John Tillotson & Mary Norton,   May 2, 1754
Joseph North & Sarah Woodruff,   June 9, 1754
Benoni Chapin of Springfield & Esther Lewis, Sept. 10, 1754
John Hills of Goshen & Jerusha Lewis,   Sept. 10, 1754
Isaac Whisck & Jerusha Woobbunn (Indians),
    under the protection of Zebulon Woodruff,
    master of said Whisck,   Sept. 17, 1754
David Humphry of Goshen & Lucy Marshall, Oct. 10, 1754
Benjamin Lewis & Sarah Hart,   Oct. 30, 1754
Medad Hart & Phebe Miller,   Nov. 17, 1754
Ambrose Hart of A. & Martha Fuller of Syms-
    bury,   March 20, 1755
Edward Little of somewhere & Anne Hart, Aug. 5, 1755
Perez Marshall & Hannah Woodford,   April 1, 1756
John Lily & Mindwell Humphrey of Symsbury,
                                          July 15, 1756
Ruben & Sarah Miller,   Jan. 16, 1757
Samuel Woodford & Lucy Thomson,   March 15, 1757
Elisha Pratt of Town & Ruth Owen,   March 15, 1759
John Mills of West Simsbury & Wait Miller, May 10, 1759
Gideon Hart & Elizabeth Hart,   Nov. 15, 1759
Timothy Barnes & Miriam Miller,   March 19, 1760
Samuel Dunning of Town & Abigail Mills of West
    Simsbury,   April 7, ——

Noah Miller & Ann Buels,   April 9, 1760
Ebenezer Tillotson of Farmington & Tamar Lewis
   of Simsbury,   Aug. 13, 1760
Obadiah Owen & Mary Hart,   Nov. 27, 1760
Daniel Hart & Comfort Stevens,   May 21, 1761
Elijah Andrews & Sarah Thomson,   Aug. 4 1761
Ezekiel Hayford of Town & Mercy Miller,   Aug. 13, 1761
Stephen Sedgwick of W. Hartford & Lucy Wood-
   ford,   Sept. 10, 1761
Samuel Fairfield of Northampton & Susannah
   Northway,   Sept. 10, 1761
Jonathan Miller & Sarah North,   Sept. 24, 1761
Simeon Marshall & Susanna Norton,   Dec. 10, 1761
William Neal of Farmington & Margaret Olds of
   Westfield,   Feb. 17, 1762
Josiah Woodruff & Abigail Hart,   Feb. 10, 1763
Benjamin Andrews & Chloe Thomson,   March 10, 1763
Israel Freeman (mulatto) & Mary Mausank (half
   Indian),   June 16, 1763
John Spalden of Canaan & Sarah Newell,   Nov. 17, 1763
Micah Segar of Simsbury & Mary Woodford,   Dec. 8, 1763
Lemuel Roberts of Simsbury & Ruth Woodford, Dec. 8, 1763
Timothy Moss of N. Cheshire & Mary Owen, Feb. 1, 1764
Dr. Thomas Mather & Huldah Bull,   March 12, 1764
Benajah Case of Simsbury & Lydia Woodruff,
                                            March 29, 1764
Samuel North of Wethersfield & Lois Woodford,
                                            June 28, 1764
Elisha Miller of A. & Sarah Fowler of Durham,
                                            Oct. 18, 1764
Dean° (?) Ebenezer Miller of A. & Mrs. Elizabeth
   Norton of Farmington,   Nov. 15, 1764
Thomas Warren of Hatfield & Lydia Northway,
                                            Nov. 15, 1764
Solomon Curtiss & Hannah Woodruff,   Dec. 6, 1764
William Dickinson of Wethersfield & Mary Olm-
   stead of Farmington,   April 4, 1765
Mather Warren of Hatfield & Esther Hart,   May 15, 1765
William Middleton of Suffield & Elizabeth Andrews
   of Farmington,   May 23, 1765

Obadiah Andrews & Hannah Hart,   Oct. 3, 1765
Eli North & Eunice Hart,   Oct. 3, 1765
Joseph Mallison of Groton & Mary Willcockson of
      West Simsbury,   Oct. 7, 1765
Timothy Porter & Hannah Andrews,   Oct. 31, 1765
Seth Gillit of Suffield & Anne Thomson,   Jan. 29, 1766
Reuben Pixly of Great Barrington & Rebeccah
      Gridley of Farmington,   Feb. 18, 1766
Ebenezer Merrels of W. Hartford & Sarah Hart,
                                          Oct. 6, 1766
James Wilcox of Simsbury & Elizabeth Bishop of
      Northington,   March 13, 1770
Rev. Rufus Hawley of Northington & Miss Debo-
      rah Kent of Suffield,   Sept. 25, 1770
Samuel Bird of Farmington & Rhoda Hawley of
      Simsbury,   May 8, 1770
Thomas Newell of ——— & Lydia Hart,   Feb. 14, 1771
Timothy Griswold of Wethersfield & Mary Newell,
                                          March 18, 1771
David Bristoll & Lois Hart,   May 30, 1771
Daniel Woodford & Ruth Thomson,   May 30, 1771
Benjamin Bishop, Jr., & Mary Ann Frasier, June 6, 1771
Abel Dego (negro) & Lucy Way (squaw),   Nov. 14, 1771
James Root & Mercy Stedman,   July 22, 1772
Gershom Orvis & widow Jemima Judd,   Nov. 11, 1772
Seth North of Kensington & Eunice Woodford, Nov. 26, 1772
Rev. Daniel Foster of the Second Society in Wind-
      sor & Rebecca Wakely Booge of Northing-
      ton,   Dec. 22, 1772
Samuel Cook Booge & Triphena Thomson,   Jan. 14, 1773
Eldad Woodruff & Dinah Woodford,   Feb. 18, 1773
John Thomas & Zilpah Woodruff,   May 19, 1773
Ezekiel Woodford & Anna Bishop,   Sept. 2, 1773
David Gleason & Susannah Hart,   Sept. 6, 1773
Solomon Woodford & Mary Ford,   Jan. 6, 1774
Elisha Woodruff of Southington & Sarah Thom-
      son of Farmington,   March 3, 1774
Noah Humphry of Goshen & Sarah Marshal, June 1, 1774
Isaac Woodford & Sarah Fuller,   July 6, 1774
Elijah Woodford & Mary Bishup,   July 7, 1774

Dudly Woodford & Elizabeth Ford,   July 7, 1774
Peter Buil Gleason of Northington & Deborah
    Hawley of Turkey Hill,   Nov. 9, 1774
James Northaway & Achsah North,   Nov. 16, 1776
John Ford & Hannah Munson,   Nov. 24, 1774
Francis Northaway & Susannah Owen,   Dec. 13, 1774
Thomas Gridly & Dorathy Woodford,   Feb. 9, 1775
Medad Woodruff & Anna Willcox,   March 1, 1775
Joshua Persons of New Cambridge & Louis Woodruff,
                        May 18, 1775
Isaac Blakesly of Woodbury & Hannah Woodford,
                        Nov. 22, 1775
Jesse Hubbard, widower, & Mary Codner, both of
    Worthington Parish,   Nov. 30, 1775
Barnabas Thomson, Jr., of Northington & Mercy
    Peck of Worthington,   Nov. 30, 1775
John Gardner & Eunice Bird,   Jan. 3, 1776
Gad Hawley of Farmington & Lydia Gillit,   Feb. 8, 1776
Uriah Whitney, widower, of Simsbury & widow Martha
    Owen,   March 20, 1776
Daniel Humphrey of Goshen & Naomy Preston,
                        June 12, 1776
Anthony Hart of Northington & Eleanor Roe of
    Simsbury,   Aug. 14, 1776
Samuel Blakesly of Woodbury & Lydia Woodford,
                        Sept. 4, 1776
Roger Woodford of Farmington & widow Elizi-
    beth Wilcox of Simsbury,   Sept. 29, 1776
Josiah Northaway & Mercy Woodford,   Dec. 5, 1776
David Orvis & Lydia Hawley,   Feb. 6, 1777
Isaiah North & Anna Bidwell,   Feb. 6, 1777
Charles Woodford & Sarah Miller,   March 13, 1777
Charles Nott of Wethersfield, widower, & widow
    Thankful Ford,   April 28, 1777
Moses Woodruff & Anna Woodford,   Oct. 16, 1777
Samuel Norton & Martha Woodruff,   May 27, 1778
Oliver Booge & Lucy Darrin,   Oct. 11, 1778
Levi Thomson & Lucy Woodford,   Oct. 4, 1778
Elisha Miller, widower, & Abigail Bunnill, widow,
                        Nov. 18, 1778

Ezra Willcox & Phebe Woodruff,	March 31, 1779
Deacon Noah Porter & Rachel Merrills,	April 8, 1779
John Phelps, widower, of Norfolk & widow Ann Northway,	May 27, 1779
Asa Thomson & Louise Willcox,	June 20, 1779
Seth Hart & Anna Miller,	Dec. 9, 1779
David Humphry of Goshen & Lucy Marshall,	Feb. 17, 1780
Lot Woodruff of Farmington & Martha Hart,	March 9, 1780
William McKinly of Goshan & Margaret North,	March 9, 1780
Eleazer Willcox & Jemima Munson,	March 16, 1780
Lot North & Silence Horsford,	Dec. 7, 1780
Samuel Pool & Lucina Fuller,	May 10, 1781
Samuel Phelps of Simsbury & Eleanor Miller,	Oct. 9, 1781
David North of Worthington & Salome Willcox,	Dec. 13, 1781
Calvin Judd & Mary Ingham,	Feb. 14, 1782
Noah Gillit & Susannah Hulbart,	Feb. 15, 1782
Munson Hart & Mary Hart,	April 28, 1782
Oliver Marshall & Charlotte Woodford,	July 11, 1782
Lent Hart & Olive Heacock,	July 18, 1782
John Tillotson of Northington & Elizabeth Brockway of West Brittain,	Oct. 24, 1782
Josiah Wilcox, Jr., & Rosannah Woodford,	Nov. 28, 1782
Truman Heacock & Sarah Hosford,	Jan. 2, 1783
Oliver Lewis of New Hartford & Lucinda North,	March 13, 1783
Jedediah Hills of West Simsbury & Abigail Kilby of Farmington,	March 13, 1783
James Gridley Hart & Lorain Darrin,	April 24, 1783
Samuel Woodford & Olive Miller,	May 8, 1783
John Buck of Farmington & Susannah Darrin,	Aug. 6, 1783
Reuben Hart & Elizabeth Kilborn,	Aug. 25, 1783
Salmon Heacock & Elizabeth Hart,	Dec. 25, 1783
Elisha Foot of Wintonbury & Rebeckah Clark Miller,	Dec. 28, 1783
Joel Marshall of Granville & Huldah Hart,	Feb. 18, 1784
Joseph Peel (?) or Peck (?) & Hannah Parsons,	April 12, 1784
Elias Tillotson & Experience Hosford,	Sept. 23, 1784

Timothy Alderman of Simsbury & Ruth Hart, Oct. 7, 1784
Ashbel Olmstead & Rachel Lusk, Dec. 29, 1784
Jonathan Alderman of Simsbury & Sally or Sable
    Thorp, May 9, 1785
Simeon Humphrey of Goshen & Lois Marshall, Aug. 21, 1785
Titus Goodwin of West Hartford & Pose (?) Hart,
    Sept. 1, 1785
Zenas Brace of West Hartford & Abi Hart. "The
    Brides are Sisters." Sept 1, 1785
Selah Woodford & Sarah Hutchinson, Oct. 5, 1785
Jesse Cowl & Annah Hart, Nov. 6, 1785
Solomon Buil, Jr., of Simsbury (widower) & the
    widow Charlotte Marshall, Jan. 31, 1786
Truman Case of Simsbury & Rhoda Lusk, March 16, 1786
Capt. Zacheus Gillit of Southington & widow Han-
    nah Stevens of Granby, Jan. 2, 1787
Josiah Fuller & Nancy Woodruff, Jan. 8, 1787
Daniel Phelps & Rhoda Eno, both of Simsbury,
    March 15, 1787
Levi Woodford of Bristol & Rebeccah Adams of
    Simsbury, July 19, 1787
Linus Hart & Mary Ann Willcox, Aug. 23, 1787
Gedor Woodruff & Corinna North, Sept. 18, 1787
Simeon Marshall, Jr., & Sarah Case, both of Sims-
    bury, Dec. 12, 1787
Isaac Gillit & Elizabith Hart, Jan. 11 or 17, 1788
Obadiah Gillit & Hannah Willcox, Feb. 21, 1788
Ebenezer Miller & Diantha Hutchinson, Sept. 25, 1788
Jesse Wilcox & Rhoda Andruss, Dec. 16, 1788
Samuel Peck & Ruina Stedman, May 15, 1789
Thomas Spring of Granby & Abigail Hawley, Oct. 6, 1789
Gedor Woodruff & Sarah Ingham, Oct. 22, 1789
Daniel Cowles, the 3d, & Eunice North, Jan. 28, 1790
John Ingham & Louis Woodruff, March 4, 1790
Thomas F. Bishop & Lucy Foot, March 11, 1790
Jacob Foot & Salle Willcox, April 21, 1790
Stephen Parsons & Atchsa Parsons, Aug. 5, 1790
Joseph Porter & Susanna Langdon, Sept. 19, 1790
Barnabas Thomson of Northington & Ede Fuller of
    Simsbury, Oct. 20, 1790

Salmon Clark & Melinda Hart,	Oct. 31, 1790
Benjamin Lewis, Jr., of West Stockbridge & Ruth Tillotson,	Dec. 26, 1790
Beniamin Landers of Wethersfield & Mary Bird Woodford,	Feb. 17, 1791
James Andruss & Eunice Gillit,	March 13, 1791
Elijah North & Mercy Horsford,	June 9, 1791
David Brown Woodruff of Northington & Ruth Leet of Guilford,	June 30, 1791
Gad Hart & Eunice Munson Woodford,	July 20, 1791
Ensign William Woodford & Mary North,	Aug. 4, 1791
Amos Gillit & Almira Heart,	Nov. 24, 179–
Ira Northway Fairfield of Williamsburg & Anna Miller,	Sept. 20, 1792
Samuel Blakesley of Hartland & Phebe Andruss,	Sept. 20, 1792
Samuel Alford & Lucy Miller,	Feb. 6, 1793
James Wilson of Tyringham & Atchsa Woodruff of Farmington,	March 18, 1793
Jordan Ingham & Mary Hart Bristoll,	April 2, 1793
Nathaniel Clark & Huldah Woodford,	May 22, 1793
Ebenezer Sanford & Rhoda North,	April 8, 1793
Benjamin Bishop of Northington & Joanna Miller of Simsbury,	—

"He is 83 or 84 years old and she is 82."

Peter Norton & Thina Thomson,	June 25, 1793
Obed Hart & Elizabeth Edson,	July 23, 1793
Joseph Drake of Torrington & Abigail Gleason,	Oct. 7, 1793
Elijah Whiting of West Hartford & Sabrah Hart,	Nov. 10, 1793
Lieut. Abraham Horsford & Mercy Thomson,	Nov. 10, 1793
Amos Fuller of Simsbury & Elisabeth Abenatha,	Nov. 10, 1793
Eldad Woodruff & Elnar Woodruff,	Nov. 14, 1793
Samuel Marshall of Granville & Lucy Andruss,	Jan. 2, 1794
Jesse Willcox (widower) of Northington & Comfort Peck (widow) of Bristol,	Feb. 5, 1794
Appleton Woodruff (widower) & Hannah Stevens (widow),	Feb. 24, 1794
Ezekiel Horsford, Jr., & Hannah Foot,	March 27, 1794

Joseph Foot & Cynthia Horsford, March 27, 1794
Isaac Woodford, Jr., & Statira Cowle, July 10, 1794
Richard (a negro) of Newington & Abigail Brawton
 (mulatto), Aug. 10, 1794
Asa Judd of Northington & Lucy Segar of Simsbury,
  Feb. 19, 1795
Chancey Woodruff & Eunice Horsford, April 3, 1795
Giles Ford & Sarah North, April 20, 1795
Ira Sturdevant & Susanna Woodford, April 20, 1795
Rufus F. Hawley of Northington & Betsey Rich-
 ards of New Hartford, Sept. 24, 1795
Horrace Wells of West Hartford & Amy Morse of
 Simsbury, Sept. 28, 1795
Capt. David Phelps (widower) & Margaret Hum-
 phrey (widow), both of Simsbury, Oct. 3, 1795
Gurden Wadsworth of Bristol & Esther Sanford,
  Oct. 4, 1795
Oliver Pomroy & Sibble Pomroy, Oct. 7, 1795
Gideon B. Hart & Marilla Woodford, Dec. 29, 1795
Samuel Andrus & Allice Hart, March 6, 1796
Amasa Frisbie & Elizabeth Woodruff, May 16, 1796
Joseph Lankton, Jr., & Chloe Harrison, both of Bris-
 tol, Jan. 11, 1797
Capt. Dudley Woodford & Candace North, Jan. 17, 1797
Michael Barber of Windsor & Elizabeth Hall Wood-
 ruff, July 20, 1797
Darius Priest of Simsbury & Sally Peck, Aug. 24, 1797
Samuel Newell & Irena Thomas, Oct. 19, 1797
Alvin Woodruff & Polly Cowles, Oct. 26, 1797
Elihu Moses of Bristol & Elizabeth Talbrett or Tal-
 briett of Northington, April 22, 1798
James Thomas & Hannah Miller, July 29, 1798
Ichabod Bartholomew & Rhoda Wood, Oct. 18, 1798
Elisha Miller, Jr., & Sarah Fitch Woodford, Nov. 22, 1798
David Hart Gleason & Isabel North, Nov. 26, 1798
Francis Northway of Westford & Elizabeth Wood-
 ford, Jan. 20, 1799
Elijah Woodford, Jr., & Rebecca Woodruff, July 13, 1799
Elijah Wright, Jr., of Wethersfield & Esther Cooley,
  July 7, 1799

Amos Gillit & Esther Bishop,   Oct. 20, 1799
Samuel Baldwin of Branford & Flora Woodruff,
                                                Nov. 28, 1799
Obed Hart & Charlotte Dorman,   Dec. 16, 1799
Samuel Peres Drake of Granby & Anna Brockway,
                                                Jan. 22, 1800
Orestes (?) Kent Hawley & Ursula Hawley,   April 6, 1800
Isaac Humaston & Abigail Allyng,   June 2, 1800
Mark Hopkins of Granby & Amanda Lee of Bristol,
                                                July 3, 1800
Isaac Bates & Lucy Woodruff,   July 27, 1800
Uriel Driggs & Hannah Ford,   Oct. 26, 1800
Rev. Rufus Hawley & Mrs. Elizabeth Curtiss, Nov. 13, 1798
Timothy Ruggles Hawley & Deborah Ingham, Oct. 3, 1790
Rufus Forward Hawley & Betsy Richards,   Sept. 24, 1795
Jesse Dudley Hawley & Lydia Root,   May 6, 1799
Orestes Kent Hawley & Betsey Austin,   July 24, 1804
George W. Hawley & Roxana Hawley,   Oct. 14, 1804
Jesse D. Hawley & Nancy Hall,   May 14, 1809
George W. Hawley & Polly Whitman,   Nov. 9, 1815

STAMFORD — NEW CANAAN.

FAIRFIELD COUNTY.

The town of New Canaan was incorporated in 1801. Previous to this date what is now New Canaan was part of Norwalk and Stamford, and called Canaan Society, incorporated 1731. The Congregational Church of New Canaan was organized in 1733 from the churches at Norwalk and Stamford. The following are the marriages recorded on the New Canaan Church book.

Josiah Weed & Abigail Boutten,	April 15, 1742
John Richards & Rebekah Fitch,	Jan. 19, 1742-3
David Holly & Sarah Little,	July 28, 1743
Peter Smith & Jemima Benedict,	Feb. 29, 1743-4
Jonathan Husted & Mary Carter,	Dec. 3, 1744
Elijah Green & Elizabeth Roberts,	Jan. 20, 1744-5
Eleazer Slosson & Sarah Raymond,	Aug. 20, 1745
Jonathan Burall & Hannah Carter,	April 7, 1746
John Benedict & Mary Benedict,	June 12, 1746
John Williamson & Mary Hoit,	Sept. 17, 1746
Peter Husted & Anne Seymour,	Oct. 23, 1746
David Stevens, Jr., & Susanna Seeley,	Sept. 1, 1747
Moses Comstock & Elizabeth St. John,	June 30, 1748
Israel Lockwood & Susanna Smith,	Sept 1, 1748
Nathanael Cryssey & Martha Bishop,	Sept. 29, 1748
William Bolt & Lydia Fitch,	Dec. 8, 1748
Benjamin Bolt & Hannah Keeler,	Dec. 29, 1748
James Hays & Eunice Wood,	Feb. 9, 1748-9
David Benedict, Jr., & Anna Hoit,	Feb. 20, 1748-9
Ezra Boutten & Mary Boutten,	June 28, 1749
Pierson Bishop & Hannah Finch,	Aug. 17, 1749
Hezekiah Boutten & Abigail Penoyr,	Oct. 12, 1749
Ebenezer Crofoot & Sarah St. John, in Norwalk,	Nov. 1, 1749
Reuben Lockwood & Elizabeth Stevens,	Dec. 21, 1749
Eliphalet Seeley, Jr., & Sarah Schrivner,	May 10, 1750
Samuel Finch & Abigail Resco,	May 15, 1750
John Finch & Sarah Penoyr,	June 14, 1750
Abram Hoit & Dorothy Keeler,	June 20, 1750
Stephen Benedict & Ruth Keeler,	July 31, 1750
Samuel Seymour, Jr., & Sarah Betts,	March 17, 1750

"Here the names of 14 couples were torn out of the original records."

John Fanshee or Fansher, Jr., & Hannah Weed,

	June 26, 1754
John Fanshee or Fansher, Jr., & Hannah Weed,	
Jehiel Boutton & Anne Finch,	July 4, 1754
Daniel Finch & Abigail Hoit,	Sept. 16, 1754
Jeremiah Beard Eells & Lois Benedict,	Nov. 28, 1754
John Utter & Mary Rusco,	Jan. 2, 1755
Nathaniel Boutton, Jr., & Lydia Penoyr,	April 10, 1755
Andrew Seymour & Sarah Cryssey,	Jan. 15, 1756
Thomas Rusco & Anne Dibble,	Feb. 26, 1756
Jonathan Kellogg (alias Green) & Susanna Chichester,	March 29, 1756
Ephraim Smith & Mehetable Parsons,	Oct. 20, 1756
Wicks Seeley & Mary St. John,	Nov. 4, 1756
Nathan Schofield, Jr., & Mercy Stevens,	Dec. 30. 1756
Jacob Weed & Abigail Tuttle,	Feb. 10, 1757
Jehiel Weed & Lydia Hoit,	March 2, 1757
John Ambler of Stamford & Sarah Weed,	March 3, 1757
David Waterbury, Jr., & Prue Smith,	March 7, 1757
Caleb St. John & Mary Seeley,	March 10, 1757
Capt. Samuel Hanford & widow Mercy Kellogg,	March 22, 1757
Elijah Hoit & Mary Raymond,	June 28, 1757
Hezekiah Green & Susanna Hoit,	Aug. 18, 1757
Joseph Clinton & Phebe Benedict,	Dec. 1, 1757
Timothy Betts & Anne Wairing (?),	Oct. 4, 1757
Matthew Seymour & Dinah Boutton,	Feb. 28, 1758
John Rusco & Jehannah Arnold,	March 9, 1758
David St. John & Jemime Penoyr,	March 9, 1758
Jedidiah Smith & Abigail Benedict,	March 16, 1758
John Levake (?) & Esther Benedict,	March 16, 1758
James Young & Mary Sherman Crane,	March 16, 1758
Matthias St. John & Naomy Weed,	June 28, 1758
Daniel Schofield & Mary Stevens,	Oct. 23, 1758
Daniel St. John, 3d, of Norwalk & Ruth Benedict,	March 3, 1759
Nathan Lounsbury & Elizabeth Talmadge,	March 6, 1759
Hezekiah Benedict & Rachel Benedict,	April 5, 1759
Samuel Lawrence & Rhoda Benedict,	April 5, 1759
Thaddeus Seymour & Molly Smith,	April 12, 1759
Moses Ferris of Horsebeck & Sarah Kellogg,	April 20, 1759

David Stevens, Jr., & Mary Talmadge, Aug. 16, 1759
Eliakim Smith, Jr., & Catharine Hanford, Aug. 20, 1759
Levi Monger of Salisbury & Elizabeth Smith, Nov. 8, 1759
Ebenezer Mead, Esq., & Naomy Weed, Dec. 19, 1759
Thomas Risco, Jr., & Elizabeth Raymard, Jan. 1, 1760
Daniel Smith of Norwalk & Ruth Fitch, May 22, 1760
Joseph Stevens & Sarah Lockwood, July 10, 1760
Abraham Dan & Rebecca Rusco, Oct. 2, 1760
Daniel Mills of Bedford & Bethiah Cryssey, Jan. 1, 1761
Nathan Fitch & Mehetabel Hoit, Jan. 8, 1761
Zuriel Finch & Susanna Betts, Jan. 15, 1761
Matthew Hoit & Mary Lockwood, Jan. 21, 1761
Caleb Benedict, Jr., & Deborah St. John, Jan. 28, 1761
Timothy Hoit & Sarah Benedict, Feb. 4, 1761
Joseph Blatchley & Mercy Seeley, Feb. 17, 1761
Samuel Hanford, Jr., & Elizabeth Seeley, March 5, 1761
Israel Benedict of Danbury & Margaret Weed, June 3, 1761
Joseph Riggs & Mary Keeler, Aug. 4, 1761
Moses Hanford & Mercy Kellogg, Oct. 1, 1761
Daniel Wairing (?) & Hannah Raymond, Oct. 8, 1761
Thomas Seymour, Jr., & Sarah Westcot, Nov. 24, 1761
David Waterbury of the Patent & Martha Hait,
Dec. 16, 1761
Daniel Richards & Abigail Wairing, Dec. 31, 1761
Jesse Smith, Jr., & Ruhamah Hoit, Jan. 14, 1762
James Canfield (so called) of Salem & Dinah Keeler,
April 29, 1762
William Reed, Jr., & Hannah Kellogg, Sept. 29, 1762
Abijah St. John of Wilton & Ruth Hoit, Sept. 30, 1762
Timothy Betts & Lydia Finch, Oct. 21, 1762
Timothy Reed & Susannah Weed, Nov. 18, 1762
Jonathan Slosson & Lydia Lockwood, Dec. 2, 1762
Joseph Durand & Patience Weed, Dec. 22, 1762
Daniel Couch of Reading & Sarah Howes, Feb. 16, 1763
Seymour Fitch & Elizabeth Hoit, April 7, 1763
Eleazer Slawson & Susanna Benedict, April 27, 1763
James Benedict & Thankful Lockwood, May 25, 1763
Samuel Benedict, Jr., & Dinah Hoit, Sept. 8, 1763
Stephen Rusco & Ruth Boutton, Sept. 29, 1763
Stephen Benedict & Hannah Finch, Oct. 13, 1763

Eleazer Boutton, Jr., & Dinah Benedict,   Nov. 10, 1763
Stephen Benedict of Norwalk & Abigail Howe,
                                               Nov. 17, 1762
Jesse Benedict of Norwalk & Esther St. John,
                                               March 22, 1764
Emanuel Cornel (?), or Correil, from Portugal, &
    Hannah Williamson,   April 9, 1764
Jacob Selleck & Hannah Fitch.   April 10, 1764
John Hoit of Pound Ridge & Bethiah Johnes of
    Stamford,   April 19, 1764
Daniel Chichester & Rachel Roberts of Stamford,
                                               June 12, 1764
Stephen Hanford & Jemima Kellogg,   June 27, 1764
Titus Finch & Hannah Benedict,   Nov. 1, 1764
William Brown of Pound Ridge & Eunice Slosson,
                                               Nov. 8, 1764
Nathaniel Gray & Hannah Bouton,   Nov. 15, 1764
Uriah Benedict & Mary Howes,   Nov. 22, 1764
Daniel Reed of Middlesex & Susanna Weed, Dec. 13, 1764
Seymour Boutton & Esther Levake (?),   Jan. 16, 1765
Luke Raymond & Lydia Betts,   March 8, 1765
Benjamin Reed of Middlesex & Bethiah Weed,
                                               April 25, 1765
Justus Hoit & Elizabeth Fitch,   May 29, 1765
Eliakim Wood & Elizabeth Husted,   July 9, 1765
Simeon Hanford & Mary Fitch,   Aug. 8, 1765
Seth Finch & Adah Hoit,   Oct. 23, 1765
Edward Johnes & Rhoda Hays of Norwalk, Nov. 21, 1765
Samuel Cooke Silliman & Elizabeth Stratten, Nov. 26, 1765
William Fansher & Sarah Smith,   Jan. 2, 1766
Daniel Olmstead & Jemima Smith,   Jan. 9, 1766
Ezra Benedict & May Benedict,   Feb. 6, 1766
James Richards, Jr., & Ruth Hanford,   Feb. 27, 1766
Enos Weed, Jr., & Rhoda Silliman,   Feb. 27, 1766
James Weed & Sarah Richards,   June 24, 1766
Samuel Betts of Wilton & Hannah Keeler,   July 2, 1766
Isaac Kellogg & Hannah Fitch.   Oct. 10, 1766
Benajah Hoit & Mary Doolittle,   Dec. 31, 1766
Jesse Ogden & Esther Schrivner, both of Wilton,
    married at Wilton,   May 21, 1767

Stephen DeForest & Sarah Nichols,   May 28, 1767
John Keeler of Wilton & Hannah Boulton,   July 14, 1767
Eliphalet Brown, Jr., of Pound Ridge & Rebecca
   Slauson,   July 24, 1767
Jonathan Dibble of Pound Ridge & Rachel Slosson,
                                  Aug. 27, 1767
Benajah Holt & Hannah Green,   Oct. 8, 1767
Goold Selleck Pennoyr & Sarah Seeley (alias
   Leeds),   Nov. 20, 1767
Ebenezer Abbot, Jr., & Esther Middlebrook, both
   of Wilton,   Feb. 11, 1768
Elijah Hoit & Abigail Bishop,   Feb. 25, 1768
Samuel Northrup of Ridgefield & Elizabeth Keeler
   of Wilton,   March 30, 1768
Peter Weed & Esther Boutton,   June 1, 1768
Nehemiah Smith & Hannah Richards,   Nov. 30, 1768
Josiah St. John of Norwalk & Mary Fitch, Dec. 27, 1768
Nathan Fitch & Mary Reed,   March 7, 1769
Jacob Reed & Ruhannah Benedict,   March 7, 1769
Josiah Nichols & Elizabeth Boutton,   Aug. 14, 1769
David June & Prudence Ambler, both of Pound
   Ridge,   Nov. 2, 1769
Ezra Seymour & Abigail Waterbury of Stamford,
                             Nov. 23, 1769
Ephraim Lockwood, Jr., & Sarah Slosson, March 7, 1770
Seth Weed & Hannah Andrews,   Jan. 3, 1771
Jonathan Hoit & Hannah Abbot,   Feb. 17, 1771
John Baxter, of Salem & Lydia Reed,   March 4, 1771
Elijah Dean of Salem & widow Abigail Smith,
                               July 4, 1771
Samuel Benedict & widow Mary Rusco, Nov. 6, 1771
Thomas Grumman & Deborah Deolf of Norwalk,
                           Aug. 27, 1772
John Benedict & Hannah Carter,   Sept. 23, 1772
Abijah Wallace of Salem & Elizabeth Keeler of
   Wilton,   April 18, 1773
Phinehas St. John & Esther Whitney, both of Nor-
   walk,   Oct. 28, 1773
David Hoit, Jr., & Rebecca Webster,   Nov. 24, 1773
Theophilus Hanford, 3d, & Esther Dean, Nov. 24, 1773

3

Simeon Steward of Wilton & Jemima Dean of Norwalk,   Nov. 24, 1773

Samuel Olmstead & Anne Dunning, both of Wilton,
   Nov. 25, 1773

Uriah Hoit of Canaan & Elizabeth Lockwood of Salem,   Jan. 31, 1774

Nathan Kellogg & Rachel Carter,   April 23, 1774

John Green & Eunice Hoit,   Aug. 15, 1774

Samuel Baker & widow Rhoda Weed,   Oct. 20, 1774

William Hoyt of Canaan & Sarah Youngs of Middlesex,   Nov. 18, 1774

Hezekiah St. John & Mary Weed,   Nov. 24, 1774

Aaron Comstock & Anne Hanford,   Nov. 24, 1774

Rev. David Close of Fredericksburgh & Hannah Comstock,   Dec. 7, 1774

Joseph Blatchley & Cata Smith,   Jan. 3, 1775

Benjamin St. John & widow Elizabeth Everitt,
   March 9, 1775

Samuel Seeley & Elizabeth St. John,   Nov. 8, 1775

Enos Tuttle & Abigail Penoyr,   Jan. 16, 1776

Richard Dunning of Wilton & Helen Raymond,
   April 3, 1776

Jacob Silleck & Sarah Fitch,   May 2, 1776

Samuel Penoyr, Jr., & Parnell Tuttle,   May 23, 1776

Levi Tuttle of Canaan & Sarah Silleck of Middlesex,   June 10, 1776

Henry Hoyt of Stamford & Miss Debby Hanford,
   March 27, 1783

Seymour Fitch & Patty St. John,   July, ——

Samuel Hoit of Stamford & Anne Seymour,   Sept. 25, 1783

Israel Slauson of Pound Ridge & Mary Defrees,
   Oct. 9, 1783

Jonathan Bell of Middlesex & Anne Benedict, Oct. 16, 1783

Nathan Wells of Redding & Rebecca Jones,   Oct. 13, 1783

Sylvanus Seeley & Mary Hoit,   Nov., ——

David Smith & Mary Blakesley,   Nov., ——

David Webb of Stamford & Sarah Davenport, Dec. 4, 1783

Noah Hoit & Mary Seeley,   Dec. 10, 1783

Jesse Richards & Lydia Hickok,   Dec. 11, 1783

Jonathan Weed & Suke St. John,   Dec. 28, 1783

Caleb Benedict, Jr., & Rebecca Seeley,   Jan. 1, 1784
Andrew Massey of Ireland & Deborah Abbot,   Jan. 1, 1784
Seymour Fitch, Jr., of Canaan & Dinah Hoit of
    Wilton,   Jan. 1, 1784
John Seymour of Norwalk & Elizabeth Wood of
    Huntington, L. I.,   Feb. 4, 1784
David Chichester & Mary Nichols,   Feb. 7, 1784
Nathaniel Seymour & Mary Carter,   March 15, 1784
Robert North of L. I. & Betsey Carter,   March 15, 1784
Matthias St. John, Jr., & Esther Raymond,   April 4, 1784
Elijah Lounsbury of North Stamford & Clarissa
    Hoit,   May 5, 1784
Uriah Selleck of Middlesex & Hannah Smith, May 19, 1784
Joseph Crawford & Sukey Reed,   May 20, 1784
Joseph Stevens, Jr., & Deborah Seeley,   May 27, 1784
Stephen Fitch of Canaan & Charlotte Selleck of
    Middlesex,   June 3, 1784
Justin St. John & Ann Kellogg,   Oct. 13, 1784
Josiah Scofield of North Stamford & Mrs. Abigail
    Weed,   Oct. 14, 1784
John Butler & Patty Eells,   Nov. 17, 1784
Josiah Jones & Betsey Howes,   Jan. 6, 1785
Matthew Marvin & Mary Weed,   ——
Jonathan Weed of North Stamford & Rachel Jones,
                                                         Jan. 7, ——
Samuel Hanford, 3d, & Abigail Richards,   March 1, ——
Mise (?) Richards & Nanny Pratt,   Feb. 27, 1785
Mr. Griffith of Norwalk & Betsey St. John, March 24, 1785
Ezekiel Baker & Ann Weed,   April, ——
James Wairing of Stanwich & Thankful Raymond,
                                                        June 11, ——
Silas Benedict & Mercy Hoit,   Oct. 22, 1785
Thaddeus Hoit & Jemima Benedict   Oct. 29, 1785
Dr. Joseph Silliman & Patty Leeds,   Nov. 2, 1785
—— Weed & Susannah Hoit, both of North Stam-
    ford,   Nov. 2, 1785
Benjamin Wairing & Martha Chichester,   Jan. 4, 1786
Caleb Benedict & Hannah Penoyer,   Jan. 7, 1786
Eleazer Bouton, Jr., & Deborah Benedict,   Jan. 22, 1786
—— Beers of Salem & Jemima Abbot,   Feb. 8, 1786

Isaac Tucker & Sarah Stevens,	Feb. 16, 1786
David Bouton & Dinah Hanford,	July 9, 1786
Mr. Griffith of Norwalk & Polly Fancher of Pound Ridge,	——
Moses Dunning (?) of Wilton & Sarah Comstock,	Aug. 9, 1786
—— Gates & Miss Scott of Wilton,	Sept. 23, 1786
—— Dunning & Miss Keeler of Wilton,	Sept. 27, 1786
Selleck St. John & Thankful Hoit,	Oct. 23, 1786
Isaac Arnold & Phebe Hayden,	Nov. 13, 1786
Joseph Wilmuth & Mary Town from Horseneck,	Nov. 19, 1786
Phineas Hoyt & widow Taylor,	——
—— Mr. Stevens of Dantown & Miss ——,	Feb. 7, 1787
Mr. Reed of Amenia & Jemima Fitch,	Feb. 4, 1787
Daniel Weed & Miss —— Fitch,	March 18, 1787
Alexander Durand & Betsey Whaley,	April 21, 1787
Stephen St. John & Deborah Finch,	May 3, 1787
Joseph Everit & Hannah St. John,	May 3, 1787
David Stevens of Canaan & Hannah Seymour of Pound Ridge,	May 3, 1787
Elias Scofield & Abbe Weed,	Nov. 22, 1787
Pettit Lodes & Elizabeth Benedict,	Nov. 22, 1787
Mr. —— Dunning & Hannah Keeler of Wilton,	Nov. 22, 1787
Mr. Bouton & Elsa Benedict,	April, 6, 1787
Gregory Thomas & Miss Ogden, and another couple, Wilton,	May 8, 1787
Eliphalet Hanford & Nancy Hanford,	Sept. 21, 1788
Ebenezer Carter & Susannah Benedict,	Sept. 24, 1788
Deodote Davenport & Abby Hanford,	Sept. 25, 1788
Ephraim Lockwood & Mary Wairing (?),	Oct., 1788
Benj. Marvin & Sally Hoit,	Nov. 16, 1788
Jonathan Slauson & Rhoda Slauson,	Nov. 1788
Seymour Sherwood & Phebe Stevens,	Nov. 1788
Eliphalet Seeley & widow Sarah Hanford,	Oct. 4, 1789
Uriah Reed & Asabel Seeley,	April 2, 1789
David Tuttle & Sarah Richards,	Nov. 30, 1789
James Benedict, Jr., & Sarah St. John,	Jan. 28, 1790
Mr. Morris & Miss Olmstead of Wilton,	Jan., 1790
Mr. Pratt of North Salem & Mary Hoit,	Feb. 4, 1790

Enoch St. John & widow Sally Powers,   March 24, 1790
The daughter of Thaddeus Hubbel & Mr. ——— of
    Wilton,   May 19, 1790
Caleb Benedict & Sally Seymour,   June 10, 1790
Matthew Fitch & Elizabeth Seymour,   June 15, 1790
Abijah Comstock, Jr., & Betsey Raymond,   Sept., 1790
Moses Hanford, Jr., & Betsey Husted,   Sept., 1790
Samuel Hoyt of Wilton & P. Weed of Norwalk, Oct. 7, 1790
John Hanford & Sally Weed,   Dec. 28, 1790
Daniel Bouton, Jr., & Hannah Mills of North Stam-
    ford,   Dec., 1790
Stephen Dan of Salem & Sarah Jones,   Dec. 1, 1790
——— Beel of Frederickstown, N. Y., & Mercy
    Richards,   March 2, 1791
Mr. ——— Deforest & Isabel Hoit,   April 28, 1791
William Raymond & Miss Clayland,   April 21, 1791
John St. John of Wilton & Mary Crissey of North
    Stamford,   May 12, 1791
Samuel Eells & Hannah Gray,   April, 1791
Andrew Seymour & Hannah Kellogg,   June 9, 1791
Elisha Stevens & Jane Stevens,   Nov. 13, 1791
Peter Buchout of Wilton & Susa St. John,   Nov. 24, 1791
Jesse Hickok & Betsey Hoit,   Nov. 24, 1791
——— Scofield of Pound Ridge & Susannah Nicols
    of North Stamford,   Jan. 4, 1792
Mr. ——— Long & Esther Robinson, both of Wil-
    ton,   Feb. 10, 1792
Benjamin St. John & Dorcas Bouton,   June 20, 1792
Samuel Cooke Silliman, Esq., & Dinah Comstock,
                                            June 28, 1792
Abijah Silsby & Mary Benedict,   ———
Jona—— Hoit, Jr., & Peggy Taylor,   ———
Abijah St. John & Hannah Hendrick,   Sept., 1792
Stephen Camp & Rachel Hickok,   Oct., ———
Ebenezer Deforest & Polly Gilbert,   Oct. 20, 1792
Daniel Weed & Mehetable Benedict,   Oct., ———
Matthias St. John & Esther Abbot,   Nov., ———
Daniel Butler & Dinah Eells,   Nov. 17, 1792
Col. Hickok of Sheffeld & Miss Comstock of Wilton,
                                            Nov. 29, 1792

Comfort Hoit of Danbury & widow Gregory of Wilton,	Jan. 16, 1793
Peter Hoit & Esther Weed,	Feb., 1793
Stephen Bouton & Polly Jarvis,	Feb. 27, 1793
Moses Stevens of North Stamford & Hannah Beebe,	Feb. 26, 1793
—— Fitch & Damaris Weed,	Feb. 27, 1793
Jehiel Keeler & Anne Hubbel of Wilton,	March 3, 1793
Asabel Weed of Stamford & Thankful Finch,	May, 1793
Luke Keeler & Jemima Benedict,	June, 1793
Peter St. John & Rachel Johnes,	July, 1793
—— Eells & —— ——,	Nov. 14, 1793
Matthew Hoit & —— Keeler,	Nov. 14, 1793
Daniel Weed & Patty Benedict,	Nov. 12, 1793
Isaac Hoit of Salem & Huldah Weed,	——
Isaac Keeler & Catharine Tuttle,	March 2, 1794
Stephen Hoit & Polly Carter,	May 20, 1794
Isaac Benedict & Mary Davenport,	Aug. 18, 1794
Timothy Reed & Mrs. Hanford of Wilton,	Aug. 27, 1794
Eben'r Ayres & Thankful Lockwood,	Nov. 5, 1794
Seth Weed & Sally Ayres,	Nov. 26, 1794
Hezekiah Jennings & Hannah Hoit,	Nov. 27, 1794
Gilead Ambler of Danbury & Anne Hoit,	Jan. 1, 1795
—— Steward of Redding & Betsey Pennoyer,	Feb. 19, 1795
Samuel Kellogg & Patty Wilson of Pound Ridge,	March 1, 1795
Seth Hickok & Keziah Hoit,	Aug. 1, 1795
Ebenezer Carter & Rhoda Weed,	April 1, 1795
Nathan Hanford & Mary St. John,	Oct. 8, 1795
Lebbeus Reed of Canaan & Abby Davenport of North Stamford,	Oct., 1795
Nehe (?) Mead of Horse Neck & Ruth Richards,	Nov. 5, 1795
David Bishop & Mary Finch,	Nov. 22, 1795
John Tuttle & Isabel Garner,	Nov. 26, 1795
Ebenezer Hoit & Hannah Hayes,	Feb. 24, 1796
Thaddeus Hanford & Sally St. John,	March, 1796
Daniel Rumsey of Ballstown & Isabel Howes,	April 21, 1796
Ezra Ayres of Pound Ridge & Abby Kellogg,	Nov. 16, 1796

Isaac Rockwell of Salem & Polly Howes,   Sept. 15, 1796
Cook St. John & Polly Seymour,   Dec. 21, 1796
David Benedict & Hannah Fitch,   Dec. 22, 1796
Andrew Messnard & Mary Hoit,   Jan. 1, 1797
Nathan Nash of Middlesex & Barbary Brown,   Jan. 1, 1797
Darius Knight & Hannah St. John,   June 22, 1797
David Weed of North Stamford & Jerusha Wairing,
                                                Aug. 10, 1797

Jonathan Wairing & Esther Hoit,   Sept., 1797
Lewis Hoit & Elizabeth Hoit,   Sept. 17, 1797
Mr. Andras & Meriam Craft,   Sept. 10, 1797
Isaac Lewis of Huntington & Polly Craft,   Sept. 24, 1797
Samuel Crissey & Mis Hoyt of North Stamford,
                                                Sept. 28, 1797

Andrus Powers & Deborah Comstock,   Nov. 2, 1797
Amos Ayres & Hannah Lockwood,   Nov. 16, 1797
Samuel Bolt & Mary Webb,   Jan. 3, 1798
James Holmes & Anna Weed,   Dec. 27, 1797
Seth Defrees (?) & Rachel Weed,   Feb. 25, 1798
Samuel St. John & Hannah Richards,   March 1, 1798
Hezekiah St. John, Jr., & Phebe Baxter Keeler, Aug. 20, 1798
Ezra Hoit of Walton & Peninnah Hickok,   April 24, 1798
Benj. Bates of Middlesex & Esther St. John, Aug. 30, 1797
Daniel Keeler & Mary Pennoyer,   Oct. 28, 1798
Joel Hoit & Esther Richards,   Jan. 17, 1799
Seth Lockwood & Matilda Lockwood,   Jan. 20, 1799
William St. John & Susanah Brown,   April 7, 1799
Joseph Seeley, Jr., & Sally Wairing,   April 25, 1799
Moses Lyon of Wilton & Irena Benedict,   Aug. 18, 1799
Martin Hanford & Hannah Hanford,   Aug. 25, 1799
Harry Fitch & Sally Ingersol (blacks),   Nov. 27, 1799
Henry Seymour & Molly Benedict,   Nov. 28, 1799
Ezra Benedict & Hannah Comstock,   Dec. 1, 1799
Daniel Hunt of Salem & Hannah Selleck,   Dec. 25, 1799
David Hendrick & Sally Hoit,   Jan. 4, 1800

PRESTON — GRISWOLD.

NEW LONDON COUNTY.

The town of Griswold was incorporated October, 1815, and was taken from Preston. The Congregational Church in Griswold was organized November 20, 1720, as the Second Church in Preston. Rev. Hezekiah Lord pastor from 1720 to 1761. Following are the marriages.

Niclas Williams & Lydia Lonord,	Dec. 5, 1720
Jonathan Geer & Elizebeth Herrick,	June 15, 1721
Daniel Brown & Mary Breed, both of Stonington,	June 21, 1721
Jonathan Phillips & Esther Ayrs,	March 15, 1721–2
Ebeneazer Herrick & Elizebeth Guile,	March 26, 1722
David Macawithee & Abigail Park,	April 3, 1722
Isaac Read of Norwich & Abigail Lonard,	July 4, 1722
Jonathan Ayrs & Lydia Burton,	Jan. 3, 1722–3
Joseph Benjamin & Deborah Clark,	April 3, 1722
John Meach, Jr., & Sarah Hutchins,	May 1, 1723
William Adams & Susannah Woodward,	May 2, 1723
Elisha Wilcox & Mary Meach,	May 9, 1723
Ebenezer Williams & Judith Brown,	May 14, 1723
Herrington James & Ann Clark,	May 23, 1723
Samuel Clark & Jemima Gates,	June 20, 1723
Samuel Bennet & Jane Clark,	Oct. 18, 1723
Joseph Cotes & Hopstill Eliot, both of Stonington,	Nov. 7, 1723
Daniel Longbottom & Mary Caswel of Norwich,	Nov. 12, ——
Thomas Walton & Mary Downing of Norwich,	Nov. 26, ——
John Green & Mary Rich,	June 2, 1724
Ebeneazer Bundy & Martha Clark, both of Plainfield,	June 11, ——
Elijah Belcher & Abigail Kinni,	Sept. 17, ——
William Bennet & Elizebeth Green,	Feb. 17, 1725
Nathaniel Tiler & Phebe Benjamin,	Feb. 23, ——
Jacob Lamb of Groton & Jerusha Williams.	
—— Parke & Elsebeth Clark, both of Plainfield.	

—— Prentice & Mary Wheeler.

——han Jennings of Windham & Elizabeth ——.

—— —— & Zeruiah Gear.

—— Geer & Experience Lester.

—— Huntington of Norwich & Lydia Lonard.

—— Phillips of Norwich & Prudence Gates.

—— Parke of Groton & Elizebeth Benjamin.

—— Hatch & Jerusha Herrick.

—— Davison & Lydia Herrick.

—— Kinni & Sarah Herrick.

John Brand & Martha Williams,	Oct. 20, 1726
Stephen Herrick & Phebe Guile,	Nov. 9, 1726
Manaseh Minor of Volentown & Kizia Geer,	Nov. 9, 1726
Robert Gates & Mary Clark of Norwich,	Nov. 9, 1726
Thomas Branch & Zipporah Kinni,	Nov. 9, 1726
Jeremiah Hatch & Lydia Rix,	Jan. 19, 1726-7
Daniel Meach & Ame Wilcox, both of Stonington,	March 21, 1727
Samuel Gallop of Stonington & Mehetable Blunt of Norwich,	May 11, 1727
William York & Comfort Burdick, both of Stonington,	May 18, ——
Zebedee Gates & Jerusha Geer,	June 5, 1727
Isaac Williams & Dorothy Freeman,	Dec. 26, 1727
John Richards & Abigail Freeman,	Jan. 2, 1727-8
John Burlesson & Hephzibeth Brumbly,	Feb. 29, 1727-8
Thomas Ross, Jr., & Joanna Wyat,	March 28, 1728
Jabez Green & Hannah Walton of Norwich,	June 20, 1728
Silas Palmer of Stonington & Ann Green,	July 4, 1728
Robert Kennedy of Volentown & Mary Cady,	Aug. 8, 1728
Daniel Geer & Hannah Davison,	Oct. 29, 1728
Job Rogers of Westerly & Mary Stanbury of Volentown,	Nov. 6, 1728
Joseph Skinner & Martha Kinni,	April 30, 1729
John Ford of Norwich & Anna Herrick,	May 1, 1729
Silvanus Herrington of Norwich & Hannah Ayr,	July 31, 1729
Jacob Burton & Mary Herrick,	Aug., 1729
Jonathan Wheeler & Grace Benjamin,	Oct. 14, 1729
Moses Tyler & Mary Belcher,	Nov. 20, 1729

Samuel Wells of Plainfield & Hannah Wedgs, April 9, 1730
Ebeneazer Geer & Desire Herrick,   April 22, 1730
Ebeneazer Lonerd & Esther Amos,   May 6, 1730
James Babcock of Stonington & Phepe Sear,   May 7, 1730
Joseph Ayrs of Stonington & Elizebeth Herrick,   1730
Daiel Baldwin of Canterbury & H——, ⎫   Nov. 16, 1730
Joseph Clark & Elizebeth Whee——,   ⎪   Dec. 10, 1730
John Green & Elize——,   ⎪   Feb. 18, 1730–1
John Carter of Canterbury & ——,   ⎪   April 13, 1731
Jedediah Williams & ——,   ⎪   Sept. 9, 1731
Joseph Elly & Rachel ——,   ⎬   Nov. 17, 1731
Silvenas Harris & Doroth ——,   ⎪   Dec. 15, 1731
Mr. Daniel Palmer, Esq., & Mrs.   ⎪
   Mary ——,   ⎪   Jan. 13, 1731–2
Edward Pain & Lois Kinni——,   ⎪   April 6, 1732
Daniel Park & Esther Averill ——,   ⎪   April 13, 1732
Lewis Jones & Mercy Green ——,   ⎪   Nov. 3, 1732
Joseph Freeman, Jr.,& Mehetebel ——, ⎭   Nov., 1732

The records are torn here.

Thomas Dunbar of Groton & Abigail Holeman of
   Volentown,   Dec. 14, 1732
Christopher & Hannah Geer,   Feb. 7, 1732–3
Joseph Clark of Norwich & Martha Blake of
   Milton,   July 16, 1733
Samuel Lonord & Lydia Stanton,   Aug. 9, 1733
Isaac Gates & Deborah Partridge,   Aug. 21, 1733
Joshua Bennet of Stonington & Sarah Green, Oct. 3, 1733
John Brown of Stonington & Jemima Springer of
   Volentown,   Nov. 7, 1733
Samuel Williams of Norwich & Phebe Randal, Dec. 11, 1733
Luke Brumbly & Priscilla Ayrs of Volentown,
                                        Dec. 12, 1733
James Clark of Plainfield & Thankfull Woodward,
                                        Dec. 13, 1733
Oliver Perkins of Volentown & Hannah Gates,
                                     Jan. 10, 1733–4
John Mirkins of Canterbury & Elizebeth Mana-
   withy,   Jan. 23, 1733–4
William Thompson of Canterbury & Prudence
   Harrington,   Feb. 4, 1733–4
Cyprian Sterry & Elizebeth Ross,   May 31, 1734

William Bates of Warrick & Sarah Bennet, June 10, 1734
David Perry of Sherbourn & Mary Tyler, Oct. 15, 1734
John Stanton & Desire Denison, April, 1735
Eleazer Bellows of Southberry & Hannah Meach,
May 26, 1735
Joseph Parish & Mary Jones, July 3, 1735
James Geer & Mary Mackneel, Nov. 5, 1735
John Guile & Sarah Hodge, Nov. 5, 1735
William Geer & Esther Geer, Dec. 10, 1735
Thomas Clark of Norwich & Sarah Woodward,
Dec. 18, ——
Henry Putnum of Salem & Hannah Boardman,
June 23, 1736
Isaac Clark of Norwich & Susanna Geer, July, 1736
James Griffeth of Kingston & Sarah Manawithee,
Nov. 11, 1736
Isaac Burton & Hannah Burton, April 11, 1737
Thomas Johnson (transient person) & Mary Green,
July 5, 1737
Jabez Benjamin & Rhoda' Smith, Oct., 1737
Henry Walton of Norwich & Tamesen Parish, Nov. 16, 1737
Nathaniel Cogswell & Huldah Kinni, Dec. 3, 1737
Edward Herrick & Marget Avery, Dec. 9, 1737
Jabez Averill & Rachel Buxton, Jan. 5, 1737-8
Mathew Beal & Hannah Cogswell, March 17, 1738
William Denison of Stonington & Hannah Tiler,
June 20, ——
William Blogit & Mary Starkweather, June 23, ——
Ebeneazer Freeman & Mary Blogit, June 23, ——
Timothy Green & Hannah Bennet, Sept. 14, 1738
Henry Burton & Elizebeth Ray, Oct. 26, 1738
William Witter & Hannah Freeman, Nov. 7, 1738
Benjamin Kinni of Salem & Elizebeth Richards,
Nov. 21, 1738
Thomas Springer of. Voluntown & Sarah Coy, Jan. 10, 1738-9
Daniel Harris & Lydia Hill, March 7, 1738-9
William Rogers of Voluntown & Jerusha Burton,
March 22, 1739
Ebeneazer Tiler & Elizebeth Bennet, alias Green,
May 23, 1739

Thomas Baily of Groton & Huldah Stanton,   April 12, 1739
John Wedge & Zeruiah Parke,   June 27, 1739
James Freeman & Phebe Kinni,   Aug. 16, 1739
Benjamin Sheldon & Abigail Green,   Aug. 12, 1739
Nathan Leonard & Abigail Herrick,   Nov. 12, 1739
Mark Williams & Hannah Cutler,   Jan. 30, 1739-40
Stephen Johnson & Mary Kinni,   Feb. 5, 1739-40
Daniel Benjamin & Phebe Guile,   March 13, 1739-40
Joseph Kinni & Sarah Blunt,   June 10, 1740
Anthony Glass & Eunice Bennet,   June 19, 1740
Abia Coy & Ruth Wedge,   July 8, 1740
Peres Partridge & Judith Burton,   Feb. 5, 1740-1
David Randal & Kezia Davison,   Nov. 6, 1740
Abraham Guile & Lydia Ray,   June 11, 1741
Henry Skilton of South Kinston & Tabitha Avery
    of North Kinston,   July 9, 1741
Timothy Lester & Mehetabel Belcher,   Oct. 1, 1741
Robert Stanton & May Lester,   Nov. 4, 1741
Samuel Partridge & Ruth Woodward,   Nov. 5, 1741
Matthew Huntington, Jr., & Elizabeth Heath, Jan. 26, 1741-2
Theodore Preston & Eunice Bundy,   Jan. 28, 1741-2
John Lester & Mary Herrick,   Feb. 3, 1741-2
Hugh Withy & Elizabeth Withy,   March 25, 1742
Ephraim Macwithee & Mercy Luce,   March, 1741-2
Elias Bellowes & Hannah Heath,   April 19, 1742
John Quequiousupi & Margaret Moses,   April 19, 1742
Obed Benjamin & Mary Warenton,   ———
Ebenezer Joyner & Mary Bundy,   Aug. 19, 1742
Jacob Brown & Deliverance Bunny,   Nov. 11, 1742
Daniel Averill & Lucy Coggswell,   Nov. 11, 1742
Zephaniah Branch & Sarah Averill,   Nov. 11, 1742
James Downing & Mary Harris,   Nov. 11, 1742
Daniel Ellis & Elizabeth Randal,   Nov. 12, 1742
Icabod Averill & Bathsheba Pain,   Dec. 8, 1742
Aaron Geer & Mercy Fisher,   Jan. 20, 1742-3
John Tyler & Mary Coit,   Dec. 14, 1742
Isaac Herrick & Elizabeth Herrick,   March 9, ———
Asa Kinni & Bethia Kimbal,   Nov. 10, 1743
Benon Thomson & Abigail Adams,   March 28, 1744
Cyprian Stevens of Plainfield & Hannah Tracy, April 3, 1744

Moses Morse & Sarah Fish,   Aug. 2, 1744
Timothy Herrenton & Sarah Geer,   Aug. 29, 1744
Ebenezer Morgan & Desire Branch,   June 24, 1745
Robert Martin & Lydia Foster,   July 8, 1745
Jabez Stanton & Sarah Morse,   Sept. 9, 1745
Jacob Galmin (?) & Lydia Huntington,   Sept. 10, 1745
Benjamin Kinni & Thankful Rude,   Dec. 24, 1745
Daniel Starkweather & Mary Geer,   March 26, 1746
Silas Reed of Norwich & Jemima Kinni,   May 15, 1746
Peter Bundy & Priscilla Prentice,   July 14, 1746
James Wily & Sarah Macmain, both of Voluntown,
                                                            August 14, 1746
Solomon Averill & Hannah Pettingale,   Dec. 18, 1746
Daniel Bellows & Deborah Rix,   Dec. 24, 1746
Robinson Bunny & Mary Williams of Hart-
    ford,   Jan. 1, 1746–7
Stephen Geer & Ruth Clark of Norwich,
                                                            Jan. 8, 1746–7
The Rev. Mr. John, pastor, of Bridgewater, & Mrs.
    Olive Johnson of Canterbury,   Feb. 3, 1746–7
Abraham Guile & Silence Herrick,   April 21, 1747
Stephen Tucker & Mrs. Susanna Corning of Nor-
    wich,   April 23, 1747
Christopher Geer & Prudence Weakly,   June 3, 1747
Ebenezer Tyler & Sarah Streto,   Nov. 2, 1747
Perry Clark of Plainfield & Lydia Lester,   Nov. 4, 1747
Zephaniah Woodward & Mary Partridge,   Jan. 27, 1747–8
Stephen Hall of Plainfield & Esther Lenard,
                                                            March 15, 1748
John Hatch, Jr., & Sarah Richards,   April 7, 1748
Israel Burton of Voluntown & Silence Herrick,
                                                            June 23, 1748
Ezra Kinni & Sarah Denison,   Oct. 26, 1748
William Babcock of Coventry & Mary Clark,   Nov. 9, 1748
Israel Herrick & Hannah Tucker,   Nov. 17, 1748
Joseph Ayr & Lydia Davis,   Dec. 15, 1748
Israel Sabin of Plainfield & Avis Bennet,   Dec. 28, 1748
Jacob Tyler & Elizebeth Stallin (?),   Jan. 2, 1748–9
William Phillips of Plainfield & Temperance Branch,
                                                            Feb. 1, 1748–9

Ezra Gates & Mary Jones,   March 23, 1749
John Kinni of Voluntown & Ann Ayrs,   May 13, 1749
James Hopkins & Miriam Hyston,   June 21, 1749
Daniel Morse & Ann Wilcox,   June 29, 1749
James Kinni & Mary Robbins, both of Voluntown,
                                            Sept. 27, 1749
Jonathan Wheeler & Lydia Edgecomb,   Nov. 22, 1749
Moses Winter of Killingly & Kezia Cady of Volun-
    town,   Nov. 22, 1749
Joseph Gates & Abigail Baker,   Dec. 7, ——
Jonathan Phillips & Jenevereth Branch,   Dec. 13, 1749
Oliver Walton & Lucy Gates,   Jan. 5, 1749–50
John Coy & Sarah Luce,   Jan. 9, 1740–50
Ebenezer Fitch & Mary Rose, both of Norwich,
                                            Jan. 25, 1749–50
James Benjamin & Priscilla Burton,   March 3, 1749–50
Elijah Bordman & Mary Tyler,   March 15, 1749–50
Jeremiah Hatch, Jr., & Abigail Rich,   Aug. 3, 1750
Joel Starkweather & Jane Trumble,   Aug. 9, 1750
Nathaniel Prentice & Hulda Stallin,   Aug. 23, 1750
John Smith of Charlestown & Elizebeth Bundy,
                                            Oct. 24, ——
Reuben Woodward & Martha Thomson,   Nov. 28, 1750
Peter Parke & Abigail Cook,   Jan. 3, 1750–1
John Longbottom of Norwich & Hannah Jewel,
                                            Feb. 6, 1750–1
Jacob Geer & Ame Wheeler,   April 22, 1751
Nathaniel Clark of Plainfield & Thankful Gates,
                                            April 30, 1751
Samuel Andress & Assia Putnam,   June 20, 1751
Jacob Burton & Mary Benjamin,   1751
Jeremiah Ross & Bathsheba Ross,   Jan. 29, 1752
Phinehas Herrick & Sarah Lenard,   Feb. 13, 1752
John Cady of Canterbury & Deborah Benjamin,
                                            Feb. 13, 1752
William Belcher & Desire Morgan,   April 23, ——
Joseph Johnson & Abigail Belcher,   May 27, 1752
William Green & Olive Macwithy,   Nov. 13, 1752
John Harris of Plainfield & Abigail Macwithy,
                                            Nov. 30, 1752

Joseph Read of Norwich & Tabitha Herrick,	Dec. 13, 1752
Benjamin Coit & Abigail Billings,	Jan. 31, 1753
Elijah Belcher & Hannah Williams,	June 6, 1753
Jacob Rothbone & Lydia Burton,	June 24, 1753
Thomas Mordock & Elizebeth Hatch,	Nov. 8, 1753
John Starkweather & Elizebeth Belcher,	Dec. 12, 1753
Elijah Starkweather & Esther Gates,	Feb. 6, 1754
Elias Lord & Elizebeth Coit,	March 21, 1754
Joseph Kimball, Jr., & Hannah Morgan,	May 2, 1754
Samuel Coit & Mercy Clark,	May 7, 1754
Daniel Ray & Olive Geer,	Feb. 19, 1755
Obed Benjamin & Mary Herd (?),	March 27, 1755
Seth Smith of Stonington & Sarah Tyler,	April 17, 1755
Samuel Tracy & Ame Partridge,	May 15, 1755
Ebenezer Welch of Plainfield & Sarah Macwithy,	
	July 17, 1755
Nathan Huntington & Ame Brown,	Aug. 26, 1755
Samuel Smith, Jr., & Delight Gibbins,	Dec. 25, 1755
Elisha Tyler & Hannah Lester,	Dec. 31, 1755
Winter Green & Borradel (?) Bennet,	Feb. 11, 1756
Aaron Crarey & Mary Stanton,	April 8, 1756
Ebenezer Belton of Groton & Ann Williams,	May 26, 1756
Samuel Wheeler & Rachel Herrick,	Sept. 28, 1756
John Smith of Stonington & Hannah Tyler,	Oct. 28, 1756
Peter Williams & Sarah Smith,	Nov. 18, 1756
Israel Hutchinson & Phebe Benjamin,	Dec. 16, 1756
John Moredock & Jerusha Hatch,	Jan. 20, 1757
Lemuel Macwithy & Mary Mirkins,	Jan., ——
Jesse Spauldin & Mary Kimball,	March 8, 1757
James Dixon of Voluntown & Agnis Moredock,	
	March 10, 1757
Samuel Tyler & Judith Brown,	March 17, 1757
Isaac Bennet, Jr., & Elizebeth Shelden,	March 29, 1757
Caleb Lewis & Sybil Macwithy,	April 7, 1757
Jabez Weight of Norwich & Sarah Lord,	April 21, 1757
Moses Branch & Abigail Tucker,	April 21, 1757
Phinehas Gates & Esther Herrick,	June 16, 1757
Samuel Guile & Lydia Geer,	Aug. 23, 1757
Benjamin Kinni & Sarah Bump,	Sept. 13, 1757
Edward Herrick & Elizebeth Brayman,	Oct. 27, 1757

Ezekiel Spauldin of Plainfield & Sarah Morgan,
                                        Oct. 27, 1757
Elijah Hamlin of Voluntown & Mary Cook,   Feb. 23, 1758
Stephen Tucker & Mary Brown,   March 2, 1758
Jonas Frink & Freelove Brumbly,   March 8, 1758
Benjamin Dow of Voluntown & Mary Hutchinson,
                                        May 17, 1758
James Brayman & Elizebeth Huntington of Nor-
    wich,   May 18, 1758
Daniel Kinni of New Milford & Huldah Cogswel,
                                        Aug. 29, 1758
James Baldwin of Canterbury & Thankful Clark
    of Norwich,   Sept. 23, 1758
Eleazer Prentice & Sarah Stanton,   Oct. 19, 1758
Lieut. Oliver Coit & Zipporah Morgan,   Nov. 21, 1758
William Adams & Mary Cook,   Nov. 23, 1758
Ezra Williams of Norwich & Anne Snow of Win-
    dam,   1759
Joseph Prentice, Jr., & Abigail Lonord,   March 15, 1759
Samuel Adams & Sarah Clark,   March 28, 1759
Eliezer Herrick & Mary Rea,   April 12, 1759
Thomas Page & Hannah Averill,   Oct. 26, 1759
Nathaniel Geer (?) of Coventry & Esther Tyler,
                                        Nov. 1, 1759
Adam Clark of Canterbury & Mehetabel Gates, Dec. 5, 1759
Spencer Kinni & Merribi Brumbly,   Dec. 12, 1759
James Brayman & Lucy Brown,   Dec. 20, 1759
Hezekiah Meach of Stonington & Abigail Johnson,
                                        March 13, 1760
Benjamin Coit & Mary Bordman,   May 28, 1760
David Kinni of Volentown & Eunice Cogswell,
                                        Dec. 16, 1760
William Halsey of Groton & Lucy Frink,   Jan. 7, 1761
Amos Cleft & Mary Coit,   Feb. 12, 1761
Rufus Herrick & Lydia Lenord,   March 3, 1761
Joseph Hatch & Elizabeth Brown,   March 19, 1761
Abraham Dibol & Sarah Welch of Simsbury, April 15, 1761
Benjamin Clark of Canterbury & Susanna Adams,
                                        April 15, 1761
John Partridge, Jr., & Hannah Lenord,   May 14, 1761

Charles Button & Anne Wilcox,   May 27, 1761
Samuel Barret of Plainfield & Jemima Hamlin, June 1, 1761
Nathan Burton & Lydia Guiles,   Nov. 18, 1762
Jonathan Herrick & Elizabeth Clark,   Dec., 1762
Thomas Rede & Eunice Kimball,   Dec. 23, 1762
Benjamin Gallup of Voluntown & Ann Kinni, Jan. 20, 1763
John Braman & Eunice Adams of Plainfield,   Feb. 3, 1763
George Darrow of Stonington & Elizebeth Benjamin,
                                            March 7, 1763
Samuel Wilcox & Lois Cogswell,   June 23, 1763
Simeon Lyton of Groton & Mary Lester,   Oct., 1763
David Perkins of Exeter, in R. I., & Zilpha Geer,
                                            Nov. 17, ——
Nehemiah Gates & Mary Woodward,   Dec., 1763
Jeremiah Hatch & Betty Bragg,   Feb. 8, 1764
Joseph Heath of Litchfield & Mercy Adams, Feb. 9, 1764
John Coy & Meriam Mordack,   March 8, 1764
Daniel Armstrong of Norwich & Docas King of Ston-
    ington,   March 29, 1764
Stephen Geer & Phebe Killam,   June 28, 1764
Isaac Gates, Jr., & Prescilla Bundy,   June 29, 1764
Phineas Clark of Norwich & Margaret Herrick,
                                          June 29, 1764
Peter Lanman of Norwich & Sarah Coit,   Dec. 6, 1764
Daniel Peck of Lyme & Jerusha Yarrinton,   Dec. 25, 1764
Josiah Burton & Mary Lenord,   April 10, 1765
Ebenezer Treacy of Norwich & Mary Freeman,
                                          May 15, 1765
John Holly & Hannah Rose, both of Norwich, June 10, 1765
Peter Branch & Ruth Partridge,   Aug. 15, 1765
Benjamin Brayman & Abigail Fitch of Norwich,
                                          Aug. 22, 1765
Amasa McWithey & Allice Apply of Plainfield, Oct., ——
Aaron Preston of Norwich & Mary Prentice,   Oct., ——
Asa Witter & Joanna Kinne,   Oct., ——
Israel Geer & Thankfull Killam,   Oct. 14, 1765
Stephen Ginnings & Thankfull Wakely,   Nov. 14, 1765
Elisha Partridge & Margaret Moredack,   Nov. 14, 1765
Ebenezer Jonson of Canterbury & Lydia Brewster,
                                          Dec. 5, 1765

4

William Palmer of Stonington & Levinah Kinne,
                                        Dec. 12, 1765
Jesse Geer & Hannah Evens of Plainfield,   Dec. 24, 1765
Wheler Coit & Mehetabell Lester,   Dec. 26, 1765
Abel Geer & Ester Fritch of Norwich,   Feb. 5, 1766
John Coit & Mehetabel Tyler,   Feb. 6, 1766
Jesse Buck & Dorothy Wheler,   Feb. 27, 1766
John Rude of Norwich & Elizabeth Freeman,
                                        March 20, 1766
John Wells & Mary Sheldon,   March 27, 1766
Joseph Freeman, Jr., & Sara Kimball,   April 15, 1766
Asa Burton & Thankfull Kinne,   April 17, 1766
James Braymen & Prudence Gates,   April 23, 1766
Samuel Morse & Eunice Brown,   April 24, 1766
Cato (negro man) & Jenne (negro woman),   May 26, 1766
Joseph Kirtland of Norwich & Ziporah Freeman,
                                        June 12, 1766
John Guile, Jr., & Asenath Elliot,   Nov. 19, 1766
Nathan Wheler of Norwich & Jemima Benjamin,
                                        Nov. 20, 1766
Jacob Dressor of Killingly & Ester Jonson of Nor-
    wich,   Nov. 27, 1766
Qember (?) Haulkins of New London & Abigail Bliss
    of Norwich,   Dec. 7, 1766
Asa Freeman & Lucretia Bennet,   Feb. 8, 1767
Nathaniel Prentice & Mercy Green of Norwich,
                                        Feb. 18, 1767
Daniel Gates & Ziporah Leonard,   April 2, 1767
Elisha Burton & Susannah Burton,   April 9, 1767
William Tucker & Ester Morgan,   June 4, 1767
Daniel Kelly of Norwich & Elizabeth Lord, June 4, 1767
Jesse Bennet of Norwich & Lydia Green,   Nov. 19, 1767
Daniel Rose & Jerusha Brewster,   Dec. 24, 1767
William Morse & Sarah Liffingwell,   Dec. 29, 1767
Samuel Porter of Woodbury & Louis Guile,   April 5, 1768
Elisha Guile & Abigail Rea,   May 5, 1768
Nathaniel Adams & Mary Geer,   June 12, 1768
Nathaniel Lord & Abigail Tyler,   Oct. 27, 1768
Caleb Shaw & Sarah Freeman,   Nov. 3, 1768
Jonathan Williams & Anne Olin,   Dec. 8, 1768

Abel Bennet & Lydia Stanton,   Dec. 29, 1768
David Meach & Prudence Stanton,   Jan 5, 1769
Asahel Tracey & Olive Leonard,   Feb. 15, 1769
John Gates & Elizebeth Tyler,   Feb. 15, 1769
Daniel Coy & Lucy Partridge,   March 30, 1769
Joseph Kinne, Jr., & Mary Button of Stonington,
                                                April 5, 1769
Daniel Gates, Jr., & Elizebeth Gates,   April 6, 1769
Silas Glass of Canterbury & Joanna Averil,   May 25, 1769
Samuel Bliss, Jr., of Norwich & Sarah Brown, Oct. 8, 1769
Samuel Manning & Mary Gates,   Nov. 9, 1769
Jesse Seaton of Plainfield & Dorothy Gates, Nov. 15, 1769
Elias Brown & Sabra Billings,   Nov. 22, 1769
Samuel Napping of Woodbury & Lydia Burton,
                                               Nov. 22, 1769
Daniel Morse, Jr., & Patience Rude,   Nov. 23, 1769
Abel Stanton of Norwich & Olive Rude,   Nov. 23, 1769
John Thompson & Fanny McFarland, both of
    Voluntown,   Dec. 7, 1769
Mr. Daniel Tyler of Pomfret & Mrs. Mary Lestor,
                                               Jan. 24, 1770
Mr. Ebenezer Bishop of Norwich & Mrs. Jerusha
    Lord,   Jan. 25, 1770
William Huntington of Windham & Mary Cutler,
                                               Feb. 15, 1770
Standbury Button & Hannah Wilcox,   Feb. 15, 1770
Elisha Geer & Desire Stanton,   March 21, 1770
Elisha Button of Stonington & Bethia Kinne,
                                              March 21, 1770
Samuel Bishop, Jr., & Mercey Jonson, both of Nor-
    wich,   Oct. 25, 1770
Simon Brewster, Jr., & Mehetabel Belcher,   Dec. 20, 1770
Jacob Cady of Voluntown & Dorothy Morgan, Dec. 27, 1770
Daniel Morgan, Jr., & Elizebeth Lord,   Jan. 30, 1771
Stephen Johnson, Jr., of Norwich & Elizebeth
    Morgan,   Jan. 31, 1771
Stephen Pain of Pomfret & Martha Cogswell,   Feb. 6, 1771
Ebenezer Freeman & Anne Tyler,   Feb. 14, 1771
Aaron Baldwin of Canterbury & Mahetabel
    Leonard,   April 11, 1771

Nathan Lester & Elizebeth Averil,   May 2, 1771
John Youngs of Norwich & Mary Tucker,   Aug. 8, 1771
Walter Fanning & Grace Benjamin,   Nov. 7, 1771
Asa Spicer of Norwich & Mary Stanton,   Jan. 1, 1772
Joseph Tyler, Jr., & Anne Freman,   Jan. 9, 1772
John Rayment of Hartford & Sarah Olin,   March 18, 1772
John Waterman of Norwich & Mary Lord,   May 28, 1772
Lestor Stanton & Margaret Benjamin,   Aug. 6, 1772
Stephen Gates & Desire Rude,   Oct. 15, 1772
Manassah Prentice & Asenath Burton,   Nov. 19, 1772
John Theop of Dublin, in Ireland, & Huldah Brown,
                                               Dec. 21, 1772
Edward Mills of Groton & Hannah Avery of Nor-
    wich,   Dec. 24, 1772
Asa Kinney, Jr., & Thankfull Bellows,   Dec. 31, 1772
Jonathan Graves & Ziporah Tracey,   March 18, 1773
Deacon Elijah Belcher & Mrs. Judith Morse,   July 15, 1773
Henry Badger of ——— & Judith Cogswell,   Sept. 30, 1773
John Lathrop of Norwich & Lydia Freeman,   Nov. 4, 1773
Dr. John Crane of Hanover, in the Province of
    New Hampshire, & Hannah Brown,   Nov. 11, 1773
Moses Lestor & Lydia Lord,   Nov. 25, 1773
Daniel Bottom of Norwich & Elizebeth Lester, Dec. 16, 1773
Samuel Davies of Stonington & Thankfull Harris,
                                               Dec. 30, 1773
Ezra Gates & Mercy Gates,   Feb. 17, 1774
Lynne Holly & Sarah Harris,   March 16, 1774
Charles Fanning & Anne Brewster,   March 31, 1774
Charles Mile of Preston & Mary Clark of Norwich,
                                          March 31, 1774
Samuel Belcher of Brantree & Mary Lewis,   July 28, 1774
John Stanton & Huldah Freeman,   Aug. 16, 1774
Samuel Williams, Jr., of Norwich & Lydia Hatch,
                                           Aug. 30, 1774
Daniel Leonard & Mary Starkweath,   Oct. 6, 1774
Isaac Spencer of Shaftbury & Anne King,   Oct. 13, 1774
Seth Paine of Pomfret & Lydia Lestor,   Nov. 16, 1774
Ebenezer Herrick & Betty Culver.   Nov. 24, 1774
Joseph Cleft & Elisabeth Stanton of Norwich,
                                           Nov. 29, 1774

Gideon Averell & Zeruiah Cogswell,   Dec. 21, 1774
John Reed of Norwich & Rachel Averell,   Dec. 22, 1774
Jonathan Reed of Norwich & Hannah Herrick,
    Dec. 22, 1774
Joseph Wilbur of Richmond, R. I., & Elisabeth
    Herrick,   Jan. 12, 1775
Jonas Geer & Martha Burton,   Jan. 12, 1775
Allen Geer & Mary Burton,   Jan. 12, 1775
Robert Hewston of Voluntown & Sara Kinne, Feb. 23, 1775
Joseph Gates & Dorothy Seaton,   March 30, 1775
Prince (negro man servant to Jabez Read of New-
    ent) & Sarah Lias (Indian woman),   Sept. 28, 1775
Thomas Chesborough & Joanna Tyler,   Oct. 15, 1775
Daniel Clark & Elisabeth Wheler of Norwich,
    Nov. 22, 1775
Daniel Hopkins of Voluntown & Olive Kinne,
    March 13, 1776
David Reed of Norwich & Hannah Kinne, March 14, 1776
Moses Woodward & Lydia Herrick,   March 31, 1776
Joshua Gates & Mercy Bennet of Norwich,   April 4, 1776
James Bottom of Norwich & Sarah Averill, June 27, 1776
Jonas Brewster & Eunice Pellet of Canterbury,
    June 30, 1776
Mr. Timothy Lestor & Mrs. Rebecca Aysault (?),
    July 3, 1776
Gideon Averell & Elizabeth Johnson of Norwich,
    Oct. 7, 1776
Asa Frink & Esther Parker,   Oct. 17, 1776
Mr. James Geer & Mrs. Mary Kimbal,   Nov. 10, 1776
Lemuel Culver of Norwich & Mary Hortness, Nov. 17, 1776
Mr. Samuel Bliss of Norwich & Mrs. Mary Stanton,
    Dec. 30, 1776
Isaac Burton & Desire Rea,   Jan. 20, 1777
Abel Lewis of Voluntown & Jerusha Rix,   Jan. 30, 1777
Brentnal (?) Robbins of Voluntown & Mary Board-
    man,   Feb. 13, 1777
Reuben Woodward & Hannah Stanton of Norwich,
    Feb. 20, 1777
Samuel Robbins of Voluntown & Zeruiah Cook,
    March 6, 1777

Pearl Brown & Olive Belcher,   March 11, 1777
Gideon Rea & Zyporah Kimbal,   March 20, 1777
Jeremiah Philips & Margaret Stanton,   May 11, 1777
Samuel Cleveland & Mercy Williams,   May 22, 1777
Col. Samuel Mott & Miss Lydia Tyler,   Aug. 7, 1777
John Wheler & Sarah Clark of Norwich,   Oct. 29, 1777
Nicholas Randal of Voluntown & Content Philips,
                                                Nov. 20, 1777
Joseph Northrop & Sarah Hatch,   Dec. 17, 1777
Oliver Walton, Jr., & Amy Woodward,   Dec. 18, 1777
Capt. Judah Burton of Nine Partners & Miss Eunice
     Morgan,   Jan. 18, 1778
James Wiley, Jr., of Voluntown & Mary Holly, Jan. 29, 1778
Moses Fish, Jr., of Voluntown & Jerusha Phillips,
                                                Feb. 12, 1778
Jabez Stanton, Jr., of Norwich & Elisabeth Clark,
                                                Feb. 12, 1778
Nathan Wallon & Eunice Gates,   March 3, 1778
Elijah Phillips & Susanna Gates,   March 5, 1778
Silas Spaulding of Plainfield & Eunice Bliss of Nor-
     wich,   March 26, 1778
Dr. Allen Campbell of Voluntown & Sarah Kinne,
                                                June 18, 1778
Zephaniah Hartshorn & Mary Guile,   June 18, 1778
James Frink & Meribah Meach,   June 25, 1778
David Smith & Hannah Wheler, both of Norwich,
                                                July 26, 1778
Nathan Geer & Mary Gates,   Oct. 1, 1778
Asher Blount of Norwich & Sarah Gates,   Nov. 19, 1778
William Clark of Voluntown & Rachel Holly,   Jan. 7, 1779
Asa Starkweather & Amy Kimball,   Feb. 18, 1779
Mr. Mical (?) Benjamin & Miss Margaret Wither-
     son of Stonington,   Feb. 23, 1779
Asahel Mordack of Norwich, Vt., & Elizabeth
     Starkweather,   Feb. 28, 1779
Calvin Worthington of Worthington & Eunice
     Brumly,   March 14, 1779
Col. Samuel Coit & Mrs. Jemima Hall,   March 22, 1779
Asa Boudish of Voluntown & Elizabeth Medkins (?),
                                                April 15, 1779

Arpl (?) Pope of Voluntown & Anne Guile,   April 15, 1779
Benjamin Slaughter of Canterbury & ———, April 19, 1779
Elijah Button of Groton & Lucy Yarington,   June 3, 1779
Capt. John Cady of Plainfield & Miss Joanna Pem-
    berton,   July 8, 1779
Asa Burnham & Lucy Huntington of Norwich,
                                             Aug. 16, 1779
Jonathan Graves & Elizabeth Bacon,   Aug. 22, 1779
Squire Phillips & Anne Gates,   Nov. 25, 1779
Asa Partridge, Jr., & Anne Woodward,   Dec. 30, 1779
Ephraim Withey of Bennington & Alice Mulkins,
                                             Jan. 6, 1780
Caleb Hall of Plainfield & Keziah Geer,   Jan. 13, 1780
Robert Geer & Salvina Gates,   Jan. 27, 1780
Asa Baker of Norwich & Comfort Kinne,   Feb. 9, 1780
Cyrus Gates & Mercy Herrick,   Feb. 10, 1780
Jacab Gates & Peggy Stewart,   Feb. 10, 1780
John Tyler, Jr., & Mary Boardman,   Feb. 17, 1780
John Withey (?) & Thankful Kinne,   May 4, 1780
Lebeus Geer & Rachel Morgan,   June 1, 1780
James Bennet, Jr., & Lucy Avery of Norwich, June 22, 1780
Charles Champlin of Stonington & Mary Wood-
    man (?),   July 16, 1780
Richard York & Phillis Lester,   Sept. 22, 1780
Roger Coit & Olive Brewster,   Sept. 28, 1780
John Cary & Mary Reade,   Nov. 12, 1780
Isaac Coit & Ruanna Hall,   Nov. 23, 1780
Laben Hall of Plainfield, N. H., & Olive Adams,
                                             Dec. 6, 1780
Jeremiah Rose or Ross & Esther Gates,   Dec. 7, 1780
Zoath Freaker of Voluntown & Mary Geer,   Dec. 7, 1780
Nathan Gates & Martha Martin,   Dec. 13 1780
Thaddeus Cook, Jr., & Sarah Prentice,   Jan. 4, 1781
Adin Palmer & Lois Stanton,   Feb. 1, 1781
Samuel Gates of Canean, N. H., & Sarah Benjamin,
                                             Feb. 8, 1781
Joseph Guile & Sarah Herrick (?),   March 22, 1781
Oliver Gates & Jemima Freman,   April 26, 1781
Joseph Crandal of Exeter & Olive Wheler of Norwich,
                                             May 24, 1781

Jonas Leonard of Worthington, Mass., & Eunice
   Herrick, May 31, 1781
David Parke of Groton & Anne Stanton of Norwich,
   July 5, 1781
Elijah Tracey of Norwich, in Vt., & Jerusha Stark-
   weather, Oct. 18, 1781
Nathan Stanton & Cynthia Kinne, Nov. 1, 1781
Joseph Billings, Jr., & Sarah Belcher, Nov. 15, 1781
Daniel Coit & Olive Tyler, Nov. 29, 1781
Jebez Rockwell of Stonington & Deborah Bellows,
   Dec. 2, 1781
Job Terral (?) of New Milford & Kezia York, Dec. 9, 1781
Jonas Morgan & Sarah Mott, Dec. 13, 1781
Peleg Freman & Abigail Reed, Dec. 27, 1781
Benjamin Rand & Sarah Tucker, Dec. 27, 1781
James Hatch & Esther Tucker, Jan. 10, 1782
Stephen Allen of R. I. & Esther Frink, Jan. 31, 1782
Jonathan Cady & Christian Geer, March 7, 1782
Elisha Smith of (?) Coventry & Martha Brown,
   March 31, 1782
Wheeler Gallop of Voluntown & Elizabeth Cogswell,
   May 2, 1782
Elisha King of Norwich & Sabra Withey, May 2, 1782
John Ash & Priscilla Frink, May 28, 1782
John Wilson & Lydia Jewett, both of Norwich,
   Aug. 1, 1782
Lemuel Stewart of Little Hoosach, New York, &
   Rebecca Rose, Aug. 18, 1782
Jacob Meach & Sarah Plummer, Nov. 21, 1782
Elisha Lester & Betsy Freman, Jan. 3, 1783
Daniel Ramon & Lydia Leonard, Jan. 9, 1783
Loring Robbins of Voluntown & Petsy Bordman,
   Jan. 9, 1783
John Austin & Esther Herrick, Jan. 16, 1783
Robert Crary & Margaret Kimball, Jan. 23, 1783
Timothy Palmer of Norwich & Lydia Aldrich, Jan. 29, 1783
Simeon Brown of Groton & Anne Spaulding of
   Canterbury, Feb. 9, 1783
James Frink, Jr., & Judith Bromly, Feb. 20, 1783
Jonas Parke & Mary Herrick, March 5, 1783

Joseph Hart of Worthington, Mass., & Rebecca
    Harris, June 2, 1783
Caleb Gasper of Ashford & Sarah Allen, June 29, 1783
Joseph Lillibridge of Richmond, R. I., & Rachel
    Stevens, Aug. 28, 1783
Hezekiah Boardman & Hannah Cook, Oct. 2, 1783
Buel Stevens & Keziah Brown, Oct. 5, 1783
Stephen Mott of Plainfield & Naoma Bennet of
    Norwich, Oct. 9, 1783
Darius Palmer & Polly Bennet, Dec. 11, 1783
Andrew Clark of Plainfield & Jean Rose, Dec. 25, 1783
John Walton & Mary Cleft, Jan. 29, 1784
Prosper Wheeler of Norwich & Sarah Dexter of
    East Greenwich, Feb. 2, 1784
Nathaniel Brown of Stonington & Abigail Stanton,
    April 2, 1784
James or Jonas Morgan & Polly Mott, April 22, 1784
Walter Palmer of Plainfield & Hannah Gates,
    April 22, 1784
Joseph Tanner of West Greenwich, R. I., & Lydia
    Stanton, May 27, 1784
Walter Brown, Jr., & Avis Kinne, Oct. 10, 1784
Capt. Ezra Bishop & Jerusha Lord, both of Norwich,
    Oct. 21, 1784
Ephraim Herrick, Jr., & Sarah Roseter (?), Nov. 11, 1784
Thomas Austin & Abigail Weadon, Nov. 11, 1784
Reuben Palmer of Stonington & Zeruiah Stanton,
    Nov. 17, 1784
Henry Withey & Keziah Worinton or Thorinton,
    Nov. 22, 1784
James Tyler & Eunice Belcher, Nov. 25, 1784
Elias Bennet & Lydia ——— of Canterbury, Nov. 25, 1784
Dennis Meach of Worthington, Mass., & Abigail
    Billings, Dec. 2, 1784
Gideon Crandal of Westerly, R. I., & Esther Rix,
    Dec. 2, 1784
Calvin Huntly of Norwich & Eunice Guile, Dec. 2, 1784
Moses Robbins of Voluntown & Abigail Cook, Dec. 30, 1784
William Tanner of West Greenwich, R. I., & Lois
    Johnson, Jan. 6, 1785

Elias Brewster & Margery Morgan,   Jan. 26, 1785
Samuel West of New Hampshire & Jerusha Stan-
    ton,   March 10, 1785
Jonathan Hartshorn & Mary Billings,   May 17, 1785
William Stanton & Levia Gates, both of Norwich,
                                           May 22, 1785
Noah Jones of Coventry & Dolly Hillman,   May 25, 1785
Pearl Wheeler & Edy Smith, both of Norwich,
                                           June 16, 1785
Reuben Parke & Zeruiah Herrington,   June 22, 1785
Samuel Clark & Phebe Thornton of Plainfield,
                                           Aug. 25, 1785
Walter Blunt & Deborah Herrick,   Sept. 1. 1785
Nathan Belcher & Lucy Huntington,   Nov. 10, 1785
William (negro man) & Pegge (negro woman), Nov. 10, 1785
Dr. Elias Parkman & Alithina Belcher,   Nov. 24, 1785
Royal (?) Fox & Phebe Hough, both of Norwich,
                                           Dec. 12, 1785
Samuel Gallup of Voluntown & Lucy Averill, Dec. 15, 1785
Joseph Brewster & Hannah Tucker,   Dec. 25, 1785
David Kimbal & Eunice Brown,   Dec. 29, 1785
Dr. Elijah Herrick & Lucinda Prentice of Stonington,
                                           Jan. 19, 1786
Peres Main of Stonington & Rebecca Stanton, Jan. 26, 1786
Benjamin Johnson of Voluntown & Abigail Rouse,
                                           Feb. 23, 1786
Darius Smith & Affiah Wheeler, both of Norwich,
                                           March 2, 1786
Thomas Ewston (?) of Stonington, Mass., & Mehet-
    able Freeman,   March 22, 1786
Lemuel Walbridge of Coventry & Elizabeth Hil-
    lom or Hillam,   March 23, 1786
Joseph Button & Olive Prentice,   March 23, 1786
Joseph Belcher & Lucy Hall,   March 30, 1786
Elisha Prentice & Deborah Whedon,   April 6, 1786
Alexander Campbell of Voluntown & Mary Halsey,
                                           April 13, 1786
Hezekiah Clift & Lucy Walton,   April 27, 1786
George Hasard Perry of South Kingston, R. I., &
    Abigail Cheseborough of Stonington,   June 11, 1786

Daniel Coit & Mercy Brewster, Aug. 31, 1786

James Thomas & Freelove Clark, both of Norwich,
Sept. 6, 1786

John Herrick & Esther Frink, Oct. 5, 1786

Phinehas Gates & Caroline Freeman, Oct. 5, 1786

Hugh O'Donnel & Mary Gates, Nov. 2, 1786

Elias Tracey & Lydia Gates, Nov. 9, 1786

James Tyler & Clarina Punderson, Nov. 22, 1786

Lot Kinne & Betsy Robbins, Dec. 7, 1786

Henry Franklin & Sarah Dark (negroes), Dec. 7, 1786

Noah Mason & Lucretia Kinne, Dec. 14, 1786

Christian Gosner & Cynthia Branch, Dec. 14, 1786

Gideon Woodward & Zeruiah Tyler, Jan. 11, 1787

Amos Starkweather & Jemina Brown, Jan. 25, 1787

Andrew Heart (?) of Stonington & Rachel Boardman, Feb. 4, 1787

Minor Spaulding & Sarah Mott, March 11, 1787

Jeremiah Bennet of Saratoga, N. Y., & Lois Gates,
March 15, 1787

Thomas Prentice of Stonington & Anne Downer,
April 19, 1787

Frederic Faning & Joanna Ruyman of Lisbon,
May 17, 1787

Daniel Stanton & Sarah Johnson, Aug. 9, 1787

Samuel Lenord, Jr., & Elisabeth Braman, Sept. 27, 1787

William Cogswell & Abigail Belcher, Oct. 11, 1787

Renyon Covey of R. I. & Sarah Kinney, Oct. 28, 1787

Nathan Cogswell & Lydia Cleft, Nov. 15, 1787

Samuel Turner of Mansfield & Lucy Morgan, Dec. 6, 1787

Rufus Hatch & Selah Hall, Dec. 27, 1787

Col. Samuel Mott & Mrs. Abigail Stanton of Groton,
Jan. 23, 1788

Nathaniel Prentice & Lucy Campbel of Voluntown,
Feb. 7, 1788

William Peters of Plainfield & Bridget Deshon, Feb. 7, 1788

Elijah Tracey & Lois Fitch, both of Lisbon, Feb. 21, 1788

Asa Stanton & Desire Kimbal of Lisbon, March 13, 1788

William Wade of Newport, R. I., & Hannah Tracey,
April 13, 1788

Jedediah Lafford & Alice Gordon, May 22, 1788

Jonas Boardman of Norwich, Vt., & Elisabeth Jewett,
June 12, 1788
Israel Burton, Jr., & Betsey Kinne, June 12, 1788
William Beard (?) Nickolson of Newport, R I.,
& Marvel (?) Palmer, Sept. 14, 1788
Rufus Herrick & Sarah Brewster, Sept. 21, 1788
Robert Love of R. I. & Susanna Trustin or Hur-
ten, Oct. 16, 1788
Ebenezer Herrick & Polly Lamb of Stonington,
Nov. 27, 1788
William Johnson of New London & Desire Haven,
Nov. 27, 1788
Rev. Amos Chase of Litchfield & Rebecca Hart,
Nov. 30, 1788
Byron or Birnon Morgan & Mary Clark, Jan. 8, 1789
Peter Grow (?) of ——, Vt., & Diana Tracey, Jan. 29, 1789
Denison Kinne & Lois Boardman, Feb. 1, 1789
Wyat Palmer of Stonington & Keziah Starkweather,
Feb. 8, 1789
Thomas Congdon of North Kingston, R. I., &
Betsey Stewart, Feb. 19, 1789
David Budlong of Voluntown & Amy Palmer, Feb. 22, 1789
Stephen Herrington of Lisbon & Sabra Bark or
Bach, March 29, 1789
Moses Kinne of Voluntown & Adah Kinne, Aug. 9, 1789
Cesar Clark & Judith Sheldon of Southington, R. I.,
(negroes), Aug. 13, 1789
Thamar Cobb & Sarah Comstock, Oct. 8, 1789
Ebenezer Ledyard, Jr., of Groton & Lucy Coit, Oct. 14, 1789
Peleg Utly of Stonington & Abigal Herrick, Nov. 22, 1789
Elisha Kezer of Lisbon & Sarah Mulkins, Dec. 10, 1789
Abraham Yarrington & Elisabeth Freeman, Dec. 10, 1789
Amos Budington of Stonington & Elisabeth Char-
ryston, Dec. 27, 1789
Constant Murdock of Norwich, Vt., & Sarah Jewett,
Jan. 25, 1790
Nathan Kimbal, Jr., & Alice Harris of Montville,
Feb. 11, 1790
John Morse of Canterbury & Hannah Morse,
Feb. 25, 1790

Joseph Jewett & Betsey King of Lisbon,   March 4, 1790
Danil Rea & Abigail Kennedy,   May 2, 1790
Jonas Kinne & Mary Herrick,   Aug. 8, 1790
Nathan Ross or Rose of Stafford & Elisebeth
   Olin,   Aug. 12, 1790
Ebenezer Rea & Lydia Burton,   Aug. 27, 1790
Rev. John Wilder of Attleboro, Mass., & Miss
   Esther Tyler,   Sept. 2, 1790
Adam ——— (?) of Southington, R. I., & Sarah
   Franklin (negroes),   Sept. 2, 1790
John Cogswell & Elisabeth Brown,   Oct. 14, 1799
Manassah Prentice & Mehetable Presson of Lisbon,
   Dec. 2, 1790
Charles Bromley & Phebe Rea,   Dec. 16, 1790
Abraham Guile, Jr., & Sarah Rea,   Jan. 2, 1791
Hiram Herrick & Anne Bromley,   March 23, 1791
Mr. Nathan Burton & Miss Esther Kimbal,   April 17, 1791
William Cogswell & Mercy Coit,   May 22, 1791
Roger Spicer & Eunice Herrick,   July 3, 1791
Edward Swan of Stonington & Hannah Tyler,
   Sept. 28, 1791
Nathan Ayer & Alice Green,   Oct. 10, 1791
Arioch (?) Smith of Ashford & Elisabeth Cook, Oct. 19, 1791
Pearl Partridge & Ziporah Freeman,   Oct. 27, 1791
Joel Hide of Lisbon & Mary Belcher,   Nov. 6, 1791
Asa Lewis (?) of Petresbergh, N. Y., & Bridget Rise,
   Nov. 17, 1791
Lenord Stevens of Ransellearville, N. Y., & Alice
   Gates,   Dec 8, 1791
John Prentice & Betsey Clift,   Dec. 25, 1791
Elisha Clark of Plainfield & Apphia Capron,   Dec. 21, 1791
Samuel Gear, Jr., & Lucy Tracey,   Jan. 1, 1792
Ezra Baker & Polly Mattison of Groton,   Jan. 1, 1792
Gurdon Crandal & Mary Roth, both of Norwich,
   Jan. 12, 1792
Prosper Kimbal & Margery Dorrance,   Jan. 22, 1792
Peleg Wheadon & Thankfull Gates,   Feb. 5, 1792
Rufus Church (?) of ——— & Elisabeth Bark or
   Bach,   Feb. 9, 1792
Alexander Kinne & Sarah Kimbal,   Feb. 12, 1792

Jabesh Kingslay of Canterbury & Dolly Averil,
        Feb. 23, 1792
George Northrop & Ellen Withey, March 8, 1792
Ellery Morris of Exeter, R. I., & Abigail Bromley,
        March 11, 1792
Nathaniel Coit & Betsey Morgan, Feb. 14, 1792
Joseph Meach & Sally Boardman, Feb. 14. 1792
Jesse Prentice of Stonington & Elisabeth Belcher,
        March 29, 1792
Thomas Austin & Mary Gates, May 27, 1792
Capt. Ezra Kinne & Mrs. Martha Putnam, June 5, 1792
Thomas Meach & Eunice Boardman, Sept. 23, 1792
Samuel Brown Philips & Mary Parke, Oct. 11, 1792
Mr. Samuel Smith & Mrs. Jerusha Mott of Stoning-
  ton,   Oct. 21, 1792
Freeman Kinyan (?) of Exeter, R. I., & Lydia
  Withey,   Dec. 2, 1792
Stephen Tucker & Eunice Baldwin of Stonington,
        Jan. 17, 1793
Joseph Durfee (?) & Lucy Barnes, Jan. 24, 1793
——— Adams of Canterbury & Patience Rix, Feb. 7, 1793
Leffield (?) Gray of Plainfield & Parthenia Rouse,
        Feb. 14, 1793
Nathan Bach & Elisabeth Tracey, Feb. 14, 1793
James Rea & Hannah Preston, Feb. 28, 1793
Ezra Leonord of Worthington, Mass., & Dorcas
  Brown,   March 4, 1793
Mark More of Plainfield &Hager Barns, April 4, 1793
Adrian Rolestson of Franklin & Elisabeth Smith,
        April 18, 1793
James Marsh of Plainfield & Polly Bennet, May 16, 1793
Moses Tyler & Olivia Coit, May 29, 1793
——— Baldwin of ——— & Susan Stewart, ———
Stephen Guile & Lydia Davies, June 29, 1793
William Hopkins of Plainfield & Abigail Kimbel,
        Oct. 24, 1793
Darius Brown of Hopkinton, R. I., & Silence Bur-
  ton,   Jan. 9, 1794
Jonas Brewster of Worthington, Mass., & Hetty
  Brewster,   Feb. 16, 1794

Mingo Chesborough & Lucretia Buck (blacks),
                                        March 2, 1794
Mr. Daniel Dunham & Mrs. Zerviah Loring, both
    of Norwich,   March 5, 1794
Mott Witheson of Voluntown & Phœbe Freeman,
                                        March 20, 1794
Josiah Rose or Ross & Patty Stewart,   April 13, 1794
Aaron Crary of Plainfield & Harmony Averil,
                                        April 17, 1794
Dwight Ripley of Norwich & Martha Coit, April 24, 1794
John Wylie of Voluntown & Amy Tyler,   May 1, 1794
William Davies & Anne Bennett,   May 11, 1794
James More & Judith Morse,   May 29, 1794
Allen Wylie & Sarah Kinne,   June 5, 1794
Jason Stanton & Sabra Olin,   Aug. 3, 1794
Shubael Clark of ———, Mass., & Esther Tracey,
                                        Aug. 24, 1794
Nathaniel Shipman of Norwich & Abigail Coit,
                                        Oct. 14, 1794
James Braman & Mehetabel Lestor,   Oct. 15, 1794
Nathan Prentice & Betsy Clift,   Nov. 6, 1794
David Smith, Jr., & Sally (?) Rathbun of Lisbon,
                                        Nov. 19, 1794
Henry Charles of South Kingston, R. I., & Sally
    ——— (blacks),   Nov. 26, 1794
Calvin or Calum Goddard of Plainfield & Alice C.
    Hart,   Nov. 27, 1794
Elias Rose & Lucretia Woodward,   Dec. 21, 1794
Benjamin Olin & Sarah Olin,   Dec. 28, 1794
Chester Kinne of Voluntown & Silence Bliss, Jan. 1, 1795
John Casy (?) of Lisbon & Catharine Jackson
    (blacks),   Jan. 12, 1795
Stephen Withey & Lydia Geer,   Jan. 25, 1795
Samuel Millar of Worthington, Mass., & Mehetabel
    Preston,   Feb. 2, 1795
Michael Robinson of Stonington & Polly Ray, Feb. 15, 1795
John M. Hatch & Jerusha Rose,   Aug. 30, 1795
Mr. Samuel Killam of Lisbon & Mrs. Mary Presson,
                                        Nov. 29, 1795
Jonathan Hart & Abigail Prentice,   Dec. 10, 1795

The Rev. Jonathan Law Pomroy of Worthington,
Mass., & Miss Betsey Coit,   Dec. 24, 1795
Roswell Campbel of Voluntown & ——— Williams,
                                              Dec. 24, 1795
John Rodgers & Catharine Latham of Groton, Jan. 24, 1796
John ——— of Plainfield, N. H., & Bethany Coit,
                                              Jan. 28, 1796
John Baldwin, Jr., of Stonington & Nabby
    Boardman,   Jan. 31, 1796
Barton Cook, Jr., & Anna Rose,   Feb. 22, 1796
George Campbel of Voluntown & Abigail Hering-
    ton,   Feb. 25, 1796
Nathan, Burton, Jr., & Polly Rose,   March 23, 1796
Joseph Leonard & Polly Bliss,   Nov. 2, 1796
Joseph Hatch & Betsey Weadon,   Nov. 10, 1796
Henry Brewster & Rebecca Lestor,   Dec. 8, 1796
Alfred Curtis of Hampton & Edy Weadon,   Dec. 15, 1796
Ezra R. Partridge & Polly Austin,   Dec. 22, 1796
Abel Gates & Lucy Stanton,   Jan. 11, 1797
Avery Powers of Norwich, N. Y., & Prudence
    Benjamin,   Jan. 12, 1797
John Smith, Jr., of Chatham, N. Y., & Lucinda
    Parrish,   (Patty)   Jan. 17, 1797
  Esquire   J^ohn Cook & Betty^Clark of Middletown,
    Vt.,   Jan. 22, 1797
Joseph Boardman of ———, Vt. & Deborah Rix, Feb. 1, 1797
James ——— & Betsey Kegwin,   March 2, 1797
Joseph Gardner Smith & Anna Geer,   March 21, 1797
Daniel Geer, Jr., & Sally Geer,   July 6, 1797
Elijah Hatch & Emillia Rose   July 12, 1797
Elijah Belcher of Cherry Valley, N. Y., & Lydia
    Clark,   Aug. 8, 1797
Samuel Smith, Jr., of Norwich & Esther Geer, Sept. 3, 1797
Rev. Lemuel Tyler & Miss Sally Crary,   Sept. 21, 1797
Elisha Parke of Plainfield & Rachel Averil,   Sept. 21, 1797
Obadiah Lewis of Exeter, R. I., & Sarah Treat
    Partridge,   Nov. 16, 1797
Nathan ——— of Canan & Polly Green,   Nov. 21, 1797
Charles Frink of Stonington & Rebecca Johnson,
                                              Dec. 24, 1797

Dudley Morgan & Phebe Goodale, May 6, 1798
Asa Partelo of Voluntown & Mary Rose, Sept. 20, 1798
Asher Prentice of Stonington & Elisabeth Rix,
Sept. 27, 1798
John Kennedy of Voluntown & Polly Withey, Oct. 4, 1798
Isaac Burton of Canaen, N. Y., & Abigail Rea, Oct. 11, 1798
Lemuel —— of Chesterfield, Mass., & Olive Brew-
ster, Nov. 4, 1798
Shubael Meach & Sally Lord, Nov. 15, 1798
Silas Davis & Eunice Geer, Nov. 29, 1798
William Justin of Canterbury & Mercy Davis, Nov. 29, 1798
Charles Geer & Sally Graves, Jan. 3, 1799
James Rogers of Norwich & Sally Coit, Jan. 16, 1799
Rev. Gordon Dorrance (?) of Windsor, Mass., & Miss
Hannah Morgan, Jan. 20, 1799
Joshua Lad & Peace Partridge, Jan. 31, 1799
Elisha Partridge & Anne Cook, Feb. 14, 1799
Daniel James & Patience Whaley, Feb. 17, 1799
Stephen Benjamin & Barbara Phillips, March 7, 1799
Henry Babcock of Plainfield & Thankful Bennet,
March 13, 1799
—— Olin & Alice Walton, April 4, 1799
Gerdon Buck & Martha Moody, April 7, 1799
John Clark & Hannah Cook, Sept. 15, 1799
George Mattison of Lisbon & Nancy Caswell, Sept. 20, 1799
Danie Mix & Desire Austin, Nov. 3, 1799
Palmer Hewit of Voluntown & Mercy Kimbal, Dec. 5, 1799
David Kinne, Jr., of Plainfield & Margaret Ed-
monds, Dec. 25, 1799

WALLINGFORD.

NEW HAVEN COUNTY.

The town of Wallingford was named in May, 1670. The First Congregational Church in Wallingford was organized in 1675 by settlers from New Haven. The following are all the marriages recorded.

Caleb Hall, Jr., & Susanna Hall,	Feb. 8, 1759
Tyrannus Collins of Guilford & Abigail Peck,	
	April 12, 1759
Moses Tharp & widow Lucy Dayton of North Haven,	May 2, 1759
Aaron Parsons & Elizabeth Ives,	Nov. 15, 1759
James Dana & Katharine Whittlesey,	May 8, 1760
Isaac Cook Jr., & Martha Cooke,	March 6, 1760
Nathaniel Androus & Elizabeth Hitchcock, both of Cheshire,	May 15, 1760
Moses Holt & Desire Hall,	May 15, 1760
Abel Ives, Jr., & Lois Tuttle,	June 19, 1760
Levi Munson & Mary Cooly,	Nov. 27, 1760
Ambrose Ward of New Haven & Sarah Chamberlain,	Nov. 27, 1760
Samuel Peck & Susannah Doolittle,	Dec. 10, 1760
Capt. *Macock* Ward & widow Mary Hull,	Dec. 23, 1760
Hawkins Hart & Abigail Hall,	Feb. 12, 1761
Jacob Teel & widow Joanna Merriman,	March 17, 1761
Jonathan Moss & ——— Curtiss,	April 23, 1761
Daniel Hall & Sarah Atwater,	Oct. 7, 1761
Abraham Ives & widow Lucy Tharp,	Oct. 14, 1761
Elisaph Merriman & Jerusha Mattoon,	Jan. 13, 1762
Zuar Bradley of North Haven & Mary Mattoon,	
	Jan. 13, 1762
Joseph Holt & widow Elizabeth Merwin,	Feb. 9, 1762
Thomas Merwin & Hester Ives,	Feb. 18, 1762
Reuben Ives & Elizabeth Rice,	Feb. 24, 1762
Ephraim Preston & Esther Merriman,	April 5, 1762
Ebenezer Moss & Esther Preston,	April 29, 1762
Ichabod Russell of East Haven & Hannah Bartholomew,	Nov. 3, 1762

James Marks & Hannah Blakesly,	Dec. 23, 1762
Ephraim Johnson & widow Lois Beadle,	Dec. 30, 1762
Caleb Cook & Abigail Finch,	Jan. 12, 1764
Eliasaph Preston & Phebe Hart,	Feb. 16, 1764
Abraham Graves of North Guilford & Kath. Hall,	
	March 14, 1764
James Scarrit & Love Hall,	May 10, 1764
Miles Hall & Abigail Smith,	Sept. 20, 1764
Timothy Bates & Abigail Atwater,	Sept. 20, 1764
Nathan Sumners of Stratford & widow Abigail	
Ives,	Oct. 15, 1764
Silas Clarke of Farmington & Thankful Merwin,	
	Nov. 8, 1764
Oliver Parker & Lucy Parker,	Dec. 11, 1764
David Miller & Zerviah Parker,	Jan. 3, 1765
Josiah Hart, Jr., & Lydia Moss,	Jan. 10, 1765
John Sedgwick of Cornwall & Abigail Andrews,	
	Feb. 3, 1765
Samuel Waterhouse & Sarah Allen,	Feb. 5, 1765
Daniel Chiddington of Cohabit & Rebecca Hall,	Feb. 13, 1765
Amos Moss & Elizabeth Ives,	April 4, 1765
Nathaniel Jones & widow Phebe Hall,	Aug. 7, 1765
Josiah Benton of Litchfield & Mehetabel Smith,	
	Aug. 20, 1765
Ambrose Cook & Esther Peck,	Sept. 25, 1765
Joshua Parker & Mary Hitchcock,	Oct. 30, 1765
Nicholas Peck & Dinah Dowd of Goshen,	Oct. 31, 1765
John Street, Jr., & Esther Parsons,	Dec. 16, 1765
Jonathan Byington of Branford & Comfort Beardslee,	
	Dec. 25, 1765
David Sturgis of Danbury & Phebe Ludington,	Feb. 6, 1766
Daniel Ives, Jr., & widow Elizabeth Ives,	April 3, 1766
George Peckham & Rachel Bradley of New Haven,	
	May 1, 1766
Eber Hall of Guilford & Hannah Newel,	May 2, 1766
John Lewis & Thankful Hitchcock,	May 15, 1766
John Carter & Abigail Hough,	June 19, 1766
Ephraim Hough, Jr., & Eunice Andrews,	Oct. 2, 1766
Caleb Atwater & Abigail Jones,	Nov. 12, 1766
Stephen Ives, Jr., & Susanna Parker,	Nov. 20, 1766

Ichabod Parker & Susanna Cook,   Dec. 3, 1766
Joel Collins & Bethiah Hall, both of Guilford, July 29, 1767
Joseph Rice & Phebe Rich,   Nov. 19, 1767
Samuel Cook & Chloe Atwater,   Nov. 25, 1767
Titus Hall & Olive Barnes,   Nov. 26, 1767
Samuel Carter & Margaret Saxton,   Nov. 30, 1767
Amos Churchill of Middletown & Lydia Cole of
     Meriden,   Feb. 8, 1768
Ephraim Hough, Jr., & Huldah Rice, both of
     Meriden,   Feb. 10, 1768
Caleb Bull & Ruth Robinson, both of Meriden,
     Feb. 18, 1768
Solomon Doolittle & Eunice Hull,   Feb. 24, 1768
Theophilus Hall & Elizabeth Coach, both of Meri-
     dan,   March 10, 1768
Benjamin Sperry & Rhena Hull,   April 10, 1768
Joseph Hough & Ruth Beardsley,   April 21, 1768
Elisha Perkins & Mehetabel Meriam, both of
     Meridan,   June 9, 1768
David Ives & Mary Osborn,   Oct. 18, 1768
Amos Moss of Litchfield & Esther Andrews, Nov. 24, 1768
James Hough & Lucy Hall, both of Meriden, Dec. 15, 1768
The Rev. Andrew Lee of Hanover, in Norwich, &
     Eunice Hall of Meriden,   Dec. 15, 1768
Solomon Rice & Eunice Miles, both of Meriden,
     Jan. 5, 1769
Timothy Cole & Huldah Cole, both of Meriden,
     May 11, 1769
Joseph Edwards & Lucy Jerome, both of Meriden,
     May 25, 1769
Eliakim Hall, Jr., & Eunice Moss,   May 30, 1769
Jeremiah Carrington & Mindwell Cook,   Nov. 9, 1769
Joseph Parker, Jr., & Patience Parker,   June 29, 1769
Aaron Hull & Sarah Merchant,   Nov. 16, 1769
Daniel Ives, Jr., & widow Obedience Cook of
     Cheshire,   Dec. 7, 1769
Samuel Osborn & Mary Green,   Feb. 1, 1770
Benjamin Cook, Jr., & Esther Rice,   April 19, 1770
Simeon Stedman of Farmington & Sarah Parker,
     May 10, 1770

Eliada Parker, Jr., & Margery Parker,	May 10, 1770
Philip Curtiss & widow Mary Mattoon,	Dec. 27, 1770
Giles Hall, Jr., & Lois Ives,	Dec. 27, 1770
Abel Hall, Jr., & Ruth Moss,	Jan. 3, 1771
Amasa Rice & Mary Griswold,	July 10, 1771
Timothy Ward & Elizabeth Parker,	Dec. 25, 1771
Eliasaph Doolittle & Ruth Hall,	Jan. 1, 1772
John Mansfield & Sybil Sexton,	Feb. 20, 1772
David Way & Eunice Fenn,	March 12, 1772
Samuel Peck & Anna Hall,	June 10, 1772
Titus Luddington & Miriam Parker,	July 15, 1772
Jonathan Dutton & Eliz. Hall,	Oct. 21, 1772
Andrew Hall & Thankful Preston,	Oct. 21, 1772
Timothy Barnes of Litchfield & Eunice Munson,	Oct. 28, 1772
Jonathan Brooks & Katharine Roe, both of New Haven,	Nov. 5, 1772
Andrew Bartholomew & Rachel Rice,	Jan. 7, 1773
Moses Way & Sarah Miles, both of Meriden,	Feb. 11, 1773
Joel Austin & Hannah Sexton,	April 12, 1773
Samuel Doolittle & Sarah Jones,	June 7, 1773
Deacon Elijah Steel of Cornwall & Sarah Andrews,	Aug. 4, 1773
Oliver Hitchcock & widow Anne Munson,	Sept. 29, 1773
Jonathan Gaylord of Waterbury & Bethiah Parker,	Nov. 3, 1773
Ebenezer Mattoon & Martha Merriman,	Nov. 16, 1773
Lent Hough & Rebecca Tuttle,	Jan. 20, 1774
Joshua Munson & Meriam Dayton,	April 18, 1774
Deacon Benjamin Atwater & widow Elizabeth Merriman,	May 5, 1774
Samuel Hall & Elizabeth Parsons,	May 10, 1774
Elihu Yale & Lucretia Stanley,	Nov. 24, 1774
Samuel Church of Woodbury & Mary Jones,	Nov. 30, 1774
Stephen Beach & Miriam Parker,	Dec. 22, 1774
Oliver Doolittle & Lois Cooke,	Jan. 16, 1775
Ezra Doolittle & Sarah Morse,	Jan. 18, 1775
Abner Rice & Kezia Hall,	Jan. 19, 1775
Israel Williams of Waterbury & Hannah Parker,	Jan. 19, 1775

Amos Ives & Lucy Hall,   Feb. 23, 1775
Samuel Wright & Lydia Ives,   Feb. 27, 1775
Isaac Parker & widow Lois Rice,   April 27, 1775
John Ives of Meriden & Mehetabel Rose,   May 14, 1775
Titus Basset of N. Haven & Sarah Hitchcock, June 21, 1775
Eben. Culver & Eliz. Curtiss,   Oct. 23, 1775
Samuel Hull of Durham & Sarah Ives,   Jan. 4, 1776
Daniel Bradley of New Haven & Eunice Ives,

                                                     Jan. 11, 1776
Ambrose Hough & Eunice Holt,   March 14, 1776
Isaac Doolittle & Phebe Cook,   April 18, 1776
Levi Ives & Lois Hind,   May 2, 1776
Edmund Field & Susannah Wainwright,   May 2, 1776
Asaph Cooke, Jr., of East Hoosick & Thankful Par-
    ker,   June 17, 1776
Nathaniel Jones, Jr., & Content Johnson,   July 31, 1776
Gershom Mattoon & Ruth Parker,   Dec. 5, 1776
Medad Munson & Sybil Carrington,   Nov. 20, 1777
John Culver & Sarah Mattoon,   Dec. 8, 1777
Abraham Ives & widow Sabra Wainwright,   1778
Nathaniel Hart & widow Phebe Johnson,   Feb. 16, 1778
Ambrose Merriman & widow Tabitha Atkins, Feb. 18, 1778
Isaac Parker, Jr., & Anna Parker,   March 19, 1778
Joel Moss & Hannah Hall,   March 19, 1778
Oliver Stanley, Esq., & widow Desire Munson, April 20, 1778
John Culver & Sarah Mattoon,   Sept. 14, 1778
Theophilus Moss, Jr., & Bede Hull,   Oct. 22, 1778
Moses Tuttle & Damaris Hitchcock,   Nov. 26, 1778
Solomon Lindly & Thankful Tyler, both of North-
    ford,   June 7, 1779
Levi Parker & Lydia Bradly of East Haven,   July 22, 1779
Jehiel Preston & Molly Rice,   Sept. 9, 1779
Isaiah Tuttle & Hannah Jones,   Nov. 25, 1779
Joseph Rogers of Northford & Lois Hall,   Dec. 29, 1779
Joseph Doolittle, Jr., & Sarah Hart,   Jan. 27, 1780
Capt. Stephen Yale & widow Phebe Preston, Feb. 24, 1780
Joel Hough & Sarah Rice,   March 30, 1780
John Ammat of Wethersfield & widow Mary McCua (?),

                                                    April 18, 1780
Capt. Asahel Cooley & Chloe Bliss,   May 9, 1780

Orange Burnham of Cornwall & Mabel Andrews,
Nov. 23, 1780
Deodate Beman & Mary Parsons, Dec. 12, 1780
Caleb Merriman & Amy Lewis, Dec. 14, 1780
Joseph Blakesly, Jr., & Phebe Curtis, Dec. 20, 1780
John McCleave & widow Thankful Hall, Jan. 18, 1781
Benjamin Hall, 2d, & widow Mary Cook, March 29, 1781
Aaron Hall & Elizabeth Cooke, May 24, 1781
Caleb Mattoon & Hannah Spencer of Haddam,
July 16, 1781
Ambrose Avery & Hannah Mattoon, Oct. 4, 1781
Asa Thompson & Sarah Cooke, both of Cheshire,
Oct. 17, 1781
Nathaniel Merriman & Lucy Moss, Dec. 27, 1781
Gamaliel Parker & Martha Parker, May 2, 1782
Oliver Dexter & Lowly Andrews, Nov. 28, 1782
Johnson Hall & Abiah Humiston, Jan. 5, 1783
Timothy Coe of Durham & May Hall, Jan. 6, 1783
Ezra Austin of Meriden & Esther Sturgis, Jan. 9, 1783
Jonas Clarke of Cheshire & Sarah Hall, April 2, 1783
Elisha Smith & Katharine Hough, July 31, 1783
Selah Stedman & Mary Hall, Aug. 14, 1783
Charles Tuttle & Sarah Bliss, Sept. 29, 1783
Col. Isaac Lee of Farmington & widow Mary Hall,
Oct. 9, 1783
John Parsons & Asenath Carrington, Dec. 11, 1783
Hezekiah Dickeman of Mt. Carmel & Hannah
Rice, Dec. 24, 1783
Moses Hall, Jr., of Meriden & Lucy Hart, Dec. 25, 1783
Joel Cooke & Rebecca Hart, Jan. 1, 1784
John Robinson of East Haven & Lucy Spencer,
March 11, 1784
Alner Doolittle & Lydia Tuttle, both of Cheshire,
Jan. 22, 1784
Elisha Rice, Jr., of Cheshire & Jerusha Scovill of
Meriden, April 7, 1784
Josiah Hall & Phebe Dutton, both of Cheshire,
Aug. 12, 1784
John Carter & Phebe Rice, Oct. 20, 1784.
Lemuel Cooke & Betsey Bates, Dec. 20, 1784

Mansfield Munson of No. Haven & Lua Brooks of
   Mt. Carmel,   Jan. 13, 1785
Isaac Bartholomew & Damaris Hall,   March 31, 1785
Samuel Street, 3d, & Anna Munson,   May 10, 1785
Charles Lewis & Sarah Hull,   Aug. 17, 1785
Caleb Merriman & Statira (?) Hall,   Oct. 20, 1785
Seth Lankton & Sarah Sloper, both of Southington,
                                    Nov. 9, 1785
Capt. Moses Rice & widow Kezia Lewis,   Nov. 17, 1785
Abraham Bartholomew & Mary Page,   Nov. 24, 1785
John Ballard Douglas of Meriden & Katharine
   Tharp,   Jan. 18, 1786
Cone Hartman of Granville & Rhoda Parker, Feb. 22, 1786
Gad Ely & Tamar Meeker, both of Meriden,
                              March 29, 1786
Harvey Hall & Ruth Patterson,   April 13, 1786
James Clark & Betsey Parsons,   April 13, 1786
Jonathan Merrick of Branford & Sarah Atwater,
                              Aug. 10, 1786
Asahel Hall, Jr., & Ruth Johnson,   Sept. 22, 1786
Enoch Culver, Jr., & Ruth Hall,   Oct. 18, 1786
Caleb Street & Susannah Whittlesey,   Nov. 19, 1786
Joseph Hitchcock & —— Munson,   Nov. 22, 1786
Amos Moss & Ruth Hull,   Nov. 29, 1786
Stephen Hall, Jr., & Lucy Cooke,   Dec. 6, 1786
Eliada Parker of Lenox & Beulah Parker, Dec. 13, 1786
Joel Doolittle & Lois Hart,   Feb. 22, 1787
James Hough & Mary B——y,   Nov. 15, 1787
Lois Dout & Samuel Hull (?),   1788
Samuel Johnson of Meridan & Lucretia Andrews
   of Cheshire,   Jan. 3, 1788
Jehiel Merriman of Cheshire & Eunice Preston,
                              Jan. 13, 1788
Dr. Lewis of Lenox & Ruth Collins,   Oct. 22, 1788
Nathaniel Holt of Meriden & —— Dudley of
   Woodbury,   May 25, 1789
Rufus Hoadley of Northford & Obedience Ives,
                             Oct. 28, 1789
Javin (?) Manser of New Haven & Lydia Parker,
                              Nov. 1, 1789

Samuel Peck, Jr., & Abigail Hall,	Dec. 13, 1789
Ira Day & Eunice McCleave,	Dec. 20, 1789
Hall Hart of Barkhamsted & Phebe Hall,	Jan. 14, 1790
Amos Baldwin & Lois Moss,	Feb. 11, 1790
Jared Braket & Eunice Marks,	March 23, 1790
Joseph Ives & —— Ives,	March 24, 1790
Justus Tuttle & Polly Tuttle of No. Haven,	April 29, 1790
John Peck & Eunice Hall,	May 9, 1790
Samuel Doolittle & Rachel Tod of Northford,	Aug. 5, 1790
David Hall, Jr., & Thankful Moss,	Sept. 22, 1790
Jonathan Moss & Thankful Blakesley,	Nov. 4, 1790
Charles Johnson & Elizabeth Rice,	Nov. 4, 1790
Zerah Munson & Mary Alling,	Nov. 4, 1790
David Hall & Betsey Whitehead,	Jan. 20, 1791
Asahel Munson of Northford & Ruth Hart,	Jan. 27, 1791
John Phillips & Deidama Curtiss of Cheshire,	
	March 9, 1791
—— Munger of East Guilford & Esther Moss,	
	March, 1791
Samuel Hopkins of Kensington & Polly Rogers,	
	March 22, 1791
David Barns & Tintee (?) Thompson,	March 27, 1791
Samuel Canary of Middletown & —— Beach,	Nov., 1791
—— Baldwin & Mina Whitmore,	Nov. 24, 1791
David Lewis Beebee of Woodbridge & Polly At-	
water,	Feb. 1, 1792
Joseph Todd of Derby & Mamra Carrington,	May 7, 1792
Judas Tuttle & —— Smith,	July 18, 1792
John Skarot (?) & Eunice Merriman,	May 24, 1792
Jeremiah Hull & Phebe Hart,	Sept. 6, 1792
Paul Noyes of New Haven & Ro—— Benton,	Sept. 20, 1792
Ira Hall & Hanah Hough,	Oct. 11, 1792
James P——nt & L——d Todd of North Haven,	
	Oct. 11, 1792
Samuel Tuttle & Abigail Cook,	Oct. 25, 1792
Silvanus Wilson of Harwinton & Chloe Hall,	Nov. 8, 1792
Jno. Webb Blakesly & Ruth Ives,	Nov. 12, 1792
Wm. Ensworth of Canterbury & Elizabeth Worth-	
ington,	Nov. 17, 1792
Ephraim Hall & widow Waitstill Parker,	Nov. 18, 1792

—— Dibble of Saybrook & —— Ives,   Dec. 7, 1792
Levi Curtiss & Sally Francis of Meriden,   Dec. 7, 1792
Lyman Hopson of New Durham & Lois Bartholomew,
                                              Jan. 20, 1793
Nathan Harrison (?) of Branford & Lowly Cook,
                                              Jan. 24, 1793
Benajah Rice & Sarah Hough,   Jan. 31, 1793
Joel Hall & Lucrecia Street of Northford,   Feb. 4, 1793
Abrm Page & a daughter of Saml Rice,   April 10, 1793
Ephraim Cook & Sally Lewis,   May 16, 1793
Jno. Bartlett & Ruth Hall,   June 1, 1793
Johnson Doolittle & Elizabeth Doolittle,   June 5, 1793
Samuel Cooley & Polly Carter,   June 16, 1793
Augustus Cook & Sally Dutton,   June 20, 1793
A son of Timothy Hart & a daughter of widow
    Douglass,   June 20, 1793
Uriah Collins & —— Munson of Northford, Aug. 28, 1793
Dayton Johnson's eldest son & eldest daughter of
    Solomon Johnson,   1793
Solomon Carter & Polly Hough,   Nov. 13, 1793
Prindle Hall & Eunice Parker,   Nov. 25, 1793
Ha—— Munson & Jerusha Cook,   Nov. 14, 1793
Benjamin Hall's eldest son & Merriman Cook's
    daughter,   Nov. 14, 1793
Billious B. Norton & Olive Peck,   ——
Uriah Colman & widow Munson,   ——
James Curtis & Jerusha Hull,   Dec. 3, 1793
Stephen L—— & Rachel Hinman, both of Durham,
                                              Dec. 3, 1793
Augustus Hall, 2d, & Parmeli Hall,   Feb. 6, 1794
Isaac Doolittle & Esther Hill,   March 9, 1794
Joshua Austin, 2d, & Esther Norton,   Feb. 6, 1794
Samuel Doolittle & Mary Hart,   March 12, 1794
Eliakim Hall & Clarissa Cook,   March 13, 1794
David Merriman Cook & Day Hall,   April 24, 1794
Benj. Baldwin & Elizabeth Hart,   May 1, 1794
Reuben Bachelor of Litchfield & Anna Parker of
    North Haven,   May 1, 1794
Orchard Ghy & Lois Hall, both of Meriden,   May 28, 1794
Hezekiah Parker & Keziah Parker,   Sept. 18, 1794

Isaac Kirkland (a negro) & Rose Bristol of Hamden,
Oct. 30, 1794
Samuel Frost of North Haven & Ruth Merriman,
Nov. 24, 1794
Michael Johnson & ——— Cornwall, Dec., 1794
John Curtis of Durham & Lydia Hall, Dec. 29, 1794
Miles Peck & Eunice Hall, Jan. 4, 1795
Caleb Cook & Lydia Tyler, Jan. 18, 1795
James Bradley of Southington & Abigail Ives, Jan. 26, 1795
Pomp Thomson & Mina Chatfield, Feb. 17, 1795
Daniel Hotchkiss of Cheshire & Esther Moss, Feb. 19, 1795
Josiah Hall & Patty Hall, April 1, 1795
Theophilus Moss & Christian (?) Horton, April 8, 1795
Lyman Benton of Cohabit & Anna Hopson, April 27, 1795
Joseph Knevals (?) & Susana Barns both of North
Haven, July 6, 1795
Jacob Francis & Content Hall, Oct. 7, 1795
Elisha Hall & widow Lois Street of Northford, Oct. 22, 1795
William Thomas of Northford & Rhoda Ward, Dec. 5, 1795
Jared Kirtland & Lois Yale, Dec. 21, 1795
Silas Newton of Cheshire & Lucinda Parker, Dec. 24, 1795
Benajah Yale & Esther Cook, Jan. 21, 1796
Ira Day & Lucy Atwater, Jan. 31, 1796
Amos Bristol of Cheshire & Betsey Hitchcock, Feb. 14, 1796
Sylvanus Youngs of Middletown & Patty Mattoon,
Feb. 24, 1796
——— Churchel of Stratfield & Polly Merriman,
Feb. 25, 1796
Wm. Williams & Phebe Ludington, March 8, 1796
Dickiman Hall & Lucy Hough, March 13, 1796
Samuel Miller & Vinery Blakeslee, April, 1796
Joseph Hall & Sally Ghooam (?), May, 1796
Joseph Merriman of Litchfield & Betsey Smith, May, 1796
Billions Avery & Esther Street, June 7, 1796
Munson Cook & Thankful Austin, Sept. 4, 1796
Chas. Cook & Sylvia Yale, Sept. 15, 1796
Lowman Horton & Susannah Francis, Sept. 21, 1796
Erastus Hall & Polly Moss, Sept. 21, 1796
Levi Moss Bartholomew & Lucy Ives, Sept. 21, 1796
Jonathan Dickerman & Morab Rice, Oct. 2, 1796

Nehemiah Rice & Ruth Hall,	Nov. 25, 1796
—— Rice & Eunice Rogers,	Nov. 27, 1796
Lot. Gaylord & Sarah Allen,	Dec. 22, 1796
Joseph Way & Ulda Winston,	Dec. 26, 1796
—— Douglas of Northford & —— ——,	Jan. 28, 1797
Bezaleel Dayton of North Haven & Olive Johnson,	
	June 20, 1797
Ebenezer Gills & Lydia Todd,	Sept., 1797
Bates Tyler & Damaris Hall,	Sept. 10, 1797
Joseph Francis & Hannah Hall,	Sept. 21, 1797
Jeremiah Tyler & Esther Hough,	Sept. 21, 1797
Elihu Cook & Mr. Thorp's daughter,	1797
Virtue (?) Bronson & Lina Carrington,	March 13, 1798
Joseph Mansfield & Eunice Lewis,	May 20, 1798
David Way & Elizabeth Baldwin,	Aug. 20, 1798
Arad Munson (?) of Plymouth & Lidya Baldwin,	
	Nov. 4, 1798
Daniel Hitchcock of Cheshire & Lydia Ives,	Nov. 29, 1798
Elihu Cook & Sally Cooley,	Dec. 9, 1798
Daniel Allin & Thezia Doolittle,	Dec. 11, 1798
Liberty Lyman & Sarah Lyman,	Dec., 1798
Asahel Moss of Cheshire & Eunice Doolittle,	Jan. 29, 1799
Nathaniel Curtiss & Susanna Hall,	Jan. 22, 1799
John T. Meigs of East Guilford & Phebe Hall,	Feb. 14, 1799
Samuel Guy (?) & Clarissa King, both of Berlin,	Sept., 1799
Samuel Davidson & Solomon Doolittle's daughter,	
	Nov. 26, 1799
Thomas Cook & Katherine Atwater,	Nov. 28, 1799
Jotham Tuttle & —— Bradley,	Dec. 12, 1799
Isaac Peck & James Rice's eldest daughter,	Dec. 22, 1799
Andrew Bartholomew's second son & Mr. Brooks' daughter,	Dec. 25, 1799

WINDHAM — HAMPTON.

WINDHAM COUNTY.

The town of Hampton was organized in 1786. It was taken from Windham, Pomfret,, Brooklyn, Canterbury and Mansfield The Congregational Church in Hampton was organized June 5, 1723, being at that time the church in Windham Village or Canada Society Church. Rev. Samuel Moseley pastor from 1734 to 1791.

Nathaniel Johnson of Woodstock & Mary Robbins of Canterbury,	July 4, 1734
Israel Shaw of Farmington & Mary Davis of Lebanon,	Sept. 19, 1734
Jonathan Hains of Haverhill & Elizebeth Kingsbury,	Sept. 26, 1734
Seth Cutler & Elizebeth Babcock,	Oct. 22, 1734
Nathaniel Flint & Mercy Abbey,	Dec. 11, 1734
Moses Stiles & Phebee Cram,	Feb. 26, 1735
Joseph Genings & Sarah Hovey,	April 15, 1735
Joseph Preston & Phebee Farnum,	May 9, 1735
William Durkee & Elizebeth Ford,	Aug. 5, 1735
John Ford & Mary Pease,	Aug. 5, 1735
Oxonbridge Danes of Norwich & Abigail Danes,	Aug. 25, 1735
Jonathan Kingsbury & Abigail Holt,	Dec. 3, 1735
Samuel Stiles & Huldah Durkee,	Feb. 11, 1736
Nathaniel Gates of Canterbury & Ann Robbins,	Feb. 11, 1736
John Marsh & Sarah Martin,	Sept. 29, 1736
Ephraim Bemas & Lydia Thomas,	Oct. 5, 1736
John Preston & Mary Ford,	Dec. 9, 1736
Stephen Smith & Mary Preston,	Dec. 28, 1736
George Martin & Sarah Durkee,	May 12, 1737
Timothy Pearl & Mary Leach,	Nov. 15, 1737
Ezekiel Spaulding of Canterbury & Martha Kimbal,	Nov. 24, 1737
Ebenezer Adams of Canterbury & Mary Holt,	Dec. 5, 1737
James Pease of Somers & Abigail Ford,	Dec. 8, 1737
Jonathan Holt & Mary Parker,	April 12, 1738
Robert Durkee & Easter Warren,	April 27, 1738

Jonathan Shaw & Elizebeth Greene, both of Can-
terbury,   Nov. 9, 1738
Jacob Woodward & Abigail Flint,   Dec. 16, 1738
Manassah Farnam & Keziah Ford,   April 23, 1739
Daniel Plumbly of Upton & Abigail Preston, Oct. 5, 1740
John Howard & Sarah Bennett,   Jan. 5, 1741
David Fuller & Hannah Fuller,   May 18, 1741
Samuel Bell of Woodbury & Martha Warren, June 30, 1741
David Kindall & Abigail Holt,   Nov. 5, 1741
Nathaniel Flint & Sarah Bidlack,   June 16, 1742
William Farnum & Martha Fuller,   June 23, 1742
Asa Peabody & Mary Prentice,   July 13, 1742
William Holt & Hannah Holt,   July 13, 1742
James Utley & Mary Kingsbury,   Aug. 10, 1742
John Hovey & Susanna Ashley,   Nov. 8, 1742
Nathan Abbot & Eunice Marsh,   Nov. 24, 1742
Ebenezer Smith of Canterbury & Patience Robbins,
                               Jan. 31, 1743
Stephen Clark & Hannah Durkee,   Feb. 5, 1743
Robert Holt & Hannah Andross of Ashford,
                        March 28, 1743
Joseph Marsh & Anna Stedman,   April 27, 1743
Seth Tubbs of Norwich & Mary Groves, May 2, 1743
Josiah Roggers & Hannah Ford,   June 30, 1743
Zebediah Farnum & Mary Fuller,   July 27, 1743
Iccabod Roggers & Priscilla Holt,   Nov. 10, 1743
Ebenezer Woodward & Rachel Meacham, June 19, 1744
Daniel Butler & Hannah Parker,   Dec. 5, 1744
Thomas Butler & Deborah Meachan,   Feb. 7, 1745
Daniel Owen of Ashford & Abigail Pierce, April 25, 1745
James Kies & Tabitha Howard,   Nov. 5, 1745
Ezra Gears of Norwich & Elizebeth Canada, Nov. 7, 1745
Nehemiah Holt & Anne Farnum,   Nov. 25, 1745
Theophilus Clark of Ashford & Bethiah Billings,
                          Dec. 4, 1745
Ebenezer Burnham & Martha Hibbard of Canter-
bury,   Jan. 1, 1746
Bejamin Abbott of Ashford & Mary Anna Saun-
ders,   Jan. 16, 1746
John Dean of Canterbury & Rachel Bond, Jan. 22, 1746

Nathaniel Johnson of Woodstock & Jemima Farnum,
                                              Feb. 7, 1746
Ebenezer Stowel of Pomfrett & Anna Martin,
                                              Feb. 19, 1746
Nathaniel Bugbee of Ashford & Sarah Johnson,
                                              Feb. 20, 1746
Abner Ashley & Mary Cresy,   March 5, 1746
William Preston & Miss Averil,   Oct. 9, 1746
John Frame & Lydia Johnson,   Oct. 13, 1746
Samuel Ashley & Ruth Cresey,   Nov. 3, 1746
Ezekiel Holt & Lucee Durkee,   Nov. 5, 1746
Timothy Pearl & Dinah Holt,   Nov. 6, 1746
Joseph Burnham & Lucee Bennet,   Dec. 11, 1746
Dr. Solomon Wheat & Margaret Green,   Feb. 17, 1747
David Fisk & Sarah Farnum,   March 26, 1747
Joseph Sparks & Mehitabel Johnson,   April 29, 1747
Jethro Rogers & Hannah Holt,   Oct. 8, 1747
John Clark & Elizebeth Parker,   Nov. 12, 1747
Ebenezer Stoddard & Anna Stowel, both of Pom-
     fret,   Jan. 21, 1748
John Robbins & Rebecca Farnham,   Jan. 21, 1748
Nathaniel Hovey & Ruth Parker,   Jan. 21, 1748
Nathan Pearl & Elizabeth Utley,   March 14, 1748
Isaac Burnham & Eunice Holt,   March 22, 1748
Ezekiel Holt & Abia Sessions,   May 2, 1748
Joshua Farnun & Sarah Ford,   June 6, 1748
John Martin & Sarah Parker,   June 16, 1748
Benjamin Johnson of Preston & Mary Holt, Oct. 28, 1748
Samuel Robinson & Sarah Kimball,   Feb. 14, 1749
John Hibbard of Canterbury & Elizebeth Pearl,
                                              May 24, 1749
Joseph Ingalls & Sarah Abbott,   May 24, 1749
Samuel Utley & Hannah Abbott, both of Pomfret,
                                              Aug. 21, 1749
Sypperan Stephens of Plainfield & Rachel Lyon of
     Pomfret,   Aug. 9, 1749
Robert Coburn & Mary Genings,   Nov. 7, 1749
John Hammond & Abigail Fuller,   Dec. 19, 1749
Stephen Abbott & Freelove Burgess,   Jan. 3, 1750
David Canada & Deborah Genings,   Jan. 10, 1750

John Genings & Sarah Kingsbury,   Jan. 10, 1750
Jonathan Orms of Pomfret & Hannah Canada,

                                     Jan. 17, 1750
James Bidlack & Mehitable Durkee,   Feb. 14, 1750
Christopher Lewis & Mary Neff,   Feb. 23, 1750
Silas Woodward of Canterbury & Mary Bidlack,

                                     Feb. 28, 1750
John Stores of Mansfield & Mary Chaplin of Pom-
    fret,   March 14, 1750
John Pearl & Keturah Holt,   June 7, 1750
William Hibbard of Carterbury & Dorathy Burn-
    ham,   Oct. 16, 1750
Phinehas Durkee & Phebee Pearl,   Nov. 29, 1750
Jonathan Kingsbury & Hannah Clark,   Jan. 9, 1751
Samuel Coburn & Judah Webster,   Jan. 23, 1751
Daniel Kimball of Pomfret & Anne Hammond,

                                 March 27, 1751
James Stedman & Hannah Griffon,   April 11, 1751
Nathaniel Flint, Jr., & Mary Hovey,   June 3, 1751
Joseph Martin & Elizebeth Ford,   Oct. 17, 1751
Stephen Fuller & Mary Abbot,   Oct. 17, 1751
Jabez Brown of Pomfret & Mary Kimball,   Oct. 18, 1751
Joseph Ashley & Sarah Cresy of Bethney,   Nov. 25, 1751
Daniel Stoughton & Sarah Kimball of Pomfret,

                                 June 2, 1752
Zephaniah Davis & Susanna Durkee,   July 16, 1752
John Curtiss of Canterbury & Hannah Moseley,

                                 May 29, 1753
Daniel Denison & Lydia Pearl,   Nov. 27, 1753
Joseph Durkee & Elizebeth Fish,   Nov. 27, 1753
John Richardson of Pomfret & Martha Holt,   Jan. 1, 1754
Zebadiah Coburn & Elizebeth Durkee,   Jan. 22, 1754
James Oles of Ashford & Sarah Kingsley,   March 21, 1754
Jacob Woodward & Elizebeth Durkee,   March 28, 1754
Joseph Utley & Jerusha Martin,   May 29, 1754
Joseph Chaplin of Pomfret & Sarah Stedman, June 13, 1754
Benjamin Neff & Anna Neff,   June 13, 1754
Joseph Marsh & Lydia Bennet,   June 20, 1754
Robert Durkee & Sarah Durkee,   Nov. 22, 1754
Ebenezer Goodale of Pomfret & Phebe Holt,   Feb. 13, 1755

William Foster of Holliston & Hannah Durkee,
May 27, 1755

Christopher Davis & Lydia Hovey,	June 5, 1755
John Peck of Ashford & Elizabeth Denison,	June 17, 1755
Aaron Geer & Hannah Utley,	July 8, 1755
Amos Clark & Abigail Utley,	Oct. 23, 1755
Asa Farnum & Lydia Bidlack,	March 2, 1756
John Parish & Tamma Preston,	May 27, 1756
Francis Bennet & Elizebeth Howard,	June 9, 1756
Nathaniel Holt & Phebe Canada,	Dec. 16, 1756
Thomas Butler & Elizebeth Holt,	Jan. 4, 1757
Ebenezer Griffen & Elizebeth Martin,	Feb. 13, 1757
William Martin & Naomi Upton,	March 3, 1757
Andrew Burnham & Jane Bennet,	May 11, 1757
Asa Hammond & Lois Durkee,	Jan. 11, 1758
Eleazer Butler & Lydia Durkee,	Jan. 11, 1758
Zebediah Holt & Jemimah Simons,	Feb. 16, 1758

Josiah Moss of Canterbury & Mehitable Tresscot,
Feb. 22, 1758

Ephraim Stowel of Pomfret & Elizebeth Cutler,
March 9, 1758

Joseph Abbot & Elizebeth Stedman,	April 20, 1758
Simon Clark of Lebanon & Elizebeth Moseley,	May 25, 1758
John Lummus & Ruth Averel,	Sept. 21, 1758
John Webb of Norwich & Jane Fortner,	April 26, 1759
Thomas Stedman & Mehitable Griffen,	Sept. 23, 1760
Jacob Simonds, Jr., & Mehitable Preston,	Sept. 27, 1760
Solomon Smith & Eunice Bennet,	Nov. 24, 1760
James Hostun & Mary Luce,	March 12, 1761
Amos Ford & Lydia Davison,	May 25, 1761
Benjamin Durkee & Abigail Durkee,	Jan. 21, 1762

Capt. Benjamin Pierce of Brookline & Mrs. Sarah
Holt,   Jan. 28, 1762

Benjamin Jewet & Hannah Bidlack,	Feb. 10, 1762
Joseph Robinson & Rebecca Durkee,	March 10, 1762
Jonathan Fisk & Sarah Leach of Ashford,	March 18, 1762
Nathan Griggs of Pomfret & Anna Cresee,	April 9, 1762

Obadiah Johnson of Canterbury & Mary Howard,
April 24, 1762

Samuel Moseley, Jr., & Luce Stedman,   Oct. 7, 1762

6

Isaac Dodge & Sarah Utley,	Oct. 20, 1762
The Rev. Joshua Paine of Sturbrige (?) & Mary Mosley,	Nov. 11, 1762
Daniel Fuller & Patience Stedman,	Nov. 18, 1762
Hopstil Welch & Ellis Woodward,	May 12, 1763
William Preston, Jr., & Desire Williams,	Aug. 18, 1763
William Holt, Jr., & Mercy Holt,	Sept. 8, 1763
Barnabas Wood & Mary Alworth,	Oct. 20, 1763
Daniel Canada of Canterbury & Ruhamah Preston,	Nov. 17, 1763
Benjamin Martin & Lucee Clark,	July 26, 1764
Amos Kinny of Pomfret & Easther Utley,	Oct. 5, 1764
Gideon Martin & Rachel Heth,	Jan. 24, 1765
Darius Fish of Canterbury & Sarah Howard,	Feb. 7, 1765
Thomas Napin of Canterbury & Sibbel Holt,	March 7, 1765
Eleazer Write of Mansfield & Anna Marsh,	April 25, 1765
Jacob Abbee of Westminster & Sarah Richardson,	July 7, 1765
John Greenslit & Sarah Burnham,	Nov. 14, 1765
Aron Litchfield of Canterbury & Phebe Holt,	Jan. 14, 1766
Ephraim Cleveland of Canterbury & Mary Griffing,	March 6, 1766
Elijah Fitch & Hannah Fuller,	April 17, 1766
James Smith & Lois Preston,	April 30, 1766
Jonathan Utley & Mary Robbins,	May 5, 1766
Stephen Durkee, Jr., & Jerusha Simons,	May 15, 1766
Nathaniel Gates of ―――― & Ellis Robbins,	June 29, 1766
Holland Weeks of Pomfret & Hannah Moseley,	Sept. 4, 1766
John Sessions & Martha Neff,	Nov. 20, 1766
Stephen Williams of Brookline & Sarah Mosley,	Jan. 15, 1767
John Peck of Ashford & Jerusha Preston,	Aug. 25, 1767
Daniel Dunum of Lebanon & Anna Moseley,	Dec. 17, 1767
Samuel Flint & Lucee Martin,	Dec. 17, 1767
Samuel Moulton & Sarah Ringe,	Dec. 17, 1767
Joel Utley & Abigail Durkee,	Jan. 7, 1768
Jonathan Kingsbery & Anne Geers,	Jan. 14, 1768
John Collins of Stonington & Mary Smith,	Aug. 24, 1768

Nathaniel Mosley of Windham & Rosanna Alworth
    of Pomfret,   Sept. 29, 1768
Robbert Crook of Westminster & Mercy Richardson,
                                   Oct. 17, 1768
Shubel Simons & Tamma Durkee,   April 6, 1769
Henry Durkee & Sarah Holt,   Nov. 16, 1769
Samuel Cutler of Norwich & Eunice Simons, Nov. 23, 1769
Andrew Fuller & Eunice Burnham,   Jan. 18, 1770
Daniel Trobrige of Pomfret & Mary Pearl,   Feb. 15, 1770
James Butts of Canterbury & Abigail Utley, Feb. 15, 1770
William Adams of Canterbury & Sarah Night, June 12, 1770
John Abbot of Wrentham & Abigail Gould, Sept. 11, 1770
Isaac Parish & Mary Clark,   Nov. 14, 1770
Amaziah Fisk & Priscila Bingham,   Jan. 3, 1771
Hezekiah Coburn & Mary Bill,   Jan. 17, 1771
Ichabod Hyde & Abigail Burnham,   Jan. 24, 1771
John McClarren Breed of Norwich & Mrs. Mary
    Devotion,   Nov. 24, 1771
Daniel Stedman & Sarah Wilcom,   Feb. 13, 1772
James Bidlack of Canterbury & Abigail Fuller,
                             April 30, 1772
Thomas Moseley & Sarah Ford,   May 21, 1772
William Alworth of Pomfret & Bulah Moseley, Oct. 15, 1772
The Rev. James Cogswell & Mrs. Martha Devotion,
                             Jan. 21, 1773
Asa Aspenwall of Canterbury & Hannah Bennet,
                             Jan. 21, 1773
Samuel Humprey of Barrington & Mary Ashley,
                             Oct. 24, 1773
Levi Perkins of Norwich & Eleanor Howard, June 6, 1774
Phinas Ford & Mary Martin,   Feb. 22, 1774
Daniel Butler & Hannah Reed,   Feb. 24, 1774
Cornelius Adams of Canterbury & Esther Stedman,
                             April 14, 1774
Amos Woodward & Molley Derbe,   Aug. 25, 1774
Jeremiah Farnum & Lucee Durkee,   Oct. 8, 1774
Edward Cartwright & Allice Havens,   Dec. 28, 1774
John Lummus & Eunice Sessions,   Jan. 5, 1775
John Chamberlain of Armenia Precinct & Abigail
    Abbott,   Feb. 2, 1775

Peter Ingols of Pomfret & Sarah Ashley,   April 20, 1775
Josiah Collins & Hannah Abbott,   May 24, 1775
Josiah Henday of Ashford & Tamma Clark,   Nov. 16, 1775
Caleb Grosvenor of Pomfret & Olive Griffen, Jan. 11, 1776
John Downing of Norwich & Mary Parker,   Feb. 1, 1776
Benjamin Griffen & Cloe Howard,   Feb. 8, 1776
Nathan Paine of Pomfret & Patty Hovey,   March 21, 1776
Jeseph Martin & Zerviah Daly,   April 11, 1776
Joseph Burnham of Ashford & Elizabeth Durkee,
    June 13, 1776
Abiel Holt & Abigail Durkee,   July, 1776
James Butt of Canterbury & Elizabeth Coburn,
    Sept. 8, 1776
Joseph Cresey of ——— & Hannah Ashley,   Dec. 5, 1776
William Howard & Phebe Fuller,   April 10, 1777
Abljah Fuller & Abigail Meacham,   May 15, 1777
Eliphalet Martin & Eunice Clark,   May 15, 1777
Abiel Abbott & Ruth Hovey,   Nov. 13, 1777
Samuel Lamphire of Mansfield & Sarah Durkee,
    Nov. 20, 1777
James Abbott & Hannah Denison,   Jan. 1, 1778
Henry Durkee, Jr., & Sarah Lumuss,   April 23, 1778
Seth Stoel of Pomfret & Dinah Holt,   June 30, 1778
John Downing of Norwich & Mary Millar,   Aug. 27, 1778
Abel Hall of Mansfield & Susannah Clark,   Dec. 3, 1778
Thomas Utley & Abigail Hodgkins,   May 25, 1780
Benjamin Fuller & Joanna Trobridge, both of Pom-
    fret,   Sept. 28, 1780
Josiah Hammond & Elizebeth Mosley,   Sept. 28, 1780
Nathan Genings & Zerviah Richardson,   Dec. 14, 1780
Dr. Thomas Clark & Abigail Mosley,   Dec. 13, 1781
Joseph Steward of Upton & Sarah Mosley,   May 31, 1789

NORWICH — FRANKLIN.

NEW LONDON COUNTY.

The town of Franklin was organized in 1786, having been a part of Norwich. The Congregational Church of Franklin was organized January 4, 1718, and called the West Farms (Norwich) Church. Rev. Henry Willes, pastor, 1718-1758. Following are the records at Franklin.

Jacob Hazzen & Abigail Baker,	Oct. 27, 1719
Ebenezer Baker & Ruth Johnson,	Dec. 15, 1719
Thomas Wood & Experience Abell,	Jan. 26, 1720
David Birchard & Lydia Backus,	May 9, 1720
Jacob Willes & Dinah Peck,	May 17, 1720
Samuel Crocker & Jemima French,	May 25, 1720
Daniel Woodworth & Mehitabell Brown,	Dec. 15, 1720
Francis Smith & Elizebeth Gager,	May 25, 1721
Thomas Grist & Ann Birchard,	Aug. 14, 1721
John Hyde & Sarah Haskin,	Sept. 21, 1721
Thomas Wallbridge & Mary Knight,	March 29, 1722
Thomas Austin & Sarah Holmes,	June 7, 1722
Daniel Buck & Elizebeth Perkin,	June 11, 1722
Nathaniel Baker & Mary Longbotom,	Aug. 20, 1722
John Partridge & Ann Fitch,	Sept. 27, 1722
Aaron Read & Hannah Knight,	Jan. 10, 1723
Daniel White & Elizebeth Answorth,	Jan. 10, 1723
Timothy Collins & Elizebeth Hyde,	Jan. 16, 1723
James Birchard & Deborah Marks,	Oct. 1, 1723
Abner French & Sarah Sluman,	Nov. 6, 1723
Jabez Crocker & Ruth Hazzen,	Feb. 25, 1724
William Johnson & Hannah Stodard,	March 2, 1724
John Badger & Sarah Noyes,	May 13, 1724
Joshua Smith & Edne Hazzen,	Oct. 21, 1724
Evan Harris & Mary Badger,	Nov. 5, 1724
Richard Edgerton & Hannah Calkin,	Feb. 9, 1725
Daniel Palmeter & Mary Ames,	June 29, 1725
Thomas Groves & Hannah Baker,	Aug. 10, 1725
Jonathan Dyke & Mary Edgerton,	Nov. 11, 1725
Mathew Birchard & Ruth Hartshorn,	Dec. 21, 1725
Timothy Ayer & Abigail Hartshorn,	Jan. 25, 1726

John Baker & Jerusha Pitcher,	June 27, 1726
Friend Weeks & Rachell Armstrong,	Aug. 24, 1726
Daniel Johnson & Jemima Olmsby,	Nov. 9, 1726
Benjamin Armstrong & Hannah Fox,	Jan. 12, 1727
David Lambard & Lurana Bill,	Feb. 1, 1727
John Morgan & Susannah ———,	Feb. 23, 1727
John Searborn & Abigail Philmore,	April 4, 1727
Daniel Badger & Patience Durkee,	June 28, 1727
Jacob Hyde & Hannah Kingsbery,	Oct. 11, 1727
James Bill & Keziah French,	Nov. 8, 1727
Daniel Denison & Hannah Crocker,	Dec. 6, 1727
John Birchard & Jane Hyde,	March 20, 1728
Ephraim Kingsbery & Martha Smith,	July 3, 1728
John Barker & Hannah Brewster,	Nov. 6, 1728
Samuel Bushnell & Ann Cogswell,	Jan. 22, 1729
Benjamin Peck & Phebe Hatch,	May 14, 1729
John French & Phebe Hyde,	Aug., 1729
Samuel Butt & Abigail Rudd,	Sept. 24, 1729
Jarret Ingraham & Mary Taylor,	Oct. 27, 1729
Henry Legrant & Elizebeth Richley,	Oct. 28, 1729
——— Holmes & Ann Rockwell,	Dec. 3, 1729
Edward Marcy & Rebecca Haskin,	Jan. 22, 1730
Ephraim Tingly & Elizebeth Birchard,	Aug. 28, 1730
Ebenezer Wallbridge & Mary Durkee,	Dec. 2, 1730
John Barret & Hannah Downer,	Dec. 10, 1730
Samuel Ladd & Hannah Hartshorn,	Dec. 30, 1730
Nathaniel Badger & Rebecca Simons,	Jan. 6, 1731
Laurance Antiszell & Mary Armstrong,	March 15, 1731
Eleazer Hamon & Margaret Wallbridge,	March 15, 1731
Stephen Meigs & Jane Johnson,	June 1, 1731
William Wentworth & Martha Armstrong,	June 16, 1731
David Hartshorn & Sarah Birchard,	June 17, 1731
Elisha Lothrope & Margaret Sluman,	Jan. 31, 1732
John Lune & Experience Edgerton,	March 9, 1732
Isaac Woodard & Elisabeth Armstrong,	Aug. 22, 1732
Simeon Woodard & Sarah Baker,	Nov. 23, 1732
Josiah Backus & Love Kingsbery,	Nov. 30, 1732
Nathaniel Day & Ruth Filmore,	Dec. 4, 1732
Aaron Owen & Meriham Wright,	Jan. 11, 1733
Edward Waldoe & Abigail Elderkin,	Jan. 25, 1733

Moses Buzzell & Mehitabell Baker,	Jan. 30, 1733
Daniel Armstrong & Mary Guile,	April 4, 1733
Joshua Vose & Prudence Saunders,	June 18, 1733
William Edgerton & Lydia Barstow,	Nov. 6, 1733
Joseph Rudd & Sarah Mosley,	Nov. 21, 1733
Caleb Downer & Martha Smith,	Dec. 5, 1733
James Payne & Sarah Armstrong,	Jan. 15, 1734
Hezekiah Edgerton & Ann Abell,	May 13, 1734
John Gager & Jerusha Barstow,	July 3, 1734
Abner Hyde & Mehetable Smith,	Oct. 28, 1734
Samuel French & Elizabeth White,	Nov. 4, 1734
Abell Deene & Mercy Polley,	Jan. 28, 1735
Joshua Edgerton & Ruth Kingsbery,	Jan. 28, 1735
Joseph Lothrup & Mary Hartshorn,	April 17, 1735
Joshua Pettes & Elizabeth Crocker,	May 20, 1735
John Armstrong & Mary Durke,	Oct. 9, 1735
Samuel Lothrup & Charity Sluman,	Oct. 16, 1735
William Mannering of New London & Rebekah Gager,	Nov. 5, 1735
Samuel Field of Guilford & Bethiah Johnson,	Dec. 15, 1735
David Hartshorn & Olive Armstrong,	April 1, 1736
Nathan Messenger & Abigail Collam,	Nov. 11, 1736
Stephen Howard of Mansfield & Mrs. Martha Ladd,	Nov. 15, 1736
Jabez Hyde & Lydia Abell,	Dec. 8, 1736
Joseph Hastings & Zeruiah Crocker,	June 21, 1737
Andrew Veach of Lebanon & Experience Edgerton,	Aug. 18, 1737
Isaac Woodworth, Jr., & Elizabeth Fox,	Aug. 22, 1737
Joseph Lanphere of Stonington & Margaret Crocker,	Sept. 22, 1737
Isaac Williams & Lydia Taylor,	Sept. 27, 1737
Israel Lothrup & Ednah Moseley,	Oct. 5, 1737
Hopestill Armstrong & Rebecca Durke,	Dec. 22, 1737
John Rouse & Alice Hazzen,	March 16, 1738
Joseph Kingsbery, 3d, & Deliverance Squire,	March 28, 1738
Elisha Tubs & Ann Miller, both of Lyme,	July 31, 1738
Benoni Messenger & Mary Wood,	Sept. 6, 1738
John Peck & Mary Deming,	Sept. 7, 1738
James Dean & Elizabeth Rood,	Oct. 11, 1738

Joseph Shadduck & Mary Willson,	Nov. 7, 1738
Andrew Reed & —— Steal,	Sept. 26, 1739
Ezekiel Barret & Mary Lothrup,	Oct. 24, 1739
Baily Bishop & —— Downer,	Nov. 8, 1739
John Jurdan & Dorcas Burt,	Dec. 9, 1739
Aaron Cook & Submit ——,	Dec. 9, 1739
Thomas Williams & Esther Hyde,	Feb. 5, 1740
Timothy Corlis, Jr., of Haverhill & Mrs. Ann Willoughby,	June 2, 1740
Zebulon Lothrup & Lois Rodgers,	Sept. 4, 1740
Josiah Tracy & Rachel Allin,	Nov. 3, 1740
Joseph Hazzen & Elizabeth Durke,	Dec. 3, 1740
—— Story & Lydia Wood,	Oct. 6, 1741
Ichabud Hyde & Mary ——,	Oct. 21, 1741
Jonathan Ely & Bridget Callam,	Nov. 5, 1741
Noah Woodard of Canterbery & Ann Armstrong,	Nov. 25, 1741
Jonathan Peck & Bethiah Bingham,	Jan. 14, 1742
John Elderkin & Rebecca Allen,	March 2, 1742
Benjamin Atwell & Mary Story,	March 4, 1742
Jonathan Weston & Elizabeth Bosworth,	April 7, 1742
Samuel Pitcher & Hannah Fox,	Aug. 23, 1742
Jonathan Barstow & Abigail Hyde,	Sept. 7, 1742
Jedediah Lothrup & Abigail Hyde,	Sept. 27, 1742
Rev. Daniel Fuller of Willington & Mary Edgerton,	Oct. 26, 1742
Richard Haskin & ~~Julia~~ *Beula* Wood,	Nov. 23, 1742
Samuel Robbards & Zeruiah Hartshorn,	Jan. 4, 1743
William Armstrong & Mercy Pitcher,	March 16, 1743
Jabez Emerson & Sarah Downer,	March 23, 1743
Joseph Sanford & Bethiah Lothrup,	April 6, 1743
Jeremiah Bingham & Sarah White,	April 14, 1743
John Wheatly & Submit Cook,	April 25, 1743
Nathaniel Messenger & Joanna Callam,	May 19, 1743
John Packer & Elizabeth Lothrup,	June 29, 1743
James Elderkin & Betty Waterman,	Aug. 31, 1743
James Blague & Abigail Rennals,	Nov. 6, 1743
Rodolphus Hawkins & Typhena Lathrop,	March 27, 1782
Cherub Abell & Lydia Gager,	April 18, 1782
Jathbell Peck & Olive Hyde,	May 2, 1782

Jabez Lanphere & Esther Sabin,	May 16, 1782
Abel Edgerton & Mehitable Tracy,	May 16, 1782
Abel Hyde & Margaret Tracy, 3d,	May 23, 1782
Ephraim Chaffee & Olive Edgerton,	Aug. 29, 1782
Isaiah Armstrong & Artemis Philemore,	Sept. 15, 1782
Azel Peck & Dolly Kingsley,	Sept. 19, 1782
William Ellis & Anna Edgerton,	Sept. 19, 1782
Benjamin Hyde & Elizabeth Hyde,	Oct. 26, 1782
Jonathan Palmer & Lucinda Smith,	Nov. 7, 1782
Amos Ingram & Sarah Ayer,	Nov. 11, 1782
Ezekiel Hyde & Mary Closen,	Dec. 12, 1782
—— Lathrop & Polly Whetmore of Chelsea,	Dec. 14, 1782
Asa Hibbard of Windham & Abigail Armstrong,	Jan. 1, 1783
Moses Hazen & Joanna Samson,	Jan. 9, 1783
Daniel Ellis & Roxanna Peck,	March 13, 1783
David Metcalf & Anna Champion,	April 27, 1783
William Tiffany & Anna Pettis,	April 30, 1783
Levi Gager & Anna Sabin,	May 22, 1783
David Ladd & Eunice Sabin,	June 4, 1783
Benoni Muro & Margaret Edgerton,	June 12, 1783
Joseph Knight & Jane Hyde,	Sept. 14, 1783
Daniel Tracy & Lucy Tracy,	Oct. 30, 1783
Dudley Tracy & Sarah Kingsbury,	Nov. 3, 1783
Joseph Hyde & Juliette Abell,	Jan. 11, 1784
John Munsell & Dilla Edgerton,	Feb. 1, 1784
John Vaughan & Mary Hyde,	Feb. 19, 1784
Eliphelet Rudd & Sibyl Tracy,	April 1, 1784
Nathan Gile & Eunice Ladd,	April 29, 1784
Nathan Edgerton & Sally Belshaw,	May 2, 1784
Elisha Huntington & Nancy Rudd,	May 20, 1784
Cyrus Brewster & Anna Willes,	Aug. 10, 1784
Joseph Davis & Fanny Belshaw,	Aug. 25, 1784
Charles Bentley & Phebe Pember,	Sept. 2, 1784
Stephen Rogers & Ednah Hyde,	Oct. 7, 1784
Edward Corwin & Esther Barstow,	Nov. 4, 1784
Nathaniel Smith & Lurinda Armsby,	Nov. 4, 1784
Jonathan Samson & Clarissa Hyde,	Nov. 7, 1784
Jeremiah Armstrong & Anna Hazen,	Dec. 30, 1784
Billey Hale & Hannah Barker,	Jan. 1, 1785
Hayward Cheney & Cynthia Hartshorn,	March 17, 1785

Elijah Hartshorn & Jerusha Johnson,	June 30, 1785
Stephen Ellis & Rebecca Huntington,	Nov. 23, 1785
James Armstrong & Nabby Ladd,	Nov. 24, 1785
—— Hibbard of Vermont & —— Wood,	Dec. 6, 1785
Eleazer Hartshorn & Lidia Hyde,	March 16, 1786
Miner Sholes & Abigail Chappel,	March 16, 1786
—— Doubledee of Lebanon & —— Huntley of Norwich,	March 25, 1786
Ezekiel Waterman & Ruth Huntington,	April 2, 1786
Samuel Judd & Dinah Huntington,	May 19, 1786
Benjamin Storrs & Margaret Lathrop,	Sept. 14, 1786
Daniel Hyde & —— Rogers,	Sept. 21, 1786
Isaac Sargent & —— Belshaw,	Oct. 19, 1786
Darius Lathrop & Lydia McCall,	Nov. 23, 1786
—— Philemore & —— Ladd,	Dec. 21, 1786
Ezra Edgerton & Anna Edgerton,	Jan. 21, 1787
John Hartshorn & Irene Haskin,	Feb. 14, 1787
John Nott & Hannah Hyde,	April 5, 1787
Nathan Palmer & Saloma Smith,	April 12, 1787
William Crocker & Sibyl Lathrop,	May 17, 1787
Oliver Backus & Dice Hyde,	May 20, 1787
Thomas Marshall & Frelove Edgerton,	June 13, 1787
Eveter Cyrus & —— Gune (colored),	Sept. 13, 1787
Jeremiah Ingraham & Sally Ladd,	Oct. 11, 1787
Levi Hazen & Breenetta Philemore,	Dec. 16, 1787
Eleazar Bently & Elizabeth Edgerton,	Feb. 14, 1788
Andrew Ladd & Hannah Sanford,	April 17, 1788
Elihu Hyde & Hannah Abell,	April 24, 1788
Gidion Prior & Lydia Loomis,	May 8, 1788
Andrew Williams & Bethiah Tracy,	May 8, 1788
Green Marshall & Asenath Gager,	June 5, 1788
Timothy Backus & Jerusha Tracy,	July 6, 1788
John Gager & Phebe Hyde,	Aug. 11, 1788
Eleazer Tracy & Prudee Rogers,	Sept. 14, 1788
Jonathan Jilson & Lydia Pember,	Oct. 1, 1788
Benjamin Ellis & Sally Kingsbury,	Oct. 5, 1788
Eliphelet Metcalf & Bethiah Edgerton, Jr.,	Oct. 12, 1788
Jedediah Griswold & Nancy Maning,	Oct. 30, 1788
Walter Birchard & Abigail Rogers,	Nov. 2, 1788
Jeremiah Lathrop & Lucretia Smith,	Jan. 22, 1789

Hezekiah Edgerton, Jr., & Maria Brigham, April 26, 1789
Josiah Griswold & Eunice Kingsbury, Oct. 31, 1789
Stephen Nott & Abigail Bradford, Nov. 1, 1789
Gui Morris & Freelove Frank, Dec. 9, 1789
Azel Avery & Clarissa Hartshorn, Dec. 17, 1789
Seth Johnson & Daphne Edgerton, Jan. 4, 1790
Asa Backus & Parthena Jones, Feb. 10, 1790
Jabez Willes & Nabby Abell, March 10, 1790
Roswell Foard & Polly Harris, June 8, 1790
Joshua Parish & Abigail Waterman, Aug. 28, 1790
Othniel Gager & Rebekah Rudd, Aug. 25, 1790
Jabez R. Packard & Lois Hartshorn, Sept. 2, 1790
Johathan Peck & Martha Willes, Oct. 15, 1790
Ambrose Hyde & Phebe Hyde, Nov. 24, 1790
Oliver Scott & Ruth Kingsbury, Dec. 8, 1790
Simeon Hazen & Nabba Sampson, Dec. 16, 1790
Joshua Griswold & Clarissa Wright, Dec. 30, 1790
Azariah Huntington & Parnel Champion, Jan. 9, 1791
Gurdon Tracy & Eunice Packard, Jan 31, 1791
Samuel Ellis & Rachel Smith, March 17, 1791
Samuel Hutchinson & Hannah Hale, March 24, 1791
Eb. Edgerton & Eunice Smith, March 24, 1791
Samuel Whiting & Faith Manning, April 18, 1791
Reuben Ingram & Lydia Gager, April 28, 1791
Asa Crocker & Lois Crocker, May 21, 1791
Lavius Fillemore & Philura Hartshorn, Sept. 8, 1791
Aaron Fargo & Ruth Perry, Sept. 20, 1791
Azel Fitch of Lebanon & Demmis Ellis, Sept. 22, 1791
Otis Chester of Montville & Charlotte Nott, Oct. 6, 1791
Ezra Woodworth & Sukey Gager, Nov. 15, 1791
Jehiel Root of Willington & Rachel Edgerton, Nov. 24, 1791
William Gager of Lebanon & Lavinia Barker, Dec. 1, 1791
Oliver Gager of Lebanon & Sarah Lathrop, Jan. 12, 1792
Erastus Ladd & Sarah Hazen, Jan. 12, 1792
Amos Jones of Middlebury, Vt., & Lois Pember, Jan. 19, 1792
Aaron Bailey & Hannah Ladd, Jan. 19, 1792
Daniel Sampson of the Grand Isle & Anna Sampson,
 Jan. 26, 1792
Roger Wattles of Hamden, N. Y., & Sally Mason,
 Jan. 29, 1792

Jedediah Morse & Fanny Waterman,   Jan. 31, 1792
James Tracy & Ruth Calkins,   Feb. 19, 1792
Jedediah Armstrong & Anna Graves,   March 12, 1792
Hazen Ladd & Rhoda Smith,   April 9, 1792
Oliver Tracy & Lydia Rudd,   June 14, 1792
Eliel Wales of Windham & Anna Edgerton, June 28, 1792
Ephriam Bushnell & Temperance Willes,   Sept. 20, 1792
Eliekam Hitchcock of Bolton & Eunice Abell, Oct. 31, 1792
Strephon Palmer of Lebanon & Naomi Calkins, Nov. 8, 1792
Silas Hartshorn & Mrs. Eunice Backus,   Nov. 15, 1792
Erastus Tracy & Clarissa Prentice,   Nov. 29, 1792
Milton Hyde & Lovice Hyde,   Jan. 6, 1793
Enos Thompson & Sally Munsell,   March 7, 1793
Newell Robinson & Sally Giddings,   March 24, 1793
Oliver Smith & Eunice Abell,   April 7, 1793
Eliphalet Gray & Sally Owen,   April 7, 1793
Abner Ladd, Jr., & Sally Cook,   Aug. 25, 1793
Eliphalet Dewey of Lebanon & Rachel Hyde, Aug. 25, 1793
Denison Wales of Windham & Parmelia Edgerton,
                                           Sept. 19, 1793
Cato Quasho of Ellington & Selah Pedro,   Sept. 26, 1793
Eben Hyde & Anna Edgerton,   Nov. 6, 1793
Darius Peck & Mary Francis,   Nov. 14, 1793
Abell Holt of Willington & Anne Abell,   Nov. 17, 1793
Silas Hyde of Lebanon, N. H., & Sally Armstrong,
                                           Nov. 26, 1793
Nathan Williams of Lebanon & Temperance Edgerton,
                                           Dec. 21, 1793
Samuel Ladd, 3d, & Abigail Ladd,   Jan. 30, 1794
Bradford Peck & Lydia Barstow,   July 24, 1794
Ira Abell & Abigail Hyde,   Oct. 28, 1794
Jabez Abell & Elizabeth Sanford,   Jan. 18, 1795
Hezekiah Tracy & Abigail Starr,   Feb. 1, 1795
Jonathan Taylor of Mansfield & Ruth Edgerton,
                                           Feb. 12, 1795
Eliphalet Wright of Norwich & Mary Griswold, Feb. 19, 1795
John Colegrove of Coventry, R. I., & Hannah Corwin,
                                           March 5, 1795
Ebenezer Luce of Windham & Rebecah Scott,
                                           March 16, 1795

Hiel Tracy & Susanna Gifford, Nov. 8, 1795
Elias West of Bozrah & Polly Armstrong, Dec. 13, 1795
James Hyde & Betsey Starr, Feb. 18, 1796
Josiah Tracy & Polly Birchard of Bozrah, Feb. 20, 1796
Joshua Brooks of Lebanon & Lucy Abell, April 24, 1796
John Birchard of Norwich & Anna Hyde, May 8, 1796
Eliphalet Barker of Lebanon & Lucinda Andrews of
  Windham, May 22, 1796
N. Bingham of Windham & Mrs. Lucretia Edgerton,
  July 7, 1796
Gurdon Lathrop of Norwich & Jemima Pember,
  Dec. 22, 1796
Jedediah Sabin & Lydia Armstrong, Dec. 24, 1796
Asaph Smith, Jr., of Ashford & Vienna Robinson,
  Jan. 3, 1797
Cyrenus Clark of Lebanon & Rachel Tracy, Jan. 19, 1797
John Crocker of Lebanon, N. H., & Mrs. Anne Gard-
  ner of Bozrah, Feb. 1, 1797
Joshua Smith, 3d, & Elizabeth Hartshorn, Feb. 13, 1797
Azel Edgerton & Lucy Pember, March 6, 1797
Varanes Lathrop of Lebanon & Lucy Edgerton,
  March 7, 1797
Jacob Linkhorn of Windham & Elizabeth Scott,
  March 12, 1797
Carpenter Morse of Norwich and Mary Tenny,
  April 12, 1797
Jesse Lathrop of Norwich & Rhoda Hyde, April 16, 1797
Asahel Ladd & Rebekah Armstrong, April 23, 1797
Joshua Bushnell of Lisbon & Zervia Fillemore,
  May 14, 1797
Samuel Carver of Bolton & Lucy Tracy, June 7, 1797
Ezra Hunting of Norwich & Mary Deans, Oct. 8, 1797
William Thomas & Eunice Duglass of Norwich,
  Oct. 22, 1797
Jonathan Hyde of Canterbury & Hannah Bently,
  Nov. 4, 1797
Jesse Birchard of Bozrah & Harriet Smith, Nov. 4, 1797
William Bacon of Windham & Anne Clark of
  Lebanon, Dec. 14, 1797
Septa Fellemore & Eunice Edgerton, Dec. 21, 1797

Andrew Lathrop of Hartford, N. Y., & Betsey Mason,

	1798
Jabez Rudd & Elizabeth Hyde,	Feb. 25, 1798
Silas Scott & Betsey Perry,	April 16, 1798
Asahel Smith & Eunice Sampson,	May 27, 1798
Simeon Backus & Clarissa Hyde,	June 3, 1798
Eliud Smith & Betty Smith,	July 8, 1798
Ebenezer Peck & Polly Tracy,	July 15, 1798

Urlah Lathrop of Lebanon & Betsey P. Edgerton,

	Sept. 9, 1798
Jared Hyde & Polly Hartshorn,	Oct. 25, 1798
Jonathan Bushnell & Eunice Kingsley,	Nov. 26, 1798
Earl Fillemore & Betsey Mahegue,	Jan. 20, 1799

Pliny Searl of Norwich, Mass., & Susanna Carpenter, Feb. 5, 1799

James Gordon of Lisbon & Anna Lathrop of Norwich,
Feb. 17, 1799

William Bailey of Lebanon & Lucretia Tracy,
March 6, 1799

Solomon Holt of Willington & Zerviah Abell, April 7, 1799

Nathaniel Hopkins of Harwick, Mass., & Anna
Armstrong, July 7, 1799

Jacob Kingsbury & Sally P. Ellis,	Nov. 24, 1799
Ebenezer Hyde & Elizabeth Peck,	Dec. 4, 1799
Aaron Bailey & Matilda Giddings,	Dec. 25, 1799

GREENWICH.

FAIRFIELD COUNTY.

The town of Greenwich was settled in 1640. It submitted to Connecticut, October, 1662. The First Congregational Church in Greenwich was organized in 1670. There are no records of this church prior to 1787. It is said that the earlier records were taken to Long Island during the Revolution and never returned. The Second Congregational Church in Greenwich was organized in 1705. The records begin with Rev. Stephen Munson's pastorate, 1728 to 1733. The marriages are as follows.

Joseph Close, Jr., & Unis Hoit,	May 29, 1728
Elisha Mead & Mary Brown,	Nov. 18, 1728
Benjamin Mead & Martha Ferris,	Nov. 28, 1728
Charles Gorman & Rachel Defowe (?),	Dec. 30, 1728
Benjamin Brundage of Rye & Elizabith Brush,	
	Jan. 1, 1728–9
Nathaniel Reynolds & Ruth Purdy,	Jan. 29, 1728–9
Thomas Cord (?) of Stamford & Deborah Hiat of White Plains,	Feb. 5, 1728–9
Theophilus Peck & Elizabeth Mead,	Feb. 13, 1728–9
The Rev. Pastor ——— & Susanna Punderson of New Haven,	April 4, 1729
Jacob Rundal & Rebeckah Knap,	April 4, 1729
Thomas Close (?) & Hannah Lyon,	May 6, 1729
Ebenezer Hustead & Sarah Holms,	May 13, 1729
Thomas Travis of White Plains & Catharine ———,	Sept. 21, 1729
Charles Knap & ——— Wiks (?),	Nov. 13, 1729
John Benedict & Abigail Reynolds of Norwalk,	Nov. 19, 1729
Timothy Canfield of Ridgefield & Kesia Ferris,	Nov. 19, 1729
John Reynolds & Ruth Reynolds,	Nov. 19, 1729
Nathaniel Jugerson (?) of Stamford & Hannah Finch,	Nov. 19, 1729
John Finch of North Castle & Elizabeth Reynolds of Horseneck,	Dec. 4, 1729
Samuel Foster & Ellen Ducher a (Duch girl), both of White Plains,	Jan. 2, 1729–30
John Newman of Stamford & Elizabith Finch,	April 28, 1730
John Cross & Kezia Blackman,	April 22, 1730

REV. ABRAHAM TODD WAS PASTOR 40 YEARS, 1734 TO 1773, BUT NO RECORD IS TO BE FOUND OF HIS MINISTRY—MARRIAGES BEGIN AGAIN WITH REV. JONATHAN MURDOCK'S PASTORATE.

James Brown & Elizabeth Mead,	June 16, 1774
Thomas Johnson & Mindwell Rundel,	June 16, 1774
Josiah Purdy & Eunice Knapp,	June 23, 1774
Benjamin Wilson & Betsey Beard,	July 14, 1774
Stephen Knapp & Sarah Hobby,	Aug. 8, 1774
William Cornell & Hannah Finch,	Nov. 13, 1774
John Weeks & Lydia Mead,	Jan. 5, 1775
James Wilson & Mary Hoit,	Jan. 16, 1775
John Sacket & Mary Bush,	March 16, 1775
Peter Knapp & Dinah Gu——,	May 18, 1775
Hezekiah Knapp & Mary Peck,	Aug. 8, 1775
Henry Mead & Elizabeth Denton,	Sept. 10, 1775
Titus Finch & Elizabeth Worden,	Nov. 2, 1775
Richard Mead & Sarah Mead,	Jan. 3, 1776
Enoch Mead & Jemima Mead,	Feb. 1, 1776
Shubel Rundle & Hannah Reynolds,	Feb. 8, 1776
Edmund Mead & Theodora Mead,	Feb. 15, 1776
Joseph Ferris & Bathena Miller,	March 20, 1776
Sylvanus Reynolds & Mercy Mead,	May 7, 1776
James Lockwood & Anna Grigg,	Nov. 3, 1776
Solomon Mead & Eunice Mead,	Jan. 16, 1777
Thomas Wicks & Elizabeth Finch,	Jan. 29, 1777
Joseph Henning & Mary Lockwood,	April 21, 1777
Nathaniel Peck & Experience Wood,	April 21, 1777
Mordecai Wheeler & Hannah Mead,	April 21, 1777
Jonathan Reynolds & Mary Brown,	April 23, 1777
Thomas Hobby & Clements Hobby,	July 2, 1777
—— Swortout & Elizabeth Lockwood,	Aug. 10, 1777
Nehemiah Reynolds & Mary Clausen,	Aug. 13, 1777
Titus Knapp & Susanna Holmes,	Aug. 19, 1777
Joseph Knapp & Rachel Mead,	Aug. 20, 1777
Stephen Parmer & Hannah Lockwood,	Sept. 23, 1777
Peter Mead & Hannah Close,	Nov. 18, 1777
Jeffrey Wehueter (?) & Sarah Williams,	Jan., 1778
William Bush & Deborah Mead,	Jan. 11, 1778
Elisha Buerest (?) & Susanna Mead,	Jan. 22, 1778

Daniel Lyon & Betsy Lockwood Wheepley,	Feb. 5. 1778
Hercules Vessels & Elizabith Adington,	Feb. 19, 1778
Walter Butter & Hannah Hays,	March 3, 1778
Nathaniel Finch & Anne Hebberd,	March 24, 1778
Dufty (?) Jacobs & Jenne Weeks,	March 26, 1778
Amos Lockwood & Phebe Lockwood,	April 19, 1778
Isaac How, Jr., & Lucy Mead,	May 28, 1778
Enoch Docker (?) & Kezia Dayton,	Aug. 7, 1778
Abraham Jacobs & Martha Brown,	Sept. 12, 1778
Jotham Lowering (?) & Margaret Feris,	Oct. 14, 1778
Nehemiah Mead & Ester Hays,	Jan. 10, 1779
Jonathan Merrit & Rebecca Merrit,	Jan. 20, 1779
Josiah Utter & Mary Ketcham,	Feb. 4, 1779
Abraham Florence & Charity Lounsbury,	Feb. 16, 1779
Benjamin Green, Jr., & Margaret Thorn,	April 1, 1779
Absalom Holmes & Charity Mead,	April 11, 1779
Thomas Studwell & Sarah Palmer,	April 18, 1779
David Reed & Bathia Close,	March 24, 1779
John McNulty & Ruth Rich,	Aug. 23, 1779
William Brown & Mary Brown,	Aug. 27, 1779
John Mead & Mary Cho. (?),	Oct. 5, 1779
Jonas Mead & Sarah How,	Dec. 8, 1779
Abraham Hobby & Mary Mead,	Dec. 16, 1779
Gershom Lockwood & Millison Darrow,	Dec. 19, 1779
Roger Pardy & Tamer Lyon,	Dec. 21, 1779
Joel Pomeroy & Mary Johnson,	Dec. 22, 1779
William Griffin & Mary Salts,	Jan. 4, 1780
Stephen Hobby & Deborah Ferris,	Jan. 5, 1780
Zacheus Mead & Deborah Close,	Jan. 12, 1780
Reuben Bailey & Ruama Smith,	Jan. 16, 1780
John Millen & Hannah Rich,	Feb. 3, 1780
Jabez Fitch & Anna Knapp,	May 29, 1780
Josiah Haight & Anna Bloomer,	June 11, 1780

"The distress of war caused public worship to cease for a time and the omission of making records."

Josiah Mead & Mercy Burley,	Aug. 18, 1783
Abraham Merritt & Elizabeth Lyon,	Aug. 24, 1783
Benjamin Banks & Hannah Marshal,	Jan. 20, 1784
Jesper Mead & Sarah Mead,	Feb. 4, 1784

7

Benjamin Brush & Samantha Reynolds,	Feb. 5, 1784
Peter Cotan (?) & Susanna Shading (?),	Feb. 8, 1784
John Scureman (?) & Cate Hyat,	Feb. 8, 1784
Daniel Howard & Rachel Studwell,	Feb. 12, 1784
Andrew Lyon & Eunice Sniffin (?),	Feb. 12, 1784
Wandel Boos & Elizabeth Cegbay (?),	Feb. 19, 1784
William Damine & Elizabeth Fisher,	Feb. 26, 1784
Zophar Carpenter & Susa Firman,	March 2, 1784
William Nutt & Rachel Taylor,	March 2, 1784
Andrew F-ash (?) & Elizabeth Palmer,	March 6, 1784
Stephen Ward & Mary Griffin,	March 7, 1784
Joseph Mead & Hannah Mead,	March 17, 1784
Jonathan Close & Hannah Rich,	*March 15, 1739
Henry Griggs & Elizabeth Bush,	*April 21, 1739
John Griffin & Mary Ann Mead,	*April 26, 1739
James Reynolds & Abigail Knapp,	Oct. 18, 1786
Nehemiah Wilson & Rachel Avery,	Nov. 6, 1786
John Burley & Phebe T(?)reen,	Nov. 23, 1786
Job Lyon & Elizabeth Mead,	Dec. 20, 1786
Underhill Lyon & Polly Holstead (York State),	
	Jan. 4, 1787
Solomon Lockwood & Elizabeth Knap,	Jan. 21, 1787
Nathan Lockwood & Patty Mead,	Jan. 28, 1787
John Griffith & Esther Skuremond (York State),	
	Feb. 22, 1787
Caleb Knap & Hannah Knap,	March 8, 1787
Seth Clawson & Sarah Ferris,	March 11, 1787
Benaijah Boughton & Ruth Mead,	March 29, 1787
Samuel Merrit & Mercy Bloomer (York State),	
	May 17, 1787
Henry Mosier & Polly Davis,	July, 1787
Isaac Finch & Hannah Rundle,	Aug. 2, 1787
——— Heirs & ——— Brown (York State),	Sept., 1787
Samuel Rundle & Lucy Mumford Clark,	Sept. 27, 1787
Philemon Reynolds & Hannah Mead,	Oct. 21, 1787
Joshua Banks & Ruth Smith,	Oct. 24, 1787
Timothy Horton & Nancy Hawkins (York State),	
	Oct. 26, 1787
Thomas Peck & Tamar Reynolds,	Nov. 14, 1787

---

* 1789, probably—ED.

Elijah Tompkins & Sarah Barker (York State), Nov. 22, 1787
Benjamin Lyon & —— Merrit,   Dec. 12, 1787
Whitman Mead & Rachel Mead,   Dec. 19, 1787
Nehemiah Merit & Catharine Purdy (York State),
                                              Dec. 24, 1787
William Anderson & Polly Lyon (York State),Dec. 25, 1787
Samuel Travlss & Betsey Jameson (York State),
                                              Dec. 28, 1787
John Lyon & Molly Merit,   Jan., 1788
—— Merit &.—— Anderson,   Jan., 1788
Calvin Mead & Deborah Mead,   Jan. 17, 1788
Stephen Davis, Jr., & Bethiah Mead,   Jan. 21, 1788
Gilbert Close & Charlotte Peck,   April 10, 1788
A son of Judge Ward & a daughter of Judge Tomp-
  kins,   April 16, 1788
Isaac Seaman & Phebe Lyon,   May 18, 1788
Thomas Seaman & Sarah Miller,   June 22, 1788
Caleb Mead, 3d, & Orpha Hobby,   June 22, 1788
Jabez Mead & Elizabeth Hobby,   Aug. 28, 1788
Elnathan Mead & Anne Merit,   Sept. 7, 1788
David Ferris & Mary Mosier,   Sept. 21, 1788
Caleb Frost of N. Y. & Sally Holstead of Rye, Nov. 5, 1788
Elisha Maynard & Esther Horton,   Nov. 11, 1788
Isaiah Guion & Esther Palisse (?) or Palifse (?) of
  New Rochelle,   Nov. 18, 1788
Charles Mead & Rebecca Denton,   Nov. 18, 1788
Isaac Peck & Hannah Fletcher,   Nov. 20, 1788
Andrew Mead & Amah Hobby,   Nov. 26, 1788
Butler Hubbard & Clarissa Davis,   Dec. 20, 1788
Gilbert Guion & Jenny Flandrau (?),   Dec. 23, 1788
—— Brown & —— Merit,   Jan. 7, 1789
James Ward & —— Thompkins,   Jan. 7, 1789
Daniel Mosier & Sally Reynolds,   Jan. 25, 1789
Abraham Lyon & Hannah Mills,   Feb. 7, 1789
Timothy Peck & Anne Kniffen,   Feb. 26, 1789
Nathaniel Sacket & Bethiah Reynolds,   Feb. 19, 1789
Jonathan Close & Hannah Ritch,   March 15, 1789
Henry Grigg & Elizabeth Bush,   April 21, 1789
John Kniffen & Mary Ann Mead,   April 26, 1789
John Gedney & Sarah Crompton (York State), Aug. 26, 1789

Joshua Knapp, ye 3d, & Charity Mead,	Sept. 1, 1789
Gilbert Knapp & Mary Knapp,	——
Joseph Hibbard & Charity Banks,	Dec. 25, 1789
Benjamin Knapp & Rachel Mead,	Jan. 6, 1789
James Darrow & Rebecca Davis,	Jan. 10, 1789
Samuel Peck, Jr., & Mary Mead,	Jan., 1790
William Skureman (?) & Elizabeth Flandrau,	Feb. 25, 1790
David Hobby & Anne Reynolds,	Feb. 25, 1790
Jotham Holmes & Amah Knapp,	March 14, 1790
Solomon Peck & Mary Lyon,	March 18, 1790
Isaac Holly & Sarah Reynolds,	April 14, 1790
James Ward & Anne Gedney (York State),	July 25, 1790
Solomon Lockwood of Pound Ridge & Mary Close,	
	Sept. 22, 1790
—— Merit & Rebecca Bush (York State),	——
James Knap & Hannah Hobby,	Jan. 6, 1791
—— Wilson & —— Wilson,	1791
—— Cornel & —— Angevine,	1791
John Merit & Sarah Hobby,	March 4, 1791
Seymour Marshal & Nancy Sherwood,	March 10, 1791
Mathew Mead, Jr., & Nancy Hobby,	March 15, 1791
Michael Dykeman & Polly Oakley,	March 27, 1791
Hardy Mead & Rachel Brown,	April 19, 1791
Squire Hobby & Synthia Husted,	Nov, 1791
William Broadwill of New York & Prudence Mead,	
	March 18, 1792
Nath'l Briggs & Mary Lockwood,	June 27, 1792
Robert Morrel & Katurah Daton,	Aug., 1792
Edmund Knapp & Zereviah Smith,	Aug. 8, 1792
Joseph Banks & Elizabeth Anderson,	Aug. 12, 1792
Solomon Knapp & Rosanna Close,	Sept. 2, 1792
Augustus Treadwill & Martha Canady,	Nov. 18, 1792
Peter Underhill & Annie Skuirmond (?) (York State),	
	Jan. 3, 1793
—— Fisk & Abigail Denton,	Feb. 4, 1793
Daniel Denton & Abigail Mead,	Feb. 14, 1793
Billy Thields & Lavinia Peck,	March 25, 1793
Richard Wyllys & Sally Carpenter,	April 1, 1793
Robert Peck, Jr., & Levinia Peck,	April 11, 1793

Amos Hobby & Sally Hobby,   April 14, 1793
Josiah Carpenter & Charlotte Mead,   April 15, 1793
John Knapp & Martha Brown,   April 16, 1793
Zalmon Sanford & Rachel Reymond,   April 24, 1793
David Ferris, Jr., & Esther Ask (?),   May 24, 1793
Philo Johnson & Naomi Cannon,   July 24, 1793
Caleb Purdy & Polly Reynolds,   July 25, 1793
Amos Husted & Eunice Close,   Aug. 14, 1793
Henry How & Sabrina Mead,   Aug. 29, 1793
Charles Weed, Jr., of Canaan & Rachel Mead,   1794
Daniel Close & Rachel Mead,   1794
—— Palmer & —— Marshal,   1794
—— Vikars (?) & Nancy Bush,   1794
Ebenezer Davenport of Stamford & Jerusha Van
    Alstyne,   April 13, 1794
Gilbert Ireland & Lydia Mead,   April 22, 1794
William Griffith & Hetty Griffith,   May, 1794
William Morrel & —— Birley,   May, 1794
Peter Van Bomell of Poughkeepsie & Elizabeth
    Marshall,   July 27, 1794
Thomas Morrell & Charity Johnson,   Aug. 21, 1794
John Webb & Anne Marshal,   Sept., 1794
Jered Smith & Rebecca Wood of Stanwich,   Sept. 28, 1794
Reuben Finch & Abigail Reynolds,   Oct. 5, 1794
Samuel Denton & Anne Mead,   Oct. 12, 1794
Amariah Marshall & Mary Brown,   Oct. 14, 1794
Jonah Mead & Mary Mead,   Dec. 4, 1794
Lockwood Reynolds & Elizabeth Mead,   Dec. 24, 1794
Tomkins Close & Mary Reynolds,   Dec. 28, 1794
Robert Mead & Prudence Mead,   Oct., 1794
Ira Mead & —— Marshal,   Jan. 1, 1795
Israel Mead & Mary Rundle,   April, 1795
Jehial Mead, Jr., & Phebe Mead,   April 12, 1795
Jabez Peck & Mary Mead,   May 14, 1795
Henry Light & Deborah Purdy,   June, 1795
Ira Avery & Mary Wilson,   July 5, 1795
Frederick Betts & Hannah Sacket,   Sept. 27, 1795
Edward Mead, Jr., & Rebekah Knapp,   Sept. 29, 1795
Daniel Green & Francis Peck,   Sept., 1795
Peter De Wiet (?) & Sophia Mead,   Nov. 16, 1795

Abraham Wallace & Nancy Daton,	Nov., 1795
Nathaniel Knapp & Ruth Purdy,	Nov. 31, 1795
Andrew Marshall, Jr., & Maria Hobby,	Dec. 13, 1795
John McKay, Jr., & Betey Knapp,	1795
Eben. Knapp, Jr., & Ruth Reynolds,	Dec. 24, 1795
David Heusted & Hannah Mead,	Jan. 24, 1796
Zopher Mead & Huldah Mead,	Jan. 25, 1796
Darius Mead & Hannah Peck,	1796
Lewis Webb, Jr., of N. Y. & Mary Lockwood,	April 14, 1796
Samuel Boughton, Jr., of Brooklin & Marilda Mead,	April 20, 1796
Stephen Dutch of N. Y. & Ruth Close,	April 20, 1796
Stephen Hobby & Sally Ferris,	1796
Ezra Marshall, Jr., & Hannah Reynolds,	Oct. 9, 1796
Barzillia Brown & Charlotte Marshall,	Oct. 16, 1796
Philo Clerk & Betsy Timpany (?),	1796
Nehemiah Brown & Maria Seymour,	Nov. 17, 1796
Jered Peck & Tamasin Adee,	Dec. 22, 1796
Stephen Holmes & Enor Raymond,	Dec., 1796
Rev. Platt Buffott & Hannah Lewis,	Feb. 8, 1797
Ebenezer Hobby, ye 3d, & Theodocia Ritch,	Feb. 14, 1797
Warren Delancy & Rebecah Lawrence,	Feb. 14, 1797
Joshua Mead, Jr., & Mary Mead,	March, 1797
Elihu Heusted & Nancy Close,	"date forgotten"
Marshal Ferris & Lorama Palmer,	June 19, 1797
Robert Merrit & ——— Slaughter,	Aug., 1797
Capt. Nehemiah Brown & Sally Purdy,	Sept. 3, 1797
——— Knapp & Hannah Peck,	Sept. 10, 1797
Luther Peck & Rachel Peck,	Sept. 19, 1797
Luther Lyon & Ruth Peck,	Nov. 16, 1797
Stephen Waring & Polly Purdy,	Nov. 19, 1797
Stephen Holmes of N. Y. & ——— Ferriss,	Nov. 20, 1797
Justus Mead & Mary Knapp,	Dec. 24, 1797
——— Johnson & Betcy How,	Dec. 31, 1797
Caleb Hobby & Harriot Hobby,	Feb. 4, 1798
Moses Heusted & Sally Peck,	April, 1798
Thadeus Fancher & Sally Mead,	May 27, 1798
Westover Millar of Suffield & Hannah Denton,	May 6, 1798
Amos Green & Esther Grummon,	April, 1798
Richard Mead & Rachel Mead,	June 27, 1798

Thomas (?) Mead & Matilda Peck, Aug. 25, 1798
Daniel Rowell & Hannah Persons, Sept. 16, 1798
Rev. Isaac Lewis, Jr., of Newburgh & Catharine
    Evertson of Pleasant Valley, Oct. 4, 1798
Ebenezer Mead & Zetty Mead, Nov. 29, 1798
Andrew Hubbard & Polly Mead, Jan. 22, 1799
John Bart & Sarah Mesnard (?), Feb. 24, 1799
Beale N. Lewis & Eliza Crosfield of New York, April 10, 1799
Eliakim Lockwood & Sarah Marshall, April 28, 1799
Reuben Holmes, Jr., & Lucretia Davis, April 28, 1799
John R. Cozine of New York & Rebecca Bush, June 24, 1799
William Lockhart of Stamford & Sally Johnson,
                             June 27, 1799
Henry Lockwood & ——— ———, 1799
Abraham Peck & Anna Peck, Dec. 1, 1799
Robert Ross & Ann Sharpe McKnight (New York
    State), Dec. 1, 1799
Solomon Peck & Mary Ferris, Dec. 29, 1799
Noah Slites (?) (Stiles) (?) & Mary Marshall, Dec. 31, 1799
Jonathan Mead & Hannah Lyon, March 5, 1800
John Ryker of New York & Easther Davis, Aug., 1800
William Carpenter & Jane Halsted of Rye, Dec. 10, 1800
Justus Sacket & Clarissa Belcher, Dec. 25, 1800
Benjamin Palmer & Betcy Mead, Jan. 18, 1801
Daniel Carpenter & Mary Merrit, all of Rye, Feb. 1, 1801

CHATHAM — PORTLAND.

MIDDLESEX COUNTY.

The town of Chatham was organized in 1767. It was taken from Middletown. The Congregational Church of Chatham was organized October 25, 1721, by settlers of Middletown. The town of Portland was taken from Chatham in 1841, so that the old church (at Gildersleeve) now belongs in Portland territory. The marriages are as follows.

Marshall Stocking & Esther Trion,	Sept. 3, 1767
Calvin Tory & Elizabeth Youngs,	Oct. 29, 1767
William Dixon & Prudence Goodrich,	Nov. 13, 1767
James Griswold of Enfield & Mary Bidwell,	Dec. 16, 1767
Deliverance Warner & Esther Karr (?),	April 14, 1768
Nicholas Ames & Abigail Robinson,	May 19, 1768
Thomas Rogers & Sarah Bartlit,	Nov. 14, 1768
Ebenezer Hulburt & Elizabeth Bush (widow),	Jan. 4, 1769
Henry Goodale & Elizabeth Ranney,	Jan. 10, 1769
Jesse Johnson & Mary Stevenson,	Feb. 27, 1769
Aaron Wright & Phebe Schellinx (?),	March 22, 1769
Abel Sheperd & Mary Lewis,	April 16, 1769
Phineas Dean & Mary Combs,	July 13, 1769
Samuel Achan & Mary Stewert,	Aug. 31, 1769
James Smith & Mary Bliss,	Nov. 9, 1769
Samuel Waterman & Cloe Trion,	Nov. 12, 1769
Abraham Schellenx & Jane Johnson,	Nov. 12, 1769
John Wood & Hannah Storey (?),	Jan. 4, 1770
Ira Church of East Haddam & Elizabeth Leet,	April 4, 1770
Jonathan Bush & Esther Warner,	April 22, 1770
Dennis Dorothy & Lydia Wood,	May 20, 1770
Joshua Holton of Westminster & Abigail Willcox,	
	May 24, 1770
Charles Cheney & Prudence Goodrich,	Nov. 22, 1770
George Ranney, Jr., & Esther Hall,	Jan. 31, 1771
Jabez Hall & Mary Little,	May 24, 1771
Jere. Norton & widow Sybile Knowles,	June 28, 1771
William Grey & Elizabith Stevenson,	Nov., 1771
Ezra Purple & Mary Penfield,	Jan. 16, 1772
Thomas Murphy & Lydia Taylor,	Jan. 20, 1772
Abiel Cheney, Jr., & Prudence Penfield,	Feb. 20, 1772

Darius Adams & Mary White, Feb. 27, 1772
Jonathan Ufford & Mary Goodrich, March 26, 1772
Abel Strickland & Esther Bidwell, April 22, 1772
—— Sawyer of Montague & Margaret Stevenson,
Oct. 22, 1772
Chester Allen of Suffield & Anna Powell, Nov. 8, 1772
Daniel Shepherd, Jr., & Phebe Strickland, Nov. 12, 1772
Joseph Kellogg & Lucy Warner, Nov. 22, 1772
Darius Willcox of Middletown & Mary Abby, Dec. 16, 1772
—— Burnham of Hartford & widow Abigail Dixon,
Dec. 24, 1772
Jonathan Brown & Sarah Petton, Jan. 21, 1773
Samuel Shipman, Jr., of Saybrook & Sarah Stanclift,
Feb. 14, 1773
Francis Ranney & Rachel Hall, Feb. 16, 1773
Daniel Shepherd & Grace Savage, Oct. 17, 1773
Owen Shurt (?) of New York & Esther Cheney, Oct 19, 1773
Charles Holmes of Wethersfield & Martha Wetherby,
Nov. 16, 1773
Nathaniel Goodrich & Prudence Stocking, Dec. 19, 1773
Samuel Wright of East Haddam & Rebecca Dixon,
Dec. 22, 1773
Ezra White of Farmington & Lucy Stanclift, Feb. 7, 1774
Jonathan Miller of Glastonbury & Elizabeth Church,
Feb. 10, 1774
William Manly of Windsor & Molly Witon, May 31, 1774
Ephraim Bowers & Eunice Stocking, July 11, 1774
Edward Dixon of Chatham & —— Fuller of East
Haddam, July 28, 1774
Levi Goodrich of Pittsfield & Azuba Goodrich, Oct. 6, 1774
Giles Goodrich & Hannah Stanclift, Oct. 22, 1774
Barzeel Duset & Susa Stanclift, Nov. 3, 1774
Jedediah White of Mansfield & Sarah Storer, Nov. 9, 1774
Charles Davis & Anna Pelton, Nov. 15, 1774
William Dudley of Middletown & Desire Russell,
Dec. 1, 1774
Lazarus Loveland of Glastenbury & Azubah Reeves,
Dec. 1, 1774
Ephraim Bartlit of Middletown & Lucy Pelton,
Dec. 8, 1774

Elisha Fuller of Ludlow, in Springfield, & Rebecca
    Waterman,   Dec. 21, 1774
John Payne & widow Lucy Montgomery,   Jan. 12, 1775
Thomas Edy, Jr., & Elizabeth Goodrich,   Feb. 2, 1775
Jesse Buck of Weathersfield & Anne Goodrich,
                           March 9, 1775
Richard Orchard of Boston & Lucy Pelton, March 23, 1775
James Bartlit of Farmington & Temperance Schellenx,
                         March 23, 1775
Samuel Bidwell of Middletown & Christian Knowles,
                         April 6, 1775
Abner Pelton & Sarah Bidwell,   May 13, 1775
Elisha Hale & widow Hannah Brewer,   July 16, 1775
Suncon (?) Penfield & Penellope Eddy,   Aug. 10, 1775
David Bogly of Providence & Dorothy Fox, Aug. 20, 1775
John Bidwell & Sarah Penfield,   Aug. 24, 1775
William Casheen (?) & widow Abigail Bevin, Aug. 28, 1775
David Bates & Ruth Cheney,   Sept. 21, 1775
Thomas Lloyd & widow Cloe Ranney,   Sept. 21, 1775
Robert Wilkinson & Dorcas Pelton,   Sept. 23, 1775
Amos Penfield & ——— Buller,   Oct. 4, 1775
Nathaniel White & ——— Miller,   Oct. 19, 1775
Joseph Pelton, Jr., & Mary Shepherd,   1776
Jonathan Verry of Salem, Mass., & Phebe Merrick,
                         April 3, 1776
Benj. Abby & Lois Stocking,   ——— 11, 1776
——— Hulburt & Damaris Abby,   June 27, 1776
Jonathan Sexton of Windsor & Susanna Montgom-
    ery,   Oct. 23, 1776
David Hale & Prudence Eaton,   Nov. 14, 1776
Jesse Plum of Middletown & Mary Churchell, July 9, 1777
Eliphalet Wood of Long Island & Hannah Wright,
                         July 27, 1777
Gideon Hulburt, Jr., & Sarah Stocking,   Sept. 30, 1777
Amos Hulburt & Esther Geer,   Dec. 11, 1777
Elijah Brown of Hebron & Abigail Stanclift, Dec. 18, 1777
Stephen Burroughs of East Windsor & Amelia
    Montgomery,   Jan. 21, 1778
Henry Gildersleeve & Elethean Overton, both from
    Long Island,   Jan. 29, 1778

—— Fuller of East Haddam & —— Gilder-
    sleeve, a native of Long Island,   Feb. 9, 1778
Thomas Ranney & widow Mary Mighelles,   April 2, 1778
William Bevin & widow Mary Johnson,   May 28, 1778
Jonathan Hale & Mary Clark,   July 7, 1778
Aaron Palmer of Norwich & Sybell Stanclift, Oct. 29, 1778
John Eddy & widow Anne Cornwell,   Nov. 24, 1778
Dr. Thomas Welles & Hannah Diggins,   Nov. 26, 1778
Elizur Miller of Glastenbury & Dorcas Goodrich,
                           Dec. 16, 1778
John Divers & widow Elizabeth Waterman, Dec. 29, 1778
Selah Gridley of Farmington & Lois Russell, Dec. 31, 1778
Joseph Symonds of Hartford & Prudence Cooper,
                           Jan. 13, 1779
Daniel Goodrich & Bethiah Shephard,   Jan. 20, 1779
Seth Eddy & Elizabeth Waterman,   March 17, 1779
John Shepard, Jr., & Hannah Knowles, March 18, 1779
Seth Overton & Mehitable White,   April 15, 1779
John Storer & Mercy Allen,   April 23, 1779
Nathaniel Bosworth of Mansfield & Mary Ran-
    ney,   July 1, 1779
George Bush & Prudence Churchill,   Sept. 2, 1779
—— Potter & Lydia Wright,   Sept. 30, 1779
Henry McCone & Abigail West,.   Oct. 7, 1779
John Wright & Abigail Bliss,   Nov. 29, 1779
Aaron Holister of Glastonbury & Phebe Goodrich,
                          Dec. 9, 1779
Noah Sage & Honor White,   Dec. 24, 1779
Samuel Stocking & Lucy Knowles,   Dec. 30, 1779
Capt. Thomas Wadsworth of Hartford & widow
    Honor White,   Jan. 12, 1780
Daniel Hollister of Glastonbury & Sarah Goodrich,
                          Jan. 26, 1780
Joseph Sage & Ruth Goodrich,   Feb. 9, 1780
Johnson Pelton of Ashfield & Rachel Penfield, Feb. 17, 1780
Sylvanus Eaton & Sarah Goodrich,   Feb. 21, 1780
—— Knowles & Ruhamah Schellinx,   May 3, 1780
Phillip Gildersleeve & Temperance Gibbs, May 4, 1780
Gideon Schellinx & Sarah Lewis,   June 1, 1780
Miner Bates & Lucy Hale,   June 5, 1780

Ebenezor Sumner of Welles, Vt., & Jemima Hall,

June 29, 1780

Timothy Ford of New Haven & Permit Parsons,

July 12, 1780

Nathaniel Montgomery & Bathsheba Lewis,   Oct. 19, 1780

John Savage & Rachel Shepard,   Nov. 8, 1780

Moses Lewis & Mary Case,   Nov. 9, 1780

John Willcox & Ruth Penfield,   Nov. 30, 1780

Samuel Cornwall & Rachel Savage,   Dec. 15, 1780

Benjamin Hodge, Jr., of Glastonbury & Sarah
    Churchill,   April 9, 1781

Jesse Penfield & Sarah Hall,   May 17, 1781

Ephraim Whitaker & Hannah Stevenson,   May 27, 1781

Joseph Pelton of Saybrook & Prudence Pelton, Nov. 3, 1781

Eliakim Goodrich of Glastonbury & Sarah Knee-
    land,   Jan. 13, 1782

Stephen Stocking & Sarah Hills,   Jan. 31, 1782

Stephen Clark of East Hampton & Prudence Hale,

Feb. 28, 1782

Comfort Goff of Colchester & Amelia Pelton,

March 10, 1782

Joseph Shepard & Annie Bozworth,   June, 1782

Stephen Hurlburt of Weathersfield & Phebe Pelton,

Aug. 11, 1782

Andrew Cornwall & Mary Bartlett,   Sept. 30, 1782

Dan Cornwall & Rachel Hale,   Nov. 26, 1782

Giles Knowles & Sile Hall,   Jan. 16, 1783

Richard Miles of Enfield & Lydia Stevenson, Jan. 16, 1783

Daniel Cheney & Julia Cornwall,   Jan. 23, 1783

Marshal Stocking & Anna Bartlett,   Feb. 5, 1783

David Warner of Amherst & Lucy Orchard, Feb. 12, 1783

David Crosley of Hartford & Grace Stevenson, Feb. 16,1783

—— Willcox of Guilford & Sarah Nichols, April 4, 1783

Samuel Burton & widow Pelton,   July 31, 1783

David Eddy & Mercy Waterman,   Aug. 27, 1783

Nathaniel Roberts & Azubah Pelton,   Nov. 5, 1783

Timothy Russell & Elizabeth Gildersleeve, Nov. 18, 1783

Rhoderic Brady of Middletown & the widow
    Lamb,   Nov. 26, 1783

Freeman Pelton & Prudence Russell,   Nov. 30, 1783

Seth Knowles & Lucy Ranney,   Jan. 22, 1784
Benjamin Goodrich & Bethiah Churchill,   Jan. 26, 1784
Israel Slate of Barnardstown & Phebe Hurlburt,
                                               Feb. 17, 1784
Daniel Burton & Mollie Bowers,   March 7, 1784
Samuel Butler & Anne Reeves,   March 9, 1784
Jonathan Stocking & Polly Allen,   April 26, 1784
Seth Strickland & Ann Shepard,   May 17, 1784
Samuel Willcox & Sarah Gildersleeve,   June 6, 1784
Thaddeus Cotten & Loley Goodrich,   June 24, 1784
Fitch Andrus of Wethersfield & Rachel Goodrich,
                                               Sept. 2, 1784
Jesse Pelton & Phebe Penfield,   Sept. 23, 1784
John McKay of East Hartford & widow Martha
    Cooper,   Oct. 6, 1784
—— Bates of East Hampton & daughter of Elijah
    Stocking,   Oct. 6, 1784
Nathaniel Brown, Jr., & Mollie Ufford,   Oct. 12, 1784
John Andrews of Glastonbury & Lucy Eddy,   Oct. 14, 1784
Samuel Penfield & Jemima Hurlburt,   Oct. 17, 1784
Elijah Hubbard & Penelope Goodrich,   Oct. 28, 1784
Zebulon Waterman & Betss (?) Cornwall,   Nov. 4, 1784
Bethuel Goodrich & Silence Boardman,   Nov. 22, 1784
George Cooper, Jr., & Mime Miles,   Dec. 2, 1784
Uriel Penfield & Elizabeth Payne,   Dec. 9, 1784
Deliverance Cooper & Sarah Sage,   Jan. 16, 1785
Timothy Cooper & Sarah Doan,   April 24, 1785
William Williams & Lois Stevenson,   Aug. 17, 1785
Daniel Stow & Lucy Cooper,   Sept. 11, 1785
—— Bradley of East Guilford & —— Harding
    of East Hartford,   Oct. 9, 1785
Timothy Lee of Guilford & Grace Goodrich,   Oct. 19, 1785
Luther Savage & —— Goodrich of Glastonbury,
                                               Oct. 27, 1785
Hosea Goodrich & Hephziba Penfield,   Nov. 10, 1785
Will Diggins & Mary Knowles,   Nov. 10, 1785
Moses Stocking & Elizbeth Pelton,   Nov. 17, 1785
Joseph Gleason & Elizabeth Fox,   Nov. 24, 1785
Joseph Willcox & Grace Stocking,   Dec. 1, 1785
Phineas Dean, Jr., & Ruth Hall,   Dec. 15, 1785

Ansel Stocking of Glastonbury & Prudence Crosley,

	Jan. 30, 1786
Jonathan Ranney & Sarah Parsons,	Feb. 26, 1786
—— Button of Norwich & Polly Bartlett,	Feb. 16, 1786
Jeremiah Buck & Mary Butler,	March 16, 1786
Reuben Akin & Hannah Hall,	Sept. 21, 1786
Justin Smith & Mollie Fox,	Nov. 2, 1786
Chester Kimball & Lucy Fox,	Nov. 8, 1786
Richard Brown & Annie Penfield,	Dec. 27, 1786
Abner Sage & Ruth Ellsworth,	Jan. 25, 1787
Doct. Elisha Shepard & Mollie Bartlit,	March 3, 1787
Jeremiah Penfield & Elizabeth Williams,	March 15, 1787
Lt. Daniel Shepard & widow Ruth Willcox,	April 9, 1787
Amasa Payne & Chloe Hepson,	Aug. 1, 1787
John Cooper & Grace Savage,	Sept. 7, 1787

Elizur McKay of East Hartford & Abigal Fox,

	Oct. 17, 1787
Samuel Brown & Lydia Fox,	Oct. 31, 1787

Noah Brent of East Hartford & Annie Stanclift,

	Feb. 15, 1788
James Sheild & widow Mary Dean,	March 11, 1788
Elisha Clark of Preston & Hannah Pelton,	May 12, 1788
William Stratten & Ruth Goodrich,	June 2, 1788
Charles Treat & Rachel Abbe,	June 2, 1788
Nath'l Taylor & Rachel Goodrich,	July 2, 1788
William McCorney & Lucretia Butler,	Sept. 24, 1788
Charles Churchill & Ruth Shipman,	Oct. 29, 1788
—— Isan (?) & Mollie Gaines,	Dec. 24, 1788
John Ellsworth & Sarah Strong,	Nov. 28, 1788
Benj. Stocking & widow Mollie Stocking,	Jan. 1, 1788
Stephen Ranney, Jr., & Persis Crosley,	Jan. 15, 1789
Cap. Ingham & —— Starr of Middletown,	Jan. 25, 1789
David Lathrop of Windsor & Annie Chipman,	Jan. 28, 1789
Abijah White of Linerbourough & Hannah Hall,	Feb., 1789

Rev. Elijah Gridley of Mansfield & Ruth White,

	April 29, 1789
Amos Boardman & Prude Chapman,	April 30, 1789
Ignatius Perkins & Hannah Russell,	May 30, 1789
Reuben Willcox & Abigail Bates,	June 29, 1789
Richard Goodrich & —— Smith,	July 31, 1789

—— Collins & —— Goodrich, daughter of
  Solomon,   Aug., 1789
Collins Bowers & Honer McCorney,   Sept. 29, 1789
Amos Goodrich & Catherine Crittenden,   Oct. 1, 1789
—— Hill & Elizabeth Warner,   Jan., 1790
Comfort Butler & widow Eleanor Bush,   Feb. 1, 1790
David Brewer & Hannah Buck,   July 5, 1790
Ezra Bevin & Hannah Pelton,   Sept. 25, 1790
Ezekiel Goodrich & Ester Buck,   Oct. 3, 1790
Andrew Shepard & Deliverance Leland,   Dec., 1790
—— Calkins of Catskill & Sarah Reeves,   May 16, 1791
Asahel Willcox & Lucy Crittenden,   Oct. 2, 1791
Daniel Brewer & Lydia Penfield,   Oct. 2, 1791
Asahel McKay & Persis Chipman,   Nov., 1791
Isaac Hodge & Ester Warner,   Dec. 25, 1791
Elisha Hale & Submit Goodrich,   Jan. 12, 1792
David Bailey & Rachel Brewer,   Aug., 1792
Abel Lewis & Polly Crittenden,   Aug. 25, 1793
Robert Pelton & Lucy Wright,   Nov. 21, 1793
David Wilcox & Polly Chapel,   Nov. 25, 1793
Josiah Pelton & Lucy Shepard,   Dec. 19, 1793
Zenas Chapman of Lebanon & Anna Randol,   Feb. 24, 1794
Jonathan Penfield & Jane Stewart,   Feb. 27, 1794
Samuel Stewart & Elizabeth Johnson,   April 13, 1794
James Stewart & Grace Pelton,   May 4, 1794
Charles Dixon & Lucy Sage Penfield,   Nov. 16, 1794
Samuel Shepard & Lucy Ames,   May 10, 1795
Samuel Wright of East Haddam & Jerusha Bartlet,
                                             July 17, 1796
—— Hilliard of Killingworth & Hannah Bates,
                                             Oct. 2, 1796
Capt. Joseph Pelton & widow Lucinda Bidwell, March, 1798
Thomas Shepard & widow Ann Washburn,   May, 1798
Elisha Tryon of Glastonbury & widow —— Clark,
                                             June, 1798
Zacheus Goodrich of Sheffield & Mrs. Ranney of Mid-
  dletown,   July 22, 1798

WALLINGFORD — MERIDEN.

NEW HAVEN COUNTY.

The town of Meriden was organized in 1806, having been a part of Wallingford. The First Congregational Church in Meriden was organized October 22, 1729. Rev. Theophilus Hall pastor from 1729 to 1767. Following are the marriages recorded.

"An account of the number of persons that I have married; the number from October, 1729, when I was ordained, till January 1, 1736–7, according to the best of my remembrance."

Samuel Barns & his wife.
One, Judd of Waterbury & Robert Royce's daughter.
Isaac Brockett & one of Samuel Culver's daughters.
Caleb Merriman to another; Samuel Tyler to another.
One, Baldwin of Branford & Jacob Royce's widow.
Aaron Cook to his second and third wife.
Thomas Royce to his second wife.
One, Holibert of Middletown & Thomas Royce's daughter.
Giles Andrews & his wife.
Stephen Ives & his wife.
John Webb & his wife.
Lazarus Ives & Isabel, dau. of Timothy Jerome, Jan. 5, 1731
One of Joseph Curtiss' sons & Elizabeth Parker's daughter.
Hawkins Hart & his wife.
Nathaniel Pentfield & his wife.
Moses Curtiss & his wife.
John Austin & his wife.
Timothy Gailord & his wife.
Enos Curtiss & his wife.
Isaac Curtiss to his third wife.
Daniel Johnson & Joanna Preston.
John Hull & Mary Andrews.
Joseph Parker's son & his wife.
Daniel Murwine & Mehitabel Twist.
Daniel Ives & his wife.
Abraham Ives & Barbary Johnson.
John Ward & his wife.
Samuel Hough & Mehitabel Royce.

Henry Stanton & Sarah Scofield.
Jonathan Curtis & Deborah Mix.
Joseph Cowles, Jr., & Susannah Cook.
Tim Jearum, Jr., & Anna Norton.
John Prout & widow Royce.
Reuben Royce & Kesiah Moss.
Joseph Moss & Jones' daughter.
Samuel Beach & Hannah Benham.

MARRIAGES A. D. 1743, BEGINNING JANUARY 1.

Samuel Foginson & Lois Royce,	Nov. 2, 1743
David Rich, Jr., & Mehitabel Ives,	Nov. 10, 1743
Phinehas Royce of Northberry & Thankful Merriman of Wallingford,	Nov. 15, 1743
Jehiel Baldwin & Mary Way,	Nov. 30, 1743
John Way, Jr., & Hannah Royce,	Jan. 24, 1744
Thomas Berry & Rebecca Yale (second wife),	Jan. 26, 1744
Daniel Cowles of Kensington & Martha Powell,	Feb. 2, 1744
Benj. Hart & Phebe Rich,	May 24, 1744
Noah Yale & Anna Ives,	Aug. 2, 1744
Jonathan Collins & Agnes Linn,	Aug. 22, 1744
Stephen Mix & Rebecca Ives,	Sept. 19, 1744
Nehemiah Manross of (probably New Cambridge) & widow Thankful Cooper,	Jan. 3, 1745
David Ives & Elizabeth Merriman,	Feb. 28, 1745
Abel Doolittle of Westbury & Thankful Moss,	March 19, 1745
Abel Austin & Temperance Hough,	Oct. 16, 1745
Ignatius Rhody of Lynn & Mrs. Sarah Merriam,	Oct. 31, 1745
Joseph Hoult of East Haven & widow Joanna Johnson,	Dec. 19, 1737
Joseph Atkins of Middletown & Abigail Rich,	Jan., 1737
Nash Yale & Sarah Emerton or Amerton,	Feb. 28, 1737
Nehemiah Pratt of Saybrook & Deborah Hough,	June 20, 1737
Timothy Bartholomew & Mary Hull,	July 11, 1737
Jedediah Norton & widow Eunice Curtis,	Nov. 3, 1737
Eleazer Peck of Southington & widow Ann Camp,	Nov. 29, 1737

John Hendrick & Ruth, dau. of Daniel Mix,   Dec. 1, 1737
John Painter & Deborah Welshire,   March 27, 1738
Benj. Andrews of Middletown & Tabitha Sanford,
                                             May 4, 1738
Zerubbabel Jerom & Phebe Cook (a second wife),
                                             Aug. 30, 1738
Joseph Gailard & Elizabeth Rich,   Nov. 9, 1738
William Jerom & Elizabeth Hart,   Nov. 13, 1738
Ephraim Munson & Comfort Curtis,   Feb. 6, 1739
Stephen Atwater to Elizabeth Yale,   June 6, 1739
Ephraim Royce & Eunice Harriss,   June 26, 1739
Samuel Levitt & Adah Curtis,   Sept. 23, 1739
Andrew Andrews & Esther Royce,   March 17, 1740
Zebulon Frisbie & Luce Lewis,   April 2, 1740
Jonathan Preston & Sarah Williams of Waterbury,
                                             July 29, 1740
Timothy Shattuck of Middletown & Desire Hall,
                                             Nov. 5, 1740
Benj. Matthews of Cheshire & Lucy Clark of
    Northbury,   Dec. 3, 1740
Ebenezer Hawley of Farmington & Mary Hart, July 1, 1741
Daniel Luttenton of East Haven & Suzanna
    Park,   Oct. 19, 1741
John Johnson of New Haven & widow Joanna
    Royce,   Nov. 19, 1741
Benj. Brooks of Cheshire & Thankful Hickock,
                                             Dec. 15, 1741
Joseph Stone & Abigail Jearom,   Jan. 11, 1742
Thos. Heart & Hannah Coe,   April 21, 1742
Nehemiah Manross & Sarah Royce,   May 12, 1742
John Way & Phebe Ford,   June 2, 1742
Gideon Royce & Mary Dutton,   Oct. 7, 1742
John Adkins of Middletown & Elizabeth Jerom,
                                             Dec. 15, 1742
Amos Camp & widow Mary Andrews,   Dec. 30, 1745
Nathaniel Yale & Hannah Weeks,   Feb. 20, 1746
Abraham Hall & Mary Prindle,   June 23, 1746
Asa Royce & Annah Royce,   Nov. 25, 1746
Noah Austin & Abiah Hough,   Dec. 17, 1746
Amos Beach of Goshen to Sarah Royce,   Dec. 29, 1746

Gideon Royce & widow Rebecca Elenoth (second
    wife),   March 25, 1747
Mr. Walter & Suzana Smith,   May 4, 1747
Caleb Merriman & Margaret Robinson,   May 12, 1747
David Dutton & widow Juda Yale,   Oct. 13, 1747
Linus Beach of Goshen & Dinah Royce,   Oct. 21, 1747
Nathaniel Peck's son & David Cook's daughter,
                              in the summer, 1747
John Coach & Azubah Andrews,   Feb. 9, 1748
Joel Ives & Rebecca Merriam,   Feb. 10, 1748
David Way & Eunice Hall,   Oct. 5, 1748
Josiah Robinson & Eunice Ives,   Feb. 23, 1749
Jared Spencer of Haddam & Susannah Dickinson,
                                May 2, 1749
John Hall & Elizabeth Prindle,   May 4, 1749
Wm. Andrews & widow Mary Yale,   May 10, 1749
Tim Thompson of East Haven & Esther Curtis,
                                July 20, 1749
Thomas Scofel of Hadlime & Jerusha Scofel,
                                Nov. 9, 1749
Samuel Jerom & Luce Foster,   Nov. 21, 1749
John Yale, Jr., & Eunice Andrews,   Dec. 22, 1749
James Cobbon & Irania Powel,   Jan. 11, 1750
John Whiting & Sarah Foster,   Jan. 18, 1750
Jesse Merriam & Mary Johnson,   May 9, 1750
Daniel Hall & Patience Baldwin,   July 25, 1750
Joseph Francis, Jr., & Mary Tuttle,   Oct. 31, 1750
Joseph Mitchell of Deerfield & Lydia Foster, Jan. 29, 1751
John Ball & Annah Mitchell,   Feb. 14, 1751
Barzeliel Ives & Hannah Merriam,   Feb. 14, 1751
Gershom George (?) & Mary Salter of Cheshire,
                              April 24, 1751
William Merriam, Jr., & Phebe Ives,   May 29, 1751
Jacob Deming of Kensington & Mrs. Abigal Jerom,
                             March 29, 1752
Thomas Berry, 2d, & Annah Perkins,   June 3, 1752
Samuel Andrews, 2d, & Lydia Royce,   Nov. 9, 1752
Nathan Cobbin of Deerfield & Thankful Foster,
                              Nov. 27, 1752
William Hough, Jr., & Mary Hall,   Dec. 20, 1752

Benjamin Hall of Wallingford & Mary, dau. of Abi-
    jah Ives,   Dec. 27, 1752
Tim Foster, Jr., & Elizabeth Berry,   Jan. 17, 1753
Nathaniel Hart & Elce Hall,   Jan. 24, 1753
Daniel Macky of Cheshire & Hannah Yale,   Jan. 24, 1753
Joshua Curtis of Cheshire & Sarah P. Salter, Feb. 22, 1753
Stephen Royce of Cornwall & Mary How, May 3 or 8, 1753
Benjamin Tyler & Mehitabel Andrews,   June 26, 1753
Moses Blachley of Northbury & Hannah Dunbar,
                           Sept. 24, 1753
Joseph Rexford & Lydia Spencer,   Nov. 28, 1753
Benjamin Merriam & Mary Berry,   Dec. 19, 1753
Amos Hall & Mary Johnson,   Dec. 27, 1753
Abijah Ives & Josiah Mix's widow,   Aug., 1753
John Berry & Lucy Royce,   Jan. 9, 1754
Matthias Hitchcock of Cheshire & widow Sarah
    Hough,   Jan. 16, 1754
John Thomson, Jr., & Hannah Eaton of N. Haven,
                           Jan. 31, 1754
Eldad Curtis & Tabbitha Perkins,   Feb. 6, 1754
Moses Hall & Elizabeth Johnson,   March 20, 1754
John Potter of Southington & widow Elizabeth
    Spencer,   May 16, 1754
John Moss & widow Fenn,   Dec., 1754
Nathaniel Pentfield, Jr., & Lydia Barns,   Jan., 1755
Thomas Dutten, Jr., & Annah Royce,   Jan. 13, 1755
Jonathan Webb & Elizabeth Judd,   March 13, 1755
William Merriam & Mary Austin,   Sept. 24, 1755
Benjamin Whiting, Jr., & Esther Merriam, Oct. 14, 1755
James Scovill, Jr., & Hannah Hough,   Dec. 10, 1755
John Prout & Sarah Corbit,   Jan. 1, 1756
Thomas Merriam & Ann Moss,   Jan. 22, 1756
Abel Merriman & Elisabeth, dau. of Ens. Merriman,
                         March 11, 1756
Morlo A. Blachley & Stephen Ives' daughter, March 11, 1756
——— Perkins & Susannah Curtis,   March 12, 1756
James Scofel, Jr., & Hannah Hough,   March 13, 1756
Joseph Atwater, Jr., & Phebe Hall,   Aug. 18, 1756
David Wetmore & Sarah Stanton, of Middletown,
                         Sept. 16, 1756

Joshua How, Jr., & Merriam Blachley,   Oct. 19, 1756
Asa Bronson & Achsah Curtis,   Jan. 20, 1757
Timothy St. John of Norwalk & Deborah Royce,
                                                  Jan. 26, 1757
Asahel Beach & Kesiah Royce,   Feb. 10, 1757
Recompense Miller of Middletown & Isabel Ives,
                                                  Feb. 17, 1757
Gideon Horsford & Jerusha Cook,   Feb. 23, 1757
Amos Cook & Rhoda Horsford,   Feb. 23, 1757
Christopher Robinson & Sarah Mix,   April 14, 1757
Enos Tuttle & Sarah Francis,   April 21, 1757
Thomas Shyoha (?) & Mary Hull.   April 27, 1757
Moses Hull & Mary Ives,   May 5, 1757
Thomas Berry, Jr·, & Anna Merriam,   March, 1757
Denison Andrews & Abigail Whiting,   May 11, 1757
John Merriam & Mrs. Hannah Ives,   Aug. 9, 1757
Jotham Hall & Elizabeth Saxton of Middletown,
                                                  Nov. 10, 1757
Abel Cook & Mary Atwater,   Nov. 16, 1757
Gideon Barns of Canaan & Lucy Way,   Nov. 16, 1757
Thomas Atwater & Lois Hull of Cheshire,   Dec. 8, 1757
Waitstill Parker & Martha Hall,   Dec. 13, 1757
Jesse Parker & Dorathy Spenser,   Feb. 16, 1758
Divan Berry, Jr., & Lydia Yale.   Feb. 22, 1758
Elnathan Ives & Anna Yale,   March 9, 1758
Divan Berry & widow Mary Andrews (second wife),
                                                  March 28, 1758
Isaac Royce & Hannah Pentfield,   April 6, 1758
Dennis Covert of New Haven & Esther Jones, May 10, 1758
Samuel Pentfield & Rebecca Scofel,   June 1, 1758
Elisha Goodrich, Jr., & Sibil Mix,   June 29, 1758
Joseph Higbee & Abigal Ives,   Sept. 21, 1758
Elijah Powell of Middletown & Mary Andrews,
                                                  Jan. 17, 1759
John Ives & Mary Hall,   Jan. 17, 1759
Hezekiah Warner of Middletown & Lois Pentfield,
                                                  Feb. 8, 1759
Abel Curtis & Hannah Foster,   March 7, 1759
Ezekiel Royce, Jr., & Lydia Hough,   June 7, 1759
Asa Barnes & Lois Yale.   June 21, 1759

John Smith of Saybrook & Thankful Curtis,	June 28, 1759
Joseph Merriam & Sarah Austin,	Nov. 15, 1759
Daniel Hall, Jr., & Zeruiah Whitmore,	Nov. 19, 1759
William Andrews & Mary Curtis,	Dec. 27, 1759
John Hough & Lois Merriam,	Jan. 10, 1760
Barnabas Hough & Eunice Weeks,	Jan. 29, 1760
Thomas Foster & Elizabeth Berry,	Feb. 21, 1760
John Newell of Farmington & Ruth Merriam,	May 22, 1760
Bartholomew Andrews & the daughter of Andrew Andrews,	June, 1769
Benjamin Rexford & Esther Hall,	July 1, 1760
Phileomon Johnson & Sarah Hall,	Oct. 16, 1760
James Clark (a stranger) (?) & widow Yale,	Oct. 20, 1760
Allen Royce & Mindwell Cowls,	Dec. 4, 1760
John Denison of East Haven & Sarah Hough,	March 24, 1761
Daniel Mecky & Sarah Yale,	Nov. 19, 1761
Silas St. John of Sharon & Abigail Royce,	Dec. 1, 1761
James Churchill of Middletown & Sarah Penfield,	Feb. 11, 1762
Jahleel Clark & Esther Yale,	May 12, 1762
Jacob Tyler & Hannah Rigford,	May 12, 1762
Robert Royce & Jerusha Parker,	May 26, 1762
Deacon Parker of Cheshire & widow Ruth Merriam,	Sept. 30, 1762
Daniel Parker & Meriam Curtis,	Nov. 18, 1762
Matthew Grant of Torrington & Phebe Foster,	Nov. 18, 1762
William Grant of Torrington & Lois Foster,	Nov. 18, 1762
Cornelius Coverling & Sibil Iglestone,	Dec. 2, 1762
Joseph Cowles & widow Rebecca Rice,	Feb. 24, 1763
Benjamin Curtis & Mindwell Hough,	March 31, 1763
John Morgan of Middletown & Ann Hall, daughter of Israel Hall,	Oct. 18, 1763
Elijah Scofel & Jemima Shaler,	Oct. 20, 1763
Isaac Parsons & Leah Clark,	Nov. 10, 1763
Obediah Allen of Middletown & widow Hannah Mackey,	Nov. 17, 1763
David Hotchkiss of Waterbury & Abigail Douglas,	Nov. 21, 1763
Nathaniel Luttenton & Elizabeth Mackey,	Dec. 1, 1763

William Johnson & Hannah Cole,   Dec. 15, 1763
Janna Meigs of Salisbury & Rebecca Whiting, Jan. 16, 1764
Ephraim Allen of Kensington & widow Asubah Yale,
                                            Jan. 23, 1764
Eldad Peck of Kensington & Mary Foster,   Feb. 6, 1764
Jonathan Foster & Rebecca Foster,   Feb. 6, 1764
Robert Pattin & Eunice Curtis,   May 10, 1764
Isaac Hall, Jr., & Phebe Ives,   Sept. 6, 1764
Ephriam Rice & Abigal Fox of Cheshire,   Oct. 4, 1764
Daniel Bradley of Oblong & Rebecca Berry,   Oct. 11, 1764
Joseph Hall & Sarah Prout,   Oct. 15, 1764
William Barker of Branford & widow Mary Gilbert,
                                            Jan. 16, 1765
Comfort Butler & Mary Berry,   May 10, 1765
Rev. Burrage Merriam of Stepna & Mrs. Hannah
   Rice,   Sept. 12, 1765
Joseph Yale & Martha Livingston,   Nov. 27, 1765
John Miles, Jr., & Abigal Perkins,   Jan. 23, 1766
Samuel Whiting & Hannah Berry,   Feb. 27, 1766
John Butler & Lois Cole,   June 26, 1766
Thomas Mix, Jr., & Lois Collins,   Dec. 11, 1766
Samuel Collins & Phebe Ives,   Nov. 3, 1783
Lamberton Clark & Martha Rexford,   Dec. 11, 1783
Ephraim Merriam & Bulah Galpin,   Feb. 12, 1784
Levi Robinson & Elizabeth Yale,   Feb. 12, 1784
Hezekiah Miller of Middletown & Miss Bradley of
   N. Haven,   Sept. 25, 1786
Edward Collins & Mrs. Mary Hall,   Feb., 1787
Moses Sibly of Ashford & Patience Yeamans,
                                            March 22, 1787
Isaac Rice & Rachol Gain or Jain,   April 19, 1787
John Merriam & Mrs. Johnson,   July 11, 1787
Mr. Dowd & Miss Scovil,   Feb. 28, 1787
Levi Douglas & Miss Hall of Cheshire,   June 14, 1787
Samuel Hough, Jr., & Hannah Page,   July 19, 1787
Shelden Johnson & Hannah Rice,   Sept. 10, 1787
Matthew Hough & Martha Cowles,   Nov. 15, 1787
Ozias Foster & Phebe Miles,   Feb. 14, 1788
Mr. Todd & Polly Rice,   May 1, 1788
Solo Yale & Sarah Andrews,   Oct. 2, 1788

Mr. Hull & Miss Carter,	Oct. 2, 1788
Timothy Hall of Cheshire & Hannah Hall,	Nov. 27 1788
Mr. Dewolf (?) & Hannah Robinson,	April 23, 1788
Aron Lyman & widow Rebecca Hough,	June 22, 1788
Jesse Merriam, Jr., & Sally Andrews,	Oct. 6, 1788
Mr. Jerom & Polly Cobbon,	Nov. 27, 1788
Josiah Norton & Phebe Edwards,	Jan., 1789
Samuel Hally & Miss Babbit, both of Middlefield,	Feb., 1789
John Miles & Ruth Atwater,	May 4, 1789
Levi Ives & Fanny Silliman,	June 18, 1789
Amerton Yale & Mercy Scovil,	Jan., 1790
Matthew Yale & Lucy Ives,	Feb., 1790
Joel Mix & Eleanor Merriam,	April, 1790
John Richmon (?) & Rhoda Andrews (?),	May, 1790
Mr. Bacon & Mrs. Edwards,	June, 1790
Fletcher Perkins & Mrs. Damaris Miller,	Sept. 26, 1790
John Butler & Mrs. Phebe Foster,	Jan., 1791
Thos. Foster, Jr., & Hannah Yale,	Feb., 1791
Barnabas Yale & Lois Merriam,	May, 1791
Benjamin Hall & Sally Hall,	Aug. 24, 1791
Matthew Hough & the widow Woodruff,	Oct. 20, 1791
Joseph Ives & Clarissa Hall,	Nov. 4, 1791
Mr. Hotchkiss of Cheshire & Keturah Hough,	Nov. 17, 1791
Mr. Hull & Miss Rice,	Jan., 1792
Elihu Ives & Miss Hall,	Feb. 2, 1792
Joel Foster & Lucy Whiting,	Feb. 9, 1792
James Avery Hough & Sarah Todd,	April 19, 1792
Nathaniel Merriam & Eunice Curtis,	Oct., 1793
Noah Foster & Anna Ives,	1793
Aaron Johun & Miss Rice,	April, 1793
Aaron Curtis & Susanna Cutler,	Oct., 1793
Levi Hough & Lucretia Merriam,	Nov. 14, 1793
Mr. Talmage & Miss Bellamy,	Nov. 14, 1793

WINDSOR — BLOOMFIELD.

HARTFORD COUNTY.

The town of Bloomfield was incorporated in 1835; taken from Windsor. The Congregational Church in Bloomfield, called Wintonbury, was organized February 14, 1738. Rev. Hezekiah Bissell pastor from 1738 to 1783. The following marriages are recorded.

Stephen Gillet & Anne Loomis,	Sept. 22, 1738
Wm. Wallis & Anne Porter,	Nov. 10, 1738
Sam'l Filley & Jerusha Drake,	Aug. 13, 1739
Wm. Phelps & Martha Holcomb of Poquonot,	Jan. 4, 1740
Ebenezer Burr & Hephsiba Brown,	Jan. 10, 1740
Wm. Moore of Turkey Hills & Damaris Phelps of Pequonot,	Jan. 10, 1740
Nath'l Burr & Hannah Loomis,	July 8, 1740
Jonathan Bidwell & Hannah Hubbard,	Aug. 6, 1740
Jonathan Gillet & Abigail Hubbard,	Dec. 11, 1740
Noah Drake & Hannah Skinner,	Oct. 1, 1741
Abel Loomis & Eunice Porter,	Nov. 3, 1741
Jas. Stephens of New Haven & Rachel Fyler,	Nov. 30, 1741
Sam'l Webster & Elizabeth Case,	Dec. 17, 1741
Gideon Burr & Eunice Loomis,	Nov. 11, 1742
Noadiah Phelps & Naomi Case,	Feb. 24, 1743
Stephen Loomis, Jr., & Grace Loomis,	June 9, 1743
Josiah Bissell & Ruth Bissell,	Aug. 11, 1743
Benj. Case & Hannah Drake,	Nov. 10, 1743
Ezekiel Osborn & Abigail Watson,	April 12, 1744
Benedict Alford & Jerusha Ashley,	Aug. 7, 1744
Isaac Skinner, Jr., & Dorcas Drake,	Oct. 8, 1744
Reuben Cooke & Thankful Hodge,	Nov. 8, 1744
Asahel Drake & Damaris Kelsey,	Feb. 7, 1745
Jonathan Adams & Mindwell Phelps,	March 7, 1745
Isaac Phelps & Martha Mills,	Sept. 5, 1745
Reuben Loomis & Rebecca Goodrich,	Feb. 7, 1745-6
Jonah Griswold & Ruth Barnett,	Oct. 9, 1746
Hez. Drake & Mary Filley,	June, 1747
Reuben Case & Ruth Goodrich,	July 9, 1747
Silas Burnham & Hannah Norton of East Hartford,	Sept. 3, 1747

Silas Fyler & Cateran Drake,   Sept. 10, 1747
Matthew Cadwell of Hartford & Elizabeth Hub-
    bard,   Oct. 15, 1747
John Burr, Jr., & Tabitha Loomis,   Dec. 17, 1747
Solomon Clark, Jr., & Anne Ashley of Hartford,
                                             Jan. 11, 1747–8
Seth Loomis & Hester Kelsey,   Feb. 29, 1747–8
Sam'l Pierce & Loisa Hoskins,   April 19, 1748
Chas. Phelps & Hannah Cooke,   May 12, 1748
Sam'l Francis & widow Martha Case,   Oct. 13, 1748
Jedediah Loomis & Sibbel Case,   Nov. 25, 1748
Noah Marshel & Ruth Cooke of Windsor,   Jan. 26, 1749
Eliphalet Loomis & Theodotia Clark,   March 28, 1749
Job Drake & Hannah Goodrich,   April 27, 1749
Caleb Phelps & Mary Henderson of Windsor, June 21, 1749
David Filley & Margeree Brown,   Sept. 22, 1749
Isaac Fosbury of Sheffield & widow Anne Gillet,
                                             Sept. 11, 1750
Ezra Kent of Suffield & Elizabeth Gillet,   Nov. 8, 1750
Sam'l Stone Butler & Mary Goodwin,   Aug. 19, 1751
Josiah Clark & Deliverence Eggleston,   Sept. 6, 1751
John Eggleston, Jr., & Martha Clark,   Jan. 29, 1752
Alex Hoskins & Martha Parsons,   Feb. 13, 1752
Stephen Goodwin, Jr., & Abigail Gillett,   April 16, 1752
Joel Loomis of Torrington & Elizabeth Brown of
    Poquonuch,   June 4, 1752
Geo. Manley & Ruth Burr,   Aug. 13, 1752
Elijah Goodrich & Margeree Gillett,   Aug. 20, 1752
Hosea Clark & Mary Skinner,   Oct. 5, 1752
Wm. Manley, Jr., & Mary Burr,   Nov. 9, 1752
Jonah Gillett, Jr., & Sarah Goodrich   Nov. 9, 1752
Thomas Cadwell, Jr., of West Hartford & Mary
    Porter,   Dec. 21, 1752
Sam'l Burr & Christian Cadwell,   Dec. 28, 1752
Thomas Beman & Lydia Robearts,   Jan. 18, 1753
John Eggleston, Jr., & Sarah Stannard,   Aug. 31, 1753
Benj. Gillett & Elizabeth Cadwell,   Dec. 20, 1753
Joseph Atwell & Miriam Case,   Dec. 27, 1753
Stephen Goodrich & Rachel Gillett,   Jan. 3, 1754
Wm. Shepard of Hartford & Hannah Gillett, March 28, 1754

Sam'l Fitch & Martha Rowell,   April 25, 1754

" Ye groom was, as far as I could learn, more than 70 years old, and ye bride near 80, neither of which had been married before.

Elisha Grimes & Anne Humphrey,   June 20, 1754
Josiah Butler & Margeret Manley,   Nov. 13, 1754
Jonathan Filley, Jr., & Sarah Butler,   Feb. 6, 1755
Jacob Merrels of West Hartford & Mary Manley,
                                                           Feb. 17, 1755
Joel Cook & Sarah Pinney,   April 7, 1755
Hezekiah Richards of West Hartford & Sarah Case,
                                                           May 8, 1755
Henry Moore of Penn. & Elizabeth Tuller,   May 22, 1755
John Hoskins, Jr., & Jerusha Gillett,   July 10, 1755
Sanders Moore & Damaras Tuller of Scotland, Aug. 27, 1755
Isaac Graham & Sarah Moses,   Jan. 12, 1756
Elihu Lawrence of Kensington & Eunice Case, May 13, 1756
Roice Beech of Goshan & Phebe Soper,   June 9, 1756
Hezekiah Parsons & Anne Latimer,   July 16, 1756
Wm. Tuller of Scotland & Mary Matson,   Feb. 9, 1757
Robt. Joyner of Sheffield & Lucy Loomis,   March 3, 1757
Sam'l Case, Jr., & Violet Burr,   April 7, 1757
Noadiah Burr, Jr., & Abigail Peese,   May 15, 1757
Amos Lawrence of Kensington & Sarah Webster,
                                                           June 2, 1757
Aaron Drake & Chloe Gillett,   July 21, 1757
Joseph DeForest of Stratford & Mrs. Susanna Mills,
                                                           Aug. 18, 1757
Ezra Brown of Poquonock & Chloe Hoskins, Oct. 13, 1757
Joseph Eggleston & widow Naomi Phelps,   Dec. 21, 1757
Hezekiah Lattimer & Triphena Gillett,   Jan. 26, 1758
John Brown, Jr., of Poquonock & Hannah Owen,
                                                           March 2, 1758
Robert Barnett & Hannah Parson,   March 16, 1758
Joseph Nash & Ann Skinner,   March 16, 1758
Joel Griswold & Mary Evans,   May 11, 1758
Oliver Diggins & Mehitabel Porter,   Sept. 20, 1758
Joel Barber of 1st South Windsor & Mary Drake,
                                                           Nov. 23, 1758
Daniel Grayhem & Zeruiah Moses,   Feb. 6, 1759
Caleb Talcott of Bolton & Martha Parsons, March 22, 1759

Lt. Jonathan Gillet & widow Rachel Goodrich,
April 26, 1759
Jeddediah Olcott of New Hartford & Sarah Cad-
well,   Oct. 3, 1759
Samuel Loomis & Jerusha Filley,   Dec. 13, 1759
Lent (Lieut.?) Mott of Winchester & Mary Filley,
Jan 1, 1760
Roger Fyler & widow Triphena Allen,   April 7, 1760
Thomas Hoskins & Margaret Filley,   April 23, 1760
Benjamin Brown & widow Mary Brown of West
Hartford,   June 12, 1760
Samuel Barber & Hannah Olds of Suffield,   Sept. 8, 1760
Stephen Rossiter of Harwinton & Mrs. Mary
Jonson, Mr. Elihu Lawrence's sister,   Dec. 23, 1760
David Ives of Goshen & Eunice Gillett,   Feb., 1761
Abraham Pinney, Jr., & Lucretia Barnard of Sims-
bury,   June 9, 1761
Luther Barber of Norfolk & Hannah Burr,   Oct. 15, 1761
Stephen Burr, Jr., & Sarah Burr,   Oct. 22, 1761
Amos Burr & Anne Rowel,   Dec. 30, 1761
Lanchlan McLean & Lucy Humphrey,   April 11, 1762
Simeon Gillet & Rebecka Andrus,   May 20, 1762
Daniel Boadman of Wethersfield & Sarah Foot of
Simsbury,   June 9, 1762
Jonathan Eggleston & Mindwell Hoskins,   June 24, 1762
Deacon Isaac Butler of Harwinton & Thankful
Persons,   July 1, 1762
Ebenezer Manley & Marcy Gillet,   Dec. 23, 1762
Joseph Goodwin & Rosanna Gillett,   April 21, 1763
James Webster & Hannah Hubbard,   June 9, 1763
Benjamin Case & widow Mary Loomis of Sims-
bury,   June 13, 1763
Asahel Smith of Suffield & Agnes Gillett,   June 29, 1763
Pelatiah Mills, Jr., & Lois Gillett,   June 29, 1763
Henry Brace, Jr., & Abigail Hooker of West Hart-
ford,   Aug. 18, 1763
Enoch Drake, ye 3d, & Sibbel Griswold,   Aug. 25, 1763
Benjamin Newbury & Sarah Drake,   Oct. 13, 1763
Jonathan Palmer & widow Hannah Hubbard,   Jan. 19, 1764
Amos Gillett & Susanna Webster,   Feb. 23, 1764

Ebenezer Drake & Mahitabel Cook,	Feb. 23, 1764
Ashbel Grant & Elizabeth Chapman,	March 29, 1764
Jacob Drake, Jr., & Rhode Drake,	April 12, 1764
John Filley & Annie Filley,	April 26, 1764
Edward Matson of Turkey Hills & Elizabeth Matson,	May 2, 1764
Edmund Brown of Norfolk & Anna Burr,	May 9, 1764
Noah Weight of Turkey Hills & widow Elizabeth Moore of Scotland,	July 24, 1764
Alexr Hoskins, Jr., & widow Mary Drake,	Feb. 14, 1765
Elezer Merrills of West Hartford & Louis Foot,	May 29, 1765
Stephen Loomis, Jr., & Mary Mumford,	June 13, 1765
John Soper & Rosanna Blancher of West Hartford,	Jan. 8, 1766
Ebenezer Latimer & Eunice Hoskins,	Jan. 9, 1766
Sam'l Deming & Jerusha Butler,	Nov., 1765
Sam'l Mills & Kezia Filley,	March 13, 1766
Sam'l Foot, Jr., & Hannah Bidwell,	March 27, 1766
Dr. Nehemiah Palmer & widow Elizabeth Palmer of Wethersfield,	May 26, 1766
John Kelly, from Ireland, & ——— Loomis of Simsbury,	June 8, 1766
John Fitch of Windsor & Lucy Roberts of Symsbury,	Dec 29, 1766
Matthew Cadwell, Jr., & Joanna Marshall,	Feb. 12, 1767
Jas. Cadwell & Mary Foot,	Nov. 19, 1767
Abel Gillett, Jr., & Jerusha Andrus,	Jan. 7, 1768
Joel Wilson, Jr., & Grace Loomis,	Jan. 24, 1768
Ebenzer Center of West Hartford & Agnes Hubbard,	March 17, 1768
Roger Mills & Mary Webster,	March 23, 1768
Levi Soper & Hannah Mills,	April 14, 1768
Zacheus Munsel & Hannah Drake,	May 4, 1768
James Barber or Barker & Hester Allyn,	July 17, 1768
Aaron Henry & Mabel Tucker of West Hartford,	Sept. 26, 1768
John Waters & Phebe Roberts,	Sept. 29, 1768
Wm. Watson of Hartford & Deborah Griswold,	Oct. 30, 1768
Sam'l Marshall, Jr., & Sabra Mills,	Jan. 12, 1769
Rev. Theodore Hinsdale & Anne Bissell,	July 14, 1768?

Zenas Case & Mary Loomis,   March 2, 1769
Gideon Barber of Windsor & widow Mary Hoskins,
                                              Aug. 17, 1769
Rev. Wm. Russell & Abigail Newbury,   Jan. 18, 1770
Jas. Parsons & Hannah Phelps,   Jan. 25, 1770
Sam'l Goodwin & Rebecca Loomis,   Feb. 8. 1770
Dan'l Pettebone & Sarah Brown,   Feb. 15, 1770
Jonathan Ashley of Hartford & widow Mary Goff,
                                              April 11, 1770
Aaron Barnard of Simsbury & Lucy Phelps,   June 27, 1770
Sam'l Eggleston & Dorcas Loomis,   Aug. 9, 1770
John Wells, Jr., of Farmington & widow Lois Mer-
    rils,   Oct. 25, 1770
David Lane of Suffield & Lucy Gillett,   Dec. 26, 1770
Nath'l Butler & Anne Gillett,   Dec. 27, 1770
Edward Moore & widow Ruth Parsons,   Jan. 31, 1771
Chatwill Parsons & Mabel Bidwell,   April 4, 1771
Caleb Case & Christian Burr,   April 11, 1771
Roger Mills & Abigail Griswold of Poquonock,
                                              April 17, 1771
Sam'l Rowel, Jr., & Catharine Fyler,   June 9, 1771
Simeon Judd of Hartford & widow Theodotia
    Loomis,   June 20, 1771
Jonathan Bidwell, Jr., & Abigail Eggleston,   July 18, 1771
Jacob Loomis & Diadema Hubbard,   Aug. 15, 1771
Alpheus Brown & Miriam Burr,   Oct. 9, 1771
Nath'l Hubbard, Jr., & Dolle Cole of Hartford, Nov. 28, 1771
Timothy Foot & Abigail Barnes,   Dec. 12, 1771
Isaac Bartlett & Olive Rowel,   April 29, 1772
Timothy Hoskins & Rhoda Gillett,   April 30, 1772
Timothy Hubbard & Sarah Gillett,   June, 18, 1772
Henry Mumford of Hartwood & Sarah Filley,   July 1, 1772
Eli Hoskins & Martha Clark,   Aug. 13, 1772
Abijah Moore & Abigail Drake of Windsor,   Aug. 20, 1772
Oliver Woodford or Woodward & Thankful Brown, ——
Darius Segar & Eunice Drake,   Nov. 12, 1772
Joseph Drake & Lois Pierce or Pirce,   Nov. 19, 1772
Charles Seward of Torrington & Abigail Bidwell,
                                              March 11, 1773
Isaiah Burr & Eunice Rowel,   May 10, 1773

Jas. Filley, Jr., & Charity Munsil of East Windsor,
                                    June or July, 1772
Moses Merrils, Jr., & Waitstill Hath of West Hart-
    ford,   Sept. 23, 1773
Calvin Hammon of Jericho & Jerusha Brown,   Oct. 6, 1773
Aaron Booth of East Windsor & widow Ann Nash,
                                          Oct. 22, 1773
Reuben Judd, Jr., of Hartford & Ann Brown,   Oct. 31, 1773
William Kelley, Jr., & Triphena Allyn,   Jan. 27, 1774
Job Drake & Hepsibah Wallis of East Hartford, Feb. 7, 1774
Timothy Munros of New Canaan & Hepsibah Drake,
                                        March 17, 1774
James Barnett of ye nine partners & Martha Mills,
                                        March 31, 1774
Daniel Olmstead of Simsbury & Rachel Hubbard,
                                          Nov. 24, 1774
Philander Rowel & Joanna Hayse of Salmon Brook,
                                            Jan. 5, 1775
Elijah Foot & Mary Latimer,   Jan. 8, 1775
Eli Mills & Sarah Filley,   Jan. 23, 1775
Daniel Rowel, Jr., & Phebe Spencer of Suffield,
                                            Jan. 23, 1775
Isac Thrall & Rhoda Phelps,   Jan. 26, 1775
William Robe Case & Hulda Loomis,   Feb. 3, 1775
John Hubbard & Susanna Mills,   June 15, 1775
Nathaniel Austin of Toringford & Anne Bidwell,
                                          Sept. 27, 1775
Stephen Brown & Eunice Loomis, Windsor Third
    Society,   Nov. 26, 1775
Zadock Brown & Ann Eggleston,   Dec. 3, 1775
Charles Phelps, Jr., & Ann Cook,   Feb 12, 1776
Thomas Allyn, Jr., & Elizabeth Burr,   April 11, 1776
Simeon Judd of Hartford & Olive Pirce,   June 3, 1776
David Filley & Lydia —— of Hartford,   July 25, 1776
George King & Triphena Latimer,   Aug. 13, 1776
Thomas Gillett & Hannah Drake,   Sept. 12, 1776
David Schield, perph(?), of New Canaan & Hannah
    Drake,   Sept. 15, 1776
Pelatiah Cadwell & Lucy Foot,   Nov. 7, 1776
Asa Hubbard & Submit Bishop,   Nov. 20, 1776

Ammariah Watson of New Hartford & Eleanor
    Burr,   Dec. 5, 1776
David Barber, Jr., of Poquonack & Jane Filley, Dec. 15, 1776
Ebenezer Brown & Susanna Pirce,   Dec. 19, 1776
George Case & Rhoda Pirce,   Dec. 19, 1776
Increase Hopkins & Martha Person (or perhaps Par-
    sons),   March 20, 1777
Elisha Rose of Granvell & ye widow Sibble Drake,
                              April 17, 1777
Samuel Eno, Jr., & Marcy Manley,   May 7, 1777
Davis or Pavis Fyler & Abigail Allyn,   Aug. 15, 1777
Robert Sanford & the widow Mary Hopkins, Oct. 12, 1777
Captain Rueben Loomis & ye widow Mary Hubbard,
                             Nov. 23, 1777
William Gray & Ami Fosbury,   Dec. 8, 1777
Eli Cook & Rachel Russell,   Dec. 21, 1777
John Manning & Lydia Holcomb,   Dec. 29, 1777
Asa Gillett & Violet Case,   Feb. 1, 1778
Stephen Gillett & Ruth Case,   April 30, 1778
Elihu Case & Freelove Burr,   May 7, 1778
Elijah Loomis & Abigail Gillett,   May 10, 1778
Roger Rowel & Anne Bunce of New Haven, May 31, 1778
Uriah Brown & Cloe Clark of Pequonock, June 4, 1778
Aaron Crane of East Windsor & Mary Barber of
    the First Society of Windsor,   June 16, 1778
Hezekiah Parsons, Jr., & Anne Webster, June 25, 1778
Aaron Webster & Mary Sheppard,   July 1, 1778
Ashbel Webster & Anna Attwell,   July 22, 1778
Stephen Filer & Polle Colier,   July 28, 1778
Hosea Clark & Hannah Hoskins,   Oct. 4, 1778
Franciss Barnard of Scotland & Cloe Brown, Oct. 8, 1778
Silas Filer of Windsor & Lucy Drake,   Feb. 4, 1779
Solomon Allyn, Jr., & Lucina Gillett, March 29, 1779
Samuel Colton & Lois Brown,   April 8, 1779
George Clark & Charity Clark,   Aug. 15, 1779
Aaron Bates of Hartland & Sarah King, Sept. 8, 1779
Ira Clark & Bede Barnes,   Oct. 10, 1779
Darius Case & Hepsiber Foot,   Oct. 20, 1779
Thomas Rowely (or Rowly) & Mary Hale of Sal-
    mon Brook,   Nov. 4, 1779

Job Cook & Ruth Pierce,	Dec. 16, 1779
Hosiah Burr, Jr., & Hannah Rowley,	Jan. 25, 1780
Seth Gutrich & Hannah Chapman,	Feb. 10, 1780
Salem Burr & Annie Cole,	Feb. 26, 1780
Solomon Griswould & Abiah Alyn,	April 27, 1780
Moses Clark & Uslae(?) Phelps of Poquonock,	Oct. 30, 1780
Jonathan Palmer & Auria(?) Griswold,	Oct. 19, 1786
Joseph Holcomb & Olive Marshel,	Jan. 15, 1787
Jonah Gillet, Jr., & widow Eunice Whiton,	Jan. 30, 1787
Friend Griswold & Dorothy Wellor,	March 12, 1787
Elihu Mills & Mehitable Allyn,	April 2, 1787
Benjamin Creasea & Welthy Gillet,	April 5, 1787
William Delane & Lucy Skinner,	May 4, 1787
Samuel Stoton, Jr., & Cloa Gillet,	June 6, 1787
John Clark & Sarah Borker (or Barker),	July 22, 1787
Seth Talcott & Lucy Gillet,	Feb. 14, 1788

PERSONS MARRIED BY WM. F. MILLER, 1792.

Zebeston Curtis of Toringford & Hannah Parsons, dau. of Hezekiah Parsons, ensign,	Jan. 5, 1792
Oliver Roberts of Windsor & Anna Bunce,	April 15, 1792
Job Higley & Dorcas Egleston,	May 9, 1792
George Warner & Nabby Griswold Mills,	May 17, 1792
Samuel Burr, Jr., & Clarissa Barber,	Oct. 5, 1792
Joab Phelps & Heziah Burr of Wintonbury,	Oct. 14, 1792
Ahaset Nearing & Molly Loomis,	Oct. 21, 1792
Izaac Hunt of Sharon & Abigail King,	March 31, 1793
Theodore Wadsworth of Hartford & Clarissa Drake,	April 11, 1793
Abijah Cadwell & Eunice Allyn,	May 9, 1793
Joseph Wadsworth of Hartford & Dorcas Andras,	Aug. 8, 1793
Roswell Clark & Rhoda Wilson,	Aug. 25, 1793
Samuel Foot & Lucy Foot,	Feb. 17, 1794
Gurdon Filley & Eunice Phelps,	May 29, 1794
William Webber & Hannah Clark,	Aug. 7, 1794
Aaron Cadwell & Cloe Ford,	Aug. 24, 1794
Griswold Gustan of Simsbury & Sarah Brown of Farmington,	Aug. 28, 1794
Benjamin Graham & Candice Bidwell,	Nov. 27, 1794

9

Solomon Allyn & Sarah Burr,   April 14, 1795
Elisha Lord & Susannah Alcott,   Dec. 13, 1795
Bethuel Parker of Wallingford & Eunice Rogers
    of Lyme,   Feb. 4, 1796
A. Woodward of Middletown & Rockcy Burr of
    Farmington,   March 10, 1796
Uriah Cadwell & Marian Cadwell, both of West
    Hartford,   June 27, 1796
Samuel Burr, Jr., & Rhoda Cadwell,   Oct. 23, 1796
Caleb Hitchcock, Jr., & Electa Foot,   Jan. 15, 1797
David Filley, Jr., & Jerasha Rowley,   Jan. 19, 1797
John Giles of Charlemont & Deborah Clarke, Feb. 12, 1797
John Thorp & Abiah Parsons,   Feb. 16, 1797
Chestor Rice of Sandisfield & Parmela Manley,
                                               Feb. 27, 1797
Amos Gillett, Jr., & Milly Hubbard,   March 9, 1797
—— Dewey of Suffield & Mercy Marshall of
    Northington,   June 19, 1797
Grove Taylor & Elizabeth Wilson,   Sept. 10, 1797
Asahel Brace & Sally Graham of W. Hartford, Dec. 3, 1797
John Wells, Jr., of Johnstown & Mercy Gillett, Jan. 1, 1798
Selah Bernard & Elizabeth Filley,   Feb. 28, 1798
Hezekiah Goodwin & Rebekah Loomis,   Aug. 29, 1798
Dan Gregory of Granby & Peggy Combs,   Oct. 22, 1798
James Goodwin of Hartford & Eunice Roberts,
                                               March 3, 1799
Aaron Foot of Northampton, N. Y., & Esther Bar-
    ber,   April 7, 1799
Luke Filley & Mary Hall,   May 25, 1799
Joseph Filley, Jr., & Cloe Burr,   May 30, 1799
William Cooley & Lucinda Evenes of East Hart-
    ford,   June 11, 1799
Plinny Harner & Charlotte Brown,   June 17, 1799
Jonathan Allyn, Jr., & Hannah Holcomb or But-
    tles of Granby,   Sept. 12, 1799
Levi Cadwell & Rockcy Brown,   Oct. 7, 1799
Amos Sedgwick & Ruth Colten of W. Hartford, Oct. 29, 1799
Noah Burr & Lucy Cadwell,   Nov. 28, 1799
Elisha Cook & Susanna Rowley,   Jan. 16, 1800

BOLTON.

TOLLAND COUNTY.

The town of Bolton was incorporated in 1720. The Congregational Church organized October 27, 1725. Rev. Thomas White pastor from 1711 to 1763. Marriages recorded as follows.

Samuel Barthelemew of Branford & Sarah Bissell,	Jan. 7, 1738
James Olcott & Sarah Griswold,	June 15, 1738
Joseph Crane & Deborah Morey,	Aug. 24, 1738
John Chapman & Hannah Kingsbury, both of Coventry,	Oct. 10, 1738
Stephen Johns & Sarah Loomis,	Feb. 7, 1739
Jonathan Crane & Kezia Morey of Glastonbury,	May 4, 1739
Benjamin Smith & Ann Griswold,	June 26, 1739
Daniel Gilbert of Windsor & Ruth Loomis,	Aug. 27, 1735
John Crane of Coventry & Mary Pinney of Windsor,	Dec. 25, 1735
Joel White & Ruth Dart,	Jan. 22, 1736
Samuel Spencer, Jr., & Hannah Shalyer,	April 26, 1736
Comfort Brewster of Lebanon & Deborah Smith,	Dec. 3, 1736
William Burnham & Jerusha Clark, both of Hartford,	April 18, 1734
Stephen Olmstead of Hartford & Margarett Olcott,	Nov. 14, 1734
Eliphalet Youngs & Mary Rollo, both of Hebron,	Dec. 19, 1734
Ebenezer Dewey & Martha Willcox, both of Hebron,	March 12, 1735
Jerijah Loomis & Abigail Atherton of Coventry,	Aug. 13, 1735
Titus Olcott & Damaris Marshall,	Oct. 5, 1732
Elijah Hammond & Mary Kingsbury,	Oct. 12, 1732
Isaac Brunson & Abigail King,	Nov. 9, 1733
Joseph Fitch of Windsor & Sarah Shailer,	Dec. 25, 1729
Thomas Loomis & Mary Dart,	Dec. 7, 1729
Benjamin Smith & Miss Spencer,	Nov. 18, 1728
Joseph Cobb & Surviah Webster,	Nov. 17, 1763
Benj. Trumbull & Abigail Loomis,	May 29, 1764

Col. Thomas Wells & Mrs. Martha White,	Aug. 15, 1764
Abner Loomis & Martha Thayer,	Dec. 6, 1764
George Griswold & Susanna Cone,	Dec. 12, 1764
Jerijah Loomis, Jr., & Sarah Webster,	Jan. 3, 1765
Phillip Clark & Abigail Birge,	April 14, 1765
John Jones & Susanna Bates,	May 2, 1765
Rev. John Bliss & Bette White,	Jan. 15, 1766
Jordan Post & Abigail Loomis,	May 29, 1766
Rev. Samuel Clark & Jerusha White,	July 1, 1766
Aaron Strong & Margaret Howard,	Sept. 3, 1766
Ashahel Skinner & Sarah Trumbull,	Nov. 20, 1766
Thomas Coleman & Anna Shaylor,	Nov. 25, 1766
David Webster & Mary Hitchcock,	Dec. 18, 1766
Judah Strong & Martha Alvord,	Dec. 31, 1766
Nathan Darte & Dorothy Gaines,	March 19, 1767
David Norton & Susanna Bishop,	April 1, 1767
Michael Taintor & Lydia Loomis,	April 2, 1767
John Howard & Chloe Talcott,	May 12, 1767
John Post & Comfort Goodrich,	Sept. 25, 1767
Riverious Hooker & Abigail Bishop,	Nov. 20, 1767
Joseph Webster & Ruth Loomis,	March 3, 1768
Stephen Post & Mary Taylor,	Aug. 1, 1768
John Hale & Martha Schovill,	Sept. 29, 1768
Benjamin Mann & Bette Darte,	Dec. 15, 1768
Andrew Loomis & Beulah Strong,	Dec. 22, 1768
Ebenezer Hide & Lois Thatcher,	March 6, 1769
Joseph Burnham & widow Eunice Shaylor,	Aug. 16, 1769
Noah Bartlett & Sarah Scott,	Oct. 30, 1769
Hezekiah Crone & Sybyl Lamphier,	Nov. 7, 1769
Ebenezer Hibbard & Ann Spencer,	Nov. 9, 1769
Thomas Brown & Charity Cooley,	April 5, 1770
Ebenezer Carver & Esther Trumbull,	April 5, 1770
Niles Wilrich & Margaret Baxter,	Sept. 6, 1770
Ozias Tyler & Jerusha Loomis,	Oct. 30, 1770
Joseph Sutlief & Zerviah Cobb,	April 2, 1771
Daniel Griswold & widow Judith Shaylor,	May 23, 1771
William Hibbard & Bathsheba Strong,	Aug. 29, 1771
John Gibbs & widow Dorothy Dart,	Feb. 21, 1772
Jabez Emerson & Sarah Atherton,	June 18, 1772
Solomon Dewey & Christiany Cone,	July 30, 1772

Thomas Kimberly & Ann White,	Sept. 16, 1772
Elisha Taylor & Jerusha Hatchins,	Feb. 16, 1773
Jacob Williams & Mary Carver,	March 31, 1773
Eliphalet Hendee & Mary Loomis,	June 1, 1773
Jabez Crocker & Elizabeth Talcott,	Oct. 5, 1773
John Cone & Patience Strickland,	Nov. 13, 1773
Joshua Talcott & Jemima Howard,	Dec. 7, 1773
Seth Waterman & Elizabeth Loomis,	Dec. 14, 1773
John Coleman & Mary Woodruff,	Jan. 20, 1774
Zacheus Scott & Sarah Quomine (?),	April 20, 1774
Joseph Fitch & widow Susanna Cone,	June 30, 1774
Asa Kellogg & Ann Webster,	Dec. 19, 1774
Eleazer Huntington & Elizabeth Pitkin,	Jan. 4, 1775
Amos Palmer & Joanna Waldo,	Jan. 26, 1775
John Talcott & Sarah Stimpson,	May 8, 1775
Jonah Strickland & Ann Cone,	June 29, 1775
Lemuel Long & Anna Bissell,	Nov. 16, 1775
Ozias Bissell & Elizabeth Kilborn,	Jan. 25, 1776
Daniel Skinner & Ann Andrus,	Nov. 6, 1776
Joseph Carver & Martha Boardman,	Nov. 7, 1776
Abner Lamphier & Rachel Clark,	Feb. 7, 1777
Simeon Spencer & Abigail Darte,	Feb. 27, 1777
Samuel Carver & Bathsheba Griswold,	Aug. 14, 1777
James Negro & Sarah Scott,	Aug. 15, 1777
John Couch & Abigail Webster,	Sept. 18, 1777
Gurdon Woodruff & Ann Webster,	Sept. 18, 1777
Aaron Haskins & Rhoda Risley,	Sept. 30, 1777
Theophilus Huntington & Ruth Talcott,	Nov. 5, 1777
Joseph Andrus & Mercy Darte,	Nov. 27, 1777
Nathaniel Howard & Mary Grover,	Feb. 12, 1778
Anderson Miner & Martha Pitkin,	March 5, 1778
Simeon Griswold & Ann Hutchins,	May 5, 1778
Ashbel Webster & Mercy Sweetland,	. Sept. 8, 1778
William Richardson & Abigail Thayer,	Sept. 24, 1778
John Doughty & Sarah Smith,	Nov. 12, 1778
Mathew Dewolf & widow Susan Brockway,	Nov. 16, 1778
Samuel Lyman & Ruamah Allen,	Dec. 3, 1778
Elnathan Bush & widow Lydia Loomis,	Nov. 2, 1779
Abial Bill & Bette Darling,	Dec. 24, 1779

INDEX.

Early Connecticut Marriages

AS FOUND ON

ANCIENT CHURCH RECORDS

PRIOR TO 1800.

FIFTH BOOK.

EDITED BY THE

REV. FREDERIC W. BAILEY, B.D.,

OFFICIAL COPYIST OF PAROCHIAL ARCHIVES AND SECRETARY OF COMMISSION, DIOCESE OF
CONNECTICUT; EDITOR "EARLY MASSACHUSETTS MARRIAGES;" DESIGNER BAILEY'S
PHOTO–ANCESTRAL RECORD, "THE RECORD OF MY ANCESTRY;" MEMBER NEW
ENGLAND HISTORIC GENEALOGICAL SOCIETY; CONNECTICUT HISTORICAL
SOCIETY; NEW HAVEN COLONY HISTORICAL SOCIETY; SONS
OF THE AMERICAN REVOLUTION (MASSACHUSETTS).

PUBLISHED BY THE

BUREAU OF AMERICAN ANCESTRY
FOR
Family   Researches

FREDERIC W. BAILEY, MGR.
P. O. BOX 587.   NEW HAVEN, CONN.

EARLY CONNECTICUT MARRIAGES.

FIFTH BOOK.

When some six years ago we commenced the publication of this series it did not seem possible that there ever would be a call for a fifth book. The venture was made with strange misapprehension of the real nature of that interest which the American people was supposed to have in the question of ancestry. Fortunately for us, however, the value of our effort was greatly underestimated. Likewise, too, had we but faintly conceived the extent and intensity of that devotion to the study whose best encouragement came from such contributions as our own.

In the natural course of things this historic state of Connecticut has turned out a good many people. The numerous generations since the first settlement have been very prolific. Large families were the rule. Had all the children and the children's children remained at home and in the little commmonwealth it would have found us somewhat cramped for room and with serious problems to face. Fortunately as it was, however, the spirit of the times, the opportunities which fresh discovery of new fields brought, a love of adventure not unmixed with an increasing love of gain and enterprise, all these and more led these Connecticut born into Central and Western Massachusetts, up the great river into far away Vermont, over into New York, just across the border and later into the rich and fertile territory of Central and Western New York, Ohio, and portions of Pennsylvania. From these parts they spread out to every section of our country, contributing their good share to its betterment and upbuilding. Ultimately without loss of the high endeavor which inspired them from the first, lacking in some essential portions of the story of emigration, they rightly seek now to complete that interesting work.

Our humble effort, therefore, has not been without goodly fruitage if it has aided in this intention. Indeed are very sure that since these issues have appeared, the name of Connecticut has become dearer and more dear to many scattered everywhere who before never betook themselves to a study of its ancient glories.

And as to that be it said with convincing truthfulness that to one who loves genealogical research it is a new and a lasting glory to surely find the state and the particular place where first our own people made themselves a permanent abiding place. The very spot where once that early ancestor lived, toiled, suffered, died, its surroundings and environment, all things thereabouts which might possibly have been associated with his limited sphere and long life have their fascination. The intervening period of family existence when one's fathers were more often on the move is not half as attractive as that of the early beginnings when somehow we seem to feel that then and there in that atmosphere and those particular conditions and prospects our own family characteristics had for this country at least their first permanent setting.

In these recent years there has been much said and written about the abandoned farms of New England. In this discussion even Connecticut with all its prosperity and internal advantages may well share as one views with some touch of sadness the decayed and desolate homesteads found in several isolated sections of the state. Of course there is a clear explanation for this condition of things which no one can question. It is the solution of the great problem most wanted, whereby to restore to town and commonwealth an essential element of strength. The Governor of New Hampshire who inaugurated "Old Home Week" and saw it successfully established accomplished thereby a great step toward solving the question. For through that appeal to a delicate instinct which most of us feel, there came quick response; and the old tottering farm house afar away upon lonely hill that once was the center of so much joy and affection again clothed itself in much of its former beauty and freshness. There have been worthy instances of this sort in our own state where the ambitious son with that restless and resistless spirit of youth has gone forth from the parental roof in the wilds, and after the years of successful toiling that has produced its own weariness, returns at last satisfied to spend his remaining years, as also his hard accumulations, amidst the scenes and environments of early and visionary youth. Such fortunate men and wise have made the wilderness bloom and blossom as the rose.

The question of the abandoned farm seems to us at times to be more a question of the abandoned family than anything else. In other words a case wherein some well established family of to-day in the changing vicissitudes of our American life as is so common had lost all knowledge of its early career. Even the traditional had faded from view and that usual mainstay—a Bible record—but began a short and uninteresting story some two or three generations back with the bare facts of a birth. a marriage and the children; just where, it did not seem as if of enough consequence to state. There are, we feel sure, many such instances all over the land of old American families that through the changing years and circumstances have become detached from their early anchorage, while the effort to find it again has seemed so hopeless as to induce the feeling of utter despair.

It might seem therefore as if the disclosure of these early marriage records might serve a good purpose if they surely revealed the long hidden secret and fixed the locality in the minds and hearts of this generation.

In our last issue—Book IV—we had occasion in the Preface to refer to the bright prospects of some definite action by the state authorities to repair and save the old records scattered about; and could wish now it was our pleasure to report steady progress in that direction. The question seemed so vital and so completely removed from any thought of party prejudice that every member of the General Assembly might be presumed to have an interest as he had an interest in his own town's need.

A definite policy for the reconstruction of the old books seemed to be the most natural conclusion to draw from the facts in hand. From our view therefore it is a real disappointment to have to chronicle here that when the special commission had, after months of labor, made its interesting report, been given a hearing and had pressed its recommendations, said report met the same fate as many another unpopular though worthy cause. And so here seems to be the end of the suggestion which Governor Lounsbury so faithfully urged, with nothing apparently gained by the long discussion. The old records are now two years older than when this subject was first as a crying need advocated; while what is a more serious complication consists in the fact that in two old towns at least with records of very ancient date, a private corporation has seen fit to make complete abstracts of both land and probate for their own use, while the originals freely handled have suffered even more serious damage.

There would arise a very peculiar condition of things likely at last to awaken some of these conservative towns if this method were pursued to any great extent among us while the old originals (with no public copy) be left to decay and ultimately perish.

The records published herewith have for the most part been thoroughly verified and we can offer them as another contribution to the study of Connecticut genealogy. Of course there are the usual complications of varied spellings, and obscure chirography. These matters will surely correct themselves once the clue is established and the valued discovery effectually offset our seeming error.

FREDERIC W. BAILEY.

New Haven, Conn., Feb. 15, 1902.

CONTENTS.

FIFTH BOOK.

RECORDS LOST.

The following is a (revised) list of Congregational Churches so far reporting the loss of their records of Baptisms and Marriages prior to 1800.

CHURCH.	COUNTY.	ORGANIZED.	REMARKS.
Westminster, of Canterbury	Windham,	1770,	none before 1824.
Coventry,	Tolland,	1745,	none before 1818.
Hebron,	Tolland,	1716,	burned.
Ellington,	Tolland,	1736,	lost.
Sherman,	Fairfield,	1744,	burned.
East Granby,	Hartford,	1737,	
Goshen,	Litchfield,	1740,	lost.
Watertown,	Litchfield,	1739,	lost.
Canton Center,	Hartford,	1750,	before 1826, lost.
So. Manchester,	Hartford,	1779,	
North Guilford,	New Haven,	1725,	lost.
East Lyme,	New London,	1719,	lost.
Lyme (Hamburgh),	New London,	1727,	lost.
West Haven,	New Haven,	1719,	before 1815, lost.
Litchfield,	Litchfield,	1721,	before 1886, burned.
Tolland,	Tolland,	1723,	burned.
Bethany,	New Haven,	1763,	before 1823, lost.
Andover,	Tolland,	1749,	B. and M. before 1818, burned at W. Springfield, Mass.
Glastonbury,	Hartford,	1693,	before 1797, lost.
Marlborough,	Hartford,	1749,	missing.
Harwinton,	Litchfield,	1738,	nothing before 1790.
Ridgefield,	Fairfield,	1714,	nothing before 1800.
Plymouth,	Litchfield,	1740,	no marriages before 1800.
Greenwich,	Fairfield,	1670,	nothing before 1787.
Greenwich, (Stanwich),	Fairfield,	1735,	burned 1821.
Torringford,	Litchfield,	1764,	burned, nothing before 1837.
East Haddam, (Hadlyme),	Middlesex,	1745,	no marriages before 1800, baptisms begin 1745.
Monroe,	Fairfield,	1764,	no marriages before 1821, baptisms begin 1776.
Bristol,	Hartford,	1747,	no marriages before 1792, baptisms begin 1800.
Suffield (West),	Hartford,	1744,	no records before 1840.
Eastford,	Windham,	1778,	no records before 1800.
Middlefield,	Middlesex,	1745,	no records before 1808.
Salisbury,	Litchfield,	1744,	few records before 1800.
Middletown (South),	Middlesex,	1747,	few records before 1800.

MILFORD.

NEW HAVEN COUNTY.

The town of Milford was settled in 1639. The First Congregational Church was organized August 22, 1639. While the church record of baptisms begins very early, the record of marriages is very incomplete, as the following list shows.

Newton Prudden & Elizabeth Northrop,	March 18, 1784
Phineas Baldwin & Abigail Woodruff,	March 31, 1784
Jehiel Bryan & Polly Treat,	April 29, 1784
Robert Treat & Content Bryan,	April 29, 1784
Elijah Bryan & Content Fowler,	Aug. 22, 1784
Daniel Burwell & Abigail Pardee,	Sept. 16, 1784
Richard Treat & Sarah Smith,	Sept. 23, 1784
Ebenezer Nettleton & Comfort Rogers,	Nov. 25, 1784
Ebenezer Smith & Abigail Baldwin,	Jan. 2, 1785
Andrew Smith & Sarah Fowler,	Jan. 16, 1785
Caleb Nettleton & Sarah Camp,	Feb. 3, 1785
Isaac Treat & Mehetable Platt,	Feb. 9, 1785
Joseph Smith & Susannah Fowler,	April 20, 1785
William Glenney & Polly Green,	June 28, 1785
John Stone & Esther Stow,	Sept. 11, 1785
William Phillips & Urani Buckingham,	Nov. 11, 1785
John Gibbs, Jr., & Sarah Jones,	Jan. 1, 1786
John Whiting & Nancy Welch,	Jan. 29, 1786
John Ford, Jr., & Ann Smith,	Feb. 15, 1786
Fowler Bryan & Ann Nettleton,	Feb. 22, 1786
Edmond Treat, age 75, & Elisabeth Uvit, age 21,	May 8, 1786
Stephen Gunn & Martha Hopkins, second wife, and she a widow,	Aug. 3, 1786
Johnson Heacock of Washington, Ct., & Mehetable Clark,	Aug. 27, 1786
Jonah Clark & Sarah Northrop,	Sept. 6, 1786
Moses Hine of Woodbridge & Susannah Woodruff,	Nov. 23, 1786
John Nettleton & Comfort Hine,	Nov. 29, 1786
Moses Hotchkiss of Derby & Sarah Bryan,	Jan. 25, 1787
Isaac Smith & Anna Clark,	Feb. 7, 1787

Samuel Treat & Sarah Nettleton,	June 28, 1787
Rev. Isaac Foster of Great Barrington & Esther Carrington,	
	Sept. 10, 1787
William Tomlinson & Jane Treat,	Nov. 1, 1787
Benedict Arnold Law. & Henrietta Gibbs,	Dec. 24, 1787
Samuel Beach & Betsy Ward,	Dec. 26, 1787
Amos Baldwin & Nancy Smith,	Dec. 27, 1787
Miles Mallett & Mary Ann Miles,	Jan. 2, 1788
Isaac Summers & Annah Fenn,	Jan. 27, 1788
Amos Ford & Eunice Treat,	April 28, 1788
Daniel Buckingham & Susanna Fowler,	May 15, 1788
Amos Clark & Sarah Summers,	May 25, 1788
Samuel Leavenworth Perry of Ripton & Anne Davidson,	
	June 1, 1788
Aaron Botsford & Comfort Seaton,	June 22, 1788
Nathan Fowler, Jr., & Sarah Platt,	July 9, 1788
Deacon Samuel Platt & widow Sybil Nettleton,	Aug. 20, 1788
John Foot & Sarah Baldwin,	Sept. 24, 1788
Isaac Fenn & Anne Hotchkiss,	Oct. 2, 1788
William Munson & Sarah Beardsley,	Jan. 29, 1789
John Treat & Esther Hine,	Feb. 26, 1789
Amos Clark & Eunice Clark,	April 12, 1789
Ezra Talmage & Elizabeth Clark,	Nov. 5, 1789
Benjamin Nettleton & Comfort Beard,	Dec. 9, 1789
Abraham V. H. DeWitt & Patty Pond, daughter of	
Capt. Charles Pond,	Jan. 3, 1790
David Turrell & Mary Northrop,	Jan. 12, 1790
Joseph Bradley Barlow & Sarah Merwin,	April 1, 1790
Samuel Curtis & Sarah Miles,	April 4, 1790
Benjamin Hodge & Elophal Mallery,	June 2, 1790
Peleg Baldwin & Anne Turrell,	Sept. 1, 1790
Oliver Clark & Sarah Northrop,	Sept. 2, 1790
David Baldwin & Abigail Bull,	Oct. 20, 1790
Daniel Treat & Elizabeth Bristol,	Nov. 1, 1790
Hon. James Davenport & Mehetable Coggeshall,	Nov. 6, 1790
Samuel Hine, Jr., & Polly Harlakin,	Feb. 3, 1791
William Durand & Mary Baldwin,	Feb. 13, 1791
Asa Platt & Martha Woodruff,	April 6, 1791
Josiah Treat & Rebecca Treat,	May 25, 1791

Francis Voluntine & Kata Fitzgerald,	July 11, 1791
Hezekiah Peck & Sally Bull,	Aug. 27, 1791
Richard Treat Davidson & Polly Stow,	Aug. 28, 1791
Theophilis Miles & Martha Clark,	Sept. 15, 1791
Edward Green Ray & Agnis Gillett,	Nov. 3, 1791
David Tomlinson & Anne Camp,	Nov. 6, 1791
David Nettleton & Mehetable Camp,	Dec. 5, 1791
Israel Isbell & Sarah Pardee,	Jan. 15, 1792
Peares Mann of Bristol & Frances Treat,	Feb. 6, 1792
Elias Carrington & Content Baldwin,	March 25, 1792
Samuel Beech & Charlotte Andrew,	April 11, 1792
David Treat & Mehetable Platt,	May 24, 1792
Fisk Platt & Sarah Newton,	Aug. 8, 1792
Isaac Smith & Phebe Platt,	Sept. 10, 1792
Daniel Bull and Elisabeth Durand,	Oct. 14, 1792
Newton John Morris & Eunice Newton,	Nov. 8, 1792
Silas Tracy & Susanna Baldwin,	Nov. 13, 1792
John Gunn & Martha Treat,	Nov. 15, 1792
Miles Hotchkiss & Aner Hepburn of N. Haven,	Nov. 18, 1792
Peter DeWitt & Susanna Stone,	Nov. 29, 1792
Samuel Wardain of Stratfield & Nancy Mallet,	Dec. 13, 1792
Henry Turner & Avis Mallet,	May 29, 1793
Henry Ward of West Haven & Catharine Gibb,	Oct. 20, 1793
John Jones of Southbury & Mabel Pardy,	Oct. 21, 1793
Caleb Tomlinson & Loisa Hopkins,	Nov. 7, 1793
John Miles, Jr., & Eunice Woodruff,	Nov. 14, 1793
Nathaniel Hepburn & Anna Merwin,	Dec. 5, 1793
James Davidson, Jr., & Sybil Baldwin,	June 23, 1795
Richard Smith & Julia Bryan,	Aug. 30, 1795
Amiel Camp & Elizabeth Camp,	Oct. 28, 1795
Samuel Peck & Mehetable Ingersoll,	Jan. 13, 1796
Joseph Green & Nancy Mallery,	March 3, 1796
Samuel Merwin & Susannah Nettleton,	March 9, 1796
Samuel Ufford of Stratford & Susanna Clark,	April 15, 1796
Levi Nettleton & Catharine Stow,	April 15, 1796
Jonah Platt & Hannah Clark,	Nov. 5, 1796
Daniel Gardner & Elizabeth Gillett,	Nov. 9, 1796
Elijah Treat & Esther Rhodes,	Dec. 8, 1796
William H. Fowler & Sally Pond, daughter of Charles Pond,	
	Dec. 18, 1796

2

Treat Clark & Sybel Nettleton,   Dec. 18, 1796
Thomas Finch & Esther Bryan,   Dec. 20, 1796
Michael Peck, Jr., & Polly Marshall,   Jan. 1, 1797
James Peck & Polly Hepburn,   Jan. 24, 1797
Isaac Miles & Susanna Carrington, daughter of Ed.,
                                                   Jan. 26, 1797
Nehemiah Woodruff & Hannah Jones,   March 5, 1797
James Beard & Phebe Newton,   March 12, 1797
Fenn Peck & Sally Treat,   April 2, 1797
Jonathan Clark & Polly Gillett,   April 3, 1797
Joel Scribner & Mary Bull,   June 21, 1797
Amos Camp & Mehitable Smith,   June 22, 1797
Joseph Woodruff & Mabel Nettleton,   July 6, 1797
Benedict Law, Jr., & Thankful Smith of West Haven,
                                                   Aug. 6, 1797
Phineas Stow & Polly Platt,   Aug. 14, 1797
John Welch Burwell & Abigail Ellis,   Sept. 22, 1797
James Hyndman & Thankful Humeston,   Oct. 23, 1797
Joseph Fowler & Abigail Baldwin,   Nov. 12, 1797
Barzillai Benjamin & Mary Wheeler of Stratford,
                                                   Nov. 16, 1797
Capt. Charles Pond married, 2d, Mrs. Catharine
    DeWitt, widow of Garrit,   Dec. 10, 1797
Samuel Buckingham Gunn & Catharine Miles,   Dec. 24, 1797
Samuel Miles Smith & Lucretia Down,   March 5, 1798
Daniel Munson & Fanny Tolles,   March 19, 1798
John Downs & Sarah Woodruff,   March 22, 1798
Joel Baldwin & Sally Rodes,   April 1, 1798
James Ryley & Betsey Eliot Marshall,   April 29, 1798
Mordecai Howman of L. I. & Polly Buckingham,
                                                   May 17, 1798
Nehemiah Bristol & Lorania Down,   June 3, 1798
David Atwater & Charlotte Pond, daughter of Charles,
                                                   Sept. 19, 1798
Hezekiah Baldwin & Mary Ann Hine, daughter of Joel,
                                                   Nov. 7, 1798
Harry Bronson of Waterbury & Fanny Munson,
                                                   Nov. 29, 1798
Edward Brown of Campbeltown, Argyleshire, Scot-
    land, & Eunice Gillett,   Jan. 5, 1799

Lewis Alling of New Haven & Elizabeth Clark, Jan. 6, 1799
Josiah Boardman & Sarah Woodruff, daughter of
   Matthew,   Jan. 8, 1799
William Fenn & Mary Fenn,   Feb. 9, 1799
Eliphalet Sanford & Abigail Platt,   March 10, 1799
Nathan Fowler & Mehetable Platt,   May 10, 1799
Joel Woodruff & Hannah Clark,   June 30, 1799
Isaac Bristol & Abigail Pardie,   Sept. 23, 1799
Nathan Hine & Mary Smith,   Oct. 9, 1799
Stephen Summers & Jane Miles,   Dec. 15, 1799

MILFORD—Continued.

The Second Congregational Church in Milford, called Plymouth Church, was organized in
1741. The following are all the marriages recorded before 1800.

Nathan Smith of Derby & Sarah Northrop,   Nov. 4, 1747
Rev. Eleazer Wheelock of Lebanon & Mrs. Mary
   Brinsmade,   Nov. 24, 1747
John Tibbals & Deborah Downs,   June 22, 1748
Cuff & Pitty (negroes),   April 13, 1749
William Gillet & Phebe Terrel,   Sept. 7, 1749
Job Clark & Jane Northrop,   Sept. 28, 1749
Robin (Indian) & Sue,   Oct. 5, 1749
John Peck & Sarah Plat,   Feb. 15, 1750
Henry Peck & Rachel Lambert,   May 15, 1751
Daniel Allen & Darnel Smith,   Sept. 20, 1751
Elisha Gillet & Sarah Buckingham,   April 13, 1753
Jehiel Brian & Esther Buckingham,   June 4, 1753
John Gillet & Comfort Plum,   Aug. 5, 1753
Benjamin Pritchet & Martha Lambert,   Aug. 23, 1753
Daniel Judson & Lois Clark,   Dec. 26, 1754
David Heecock & Sarah Dewolf,   Feb. 2, 1755
Samuel Frost & Betty Newton,   May 1, 1755
Deacon Judson & Mrs. Abigail Clark,   Jan. 10, 1756
Nehemiah Woodcock & Elisabeth Collins,   Dec. 25, 1756
John Durand & Ann Down,   Dec. 29, 1756
Isaac Hine & Ann Bristol,   Jan. 12, 1757

Hezekiah Hine & Eunice Bristol,	Jan. 30, 1757
Benjamin Peck & Anna Smith,	Feb. 3, 1757
David Lambert & Martha Northrop,	March 8, 1757
John Woodruff & Hannah Lambert,	March 13, 1757
Abraham Bristol & Susanna Colbreath,	April 18, 1757
Nathan Nettleton & Sybel Buckingham,	Nov. 3, 1757
Elihu Sanford & Hannah Sanford,	June 28, 1758
Fitch Kimberly & Abigail Woodruff,	July 6, 1758
Abijah Buckingham & Hannah Byington,	Jan. 11, 1759
Gideon Sanford & Jane Colbreath,	Feb. 1, 1759
Abel Summers & Lois Bristol,	Dec., 1759
Andrew Baldwin & Mary Hine,	March 26, 1760
William Stevens & Abigail Sanford,	Oct. 1, 1760
Capt. Matthew Minor & Mrs. Rachel Sanford,	Dec. 17, 1760
George Leere (?) & Elizabeth Woodcock,	May 26, 1761
Nathan Fowler & Susanna Miles,	July 14, 1761
Ralph Isaacs & Mary Perrit,	Sept. 8, 1761
Fitch Welch & Martha Clark,	Feb. 16, 1762
Josiah Camp & Elisabeth Gunn,	April 7, 1762
Isaac Clark & Hannah Fowler,	July 20, 1762
Jonathan Fowler & Sarah Johnson,	Dec. 7, 1762
Samuel Sanford & Hannah Tomlinson,	Dec. 20, 1762
Hiel Bristol & Elizabeth Hine,	July 22, 1763
Nehemiah Woodcock & Hannah Bristol,	Nov. 13, 1763
John Underwood & Mary Jordan,	Dec. 22, 1763
Abraham Hine & Sarah Bristol,	May 29, 1764
Timothy Minor of Woodbury & Elisabeth Downs,	
	June 5, 1764
Samuel Terrel, Jr., & Ann Baldwin,	Aug. 19, 1764
Benjamin Peck & Sarah Smith,	Nov. 21, 1764
Peter Hepburn & Mary Cobb,	Nov. 22, 1764
David Hine & Susanna Newton,	Dec. 29, 1764
Samuel Platt, Jr., & Sybel Stronge,	March 5, 1765
Alexander Oviat & Penelope Charles,	April 1, 1765
Samuel Sanford, Jr., & Parthenia Baldwin,	July 26, 1765
Benjamin Fenn, 3d, & Sarah Treat,	Oct. 31, 1765
Barnabus Woodcock & Freelove H——,	Nov. 27, 1765
John Colbreath & Eunice Tuttle,	Dec. 5, 1765
John Jones & Sarah Hawley,	Dec. 5, 1765

(Intervening period, pages lost).

Stephen Gunn, Jr., & Sally Peck,	Nov. 5, 1794
Freegift Coggeshall & Polly Pond,	Nov. 26, 1794
Jesse Peck Lambert & Amy Clark,	Nov. 27, 1794
Elisha Treat & Mehetable Treat,	Dec. 25, 1794
John Plumb, Jr., & Sybil Smith,	Jan. 11, 1795
Richard Marks & Content Summers,	Jan. 21, 1795
—— Geneson of Southbury & widow Martha Clark,	
	Jan. 27, 1795
Amos Smith & Sally Beers,	Feb. 19, 1795
Peter Short & Frances Malery,	Feb. 19, 1795
Pomp Jesen & Sarah Ingrum,	Feb. 22, 1795
Benjamin Morehouse of Greensfarms & Temperance Cables,	
	March 15, 1795
Joseph Roads & Frances Bristol,	May 7, 1795
Samuel Downs & Jane Woodruff,	May 28, 1795
Nathaniel Nettleton & Susanna Martin,	June 14, 1795
Moses Jennings of Fairfield & the widow Martha Welch,	
	Sept. 24, 1795
Elisha Edwards of Berlin & Sally Fenn,	Nov. 26, 1795
John Welch & Anne Frost,	Dec. 31, 1795
Nando Brinsmade & Olive Mansfield,	May 19, 1796
Richard Platt, Jr., & Margaret Fowler,	June 6, 1796
Isaac Mallet & Sally Brintnal,	June 12, 1796
Lemuel Durand & Catharine Smith,	June 16, 1796
John L. Daniels & Patta Smith,	June 26, 1796
Richard Hine & Susanna Mitchel,	July 31, 1796
Beard Baldwin & Sibil Clark,	Aug. 24, 1796
Joseph Peck of Newtown & Anne Andrews,	Oct. 2, 1796
Elias Andrews & Huldah Rogers,	Oct. 6, 1796
Capt. Samuel Stow & Lovice Tomlinson,	Oct. 16, 1796
Abel Oviatt & Margaret Mallory,	Oct. 16, 1796
Andrew Hine & Abigail Prince,	Dec. 4, 1796
Josiah Rogers & Sally Andrews,	Jan. 3, 1797
John Smith, Jr., & Abigail Burn,	April 16, 1797
Capt. Samuel Tibballs & Esther Cady, alias Stone,	
	June 7, 1797
David Foster & Fally Baldwin,	Oct. 5, 1797

Major Ezra Fellows of Sheffield & widow Sarah Fenn,
                                        Oct. 23, 1797
Eli Woodruff & Polly Fenn,   Feb. 4, 1798
Jehiel Bristol & Martha Beecher of N. Haven, March 22, 1798
Enoch Clark & Margaret Butrick,   June 10, 1798
John Butric & Polly Seward,   Dec. 16, 1798
John D. Perry & Theresa Carlavan, both from the
    West Indies,   Dec. 23, 1798
Daniel Suard & Sally Way,   Dec. 23, 1798
John Lambert & Esther Woodruff,   Jan. 3, 1799
David Engersol & Patty Malery,   May 14, 1799
Jirah Bull & Elizabeth Atwater,   May 23, 1799
John Basset & Susannah Bristol,   Aug. 25, 1799

NORTH BRANFORD.

NEW HAVEN COUNTY.

The town of North Branford was incorporated in May, 1858, taken from Branford. The Congregational Church at North Branford, called Northford, was organized June 13, 1750.

Jonah Todd & Esther Harrison,   Nov. 12, 1750
Amos Seaward & Ruth Rogers,   Jan. 16, 1750-1
Benjamin Farnum & Mary Howd,   March 7, 1750-1
Berijah Tyler & Hannah Hall,   April 17, 1751
Timothy Pond & Mary Munson,   June 20, 1751
Joshua Dudley & Elisabeth Finch,   Nov. 20, 1751
Ezekiel Frisbe & Elisabeth Pardee,   Feb. 18, 1752
Josiah Bartholomew & Phebe Munson,   April 9, 1752
Abiel Linsly, Jr., & Thankful Pond,   Oct. 5, 1752
Nathaniel Tainter & Submit Tyler,   Jan. 4. 1753
Wise Barns & Hannah Bartholomew,   Jan. 18, 1753
John Thompson & Mary Hoadly,   Feb. 22, 1753
Daniel Heaton & Ruth Harrison,   Sept. 13, 1753
Ensign William Stebbins & widow Thankful Pond,
                                        May 15, 1753
Uriah Collins & Lydia Cook,   May 23, 1754
Thomas Pardee & Lois Bradley,   Nov. 28, 1754
Deacon Daniel Benton & widow Sarah Seaward, Jan. 1, 1755

Daniel Foot & Mary Ingraham,	Feb. 13, 1755
Stephen Harrison & Susanna Bartholomew,	March 17, 1755
Samuel Bartholomew & widow Hannah Tyler,	March 20, 1755
Gideon Baldwin & Thankful Barns,	April 2, 1755
Joseph Finch & widow Chloe Talmadge,	Sept. 16, 1755
Nathan Butler & Rebekah Rogers,	Dec. 18, 1755
Samuel Bishop & Hannah Page,	March 9, 1757
Titus Munson & Lydia Linsly,	Sept. 22, 1757
Deacon Merriman Munson & widow Thankful Peck,	
	Jan. 23, 1758
David Tyler & Sybil Ingraham,	Jan. 26, 1758
Abraham Post & Lydia Palmer,	March 28, 1758
Stephen Darin & Lucy Page,	Oct. 26, 1758
Daniel Linsly & Anne Tyler,	Nov. 13, 1758
Solomon Seaward & Elenor Baldwin,	Dec. 27, 1758
Stephen Todd & Rachel Johnson,	Feb. 12, 1759
Josiah Talmadge & Sybil Todd,	March 15, 1759
Phinehas Baldwin & Mary Harrison,	Sept. 6, 1759
Solomon Munson & Sarah Munson,	Oct. 11, 1759
Phinehas Baldwin & Martha Peck,	Jan. 1, 1761
Joseph Foot & Abigail Winchel,	Feb. 26, 1761
David Tyler & Sarah Bartholomew,	June 28, 1761
John Munson & Lydia Todd,	July 2, 1761
Solomon Munson & Hannah Baldwin,	Nov. 19, 1761
Wilkinson Howd & Thankful Peck,	Dec. 17, 1761
Ashbel Porter & Hannah Norris,	Nov. 24, 1762
Asa Jones & Abigail Bunnel,	Jan. 27, 1763
David Frisbe & Mary Whedon,	April 7, 1763
Jared Foot & Submit Bishop,	May 12, 1763
Daniel Maltbie, Jr., & Margaret Munson,	Dec. 22, 1763
Peter Tyler & Hannah Tyler,	Feb. 16, 1764
Benjamin Ingraham & Lydia Finch,	May 23, 1764
Samuel Foot & Anne Harrison,	Dec. 28, 1764
Samuel Brown & Mary Maltbie,	Feb. 20, 1765
John Crowfoot & Sarah Burgess,	May 9, 1765
Whitehead Howd & Dorcas Tyler,	Nov. 6, 1765
George Baldwin & Hannah Frisbie,	July 2, 1766
Joshua Austin & Susanna Page,	April 17, 1766
Moses Munson & Abigail Munson,	Jan. 22, 1767

Rufus Hoadly & Ruth Peck,	May 28, 1767
Jared Butler & Elisabeth Dorchester,	Nov. 19, 1767
Isaac Foot & Lydia Tyler,	April 24, 1768
Nathaniel Munson & Avis Hopson,	May 19, 1768
Isaac Linsly & Esther Munson,	June 30, 1768
Silas Benton & Abigail Linsly,	July 6, 1768
Phinehas Curtiss & Mary Elwell,	Jan. 16, 1769
Jonathan Tyler & Elisabeth Linsley,	Dec. 28, 1769
Jairus Bunnel & Lydia Baldwin,	March 14, 1770
Moses Page & widow Abia Butler,	Nov. 26, 1771
Edward Harrison & Sarah Dudley,	Dec. 21, 1771
Ozias Norton & Miriam Frisbe,	March 11, 1772
John Beach & Mary Todd,	Oct. 4, 1772
Jared Tainter & Rebekah Linsly,	Dec. 31, 1772
Dan Munro & Abigail Allen,	May, 1773
Elihu Baldwin & Abigail Rogers,	Nov. 25, 1773
Dick ——— (negro) & Mary Lattomore (Indian),	
	Feb. 23, 1774
John Norton & Sarah Tainter,	March 24, 1774
Stephen Olds & Clorinda Howd,	July 31, 1774
Joseph Brockway & Achsah Potter,	Oct. 24, 1774
John Baldwin & Catharine Seaward,	Nov. 10, 1774
Joseph Russel & Martha Rogers,	May 25, 1775
Joseph Jacobs & Lydia Jacobs,	June 21, 1775
Abijah Rogers & Lydia .Harrison,	Aug. 9, 1775
Levi Cooper & Thankful Dayton,	Dec. 6, 1775
Samuel Bartholomew, Jr., & Irene Munson,	May 14, 1776
Jeremiah Cornwell & Lydia Sperry,	Oct. 24, 1776.
John Augur, Jr., & Dinah Page,	Nov. 24, 1776
Stephen Cook, Jr., & Sylvia Meigs,	April 20, 1777
Capt. Stephen Cook & widow Ann Linsly,	Nov. 20, 1777
Benjamin Maltbie, Jr., & Rebekah Tainter,	Jan. 22, 1778
Stephen Williams & Eunice Tainter,	Jan. 22, 1778
William Whedon & Mary Farnum,	April 24, 1778
Jonathan Munson & Mary Tainter,	July 16, 1778
Hezekiah Reynolds & Martha Wolcott,	Sept. 16, 1778
Houston Henman & Mercy Palmer,	Jan. 21, 1779
George Howe & widow Sarah Wetherill,	Feb. 11, 1779
Josiah Fowler, Jr., & Lydia Hoadly,	Feb. 17, 1779

Charles Parmele & Mary Tyler,	May 20, 1779
Caleb Cook & Sarah Heaton,	Jan. 13, 1780
Phinehas Fowler & Dorothy Baldwin,	Jan. 19, 1780
Elnathan Tyler & Elisabeth Maltbie,	March 16, 1780
Capt. Benjamin Baldwin & Lydia Goodsell,	April 27, 1780
Jonathan Bartholomew & Anne Cook,	June 8, 1780
John Smith & Anne Cook,	Oct. 16, 1780
Capt. Amos Beecher & Rebekah Abbot,	Nov. 23, 1780
Capt. Timothy Hoadly & widow Rebekah Tainter,	
	Jan. 28, 1781
Daniel Jones & Elisabeth Frisbe,	Jan. 2, 1782
Joseph Sutby (?) & widow Catharine Baldwin,	Jan. 17, 1782
Benjamin Culver & Martha Howd,	March 7, 1782
Moses Gaylord & Jemima Tyler,	May 30, 1782
Jonathan Frisbie & Elisabeth Bartholomew,	June 22, 1782
Abiathar Rogers & Naomi Rose,	July 4, 1782
John Plymet & Abigail Foot,	Sept. 5, 1782
Timothy Bartholomew & Abigail Munson,	Dec. 5, 1782
Waitstill Munson & Elisabeth Frisbe,	Jan. 15, 1783
Abraham Corey & Elisabeth Beach,	April 24, 1783
Rev. Jason Atwater & Anne Williams,	Dec. 7, 1784
Abraham Norton & Elisabeth Farnum,	Dec. 16, 1784
Solomon Fowler & Olive Douglass,	Jan. 26, 1786
Jacob Bunnel, Jr., & Hannah Hotchkiss,	March 28, 1786
Nathaniel Johnson & Sarah Tyler,	April 13, 1786
James Linsly & Sarah Maltbie,	Sept. 28, 1786
Lieut. Robert Griffing & Elisabeth Baldwin,	Oct. 16, 1786
John Page & widow Rosanna Maltbie,	Nov. 30, 1786
Eli Smith & Hannah Howd,	Jan. 4, 1787
Jonathan Rose & Hannah Rose,	April 1, 1787
Jonathan Maltbie, A. M., & Submit Tainter,	June 17, 1787
David Staples & Clarissa Kimberly,	Oct. 17, 1790
Ebenezer Allen & Sally Kimberly,	June 5, 1791
John Maltbie & Elisabeth Ives,	Oct. 5, 1791
Jude Smith of N. Haven & Olive Foot,	Nov. 23, 1791
Philo Hopson of Wallingford & Anna Norton,	Dec. 11, 1791
Isaac Linsly & Martha Russel,	Dec. 18, 1791
Jesse Cooper & Sarah Beach of N. Haven,	Dec. 21, 1791
Samuel Foot, Jr., & Submit Foot,	Jan. 1, 1792

Phinehas Baldwin, Jr., & Molly Finch,   March 28, 1792
Mack Daniels & Elisabeth Hawkins,   June 7, 1792
Daniel Linsly & Sally Baldwin,   Sept. 23, 1792
Edward Howd & Chloe Linsly,   Dec. 6, 1792
Daniel Rose & Anna Russel of N. Branford,   Oct. 7, 1793
Joshua Atwater of Wallingford & Betsy Cook,   Oct. 22, 1793
Amos Dutton of Wallingford & Hannah Douglass,

                                               Nov. 10, 1793
Morris Maltbie & Sybil Todd,   Dec. 12, 1793
Munson Lindsly & Anna Foot,   Jan. 1, 1794
Samuel Merwin of Batavia, N. Y., & Thankful Parker
    of Wallingford,   Feb. 10, 1794
Kilburn Cook & Eunice Williams,   Feb. 13, 1794
Billy Evarts & Eunice Tyler,   June 1, 1794
Levi Fowler & Fanny Clark,   Oct. 2, 1794
Stephen Frisbie of Branford & Anna Kirkum of N.
    Guilford,   Oct. 20, 1794
Rheuben Harrison & Sarah Foot,   Jan. 1, 1795
John Elliot & Sarah Harlow,   Jan. 21, 1795
Benjamin Munson & Betsey Humaston,   Jan. 29, 1795
Constant Abbot & Thankful Hammond,   Oct. 18, 1795
Amaziah Rose & Abigail Munson,   Dec. 23, 1795
John Gills of North Haven & Lucy Foot,   Feb. 29, 1796
Jesse Mix & Rebecca Gilbert of New Haven,   April 9, 1796
Capt. Isaac Foot & Phebe Benton,   Sept. 20,1796
Bela Peck & Eunice Munson of Wallingford,   Nov. 6, 1796
Dr. Benjamin Rockwell of Norwalk & Rebecca Foot,

                                               Nov. 27, 1796
Eli Smith & Polly Whitney,   April 16, 1797
Col. Jonathan Todd & Sally Fowler,   Jan. 11, 1798
John Street & Lois Page,   Dec. 30, 1798
Lemuel Lewis of Southington & Sally Lindsly,   Jan. 9, 1799
Isaac Fowler of Guilford & Assene Hopson of Wal-
    lingford,   Feb. 16, 1799
Ruphas Foot & Elisabeth Harrison,   March 12, 1799
Thomas Dawson & Chloe Howd,   Oct. 22, 1799
Augustus Russell & Lydia Rose of North Branford,

                                               April 6, 1800

Mansfield Sperry & Assene Sperry of Woodbridge,
Aug. 10, 1800
Moses Barns & Sally Bartholomew,   May 26, 1800
Charles Anthony & Nabby Baldwin of Wallingford,
Oct. 30, 1800
Timothy Eliott, Jr., & Lydia Bartholomew,   Dec. 14, 1800

KENT.

LITCHFIELD COUNTY.

The town of Kent was incorporated in October, 1739. The Congregational Church was organized April 29, 1741.

Samuel Beats (?) & Rachel Fuller,   July 16, 1741
Theo. Skeel & Prudence Slosson,   Sept. 25, 1741
Barnabas Delano & Ruth Pack,   May 4, 1742
Samuel Crippin of Sharon & Keziah Algur of Statekook (?),
Feb. 23, 1742-3
Sylvanus Hatch & Mehetable Hubble,   April 14, 1743
Jonathan Skeel & Abigail Slosson,   May 11, 1743
Ebenezer Pack of Cornwell & Mercy Castle,   Nov. 8, 1743
Amos Barnum & Jemima Hall,   April 11, 1744
Ebenezer Barnum, Jr., & Elizabeth Skiff,   July 25, 1745
John Cahoon & Grace Fuller,   Dec. 25, 1745
Jabez Rowley, Jr., & Mary Hambleton,   April 17, 1746
John Beeman & Sarah Thomson,   Nov. 5, 1746
Joseph Crippin of Sharon & Tabitha Rowley,   May 7, 1747
Gideon Roots of Woodbury & Mercy Roberts,   May 28, 1747
Abel Comstock & Judith Pain,   Sept. 17, 1747
John Beach of Stratford & Rebekah Berry,   Aug. 23, 1748
Daniel Slosson & Eunice Lasells,   Aug. 23, 1748
Josiah Thomas, Jr., & Sarah Judd,   Oct. 12, 1748
William Tanner of Cornwell & Hannah Newcomb,
March 23, 1749
Jonas Beemas of Worcestershire & Abiah Matthews
of Dover, N. Y.,   April 18, 1749
Reuben McWethy & Zerviah Whitney of Plainfield,
Nov. 1, 1749

John Beebe, Jr., & Mary Hill,   Nov. 9, 1749
Asa Parish & Mindwell Fuller,   Nov. 23, 1749
James Walling & Hannah Pratt,   Feb. 22, 1749
Ephraim Hubbell, Jr., & Alice Spooner,   April 4, 1751
Joseph Fuller, Jr., & Zerviah Hill,   Aug. 10, 1752
Miles Washburn & Sarah Lyon,   Oct. 12, 1752
Reuben Sackett & Mercy Finney of East Greenwich
    in Kent,   Dec. 21, 1752
Moses Palmer & Phebe Brownson of East Greenwich
    in Kent,   Jan. 4, 1753
Jeremiah Fuller & Lydie Mills,   Jan. 11, 1753
Levi Crocker & Freelove Pain of East Greenwich in Kent,
                                                          Feb. 27, 1753
Benjamin Johns of New York Province & Eunice Rowlee,
                                                          April 24, 1753
John Vaughan of Lebanon & Anna Beebe,   June 30, 1753
John Hambleton & Susanna Slosson,   Dec. 5, 1753
Gershon Comstock & Lydia Pratt,   Feb. 20, 1754
George Bugby & Dorothy Palmer of Nine Partners,
                                                          April 9, 1754
Simeon Kelsey & Nelly Sackett of Dover, N. Y., Aug. 22, 1754
John Swan, Jr., & Elizabeth McWealthy,   Aug. 27, 1754
David Bates of Kent & Nelly Ousterhout of Dover,
                                                          Sept. 15, 1754
Thomas Burns of Kent & Elisabeth Printrupp (?) of
    Nine Partners,   Oct. 8, 1754
Jedediah Hubbell of Kent & Lucia Noble of New Preston,
                                                          Dec. 25, 1754
Benjamin Eaton of Holland & Hepzibah Skiff, Jan. 29, 1755
David Ferris of New Milford & Abigail Comstock,
                                                          Feb. 26, 1755
Nathaniel Porter of Sharon & Zerviah Wadsworth of
    Dover, N. Y.,   March 13, 1755
Noah French & Hannah Riggs, both of Derbe, June 12, 1755
Rev. Cyrus Marsh & Mrs Abigail Marvin of Sharon,
                                                          Aug. 5, 1755
Rev. Cyrus Marsh & Mrs. Susanna Dow of Plainfield,
                                                          April 25, 1757
                (Next record begins 1813).

NORTH CANAAN.

LITCHFIELD COUNTY.

The town of North Canaan was incorporated in May, 1858, taken from Canaan. The Congregational Church in North Canaan was organized December 5, 1769.

Robert Rood & Mary Rowe,	May 5, 1770
Paul Raymond of Richmond & Rachel Stevens,	Oct. 11, 1770
Abel Stevens & Rachel Fellows,	Oct. 11, 1770
Daniel Richards of Sheffield & Sarah Freeman,	Nov. 13, 1770
Asa Lawrence & Lucy Miller,	Jan. 29, 1771
John Watson of Norfolk & Sarah Douglas,	Jan. 31, 1771
Elisha Freeman & Chloe Stevens,	May 5, 1771
Rozil Fellows & Mary Partridge,	July 5, 1771
William Hamilton of Norfolk & Dorothy Cornish,	July 4, 1771
Ira Rowlinson & Hannah Lane,	July 18, 1771
Ezekiel Hamilton of Norfolk and Mary Stevens,	Aug. 1, 1771
John Freeman & Anne Fellows,	Oct. 23, 1771
Elihu Higby of Middletown & Martha Green,	Dec. 22, 1771
Samuel Ward & Hannah Lee,	Dec. 25, 1771
Daniel Richards of Sheffield & Huldah Fellows,	Feb. 6, 1772
Oliver Wilcox & Rebecca Doolitle, both of Goshen,	Jan. 10, 1773
Robert Green of Sheffield & Mary Shailor of Haddam,	Jan. 10 (?) 18, 1773
Asa North & Susanna Newell,	Feb. 11, 1773
Jeremiah Baker & Anna Stevens,	March 4, 1773
Nathan Newel & Lydia Rood,	March 15, 1773
Dan Huxley & Ruhamah Holcomb,	March 25, 1773
Isaac Craw of New Marlboro & Elisabeth Miller,	June 3, 1773
Stephen Harrison & Susanna Franklin,	July 29, 1773
Zebulon Stevens & widow Thankful Partridge,	Oct. 13, 1773
Phineas Derby & Sarah Stevens,	Nov. 25, 1773
Robert Bra(?)ford & Sarah Cornish,	Dec. 4, 1773
Edward Brownell & Susanna Wells,	Jan. 26, 1774
John Franklin, Jr., & Lydia Doolittle,	Feb. 2, 1774
Andrew Lester of Canterbury & Lydia Partridge,	July 28, 1774

Wooden Sperry & Anna Lawrence,   Sept. 8, 1774
Samuel Barnett & Lydia Hyde,   Nov. 10 or 16, 1774
William Jackway & Rachel Root,   Nov. 30, 1774
Samuel Green of Canaan & Anna Clark of Sheffield,
                                             Feb. 23, 1775

CORNWALL.

LITCHFIELD COUNTY.

The town of Cornwall was incorporated May, 1740. The Congregational Church at same time, May, 1740. "The first vote passed at this town meeting, after the election of town officers, was 'to provide for the preaching of the Gospel among them.'"

Samuel Smalley & Hannah Duglas,   Jan. 19, 1756
Daniel Elmer & Ruth Ford,   Nov. 14, 1756
Able Abbit & Hannah Dibble,   Feb. 16, 1757
Nathan Abbit & Mercy Daily,   Feb. 23, 1757
Timothy Cole & Rebekah Dibble,   April 5, 1757
Benoney Peck & Mehitable Millard,   April 7, 1757
Elijah Strong & Elizabeth Dailey,   May 5, 1757
John Clother & Eunice Squire,   July 5, 1757
Gilbert Harrison & Thankful Townsend,   July 28, 1757
Hezekiah Ford & Deborah Chandler,   Dec. 7, 1757
Moses Dean & Hannah Tanner,   May 17, 1757
Edward Bumpus (?) & Susannah Dean,   March 8, 1758
Jonathan Chandler & Sarah Bierce,   April 13, 1758
Thomas Carter & Abigail How,   Aug. 31, 1758
John Pierce & Luce How,   Aug. 31, 1758
John Tanner & Jemima Bishop,   Sept. 14, 1758
Neamiah Bierce & Mary Bishop,   Sept. 14, 1758
Talmage Bishop & Lovis Burr,   Nov. 22, 1758
William Pierce & Sarah Bishop,   March 9, 1758
Solomon Johnson & Ellaner Pierce,   Sept. 28, 1758
John Dibble & Ester Mackquaver,   May 7, 1759
William Johnson & Mercy How,   May 31, 1759
Captain John Jeffers & Mary Howland,   July 22, 1760
Doctor Thomas Russel & Mary Patterson,   Oct. 7, 1760
John Millard, Jr., & Christiana Rust,   1760
Nathan Millard & Submit Bayley,   June (?) 29, 1761

Samuel Scophel & Mary Rowland,	1761
Cele Abbit & Ann Jones,	1761
Jethro Bonney & Rachel Bailey,	1761
Ambros Clother & Mary May,	1761
John Pangborn & Sarah Wood,	Nov., 1761
Daniel Squire & Hannah Abbit,	Feb. 19, 1761
Joshua Harris & Ruth Symmons,	1761
Noah Bull & Mary Jeffers,	1761
Isaac Bates & Jemima Carter,	1761
Elijah Dickerson & Rachel Harris (?),	1761
——— Boogue & widow Hannah Smalley,	1761
Clemens Dibble & Rhode Dibble,	March 13, 1762
Thomas Fleming & Mary Dean,	Aug., 1762
Benjamin Dean & Ruth Tanner,	Oct. 14, 1762
Israel Dibble & Elizabeth Millard,	March 3, 1763
Martin Dudley & Anna Dudley,	June 21, 1763
John Bishop & Mary Perce,	Oct. 2, 1763
Jesse Squire & Lidea Clother,	Dec. 15, 1763
Timothy Spaulding & Mary Squier,	Jan. 25, 1764
Levi Pierce & Elisebeth Mackgalpin,	Aug. 4, 1764
Esquire ——— Judd of Westbury & Mrs. Ann Sedgwick,	Aug. 4, 1764
Levi Bonney & Mary May,	Oct. 4, 1764
Isaac Balding & Elisebeth Penick (?),	Nov. 15, 1764
Samuel Emmons & Hanar (?) Jennings,	June 12, 1764
Zachariah Jones & Jane Dibble,	May 3, 1766
Andrus Young & Marget Mitchel,	June 17, 1766
Timothy Spaulding & Abigail Brunson,	Jan. 13, 1769
Ebenezer Sherwood & Hannah Bradford,	Jan. 2, 1772
Consider Tanner & Rachel Benedict,	March 3, 1772
Mathew Lyon & Mary Horsford,	June 23, 1773
Edward Rogers & Hannah Jackson,	July 18, 1773
David Dibble & Mehitable Garnsey,	Oct. 28, 1772
Salmon Emmons & Hannah Jeffers,	Nov. 5, 1772
John Hart & Ester Hand,	Nov., 1774
Joseph Wadsworth & Eunis Duglas,	Nov., 1774
Daniel Bishop & Eunis Paterson,	Nov. 27 (?), 1774
Thomas White & Ann Abbit,	Sept., 1774
Rufus Pain & Agnis Findla (?),	Feb. 17, 1774

Samuel Brunson & Johannah Balding,	March, 1775
Lemuel Gillet & Mercy Jackson,	May 29, 1775
Linus Beech (?) & Elisebeth Abbit,	May 31, 1775
James Berce & Elisbeth Gillit,	March, 1776
Thomas Dean & Olive Willobey,	April 23, 1776
Joshua Hartshorn & Huldah Dibbil,	Oct. 29, 1776
Bial Tanner & Huldah Jackson,	May 12, 1777
Solomon Emmons & Sabra Canfield,	May 22, 1778
Jonathan Bell & Susannah Canfield,	May 19, 1779
Ichabod Brown & Submitte Millard,	June 26, 1780
John Dean & Martha Scott,	Oct. 12, 1780
Theophilus Bisshop & Sarah Beach,	Dec. 7, 1780
Abner Lasel (?) & Cloe Millard,	May 11, 1781
Elias Hart & Philomele Burnham,	June 14, 1781
Benjamin Abbit & Huldah Beach,	June 27, 1781
Joel Tuttle (?) & Rebekah Bierce,	Oct. 2, 1781
Jones Cole & Anner Stetson,	July 25, 1782
Darius Hand & Elizebeth Catlin,	Nov., 1782
John Dibble, 2d, & Elisebeth Carter,	Nov. 6, 1782
Israel Everest & Anna How,	March 30, 1783
Silas Hart & Anne Pierce,	April 17, 1783
David Crocker & Hannah Beach,	June 11, 1783
William Chistester & Martha Dean,	Oct., 1783
Aaron Balding & Spedy Hart,	Oct. 1, 1783

Solomon Johnson & Rebecah Pain,
Thanksgiving Day, Dec. 11, 1783

Asaph Emmons & Nance Sealey,	Aug. 11, 1784
Benjamin Gold & Elliner Johnson,	Nov. 26, 1784
Samuel Scophel & Mary Emmons,	Dec. 2, 1784
Curtiss Lake & Marget Clarey (?),	Dec. 2, 1784
Jasper Pratt & Abigal Butler,	Dec. 30, 1784
Elisha Bradford & Lucy Rosseter,	Aug. 20, 1786

——— Bayley of Danbury & widow Mary Dibble,
Nov. 24, 1786

William Bayley of Sharon & widow Mabel Dibble,
Nov. 26, 1786

Aron Morrils of Goshen & Ruth Page of Litchfield,
Nov. 15, 1786

——— Everett (?) of Sharon & Rhoda Peck,	Nov. 17, 1786

William Bierc & Abigal Bell, Jan. 17, 1787
———— Luddenton & Polle Stuart (?), Nov. 24, 1787
Jabez (?) Swift & Abigal Johnson, Nov. 28, 1787
David Patterson & Abigal Jones, Dec. 6, 1787
Joel Millard & Asuba Sherwood, Jan. 16, 1788
William Brace & Mary Moss, Jan. 22, 1788
———— Warner & Rachel Crocker, Jan. 23, 1788
Thomas Ruggles Gold & Salle Sill, Feb. 14, 1788
Nathaniel Peck & Elizebeth Beach, Feb. 24, 1788
———— Lindley & a daughter of Mr. Rous, March 6, 1788
———— Chickeston & Huldah ————, May, 1788
Neamiah Clark & Lorain Pierc, April 9, 1788
Hebe—k (?) Crooner & widow Hannah Sherwood,
Sept. 30, 1788
Hezekiah Gold, Jr., & Rachel Wadsworth, Oct., 1788
Samuel Rexford & Lidea Millard, Nov. 6, 1788
General Heman Swift & Elliner Johnson, Dec. 8, 1788
James Wright & Hannah Wood, Nov. 23, 1788
Seth Abbit & Salle Beebe of Danbury, Jan. 1, 1789
Ebenezer Birdsey & Sarah Bell, March 8, 1789
Isaac Dibble & Rebecah Dibble, July 20, 1789
———— Hays of New York state & ———— Dean, Dec. 24, 1789
Joseph M. Wood & Mary Wood, Oct. 14, 1789
Theodore Abbit & Rhode Preston, July 11, 1790
Rouel Hotchkiss & Anner Brunson, March 2, 1790
Shepherd & Ruth May, March 18, 1790
Samuel Abbit & Mary Wood, March 19, 1790
Benjamin Bell & Jane Patterson, Feb. 29, 1792
Eli Bierce & Charry Landern, June 20, 1792
Doctor Jon. Calhoon & Polly Swift, July 1, 1792
Joseph Judson & Hannah Paterson, July 8, 1792
Austine Bierce, Jr., & Zerviah Bryant, Nov. 27, 1792
Cesar, a free negro man from Litchfield, & Peg, a
negro woman, freed by the Rev. Mr. Gold's heirs,
Nov. 29, 1792
Charles Jackson & Abigail Andrews from Wallingford,
Oct. 1, 1793
MacAlpine Pierce & Patience Barnes of Canaan, Oct. 2, 1793
Caleb Andrews & Patience Jackson, Oct. 17, 1793

Ebenezer Jeffers & Mary Frost Clarke,   Nov. 12, 1793
Joshua Bradford Sherwood & Anne (?) Bonney, Nov. 12, 1793
Henry Sedgwick & Hannah Rogers,   Dec. 17, 1793
Samuel Buster (?) of Canaan & Elizebeth Stewert, Feb. 6, 1794
Ichabod Wickwire & Submit Ford,   Feb. 27, 1794
Samuel Pratt & Rhode Dean,   March 27, 1794
Daniel Brunson & Rhode Holdcomb,   June 5, 1794
Henry Dibble & Anne Wicks,   June 12, 1794
Amos Dewey & Sary Abbot,   July 3, 1794
Ziba Hyne & Sarah Holister,   July 21, 1794
Heman Swift, Jr., & Polly Peck,   Aug. 10, 1794
Miles Lewis of Canaan & Rhoda Swift,   Oct. 16, 1794
Silas Paterson & Nabby Bonny,   Oct. 16, 1794
Hercules Weston & Abbilene Mills of Kent,   Nov. 19, 1794
Daniel Rogers & Polly Abbot,   Dec. 7, 1794
Silas Mechorn (?) & Lucy Wood,   Dec. 7, 1794
Arvin Skiff of Sharon & Sally Jeffers,   Aug. 1, 1795
Trustian Parmely & Martha Dean,   Aug. 23, 1795
Roger Catling, Jr., & Sally Clarke,   Nov. 12, 1795
William Dean & Parthene Bailey,   Aug. 25, 1796
Martin Everit of Sharon & Ester Carter,   Dec. 22, 1796
Niles Squire & ———— ———— of Goshen,   April 27, 1797
John Pierce, Jr., & Sarah Judson,   Oct. 10, 1797
William Piersons of Derby & Betsey Sawyer,   Dec. 31, 1797

UNION.

TOLLAND COUNTY.

The town of Union was incorporated October, 1734. The Congregational Church in Union
was organized December 13, 1738.

Isaack Holliday of Suffield & Martha Bishop,   Oct. 18, 1759
John Fuller of Wendham & Thankful Watkins of Ashford,
                                                     Nov. 8, 1759
John Rosebroock of Brimfield & Sarah Cram of Brimfield,
                                                    April 10, 1760
William Martin of Woodstock & Elizabeth Crawford,
                                                    June 12, 1760

David Strong of Stafford & Sarah Warner,   Nov. 27, 1760
Archibal Cay or Coy & Elizabeth Badrisr (?),   Dec. 25, 1760
John Hendrick & K—— Abbot,   March 24, 1761
William Moore of Union & Sarah Rosebrook of Brimfield,
                            Sept. 20, 1762
Joseph (?) Fairbanks & Tabitha Merry (?),   Nov. 4, 1762
Moses Peck & Sybbel Mo——,   Feb. 24, 1763
Samuel Marcy & Louis Pec—k,   April 10 (?), 1763
Daniel Loomis & Sarah Crawford,   Feb. 9, 1764
Ephraim Badger & Keziah Wakefield,   Sept. 6, 1764
James Enos & Silence Sessions,   Oct. 18, 1764
Timothy Walker & Rebecca Walker,   Nov. 28, 1764
Jonah Loomis of Union & Mehetable Cram of South
  Brimfield,   Nov. 29, 1764
—————— ——— & Susanna Nicols,   Dec., ——
Samuel Peck of Union & Abigail Fuller of Killingly,
                    ——ember 12, 176—
Amos Hutchinson of Union & Mary Brown of Ashford,
                    March 20, 1766
Josiah Burley & Hannah Hiscock,   ——ember 12, 1765
Thomas Hill of Ashford & Ruth Wyman,   April 10, 1766
Calvin Sprague & Elisabeth Wright,   —— 4, 1766
Sam Abbott of Ashford & Elizabeth Moore,   Oct. 9, 1766
Thomas Denison of Ashford & Eunice Hutchinson,
                    Nov. 4, 1766
Jeremiah Badger & Zurviah Peck,   Jan. 15, 1767
Elias Underwood & Anner Crouch, both of Woodstock,
                    Jan. 22, 1767
Ebenezer Jackson of Woodstock & Abigal Walker,
                    May 6, 1767
Gershom Rosebrook of South Brimfield & Jane Craw-
  ford,   1767
David Bratten of Palmer & Martha Lawson, —— 22, 1767
Thomas Sprague & Hannah Cob,   —— 28, 1768
John Gyson (?) of Windham & Mary Hutchinson,   1768
Asa Houghton of Union & Sybil Davis of South Brimfield,
                    —— 24, 1768
James Paul & Zurviah Marcy,   Dec. 28, 1768
Joseph Bartholomey & Laurana Turner,   —— 10, 1769

Samuel Nelson of South Brimfield & Dorothy Fuller,

—— 11, 1769

Ebenezer Sessions of Union & Huldah Howard of Ashford,

1769

Daniel Badger & Gonard (?) Walker,	Oct. 5, 1769
Caleb Abbott & Margaret Paul,	Nov. 23, 1769
Samuel Abbott & Rachel Ward,	Jan. 15, 1770
William Abbott & Mary Coy,	Nov. 15, 1770

James King of Palmer & Jane Moor of Windham,

Jan. 24, 1771

Elija Hulburt of Woodstock & Sarah Standly,	Feb. 19, 1771

John Nelson of South Brimfield & Hannah Tw——,

April 30, 1771

James Bartlit & Experience Houghton,	June 13, 1771
Simond Walker & Elisabeth Walker,	Sept. 12, 1771
Abel Allen & Rhoda Batchelor,	Oct. 31, 1771
Henry Martin of Woodstock & Mary Sessions,	Nov. 14, 1771
Nathan Hiscock & Rebecka Keene,	Jan. 9, 1772
William Moor & Margaret Crawford,	Feb. 13, 1772
Noah Loomis & Sybil Williams,	Feb. 4, 1773
Elija Loomis & Alithea Burley,	Jan. 27, 1774
Simeon Wright & Sophia Child,	Oct. 6, 1774
John Bliss of Brimfield & Ester Wales,	Nov. 24, 1774
Samuel Burley & Rachel Roberts,	May 16, 1775

Jotham Bigelow of New Guilford & Sarah Lo—— of Union,

June 8, 1775

Ebenezer Lille of Union & Jerusha Williams of Woodstock,

Sept. 21, 1775

Ebenezer Child & Allis Cobb,	Nov. 1, 1775
Nat. Sessions & Irena Wales,	Nov. 16, 1775

Nathaniel Newel & Silence Reep or Keep or Rees,

Dec. 13, 1775

John Crawford & Dorcas Ward,	Dec. 14, 1775
James Armour, Jr., & Eunice Arnold,	Oct. 18, 1776
Jonathan Badger & Abigail Rice,	Dec. 5, 1776
Benjamin Ayard (?) of Stafford & Sarah Hiscock,	Jan. 23, 1777
Daniel Haradon of Woodstock & Olive Walker,	March 2, 1777
Nathan Mors (?) of Ashford & Molly Bugbee,	May 8, 1777
John Ruby & Esther How,	June 19, 1777

James Armour & Hannah Mckneil, Dec. 17, 1777
Noah Loomis of Orandon (?) & Dorcas Crawford,
Feb. 24, 1778
John Joslin of Killingly & Deb. Aldridge, Nov. 19, 1778
Abel Simons of Enfield & Elizabeth Coburn, 1779
Nathaniel Draper of Pomfret & Hannah Robbi—,
Dec. 16, ——
John Harris of Ashford & Nabby Bates, Feb. 17, 1780
Francis Pierce & Phebe Ainsworth, April 27, 1780
Jonathan Ripny (?) of Suffield & Hannah Strong (?),
May 9, 1780
Parley Herring of Killingly & Elizabeth Lille, July 26, 1780
Clark Robbins & Zilpha Keys, both of Ashford, Nov. 16, 1780
Abram Lupliny (Lafling) (?) & Elisabeth Paul, Dec. 14, 1780
John Lawson & Keziah Whitney, June 5, 1781
Penuel Chils & Charlotte Lomis, Oct. 11, 1781
John Harkness of Pelham & Rachel Mackneel, Nov. 22, 1781
Samuel Laflin & Martha Carpenter, Jan., 1782
James Lafling of South Brimfield & Rebeca Wood,
Jan. 31, 1782
Samuel Cody & Susanna Armstrong, June 6, 1782
Robert Lawson & Anna Horton, May 30, 1783
Jonah Cooly of Springfield & Abigail Reep (?) (Russ ?),
March 5, 1783

BETHLEHEM.

LITCHFIELD COUNTY.

The town of Bethlehem (Bethlem) was incorporated May, 1787. Formerly a part of
Woodbury. The Congregational Church was organized March 27, 1739.

Samuel Church & Sary Porter, June 2, 1740
Isaac Hill & Cat. Perry, Nov. 16, 1741
Eben Thompson & Mary Judd, Oct. 29, 1742
Caleb Wheelor & Lydia Clark, June, 1744
Eliphalet Clark & Abigal Garnsey, Nov. 8, 1744
Nathaniel Porter & Deborah Hard, June 20, 1745
Dan Everet & Elise Steel, March 25, 1747

Hezekiah Hooker & Elizabeth Stone,	Jan. 30, 1746
John Twiss & Sary Munger,	May 19, 1743
Daniel Dudly & Mary Hendee,	Sept. 6, 1747
Amos Roots & Mercy Martin,	Sept. 16, 1747
Samuel Martin & Mary Steel,	Sept. 29, 1747
Jacob Frisby & Ruth Porter,	Nov. 18, 1747
Ezra Terril & Rebeccah Andrass,	Dec. 29, 1747
Josiah Whittlesy & Elizabeth Jackson,	June 5, 1748
David Hotchkiss & Submit Hill,	Nov. 10, 1748
John Porter & Deborah Hand,	Jan. 15, 1751
Ahira Hill & Hanna Lewis,	Jan. 29, 1751
John Stodard & Mary Atwood,	April 15, 1751
Samuel Slater & Ann Stone,	April 25, 1751
Wil. Andrass & Mahit. Lewis,	July 3, 1751
Seth Avered & Eunice Minor,	Feb. 26, 1752
John Barns & Rachel Judd,	Feb. 19, 1752
Ben Wheelor & Consider Spencer,	April 21, 1752
Eben Garnsey & Ann Garnsey,	Nov. 5, 1752
David Crissy & Hannah Wilmot,	Nov. 15, 1753
James Hooker & Dorothy Parmerly,	April 1, 1754
Thomas Porter & Beulah Miner,	July 24, 1754
Ezekiel Steel & Rosamond Dudly,	1755
Waitful Goodrich & Mary Hooker,	June 5, 1755
Benjamin Peet & Elizabeth Hendee,	Oct. 27, 1756
Joseph Curby & Rachel Hand,	March 24, 1757
Preserved Whelor & Lucy Parks,	May 1, 1757
Mr. Roots & Elisabeth Garnsey,	Sept., 1757
Joseph Waugh & Elisabeth Miner,	Feb., 1758
Simeon Whelor & Cloe Way,	March 16, 1758
Philemon Way & Jane Crissy,	
Isaac Miner & Mary Butler,	April, 1758
Ozias Pettebone & Sibbel Garnsey,	May 11, 1758
Robert Hanna & Mable Bishop,	July 4, 1758
Abel Barns & Gift Gay,	Aug. 9, 1758
Stephen Galpin & Lydia Stone,	Dec. 26, 1758
Joseph Whelor & Lucy Hotchkiss,	Jan. 4, 1759
Titus Tyler & Susannah Berry,	Jan. 15, 1759
Abijah Mitchel & Anne Berry,	May 15, 1759
—— Farnum & Roseman Steel,	Dec., 1762

Elisha Steel & Susannah Strong,	March 10, 1763
John Whelor & Louis Dudley,	April 14, 1763
Elisha Clark & Irena Meigs,	Dec. 15, 1763
Ichabod Loomiss & Mindwell Lewis,	Jan., 1767
Abiram Peet & Ann Lewis,	Nov. 19, 1767
Francis Blois & Esther Thomson,	Feb. 22, 1768
Levi Hart & Rebecca Bellamy,	Sept. 6, 1769
Joseph Throop & Sary Kasson,	Nov., 1769
Solomon Garnsey & Sary Kasson,	Nov., 1769
Attwood Bird & Jane Miller,	Nov., 1769
Samuel Veal & Sary Berry,	July, 1766
—— —— & Agapa Munger,	Aug., ——
Simeon Martin & Ann Atwood,	Nov., 1767
James Edmand & Ruth Kasson,	Nov. 1, 1768
Timothy Hand & Rhoda Bradley,	Nov. 20, 1768
Ezekiel Lewis & Ann Bird,	March 23, 1769
Samuel Camp & Hannah Garnsey,	Sept. 21, 1769
Asaph Parmely & Sary Everet,	Nov., 1769
Joseph James Judson & Lydia Hull,	Nov., 1769
Elizur Andrass & Ann Clark,	Nov. 21, 1769
Aaron Peirce & Thankful Frost,	Nov. 23, 1769
Amos Allen & Anna Rogers,	May, 1770
Solomon Butler & Phebe Beach,	——
David Bellamy & Silence Leavit,	July 9, 1772
Abijah Garnsey & Lucy Bellamy,	Aug., 1772
Elex. Kasson & Comfort Thomson,	Nov. 3, 1772
David Lyman & Mary Brown,	——
Levi Thomson & Rebecca Levit,	Dec. 3, 1772
Jonas Spaldin & Lucy Bishop,	July 29, 1773
John Porter & Rebecca Joslin,	June 23, 1774
Paul Clark & Sary Wheler,	Nov. 17, 1774
John Monson & Damaris Martin,	Feb. 23, 1775
Judah Lewis & Submit Brace,	Feb. 26, 1775
—— Knap & Jerusha Galpin,	March 21, 1775
Abner Judson & Mary Ann Minor,	May 1, 1791
Amos Frisbie & Lucy Roberts,	Jan. 1, 1791
David Towner & Betty Bishop,	Nov. 6, 1791
Elisha Stoddard & Mary Crane,	Nov. 22, 1791
Bristol Hall & Jane Gordon,	Dec. 30, 1791

Andrew Davidson & Hannah Hine,	March 6, 1792
Friend Webster & Philena Brown,	April 5, 1792
Timothy Lindley & Irene Jackson,	April 22, 1792
Joseph Mason & Mehitibel Seymour,	Nov. 26, 1792
Oliver Parmelee, Jr., & Kezia Allen	Nov. 29, 1792
George Dixon Kasson & Selina Camp,	Dec. 19, 1792
Elijah Andrews & Hannah Hawley,	Jan. 13, 1793
Salmon Bronson & Katherine Noble,	Feb. 4, 1793
Elisha Steel, Jr., & Anna Brown,	Feb. 18, 1793
Enos Hinmon & Sarah Hitchcock,	March 10, 1793
Erastus Griswold & Anna Lewis,	April 2, 1793
Charles Webster & Lydia Egleston,	May 12, 1793
Lewis Stiles & Sarah Way,	Sept. 15, 1793
Samuel Bloice & Deborah Allen,	Nov. 14, 1793
Jonathan Steel & Fanny Warner,	——
Thaddeus Hurlbut & Salindy Higgins,	Dec. 25, 1793
Amos (negro) & Sally (mulatto),	Jan. 10, 1794
Joseph Minor & Phelena Martin,	Jan. 14, 1794
Daniel Atwood & Polly Brown,	May 15, 1794
Horace Brace & Polly Ambler,	June 1, 1794
Captain Jonathan Smith & Sarah Steel,	June 5, 1794
Jacob Frisbie & Mary Repner,	July 23, 1794
Edward Perkins & Lucinda Stoddard,	July 24, 1794
Levi Austin & Polly Martin,	Nov. 16, 1794
Elijah Weller & Eunice Hawley,	Dec. 7, 1794
William Orton & Ruana Lewis,	Dec. 24, 1794
Caleb Walker & Nabbe Mallory,	Feb. 6, 1795
James Walling & Margaret Hannah,	Feb. 19, 1795
Philemon Way & Mary Thomas,	March 1, 1795
David Camp & Abiah Camp,	June 22, 1795
Isaac Merwin & Abigal Brownson,	Dec. 22, 1795
Moses Parmelee & Sarah Treat,	Dec. 23, 1795
Elisha Brace & widow Lucy Bird,	March 17, 1796
George D. Kasson & Lucy Steel,	May 16, 1796
John Wright Johnson & Sally Maria Wetherill,	May 30, 1796
Silas Swift & Sally Parmelee,	June 1, 1796
Chandler Rogers & Agnes Prindle,	Incog.
—— Monson & Eliza Munger,	Nov. 2, 1796
Amos Thompson & Dotha Brace,	Nov. 20, 1796

Joseph Palmer & Nabby Weller,	——	
Matthew Billings & Anne Barlow,	Nov. 27,	1796
Milo Foot & Polly Hicthcok,		
Calvin Hinman & Sarah Wheeler,	Dec. 22,	1796
Harvey Steel & Phebe Camp,	Jan.,	1797
Salmasius Bordwell & Rhoda Martin,	Jan. 7,	1797
Hart Scott & Miss Anna Stow of Watertown,	——	
Eliphet Gillet & Nabby Hannah,	April,	1797
Solomon White & Esther Codger,	Sept.,	1797
Ager Judson & Betsey Lang,	Oct. 22,	1797
Jonathan Garnsey & Mary Judson,	Nov. 9,	1797
David Bird & Betty Church,	Nov. 12,	1797
—— Emons & —— Webster,	——	
Almon Beardsley & Rebecca Barton,	Dec. 10,	1797
Samuel Atwood & Irene Orton,	Jan. 11,	1798
Bela Thompson & Amy Clark,	Jan. 28,	1798
Tapping Reeve, Jr., & Betsey Thompson,	April 30,	1798
Robert Crane, Jr., & Sybilla Hill,	Aug.,	1798
Elisha Atwood, Jr., & Lucy Carr,	Sept. 6,	1798
Abner Allen & Susanna Mitchell,	Oct. 4,	1798
—— Maltby & —— Leavenworth,	Dec.,	1798
Eleazer Crane & Nancy Prudden,	——	
Jacob Beach & Elizabeth Farrin,	Dec. 17,	1798

KILLINGLY—PUTNAM.

WINDHAM COUNTY.

The town of Putnam was incorporated in 1855. It was formed by taking parts of Thompson, Pomfret and Killingly. The old Congregational Church at North Killingly, organized in October, 1715, thus came within its limits. Rev. J. Fisk the first pastor.

William Larned & Hannah Briant,	Nov.,	1715
Benjamin Leavens & Elizabeth Church,	Dec. 21,	1715
Jacob Comins & Martha Brooks,	March 28,	1716
Timothy Parkhurst & Elizabeth Cady,	Jan. 15,	1717
Eleazer Bateman & Mary Aspinwall,	Jan. 22,	1717
Edward Converse & Elizabeth Cooper,	Aug. 6,	1717
Ebenezer Brook & Sarah Childs,	Aug. 14,	1717

William Spalding & Lydia Blanchard,	April 8, 1718
Samuel Bixby & Martha Underwood,	May 14, 1718
John Upham & Mary Lorton,	June 9, 1718
James Wilson, Jr., & Mehitable Leavens,	Nov. 17, 1718
Thomas Whitmore, Jr., & Elizabeth Lee,	Dec. 5, 1718
Daniel Fitch & Anna Cooke,	March 5, 1719
Joseph Covell, Jr., & Hannah Lamb,	April 9, 1719
James Craft of Rox. & Susannah Warren of Pomfret,	
	Oct. 29, 1719
Nicholas Blanchard of Stafford & Hannah Jarett of Swansea,	Nov. 23, 1719
Moses Barrett & Abigail Trott,	March 15, 1720
Moses Sweney & Mary Reed,	May 23, 1720
Daniel Bemis of Windham & Ruth Winter of Killingly,	
	July 18, 1720
Jabez Allen & Mehitable Moffatt,	July 20, 1720
Jacob Cummins & Abigail Wilson,	Nov. 9, 1720
James Barnes & Elizabeth Lorton,	Dec. 29, 1720
Samuel Utter & Jonanna Preston,	May 5, 1721
Jabez Brooks & Mary Bateman,	Dec. 20, 1721
David Cady & Hannah Whitmore,	Oct. 18, 1722
Samuel Whitmore & Mary Haskell,	Nov., 1722
Joseph Warren of Plainfield & Martha Bateman,	Jan. 2, 1723
Edward Russell of East Haven & Katherine Utter,	
	Jan. 3, 1723
Isaac Jewett & Annie Bloss,	Jan. 9, 1723
Nathaniel Blanchard & Katharine Briant,	Feb. 24, 1723
Stephen Cady & Abigail Lee,	March 20, 1723
Daniel Whitmore & Dorcas Converse,	March 20, 1723
Thomas Converse & Martha Cluffe,	April 11, 1723
Caleb Bixby & Sarah Blanchard,	April 17, 1723
Robert Plank & Hannah Cooper,	June 20, 1723
William Whitney & Mary Whitmore,	July 16, 1723
'Ephriam Warren, Jr., & Tabitha Russell,	Dec. 4, 1723
Eleazer Brooks & Hannah Leavens,	Jan. 16, 1725
Jaazaniah Hosmer & Rachel Pierce,	March 11, 1725
John Lee & Margaret Wilson,	March 13, 1725
Samuel Danielson & Sarah Douglas of Plainfield,	
	March 26, 1725

William Moffatt, Jr., & Deliverance Parks, Nov. 5, 1725
Sterling Heath of Pomfret & Hannah Cutler, Nov. 26, 1725
Benjamin Lovejoy of Plainfield & Sarah Whitmore,
March 3, 1725
William Ford of Providence & Abigail Robinson,
March 18, 1725
Benjamin Barrett & Mary Parks, April 8, 1725
Urian Hosmer & widow Elizabeth Leavens, May 12, 1725
Richard Bloss, Jr., & Ruth Mackintyre, Nov. 10, 1725
Moses Learned of Framingham & Lydia Bryant, Dec., 1725
John Moffitt & Elizabeth Firman, Feb. 2, 1726
Samuel Daily & Sarah Cooper, March 3, 1726
Joshua Hall & Abigail Mackintyre, May 24, 1726
John Felshaw & Elizabeth Robinson, Dec. 23, 1726
Samuel Bloss & widow Martha Barker, Sept. 4, 1727
Nathaniel Colton & Sarah, daughter of James Mighill,
Jan. 25, 1728
Stephen Cummins (?) & Mary, daughter of Benjamin
Bixby, Feb. 13, 1728
Ephraim Guile & Abigail Converse, June 15, 1730
David Town of Oxford & Sarah Gary of Pomfret,
April 21, 1740
Isaac Stone & Mary Jewett, April 22, 1740
Rev. Mr. Marston Cabot & Mrs. Mary Dwight, July 22, 1740
Nathaniel Patten & Anne Hutchins, Oct. 18, 1740
James Johnson & Susanna Waters, Dec. 19, 1732
Benjamin Cady & Elizabeth Church, Nov. 29, 1733
Hezekiah Cutler & Susanna Clark, Dec. 5, 1734
Barachiah Johnson & Barthsheba Cady, ·Dec. 16, 1734
John Church & Amey Winter, Jan. 1, 1735
Rev. Mr. James Osgood of Stoneham & Mrs. Sarah Fisk,
Nov. 10, 1735
Joseph Hutchins & Zerviah Leavens, Jan. 22, 1736
Samuel Knight & Rachel Leavens, Feb. 12, 1736
Andrew Philips & Mary Lock, Feb. 23, 1736
Phineas Green & Elizabeth Cutting, June 29, 1736
Joseph Cheney of New Medfield & Abigail Warren,
Oct. 21, 1736
Eleazer Bateman & Mrs. Hannah·Cutler, Nov. 2, 1736

Ebenezer Plummer & Abigail Jewett,   Nov. 4, 1736
John Church & Susanna Morris,   Dec. 15, 1736
Daniel Russell & Phebe Roberts,   July 13, 1737
Ebenezer Fay of New Medfield & Abigail Waters,
             May 19, 1737
Stephen Mackintyre of New Sherbourne & widow
  Tryphena Place of Gloucester,   Feb. 1, 1738
Josiah Spalding & Hannah Grover,   May 18, 1738
Aaron Allen of ——— & Hannah Waters, Oct. 4, 1738
Joseph Symonds & Hannah Abbe,   Nov. 17, 1738
Wyman Hutchins & Abigail Cutler,   Jan. 1, 1739
John Roberts & Abigail Whitney,   April 25, 1739
William Robinson & Hannah Cutler,   May 30, 1739
Richard Abbe of Ashford & Hannah Simmons, Nov. 21, 1739
Ebenezer Stearns of Plainfield & Mary Gould, Feb. 28, 1740
Jonathan Bullard of Sherbourne & widow Sarah Wood,
            March 18, 1740
John Mashcraft of Woodstock & Sarah Wilson, May 28, 1740
Nathan McKee & Mary Whitney,   Nov. 19, 1740
Robert Latham & Eunice Bruce,   Nov. 21, 1740
Benjamin Leavens & Elizabeth Cady,   Dec. 4, 1740
David Roberts, Jr., & widow Mercy Heminway of
  Woodstock,   June 23, 1741

AN ACCOUNT OF PERSONS MARRIED BY REV. AARON BROWN.

Isaac Learned of Oxford & Mary Leavens, Feb. 14, 1754
Giles Roberts & Zerviah Buck,   April 3, 1754
Ezekiel Mighill & Margaret Wilson,   May 23, 1754
Benjamin Leavens & Dorothy Perrin of Pomfret, July 18, 1754
John Eaton & Eunice Gould,   Oct. 9, 1754
John Ranne of Middletown & Sybil Wilson, Nov. 7, 1754
Rev. Aaron Brown & Mrs. Damris Howe, Nov. 21, 1754

BY REV. NEHEMIAH BARKER.

Jonathan Wilson & Lucy Hosmer of Woodstock,
            Dec. 11, 1754
Samuel Allen & Ruth May,   Jan. 27, 1755
James Collar & Huldah Simmons,   April 17, 1755

Obadiah Clough & Elizabeth Whitmore,   July 31, 1755
John Adams & Jerusha Cady,   Sept. 4, 1755
John Weld & Chloe Perrin of Pomfret,   Sept. 4, 1755
Samuel Narramore of Pomfret & Deborah Cotton,
                                                  Oct. 23, 1755
Joseph Griffin of Pomfret & Sarah Brown,   Oct. 23, 1755
Hezekiah Green & Alice Leavens,   Dec. 11, 1755
Elisha Lawrence & Phebe Wilson,   March 4, 1766
James Bloss & Elizabeth Clough,   June 8, 1766
Phinehas Green of Spencer & Judith Sprague,   Aug. 6, 1766
Daniel Waters & Lucy Spalding,   Sept. 21, 1766
Robert Burch & Damaris Cady,   Nov. 11, 1766
Barachiah Cady & Elizabeth Covell,   Nov. 18, 1766
Henry Carpenter & Phebe Brooks,   Nov. 29, 1766
Joseph Brown & Hannah Carrol, both of Thompson Parish,
                                                  Nov. 30, 1766
John Whitmore & Grace Child,   Jan. 11, 1757
Timothy Parkhurst & Joanna Cady,   March 29, 1757
Nathaniel Collar & Miriam Dickerman,   April 4, 1757
John Streeter of Sturbridge & Margaret Heminway,
                                                  April 5, 1757
Ebenezer Brooks, Jr., & Mary Glazier of Northlake,
    alias Brookline,   May 4, 1757
James White of Pomfret & Jemima Town of Thomp-
    son Parish,   May 18, 1757
Timothy Atwood & Elizabeth Converse,   May 25, 1757
John Cady & Hannah Mighill,   June 9, 1757
James Bruce & Elizabeth Bateman,   Dec. 21, 1757
Benjamin Shepard of Brookline & Martha Whitmore,
                                                  Dec. 22, 1757
Samuel Bloss, Jr., & Mary Winter,   April 27, 1758
David Buck & Anna Russell,   June 22, 1758
Richard Bloss & Sarah Barrett,   June 29, 1758
Josiah Chaffee of Woodstock & Sarah Cady,   July 13, 1758
Samuel Sabin & Sarah Wilson,   Aug. 9, 1758
Simeon Lee of Pomfret & Mehitable Cutler,   Oct. 11, 1758
Jesse Converse & Damaris Chandler,   Nov. 23, 1758
Jeremiah Fitch of Coventry & Abigail Whitmore,
                                                  Feb. 21, 1759

Samuel Harrendon & Percy Russell,	March 14, 1759
Asahel Blanchard & Priscilla Brooks,	April 30, 1759
James Chaffee of Woodstock & Rhoda Cady,	Aug. 5, 1759
Samuel Buck & Martha Bloss,	Jan. 1, 1760
William Blackmar & Lydia Ricard,	Feb. 3, 1760
Joseph Moffat & Anna Green,	Sept. 27, 1761
Abel Cady & Sarah Cady,	Oct., 1761
John Winter & Mary Robinson,	Dec., 1761
Josiah Brown & Mary Lawrence,	Feb. 7, 1762
Justin Cady & Keziah Covell,	Feb., 1762
Jacob Brown & Lucy Russell,	Jan., 1763
Ephraim Joy & Elizabeth Pool,	Feb. 18, 1763
Thomas Sumner & Mary Leach,	April 19, 1763
Amasa Grover & Elizabeth Jeffers,	April 28, 1763
James Blackmar of Gloucester, R. I., & Sarah Wilson,	
	June 18, 1763
Benoni Cutler & Lurana Leavens,	Dec. 22, 1763
David Perry & Anna Bliss,	Jan., 1764
Isaac Allen & Amy Dean,	Jan. 30, 1764
Isaac Church & Elinor Daniels,	Sept. 5, 1765
Isaac Cady Howe & Damaris Burch,	Sept. 12, 1765
Benjamin Wood & Sarai Cady,	Sept. 16, 1765
Jacob Whitmore & Hannah Brown,	Sept. 18, 1765
Asa Lawrence & Lucy Joy,	March 18, 1765
Darius Priest & Hepzibah Graves,	April 6, 1765
Jonathan Howe of Plainfield & Grace Campbell,	June 4, 1766
John Fuller & Sibyl Richmond,	Aug. 7, 1766
Joseph Cady, Jr., & Susanna Sanders (Alexander),	
	Sept. 21, 1766
Isaac Cady & Sabra Green,	Nov. 16, 1766
Jonathan Cady & Rebecca Cady,	Nov. 20, 1766
John Robarts & Hannah Mac. ———,	Aug. 2, 1767
Eleazer Moffat & Lucy Comings,	Jan., 1767
John Bateman & Sarai Kee,	Sept. 17, 1767
Timothy Houghton & Damaris Howe,	Feb. 11, 1768
Oliver Richmond & Mary Bateman,	Feb., 1768
William Givens & Mary Cutler,	March 13, 1768
John Kibbe & Elizabeth Bruce,	June 10, 1768
Daniel Harrenden of Canterbury & Margaret Cutler,	
	Sept. 4, 1769

Benjamin Joy & Elizabeth Leonard,	Oct. 30, 1769
Nathaniel Grow & Betty Cady,	Nov. 9, 1769
David Chandler of Pomfret & Mary Parks,	Jan. 15, 1770
John Wade & Sarai Sawyer,	Feb. 1, 1770
Daniel (?) Clark & Molly Adams,	Feb. 13, 1770
Abiel Blanchard & Elizabeth Church,	March 15, 1770
Sylvanus Perry & Rebecca Bliss,	April 4, 1770
Ebenezer Hardwood of Uxbridge & Margaret Wilson,	
	May 2, 1770
Samuel Felshaw & Sabra Russell,	June, 1770
Joseph Lee & Hannah Leavens,	July 15, 1770
Thadeus Fairfield of Belchertown & Keziah Lee,	
	Aug. 30, 1771
Zaccheus Brown & Elizabeth Goodspeed,	Aug. 30, 1771
Battel Robinson & Prudence Leach,	Jan. 15, 1772
Benjamin Brown & Sarai Smith,	June 18, 1772
William Dixon & Priscilla Danielson,	Sept. 20, 1772
Cornelius Sawyer & Anna Williams,	Nov. 5, 1772
Nathan Draper & Hannah Whitmore,	Dec., 1772
James Downing of Pomfret & Elizabeth Gay,	Jan. 31, 1773
Ebenezer Gay & Elizabeth Leavens,	March 5, 1773
John Parkhurst & Chloe Guernsey,	June 17, 1773
Charles Leavens & Lida Grover,	June 27, 1773
Nathan Hartwell & Lida Covell,	June 30, 1773
Silas Robbins & Sarai Moss,	July, 1773
Nathan Young & Sabra March,	Sept. 7, 1773
Peter Olney & Tabitha Clark,	Dec. 23, 1773
Ebenezer Kimball & Rebecca Knight,	June 19, 1774
Isaiah Robinson & Sarai Robbins,	Nov. 20, 1774
Abraham Fairman of Pomfret & Keziah Olney,	Dec. 3, 1774
Perley Howe & Abigail DeWolf,	Jan. 29, 1775
William Parks & Lodema Cutler,	Feb. 1, 1775
Benjamin Hatch of Hanover & Lucy Parks,	Feb. 9, 1775
David Paul & Mary Evans,	Feb. 16, 1775
John Wilson of Plainfield & Ruth Joy,	March 5, 1775
Ebenezer Brown & Molly Redway,	March 26, 1775
Samuel Pool & Ruth Whitmore,	May 18, 1775
Daniel Hulett & Abigail Paul,	Aug. 3, 1775
Benjamin Cutler & Olive Buck,	June 27, 1784

——— Warren & Eunice Bassett,   Aug., 1784
Oliver Torrey & Tamer Davis,   Sept. 13, 1784
Samuel Walding & Betty Burch,   Sept. 30, 1784
Jonathan Whitney & Olive Cady,   Nov., 1784
Daniel Whitmore & Phebe Green,   Dec. 16, 1784
Jacob Warren & Susanna Harrington,   Dec. 16, 1784
——— Whitney & Anna Ames,   Dec. 16, 1784
Mauessah Cady & Elizabeth Harrington,   Jan. 27, 1785
Esek. Eddy & Anna Cutler,   Feb. 8, 1785
Isaac Cutler & Th. Peck,   Feb. 8, 1785
Benoni Page & Abigail Slaughter,   March 28, 1785
Abraham Slaughter, Jr., & Hannah Moffatt,   March 28, 1785
——— McCall & May Cutler,   April 12, 1785
Col. Whitney & Sarah Cady,   Oct. 19, 1785
Mr. Phillips & El. Howe,   Oct. 19, 1785
Robert Burch & Polly Felshaw,   1786
Daniel Davis & Deborah Talbot,   July 16, 1786
David Buck & Zerviah Leonard,   Aug. 3, 1786
            (Part of Record here illegible).
William Davis & Sally Adams,   1787
——— Cotney & B. Cady,   1789
P. Cutler & ——— Drinkwater,   1789
——— Talbot & Covill,   1789
——— Smith & ——— L. Brown,   1789
Aaron Buck & Anna Laurence,   Oct., 1790
Talbot & Starkweather,   1791
T. Adams & Lucy Torrey,   1792
——— Davis & H. Talbot,   Oct., 1792
D. Copp & Betsey Torrey,   1792
Lemuel Felshaw & Sally ———,   1792
Joseph Cady & Laurence Kingsbury,   1792
——— ——— & Lucy Laurance,   1792
Dr. Grosvenor & Abilene Howe, Home (?),   June 25, 1795
Joseph Heath & ——— Kelly,   1795
——— Carder & ——— Durfee,   1795
——— Hall & ——— S. Larned,   1795
——— Martin & Betsey Laurence,   Nov., 1795
——— Cutler & Blackmar,   1795
——— Durfee & ——— Carder,   1796

Erastus Larned & Freelove Wilkinson, 1796
Joseph Talbot & ——— Tucker, 1796
Luther Hawkins & ——— Lee, Oct. 20, 1797
Joseph Starkweather & widow ———, June 8, 1799
——— Wood & Betsey Howard, Aug., 1799

LEBANON—(Goshen).

NEW LONDON COUNTY.

The town of Lebanon was incorporated in October, 1700. The First Congregational Church was organized in 1700, the records of which were published in Book II of this series. The Second Church of Lebanon was organized November 26, 1729, and located in the district of Goshen, now at Bozrahville.

Moses Woodworth of Norwich & Mehitable Gay,
May 21, 1730
Ashahel Lee & Hannah Stark, Dec. 2, 1730
Samuel Smith & Betty Church, both of Colchester,
Jan. 7, 1731
John Bentley of Lebanon & Mary Roberts of Colchester,
July 12, 1731
William Lothrop of Norwich & Mary Hunter, alias Kelsey,
Aug. 5, 1731
Daniel Clark & Esther Bridges, Nov. 11, 1731
Oliver Brewster & Martha Wadsworth, March 22, 1732
Joseph Gillet of Litchfield & Deborah Chappel, Nov. 9, 1732
Amos Spafford & Hannah Vetch, Jan. 4, 1733
Israel Foster & Ruth Bridges, April 10, 1733
John Lambert of Canterbury & Sarah Archer, June 21, 1733
Philip Gay & Margaret Harden, Oct. 11, 1733
Nathaniel Bozworth & Berthia Hinckley, Nov. 22, 1733
John Brown & Anne Brown, June 27, 1734
Thomas Loomis & Susannah Clark, Nov. 7, 1734
Samuel Hills, Æt. 62, & Abigail Hinckley, Æt. 42,
Feb. 25, 1735
Phineas Foster & Lydia Hills, May 1, 1735
William Batharick & Abigail Hills, Nov. 12, 1735
Thomas Rist of Uxbridge & Mary Fowler, Nov. 20, 1735

Ephraim Hills & Hannah Bentley, Feb. 19, 1736
Peter Hartwell & Mary Coleman of Colchester, April 22, 1736
David Lyman of Crank Lacy & Anna Lee, May 27, 1736
Richard Murch of Mansfield & Mary Lee, April 14, 1737
Abraham Whitman of Norwich & Susannah Stark (Baptist),
April 19, 1737
Samuel Gay, Jr., & Mary Walker, June 27, 1737
Nathaniel Fitch, Jr., & Susannah Vetch, Sept. 22, 1737
Josiah Dean, Jr., & Thankful Thomas, Nov. 10, 1737
Edward Kellogg & Jemima Bartlett, Jan. 4, 1738
Nehemiah Fitch & Anne Metcalf, Jan. 26, 1738
Eliphalet Clark & Mary Bridges, June 15, 1738
Ebenezer Baldwin of Norwich & Berthia Barker,
Oct. 10, 1738
John West, Jr., & Rebecca Abel, Nov. 16, 1738
Nathan West & Mary Hinckley, Dec. 7, 1738
Ebenezer McCall & Rachel Ordaway, Jan. 25, 1739
Marshall Hackley & Hannah Abell, Oct. 3, 1739
Joseph Tracy, Jr., of Norwich & Anne Hinckley,
Nov. 5, 1739
Nathaniel Clark & Martha Wilt, Nov. 5, 1740
Samuel Gustin of Lyme & Mary Thomas, Dec. 31, 1740
Amos Randall & Berthia Abel, Feb. 19, 1741
Daniel Polley of Hebron & Rachel Loomis, Aug. 20, 1741
Simon Chalcom & Ruth Raymond, Jan. 7, 1742
Jeremiah Fuller & Berthia Dean, Feb. 24, 1742
Samuel Law & Mary Langrel, Feb. 24, 1743
Gershom Matoon & Abigail Chappel, May 12, 1743
David Bosworth & Mary Strong, June 27, 1743
Zebulon West, Esq., of Tolland & Mrs. Sarah Sluman,
Feb. 22, 1744
Nathan Ingraham of Colchester & Mary Pitts, April 17, 1744
Elias Worthington & Rhoda Chamberlin of Colchester,
Sept. 20, 1744
Jonathan Williams & Mary Whitney, Sept. 26, 1744
David Roberts & Mary Webster, Jan. 3, 1745
Daniel Rowley of Moodus & Berthia Langrel, Jan. 24, 1745
Asa Foster & Hannah White, Feb. 4, 1745
John Lane, Esq., of Killingworth & Mrs. Deborah West,
May 15, 1745

David Bartlett of Northampton & Elizabeth Bascom,

Feb. 18, 1746

John Badger of Norwich Farms & Mary Lamb, Aug. 27, 1746

Brotherton Martin & Betty Bartlett, Oct. 2, 1746

Jonathan Jones of Coventry & Abigail (?) Strong,

March 12, 1747

Benajah Ackley of East Haddam & Lurany Bill, May 21, 1747

James Gould & Betty Chappel, May 25, 1747

Stephen Strong, Jr., & Elizabeth Barstow of Pembroke,

May 28, 1747

Mason Wattles & Irena Chandler, June, 1747

Caleb West & Hannah Tuttle, Aug. 12, 1747

Henry Brisco & Beulah Cutting, Dec. 10, 1747

John Ellis of Norwich & Margaret Kellogg, Jan. 23, 1771

Levi Case of Hebron & Hannah Pierce of Lebanon,

Feb. 7, 1771

John Webster & Amy Webster Martin, Aug. 5, 1771

Samuel Loomis & Vine Palmer, Sept. 24, 1771

Jonathan Wise & Mary Loomis, Nov. 20, 1771

Michael Stewart & Mehitabel Bettis of Charlestown,

Nov. 28, 1771

Joseph Finney & Mary Brown, April 2, 1772

Ichabod Brewster & Lucy Clark, Nov. 19, 1772

William Gay & Cloe Cuttin, Dec. 17, 1772

John Castwell of Chatham & Berthia Hinckley, Jan. 21, 1773

David Bosworth, Jr., & Mindwell Fitch, March 4, 1773

Jobin Bozworth & Luna West, March 4, 1773

Simon Abel & Rachel Partridge Brewster, April 1, 1773

Daniel Strong, Jr., & Desire Bartlett, Sept. 29, 1773

Elihu Thomas & Hannah Strong, Sept. 30, 1773

Hobart McCall & Lucy Strong, Sept. 30, 1773

Sluman Wattles & Mercy (?) McCall, Oct. 5, 1773

Judah Bartlett & Caroline Wattles, Oct. 6, 1773

Phineas Lamphear of Pansborough, Ms. Bay, & Elizabeth Lyman, Jan. 13, 1774

Joseph Sprague & Mary Jackson, March 10, 1774

Isaiah Loomis & Abigail Williams, Dec. 7, 1774

Zebulon Ames of Lebanon & Sybil Lathrop of Norwich,

May 8, 1774

John Bartlett & Desire Loomis,   Dec. 8, 1774
Jacob Clark & Caroline Williams,   Dec. 22, 1774
Daniel Jones of Colchester & Submit Hills,   Dec. 23, 1774
John Robinson & Delight Bartlett,   Dec. 28, 1774
Solomon Abel & Aseneth Wood,   Dec. 29, 1774
William Stanton of Stonington & Hannah Loomis,

                                                        Feb. 15, 1776
Jesse Doubleday & Rachel Woodworth,   Nov. 14, 1776
Nathan Delano & Sarah Eells,   Dec. 15, 1776
Jabez Foster & Esther Bliss,   Dec. 25, 1776
Jacob Buell & Betty Wright,   Dec. 31, 1776
Joseph Howes & Martha Howard,   Jan. 1, 1777
Thomas Loomis, Jr., & Mary Williams,   March 19, 1777
Nathan Bingham of Norwich & Susannah Stark,

                                         March 27, 1777
Capt. Daniel Smalley, age 80 yrs., & Hannah Boyington,

                                        May 22, 1777
Diah Stark of Hebron & Hannah Rose,   May 29, 1777
Chandler Bartlett & Delight McCall,   Aug. 7, 1777
Joseph Smith of Norwich & Judith Tilden,   Aug. 11, 1777
Otis Bigelow & Betty Bartlett,   Dec. 18, 1777
John Shappley & Hannah Bartlett,   Dec. 18, 1777
Benjamin Hawley of Spencertown, N. Y., & Theodosia
    Fitch,   Feb. 5, 1778
Thomas Scott of Norwich & Betty Abel,   Dec. 11, 1777
Eliphalet Murdock of Windham & Anna McCall,

                                       March 25, 1778
Oliver Wattles & Theoda Partridge,   April 2, 1778
Samuel Robinson & Drusilla or Priscilla Metcalf, Sept. 9, 1778
Peter Huxford of Glastonbury & Bathsheba Chappel,

                                       Oct. 8, 1778
William Hyde & Zerviah Fitch Hyde,   Dec. 24, 1778
Charles Lathrop & Lucy Starkie,   Jan. 21, 1779
Abraham Warner of New Canaan, N. Y., & Theoda Hunt,

                                       Feb. 17, 1779
Daniel Judd of Colchester & Hannah Hinckley, Feb. 21, 1779
Andrew Hackley of N. Lebanon, N. Y., & Hannah Metcalf,

                                       Feb. 27, 1779
Oliver Seabury & Abigail Tisdale,   July 15, 1779

Charles Thacher & Hannah Hunt, July 22, 1779
Jonathan Webster & Dorothy Hills, May 25, 1748
Christopher Pease & Hannah Hills, the 3rd, June 9, 1748
Nathan Stark & Anna Fitch, Nov. 2, 1748
Nehemiah Huntington of Norwich & Lois Hinckley,
March 14, 1749
Ephraim Wilcox & Abigail Bascom, April 6, 1749
Ichabod Robinson & Mary Hyde, May 25, 1749
Simeon Bettis of Canterbury & Mehitabel Archer,
Nov. 16, 1749
Joseph Richardson & Elizabeth Wise, Nov. 23, 1749
Joseph McCall & Hannah Clark, Dec. 26, 1749
Crippen Hurd of East Haddam & Mary Archer, Jan. 18, 1750
Joseph Tilden & Elizabeth White, June 14, 1750
Benjamin Baldwin & Ruth Porter, Sept. 27, 1750
Samuel Wise & Grace Webster, Dec. 3, 1750
Daniel Clark & Mary Tuttle, Dec. 13, 1750
Elijah Mason & Martha Clark, Oct. 17, 1751
Jonathan Edgerton & Freedom Buel, Oct. 31, 1751
Hezekiah Cooley of Springfield & Charity Clark,
Feb. 26, 1752
James Hills & Keziah Cutting, Oct. 4, 1753
Isaac Williams & Olive Smith, Nov. 1, 1753
Lazarus Puffer & Sarah Reynolds, Nov. 12, 1753
William Hyde of Norwich & Abigail Langrel, March 28, 1754
Jeremiah Mason, Jr., & Elizabeth Fitch, May 9, 1754
Hubbell Wells of Colchester & Zerviah Chandler,
May 16, 1754
Leonard Hills & Eleanor Root of Hebron, Aug. 28, 1754
Simeon Metcalf & Hannah Brewster, Oct. 16, 1754
Samuel Allen of Hebron & Mary Bascom, Nov. 21, 1754
Jared Clark & Mary Abel, Dec. 12, 1754
Elias Bliss & Zerviah Davenport, Dec. 30, 1754
Joshua Carpenter & Submit Webster, Jan. 15, 1755
Elisha Dunk of Hebron & Esther Porter, Jan. 23, 1755
Ezekiel Welles & Mary Foster, Feb. 5, 1755
Elijah Webster, Jr., & Abiah Metcalf, March 26, 1755
William Bentley, Jr., & Margaret Tracy of Norwich,
Aug. 25, 1755

James Barnaby & Hannah Hills, the 3rd,	Aug. 27, 1755
Bezaleel Badger & Abigail Wattles, Jr.,	Feb. 19, 1756
Ebenezer Cole, Jr., & Abigail Wise,	Feb. 19, 1756
Abiel Stark & Cloe Hinckley,	Feb. 26, 1756
Ebenezer Coleman of Hebron & Beulah Brisco,	July 1, 1756
Samuel Hills, Jr., & Sarah Lillie,	Oct. 28, 1756
Patrick Butler & Mercy Bartlett,	Dec. 16, 1756
Andrewson Dana of Ashford & Susanna Huntington,	
	June 2, 1757
Elijah Taylor & Prudence Lamb,	Feb. 11, 1757
Zephaniah Stark & Hannah Edgerton,	Oct. 26, 1757
John Waddams of Glastonbury & Eunice Porter,	Nov. 3, 1757
Elezer Booge (?) of East Haddam & Lydia Burt,	
	March 9, 1758
John Chamberlain of Colchester & Lydia Welles,	
	March 22, 1758
Rev. David Ripley of Abington & Betty Elliot,	Dec. 12, 1758
Stephen Lee & Mary Gay,	Feb. 22, 1759
Caleb Root of Hebron & Patience Porter,	Jan. 10, 1760
Abner Hills & Mary Comstock,	April 15, 1760
Ozias Coleman of Colchester & Huldah Brewster,	
	June 24, 1760
William Hyde & Alice Otis,	July 10, 1760
David Pratt of Colchester & Keziah Bill,	July 17, 1760
Joseph Peabody of Norwich & Anne Fitch,	Sept. 11, 1760
Amos Bliss & Mary Davenport,	Sept. 11, 1760
Peleg Thomas & Molly Bartlett,	Nov. 18, 1760
Reuben Porter & Sarah Bliss,	Feb. 26, 1761
Ephraim Carpenter & Mary Wheeler,	May 21, 1761
Jacob Elliot, Jr., & Martha Blackleach of Ripton,	
	May 27, 1761
Gideon Arnold of New Hampton & Lucy Hinckley,	
	Sept. 2, 1761
Caleb Gifford & Delight Spafford,	Oct. 14, 1761
Abijah Thomas & Rachel McCall,	Oct. 15, 1761
David Cole of Colchester & Abigail Bliss,	Feb. 9, 1762
Isaac Peabody & Molly Clark,	Feb. 24, 1762
Caleb Hyde & Elizabeth Sackett,	May 6, 1762
Jonathan Webster & Ruth Holdridge,	Nov. 24, 1763

Aaron Thorp & Susanna Loomis, Jr.,   Feb. 15, 1763
Lemuel Clark of Mansfield & widow Jerusha Bill,
                                                   March 9, 1763
Robert Patrick & Lois Buel,   Dec. 6, 1763
Nehemiah Fitch & Rebecca Peabody,   Dec. 28, 1763
Simeon Gay & Ruth Goward or Gowdy of Hebron,
                                                   March 1, 1764
John Strong of Hebron & Thankful Bascom, March 13, 1764
Zebulon Gay of Hebron & Lydia Tyler,   April 3, 1764
Israel Everit, Jr., & Lucy Thomas,   May 24, 1764
Reuben Whitney & Mary Harman,   Aug. 14, 1764
Benjamin Archer, Jr., of Hebron & Jerusha Archer,
                                                   Oct. 3, 1764
Parker Peabody & Sarah Spafford,   Dec. 13, 1764
John Archer & Hepzibah Walters,   April 25, 1765
Sylvanus White & Hannah Thomas,   Oct. 29, 1765
Amos Thomas, Jr., & Betty Brewster,   Oct. 30, 1765
Ezekiel Chapman of Colchester & Jerusha Lee, Dec. 14, 1768
David Webster & Bridget Holdridge of Hebron, Oct. 30, 1765
Daniel Douglass of Norwich & Martha Law,   Oct. 31, 1765
Thomas Bettis of Colchester & widow Jemima Kellogg,
                                                   Nov. 18, 1767
Joseph Richardson & Sarah Marriner of Colchester,
                                                   Jan. 1, 1768
Samuel Hewitt & Betty Archer, both of Hebron, Jan. 1, 1768
Alpheus Phillips & Jemima Brown of Colchester,
                                                   Nov. 16, 1768
Abner Kellogg & Lydia Bartlett,   Nov. 24, 1768
Israel Lee, Jr., & Sarah Law,   Dec. 14, 1768
Richard Otis of Colchester & Mary Hinckley, March 2, 1769
Daniel Pain & Elizabeth Wright,   May 4, 1769
Simon Williams & Esther Clark,   May 8, 1769
Ephraim McCall & Elizabeth Clark,   Sept. 17, 1769
Benajah Bennett & Zerviah Crane,   Oct. 1, 1769
Ezra Lee & Sarah Hackley,   Nov. 15, 1769
Elijah Palmer & Mary Dodge of Colchester,   March 4, 1770
Ichabod Bozworth & Abigail Chappel,   April 4, 1770
James McCarter & Lurany Hennessy,   May 2, 1770
Amos Peabody & Abigail Swift,   Oct. 25, 1770

John Law & Betty Woodworth,	Sept. 30, 1779
Alexander Elmer & Elizabeth Huntington,	Dec. 29, 1779
Asa Tiffany & Lucy Mason,	Feb. 2, 1780
James Lathrop & Molly Stark,	May 4, 1780
Joseph Waterman & Rebecca Blackman,	July 13, 1780
Ozias McCall & Elizabeth Williams,	Oct. 19, 1780
Isaac Bartlett & Sarah Lee,	Oct. 27, 1780
Josiah Huntington & Abigail Gilbert,	Nov. 9, 1780
Thomas Hyde & Priscilla Hinckley,	Nov. 23, 1780
Charles Wattles & Olive Williams,	Dec. 6, 1780
John Burchard of Norwich & Ann Law,	Jan. 18, 1781
James Clark, Jr., & Anna Lyman Tiffany,	Jan. 18, 1781
William Whitney of Norwich & Ruth Berthia Thomas,	
	April 12, 1781
Andrew Fitch & Abigail Mason,	May 17, 1781
Capt. Sylvanus Ticknor of East Haddam & Wealthy Gilbert,	
	May 23, 1781
Palmer Smith of Dresden, N. H., & Sarah Loomis,	
	June 21, 1781
Joshua Wattles & Sarah Ann Hyde,	Dec. 9, 1781
Richard Lyman & Philamelia Loomis,	Dec. 17, 1781
Oliver Strong & Freedom Edgerton,	Dec. 20, 1781
Isaac Brown of Colchester & Hannah Hills,	March 7, 1782
Joseph Babcock of Windham & Molly McCall,	May 1, 1782
William Webb of Windham & Lois Strong,	May 16, 1782
Solomon Hyde of Norwich & Susannah Rogers,	May 30, 1782
Simon Loomis & Sarah Holbrook,	Oct. 23, 1783
Philip Harris, Jr., & Lois Metcalf,	Dec. 11, 1783
Nathan Woodworth & Amy Avery,	March 25, 1784
William Williams & Lydia Williams,	May 20, 1784
David Dean & Mary Palmer,	Oct. 14, 1784
Justin Lewis of New Hartford & Nabby Kaples,	Oct. 21, 1784
Joseph Metcalf & Clarissa Thomas,	Nov. 25, 1784
Hallet Gallop & Mary Bartlett,	Dec. 23, 1784
Eliphalet Dewey & Susanna Williams,	Dec. 30, 1784
Zebediah Lathrop of Norwich & Abigail Harris,	June 6, 1785
Luke Metcalf & Nabby Frink,	Sept. 1, 1785
Jabish Metcalf & Violete Thomas,	Aug. 11, 1785
David Young of Windham & Mary Chappel,	Nov. 10, 1785

Christopher Raymond of New London & Nancy Mason,
Jan. 24, 1786
Ezekiel Avery of New London & Lucinda Roders,
March 24, 1786
Elihu Thomas & Elizabeth Hinckley,   June 1, 1786
Timothy Holbrook & Lucy Fargo,   Oct. 5, 1786
Elijah Howard of Bolton & Clarinda Waterman, Oct. 18, 1786
John G. Hillhouse of Montvill & Betsy Mason, Dec. 28, 1786
Christopher Hann & Rhoda Polly,   March 15, 1787
James Thorp & Lydia Lisk,   June 6, 1787
Abel Buel & Betsey Dewey,   Sept. 6, 1787
Jacob Mantle & Berthia Langrel Hills,   Sept. 13, 1787
Edward Culver Sumner & Abigail Clark,   Nov. 15, 1787
Bezaleel Dewey & Sybil Metcalf,   Dec. 9, 1787
Abijah Thomas, Jr., & Lydia Thomas,   April 28, 1788
Aramel Hinckley & Lydia Strong,   July 10, 1788
Peter Metcalf & Abigail Badger,   Oct. 16, 1788
Francis Becket of Colchester & Betsy Richardson,
Nov. 27, 1788
William Beadle of Colchester & Rhoda Hinckley,
March 3, 1789
Daniel Tillotson & Molly Butler,   Jan. 14, 1790
Abver Hills, Jr., & Joanne Strong,   Jan. 14, 1790
Samuel Skinner of Woodstock & Abigail Dean, June 28, 1790
James Downe of Bozrah & Arthusa Thorp,   Sept. 23, 1790
Timothy Hinckley & Salome Strong,   Nov. 10, 1790
Andrew Champion of East Haddam & Lucy Bartlett,
Jan. 27, 1791
John Palmer of Colchester & Lucy Thomas,   Feb. 10, 1791
Jehiel Johnson of Bozrah & Jerusha Lathrop, March 10, 1791
Charles Lathrop & Lucy Williams,   July 2, 1791
Joshua Brown of Bozrah & Olive Lamphear,   Aug. 18, 1792
Jared Hinckley & Hannah Sluman,   Aug. 16, 1792
Otis Bigelow, Jr., & Henrietta Butler,   Jan. 17, 1793
James Stark & Ruth Yeomans,   Nov. 14, 1793
Denison Palmer of Colchester & Delight McCall Thomas,
Jan. 1, 1794
Abel Metcalf & Clarissa Bozworth,   Feb. 4, 1794
John N. Peabody of New Canaan, N. Y., & Polly Mason,
June 5, 1794

Andrew Huntley & Zelinda Bozworth,	April 3, 1794
Jonathan West & Emma Newcomb,	Nov. 14, 1798
Thomas R. Palmer of Colchester & Ruth Thomas,	
	Nov. 24, 1798
James Williams & Susannah Loomis,	Dec. 16, 1798
Job Lathrop of Canterbury & Deborah Jeffers,	Oct. 23, 1799

NORWICH—BOZRAH.

NEW LONDON COUNTY.

The town of Bozrah was incorporated May, 1786, originally a part of Norwich. The Congregational Church in Bozrah was formed January 3, 1739.

Daniel Palmiter & Mary Eams,	June 12, 1740
Jabez Crocker & Experience Fox,	Nov. 5, 1740
Zacharias Doud & Ruth Howard,	Nov. 18, 1740
Daniel Woodworth & Sarah Colver,	Nov. 27, 1740
Stephen Starke & Mary Pembleton,	Feb. 26, 1741
John Starke & Sarah Hough,	June 1, 1741
Icabod Starke & Mehitable Hough,	May 14, 1741
James Walters & Sarah Birchard,	June 3, 1741
Elisha Gay & Anna Reed,	Oct. 13, 1741
Jedediah Hide & Jerusha Tracy,	May 17, 1742
Silas Crane & Lucy Waterman,	Sept. 20, 1742
Elisha Lothrup & Hannah Hough,	Jan. 23, 1743
Lemuel Colver & Mary Webb,	March 7, 1743
Gideon Rudd & Thankful Allen,	May 25, 1743
Abiel Marshel & Ann Waterman,	July 12, 1743
Thomas Perkins & Elizabeth Loomis,	Nov. 1, 1743
John Wattles & Sarah Slewman,	Jan. 25, 1744
Eldad Sabins & Abigail Fox,	Jan. 31, 1744
John Hackley & Edna Lothrup,	Feb. 2, 1744
William Fox & Hannah Lyon,	Feb. 23, 1744
Joseph Throop & Susannah Gallop,	March 29, 1744
Ebenezer Smith & Lucy Polley,	Oct. 4, 1744
James Lamb & Susannah Weightman,	Oct. 31, 1744
Elisha Edgerton & Zerviah Abel,	Dec. 31, 1744
Nathaniel Ingraham & Sarah Pitts,	Sept. 26, 1745

Richard Williams & Ann Brown,	Nov. 27, 1745
Daniel Waterman & Ann Ford,	Feb. 20, 1746
Ezra Lothrup & Esther Clerk,	Feb. 25, 1746
John Squire & Lydia Airs,	March 26, 1746
John Lewis & Sarah Cross,	April 23, 1746
Joseph Fox & Hannah Crocker,	Oct. 13, 1746
John Brown & Almy Jenkins,	Oct 16, 1746
Jeremiah Gifford & Anne Cole,	Nov. 25, 1746
Hezekiah Edgerton & Freelove Helyard,	Dec. 17, 1746
Caleb Fitch & Ruth Woodworth,	April 5, 1747
Nathan Reed & Mary Gay,	May 21, 1747
John Tracy & Margaret Huntington,	Feb. 13, 1747
Benjamin Waterman & Experience Hide,	Feb. 1, 1748
James Fox & Ann Hide,	March 10, 1748
Ebenezer Palmiter & Mary Palmiter,	May 1, 1748
David Hough & Desire Clarke,	May 19, 1748
Benjamin Sprague & Abigail Tredaway,	May 29, 1748
Nathaniel Collens & Hannah Birchard,	June 3, 1748
John McCall & Elizabeth Ford,	Sept. 8, 1748
Christopher Huntington & Sarah Bingham,	Sept. 29, 1748
David Bentley & Ann Baldwin,	Dec. 1, 1748
Samuel Loomer & Zerviah Johnson,	Sept. 14, 1749
Stephen Loomer & Hannah Chapman,	Oct. 11, 1749
David Clarke & Jane Wightman,	Nov. 5, 1749
Abner Huntington & Mary Wightman,	Nov. 16, 1749
James Fox & Grace Chapman,	Jan. 24, 1750
Solomon Hewett & Abiah Johnson,	Nov. 6, 1750
William Haze & Mary Post,	Dec. 19, 1750
David Johnson & Joannah Palmiter,	Dec. 20, 1750
Jacob Walters & Hepsiba Wise,	March 26, 1751
Wigglesworth Law & Ann Tuttle,	May 2, 1751
Ezra Selden & Elizabeth Rogers,	May 6, 1751
Thomas Woodworth & Zerviah Fox,	July 29, 1751
Jonathan Blackman & Sarah Comstock,	Nov. 7, 1751
Matthew Polley & Martha Hosmer,	Dec. 30, 1751
Samuel Thomson & Lucy Armstrong,	Dec. 18, 1751
Jabez Crocker & Mary Waterman,	Jan. 28, 1752
Asa Baker & Elizabeth Abel,	Jan. 28, 1752
John Polley & Thankful Walters,	March 16, 1752

Jedediah Lothrop & Jemima Birchard,	May 18, 1752
Abiel Squire & Rebekah Lothrop,	June 8, 1752
Joseph Peck (?) & Joannah Rudd,	June 9, 1752
John Lothrop & Sarah Peck,	July 15, 1752
Simeon Leros or Lews & Abia Hough,	Oct. 14, 1752
Jabez Edgerton & Martha Willes,	Oct. 19, 1752
Obediah Smith & Irene Backus,	Jan. 15, 1753
Benjamin Spicer & Jemima Johnson,	March 29, 1753
Elisha Edgerton & Elizabeth Lord,	May 9, 1753
Joshua Calkin & Temperance Edgerton,	Aug. 15, 1753
Jonathan Fitch & Ann Calkin,	Oct. 19, 1753
Ezekiel Lothrop & Abigail Lyon,	Oct. 19, 1753
John Hough & Abigail Baldwin,	Nov. 11, 1753
James Dyar & Anne Whiting,	Dec. 8, 1753
Eliphalet Gustin & Freelove Whitman,	March 11, 1754
Jabez Hough & Phebe Harris,	March 12, 1754
Stephen Chapman & Elizabeth Ingraham,	April 18, 1754
Marshal Hackley & Sarah Deatrick (?),	April 24, 1754
Jabez Backus & Esther Lothrop,	April 24, 1754
Stephen Lee & Lydia Metcalf,	Sept. 3, 1754
Zebulon Metcalf & Lydia Boarn,	Oct. 24, 1754
Jonathan Harris & Martha Woodworth,	Nov. 13, 1754
Mathew Polley & Susannah Spicer,	Nov. 14, 1754
Benjamin Metcalf & Mary Mattoon,	Feb. 27, 1755
John Vargison & Ann Ford,	March 24, 1755
Abel Metcalf & Abigail Thorp,	Aug. 12, 1755
John Hewett & Mahitabel Wentworth,	Aug. 26, 1755
Andrew Lothrop & Deborah Woodworth,	Oct. 15, 1755
Jonathan Rathborn & Katherine Weightman,	Oct., 1755
James Ford & Rachel Backus,	Nov. 12, 1755
Nathaniel Rudd & Alice Kingsley,	Nov. 12, 1755
John Teniss & Experience Rudd,	March 12, 1756
Caleb Whiting & Lois Lyon,	March 18, 1756
David Chapman & Abigail Willet,	May 26, 1756
Jabez Post & Martha Hide,	Aug. 12, 1756
Hezekiah Reynolds & Freelove Wilke,	Sept. 28, 1756
Ezra Birchard & Martha Barret,	Oct. 17, 1756
Sabin Durkee & Ruth Crocker,	Nov. 9, 1756
Zebedee Wood & Esther Hough,	Nov. 10, 1756

Nathan Edgerton & Lucy Smith,	Nov. 17, 1756
John Griswold & Ruth Hewett,	Nov. 23, 1756
James Crocker & Rhoda Johnson,	Feb. 23, 1757
Elisha Hewett & Tryphena Bingham,	March 2, 1757
Theophilus Abel & Mary Pebody,	March 31, 1757
John Lee & Elizabeth Griswold,	April 14, 1757
Stephen Utley & Zeporah Hastings,	April 28, 1757
Elijah Warren & Ann Grover,	April 28, 1757
James Bramble & Elizabeth Pettice,	Aug. 10, 1757
Lemuel Woodworth & Elizabeth Hunt,	Oct. 10, 1757
Zebdiel Rodgers & Elizabeth Tracy,	Nov. 10, 1757
Elisha Rudd & Ruth Kingsley,	Nov. 15, 1757
Salvester Randal & Martha Weightman,	Nov. 16, 1757
John Tracy & Bethiah Johnson,	Jan. 19, 1758
John Betty & Almy Bentley,	March 15, 1758
Jonathan Lothrop & Thoda Woodworth,	March 16, 1758
Benajah Lamphire & Jerusha Woodworth,	March 16, 1758
Ezekiel Vergeson & Sarah Jones,	March 26, 1758
Benjamin Woodworth & Elizabeth Simins (?),	May 4, 1758
Andrew Metcalf & Zerviah Hide,	Sept. 20, 1758
Daniel Osgood & Ruth Eames,	Oct. 12, 1758
Simeon Edgerton & Abiah Hough,	Nov. 23, 1758
Joseph Kellog & Mary Cushman,	May 31, 1759
Samuel Gay & Miriam Collins,	June 21, 1759
Caleb Owen & Priscilla Throop,	Aug. 16, 1759
John Vergeson & Susannah Jones,	Sept. 10, 1759
Nathaniel Pebody & Elizabeth Smith,	Nov. 13, 1759
Richard Downer & Margaret Caruthers,	Dec. 12, 1759
Oliver Wells & Azuba Fitch,	Feb. 7, 1760
Ozias Backus & Lydia Waterman,	May 5, 1760
Samuel Abel & Elizabeth Waterman,	May 29, 1760
Jacob Worthington & Phebe Birchard,	May 29, 1760
Schubal Smith & Hannah Waterman,	June 11, 1760
Palmer Carew & Sarah Chapman,	Oct. 23, 1760
John Brown & Zerviah Wentworth,	Oct. 30, 1760
George Harris & Anna Lothrop,	Dec. 3, 1760
William Fitch & Elizabeth Haughton,	Feb. 10, 1759
Daniel Johnson & Elizabeth Wentworth,	Feb. 18, 1761
John Birchard & Ann Waterman,	April 28, 1761

William Hinson & Azuba Raymond,	May 7, 1761
David Wedge & Sarah Hawlee,	July 12, 1761
Rufus Welch & Abigail Smalle,	July 30, 1761
Jonathan Avery & Jerusha Davies,	Aug. 25, 1761
Isaac Dean & Martha Lothrop,	Oct. 3, 1761
James Huntington & Hannah Maples,	Oct. 11, 1761
Samuel Lothrop & Lois Lothrop,	Dec. 31, 1761
Elias Lothrop & Hannah Gorton,	Jan. 28, 1762
Thaddeus Lothrop & Ann Gorton,	Jan. 28, 1762
Joseph Edgerton & Lucy Lyon,	Feb. 11, 1762
Stephen Gifford & Sarah Waterman,	April 8, 1762
Caleb Tennant (?) & Sarah Wightman,	Sept. 8, 1762
Daniel Loomer & Eunice Buel,	Sept. 26, 1762
Isaiah Abel & Rhoda Pettice,	Nov. 5, 1762
Labbeus Backus & Hannah Ford,	Nov. 24, 1762
Abraham Acley & Lydia Parks,	Dec. 5, 1762
Waters Clarke & Lucy Hill,	Dec. 9, 1762
Vine Welch & Lydia Williams,	Dec. 28, 1762
Ebenezer Wel & Deborah Tracy,	Feb. 10, 1763
Ezekiel Gardiner & Lydia Eames,	April 26, 1763
David Avery & Lydia Lord,	June 29, 1763
Nathan Lee & Sarah Metcalf,	Oct. 7, 1763
Daniel Die & Elizabeth Guard,	Jan. 5, 1764
David Hough & Jemime Baldwin,	May 24, 1764
Ebenezer Baldwin & Esther Backus,	July 11, 1764
Ichabod Ford & Ruth Backus,	Sept. 13, 1764
Charles Hinkley & Elizabeth Throop,	Oct. 24, 1764
John Isham & Eunice Baldwin,	Sept. 7, 1764
Gideon Baker & Rhoda Crocker,	Sept. 8, 1764
Thomas Harris & Sarah Whiting,	Feb. 7, 1765
Jesse Birchard & Lydia Backus,	Aug. 23, 1765
Zerobabel Weightman & Sarah Gardiner,	Nov. 14, 1765
John Waterman & Mary Fitch,	Dec. 12, 1765
Simeon Abel & Martha Crocker,	Feb. 13, 1766
Uriah Waterman & Ann Abel,	Oct. 14, 1766
Ebenezer Backus & Elizabeth Waterman,	Oct. 14, 1766
Andrew Perkins & Ann Turner,	Oct. 21, 1766
Amma Fitch & Lois Waterman,	Feb. 25, 1767
Joseph Chapman & Lois Birchard,	May 23, 1767

David Kilborn & Lydia Abel,	Nov. 5, 1767
Ichabod Ford & Marget Fish,	Nov. 11, 1767
Joseph Harris & Sybil Throop,	Nov. 19, 1767
John Randal & Kathrine Lamb,	Oct. 27, 1768
Joseph Gay & Martha Lothrop,	Dec. 4, 1768
Christopher Calkin & Hannah Lothrop,	July 9, 1769
Samuel Willard & Sarah Starke (?),	Sept. 24, 1769
William Throop & Prudence Hide,	Nov. 9, 1769
Jesse Brown & Ann Rudd,	Dec. 21, 1769
Nathan West & Sarah Chapman,	June 12, 1770
James Saxton & Deborah Fox,	June 26, 1770
Jesse Brown & Abigail Park,	Sept. 26, 1770
Joseph Davis & Mary Rudd,	Oct. 11, 1770
Ebenezer Peck & Lydia Park,	Dec. 3, 1770
Jedadiah Lothrop & Almy Gardiner,	Dec. 13, 1770
Elijah Huntington & Lydia Baldwin,	March 27, 1771
Ebenezer Peck & Martha Wentworth,	Aug. 18, 1771
Samuel Empsted & Mary Walters,	Oct. 16, 1771
Jabez West & Abagail Throop,	June 3, 1772
James Weightman & Hannah Weightman,	Sept. 24, 1772
Simeon Backus & Eunice Waterman,	Oct. 28, 1772
Stephen Woodworth & Eunice Lothrop,	Oct. 29, 1772
Benjamin Dike & Ann Sabin,	Feb. 10, 1773
Lemuel Hough & Hannah Lothrop,	Feb. 18, 1773
Joseph Johnson & Temperance Calkin,	May 27, 1773
Samuel Gager & Hannah Calkin,	July 29, 1773
William Whiting & Alathea Woodworth,	March 8, 1774
Matthew Birchard & Anne Pelton,	May 16, 1774
Andrew Smith & Alice Baker,	May 17, 1774
John Weightman & Susannah Weightman,	Aug. 1, 1774
Eliphalet Baldwin & Sybil Wood,	Oct. 6, 1774
Solomon Giddeen & Sarah Waterman,	Oct. 20, 1774
Elihu Avery & Mercy Gardiner,	Dec. 15, 1774
Benjamin Woodworth & Sybil Fox,	Jan. 26, 1775
Benjamin Cocking & Elizabeth Birchard,	March 9, 1775
William Edgerton & Lucy Birchard,	April 27, 1775
Thomas Baldwin & Ruth Huntington,	Sept. 21, 1775
Vaniah (?) Hyde & Rebeckah Barker,	Oct. 5, 1775
John Dabridge & Elizabeth Waterman,	Nov. 15, 1775

Silas Hartshorn & Anne Huntington,	June 18, 1776
Joseph Fish & Abigail Lothrop,	July 4, 1776
Jonathan Davis & Sarah Dennison,	Dec. 5, 1776
Samuel Gager & Zerviah Gustin,	Dec. 19, 1776
Elijah Treadway & Deborah Harris,	Nov. 18, 1777
Job Talcott & Abigail Huntington,	April 3, 1778
Oliver Clarke & Bettey Fish,	April 15, 1778
Ebenezer Backus & Phebe Calkin,	May 28, 1778
Jonathan Rudd & Mary Huntington,	June 25, 1778
Amos Tooly & Elizabeth Fergo,	July 9, 1778
Azariah Hilyard & Demis Bentley,	Oct. 22, 1778
Joshua Backus & Hannah Calkin,	Nov. 19, 1778
Samuel Campbel & Anne Whiting,	Feb. 10, 1779
William Cardwell & Sybial Griswold,	April 11, 1779
Zerobabel Weightman & Anna Harris,	May 2, 1779
Walter Lothrop & Esther Fox,	May 13, 1779
George Bentley & Lucy Gardiner,	May 16, 1779
William Fox & Jemima Spicer,	Sept. 8, 1779
Thomas Huntington & Nabbe Backus,	Oct. 14, 1779
Charls Woodworth & Joannah Woodworth,	Nov. 4, 1779
Asa Bruster & Betty McCall,	Nov. 25, 1779
Joseph Kilborn & Lucy Whiting,	March 12, 1780
Joseph Hyde & Lusa Waterman,	Sept. 6, 1780
Thomas Walsworth & Hannah Crocker,	Nov. 7, 1780
Caleb Tenent & Eunice Colon,	Nov. 14, 1780
John Gardiner & Phebe Lothrop,	Dec. 13, 1780
David Lamb & Almy Weightman,	March 5, 1781
Jehiel Pettis & Elizabeth Lord,	Aug. 16, 1781
Enoch Hail & Octuna Throop,	Aug. 30, 1781
Elisha Tracy & Lois Huntington,	Oct. 19, 1781
Joseph Perkins & Mary Waterman,	Oct. 26, 1781
William Smith & Betty Crocker,	Nov. 15, 1781
Ebenezer Metcalf & Hannah Hackley,	Nov. 22, 1781
Olive Lothrop & Eunice Hough,	Dec. 13, 1781
Jesse Brown & Lucy Rudd,	Dec. 26, 1781
Martin Dewey & Hannah Waterman,	Feb. 7, 1782
Ignatius Waterman & Mary Birchard,	Feb. 29, 1782
Guy & Time,	Sept. 26, 1782
Asa Lothrop & Allice Fox,	Oct. 17, 1782

Capt. John Hough & Mrs. Ann Baldwin,	Oct. 24, 1782
John Hough & Susannah Johnson,	Nov. 21, 1782
Thomas Adgate & Mary Abel,	Dec. 27, 1782
Ezekiel Lothrop & Lydia Crocker,	April 3, 1783
Aururo Hickley & Mary Crocker,	Nov. 27, 1783
Jabez Cotton, A. M., & Mrs. Mary Baldwin,	Jan 27, 1784
David Bingham & Zerviah Sabin,	Jan. 29, 1784
Zefamah Lothrop & Rachel Wood,	Jan. 29, 1784
Menassah (?) Torrey & Lucy Lothrop,	June 17, 1784
Noah Davenport & Lydia Metcalf,	Sept. 23, 1784
Dan Lee & Keziah Fox,	Nov. 25, 1784
Uriah Lothrop & Lois Hinckley,	Dec. 30, 1784
William Harris & Eunice Crocker,	Nov. 23, 1786
Zeba Woodworth & Lucretia Osgood,	Dec. 6, 1786
Hubbard McCall & Sarah Throops,	May 24, 1787
James Lathrop & Lucy ——,	June 7, 1787
William Day & Phebe Backus,	June 8, 1787
Daniel Gardiner & Anne Crocker,	July 1, 1787
Uriah Downer & Desire Hough,	Nov. 15, 1787
Ebenezer Backus & Elizabeth Crocker,	Dec. 30, 1787
Asahel Birchard & Elizabeth Fox,	Jan. 1, 1788
Jesse Johnson & Elizabeth Harris,	Jan. 13, 1788
Samuel Tillotson & Anne Johnson,	July 24, 1788
Jesse Abell & Elizabeth Lathrop,	Nov. 11, 1788
Dan Throop & Mary Gager,	Nov. 12, 1788
Israel Birchard & Lydia Birchard,	Dec. 25, 1788
Rufus Backus & Clarinda Throgs,	Jan. 18, 1789
Durkie Calkins & Abagail Browning,	Feb. 15, 1789
Caleb Whiting & Mary Loomer,	March 26, 1789
Amos Whitman & Lucretia Whipple,	June 14, 1789
Elderkin Spicer & —— Lathrop,	Sept. 3, 1789
Lemuel Gardiner & Jemima Lathrop,	Oct. 28, 1789
James Deans & Ann Crocker,	Nov. 3, 1789
Azel West & Sally Wightman,	Jan. 14, 1790
William Lathrop & Lydia Harris,	Feb. 8, 1790
Josiah Eames & Lucretia Whipple,	March 4, 1790
John Perkins & Polly Cardwell,	Aug. 19, 1790
William Thomas Avery & Phebe Throgs,	Jan. 30, 1791
Oliver Wattles & Abagail Lathrop,	June 2, 1791

William Collies & Jemima Loomer,	Jan. 28, 1792
Thomas Crocker & Betsey Caulkins,	April 15, 1792
Ishmael Spicer & Martha Abell,	Nov. 29, 1792
Samuel Gager & Fanny Woodworth,	Nov. 29, 1792
Jonathan Caswell & Lydia Abell,	Feb. 28, 1793
——— ——— & Hannah Williams,	Oct. 6, 1793
Peleg Berry & Betsey Woodworth,	Oct. 19, 1794
Israel Lathrop & Deborah Lathrop,	Nov. 18, 1794
Daniel Woodworth & Bathsheba Gardiner,	Jan. 5, 1795
Reuben Bloomer & Lois Abell,	Jan. 29, 1795
Abiel Hyde & ——— Leffingwell,	June, 1795
Gurdon Gifford & Serviah West,	Dec. 10, 1795
Daniel Harris & Sarah Hunt,	Dec. 24, 1795
Simeon Abell & Lucy Leffingwell,	March 12, 1796
Samuel Bragg & Polly Reed,	March 31, 1796
Benjamin Avery & Lois Loomer,	April 21, 1796
James Lamphier & Hannah Eames,	May 8, 1796
Ezra Lathrop & Rebecca Huntington,	Oct. 18, 1796
Stephen Strong & Clorina Mason,	Dec. 25, 1796
Elisha Ford & Sibbil Hammond,	Jan. 7, 1797
Chandler Woodworth & Hannah Hyde Metcalf,	Feb. 28, 1797
Andrew Lathrop & Sibbel Downer,	June 1, 1797
Azel Dean & Huldah Crocker,	Aug. 15, 1797
Rufus Parsons & Ruth Crocker,	Sept. 17, 1797
Benjamin Culver & Dorilly Baldwin,	Sept. 24, 1797
Amos Randall & Peda Abell,	Dec. 17, 1797
Oliver Lamphear & Molly Ford,	Jan. 18, 1798
Timothy Whitman & Mary Randall,	Jan. 21, 1798
Isaac Hall & Eda Wentworth,	April 1, 1798
Sterling Yeomans & Nancy Whitman,	June 10, 1798
Timothy Thore & Eunice Johnson,	Aug. 13, 1798
Daniel N. Throops & Patty Birchard,	Sept. 2, 1798
Benjamin Norris & Sarah Baldwin,	Sept. 19, 1798
Thomas Bettes & Anna Story,	Dec. 16, 1798
Jabez Birchard & Polly Downer,	Jan. 31, 1799
William Gager & Harriet Baldwin,	March 21, 1799
Labean Otis & Nancy Bill,	May 16, 1799
Peter Yates & Lucinda Henson,	March 29, 1799

FAIRFIELD—EASTON.

FAIRFIELD COUNTY.

The town of Easton was incorporated in May, 1845, being previously a part of Weston, Weston, incorporated in 1787, was taken from Fairfield. The Congregational Church of Easton was formed December 13, 1763. It was then in North Fairfield District.

Abel Adams & Lucretia Crane,	Nov. 25, 1773
Joseph Atwell & Hannah Lion,	Nov. 9, 1791
Erva Adams & Elizabeth Bradley,	Oct., 1792
Timothy Blackman & Rhoda Risdon (?),	March 21, 1764
Nehemiah Blackman & Abiah Booth,	July 25, 1764
Heze—— Osborn & Ruth Burton,	Oct. 18, 1764
Nathaniel Barley (?) & Jane Bradley,	April 24, 1765
Stephen Bennit & Ann Seley,	June 20, 1765
Nathan Bennit & Abigail Sherwood,	June 25, 1767
Joseph Bradlee & Martha Bates,	Dec. 10, 1767
Najer Bennit & Sarah Gilbert,	Aug., 1768
Jared Baldwin & Dammores Booth,	—— 1, 1755
Abijah Beardslee & Bethiah Sherwood,	Oct. 24, 1769
Benjamin Bradlee & Abigail Demmon,	Feb. 7, 1770
Aaron Banks & Sarah D——,	Nov., 1772
Seth Bradley & Dorothy Bradlee,	Feb. 18, 1773
Daniel Blackman & Mary Hubbel,	July, 1773
Stephen Barlow & Phebe Jackson,	Aug. 12, 1773
Hezekiah Burr & Ester Downs,	Sept. 15, 1773
Gabriel Baldwin, son of Jared, & Sarah Summers, daughter of Zechariah,	May 1, 1788
David Baker & Lucia Squire,	March 1, 1789
Gersham Bradlee & Sarah Davis,	April 22, 1789
Peter Buckley & Eunice Lion,	Nov. 25, 1789
Abraham Bennit & Cate Hubbel,	Dec., 1790
Isaac Bennit & Polly Johnson,	Dec., 1790
Joseph Burr & Sarah Hill,	Dec., 1790
John Baldwin & Noami Brinsmade,	Dec., 1790
Isaac Bradlee & Sarah Williams,	Sept., 1791
Martin Beers & Rachel Williams,	Dec. 3, 1791
Silvester Booth & Sarah Beers,	Jan., 1792

Joseph Banks & Abigail Bradlee,	Feb., 1792
Stephen Blackman & Charity Wheeler,	Nov., 1792
Justus (?) Bennit & Eunice Mallet,	Dec. 24, 1795
Wakeman Bradley & Sarah Wheeler,	Oct., 1796
Aaron (?) Bradley & Jane Nichols,	Dec. 11, 1796
Wolsey Bradley & Maretta Treadwell,	Dec., 1814
Daniel Cable & Eunice Turney,	Nov. 22, 1769
——— Chambers & Naomi Waklee,	March, 1773
William Cole & Rachel Johnson,	Dec. 20, 1795
Wheeler Cable & Huldah Fairchild,	Feb. 29, 1796
Nehemiah Davis & Ruth Dimon,	March 8, 1789
John Dimon & Sarah Thorpe,	Dec., 1789
Jimie (?) W. Elkinson (?) & Hannah Parrott,	Nov. 10, 1795
Nehemiah Fanton & Sarah Hull,	Jan. 1, 1772
Hezekiah Fanton & Ruth Merwin,	Jan. 14, 1773
Joshua Ferry & Sarah Patterson,	May, 1789
Rowland Fanton & Polly Burr,	Jan., 1792
Andrew Gilbert & Eunice Waklee,	Sept. 10, 1769
David Gorham & Abigail Cable,	March 25, 1770
——— Gregory & Rhoda Hall,	March, 1772
Samuel Goodsel & Eunice Cable,	March, 1790
Thomas Gilbert & Anna Bennit,	Feb., 1791
Abel Turril & Hannah Hoit,	Dec. 21, 1764
John Hoit & Hannah Treadwell,	Nov. 1, 1764
Nathaniel Hubble & Sarah Burton,	Oct. 19, 1766
Seth Hubbel & Lois Jackson,	Nov. 11, 1771
Aaron Hall & Rebecca Summers,	Feb. 18, 1773
Abel Hill & Anna Lyon,	May, 1773
Daniel Hoit & Sarah Wheeler,	June 10, 1773
James Husted & Ruth Bennit,	Nov. 23, 1773
Augustus Hill & Susanna Lyon,	Nov. 24, 1773
John Hall & Hannah Wheeler,	March 7, 1791
Ebenezer Hall & Lydia Booth,	Oct. 26, 1791
Abel Hall & Sarah Sherwood,	Nov., 1792
Josiah Hall & Betsey Burr,	Nov., 1795
Benajah Hill & Molly Jackson,	Nov., 1795
Walter Hull & Anne Gilbert,	Sept., 1796
David Jennings & Mary Staples,	May 19, 1765
John Jewill & Hannah Seley,	June 22, 1769

Ezra Jennings & Martha Bennit,	Nov. 23, 1769
Ebenezer Jennings, Jr., & Sarah Bennit,	March, 1772
John Jones & Hannah Williams,	April 17, 1772
Philemon Jennings & Molly Beach,	April 23, 1789
Seley Jewell & Lucretia Robertson,	Oct., 1789
James Jennings & Deborah Burr,	March 16, 1820
Samuel Lacey & Huldah Sanford,	May 9, 1765
Ebenezer Lord & Ruth Lacey,	Oct. 29, 1771
Joseph Lacey & Mary Bennit,	Feb. 17, 1772
Daniel Lyon & Phebe Seley,	Feb., 1774
Walter Lyon & Priscilla Redfield (?),	Nov. 25, 1789
Nathaniel Lyon & Kate Sherwood,	Jan., 1792
Thomas Merwin & Ruth Silliman,	Feb. 12, 1767
Stephen Morgan & Molly Wakeman,	March 5, 1771
Ogden Meeker & Ruth Lions,	May, 1789
Robert Mills & Desire Robertson,	Aug., 1790
David Murwin & Grisel Burr,	Dec. 7, 1791
James Adiar Merwin & Cate Demmores,	Sept., 1792
——— Meeker & Mary Meeker,	Oct., 1796
Hezekiah Morgan & widow Hill,	Dec. 27, 1796
Peter Nichols & Hannah Burr,	June 15, 1773
Jesse Nichols & Abigail Hill,	Nov., 1792
Hezekiah Osborn & Ruth Burton,	Oct. 18, 1764
Peter Ockly & Ester Fanton,	Nov. 11, 1774
Hezekiah Patterson & Mehitable Jackson,	Feb. 25, 1772
Zophar Platt & Rebecca Fairchild,	Feb. 2, 1773
Nathaniel Picket & Mary Squires,	April, 1773
Daniel Persoll (?) & Hannah Buckley,	Jan. 2, 1792
Walker Perry & Betsey Burr Sturgis,	May, 1793
Jesse Platt & S——— Jackson,	Nov., 1795
James Parrott & Catharine Gilbert,	Nov., 1795
Timothy Blackman & Rhoda Risdon (?),	March 21, 1764
James Rowell & Jemima Beach,	March 20, 1771
Jabez Rowland & Sarah Lacey,	May 2, 1771
Daniel Rowland & Anne Turril,	Dec. 27, 1773
Noah Rockwill & Ester Wescote,	April, 1789
Ezekiel Robertson & Olive Hall,	Oct., 1791
David Sanford & Polly Silliman,	March 22, 1764
Samuel Seeley & Sarah Silliman,	Nov. 22, 1764

Huldah Sanford & Samuel Lacey,	May 9, 1765
Amos Sherwood & Cate Leanil (?),	April 30, 1767
Ebenezer Speer & Mary Stocker,	Nov. 2, 1767
David Stratton & Hannah Sanford,	June 23, 1768
Nathaniel Seley & Rhoda Bennit,	July, 1768
Josiah Sanford & Mary Thorpe,	Nov. 16, 1769
Amos Sherwood & Molly Fanton,	Nov. 18, 1770
Eleazer Sherwood & Mary Squire,	Dec., 1770
Jonathan Squire & Thankful Wheeler,	Dec., 1771
Benajah Starke & Bette Beach,	Jan. 16, 1772
Zechariah Summers & Martha Burr of Redding,	1765
Freeman Seeley & Anna Hains,	Dec., 1790
Asa Silliman & Anne Jackson,	Oct., 1792
Burr Silliman & Eunice Hurlburt,	Oct., 1795
Elihu Sherwood & Charity Jackson,	Nov., 1795
Ephraim Sanford & Polly Bradley,	Dec. 22, 1795
Beach Sherman & Rhoda Hubbel,	Nov., 1796
Samuel Sanford & Polly Silliman,	Dec. 11, 1796
Asiel Turril & Hannah Hoit,	Dec. 21, 1763
Hannah Treadwell & John Hoit,	Nov. 1, 1764
Hezekiah Thorpe & Sarah Winton,	Feb. 28, 1765
John Thorpe & Abigail Gilbert,	July 9, 1767
Enoch Turrel & Sarah Lacey,	Feb., 1769
Jabez Thorpe & Mary Bradley,	Aug. 16, 1769
John Turrel & Deborah Middlebrook,	Aug. 17, 1769
Benjamin Turney & Sarah Lion,	July, 1771
Samuel Thorpe & Huldah Barton,	Feb. 20, 1772
Stephen Turrel & Abigail Hubbel,	May, 1773
Elisha Thorpe & Sarah Wakeman,	July, 1773
Ephraim Terrill & Deborah Rowell,	Sept., 1790
Jabez Treadwell & Lucy Crofutt,	Sept., 1792
Elijah Turney & Eunice Thorpe,	Nov., 1796
David Thompson & Hannah Thorpe,	Dec. 22, 1796
Sarah Winton & Hezekiah Thorpe,	Feb. 28, 1765
Benjamin Whitehead & Mable Jackson,	Nov. 20, 1766
John Wheeler & Ruth Seley,	July 12, 1767
Aaron Wood & Dorothea Mead,	Jan., 1770
Noah Wakeman & Lydia Wheeler,	Oct., 1770
Ichabod Wheeler & Katharine Wakeman,	April 28, 1771

Caleb Wheeler & Mary Sanford,	Oct.,	1771
Nathan Wheeler & Deborah Sanford,	Feb. 10,	1773
Eliphalet Wakeman & Katharine Bennit,	March 11,	1773
Hezekiah Weeb (?) & Abigail Whitehead,	Sept. 14,	1773
Gideon Wheeler & Ruth Burton,	June 7,	1789
Samuel Whitney & Sarah Thorpe,	Sept.,	1789
James Wakeman & Elizabeth Demon,	Dec.,	1789
Moses Wakeman & Sarah Williams,	March,	1790
Samuel Woodkins & Elizabeth Bates,	Jan. 20,	1790
Stephen Wakeman & Sarah Jennings,	Sept.,	1792
Brown Whitehead & Asenath Bennit,	Oct.,	1792
Obadiah Wheeler & Sarah Gilbert,	Nov.,	1792
Stephen Wheeler & Eleanor Wakeman,	April,	1793
Abel Wheeler & Betsey Seley,	Jan. 10,	1796

FAIRFIELD—WESTON.

FAIRFIELD COUNTY.

The town of Weston was incorporated in October, 1787, taken from Fairfield. The Congregational Church in Weston was organized August 17, 1757, and called Norfield.

Justis Olmstead & Mercy Morehouse,	Oct. 12,	1757
Joseph Morehouse & Hannah Banks,	Jan. 12,	1758
Thomas Downs & Eunice Barlow,	Aug. 27,	1758
Ebenezer Davis & Mary Hays,	Jan. 3,	1759
Gershom Fanton & Anna Sturges,	Jan. 18,	1759
Nehemiah Cable & Martha Bradley,	Feb. 22,	1759
Daniel Godfrey & Eunice Bulkley,	March 22,	1759
Isaac Bulkley & ———— ————,		——
Jonathan Fanton & Elizebeth Downs,		1759
———— Cough from Greenfield & ———— ————,	June 22,	1759
Gideon Wakeman & Anna Adams,	Oct. 24,	1759
George Patchen & Elizebeth Williams,	Dec.,	1759
John Thomson & Betty Cable,	May 22,	1760
Lemuel Wood & Sarah Whitlock,	June 3,	1760
Daniel Beers & Abigail Dikeman,	Sept. 3,	1760
Hezekiah Lyon & Rachel Dikeman,	Oct. 17,	1760
John Thorp & widow Mary Whitlock,	Oct. 17,	1760

"———— Cough from Wilton & Darrow & Steward,"

	Nov., 1760
Reuben Solomon & Prudence Bennett,	Dec. 3, 1760
Thaddeus Betts & Anna Patchen,	Dec. 3, 1760
David Morehouse & the daughter of Eli Handford,	
	April 23, 1761
John Bryant & woman bought by Mr. Steward,	Oct., ————
John Dimon & Abigail Fanton,	Nov. 26, ————
James Disbrow & Elizabeth Cable,	April, ————
John Coley & Anna Ogden,	April 7, ————
Jonathan Squires & Elizabeth Morehouse,	May, 1761
Peter Tuttle & Anna Gellet,	Nov. 22, 1762
Nathan Price & Jamima Jecock (?),	Sept. 15, 1763
Beniah Manrow & Betty Guyer,	Feb. 1, 1764
John Sillimon Andrews & Eunice Lyon,	Feb. 8, 1764
David Morehouse & Lyda Rowe,	Feb. 17, 1764
John Olmstead & Abigail Lyon,	May 6, 1764
Brush Marvin & Abigail Squires,	Oct. 2, 1764
Abner Booth & Mercy Olmstead,	Dec. 2, 1764
Timothy Sherwood & Martha Squires,	March 21, 1765
John Adams & Sarah Coley,	Aug. 31, 1765
Nehemiah Gray & Sarah Downs,	Oct. 18, 1765
Jesse Guyer & Mary Squires,	Nov. 20, 1765
Andrew Sturges & Abigail Finch,	Feb. 27, 1766
Josiah Couch & Eunice Frost,	April 21, 1766
Peter Moseman & Ellen Allen,	Aug. 26, 1766
Elias Scribner & Lydia Bennitt,	Sept. 24, 1766
David Couch & widow Mary Gorham,	Oct. 1, 1766
Elias Morehouse & Sarah Patchin,	Nov. 5, 1766
John Fitch & Elizabeth Lockwood,	Nov. 6, 1766
Ebenezer Bixby & Mary Morehouse,	Jan. 1, 1767
Thomas Gray & Mary Mills,	March 1, 1767
Ephraim Lockwood & Anna Whitlock,	March 19, 1767
Ebenezer Hubbil & Lydia Couch,	April 8, 1767
Oliver Sanford & Rachel Coley,	April 9, 1767
Silas Olmsted & Lydia Sloan,	May 10, 1767
James Anthiny & Hannah Squires,	May 12, 1767
Stephen Goreham & Sarah Sturges,	May 21, 1767
Jaber Sherwood & Damaras Cable,	June 3, 1767

Peter Merwin & daughter of Mr. Rowland,	Sept. 24, 1767
Jonathan Cable & Rebeccah Chard (?),	Sept. 30, 1767
John Olmstead & Anna Andrews,	Jan. 26, 1768
Samuel Higgins, Jr., & Fannie Dunning,	Nov. 8, 1768
Michael Lockwood & Abigail Adams,	Nov. 9, 1768
Jehial Smith & (?)ene Davis,	Nov. 21, 1768
Mathew Sherwood & Mary Rowe,	Nov. 27, 1768
Jared Marvin & Hannah Dunning,	Dec. 1, 1768
Thomas Lyon & Thankful Rusique,	May 10, 1769
William Downs & Hannah Bulkley,	Feb. 11, 1769
Silas Fairchild & Sarah Goodsell,	Jan. 11, 1770
David Manrow & widow Jackson,	Jan. 16, 1770
Ebenezer Gorham & Martha Lyon,	Jan. 31, 1770
Nathan Sturges & Mary Ogden,	April 22, 1770
Sealy Squires & Esther Taylor,	Sept. 13, 1770
Elijah Gray & Esther Sturges,	Sept. 20, 1770
David Morehouse & Ann Squires,	Nov. 15, 1770
Jonathan Squires & Mary Gray,	Jan. 20, 1771
Benjamin Allen & Rhoda Allen,	Feb. 25, 1771
John Whitlock & Ellenar Coley,	March 6, 1771
Alexander Rusique & Eunice Blackman,	July 26, 1771
Joseph Ogden & Rachel Andrews,	Oct. 3, 1771
Ebenezer Wakeman & Anna Banks,	Nov. 17, 1771
William Rusique & Susannah Patrick,	Dec. 16, 1771
Joseph Dixon & Susannah Lockwood,	March 5, 1772
Joel Guilburt & widow Mary Guyer,	June 3, 1772
Abel Bradley & Hannah Morehouse,	Nov. 28, 1772
Stephen Hurlbutt & Sarah Ogden,	Dec. 24, 1772
———— ———— (?), son of Reuben, & Susannah Guilburt,	
	Oct. 6, 1773
Thomas Banks & Sarah Dean,	Nov. 21, 1773
James Sturges & Mary Dikeman,	Sept. 14, 1773
Jonathan Cole & Lois Squires,	Feb. 3, 1774
John Gray & Eunice Morehouse,	Feb. 3, 1774
Elisa Brown & Abigail Sturges,	July 7, 1774
David Coley, Esq., & Anna Morehouse,	Sept. 4, 1774
Samuel Lyon & Phebe Canfield,	Oct. 14, 1774
Daniel Smith & Chloe Finch,	Nov. 15 or 13, 1774
Peter Guyre & Eunice Cohoon,	Dec. 21, 1774

Coffee, a free negro, & Bett, servant of Deacon An-
drews, daughter of Jack and Dinah,   Feb. 2, 1775
John T—— & Sarah Whitlock,   Feb. 8, 1775
Albin Cole & Esther Squires,   May 12, 1775
Joseph Gorham & Mary Roberts,   June 11, 1775
John Hanford & Rebeccah Goreham,   Aug. 6, 1775
Jacob Ressoe (?) & Hannah Nothing (?),   Aug. 29, 1775
Ezra Benedict & Mable Morehouse,   Nov. 2, 1775
Jonathan Squires & Mary Reeves,   Nov. 19, 1775
John Lockwood, Jr., & Eunice Squires,   Jan. 4, 1776
David Burr & Jane Banks of Greenfield, Conn.,   Nov. 3, 1776
David Bulkley & Sarah Beers,   May 19, 1777
—————— Fairchild of Newtown & Mary Beers,   June 23, 1777
Nathan Whitlock & Hester Dean,   Aug. 27, 1777
Samuel Rowland & Mable Andrews,   Sept. 25, 1777
Isaac Isaacs (Cole) & —————— St. John's daughter,
    April 15, 1778
David Price & Rachel Smith,   June 17, 1778
Joseph Whitlock & Susannah Downs,   Sept. 10, 1778
Lieut. Jonah Rockwell & Betty Rowe,   Oct. 22, 1778
Robert Harris & Eunice Gray,   Nov. 15, 1778
Prudence Beers & Eunice Ogden,   Nov. 19, 1778
Jonathan Godfrey & Mary Rockwell (?),   Nov. 22, 1778
Ebenezer Banks & Huldy Sherwood,   Dec. 27, 1778
Seth Squires & Hannah Canfield,   Dec. 31, 1778
John Finch & widow Mary Ogden,   Jan. 7, 1779
Squire Adams & Mary Godfrey,   Jan. 24, 1779
Joshua Adams & Sarah Adams,   Jan. 31, 1779
Ezra Elwell & Mercy Finch,   April 9, 1779
Thomas Elsner & Ann Philo of Norwalk, Conn.,   June 23, 1779
William Green & Huldah Squires,   Nov. 10, 1779
Michael —————— & Hannah Hurlbutt,   Feb., 1780
James Beers & Eunice Waterbery,   Feb., 1780
Belah Nash & Sarah Guilbert,   April 6, 1780
Nathan Gray, Jr. (?), & Eunice Bulkley,   May 4, 1780
James Bennit & Anna Godfrey,   June 7, 1780
Elias Godfrey & Eunice Cable,   June 8, 1780
David Smith & Lois Taylor,   July 12, 1780
Jared Duncan & Dolly Osborn,   Aug. 30, 1780
*Amos Stewart, man of Deacon Andrews & Prisilla,
a servant girl in Wilton*   *July 3, 1777*

Samuel Smith & Betty Squires,	Oct. 12, 1780
Jaber Morehouse & R—— Sturges,	Dec. 28, 1780
Albert Lockwood & Grace Godfrey,	April 12, 1781
Nathan Thorps & Hulda Rowland,	June 5, 1781
Ezekiel Sturges & Hannah Moris,	June 14, 1781
Jonathan Coley & Betty Guilbert,	June 29, 1781
David Godfrey & Salome Finch,	June 29, 1781
Ebenezer Abbott & Elizabeth Godfrey,	Oct. 15, 1781
Russel Disbrow & Cloe Canfield,	Oct. 25, 1781
Thomas Squires & widow Hannah Rowe,	Nov. 14, 1781
William P—— & Abigail Coley,	Dec. 16, 1781
Jeremiah Rowland & El—— Downs,	Jan. 27, 1782
Ry—— Van—— & Mercy Taylor,	Jan. 31, 1782
Nathan Morehouse & Mary Ogden,	March 9, 1782
Samuel Ogden & Anne Morehouse,	April 18, 1782
Daniel Sturges & Abigail Steward,	June 22, 1782
Silleman Adams & Rhoda Taylor,	Sept. 19, 1782
Eliphalet Hull & Eunice Downs,	Dec. 8, 1782
Stephen Williams & Mille Morehouse,	Jan. 20, 1783
Gershom Cable & widow Biah Meaker,	July 23, 1783
David Coley, Jr., & Lydia Sturges,	June 29, 1786
Jonathan Perry & Mahitabel Squires,	Sept. 20, 1786
The same Jonathan Perry & Hannah Jackson,	April 19, 1787
Wakeman Hill & Sarah Sturges,	Aug. 2, 1787
Samuel Burr Sherwood & Charity Hull,	Sept. 3, 1787
Ezra Beers & Lucretia Squires,	Sept. 16, 1787
Francis Newel & Abiah Fuller of Wilton,	Sept. 26, 1787
James Batterson & Nancy Williams of Wilton,	Nov. 29, 1787
Asa Olmsted & Betty Steward of Wilton,	Dec. 5, 1787
Levi Lyon & Abigail Squires,	Jan. 11, 1788
Joseph Morehouse & Elen Bixby,	Jan. 24, 1788
Ebenezer Thorp & Rhoda Lockwood,	Feb. 19, 1788
Obediah Wood & Mary Sherwood,	Sept. 4, 1788
Joshua Chapman & Lucy Adams,	Nov. 26, 1788
Noah Dimon & Molly Marvin,	Dec. 31, 1788
John Allen & Anna Seely,	July 5, 1789
Ebenezer Davis & Mary Dimon,	Aug. 1, 1789
Josiah Bennit & Mary Hilton,	Sept. 13, 1789
James Gray & Elizabeth Orsborn,	Nov. 5, 1789

James Dann & Sarah Canfield of Wilton,	Dec. 31, 1789
Daniel Dikeman & Elen Godfrey,	Feb. 10, 1790
Albin Bixby & Mary Sturges,	March 29, 1790
Banks Morehouse & Eunice Morehouse,	May 27, 1790
Hezekiah Andrews & Sarah Beers,	Aug. 5, 1790
Jabez Bennit & Mary Bennit,	Sept. 16, 1790
Silliman Andrews & Mary Thorp,	Sept. 23, 1790
Thomas Whelply & Mary Hubbel,	Nov. 21, 1790
William Scofield & Hannah Abbot,	Nov. 21, 1790
Joseph Sturges & Amelia Ogden,	Nov. 28, 1790
Jonah Rockwell & Urane Elwood,	March 2, 1791
William Downs & Elizabeth Gray,	March 12, 1791
Ralph Smith & Betty Parsons,	May 7, 1791
Benjamin Allen & Rhuamy Bulkley,	May 19, 1791
Samuel Coley & Rhuamy Coley,	June 23, 1791
Ebenezer Manrow & Sarah Hendrix (?),	June 30, 1791
William Greffeth (?) & Betsy King,	Oct. 16, 1791
Isaiah Mallery & Abigail Bennit,	Oct. 26, 1791
Daniel Mallery, Jr., & Mary Adams,	Jan. 15, 1792
Job Lockwood & Hannah Sturges,	April 28, 1792
Thomas Wood & Sarah Rowland,	May 3, 1792
Aaron Morehouse & Parthena Gilbert of Wilton,	June 6, 1792
Samuel Marvin & Anna Burr,	June 28, 1792
Peter Lockwood & Belinda Smith,	July 28, 1792
Thomas Downs & Betsy Thorp,	Aug. 14, 1792
Nehemiah Bradley & Esther Cable,	Sept. 13, 1792
Burton Osborn & Sarah Godfrey,	Nov. 14, 1792
Claudius H—— (?) & Esther Squires,	Nov. 14, 1792
Samuel Guyre & Rebecca Bennit,	Nov. 27, 1792
Deacon Joseph Hyde & widow Tamisin Higgins,	
	Dec. 18, 1792
Elijah Betts, Jr., & Betty Patchen of Wilton,	Dec. 19, 1792
Miles Merwin & Elizabeth Dimon,	Dec. 20, 1792
Gershom Davis & Sarah Sherwood,	Feb. 13, 1793
Hezekiah Mills & Adria Squires,	March 15, 1793
Joseph Bunnel & Esther Gilbert,	April 7, 1793
Ezekiel Morgan & Sarah Whitlock,	May 2, 1793
James Davis & Lydia Fitch of Wilton,	May 2, 1793
Elijah Fitch, Jr., & Mary Olmstead,	May 30, 1793

Thomas Whitlock & Betty Disbrow,	July 15, 1793
Ebenezer Hubbell & Esther Gray,	Aug. 7, 1793
David Duncan & Huldah Smith,	Sept. 26, 1793
Nathan Marvin & Molly Burr,	Nov. 8, 1793
Lewis Handford & Mary Betts of Wilton,	Nov. 12, 1793
Aaron Dean & Huldah Hawley,	Nov. 24, 1793
Levi Davis & Nancy Carley or Curley,	Nov. 24, 1793
John Guyre & Huldah Whitlock,	Jan. 22, 1794
Ebenezer Lockwood & Hannah Jennings,	Jan. 30, 1794
Nathan Morehouse & Mercy Sturges,	Feb. 27, 1794
Nathan Wakeman & Mercy Coley,	March 1, 1794
Joel Davis & Mary Hull,	March 19, 1794
Simon —— & Elizabeth —— (free negroes),	July 21, 1794
Daniel Cole & Anna Whinkkler,	July 26, 1794
Daniel Duncan & Anna Lockwood,	Nov. 20, 1794
Daniel Sturges & Eunice Thorp,	April 16, 1795
Eli Goold & Mary Cable,	April 30, 1795
David Sherwood & Hannah Dan,	Aug. 4, 1795
Joseph Johnson & Hannah Banks of Greenfield,	Aug. 18, 1795
Ezekiel (servant of Joseph Hide) & Cloe (a free girl),	Aug. 18, 1795
James Parson & Ruamy Beers,	Aug. 20, 1795
Silliman Godfrey & Jemima Orsborn,	Aug. 23, 1795
Eliphalet Beers & Anna Cable,	Sept. 30, 1795
Jabez Gray & Rachel Chubb,	Dec. 20, 1795
Nathaniel Gilbert & Huldah Manrow,	March 17, 1796
Jared Beers & Sarah Parsons,	April 3, 1796
Daniel Squire & Abigail Downing,	Sept. 22, 1796
Joseph Elwood & Charlotte Squire,	Oct. 19, 1796
Stephen Perry & Lois Bulkley,	Oct. 27, 1796
Phineas Chapman & Ruth Treadwell,	Dec. 15, 1796
Aaron Dimon & Urane Beers,	Dec. 21, 1796
David Stewart & Phebe Roberts,	Dec. 25, 1796
Samuel Brown & Polly Whinkler,	Dec. 29, 1796
Jonah Rockwell & Huldah Green,	Jan. 15, 1797
Barney Lockwood & Elizabeth Squires,	Feb. 16, 1797
Elijah Gray & Lydia Taylor,	Feb. 19, 1797
Ebenezer Coley & Mary Godfrey,	March 23, 1797
Hull Fanton & Margery Collier,	June 22, 1797

Jabel Sturges, Jr., & Betty Cole,	July 5, 1797
Burr Rowland & Abigail Bennit,	Nov. 9, 1797
Isaac Scudder & Sarah Banks,	Dec. 24, 1797
David Banks & Lois Lyon,	Jan. 18, 1798
Thomas Rodgers & Meriam Rockwell,	Feb. 12, 1798
Eliphalet Taylor & Clarissa Osborn,	Feb. 22, 1798
Robert Sturges & Abigail Goodsell,	Feb. 25, 1798
Daniel Jackson & Cynthia Patchen,	Feb. 28, 1798
Samuel Meaker & Deborah Gray,	March 5, 1798
Lemuel Wood, Jr., & Sarah Smith,	March 6, 1798
Abraham Andrews & Sally Hull,	April 5, 1798
David Bulkley & Mercy Morehouse,	April 7, 1798
Noah Lee & Elen Godfrey,	May 3, 1798
Elias Bennet & Elizabeth Squires,	May 19, 1798
Hezekiah Sherwood & Mable Banks of Greenfield,	Aug. 2, 1798
John Lockwood, 3d, & Polly Sturges,	Aug. 5, 1798
Silliman Fanton & Mary Coley,	Aug. 16, 1798
Joseph Burr & Betty Morehouse,	Aug. 19, 1798
Bebe Gray & Elen Sherwood,	Sept. 27, 1798
Ebenezer Gilbert & Betty Manrowe,	Nov. 11, 1798
Isaac Bedient & Hannah Bennit,	Jan. 6 or 16, 1799
Joseph Whitlock & Sarah Raymond,	March 11, 1799
Levi Thorp & Tamisin Rockwell,	March 14, 1799
Jesse Crossman & Betsy Brown,	April 23, 1799
Peter Thorp, 2d, & Rachel Hull of Greenfield,	April 30, 1799
Samuel Lord & Eunice Beers,	June 9, 1799
Thomas Selleck & Esther Fitch (free negroes),	June 13, 1799
Daniel Duncan, Esq., & Elizabeth Williams,	July 6, 1799
Wakeman Bradley & Katharine Andrews,	Sept. 8, 1799
John Basset & Urane Thorp of Greenfield,	Nov. 17, 1799
John Meaker & Sally Duncan,	Nov. 29, 1799
Walker Wakeman & Molly Orsborn,	Dec. 18, 1799
Joseph Lyon & Jane Rowland,	Dec. 25, 1799

WASHINGTON.

LITCHFIELD COUNTY.

The town of Washington was incorporated January, 1779, taken from Woodbury, Litchfield, Kent and New Milford. The Congregational Church in Washington, located at New Preston, was organized in 1757.

David Bostwick & Hannah Hill,	April 5, 1770
Abraham Dayton & Abigail Cogswell,	April 8, 1770
John Barlow & Anna Casswell,	May 27, 1770
Abraham Barns & Abigail Kinne,	June 15, 1770
John Peet, 3d, & Deborah Leach,	Sept. 30, 1770
Titus Allen of Litchfield & Phebe Morris,	Nov. 22, 1770
Benjamin Lamkin of Stratford & Esther Kinne,	Jan. 24, 1771
Gideon Morgan & Patience Cogswell,	June 16, 1772
Samuel Hill & Anna Terrill,	June 18, 1772
Jonah Rude of New Preston & Eleanor Foot of Judea,	
	Aug. 26, 1772
Elijah Couch of Reading & Mary Bosworth,	Nov. 5, 1772
Daniel Toneray (?) of Oblong & Huldah Tracy,	Dec. 27, 1772
John Barlow & Temperance Branch,	Jan. 24, 1773
Salmon Crittenden & Rebecca Peet,	April 14, 1773
Joseph Whitney of New Preston & Sarah Weeks of	
Cornwall,	Sept. 2, 1773
Samuel Allan & Mary Caswell,	Sept. 26, 1773
Joel Terrill & Olive Dibble,	Oct. 3, 1773
Daniel Owen, Jr., & Ruth Peet,	Oct. 25, 1773
George Keith & Elizabeth Reynolds,	Oct. 25, 1773
Benjamin Adams & Chloe Hatch,	.Dec. 30, 1773
Martin Bostwick of New Preston & Phebe Washburn	
of Kent,	Jan. 6, 1774
David Olmstead & Sarah Waller,	Feb. 7, 1774
Abel Terrill & Jerusha Peet,	March 24, 1774
Jonah Daton of New Milford & Jane Terrill,	April 6, 1774
David Washburn & Phebe Terrill,	May 31, 1774
Daniel Hill & Love Waller,	June 16, 1774
David Bosworth & Elizabeth Curtis,	July 1, 1774
Elijah Dean & Sarah Palmer,	Sept. 8, 1774

Isaac Pratt of Litchfield & Abigail Barlow,   Nov. 10, 1774
Thomas Morris, Jr., & Rachel Budd,   Nov. 15, 1774
Serajah Blackman & Sarah Stockwell,   Nov. 24, 1774
Joel Murray & Abigail Peet,   Dec. 29, 1774
Benjamin Jones of New Concord & Thankful Whitney,
                                                     Jan. 17, 1775
David Henderson & Mary Duane,   May 18, 1775
Isaac Mallory of New Preston & Silence Hurd of Judea,
                                                     Aug. 2, 1775
Caleb Rude, Jr., & Antha Keeney,   Aug. 14, 1776
Isaac Ball of Stockbridge & Rachel Terrell,   Dec. 10, 1776
Semour Crittenden of Lenox & Sibil Kinne, March 16, 1777
Pearly Kinne of New Preston & Sarah Hine of Judea,
                                                     March 16, 1777
Byal Bristol of New Preston & Mehitable Canfield of
    New Milford,   May 9, 1777
Elijah Couch of Reading & Eunice Coplee of Judea,
                                                     July 20, 1777
Epaphras Bell of Fort Edward & Lucy Cary, Aug. 17, 1777
Ebenezer Couch & Sarah Bostwick,   Nov. 4, 1777
Stiles Beardsley & Bathsheba Bosworth,   Nov. 9, 1777
Archibald Fipping of New Milford & Mary Beeton (?)
    of Stratford,   March, 1778
Jesse Baker of Judea & Ruth Cary,   April 16, 1778
James Graham of Farmington & Eunice Guthrie,
                                                     April 30, 1778
Heath Kelsey of Kent & Rhoda Guthrie,   April 30, 1778
Eli Taylor & Huldah Swetland,   May 19, 1778
Israel Camp & Bette Hurlburt,   Oct. 13, 1778
Wells Beardsley & Andrea Fowler,   Nov. 26, 1778
Joseph Guthrie & Hannah Cogswell,   Dec. 10, 1778
William Stone of Litchfield & Rachel Curby, March 10, 1779
Eliphalet Richards of New Hartford & Abigail Whittlesey,.
                                                     Sept. 2, 1779
Julius Caswell & Amy Averill,   Oct. 28, 1779
Elijah Barns of New Preston & Mercy Farnham of
    Salisbury,   Dec. 9, 1779
Thomas Runnolds of Kent & Sibil Fisher,   Dec. 28, 1779
William Beardsley & Susanna Whitney,   June 25, 1780

Robert Osborn & Mary Taylor, Nov. 6, 1780
Jonas Newton of Arlington & Rachel Stuart, Dec. 7, 1780
John Beckwith of New Canaan & Chloe Bosworth,
Jan. 15, 1781
Nathaniel Tibbals & Mollie Kinne, July 8, 1781
Rev. Seth Swift of Williamstown & Lucy Elliot, Sept. 7, 1781
Goodman Noble & Sarah Tiley, both of New Milford,
Oct. 24, 1781
Nathaniel Chaffee of Rehoboth & Huldah Dean, Dec. 27, 1781
Lyman Kinne of New Preston & Sarah Stone of New
Milford Jan. 3, 1782
David Austin of New Preston & Hannah Buckley of
East Greenwich, March 3, 1782
Stephen Noble & Abigail Crocker, April 19, 1782
John Jones & Esther Stone, May 2, 1782
Solomon Murray & Martha Averill, Aug. 14, 1782
Sylvester McKay & Elizabeth Bostwick, Sept. 13, 1782
Eleazar Hendricks & Martha Stone, Oct. 2, 1782
Gideon Lawrence of Kent & Berthia Keeney, Oct. 10, 1782
Zeckeriah Price & Ruth Averill, Oct. 20, 1782
William Bradley of New Preston & Anna Cheeney of Kent,
Oct. 24, 1782
Reuben Curby of Litchfield & Anne Guthrie, Oct. 29, 1782
David Tibbals & Anne Rude, Dec. 5, 1782
Daniel Averill of New Preston & Phebe Andres of Kent,
Jan. 8, 1783
Abram Guthrie & Keziah Mallory, Jan. 9, 1783
John Torrence & Rhoda Lacey, Feb. 23, 1783
David Hubbell of Newtown & Elizabeth Taylor,
March 2, 1783
John Couch of New Preston & Lois Stone of New
Milford, March 9, 1783
Lemuel Beeman of East Greenwich & Lydia Cogswell,
March 11, 1783
Samuel Sturtevant & Sarah Morris, Sept. 9, 1783
Eponetus (?) Platt of New Milford & Molly Stone, Oct. 8, 1783
B. Ruggles Bostwick of New Milford & Rachel Stone,
Nov. 30, 1783
Amos Jones of Hartland & Thankful Whitney, Dec. 9, 1783

Nathan Tibbals, Jr., & Hannah Cogswell,   Dec. 25, 1783
Tracy Beeman of Kent & Polly Cogswell,   Jan. 8, 1784
Jeremiah Crandall of Pawling's Precincts & Freelove
    Keeney,   Jan. 12, 1784
Jesse Benedict of Ridgefield & Urania Waller,
                                                  March 25, 1784
Daniel Averill, Jr., & Eunice Calhoun,   May 17, 1784
Joseph Badger & Lois Noble,   Oct. 1, 1784
Daniel Campbell of Sharon & Lydia Blackman, Dec. 2, 1784
Joseph Cary & Sarah Bostwick,   Jan. 20, 1785
Joseph Whittlesey & Mary Camp,   Oct. 6, 1785
Henry Gosley & Sarah Kimbal,   Oct. 6, 1785
David Reynolds & Jane Brown,   Nov. 13, 1785
Henry Whitlock of Ridgefield & Anne Couch, Dec. 30, 1785
Samuel Beeman & Beulah Porter, both of Kent, Feb. 5, 1786
Eli Phelps of Stockbridge & Mehitable Bostwick,
                                                  Feb. 19, 1786
Samuel Bradley of Ridgefield & Hannah Bostwick,
                                                  Feb. 22, 1786
Thomas Porter, Jr., & Deborah Cummings, both of
    East Greenwich,   March 27, 1786
Eliakim Sharp & Hannah Guthrie,   March 29, 1786
Gillet Jones & Bette Mallory,   May 4, 1786
Benjamin Morehouse & Jane Hill,   Nov. 30, 1786
William McDonald of York City, State of N. Y., &
    Abigail Fowler,   Jan. 8, 1787
Hezekiah Ackley & Jemima Whittlesey,   Jan. 11, 1787
Sylvester Kinne & Sally Stewart,   Sept. 24, 1787
Arthur Knowles of New Milford & Urania Lamson,
                                                  Oct. 19, 1787
Gideon Benedict Knowles & Comfort Waller,   Nov. 15, 1787
Francis Hall & Elizabeth Reynolds,   Nov. 19, 1787
Reuben Wells of Susquehannah & Abigail Terrill,
                                                  March 5, 1788
Reuben Dayton & Sarah Morehouse,   June 23, 1788
Aaron Coleman of Kent & Armilla Noble,   Nov. 25, 1788
Stephen Guthrie & Sally Chappell,   Jan. 11, 1789
Daniel Terrill of Shoreham & Temperance York, Jan. 28, 1789
Ebenezer Strong of Warren & Mary Hine of New Milford,
                                                  Feb. 25, 1789

Joshua Keeney of Susquehannah & Phebe Sturtevant,
Feb. 14, 1790
Jonathan Warner of New Canaan & Clarina Elliot,
Feb. 23, 1790
Henry Strait & Olive Terrill, March 2, 1790
Nathaniel Beecher & Hannah Strait, April 7, 1790
Ebenezer Smith of Ridgefield & Elizabeth Bostwick,
April 7, 1790
John Keeney of New Preston & Chloe Ingraham of
New Milford, July 13, 1790
Pierce Freeman & Rebecca Moody, July 26, 1790
Justis Dimon & Olive Stone, Aug. 19, 1790
Truman Mallory & Amey Sharp, Oct. 21, 1790
Stiles Goodsell & Chloe Stone, Oct. 28, 1790
Gideon Orton of Litchfield & Polly Ross of Kent,
Nov. 21, 1790
William Cogswell of New Preston & Amaryllis Johnson
of Southbury, Jan. 30, 1791
William David Willockson & Sally Partridge, Feb. 7, 1791
Isaac Blackman & Lydia Taylor, Feb. 18, 1791
Isaiah Johnson of Montgomery, N. Y., & Sally Whit-
tlesey, March 3, 1791
Elijah Curtis of New Milford & Jane Cogswell,
March 24, 1791
Stephen Cogswell & Anne Camp, May 22, 1791
James Chapel of Richmond & Sylvia Wheaton, Nov. 24, 1791
Samuel Young & Tryphena Barns, Nov. 24, 1791
Aaron Bliss of Brimfield & Rachel Fowler, Jan. 19, 1792
Stephen Strong of Warren & Lydia Hine of New
Milford, Feb. 2, 1792
Daniel Lyon of Warren & Mabel Barns, March 14, 1792
John Whittlesey of Salisbury & Abigail Johnson of
New Milford, May 24, 1792
Nathaniel Averill of Washington & Polly Whittlesey
of Salisbury, Sept. 25, 1792
Gold Camp & Rebecca Brown, Nov. 25, 1792
John Morehouse, Jr., & Sarah Strait, Jan. 22, 1793
George King & Nancy Gallaspie, Aug. 8, 1793
Richard Eliot & Joanna Hill, Oct. 6, 1793

Elihu Bishop of Washington & Polly Taylor,   Jan. 12, 1794
Reuben Kirby of Clinton & Naomi Patterson,   Jan. 22, 1794
Benjamin Adams of New Preston & Sarah Gridley of
    Kent,   July 1, 1794
Elijah Bunnell of Litchfield & Mary Pratt,   Feb. 21, 1795
Eleazer Beecher of New Milford & Mary Ann Barlow,
                                      April 16, 1795
John Beecher of New Milford & Abigail Barlow,
                                      April 16, 1795
David Waller & Abigail Terrill,   May 21, 1795
Philo Barnum of New Preston & Lois Kinney of New
    Milford,   June 17, 1795
Matthus Mallet of New Milford & Anna Morehouse,
                                       July 5, 1795
Daniel Ingraham & Huldah Sweatland,   Oct. 25, 1795
Elnathan Peet & Sally Tucker,   Oct. 25, 1795
Nathaniel Wilson of Fairfield & Rachel Benedict,
                                  April 24, 1796
Henry Dains of New Preston & Zilpha Cogswell of Warren,
                                  June 15, 1796
Samuel Titus & Polly Sanford, both of Kent,   July 5, 1796
Nehemiah Patterson & Marsena Daton,   Jan. 2, 1797
Dimon Bostwick & Lois Olmstead,   Feb. 19, 1797
Leman Terrill & Lucy Terrill,   March 5, 1797
Daniel Morehouse & Elizabeth Tucker,   April 11, 1797
Tobias Lanson of Litchfield & Anna Charles,   July 11, 1797
Martin Whittlesey & Lorana Dayton,   Dec. 19, 1797
Joel Stone of New Milford & Chloe Brown,   Dec. 21, 1797
Roger Averill & Anna Cogswell,   Dec. 31, 1797
Philo Barnum & Abigail Hull,   Jan. 14, 1798
Curtis Hicok & Sally Brown, both of Washington,
                                  May 21, 1798
John Beecher of New Milford & Clarina Barlow, May 21, 1798
Job Picket & Mary Terrill,   Nov. 29, 1798
Samuel Knapp of Norfolk & Lois Lake of New Milford,
                                  Feb. 20, 1799
James Young of Kent & Naomi Clark of Warren,
                               March 10, 1799
Aaron Beeman & Jerusha Beeman, both of Kent,
                               March 10, 1799

Reuben Tucker & Sally Richmond, both of New Milford,
                                        March 24, 1799
Gidion Beeman of Warren & Patience Cogswell, July 18, 1799
Rufus Beeman of Warren & Polly Hungerford, Aug. 8, 1799
Josiah B. Benedict of Ridgefield & Esther Terrill,
                                        Aug. 8, 1799
John Hathaway of Partridgefield & Abigail Calhoun
    of Washington,   Aug. 8, 1799

HARTLAND.

HARTFORD COUNTY.

The town of Hartland was incorporated May, 1761. The Congregational Church, located at East Hartland, was organized May 1, 1768.

Jedidiah Bushnell & Debborah Giddings,   Oct. 27, 1768
Josiah Harvey of East Hartland & Elizabeth Bates of
    Granville, Mass.,   Nov. 1, 1768
John Wilder & Hannah Andrews   Feb. 15, 1770
Benjamin Brown of Windsor & Abigail Parker of Hartland,
                                         Nov. 13, 1770
Jonathan Couch of Symsbery & Ruth Giddings of Hartland,
                                         Nov. 18, 1770
Nathaniel Buttler & Lydia Bemon of Hartland, March 6, 1771
Nehemiah Andrews, Jr., & Hephzebah Rowling,
                                         March 14, 1771
Joseph Perkins & Lois Couch,   Nov. 25, 1771
Timothy Couch & Eunice Perkins,   Jan. 23, 1772
Daniel Wilcocks of Simsbury & Isabel Hambleton of
    Hartland,   June 18, 1772
Thomas Jones of Barkhamstead & Susanna Adams of
    Hartland,   Nov. 23, 1773
Frederic Shipman & Elisabeth Phelps,   Oct. 5, 1774
Samuel Andrews & Ruth Hutchens,   Jan. 25, 1775
Amos Rose & Abigail Hitchcock, both of Granville, Mass.,
                                         Feb. 16, 1775
Samuel Crosby & Lydia Allen,   March 23, 1775
Eliphalet Parker & Jael Leavitt,   May 17, 1775

Barzeliel Gates of East Haddam & Helen Wilder of
    Hartland, July 6, 1775
David Gilbert & Elizabeth Wilder, Dec. 21, 1775
Eli Andrus & Abigail Hutchins, Jan. 8, 1776
Eliphaz Perkins & Mary Daniels, Jan. 11, 1776
Elisha Giddings & Susanna Perkins, April 22, 1776
Oliver Hitchcock, Jr., of Wallingford & Mercy Parker
    of Hartland, Oct. 3, 1776
Phineas Williams & Anna Bartlett, both of Granville, Mass.,
Nov. 29, 1776
Ephraim Wright of Spencertown & Olive Reeves of
    Hartland, Jan. 23, 1777
Eliphalet Parker & Ruth Couch, Feb. 6, 1777
Reuben Daniels & Sarah Meeker, Sept. 3, 1777
Thomas Jones of Hartland & Rebecca Knap (?), of
    West Springfield, Sept. 4, 1777
Edward Brockway & Hannah Parmer, Oct. 23, 1777
Samuel Clark & Hepzibah Jones, Nov. 9, 1777
George Shepherd & Elizabeth Crane, both of Barkhamstead,
Dec. 4, 1777
Timothy Stanley of Groton & Lydia Cowdery of
    Hartland, Dec. 18, 1777
Jonathan Cook & Deborah Leonard, both of Loudon,
    in the State of Massachusetts Bay, March 4, 1778
Ebenezer Crane of Barkhamstead & Jemima Tiffany
    of Hartland, May 21, 1778
Elishama Porter & Elizabeth Benjamin, May 28, 1778
Lieut. Amos Palmerly of Litchfield & widow Eunice
    Gilbert of Hartland, Dec. 3, 1778
Isaiah Clark of Hartland & Eunice More of Simsbury,
Dec. 24, 1778
Lieut. Israel Jones of Barkhamsted & Rhoda Parsons
    of Granville, Mass., Jan. 19, 1779
David Banning & Mary Rathbone, Feb. 3, 1779
Ezekiel Kellogg & Caroline Ensign, Feb. 4, 1779
Simeon Ward of Barkhamstead & Rachel Beech of Hartland,
March 29, 1779
Jonathan Bill, Jr., & Elizabeth Sparrow, April 22, 1779
Phineas Perkins, Jr., & Phebe Hall, May 4, 1779

Elijah Coe & Margaret Hutchins,	May 20, 1779
Zebulon Mack & Mary Bill,	Aug. 4, 1779
Timothy Spelman of Granville, Mass., & Hannah Hayes of Hartland,	Oct. 13, 1779
Joshua Giddings, Jr., of Hartland & Submit Jones of Barkhamstead,	Oct. 28, 1779
Reuben Smith & Ruth Wilcox, both of Granville, Mass.,	Nov. 10, 1779
Samuel Church of Granville, Mass., & Phebe Ma—— (?) of West Springfield,	. Nov. 18, 1779
Daniel Scoville of Granville & Elizabeth Granger of Sandisfield,	Nov. 25, 1779
Peter Gibbons, Jr., of Granville & Hannah Couch of Hartland,	Feb. 3, 1780
Robert Hills & Sybil Glawson, both of Symsbery,	March 23, 1780
Gordon Mack & Asenath Palmer,	Aug. 1, 1780
Joseph Wolf & ——— Gibbons of Granville,	Oct. 12, 1780
Phineas Coe & Rhoda Banning,	Oct. 15, 1780
Elihu Achley of Symsbury & Thene Hayse of Hartland,	Nov. 23, 1780
Daniel Bill of Hartland & Mindal Brainard of East Haddam,	July 29, 1781
Abijah Spencer & Hannah Bill,	March 5, 1782
Thomas Bushnell & Rebeckah Andrews,	March 14, 1782
Jonathan Emmons, Jr., & Mary Brainard,	April 4, 1782
Darius Case of Simsbury & Mary Giddings of Hartland,	May 7, 1782
Russel Borden & Fairvine (?) Wilson,	Nov. 28, 1782
Ashbel Irving of Suffield & Jemima Smith of Hartland,	Dec. 19, 1782
Asa Cowdery & Abigail Ensign,	Jan. 9, 1783
Elijah Adams & Sarah Emmons,	April 16, 1783
Thomas Beman, Jr., & Ann Fuller,	April 17, 1783
Daniel Adams & Sarah Mack,	Aug., 1783
Gideon Perkins & Sarah Harger,	Oct. 14, 1783
Peletiah Daniels, Jr., & Hulda Gates,	Oct. 14, 1783
Benjamin Mack & Isabel Bawstick,	Oct. 30, 1783
Asa Andrews & Lucy Achley,	Nov. 27, 1783

Anjus McCloud & Sarah Giddings, Feb. 18, 1784
Micah Schovil, Jr., & Hannah Meeker, March 4, 1784
Ichabod Fuller & Affia Spa—w (?), March 4, 1784
Ambrose Cowdry & Mary Green Reed, Aug. 18, 1784
Dr. Amherst Coult of Lyme & Miriam Giddings of
    Hartland, Sept. 12, 1784
Isaach Jones of Barkhamsted & Abigail Brockway of
    Hartland, Dec., 1784
Ashur French & Anna Carter, Dec. 30, 1784
Judah Holcomb of Symsbery & Martha Benjamin of
    Hartland, June 16, 1785
Ebenezer Hathaway of Suffield & Mahittable Cowdry
    of Hartland, July 27, 1785
Daniel Bushnel & Rebeckah Banning, March, 1786
William Bushnel & Mary Borden, July 25, 1786
Obediah Gildersleaves & Cloe Bushnell, Dec. 3, 1786
Jonathan Bill & Caroline Kellogg, Dec. 7, 1786
Moses Brockway & Cloe Giddings, Sept. 26, 1787
John Treat & Abigail Huthens, Dec. 6, 1787
Joshua Bill & Lydia Spencer, Dec. 13, 1787
Ozias Holcomb, Jr., of Granby & Ruth Perkins of
    Hartland, Jan. 1, 1788
Jesse Spencer & —————— ——————, Jan. 30, 1788
Liberty Cressie & Statira Brainard, May 22, 1788
Havilah Smith & Louisa Hutchens, Nov. 27, 1788
Asa Haines & Molly Tuller, Nov. 27, 1788
Aaron Spencer & Mindel Phelps, Feb. 10, 1789
Benjamin Hutchens & Jerusha Bradley, Feb. 15, 1789
John Olmstead of Cochester & Ruth Hutchens of
    Hartland, May 13, 1789
Benjamin Reed & Dameras Cowdry, April 29, 1790
David Shipman & Tabitha Meacham, Jan. 6, 1791
Charles Jones of Hartland & Hannah Reed of Granby,
    Feb. 3, 1791
Eben Warner Judd of Vermont & Lydia Giddings of
    Hartland, Feb. 27, 1791
Simon Achley & Lydia Emmons, Nov. 15, 1791
Benjamin Schovil & Temperance Spencer, Dec. 8, 1791
Abner Johnson of Southwick & Elizabeth Gales of
    Hartland, May 2, 1792

Richard Hayes & Mary Lane, Nov. 1, 1792
Jesse Cornwall of Granville & Phebe Hall of Hartland,
Nov. 11, 1792
Benjamin Hayes of Granby & Hannah Tuller of Hartland,
Nov. 20, 1792
Jeames Barlow & Rhoda Pratt, both of Granville,
Feb. 21, 1793
Medad Canfield of Granville & Hepzibah Andrews of
Hartland, March 31, 1793
Stephen Dewolf of Granby & Deborah Church of
Hartland, Nov. 19, 1793
John Carrington & Cynthia Fuller, Dec. 12, 1793
Ozias Robertson of Granville & Lydia Bill of Hartland,
Dec. 31, 1793
Samuel Emmons & Prudence Harris, both of Bark-
hamstead, Jan. 23, 1794
David Mecher, formerly of Hartland, & Lois Adams
of Granby, July 23, 1794
Isaac Roberts & Abigail Fox, both of Granville, Sept. 4, 1794
Amos Perkins of Hartland & Olive Adams of Granby,
Sept. 9, 1794
Harris Emmons & Sebra Merrit, both of Barkhamstead,
Oct. 2, 1794
Shayler Fitch & Louisa Borden, both of Barkhamstead,
Oct. 12, 1794
Phineas Meacham & Lois Beman, Oct. 19, 1794
Gad Ferry & Hannah Pease, both of Barkhamstead,
Oct. 27, 1794
Aron Cowles of Hartland & Jemima Chapman of
Barkhamstead, Nov. 27, 1794
Martin Daniels & Lucretia Mory, Dec. 24, 1795
William Clark Jones of Snowbush & Rany Brockway
of Hartland, Feb. 4, 1796
Ozni Miller & Hannah Clark, Feb. 18, 1796
Elijah Clark & Katharine Frances, Feb. 18, 1796
Martin Meacham & Anna Fuller, March 31, 1796
Rev. Timothy Mather Cooley & Content Chapman,
both of Granville, May 4, 1796
Aaron Brockway & Mary Williams Emmons, June 30, 1796

Dennis Clark Palmer & Phebe Edwards, Sept. 5, 1796

Robert Robbins of Sandisfield & Lucy Wright of Hartland,
Sept. 27, 1796

Daniel Clark Judd of Williamstown & Deby Hatch of
Granville, Sept. 29, 1796

Titus Haize of Granby & Ruth Jones of Barkhamstead,
Nov. 10, 1796

Daniel Wait of Southwick & Huldah Gates of Hartland,
Nov. 10, 1796

Ezekiel Kellogg of Granby & Luna Clark of Hartland,
Dec. 8, 1796

———— Buttolf & Louisa Reed, both of Granby, Dec. 21, 1796

Calvin Cone of Barkhamstead & Mary Bushnell of
Hartland, Dec. 22, 1796

Warren Higley of Simsbury & Lucy Sawyer of Hartland, Jan. 9, 1797

Hector Hamilton & Elizabeth Clark, both of Granville,
July 21, 1797

———— Tylor of New Hartford & Statira Emmons of
Hartland, Nov. 9, 1797

Russel Smith of Granby & Lucy Gates of Hartland,
Dec. 26, 1797

Marvin Gates & Rachel Coe, both of Granville, Jan. 16, 1798

Thomas Hatch of Barkhamstead & Cynthia Holmes
of Hartland, March 4, 1798

Francis Peebles & Marjery Baldwin, both of Granville,
Aug. 9, 1798

Newton Hayes & Sally Wilcox, both of Granville,
Dec. 25, 1798

Charles Merry of Genesee & Martha Brockway of
Hartland, Jan. 6, 1799

Philander Humphrey & Anna Selby, May 7, 1799

Judson Spelman & Abigail Basset, June 20, 1799

William Wright & Prudence Spelman, Nov. 28, 1799

NORWICH—LISBON.

NEW LONDON COUNTY.

The town of Lisbon was incorporated in May, 1786, taken from Norwich. The Congregational Church in Lisbon (Newent Society), located at Jewett City, was organized December, 1723. Rev. Daniel Kirtland, Pastor.

Samuel Parish, Jr., & Mary Rudel,	July 6, 1724
Jonathan Knight & Abigail Longbottom,	May 3, 1726
Thomas Tudd & Martha Perkins,	April 19, 1727
Benjamin Barnum & Mary Kinsman,	April 20, 1727
William ——— of Lebanon & Abigail Heth,	April 22, 1727
Sylvanus Harrington & Elizabeth Lambert,	June 26, 1727
Joseph Lane of Windham & Elizabeth Rudd,	July 17, 1727
Joseph Lothrup & Martha Perkins,	Nov. 22, 1727
John Bishop & Temperance Lothrup,	Nov. 22, 1727
John Deming of Wethersfield & Elizabeth Bush,	Nov. 22, 1727
Jacob Read of Norwich & Sarah Gale of Canterbury,	Dec. 12, 1728
Ebenezer Leatch & Sarah Butt, both of Canterbury,	Jan. 27, 1728-9
Solomon Lothrop & Martha Tudd,	Feb. 6, 1728-9
James Longbottom & Priscilla Lovit,	March 27, 1729
Benjamin Knight & Hannah Jewett,	Nov. 5, 1729
Joseph Safford & Anna Longbottom,	Nov. 5, 1729
Samuel Linkon of Windham & Experience Lam of Stonington,	Nov. 14, 1729
Capt. Samuel Griswold & Hannah Tracy,	Nov. 18, 1729
Roger Haskel & Mary Walbridge,	Dec. 9, 1729
Salmon Wheat & Mary Geal, both of Canterbury,	Jan. 1, 1729-30
Isaac Canedy & Phebe Leonard,	Jan. 1, 1730
Jonathan Burley of Norwich & Elizabeth White of Canterbury,	March 30, 1730
Sylvanus Jones & Keziah Cleveland,	April 9, 1730
Thomas Perkins & Sarah Jewett,	June 29, 1730
Jacob Perkins & Jemimah Leonard,	Oct. 14, 1730
Samuel Manning of Windham & Sarah Gail of Canterbury,	June 10, 1731

Samuel Smith, residing in Norwich, & Esther Lothrop,

                        July 15, 1731

Joseph Bell of Lebanon & Mehetabell Heth,   Aug., 1731

Samuel Bishop, Jr., & Abigail Corning,   Oct. 6, 1731

James Tyler, Jr., of Preston & Esther Bishup,   Oct. 7, 1731

Richard Bushnell & Lucy Perkins,   Oct. 14, 1731

Ebenezer Bettis of Woodstock & Lurana Knight,

                        Nov. 11, 1731

Benaiah Gears of Preston & Elizabeth Clark,   Jan. 26, 1731-2

Ebenezer Harris & Sarah Trall of Plainfield,   June 5, 1732

Joel Parish & Rebecca Green, both of Canterbury,

                        June 27, 1732

Daniel Davis of Canterbury & Elizabeth Lothrop,

                        Sept. 21, 1732

Moses Kinney of Preston & Abigail Read,   Sept. 27, 1732

James Longbottom & Elizabeth Jackson,   Nov. 6, 1732

Joseph Knight & Sarah Read,   Dec. 7, 1732

Umfry Cram of Windham & Hannah Blunt,   Feb. 22, 1733

Jedidiah Hide & Jerusha Perkins,   July 17, 1733

Josiah Heth & Rebecca Handy,   Dec. 17, 1734

Paul Hibbard of Windham & Deborah Lawrence,

                        Jan. 6, 1735-6

Benjamin Parish of Preston & Mary Rude of Canterbury,

                        Jan. 29, 1735-6

John Safford & Lydia Hibbard,   Feb. 26, 1735-6

David Downing & Anne Blunt,   Nov. 11, 1736

Joseph Connant of Stafford & Thankful Gail of Canterbury,

                        March 17, 1737

Lemuel Bingham of Windham & Hannah Perkins,

                        April 28, 1737

Zebediah Gates of Preston & ———,   June 15, 1737

Nehemiah Parish & Ruth Green,   1737

Nathan Bushnell & Margary Jackson,   Nov. 13, 1737

Jacob Read & Esther Read,   Dec. 23, 1737

Henry Baldwin of Bolton & Mercy Read,   Nov. 21, 1738

Jonathan Rudd of Windham & Esther Tyler,   Dec. 6, 1738

Mathew Perkins & Hannah Bishop,   April 19, 1739

Caleb Bishop & Keziah Hebard,   April 19, 1739

Gersham Hail & Mercy Holland, both of Canterbury,

                        May 17, 1739

"The recording of many marriages since is omitted
here because the pastor gave certificates of them
to ye town clerk."

David Palmer & Hannah Lawrence,   Feb. 28, 1740

REV. PETER POWERS, PASTOR.

Jupiter, negro servant of Daniel Bishop of Newent, &
    Hannah, a free Indian woman of Preston,   Dec. 3, 1756
William Bauldwin of Canterbury & Ruth Asten, Jan. 11, 1757
James, Winchester & Anna Longbottom,   March 15, 1757
Joseph Perkins, Jr., & Joannah Burnham,   May 10, 1757
Timothy Babcock of Stonington & Thankful Read,
                                                Oct. 20, 1757
Job Woodard & Theudee Walbridge,   Feb. 27, 1758
Lemuel Buzel & Anna Lovett,   March 8, 1758
Joseph Jackson & Elizabeth Jones,   March 29, 1758
David Lopham & Mary Jones,   March 29, 1758
James Woodworth & Hannah Hackstone,   March 30, 1758
Simon Chapman & Alice Rows (?),   April 5, 1758
Samuel Lovett, Jr., & Abigail Sprague,   April 20, 1758
William Vincent of Westerly & Zerviah Rudd, June 20, 1758
Hezekiah Wright & Abigail Dexter (free Indians),
                                                Aug. 21, 1758
John Eames & Betty Longbottom,   Nov. 23, 1758
Nathaniel Preston & Mary Hale,   April 19, 1759
Cornelius Cady & Elizabeth Safford,   June 25, 1759
Jonathan Lawrence & Zerviah Ormsby,   Aug. 29, 1759
William Witter, Esq., of Preston & widow Elizabeth
    Lothrop,   Oct. 4, 1759
Reuben Peck of Canterbury & Charity French, Dec. 6, 1759
Nathan Walden & Bethiah Munsil,   Dec. 27, 1759
Isaac Allen & Sarah French,   Jan. 30, 1760
David Thompson of Ashford & Patience Russ of Can-
    terbury,   Feb. 27, 1760
Abner French & Phebe Birchard,   April 3, 1760
Moses Haggett, Jr., of Norwich & Elizabeth Green of
    Canterbury,   May 22, 1760
Jabez Fitch, Jr., & Hannah Perkins,   June 3, 1760
Capt. John Safford & widow Mary Lawrence,   Aug. 13, 1760

Daniel Gatt or Gott of Hebron & Charity Russ of Can-
    terbury,   Aug. 13, 1760
Samuel Safford & Mary Lawrence,   Sept. 25, 1760
Nathan Bushnell & Ruth Bushnell,   Nov. 19, 1760
Bildad Curtiss of Coventry & Zerviah Bishup, Nov. 26, 1760
Rev. Timothy Allen of Ashford & widow Dorothy Read,
                                   Jan. 6, 1761
Samuel Noulding of Canterbury & Mary Butt, Jan. 14, 1761
Reuben Bishup & Hannah Bishup,   Feb. 18, 1761
Caleb Austin of Canterbury & Hephzibah Jones,
                               April 15, 1761
Joseph Read of Norwich & Mary Fenn of Westerly,
                               July 7, 1761
Samuel Fuller of Pomfret & Sarah Read,   Oct. 22, 1761
Capt. David Homes, M. D., of Woodstock & Temper-
    ance Bishop, Jr.,   Nov. 12, 1761
Thomas Moorey of Lebanon & Sarah Crosby, Nov. 26, 1761
Jonathan Pitcher & Elizabeth Walden,   Dec. 18, 1761
Samuel Anderson & Deliverance Butt,   Jan. 20, 1762
Elijah Geer of Preston & Margaret Ross, Jan. 20, 1762
Henry Walton of Norwich & Hannah Mott of Voluntown,
                                 Jan. 21, 1762
Charles Putnam of Preston & Martha Ross, May 27, 1762
Thomas Rathbun & Priscilla Bauldwin,   July 19, 1762
Silas Gates of Preston & Mary White of Canterbury,
                               Sept. 23, 1762
Josiah Safford & Deborah Sprague,   Oct. 20, 1762
John Green of Ulster Co. & Abigail Rude, Dec. 27, 1762
Joseph Jones & Mary Downing,   Feb. 8, 1763
Amariah Branch of Preston & Sarah Huntington,
                               May 19, 1763
Samuel Lovet, Jr., & Charity Perkins,   June 30, 1763
Manchester Hawly of Norwich & Mabel Park of Preston,
                               Aug. 4, 1763
Daniel Comstock & Mary Bishop,   Oct. 27, 1763
Jedidiah Palmer & Esther Read,   Nov. 17, 1763
Samuel Lothrup & Sarah Oakman,   Nov. 24, 1763
Capt. James Grant & widow Temperance Bishop,
                               Dec. 14, 1763
Cyprian Downes & Hannah Jewet,   June 21, 1764

REV. JOEL BENEDICT, PASTOR.

Elijah Fay of Bennington & Deborah Lawrence,
March 21, 1771
Lemuel Robins of Windham & Sarah Rude, Dec., 1771
Gamaliel Ripley of Windham & Judith Perkins, Jan. 23, 1772
James Miller, a transient person, & Anne Rude, Jan. 23, 1772
John Babcock of Stonington & Elizabeth Palmer, Sept. 3, 1772
Jedidiah Read & Judith Bottom, Oct. 20, 1772
Luke Burdick of Hopkinton, R. I., & Sarah Haskel,
Nov. 8, 1772
John Rubins & Olive Knight, April 18, 1773
Elkanah Hunt of Stonington & Temperance Grant,
Sept. 16, 1773-5
Solomon Perkins & Susannah Fitch, Nov. 25, 1773-5
William Tracy & Mary Burnham, Jan. 9, 1774
Samuel Smith & Eunice Tupper, April 14, 1774
Nathaniel Padock of Philip's Patent & Mary Crane of
Salem, N. Y., May 1, 1774
Daniel Bennet of Preston & Hannah Reed, May 1, 1774
Israel Kense of Preston & Ruth Tracy, Jan. 5, 1775
Jedediah Williams & Lucy Bennet, Jan. 5, 1775
Jedediah Kimbal & Eunice Love, July 2, 1775
Thomas Hutchins & Sarah Butts, Jan. 18, 1776
Jacob Galusha of Salisbury & Abigail Porter, Feb. 25, 1776
Ezekiel Bushnell & Sela Darby, Sept. 8, 1776
Abiel Cheney & Lurinda Clement, Dec. 15, 1776
David Breed & Elizabeth Clement, Dec. 15, 1776
Zephaniah Frank of Voluntown & widow Anna Bingham,
Jan. 16, 1777
Abraham Bishop of Lyme & Patience Downing, Feb. 6, 1777
Jabez Fox of Windham & Jerusha Perkins, Feb. 26, 1777
Gideon Porter & Abigail Bottom, March 13, 1777
Thomas Munroe & Susanna Lathrop, April 13, 1777
John Bishop & Lucretia Darby, April 13, 1777
Elias Burnham & Sarah Calkins, Dec. 25, 1777
David Fasset of Bennington & Sabra Safford, Jan. 22, 1778
Jonathan Corwin & Hannah Hazen, Feb. 4, 1778
Timothy Cady of Pomfret & Lois Harrington, March 12, 1778
Enoch Baker & Anna Calkins, April 19, 1778

Thomas Munroe & Esther Baldwin, May 7, 1778
Yet Once Barstow & Hannah Corbin, May 19, 1778
John Fuller & Wealthy Hazen, May 21, 1778
Josiah Butt of Canterbury & Eunice Knight, May 28, 1778
Rufus Morse of Canterbury & Lida Rathbon, Sept. 13, 1778
John Jackson & Mary Lewis, March 10, 1779
William Sheldon & Ruth Bishup, Oct. 26, 1779
Joseph Gorton & Susanna Lawrence, Nov. 4, 1779
Elisha Conors of Killingly & Mary Bishup, Dec. 2, 1779
Theophilus Waley & Mary Kilburn, Dec. 30, 1779
Pember Calkins of New London & widow Joanna Perkins,
Jan. 6, 1780
Elijah Park of Canterbury & Anna Smith, March 16, 1780
Daniel Preston & Deborah Kilburn, Nov. 30, 1780
John Hart of Southington & Mary Smith, June, 1780
David Avery & Sarah Palmer, Jan. 11, 1781
Farwell Coit of Preston & Anna Tracy, 178—
Zacheus Waldo of Windham & Esther Steven, 178—
William Conner of Norwich & Miriam Tyler of Preston, 178—
Elijah Lester of Preston & Damaris Lord of Norwich, 178—
Aaron Overton & Sarah Ayers, April 3, 1783

REV. DAVID HALE, PASTOR.

Ezra Walton of Preston & Phebe Coie or Cort, Jan. 27, 1791
Frederic Perkins & Sarah Kinsman, March 29, 1791
Joseph Hebbard of Canterbury & Lydia Baldwin,
April 7, 1791
Caleb Bishup & Zipporah Tracy, April 21, 1791
Christopher Starr of Norwich & Olive Perkins, May 1, 1791
Joseph Shepherd of Plainfield & Hannah Kirtland,
Dec. 18, 1791
Samuel Bishup & Lucy Lord, Jan. 3, 1792
Cyrus Bishup & Susanna Bishup, Jan. 17, 1792
George James of Newport & Sally Allerton, April 3, 1792
John Kinsman & Rebecca Perkins, Oct. 4, 1792
Grover LeHomedieu of Norwich & Betsey Tracy, Oct. 7, 1792
Jonathan Harrinton of Lisbon & Elizabeth Tucker
of Voluntown, Oct. 28, 1792
Roger Adams & Polly Willoughby, May 7, 1793
Stephen Tanner of Preston & Betsy Rose, June 2, 1793

Joseph Avery of Lisbon & Lydia Leffingwell of Bozrah,

June 6, 1793

Reuben Hard of Plainfield & Elizabeth Tyler, Aug. 18, 1793

Elisha Bartholomew of Woodstock & Betsy Bingham,

Nov. 14, 1793

Elisha Burnham & Sarah Tracy, Nov. 23, 1793

Jared Baker of Montville & Nabby Welby, Dec. 26, 1793

Mint Fagans & Daffa Oseford (negroes), Dec. 29, 1793

Asa Bennet of Preston & Amy Kimbal, March 20, 1794

Henry Eldridge of South Kingston, R. I., & Hannah

Rathbon, Oct. 27, 1794

Caleb Smith & Mercy Kinne, both of Preston, May 11, 1795

Thomas Serjeant of Springfield & Lydia Adams, Oct. 3, 1795

Thomas Smith of Canterbury (76) & Amy Smith (55),

Oct. 18, 1795

John Greenslit & Eunice Hall, Oct. 29, 1795

Darius Bingham & Sally Bottom, Dec. 17, 1795

Daniel Bishup of West Springfield & Lucy Read, Jan. 26, 1796

Rufus Austin of West Greenwich, R. I., & Eunice Rathbun,

Feb. 21, 1796

John Wilson of Preston & Mary Baldwin of Canterbury,

March 15, 1796

John Fitch, Jr., of Canterbury & Eunice Baldwin, April 12, 1796

Solomon Morgan of Vergennes, Vt., & Hannah Willaby,

April 19, 1796

Freeman Tracy & Charity Lathrop, May 17, 1796

Amos D. Allen of Windham & Lydia Tracy, Aug. 18, 1796

Nathaniel Frink & Polly Bingham, Dec. 15, 1796

Samuel Lovett, Jr., & Joanna Perkins, Jan. 1, 1797

Daniel Lathrop & Hannah Bishop, Feb. 14, 1797

Asa Apley of Canterbury & Hannah Read, March 23, 1797

Prince Kinsman & Jane Mingo (negroes), March 23, 1797

Gurdon Goodell & Phebe Walton, Aug. 20, 1797

Elisha Day of Haddam & Anna Hazen, Aug. 24, 1797

Benjamin Austin of Preston & Sally Lathrop, Aug. 27, 1797

John Sherman of Mansfield & Abigail Perkins, Feb. 10, 1798

Joseph Huntly of Lyme & Elner Greenslet, April 1, 1798

Nathan Geer & Olive Gates, both of Preston, Oct. 23, 1798

Manassah Prentice of Preston & Susa Lathrop, Feb. 27, 1799

Russel Rose & Rebecca Lathrop,   Nov. 10, 1799
Jehu O—ry (?) & Violet French,   Nov. 17, 1799
Nathaniel Norman of Norwich & Lydia Frink, Dec. 12, 1799
Russel Green of Plainfield, N. H., & Ruby Lathrop,

Dec. 24, 1799
Edward Paine of Pomfret & Judith Lathrop,   March 12, 1800

SOMERS.

TOLLAND COUNTY.

The town of Somers was incorporated in July, 1734, by Massachusetts. It was annexed to Connecticut in May, 1749. The Congregational Church of Somers, formerly called East Enfield, was organized March 15, 1727.

Joseph Fish & Mary Sittson,   Oct. 5, 1727
Samuel Bartlett & Rebekah Kebbe,   Jan. 16, 1728
Joseph Hunt & Ann Wood,   Jan. 29, 1728
Elisha Kebbe & Mehitable Felt,   May 3, 1728
Edward Farrington & Ruth Killum,   June 26, 1728
Samuel Gibbs & Rebekah Gary,   Sept. 8, 1728
Joseph Gary & Unice Gary,   Oct. 30, 1728
Joseph or Thomas Roe & Elizabeth Purchase,   Dec. 26, 1728
Samuel Allis of Enfield & Hannah Sheldon,   Nov. 4, 1729
John Atcherson of Brimfield & widow Ann Hunt, Aug. 5, 1731
Ebenezer Buck & Abigail Felt of Enfield,   Nov. 15, 1731
James Kebbe & Annah Kebbe of Enfield,   Sept. 28, 1732
Eben Spencer (?) & Elisabeth Root, both of Enfield,

Feb. 14, 1733
Joseph Jones & Sarah Wood, both of Enfield,   April 8, 1734
William Collins & Ann Jones, both of Enfield,   May 3, 1734
Joseph Phelp of Coventry & Naomi Kebbe,   Aug. 14, 1734
Benjamin Thomas of S. & widow King of Stafford,

Nov. 7, 1734
David Rose of Durham & Elizabeth Fowler,   Dec., 1734
Jonathan Purchase & Margaret Worthington of Springfield,

Dec., 1734
Daniel Wood & Lydia Dorchester,   Dec. 8, 1735
Joseph Diggens & Elizabeth Houghton, both of Windsor,

Dec. 17, 1735

Joseph Felt & Hannah Bigsby,   Aug. 10, 1736
Benjamin Grant of Ellington & Ann Hunt,   Feb. 10, 1737
Samuel Haidon of Windsor & Abigail Hall,   Nov. 17, 1737
Thomas Purchase & Sarah Persons,   April 7, 1738
Nathaniel Miles of Enfield & Sarah Sitton,   May 4, 1738
Zabulon Cross of Mansfield & Mary Wardwell, June 30, 1738
Hezekiah Spencer & Mary Root,   March 15, 1739
Moses Allyn & Hannah Millar,   Oct. 11, 1739
Moses Bronson of Tolland & Phebe Warner of Stafford,
                                                                              Feb. 28, 1740
George Cooley & Hannah Pease,   March 31, 1740
Benjamin Thomas, Jr., of Stafford & Elisabeth King,
                                                                              May 14, 1740
Ebenezer Tiffany & Abigail Jones,   Aug. 20, 1741
Samuel Cravath of Middletown & Eunice Hall, Aug. 31, 1741
Samuel Hall & Hannah Persons,   Oct. 1, 1741
Daniel Kebbe of Enfield & Mary Pratt   Oct. 29, 1742
Moses Thomas of Hartford & Sarah Horton,   Oct. 6, 1742
Nathaniel Bliss of Longmeadow & widow Mary Cooley,
                                                                              Dec. 1, 1742
Abraham Cary of Ellington & Abigail Pease,   Dec. 23, 1742
Samuel King & Hannah Bush,   Aug. 23, 1743
Daniel Reed & Elizabeth Pease,   Dec. 1, 1743
Simeon Dwight of Brookfield & Cybyl Dwight, Dec. 14, 1743
Jonathan Osborn of S. & Bethiah Pain of Stafford,
                                                                              Dec. 15, 1743
Jacob Kebbe, Jr., & Abigail Warner,   April 5, 1744
Phinehas Felt & Mary Parsons,   May 24, 1744
Aaron Stebbins of Springfield & Mary Wood,   Oct. 14, 1744
Zabulon Jones & Annah Kebbe,   Oct. 31, 1744
Samuel Davis of Stafford & Martha Wood,   March 8, 1745
Luke Persons, Jr., & Mary Dickinson,   July 31, 1745
Thomas Whipple, Jr., & Abigail Wood,   Sept. 5, 1745
Alexander Brown & Grace Kebbe,   April 18, 1745
Jonathan Rockwell of Windsor & Margaret Bush,
                                                                              Nov. 5, 1745
Samuel Wardwell & Elisabeth Osborn,   March 27, 1746
Jacob Ward, Jr., & Irene Jones,   Aug. 22, 1746
Robert Pease, Jr., & Hannah Sexton,   Sept. 4, 1746

Reuben Chapin of Salisbury & Rebecca Kebbe, Nov. 5, 1746
John Abbe of Enfield & Sarah Cooley, Jan. 26, 1775
Elijah Allen of Union & Anne Gibbs, March 16, 1785
John Abbe, 3d, of Enfield & Hannah Billings, Nov. 25, 1788
Walter Ainsworth & Lois Wood, July 22, 1794
Benjamin Alfred of W. Springfield & Elizabeth Chapin,

Jan. 25, 1795
Daniel Burbank of Enfield & Rachel Dwight, Dec. 22, 1774
Eli Banister of Springfield & Hannah Wright, May 25, 1775
Jacob Brown & Kezia Wood, Jan. 28, 1778
Samuel Benton of Tolland & Mercia Jones, Aug. 13, 1778
Daniel Benton of Tolland & Betty Richardson, Feb. 18, 1779
Seth Burbank of Enfield & Joanna Dwight, June 13, 1782
Ebenezer Brown & Irene Wood, both of Longmeadow,

Dec. 8, 1783
Samuel Blair of New Braintree & Irene Whitaker,

May 27, 1784
Samuel Barnes of East Haddam & Sally Newcomb,

Aug. 2, 1784
Bernard Berton of Norwich, Mass., & Esther Davis,

Oct. 18, 1787
Joseph Bumstead of Wilbraham & Mary Davis, Sept. 30, 1788
Elain Buel & Hannah Cooley, July 7, 1793
Joseph Billings & Abi Pomeroy, Aug. 28, 1794
Josiah Brown of Williamstown, Vt., & Editha Ban-
    croft of E. Windsor, Jan. 31, 1799
Diodate Brockway & Miranda Hall, both of Ellington,

Oct. 30, 1799
Alpheus Colton of Longmeadow & Lois Spencer,

Aug. 31, 1786
Aaron Coy of Granby & Mary Bicknel, June 19, 1787
Reuben Carpenter of Wilbraham, Mass., & Anna
    Stacy of Wilbraham, Mass., April 16, 1788
Elisha Cook of Ellington & Hulda Pratt, March 19, 1791
Joseph Collins, Jr., & Betsey Billings, Feb. 10, 1795
Asa Cooley & Sarah Pratt, Feb. 12, 1795
John Cooley & Polly Tainter, Jan. 4, 1796
Joseph Cooley & Lydia Walker, April 21, 1796
Simeon Cooley of E. Windsor & Clarissa Percival,

Nov. 28, 1799

Rufus Collins of Lebanon Crank & Rebekah Parsons,
Nov. 9, 1774

Bliss Corliss & Phebe Kibbe, Oct. 26, 1775

Eleazer Collins of Lebanon Crank & Hannah Russell,
May 29, 1776

Ebenezer Crocker & Sarah Langdon, both of Wilbraham, Mass., March 4, 1776

Lieut. Elias Chapin & Submit Davis, Aug. 27, 1778

Eliphalet Coleman of Coventry, Conn., & Ruth Brown
of Longmeadow, Mass., Dec. 16, 1778

Asa Cady of Stafford, Conn., & Martha Wood, Jan. 6, 1780

Jonathan Chaffee of Wilbraham, Mass., & Olive Davis,
Oct. 17, 1782

Abner Cooley of Monson, Mass., & Maria Chapin of
Wilbraham, Mass., Oct. 16, 1783

Jeremiah Chapin & Chloe Cooley, Sept. 12, 1785

Stephen Chapel of Coventry, Conn., & Lucy Russell,
Oct. 25, 1785

Jesse Cogsdel & Sibel Tiffany, both of Ellington, Conn.,
Feb. 2, 1786

Elihu Church of Middlefield & Lydia Sheldon, June 26, 1786

Seth Dwight & Esther Pease, Dec. 9, 1779

Joseph Diggins & Elizabeth Houghton, both of Windsor,
Dec. 17, 1735

Jesse Davis of Stafford & Mary Billings, March 28, 1782

Job Davis & Love Snow, Nov. 30, 1786

Stephen Douglass of Westfield, Mass., & Hannah Sexton,
April 5, 1795

Daniel Davis of Stafford, Conn., & Margaret Chapin,
Sept. 26, 1798

Lieut. Nathaniel Ely of Longmeadow, Mass., & Elizabeth Raynolds, Feb. 16, 1786

Deacon Nathaniel Ely of Longmeadow, Mass., & Mrs.
Marth Raynolds, Nov. 15, 1787

Joseph Fisk & Mary Sitson, Oct. 5, 1727

Edward Farrington & Ruth Killam, June 26, 1728

Thomas Faxton of Deerfield, Mass., & Rachel Davis,
Oct. 15, 1777

John Firman & Elizabeth Pelton, Oct. 19, 1783

Timothy Flower of West Springfield, Mass., & Hannah
   Spencer,   March 24, 1784
David Fowler & Experience Field,   Sept. 15, 1785
John Fowler & Jerusha Russell,   Dec. 10, 1795
Isaac Fuller & Elenor Jones,   Aug. 11, 1796
Elam Felt of Hamilton, N. Y., & Elizabeth Davis,
                           Jan. 25, 1795
John French of Washington, N. Y., & Annie Phelps,
                           Jan. 21, 1799
Samuel Gibbs & Rebekah Gary,   Sept. 8, 1728
Joseph Gary & Eunice Gary,   Oct. 30, 1728
Solomon Gains of Enfield, Conn., & Sarah Ford,
                         Nov. 20, 1777
Ebenezer Grover of Tolland, Conn., & Mary Palmer
   of Wilbraham, Mass.,   April 16, 1778
Timothy Grover of Tolland, Conn., & Phalle Richardson,
                         Jan. 25, 1781
John Gowdy & Susanna Ward,   Feb. 14, 1782
William Gurley of Mansfield, Conn., & Sibel Chapin,
                         May 2, 1782
Jard Green of Granby, Conn., & Mercy Sweatland of
   Longmeadow, Mass.,   Jan. 23, 1785
Nathan Gilligan & Desire King, both of Ellington,
                         Aug. 11, 1791
Asa Goodwin of New Hartford, Conn., & Polly Pease.
                         Nov. 14, 1793
Joseph Hunt & Ann Wood,   Jan. 29, 1728
Samuel Hayden of Windsor, Conn., & Abigail Hall,
                         Nov. 17, 1737
Job Hulburt & Dorcas Spencer,   Oct. 31, 1776
Azariah Hall of Mansfield, Conn., & Keturah Pease,
                         Dec. 9, 1779
Zadock Hall & Elizabeth Coy,   April 19, 1781
Joseph Holcomb of Simsbury, Conn., & Sarah Ford,
                       March 9, 1784
Josiah Hollister of Oxford & Aseneth Sweatland,
                       April 25, 1787
Joseph Howard of Longmeadow, Mass., & Submit Luce,
                       April 3, 1788

Alpheus Hall & Hannah Sikes,   Sept. 7, 1789
Luke Hall, Jr., & Ruby Pease,   Jan. 8, 1795
Stephen Hudson & Lois Root,   March 2, 1795
Elam Hale of Longmeadow & Elizabeth Pease, May 31, 1798
Ebenezer Jennings of Windham, Conn., & Abi Sweat-
    land of Springfield, Mass.,   Oct. 21, 1783
Benjamin Jennings & Susannah Davis,   Sept. 13, 1784
Eli Jones of Hebron, Conn., & Abigail Pomeroy,
                                                         Jan. 16, 1798
Elisha Kibbe & Mehitable Felt,   May 3, 1728
James Kibbe & Annah Kibbe of Enfield, Conn., Sept. 28, 1732
Samuel Kelsey & Betsey Hollister,   Nov. 4, 1779
Amos Kellogg of Colchester, Conn., & Mary Pomeroy,
                                                         June 28, 1781
Asa Kibbe of Wilbraham, Mass., & Jerusia Coy,
                                                         Aug. 14, 1783
Bildad Kibbe & Azuba Pease,   Sept. 9, 1784
Moses Kibbe & Mary Pratt,   April 27, 1786
Joshua Luce & Anna Horton,   July 27, 1780
Philip Loomis & Lydia Purchis,   Aug. 31, 1780
John Ladd of Tolland & Esther Wood,   Dec. 11, 1783
Joshua Luce & Sarah Walden,   March 13, 1794
Rubin Luce of Tolland & Rhoda Parsons,   Feb. 9, 1795
Noah Levings of Hoosack, N. Y., & Polly Kibbe,
                                                         Feb. 1, 1796
Martin Loomis of East Windsor & Phila Inman,
                                                         Sept. 29, 1797
Caleb Lyman of Hadley, Mass., & Amber Cooley,
                                                         Aug. 30, 1798
Ebenezer Magriggery of Enfield, Conn., & Susanna Bradley,
                                                         Nov. 20, 1777
Joel Magriggery of Enfield, Conn., & Martha Bellows,
                                                         Aug. 28, 1783
John McKinney & Violetta Chapman, both of Elling-
    ton, Conn.,   Nov. 6, 1783
David Marchies of Stafford & Lucy Kibbe,   April 29, 1784
John McGregory of Newport, N. H., & Lucy Chapin,
                                                         Sept. 30, 1784
John McCray & Charlott Welles, both of Ellington, Conn.,
                                                         Feb. 23, 1786

Simeon Meacham of New Lebanon, N. Y., & Mary
　　Prentice,　　　　　　　　　　　March 6, 1788
Isaacher Meacham of New Lebanon, N. Y., & Dorothy
　　Rumrell of Enfield, Conn.,　　　　　Nov. 23, 1791
David Markham of Enfield, Conn., & Caroline Billings,
　　　　　　　　　　　　　　　　Jan. 2, 1793
Israel Markham of Enfield, Conn., & Lusina Kibbe
　　of Longmeadow, Mass.,　　　　　　Sept. 4, 1794
Andrew Meacham of Middlefield, Mass., & Sally Wood,
　　　　　　　　　　　　　　　　Nov. 12, 1794
John Newton of Stafford, Conn., & Ruth Bradley,
　　　　　　　　　　　　　　　　Nov. 20, 1777
Sylvester Noble of New Canaan, N. Y., & Betsey Kibbe,
　　　　　　　　　　　　　　　　Jan. 2, 1792
Jacob Orcutt & Mirriam Cooley,　　　　March 13, 1776
Jonathan Porter of Hatfield, Mass., & Ruth Chapin,
　　　　　　　　　　　　　　　　Jan. 24, 1776
Isaach Pease of Enfield, Conn., & Submit Spencer,
　　　　　　　　　　　　　　　　Dec. 19, 1776
Gideon Pease of Enfield, Conn., & Deborah Meacham,
　　　　　　　　　　　　　　　　Dec. 30, 1778
Ebenezer Pierce of Enfield, Conn., & Freelove Shepherd,
　　　　　　　　　　　　　　　　April 9, 1779
Elisha Pilkin of Hartford, Conn., & Elizabeth Kings-
　　bury of Enfield, Conn.,　　　　　　May 30, 1780
John Pierce of East Windsor, Conn., & Flavia Dewey,
　　　　　　　　　　　　　　　　April 12, 1781
Rufus Pease of Enfield, Conn., & Ruth Cooley, Jan. 23, 1783
David Pease of Enfield, Conn., & Jerusha Spencer,
　　　　　　　　　　　　　　　　Jan. 30, 1783
Alpheus Pease & Olive Anderson,　　　Oct. 14, 1784
John Philips & Olive Lord,　　　　　　Dec. 2, 1784
Levi Pease of Suffield, Conn., & Mary Gibs,　Dec. 27, 1784
Solomon Parsons & Anne Phillips,　　　April 7, 1785
Reuben Porter & Rhoda Goodale, both of Ellington, Conn.,
　　　　　　　　　　　　　　　　March 30, 1786
Samuel Pease of Enfield, Conn., & Elizabeth Sexton,
　　　　　　　　　　　　　　　　June 15, 1786
Josiah Phelps of Stafford, Conn., & Roxa Newcomb,
　　　　　　　　　　　　　　　　Jan. 31, 1788

Levi Pratt & Sally Fowler,	Aug. 11, 1788
Isaach Pease of Enfield & Ruth Cooley,	Aug. 30, 1788
Eleazer Pinney of Ellington & Rhoda Tiffany,	Feb. 12, 1789
George Perkins of Enfield, Conn., & Lucy Cooley,	
	Nov. 26, 1789
Joseph Parsons & Eunice Fobes,	Aug. 4, 1790
John Pomroy, Jr., & Sarah Parsons,	April 14, 1791
Daniel Perkins, Jr., of Enfield, Conn., & Persis Billings,	
	Jan. 1, 1795
Hiram Pomeroy & Ruby Parsons,	July 10, 1796
Ebenezer Pratt, Jr., of Somers & Abiah Richardson	
of Longmeadow, Mass.,	Dec. 5, 1797
Samuel Pomeroy & Catharine Day,	Dec. 28, 1797
Ashbel Pratt, Jr., & Lois Cooley,	Nov. 27, 1798
John Putnam & Prudence Walden,	April 7, 1799
John Parsons of Sherburn, N. Y., & Flavia Billings,	
	Oct. 17, 1799
Joseph Roe & Elizabeth Purchas,	Dec. 26, 1728
David Rose of Durham & Elizabeth Fowler,	Dec., 1734
Jesse Richardson & Anna Jones,	Nov. 12, 1778
David Richardson, Jr., & Eunice Wood,	Nov. 30, 1780
John Russell & Lois Johnston, both of Wilbraham, Mass.,	
	Jan. 30, 1783
Joseph Root & Elizabeth Pomeroy,	Sept. 23, 1784
David Richardson, Jr., & Sarah Hudson,	June 15, 1785
Thomas Root of Enfield, Conn., & Azuba Chapin,	
	Feb. 23, 1786
Persevid Redway of Albany, N. Y., & Azubah Jones,	
	June 29, 1789
Eben Spencer & Elizabeth Root, both of Enfield,	
	Feb. 14, 1733
William Scott of Palmer, Mass., & Susa Newcomb,	
	Nov. 27, 1792
Elias Sanford of Litchfield, Conn., & Allice Fuller,	
	Jan. 23, 1776
Stephen Stebbins & Chloe Hall, both of Wilbraham, Mass.,	
	May 23, 1776
Daniel Sweatland of Springfield, Mass., & Hannah	
Bellows of Wilbraham, Mass.,	Dec. 7, 1780

Isaach Shepard & Elizabeth Brace,   April 26, 1781
Cornelius Sawyer of Redding & Alice Forbes, May 22, 1782
Benjamin Sweatland & Rosanna Hancock, both of
    Springfield, Mass.,   June 6, 1782
Asahel Sexton of Enfield, Conn., & Miriam Coy,
                                            Jan. 6, 1783
David Stebbins of Wilbraham, Mass., & Mary Charter
    of Ellington,   March 11, 1790
Jonathan Shearer of Palmer & Hannah Dickenson,
                                           May 24, 1790
Ebenezer Sheldon of Suffield, Conn., & Love Davis,
                                           Jan. 24, 1793
David Sheldon of Suffield & Betsey Hall,   Jan. 16, 1794
Daniel Spencer & Polly Hall,   Jan. 23, 1794
Oliver Skinner of East Windsor, Conn., & Mary Brunson,
                                           March 9, 1797
Peter Smith of Ellington, Conn., & Polly Pratt of
    Longmeadow, Mass.,   May 4, 1797
Jacob Shepherd, Jr., & Chloe Jones,   Feb. 22, 1798
John Spencer & Hannah Shepherd,   May 10, 1798
Abel Sexton & Ruth Phelps,   Oct. 24, 1798
James Storms & Jenney Snow (blacks) of Ellington,
                                           Sept. 27, 1798
Ezekiel Spencer, Jr., & Dolly Sexton,   Oct. 24, 1798
Samuel Snow of South Wilbraham & Love Dickinson,
                                           Nov. 29, 1798
Theophilius Sweatland & Anne Brown, both of Long-
    meadow, Mass.,   Dec. 19, 1799
Joseph Talcott of Enfield, Conn., & Mary Thomas of
    Stafford,   March 13, 1777
Jonathan Tainter of Westbourough & Jemima Root,
                                           April 8, 1777
Timothy Torry of Stafford & Chloe Kibbee, Sept. 30, 1784
Jared Tuttle of Barkhamstead & Roxanna Ward, July 28, 1785
Nathaniel Tiffany, Jr., & Lucy Inman,   March 22, 1786
Thomas Tupper of Stafford & Martha Wood,   Feb. 7, 1799
Stephen Warner & Mary Pratt,   Sept. 22, 1774
Ebenezer Wardwell & Esther Kibbee,   March 22, 1775
Thomas Wilkinson of Enfield, Conn., & Sarah Hall,
                                           Jan. 16, 1777

Timothy Wheeler & Rhoda Thomas, both of Stafford, Conn.,
June 25, 1777
Samuel Wright, Jr., & Ruth Kibbe,   Nov. 20, 1777
John Ward & Hannah Booth, both of Enfield, April 12, 1780
James Ward, Jr., & Hulda Gibbs,   Jan. 25, 1781
Stephen Whitaker & Sarah Pratt,   Nov. 8, 1781
Oliver Wait of Whately, Mass., & Hannah Perry of
Wilbraham,   Oct. 30, 1783
John Williams of Wilbraham & Sarah Parsons,   Oct. 14, 1784
John Ward of Enfield, Conn., & Naomi Butler,
March 24, 1785
James Ward & Deborah Billings,   Oct. 22, 1786
Nathan Wardwell of Newport, N. H., & Agness Brown
of Enfield, Conn.,   Feb. 17, 1789
Aaron Warriner of Wilbraham, Mass., & Phebe Han-
cock of Longmeadow,   April 2, 1789
Samuel Wells of East Hartford & Dolly Prentice,
Dec. 22, 1789
Josiah Wood of Somers & Lucy Hancock of Long-
meadow, Mass.,   Jan. 22, 1791
Noah Wood & Aseneth Caulkins,   March 12, 1795
Daniel White of Whitestown, N. Y., & Lucy Allis,
March 8, 1796
Amos Ward & Abigail Shepherd,   Aug. 31, 1797
Samuel White of Thetford, Vt., & Cynthia Allis, Jan. 21, 1798
Luke Wood & Anna Pease,   Feb. 27, 1799

STRATFORD.

FAIRFIELD COUNTY.

Stratford was settled in 1639. The Congregational Church was organized in 1640. The following are all the marriages recorded.

Daniel Burch & Rachel Foot,   July 19, 1733
Ichabod Clark, & ——— ———   Oct. 4, 1733
John Arnold & Mary Blakeman,   Oct. 18, 1733
Zachri Booth & An—— ———,   Jan. 1, 1733-4
John Burret & ——— ———,   Jan. 3, 1733-4

Daniel Tompson & ——— ———,	March 17, 1735
Sergt. John Sherwood & Mary Walker,	June 14, 1733
Josiah Patterson & Phebe Wells,	May 24, 1753
Warman Duncan & Ruth Curtiss,	Sept. 30, 1753
Curtiss Fairchild & widow Mary Curtiss,	——— 3, 1753
John Beers & Susanna Foot,	April, 1754
William Southworth & Charity Curtiss,	July 14, 1754
Jeremiah Curtiss & Elizabeth Miner,	Oct. 2, 1754
Benjamin Judson & Elizabeth Curtis,	Nov. 13, 1754
Abraham Tomlinson & Rebeckah Gould,	Dec. 24, 1754
Nathaniel Sherman & Jerusha Thompson,	Dec. 26, 1754
Joseph Loring & Zerviah Shelley,	1755
Isaac How & Martha Pierc (?) or Price,	April, 1755
Philo Treat & Mary Hull,	June, 1755
*J. Bailey & Rhoda Fairchild,	Aug. 15, 1784
James Beach & Anna Lewis,	Sept., 1784
Legrand Wells & †Mary Wells,	Dec., 1784
Hezekiah Boothe & Mary Lewis,	Jan., 1785
Daniel Rider & Lucretia Lambson,	Jan., 1785
Isaac Hubbel & Ellen Wells,	Dec., 1785
Col. Thompson & widow Ufford,	Feb., 1785
Mathew Beers & Sarah Curtiss,	March, 1785
Agur Curtiss & Huldah Lewis,	March, 1785
Rev. ——— Rexford & widow Tomlinson,	Jan., 1786
Thaddeus Birdsey & Helen Lewis,	Feb., 1786
A stranger & ——— Munson,	March, 1786
Peter Pixley & Betsey Curtiss,	May, 1786
Jabez Beers & Betsey Hawley,	May, 1786
Ebenezer Hawley & Esther Ward,	Nov., 1786
Dr. William A. Tomlinson & Phebe Lewis,	Nov., 1786
Samuel Hawley & Charity Judson,	Dec., 1786
Aaron Benjamin & Dorothy Brooks,	Jan., 1787
Solomon Curtiss & Jerusha Wheeler,	March, 1787
Elnathan Wheeler & Phoebe Peck,	Oct., 1787
Asaph Benjamin & Hannah Plant,	Oct., 1787
William Roberts & Polley King,	Nov., 1787
Abel De Forrest & Polley Hawley,	Nov., 1787

---

* " Thomas on Town Records."
† " Is Caty on Town Records."

John Brooks & Polley Coe,	Nov., 1787
Peter Hibbard & Anna Booth,	Dec., 1787
Lyman Bevans & Betsey Lambson,	Dec., 1787
Wakeman Hubbel & Naomi Sherman,	Jan., 1788
Lewis Judson Burton & Anna Booth,	Nov., 1788
Capt. Benton & Betsey Jones,	Dec., 1788
Joel Wilcockson & Sarah Booth,	Jan., 1789
Wells Curtis & Betsey Clark, a couple at Greenfield, Feb., 1789	
Charles Butler & Polly Thomson,	May, 1789
William Thompson & Phebe Lewis,	May, 1789
Isaac Brownson & Anna Olcott,	Aug. 30, 1789
Ephraim Peck & Rachel Bennet,	Oct. 29, 1789
Isaac Jones & Ruth Curtiss,	Nov. 22, 1789
Nathan Sherwood & Esther Finch,	Nov. 26, 1789
Abijah Beardsley & Sarah Anne Wilcockson,	Feb. 21, 1790
Samuel Hawley & Lucy Hawley,	Aug. 11, 1790
Rev. Payson Williston & Sarah Birdsey,	Sept. 12, 1790
Isaac Nicoll & Anne Hawley,	Oct. 4, 1790
Thomas Burrit & Abigail Curtiss,	Dec. 12, 1790
Pixley Judson & Catharine Nicholl,	Dec. 29, 1790
Isaac Judson Curtiss & Charity Booth,	Jan. 2, 1791
Azariah Clark & Nancy Ferguson,	Jan. 25, 1791
Joseph Northrop & Charity Benjamin,	Jan. 30, 1791
Daniel Booth, Jr., & Betsey Booth,	Feb. 6, 1791
Joel Curtiss & Sally Beardsley, "92 years old in 1859,"	
	Feb. 19, 1791
John Burr & Jerusha Beardsley,	March 14, 1791
Victory Wetmore & Katee Maria McEwen,	April 3, 1791
Eli (?) Booth & Charity Osborn,	Sept. 22, 1791
Alexander Clark & widow Ruth Wright,	Oct. 30, 1791
Joseph Shelthon & Chary Lewis,	Nov. 24, 1791
S. Conway Whiting & Hannah Curtiss,	Nov. 24, 1791
James Ross Edwards & Alice Coe,	Jan. 22, 1792
Robert Daskum, Jr., & Grissel Patchen,	Jan. 24, 1792
Joseph Lewis, Jr., & widow Charity Paterson,	Feb. 5, 1792
Hilkiah Booth, Jr., & Amee Curtiss,	Feb. 29, 1792
Everett Curtiss & Lucy Paterson,	May 16, 1792
Joseph Thompson & Hellen Curtiss,	June 6, 1792
Isaac Thompson & Sally Thompson,	July 25, 1792

James Humphrey & Abiah Barlow,	Aug. 29, 1792
Ebenezer Wheeler & Naomi Wheeler,	Sept. 1, 1792
Charles Hammond & Anne Wheeler,	Sept. 27, 1792
William Boothe & Mary Ann Lewis,	Nov. 15, 1792
Lewis Sherman & Martha Curtiss,	Oct. 26, 1793
Judson Curtiss & Sarah Lewis,	Oct. 27, 1793
Lewis Beers & Phoebe Curtiss,	Nov. 11, 1793
David Thomson & Bettee Peck,	Nov. 17, 1793
William Satterly & Nancy Curtiss,	Dec. 1, 1793
Elisha Treat Mills & Caty Lewis,	Dec. 9, 1793
Josiah Coe & Esther Curtiss,	Dec. 24, 1793
Abijah Uffoot & Elizabeth Lewis,	Jan. 22, 1794
Samuel Curtiss, Jr., & Temperance Anne Patterson,	
	Jan. 23, 1794
Josiah (?) Hawley & Betty Clark,	April 12, 1794
Russel Edwards & Sarah DeForest,	April 16, 1794
John White of Hartford & Betsey Shelton of Huntington,	July 21, 1794
Isaac Beach & Betsey Silliman,	Dec. 7, 1794
William Walker & Eunice Hawley,	Dec. 15, 1794
Samuel Wheeler, Jr., & Betsey Curtiss,	Dec. 25, 1794
Levi Curtiss & Betsey Uffoot,	Jan. 28, 1795
Nathan Curtiss & Sally Peck,	Jan. 31, 1795
Elijah Judson & Rebeckah Booth,	March 1, 1795
John Wells & Polly Wells,	April 29, 1795
—— Stephenson & Sally Lewis,	May 23, 1795
Silas Booth & Ruth Jones,	May 25, 1795
Stephen Thomson & Nabby Beach,	July 25, 1795
Joseph Benjamin & Betty Curtiss,	July 25, 1795
Daniel DeForest & Phebe Uffoot,	Oct. 6, 1795
William Beers & Mary Uffoot,	Oct. 14, 1795
Robert Seilby (?) & Aner Willoughby,	Oct. 25, 1795
Joel Hawley & Phebe Beers,	Dec. 1, 1795
Josiah Coe & —— Beach,	Dec. 24, 1795
Robert Fairchild & Esther Brooks,	Feb. 9, 1796
Joseph Tomlinson & Sarah Curtiss,	March 20, 1796
Joseph Curtiss & Naomi Curtiss,	March 23, 1796
Dr. Ezra Curtiss & Nancy Uffoot,	May 9, 1796
—— McDonald & —— Lawson,	July 17, 1796

Benjamin Judson, Jr., & Polley Harlow,	Aug. 28, 1796
Daniel Swan Messer & Chloe Silliman,	Sept. 25, 1796
Isaac Coe & Polley Curtiss,	1796
Stephen Montross & Catee Waklee,	—— 29, 1796
David Brooks & Abigail Hawley,	Nov. 13, 1796
Isaac Judson Booth & Sally McEuen,	Dec. 11, 1796
Abel Curtiss & Sally Burton,	Dec. 18, 1796
Philo Curtiss & Betsey Frost, daughter of Stephen,	
	March 20, 1797
Lewis Wheeler & Hannah Beers,	Oct., 1797
Daniel Judson, Jr., & Sally Plant,	Sept. 12, 1797
Joseph Curtiss & Esther Blackman,	Nov. 13, 1797
Agur Lewis & Charity Birdseye,	Nov. 15, 1797
Silas Curtiss & Hellen Judson,	Dec. 24, 1797
Samuel O. Wilcockson & Anne Curtiss,	Jan. 3, 1798
Ralph Snow & Theodocia Brooks,	Jan. 1, 1798
Samuel McEuen & Sally Uffoot,	June 2, 1798
Ephraim Lewis & —— Curtiss,	June, 1798
Everit Birdseye & Polly McEuen,	Nov. 25, 1798
Benjamin Uffoot & Phoebe Curtiss,	Dec. 3, 1798
Abraham C. Lewis & Elizabeth Beers,	Jan. 27, 1799
Reuben Wheeler & Elizabeth Booth,	April 20, 1799
James B. Lewis & Polley Beardsley,	June 1, 1799
David Mills of Morristown & Abigail Parish,	June 17, 1799
Littleton Furness of Maryland & —— Judson,	
	June 20, 1799
Elisha Wheeler & Dorothy Birdseye,	Jan. 5, 1800

GLASTONBURY.

HARTFORD COUNTY.

The town of Glastonbury was incorporated May, 1690, taken from Wethersfield. The First Congregational Church in Glastonbury was organized July, 1692. Its early records are lost. The Second Congregational Church was organized at East Glastonbury in 1727, formerly called Eastbury. The following are the marriages recorded.

James Wire & Hannah House,	Oct., 1769
Rhuben Kenney & Jemima Webster,	Feb. 22, 1769
Ephraim Baker & Martha Scott,	March 26, 1770
Lazarus House & Rebeccah Ripley,	July, 1770

David Loveland & Mehitable Haurlburt,   1770
Martain Woodruff & Freelove Goodale,   Jan. 7, 1770
Ebenezer Coleman & Rachel Wright,   May 2, 1771
Peter Pease & Ann Densmore,   Oct., 1771
Elizur Goodrich & Sarah Kimberly,   Nov. 14, 1771
Nehemiah Andrews & Elizabeth Fox,   Dec., 1771
Isaac Tryon & Elizabeth Kimberly,   Dec. 25, 1771
Edmund Grover & Jemima Wickham,   Sept., 1771
John Gains & Sarah How,   Jan. 19, 1771
Theodore Holester & Annah Loveland,   March 27, 1773
Thomas Forbs & Lucy Loveland,   Oct. 27, 1773
Ebenezer Fox & Mary How,   Dec. 27, 1773
Benoni Dewolf & Mary Preston,   Dec. 28, 1773
David Hubbard & Jemima Hollester,   March 8, 1774
Samuel Kelsey & Betty Hollister,   Sept., 1774
Elisha Hills & Rebecah Loveland,   Nov. 24, 1774
John Andrews & Prudence Fox,   Oct. 17, 1775
David Andrews & Rebeccah Straton,   Oct. 17, 1775
Nehemiah Holister & Abigail House,   Jan. 24, 1776
William Smithers & Sarah Goff,   Feb. 15, 1776
Israel Fox & Sarah Strickland,   Feb. 22, 1776
Hezekiah Wright & Onnor Stratton,   March 10, 1776
David Fox & Hapsabeth Brooks,   May 23, 1776
Benjamin Skinner & Easter Chamberlain,   June 6, 1776
Stephen Fox & Sarah Andrews,   July, 1776
Philip Scovel & Mercy Fox,   Jan. 18, 1777
Eliezar Hubbard, Jr., & Sarah House,   Aug. 7, 1777
Samuel Hills, Jr., & Abigail Hubbard,   Sept. 3, 1777
John How & Elizabeth Holester,   Nov. 20, 1777
Timothy Branerd & Jemimah Hubbard,   "being
   Thanksgiving Day,"   Nov. 20, 1777
Elijah Hammond & Abigail Terry,   Jan. 1, 1778
Benjamin Andrews, Jr., & Abigail Covel,   Jan. 8, 1778
Amos Fox & Mary Stratton,   Jan. 8, 1778
John Follon & Beriah Dickerson,   July 9, 1778
Doctor Asaph Coleman & Eunice Holester,   Nov. 11, 1778
Joseph Holester & Patience Holester,   Nov. 19, 1778
Edward Potter & Sarah Brooks,   Jan. 6, 1778
Elisha How & Anna Holester,   March 10, 1779

Noah Fox & Terety (?) Goodale, March 17, 1779
Israel Hills & Ruth Holester, May 20, 1779
Philip Squires & Hannah Daniels, Dec. 6, 1779
Enoch Smith & Hannah Nye, Jan. 12, 1780
Thomas Beal & Hannah Riley, Feb. 3, 1780
Ebenezer Goodale & Jerusha Hodge, Feb. 10, 1780
Josiah White & Hannah Hills, April 25, 1780
William Buck & Ruth Strickland, April 26, 1780
Simeon Fox & Mary Dewolf, Aug. 13, 1780
Josiah Holester & Mary House, Aug. 16, 1780
Crummal Price & Jerusha Pease, Sept. 25, 1780
Benjamin Tucker & Anna Fox, Sept. 28, 1780
Stephen Strickland & Rhoda Holester, Nov. 2, 1780
Charles Treat & Doretha Fox, Nov. 25, 1780
David Kenney & Jerusha Morley, Nov. 30, 1780
James McLean & Abigail Strickland, Dec. 26, 1780
Josiah Brooks & Abigail Goslee, Jan. 4, 1781
William Dutton & Easter Riley, Aug. 6, 1781
Zebulon Bidwell & Sarah Hale, Aug. 15, 1781
James Wright & widow Mable Loveland, Aug. 28, 1781
Eli Hodge & Sarah Goolee, Sept. 27, 1781
David Nye & Onnor Tryon, Oct. 12, 1782
Samuel Pease & Rhodea Hodge, Oct. 25, 1781
James Heney (?) & Anna Brooks, Oct. 25, 1781
Lemuel Fox & Prudence Brooks, Dec. 28, 1781
Ezekiel Morley & Deliverance Sweetland, Feb. 28, 1782
Daniel House & Ruth Holester, Feb. 28, 1782
Nehemiah Strickland & Phebe Brainard, March 20, 1782
Abner House & Cloe Holester, March 21, 1782
Levi Hills & Olle Holester, March 28, 1782
Elijah Andrews & Mable Fox, May 2, 1782
Asa Smith & Sarah Goodrich, May 2, 1782
James Rogerson (?) & Eunice Fuller, May 30, 1782
David Holester & Hope Clerk, June 6, 1782
Daniel Chamberlain & Hannah Emerson, July 18, 1782
Russel Kenney & Sarah Cornley or Comley, Nov. 8, 1782
George Tryon & Flore Strickland, Dec. 6, 1782
Jonathan Treat, Jr., & Cloe Fox, Feb. 19, 1783
Asa Goslee & Ester Strickland, Feb. 20, 1783

8

Jonathan Dart & Susannah Smith,	Oct. 9, 1783
Roger Alger & Susanna Wolf,	Dec. 21, 1783
Jonathan Covel & Rhoda Kimberly,	Dec. 11, 1783
Samuel Risley & Experience Holester,	Dec. 8, 1783
Daniel Loveland & Ruth Kenny,	Jan. 12, 1784
Thomas Sparks & Jemima Fox,	Aug. 5, 1784
Asa Goodrich & Anna Clark,	Aug. 12, 1784
Isaac Loveland & Judah Holden,	Dec. (?), 1784
Allen Goodrich & Lucy Hollester,	Dec. 2, 1784
Nathan Loveland & Deborah Dogg,	Dec. 2, 1784
Amos Loveland & Jemimah Dickerson,	Jan. 13, 1785
Jonathan Shirtliff, Jr., & Mary Goslee,	April 14, 1785
Thomas Blish & Prudence Hubbard,	April 21, 1785
Timothy Lockwood & Meriba Simons,	June, 1785
Joshua Hills & Zeuby Simons,	Sept. 2, 1785
Elijah Covel & Lydia Hodge,	Sept. 22, 1785
William Phelps & Anna Hodge,	Oct. 23 (?), 1785
David Pease & Polly Chapel,	Nov. 23, 1785
Zebulon Robbins & Hannah Holmes,	Jan. 28, 1786
Timothy Hale, Jr., & Anna Andrus,	Feb. 1, 1786
Joel House & Loise Risley,	Feb. 9, 1786
Capt. Jedediah Post & Mrs. Hannah Hubbard,	Feb. 15, 1786
Daniel Hills & Ruth Dickerson,	Feb. 23, 1786
Daniel Wright & Mabel Loveland,	March 13, 1786
Thomas Fox & Cloe Fox,	Feb. 7, 1786
William Miller & Easter Kilborn,	June 18, 1786
Benoni Gillet & Penelope Hubbard,	June 22, 1786
Jesse Tryon & Jemima Goodrich,	Sept. 22, 1786
James Bailey & Patience Williams,	Oct. 11, 1786
Mr. Charles Williams & Mrs. Sarah Goodrich,	Oct. 31, 1786
John Rogers & Rachel Scott,	Nov. 19, 1786
William Andrus & Lucy Goslee,	Dec. 3, 1786
Abner Loveland & Lois Hodge,	Jan. 11, 1787
David Loveland & Penelope Loveland,	June 21, 1787
Eliazer Fox & Olivilee (?) Blare,	June 29, 1787
John Loveland & Elizabeth Wickham,	June 29, 1787
John Hills & Ruth Smith,	July 1, 1787
Mr. Richard Risley & Mrs. Mary Branard,	Aug. 15, 1787
Jonathan Holden, Jr., & Lydia Chapel,	Aug. 16, 1787

Benjamin Brower (?) & —— Webster,	Aug. 26, 1787
Thomas Risley, Jr., & Thankful Andrus,	Sept. 28, 1787
James Covel & Lucy Hale,	Oct. 28, 1787
Asahel Holester & Elizabeth Wire,	Dec. 2, 1787
Reuben Bebe & Elizabeth Holester,	Feb. 10, 1788
Samuel Keney & Jedidah Simons,	Feb. 28, 1788
William Kenny & Hannah Smith,	March 12, 1788
Mat. House & Loise Hubbard,	March 14, 1788
Nehemiah Holester & Elizabeth Fox,	April 2, 1788
Henery Turner & Mary Risley,	May 4, 1788
Thomas Goodale & Anna Kenney,	June 19, 1788
Frary Talcott & Ruth House,	July 9, 1788
Caleb Williams & Abigail Andrus,	Nov. 6, 1788
Amasa Fox & Abigail Weir,	Nov. 6, 1788
Isaac Williams & Ruth Goodale,	—— 8, 1788
Daniel Hutson & widow Dorotha Hubbard,	Dec. 10, 1788
Avery Goodale & Betty Dealing,	Feb. 5, 1789
Josiah Robbins & Christiana Morley,	June 4, 1789
Nathan Dickerson & Elizabeth House,	Aug. 6, 1789
William Dewolf & Anna Brewer,	Oct. 1, 1789
Lebeus Hills & Polly Gibson,	Oct. 22, 1789
Jabez Talcott & Ruth Kimberly,	Nov. 20, 1789
John Talcott & Mercy Hubbard,	Nov. 25, 1789
Hoel Strickland & Cloe Kimberly,	Nov. 24, 1789
John Darling & Jerusha Andrus,	Feb. 8, 1790
William Holester & Rachel Holden,	Feb. 21, 1790
Elijah Welles & Anner Talcott,	March 26, 1790
Josiah Goodale & Rebecca Brooks,	May 11, 1790
William Tubbs & Jemima Goff,	Sept. 9, 1790
Aaron Hills & Asenah Smith,	Nov. 11, 1790
Amasa Dodge & Mary Wickham,	Nov. 11, 1790
Solomon Williams & Pegy Standliff,	Dec. 27, 1790
Benoni Buck & Lucretia Holester,	Jan. 2, 1791
Francis Loveland & Hannah Stevens,	Jan. 6, 1791
Seth Goodrich & Mary Grover,	March 24, 1791
David Damon & Beriah Follon (?),	May 27, 1791
Jabin Strong & Ruth Hunter,	May 27, 1791
Nathaniel Holester, Jr., & Prudence Strickland,	June 5, 1791
Simeon Daniels & Mable Treat,	June 16, 1791

James Fuller & Rhoda Rogers,   Aug. 4, 1791
Abijah Miller & Lucy Strong,   Aug. 18, 1791
John Nichols & Ruth Wickham,   Aug. 18, 1791
Eliezer Bell, Jr., & Polly Atkins,   Aug. 29, 1791
Jacob Humerson & Anner Hubbard,   Sept. 1, 1791
Ebenezer Smith & Betsey Risley,   Sept. 22, 1791
Joseph Henderson & Sarah Bell,   Sept. 26, 1791
Joseph Taylor & Elizabeth Ingram,   Oct. 21, 1791
Aaron Plush & Roxey Webster,   Nov. 3, 1791
Ebenezer Chapman & Rhodea Hale,   Nov. 10, 1791
Reuben Abbe & the widow Eunice Williams,   Nov. 10, 1791
David Hurlburt & widow Ruth Fox,   Nov. 13, 1791
Moses Goodale & Betty Andrus,   Nov. 17, 1791
Abel Hodge & Submit Brooks,   Nov. 24, 1791
Frederick Goodrich & widow Sarah Bulkley,   Nov. 24, 1791
Joseph Daniels & Phebe Chapman,   1791
George Hunt & Jemimah Holester,   Jan. 4, 1792
Elijah H. Goodrich & Mable Nicholson,   Jan. 12, 1792
Joseph De Wolf & Anna T—ori— (?),   Jan. 24, 1792
Benajah Skinner & Martha Baker,   Feb. 9, 1792
Cornwell Mark & Sarah Goodrich,   Feb. 13, 1792
Martin Daton & widow Ruth Talcott,   April 3, 1792
Ephraim Hale & Betty Morley,   April 5, 1792
William Goodale & Prudence Baker,   June 20, 1792
Gilbert Wier & Sarah Holester,   July 1, 1792
Ashbel Auger & Mary Bidwill,   July 3, 1792
Thomas Hale & Lucretia House,   July 3, 1792
Eliezur Andrus & Sarah Norton,   July 8, 1792
Bliss Webb & Florinday Holmes,   Aug. 5, 1792
Nathaniel Spelman & Lydia Wier (?),   Aug. 21, 1792
Andrew Warner & Gillet Goodale,   Nov. 11, 1792
Jonathan Treat & Caturah Wier,   Nov. 14, 1792
Asa Cook & Edit Holester,   Nov. 18, 1792
Zadock Andrus & Ruth Brooks,   Feb. 1, 1793
Israel Lucas & Dorotha ———, "her surname forgot,"
                                                Feb. 25, 1793
Abihu Acklen & Anna Wier,   April 23, 1793
William White & Polly Hunt,   March, 1793
David Curtis & Louice Tom, "her Christian not re-
     membered,"   May 23, 1793

Jeremiah Hurlburt & Rhodea Kenny,	June 23, 1793
Jeremiah Hugeson & Lucy Hall,	July 7, 1793
Timothy Balch & Anna Whitman,	July 22, 1793
Samuel Brooks & Elizabeth Hollister,	Sept. 18, 1793
Abijah Keney & Hannah Swetland,	Sept. 22, 1793
William Whitford & Lucy Welding	Feb. 18, 1794
John Holden, Jr., & Sarah Welding,	May 18, 1794
Miles Lee & Sybil Eells,	May 20, 1794
Russell House & Sarah Welles,	May 22, 1794
Isaac Wickham & Ruth Bidwell,	June 8, 1794
Joseph Freman & Amelia Freman (negroes),	June 26, 1794
William Dean & Hope Sterns,	Sept. 17, 1794
Darius Pease & Margaret Wier,	Oct. 5, 1794
William Heldreth, Jr., & Ruth Mason,	Oct. 8, 1794
Oliver Phelps & Polly Hills,	Nov. 28, 1794
Jered Hollister & Elizabeth Algar,	Dec. 7, 1794
Samuel Jones & Sarah Duey (?),	Dec. 17, 1794
Benjamin Risley & Anna Benton,	March 13, 1795
Moses Hills & Lucy Goodale,	March, 1795
Elisha McCaul (?) & Dorothy Holester,	April 2, 1795
Roger Jones & Sarah Dickinson,	April 8, 1795
John Lucus & Ruth Thomas,	May 14, 1795
Abial Dart & Hope Fox,	Aug. 23, 1795
George Simons & Ruth Holmes,	Aug. 27, 1795
Justus Weldin & Roxany Stevens,	Sept. 7, 1795
Jeremiah Wier & Elizabeth Fox,	Oct. 4, 1795
Eliezur Hubbard & Ruth Stilman,	Dec. 7, 1795
Ambrose Hitchcox & Olive Andrus,	Dec. 23, 1795
Moses Goodale & Anna Andrews,	Dec. 24, 1795
Gi—— (?) Goodale & Penelope Holester,	Dec. 24, 1795
James Buck & Ruth Matson,	Dec. 24, 1795
Thomas Goslee & Electa Hunt,	Jan. 10, 1796
Ambrose Dodge & Mary Holester,	Aug. 21, 1796
Israel Wier & Charity Loveland,	Sept. 3, 1796
Henery Daton & widow Bethia Holester,	Oct. 17, 1796
Wait Hale & Abigail Holester,	Nov. 19, 1796
Job Hurlburt & Penelope Goslee,	Dec. 22, 1796
John Henney or Kenney (?) & Martha Harris,	Jan. 26, 1797
Joseph Wiers, Jr., & Mille Andrus,	Feb. 12, 1797

William Goodale & Hannah Furbs (?),	March 23,	1797
Israel Fox, Jr., & Rhoda Goslee,	July 30,	1797
Samuel Findley Jones & Anna Strong,	Sept. 10,	1797
Randolph Wright Field & Hannah Dwight Holester,		
	Sept. 14,	1797
Eliezur Andrus & Sarah Wier,	Oct.,	1797
Josiah or Thomas Curtis & Mahitibel Not,	Oct. 10,	1797
William Case & Phebe Holester,	Oct. 13,	1797
Elisha Furbs & Hannah Loveland,	Nov. 11,	1797
Phelix Linzley & Mary Morley,	Nov. 27,	1797
Charles Dewolf & Susannah Lucas (?),	Jan. 10,	1798
Nathaniel Curtis & Britty (?) Holester,	Jan. 11,	1798
Nathan Thomson & Abigail Daton,	Feb. 18,	1798
John Couch (?) & Ruth Fox,	March 4,	1798
Gurdon Wells & Poly Nickelson,	March 25,	1798
Moses Giles & Ruth Jones,	April 22,	1798
Joseph Tanto & Anna Stodard,	May 7,	1798
William Benton & Roxey Briant,	July 4,	1798
Richard Parker & Lydia Hostford,	Oct. 10,	1798
James Goslee & Mercy Welles,	Aug.,	1798
Benjamin Mosely & Polly House,	Oct. 11,	1798
Joshua Smith & Katurah Loveland,	Oct. 21,	1798
Roger Daniels & Deborah Loveland,	Oct. 23,	1798
Timothy Holester & Betty Treat,	Nov. 14,	1798
Roger Collins & Betsey Smith,	Nov. 15,	1798
John Brown & Sarah Fox,	Nov. 28,	1798
Simon Alington & Roxy Risley,	Nov. 28,	1798
Asa Loveland & Mary Stodard,	Nov. 28,	1798
Walter Hinkley & Mercy Gibson,	Dec. 20,	1798
Samuel Holester & Cloray Shipman,	March 28,	1799
Harvey Horton & Betsey Fuller,	May 19,	1799
Walter Wier & Clarissa Hurlburt,	July 9,	1799
David Carrier & Elizabeth How,	July 14,	1799
Elisha Couch, Jr., & Lucy Loveland,	Sept. 8,	1799
Henery Sumner & Polly Goslee,	Sept. 11,	1799
David Elizur Hubbard & Pamela Holester,	Oct. 6,	1799
Jonathan Deling (?) & Betsey Dickinson,	Oct. 7,	1799
Stephen Shipman & Elizabeth Ferris,	Dec. 13,	1799

INDEX.

Early Connecticut Marriages

AS FOUND ON

ANCIENT CHURCH RECORDS

PRIOR TO 1800.

SIXTH BOOK.

EDITED BY THE

REV. FREDERIC W. BAILEY, B.D.,

LATE OFFICIAL COPYIST OF PAROCHIAL ARCHIVES AND SECRETARY OF COMMISSION, DIOCESE
OF CONNECTICUT; EDITOR "EARLY MASSACHUSETTS MARRIAGES;" DESIGNER BAILEY'S
PHOTO-ANCESTRAL RECORD, "THE RECORD OF MY ANCESTRY;" MEMBER NEW
ENGLAND HISTORIC GENEALOGICAL SOCIETY; CONNECTICUT HISTORICAL
SOCIETY; NEW HAVEN COLONY HISTORICAL SOCIETY; SONS
OF THE AMERICAN REVOLUTION (MASS.).

PUBLISHED BY THE

BUREAU OF AMERICAN ANCESTRY
FOR
Family   Researches

FREDERIC W. BAILEY, MGR.

P. O. BOX 587.   NEW HAVEN, CONN.

PREFACE.

With considerable satisfaction we are able to present herewith our Sixth Book of Early Connecticut Marriages, and, thanks to our interested patrons who have regularly purchased these issues, our Yankee grit has won, and still more of these perishing records are secured in type. It looks now as if the work begun but feebly, some eight years ago, was nearing its completion. Our only hope is that it may be our privilege to bring them all out from their obscurity into ultimate service whereby additional links may be supplied to those who would find a real Connecticut anchorage.

As these records have been copied, it has produced in us, as it must produce in those who possess the books, no end of amazement at the vast number of such records found in different localities at such early periods, all in possession of church authorities. Surely we all owe a debt of gratitude not only to the faithful clergy of these early years for so regularly recording, but also to those clerks who felt a real sacred obligation attached to their position in guarding these perishing books with a jealous care. We fear there is not the same sense of responsibility felt to-day in such matters, though the examples here set ought to inspire all with a like devotion, especially as is realized the exceeding value of all such records. Nor is it too late for even town clerks to learn a lesson from what has proved to be a most valuable possession of the State. Because a record is old is no evidence that such is either useless or worthless, but rather, in that such is old and perishing, should be reason for greater care and more delicate handling.

And so we are coming by slow degrees to view it, till ere very long the ancient in all our towns shall have the respect due to age and the attention as deep and as absorbing as the valued message it conveys.

FREDERIC W. BAILEY.

New Haven, Conn., April 15, 1904,

CONTENTS.

SIXTH BOOK.

RECORDS LOST.

The following is a (revised) list of Congregational Churches so far reporting the loss of their records of Baptisms and Marriages prior to 1800.

CHURCH.	COUNTY.	ORGANIZED.	REMARKS.
Westminster, of Canterbury,	Windham,	1770,	none before 1824.
Coventry,	Tolland,	1745,	none before 1818.
Hebron,	Tolland,	1716,	burned.
Ellington,	Tolland,	1736,	lost.
Sherman,	Fairfield,	1744,	burned.
East Granby,	Hartford,	1737,	
Goshen,	Litchfield,	1740,	lost.
Watertown,	Litchfield,	1739,	lost.
Canton Center,	Hartford,	1750,	before 1826, lost.
So. Manchester,	Hartford,	1779,	
North Guilford,	New Haven,	1725,	lost.
East Lyme,	New London,	1719,	lost.
Lyme (Hamburgh),	New London,	1727,	lost.
West Haven,	New Haven,	1719,	before 1815, lost.
Litchfield,	Litchfield,	1721,	before 1886, burned.
Tolland,	Tolland,	1723,	burned
Bethany,	New Haven,	1763,	before 1823, lost.
Andover,	Tolland,	1749,	B. and M. before 1818, burned at W. Springfield, Mass.
Glastonbury,	Hartford,	1693,	before 1797, lost.
Marlborough,	Hartford,	1749,	missing.
Harwinton,	Litchfield,	1738,	nothing before 1790.
Ridgefield,	Fairfield,	1714,	nothing before 1800.
Plymouth,	Litchfield,	1740,	no marriages before 1800.
Greenwich,	Fairfield,	1670,	nothing before 1787.
Greenwich, (Stanwich),	Fairfield,	1735,	burned 1821.
Torringford,	Litchfield,	1764,	burned, nothing before 1837.
East Haddam, (Hadlyme),	Middlesex,	1745,	no marriages before 1800, baptisms begin 1745.
Monroe,	Fairfield,	1764,	no marriages before 1821, baptisms begin 1776.
Bristol,	Hartford,	1747,	no marriages before 1792, baptisms begin 1800.
Suffield (West),	Hartford,	1744,	no records before 1840.
Eastford,	Windham,	1778,	no records before 1800.
Middlefield,	Middlesex,	1745,	no records before 1808.
Salisbury,	Litchfield,	1744,	few records before 1800.
Middletown (South),	Middlesex,	1747,	few records before 1800.

NEW HAVEN.

NEW HAVEN COUNTY.

(See Book I.)

New Haven was settled in 1638 and named August, 1640. The records of the First Congregational Church were published in Book I. The North Congregational Church, or the United Society, was organized May 7, 1742, as the "Church of Christ in White Haven Society." The records follow. In June, 1771, there was a secession from this church called the Church of Christ in the Fair Haven Society, which in November, 1796, reunited with the former organization. The records of that society also follow.

John Bishop & Rachel Ruggels of N. Milford,   Jan. 1, 1751
Thomas Pursel & Mary Newell,   March 30, 1752
Joseph Thompson & Lydia Gilbert,   April 2, 1752
Jehiel Tuttle & Charity Dayton of North Haven, May 14, 1752
Joseph Mix, Jr., & Sarah Morris,   May 21, 1752
Samuel Allen & Mary Leeke,   June 18, 1752
Stephen Johnson & Sarah Hull,   Oct. 25, 1752
Joseph Talmage & Sarah Parmely,   Nov. 2, 1752
David Austin & Mary Mix,   Dec. 1, 1752
James Searles & Hannah Blin,   Feb. 1, 1753
James Renalls of Weathersfield & Mehitable Blakeley,
  March 2, 1753
Joseph Josling & Sarah Parmele,   April 3, 1753
Robin, servant of A. Thompson, & Rose, servant of
  Aaron Day,   Aug. 16, 1753
Samuel Gridley of Huntington & Deborah Jones, Oct. 3, 1753
Joseph Beacher & Esther Potter,   Feb. 28, 1754
Isaac Dickerman, Esq., & Elizabeth Morris,   June 12, 1754
Hezekiah Hotchkiss & Mary Wood,   June 19, 1754
Israel Woodin & Lydia Basset,   June 24, 1754
Joseph Wise & Ells Marks,   July 8, 1754
Ezra Dogge & Susanna Hotchkiss,   July 17, 1754
Timothy Munson & Sarah Bishop,   July 17, 1754
Isaac Quintard of Stratford & Lucretia Burroughs,
  Oct. 10, 1754
Nathan Dummer & Triphena Austin,   Oct. 24, 1754
Nathaniel Brunson of Farmington & Mercy Allen,
  Dec. 18, 1754

John Hitchcock of New Milford & Sibyl Sherwood of
    Woodbury,   Dec. 20, 1754

Stephen Russel of New Haven & Ruth Butler of Mid-
    dletown,   Feb. 13, 1755

Moses Beacher & Anne Johnson,   March 12, 1755

William Hodge of West Haven & Luce Smith of
    West Haven,   June 12, 1755

Mathew Gilbert, Jr., & Sarah Thompson,   June 12, 1755

Thomas Davis & Lois Tuttle of North Haven, July 1, 1755

James Blakeslee of Waterbury & Anne Bradley, July 14, 1755

John Hotchkiss & Susanna Jones,   Aug. 28, 1755

Dennis Couert (?) & Rhoda Potter,   Feb. 12, 1756

Zebulun Crudendon & Doritha Parmele, both of Guilford,
                               June 17, 1756

Hezekiah Bradley & Unice Johnson,   Aug. 12, 1756

William Allen & Eliza. Stacey,   Sept. 16, 1756

Enos Johnson & Abigail Leeke,   March 2, 1757

Charles Cooke & Ruth Russel,   Aug. 25, 1757

Charles Sabin & Sarah Todd,   Sept. 8, 1757

Thomas Ivers of Bolton & Jane Jones,   Dec. 1, 1757

Nathaniel Hatch of Mansfield & Ashseh (?) Pamele,
                               Dec. 6, 1757

Edward Meloy & Mary Pamele,   Feb. 7, 1758

Joseph Peck & Lidia Parde of West Haven, Feb. 22, 1758

James Bishop & Patience Todd of North Haven,
                             March 1, 1758

William Dinslo & Sarah Dormon,   March 23, 1758

Archebald McNeal of New Haven & Sarah Clark of
    Darbe,   May 2, 1758

William Manser (?) of New Haven & Lois Potter of
    North Haven,   May 30, 1758

Abraham Thompson & Rachel Warner,   June 13, 1758

Josiah Ingraham & Rebeca Sherman,   Dec. 7, 1758

Josiah Parde & Sibyl Johnson,   Dec. 13, 1758

David Jackson of Newtown & Rachel Sperry, Feb. 1, 1759

Judah Thompson & Sarah Morris,   Feb. 14, 1759

Joseph Potter & Jemima Smith,   April 26, 1759

Michael Gilbert & Elizabeth Potter,   April 26, 1759

Thomas Humpreville & Elizabeth Morris, May 13, 1759

Solomon Lewis & Rhode Woodin,   Oct. 4, 1759
Roger Dearing Phips, Falmoth, & Phebe Brown,
  Nov. 15, 1759
Samuel Austin & Lidiah Woolcott,   Dec. 6, 1759
David Allen & Patience Sanford,   Jan. 3, 1760
Eliheu Crane of Newark & Hannah Mix,   Feb. 17, 1760
Samuel Horton & Susanna Howel,   Aug. 7, 1760
Enoch Bauldwin of Amity & Mary Allin,   Sept. 17, 1760
Alexander Buckland of Windsor & Sarah Smith,
  Oct. 1, 1760
Nehemiah Strong & Lidia Bur,   Nov. 27, 1760
Ebenezer Warner & Susanna Tuttle,   Jan. 27, 1761
Joel Munson of Mount Carmel & Sarah Dickerman,
  widow,   Feb. 4, 1761
Timothy Woodin & Sarah Ford,   Feb. 5, 1761
Abel Mix of New Haven & Ruth Hawley of Farmington,
  Feb. 23, 1761
Zadock Allen & Desire Warner,   March 19, 1761
Thomas Leek & Mary Johnson,   April 22, 1761
Joseph Mansfield & Hanah Punderson,   May 28, 1761
Joseph Gilbert & Doritha Munson,   Aug. 27, 1761
Isaac Townsend of New Haven & Elizabeth Hitchcock
  of Springfield,   Sept. 24, 1761
John Bradley & Deborah Tuttle,   Oct. 22, 1761
Jonathan Mansfield, Jr., & Mary Dorchester,   Nov. 10, 1761
John Storer, Jr., & Hannah Brown,   Nov. 11, 1761
Silvanus Bishop of Durham & Sarah Beecher, Nov. 16, 1761
Aaron Hayes of Symesbury & Hannah Parde of East
  Haven,   Jan. 7, 1762
Rubin Blakeslee & Rhode Griswold,   Jan. 20, 1762
John Cornel & Lydia Austin,   July 1, 1762
John Warner & Phebe Basset,   Sept. 2, 1762
Isaac Johnson of Stratford & Phebe Grant,   Sept. 15, 1762
Timothy Mix, Jr., & Margaret Storer,   Sept. 30, 1762
Asher Blakeslee of Waterbury & Mary Hummason of
  Litchfield,   Oct. 26, 1762
John Austin & Permit Anne Mix,   Oct. 28, 1762
Isaac Bradley & Lois Lewis,   April 7, 1763
Charles Munson & Hannah Munson,   June 14, 1763

Josiah Parde & Rebecca Beacher,   Aug. 10, 1763
Icabod Page & Ruth Hotchkiss,   Nov. 15, 1763
Moses Ford & Unice Potter,   Nov. 17, 1763
Jonathan Beacher & Lois Hull,   Dec. 29, 1763
Benjamin Allin & Lidia Tuttle,   March 7, 1764
Joel Ford & Thankful Potter,   March 15, 1764
Caleb Turner of North Haven & Mable Brown,
                                                   March 29, 1764
Charles Cook of Mt. Carmel & Sibyl Munson of
    White Haven,   Aug. 2, 1764
William Lucas of New Haven & Hulda Ranney of
    Middletown,   Aug. 21, 1764
Abel Burrit of Stratford & Unice Austin of White
    Haven,   Sept. 19, 1764
John Russel of East Haven & Hannah Griswold of
    White Haven,   Sept. 27, 1764
David Beecher & Mary Austin,   Oct. 18, 1764
Caleb Gilbert & Unice Basset,   Oct. 18, 1764
John Lothrop & Mary Jones,   Oct. 31, 1764
Jabez Johnson & Abigail Durrow of East Haven,
                                                   Nov. 8, 1764
James Storer & Electa Bradley,   Nov. 15, 1764
Hezekiah Pamele & Elizabeth Cook,   Dec. 6, 1764
Nathan Beers & Abigail Allen,   Jan. 20, 1765
Elisha Boxford (or Roxford) of Stratford & Lydia
    Munson,   Jan. 30, 1765
Abraham Auger of Amity & Sarah Allcock   Feb. 17, 1765
Joseph Denison of Middlefield & Rhoda Wilmot,
                                                   March 27, 1765
Israel Munson & Anna Griswold,   April 11, 1765
Moses Parde of East Haven & Sarah Wilmot,
                                                   May 2, 1765
Stephen Ingraham & Sarah Talmage,   May 23, 1765
John Cornwell & Abigail Maultbee,   May 27, 1765
Ruben Beacher & Sarah Dorchester,   July 18, 1765
Jeremiah Osborn & Anne Munson,   Oct. 24, 1765
Isaac Thompson & Elizabeth Thompson,   Nov. 14, 1765
John Ball & Sarah Johnson,   Jan. 16, 1766

James Hull & Mary Ball,	Jan. 16, 1766
Erastus Bradley & Lidia Beecher,	Jan. 30, 1766
Charles Prindle & Ruth Storer,	March 19, 1766
Nicholas Streat of East Haven & Hannah Austin,	
	April 23, 1766
Philip Rexford & Mary Ball,	May 4, 1766
Asa Sperry of Amity & Ester Tuttle,	Nov. 20, 1766
Stephen Brown & Elizabeth Phips,	Dec. 3, 1766
Joseph Trowbridge & Sarah Sabins,	Dec. 10, 1766
Zuriel Kimberly & Martha Hitchcock of Mt. Carmel,	
	Dec. 15, 1766
John Peirpoint & Sarah Beers,	Dec. 28, 1766
Isaac Beers & Mary Mansfield,	Dec. 29, 1767
Aaron Potter & Mary Allen,	Feb. 5, 1767
Benedict Arnold & Margaret Mansfield,	Feb. 11, 1767
Cuff, servant of Samuel Bird, & Lilly, servant of	
Thomas Darling,	May 2, 1767
Samuel Woodin & Elizabeth Punderson,	July 2, 1767
Edward Larkins & Unice Thompson,	Aug. 13, 1767
Timothy Andrews of Mt. Carmel & Sarah Ball,	
	Sept. 24, 1767
Jabez Colt & Sarah Mix,	Nov. 11, 1767
Curtis Hall of Farmington & Rachel Beecher,	Jan. 17, 1771
Nathan Dummer & Esther Dorman,	Jan. 17, 1771
Ashbell Stilman & Mary Storer,	March 21, 1771
Jeremiah Atwater, Jr., & Lois Hurd,	Aug. 14, 1771
Timothy Prout Bontacue & Elizabeth Upson,	Nov. 5, 1771
Gabriel Allen & Sarah Churchill,	Nov. 10, 1774
James Gourlie & Sarah Sloan,	Nov. 22, 1774
Joel Northrop of New Milford & Mable Sarah Bird,	
	May 17, 1777
Abraham Pinto of New Haven & Mary Gault or Gautt	
of Boston,	Dec. 30, 1779
Eldad Mix & Mary Hitchcock,	July 15, 1780
Jonathan Smith of West Haven & Susannah Tuttle of	
North Haven,	Aug. 12, 1783
Frederick Hendrick & Sarah McDaniel,	Feb. 1, 1784
Samuel Wood & Sarah Brown,	March 17, 1784

FROM FAIR HAVEN CHURCH RECORDS.

John Knott & Esther Atwater Hotchkiss,	April 16, 1788
William Trowbridge & Lucy Peck,	July 27, 1788
Caleb Miller & Phebe Wooden,	Aug. 3, 1788
Abraham Johnson & Mrs. —— Johnson,	Oct. 16, 1788
—— Barnett & —— Johnson,	Oct. 19, 1788
Charles Northrop & Rachel Church,	Oct. 20, 1788
Noah Johnson & Sally Hill,	Oct. 30, 1788
Adrian Forbes & Esther Everton,	Nov. 3, 1788
James Law (or Lane) & Elizabeth Smith,	Nov. 23, 1788
Samuel Thomas & Lois Howel,	Nov. 23, 1788
Peter Gold & Laura Byington,	Dec. 18, 1788
Hezekiah Bradley & Lucy Hull,	Dec. 21, 1788
—— Pe—— & Azubah Atkins,	Dec. 25, 1788
Rossiter Griffin & Mrs. Hobby,	Jan. 5, 1789
Isaac Gorham & Eliza Brown,	March 10, 1789
John Tappin & Lydia Atwater,	March 14, 1789
Nathaniel Jacobin & Mrs. Sarah Bristol,	April 13, 1789
Amos Hill & Miss Jerusha Towner,	Nov. 22, 1789
Kneeland Townsend & Miss Susanna Hampton (?),	
	Dec. 13, 1789
Alexander Booth & Miss Huldah Thompson,	Dec. 30, 1789
Ward Atwater & Alia Atwater,	March, 1786
Benjamin Ally & Esther Bradley,	March, 1786
Noah Barber & Temperance Wise,	March, 1786
Nicholas Tuttle & Betsey Payne,	Aug. 9, 1787
Christopher Fry & Betsey Humphrey,	Dec. 9, 1787
Moses Merriman & Lois Wantwood,	Nov., 1787
Thomas Goward & Lydia Thompson,	Nov., 1787
Eber Sperry & Pamelia Page,	Dec. 17, 1787
John Gabriel & —— Ayres,	Jan. 3, 1788
Rev. David Higgins & Miss Eunice Gilbert,	Jan. 17, 1788
Solomon Phipps & Mrs. —— Dwight,	Feb. 3, 1788
Merit Carrington & Rebecca White,	Feb. 3, 1788
Prat Jones & Sarah Dickerman,	March 12, 1788
Lewis Hepburn & Huldah Hotchkiss,	April 4, 1788
Diman Bradley & Bule Turner,	Jan. 14, 1784
Henry Daggett & Anne Ball,	July 7, 1784

Abner Tuttle & Elizabeth Mix,	June 5, 1783
John Thomas & Susanna Mahan,	June 17, 1783
James Dixon & Mary Smith,	July 11, 1783
Asa Potter & Phebe Mansfield,	Sept. 4, 1783
Thomas Kirkland & Cyble Sabens,	Sept. 20, 1783
John Manser & Elizabeth Wooden,	Oct. 16, 1783
James Peck & Sibyll Ford,	Oct. 30, 1783
John Lewis & Sarah Storer,	Oct. 30, 1783
John Waters & Rachel Redmon,	Nov. 3, 1783
John Johnson & Huldah Chittendon,	Dec. 21, 1783
Roger Alling & Esther Smith,	Sept. 27, 1783
Harthan Ramsdell & Katharine Burn,	Jan. 1, 1784
Elijah Hotchkiss & Rebecca Osborne,	March 3, 1782
John Dorman & Sybell Gilbert,	March 7, 1782
John Mason & Sarah Sears,	April 6, 1782
Ezra Lines & Lue Wheton,	June 4, 1782
Hathen Ramsdle & Sarah Danelson,	June 20, 1782
Solomon Meers of Hartford & Sally Daggett of New Haven,	June 22, 1782
Sturges Burr & Betsey Judson of Newtown,	Aug. 17, 1782
Daniel Hotchkiss & Ana (?) Andrus,	Aug. 20, 1782
Jared Thompson & Lydie Hotchkiss,	Sept. 26, 1782
Alexander Bradly & Lydia Bradly,	Nov. 28, 1782
Jared Bradly & Susanna Smith,	Dec. 8, 1782
Abner Scott of Waterbury & Aletheah Bradley of New Haven,	Feb. 5, 1783
Timothy Gorham & Mary White,	March 3, 1783
Timothy Atwater & Cloe Auger,	Feb. 3, 1773
Elijah Thompson & Mable Alling,	May 20, 1773
Jabez Brown & Rebecca Smith,	Nov. 18, 1773
Elijah Osborn & Phebe Tuttle,	Jan. 2, 1774
Amos Gilbert & Elizabeth Ann Alling,	April 14, 1774
Ashbel Beecher & Mary Thomas,	Nov. 4, 1774
Joseph Peck & Sarah Allcock,	Dec. 27, 1774
Asahel Todd & Phebe Phips,	Jan. 22, 1775
Person Stilman & Elizabeth Allin,	Feb. 8, 1775
Joseph Thomas & Anne Hodge,	Feb. 9, 1775
Timothy Ohara & Eleanor Pattlebee,	Feb. 26, 1775
Daniel Carrington & ——— Talmadge,	June 22, 1775

Abner Bristo & Eunice Dorchester,	Aug. 1, 1775
Charles Sabens & Jemima Barnard,	Nov. 14, 1775
Job Potter & Mary Bradley,	Nov. 16, 1775
Daniel Goff Phipps & Anny Townsend,	March 3, 1776
Timothy Johnson & Martha Humerston,	March 5, 1776
Henry Yorke & Susanna Chataton,	May 5, 1776
Samuel Denten & Unice Humerton,	June 11, 1776
Samuel Gorham & Sarah Lines,	Dec. 8, 1776
David Molthrop & Hephzibath Hotchkiss,	Jan. 1, 1777
James Murray & Katharine Scovert (?),	May 28, 1777
John Troop & Susanna Bills,	May 30, 1777
Titus Smith & Martha Belding of West Haven,	July 23, 1777
Stephen Mix & Esther Reed,	Nov. 19, 1777
William Osborn & Dorcas Peck,	Dec. 10, 1777
Medad Beecher & Eunice Johnson,	Dec. 14, 1777
Silas Hotchkiss & Esther Gilbert,	Dec. 17, 1777
David Warner & Sarah Wooden,	Dec. 30, 1777
Isaac Augur & Esther Dorman,	Jan. 1, 1778
Edmund Smith & Mariam Malery,	Jan. 25, 1778
Samuel Mix & Martha Burret,	April 5, 1778
William Noyes & Rebecca Alling,	June 23, 1778
Hezekiah Augur & Lydia Atwater,	Oct. 28, 1778
Jabeth Turner & Rebecca Woolcutt,	Oct. 29, 1778
Daniel Hubbard & Sarah Alling,	Nov. 26, 1778
Samuel White, Jr., & Sarah Barnes,	Dec. 28, 1778
Hezekiah Reed & Sarah Noyes,	Jan. 21, 1779
Jehial Arnold & Hanah Thompson,	May 6, 1779
William McNeil & Hulda Augur,	Sept. 25, 1779
James Howell & Rhoda Augur,	Oct. 31, 1779
Elihu Hotchkiss & Naomi Gilbert,	Dec. 14, 1779
John Stone & Mary Mansfield,	Jan. 25, 1780
John McCoy & Abigail Broughten,	Feb. 13, 1780
William Steward & Sarah McCone,	Feb. 17, 1780
Charles Fryers & Susanna Jonsen (?),	Feb. 23, 1780
John Peck & Louis Osborne,	March 12, 1780
Timothy Gilbert & Triphena Dummer,	March 15, 1780
Silas Graves & Mary Hubbard,	March 29, 1780
James Thompson & Lorinda Hotchkiss,	April 19, 1780
Zophar Atwater & Lucy Osborne,	April 27, 1780

Abijah Treet & Margaret Spery,	July 12, 1780
Josiah Burr & Mary Burr,	Sept. 7, 1780
Phineas Andrus & Hephzibath Molthrop,	Nov. 14, 1780
Benjamin Grannis & Bathsheba Howel,	Sept. 29, 1780
James Gilbert & Sarah Cooper,	Oct. 5, 1780
Cebria Chaplin & Sarah Plimate (?),	April 22, 1781
John Gilbert & Marian Phips,	July 30, 1781
Holbrook Atwater & Mehitable Alling,	Aug. 2, 1781
Stephen Munson & Mary Goodyear,	Aug. 16, 1781
Mark Leavenworth & ———,	Sept. 23, 1781
Thomas Bassel & Lydia Allcock,	Sept. 28, 1781
Joseph Dorman, Jr., & Patience Heaton,	Oct. 17, 1781
Isaac Munson & Elizabeth Phips,	Oct. 30, 1781
Mathew Gilbert & Phebe Dorman,	Jan. 2, 1782
Stephen Alling & Lidia Thompson,	Feb. 2, 1782

NORTH HAVEN.

NEW HAVEN COUNTY.

The town of North Haven was incorporated October, 1786, taken from New Haven. The Congregational Church was organized in 1718. The following are the records.

Joseph Basset & Cloe Sanford,	Dec. 24, 1760
Elihu Sperry & Martha Pain,	Feb. 11, 1761
Abraham Basset & Lydia Smith,	Dec. 12, 1761
Noah Woolcot & Thankful Hitchcock,	March 4, 1761
Deacon Isaiah Tuttle & Deborah Clark,	May 7, 1761
Ensign Ezra Tuttle & Susanna Tuttle,	May 27, 1761
Jesse Goodyear & Hannah Bradley,	June 25, 1761
Ebenezer Durham & Dinah Thorp,	July 13, 1761
Seth Blakeley & Phebe Todd,	Sept. 7, 1761
Abel Bishop & Cloe Todd,	Sept. 7, 1761
Jesse Todd & Lydia Cooper,	Nov. 26, 1761
Josiah Andrews & Rebeckah Bishop,	Jan. 6, 1762
Elisha Mallery & Esther Chatterton,	Jan. 14, 1762
Capt. Castle & Joel Morrison's daughter,	April 8, 1762
One Beather of New Chesire & widow Dorcas Tuttle,	
	April 20, 1762

Abner Todd & ——— Tuttle,   May 6, 1762
William Marks, Middletown, & Lydia Batchelor, N. H.,
                                             June 3, 1762
John Hays & Phebe Thorp,   June 3, 1762
Caleb Cooper & Eunice Barns,   Nov. 4, 1762
Jonathan Bull & Cloe Blakesley,   Nov. 14, 1762
Ebenezer Harrison & Temperance Lete, Branford,
                                             Nov. 16, 1762
Noah Ives & Abigail Pierpoint,   Dec. 23, 1762
Joseph Bradley & Mabel Goodyear,   Dec. 27, 1762
Joel Thorp & Mary Standley,   Dec. 29, 1762
Titus Barnes & Eunice Brocket,   Jan. 26, 1763
Ely Bradly & Esther Goodyear,   March 8, 1763
Nathaniel Yale & Huldah Foster,   April 18, 1763
Joseph Tyler & Rachel Tuttle,   June 23, 1763
Obed Bradley & Mary Alcock,   June 29, 1763
Benjamin Bishop & Rebeckah Mansfield,   Nov. 17, 1763
Abel Bishop & Mary Barns,   Dec. 15, 1763
Jesse Alcock & Patience Blakesley,   Dec. 25, 1763
Titus Thorp & Merriam Bishop,   Feb. 16, 1764
Stephen Cooper & Bede Goodyear,   March 8, 1764
James Hill & Rachel Tuttle,   May 24, 1764
Joseph Ives & Abigail Grannis,   Dec. 6, 1764
Abraham Chatterton & Ann Sperry, Mt. Carmel,
                                             Feb. 6, 1765
Thomas Cooper & Mary Shepherd,   March 14, 1765
Nathaniel Beech & Phebe Potter,   March 14, 1765
Ichabod Brocket & Susannah Frost,   March 20, 1675
Wise Barns & Jerusha Barns,   May 15, 1765
Isaac Dickerman & Cibel Sperry, M. C.,   Aug. 21 1765
Seth Todd & Mary Ives,   Sept. 9, 1765
Amasa Hitchcock & ——— Bradley,   Oct. 2, 1765
——— Horton & Elizabeth Bishop,   Oct. 9, 1765
Benjamin Pierpoint & Sarah Blakslee,   Oct. 17, 1765
Joel Todd & Elisabeth Peck, M. C.,   Oct. 30, 1765
Giles Pierpoint & Elisabeth Cooper,   Jan. 22, 1766
Stephen Jacobs & Lydia Turner,   Jan. 22, 1766
David Sperry & ——— Peck, M. C.,   Dec. 3, 1766
Joy Bishop & Abigail Tuttle,   Jan. 1, 1767

Capt. Phinehas Castle & Mary Dickerman,	Feb. 12, 1767
Abel Bradley & Hannah Todd,	Feb. 19, 1767
John Cooper & Zurviah Barns,	April 8, 1767
Abel Smith & Lydia Tuttle,	June 25, 1767
Samuel Woodin & Esther Joslin,	Aug. 6, 1767
Ebenezer Heaton & Susannah Brocket,	Aug. 7, 1767
Enos Dickerman & Lois Allen,	Oct. 22, 1767
William Philip Daggett & Beede Mansfield,	Nov. 8, 1767
Solomon Tuttle & Eunice Tuttle,	Nov. 11, 1767
James Dickerman & Lois Bradley,	Dec. 26, 1767
Samuel Sacket & Abigail Blakeslee,	Dec. 24, 1767
John Blakslee & Ann Allen,	Feb. 16, 1768
Elias Beach & Elisabeth Gilbert,	March 9, 1768
James Bishop & Hannah Dickerman,	March 15, 1768
Ebenezer Blakslee & Martha Beech,	April 13, 1768
Jeremiah Ives & Hannah Basset,	June 7, 1768
Jacob Thorp & Enice Eishop,	June 26, 1768
Edmund Todd & Hannah Tuttle,	Aug. 23, 1768
Ebenezer Barns & Luranda Shattuck,	Sept. 19, 1768
Levi Ray & Mary Cooper,	Oct. 30, 1768
Josiah Mansfield & Hannah Cooper,	Feb. 7, 1769
John Hulls & Martha Pardee,	Feb. 9, 1769
Stephen Ives & Sarah Ames,	Feb. 12, 1769
Alexander Turner & Meriam Basset,	Sept. 21, 1769
Amasa Hall & Thankful Todd,	Nov. 23, 1769
Christopher Brocket & Elisabeth Tuttle,	Nov. 23, 1769
Hezekiah Tuttle & Lois Clark,	Dec. 7, 1769
Benjamin Brockett & Althea Ray,	Jan. 3, 1770
James Ives & Lois Turner,	Jan. 15, 1770
Hezekiah Basset & Sarah Ives,	Feb. 15, 1770
Joseph Dickerman & Lucy Thorp,	March 8, 1770
Stephen Jacobs & Mary Ives,	July 12, 1770
Elisha Alderman of Simsbury & Sarah Barns,	Oct. 1, 1770
Uzel Mansfield & Rachel Sperry of Mount Carmel,	
	Oct. 1, 1770
Stephen Brocket & Mabel Barns,	March 27, 1771
Joseph Turner & Susannah Beech,	April 3, 1771
Abraham Heaton & Mabel Cooper,	May 27, 1771
Stephen Hitchcock & Sarah Brocket of M. C.,	Sept. 16, 1771

Hezekiah Pierpoint & Mahitebel Cooper,   Sept. 26, 1771
Jonathan Barns & Ester Barns,   Nov. 7, 1771
Elisha Horton & Ruth Bishop,   June 24, 1772
Caleb Street of Wallingford & Mabel Sanford, Oct. 29, 1772
James Parde & Mary Smith,   Nov. 2, 1772
Joel Ives & Mary Heaton,   Dec. 2, 1772
William Rexford & Denis Sperry of Mount Carmel,
                                              Dec. 30, 1772
Enoch Ray & Abigail Frost,   Jan. 7, 1773
Caleb Andrews & Anna Woolcot,   June 22, 1773
Titus Frost & Mabel Stiles,   July 29, 1773
Obed Blakeslee & Sarah Gilbert,   Dec. 16, 1773
Daniel Basset & Eunice Turner,   Jan. 6, 1774
John Lothrop & Mrs. Mary Bonticue,   Jan. 13, 1774
James Bishop, 1st, & Mrs. Mary Molthrop,   Feb. 23, 1774
Elihu Sperry & Abigail Barns,   March 10, 1774
John Cory & Rebeckah Thomas,   July 7, 1774
Daniel Doolittle & Abigail Johnson,   Aug. 24, 1774
Samuel Orell & Lois Pain,   Sept. 5, 1774
Justus Johnson Fitch & Susannah Turner,   Sept. 29, 1774
Samuel Thorp & Dorcas Turner,   Sept. 29, 1774
Timothy Andrus & Mary Pierpoint,   Oct. 20, 1774
Oliver Smith & Thankful Brocket,   Nov. 17, 1774
Samuel Basset & Catharine Tuttle,   Nov. 17, 1774
Andrew Clark of Wallingford & Mary Robinson of
    N. Haven,   Nov. 24, 1774
Jesse Woolcot & Mehitabel Brocket,   Nov. 24, 1774
Joseph Gilbert & Mabel Heaton,   March 1, 1775
Isaiah Brocket & Sarah Cooper,   Aug. 23, 1775
Elias Townsend & Huldah Shepherd of New Haven,
                                              Jan. 1, 1776
——— Carter of Farmington & Abigail Molthrop of
    New Haven,   Jan. 10, 1776
Richard Waters of Derby & Eunice Ball of New Haven,
                                              March 17, 1776
Caleb Clark & Elizabeth Smith, both of New Haven,
                                              Dec. 2, 1776
——— Andrus of Mount Carmel & Mabel Barns of
    N. Haven,   Dec. 25, 1776

Joseph Hull & Sarah Pardee,	Jan. 1, 1777
Samuel Pierpoint & Sarah Woolcot,	Jan. 12, 1777
Jacob Brocket & Ruth Humaston,	Jan. 15, 1777
Benjamin Basset & Hannah Tuttle,	Jan. 15, 1777
James Humaston & Phebe Basset,	Feb. 26, 1777
James Smith & Martha Frost,	March 19, 1777
Jonathan Heaton & Isabel Hitchcock,	April 23, 1777
Ebenezer Todd & Patience Jacobs,	Oct. 13, 1777
Eden Johnson & Cibel Thorp,	Nov. 6, 1777
William Walter & Theodosia Pierpoint,	Nov. 17, 1777
Joseph Chene & Rebekah Sely,	Nov. 20, 1777
John Heaton & Lois Ray,	Dec. 31, 1777
Michael Ames & Abigail Brockett,	Jan. 22, 1778
John Potter & Abigail Forbes,	Feb. 5, 1778
Simeon Bishop & Patience Winston,	Oct. 14, 1778
Solomon Barns & Lydia Smith,	Oct. 22, 1778
Yale Todd & Phebe Brown,	Nov. 2, 1778
Stephen Hitchcock & Mrs. Abigail Pardee,	Nov. 5, 1778
Zophar Barns & Mary Barns,	Nov. 9, 1778
Alsup Talmage & Thankful Cooper,	Dec. 2, 1778
James Ives & Mary Brockett,	June 16, 1779
Monson Brocket & Hannah Allea,	Dec. 9, 1779
Solomon Jacobs & Esther Clenton,	Dec. 30, 1779
Josiah Rogers Dea. of Farmingbury & Mrs. Mary Smith, N. Haven,	April 12, 1780
John Sanford & Susannah Thorp,	June 21, 1780
Isaac Thorp & Bathsheba Towner,	Aug. 2, 1780
Joatham Blakslee & Mary Woodin,	Jan. 1, 1781
Abel Tuttle & Sally (Sarah) Bishop,	Jan. 18, 1781
Ebenezer Pardee & Jemima Barns,	March 22, 1781
Zebulun Jacobs & Esther Brocket,	April 7, 1781
Nathan Broughton & Elisabeth Clark,	May 2, 1781
Levi Bradley of Mt. Carmel & Esther Cooper,	Nov. 8, 1781
Lieut. David Bishop & Ruth Tuttle,	Dec. 13, 1781
Thomas Pierpoint & Elisabeth Bishop,	Dec. 13, 1781
Justus Cooper & Lois Bradley,	Jan. 17, 1782
Samuel Grigs & Anna Smith,	Jan. 4, 1782
Joel Jacobs & Sarah Stow,	Feb. 13, 1782
Newman Bishop & Mary Tuttle,	Feb. 14, 1782

Caleb Humaston & Sarah Bishop,   Feb. 14, 1782
Solomon Talmage of Northford & Lucretia Todd of
    New Haven,   May 2, 1782
Andrew Porch & Anna Brockett,   Sept. 12, 1782
Amasa Allen of ———— & Esther Todd,   Oct. 24, 1782
Amos Blakslee & Eunice Cooper,   Nov. 7, 1782
Justus Barns & Susanna Pardee,   March 6, 1783
Ezra Pierpoint & Mary Blakslee,   March 31, 1783
Wait Chatterton & Susanna Dickerman,   April 17, 1783
Bethuel Todd & Esther Ives,   June 25, 1783
Isaac Cooper & Lydia Cooper,   July 21, 1783
Dan Ives & Mary Baldwin,   Dec. 31, 1783
———— Butler of Farmington & Hannah Hulls,
    N. H.,   Oct. 6, 1783
William Southworth of Saybrook & Rhoda Blakslee
    of N. H.,   Nov. 11, 1783
Capt. Joshua Barns & Rebekah Hill,   Nov. 25, 1783
Thadeus Todd & Penniah Brocket,   Dec. 4, 1783
John Frost & Phebe Cooper,   Feb. 5, 1784
William Rozel Cook & Mrs. Sarah Blakslee,   June 10, 1784
Lieut. David Atwater & Mrs. Abiah Barns,   June 10, 1784
James Sisson of Newport in R. I. & Miss Sarah
    Mansfield of New Haven,   August 21, 1784
Jonathan Tuttle & Cibel Cooper,   Oct. 25, 1784
Caleb Todd & Hannah Goodsel,   Oct. 25, 1784
William Marry & Sarah Clark,   Nov. 11, 1784
George Lewis Hotchkiss of New Haven & Eunice
    Cook of Wallingford,   Feb. 6, 1785
Theophilus Bradley & Sarah Gills,   Feb. 28, 1785
Ezekiel Jacobs & Elenor Walters,   March 3, 1785
Nathaniel Johnson of Northford & Cibel Brocket of
    N. H.,   April 4, 1785
Zuar Bradley & Hannah Thorp,   April 6, 1785
Giles Eaton & Lucy Grannis,   May 9, 1785
David Pardy & Polly Spencer,   May 19, 1785
Seth Strong of N. Y. & Hannah Barns of New
    Haven,   June 16, 1785
Richard Mansfield & Mary Stiles,   June 23, 1785
Eliada Sanford & Nancy Todd,   July 6, 1785

John Cooper & Hannah Pardee,	July 14, 1785
Ensign Thomas Cooper & Mrs. Bede Daggett,	Oct. 24, 1785
Jacob Molthrop & Abigail Pardee,	Dec. 22, 1785
John Brockett of Westfield & Sarah Smith of N. Haven,	Dec. 26, 1785
Eli Todd & Patience Basset,	Jan. 17, 1786
Bethuel Turner & Bede Bradley,	Feb. 23, 1786
Oliver Todd & Betsey Smith,	May 1, 1786
Giles Heaton & Mary Grannis,	May 22, 1786
Jery Barns & Silence Brocket,	June 22, 1786
Jabez Spencer & Joanna Ives,	June 28, 1786
Jared Norton & Sarah Brocket,	Oct. 4, 1786
Jared Thompson & Lydia Blakslee,	Oct. 12, 1786
David Bradley & Martha Sperry,	Nov. 23, 1786
Abraham Sely & Eunice Butler,	Jan. 25, 1787
Abraham Blakslee & Mabel Pierpoint,	Feb. 1, 1787
John Brockett & widow Mehitable Cooper,	Feb. 7, 1787
Isaac Basset & Rosanna Pardee,	Feb. 12, 1787
Obed Basset & Susanna Bradley,	Feb. 12, 1787
Phelemon Blakslee & Lydia Brocket,	Feb. 22, 1787
Isaac C. Stiles & Eunice Blakslee,	April 3, 1787
Thomas Cooper & Mary Bishop,	Aug. 13, 1787
Asahel Stebbins & Elisabeth Brocket,	Jan. 10, 1788
Tru. Todd & Bede Humaston,	May 29, 1788
Solomon Barns & Mary Pardee,	May 29, 1788
Lemuel Tuttle & Lydia Basset,	June 12, 1788
John Barns & Cloe Bishop,	Aug. 13, 1788
Jesse Basset & Abi Blakslee,	Jan. 1, 1789
Thomas Smith & Sarah Frost,	Jan. 15, 1789
John Pierpoint & Ruth Stiles,	Feb. 26, 1789
Jonathan Dickerman & Mrs. Deborah Todd,	April 30, 1789
Ebenezer Buck & Adah Robinson,	July 23, 1789
Daniel Tuttle & Hannah Mansfield,	Oct. 6, 1789
John Pardee & Elisabeth Brocket,	Oct. 8, 1789
Rev. Samuel Tyler & Miss Ruth Fowler,	Dec. 3, 1789
David Bishop & Lucy Smith,	Dec. 14, 1789
Joel Sackitt & Lydia Todd,	Dec. 6, 1789
David Tuttle & Sarah Basset,	Dec. 24, 1789
Joel Todd & Amelia Sackitt,	Feb. 9, 1790

Reuben Tuttle & Thankful Todd,	March 10, 1790
Austin Goodyear & Susannah Pardee,	April 29, 1790
Javan Goodin & Desire Barns,	June 23, 1790
Samuel Todd & Lowly Humaston,	July 1, 1790
Jesse Bull & Chloe Brocket,	July 8, 1790
Eli Jacobs & Lydia Tyler,	Aug. 11, 1790
Solomon Sackit & Ruth Turner,	Sept. 1, 1790
Joel Pierpoint & Hannah Clenton,	Sept. 20, 1790
Thomas Beach & Euneshea Clenton,	Jan. 13, 1791
Isaac Chitsey & Lydia Smith,	Jan. 26, 1791
Merriman Monson & Mabel Smith,	Feb. 9, 1791
Joshua Tuttle & Cynthia Todd,	March 17, 1791
Philemon & Hannah Tuttle,	March 21, 1791
Joseph Goodyear & Susannah Atwater,	March 31, 1791
Enos Mansfield & Elisabeth Jacobs,	April 4, 1791
Stephen Jacobs & Naomi Gills,	May 19, 1791
Joel Atwater & Sarah Thomas,	Aug. 2, 1791
Titus Todd & Elisabeth Todd,	Sept. 29, 1791
George Augustus Bristol & Abigail Basset Munson of Hamden,	Oct. 6, 1791
Seth Plum & Sarah Tuttle,	June 11, 1792
Jesse Tuttle & Eunice Gilbert, Hamden,	Oct. 8, 1792
William Wilson & Lucy Ball,	Jan. 10, 1793
Timothy Heaton & Catherine Walter,	Feb. 4, 1793
William Waterman & Meriam Thorpe,	Oct. 16, 1793
Samuel Mix, Jr., & Susannah Humaston,	Nov. 14, 1793
Rev. Aaron Woodward of Norwalk & Miss Martha Trumbull, N. H.,	Jan. 20, 1794
Jared Sperry & Esther Sanford of Woodbridge,	Feb. 2, 1794
Newbury Button & Bede Pierpont,	May 29, 1794
John Core & Mary Bishop,	April 27, 1794
Jesse Basset & Esther Basset,	Oct. 20, 1794
Augustus Hall of Wallingford & Ruth Thorpe,	Oct. 22, 1794
Samuel Todd & Sarah Brockett,	Feb. 19, 1795
Jesse Mansfield & Keziah Stiles,	June 28, 1795
Titus Mansfield & Hannah Ives,	July 16, 1795
Isaac Hammack & Hannah Shapla of New Haven,	Sept. 1, 1795
Jesse Tuttle & Esther Pierpont,	Sept. 30, 1795

Samuel Mix, Esq., & Mrs. Sarah Ives,   Oct. 4, 1795
Jacob Thorpe & Susannah Thomas,   Dec. 23, 1795
Edward Turner & Cloe Humaston,   Jan. 10, 1796
Medad Bradley & Sally Basset Humaston,   Feb. 15, 1796
Stephen Bunnel & Patty Blakslee,   May 2, 1796
Enos Todd & Mrs. Lydia Todd,   May 16, 1796
———— Ives of Torrington & Mrs. Lydia Mix, N. H.,
    Sept. 28, 1796
Joel Ford, Jr., & Eunice Ford of Hamden,   Oct. 30, 1796
Joseph Knevels & Elisabeth Hill,   Nov. 3, 1796
Joel Heaton & Abigail Barns,   Nov. 24, 1796
Ichabod Wright & Damoris Cook,   Nov. 17, 1796
Abijah Cornwall & Eunice Ives,   1796
Nathl. Bunnell & Thankful Bristol,   Nov. 27, 1796
Amasa Hitchcock, Jr., & Abigail M. A. Foot,   Dec. 4, 1796
Roger Peck & Mary Atwater,   Dec. 19, 1796
Joel Humaston & Emelia Mix,   Jan. 12, 1797
Eli Jacobs & Ruth Bradley,   Jan. 16, 1797
John Bristol & Abigail Dickerman of Hamden,   Feb. 8, 1797
Timothy Eaton Heaton of N. H. & Lydia Ives of
    Hamden,   Sept. 7, 1797
Enos Dickerman of Cheshire & Molly Todd, N. H.,
    Sept. 7, 1797
Josiah Ames of Middletown & Sally Stacy, N. H.,
    Dec. 8, 1797
John Potter of Branford & Mabel Basset, N. H.,
    Jan. 15, 1798
Sebe Thorpe & Zipporah Lynes,   March 1, 1798
John Hunt of New Haven & Polly Merriman of Wal-
    lingford,   Dec. 27, 1798
Lent Hough of Wallingford & Mrs. Mary Andrus,
    N. H.,   Jan. 6, 1799
Samuel Chapman & Clarrissa Todd,   Jan. 23, 1799
Ebenezer B. Munson & Rebekah Dickerman, both of
    Hamden,   Feb. 6, 1799
Capt. Gideon Todd & Mrs. Eunice Brocket,   March 7, 1799
Oliver Blakslee & Mrs. Susanna Tuttle,   March 20, 1799
Eliezer Todd & Cloe Stacy,   Aug. 29, 1799
Giles Ives & Abigail Gilbert,   Oct. 9, 1799

Ephraim Cook of Cheshire & Sukey Ives of N. H.,
Oct. 16, 1799
Elam Bradley & Lowly Dickerman, both of Ham-
den,   Nov. 6, 1799
Alien Todd & Polly Ray,   Nov. 20, 1799

EAST HAVEN.

NEW HAVEN COUNTY.

The town of East Haven was incorporated May, 1785, and taken from New Haven. The
Congregational Church in East Haven was organized October 8, 1711. The following are all
the early marriages recorded.

Thomas Robinson & Mary Butler,	Nov. 11, 1755
William Everton & Izabel Holbrook,	Nov. 14, 1755
Elias Forbs & Abigail Sheppard,	Nov. 26, 1755
Jacob Goodsell & Lydia Denison,	Dec. 4, 1755
Enos Hotchkiss & Elizabeth Sheppard,	Feb. 5, 1756
Joshua Austin & Abigail Hitchcock,	May 6, 1756
John Mulloon & Phebe Nails,	July 4, 1756
Ebenezer Robbards & Elizabeth Jacobs,	Dec. 15, 1756
George King & Patience Conkling,	Dec. 27, 1756
James Thomson & Elizabeth Bishop,	Feb. 9, 1757
Joshua Sperry & Zurviah Robbison,	March 16, 1757
Caleb Hitchcock & Sarah Sheppard,	May 26, 1757
Amos Luddington & Mary Thomson,	June 7, 1757
Jehiel Forbs & Mabel Morris,	Nov. 2, 1757
Timothy Andrews & Anna Holt,	Jan. 25, 1758
David Slusher & Martha Nails,	Feb. 16, 1758
John Prindle & Dorothy Tuttle,	Feb. 22, 1758
Abraham Selee & Mary Barns,	Feb. 23, 1758
Aaron Page & Desire Grannise,	May 22, 1758
Jack & Nanna (negroes),	May 23, 1758
Aaron Williams & Sarah Robinson,	May 25, 1758
Benjamin Russel & Mary Utter,	July 13, 1758
Anthony Thomson & Sarah Pardy,	July 20, 1758
David Bishop & Sarah Austin,	Nov. 9, 1758
Phineas Curtis & Hannah Russel,	May 28, 1759

Daniel Oles & Sarah Row,	Jan. 7, 1759
Simeon Bradley & Abigail Denison,	July 26, 1759
Aaron Blakesley & Avis Fintch,	Aug. 2, 1759
Caleb Chidsey & Mabel Moulthrop,	Sept. 3, 1759
Samuel Thomson & Desire Moulthrop,	Sept. 12, 1759
Richard Darrow & Margaret Dorson,	Nov. 6, 1759
Azariah Bradley & Elizabeth Thomson,	Nov. 7, 1759
Deodate Davenport & Mrs. Mercy Morris,	Jan. 10, 1760
Pater & Betty, servants of Heminway,	Jan. 17, 1760
Eli Tully & Sarah Granger,	March 31, 1760
Bornsell (?) Huse & Mercy Collins,	April 15, 1760
Stephen Smith & Sarah Dawson,	Nov. 20, 1760
Enos Clark & Desire Russel,	Dec. 11, 1760
Jared Robinson & Mary Thompson,	Dec. 24, 1760
Israel Potter & Mary Dorson,	Feb. 4, 1761
John Pardee & Sarah Russel,	Aug. 18, 1761
Ebenezer Chidsey & Elizabeth Grannise,	1761
Benjamin Multhrop & Thankful Grannise,	1761
John Hemminway & Jemmima Hitchcock,	1761
Joseph Tuttle & Mary Granger,	Oct. 20, 1761
Aaron Buckley & Lydia Ludinton,	Oct. 20, 1761
Isaac Multhrop & Jemima Grannise,	Nov. 11, 1761
John Sheppard & Mary Patterson,	Jan. 23, 1762
Abram Bradley & Anna Heminway,	June 23, 1762
Isaac Smith & Mabel Chidsey,	Sept. 23, 1762
Caleb Chidsey & Elizabeth Penfield,	Dec. 9, 1762
George How & Abigail Forbes,	Dec. 9, 1762
David Granniss & Mary Sheppard,	Dec. 9, 1762
Nathaniel Cook & Ann Harrison,	Dec. 15, 1762
John Woodward, Jr., & Ruth Curtiss,	1763
Jesse Ives & Sarah Bellamy,	Aug. 24, 1763
Israel Linsley & Hannah Multhrop,	Sept. 15, 1763
John Barns & Abigail Collins,	Oct. 10, 1763
Matthew Man & Hannah Goodsell,	Oct. 13, 1763
John North & Anna Russell,	Nov. 17, 1763
Azariah Bradley & Lydia Woodward,	Jan. 18, 1764
Josiah Bradley & Comfort Hitchcock,	Feb. 2, 1764
Dr. Jared Potter & Sarah Forbes,	April 19, 1764
Samuel Barns & Hephziba Collins,	May 30, 1764

3

John Woodin & Hannah Holbrook, Nov. 7, 1764
Joseph Russel & Abigail Grannise, Nov. 7, 1764
Gaskel Woodward & Anne Butler, Nov. 8, 1764
Stephen Sheppard & Anna Grannise, March 13, 1765
Samuel Smith & Mary Dawson, April 11, 1765
John Sheppard & Elizabeth Bradley, April 18, 1765
Penfield Goodsell & Hannah Thompson, April 19, 1765
Ichabod Barns & Esther Talmage, Aug. 12, 1765
James Walker & Abigail Everton, Aug. 30, 1765
Timothy Bradly & Sarah Goodsell, Sept. 12, 1765
Timothy Way & Abigail Dorson of Branford, Oct. 2, 1765
Samuel Holt & Mary Rowe, Oct. 10, 1765
Solomon Multhrop & Lois Rowe, Oct. 10, 1765
Charles Page & Lois Multhrop, Oct. 31, 1765
Dan Holt & Anna Hitchcock, Dec. 5, 1765
David Engolston & Elizabeth Higgins, Dec. 5, 1765
Gurdon Bradley & Mary Woodward, Jan. 30, 1766
George Lancraft & Sarah ———, Feb. 6, 1766
Joseph Multhrop & ——— ———, 1766
John Fuller & Lydia Multhrop, March 13, 1766
Abram Chidsley & Hannah Goodsell, March 27, 1766
Isaac Forbes & Hannah Heminway, May 1, 1766
Timothy Cooper & Abigail Holbrook, June 19, 1766
Michael Todd & Mary Rowe, Sept. 15, 1766
Israel Bishop & Hannah Peck of New Haven, Sept. 15, 1766
Thomas Smith & Anne Smith, Nov. 20, 1766
John Page & Lois Brewster Pogue, Nov. 27, 1766
Dan Bradley & Mehitable Heminway, Feb. 12, 1767
Samuell Thompson & Mary Potter, April 7, 1767
Timothy Way & Rhoda Rose, Dec. 18, 1767
William Scot & Mary Basset, Nov. 17, 1767
Daniel Goodrich & Mary Page, Jan. 14, 1768
David Down & Susannah Dorson, Feb. 9, 1768
Zebulon Farron & Desire Heminway, March 3, 1768
Asa Bradley & Anna Morris, May 12, 1768
Jared Bradley & Sarah Smith, April 8, 1768
Jacob Shepherd & Patience Bradly, Aug. 3, 1768
Jedediah Deisher & Sarah Whedon, Aug. 28, 1768
Ichabod Foot & ——— Smith, Aug. 21, 1768

Abner Bean & Kezia Potter,	Sept. 6, 1768
Stephen Pardee & Abigail Smith,	Dec. 1, 1768
Moses Perkins & Mary Smith,	March 23, 1769
Benjamin Bishop & Abigail Hotchkiss,	May 5, 1769
Joseph Chidsey & Sarah Goodrich,	May 17, 1769
Elisha Andrus & Sarah Multhrop,	Aug. 31, 1769
Jacob Eaton & Sarah Heminway,	Sept. 21, 1769
Abijah Bradley & Sarah Thompson,	1769
Jehu Robinson & Elizabeth Augur,	1769
James Chidsey & Mehitable Grannise,	Nov. 17, 1769
Stiles Curtiss & Hannah Bishop,	Nov. 27, 1769
Joseph Heminway & Elizabeth Woodward,	Dec. 21, 1769
Thomas Allen & Dorothy Mallery,	Dec. 7, 1769
John Chidsey & Anna Luddinton,	March 8, 1770
Cajol & Jenny (negroes),	April 4, 1770
Isaac Page & Sarah Bradley,	Aug. 8, 1770
Nicholas Charlihan & Susan Jackson,	Aug. 29, 1770
Levy Chidsey & Hannah Potter,	Sept. 10, 1770
Edward Goodsell & Lydia Luddinton,	Oct. 4, 1770
Elihu Multrop & Mary Hotchkiss,	Nov. 21, 1770
Samuel Heminway & Hannah Morris,	Jan. 1, 1771
Levy Pardee & Sarah Chidsey,	Jan. 3, 1771
David Beecher & Lydia Morris,	May 15, 1771
Jesse Denison & Mabel Woodward,	May 20, 1771
Abraham Heminway & Anne Smith,	Aug. 11, 1771
John Deliverance & Sarah Adams,	Oct. 17, 1771
Gershom Scot & Sarah Morris,	Nov. 6, 1771
Ambrose Smith & Mary Smith,	Nov. 14, 1771
William Day & Abigail Woodward,	Nov. 14, 1771
Ebenezer Burrington & Mary Multrup,	Dec. 30, 1771
Timothy Dorson & Anne Holt,	Jan. 2, 1772
Josiah Talmage & Mary Basset,	June 29, 1772
Zaccheus How & Esther Thompson,	Dec. 7, 1772
Samuel Crumb & Rachel Andress,	Dec. 15, 1772
John Goodsell & Abigail Chidsey,	Jan. 12, 1773
Jehiel Holmes & Martha ——ink,	Feb. 10, 1773
Samuel Brittain & Eunice ——,	Sept. 15, 1773
Ezra Rowe & Hulda Chidsey,	1773
Joel Tuttle & Anne Woodward,	Jan. 6, 1774

Joseph Multhrop & Lorana Grannise,	May 26, 1774
Joseph Mallery & Eunice Barns,	Feb. 23, 1774
Jared Heminway & Huldah Woodward,	June 9, 1774
Stephen Brackett of New Haven & widow Goodsell of Northbury,	June 23, 1774
Amos Ford & Abigail Thomson,	Oct. 5, 1774
Freemen Huse & Mary Richards,	Nov. 24, 1774
Elam Luddinton & Rachel Tuttle,	Dec. 8, 1774
Charles Bishop & Mary Forbes,	Dec. 13, 1774
Andrew Davidson & Elizabeth Bradley,	Dec. 15, 1774
Benjamin Mallery & Eunice Talmadge,	Dec. 19, 1774
Samuel Smith & Anne Multrup,	March 9, 1775
Ichabod Bishop & Mehitable Bradley,	March 9, 1775
Nehemiah Smith & Lois Potter,	May 22, 1775
Moses Thompson & Desire Multrop,	May 23, 1775
Enos Hull & —— Frost of New Haven,	June 8, 1775
Jesse Upson & Elizabeth Smith,	Nov. 17, 1775
Isaac Hotchkiss & Lydia Fields,	Dec. 4, 1775
Abram Barns & Hannah Grannis,	Jan. 5, 1776
Isaac Barns & Lois Pardee,	Feb. 12, 1776
John Goodsell & Abigail Chidsey,	April 7, 1776
George King, 2d, & Elizabeth Tuttle,	May 30, 1776
Abram Beecher & Esther Thomas of New Haven,	June 12, 1776
Pomp & Dinah (negroes),	Oct. 2, 1776
Moses Heminway & Martha Tyler,	Oct. 16, 1776
Jedidiah Andress & Anna Bradley,	Nov. 19, 1776
Timothy Andress & Dorcas Smith,	Dec. 16, 1776
Joseph Smith & Lydia Grannis,	Feb. 4, 1777
Nathaniel Barns & Abigail Heminway,	March 16, 1777
James Stanclift & Mary Russell,	March 27, 1777
Enos Heminway & Sarah Heminway,	April 23, 1777
Amos Mallery & Abigail Brown,	June 4, 1777
Ephraim Hough & Lydia Goodsell,	June 5, 1777
Eliphalet Luddinton & Sarah Potter,	June 9, 1777
Stephen Thompson & widow Mary Baldwin,	June, 1777
Nathaniel Grannise & Marther Smith,	July 28, 1777
Jacob Pardee & Lydia Heminway,	Nov. 30, 1777
Abijah Pardee & Rosannah Multrup,	Dec. 9, 1777

Samuel Bradley & Abigail Thompson,	Dec. 18, 1777
Isaac Bradley & Mary Fields,	Feb. 5, 1778
Jedediah Andress & Abigail Barns,	Feb. 15, 1778
Asa. Mallery & Hannah Chidsey,	Feb. 26, 1778
Ephriam Chidsey & Desire Denison,	Feb. 26, 1778
Capt. Amos Morris & Mrs. Lois Clark of Southerton,	
	March 4, 1778
Levy Potter & Sarah Thompson,	1778
Nicodemus Baldwin & Martha Harrison,	June 10, 1778
Jacob Smith & Lois Bishop,	July 15, 1778
John Huse & Mary Grannise,	July 15, 1778
John Fowler (?) & Esther Hotchkiss,	July 29, 1778
William Broughton & Mary Potter of New Haven,	
	Jan. 11, 1779
Roswell Bradley & Elizabeth Auger,	Feb. 25, 1779
Cork & Sybill, servants of Jehoel Forbes,	April, 1779
John Morris & Desire Street,	Aug. 8, 1779
Jesse Luddinton & Thankful Chidsey,	Aug. 20, 1779
Darius Hicock & Lucinda Street,	Sept. 13, 1779
Samuel Holt & Lydia Davenport,	Oct. 23, 1779
Stephen Thompson, Jr., & Lois Bradley,	Dec. 27, 1779
Richard Barret & Sarah Chidsey,	Jan. 13, 1780
Stephen Woodward & Elizabeth Morris,	Jan. 20, 1780
Joseph Hotchkiss & Temperance Andrus,	Jan. 27, 1780
Earls Thorp of Southington & Lydia Denison,	Jan. 27, 1780
Elihu Bradley & Sybil Grannis,	May 22, 1780
John Davenport & widow Anne Pierpoint,	Oct. 15, 1780
David Munson & widow Huldah Ives of New Haven,	
	Oct. 15, 1780
Joshua Barns & Marsey Tuttle,	Feb. 15, 1781
Elijah Bradley & Esther Thompson,	March 29, 1781
Nathaniel Dayton & Mabel Cooper,	April 8, 1781
Edmund Bradley & Lydia Chidsey,	April 12, 1781
John Wise & Isabel Goodsell,	May, 1781
Stephen Bradley & Mehitable Luddinton,	1781
Jesse Mallery & Hannah Luddinton,	1781
—— Potter & Bedee Potter (?),	1781
Benjamin Barns & Abigail Goodsell,	Nov. 29, 1781
Daniel Smith & Rachel Bishop,	Nov. 12, 1781

John Potter & Sena Linsley, both of Branford, Nov. 27, 1781
Stephen Rowe & Abigail Huse,   Dec. 6, 1781
Chandler Robinson & Lois Grannise,   Dec. 26, 1781
Capt. Samuel Forbes & widow Elizabeth Bradley,
                                            Dec. 8, 1781
Dan Goodsell & Desire Potter,   March 18, 1782
Chauncey Denison & Sarah Grannise,   April 18, 1782
Lemuel Shepherd & Lorana Mallery,   May 3, 1782
Joseph Brockett & Rebecca Tuttle,   May 8, 1782
Eliphalet Pardee & Abigail Bishop,   Oct. 24, 1782
Mr. Brockway & Sarah Scot,   Oct. 24, 1782
Leavit Pardee & Elizabeth Heminway,   Nov. 18, 1782
Joel Mulford & Polly Bishop,   Nov. 21, 1782
Joel Thompson & Lois Chidsey,   Dec. 23, 1782
Hezekiah Todd & Mary Holt,   Jan. 2, 1783
Joseph Pardee & Sarah Fields,   Feb. 15, 1783
William Collins & Esther Morris,   Feb. 10, 1783
Thomas Shepherd & widow Lydia Goodsell,   Feb. 24, 1783
Eliphalet Fuller & Anna Bradley,   April, 1783
John Thompson & Dorcas Andrus,   Sept. 4, 1783
Arthur Multrop & Mary Chidsey,   Oct. 13, 1783
Timothy Way & Hannah Shepherd,   Jan. 28, 1784
Roger Lord & Ruth Hotchkiss,   June 26, 1784
Jared Pardee & Rebecca Brown,   July 19, 1784
Francis Hail & Olive Harrison, both of North Bran-
    ford,   Oct. 17, 1784
———— Brown of Branford & Anne Huse,   Oct. 28, 1784
Stephen Williams Stebbins & Eunecia Street, Sept. 11, 1784
Capt. Amos Morris & widow Esther Smith,   March 8, 1784
William ———— & Ellinor Smith,   Dec. 9, 1784
Jacob Heminway & Abigail Linsley,   Dec. 28, 1784
Ira Smith & Sarah Davenport,   Dec. 28, 1784
Daniel Tuttle & Anny Granniss,   March 24, 1785
Job Smith & Lucretia Smith,   June 27, 1785
William Bradley & Polly Multhrop,   Oct. 6, 1785
Stephen Foot & Mary Pardee,   Oct. 10, 1785
Samuel Shepherd & Abigail Multrup,   Nov. 17, 1785
Giles Brocket & Sarah Smith,   Nov. 17, 1785
Ephraim Chidsey & Hannah Barns,   Jan. 16, 1786

Jonathan Ingersoll & Grace Isaacs,	April 5, 1786
Charles Wetmore & Lydia Grannise,	April 14, 1786
Jacob Heminway & widow Abigail Bradley,	April 19, 1786
John Tyler & Mabel Bradley,	April 20, 1786
Samuel Thompson, Jr., & Sarah Holt,	April 20, 1786
John Mitchiel & Easter Nails,	June, 1786
Christopher Tuttle & Abigail Luddington,	Sept., 1786
—— Twist & Lois Austin,	Sept. 9, 1786
Ely Multrup & Mary Multrup,	Jan., 1787
Samuel Heminway & widow Sarah Bradley,	May 28, 1787
Phineas Curtiss & Mary Chidsey,	July 16, 1787
Daniel Austin & Sarah Pardee,	Sept. 5, 1787
George Oswell & Pamela Nails,	Sept., 1787
William Bailey & Eunice Luddington,	Oct. 4, 1787
Joseph Shepherd & Abigail Russel,	Nov. 11, 1787
Samuel Luddington & Desire Barns,	Dec. 4, 1787
Robert Dorson & Mary Russel,	Dec. 6, 1787
—— Freeman & Blossom, servants of Peleg Bishop,	
	Dec. 6, 1787
William Walker & Eunice Chidsey,	Dec. 9, 1787
Jesse Bradley & Lydia Holt,	May 4, 1788
Asaph Hotchkiss & Hannah Russel,	May 15, 1788
Samuel Hathaway & Lorinda Morris,	Nov. 11, 1788
Russel Granniss & Sarah Granniss of Southernton,	
	Dec. 4, 1788
Daniel Holt & Hannah Holt,	Jan. 10, 1789
Titus Allin & Lucinda Hickcox,	Jan. 27, 1789
Laban Smith & Mary Bradley,	Feb. 12, 1789
Eli Gilbert & Lydia Pardee,	Feb. 16, 1789
Russel Grannis & Molly Bradley,	May 28, 1789
Peter & Jenne,	July, 1789
Jacob Barns & Hannah Chidsey,	July 30, 1789
Roger Allin & Rhoda Tuttle,	Aug. 13, 1789
David Green & Zurviah Broton (?),	Aug. 15, 1789
John Shepard & Anne Goodsell,	Dec. 30, 1789
Collins Huse & Abigail Bradley,	Jan. 2, 1790
Levy Goodsell & Eunice ——,	Jan. 3, 1790
Chandler Pardee & Lydia Hotchkiss,	Feb. 4, 1790
Adoniram Bickford & Sally Mallery,	March 7, 1790

Deodate Beemen of Wallingford & Zina Rose of
    Bradford,   Sept. 2, 1790
Hiel Hall & Sarah Olds,   Oct., 1790
Philemon Auger & Mary Shepard,   Jan. 5, 1791
Levy Barns & Huldah Grannis,   Jan. 7, 1791
Leavit Bradley & Esther Bradley,   Jan. 20, 1791
Amos Luddington & Huldah Chidsey,   Feb. 12, 1791
Stephen Heminway & Esther Bradley,   Feb. 21, 1791
Allin Frost & Mary Walker,   April 20, 1791
Stepha & Pink, servants of Capt. Forbes, May 15, 1791
Levy Fuller & Pamela Roswell,   July 25, 1791
Nathaniel Yale & Abigail Bradley,   Aug. 11, 1791
Amos Broughton & Mary Allin,   Sept. 19, 1791
Jonathan Goodsell & ———— Bradley,   Oct. 17, 1791
David Burnam & Rachel Luddington,   April 12, 1792
Enos Bradley of Hamden & Sarah Bishop, April 30, 1792
Jared Andrus & Dorothy Phelps,   May 28, 1792
Josiah Multhrop & widow Lydia Smith,   July 4, 1792
Noah Wolton & Nabby Chidsey,   Aug. 13, 1792
Thomas Smith & Desire Thompson,   Oct. 16, 1792
Reuben Moulthrop & Hannah Street,   Nov. 18, 1792
Timothy Way & Hannah Fuller,   Nov. 25, 1792
Nehemiah Smith & Irene Bradley,   Jan. 2, 1793
Eli Potter & Patty Davenport,   1793
Joseph Northrop & Huldah Bradley,   1793
Amos ———— & Elizabeth Bradley,   May 5, 1793
Holt Dorson & Irene Shepard,   May 20, 1793
Herman Hotchkiss & Elizabeth Ford,   July 28, 1793
Thomas Potter & Anna Shepard,   Sept. 16, 1793
Henry Hotchkiss & Liza Barnes,   Oct. 13, 1793
C—— Rogers & Carolina Barker,   Oct. 17, 1793
Roswell Davenport & Esther Heminway, Oct. 23, 1793
Lyman Foot & Lucretia Page,   Nov. 4, 1793
John Forbes & Anne Holt,   Dec. 16, 1793
John Woodward, Jr., & Polly Davenport, Jan. 15, 1794
Joel Bradley & Lovisa Bradley,   Jan. 30, 1794
Jehiel Forbes & Huldah Bradley,   Feb. 20, 1794
Morris Scot & Mary Goodsell,   April 2, 1794
Hezekiah Woodward & Sene Bradley,   April 13, 1794

Zebulon Bradley & Elizabeth Goodsell, May 11, 1794
Caleb Smith & Lydia Chidsey, May 29, 1794
Chauncey Barns & Sally Smith, May 29, 1794
Joseph Trowbridge & Abigail Russell of Branford,
June 18, 1794
Eleazer Heminway & Mary Woodward, June 22, 1794
Ammi Bradley & Lydia Grannis, June 26, 1794
John Tyler of New Haven & Sally Smith, Aug. 26, 1794
Deacon Stephen Smith & Elizabeth Thompson, Oct. 7, 1794
Isaac Forbes & Anne Bradley, Dec. 8, 1794
William Smith & Anna Chidsey, Jan. 11, 1795
Phinehas Clark & Dorinda Farran, Feb. 19, 1795
Heman Atwater & Huldah Heminway, May 10, 1795
Titus Sanford of North Haven & Lydia Hotchkiss,
May 20, 1795
Lot Siser & Mehitable Farran, June 9, 1795
William Armstrong & Polly Banks of New Haven,
July 2, 1795
Wyllis Heaton & Mela Potter, July 6, 1795
Josiah Tuttle & ——— Gates, Sept. 19, 1795
Heminway Holt & Lorinda Bradley, Dec. 2, 1795
Abiah Heminway & Huldah Pardee, Dec. 31, 1795
Josiah Howd of Branford & Sarah Luddington,
March 2, 1796
Samuel Holt & Abigail Bradley, May 12, 1796
Wilke Edwards & Polly Smith, Aug. 24, 1796
John McKoy & Cate McKoy, both of New Haven,
Nov. 5, 1796
Levy Baldwin of Branford & Anne Chidsey, Nov. 6, 1796
Jared Thompson & Grace Hunt, Jan. 30, 1797
John Heminway, Jr., & Hannah Thompson, Feb. 25, 1797
Jeremiah Johnson & Lydia ——— of Branford, March 4, 1797
Joseph Holt & Anna Goodsell, March 20, 1797
Samuel Mallery & Bethiah Johnson, June 26, 1797
Dr. Bela Farnum & Anne Morris, Nov. 13, 1797
Abraham Thompson & Mary Smith, Nov. 16, 1797
Moses Augustinus Street & Lois Smith, Dec. 10, 1797
James Thompson & Lydia Chidsey, Jan. 5, 1798
Joseph Shepard & Huldah Thompson, Jan. 4, 1798

James Heminway & Elizabeth Bradley,	Feb. 19, 1798
Justice Potter & Anna Moriah Street,	June 5, 1798
Jared Luddington & Sarah Goodsell,	June 11, 1798
Stephen Shepard & Sally Grannis,	Feb. 18, 1797 (?)
John Northrop & Lucy Russell, both of Woodbridge,	
	Feb. 25, 1799
Azahel Bradley & Seney Grannis,	March 14, 1799
Eleazer Heminway & Desire Bradley,	Oct. 16, 1799
Asa Luddington & Betsey Luddington,	Oct. 29, 1799
Thomas Rocke & Pegge Rogers from New Haven,	
	Nov. 30, 1799

FAIRFIELD.

FAIRFIELD COUNTY.

(See Books III and V.)

The town of Fairfield was settled in 1639 and named in 1645. The First Congregational Church of Fairfield was organized in 1650. The following marriages are recorded.

Joseph Squire & Sarah Jennings,	Nov. 19, 1726
Peter Hepburn & Sarah Clark,	March 13, 1727
Lotrop Lewis & Mrs. Sarah Wakeman,	July 26, 1727
Daniel Bulkley & Hannah Johnson,	May 21, 1728
Samuel Jennings, Jr., & Johanna Risden,	Oct. 2, 1728
Gershom Scott of Waterbury & Mary Fanton,	Nov. 18, 1728
Andrew Sinclair & widow Abigail Cosier,	Dec. 24, 1729
Peter Penfield & Mrs. Mary Allen, married by Joseph Webb,	May 28, 1730
Nathan Stephens of Danbury & Phebe Lyon,	Jan. 31, 1733
Job Gorham of Barnstable & Bethiah Freeman,	Nov. 24, 1735
Rev. Nathaniel Hunn & Ruth Read,	Sept. 14, 1737
David Allen & Sarah Gold,	Oct. 11, 1739
Samuel Sturgis & Ann Burr,	Jan. 17, 1739
John Thompson of Stratford & Mrs. Mehitable Webb,	July 7, 1741
Stephen Jennings & Hannah Sturgis,	Aug. 20, 1741
Daniel Sturgis & Mary Beers,	Nov. 5, 1741
Benjamin Fayerweather & Elizabeth Beach,	Jan. 7, 1742

Thomas Chambers of Newtown & Mary Bulmore,

	Oct. 11, 1742
Jacob Levet & Catee Gold,	Oct. 18, 1742
Micah Perry & Grace Sturgis,	Dec. 8, 1742
John Turney & Esther Gold,	Dec. 28, 1742
Thomas Gibbs of Milford & Hannah Allen,	March 24, 1743
Edward Treadwel & Sarah Trowbridge,	May 26, 1743
Samuel Beers & Thankfull Osborne,	Nov. 10, 1743
Jabes Barlow & Elizabeth Hunt,	March 1, 1743
Andrew Bearsly & Sarah Squire,	March 1, 1744
Nathan Thompson & Abigail Gold,	July 19, 1744
James Adair & Ann McCarty,	Oct. 18, 1744
Daniel Perry & Sarah Wilson,	Jan. 1, 1745
David Rowland & Deborah Sloss,	Dec. 1, 1745
John Jennings, Jr., & Sarah Jennings,	Jan. 30, 1746

Samuel Galpine of Woodbury & Ann Sherwood,

	Feb. 4, 1746

Rev. Thomas Arthur of New Brunswick & Sarah Burr,

	Sept. 16, 1746
Nathaniel Pierson & Hannah Beers,	Oct. 14, 1746
Joseph Morehouse & Elisabeth Silliman,	March 26, 1747
Joseph Frost, Jr., & Esther Dimon,	Oct. 19, 1747
Jabes Bulkley & Elisabeth Osborn,	Nov. 5, 1747
Stephen Turney & Sarah Squire,	Dec. 17, 1747
James Smedley & Mary Dimon,	Jan. 4, 1748

Thomas Hawley of Ridgefield & Elisabeth Gold,

	Jan. 13, 1748
Nathaniel Seely & Rebecca Hubbel,	Jan. 14, 1748
John Hyde, Jr., & Abigail Ogden,	Jan. 21, 1748
John Clugstone & Elisabeth Rowlandson,	March 24, 1748
Jabes Patchin of Wilton & Hannah Squier,	Aug. 11, 1748
Ebeneser Wakeman & Ann Hill,	Sept. 4, 1748
Anthony Annable & Sarah Middlebrook,	Jan. 16, 1749
Gamaliel French of Stratfield & Sarah Redfield,	Aug. 7, 1749
Lieut. Gideon Allen & Mrs. Jane Dimon,	Aug. 10, 1749
Ebeneser Middlebrook & Sarah Buckley,	Sept. 20, 1749
Gephaniah Clark & Olive Osborn,	Oct. 31, 1749
David Rowland & Mrs. Elizabeth Hill,	Feb. 14, 1750
David Ogden, Jr., & Jane Sturgis,	April 5, 1750

Ebeneser Knap & Elisabeth McRaa,	Dec. 31, 1750
John Allen & Abigail Jessup,	Jan. 17, 1751
Daniel Kellogg of Norwalk & Hannah Fairchild,	
	March 19, 1751
Thomas Minor of Woodbury & Tabitha Treadwell,	
	Sept. 7, 1751
Hezekiah Sturgis & Abigail Dimon,	Nov. 21, 1751
David Burr & Eunice Osborn,	Dec. 11, 1751
Ichabod Wheeler & Deborah Burr,	Jan. 1, 1752
John Parrit & Sarah Hubbel,	Jan. 17, 1752
Ebeneser Wakeman & Sarah Hanford,	May 10, 1752
Lyman Hall & Abigail Burr,	May 20, 1752
Sturgis Lewis & Ann Burr,	Oct. 10, 1752
Thaddeus Betts of Ridgefield & Mary Gold,	Nov. 8, 1752
Daniel Jennings, Jr., & Eunice Burr,	Dec. 21, 1752
David Hubbel & Martha Gold,	Feb. 5, 1753
Peter Hull & Ann Dimon,	Feb. 22, 1753
Jesse Hunt & Sarah Staples,	March 22, 1753
Abraham Betts of Norwalk & Mary Bedient,	April 19, 1753
Samuel Burr, Jr., & Eunice Sturgis,	May 31, 1753
Nathan Hill & Eunice Wakeman,	July 3, 1753
Benjamin Osborn & Mary Dimon,	Oct. 16, 1753
Elnathan Williams & Hannah Thorps,	Dec. 5, 1753
Johnathan Lewis & Sarah Osborn,	Jan. 10, 1754
Ebeneser Meeker, Jr., & Elisabeth Jennings,	Jan. 30, 1754
David Wakeman & Mary Jennings,	Feb. 17, 1754
Benjamin Wynkoops, Jr., & Grissel Frost,	March 6, 1754
Jabes Thorps & Ann Sturgis,	March 7, 1754
Capt. Samuel Burr & Mrs. Ruth Bulkley,	March 14, 1754
Peter Thorp & Abigail Ward,	April 18, 1754
Gideon Welles & Catharine Wynkoop,	May 1, 1754
Samuel Sherwood & Rachel Hyde,	June 6, 1754
Joseph Bartram & Rebecca Squier,	Nov. 7, 1754
Moses Dimon, Jr., & Grace Dimon,	Nov. 13, 1754
Abel Gold & Ellen Burr,	Dec. 19, 1754
Amos Williams & Elinor Davis,	Jan. 22, 1755
James Hall & Abigail Beers,	April 3, 1755
Asa Spalding & Grace Rowland,	Sept. 4, 1755
John Bulkley & Martha Hubbel,	Jan. 8, 1756

Samuel Silliman & Elisabeth Burr,	Jan. 21, 1756
Daniel Burr & Ann Silliman,	Jan. 22, 1756
Matthew Jennings & Rebecca Morehouse,	Feb. 5, 1756
Nathan Adams & Mary Hubbel,	Feb. 11, 1756
Hesekiah Platt & Sarah Lord,	March 31, 1756
James Bulkley & Elisabeth Whitehead,	April 8, 1756
Nathan Bulkley & Sarah Perry,	April 15, 1756
Nathan Beers & Abigail Squire,	July 22, 1756
Edmund Hunt & Abigail Smedley,	Aug. 12, 1756
Gershom Hubbel & Sarah Wakeman,	Nov. 2, 1756
Robert Silliman & Mrs. Mary Morehouse,	Dec. 14, 1756
Thomas Hill, Jr., & Ellen Sturgis,	Jan. 20, 1757
Daniel Osborn & Elisabeth Burr,	Jan. 19, 1758
John McDonald & Elisabeth Fraser,	Feb. 21, 1758
Cornelius Wynkoop, Jr., of New York & Abigail Osborn,	
	March 12, 1758
Abel Wheeler & Rebecca Whitear,	March 27, 1758
Abel Jennings & Sarah Holingsworth,	Aug. 16, 1758
Moses Bulkley & Abigail Sturges,	Aug. 29, 1758
Ebeneser Burr & Amelia Silliman,	Feb. 26, 1759
Thaddeus Burr & Eunice Dennie,	March 22, 1759
Moses Jennings & Abigail Burr,	Oct. 11, 1759
Peter Hull & Jerusha Sturgis,	Nov. 8, 1759
Matthew Curtis of Newtown & Abigail Thompson,	
	Dec. 5, 1759
Johnathan Sturgis & Deborah Lewis,	Oct. 26, 1760
Mordicai Bedient & Abigail Raymon,	April 26, 1761
Daniel Wakeman & Esther Hill,	May 28, 1761
David Rice & Rebecca Middlebrook,	June 4, 1761
Jonathan Ogden & Sarah Ogden,	June 11, 1761
Jonathan Darrow & Elisabeth Bulkley,	Dec. 9, 1761
Elijah Abel & Grissel Burr,	Dec. 31, 1761
Noah Lane of Killingworth & Grace Buddington,	
	March 3, 1762
Justin Hobart & Hannah Penfield,	March 18, 1762
——inson & Ruhamah Lynde,	May 4, 1762
George Wakeman & Sarah Hill,	June 17, 1762
Ephraim Burr, Jr., & Eunice Wilson,	Aug. 12, 1762
Peter Jennings & Eunice Smith,	Nov. 3, 1762

Joseph Sturgis & Sarah Dimon,	Nov. 11, 1762
David Dimon & Anne Allen,	Nov. 15, 1762
Hesekiah Nichols & Ann Penfield,	Nov. 25, 1762
Jeremiah Jennings & Elisabeth Smith,	Dec. 8, 1762
John Smedley & Eunice Wynkoop,	Jan. 13, 1763
Andrew Morehouse & Ann Knap,	Jan. 27, 1763
Joseph Sprague & Elisabeth Squire,	Jan. 31, 1763
Capt. Isaiah Burnham of Kensington & Mrs. Mary Smith,	April 14, 1763
Nehemiah Burr & Sarah Osborne,	April 21, 1763
Thomas Fitch, Jr., of Norwalk & Sarah Hill,	April 28, 1763
Ebeneser Silliman, Jr., & Ruth Silliman,	May 5, 1763
Peter Penfield, Jr., & Hannah Lewis,	Aug. 1, 1763
Andrew Hill & Abigail Lewis,	Dec. 1, 1763
David Silliman & Lydia Penfield,	Dec. 21, 1763
Stephen Adams & Hester Hill,	May 9, 1764
Jesse Raymond of Middlesex & Jemima Gold,	May 22, 1764
Isaac Tucker & Mary Wakeman,	June 1, 1764
Eleaser Osborne, Jr., & Sarah Burr,	June 3, 1764
Woolcot Hawley (or ly) & Ellen Osborne,	Nov. 29, 1764
Seth Warner & Mrs. Sarah Wakeman,	Dec. 13, 1764
William Dimon & Esther Sturgis,	Jan. 3, 1765
Abraham Andrews & Catherine Wakeman,	Feb. 14, 1765
Gould Hoyt of Norwalk & Elisabeth Dimon,	June 13, 1765
Gershom Burr & Priscilla Lothrop,	Dec. 12, 1765
Ebeneser Burr, 3rd, & Hannah Morehouse,	Jan. 9, 1766
Capt. Johnathan Camp of Norwalk & Abigail Shawe,	April 17, 1766
Paul Nichols & Sarah Middlebrook,	Aug. 14, 1766
Samuel Andrews & Hannah Wakeman,	May 24, 1767
John Whitear & Abigail Rowland,	June 11, 1767
Hesekiah Fitch & Jerusha Burr,	Sept. 21, 1767
Isaac Turney & Elisabeth Hubbel,	Jan. 21, 1768
Nathaniel Lothrop of Plimouth & Ellen Hobart,	May 10, 1768
Gideon Beebee & Betty Sherwood,	May 10, 1768
Andrew Jennings & Abigail Hunt,	Aug. 17, 1768
Johnathan Maltby & Elisabeth Allen,	Oct. 23, 1768
David Jennings & Mehitable Squire,	Nov. 3, 1768

Daniel Wilson & Sarah Squire,   April 20, 1769
George Morehouse & Sarah Davis,   Jan. 19, 1770
William Beadle & Lydia Lothrop,   April 15, 1770
Oliver Burr & Elisabeth Smith,   April 23, 1770
Johnathan Cole & Lois Bulkley,   May 15, 1770
Jabes Thorp & Martha Osborne,   June 14, 1770
Abijah Morehouse & Mary Allen,   Nov. 1, 1770
John Penfield & Eunice Ogden,   Nov. 1, 1770
Isaac Jennings & Abigail Gold,   Nov. 15, 1770
Daniel Dimon & Lois Bradley,   Dec. 6, 1770
James Goodsel & Esther Adair,   Dec. 20, 1770
Samuel Sturges & Abigail Hill,   Jan. 9, 1771
David Edwards of North Stratford & Lydia Osborn,
                                                                          Jan. 23, 1771
Johnathan Darrow, Jr., & Elisabeth Bulkley,   Jan. 31, 1771
Samuel Smedley & Esther Rowland,   April 9, 1771
David Osborn & Mary Beers,   July 11, 1771
Jehiel Thorp & Ellen Perry,   Dec. 17, 1771
Josiah Bulkley & Abigail Beers,   Dec. 25, 1771
John Pierson & Jane Sturgis,   March 5, 1772
Levi Mallery & Sarah Annable,   Aug. 3, 1772
Nathan Lewis & Esther Bulkley,   Dec. 24, 1772
Gershom Osborn & Grissel Sherwood,   Dec. 29, 1772
Elisha Alvord & Mary Beers.   Jan. 20, 1773
Andrew Wakeman & Hannah Allen,   April 14, 1773
Ebeneser Bradley & Mary Burr,   June 6, 1773
Tappan Reeve of Litchfield & Sarah Burr,   June 24, 1773

MARRIED BY ANDREW ELIOT.

Stratton Osborn & Rhoda Patchin,   June 29, 1774
William Silliman & Anne Allen,   Sept. 22, 1774
John Redfield & Lucretia Macquand,   Dec. 25, 1774
Nicholas Darrow & Elisabeth Beers,   Jan. 26, 1775
Toney (negro), servant of Jeremiah Sherwood, &
     Nanny (negro), servant of Andrew Eliot,   Feb. 25, 1775
Toney (negro), servant of Abel Gould, & Dorcas
     (negro), servant of Nathan Bulkey,   March 9, 1775
Capt. Johnathan Dimon of Greenfield & Elizabeth
     Wakeman,   April 16, 1775

Stephen Jackson of Reading & Elizabeth Hull,   May 17, 1775
Deodate Silliman & Catharine Silliman,   May 25, 1775
Isaac Jarvis & Abigail Squire,   July 11, 1775
Jack (negro), servant of David Barlow, & Mary
     (negro), servant of Deacon Hill of Greenfield,
                                                July 18, 1775
John Hancock & Dorothy Quincy, both of Boston,
                                                Aug. 28, 1775
Robert Harris of Norfield & Mary Bulkeley,   Oct. 26, 1775
Jabes Hubbel & Abigail Gray,   Dec. 28, 1775
Joseph Bulkeley & Elisabeth Lewis,   March 24, 1776
Samuel Wheeler of Stratford & Sarah Morehouse,
                                                June 20, 1776
Ebenezer Squire & Mary Wheeler,   June 20, 1776
Ebenezer Sturges & Sarah Bulkley,   July 4, 1776
Peter Hendrick & Sarah Allen,   July 11, 1776
Moses Sturges & Elizabeth Bradley, both of Greenfield,
                                                July 18, 1776
David Downs & ———— ————, both of Greenfield,
Nathan Thorp & Patience Wheeler,   Nov. 10, 1776
Peter Burr, Jr., & Esther Jennings,   Nov. 17, 1776
Johnathan Bulkeley, Jr., & Lydia Bulkeley,   Dec. 12, 1776
Amos & Nance (negroes), servants of Ebenezer Hill
     of Greenfield,
Nathan Beers & Mehitabel Perry,   Nov. 27, 1777
Stephen Stratton of Greenfield & Sarah Darrow, Dec. 25, 1777
Abel Gold & Amelia Burr,   Jan. 18, 1778
Johnathan Darrow & Molly Thorp,   Feb. 8, 1778
Nehemiah Fowler & Abiah Wheeler,   March 1, 1778
Joseph Bulkeley & Grizzel Thorp,   July 27, 1778
Jesse Nichols & Mabel Bulkley of Greenfield,   Nov. 22, 1778
Isaac Lewis of Stratford & Mary Morehouse,   Nov. 26, 1778
Jedediah Hull of Greenfield & Mary Osborn,   Dec. 10, 1778
Stephen Osborn & Grizzel Osborn,   Dec. 17, 1778
Nathaniel Perry & Eunice Sturges,   Jan. 21, 1779
John Williams, Jr., & Anne Mitchel,   Jan. 24, 1779
Josiah Beardslee of Greenfield & Abigail Bulkley,
                                                Jan. 28, 1779
Robin, servant of Samuel Squire, & Dorcas, servant
     of Elijah Abel,   Feb. 18, 1779

Samuel Stratton of Greeenfield & Grace Darrow,
March 30, 1779
John Wasson & Elizabeth Bartram, April 18, 1779
Stephen Keeler of Norwalk & Margaret Pynchon,
April 28, 1779
Wright White & Esther Hughes, June 10, 1779
Jabez Hubbel & Rhoda Osborn, June 24, 1779
Dr. Hosea Hurlbut & Rachel Hubbel of Greenfield,
Jan., 1780
Dimon Sturges & Sarah Perry, Feb. 13, 1780
Abraham Morehouse & Ruth Wilson, Feb. 17, 1780
Phillip Hubbard & Ambrillis Morehouse (free negroes),
Feb. 21, 1780
William Gates of Long Island & Margaret McRaa,
Feb. 24, 1780
Ebenezer Knapp & Mary Wilson, April 20, 1780
Tego (negro), servant of Ozias Burr of Stratfield, &
Sue (negro), servant of Gold Silliman, June 5, 1780
Isaac Sherwood of Stratfield & Drusilla Sherwood,
June 15, 1780
Benjamin Knapp & Elizabeth Wilson, July 13, 1780
Callico (negro), servant of Daniel Wilson, & Dinah
(negro), servant of Matthew Jennings, Sept. 20, 1780
Reuben Sherwood & Abigail Perry, Nov. 5, 1780
Capt. Eliphalet Thorp & Mrs. Sarah Ogden, Nov. 30, 1780
Major William Silliman & Phebe Jennings, Dec. 7, 1780
Samuel Squire & Abigail Squire, Dec. 28, 1780
Nathaniel Wilson, Jr., & Ruth Silliman, Feb. 15, 1781
William Sisco & Hannah Taylor, April 15, 1781
Priamus & Luce (negroes), servants of Thaddeus Burr,
April 17, 1781
Samuel Burr & Abigail Jennings, June 21, 1781
Priamus (negro), servant of Joseph Hill of Green-
field, & Nancy (negro), servant of Thomas
Edwards of Chestnut Hill, Oct. 14, 1781
John Hayes & Sarah Adams, Oct. 18, 1781
Stephen Adams, Jr., & Ellen Burr, Oct. 25, 1781
George Squire & Irene Hayes, Nov. 7, 1781
Gold Curtis of Newton & Elizabeth Gold, Dec. 2, 1781

4

Aaron Turney & Sarah Staples,   Jan. 24, 1782
William Morehouse & Anne Burr,   Dec. 6, 1781
Jacob June of Courtland Manor, N. Y., & Elizabeth
     Penfield,   Feb. 24, 1782
Nathaniel Penfield & Rachel Marquand,   Feb. 24, 1782
William Burr & Eunice Thorp,   March 6, 1782
Aaron Fox & Elizabeth Price,   March 14, 1782
Talcot Gold & Anna Barlow,   March 18, 1782
Solomon Sturges & Amelia Sherwood of Greenfield,
     March 28, 1782
Ebenezer Silliman of North Fairfield & Sarah Penfield,
     March 31, 1782
David Lacy of Stratfield & Katherine Silliman, April 11, 1782
Abraham Cooper Woodhull of Brookhaven, L. I.,
     & Eunice Sturges,   April 17, 1782
John Perry & Hannah Thorp,   April 28, 1782
Joseph Wyatt of Newport, R. I., & Huldah Meason,
     May 5, 1782
Benjamin Sherwood of Greenfield & Anna Hull, May 26, 1782
Ezekiel Oysterbanks of Greenfield & Esther Beers,
     June 20, 1782
George Allen & Huldah Knap,   July 21, 1782
Sylvanus Middlebrook of Greenfield & Elizabeth Wilson,
     Sept., 1782
Jabez Perry & Susanna Jennings,   Nov. 4, 1782
James Knap & Mary Brown,   Dec. 17, 1782
Peter Hull & Mary Redfield,   Dec. 17, 1782
Joshua Davis of Long Island & Abigail Redfield of
     Greenfield,   Jan. 1, 1783
David Ogden of Greenfield & Sally Perry,   Jan. 8, 1783
William Pike of Roxbury & Molly Darrow,   April 17, 1783
Stephen Runnels of Lee, N. H., & Anne Nichols,
     May 1, 1783
Benjamin Sturges & Thankful Darrow,   Sept. 11, 1783
David Judson & Esther Bulkley,   Nov. 13, 1783
Joseph Noyes & Amelia Burr,   Dec. 11, 1783
Gideon Hawley of North Stratford & Hannah Penfield,
     Jan. 18, 1784
Aaron Rawlings of New Market, in N. H., & Mary
     Jennings,   Jan. 18, 1784

Benjamin Dickinson of Long Island & Esther Ogden,
April 8, 1784
Caleb Brewster of Brook Haven, L. I., & Anna Lewis,
April 18, 1784
Thomas Hill & Catherine Jennings,   June 20, 1784
Gideon Hawley & Levina Darrow, both of Stratfield,
Oct. 9, 1784
Aaron Whaley of Greenfield & Hannah Silliman,
Oct. 28, 1784
Stephen Stirling & Sarah Sherman, both of Stratfield,
Nov. 3, 1784
Silliman Wilson & Rhoda Silliman,   Dec. 2, 1784
Hezekiah Burr, Jr., & Mary Annable,   Dec. 5, 1784
Rev. William Lockwood of Milford & Sarah Sturges,
Dec. 16, 1784
Abel Turney & Deborah Bulkley,   Dec. 26, 1784
Daniel Osborn, Jr., & Deborah Gold,   Jan. 4, 1785
John Redfield & Esther Thorp,   Jan. 12, 1785
Capt. Samuel Keeler & Mrs. Anna Thacher, March 3, 1785
Thomas Staples, Jr, & Martha Treadwell, Nov. 15, 1785
Wright Weeks of Huntington, L. I., & Mary Perry,
Nov. 24, 1785
Galmon Sherwood of Greenfield & Sarah Ogden,
Nov. 24, 1785
Eleazar Bulkley & Mary Ogden,   Dec. 22, 1785
Joseph Beers & Mary Buddington,   Feb. 2, 1786
Hezekiah Gold & Ellen Hobart,   Feb. 4, 1786
John Noyes & Eunice Sherwood of Norfield, March 8, 1786
Sturges Ogden & Loe Thorp,   March 30, 1786
Joel Burr of Reading & Elizabeth Gold, April 13, 1786
Paul Sheffield of Stonington & Mabel Thorp, July 4, 1786
William Robinson & Abigail Smith of New London,
Sept. 14, 1786
James Penfield, Jr., & Mary Tucker,   Dec. 24, 1786
Nathan Adams Hayes & Pebe Sturges,   Feb. 15, 1787
Daniel Osborn, Jr., & Mary Bartram,   April 7, 1787
Jesse Lyon of Greenfield & Sarah Godfrey, May 1, 1787
Gamaliel Bradford Whiting & Mary Dimon, Oct. 29, 1787
Miah Perry & Elizabeth Dimon,   Oct. 31, 1787

William Sturges & Mary Osborn, Nov. 11, 1787

Edward Sturges & Elizabeth Ogden of Greenfield,
Jan. 24, 1788

James Vander Speagle Wynkoop & Sarah Price of
Greenfield, April 20, 1788

Peter Whitney & Grace Bulkley, April 27, 1788

Robert Jennings & Abigail Barlow, May 4, 1788

Gold Silliman & Esther Spalding, Nov. 26, 1788

Allen Nichols & Abigail Sturges, Dec. 18, 1788

John Walker Odell & Clary Gregory, both of Stratfield,
Feb. 19, 1789

Elijah Morehouse & Hannah Bulkley, March 15, 1789

Abraham Gold & Anna Osborn, April 5, 1789

William Squire & Esther Gold, May 7, 1789

Barlow Sturges & Eunice Osborn, June 21, 1789

Samuel Squire & Ellen Gold, July 20, 1789

Jesse Wilson & Sarah Jennings, Aug. 2, 1789

David Barlow & Hannah Patchin, Aug. 16, 1789

William Henry Capers of South Carolina & Abigail
Burr, Sept. 9, 1789

Barnabas Hedge of Plymouth, Mass., & Eunice
Dennie Burr, Sept. 9, 1789

Gershom Burr & Susanna Young of Stratfield, Sept. 10, 1789

Abijah Knap & Esther Burr, Nov. 24, 1789

David Russel of Bennington, Vt., & Martha Pynchon,
Nov. 26, 1789

Ebenezer Plat of Reading & Abigail Truby, Dec. 8, 1789

Silliman Gray of Greenfield & Anna Hubbel, Dec. 20, 1789

William Hayes & Jane Redfield of Greenfield, Dec. 22, 1789

York (negro), servant of Samuel Smedley, & Kate
(negro), servant of Nathan Bulkley, Jan. 21, 1790

Isaac Gold & Ellen Jennings, Feb. 7, 1790

Nehemiah Hayes & Eunice Wilson, Feb. 20, 1790

Jesse Bradley of Greenfield & Mary Morehouse,
March 18, 1790

James Bulkley, Jr., & Sarah Smith of Norwalk, Dec. 16, 1790

Silliman Meeker of Green'sfarms & Sarah Thorp, Jan. 9, 1791

Abraham Morehouse, Jr., & Sarah Bulkley, Feb. 3, 1791

Christopher (negro), servant of Johnathan Maltby, &
Dinah (negro), servant of Gershom Burr, Feb. 11, 1791

Peter Jennings, Jr., & Hannah Tucker,   Feb. 13, 1791
Esekiel Lovejoy of Stratford & Hannah Hawley,
                                                 Feb. 20, 1791
Nathan Oysterbanks & Livia Drusilla Soards, March 9, 1791
William Jennings & Charlotte Wilson,   April 3, 1791
Squire Parrot & Rhoda Knap,   May 22, 1791
Andrew Wakeman & Eunice Smedley,   June 16, 1791
Samuel Staples & Esther Parsons,   June 16, 1791
Barnabas Lothrop Sturges & Mary Sturges,   Sept. 29, 1791
John Wheeler of Weston & Abia Turney,   Nov. 23, 1791
Seth Sturges, Jr., & Grizzel Gold,   Dec. 4, 1791
Ebenezer Silliman & Anna Gold,   Jan. 9, 1792
Walter Staples & Mary Lord of Weston,   Jan. 22, 1792
John Wheeler & Lydia Squire,   Feb. 2, 1792
William Thorp & Mary Tucker,   March 5, 1792
Daniel Young, Jr., of Stratfield & Eunice Hubbel,
                                                 March 8, 1792
Stephen Burroughs of Stratfield & Mary Jennings of
    Boston,   March 27, 1792
James Knap & Abigail Penfield,   Aug. 19, 1792
Daniel Wilson, Jr., & Anna Jennings,   Aug. 22, 1792
Nathaniel Lewis Sturges & Sarah Bulkley,   Sept. 20, 1792
Samuel Squire, 3rd, & Lucy Squire,   Oct. 18, 1792
Moses Hubbel of Greenfield & Anna Silliman, Nov. 25, 1792
Nathan Lewis of Derby & Jerusha Bartram,   Dec. 2, 1792
Titus (negro), servant of Peter Burr, & Nance (negro),
    servant of Ezekiel Hull,   March 6, 1793
William Pitt Beers & Anna Sturges,   June 9, 1793
Libbens Brown & Hannah Godfrey,   July 29, 1793
Johnathan Sturges, Jr., & Priscilla Lothrop Burr,
                                                 Aug. 12, 1793
Stephen Middlebrook, Jr., of North Stratford & Ellen
    Gold,   Oct. 7, 1793
David Sturges & Thankful Osborn,   Nov. 10, 1793
Gershom Beers & Sarah White of Greenfield, Nov. 10, 1793
Seth Silliman, Jr., & Elizabeth Morehouse of Stratfield,
                                                 Nov. 18, 1793
Richard Bangs & Elizabeth Bulkley,   Dec., 1793
Medad Gold of Greenfield & Elizabeth Jackson, Jan. 30, 1794

Ebenezer Burr, 4th, & Sarah Dimon,   June 5, 1794
Jason Gold & Catharine Carson,   Aug., 1794
Nathan Perry of Greenfield & Ruth Morehouse, Sept. 11, 1794
Benjamin Wilson & Martha Perry,   Oct. 16, 1794
Abraham Willey of Danbury & Mary Penfield, Oct. 22, 1794
Samuel Rowland & Sarah Maltby,   Oct. 30, 1794
Priamus (negro), servant of Moses Jennings, & Caty
    (negro), servant of Mrs. Sarah Sturges,   Nov. 27, 1794
Hezekiah Osborn & Nancy Perry,   Dec. 16, 1794
Nathan Guyer & Elizabeth Jennings,   Jan. 7, 1795
James Wilson & Sarah Wilson,   Feb. 8, 1795
Ephraim Penfield & Esther Turney,   May 7, 1795
Nehemiah Phippeny & Jehanna Parmiter,   June 14, 1795
John Gold Allen & Elizabeth Nichols,   Nov. 5, 1795
Joseph Hayes & Grizzel Burr,   Nov. 22, 1795
Amos Wilson & Phebe Bangs of Stratfield,   April 3, 1796
Ozias Burr, Jr., of Stratfield & Lois Jennings, April 21, 1796
Jesup Wakeman & Esther Dimon,   May 29, 1796
Francis Botsford & Ruth Nichols, both of Stratfield,
                                                     May 29, 1796
Elijah Turril & Clary Meeker,   July 16, 1796
Isaac Marquand & Mabel Perry,   Aug. 16, 1796
Elijah Bibbins & Lucretia Jennings,   Sept. 22, 1796
Job Bartram & Ruthy Holbertson,   Nov. 6, 1796
Sturges Thorp & Nancy Sturges,   Nov. 11, 1796
Lewis Goodsell & Debby Jennings,   Dec. 18, 1796
Stephen Beers & Lydia Hobart,   Dec. 21, 1796
Jesse Wheeler of Greenfield & Anna Ogden,   Dec. 29, 1796
John Alvord of Greenfield & Elizabeth Bulkley, Feb. 5, 1797
James Johnson, Jr., of Weston & Elizabeth Burr,
                                                     May 23, 1797
Isaac Bulkley & Abigail Turney,   July 13, 1797
Thomas Bartram & Sarah Burr,   Nov. 16, 1797
Johnathan Warren of Troy, N. Y., & Ellen Allen,
                                                     Feb. 13, 1798
Edward Allen Morehouse & Betsey Webb of Greenfield,
                                                     Sept. 2, 1798
Selleck Burr of Greensfarms & Abigail Jennings, Oct. 21, 1798
John Morehouse & Hannah Gold,   Oct. 21, 1798

Ethan Sherwood & Abigail Bibbins,	Nov. 4, 1798
Aaron Hubbel & Betsey Jennings,	Jan. 30, 1799
Peter Sturges of Greenfield & Clarina Bulkley,	July 7, 1799
Philo Ruggles of New Milford & Ellen Bulkley of Greenfield,	July 21, 1799
John Wheeler & Catherine Holberton,	Aug 21, 1799
Abel Ogden & Betsey Sherwood,	Nov. 28, 1799
Andrew Mallery & Sarah Hubbel,	Dec. 14, 1799

STAMFORD.

FAIRFIELD COUNTY.

(See Book IV.)

Stamford was settled in 1640 under New Haven jurisdiction. Was named April, 1642. The First Congregational Church was organized May, 1641. See Book IV, New Canaan Society.

Ezekiel Smith & Martha Holly,	July 9, 1747
Charles Webb & Mercy Holly,	July 16, 1747
Gideon Lounsbery & Deborah Buxton,	Jan. 14, 1748
Benjamin Weed, Jr., & widow Sarah Smith,	Jan. 14, 1748
Daniel Smith & Deborah Webb,	Feb. 4, 1748
Nathaniel Weed, Jr., & Mercy Brown,	July 28, 1748
John Belding & Elizabeth Hays,	Nov. 10, 1748
Andrew Bishop & widow Hannah Thorp,	Dec. 1, 1748
Uriah Crofford of North Castle & Phebe Lewis,	Jan. 5, 1749
John Delevan & Marcy Hart,	Jan. 5, 1749
Lieut. Samuel Knapp & widow Mercy Benton,	March 15, 1749
Joshua Ambler & Bethiah Weed,	April 6, 1749
Reuben Knapp & Mary Bouton,	June 2, 1749
Nathan Middlebrook of Fairfield & Elizabeth Hoit,	Nov. 2, 1749
Israel Weed & Abigail Waterbery,	Jan. 3, 1750
John Knapp & Hannah Blackman,	Jan. 11, 1750
Epenetus Lounsbery & Elizabeth Finch,	Jan. 26, 1750
Richard Davis of Stanwich & Bethiah Brown,	March 1, 1750
Nehemiah Weed & Susanna Pettit,	April 5, 1750

David Scofield & Eunice Seely,   May 18, 1750
Nathaniel Palmer of Greenwich & Elizabeth Knapp,
                                                  April 4, 1751
Gideon Weed & Sarah Waterbery,   Aug. 15, 1751
David Waterbery & Jemima Knapp,   Dec. 12, 1751
Thomas Waterbery & Mary Brown,   April 20, 1753
Eli Scofield & Susanna Bell,   Oct. 3, 1753
Nathaniel Dodge of Bedford & Jane Finch,   Dec. 5, 1753
John Dibble & Rebecca Merril,   Dec. 18, 1753
Hezekiah Holmes of Bedford & Elizabeth Finch,
                                                  March 28, 1754
Dr. Thaddeus Betts of Ridgefield & Elizabeth Maltbie,
                                                  May 15, 1754
Gideon Seely & Deborah Lockwood,   July 11, 1754
Nathan Brown & Mary Holly,   Oct. 15, 1754
Nathan Middlebrook & Sarah Clauson,   Feb. 6, 1755
Jacob Brown & Hannah Webb,   May 1, 1755
Samuel Johnson of Greenwich & Abigail Knap, July 31, 1755
William Wordwell, Jr., & Abigail Bishop,   Oct. 1, 1755
Rev. Moses Mather & Elizabeth Whiting,   Jan. 1, 1756
Nehemiah Mead of Horseneck & Sarah Knapp, Jan. 22, 1756
Abraham Bell & Mary Holly,   March 4, 1756
Nathaniel Weed of Canaan & Mercy Waterbery, June 17, 1756
Samuel Jeffers & Mercy Holmes,   Sept. 22, 1756
David Brown & Rebecca Slauson,   Jan. 25, 1757
Israel Leeds & Elizabeth Knapp,   Jan. 27, 1757
Josiah Scofield, 3d, & Mary Smith,   Feb. 3, 1757
Jonathan Smith & Abigail Dibble,   March 16, 1757
Samuel Brown & Susanna Knapp,   April 21, 1757
Charles Knapp, Jr., & Deborah Hustead,   April 28, 1757
Israel Smith & Abigail Holly,   May 30, 1757
John McKenzie, soldier, & Jannet Cameron,   Dec. 22, 1757
David Hoit, Jr., & Sarah Lockwood,   March 16, 1758
Reuben Dibble & Anne Sherwood,   March 16, 1758
Nathan Hart, Jr., & Sarah Jeffers,   March 23, 1758
Jack, servant of Capt. Weed, & Sylvia, our servant,
                                                  March 27, 1758
Roger Sutherland of North Castle & Mary Scofield,
                                                  April 20, 1758

William Gale & Rebecca Jaggar, July 4, 1758
John Weed & Sarah Clock (?) or Clark, July 27, 1758
William Blair, soldier, & Elizabeth Davis, Dec. 24, 1758
Abraham Smith & Mary Gale, Jan. 28, 1759
James Jones, soldier, & Mary Smith, Feb. 7, 1759
James Spaulding, soldier, & widow Lucretia Ferris,
Feb. 26, 1759
Silvanus Brown & Rebecca Newman, March 4, 1759
Jonathan Scofield & Mary Stuart, March 25, 1759
Joseph Hoit, Jr., & Deborah Bell, April 1, 1759
Silas Scofield & Mary Weed, April 6, 1759
Samuel Cressy & Hannah Buxton, April 6, 1759
Nathan Scofield & Hannah Clauson, April 29, 1759
Nathan Webb of Goshen & Sarah Bishop, Nov. 4, 1759
Josiah Waterbery & Sarah Hustead, Nov. 22, 1759
Philip Kennedy & Abigail Weed, Dec. 22, 1759
Nehemiah Bates, Jr., & Mary Smith, Jan. 31, 1760
Gideon Hoit & Elizabeth Weed, Feb. 7, 1760
Hezekiah Gray of Fairfield & Abigail Waterbery,
April 24, 1760
Capt. David Waterbery & widow Lounsbery, June 5, 1760
Elijah Seeley & Elizabeth Weed, June 12, 1760
George Niell & Abigail Weed, Aug. 12, 1760
Samuel Scofield & Hannah Scofield, Aug. 14, 1760
Titus Finch & Thankful Dean, Aug. 28, 1760
Lieut. Nathan Ferris & Abigail Hustead, Nov. 14, 1760
Sacket Reynolds of Horseneck & Mary Jones, Nov. 21, 1760
George Merrit & Hannah Wright, April 9, 1761
Isaac Hoit & Mary Shelding, Aug. 6, 1761
Silvanus Hoit & Elizabeth Buxton, Aug. 20, 1761
Samuel Garnsey & widow Mary Shelding, Sept. 22, 1761
Nathan Knapp & Rebecca Wordwell, Sept. 23, 1761
Peter Ferris of Stanwich & Martha Weed, Oct. 1, 1761
John Knapp, Jr., & widow Rhoda June, Nov. 10, 1761
David Potts & Hannah Weed, Nov. 19, 1761
Zophar Catchum of Crum Pond & Mary Bishop,
Nov. 26, 1761
Charles Smith of Stanwich & Hannah Weed, Dec. 17, 1761
Zophar Wilmoth & Sarah Webb, Dec. 29, 1761

John Hoit, Jr., & Abigail Hoit,	Dec. 31,	1761
Eliphalet Kellogg of Canaan & Sarah Brown,	Dec. 31,	1761

Joe (negro), servant of Ensign Weed, & Dinah, servant
of N. Middlebrooks, Jan. 4, 1762

Peter Weed & Abigail Hustead,	Jan. 7,	1762

Jonathan Whiting of Horseneck & Rachel Smith,
Jan. 14, 1762

Ensign Israel Smith & Deborah Holmes,	Jan. 21,	1762

Capt. Charles Weed of Canaan & Elizabeth Hoit,
Jan. 28, 1762

Simon Ingersoll of Stanwich & Elisabeth Scofield,
March 29, 1762

Isaac Lockwood & Rebecca Seely,	April 15,	1762
Epenetus Webb & Sarah Judson,	May 30,	1762
Jonathan Sherwood & Phebe Knapp,	July 22,	1762
Samuel Penoyer of Canaan & Martha Leeds,	Nov. 11,	1762
Hezekiah Scofield & Mary Thorp,	Dec. 23,	1762
Joshua Pardee & Elisabeth Webb,	Jan. 13,	1763

John Ingersoll of Bedford & Thankful Garnsey,
March 13, 1763

Adam Babcock of New Haven & Abigail Smith,
Oct. 11, 1763

Abraham Slosson of Bedford & widow Mary Scofield,
Nov. 10, 1763

Epenetus Webb, Jr., & Mary Loder,	Dec. 29,	1763
Aaron Weed & Elizabeth Penoyer,	Jan. 11,	1764

Joseph Hustead, Jr., & Sarah Rogers of Greenwich,
Jan. 12, 1764

Samuel Waring & Ruth Scofield,	Feb. 23,	1764
Edmund Lockwood, Jr., & Abigail Brown,	March 31,	1764
Abraham Scofield, Jr., & Sarah Lockwood,	April 26,	1764
John Lockwood, Jr., & Hannah Hoit,	May 31,	1764
Benjamin Bishop, Jr., & Mary Scofield,	Sept. 24,	1764
Reuben Ayres & Abigail Scofield,	Nov. 29,	1764
James Hoit & Hannah Jones,	Jan. 22,	1765
Hezekiah Weed & widow Mary Belding,	Feb. 7,	1765
Silas Davenport & Mary Webb,	March 7,	1765
Amos Smith & Deborah Knapp,	Oct. 17,	1765
David Whiting & Mary Weed,	Oct. 24,	1765

Silas Hoit of S. & Sarah Lockwood of Greenwich,
	Nov. 14, 1765
John Smith, Jr., & Martha Smith,	Dec. 25, 1765
Benjamin Lounsbery & Rebecca Whiting,	Jan. 16, 1766
John Pardee & Sarah Webb,	Jan. 23, 1766
Ebenezer Scofield of Salem & Hannah Seely,	Jan. 23, 1766
Samuel Webb & Mary Knapp,	March 6, 1766

John Morehouse of Middlesex & Sarah Wardwell,
| | April 24, 1766 |
| John Bishop & Elisabeth Cressey, | June 18, 1766 |

Enoch McKenzie & widow Sarah Middlebrook,
	June 22, 1766
William Hoit & Mary Weed,	Dec. 4, 1766
David Smith & Lydia Smith,	Jan. 1, 1767
Justus Weed & Sarah Knapp,	Jan. 28, 1767
Samuel Garnsey & widow Mary Shelding,	Feb. 1, 1767

Theophilus Hunt of Bedford & Millisent Lockwood,
	March 13, 1767
Silvanus Knapp & Abigail Weed,	May 7, 1767
Joseph Webb, Jr., & Mary Hastead,	July 28, 1767

Rev. C. Jefferey Smith of Brookhaven & Miss Elizabeth Smith,
	Aug. 20, 1767
Charles Bishop & widow Joanna Scofield,	Sept. 3, 1767
Timothy Curtis, Jr., & Rebecca Scofield,	Oct. 18, 1767
Jesse Reed of Middlesex & Mercy Weed,	Dec. 4, 1767
John Scofield, 4th, & Susanna Weed,	Feb. 18, 1768
John Judson & Charity Smith,	March 17, 1768
Jacob Scofield & Joanna Scofield,	April 7, 1768

Nathaniel Hustead of S. & Hannah Webb of Stanwich,
	April 14, 1768
Hezekiah Reed of Danbury & Phebe Ayres,	May 5, 1768
Isaac Hoit & Sarah Hoit,	May 26, 1768
John Waterbery & Martha Winchel,	Oct. 28, 1768
David Webb & widow Sarah Maltbie,	Nov. 6, 1768

Nehemiah Dibble of Danbury & Rebecca Hutton,
| | Dec. 21, 1768 |

David Fanshaw of Pound Ridge & Martha Bellamy,
| | Jan. 1, 1769 |
| Caleb Stevens of Danbury & Mary Weed, | Jan. 10, 1769 |

Jehiel Tyler of Salem & widow Rhoda Knapp, Jan. 19, 1769
Silvanus Scofield & Sarah Weed, Jan. 19, 1769
Jacob Wardwell & Hannah Whitney, Jan. 30, 1769
John Holmes, Jr., & Sarah Hoit, Jan. 31, 1769
Titus Lockwood & Hannah Dan, Feb. 13, 1769
David Bates of Middlesex & Thomasine Knapp, Feb. 23, 1769
Miles Weed, Jr., & Mary Gray, March 22, 1769
Abraham Scofield & Abigail Hoit, April 26, 1769
Ethan Smith & Hannah Scofield, May 7, 1769
David Dibble & widow Sarah Nettleton, June 15, 1769
Eli Reed of Middlesex & Bethiah Weed, Oct. 4, 1769
John Broome of New York & Rebecca Lloyd, Oct. 19, 1769
Eliphalet Weed & Martha Hoit, Dec. 25, 1769
Elijah Weed of S. & Mary Webb of Stanwich, Jan. 25, 1770
Peter Knapp, Jr., & Sarah Reynolds, Feb. 1, 1770
Monmouth Lounsbery of S. & Sarah Davenport of Canaan,
April 18, 1770
Deacon Stephen Ambler of S. & widow Mercy
Benedict of Canaan, June 28, 1770
Amos Green & Rebecca Brown, Sept. 17, 1770
John Waring of Stanwich & Mary Ayres, Oct. 11, 1770
James Rogers & Martha Holly, May 21, 1771
Edward Lockwood & Elisabeth Bishop, June 25, 1771
Epenetus Scofield & Susanna Bates, July 11, 1771
Benjamin Trion & Rebecca Bell, Sept. 8, 1771
Joseph Smith & Hannah Hoit, Feb. 20, 1772
Jeremiah Curtis & Mary Waterbery, March 2, 1772
John Davenport of Canaan & Prudence Bell, June 4, 1772
Abner June of Stanwich & Sarah Smith, June 11, 1772
Samuel Smith of Stanwich & Azubah June, July 23, 1772
Jesse Waring of Stanwich & Ruth Weed, Nov. 5, 1772
Hanford Hoit & Sarah Knapp, Nov. 23, 1772
Jabez Weed & Hannah Bishop, Jan. 21, 1773
Jesse Bell & Mary Scofield, Jan. 25, 1773
Joseph Seely of Canaan & Hannah Hoit, March 1, 1773
Noah Bell & Prudence Scofield, March 25, 1773
Silvanus Stevens of Canaan & Hannah Scofield, April 5, 1773
Gilbert Benedict of Danbury & Mercy Weed, April 14, 1773
Benjamin Ingersoll of Stanwich & Mercy Webster,
June 2, 1773

Joseph Hoit of S. & Sarah Weed of Middlesex, June 24, 1773
Titus Knapp of Greenwich & Rachel Mead of Greenwich,
Oct. 14, 1773
Josiah Jones & Sarah Smith, Nov. 2, 1773
Jacob Scofield & Mercy Scofield, Nov. 25, 1773
Henry Livingston, Jr., of Poughkeepsie & Sarah Welles,
May 18, 1774
Joshua Ambler of Pound Ridge & widow Milliscent
Weed, May 24, 1774
Samuel Benedict of Danbury & Sarah Weed, Oct. 25, 1774
Billy Scofield of Pound Ridge & Elizabeth Ayres,
Nov. 3, 1774
Street Raymond & Mary Hutton, Dec. 28, 1774
Ebenezer Weed, 3d, & Hannah Ambler, Jan. 4, 1775
Jesse Waring of Stanwich & Jemima Lounsbery, Jan. 5, 1775
Selleck Jones & Rebecca Judson, Jan. 15, 1775
David Weed, 4th, & Rebecca Brown, Jan. 19, 1775
David Stevens of Canaan & widow Elenor Holly,
Feb. 15, 1775
Dr. James Cogswell & Elizabeth Davenport, May 4, 1775
Abraham Dayton & Ann Whelply of Greenwich, July 4, 1775
Myer Scofield & Thankful Scofield, Aug. 17, 1775
Benjamin Smith of Stanwich & Abigail Hoit, Dec. 7, 1775
Joshua Smith, Jr., of Stanwich & Mary Smith, Dec. 28, 1775
Lewis Smith of S. & Ruamah Palmer of Greenwich,
Jan. 21, 1776
Jonathan Taylor & Rebecca Palmer, both of Greenwich,
Jan. 21, 1776
Samuel Wheaton & Mary Skelding, April 22, 1776
John Holmes & widow Deborah Bell, May 13, 1776
Isaac Jones & Sarah Finch, July 5, 1776
Nathan Dan & widow Sarah Wheeler, July 12, 1776
Ezra Scofield & Mary Stuart, Aug. 7, 1776
Hon. Abraham Davenport & Mrs. Martha Fitch, Aug. 8, 1776
Isaac Smith & Eunice Scofield, Aug. 11, 1776
Daniel Provost & Elizabeth Bishop, Feb. 17, 1784
Solomon Smith of Huntington & Thamar Platt, Feb. 23, 1784
Isaac Ambler & Anna Skelden (?), Feb. 25, 1784
Zebulon Newman of Bedford & Eunice Lounsbury,
March 16, 1784

William Blake & Sarah Simkins,   March 21, 1784
Jabez Clark of Pound Ridge & Lois Weed,   March 25, 1784
Daniel Smith & Mary Lockwood,   April 12, 1784
Jacob Ambler & Lydia Weed,   May 6, 1784
Stephen Selleck & Elizabeth Smith,   May 27, 1784
Nicholas Downing & Polly Phiney,   May 30, 1784
Jerom (?) Bates & Mary Gray,   June 6, 1784
Jacob Smith & Hannah Thorp,   July 21, 1784
Gabriel Smith & Martha Bellamy,   July 29, 1784
Jonas Clock (?) & Sarah Weed,   Sept. 16, 1784
Stephen Batterson of Fairfield & Sarah Wardwell,
                                              Oct. 19, 1784
Samuel Hoit, 4th, & widow Mary Hoit,   Nov. 11, 1784
John Hadley of Greenwich & Sarah Purdy,   Nov. 24, 1784
Samuel Black & Hannah ———,   Dec. 2, 1784
Jonathan Waring & widow Mary Whiting,   March 23, 1785
Henry Hubbard & Hannah Smith,   June 27, 1785
Samuel Comstock & Elsa Thorp,   July 13, 1785
Daniel Knap & Sarah Garnsey,   Feb. 18, 1786
Jonas Scofield & Sarah Hoit,   July 13, 1786
Moses Nichols & Sarah Webb,   Aug. 31, 1786
Samuel Smith of Peekskill & Hannah Smith,   Sept. 18, 1786
Jonathan Hoit & Elizabeth Waterbery,   Oct. 29, 1786
William Hoit & Anna Heusted,   Dec. 20, 1786
Joseph Selleck & Phebe Clock,   Dec. 31, 1786
Jonathan Waterbury & Sarah Hoit,   Jan. 4, 1787
Peter Smith & Nancy Lintwright (?),   Jan. 17, 1787
John Woodin of L. I. & Sarah Webb,   June 3, 1787
Jacob Waterbury & Rebecca Weed,   July 1, 1787
Frederic Weed & ——— Hoit,   Sept. 23, 1787
George Mills & Abigail Hoit,   Nov. 8, 1787
William Webb & Susannah Weed,   Dec. 6, 1787
James Weed & Sarah Waterbery,   Jan. 8, 1788
Elisha Finney of Farmington & Polly Sturgis, Jan. 31, 1788
Upral (?) Knap & Abigail Hoit,   Feb. 14, 1788
Miles Weed & Hannah Scofield,   March 14, 1788.
Uriah Seymour & Olive Waterbury,   May 11, 1788
Isaac Hart or Hoit & Elizabeth Hoit,   May 23, 1788
Dr. Michael Henry of Lansingburgh, N. Y., & Abba
      Hazard of Waterford, N. Y.,   July 10, 1788

Jonathan Brown & Martha Brown, Sept. 25, 1788
Eben Smith of Stanwich (?) & Mary Hoit, Nov. 20, 1788
Deacon Joshua Ambler & Mrs. Martha Weed, Dec. 9, 1788
Irenia How of Ballston & Sarah Smith, Dec. 11, 1788
Josiah Lockwood & Olive Scofield, April, 1789
Frederick Hoyt & Abigail Lockwood, May 10, 1789
Solomon North of Wethersheld & Jerusha Leeds,
Sept. 20, 1789
Ebenezer Wooster & Elizabeth Waterbury, Nov. 10, 1789
Waren Hoyt & Mary Knapp, Nov. 22, 1789
Nathaniel Mills & Hannah Smith, Nov. 26, 1789
Ebenezer Jones & Rue Waterbury, Dec. 3, 1789
Isaac Peck of Greenwich & Rebecca Wordwell, Jan. 1, 1790
John Hoyt, 3d, & Abigail Smith, Jan. 21, 1790
John Skilding & Ruah Ambler, March 28, 1790
Samuel Hoyt & Betsey Webb, Nov. 8, 1790
James Judson & Anna Morehouse, Nov. 20, 1790
Solomon Smith & Mary Judson, Jan. 20, 1791
Samuel Hutton Pratt & Mary Raymond, Jan. 23, 1791
Abraham Lockwood & Susannah Finch, Feb. 2, 1791
Daniel Cotton & Eliza Watson, both of N. Y. City,
May 24, 1791
Gabriel Smith (?) of Bedford & Rachel Newman,
May 29, 1791
James (?) Wilmut & Abigail Lockwood, June 23, 1791
John Larkim (?) & Elizabeth Hoyt, Sept. 4, 1791
Samuel Sturgis of Charleton, N. Y., & Betsey Lockwood,
Sept. 5, 1793
John Pardee & Betsey Knapp, Sept. 19, 1793
Eliphalet St. John & Sally Knapp, Oct. 2, 1793
Abraham Davenport & Polly Brown, Oct. 26, 1793
Enos Weed & Keziah Powers, Nov. 14, 1793
Joshua Scofield & Hannah Hoyt, Feb. 2, 1794
Ephraim Marvin of Frederickstown & Mary Smith,
March 27, 1794
William June, Jr., & Mary Nichols, Oct. 23, 1794
Amos Mead of Greenwich & Mrs. Martha Davenport,
Jan. 13, 1795
Strong Sturgis & Betsey Weed, Feb. 19, 1795

Seth Newman & Sabra He—ie— (?),	March 26, 1795
William Green & Polly Guernsey,	May 3, 1795
Solomon Smith & Susannah Smith,	May 12, 1795
Joseph Bishop & Sally Lounsbury,	Nov. 22, 1795
Timothy Raymond & Sarah Scofield,	Feb., 1796
Henry Brown & Sarah Raymond,	March 8, 1796
William Bishop & Susannah Scofield,	March 31, 1796
Rufus Newman & Polly Knapp,	April, 1796
Benjamin Perrine & Sarah Judson,	Oct., 1796
Jacob Bates & Mary Lawrence,	Nov. 25, 1796
—— Finch & —— Scofield,	Dec. 1, 1796
Deodate Finch & Mary Waterbury,	——
Salmon Hoyt & Hannah Husted,	Dec. 21, 1796
Charles Weed & Mary Selleck,	Dec. 25, 1796
Phineas Scofield & Mercy Finch,	Jan. 12, 1797
Warren Weed & Anna Clark,	Jan. 19, 1797
John Warring & Hannah Greene,	Feb. 23, 1797
James Finch & Rebekah Brown,	March 15, 1797
Jonathan Miller & Rhoda Finch,	April 6, 1797
Josiah Lockwood & Polly Burne,	1797
John Weed, 4th, & Lucretia Dana,	Nov. 7, 1797
John Hoyt, Jr., & Rebecca Jeffery,	Nov. 12, 1797
Nathan Hoyt Reed & Mary Hoyt,	1797
John Freeman (a black man) & Lucy Silleck,	Dec. 19, 1797
Abel Knapp & Charity Judson,	Dec. 24, 1797
Jonathan Jesup, Jr., & Rhua Lockwood,	Dec. 25, 1797
Henry Ingghram & Ruth Cur—— (?),	Jan. 24, 1798
Joseph Wardwell, Jr., & Elizabeth Scudder,	July 11, 1798
Shadrack Hoyt & Mary Webb,	Sept. 8, 1798
Samuel Lockwood & Sally Lockwood,	Sept. 9, 1798
Thaddeus Hoyt, Jr., & Rebekah Lockwood,	Dec. 13, 1798
John Judson, Jr., & Polly Wardwell,	Dec. 23, 1798
Messenger Palmer & Abigail Smith,	March 21, 1799
Asa Ferris & Polly Hoyt,	March 21, 1799
Isaac Wardwell & Hannah Knapp,	March 23, 1799
Benjamin Reed, Jr., & Prudence Smith,	April 4, 1799
John Bell & Polly Lounsbury,	Oct. 21, 1799
Augustus Lockwood & Elizabeth Peck,	Jan. 1, 1800

STAMFORD—DARIEN.

FAIRFIELD COUNTY.

(See Book IV.)

The town of Darien was incorporated May, 1820, and taken from Stamford. The Congregational Church in Darien—formerly called Middlesex—was organized June, 1744. It is recorded that "one Sunday during the Revolution the church was suddenly surrounded by Tories and the British, and forty men (nearly all who were in church, including Dr. Mather, the pastor), and as many horses, were carried off to Long Island. Many of them never returned." The marriages recorded follow.

Nathaniel Sellek, Jr., & Sarah Sellek, daughter of Nathan,
Aug. 7, 1744

Eliphalet Brown of North Castle and Thankful
Wood, daughter of Isaac Wood of Norwalk, Oct. 4, 1744

Elijah Johnes & Martha Reed, July 4, 1745

John Bates, ye fourth, & Martha Seley, daughter of
Eliphalet, both of Stamford, Aug. 22, 1745

Nathan Sellik, Jr., & Katharine Clock, daughter of
John Clock, Sept. 17, 1745

Stephen Jackson of Fairfield & Mary Waterbery,
daughter of David of Stamford, Oct. 3, 1745

John Bates, ye third, & Mary Ferris, Jan. 22, 1745-6

David How & Rebekah Whiting, daughter of Joseph,
March 21, 1745-6

Daniel Reed, Jr., of Norwalk & Mary Bell, daughter
of Lieut. Jonathan Bell of Stamford, May 22, 1746

Samuel Buckston & widow Rebekah Greavs (?),
Oct. 16, 1746

Joshua Morehouse, Jr., & Abigail Bishop, daughter
of John, Oct. 29, 1746

Thomas Slason & Mary Bates, daughter of John, the
second, March 5, 1746-7

Taddeus Raymont & Mary Hanford, daughter of
Thomas, deceased, both of Norwalk, Oct. 27, 1747

Eliakins Reed & Sarah Richards, daughter of Samuel,
both of Norwalk, June 16, 1748

Eleazar Green & Sarah Sellik, daughter of Nathaniel,
Sept. 13, 1748

Bethel Hecock of Norwalk & Mary Pettit, daughter of
    Jonathan Pettit of Sharon,   Nov. 23, 1748
Gershom Raymont & Abigail Taylor, both of Norwalk,
                        April 13, 1749
John Smith of Norwalk & Elizabeth Green of Stamford,
                        Oct. 9, 1749
John Morehouse & Molley Reed, daughter of Samuel,
                        Nov. 9, 1749
David Sellik, Jr., & Sarah Bates, daughter of John, 2d,
                    Jan. 18, 1749-50
Samuel Andras & Hannah Bishop, daughter of Dr. Isaac,
                      May 17, 1750
Albert Clock of Stamford & Comfort Clark of Bedford,
                      Aug. 29, 1750
Denny Chapman of Green's Farms & Desire Love-
    well, from the Cape Codd,   Oct. 4, 1750
Nathan Weed of Stamford & Judah Kelluk of Norwalk,
                    Oct. 16, 1750
Joshua Scofield, Jr., of Stamford & Mary Smith of
    Norwalk,   Oct. 25, 1750
John Guyer of Redden & Sarah Brinsmayd, daughter
    of Samuel of Norwalk,   Nov. 21, 1750
Samuel Moger (?) & Rachel Waterbery,   Jan. 9, 1750-1
Samuel Raymond of Norwalk & Abigail Bates of
    Stamford,   Feb. 21, 1750-1
Abraham Reed of Norwalk & Hannah Bell,   May 9, 1751
James Green of Stamford & Phebe Green of Ridgefield,
                    May 27, 1751
Daniel Lockwood & Thankful Richards, both of Nor-
    walk,   Aug. 20, 1751
Joseph Ambler of S. & Elisabeth Reed of Norwalk,
                    Oct. 17, 1751
Cornelius Smith of Bedford & Hannah Waterbery,
                    Dec. 4, 1751
John Reed & Elisabeth Richards, both of Norwalk,
                    Jan. 9, 1751-2
John Raymond & Lydia Reed, both of Norwalk,
                    April 16, 1752
Jonathan Waterbury & Abigail Whiting,   May 6, 1752

James How of S. & Sarah Waring of Norwalk,
Aug. 20, 1752
Daniel Frith of Barmoodos & Rebekah Scofield of S.,
Nov. 23, 1752
Peter Selleck & Martha Whiting, Jan. 18, 1753
Samuel Bates & Anne Morehouse, March 19, 1753
William Matthias & Hannah Benchgood, March 20, 1753
Bethel Selleck of S. & Ruth Brinsmayd of Norwalk,
May 18, 1753
Ketchel Bell of Cornwell & Sarah Whiting of S.,
Nov. 14, 1753
John Selleck & Sarah Weed, April 1, 1754
Bushuel Fitch of Norwalk & Abigail Reed, Nov. 12, 1754
Joseph Waring & Elisabeth Byxbe, both of Norwalk,
Nov. 12, 1754
Ezra Selleck & Elisabeth Bates, Feb. 6, 1755
Benjamin Waterbury & Abigail Sherwood, May 28, 1755
Nathan Waring of Norwalk & Elisabeth Bell, July 25, 1755
Silvanus Fancher of S. & Priscilla Smith of Norwalk,
Oct. 2, 1755
John Dalglish (?) of Hannover & Esther Reed of Nor-
walk, Oct. 29, 1755
Jonathan Scofield of S. & Elisabeth Smith of Norwalk,
Oct. 30, 1755
Waterbery Hoyt of S. & Hannah Reed of Norwalk,
Dec. 18, 1755
Abraham Selleck & Deborah Whiting, May 3, 1756
John Farim, or Farnim, of Fairfield & Thankful Dib-
ble of S., May 11, 1756
Jonathan Chipman of Salisbury & Katharine Reed of
Norwalk, Oct. 5, 1756
Thaddeus Bates & Sarah Sturges, Jan. 5, 1757
Nathan Hubbel of Norwalk & Sarah Bates, Dec. 2, 1756
Samuel Fairchild & Hannah Tuttle, both of Norwalk,
Jan. 6, 1757
Peter James of S. & Mercy Nash of Norwalk, March 31, 1757
Zaccheus Hoyt of Norwalk & Elisabeth Green, July 16, 1766
John Munro & Katharine Reed, both of Norwalk,
Oct. 30, 1766

Samuel Bishop & Anne Bell,　　　　　　　　Nov. 6, 1766
Ely Tuttle & Sarah Smith, both of Norwalk,　　Dec. 7, 1766
Robert Peck of Greenwich & Anne Reed of Norwalk,

　　　　　　　　　　　　　　　　　　　　　Jan. 15, 1767
Gershom Morehouse of S. & Phebe Benedict of Nor-
　　walk,　　　　　　　　　　　　　　　　June 6, 1767
Jesse Tuttle & Mercy Selleck, both of Norwalk, Oct. 1, 1767
Jesse Bell & Comfort Garnsey,　　　　　　　Nov. 9, 1767
Elijah Reed of Norwalk & Esther Bates,　　　Dec. 3, 1767
Silvanus Weed & Mary Stason (?),　　　　　Dec. 17, 1767
Matthew Clark & Zerviah Youngs,　　　　　Jan. 8, 1768
Eleazar Bouton & Mary Green,　　　　　　　Jan. 14, 1768
Jonathan Clock & Sarah Green,　　　　　　　Feb. 1, 1768
Isaac Holly & Sarah Selleck,　　　　　　　　Feb. 11, 1768
Silvanus Selleck of S. & Tabitha Pierce of Stratford,

　　　　　　　　　　　　　　　　　　　　March 12, 1768
Samuel Richards, Jr., & Esther Haden (?), both of
　　Norwalk,　　　　　　　　　　　　　　Nov. 24, 1768
John Benedic of Norwalk & Mercy Pettit of S., Dec. 8, 1768
John Bell & the widow Canaday,　　　　　　Dec. 18, 1768
Daniel Selleck & Mary Brown,　　　　　　　Sept. 21, 1769
David Ferris of North Castle & Mary Reed of Nor-
　　walk,　　　　　　　　　　　　　　　　Dec. 6, 1769
Deliverance Brown of Greenwich & Hannah Reed of
　　Norwalk,　　　　　　　　　　　　　　Dec. 6, 1769
Samuel Hayden, Jr., & Mary Waring, both of Nor-
　　walk,　　　　　　　　　　　　　　　　Dec. 28, 1769
Obadiah Stevens & Sarah —ildin, both of S.,　Feb. 1, 1770
Matthew Fitch & Sarah Reed, both of Norwalk, Dec. 27, 1770
Jonathan Bates & Lidia Scofield,　　　　　　Jan. 7, 1771
Simeon Selleck & Mary Belden,　　　　　　Feb. 28, 1771
William Fancher & Esther Suard (?), both of Stamford,

　　　　　　　　　　　　　　　　　　　　July 2, 1771
Thomas Hoit & Rebeckah Green,　　　　　　Dec. 30, 1771
Jonathan Scofield & Jemima Finch,　　　　　March 21, 1772
Edward Selleck & Elisabeth Selleck,　　　　March 24, 1772
Benjamin Peck of Greenwich & Hannah Reed of Nor-
　　walk,　　　　　　　　　　　　　　　　Aug. 12, 1772
Eliakim Reed & Rebekah Fitch, both of Norwalk,

　　　　　　　　　　　　　　　　　　　　Sept. 14, 1772

Ebenezer Weed & Lydia Selleck,   Oct. 1, 1772
Jacob Waring & Sarah Bates,   Dec. 24, 1772
David Hoyt & Katharine Waring, both of Norwalk,
                                    Jan. 14, 1773
Benjamin Scofield & Rebekah How,   March 10, 1773
Gershom Richards & Elisabeth Richards, both of
   Norwalk,   March 15, 1773
Ray Selleck of S. & Mary Mills of Norwalk, March 17, 1773
Nathaniel Clock & Sarah How,   April 28, 1773
Epinetus Kellogg & Rebekah Richards, both of Nor-
   walk,   Sept. 16, 1773
Scudder Weed of S. & Abigail Waring of Norwalk,
                                    Oct. 7, 1773
Abraham Reed of Norwalk & Thankful Weed of S.,
                                  Nov. 4, 1773
Benjamin Betts of Norwalk & Jane Selleck,   Dec. 23, 1773
Peter Quintard of Norwalk & Ruth Stevens,   May 23, 1774
Solomon Whitmore & Elisabeth Reed, both of Nor-
   walk,   May 26, 1774
Denne Parketing & Hannah Slason (?),   May 30, 1774
Abraham Youngs & Mary Scofield,   July 18, 1774
Nathan Tuttle of Norwalk & Abigail Scofield, July 28, 1774
Jesse Hanford of Norwalk & Mary Gorum,   Aug. 8, 1774
Moses Waring & Mary Besse, both of Norwalk, Oct. 5, 1774
Zephaniah Weed & Martha Slason,   May 21, 1775
Jonas Weed & Sarah Waring,   April 20, 1775
——— Crisy & Rebekah How,   Oct. 26, 1775
Paul Raymond & Elisabeth Reed, both of Norwalk,
                                  Jan. 11, 1776
Josiah Weed & Sarah Ceely, both of Canaan Parish,
                                  ——— 18, 1776
Thomas Comstock of Norwalk & Phebe Selleck,
                                  Feb. 1, 1776
Bowers How & Thankful Bishop,   July 15, 1776
Joseph Warring & Anne Bates,   Oct. 17, 1776
Edmond Richards & Ruth Waring, both of Norwalk,
                                  Oct. 28, 1776
Richard Young & Rebecca Whitmore,   Dec. 12, 1776
Samuel Richards of S. & Elisabeth Waring of Nor-
   walk,   March 6, 1777

Nathaniel Hoit & Sarah Waterbery,	March 13, 1777
Stephen Bishop & Puella Hoit,	April 24, 1777
Peleg Bessey & Hannah Waring, both of Norwalk,	
	June 26, 1777
Joseph Clark of Bedford & Hannah Clock of S.,	
	Sept. 25, 1777
Elijah Allen of Cornwal & Sarah Bishop of S.,	Oct. 30, 1777
Jacob Bishop & Lydia Weed,	Nov. 12, 1777
Daniel Hoit of Norwalk & Mary Fancher,	Nov. 12, 1777
Seth Weed & Mary Brown,	Nov. 27, 1777
William Fancher & Thankful Smith, both of Norwalk,	
	Dec. 8, 1777
Jesse Raymond of Norwalk & Hannah Mather,	Dec. 28, 1777
Benjamin Belden & Anna Selleck,	Jan. 29, 1778
Ely Reed of Norwalk & Mellacent Slason,	March 12, 1778
Nathaniel Selleck & Azubah Raymond,	March 26, 1778
Isaac Squire of Norwalk & Susannah Youngs,	
	March 26, 1778
Jesse Smith of Long Island & ―――― Brown,	April 1, 1778
James Shaw & Hannah Weed,	April 9, 1778
Stephen Weed of Norwalk & Elisabeth Besse of Norwalk,	May 14, 1778-9
Jacob Hoit of Bedford & Anne Bishop,	May 20, 1778-9
Samuel Lewis & Abigail Waterbery,	July 2, 1778-9
James Waring & Polly Suard (?), both of Norwalk,	
	Oct. 27, 1778-9
―――― Glommer of N. Y. State & Lydia Raymond of Norwalk,	Oct. 29, 1778-9
Isaac Waring & Eunis Fowler Whitmore, both of Norwalk,	Nov. 26, 1778-9
John Waterbery & Abigail Weed,	Dec. 8, 1778
Daniel Moss of New Haven & Lydia Smith of Norwalk,	Feb. 3, 1779
Isaac Richards & Hannah Benedict, both of Norwalk,	
	Oct. 14, 1779
Hezekiah Weed & ―――― Knap,	Oct. 28, 1779
Nathaniel Ceely & Mary Bell,	Nov. 25, 1779
Obadiah Wheeler of Norwalk & Elisabeth Matthias of Stamford,	Nov. 29, 1779

Judd Abbot of Norwalk & Sarah Weed,   Dec. 30, 1779

Thomas Menter (?) of Lyme & Hannah Tomson,

    April 22, 1780

Thaddeus Bell & Betsey How,   May 4, 1780

Amos Roberts of Greenwich & Deborah Selleck,

    June 1, 1780

Daniel Gorum & Jane Bates,   July 22, 1780

Samuel Hutton & Abigail Lockwood,   Aug. 24, 1780

Gershom Slason & Elisabeth Marshall,   Oct. 12, 1780

Isaac Nickason & Abigail Dibble,   Dec. 4, 1780

Elias Reed of Norwalk & Hannah Scofield,   Jan. 3, 1782

Noyes Mather & Cloe Waterbery,   Feb. 13, 1782

John Carter of Norwalk & Hannah Bates,   May 29, 1782

Joseph Scidmore of L. I. & Polley Bates,   Sept. 23, 1782

Abraham Waring of Danbury & Anne Crawford of

    Norwalk,   Nov. 5, 1782

Edward Raymond & Deborah Whiting,   Dec. 9, 1783

Jesse Waring of Norwalk & Hannah Bates,   Jan. 15, 1784

Henry Weed & Mary Selleck,   June 7, 1784

Jeremiah Andrus & Sarah How,   June 30, 1784

Jonathan Bishop & Sarah Waterbury,   July 29, 1784

William Waterbury & Elisabeth Scofield,   Aug. 26, 1784

Solomon Waring & Mary Hiccoc, both of Norwalk,

    Sept. 12, 1784

Abraham Slason & Dorothy Whiting,   Sept. 19, 1784

Ebenezer How & Sarah Bell,   Jan. 3, 1785

Aquilla Sturges & Sarah Little,   March 1, 1785

———— of New Fairfield & Esther Brown, daughter

    of Nathan,   July 4, 1785

Youngs Platt & Hulda Waterbery,   1785

Epinetus Waterbery & Elisabeth Bates,   Jan. 1, 1786

Jesse Selleck & Elisabeth How,   Jan. 26, 1786

Ephraim Page of New Fairfield & Priscilla Raymond

    of Norwalk,   Feb. 20, 1786

John Holly & Tammey (?) Tomson,   March 9, 1786

Elias Sanford of Readding & Hannah Youngs, Aug. 31, 1786

Stephen Selleck & Lattey (?) Bates,   Sept. 3, 1786

John Bell & Deborah Clock,   Nov. 9, 1786

James Little of S. & Joannah Nickerson of Bedford,

    Dec. 4, 1786

Isaac Richards of Norwalk & Ennis Taylor,	Dec. 7, 1786
James Weed & Lydia Slason,	Jan. 1, 1787
Gershom Raymond & Mary Whiting,	Jan. 4, 1787
Joseph Byxbee & Nancy Slason, both of Norwalk,	
	Jan. 11, 1787
Date Weed & Sarah Holly,	April 9, 1787
Nathaniel Slason & Hannah Smith,	April 25, 1787
Thomas Provost & Elisabeth Slason,	May 10, 1787
Stephan Raymond of Norwalk & Molley Selleck,	
	May 28, 1787
Silvanus Fancher, Jr., of S. & Sarah Smith of Pound	
Ridge,	June 18, 1787
Abraham Clock & Betty Waring,	June 25, 1787
Nathan Knap & Sarah Morehouse,	July 26, 1787
Nathan Weed, Jr., & Mary Scofield,	Sept. 3, 1787
Ebenezer Little of S. & Hannah ——tter (?) of Canaan,	
	—— 8, 1787
Charles Slason & Deborah Weed,	—— 15, 1787
Nathan How & Mellasent Beel (?),	—— 22, 1787
Joshua Morehouse & Sarah Waterbery,	1787
Jesse Crissey & Bethia Weed,	Jan. 2, 1788
Jonathan Slason & Hannah Slason,	April 16, 1788
David Fancher & Mary How,	May 26, 1788
John Dean of Brooklin & Sarah Scofield,	June 23, 1788
Jonas Weed & Hannah Waterbery,	July 7, 1788
Deodate Waterbery & Mary Warring,	Nov. 25, 1788
Henry Whitney & Prudence Grey,	Jan. 8, 1789
John Clock & Sarah Fancher,	Jan. 26, 1789
Henry Scofield of S. & Mary Reed of Norwalk,	April 27, 1789
Joseph Deforrest of Danbury & Elisabeth Scofield,	
	May 21, 1789
Noah Smith & Rhoda Hays, both of Norwalk,	Jan. 12, 1790
Gideon Weed & Anna Hoit,	Jan. 28, 1790
James Lockwood & Elisabeth Richards, both of Norwalk,	
	March 31, 1790
Samuel Mather & Sarah Scofield,	May 2, 1790
Jesse St. John of Norwalk & Anna Weed,	Sept. 28, 1790
Nathan Smith of L. I. & Sarah Tuttle of Norwalk,	
	Oct. 3, 1790

William Waterbery & Sarah Waterbery, Nov. 21, 1790
Samuel Hoyt & Hannah Waterbery, Nov. 29, 1790
Stephen St. John & Mary Fitch, both of Norwalk,
Dec. 27, 1790
James Little, Jr., & Lidia Nickerson, Jan. 13, 1791
Jesse Mott & Katharine Jackson, both of Norwalk,
Feb. 15, 1791
Samuel Richards & Mercy Webb, both of Norwalk,
March 14, 1791
Gilbert Woolsey & Roda Marshal, Sept. 12, 1791
Philip Grey & Hannah Matthias, Nov. 7, 1791
Elisha Seely & Betsey Brown, both of Norwalk, Dec. 8, 1791
John Brown & Rebecca Waterbery, Dec. 19, 1791
——— Waterous of Canaan & Bethia (?) Selleck,
Jan. 5, 1792
Samuel Waring, Jr., & Elizabeth Hoit, Jan. 8, 1792
Seth Weed & Sarah Wyat, Jan. 12, 1792
Baldwin Reed of Salisbury & Hannah Reed of Nor-
walk, April 2, 1792
Uriah Waterbery & ——— Holms, Oct. 11, 1792
Thather (?) Hays of Salem & Mary Weed, Nov. 5, 1792
William Weed & Mercy Selleck, Nov. 27, 1792
James Wordwell & Hannah Weed, Dec. 1, 1792
Benjamin Little & Rebecca Slason, Dec. 27, 1792
Cary Bell & Rebecca Fancher, May 20, 1792
Isaac Selleck & Sarah Waterbery, July 1, 1793
Moses Waterbery & ——— Weed, July 22, 1793
William Penoyer & Betsey Morehouse, Sept. 25, 1793
Nathaniel Waterbury & Abigail Weed, Jan. 1, 1794
Nathaniel Crissey & Hannah Bishop, Jan. 16, 1794
Nathaniel Benedic & Hannah Selleck, both of Norwalk,
April 2, 1794
David Comstock of Norwalk & Deborah Weed, Jan. 5, 1795
Henry Clock & Hannah Waring, May 18, 1795
Silvanus Weed & Ruannah How, June 23, 1795
William Jonson of Greenwich & Lucy Dic (?), July 21, 1795
James Waring & Hannah Selleck, Sept. 3, 1795
David Streat (?) & ———attey Lawrance, Oct. 12, 1795
Jessey Penoyer & Annie Weed, Oct. 12, 1795

Nathaniel Slason & Anna Clock,   Dec. 18, 1795
Benjamin Little & Esther Weed,   Feb. 29, 1796
Joseph Richards & Lydia Waterbury,   March 16, 1796
David Foster & Sarah Weed,   April 25, 1796
Charles Selleck & Hannah Mather,   June 2, 1796
Joseph Washburn of N. Y. & Polley Waring, July 28, 1796
Peter Weed & Hannah Fancher,   Sept. 23, 1796
Lewis Richards & Katharine Clock,   Oct. 6, 1796
Jacob How & Elisabeth Slason,   Oct. 24, 1796
John Scofield & Elisabeth Reed,   Dec. 21, 1796
Isaias (?) Waring of Norwalk & Lydia Scofield, Jan. 1, 1797
Barnabas Marvin, Jr., & Hannah Richards, both of
      Norwalk,   April 27, 1797
Josia Hoit, Jr., & Polly Waring,   June 19, 1797
William Furman of N. Y. & Mercy Scofield,   June 19, 1797
Philo Bets & Hannah Raymond, both of Norwalk,

                                                       Oct. 11, 1797
Robert Pelton & Mary Slason,   Oct. 11, 1797
Samuel Waterbery & Hannah Bates,   Oct. 28, 1797
Samuel Pelton & Rachel Bates,   Oct. 28, 1797
Enos Wilmut & Hannah Clock,   Feb. 15, 1798
Phineas Waterbery & Anna Lockwood,   Feb. 26, 1798
Noyes Richards & Sarah Mather,   April 9, 1798
Ezra Mills & Katharine Roberts,   Sept. 5, 1798
Elias Marcial of S. & Hannah Picket of Norwalk,

                                                        Oct. 1, 1798
Ebenezer Peck of Greenwich & Elisabeth Ramond,

                                                       Nov. 8, 1798
John Scot & Betsey Mills, both of Norwalk, March 8, 1799
Robert Scofield & Hannah Bell,   April 16, 1799
Selleck Weed & Mersay Hoyt,   April 29, 1799
John Sears of the Jarsey & Abigail Brown,   June 7, 1799
Isaac Hoit & Mary Selleck,   Oct. 23, 1799
Ezra Waterbery & Mercy Selleck,   Dec. 30, 1799
Isaac Weed & Eunice Bates,   Feb. 20, 1800
Isaac Selleck & Eunice Youngs,   June 29, 1800
Selleck Bates & Sarah Bates,   Nov. 13, 1800

KILLINGWORTH—CLINTON.

MIDDLESEX COUNTY.

(See Book III.)

The town of Clinton was incorporated May, 1838. Taken from Killingworth. The First Church of Killingworth is located herein. It was organized in 1667. See Book III for records of the Second Church. The following marriages are recorded by the First Church.

Joseph Carter of Saybrook & Lucy Wilcocks,	Jan. 27, 1764
Oliver Stevens & Elizabeth Platt,	March 8, 1764
Jacob Parson & Anna Tooly,	April 12, 1764
Nathan Wright & Lucy Gray,	Nov. 6, 1764
Richard Redfield & Lydia Willcocks,	Dec. 9, 1765
Amos Carter & Anna Willcocks,	Jan. 10, 1765
John Rosseter & Submit Wright,	Feb. 21, 1765
Tom, servant of Theoph. Morgan, Jr., & Flora, servant of Mrs. Sarah Eliot,	June, 1765
Ebenezer Merret & Hannah Marvin,	June, 1766
Charles Hazelton & Esther Keley,	Feb. 9, 1767
Robert Street & Lydia Keley,	———
Seth Barber & Mary Norton,	May 27, 1767
Jesse Willcocks & Thankful Stevens,	June 11, 1767
Cornelius Chatfield & Ruth Morris,	1767
William Ayers & widow Sarah Hull,	1768
Hill Buel & Hannah Redfield,	Jan. 9, 1769
Phineas Bradley & Hannah Buel,	Feb. 1, 1769
William Griffing & Eunice Crane,	April 12, 1769
Samuel Hull & Betty Keley,	1770
Capt. Stephen Lane & Phebe Hull,	1770
Jesse Lane & Esther Wright, Jr.,	Feb., 1770
Giles Porter & Sarah Wellman,	Sept., 1770
Samuel Stannard & Jemima Willcocks,	Oct. 22, 1770
Jonathan Robbins & Lydia Stevens,	Dec. 4, 1770
Josiah Morehouse & Sarah Lewis,	Dec. 6, 1770
Sylvester Redfield & Martha Merrel,	Dec. 16, 1770
Hubbel Carter & Hannah Williams,	Jan., 1771
Samuel Merrel & Artemelia Redfield,	Feb. 13, 1771
Lemuel Tooly & Margaret Daily,	Sept. 26, 1771

Augustus Eliot & Mary Lewis,	Nov. 15, 1771
Daniel Peck & Hannah Redfield,	Nov. 18, 1771
Samuel Keley, 3d, & Mercy Wellman,	Jan. 16, 1772
Hill Farnam & Mary Elderkin,	Feb. 23, 1772
Benjamin Griffith, Jr., & Elizabeth Holmes,	Aug. 2, 1772
Elias Isbel & Temperance Ward,	Sept. 24, 1772
Oliver Hull & Martha Buel,	Sept. 28, 1772
Jacob Scranton & Mehitable Burris,	Dec. 7, 1772
—— Judson & Abigail Willcocks,	1773
Elisha Spencer & Mary Rossiter,	
Reuben Hopkins & Hannah Eliot,	Nov. 25, 1773
Ebenezer Bushnel & Sarah Carter,	Feb. 10, 1774
Lemuel Wheeler & Amelia Morgan,	May 16, 1774
Samuel Green & Abigail Buel,	Oct. 25, 1774
Jeremiah Stevens & Patience Holmes,	Oct. 27, 1774
William Burrall & Betsey Morgan,	Nov. 2, 1774
Nathaniel Redfield & Molly Hurd,	Dec. 14, 1774
Enoch Smith & Anna Lane,	Jan. 30, 1775
William Burris & Sarah Willcocks,	Feb. 6, 1775
Ensign Job Wright & Sarah Stevens,	Feb. 9, 1775
James Hambleton of Haddam & Jemima Stevens,	
	May 23, 1775
Caleb L. Hurd & Mary Griswold,	June 4, 1775
Asa Wright & Grace Williams,	Aug. 3, 1775
Evans Chance & Hannah Buell,	Oct. 29, 1775
Rue Hurd & Anne Finlon, or w,	Nov. 5, 1775
Jedediah Pierson, Jr., & Beulah Spencer,	Dec. 14, 1775
Levi Keley & Lucy Hull,	April, 1776
Jonathan Buel & Hannah Baley,	March, 1776
Samuel Smith & Sarah Buel,	Aug. 15, 1776
Najah Bennet & Mary Stevens,	Jan. 15, 1777
Samuel Crane, Jr., & Jerusha Wellman,	Jan. 14, 1779
Jedediah Chapman, Esq., of Saybrook & widow Hester Wright,	Feb. 18, 1779
Achilles Mansfield & Sarah Huntington,	March 10, 1779
Moses Blachley of E. Guilford & Anna Kelley,	April 25, 1779
Job Buel, 2d, & Ruth Redfield,	June 16, 1779
Daniel Willcox & Polly Redfield,	July 18, 1779
Allen Leet & Abigail Kelley,	Oct. 21, 1779

John Hurd & Amanda Farnham, Nov. 18, 1779
Zachariah Doud of E. Guilford & Mary Kilburn,
March 30, 1780
Jeremiah Atwater of New Haven & Catharine Gale,
April 6, 1780
William B. Grinnel & Sarah Griffin, May 24, 1780
Phineas Pierson & Siba Dudley, Sept. 24, 1780
James N. Griffin & Polly Stevens, Nov. 7, 1780
Daniel Everts of Salsbury & widow Molly Redfield,
Nov. 8, 1780
Nehemiah Marsh of Canaan & Ruth Rosseter, Nov. 16, 1780
Jonathan Boardman of Haddam & widow Cloe Gris-
would, Dec. 27, 1780
James Lewis & Abigail Kelley, March 18, 1781
Hezekiah Hotchkiss of New Haven & Grace Willcox,
May 6, 1781
John Willcox & Margaret Kelley, June 17, 1781
George Fowler & Sarah Griswold, June 20, 1781
David Surrunborough of N. Y. State & Matilda Teal,
Oct., 1781
Joseph Youngs & Cloe Griswould, Oct., 1781
Timothy Teal & Phebe Hull, Dec. 13, 1781
Elijah Dwolf (?) & Lois Buel, Dec. 20, 1781
John Hill of E. Guilford & Abigail Grey, Jan. 16, 1782
Lemuel Davies & Jemima Kelley, Feb. 7, 1782
John Dudley of New Port & Lydia Stevens, June 20, 1782
Edward Griffin & Submit Dwolf, July, 1782
David Griffin & Freelove Hillyard, Aug., 1782
Eliakim Stannard of Saybrook & Bethiah Kelley, Aug., 1782
William Woodstock of the Army & Elizabeth Sims,
Jan. 22, 1783
Ethan Kelley & Sarah Allen, Jan. 23, 1783
John Chittendon & Rebekah Merril, Feb. 26, 1783
Stephen Palmer & Hannah Wellman, Feb. 26, 1783
Edward Griswould & Asenah Hurd, June 19, 1783
Constant Pamerly & Esther Farnham, Aug. 28, 1783
Benjamin Wright & Ruth Grinnel, Oct. 5, 1783
Timothy Todd & Phebe Buel, Nov. 27, 1783
George Hull, 2d, & Jemima Wellman, Dec. 11, 1783

Dr. John Redfield of Guilford & Mary Gale, March 31, 1784
James Buel & Susanna Porter, April 8, 1784
Joseph Hull & Mary Teal, Sept. 16, 1784
James Brown Ketchum of N. Y. & Pameliah Willcox,
Oct. 30, 1784
Theophilus Morgan, 2d, & Abigail Lane, Nov. 25, 1784
Onis or Enis Farnham & Esther Rossiter, Dec. 12, 1784
Joseph Teal & Anna Griswould, Dec. 2, 1784
John Burrows & Louicy Grinnel, Dec., 1785
Constant Chapman of Saybrook & Jemima Kelley,
Jan. 27, 1785
Joseph Willcox & Phebe Morgan, Jan. 30, 1785
Jared Elliott, Jr., & Clarissa Lewis, Jan. 30, 1785
Jesse Chalker of Saybrook & Elizabeth Buel, March 3, 1785
Ezra Kelley, 2d, & Phebe Carter, March 16, 1785
Augustus Redfield & Anna Grinnel, March 17, 1785
David Buel, 2d, & Jane Carter, Aug. 4, 1785
Asahel Fuller of ———— & Martha Griswould, Sept. 29, 1785
Daniel Redfield & Jerusha Wright, Sept. 29, 1785
Gilbert Graves of E. Guilford & Elizabeth Kelley,
Oct. 20, 1785
Phineas Post of Saybrook & Jane Kelley, Oct. 27, 1785
Solomon Davies & Hannah Parmer, Jan. 30, 1786
John Griswould & Hannah Peck, Feb. 1, 1786
Jeduthun Bemies of Western & Polly Allen, Feb. 9, 1786
Jared Griffin of Branford & Sally Merrils, May 10, 1786
Benjamin Dwolf & Jerusha Carter, May 15, 1786
Samuel Redfield, 2d, & Martha Lane, June 11, 1786
Josiah Hull & Fanny Griffith at North Killingworth,
July 9, 1786
Nathan Kelley & Molly Hull, Aug. 1, 1786
William Leffingwell & Sally Maria Beers at N. Haven,
Sept. 12, 1786
Reuben Kelley & Elizabeth Post, Sept. 12, 1786
Gideon Post of Salsbury & Nancy Hurd, Nov., 1786
John Hopson of Guilford & Eunice Willcox, Dec. 31, 1786
George Bushnell of N. Y. State & Juliana Griswould,
Jan. 14, 1787
Josiah Carter & Lucy Dewolf, Feb. 6, 1787

Roswell Redfield & Juliana Stevens,   March 11, 1787
John Graves & Hannah Crane,   June, 1787
Phineas Bushnel of Saybrook & Hepzibah Lewis,
    Aug. 14, 1787
Nathaniel Buel & Abigail Chatfield,   Aug. 14, 1787
Nathan Willcox & Elizabeth Eliott,   Oct. 15, 1787
James Ward, 2d, & Rachel Hurd,   Jan. 16, 1788
George Morgan & Betsey Redfield,   March 25, 1788
Nathaniel Stevens, 2d, of Guilford & Rebecca Buel,
    March 25, 1788
David Rossetter & Abigail Buel,   May 8, 1788
John Spencer & Dothy Stevens,   July 16, 1788
Zadock Wellman & Martha Chatfield,   Aug. 27, 1788
David Hoit of Manchester & Sarah Fowler,   Jan. 25, 1789
Hiel Buel & Lucy Griswould,   March 28, 1790
George Elliot, 2d, & Patience Lane,   Dec. 23, 1790
Levi Griswould & Abigail Kelley,   Jan. 23, 1791
Samuel Buel & Anner Holmes,   Feb. 2, 1791
Martin Everts of Guilford & Betsey Redfield,   Feb. 2, 1791
Zina Kelley & Hannah Stannard of Saybrook, Feb. 13, 1791
Noah Kelley & Margaret Grinnel,   Feb. 14, 1791
Elisha Marshal of Windsor & Anna Carter,   Feb. 16, 1791
Levi Ward & Mehitable Hand of Guilford,   March 28, 1791
William White & Juliana Pierson, N. Killingworth,
    April 10, 1791
Jonathan Kilburn of Haddam & Elizabeth Farnham,
    April 21, 1791
Benjamin Crane & Elizabeth Dibble,   May 26, 1791
Elias Crane & Mary Rossetter,   May 27, 1791
Job Tuly & Lydia Field,   Nov. 27, 1791
Rufus Kelley & Deborah Buel,   Dec. 25, 1791
Cornelius Chittenden & Rachel Porter,   Dec. 29, 1791
Milton Graves of E. Guilford & Lucy Buel,   Feb. 1, 1792
Francis Griswold & Sarah Buel,   Feb. 2, 1792
Ebenezer Redfield & Phebe Dibble,   Feb. 4, 1792
Jedediah Smith of Canaan & Lydia Crane,   Feb. 5, 1792
Lemuel Wellman & Elizabeth Buel,   March 1, 1792
David Dibble, 2d, & Phebe Redfield,   April 11, 1792
Timothy Crane & Grace Hull,   May 3, 1792

Ezra Crane & Elizabeth Lane,	May 26, 1792
Christopher Ely of Lyme & Martha Elliot,	May 28, 1792
Aron Baldwin & Lucy Redfield,	Sept. 22, 1792
Ariel Bradley of Salsbury & Cloe Lane,	Sept. 27, 1792
John Wright & Cloe Hull,	Oct. 1, 1792
John Turner & Elizabeth Chatfield, N. Killingworth,	
	Dec. 26, 1792
Hezekiah Lane & Rebecca Carter,	Dec. 26, 1792
Thomas Skinner of Haddam & Eunice Crover (?) of Guilford,	July, 1793
Samuel Beebe of Saybrook & Susanna Chatfield,	
	Sept. 17, 1793
Abner Farnham & Grace Lane,	Feb. 24, 1794
George Hull & Temperance Northam,	March 2, 1794
Russel Doud of Guilford & Phebe Hurd,	March 12, 1794
Moses Frances of Granby & Elizabeth Keley,	May 22, 1794
Robert Griffing & Abigail Peck,	June 28, 1794
Thomas Griffeth & Hannah Tooly,	Aug. 14, 1794
Samuel Kelley, 2d, & Julia Hull,	Oct. 13, 1794
Bildad Seymor of Colebrook & Jemima Hurd,	Oct. 16, 1794
Nathan Lane & Mary Kelley, or Kellcey,	Nov. 26, 1794
Caleb Hubbard of York State & Mary Hull,	Dec. 2, 1794
Micajah Griffin & Julia Crane,	Dec. 21, 1794
Thomas Homes & Mehitable Buel,	Dec. 28, 1794
Josiah Carter & Avis, or Nois, Kelley,	Feb., 1795
Peter Ward & Sarah Hilliard,	March 2, 1795
Jared Buel & Lydia Kelley,	March 22, 1795
Gideon Kelley & Polly Dibble,	May 25, 1795
John Wellman & Lucy Stevens,	June 18, 1795
Dorance Kirtland & Fannie Field of Saybrook,	June 26, 1795
Benajah Leffingwell of Norwich & Polly Morgan,	
	Aug. 27, 1795
Benjamin Grannis of New Haven & Polly Willcox,	
	Sept. 20, 1795
John Shelden of Massachusetts & Sarah Stevens,	
	Sept. 27, 1795
Abel Meggs of Guilford & Deborah Carter,	Dec. 16, 1795
Ebenezer Nichols & Hannah Grinnel,	June 15, 1796
Joseph Hull & Martha Carter,	Nov. 10, 1796

Ashiel Griswold & Abigail Judson,	Nov. 13, 1796
George Merril & Hannah Willcox,	Nov. 13, 1796
Stephen Willcox & Sarah Davis,	Jan. 10, 1797
James Dee of Saybrook & Cloe Merrils,	Jan. 15, 1797
John Ely & Abigail Lay at Pt. Change,	June 7, 1797
Wise Chittenden & Hulda Buel,	Oct. 5, 1797
Erasmus Sawyear of Haddam & Easter Kelley,	Oct. 9, 1797
Enoch Smith & widow Hannah Peck,	Dec. 30, 1797
Elijah Griffeth & Sally Hurd,	Jan. 13, 1798
Lewis Post & Weltha Hurd,	Jan. 25, 1798
Benona Hillard & Patience Pierson,	Jan. 29, 1798
Samuel Elliot & Jane Towner,	Feb. 15, 1798
William Carter & Catharine Rutty (?),	June 11, 1798
Joseph Willcox, 3d, & Mabel Carter,	Aug. 9, 1798
John Wright & Amanda Hurd,	Sept. 23, 1798
Hiel Brockway of Lyme & Phebe Merrell,	Oct. 7, 1798
Joel Kelley & Submit Porter,	Jan. 7, 1799
Jonathan Wright & Hannah Carter,	March 11, 1799
Is—hi (?) Parmele & Esther Buel,	March 13, 1799
John Niles of York State & Hannah Elliot,	May 13, 1799
Abner Kirtland of Saybrook & Hester Wright,	Sept. 29, 1799
Partridge G. Lane & Thankful Hull,	Dec. 7, 1799
Samuel Shelden of Mass. & Thankful Stevens,	Dec. 29, 1799

WETHERSFIELD—ROCKY HILL.

HARTFORD COUNTY.

(See Book III.)

The town of Rocky Hill was incorporated May, 1843, and taken from Wethersfield. The Congregational Church at Rocky Hill—formerly called Stepney—was organized June 7, 1727, being the Third Society of Wethersfield. The marriages recorded as below.

John Wells & Martha Belding,	Nov. 26, 1766
Thomas Russel & Elizabeth Goodrich,	winter, 1766
John Morton & Mary Marsh,	March 26, 1766
Daniel Warner & widow Sarah Griswold,	Sept. 24, 1766
David Smith & Temperance Goodrich,	Sept. 25, 1766
Elisha Calendar & Sarah Crane,	Sept. 25, 1766

Nathaniel Robbins & Elizabeth Deming, Oct. 29, 1766
Ebenezer Miller of Middletown & Jerusha Goodrich,
June 18, 1767
Ebenezer Stoddard & Deborah Williams, Oct., 1767
Eben. Welton of Farmington & Olive Collins, Nov., 1767
Roger Bull & Ruth Russel, Nov. 19, 1767
George Stomer & Margaret Ebro, 1767
Joseph Edwards of Middletown & Eleanor Bulkley,
Feb. 10, 1768
Abijah Marks & Rhoda Latimore, April 21, 1768
Dick, servant Elias Williams, & Rose, servant David
Webb, May, 1768
Solomon Belding & Elizabeth Rockwell, June 27, 1768
John Grimes & Bina Smith, Oct., 1768
Eliel Williams & Comfort Morton, Jan. 26, 1769
Peter Bulkley & Christian Smith, Jan. 26, 1769
David Belding & Hepzibah Goodrich, Aug. 3, 1769
Alexander Grimes & Mary Dunn, Aug. 17, 1769
Samuel Foster & Elizabeth Webb, Sept. 4, 1769
Josiah Butler & Martha Riley, Oct. 16, 1769
Elisha Butler & Eunice Williams, Oct. 19, 1769
Daniel Griswold & Jerusha Gibbs, Nov. 23, 1769
Eben. Ranney of Middletown & Lois Blyn, Nov. 30, 1769
Bildad Belding & Mary Riley, Feb. 14, 1770
David Riley & Rachel Curtiss, April 12, 1770
Jacob Webster of Glastenbury & Abigail Goodrich,
May 13, 1770
James Hale & Sarah Forbes, Dec. 30, 1770
John Robbins & Sarah Wright, Jan. 10, 1771
Josiah Grimes, Jr., & Abigail Goodrich, Jan. 17, 1771
Michael ——— & Lydia Taylor, Jan. 23, 1771
Oliver Goodrich, Jr., & Sarah ———, 1771
Isaac Buchork & ——— Deming, April 16, 1771
Jesse Williams & Lois Collins, Sept. 19, 1771
Abner Belding & Mary Standish, Oct. 24, 1771
Edward Bulkley & Rachel Pomeroy, Oct. 27, 1771
Appleton Holmes & Lydia Goodrich, Nov. 14, 1771
Simon Giffin & Lydia Crane, Dec. 12, 1771
Simeon Richards & Anna Wright, Feb. 6, 1772

Wait Dickeman & Abigail Russel,	March 19, 1772
Josiah Wolcott & Prudence Warner,	March 25, 1772
James Mitchel & Hannah Warner,	March 30, 1772
Simeon Robbins & Sarah Rose,	April 8, 1772
Seth Belding & Christian Dickenson,	April 16, 1772
John Wright & Martha Robbins,	April 16, 1772
Nathaniel Hurlburt, Jr., & Susanna Adams,	April 27, 1772
Joseph Riley & Chloe Griswold,	Sept., 1772
Justus Blyn & Margaret Crawfoot,	Sept., 1772
Ozias Dickenson & ——— Goodrich,	Oct., 1772
Joseph Neff (X) & Esther Webb,	Nov. 5, 1772
James Belding & Dorcas Goodrich,	Nov. 5, 1772
Jacob Robbins & Chloe Williams,	Dec. 10, 1772
James Stanley & Sarah Butler,	Jan. 21, 1773
David Riley & Sarah Goodrich,	May 17, 1773
Israel Cowing & Lois Standish,	May 27, 1773
John Gibbs & Elizabeth Weed,	May 13, 1773
Josiah Grimes, Jr., & Mehitable Warner,	June 14, 1773
Samuel Burr of Hartford & Rebecca Stillman,	June 17, 1773
Ashbel Riley & Jane Aurolt (?),	July 27, 1773
John Mygate & Elizabeth Bulkley,	Aug. 26, 1773
Moses Lockwood & Sarah Bunce,	Sept. 9, 1773
John Taylor of Glastonbury & Phebe Chambers,	
	Sept. 25, 1773
Amos Belding & Comfort Blyn,	Oct. 25, 1773
Hosea Blyn & Ruth Smith,	Nov. 8, 1773
Edward Bulkley & Prudence Williams,	Nov. 2, 1773
George Wolcott & Elizabeth Nott,	March, 1774
Micah Goodrich & Elizabeth Hills,	March 17, 1774
John Saunders of Litchfield & Martha Russel,	
	March 17, 1774
Thomas Bunce & Eunice Dickenson,	April 7, 1774
Lemuel Hurlburt & Tabitha Nott,	Dec. 22, 1774
Solomon Griswold & Sarah Deming,	Feb. 2, 1775
John Bulkley & Mary Robbins,	March 2, 1775
James Price & Elizabeth Boardman,	Dec. 4, 1775
Benjamin Butler & Eunice Robbins,	Dec. 13, 1775
Jonathan Price & Patience Collins,	Dec. 11, 1775
William Bulkley & Olive Williams,	Jan. 31, 1776

Eli Deming & Sarah Ames,	Feb. 8, 1776
Joseph Bulkley & Mary Williams,	May 3, 1776
Solomon Bulkley & Martha Williams,	June 6, 1776
Jona'n Hand of Long Island & Abigail Weed,	Feb. 7, 1781
Justus Bulkley & Mabel Boardman,	March 22, 1781
Eben. Curtiss & Rebecca Dickenson,	April 4, 1781
Giles Wright & Abiah Dickenson,	April 12, 1781
Roger Brown of Stamford & Mehitable Nott,	April 22, 1781
Hosea Bulkley & Abigail Griswold,	May 1, 1781
Robert Hurlburt & Mehitable Collins,	July 5, 1781
Elijah Boardman & Mercy Nott,	Sept. 16, 1781
Joshua William A. B. & Mary Webb,	Oct. 24, 1781
Josiah Dickeman & Lucy Belding,	Dec. 6, 1781
Samuel Dimock & Rebecca Bulkley,	July 4, 1782
Jeremiah Parker of L. I. & Eunice Goodrich,	July 11, 1782
Thomas Belding & Mehitable Harris,	Aug. 8, 1782
Levi Warner & Anna Butler of Middletown,	Sept. 1, 1782

Newport, servant of Elisha Calender, & Rose, servant
of Elisha Wolcott,   Oct. 10, 1782

Thomas Coit of Norwich & Sarah Chester,	Oct. 16, 1782
John Treat & Prudence Hanmore,	Oct. 16, 1782
Charles Bulkley & Eunice Robbins,	Oct. 24, 1782
Elvin Bigalow of Hartford & Hannah Curtiss,	Oct. 24, 1782
Ezekiel Goodrich & Elizabeth Warner,	Jan. 1, 1783
Amasa Adams & widow Sarah Griswold,	Jan. 15, 1783
Elisha Wetherel & Mary Bulkley,	Jan. 26, 1783
Silas Belden & Ruth Beckley,	March 4, 1783
William Williams & Sarah Williams,	March 20, 1783
Jonathan Price & Jemima Goodrich,	April 17, 1783

Samuel Lee of New Hartford & Mehitable Robbins,
                                                        May 22, 1783
Hartwell Barnes of Farmington & Hannah Clark,
                                                        May 27, 1783
Elisha Boardman of Middletown & Mary Wright,
                                                        May 29, 1783

William Goodrich & Mehitable ——lk——,	Aug. 28, 1783
Simeon Butler & Anna Marsh,	Sept. 18, 1783
Filer Goodrich & Lucretia Williams,	Oct. 9, 1783

Solomon Savage of Middletown & Lydia Bulkley,
                                                        Nov. 27, 1783

Jesse Sanford & Eleanor Collins,   Dec. 23, 1783
Jeremiah Rash (?) & Anna Collins,   Jan. 22, 1784
Levi Smith & Sarah Collins,   Jan. 29, 1784
Richard Butler & Lois Goodrich,   Feb. 5, 1784
George Abby of Chatham & Mary Brooks,   Feb. 5, 1784
Simeon Williams & widow Eunice Butler,   Feb. 15, 1784
John Williams & Eunice Bull,   May 6, 1784
Daniel Wright of Farmington & Sarah Wilkinson,
                                                     June 24, 1784
Jason Bordman & Hepzibah Curtiss,   July 7, 1784
Samuel Stebbins & Sarah Boardman,   Aug. 12, 1784
John Sutler of Claverack & Anna Reynolds,   Sept. 13, 1784
Solomon Blyn & Desire Andrews,   Sept. 30, 1784
William Weare & Martha Miller,   Oct. 30, 1784
Eli Goodrich & Rhoda Williams,   Nov. 11, 1784
John Robbins, Esq., & Mary Russel of late Rev.
     Mr. Russel,   Nov. 25, 1784
William Nott & Elizabeth Goodrich,   Nov. 28, 1784
Israel Goodrich & Mercy Whit——,   Jan. 4, 1785
Anthony Sizer (?) & Lucretia Wa—— of Middletown,
                                                     Jan. 4, 1785
Oliver Beckley & Lucinda Beldin,   Jan. 19, 1785
David Beckley, Jr., & Eunice Williams,   March 31, 1785
Theodore Wolcott & Rhoda Good——,   April 11, 1785
Isaac Lewis & Lydia Judd, both of Southington,
                                                     June 25, 1785
Benjamin Ames & Lois Warner,   Sept. 8, 1785
Richard Belden & Mercy Collins,   Sept. 28, 1785
Samuel Reading & Hulda Miller, Middletown,   Oct. 2, 1785
Ephraim Covel of Glastenbury & Abigail Riley, Oct. 19, 1785
Eben Mitchel Holden of Granby & Hepzibah Good-
     rich,   Nov. 3, 1785
Abra'm Belding & Mary Wright,   Nov. 13, 1785
Joseph Higgins & Nancy Williams,   Dec. 18, 1785
Jacob Griswold & Rachel Warner,   Dec. 25, 1785
John Myears of Penn. & Mahitable Riley,   Jan. 5, 1786
Joseph Brooks & Lucy Smith of Glastenbury, —— 17, 1786
Zadoch Selah of Stamford & Nancy Miller,   —— 23, 1786
Alfred Riley & Mehitable Goodrich,   —— 23, 1786

Wait Curtiss & Milicent Goodrich,	March 16,	1786
Levi Williams & Jerusha Williams,	April 13,	1786
Thomas Holmes & Hannah Goodrich,	May 3,	1786
Josiah Wells & Mary Tucker,	May 11,	1786
Andrew M'Comb of Salem, Mass. & Rebecca Goodrich,		
	May 28,	1786
Aaron Bull & Lydia Williams,	Aug. 9,	1786
Gideon Goff & Anne Nott,	Aug. 21,	1786
Thomas Palmer (a free negro) & Jinny, servant of		
John Robbins, Esq.,	Aug. 23,	1786
Stephen Tilden of Lebanon & Dorothy Goodrich,		
	—— 16,	1787
Jonathan Bulkley & Mary Edwards,	Jan. 16,	1787
Jonathan Collins & Chloe Curtiss,	—— 25,	1787
Eli Marsh & Azubah Butler,	—— 25,	1787
L. D. & Mary Beckley of Worthington,	——	
David Miller & Mercy Mildrum,	——	
Elias Williams & Mary Dimock,	——	
Gideon Goodrich & Eunice Warner,	——	
Joseph Cleveland of Tratown, Mass., & Rebecca Collins,	——	
Jonas Becket of Bristol & Hannah Deming,	——	
Isaac Goodrich & Honor Goodrich,	——	
Moses Wilcox of Colebrook & Lydia Lancy,	——	
James Hammond of Hartford & Rebecca Wilkinson,	——	
Calvin Winchel of Berlin & Chloe Goodrich,	——	
Hubbard Goodrich & Susanna Graves of Granville, Mass.,	——	
Silas Walton & Rosetta Belding,	——	
Stephen Butler & Ruth Russel,		1788
Ichabod Goodrich & Bina Goodrich,	——	
Elijah Robbins & Martha Griswold,		
John Belding & Dorothy Holmes,		1788
James Prickard of Boston & Wealthy Goodrich,		1788
Elisha Coleman & Hannah Loveland,	—— 5,	1788
Jacob Riley & widow Ruth Bull,	——	
James Adam & Martha Wright,	——	
Levi Holmes & Molly Corey,	——	
—— Bordman & Rachel Riley,		1789

Thomas Riley & Honor Belding,	March 5,	1789
Moses Williams & Mary North,	July 2,	1789
Jonathan Curtiss & Hannah Wright,	Aug. 5,	1789
Joseph Dimock, Jr., & Sarah Warner,	Aug. 12,	1789
Jasper Lacy of Suffield & Abigail Bulkley,	Sept. 9,	1789
Dennis Myers & Reny Robinson,	Sept. 13,	1789
Wait Robbins & Mabel Bulkley,	Nov. 9,	1789
Jonathan Hand & Hannah Beachgood,	Feb. 7,	1790
Giles Savage of Middletown & Olive Smith,	March 14,	1790
Justus Robbins & Clarinda Huntington,	March 31,	1790
Jason Robbins & Honor Riley,	April 1,	1790
Frederic Bordman & Chloe Bulkley,	July 28,	1790
George Price & Mahetabel Foster,	Aug. 8,	1790
Levi Bordman & Elisabeth Warner,	Sept. 2,	1790
John Riley, Jr., & Huldah Robbins,	Oct. 31,	1790
Ezekiel P. Belden & Mary Parsons of Amherst, Mass.,		
	Nov. 1,	1790
William Ames & Jerusha Goodrich,	Nov. 4,	1790
Josiah Butler of Middletown & Elisabeth Russel,		
	Nov. 11,	1790
Josiah Gilbert of Berlin & Hannah Tryon of ——,		
	Nov. 11,	1790
David Blyn & Prudence Goodrich,	Dec. 14,	1790
Benjamin J. Griswold & Abigail Grimes,	Jan. 13,	1791
Silas Goff & Rosanna Goodrich,	Jan. 13,	1791
Levi Goff & Elizabeth Belden,	Jan. 27,	1791
John Wright & Sarah Culver of Bristol,	March 24,	1791
William Webb & Charlotte Griswold,	April 10,	1791
Luther Patterson of Berlin & Abigail Miller,	April 28,	1791
Charles Morgan of Hartford & Elizabeth Bordman,		
	May 15,	1791
Pownal Deming of Hartford & Mehetable Bordman,		
	May 29,	1791
Bishop Phelps of —— & Patty Storrs,	Oct. 2,	1791
Reuben Robinson of Berlin & Hannah Curtis,	Oct. 5,	1791
Roger Riley & Augusta Griswold,	Oct. 24,	1791
Luman Savage of Berlin & Sarah Goff,	Nov. 24,	1791
Benajah Bowers of —— & widow Esther Benton,		
	Nov. 27,	1791

James Riley & Esther Goodrich.	Jan. 8, 1792
Asahel Savage & Abigail Deming,	March 22, 1792
Justus Belden & Mary Riley,	April 17, 1792
Frederic Riley & Rachel Williams,	April 23, 1794
Enos Robbins & Dorothy Williams,	—— 27, 1794

REV. CALVIN CHAPIN ORDAINED, APRIL 30, 1794.

Moses Dickinson & Sarah Wright,	—— 13, 1794
Richard Williams & Hannah Danforth,	Sept. 28, 1794
Luther Wilcox of Middletown & Huldah Pulsifer of Glastenbury,	Oct. 1, 1794
Asahel Merriam & Hannah Robbins,	Oct. 1, 1794
George Risley & Jinny Scovel,	Oct. 22, 1794
Holmes Greenwood & Mary Goodrich,	Nov. 11, 1794
Amos Miller & Abigail Goodrich,	Dec. 7, 1794
Thomas Matson of Glastonbury & Abial Collins,	Dec. 21, 1794
Humphry Woodhouse & Rebecca Adams,	Jan. 1, 1795
William Holden of Granville, Mass., & Prudence Belden,	Feb. 21, 1795
Rev. Calvin Chapin & Jerusha Edwards of New Haven, by Doctor Edwards,	—— 2, 1795
Chester Williams & Patty Goodrich,	Aug. 16, 1795
Noah Shepard of Chatham & Ruth Corey of Wethersfield,	Aug. 30, 1795
Daniel Deming & Fanny Calendar,	Oct. 11, 1795
Aaron Hosford, Jr., & Roxy Goodrich,	Nov. 8, 1795
Daniel Edwards, Jr., of Middletown & Onner Bulkley,	Nov. 16, 1795
Russel Bull & Lucy Warner,	Dec. 17, 1795
Edward Culver & Hetty Williams, daughter of Eliel & Comfort (Morton) Williams,	Jan. 21, 1796
Elizur Goodrich & widow Martha Bulkley,	March 6, 1796
Charles Lyon & Lois Grimes,	March 13, 1796
Thomas Morton & Olive Dickinson,	April 14, 1796
William Ames & Lydia Callender,	April 14, 1796
Josiah Edwards & Rhoda Bulkley,	April 14, 1796
Theodore Blyn & Hannah Misner,	May 21, 1796

Mingo Horkins of Simsbury & Violet London,   July 3, 1796
Simeon Robbins, Jr., & Martha Danforth, daughter of
    Thomas & Elisabeth (Tallman) Danforth,   July 7, 1796
Leonard Miller & Lydia Belden,   Aug. 7, 1796
Jonathan Thayer & Honor Edwards,   Sept. 1, 1796
John Leeds of Stamford & Honor Williams,   Dec. 5, 1796
Salmon Booth of Berlin & Lois Wright,   April 19, 1797
William Blynn & Sally Treat of Glastonbury,   May 10, 1797
Amos Sanford & Lydia Blyn,   May 10, 1797
Samuel Wheat of Chatham & Mabel Collins of
    Glastonbury,   July 5, 1797
Aaron Belden, Jr., & Rhoda Wright,   July 30, 1797
Lemuel Goodrich & Harriet Deming,   Aug. 20, 1797
Samuel Smith of Middlebury & Amelia Goodrich of
    Glastenbury,   Sept. 28, 1797
Luther Goodrich & Elizabeth Bell of Glastenbury,
    Nov. 1, 1797
Asahel Tenan of Chatham & Edna Chapman of Glas-
    tenbury,   Nov. 1, 1797
Luther Goodrich of East Haddam & Sally Danforth,
    daughter of Thomas & Elisabeth (Tallman) Dan-
    forth,   Nov. 16, 1797
Joel Morgan of West Springfield & Eunice Goodrich,
    Dec. 3, 1797
Justus Belden & Hannah Marton,   Dec. 3, 1797
Silas Williams & Sally Griswold,   Dec. 24, 1797
Josiah Butler & Mary Robbins, daughter of Simeon,
    Sen.,   Dec. 24, 1797
Rufus Russel & Abigail Riley,   Jan. 15, 1798
Joseph Bunce & Rhoda Porter,   Jan. 29, 1798
Russel Mackee of East Hartford & Nabby Ames, Feb. 4, 1798
—— Bulkley of Somers & Anna Howard,   Feb. 6, 1798
Alpha Tucker of Bolton & Elizabeth Misner,   Feb. 12, 1798
Elizur Dickinson & Polly Bunce,   March 11, 1798
Thomas Steel, Jr., of Lenox, Mass., & Candace Bord-
    man,   May 13, 1798
Seth Dickinson & Jerusha Goodrich,   May 20, 1798
Asa Robbins of the old Society & Ab—— Daniels of
    New London,   June 21, 1798

Wait Goodrich & Olive Williams, daughter of Eliel W.,

June 26, 1798

Davis Dimock & Eleanor Williams,   July 8, 1798

Charles Bulkley of Williamstown, Mass., & the widow

Prudence Bulkley,   August 27, 1798

Joseph Clough of Springfield, Mass., & Fanny Good-

rich,   Sept. 10, 1798

Ethan Holmes & Christain Blin,   Oct. 21, 1798

John Benton & Mitty Warner,   Nov. 29, 1798

Samuel Dimock & Mary Goodrich,   March 25, 1799

Luther Colton of Long Meadow & widow Mehitable

Deming,   April 2, 1799

——— Clark of Berlin & Asenath Miller,   April 16, 1799

Wyllys Williams & Rhoda Bulkley,   June 19, 1799

Austin Mygatt of Berlin & Rhoda Russel,   July 22, 1799

Ezekiel Tryon & Betsey Harris, both of Glastenbury,

Aug. 11, 1799

——— Bidwel & Betsey Strong, both of Glastenbury,

Oct. 2, 1799

Seth Hart & widow Lydia Bull,   Nov. 10, 1799

Daniel Hubbard of Berlin & Sarah Belden,   Dec. 15, 1799

ASHFORD.

WINDHAM COUNTY.

(See Book I.)

The town of Ashford was named in 1710. The First Congregational Church records may be found in Book I. The Second Church at Westford, organized February 11, 1768, furnishes the following marriages.

Cyrill Brown of Woodstock & Mary Allin,   Sept. 15, 1768

William Walker & Hannah Smith,   Sept. 15, 1768

Samuel Walker & Bethiah Crary,   Nov. 17, 1768

Francis Curtis & Betty Robins,   Nov. 17, 1768

Ransom Curtis & Ellice Whiton,   Dec. 8, 1768

John Walker & Mary Ann Cilborne,   March 2, 1769

Abraham Foster & Bethiah Old,   Sept. 21, 1769

Samuel Knox, Jr., & Phebe Preston,   Oct. 12, 1769

Goold Stiles & Delight Broton, both of Willington,
Feb. 7, 1770
Joseph Farnam & Katharine Spring, March 15, 1770
Squir Hill & Dorothy Walker, Oct. 25, 1770
Peter Post of Hebron & Mrs. Ruth Walker, Nov. 28, 1770
Jacob Orcut of Willington & Abigail Chaffee, Jan. 1, 1771
Enos Preston & Abigail Kendal, May 28, 1771
David Robins & Lucy Knox, Nov. 6, 1771
Henry Cleaveland of Mansfield & Elizabeth Rice of
Willington, Dec. 26, 1771
James Jalley & Eunice Fox, March 2, 1772
Nathan Lamb of Palmer & Abiah Preston, April 8, 1772
Benjamin Chapman & Loas Hill, Aug. 27, 1772
Doctor Thomas Huntington & Molly Ward, Jan. 7, 1773
William Knox & Hannah Robbins, April 7, 1773
Henry Curtis & Elizabeth Davison, Sept. 6, 1773
Hovey Preston & Phebe Barney, Nov. 23, 1773
John Ward & Jennet Knox, Dec. 7, 1773
Amasa Coy of Union & Sarah Hill, Feb. 10, 1774
Jonathan Sibley of Willington & Patty Brooks, Nov. 17, 1774
Elias Burbank of New Molbury & Mrs. Meriam Dim-
mick, Dec. 15, 1774
Timothy Roberson of Woodstock & widow Anne
Chaffee, Jan. 5, 1775
James Averel & Mrs. Mary Parsons of Somers, March 6, 1775
Lemual Griggs of Stafford & Hannah (Grosevarnor (?),
March 23, 1775
Jonathan Hayward & Lydia Davison, Nov. 14, 1775
Capt. Jedediah Amidown of Willington & Hannah
Walker, June 11, 1778
John Pool, Jr., of Willington & Elizabeth Burdwin,
July 3, 1778
Stephen Convers & Sarah Kimbal, Oct. 12, 1778
Rev. Nicholas Dudley of Townsend, Vermont, & Pris-
cilla Whiton, Nov. 12, 1778
Samuel Horris, or Harris, of Mansfield & Elizabeth
Walker, Nov. 26, 1778
John Thompson & Lois Cushman, Jan. 14, 1779
William Heth & Catherine Robbins, Feb. 4, 1779

Amos Smith & Anne Chaffee,	May 18,	1779
Lovel Bullock of Gilford, Vermont, & widow Jennet Ward,	June 14,	1779
Thomas Davison & Eunice Pearl of Willington,	Aug. 26,	1779
William Davison & Molly Chapman,	Aug. 31,	1779
Zere Preston & Mary Ann Walker,	Oct. 7,	1779
Capt. Henry Wells of Hopkinton & Nancy Shirtleff,	Nov. 29,	1779
Elezer Heth & Abigail Robbins,	Dec. 16,	1779
Titus Darrow of Enfield & Anna Hill,	Jan. 17,	1780
Samuel Kymbol & Betty Pearl of Willington,	April 26,	1781
Ebenezer Humphrey & Lucy Robbins,	June 19,	1781
Emery Russel of Springfield & Elenor Smith,	Nov. 1,	1781
Christopher Chapman & Abigail Chaffee of Woodstock,	Dec. 4,	1781
Amos Bugbie & Martha Woodward,	March 21,	1782
John Davis of Willington & Tryphena Oulds,	March 28,	1782
Samuel Strickland of Stafford & Esther Brooks,	April 11,	1782
Jedediah Wadkins & Abigail Gould,	July 3,	1782
Elijah Hanks & Mary Walker,	Aug. 14,	1782
Jacob Goodell of Monson, Mass., & Mrs. Mary Preston,	Nov. 2,	1782
Levi Wakefield of Stafford & Grace Walker,	Feb. 20,	1783
Stephen Butler & Mehitophel Robinson, both of Mansfield,	March 6,	1783
John Woodward & Hannah Bicknell,	April 24,	1783

LITCHFIELD—MORRIS.

LITCHFIELD COUNTY.

The town of Morris was incorporated May, 1859, previously a part of Litchfield. The Congregational Church in Morris, formerly called Litchfield South Farms, was organized in 1768. The few marriages recorded are as follows.

Eliad Gibbs & Nancy Riggs,	1787
John Waugh & ——— Smith,	1787
Alexander Long & Achsah Hollibart,	1788
Alexander Ranne & Mrs. Zerepta Butler,	1788

Jonah Brooks & Lucy Church,	1788
—— Janes & Meriam Marsh,	1789
—— Hatch & —— Camp,	1789
—— Lovel & Polly Cole,	1789
David Pamila & Mrs. L. Barnard,	1789
John Farnum & Lecty Lindsley,	1790
Dr. Israel Spencer & Polly Waugh,	1790
Ebenezer Benton, Jr., & Lois Farnum,	1790
James Woodruff & Mrs. Salley Bartholimew,	Aug. 1, 1790
Thomas Sterling & Mahitabel Norton,	Aug. 23, 1790
Jesse Spencer & Mrs. Lucy Woodruff,	Oct. 14, 1790
John Perkins & Elisabeth Gibbs,	Nov. 10, 1790
Samuel Ensign, Jr., & Abigail Gibbs,	Jan. 7, 1791
Elisha Mansfield & Becky Camp,	Jan. 11, 1791
—— Norsford & Salley Smedley,	Feb. 2, 1791
Samuel Frost & Electy Harrison,	March 14, 1791
Joseph Mansfield & Mary Ann Harrison,	April 6, 1791
Isaac Ensign & Sabre Camp,	June 5, 1791
Timothy Foot & Abigail Stoddard,	Oct. 2, 1791
—— Kilburne & Becky Waugh,	Oct. 6, 1791
Elijah Smedley & Lucy Gibbs,	Oct. 15, 1791
Orrange Emons & Polly Doolittle,	July, 1792
—— Smith & Betsey Sears,	Aug. 3, 1792
Arthur Bostic & Lotty Griswold,	March 21, 1793
Roger Marsh & Phebe Orton,	Aug. 20, 1794
Nathan Woodruff & Chary Deforest,	Jan. 26, 1795
Dan Waugh & Anne Smedley,	Feb. 16, 1795
Stephen Foot & Rhoda Hand,	March 25, 1795
Joseph Burgess & Esther Bishop,	May, 1795
—— Bunael & Damaris Orton,	Dec. 24, 1795
Hezekiah Murray & Eunice Camp,	May 29, 1796
Simeon Harrison & Hannah Harrison,	June 2, 1796
Moody Chase & Lucy Farnum,	June 6, 1796
Mr. Westover & Miss Kilborn,	June 25, 1796
Isaac Stodderd & Lovicy Emons,	July 14, 1796
Mr. Martin of Woodbury & Miss Hand of Bethlem,	
	Jan. 9, 1797
Gideon Gallop & Lucy Waugh,	Jan. 26, 1797
John Clinton & Arhoda Peck,	June 22, 1797

Isaac Woodruff & Clarissa Peck,	June 22, 1797
John Clark & Ireny Gibbs,	Aug. 23, 1797
Clement Chase & Lucy Murray,	Sept. 10, 1797
Marvin Sanford & Anna Lindley,	Sept. 10, 1797
Leman Woodruff & Rebecca Harrison,	Oct. 31, 1797
Mr. Clark & Miss Frisbie, both of Bethlem,	Nov., 1797
Charles Goodwin & Ursule Hungerford,	Dec. 4, 1797
David Little & Susanna Waugh,	Dec. 10, 1797
Luman Westover & Sabre Smedley,	April 25, 1798
Enos Stoddard & Orrelia Bacon,	May 14, 1798
Joseph Bradley & Lucy Stoddard,	May 24, 1798
John Mansfield & Dolly Steel,	May 27, 1798
Henry Thomson & Mrs. Lotty Bostwick,	Sept., 1798
Thomas Doolittle & Polly Clark,	Sept., 1798
John Peck & Sally Beckwith,	Oct. 28, 1798
Stephen Sanford & Olive Woodruff,	Jan. 20, 1799
Heman Bissel & Susanna Camp,	June 9, 1799
Samuel Orton & Martha Bunts,	Sept., 1799
——— Allen & Rachel Hand,	Oct., 1799
Martin Kellogg & Elizabeth Waugh,	Nov., 1799
Norman Barns & Abigail Griswold,	Dec. 25, 1799

NORWICH—LISBON.

NEW LONDON COUNTY.

(See Books IV and V.)

The town of Lisbon was incorporated May, 1786. Taken from Norwich. The First Congregational Church in Lisbon was organized in 1723. See Book V. The Church in Hanover of Lisbon was organized in 1766 and furnishes the following marriages.

Moses Martin & Hannah Jupiter,	Dec. 13, 1769
Nathan Carver & Martha Chapman,	April 15, 1770
Joshua French & Hannah Hartshorn,	Feb. 20, 1771
James Bennett & Lydia Williams,	Feb. 24, 1771
Joshua Tracy & Sarah Perkins,	March 6, 1771
Thomas Cotton & Lydia Bates,	April 11, 1771
James Apley & Abigail Williams,	May 29, 1771
Daniel Kirtland & Abigail Knight,	June 23, 1771

Roger Warbey & Molly Mooch (Indians),	Nov. 28, 1771
James Adams & Jerusha Knight,	Feb. 16, 1772
Ebenezer Babcock & Eleanor Knight,	June 11, 1772
Nathaniel Tracy & Susanna Bingham,	July 19, 1772
Rev. John Staples & Susanna Perkins,	Aug. 13, 1772
Elisha Babcock & Elizabeth Wentworth,	Aug. 16, 1772
Jedediah Lathrop & Cirel Perkins,	Oct. 29, 1772
Ezekiel Perrigo & Alice Webb,	Oct. 29, 1772
Elisha Griswold & Lydia Burchard,	Dec. 13, 1772
John Flint & Sarah Tilden,	Dec. 30, 1772
Daniel Ladd & Elizabeth Cada,	Jan. 7, 1773
Zebidee Young & Ann Green,	April 4, 1773
Jesse Finney & Hannah Griswold,	Sept. 30, 1773
Adam Stephens & Patience Rathbun,	Oct. 21, 1773
Jacob Mott & Elizabeth Bates,	Oct. 28, 1773
Benjamin Baker & Lucy Longbottom,	Nov. 25, 1773
Jeremiah Mott & Abigail Stevens,	Nov. 25, 1773
Constant Reynolds & Mary Herrington,	Dec. 2, 1773
Daniel Frost & Phebe Farnam,	Dec. 16, 1773
John Albee & Delight Tilden,	March 2, 1774
Daniel Haynes & Hannah Hunt,	April, 1774
Nathaniel Babcock & Irena Kingsley, Jr.,	April, 1774
David Bottom, Jr., & Eunice Bingham,	Jan. 17, 1775
Nathaniel Fuller & Elizabeth Barber,	Jan. 22, 1775
Daniel Fitts, Jr., & Elizabeth Fuller,	Jan. 23, 1775
Timothy Green & Sarah Rude,	Feb. 19, 1775
Joseph French & Mary King,	March 15, 1775
Silvanus Wentworth & Anna Fuller,	May 21, 1775
William Perigo, Jr., & Lydia Downing,	Dec. 21, 1775
Jeduthun Spencer & Abigail Brown,	Aug. 13, 1776
Robert McThorn & Sarah Perkins,	Aug. 22, 1776
Jabez Fox & Jerusha Perkins,	1777
Ebenezer Webb & Abigail Rude,	1777
Luther Waterman & Phebe Barker,	Jan. 1, 1778
Chirstopher Webb & Olive Brown,	Jan. 8, 1778
John Mott & Eunice Thompson,	April 16, 1778
Lebbens Horton & Rahdilla (?) Griswold,	May 7, 1778
Joseph Burt & Eunice Knight,	May 28, 1778
Samuel Coburn & Anna Webb,	May 31, 1778

Joshua Phinney & Abigail Kingsley,	Oct. 4, 1778
Elijah Wentworth & Ruth Griswold,	Oct. 6, 1778
Jonathan Witter (?) & Lydia Perigo,	Nov. 5, 1778
Richard Winchester & Lydia Dodge,	Nov. 17, 1778
James Snow & Rachel Spalding,	Nov. 18, 1778
Daniel Fisher & Mary Whitney,	Nov. 26, 1778
Daniel Kingsbury & Martha Adams,	Dec. 10, 1778
Levi Case & Roxanna Davidson,	Jan. 11, 1779
Paul Palmer & Sarah Penney,	March 14, 1779
John Hutchins & Sarah Ladd,	March 18, 1779
Gideon Burt & Anna Knight,	Oct. 28, 1779
Benjamin Seabury & Lucretia Kingsbury,	Nov. 11, 1779
Zadoc Brewster & Lucy Knight,	Nov. 21, 1779
Ebenezer Griswold & Sarah Kingsbury,	April 25, 1780
Ephraim Campbell & Ruth Bushnell, Jr.,	May 14, 1780
Uriah Egerton & Anna Smith,	May 16, 1780
Benjamin Hopkins & Dille Prior,	June 19, 1780
Jonah Gross & Sarah Ladd,	June 22, 1780
Samuel Tracy, 3d, & Hannah Storey,	July 3, 1780
Dyer Kingsley & Priscilla Bottom,	Oct. 25, 1780
Ezekiel Phillips & Susanna Scott,	Feb. 7, 1781
Amaziah Winchester & Mary Hatch,	April 25, 1781
Isaac Hyde & Sybil Peck,	May 10, 1781
John Tracy, 4th, & Esther Pride,	May 24, 1781
Isaiah Williams & Alice Brown,	June 14, 1781
James Moss & Louisa Brewster,	July, 1781
John Green & Martha Knight,	Aug. 5, 1781
Nathaniel Brewster & Ruth Dimmock,	Oct. 25, 1781
William Davis & Mary Rathbun,	Oct., 1781
Francis Perkins & Esther Colburn,	Nov. 29, 1781
David Clark & Zerniah Bottom,	March 28, 1782
Enos Wood & Asenath Hazen,	May 2, 1782
Asa Palmer & Mary Kingsbury,	May 30, 1782
Jabez Edwards & Sarah Downing,	Aug. 22, 1782
Solomon Wood & Parthena Hutchins,	Oct. 9, 1782
Alpheus Kingsley & Eunice Williams,	Nov. 21, 1782
Benjamin Peck & Sarah Brown,	Dec. 5, 1782
Ebenezer Cressy & Lydia Stevens,	Dec. 31, 1782
Gershom Hale & Esther Bennett, Jr.,	Jan. 23, 1783

William Haridan & Esther Bennett,	Sept. 11, 1783
Ebenezer Perigo & Mary Rude,	Oct. 9, 1783
Cromwell Bennett & Huldah Bushnell,	Dec. 3, 1783
Reuben Adams & Abigail Lovett,	Dec., 1783
John Cleveland & Jerusha Bushnell,	Dec. 11, 1783
Nathan French & Lydia Tracy,	Jan. 1, 1784
Elkanah Smith & Jane Williams,	Jan. 29, 1784
Eleazar Coffin & Eunice Hazar,	Feb. 12, 1784
Roger Burnham & Clarissa Dimmock,	Feb., 1784
Jesse Bottom & Betty Bennett,	Feb. 19, 1784
Thomas Sly & Anna Rude.	March 21, 1784
Nathaniel Bishop & Anne Haskel,	April 1, 1784
Asa Rathbun & Ruth Kimball,	April 29, 1784
Caleb Bishop & Abigail Rude,	May 3, 1784
Daniel Fitch & Mehitabel Bushnell,	May 4, 1784
Jonas Bond & Mary Wood,	May 19, 1784
John Butt & Susanna Knight,	June 24, 1784
Eleazar Cutler & Hannah Kelley,	Sept. 28, 1784
Wesley Perkins & Sylvina Bottom,	Sept. 29, 1784
Leonard Perkins & Grace Brewster,	Nov. 17, 1784
Daniel Smith & Eunice Pettengel,	Dec. 2, 1784
Jason Bushnell & Hannah Kirtland,	Jan. 20, 1785
Thomas Jewet & Prudence Rude,	Feb. 3, 1785
Jabez Hazen & Peggy Lord,	Feb. 24, 1785
Reuben Finney & Abigail Darbe,	March 30, 1785
Asa Bushnell & Lydia Farnham,	May 29, 1785
Joshua Button & Sarah Smith,	June 14, 1785
Caleb Faulkner & Martha Chadle,	July 13, 1785
Benjamin Smith & Sarah Lyon,	Sept. 22, 1785
Hezekiah Kingsley & Rhoda Peck,	Dec. 8, 1785
John Gallup & Lydia Clark,	Jan. 12, 1786
Othniel Luce & Joanna Kimball,	Feb. 16, 1786
John Norman & Mary Preston,	March 16, 1786
Rufus Kingsley & Lucinda Cutler,	Oct. 12, 1786
Benjamin Wood & Ruhama Bennet,	Nov. 23, 1786
Guy Lester & Cynthia Lawrence,	Dec. 13, 1786
Stephen Richardson & Hannah Rudd,	Dec. 21, 1786
John Bushnell & Edna Brewster,	March 8, 1787
John Austin & Content James,	April 15, 1787

Oliver Spafford & Bethiah William,	May 24, 1787
James Barber & Ruth Stephens,	July 12, 1787
Henry Badger & Eunice Bottom,	Sept. 18, 1787
John Dodge & Martha Shaw,	July 19, 1787
John King & Jane Knight,	Nov. 22, 1787
Benjamin Greenslit & Martha Corey,	Nov. 22, 1787
Zaccheus Abell & Eunice Coburn,	Dec. 6, 1787
Daniel W. Knight & Elizabeth Coburn,	Dec. 6, 1787
Ezekiel Jones & Sarah Davis,	Dec. 24, 1787
Uriah Kingsley & Ruth Y. Bishop,	Jan. 31, 1788
Darius Bottom & Lydia Lawrence,	Feb. 12, 1788
Eli Smith & Anna Bottom,	March 27, 1788
Daniel Denison & Lucy Clarke,	April 24, 1788
Peter Rose & Kesia Kimball,	May 1, 1788
Daniel Bottom & Betsey Hyde,	May 15, 1788
Joseph Bottom & Betsey Cutler,	Oct. 26, 1788
Barnabas Huntington & Abigail Perkins, Jr.,	Nov. 13, 1788
Alexander Gordon & Sarah McKown,	Nov. 27, 1788
Jared Mott & Esther Stanton,	Nov., 1788
Pratt Allen & Rhoda Witter,	Nov., 1788
Thomas Simons & Rebekah Rathbun,	Jan. 13, 1789
Elisha Lillie, Jr., & Lemina Story,	Jan. 22, 1789
Silas Perkins & Abigail B. Bushnell,	Feb. 19, 1789
Isaac Baldwin & Alice Haskell,	Feb. 24, 1789
Samuel Barstow & Anna Fitch,	April 16, 1789
David Knight & Mary Hall,	April 28, 1789
Joseph Phelps & Sarah Hartshorn,	July 1, 1789
Shubeal Button & Amelia Jackson,	July 16, 1789
Samuel James & Lusa Bottom,	Oct. 1, 1789
Oliver Johnson & Martha Perkins,	Oct. 14, 1789
Levi Stevens & Nancy Haskell,	Nov. 24, 1789
Comfort Eames & Joanna Pemroy,	Nov. 25, 1789
David Tracy & Susanna Capron,	Dec. 3, 1789
Chester Lewis & Elizabeth Manning,	Feb. 11, 1790
William Edwards & Anne Downing,	Feb. 16, 1790
Phineas Adams & Lydia Bishop,	April 4, 1790
John Perigo & Lucy Bingham,	April 22, 1790
Simon Kingsley & Anna Williams,	April 25, 1790
Erastus Adams & Polly Brown,	April 29, 1790

Jared Webb & Prudence Mudge,	June 3, 1790
Obadiah Spicer & Anna Rathbon,	July 25, 1790
Jonathan Starr & Mary Bishop,	Aug. 9, 1790
Joseph Whipple & Huldah Clark,	Feb. 3, 1791
Calvin Palmer & Hannah Hartshorn,	Oct. 6, 1791
Simeon Palmer & Clarissa Farnam,	Dec. 1, 1791
Benjamin Burnham, Jr., & Tabitha Perkins,	Jan. 26, 1792
Shubael Durkee & Cynthia Perigo,	Nov. 11, 1792
Roswell Ripley & Susanna Kelley,	Dec. 9, 1792
Joshua Willes & Elizabeth Bushnell,	Feb. 14, 1793
Henry Wethy & Esther Dimmock,	Feb. 21, 1793
George Perigo & Anna Tubbs,	March 7, 1793
Erastus Farnham & Zerviah Knight,	March 21, 1793
Moses Stevens & Susanna Symonds,	June 23, 1793
Increase Hewitt & Clorinda Cutler, or Cutter,	May 19, 1793
Asa Bingham & Hannah Lord,	Dec. 12, 1793
Arza Tracy & Eunice Cutler, Jr.,	June 23, 1794
Crane Knight & Margey Bushnell,	June 23, 1794
Adonijah Knight & Ruby Farnam,	March 27, 1794
Enoch Allen & Betsey Witter,	April 14, 1794
John Williams & Temperance Tubbs,	Aug. 17, 1794
William Perkins & Mary Lee,	Feb. 12, 1795
Daniel Fitch & Zipporah Allen,	March 26, 1795
Asa Phinney & Lydia Appley,	May 28, 1795
Nathaniel Cutler & Mary Kingsley,	Oct. 22, 1795
Vine Cutler & Betsey Bushnell,	Dec. 11, 1795
Rev. Ezra Witter & Eunice Lee, Jr.,	Jan. 21, 1796
Tully Lee & Lois Abell,	May 19, 1796
Joseph Lyon & Susanna Kingsley,	March 6, 1797
Theodore Perkins & Lydia Trift,	Nov. 6, 1797
Solomon Read & Alice Williams,	Feb. 1, 1798
Nathan Brooks & Sally Bingham,	March 6, 1798
Adonijah Kingsley & Hannah Perigo,	Aug. 15, 1798
Edward Parker & Lois Wilson,	Aug. 16, 1798
Azariah Armstrong & Patty Waterman,	Aug. 19, 1798
John Lee & Mary Griffin,	Sept. 30, 1798
Shubael Lamb & Clarissa Bushnell,	Feb. 26, 1799
Jedidiah Brewster & Asenath Budwell,	April 10, 1799
Septimius Lathrop & Elizabeth Perkins,	May 26, 1799

John Kelley & Clarissa Harland,	July 4, 1799
Joseph Symons & Ruth Cutler,	Sept. 8, 1799
Enos Woodworth & Clarissa Burnham,	Oct. 19, 1799
Tracy Robinson & Sally Cleaveland,	Nov. 3, 1799
Oliver Abell & Mary Lord, Jr.,	Nov. 19, 1799
Daniel Fuller & Delight Smith,	Nov. 28, 1799
Charles Lord & Abigail Lee,	Dec. 19, 1799

MIDDLETOWN.

MIDDLESEX COUNTY.

(See Book II.)

Middletown was incorporated September, 1651, and named in 1653. The First Church in Middletown was organized November 4, 1668. The following cover the records.

David Fellows of Canaan & Susanna Baker,	June 2, 1762
Abijah Russell & Jemima Tryol,	July 1, 1762
Charles Hamlin & Elizabeth Rogers,	Aug. 1, 1762
James Hopkins & Mehetable Merriman,	Aug. 5, 1762
Rev. Roger Newton of Greenfield & Mrs. Abigaile Hall,	
	Aug. 26, 1762
John Crane of Wethersfield & Ruth Marcam,	Aug. 26, 1762
Josiah ——— & Elizabeth ———,	Sept. 16, 1762
Asa Fuller & Mary Goodwin,	Oct. 17, 1762
Abijah Curtis of Newton & Sarah Birdsey of Middlefield,	
	Oct. 29, 1762
Jonathan Southway & Martha Sage,	Nov. 29, 1762
Benjamin Still (lately moved into the place) & Christian Prior,	
	Dec. 21, 1762
Jonathan Allen of Northampton & Sarah Miller of Middlefield,	
	Dec. 28, 1762
Isaac Miller & Hannah Coe, both of Middlefield,	
	Dec. 28, 1762
Joseph Emmons of East Haddam & Louise Gilbert,	
	Jan. 6, 1763
Sam. Rockwell & widow Abigail Gobafon,	Jan. 20, 1763
Gale Goodwin & Abigail Starr,	March 1, 1763

Abiatha Squires of Durham & Mary Dudley,   March 9, 1763
Return Meigs & Jane Doane,   March 20, 1763
Beriah Wetmore, Jr., & widow Abigail Bacon,   June 2, 1763
Widower Robert Lee & widow Hannah Cornwall,
                                              June 20, 1763
Deacon Jonathan Allen & widow Rebecca Wetmore,
                                               July 6, 1763
William Weir & Rachel Arnold,   July 6, 1763
John Alvord & Relief Crosby,   Aug. 11, 1763
Noah Higby & Mary Cooper,   Aug. 28, 1763
Seth Thair & Ester Foster,   Sept. 1, 1763
Abner Mitchell & ——— Johnson,   Sept. 4, 1763
Elisha Roberts & Mindwell Egelstone,   Sept. 12, 1763
Jacob Glazier & Mary Strickland,   Sept. 13, 1763
Benjamin Clark & Abia Hall,   Sept. 15, 1763
Martin McManary & widow Mabel Blague,   Sept. 28, 1763
Thaddeus Bow & Mary Horton,   Sept. 29, 1763
Theophilus Canda, widower, to Anne Cornwall, widow,
                                               Sept. 29, 1763
Dr. Robert North & Dinah Camp of Middlefield, Oct. 6, 1763
Cruele William Marks & Elizabeth Kelsey,   Oct. 13, 1763
Elihu Cotton & Jane Gilbert,   Oct. 27, 1763
Domey Butler & Mindwell Clark,   Nov. 17, 1763
Jonathan Johnson & Agnes Kent,   Dec. 6, 1763
Elisha Fairchild & Abigail Crowell,   Dec. 10, 1763
Jeremiah Bacon & Hannah Condar,   Dec. 10, 1763
George Kilborn & Abigail Pierpont,   Nov. 10, 1763
Josiah Ward & Mary Hedges,   Jan. 12, 1764
John Nebling of Newport, R. I., & Katherine Harket,
                                               Jan. 21, 1764
Ezekial Cogswell & Margaret DeWolf,   Jan. 26, 1764
Daniell Brooks & Elizabeth Barn,   Feb. 2, 1764
Ebenezer Hubbard & Lydia Wetmore,   Feb. 16, 1764
Sam. Kellogg of Hoosick & Chloe Bacon,   March 4, 1764
Noadiah Hubbard & widow Phebe Crowel,   March 15, 1764
Nathan. Stevens & Lonis Camp, both of Middlefield,
                                               March 20, 1764
Edward Crowel & Lucy Eglestone,   April 26, 1764
John Plum & Dorothy Gilbert,   May 9, 1764

Amos Barns & widow Sarah Crowel,   May 17, 1764
Asa Bart of Bedford & Ruth Hubbard of Middlefield,

                                               May 21, 1764
Joshua Miller & Anna Starr,   June 10, 1764
Charles Tryon & Lancent Brockway,   July 12, 1764
Daniel Cudra & Mary Mitchel,   Aug. 2, 1764
Hezekiah Hale & Jerusha Parsons, both of Middlefield,

                                            Sept. 6, 1764
Joseph Russell of Oxford in Derby & Elizabeth Clark,

                                         Sept. 25, 1764
Hezekiah Hubbard & Ester Foster,   Oct. 8, 1764
Sam. Willis, Jr., & Lucy Brewster,   Oct. 11, 1764
Benjamin Tarbox & Martha Gilbert,   Nov. 1, 1764
Jabez Johnson, son of Caleb Johnson, & Mercy Francis,
    both of Durham,   Nov. 15, 1764
James Bishop of Guilford & Hannah Bishop, Nov. 19, 1764
Isaac Howe of ——— & Mary Conda,   Nov. 22, 1764
Sylvanus Waterman & Abigail Gleason,   Nov. 22, 1764
Thom. Padget & Eliz. Willis,   Nov. 27, 1764
Ezra Turner & Abigail Cooke,   Nov. 27, 1764
Widower Joseph Clark, Sr., & widow Phebe Comace,

                                         Dec. 3, 1764
Abner Lucas & Mercy Talbot,   Dec. 13, 1764
Noah Roberts & Eliz. Parsons,   Dec. 13, 1764
Francis Getean of Framingham & Canca Macky, Jan. 10, 1765
Prince Winborn & Ester Johnson,   Jan. 17, 1765
Daniell Cruttenden of Haddam & Rhoda Tryon, Jan. 17, 1765
Return Jonathan Meigs & Joanna Winborn,   Feb. 14, 1765
Eli Waples of Washington & Eliz. Foster,   March 7, 1765
Samuel Hubbard of Kensington & Jane Higbe, May 23, 1765
Walter Huet of Canaan & Thankful Bacon,   May 30, 1765
Abijah Savage & Martha Jowey,   Aug. 20, 1765
William Kelly & Hannah Ward,   Sept. 2, 1765
John Foster & Sarah Willis,   Sept. 17, 1765
Widower Elijah Johnson & widow Mary Witmore,

                                         Sept. 26, 1765
Abner Cone of Haddam & Hannah Cornwell,   Oct. 3, 1765
Joseph Williams & widow Mary Spelman,   Nov. 11, 1765
Ephraim Fenno & Mary King,   Nov. 14, 1765

Howard Collins Whitmore & Mary Ward,	Nov. 14, 1765
William Danils & Ruth Miller,	Nov. 28, 1765
Eliphalet Terry of Enfield & Mary Hall,	Dec. 3, 1765
Thom. Balding & Mary Arnold,	Dec. 15, 1765
John White & Abigaile Gilbert,	Dec. 15, 1765
Sam. Carrier & Rebeccah Seyeres,	Dec. 16, 1765
Nathan'll Johnson & Elizabeth Green,	Jan. 1, 1766
Dan'l Higbe & Martha Ives,	Feb. 6, 1766
John Migholls & Mary Clough,	Feb. 6, 1766
Solomon Hubbard & Rachel Tryon,	March 20, 1766
Clothier Prior & Anna Brambel,	April 17, 1766
Ebenezer Bacon & Meliscent Cornwell,	May 22, 1766
Thom. Rich & Ruth Prior,	May 29, 1766
Thom. Powers & Mary Cole,	May 29, 1766
Andrew Campbell & Ruth Roberts,	Aug. 26, 1766
Chas. Loveland & Mary Gleason,	Sept. 7, 1766
Peter Stow & Mary Cotton,	Sept. 14, 1766
Sam. Bill & Martha Goodwin,	Sept. 25, 1766
Ambrose Atwater of Wallingford & Sarah Tryon,	Oct. 2, 1766
Isaac Hedges & Anna Roberts,	Oct. 2, 1766
John Ward, Jr., & widow Ester Loveland,	Oct. 16, 1766
Micajah Tuels & widow Mary Fairbanks,	Nov. 13, 1766
John Delliber of Hartford & widow Azubah Dowd,	Nov. 20, 1766
Josiah Boardman, Jr., & Hannah Penfield,	Dec. 18, 1766
Sylvanus More of Sheffield & Deborah Markham,	Jan. 18, 1767
Elisha Smith of Sandersfield & Ruth Johnson,	March 24, 1767
Sam. Chamberlain & Ester Hedges,	April 15, 1767
Fenner Arnold & Hannah Turner,	May 5, 1767
Wm. Henshaw & Eliz. Gilbert,	May 14, 1767
Jonathan Fowler of Guilford, widower, to widow Sarah Rogers,	May 21, 1767
Dan. Plum & Mary Dowd,	June 11, 1767
Thom. Waters of Hartford & Eliz. Graves,	July 15, 1767
Ichabod Brooks & Sarah Hurlbutt,	Aug. 23, 1767
Jeremiah Wadsworth & Mehitabel Russel,	Sept. 29, 1767
Elijah Blackman & Elizabeth Hall,	Oct. 20, 1767

Thom. Welch & Esther Cotton,	Oct. 29,	1767
Isaac Mattoon of Wallingford & Martha Foster,	Oct. 29,	1767
Thom. Wright of Weathersfield & Martha Butler,		
	Nov. 4,	1767
James Pelton of Guilford & Ruth Johnson,	Nov. 19,	1767
Oliver Hubbard & Huldah Sears,	Nov. 19,	1767
Timothy Clark & Ruth Warner,	Jan. 7,	1768
Seth Doolittle & Hannah Dowd,	Feb. 4,	1768
Amaziah Waterman of Chatham & Lucy Rockwell,		
	Feb. 14,	1768
Timothy Brownson of Farmington to ——— ———,		
living in Westfield at her sister Higbe's,	Feb. 18,	1768
Nathan. Miller & Hannah Roberts,	March 30,	1768
Ebenezer Allen & Eliz. Pousley,	June 2,	1768
Sam. Warner & Sarah Cruttendon,	June 2,	1768
Israel Carrier & Mary Clark,	June 5,	1768
Caleb Tryon & Lydia Hubbard,	July 7,	1768
William McManery & Eliz. Hulett,	July 10,	1768
John Willson & Mary Strong,	Aug. 18,	1768
Nathan Williams & Lois Sage, both of the Upper		
Houses (Cromwell),	Aug. 18,	1768
Ed. Ward of Middlefield & Lydia Adkins,	Aug. 25,	1768
Jonathan Hubbard & Esther Starr,	Sept. 8,	1768
Sam. Brooks & Sarah Hedges,	Sept. 19,	1768
Job Talbot & Eliz. Payton,	Sept. 19,	1768
Giles Meigs & Experience Allen,	Oct. 13,	1768
Wm. Spencer & Eliz. Griffin,	Oct. 16,	1768
James Starr & Anna Kent,	Oct. 20,	1768
Sam. Starr & Sarah Ward,	Oct. 30,	1768
Bezaleel Fisk & Margaret Rockwell,	Nov. 13,	1768
Seth Wetmore, Jr., & Mary Wright,	Nov. 14,	1768
Prosper Hubbard & Eliz. Norton,	Nov. 17,	1768
Sam. Adkins, Jr., & Eliz. Roberts,	Nov. 17,	1768
John Roberts & Hannah Preston,	Jan. 5,	1769
Daniel Clark & Mehitabel Whitmore,	Jan. 19,	1769
Seth Johnson & Jemima Miller,	Feb. 2,	1769
John Tryon & Rhoda Lucas,	April 20,	1769
Daniel Stow & Prudence Gilbert,	May 4,	1769
Dan. Cornwell & Priscilla Starr,	May 7,	1769

Ozias Cone of Haddam & Mary Doane,   May 29, 1769
John Petton of Guilford & Huldah Johnson,   July 24, 1769
William Bivens , Jr., & Rachel Powers,   Aug. 24, 1769
Thom. Goodwin & Abia Sage,   Aug. 31, 1769
Thom. Hulett & Mary Willis,   Oct. 29, 1769
Joseph Barns, Jr., & Thankful Ward,   Nov. 16, 1769
John Hulett & Joanna Pierce,   Nov. 16, 1769
John Rockwell & Dorothy Wetmore, both of Middlefield,
                                   Nov. 22, 1769
Joseph Copley & Sarah Boe,   Nov. 23, 1769
Simeon Morgan & Sibil Foster,   Nov. 23, 1769
Stephen Parsons & Eliz. Hamilton, both of Middlefield,
                                   Nov. 30, 1769
William Wood, Jr., & Chloe Warner,   Dec. 11, 1769
Chauncy Whittlesey & Lucy Wetmore,   Feb. 14, 1770
Joseph Graves, Jr., & Lois Higbe,   Feb. 15, 1769
John Crawford & Eliz. Barns,   March 1, 1770
Caleb Strong & Amia Lee,   March 29, 1769
Chancy Whittlesey & Lucy Wetmore,   Feb. 14, 1770
Joseph Graves, Jr., & Lois Higbe,   Feb. 15, 1770
John Crawford & Eliz. Barns,   March 1, 1770
Caleb Strong & Anna Lee,   March 29, 1770
Dan. Sumner, widower, & widow Susannah Ward,
                                   April 16, 1770
Sam. Markham & Eliz. Miller,   April 26, 1770
Hosea Miller & Mary Stow,   May 15, 1770
James Egelstone & Lydia Wetmore, both of Middlefield,
                                   June 12, 1770
Timothy Starr & Abigail Hamlin,   June 14, 1770
Seth Roberts & Martha Lewis,   Aug. 6, 1770
Reuben Smith of Litchfield & Abigail Hubbard, Oct. 22, 1770
Jonathan Gilbert, Jr., & Lucy Ward,   Dec. 6, 1770
Israel Bunnel of Cheshire & Jerusha Dowd, Dec. 12, 1770
Jesse Roberts & Lucy Willson,   Dec. 27, 1770
Elias Squires & Eliz. Higbe,   Dec. 27, 1770
Bazaleel Latimore of Wethersfield & Lydia Tarbox,
                                   Dec. 27, 1770
Isaac Jones of New Haven & Lucy Goodrich of Pitts-
    field,   Dec. 27, 1770

Jonathan Johnson & Mary Whitmore,	Jan. 1, 1771
Asa Moore of Worcester & widow Lucy Wright,	Feb. 14, 1771
Sam. Bull & Lydia Gleason,	March 10, 1771
Wm. Harris, Jr., & Melliscent Hubbard,	March 19, 1771
Hezekiah Hulbert, Jr., & Hannah Johnson,	April 12, 1771
Alberk Black of Hartford & Eliz. Johnson,	April 30, 1771
Dan. Hall & Rachel Blake,	May 12, 1771
———— Norton of Guilford & Eliz. Roberts,	May 15, 1771
James Jones & Susanna Loveland,	May 16, 1771
Sam. Cunningham & Phebe Foster,	June 6, 1771
John Dunbar & Esther Adkins,	June 13, 1771
Jeremiah Weston of Kensington & Lucy Plum,	June 20, 1771
Ebenezer Bernard of Hartford & Eliz. Lane,	Oct. 10, 1771
David Bates of Granville & Ruth Ward,	Oct. 21, 1771
Sam. Hamlin & Thankful Ely,	Oct. 31, 1771
Isaac Williams & Lois Fairchild,	Nov. 3, 1771
Sam. Foster & Eliz. Willis,	Nov. 7, 1771
Josiah Churchill & Rhoda Bacon,	Nov. 11, 1771
Timothy Moss of Farmington & Mary Churchill,	
	Nov. 11, 1771
Seth Johnson & Rebecca Norton,	Nov. 14, 1771
Elijah Cole of Kensington & Sarah Lawson,	Dec. 3, 1771
Joseph Diggins of Windsor & Esther Elton,	Dec. 25, 1771
Joshua Kornwall & Rhoda Doud,	Jan. 1, 1772
Hugh Brown & Olive Sage,	Jan. 2, 1772
Elijah Hubbard & Hannah Kent,	Jan. 5, 1772
Epheraim Higbe & ———— Cornwall,	Jan. 16, 1772
John Elsworth & Martha Hall,	Jan. 23, 1772
Chas. Goodrich of Pittsfield & Hannah Ward,	Feb. 17, 1772
Rich. Stephens of Sheffield & Esther Ward,	March 5, 1772
Ebenezer Blake & Eliz. Cole,	April 7, 1772
Jacob Miller of Middlefield & Mary Crowell,	July 6, 1772
Timothy Brooks & Eliz. Lucas,	Aug. 27, 1772
Moses Mitchel of Meriden & Lucy Warner,	Aug. 27, 1772
Jedediah Hubbel of Lanesborough & Submit Alvord,	
	Sept. 3, 1772
Amos Tryon & Mary Hubbard,	Sept. 17, 1772
Timothy Powers & Eliz. Gilbert,	Oct. 29, 1772
Luke Osborn & Dorcas Bacon,	Oct. 29, 1772

Thom. Foster & Margaret Lee, Oct. 29, 1772
Thom. Right & Anne Chremer, Nov. 2, 1772
Elisha Russell & Anne Winship, Nov. 8, 1772
John McGras & Theoditia Cunningham, Nov. 15, 1772
Lot Pain of Chatham & Barbary Chremer, Feb. 18, 1773
Thos. Barns, Jr., & Sibel Adkins, Feb. 18, 1773
Ed. Rockwel, Jr., & Lucy Strong, March 25, 1773
Dan. Starr & Mabel Bow, March 25, 1773
Sam. Marshal & Hannah Doane, April 8, 1773
Nath'n Hubbard of Granville & Lucy Johnson, April 15, 1773
Jonathan Miller & Priscilla Tupper, April 29, 1773
Enoch Johnson & Sarah Warner, April 29, 1773
Sam. Tuells & Lucy Merriman, June 3, 1773
Elnathan Lucas & Margaret Ward, June 17, 1773
Jeremiah Lawrence of Canaan & widow Eliz. Higbe,
June 6, 1773
Sam. May of Weathersfield & Rhoda Roberts, Aug. 24, 1773
Roland Richardson & Eliz. Pierpont, Aug. 29, 1773
Ed. Roberts & Eunice Barns, Sept. 20, 1773
Oliver Wetmore & Lucy Sarah Brewster, Oct. 13, 1773
Sam. Johnson, Jr., & Lucy Adkins, Oct. 14, 1773
Josiah Starr & Mary Warner, Nov. 24, 1773
Giles Clark & Eliphal Johnson, Nov. 25, 1773
John Prout & Rachel Hedges, Dec. 21, 1773
Widower Ephraim Stone & widow Elizabeth Sizer,
Jan. 12, 1774
John Scot & Lucretia Warner, Jan. 20, 1774
Jonathan Roberts, Jr., & Lucy Fairchild, Feb. 2, 1774
John Babb & Mary Rand, Feb. 24, 1774
Thos. Hulbert, Jr., & Abigail Johnson, March 2, 1774
Hez. Goff, Jr., & Anner Ward, March 10, 1774
James McAlister of Enfield & Mary Anne Henry,
April 13, 1774
James Treadway & Phebe Foster, April 25, 1774
Josiah Hubbard of Westbury & Mary Hale, May 31, 1774
Sam. Rogers & Mehitabel Hubbard, June 16, 1774
Cuff (negro servant) & Zipporah, July 7, 1774
Joseph Johnson (Frenchman) & Tabitha Starr, Sept. 15, 1774
Bennet Egleston & Hannah Gill, Sept. 19, 1774

Oliver Stanley, Esq., of Wallingford & Sarah Chauncey,

                                    Oct. 6, 1774
Nathan'll Lewis & Hannah Rockwell,   Oct. 9, 1774
Hon. Wm. Cushing of Scituate & Hannah Phillips,

                                    Oct. 11, 1774
William Paddock & Lucy Loveland,   Oct. 13, 1774
Sol'o. Stow, Jr., & Abigail Pousley,   Dec. 4, 1774
Henry Hedges, Jr., & Chloe Adkins,   Dec. 15, 1774
John Gilbert & Anna Starr,   Dec. 15, 1774
Return Jonathan Meigs & Grace Starr,   Dec. 22, 1774
David White of Chatham & Marianna Stocking, Dec. 29, 1774
Ed. Hallam of New London & Mary Sage,   Jan. 8, 1775
Elisha Lean & Martha Johnson,   Jan. 12, 1775
Rob. Rand & Hepzibah Adkins,   Jan. 12, 1775
Hanover Knapp & Susanna Foster,   Feb. 16, 1775
Samuell Bull & Rebecca Cotton,   Feb. 26, 1775
Joseph Smith & Eliz. Taylor,   March 12, 1775
Robert Cook of Farmington & Martha Norton,

                                    March 30, 1775
John Cotton, 3d, & Mary Sears,   April 9, 1775
Widower Joseph Ward & widow Hannah Lee, April 17, 1775
Moses Griswold & Mary Bates,   May 15, 1775
Isaac Bow & Eliz. Lee,   May 18, 1775
Timothy Nall & Cornelia Joice,   June 2, 1775
Joseph Pierson of Derbe & Sarah Sizer,   June 2, 1775
Selden Nott of Saybrook & Sarah Nott,   June 11, 1775
Thos. Danforth, Jr., & Eliz. Tellman of N. London,

                                    July 12, 1775
John Cande & Hannah Gilbert,   Sept. 14, 1775
Sam. Tracy & Lucy Ward,   Sept. 17, 1775
John Banks & Hannah Pelton,   Oct. 24, 1775
Wm. Chamberlain of Colchester & Mary Roberts,

                                    Nov. 30, 1775
Dan. Miller & Eliz. Hall,   Dec. 14, 1775
Amos Sage & Mary Lewis,   Dec. 14, 1775
John Paddock & Mary Loveland,   Jan. 4, 1776
Stephen Clay of Chatham & Margaret Hebbard, Jan. 23, 1776
George Phillips & Esther Arnold,   March 17, 1775
Jonah Strickland of Chatham & Amia Hulett, April 18, 1776

Benjamin Birdsey & Abigaile Merriman,   May 12, 1776
Seth Coe & Mary Miller, both of Middlefield,   June 12, 1776
Elisha Sage & Martha Montague, both of Upper Houses,
                                                June 27, 1776
Josep Prior & Mary Bun,   July 4, 1776
John Davies & Hannah Pierce,   July 21, 1776
Dan. Hurlbut Cone & Eliz. Atkins,   Aug. 18, 1776
Adonijah Foot of Colchester & Abigail Roberts,
                                                Oct. 17, 1776
Thompson Phillips & Abigail Cornell,   Nov. 24, 1776
Collins Roberts & Mercy Ames,   Dec. 1, 1776
Abel Wilcocks & Experience Ramsdell,   Dec. 4, 1776
Benj. Atkins, Jr., & Sarah Ward,   Dec. 8, 1776
Thos. Cooper of Chatham & Sarah Ward,   Dec. 26, 1776
Elihu Cotton & Rebecca Hurlbutt,   Jan. 19, 1777
Ebenezer Billings of Greenfield & Esther Joyce, Jan. 26, 1777
Nehemiah Hubbard, Jr., & Cornelia Willis,   Feb. 13, 1777
Peter Burnham of Weathersfield & Eliz. Ward of Mid-
      dlefield,   March 13, 1777
Josiah Atkins & Chloe Roberts,   March 14, 1777
Elijah Fellows of New York & widow Miriam Ranny
      of Upper Houses,   March 20, 1777
Widower Dan. Savage & widow Abia Lincoln,   May 8, 1777
Ebenezer Bivins & Ruhamah Brooks,   May 15, 1777
Wm. Cone & Abiah Atkins,   May 29, 1777
Jabez Stocking & Anne Sheldon,   June 5, 1777
Sam. Beaman & Mary Ward,   June 5, 1777
Giles Meigs & Anne Pinto of New Haven,   June 8, 1777
Ebenezer Egleston & Abigail Cande,   June 10, 1777
Seth Duning & Hannah Gilbert,   June 11, 1777
Nath'll Cornwell & Annie Plum,   June 12, 1777
Hezekiah Hurlbut, Jr., & Hannah Clark,   June 12, 1777
Amos Bow & Thankful Egleston,   June 15, 1777
Ishmael Hardy & Hope Still Brewster,   July 27, 1777
Andrew Cambell & Mary Green,   July 27, 1777
John Prior & Letitia Lane,   July 31, 1777
John Smith & Mary Eliot,   Aug. 10, 1777
Wm. Warner & Hope Phillips,   Aug. 24, 1777
Stephen Pierce & Phebe Pelton,   Aug. 25, 1777

Widower Hezekiah Hale & widow Rachel Bivins,

	Aug. 30, 1777
Sam. Ward, Jr., & Anne Johnson,	Sept. 7, 1777
Lloyd Bowers of Swansey & Margaret Phillips,	Oct. 8, 1777
Joshua Miller & Mary Atkins,	Oct. 28, 1777
John Patterson & Prudence Ward,	Nov. 16, 1777
Elias Sears & Patience King,	Dec. 16, 1777
Joseph Stocking & Hannah Gill,	Dec. 21, 1777
Giles Southmay & Lois Rockwell,	Jan. 29, 1778
Caleb Bull, Jr., of Hartford & Mary Otis,	Feb. 12, 1778
Daniel Hurlbut & Hannah Higbe,	April 9, 1778
Sam. Doolittle & Anne Arnold,	April 16, 1778
Thos. Tryon & Rachel Hammond,	April 23, 1778
Rowland Allen & Huldah Kirbe,	April 23, 1778

Punch (negro servant) & Betsey Collins (free molatto),

	May 5, 1778
Amos Roberts & Susanna Prout,	May 17, 1778
James Francis, soldier, & Mary Sizer,	June 9, 1778
Wm. Bacon & Rhoda Lee,	June 10, 1778
Julius Riley & Mabel Atkins,	June 5, 1778
John Bukanan of Enfield & Jane Henry,	July 14, 1778
Simon Hoffman & Hannah Eglestone,	Aug. 25, 1778
David Harris & Mary Prout,	Sept. 22, 1778
Ed. Powers & Deborah Roberts,	Nov. 3, 1778
Frederick Bigelow & Abigail Foster,	Nov. 11, 1778
Jonathan Sizer & Eliz. Pelton,	Nov. 29, 1778
Elisha Johnson & Sarah Blake,	Dec. 10, 1778
Jacob Gelson & Catherine Trow,	Dec. 27, 1778
Cable Hubbard, Jr., & Eliz. Johnson,	Dec. 31, 1778
Seth Paddock & Phebe Johnson,	Jan. 7, 1779

Widower Abel Curtis of Meriden & widow Patience

Wickham,	March 10, 1779
Solomon Crowel & Anner Tryon,	March 11, 1779
Sam. Gaylord & Azubah Atkins,	May 13, 1779
Timothy Johnson & Grace Johnson,	May 19, 1779
Levi Dudley & Eliz. Atkins,	May 30, 1779

Francis Somers (a German deserter from ———

Newport) & Mary Gibb,	June 6, 1779

Widower Benj. Griffin & widow Mary Whitmore

(widow of Ed. Collins Whitmore), July 26, 1779
Sam. Jabe of Waterbury & Eliz. Elton, July 28, 1779
Nath'l Newel & Anne Gilchrist, Aug. 1, 1779
Dan. Hamlin & Ruth Ward, Aug. 1, 1779
Timothy Prout & Leber Turner, Aug. 2, 1779
Widower Wm. Miller, Jr., & widow Lucy Bartlett
   (of Ephraim), Oct. 7, 1779
David Wells of Shelburn, Mass., & Phebe Hubbard,
    Oct. 21, 1779
Elisha Cotton & Sarah Alvord, Oct. 21, 1779
Nathan'll Riley & Abigail Atkins, Oct. 28, 1779
Sam. Cotton & Sarah Banks, Dec. 30, 1779
John Redfield, Jr., of Guilford & Eunice Joyce, Jan. 13, 1780
Constant Johnson & Thankful Whitmore, Jan. 27, 1780
Moses Lucas & Mary Foster, Jan. 27, 1780
Sam. Canfield & Mehitable Lord, Feb. 24, 1780
Stephen Miller & Lucy Roberts, April 2, 1780
Widower Josiah Wells of Weathersfield & widow Ruth
   Rutch, April 13, 1780
Ed. Bow & Ruth Hubbard, April 21, 1780
John Ward & Rhoda Atkins, July 7, 1780
Jonathan Clark & Mary Mattoon, July 13, 1780
Sam. Johnson & Sarah Sage, Aug. 6, 1780
Comfort Williams & Patty Doolittle, Aug. 10, 1780
Timothy Starr, Jr., & Mary Fosdick, Aug. 20, 1780
Ashbel Kellogg of New Hartford & Lucy Cotton,
    Sept. 20, 1780
Widower Sam. Brook & Sibil Johnson, Oct. 25, 1780
Widower Marshal Merriam of Wallingford & widow
   Mary Doud, Oct. 30, 1780
Dudley Roberts of Farmington & Mary Stead, Nov. 27, 1780
Dan. Russell & Eliz. Lord, Dec. 11, 1780
Elijah Cornwall & Susannah Strong, Dec. 28, 1780
Eldad Grannis of Cheshire & Sarah Lane, Jan. 7, 1781
John Meigs & Eliz. Henshaw, Jan. 18, 1781
Jonathan Taylor & Hannah Tuels, Feb. 15, 1781
Jacob Hubbard & Sarah Hobby, Feb. 18, 1781
Dan. Sizer & Mary DeWolf, Feb. 22, 1781
James French & Eliz. Strong, March 28, 1781

John Dodd & Hannah Ranny,	April 4,	1781
Thos. Hurlbut & Catherine Clark,	April 5,	1781
Theophilus Botsford & Dolly Bidwell,	April 10,	1781
Joseph Danforth & Sarah King,	April 12,	1781
Oliver Boardman & Sarah Danforth,	May 1,	1781
Dan. Jones of Meriden & Margaret Lucas,	May 14,	1781
Thomas. Goodwin, Jr., & Mary Starr,	May 28,	1781
Andrew Jhonnot & Sally Overwyk,	May 29,	1781
Dan. Clark & Desire Higgins,	June 21,	1781
Nathan Starr & Polly Pomeroy,	July 5,	1781
Francis Clark & Mary Johnson,	July 12,	1781
Justus Starr & Sarah Fosdick,	Aug. 12,	1781
Richard Spelman & Rhoda Camp of Durham,	Aug. 17,	1781
Thos. Alvord & widow Anner Lucas,	Sept. 6,	1781
Widower Solomon Hubbard & Thankful Prior,	Sept. 6,	1781
Widower Jeremiah Bacon & widow ——— Porter,		
	Oct. 11,	1781
Widower Wm. Warner & Sarah Dow,	Nov. 14,	1781
James Nichols & Bethiah Clay,	Nov. 15,	1781
Richard Waves & Olive Rider,	Nov. 22,	1781
George Hubbard, Jr., & Mabel Miller,	Dec. 3,	1781
Asa Gilbert & Abigail Rogers,	Dec. 11,	1781
Asher Miller & widow Sarah Ward,	Dec. 12,	1781
Joel Fairchild & Sane Roberts,	Dec. 24,	1781
Marriel William Starr & Eliz. Starr,	Dec. 27,	1781
Elijah Hubbard & Abigail Dickinson,	Jan. 1,	1782
George Cotton & Eliz. Gilchrist,	Jan. 3,	1782
Amos Galpin of Litchfield & Jane Doane,	Jan. 15,	1782
Isaac Hubbard & Ruth Coleman,	Jan. 24,	1782
David Robert Hubbard of Shelburne & Lucy Hubbard,		
	Feb. 14,	1782
Jabez Brooks, Jr., & Rhoda Crowell,	Feb. 25,	1782
John Frothingham & Deborah Miller,	March 21,	1782
Sam. Beckwith of Hartford & Eliz. Woodward,	April 30,	1782
Josiah Griswold & Lucy Talbot,	May 2,	1782
Sam. Paddock & Mehitabel Loveland,	May 13,	1782
Abijah Hubbard & Sarah Tryon,	May 28,	1782
Noadiah Rockwell & Alice Hall,	May 29,	1782
Allen Gilbert & Mary Hall,	June 20,	1782

Ezekiel Woodruff of Litchfield & Sarah Hall, June 30, 1782
James Beers of Stratford & Rebecca Higgins, July 15, 1782
Sam. Williams of Kensington & Abigail Davis, July 25, 1782
Henry Johnson & Huldah Grier, July 25, 1782
Nathaniel Brown, Jr., & Mehitabel Hubbard, Aug. 5, 1782
Michael Melony & Polly Redfield, Aug. 11, 1782
Noyes Robbarts & Martha Arnold, Aug. 15, 1782
Elisha Atkins & widow Abigail Eglestone, Aug. 15, 1782
Lebbeus Brockway of Lyme & Elizabeth Pettis, Aug. 15, 1782
Rob. Shattuck & Lucy Neuf, Aug. 29, 1782
Widower Ed. Crowell & Maihel Roberts, Sept. 19, 1782
Amos Treadway, Jr., & Susannah Cotton, Sept. 22, 1782
Daniel Eells & Martha Hamlin, Oct. 3, 1782
Joshua Ward & Mary Stow, Oct. 24, 1782
David Clark & Jane Turpin, Oct. 31, 1782
James Fosdick & Mary King, Dec. 19, 1782
William Jobason & Jemima Hubbard, Dec. 25, 1782
Lamerton Clark & Eliz. Pease, Dec. 26, 1782
Stephen Penfield & Lydia Knowles of Chatham, Jan. 3, 1783
John Caton & Rebeccah Griswold, Jan 14, 1783
Israel Driggs & Persis Roberts, Jan. 23, 1783
Gregory Powers & widow Sally Jhonnot, Feb. 3, 1783
John Starr & Bathsheba Cotton, Feb. 6, 1783
London Bailey & Mary Griswold, March 4, 1783
Ashbel Bidwell & Mary Whiton, March 10, 1783
Capt. Joseph Walker of Stratford & Susanna Otis,
March 16, 1783
John Stowe & Esther Roberts, April 3, 1783
William Summer & Rebecca Arnold, May 1, 1783
Benjamin Tuells & Ruth Nicholls, May 5, 1783
Oliver Prout & Lucy Prier, June 5, 1783
Patrick Derby & Eliz. Ward, June 5, 1783
Rob. Cone & Margaret Paget, July 29, 1783
Stephen Ranny, Jr., & Esther Sage, Aug. 28, 1783
Sam. Frothingham & Abigail Kelly, Sept. 15, 1783
Joseph Bacon, Jr., & Eleanor Loomis, Sept. 15, 1783
Timothy Boardman of Rutland & Mary Ward, Sept. 20, 1783
William Cook & Eliz. Thayer, Oct. 6, 1783

8

Simeon Birge, Torringford, & Experience Hamlin,
                                        Oct. 8, 1783
Thaddus Baw & Mabel Stow,   Oct. 16, 1783
Isaac Miller & Irene Miller,   Oct. 16, 1783
Ed. Miller & Eliz. Rockwell,   Oct. 16, 1783
John Ward, 4th, & Lucy Pierpoint,   Nov. 17, 1783
Ithamar Atkins & Anne Hubbard,   Nov. 27, 1783
Elijah Griswold & Anne Brooks,   Dec. 8, 1783
Zebadiah Lathrop of Norwich & Sarah Stow, Dec. 11, 1783
Widower Sam. Blake & Margaret Johnson, Jan. 1, 1784
Joseph Treat of Weathersfield & Mary Fairbanks,
                                        Jan. 5, 1784
David Atkins & Cornelia Claver,   Feb. 12, 1784
David Baker & Olive Griswold,   Feb. 19, 1784
Josiah Treadway & Urania Cook,   March 3, 1784
Sam. Cotton & Lucretia Hamlin,   March 11, 1784
John Hands & Sarah Rockwell,   March 20, 1784
Michael Braddock & Hannah Goff,   March 30, 1784
Thos. Kirby, Jr., & Rebekah Hamlin,   May 19, 1784
Widower Abner Smith & widow Deborah Brainard,
                                        May 25, 1784
John Crowel, Jr., & Ruth Starr,   June 14, 1784
Mansah Hubbard, Jr., & Thankful Miller, July 13, 1784
Sam'l Loveland & Dorcas Jones,   Sept. 30, 1784
James Brattle of Pittsfield & Edith Ward, Oct. 6, 1784
Grave Rockwell & Esther Strong,   Oct. 6, 1784
Abner Hubbard & Esther Hamlin,   Oct. 7, 1784
Wm. Parker & Hannah Hubbard,   Oct. 7, 1784
Jacob Hall & Patience Starr,   Nov. 9, 1784
John Rogers, Jr., & Lucy Ames,   Nov. 30, 1784
Sam. Simmons, Jr., & Sarah Pelton of Chatham,
                                        March 3, 1785
Dr. Lemuel Hayward of Boston & Sally Henshaw,
                                        March 6, 1785
Enoch Tuells & Anner Dowey,   March 12, 1785
Joshua Buffum & Mary Bill,   March 13, 1785
Sam. Bow & Mary Arnold,   March 17, 1785
Timothy Whitmore & Lydia Lucas,   April 7, 1785
Elnathan Stephens of Durham & Sarah Prout, April 14, 1785

Wm. Wells of New Haven & Abigail Starr,   April 23, 1785
Rob. Paddock & Martha Loveland,   May 5, 1785
Jesse Hubbard & Eunice Coe,   June 1, 1785
Widower Jehosophat Starr & widow Mary Hubbard,
  July 12, 1785
Sam. Crowel & Sarah Hall,   July 13, 1785
Henry Mansfield of New Haven & Mary Hanns, Aug. 3, 1785
Obadiah Johnson & Martha Bill,   Aug. 4, 1785
Widower Sam. Goodwin & widow Margaret Clark,
  Aug. 18, 1785
David Hall & Hannah Crowell,   Aug. 23, 1785
Jacob Hubbard & Sarah Hall,   Sept. 3, 1785
Thaddeus Nichols & Aner Cone,   Sept. 7, 1785
Jacob Bow & Zerviah Brainard,   Sept. 19, 1785
Abraham Aholiab (?) Johnson of Killingly & Hannah
  Bacon,   Sept. 21, 1785
Ezekial Lyman of Lebanon & Mabel Mitchel,   Sept. 22, 1785
David Tryon, Jr., & Deborah Brainard,   Sept. 27, 1785
Asahel Ripuce of Hartford & Mary Higbe,   Oct. 12, 1785
Abraham Bow & Eliz. Arnold,   Oct. 18, 1785
Ephraim Baily of Haddam & Azibah Roberts,   Dec. 8, 1785
Isaac Bacon & Dorothy Stow,   Dec. 14, 1785
Jonathan Gilbert, Jr., & Thankful Wetmore,   Dec. 15, 1785
Thos. Child of Haddam & Hannah Tryon,   Jan. 19, 1786
Eli. Sizer & Dida Prier,   Feb. 9, 1786
Thomas Burnet of Hartford, N. Hampshire, & Mabel
  Sentow,   Feb. 14, 1786
Levi North of Berlin & Rachel White,   April 20, 1786
Sam. Prier & Rachel Cotton,   May 1, 1786
Rev. Cypriam Strong & Miss White, daughter of
  Ebenezer White of Chatham,   May 4, 1786
David Goff & Lucy Davis,   May 4, 1786
Comfort Tuells & Anne Simmins,   May 4, 1786
Peter Allen & Naomi Abbot,   May 21, 1786
Peter Vandemsen & Lydia Brewster,   June 6, 1786
William Bacon & Bathsheba Cook,   June 29, 1786
John Randall of Norwich & Sarah Tupper,   July 4, 1786
Isaac Pierson of Derby & Lucretia Sizer,   Aug. 8, 1786
Widower Amos Bow & widow Mary Roberts, Aug. 10, 1786

Joseph Parker & Sarah Goff,	Aug. 31, 1786
Wil. Williams & Abigail Treadway,	Sept. 10, 1786
Adonijah Roberts & Clarinda Parmele,	Sept. 26, 1786
Caleb Miller & Molly Ames,	Oct. 2, 1786
Reuben Willcocks & Hannah Johnson,	Oct. 26, 1786
Peleg Redfield & Eliz. Pratt,	Oct. 31, 1786
Samuel Kirtland of Saybrook & Mehitabel Lord,	Nov. 1, 1786
Giles Hubbard & Rebekah Carrier,	Nov. 23, 1786
William Shiver & Rebekah Maclive,	Nov. 27, 1786
David Hall of Meriden & Hannah Doolittle,	Dec. 7, 1786
William Southmayd, Jr., & Desire Clay,	Dec. 26, 1786
Samuel Winship & Eunice Paddock,	Dec. 28, 1786
William Sage, Jr., & Eliz. Cook,	Jan. 23, 1787
Thos. Cooke of Haddam & Olive Prout,	Jan. 25, 1787
John Becker & Susannah Bates,	Feb. 12, 1787
Elihu Cotton & Mary Sevril,	Feb. 26, 1787
Philip Dejeon & Sarah Starr,	March 22, 1787
Elijah Tryon & Prudence Tryon,	May 8, 1787
Nathaniel Willey & Mary Maqusugh of Middlefield,	
	June 4, 1787
Dan. Kelly & Jemima Stow,	June 28, 1787
Nathaniel Roberts, Jr., & Sarah Whiton,	July 12, 1787
William Daniels, Jr., & Prudence Pierce,	Aug. 16, 1787
Benj. Hands & Hannah Wetmore of Middlefield,	
	Sept. 27, 1787
George Paddock & Mary Wetmore,	Oct. 11, 1787
Wm. Cleaver, Jr., & Jemima Hunt,	Oct. 25, 1787
Giles Starr & Martha Nichols,	Nov. 22, 1787
Caleb Cornwall & Huldah Johnson,	Dec. 20, 1787
Eber Blaksley, Jr., & Sarah Ward,	Jan. 31, 1788
Gideon Mallory of Woodbury & Sarah Brown,	Feb. 14, 1788
John Chramer & Eliz. Nott,	Feb. 19, 1788
William Stors Armstrong & Patty Pierce,	Feb. 22, 1788
Ebenezer Washburn & Eliz. Clark,	March 10, 1788
Rev. Izrahiah Wetmore of Stratford & Anne Ward,	
	March 10, 1788
Tristram Neill of Newport & Sarah Bill,	March 10, 1788
Jacob Webster (negro) & Rhoda (negro),	May 1, 1788
Josiah Tryon & Mabel Johnson,	May 22, 1788

Sam. Squire of Durham & Eliz. Sexton,   June 12, 1788
John Valentine & Sarah Goodale of Chatham, June 16, 1788
John Russel & Abigail Warner,   June 29, 1788
Allen Hall & Lydia Frothingham,   July 5, 1788
John Hall & Elizabeth Allen Southmayd,   July 23, 1788
Alex. Mekee of East Hartford & Persis Cooper of
    Chatham,   July 27, 1788
Elijah Gaylord & Mary Cotton,   July 31, 1788
William Crosby of Chatham & Betsey Starr,   Aug. 6, 1788
Oliver Prier & Anna Tryon,   Aug. 14, 1788
Asa Arnold of Smithfield, R. I., & widow Sarah Jacobs,
                                               Sept. 14, 1788
Noah Washburn of Hartford & Sarah Foster,   Sept. 18, 1788
Jesse Tryon & Sarah Crowel,   Oct. 2, 1788
James McThain & Rebecca Ward,   Oct. 5, 1788
Elias Hubbard & Mary Sears,   Oct. 7, 1788
Thos. Smith of Baltimore, Md., & Eliz. Wetmore,
                                                Oct. 8, 1788
Nathaniel Gouge & Susannah Johnson,   Nov. 6, 1788
Jonathan Miller & Anner Weston,   Oct. 27, 1788
William Hubbard & Anne Prier,   Jan. 1, 1789
Michael Olmstead of East Hartford & Abigail Menow,
                                               Jan. 20, 1789
James Bliss of Norwich, Vt., & Mehitabel Johnson,
                                              March 26, 1789
Churchill Edwards & Jemima Sizer,   March 26, 1788
Sam. Bill & Sarah Mighels,   March 29, 1789
William Bowers of Swanzey & Martha Hall,   April 4, 1789
William Gilbert & Hope Burr,   April 6, 1789
Sam. Starr & Sarah Barns,   April 11, 1789
Asa Roberts & Chloe Blake,   April 23, 1789
Dan. Sexton & Sarah Weston,   May 28, 1789
Acetas Bailey of Chatham & Jemima Tryon,   June 4, 1789
Hesekiah Johnson & Abigail Wetmore, both of Mid-
    dlefield,   July 8, 1789
John Dobson of the Barbadoes & Abigail Rockwell,
                                               Aug. 26, 1789
Eliezer Merrils Roberts & Polly Revel,   Sept. 6, 1789
Charles Campbell & Olive Ward,   Sept. 23, 1789

Thos. Starr & Polly Fuller,	Oct. 5,	1789
Joseph Starr, Jr., & Nancy Cornwall,	Nov. 15,	1789
Seth Clark & Chloe Bailey,	Nov. 16,	1789
Moses Ward & Phobe Clark,	Nov. 22,	1789
Nathaniel Jones of Hartford & Polly Cornwell,	Dec. 17,	1789
Henry Powers & Hannah Miller,	Dec. 21,	1789
Dr. Ebenezer Tracy & Maria Ward of Shrewsbury, Mass.,	Jan. 14,	1790
Ebenezer Frothingham, Jr., & Polly Boardman,	Jan. 16,	1790
John Atkins & Lucretia Fosdick,	Jan. 21,	1790
Hezekiah Geer & Sarah Gilbert,	Feb. 9,	1790
William Hubbard & Naomi Stow,	March 15,	1790
Nathan Sears & Diana Roberts,	March 18,	1790
Fenner Roberts & Mehitabel Barns,	March 29,	1790
Felix Guild & Lydia Day of Spenser Town, N. Y.,	April 1,	1790
Gurdon Saltonstall of New London & Hannah Sage,	April 3,	1790
Eliphlet Lyman of Lebanon & Mary Lee,	May 3,	1790
Peleg Simmons & Amia Barret,	May 24,	1790
Elias Sears & Lucy Gilbert,	May 31,	1790
Israel Bliss of Lebanon & Dorothy Johnson,	June 10,	1790
Jesse Peck of Wallingford & Sarah Barns,	June 10,	1790
John Danels & Anner Lucas,	July 1,	1790
Jesse Coe & Olive Roberts,	July 19,	1790
Reuben Barns & Eliz. Whittlesey,	Aug. 15,	1790
John Dean & Bethiah Cook,	Aug. 24,	1790
Thomas Savage & Rebecca Plum,	Sept. 2,	1790
Sam. Chamberlain & Susanna Jones,	Sept. 12,	1790
Russel Wood of Lyme & Esther Bates,	Sept. 14,	1790
Ebenezer Prout & Thankful Prier,	Oct. 4,	1790
George Barns & Sarah Roberts,	Nov. 11,	1790
Oliver Bailey & Anner Miller,	Jan. 20,	1791
Joel Coe of Durham & Sally Talcott,	Jan. 31,	1791
David Ward & Rhoda Coe, both of Middlefield,	Feb. 3,	1791
Aaron Roberts & Hannah Ames,	Feb. 6,	1791
Hezekiah Rice of Whitestown, N. Y., formerly of Meriden, & Lydia Stow of Middlefield,	Feb. 10,	1791
Sam. Hubbard & Huldah Crowell,	March 3,	1791

David Taylor of Hartford & Hannah Stow,	March 13,	1791
Charles Tryon, Jr., & Martha Churchill,	March 14,	1791
Elijah Prier & Lucy Bailey,	March 17,	1791
Seth Wetmore & Lucretia Scott,	March 27,	1791
Elijah Bow & Eliz. Stow,	March 30,	1791
Oliver Hubbard & Eliz. Hubbard,	March 31,	1791
Ebenezer Arnold, Jr., & Persis Hubbard,	April 7,	1791
Enos Trion of Wallingford & Mary Mitchell,	April 9,	1791
Peter Lurg & Lucy Kelly,	April 14,	1791
David Rund & Hannah Fuller,	April 14,	1791
Charles Ranney & Mabel Stow,	May 5,	1791
Stephen Miller, Jr., & Abia Roberts,	June 16,	1791
Joshua Johnson & Sarah Chamberlain,	June 30,	1791
James Flaskey of New Lebanon & Hannah Comstock of Norwalk,	July 11,	1791
Jared Ball of New Haven & Mary Seannay of New Milford,	July 21,	1791
Dudley Chase Piper of Boston & Prudence Plum,	July 23,	1791
Robert Hammond of Colerain & Hannah Moger of Springfield (going in the western expedition with Capt. Buell),	July 26,	1791
Hosea Roberts & Lucy Smith of Chatham,	Aug. 12,	1791
Stephen Clark & Mary Bliss of Chatham,	Aug. 14,	1791
William Barris & Margery Bartlett,	Sept. 20,	1791
Fenner Ward of Guilford & Anne Meigs,	Sept. 22,	1791
Widower Prosper Hubbard & widow Naomi Savage,	Sept. 25,	1791
Enoch Hubbard & Sarah Brainard,	Oct. 6,	1791
Tony (negro servant) & Abigail J. Adams (molatto),	Oct. 12,	1791
Elijah Lee of Hadley & Abia Ward,	Oct. 20,	1791
Caleb Barns & Eliz. Gray,	Oct. 23,	1791
Enoch Huntington, Jr., & Sarah Ward,	Nov. 6,	1791
Constant Rogers & Mercy Starr,	Nov. 13,	1791
George Lucas & Sarah Simmons,	Nov. 20,	1791
Patrick Murray & Ruth Redfield,	Nov. 26,	1791
Josiah Johnson & Anne Hedges,	Jan. 2,	1792
Oliver Clark, Jr., & Eunice Johnson,	Jan. 17,	1792

Jonathan Whitmore & Priscilla Bidwell,	Jan. 18, 1792
Sylvester Butler & Lydia Wetmore,	Jan. 26, 1792
Abraham Hedges & Thankful Barns,	Feb. 2, 1792
Elisha Wetmore & Cynthia Guild,	Feb. 2, 1792
William Miller & Anne Bow,	April 30, 1792
Jonathan Lewis & Abigail Bow,	May 6, 1792
John Baigden & Sarah Cone,	June 3, 1792
John Miller of Elizabethtown, N. J., & Hannah Butler,	
	June 14, 1792
Stephen Wilder of N. Hamp. & Huldah Lucas,	June 19, 1792
Richard Yale & Polly Miles,	June 19, 1792
Timothy Sizer & Molly Hamlin,	June 21, 1792
Widower Simon Rereding & widow Eliz. Munroe,	
	July 4, 1792
Theodore Ellsworth of Chatham & Rebecca Lucas,	
	July 21, 1792
Theodore Dwight of Hartford & Abigail Alsop,	Sept. 9, 1792
Jacob Egleston & Sarah Whitmore,	Oct. 3, 1792
Thomas Warren & Tabitha (negroes),	Sept. 25, 1792
Rich. Nichols & Eliz. Isaacs,	Sept. 25, 1792
Nehemiah Beach Basset & Martha Savage,	Oct. 4, 1792
Sam. Johnson & Hope Warner,	Oct. 13, 1792
Levi Carrier & Persis Miller,	Nov. 22, 1792
Amos Johnson, Jr., & Desire Atkins,	Nov. 29, 1792
Isaac Ward & Diana Johnson,	Jan. 27, 1793
Ashbel Hubbard & Keturah Clark,	Feb. 7, 1793
David Jones of Wallingford & Dorothy Wetmore,	
	April 3, 1793
William Coulman & Hope Cone,	April 3, 1793
Rufus Hall of Wallingford & Sally Bates,	April 29, 1793
William Danforth & Huldah Scovil,	May 4, 1793
Thomas Lewis & Hannah Belden, both of Berlin,	
	May 15, 1793
Stephen Russel of N. Jersey & Lucretia Fisher,	May 2, 1793
Henry Johnson of N. London & Polly Jenison,	June 13, 1793
Ebenezer Hart & Mary Hands,	June 16, 1793
William Turner & Mia Goodwin,	July 1, 1793
Gilbert Fowler of New York & Hannah Kelly,	July 13, 1793
Caleb Bailey & Eliz. Tuells,	July 18, 1793

James Ward, Jr., & Eunice Birdsey, July 30, 1793
John Fisk & Poly Merrils, Aug. 10, 1793
John Hands & Eliz. Rockwell, Aug. 12, 1793
Wickham Roberts & Sarah Johnson, Aug. 29, 1793
Elijah Davis & Margaret Bennet, Aug. 30, 1793
Timothy Arnold of Great Barrington & Mary Birdsey,
  Oct. 6, 1793
Stephen Blake & Pharasenah Clark, Oct. 31, 1793
Zadoch Hubbard & Abigail Button, Nov. 4, 1793
William Roberts & Beulah Hedges, Nov. 21, 1793
Ichabod Miller & Sarah Birdsey, Nov. 28, 1793
Capt. Elisha Hubbard & Martha Roberts, Dec. 2, 1793
Joseph Colville Clark & Eliz. Clark, Dec. 9, 1793
Oliver Bidwell & Joanna Winborn Foster, Dec. 19, 1794
Seth Miller & Abigail Roberts, Dec. 30, 1793
Walter Griswold & Abigail Bates, Jan. 26, 1794
Nodiah Hubbard, Jr., & Eunice Ward, Jan. 30, 1794
William Atkins & Submit Clark, Feb. 9, 1794
Dan. Alvord, Jr., & Mindwell Cornwall, Feb. 9, 1794
Joseph Paddock & Louisa Strong, Feb. 20, 1794
Ichabod Blackstone & Catherine Gomey (free negroes),
  March 13, 1794
David Warner of Saybrook & Eunice Prout, March 27, 1794
William Birdsey & Eliz. Ward, April 3, 1794
Jabez Hall & Susanna Rees, April 8, 1794
Thomas Mather of Albany & Eliz. Hubbard, May 5, 1794
Thomas Burnham of Hartford & Phoebe Fairchild,
  June 15, 1794
John Bacon & Olive Ward, June 16, 1794
Sam. Chipman of Chatham & Anner Fraser, July 2, 1794
Prince Hull (free negro) of Hartford & Tryphosa
  Limbo (free negro) of Glastonbury, July 17, 1794
Joseph Blake of Whitestown, N. Y., & Prudence White,
  Sept. 8, 1794
Thomas Pierce of Beverley, Mass., & Nancy Alfred,
  Sept. 14, 1794
Abijah Hart of New York & Anner Hall, Sept. 22, 1794
Hezekiah Sumner of Sandisfield & widow Mary John-
  son (widow of Joseph), Oct. 1, 1794

Jesse Miller of Chatham & Patty Roberts,   Oct. 2, 1794
Calvin Johnson & widow Abia Miller,   Oct. 8, 1794
Gershom Thayer & Sarah Arnold,   Oct. 9, 1794
Joseph Kelsey & widow Patty Irons,   Oct. 16, 1794
Zadock Bailey & Lucy Treadway,   Oct. 30, 1794
Benj. Dewolf & Peggy Higbe,   Nov. 20, 1794
Elisha Fairchild & Lucretia Hubbard,   Nov. 26, 1794
Elisha Hall of Meriden & Mary Roberts of Middlefield,
                                                    Nov. 28, 1794
David Osborn of Stratford & Polly Cotton,   Dec. 6, 1794
Widower Gamaliel Loomis of Dartmouth, N. Hamp.,
    & widow Hannah Adams,   Dec. 8, 1794
Jacob Johnson & Anner Miller,   Dec. 11, 1794
Jacob Webster (free negro) & Jenny,   Dec. 11, 1794
James Pigot & Abigail Nott,   Dec. 26, 1794
Jesse Swaddle of Chatham & widow Hannah Powers,
                                                    Jan. 5, 1795
Tryon Cook of New Durham, N. Y., & Mary Griffin,
                                                    Jan. 23, 1795
Philo Beers (late of Wallingford) & Mary Lane of New
    Haven,   Feb. 19, 1795
Dan. Tallcott & Hannah Coe, both of Middlefield,
                                                    Feb. 22, 1795
Amos Miller & Elizabeth Coe, both of Middlefield,
                                                    Feb. 22, 1795
Elisha Tallcott & Dolly Wetmore, both of Middlefield,
                                                    Feb. 22, 1795
John Pratt & Eliz. Cooper,   Feb. 28, 1795
Elisha Cook of New Durham, N. Y., & Wealthy
    Bishop of Durham, Conn.,   March 7, 1795
Oliver Barns & Hannah Driggs,   April 4, 1795
Barnabas Chipman of Chatham & Abigail Cone,
                                                    May 12, 1795
Jonathan Simons of Hanover, N. Hamp., & Polly Doyle,
                                                    May 13, 1795
Widower Noadiah Hubbard & widow Sarah Seward
    of Haddam,   May 21, 1795
John Southmayd & Hannah Paddock,   June 3, 1795
Joshua Rockwell, Jr., & Nabby Partridge,   June 14, 1795

Simeon Gardner of New Lebanon, Mass., & Dorcas
    Banks,   June 15, 1795
Eliphalet Bailey of Chatham & Olive Tryon,   June 18, 1795
Barachiah Fairbanks, Jr., & Huldah Sizer,   June 18, 1795
Dan. Nice of New York & Sally Lane,   July 26, 1795
Joseph Bradford of Haddam & Martha Miller of Mid-
    dlefield,   Aug. 1, 1795
Rev. Joseph Washburn of Farmington & Sarah Boardman,
                                  Aug. 16, 1795
Dennis Billings of Hartland & Esther Hatch, Aug. 20, 1795
Jeremiah Norton of Chatham & Phila Bailey, Sept. 20, 1795
Jeremiah Markham, Jr., & Sarah Clark, daughter of
    Oliver Clark of Durham,   Oct. 1, 1795
Wm. James of Hartford & Polly Clark,   Oct. 3, 1795
Col. Howell Woodbridge of Glastonbury & Eunice
    Dickinson,   Oct. 19, 1795
Sam. Plum & Rhoda Gilbert,   Oct. 27, 1795
Remembrance Simmons Kine & Rhoda Barns, Nov. 1, 1795
Giles Lyman of Belchers, Mass., & Mary Hubbard,
                               Nov. 10, 1795
Elisha Spaulding of Plainfield, N. Hamp., & Prudence
    Tryon,   Nov. 26, 1795
Hezekiah Lord & Ruth Campbell,   Dec. 7, 1795
John Thompson of Norwich & Susannah Butler,
    widower and widow with two children each, Dec. 19, 1795
Wm. Cole & Lois Miller,   Dec. 31, 1795
Comfort Goodwin & Eliz. Pin,   Jan. 2, 1796
Widower Benj. Conklin of Hartford & widow Martha
    Ranny,   Jan. 28, 1796
Simon House of Hebron (Andover Society) & Lucy
    Huntington,   Feb. 2, 1796
Asa Hubbard & Sally Sears,   Feb. 7, 1796
David Bliss of Lebanon & Eliz. Johnson,   Feb. 24, 1796
Jabez Barns & Mary Crowell,   Feb. 24, 1796
Ebenezer Chamberlain & Susanna Jones,   Feb. 27, 1796
Henry Duc (Frenchman) & Lucy Sumner, daughter
    of Eliz., widow of Col. John Sumner, March 5, 1796
Wm. Brenton Hall & Mehetabel Parsons, March 7, 1796
Bliss Lee & Martha Barnes,   March 10, 1796

Carl Bishop of Norwich & Lucretia Miller,	March 26,	1796
Abner Bow & Rhoda Tryon,	April 6,	1796
Wm. C. Hall & Olive Cooper,	April 9,	1796
Anson Hubbard & Rebecca Hedges,	April 14,	1796
Enoch Daniels & Humility Whitmore,	May 15,	1796
Jonathan Smith & Rebecca Woodward,	May 19,	1796
Hinkman Roberts & Mary Johnson,	May 26,	1796
Hezekiah Hulbert & Catherine Hulbert,	June 2,	1796
Peter Carlton & Lucretia Russell,	June 24,	1796
John Ward Lucas & Esther Stow,	June 30,	1796
Joseph Whitmore & Huldah Roberts,	July 27,	1796
Archibald Cunningham & Sarah Miller,	Aug. 16,	1796
Wm. Knap & Katherine Whitehead,	Aug. 19,	1796
Jesse Johnson & Lydia Barns,	Aug. 22,	1796
Asahel Ward & Patty Hamlin,	Aug. 28,	1796
Moses Carpenter & widow Mary Yale, daughter of		
Wilson Mighels,	Sept. 1,	1796
David Hubbard & Hannah Clark,	Sept. 3,	1796
Isaac Smith & Hannah Brown of Chatham,	Sept. 12,	1796
David Strong & Clarissa Campbell,	Sept. 24,	1796
Obadiah Bow & Hester Markham,	Sept. 29,	1796
Aaron Root of Pittsfield, Mass., & Clarissa Pomeroy,		
	Oct. 23,	1796
Allyn Southmayd & Lucy Meigs,	Oct. 29,	1796
Ephraim Corben of Great Barrington & Rachel Bivins,		
	Nov. 23,	1796
Josiah Hubbard of Litchfield & Susanna Marks,		
	Nov. 24,	1796
Wm. Bivins & Meliscent Turner,	Nov. 30,	1796
Edward Roberts & Sarah Hedges,	Dec. 8,	1796
David Fairbanks & Anna Roberts,	Dec. 8,	1796
Phineas Brainard & Mabel Lucas,	Dec. 20,	1796
Evan Rogers of Baltimore, Md., & Clarissa Starr,		
	Dec. 23,	1796
Oliver Wetmore & Esther Southmayd,	Jan. 15,	1797
David Miner & Mary Meigs,	Jan. 21,	1797
Fairchild Hubbard & Phoebe Ward,	Jan. 22,	1797
Wm. Belcher of Chatham & Nelly Doyle,	Feb. 5,	1797
Lathrop Lee & Abigail Barns,	Feb. 23,	1797

Nathan'll Bishop of Richmond, Mass., & Nancy Pomery,
　　　　　　　　　　　　　　　March 2, 1797
Benj. Wetmore & Thankful Griswold Lucas, March 2, 1797
Widower John Crowel & widow Mary Starr,　March 9, 1797
Seth Coe & Eunice Roberts,　　　　　　　March 23, 1797
Amos Coe & Huldah Roberts,　　　　　　April 6, 1797
Joseph Austin & Polly Clark,　　　　　　April 13, 1797
Ebenezer Southmayd & Eliz. Starr,　　　　April 16, 1797
Josiah Kyes & Dorcas Hubbard,　　　　　April 18, 1797
Daniel Johnson & Lucretia Prout,　　　　April 27, 1797
Reuben Hall of Wallingford & Sally Miller,　May 25, 1797
Hezekiah Ranney, Jr., & Mary Richardson,　May 30, 1797
Joseph Hall of Wallingford & Mary Cornwall, May 31, 1797
Widower Seth Roberts & widow Dorcas Loveland,
　　　　　　　　　　　　　　　June 17, 1797
Jonathan Bill & Lucy Paddock,　　　　　July 3, 1797
Widower Wm. Devoll of Sag Harbor, L. I., & widow
　　Eliz. Giles,　　　　　　　　　　　July 13, 1797
Sam. Tiffin & Phoebe Parsons,　　　　　July 30, 1797
Elijah Kelly & Eliz. Brigden,　　　　　July 30, 1797
James Wells (negro) & Sylvia (negro),　　Aug. 1, 1797
John Ward & Hannah Hubbard (natural daughter of
　　Rebecca Ward and granddaughter of Lt. Thos.
　　Ward; her mother married James McKain),
　　　　　　　　　　　　　　　Aug. 20, 1797
Moses Tufts & Thankful Marks of Meriden,　Aug. 27, 1797
Thos. Hillhouse of Troy. N. Y., & Harriet Homer,
　　　　　　　　　　　　　　　Sept. 2, 1797
Mathew Talcot Russell & Mary Huntington, Jr.,
　　　　　　　　　　　　　　　Sept. 17, 1797
Thos. Ault (Englishman) & Phoebe Ward (a widow
　　with one child),　　　　　　　　Sept. 23, 1797
Luther Seymour & Rebecca Curtiss, both of Farmington,
　　　　　　　　　　　　　　　Sept. 27, 1797
Dan. Whitmore, Jr., & Mary Lucas,　　　Oct. 9, 1797
David Clark & Lucy Stow,　　　　　　　Oct. 14, 1797
Amasa Smith & Mary Williams,　　　　　Oct. 14, 1797
Jonathan Miller, Jr., & Lucy Harris,　　　Oct. 23, 1797
Nathan'll Cornwall & Lois Tryon,　　　　Oct. 26, 1797

George Risley of East Hartford & Eliz. Bacon, Oct. 26, 1797
Joseph Wright Alsop & Lucy Whittelsey, Nov. 5, 1797
Stephen Stow & Sally Tallcot, both of Durham, Nov. 6, 1797
Sam. Canfield & Margaret Hamlin, Nov. 11, 1797
Charles Tryon, Jr., & Sarah Smith, Nov. 19, 1797
David Stow, Jr., & Mabel O. Daniels, Jan. 1, 1798
Wm. Scovil & Rebecca Gauge, Jan. 8, 1798
Jesse Miller & Susanna Wetmore, both of Middlefield,
Jan. 13, 1798
Kirtland Field of Guilford & Abigail Brooks, March 14, 1798
Timothy Roberts, Jr., & widow Rhoda Bow, March 22, 1798
Widower Thos. Goodwin, Jr., & widow Margaret Dairs,
April 5, 1798
Dr. Wm. Dix of Boston & Mary Ruggles, May 31, 1798
Sam. Huggins of New Haven & Martha Dandridge
Starr, June 30, 1798
Gershom Birdsey & Lucy Coe, Aug. 9, 1798
Joseph Boardman & Anna Meigs, Sept. 27, 1798
Jabez Deling of Glastonbury & Eliz. Bailey, Oct. 9, 1798
George Geer & Olive Arnold, Nov. 29, 1798
James Shey, Esq., of Upton-upon-Severn, County of
Worcester, Eng., & Martha Russel, daughter of
Wm. Russel, Esq., late of Birmingham, Eng.,
Dec. 13, 1798
Timothy Cornwall, son of Timothy, & Anne, daughter
of Sam. Chamberlain, Dec. 25, 1798
Amasa Waters of Johnstown, N. Y., & Lucy Plum,
daughter of Hass Plum, Dec. 30, 1798
James Manwaring of New London & Hannah Campbell,
Jan. 1, 1799
David Miller of Middlefield & Ruth Daniels, Jan. 3, 1799
Seth Birdsey & Ruth Ward, Jan. 10, 1799
Jabez Lyman of Royalton, Vt., & Lois Johnson, Jan. 24, 1799
Timothy Southmayd & Rebecca Bull, Feb. 13, 1799
Daniel Hancock of Hartford & Katherine Hurlbut of
Weathersfield, Feb. 23, 1799
Gurdon Whitmore, Jr., & Olly Tryon, Feb. 24, 1799
Partridge Johnson & Sarah Davis, May 13, 1799
Wm. Roberts & Sarah Bailey, both of Haddam, April 6, 1799

Joshua Arnold & Eliz. Ward,   May 16, 1799
Henry Williams Jones of Brattleborough, Vt., &
    Martha Smith,   May 25, 1799
Jonathan Shency of Berlin & Rhoda Roy,   June 16, 1799
James Crowell & Phoebe Crowel,   June 20, 1799
Widower Patrick O. Daniels & widow Molly Francis,
                                           June 30, 1799
Nathan'll Elton of Canaan & Hannah Loury, July 7, 1799
Rev. Thomas Welles Bray of Cohabit (widower) &
    widow Anne Bates of Durham,   July 9, 1799
James Wright & Jane Blake,   Sept. 1, 1799
William Butler & Lois Arnold,   Sept. 5, 1799
Christopher Mungus & Mary Eglestone,   Oct. 14, 1799
Stephen Ball of New Haven & Nabby Scott,   Nov. 5, 1799
Gideon Gates of East Haddam & Ruth Blakeslee,
                                           Nov. 23, 1799

EAST HADDAM.

MIDDLESEX COUNTY.

(See Book I.)

Was taken from Haddam and incorporated in 1734. The first Congregational Church was formed in East Haddam, May 3, 1704. The Second Church records—Millington—appear in Book I. The following marriages are from the First Church records.

Thomas Gates, Jr., & Sarah Rowley,   May 31, 1751
Thomas Borall & Abigail Boogue,   June 24, 1751
Daniel Brainerd & Esther Gates,   Aug. 15, 1751
Caleb Chapman, Jr., & Elizabeth Clark,   Oct. 4, 1751
Daniel Lord & Lydia Chapman,   Oct. 11, 1751
Gideon Spencer & Elizabeth Hurd,   Nov. 7, 1751
Hezekiah Mack & Rachel Church,   ——
Elisha Cone & Abigail Olmsted,   Jan. 2, 1752
Adonijah Robards & Rachel Emons,   March 19, 1752
David Willie & Rachel Spencer,   Aug. 20, 1752
Thos. Cone, Jr., & —— Warner,   Nov. 23, 1752
Stephen Nolton & Abigail Rowley,   Dec. 21, 1752
Bethiah Bishop & Ruth Snow,   Jan. 3, 1753

Abraham Williams & Sarah Williams,	Feb. 1, 1753
David Stockin & Abigail Spencer,	June 14, 1753
Judah Gates & Abigail Hurd,	Dec. 12, 1753
John Hervey & Sarah Emons,	Dec. 27, 1753

Peter, a negro servant of Capt. Jabez Chapman, &
  Catherine, a negro wentch of Job Spencer's, Dec. 27, 1753

Jabez Chapman, Jr., & Sarah Olmsted,	Feb. 14, 1754

Felt, a negro man, & Sarah, an Indian woman, servants
  to Jonathan Cone,   March 12, 1754

John Darbe of Hebron & Hannah Rowley,	Aug. 8, 1754
Azeriah Heath & Hannah Lamb,	Oct. 16, 1754
Timothy Brainerd & Mary Smith,	Oct. 24, 1754
John Persivell & Mary Brainerd,	Nov. 7, 1754

Dudley Brainerd of Middle Haddam & Mindwell Ackley,
                                                     Nov. 13, 1754
Ezekiel Chapman of East Haddam & Abigail Niles
  of Colchester,   Jan. 30, 1755

James Green & Ruth Marshel,	Feb. 13, 1755
Seth Bush & Elizabeth Ball,	March 7, 1755
Josiah Arnold & Hannah Cone,	May 29, 1755

Gideon Webb of Haddam & Temperance Huff of
  Chester in Saybrook,   July 27, 1755

Silvanius Tinker & Abigail Olmsted,	Sept. 25, 1755
Eleazer Brainerd & Mary Bate,	Oct. 2, 1755
Benjamin Ackley, Jr., & Hannah Higgins,	Jan. 15, 1756
Thomas Olocoat & Mary Persavell,	April 7, 1756
Benjamin Bragg & Experience Ackley,	April 19, 1756
Israel Champion & Mehetable Fuller,	April 29, 1756
Nathan'll Cowdry & Mary Gates,	May 27, 1756
John Bates & Phebe Clark,	July 8, 1756
Hezekiah Ackley & Abigail Done,	Sept. 15, 1756
Abner Brainerd & Elizabeth Champion,	Dec. 29, 1756

The Rev. Mr. Elijah Mason of Malborough & Mrs.
  Mary Champion,   Feb. 16, 1757
Sam'll Huntington, Esq., of Canterbury & Mrs.
  Dorothy Gates,   May 25, 1757

Joel Cone & Hannah Brainerd,	June 9, 1757
Joseph Hull of Killingworth & Sarah Hurd,	Jan. 18, 1758

The Rev. Mr. Benjamin Bowers of Middle Haddam
  & Mrs. Ann Hosmer,   July 31, 1759

James Ackly, Jr., of Colchester & Ruth Ackly, Dec. 19, 1759
Joseph Warner & Elizabeth Cone, Jan. 24, 1760
David Belden & Mary Ackly, April 17, 1760
Abraham Waterhouse of Saybrook in Chester &
  Elizabeth Chapman, June 19, 1760
Thomas Spencer & Thankful Ackly, Aug. 27, 1760
Thomas Fuller, 2d, & Mary Hosmer, Nov. 6, 1760
Cornelius Anable & Lucy Green, Nov. 10, 1760
Israel Smith of Mansfield & Esther Andress, Dec. 18, 1760
Thomas Clark of Haddam & Susannah Swaddle,
  March 4, 1761
Eliakim Spencer & Dorothy Gates, April 16, 1761
Robert Hurd, Jr., & Elioner Andress, April 23, 1761
Matthew Smith, Jr., & Thankful Ackly, May 13, 1761
George Cone, Jr., & Elizabeth Brainerd, May 21, 1761
Timothy Gates & Hannah Persevell, June 17, 1761
William Marshal & Lydia Warner, July 26, 1761
Sam'll Phil's Lord & Rachel White, Aug. 30, 1761
Elizur Holester of Eastbury & Sarah Gates, Oct. 29, 1761
Abner Brainerd & Elizabeth Burr, Nov. 16, 1761
Phineas Tinker of Lyme & Charity Marshell, Nov. 24, 1761
Timothy Rowley of ye Oblong & Bathia Crocker, Dec. 3, 1761
Daniel Stewart of Litchfield & Phebe Chapman, Jan. 11, 1762
Peirce Mobs & Eunice Sawer, Jan. 27, 1762
Frederick Spencer & Hannah Chapman, April 1, 1762
Zaccheus Spencer & Hannah Dible, April 9, 1762
John Bates & Ann Crocker, May 27, 1762
Benjamin Read & Hannah White, June 10, 1762
Daniel Gates & Zinorah Fuller, Aug. 12, 1762
Nehemiah Higgins of Durham & Thankful Hurd,
  Feb. 10, 1763
Asaal Brainerd of Middle Haddam & Experience Ackly,
  March 30, 1763
Samuel Olmsted, Jr., & Esther Robards, March 31, 1763
Thomas Hunt of Glassenbury & Sarah Gates, April 26, 1763
James Olmsted & Ann Cone, June 23, 1763
Rowland Persevell & Sible Fuller, June 30, 1763
John Wetmore & Martha Stanclift, Sept. 15, 1763
Samuel Pennick of Goshon & Mercy Chapman, Sept. 22, 1763

9

Amasa Brainerd & Jedida Osborn,	Dec. 22, 1763
——— Whitmore of Middletown & Sarah Hall,	Jan. 10, 1764
Timothy Chapman & Sarah Fuller,	Jan. 26, 1764
Neodiah Gates & Martha Fuller,	Feb. 23, 1764
Robinson Williams & Abigale Burr,	March 27, 1764
James Cone, Jr., & Ellice Crocker,	May 3, 1764
Benjamin Barney of Norwich & Elizabeth Ackly,	
	Aug. 16, 1764
Isaiah Chapman & Hazediah Sawer of Lyme,	Oct. 29, 1764
Jehiel Saxton & Rhoda Ackly,	Jan. 15, 1765
Elijah Ackly, Jr., & Ann Osborn,	Jan. 31, 1765
Ezekiel Crocker & Lydia Arnold,	March 28, 1765
Capt. Jonathan Olburd (Olvard or Alvord) & the widow	
Mary Brainerd,	Nov. 21, 1765
David Belden & Ann Lisk,	Dec. 12, 1765
Timothy Booge & Rebeccah Stanclift,	May 7, 1766
Jonathan Kilborn, Jr., & Hannah Chapman,	Oct. 2, 1766
Zacheriah Spencer & Mary Wright,	Nov. 13, 1766
Judah Spencer & Susannah Bebe,	March 5, 1767
John Harvey & Sarah Phelps,	March 26, 1767
Ezra Caswell of Norwich & Elisabath Pratt,	March 27, 1767
Jonathan Sheperson & Susanna Lord,	April 29, 1767
John Willie & Elisabeth Marshall,	April 30, 1767
Elijah White, Jr., & Elisabeth Arnold,	May 11, 1767
Jonah Spencer & Abigail Calking,	Aug. 20, 1767
William Gilbert & Dorcas Dimock,	April 26, 1768
John Gilbert & Mehetable Cone,	April 26, 1768
Isaac Chapman & Tabaitha Chapman,	May 5, 1768
Abihu Mack & Anne Fuller,	July 12, 1767
Daniel Warner, Jr., & Elisabeth Clark,	July 28, 1767
Gershom Crocker & Ann Fisher,	Jan. 17, 1769
Caleb Stockin & Elise Williams,	Jan. 23, 1769
David Brainerd Spencer & Huldah Brainerd,	Feb. 2, 1769
Asahel Rogers & Sarah Scovell,	March 15, 1769
Ozias Chapman & Abigail Fuller,	Aug. 10, 1769
Zechariah Williams & Sible Lamb,	Nov. 21, 1769
Simeon Olmsted of Northfield & Anne Olmsted,	
	Nov. 23, 1769
Levi Austin of Richmond & Mary Gates,	Nov. 30, 1769

James Taylor & Deborah Lord, Dec. 14, 1769
Benjamin Stewart of Hebron & Lois Chapman,
Dec. 14, 1769
Bennaiah Collins of Liverpool & Susannah Tracy,
March 28, 1770
Ezra Waterman of Colchester & Mary Brewster,
April 5, 1770
Joshua Gates, Jr., & Sarah Minor, May 30, 1770
John Jack & Esther Jones, both of Morristown, East
Jersey (?), June 5, 1770
Matthew Cone & Lydia Gates, Sept. 13, 1770
Benjamin Emmons & Esther Marvin, Nov. 15, 1770
Eliphalet Fuller & Thankful Sparrow, Nov. 22, 1770
Nathan Burnham & Mary Anneble, Feb. 7, 1771
Samuel Crowell of Liverpool & Jerusha Tracy,
March 14, 1771

EAST HADDAM, OCT. 28, 1772.

The following records are entered by Elijah Parsons, who was this Day ordained Pastor of the First Church of Christ in this Place.

John Spencer & Susanna White, Oct. 28, 1772
Abner Hall & Phebe Percivall, Nov. 29, 1772
Jacob Hart & Rebecca Gates, Jan. 24, 1773
Robert Richards & Rosanna Phelps, two transient
persons, March 10, 1773
Joseph Church & Joanna Spencer, March 18, 1773
Charles Clark & Hannah Heath, Aug. 26, 1773
Zechariah Gates & Martha Annible, Sept. 5, 1773
Capt. Joshua Brainerd of Chatham & widow Martha Cone,
Oct. 31, 1773
Ebenezer Cone, Jr., & widow Mary Brainerd, Nov. 7, 1773
Elijah Parsons of East Haddam & Elizabeth Rogers
of Boston, by Rev. John Hunt, Sept. 16, 1773
Sam'l Jones of Barkhamstead & Ruth Ackley, Dec. 7, 1773
Joseph Adams of Canterbury & ——— Chapman,
Nov. 25, 1773
Aaron Chapman & Polly Northum, Jan. 2, 1774

Phineas Gates & Anne Taylor,	Dec.,	1773
Judah Cone of Had Lyme & Lydia Cone,	April 10,	1774
Doct. Francis Percival & Miriam Chapman,	May 24,	1774
—— Bryant of Richmond & Eliza'th Cone of Millington,	May 26,	1774
Darius Morris of Wilbraham & Elizabeth Fisher,	Nov. 15,	1774
Reuben Spencer & Elizabeth Cone,	March 17,	1775
John Brainerd & —— Smith,		——
Capt. David Miller & widow Elizabeth Ely,	May 24,	1775
William Cone, Jr., & Azuba Olmsted,	April 23,	1775
Joshua Brainerd & Elizabeth Gates,*	May,	1775
John Gould of Lyme & Mary Sears,	June 15,	1775
Timothy Judd of Colchester & Elizabeth Bebee,	Sept.,	1775
Isaac Humphrey of Killingly & Mary Chapman,	Oct. 5,	1775
Joseph Woodwell & —— Annable,	Oct. 12,	1775
Ebenezer Cone, 3d, & Tryphena Tracy,	Nov. 21,	1775
John Wales of Hopkinton & Lydia Hurd,	Oct. 17,	1775
Israel Dewey of Colchester & Bethiah Ackley,	Dec. 14,	1775
Caleb Chapman, Jr., of East Haddam & Hannah Brown of Chatham,	Dec. 18,	1775
Amasa Spencer & Mary Gates,	Feb. 1,	1776
Phineas Cone & Azuba Stocking,	Feb. 13,	1776
Amos Booge & Hannah Fuller,	Feb. 28,	1776
Peter Spencer, Jr., & Mehetable Cone, both of Millington,	March 6,	1776
Gideon Cook & Huldah Lisk,	March 20,	1776
Gabriel Ely & Huldah Stocking,	June 30,	1776
Capt. Daniel Pratt of Colchester & Abigail White,	July,	1776
Samuel Judd of Colchester & Phebe Beebe,	Nov. 11,	1776
John Wright of Colchester & Lucy Sears,	Nov. 21,	1776
Zachariah Cone & Jemima Hall,	Dec. 5,	1776
John Carpenter of Brimfield & Lavina Chapel,	Feb. 27,	1777
Hezekiah Mack & Anne Spencer,	March 20,	1777
—— Banning of Hartland & Annar Sparrow,	April 3,	1777
John Peck & Mary Lord,	April 21	1777
Noadiah Emmons & Elizabeth Brainerd,	May 1,	1777

* Editor.—Name said to be Abigail Gates, widow of Judah Gates.

Ephraim Fuller & Mary Brainerd,	May 15, 1777
Lemuel Scovil & Kezia Briggs, both of Chatham, July 8, 1777	
Uzziel Clark & —— Knowlton,	Nov. 20, 1777
Joseph Hungerford & Hannah Green,	Nov. 20, 1777
Joseph Selden & Abigail Beckwith, both of Had Lyme,	
	Nov. 25, 1777
Amos B. West & Anna Spencer,	Dec. 14, 1777
—— Stewart of Millington & —— Comstock of	
Had Lyme,	Dec., 1777
Matthew Smith, 3d, & Asenith Annable,	Dec., 1777
Plinny Hollister & —— Griswold of Eastbury,	
	March 18, 1778
Abel Flint of Lebanon & Martha Hosmer,	March, 1778
Edward Howell of Long Island & Abigail Kirtland,	
	April 15, 1778
Whacket & Base, two free negroes, and Peter & Peg,	
two other free negroes,	May, 1778
Gurdon Percival & Sarah Chapman,	Oct., 1778
Asa Chapman & Elizabeth Williams,	Nov. 26, 1778
Elijah Wilder & Hannah Spencer,	1778
William Lee of Middletown & Prudence Ackley, Dec. 22, 1778	
Timothy Tiffany of Lyme & Mary Foster,	Jan., 1779
Noah Stone of Guilford & Mary Hurd,	May 14, 1779
Peter Foster of Long Island & —— Vail,	May, 1779
Sam'l Phelps of Lyme & Lovina Cone,	Oct. 31, 1779
Rufus Glass & Huldah Fuller,	Nov. 16, 1779
Ephraim Selby & Olive Spencer,	Nov. 18, 1779
Josiah Lyon & Susanna Selby,	Nov. 18, 1779
Knowles Shaw of Wilbraham & Margaret Hungerford,	
	March 13, 1780
Pomp, a free negro of Richmond, & Peg of East	
Haddam,	Jan., 1780
Job Beckwith & Mehitable Champion,	March, 1780
Jabez Comstock & Dorothy Hunn,	May, 1780
Elijah Spencer & Abigail Annible,	Aug. 10, 1780
Daniel White & Hannah Brainard,	Aug. 31, 1780
Rev. Joseph Vaill & Sarah Fowler,	Oct. 12, 1780
—— Hull of Killingworth & Esther Hurd,	Dec., 1780
Timothy Fuller & Hannah Fuller,	1781

Sam'l Fox & Miriam Scovil, Feb., 1781
Daniel Jones & Olive Tinker, March, 1781
John Mitchel & Louis Gates, April, 1781
Amos & ———, two free negroes, April, 1781
Jn'o Percival, 3d, & Dorothy Burt, May 24, 1781
Daniel Stewart & Olive Scovil, May, 1781
Jabez Chapman, Jr., & Polly Rogers, May 29, 1781
Edward Johnson & Sarah Hurlburt, July, 1781
William Gelston & Sena Sears, July, 1781
Sam'l Palmes & Mary Foster, Sept. 19, 1781
John Andrews & Lucy Cone, Sept. 26, 1781
Capt. Henry Champion of Colchester & Abigail Tinker,
Oct., 1781
Isaac Taylor & Sarah Fuller, Nov. 8, 1781
William W. Fuller & Susanna Knowlton, Nov. 8, 1781
Stephen Higgins & Temperance Winslow, Nov. 15, 1781
——— Johnson of Killingworth & Esther Brainerd, 1781
Abraham Osborne of Long Island & Dorothy Booge,
Jan. 11, 1782
Thomas Hall, Jr., & Polly Smith, Jan. 20, 1782
Wm. Bradford & Elizabeth Sears, Jan., 1782
Nero Thompson & Lydia Ding, both free negroes,
Feb. 4, 1782
Ebenezer Cone & Temperance Foster, Feb., 1782
Jack Day & Desire Bates, two free negroes, Feb., 1782
Watrous Beckwith & Mary Brainerd, March, 1782
William Silliman & Dorothy Huntington, March, 1782
Joseph Beckwith & Olive Cone, May 26, 1782
John P. Albertson & Rachel Hall, June, 1782
Simeon Spencer & widow ——— Bramble, July, 1782
Squier Haskil & Esther Humphrey, Nov. 14, 1782
Samuel Chapman & Zilpa Gates, March 6, 1783
Elijah Graves & Elisabeth Warner, March 27, 1783
——— Mitchel of Chatham & ——— Thornton, April, 1783
Joseph Warner, Jr., & Sarah Osborne of Long Island,
April, 1783
Abraham Annible & Abigail Harris, May, 1783
David Brainerd & Rachel Smith, June 5, 1783
Adonijah Foot, Jr., of Colchester & Sarah Foster
from Long Island, June 19, 1783

Joshua Brainerd, Jr., & —— Foster of Chatham,
March, 1783
Jehiel Isham of Colchester & Sarah Mobs, Sept. 18, 1783
Jonathan Bebee, in the 87th year of his age, & Remem-
ber Nye, in her 85th year, Oct. 7, 1783
Robinson Williams of Colchester & Mary Lord, Oct. 23, 1783
Jared Hinckley of Lebanon & Mary Sheman, Nov., 1783
Capt. David Brainerd Spencer & Mary Fuller, also
Jehiel Fuller & Reliance Smith, June 24, 1783
Calvin Smith & Anna Annible, Jan., 1784
Wm. Baxter & Abigail Dewey, March 7, 1784
Samuel Chapman & Olive Green Fuller, March 25, 1784
Caleb Chapman, Jr., & Patty Gates, March 25, 1784
Philip White & Olive Rowley, March 25, 1784
Joshua Tinker of New London & Dorothy Cowdery,
April 8, 1784
Israel Cone & Lucy Ackley, April 13, 1784
Benjamin Trowbridge of Chatham & Sarah Harvey,
June 2, 1784
Sam'l Phelps of Lyme & Hannah Warner, June 17, 1784
Jonathan Wright of Litchfield & Tryphena Cone,
June 27, 1784
Abel Bingham & Jemima Ely, Sept. 9, 1784
Daniel Metcalf of Lebanon & Mary Cone, Nov. 11, 1784
Isaac Chalker Ackley & Ruth Burr, April 27, 1785
Daniel Cone & Olive Ackley, April 28, 1785
Hezekiah Comstock of Lyme & Annar Cone, May 19, 1785
Asa Deming & Clarissa Lyon, Oct., 1785
Josiah Lyon & Mercy Andrews, Oct., 1785
Lemuel Hungerford & Abigail Bebee, Nov. 9, 1785
John Arnold & Elizabeth Fuller, Nov. 13, 1785
Jeremiah Gates & Mary Chapel, Nov. 24, 1785
Elisha Peck of Lyme & Olive Emmons, Nov. 27, 1785
—— Dart of Chatham & Polly Kilborn, Dec. 4, 1785
Wm. Sabin of Colchester & Hannah Cowdery, Feb. 23, 1786
Oliver Gates & Mary Gates, May 4, 1786
Amasa Mitchel & Huldah Stocking, June 8, 1786
Elisha Cone & Betsey Tracy, Sept. 28, 1786
John H. Smith & Anne Champion, Oct., 1786

Selden Potter of Colebrook & Mary Rowley of Chatham,

	Nov. 2, 1786
Jonathan Spencer & Rebecca Spencer,	Dec. 14, 1786
Jonathan Northum & Patty Cone,	Dec. 21, 1786
Isaac Chapman & Abigail Brooks,	Dec. 24, 1786
Rowland Percival & Silence Gates,	Jan., 1787
Gabriel Ely & Olive Green Chapman,	March 25, 1787
David B. Hollister & Dorothy Brainerd,	March 26, 1787
Eleazer Cole of East Hartford & Mary Spencer,	May, 1787
Abraham Williams & Olive Chapman,	Aug. 19, 1787
Bezaleel Brainard, Jr., & Lydia Deming,	Oct. 21, 1787
Elijah Crosby & Phebe Church,	Oct. 31, 1787
Judah Willey & Hannah Saunders,	Nov. 4, 1787

Alexander Alvord of Colchester & Abigail Stocking,

	Dec. 12, 1787
Samuel Huntington & Patty Sears,	Jan. 24, 1788
Irad Fuller & Thankful Smith,	Jan. 29, 1788
Timothy Chapman, Jr., & Olive Fuller,	Jan. 29, 1788
Jeremiah Gates of Chatham & Ruth Williams,	May 25, 1788
Eddy Burnham & Mary Emmons,	June 30, 1788
Sterling Clark & Sarah Warner,	Oct. 29, 1788
John Mobs & Hannah Sheppardson,	Nov. 3, 1788
Nathaniel Hungerford, Jr., & Dorothy Gates,	Nov. 5, 1788
Benjamin Fuller of Ludlow & Anise Fuller,	Nov. 19, 1788
Dr. Amos Skeel of Chatham & Mercy Cone,	Dec. 10, 1788
Walter Cone & Dorothy Palmer,	March 26, 1789
Samuel Hall, Jr., & Hannah Cone,	July 7, 1789
Amasa Spencer of West Stockbridge & Sybil Cone,	June, 1789
Calvin Spencer & Mehitable Brainerd,	Nov. 1, 1789
Stephen Fuller & Hannah Smith,	Nov. 8, 1789
Jared Spencer & Nancy Green,	Nov. 30, 1789

Col. Elias Worthington of Colchester & Dorothy Cone,

	Jan. 10, 1790
Avery Bebee & Lucy Beckwith,	Jan. 14, 1790
Joshua Cone & Cloe Chapman,	Jan. 17, 1790
Jonah Gates & Esther Smith,	Feb. 25, 1790
Oliver Warner & Charity Brainerd,	June 6, 1790
Augustus Hills & Jane Moseley (free negroes),	June, 1790
Green Hungerford & Alice Willey,	Jan. 11, 1791

Josiah Griffing & Dorothy Gates,	Feb. 22,	1791
Ira Johnson & Mary Rollo,	Feb. 23,	1791
Jacob Comstock & Sarah Been Foster,	March 17,	1791
Joseph White of Chatham & Hannah Gates,	March 29,	1791
Jabez Fuller & Lydia Smith,	April 3,	1791
Abner Brainerd of Chatham & Lucy Fuller,	April 24,	1791
Thomas Moseley & Phebe Throop,	Oct. 20,	1791
William Green & Indiana Tinker,	Oct. 26,	1791
James Mitchel & Abigail Spencer,	Dec. 5,	1791
Isaac Ackley & Mary Brainerd,*	Jan. 2,	1792
Daniel Janes of Canaan & Temperance Tinker,	Feb. 6,	1792
John Isham of Colchester & Esther Annable,	March,	1792
Duell Rowley & Deborah Fuller,	Sept. 6,	1792
Silas Loomis of North Bolton & Betsey Emmons of		
Millington,	Sept. 6,	1792
Ephraim Foot of Colchester & Lydia Ackley,	Oct. 4,	1792
Capt. Jonathan Kilborn & Elizabeth Brainerd,†	Jan. 23,	1793
Noadiah Gates, Jr., & Anna Emmons,	April 14,	1793
Sylvanus Lindsley & Abigail White,	April 28,	1793
Benjamin Manwaring of Lyme & Sabra Hurd,	June 24,	1893
Thomas Fuller, 2d, & Statira Chapman,	Aug. 29,	1793
Rufus Dewy & Polly Kilborn,	Dec. 12,	1793
Elizur Gates & Abigail Rowley,	Dec. 25,	1793
Isaac Bigelow of Springfield & Tabitha Chapman,		
	Aug. 24,	1794
Asa Isham of Colchester & Sally Chapman,	Dec. 21,	1794
Henry White of Hadley & Almira Tinker,	Feb. 1,	1795
Samuel Spencer & Anna Olmsted,	Sept. 24,	1794
William Chapman & Lucy Higgins,	Oct. 15,	1795
Charles Northum & Sally Harvey,	Nov. 18,	1795
Gurdon Chapel & Olive Gates,	Nov. 23,	1795
Calvin Chapel & Mary Brooks,	Feb. 16,	1796
Reuel Eddy & Salina Gates,	Feb. 23,	1796
William Palmer & Dorothy Smith,	March 3,	1796
Rev. Amos Bassett of Hebron & Sarah Tinker,		
Edmund Doolittle & Lydia Gates,	——	
	March 30,	1796

* EDITOR.—Said to be Abigail Brainerd, widow of Joshua Brainerd.
† EDITOR.—Widow of Lieut. Abner Brainerd.

Gamaliel Thatcher & Sally Johnson,   Aug. 5, 1796
Samuel Huntington, Jr., & Demise Huntington from
    Hebron,   Oct. 7, 1796
Thomas Ackley & Huldah Hurd,   Dec. 14, 1796
Simeon Metcalf & Lydia Marshal,   Jan., 1798
Moses Knowlton Bartlet of Wilbraham & Mary
    Wright of East Haddam,   March 6, 1798
Hezekiah W. Percival & Phebe Foster,   March 18, 1798
Elijah Payne of Bolton & Mary Gates,   April 12, 1798
Solomon Huntington & Elizabeth Fowler,   April 12, 1798
Ezekiel Lord of Colchester & Sarah Woodwill,   Sept. 16, 1798
Samuel Fay of Thompson & Betsey Chapman,   Oct. 28, 1798
Amos White, Jr., & Hannah White,   March 17, 1799
Gurdon Fowler of Bolton & Anne Ackley,   June 13, 1799
Asa Spencer & Polly Ackley,   Aug. 23, 1799
Darius Gates & Anna Brainerd,   Oct. 7, 1799
Nathaniel Leet (?) of West Stockbridge & Demise
    Wickham,   Feb. 2, 1800
Joseph Brooks & Betsey Cone,   Feb. 27, 1800
Joseph S. Brainerd & Hannah Hungerford,   May 25, 1800
Timothy Fuller Andrews & Rhoda Spencer,   July 5, 1800
Sylvester Williams & Polly Brainerd,   Sept. 7, 1800
Henry Snow of Chatham & Anne Cook,   Oct. 9, 1800
Abner Hurd & Olive Daniels,   Nov. 16, 1800
Deacon Caleb Gates & Elizabeth Percival,   Dec. 4, 1800

INDEX.

EARLY CONNECTICUT MARRIAGES

AS FOUND ON

ANCIENT CHURCH RECORDS

PRIOR TO 1800.

SEVENTH BOOK.

EDITED BY THE

REV. FREDERIC W. BAILEY, B.D.,

LATE OFFICIAL COPYIST OF PAROCHIAL ARCHIVES AND SECRETARY OF COMMISSION,
DIOCESE OF CONNECTICUT; EDITOR "EARLY MASSACHUSETTS MARRIAGES;"
DESIGNER BAILEY'S PHOTO-ANCESTRAL RECORD, "THE RECORD OF MY
ANCESTRY;" MEMBER NEW ENGLAND HISTORIC GENEALOGICAL
SOCIETY; CONNECTICUT HISTORICAL SOCIETY; NEW
HAVEN COLONY HISTORICAL SOCIETY; SONS OF
THE AMERICAN REVOLUTION (MASS.).

PUBLISHED BY THE

BUREAU OF AMERICAN ANCESTRY
FOR
Family   Researches

FREDERIC W. BAILEY, MGR.
P. O. BOX 587   NEW HAVEN, CONN.

PREFACE.

EARLY CONNECTICUT MARRIAGES, BOOK VII.

So often is it such undertakings as this are left very incomplete that we have special reason for gratification in the final accomplishment of a task begun some ten years ago with timid heart. It was a large task then set ourselves; but the years and the accomplishment alone have revealed its full meaning. And now we are exceeding glad of the effort in that so many in all parts of the country have received some benefit therefrom.

As to the records herein, so far as can be discovered they are the only existing ones of this period not before appearing in print. It is possible the coming years may reveal others as in the case of Glastonbury and gradually our list of "Church Records Lost" see some reduction. Let us hope so. Our own search has failed to find more. Any information that would lead to the discovery of a single additional book would be gladly welcomed. For the value of such records lies but in their ability to disclose additional family data whereby to anchor another American family to the good old state of Connecticut and to the churches that have in all the years fostered the Christian manhood and womanhood shared by the generations of to-day.

In addition to the records of Congregational churches it is our pleasure to supply herein those of the Episcopal Church also. Unfortunately they are comparatively few though the Church was early established here and might but for the trials of the Revolution which scattered so many of its adherents have contributed much more to the result. However herein are published all that can be found to date.

New Haven, Conn.; August 1, 1906.

FREDERIC W. BAILEY.

New Haven, Conn., August 1, 1906.

CONTENTS.

SEVENTH BOOK.

RECORDS LOST.

The following is a (revised) list of Congregational Churches so far reporting the loss of their records of Baptisms and Marriages prior to 1800.

CHURCH.	COUNTY.	ORGANIZED.	REMARKS.
Westminster, of Canterbury,	Windham,	1770,	none before 1824.
Coventry,	Tolland,	1745,	none before 1818.
Hebron,	Tolland,	1716,	burned.
Ellington,	Tolland,	1736,	lost.
Sherman,	Fairfield,	1744,	burned.
East Granby,	Hartford,	1737,	
Goshen,	Litchfield,	1740,	lost.
Watertown,	Litchfield,	1739,	lost.
Canton Center,	Hartford,	1750,	before 1826, lost.
So. Manchester,	Hartford,	1779,	
North Guilford,	New Haven,	1725,	lost.
East Lyme,	New London,	1719,	lost.
Lyme (Hamburgh),	New London,	1727,	lost.
West Haven,	New Haven,	1719,	before 1815, lost.
Litchfield,	Litchfield,	1721,	before 1886, burned.
Tolland,	Tolland,	1723,	burned.
Bethany,	New Haven,	1763,	before 1823, lost.
Andover,	Tolland,	1749,	B. and M. before 1818, burned at W. Springfield, Mass.
Marlborough,	Hartford,	1749,	missing.
Harwinton,	Litchfield,	1738,	nothing before 1790.
Ridgefield,	Fairfield,	1714,	nothing before 1800.
Plymouth,	Litchfield,	1740,	no marriages before 1800.
Greenwich,	Fairfield,	1670,	nothing before 1787,
Greenwich, (Stanwich),	Fairfield,	1735,	burned 1821.
Torringford,	Litchfield,	1764,	burned, nothing before 1837.
East Haddam, (Hadlyme),	Middlesex,	1745,	no marriages before 1800, baptisms be bin 1745.
Monroe,	Fairfield,	1764,	no marriages before 1821, baptisms begin 1776.
Bristol,	Hartford,	1747,	no marriages before 1792, baptisms begin 1800.
Suffield (West),	Hartford,	1744,	no records before 1840.
Eastford,	Windham,	1778,	no records before 1800.
Middlefield,	Middlesex,	1745,	no records before 1808.
Salisbury,	Litchfield,	1744,	few records before 1800.
Middletown (South),	Middlesex,	1747,	few records before 1800.

STRATFORD.

FAIRFIELD COUNTY.

(See Book V.)

Christ Episcopal Church in Stratford was organized in April, 1707, the first in the Connecticut Colony (the error in Preface II here corrected). Here too was the first edifice for divine worship erected in 1724. The records begin with the rectorship of the Rev. Samuel Johnson. Following are the marriages:

Abraham Beardslee & Hester Jeanes(?),	April 12, 1723
William Luce & Sarah Clarke,	Aug. 26, 1724
Edward Jessop & Sarah Blackleach,	Dec. 7, 1724
Joshua Jennings & Rebecca Adams, at Fairfield,	Feb. 3, 1724–5
John Outman & Elizabeth Jeanes,	Dec. 31, 1725
David Bostick & Elizabeth McKenzie, at Fairfield,	Sept. 3, 1726
Christopher Eliot & Judith F or Jilluid(?),	Dec. 8, 1716
Benjamin Jones & Martha Hodges,	Jan. 19, 1726–7
Nicoll Floyd & Tabitha Smith, at Smithtown, L. I.,	Apr. 6, 1727
Nehemiah Loring & Deborah Watkins,	Oct. 29, 1727
Henry Caner & Anne McKenzie, at Fairfield,	Aug. 25, 1728
John Kees & Frances Gilberts,	Dec. 25, 1728
Nath'l Browne & Olive Browne,	March 20, 1728–9
Mordechai Markes & Elizabeth Vosien (?)	Dec. 15, 1729
Israel Beardsley & Elizabeth —lagge(?),	May 30, 1730
Edward Lewis & Hannah Hawkins at Darby,	July 26, 1731
Samuel Clark & Elizabeth Loring,	Oct. 26, 1731
Samuel Benjamin & Elizabeth Bostwick,	March 22, 1731–2
Jacob Lane & Hannah Beardsly,	Aug. 2, 1733
James Bayle & Deborah Tyler,	Aug. 20, 1733
Augustus Lucas & Mary Caner at N. Haven,	March 10, 1734–5
Benjamin —— & Elizabeth ——,	April 8, 1734–5
Jehoshaphat Prindle & Hannah Smith, at W. Haven,	May 6, 1735
Nathan Grey & Mary Hurlbut,	July 23, 1735
Samuel Humphrey & Susan Thomas, at Darby,	Aug. 18, 1735
Samuel Hull & Sarah Harger, at Darby	Sept. 25, 1735
Daniel Thomas & Sarah Brown,	Dec. 25, 1735
Sam'l French & Elisabeth Clarke,	Jan. or June 2, 1736

Jeremy French & Hannah Edwards,	July 28, 1737
James Moor & Rachel Grant,	May 25, 1737
John Mitchel & Sarah Baldwin at Ripton,	Nov. 10, 1737
Jacob Baldwin & Sarah Marchant,	March 2, 1738
Barzillai D—an & Mary Brown,	Oct. 5, 1738
John Banks & Sarah Hitchcock,	Oct. 31, 1738
William Bennet & Elisabeth Smith,	April 10, 1739
James Poison? & Sarah Pingeky?	Aug. 14, 1739
David Peat & Thankful Whipp—,	Nov. 29, 1739
Geo. McKune & Elisabeth Beardsley,	Dec. 25, 1739
Benja. Booth & Mary French,	Aug. 10, 1740
—— Church & Katharine ——,	Aug. 17, 1740
Paul Maverick & Gloriana Margaretta ——	Dec. 25, 1740
Gideon Canby & Sarah Smith,	March 11, 1740–1
Sam'l Beardsley & Ann French,	Nov. 19, 1741
John Seers & Frances Plumb,	Dec. 4, 1741
Sam'l Preston & Susanna Wilcoxson,	April 19, 1741
Jabez Beardsley & Patience Hubbel,	April 20, 1741
William Scovil & Elisabeth Browne,	June 16, 1742
Ephraim Osborn & Abia Hawl—,	April 24, 1743
Joseph Smith & Abigail Smith,	Aug. —, 1743
Ebenezer Sherman & Mary ——,	Dec. 18, 1744
Abel Birdsey & Phebe Thomson,	Jan. —, 1745–6
John Wooster & Eunice Hull,	June 18, 1746
Ephraim Beers & Betty Pearce,	June 19, 1746
Jeremy Judson Curtis & Mary Edwards,	July 18, 1746
Samuel Stevens & Rhoda Clinton, at Darby	Nov. 3, 1746
William Watkins & Mary French,	May 16, 1747
John Oatman & Elisabeth Bennet (Smith)	Aug. 20, 1747
Peter Mitchel & Elisabeth Lamson,	Sept. 17, 1747
Benjamin Arnold & Mary Munson,	Nov. 9, 1747
Sam'l Gorham & Anna Greenman,	Dec. 8, 1747
Ephriam Smith & Elizabeth Dunster,	March 9, 1747–8
Samuel Johnson & Anne Beach,	Nov. 5, 1749
Richard Mansfield & Mrs. Anne Hull at Darby,	Oct. 10, 1751
Nath'l Jones & Martha Wakeley at Ripton,	Feb. 20, 1752
Phillip Benjamins & Prudence Miner,	—— —,1752
William Russel & Hannah Brinsmade,	March 9, 1753

Sam'l Cole & Mary Dean,	April 6, 1753
Abijah Beach & Mary Brewster,	April 15, 1753
Benedict Lillingstone & Abigail Laborie,	June 10, 1753
Ebenezer Plummer & Elisabeth Shelton at Ripton, Sept.	— 1754
Geo. Benjamin & Mary Howe (at Church)	Feb. 8, 1756
Sherman Lewis & Mary Jones (at Church)	April 11, 1756
David Bosch? of Horse Neck & Sarah Isaacs of Norwalk	
at Norwalk,	July 25, 1756
Col. Edmund Lewis & Mrs. Frances Kees,	Nov. 10, 1756
Ebenezer Allen & Dinah Fairchild,	Dec. 12, 1756
John Backhus & Sarah Benjamins (at Church)	July 17, 1757
Abel Beach & Mary Lewis (at Church)	July 17, 1757
Alexander Fairchild & Ann Benjamins	Aug. 14, 1757
John Willoughby & Gloriana Edwards,	Sept. 1, 1757
Philip Nicolls & Mary Prince (at Church)	Oct. 16, 1757
Joseph Wooster, Esq., & Lucy Niccolls,	Dec. 14, 1757
Daniel Shelton & Mary French,—	March 13, 1758
Isaac Niccolls & Sarah Lewis (at Church)	Oct. 15, 1758
Alexander Z (?) uil (?) & Frances Rush,	Jan. 7, 1759
John Lamson & Mary Burritt	April 20, 1759
Josiah Hubbell & Sarah Edwards,	Oct. 28, 1750
Jonathan Blakeley & Martha Parker, at Wallingford, Nov. 15, 1759	
Edmund Burritt & Mary Lamson,	Jan. 27, 1760
Stephen Burroughs & Elisabeth Browne,	May 22, 1760
William Wells & Anna Edwards,	May 14, 1761
Rev. Dr. Sam'l Johnson & Mrs. Sarah Beach,	June 19, 1761
Brewster Dayton & Isabella Miner,	Aug. 13, 1761
Wolcott Chauncey & Anne Browne,	July 29, 1762
Ebenezer Coe & Sarah Backhus,[née Benjamin]	Jan. 9, 1763
Charles Burrough & Lettice Selby,	Feb. 10, 1763
Archibald Jones & Hannah Russell,	April 3, 1763
William McIntosh & Eunice Hawley,	April 14, 1763
Henry Beardsley & Lucretia Graveston,	April 19, 1763
Edward Hawley & Abigail Southward,	Nov. 13, 1763
Samuel Jones, Jr., & Mary Russell,	Jan. 5, 1764
John Selby & Asenath Fairchild	Jan. 22, 1764
Richardson Miner & Tabitha Curtiss,	Jan. 23, 1764
Peter Finch & Phebe McCune,	March 15, 1764

Jabez Hurd & Sarah Caldwell,	April 19, 1764
William Edwards & Elizabeth Russel,	Aug. 28, 1764
Benjamin Edwards & Mary Sherwood,	Sept. 5, 1764
Isaac Hitchcock & L. Mary Ann Dean,	
Amos Belden & Abigail Fulsom,	} Dec. 16, 1764
(both couples together at Church)	
Peter Mallet & Eunice Curtis,	March 7, 1765
Eliphalet Curtis & Ruth Burton,	Nov. 9, 1765
Cyrus Fulson & Mary Curtiss,	March 9, 1766
Sam'l Whitney & Martha Howes,	May, 4, 1766
Ebenezer Shelly & Abigail Bundy,	July 13, 1766
Jonathan Peck & Mehetabel Blackman,	Nov. 22, 1766
Thomas Stewart & Mary Burret,	Dec. 1, 1766
Timothy Sherman & Naomi Lewis,	March 22, 1767
Ephraim Osborn & Martha Sherman,	April 13, 1767
Elisha Wilcox & Sarah Nicholls,	July 19, 1767
Henry Van Dyck & Huldah Lewis,	Aug. 9, 1767
Jonathan Mallery & Anne Conn,	March 27, 1768
John Curtis Fairchild & Ruth Lamson,	Nov. 6, 1768
Thomas & Mime,(negroes),	April 16, 1769
Thaddeus Clarke & Phebe Hurd,	Aug. 3, 1769
Ebenezer Kneeland & Charity Johnson,	Oct. 29, 1769
Everet Birdsey & Phebe Thomson,	Nov. —, 1769
John Bassett & Sarah Arnold,	Aug. 1, 1770
Isaac Peet & Abigail Lewis,	Aug. 19, 1770
Silas Hubbell & Elisabeth Lamson,	Aug. 30, 1770
Phineas Blackman & Elizabeth Wattaker,	Feb. 7, 1771
John Sterling & Glorianah Fulson,	March 10, 1771
Daniel Booth of N. Town & Huldy Thomson,	Oct. 9, 1771
Mack & Phillis (nogroes),	Nov. 24, 1771
Nathaniel Nichols & Mehitabel Bryant,	Dec. 8, 1771
Josiah Borough & Sarah Clarke,	Dec. 15, 1771
William Prince & Ruth Nichols,	Dec. —, 1772
Rev. Sam'l Peters & Miss Mary Birdseye,	April 20, 1773
Robert Linus & Mary Dunlap,	May 29, 1773
Edward DeFrost & Jerusha Cannon,	Feb. 16, 1785
Phinehas Blackman & Lettice Borrough,	Feb. 24, 1785
William Welles & Mary Silby,	Sept. 20, 1785

Daniel Crommelin Virplank & Elizabeth Johnson, Oct. 29, 1785
Alexander Fairchild & Mary Plum, Feb. 8, 1786
John Thompson & Ellis Benjamin, Feb. 19, 1786
John Booth & Jerusha Lewis, Oct. 15, 1786
Hezebiah Wetmore & Sarah Hoyt, July 17, 1787
Lewis Nicols & Amy Curtis, Aug. 7, 1787
William Clarke & Mary Benjamin, May 25, 1788
Sam'l Southard & Mary Ann Fulsom, Sept. 6, 1788
Isaac Fintch & ———, Sept. 19, 1788
Isaac Bateman & Hellen Nichols, Oct. 19, 1788
Bruster Daton & Bitza Wiloby, Dec. 24, 1788
Elisha Wilcox & Ruth Walker, Jan. 1, 1789
James Cannon & Mary Burret, Aug. 27, 1789
Peter DeWites & Lucretia Benjamin, Aug. 29, 1789
John Beardsley & Margaret Plumb, Nov. 2, 1791
Jacob Hurd & Jane Townshend (free negroes), by the
    Rev. Asbbel Baldwin, Nov. 24, 1791
Lyman Edwards & Sarah Guire, 1794
Salmon Orsborn & Ruth Lyon, 1794
Elijah Mallet & Sarah Sanford, 1794
Benjamin Fullen (?) & Sarah Blackman, 1701
Joseph Alin (?) & Betsey Sacket, 1794
Botsford Farman & Sarah Clark, 1794
John Fairchild & Abigail Patterson, 1795
Curtis Fairchild & Betsey Whiting, 1795
John Silbey & Betsey Hubbel, 1795
Elisha Burr ⊗ & Mary Orsborn, 1795
Sam'l Clark & Eunice Riggs 1796
Sam'l Wells & Polly ———, 1796
William Curtis & Fanny Curtis, 1796
Waterous Clark & Eunice Clark, 1797
William Murrill (?) & Eunice Edwards (Edwards crossed,
    Deforest added), 1797
Timothy Johnson & Peggy Johnson, 1797
Isaac Burrows & Rebecca Hurd, 1799
Ephraim Burit, Jr., & Nancy Satterley (?), 1799
Thomas Scott & Mary Curtis, 1799
Zophar Thorp & Eunice Meritt, 1800

James Beach & Susanne Seeley,	1800
Robert Dascomb & Sarah Peet,	1800
Joseph Hubbel & Charity Edwards,	1800
Hezekiah Nicols & Prudence Polly Shelton,	1800

STRATFORD—HUNTINGTON.

FAIRFIELD COUNTY.

(See Book V.)

Huntington was incorporated in Jan. 1789, and taken from Stratford. St. Paul's Episcopal Church of Huntington was set off from Christ Church, Stratford, as the Parish of Ripton in April, 1749. The Rev. Abram Lynson Clark was rector from 1787 to 1792. The following are his records:

Nehemiah Rice & Abigail Blackleach,	Oct. —, 1787
Selah Shelton & Phebe French,	Oct. 18, 1787
Sam'l Hurd & Elisabeth Clark,	Nov. —, 1787
Lewis Beardslee & Martha Lane,	Dec. 2, 1787
Abraham Marks & Content Murren of Milford,	March 2, 1788
Josiah Wakelee & Hannah Beardslee,	April 3, 1788
Abraham Hurd & Rebeckah Clark,	April 12, 1788
Ellis Gratlove & Fanny Shelton,	May 11, 1788
James Wakelee & Ameritta Patterson,	July 6, 1788
Hezekiah Clark & Sally B. Marks,	July 6, 1788
Thomas Hubbel & Sarah French,	Jan. 28, 1789
John Whinton & Rebeckah Hall, Tashua,	Feb. —, 1789
Peet Seeley & Rebecca Peltor Peet, Northside,	Feb. —, 1789
Daniel Lyon & Anar Summers, Tashua,	March —, 1789
Sam'l Sanford & Charity Bristol, Newtown,	May —, 1789
Zechariah Shelton & Elisabeth Marks,	July —, 1789
Sam'l Wells & Caty Lewis,	Oct. —, 1789
Joel Fairchild & Clara Hall, both of Tashua,	Nov. —, 1789
Ely Mitchel & Charity Barlow,	Dec. —, 1789
Jared Stone & Polly Newton,	Dec. —, 1789
Gershom Shelton & Betsey Beardslee,	Dec. —, 1789
Benedict Laboree & Sally Clark,	March —, 1790
Jacob Clark & Rosana Wilson,	May, —, 1790
Charles Lane & Mary Shelton,	May —, 1790

Zachariah Mallett & Abigail Osburn of Tashua,	May 16, 1790
Lewis Shelton & Charity Edwards,	Aug. —, 1790
Ephraim Lewis & Mehitable Nichols,	Sept. —, 1790
David Walker & Elizabeth Shelton, Northside,	Nov. 24, 1790
James B. Gilbert & Sarah Lovring,	Dec. 12, 1790
Luke Beardslee & Sarah Lane,	Jan. 9, 1791
Ezra Lake & Hannah Thompson,	Feb. —, 1701
Jabez Beardslee & Eunis Summers,	Sept. 10, 1791
Ephraim Stebbins & Abigail Wilson,	Oct. 23, 1791
Elim Wooster & Alethea Hurd,	1792
—— Judson & Charlotte Clark,	1792
John Seeley & Anna Gilbert,	1792
Agur Tomlinson & Mabel Peet,	July 8, 1792
—— Grey & Abigail Beardslee,	July 8, 1892
Andrew Curtis & Eunis Hall, by William Green,	Aug. —, 1792

John Powell & Ruth Dart,

——than Nicolls Walkir & —— Shelton.

STAMFORD.

FAIRFIELD COUNTY.

(See Book IV.)

While Episcopal services were held in Stamford as early as 1726-7, the records of St. John's Episcopal Church begin April 15, 1754. The Rev. Ebenezer Dibble, D. D., was rector from 1747 to 1797. The following cover the marriages recorded:

Stephen Fowler & Hannah Fowler, both of North Castle,
                                        March 28, 1758

John Ketchum & Elizabeth Brown, both of Norwalk,
                                        June 27, 1758

John Hay a soldier under command of Capt. Barbet of ye
    48th Reg., & Hannah Welch,   Dec. 25, 1758

Thomas Beckett a soldier under command of Capt. Barbet
    of ye 48th Reg., & Mary Dibble,   Jan. 4, 1759

Bezaleel Brown & Rachel Mead, both of Greenwich, Feb. 11, 1759

James King of New Castle in one of ye Southern Provinces
    as he says, & Keziah Cory of Greenwich, Ct.
                                        Aug. 23, 1759

Lemuel Raymond of Salem & Lydia Seely,   Dec. 13, 1759
Platt Townsend of Oyster Bay, L. I., & Elisabeth Hubberd,
                                                April 6, 1760
Nath'l. Sacket & Widow Sarah Lockwood both of Greenwich,
                                                Aug. 10, 1760
Nathan Smith of Stamford & Elizabeth Betts of Greenwich,
                                                July 6, 1761
Stephen Platt & Jane Rogers,   Aug. 1, 1761
Selleck Holly & Abigail Waterbury,   Aug. 22, 1761
Nath'l Seely & Elisabeth Scofield,   Nov. 10, 1761
Fyler Dibblee & Polly Jarvis,   June 18, 1763
Wm. Hunt of Westchester & Susanah Fowler of No. Castle,
                                                July 23, 1761
Henry Johnson & Anna Peck of Greenwich,   Oct. 18, 1761
Israel Knap & Elisabeth Hugford relict widow of Dr. Hug-
    ford of Greenwich,   Jan. 7, 1762
Sands Sutton & Mary Fowler of No. Castle,   Feb. —, 1762
Nath'l. Jessup & Sarah James of Greenwich,   April, 1762
William Dodge of New York & Jamima Meed of Greenwich,
                                                July 25, 1762
Silas Lockwood & Deborah Lockwood of Greenwich, Oct. 1, 1762
Sylvanus Hart & Mary Bets of Canaan Parish,   Feb. 19, 1764
Wm. Woodward & Amelia Medows of Rye   Oct. 21, 1762
Basil Bartow of Westchester & Clarena Punderson of Rye,
                                                Nov. 4, 1762
James Macdonald of Bedford & Elizabeth Belding, Dec. 20, 1762
Epinetus How & Elisabeth Cramner,   June 27, 1763
William Thomson & Hannah Panybon (?),   Jan. 1, 1763
William King & Olive Boardman,   Jan. 11, 1765
Zephaniah Hubs & Elisabeth Purdy of Rye,   Oct. 29, 1764
Jeremiah Anderson of Greenwich & Susanna Wilson of Rye,
                                                Jan. 13, 1765
Jas. Crawford of Old Pound Ridge & Rachel Benedict of
    Ridgefield,   Feb. 21, 1765
John Smith of Bedford & Ann Crawford of Old Pound
    Ridge,   Feb. 21, 1765
Daniel Haviland & Esther Lawrence of Rye,   March 6, 1765
Wm. Miller & Mary Haviland of Rye,   March 21, 1765

Ebenezer Haviland & Thamar Bud of Rye, March 25, 1765
Dr. Edward Joyce of New York & Sarah Sacket of Green-
wich, March 30, 1765
Nicolas Falch of New York & Sarah Harisan residing at
Greenwich, lately from New York, April 14, 1766
John Aspinwall of Flushing & Rebecka Smith of Queens
Village, June 5, 1766
Daniel Ghorum & Abigail Waterbury, Jan. 25, 1766
Eliot Green & Marcy Seely, April 23, 1766
Jacob Slauson & Kezia Weed, March 19, 1767
Nath'l. Munday & Sarah Jarvis, April 23, 1767
Tom & Tim slaves of John Holly & Abraham Bates May 31, 1767
Cesar & Candace black slaves of Sands Selleck & Mr. Dibblee,
June 23, 1767
Alexander Bishop, Jr., & Mary Bates, Sept. 18, 1768
David Picket & Sarah Lewis, March 18, 1769
Samu'l Whiting of Stamford & Abigail Ferris of Greenwich,
June 4, 1767
Simeon Raymond of Norwalk & Sarah Sangbon,
January 12, 1768
Thaddeus Duning of Norwalk & Mary Goold, Jan. 14, 1769
Lewis Marvin of Rye & Sarah Middlebrooks, Feb. 18, 1769
Joseph Smith of Canaan Parish, Norwalk, & Mary Water-
bury, Feb. 25, 1769
John How of Woster, Mass. Bay Gov., & Mary Williamson,
March 22, 1769
Jonathan Heusted of Canaan Parish, Norwalk, & Hannah
Waterbury, April 6, 1769
Abraham Lockwood & Mary Lockwood both of Greenwich,
April 30, 1769
Dunlap Cogsil & Abigail Hart of Bedford and Stamford,
Dec. —, 1769
Stephen Hanford of Canaan Parish, Norwalk & Sarah Ghorum
of Middlesex Parish, Stamford, Feb. 25, 1770
Matthew Partilow & Alethea Wheeler, Sept. 21, 1769
Munson Jarvis & Mary Arnold, March 4, 1769
Jacob Howe & Sarah Bates, May 20, 1769
Newman Holly & Sarah Blackburn, Feb. 19, 1772

Alexander Bishop & Hannah Holly,	April 20, 1772
Joseph Wilmot & Hannah Holly, the reputed daughter	
of Capt. John Holly of Stamford,	May 17, 1772
Levy Bouton & Hannah Waterbury,	Jan. 14, 1773
James Talmage, Jr., & Bethya Waterbury,	July 10, 1773
Abijah Bishop & Susanna Holly,	Sept. 13, 1773
Nath'l. Ghorum & Mary Whiting,	Sept. 16, 1773
William Frost & Sarah Scofield,	Nov. 4, 1773
Sam'l Hecock & Zilpha Scofield,	Nov. 4, 1773
Obediah Seely ye 3d. & Hannah Lounsbery,	Nov. 5, 1773
Uriah Hart & Jane Hoit,	Nov. 5, 1773
Thos. Slauson & Hannah, Hull	March 17, 1774
Jonathan Lewis & Millisen Weed,	March 20, 1773
Seymour Talmage & Sarah Hoit,	April 7, 1773
Joel Harvey, Jr., of Sharon & Jane Dibblee,	May 2, 1770
Abijah Nash of Norwalk & Sarah Whitney,	Nov. 5, 1770
Angus McCall & Mary Rich, both of Greenwich,	May 16, 1771
Thos. Sanders of New York & Mary Hubberd,	June 18, 1772
Silas Hamlin of Amenia Precinct, N. Y., & Polly Lines	
daughter of David Lines	Nov. 18, 1772
Cornelius Lane & Margaret Mesnard, both of Greenwich,	
	April 4, 1773
John Leeks of New Haven & Hannah Quintard,	June 12, 1774
Jas. Bettis of Danbury & Pegge Whitney of Norwalk,	
	Jan. 25, 1775
John Kellog of Norwalk & Sarah Bishop,	April 16, 1775
Robt. Escot resident of Stamford, an Englishman from	
London & Rhoda Whitney,	Sept. 24, 1775
Jas. Harvey of Sharon & Rheuamah Smith,	Oct. 13, 1776
Ebenezer Dibblee & Esther Hervey, both of Sharon,	Nov. 14, 1776
John Smith & Anna Lowre, both late of N. Y., now of S.	
	Feb. 23, 1777
Capt. David Hart of S. & Anna Peck of Greenwich,	Mar. 5, 1777
Silas Bets, Jr., of Greenwich & Abigail Smith,	May 20, 1777
John Cleaveland a soldier, lately of Canaan upper town,	
& Sarah Safield (or Scofield),	Aug. 7, 1777
Thos. Peck & Widow Mary Ferris, both of Greenwich,	
	Dec. 30, 1777

Major William Stevens of Westchester, N. Y., & Margaret
  Thomas of Rye, N. Y.   Feb. 15, 1778
James, negro servant of Esq. Palmer's, Greenwich, & Lucy
  negro servant of Mrs. Hubberd's   Feb. 20, 1778
Chas. Wright of Greenwich, Ct., & Elisabeth Hunnewell of
  Westchester, N. Y.,   July 16, 1778
Nath'l. Mandevil of Peakskill, N. Y., & Rheuamah Holly,
                                               Dec. 16, 1778
Juba Freeman, a negro of Milford in the Continental service,
  & Betty servant to Mrs. Hayes,   Dec. 30, 1778
John Haviland & Hannah Purdy, both of Harrison Pur-
  chase, N. Y.,   Feb. 24, 1779
Joseph Smith late of Huntington, L. I., & Hannah Whitney,
                                               April 18, 1779
Jas. Parker a foreigner & Mabel Tuttle of Norwalk, Sept., 1779
Azariah Wetmore & Susannah Thale, both of Rye, Jan, 29, 1780
Elisha Ely of Lime, a Capt. in Col. Megg's Reg., & Susannah
  Bloomer of Rye, N. Y.,   April 10, 1780
Scudder Weed of S. & Mary Lockwood ("her maiden name")
  of Norwalk,   May 6, 1780
Joel Jones of Amenia Precinct, N. Y., & Elisabeth Rogers
  of Sharon, Ct., grand daughter of Mr. Hervey, Oct. 8, 1780
Lot Norton, Esq. of Salsbury & Mary Davis of Sharon,
                                               Oct. 8, 1780
Abraham Bush of Rye & Mary Lyon of Rye (or Greenwich),
                                               Nov. 26, 1780
Thos. Brown of Greenwich & Abigail Holly,   Dec. 7 or 9, 1780
Ashur Taylor & Mary Ghorum, both of Norwalk, March 18, 1781
Nath'l Jarvis Street & Jane Nash, both of Norwalk, April 11, 1781
William Nash & Elizabeth Waring, both of Norwalk, Apr. 11,1871
John Ward & Ann Street, both of Norwalk,   April 11, 1781
Aaron Keeler & Mary James both of Norwalk,   May 20, 1781
Jonathan Cowder a refugee from N. Y., resident in S. & Sally
  Hoit,   May 31, 1781
Amos Lounsbury of S. & Betsy Lockwood of Greenwich,
                                               June 14, 1781
Nath'l. Webb, Jr., of S. & Easter Lockwood of Greenwich,
                                               June 28, 1781

Sam'l Bush of Greenwich & Anna Hubberd   Oct. 11, 1781
Moses Webb, of S. & Polly Street of Norwalk,   Nov. 22, 1781
Reuben Rundle, Jr., of Greenwich & Sarah Holly, Jr.,
                                                  Dec. 23, 1781
Sam'l Cannon & Sarah Belding both of Norwalk, Dec. 26, 1781
Wm. Chapman of Long Island & Margaret Loder, Jan. 1, 1782
Jehiel Wetmore & Elisabeth Bush, both of Rye, March 12, 1782
Absolam Gidvey of Philips Manor (or White Plains) & Anna
        Haynes of Rye,   Feb. 10, 1784
Joseph Clinton & Abigail Camp, both of Norwalk, March 14, 1784
Noah Lockwood & Catharine Colby or Colly, both of
        Greenwich,   Sept. —, 1784
Nath'l. Ferris & Wid. Mary Peck both of Greenwich,
                                                  Dec. 15, 1784
William Knap of Greenwich & Easter Isaacs late of Norwalk,
                                                  Dec. 19, 1784
Hughes Maginnis residing at Norwalk & Rebecca Selleck,
                                                  Jan. 26, 1785
Dr. Donald Mackentire & Easter Hains both of Rye,
                                                  March 10, 1785
Thos. Hoit of Rye & Jane Sniffin of White Plains, March 21, 1785
Eliakim Ford of N. Y., & Hannah Lockwood of Greenwich,
                                                  June 19, 1785
John Purdy & Mary Purdy, both of Rye,   Dec. 19, 1785
Gen'l? John Meed of Greenwich & Wid. Mehitabel Peck,
                                                  Jan. 8, 1786
Abraham Knox of Cortland Manor & Pamelia Purdy of
        White Plains,   Jan. 29, 1785
John Hawkins of Rye & Hellina Dewsonbury of Harrison
        Purchase,   Jan. 29, 1785
Sam'l Seely of Old Pound Ridge, & Abigail Seely, Feb. 2, 1785
Elias Purdy & Rachel Merret, both of Rye,   Jan. 27, 1785
Samuel Lyon of King Street, Greenwich and Elisabeth Lyon
        of Byram,   March 26, 1785
Isaac Dickinson of St. Johns, N. B., & Phebe Scofield,
                                                  March 27, 1785
Jonathan Purdy & Abigail Purdy,, both of White Plains
                                                  May 21, 1785

—— Griffin of Rye or Maroneck, Nov. —, 1785
Joseph Knap & Clarissa Perrot, both of Greenwich, Jan, 21, 1787
Ebenezer Burling of East Chester & Eve Bloomer of
    Manaroneck, Feb. 25, 1787
Elijah Crawford & Sarah Sniffen, both of White Plains,
    Aug. 8, 1787
Francis Wilmot of Greenwich, & Esther Reed a widow,
    Nov. 12, 1787
Josiah Brown & Mary Sacket, both of Greenwich, Jan. 27, 1788
Lewis McDonald late of Bedford residing in Greenwich,
    & Clay Feris of Greenwich, Feb. 14, 1788
Elliott Palmer & Elisabeth Lyon, both of Greenwich, June 29, 1788
Ebenezer Purdy & Eunice Purdy, both of White Plains,
    Dec. 2, 1788
Deacon Ambrose Todd (or Food) of Simsbery, & Levina
    Jarvis, Dec. 25, 1788
Roger Purdy & Anna Purdy, both of Rye, March 2, 1789
Thos. Kenworthy, resident of S. late of Manchester, Eng., &
    Martha Lowder of S., Feb. 4, 1790
Henry Davis of Poughkeepsie & Mary Bush of Greenwich,
    Feb. 7, 1790
Thos. Clap of St. Johns, N. B., & Ruth Scofield, Feb. 11, 1790
Sam'l Heviland of the Oblong, N. Y., & Judith Purdy of
    White Plains, Feb. 16, 1790
Ebenezer Adams of Greenwich & Elisabeth Matthias, Jan., 1791
Albert Rykman of N. Y., & Sally Burwell Jarvis, Sept. 16, 1792
Seth Hamilton of Reading & Lydia Seely, widow, Nov. 8, 1792
Thos. Robert Smith of N. Y., & Hannah Holly, April 12, 1794
Nath'l. Brown & Elisabeth King, both of Greenwich, June 1, 1796
Ezekiel Stone of Stockbridge, Mass., & Sally Seely, Sept. 6, 1796
Thos. Hitchkock & Polly Tenpenny, both of Greenwich,
    Nov. 27, 1796
Elijah Reynolds & Priscilla Lockwood, both of Green-
    wich, May 9, 1797
Alexander Stephenson & Ruhamah Dibblee, both of North
    East Town, Dutches Co., N. Y., Oct. 18, 1797
David Holly Bishop of Stamford & Hannah Bishop, Jan. 21, 1799
Abijah Bishop & Hannah Lounsbery, of Stamford, Nov. 20, 1800

NEW HAVEN.

NEW HAVEN COUNTY.

(See Book I.)

Trinity Episcopal Church, New Haven, was organized before 1752—the exact time of its formation is in doubt. The records begin with the rectorship of the Rev. Bela Hubbard.

David Cook & Ann Bradley,	Nov. 15, 1768
William Sherman & Easter White,	Jan. 17, 1768
John Prindle & Susannah Smith,	Feb. 17, 1768
Ulrick Winegar of America & Sarah Toles,	March 6, 1768
Martin Clock & Mehitable Sperry of Amity,	March 17, 1768
Jeremiah Parmelee & Sarah Doolittle,	Nov. 21, 1768
William Harison & Sarah Perkins,	Dec. 1, 1768
Simeon Perkins & Triphena Bennam,	Feb. 22, 1771
Elias Shipman & Easter Whiting,	March 13, 1771
Oliver & Fanny Bailey,	June 18, 1769
Robert Grant & Fanny Bailey,	Sept. 6, 1772
Anthony Perit & Mary Sanford,	Jan. 31, 1773
Philip Maighan & Susanna Killum,	March 7, 1773
Nathaniel Black & Molly Cables,	March 7, 1773
William Powell & Miriam Tyler,	Oct. 17, 1773
Daniel Lyman & Statira Camp,	Nov. 15, 1773
John Wright & Ann Sawyer,	July 3, 1774
Nathan Hertland & Abigail Smith, both of West Haven,	
	Dec. 11, 1774
Timothy & Kate, free negroes,	Feb. 23, 1775
John Umphervile & Easter Sperry,	June 7, 1775
Dr. Daniel Bonticue & Rebceca Rhodes, late wife of Dr.	
John Rhodes, dec.,	Sept. 12, 1775
Patrick Colonell & Wid. Margaret Yeomans,	Oct. 30, 1775
George Cook & Mary Browne,	July 20, 1776
Thomas Robinson & Hannah Warner,	Oct. 31, 1776
William Daily & Thankful Woolsey,	July 25, 1777
John Jiles & Susanna Jocelin,	Oct. 14, 1777
Michael Lynch & Polly Crane of Long Island,	Oct. 30, 1777

Oliver Bailey & Elisabeth Waterhouse,   Nov. 20, 1777
Thomas Osborn of Oxford in Derby & Wid. Comfort Alling,
                                               Feb. 20, 1778
Nathan Thompson & Elisabeth Barnet (or Barret) March 2, 1778
William Stevens & Sarah,   April 5, 1778
Samuel Downs & Widow Rachel Smith of West Haven,
                                               June 29, 1779
Frederic Stein & Widow Christine Gatler,   Dec. 17, 1780
Ebenezer Umperville, Jr., & Esther Downs,   Jan. 29, 1781
Samuel Storer & Polly Augusta Bonticue,   July 22, 1781
Elijah Stone & Lavinia Fairchild,   1781
———— Malbone & Mary Isaacs,   Oct. —, 1781
Thaddeus Perit of N. H., & Sophia Webster of Philadel-
     phia, at Branford,   March 16, 1782
Thomas Green & Abigial Miles,   March 21, 1782
Samuel Redfield & Nancy Fairchild, at Guilford, May 26, 1782
Sharper, a negro serv't, & Wid. Elisabeth Wilford, Jr.,
                                               June 13, 1782
Ephraim Beardsley & Frances Chapman, at Stratford,
.   Sept. 12, 1782
Levi Trowbridge & Hannah Smith,   Dec. 29, 1782
John Coil & Abigail Jocelin,   Jan. —, 1783
Benjamin Matthews & Sarah Perkins,   April 27, 1783
Russel Clarke & Content Ward,   June 14, 1783
Major Roger Alden & Gloriana Ann Johnson,   Sept. 7, 1783
Shadrack Osborn of Woodbury & Aletta Blaggs,   Oct. 16, 1783
Walter Bradley of Fairfield & Sarah Bradley,   Dec. 6, 1873
Sharper Rogers, a free negro man to Phillis, belonging to
John Whiting, Esq.,   Jan. —, 1784
A negro couple,   Feb. 7, 1784
Nathaniel Ingram & Juliana Redfield,   Feb. 29, 1784
David Lambert of Milford & Lois Brindle of West Haven,
                                               April 7, 1784
Caleb Ray & Elisabeth Davis,   May 26, 1784
Thomas Summers & Elsa Slowly,   June 23, 1784
Abraham Foot & Mary Ponsonly of Branford,   July 20, 1784
James Discon & Mary Smith,(This marriage is subject to
     criticism),   July —, 1784

Samuel Post & Mary Davis,	Aug. 21, 1784
James Sanderson & Sophia Jackson, negroes,	Oct. 18, 1784
Anthony Perit & Betsey Quintard,	Nov. 11, 1784
William Bonticue & Hannah Storer,	Nov. 13, 1784
Aaron Thomas & Martha Toles,	Dec. 16, 1784
Jared Humiston & Mary Ann Gochee,	Dec. 28, 1784
Chas. Prindle, Jr., & Sybel Clark,	Jan., 1785
Ebenezer Thompson & Lidea Richards, at West Haven,	
	June 9, 1875
Arthur Keef & Lois Joiclyn,	June 13, 1785
John Graham & Hannah Hunswell,	July 28, 1785
Elijah Forbes & Eunice Chester,	Sept. 4, 1785
Leonard Vollum & Esther Umpherville,	Oct. 2, 1785
Peter Totton & Grace Mansfield,	Oct. 15, 1785
Benjamin ——— & Hannah Upson,	April 15, 1786
Timothy Chittenden & Hannah Trowbridge,	June, 1785
Ambrose Ward, Sr., & Mary Chapel,	June, 1786
Robert Anderson & Ruth Crane,	July 18, 1786
William Wallace & Elisabeth Griffeth,	Sept. 28, 1786
Elijah Turner & Rebecca Mix,	Oct. 13, 1786
William Mowatt & Esther Thompson,	Nov. 27, 1786
Ambrose Ward, Jr., & Rebecca Parmeley,	Nov. 27, 1786
Lemuel Taylor of Danbury & Adah Cornwell of Middletown,	
	March 8, 1787
Luther Collens & Mary Doolittle,	Aug. 16, 1787
John Brainard & Abigail Mary Woodhull,	Sept. 19, 1787
James Sheppard of Boston & Mary Wood of L. I.,	
	Jan. 13, 1788
John Ward & ——— Richards in West Haven,	Feb. 14, 1788
Philip Worthly & Elisabeth Stone,	March 11, 1788
Capt. Joseph Julian & Hannah Lindslee, at Branford,	
	March 30, 1788
Joseph Prindle & Lois Beecher,	April 9, 1788
Nathaniel Lyon & Lucy Boothe,	Sept. —, 1788
John ——— & Anne Page,	Oct. —, 1788
Jeremiah Thompson of Cumberland, Eng., & Tempr. Bills	
of N. H.,	Dec. 9, 1788
——— ——— & Mary Storer,	Dec. 15, 1788

Christopher Putts of Old England & Wid. Abigail Smith
   of West Haven,   Jan. 3, 1789
Rev. R. Ives & Miss Susanna Anna Maria Marshall, Jan. 21, 1789
Isaas Tomlinson & Sarah Ward,   March 15, 1789
Jacob Morgan of Amety & Widow Elisabeth Bonticue,
                          May 22, 1789
Constant Abbott of Wallingford & Sarah Hoy, June 25, 1789
Eneas Alling & Elisabeth Morrison,   Oct. 24, 1789
Thadeus Perit & Desire Sanford,   Nov. 26, 1789
Michael Kenney, of Ireland & Rachel Osborn, Dec. 1, 1789
Elihu Lyman & Polly Forbes,   Dec. 26, 1789
James Cochran & Elisabeth Beecher,   Feb. 14, 1790
Eli Smith & Widow Lidea Thompson,   March 14, 1790
Christopher Kelby Allicock & Elisabeth Tretton, March 27, 1790
John ———— Wittee & Julian ————,   April 17, 1790
Nathaniel Woodruff & Abigail Cooper,   Oct. 16, 1790
Joseph Skattes Potter & Elice Hatch,   Nov. 14, 1790
Stephen Chatterton & Axsa Hatch,   Jan. 10, 1791
Asahel Thomas & Hanah Merwin,   Jan. 27, 1791
Richard Hoods & Abigail Ray,   Feb. 12, 1791
John Commodore & Sybel Rice, free negroes, March 16, 1791
London Facapana & Cato Aspenwall,   June —, 1791
———— Clarke & Lois Richards,   Oct. 2, 1791
Samll, Wm. Johnson, Esq., of Stratford & Susan Edwards,
                       Nov. 27, 1791
Benjamin Browne & Theda Chatterton,   Oct. 20, 1792
John Benners & Anna Maria Heyligar,   Oct. 22, 1792
Major Cook & Elisabeth Chappel,   Oct. 22, 1792
Samuel Hughs & Philomela Miles,   Nov. 10, 1792
Uri Tuttle & Margaret Morrison,   Jan. —, 1793
William Bryan & Rinda Benham,   May 18, 1793
Willard Bristol & Betsey Ward, at West Haven, June 22, 1793
Ebur Hubbard of Cohabit, age 60 & Widow Jerusha Tyler of
   Branford, age 46,   Oct. 31, 1793
John Bird & Elisabeth Danielson,   Nov. 2, 1793
John Bell & Elisabeth ————,   Nov. —, 1793
Abraham Bradly 2d & Mary Sherman,   Nov. 23, 1793
Stephen Foster & Ruth Cambridge,   Feb. 27, 1794

Wm. Powers & Elisabeth Whiting,	Feb. 27, 1794
Joseph Lucius Wooster & Elisabeth Beers,	Feb. 28, 1794
John Woodworth & Anna Hubbard,	March 8, 1794
Philemon Peckham & Anne Howell,	April 19, 1794
Cornelius Hendricks of Damarary & Lucy Davis,	Aug. 2, 1794
Chauncy Smith & Sarah Thomas at West Haven,	Oct. 22, 1795
Noah Barber & Phebe Browne,	Jan. 1, 1795
Clement Seth ——— of Fort Edward & Cloe Roberts,	
	Jan. 2, 1795
Elias Quy & Sarah Phagan,	Jan. 9, 1795
Ezra Lines & Abigail Hood,	Jan. 29, 1795
Stephen Prindle & Mary Andrew, at Bryant Farms, Milford,	
	Jan. 25, 1795
Timothy Phelps & Jennet Broome,	March 21, 1795
Isaac Ludington of East Haven & Sarah Frisbie of Branford, at home of Thos. Frisbie, Branford,	April 9, 1795
Josias Wiggins, N. Y., & Catharine Roberts	April 29, 1795
Oliver Leicester Phelps & Elisabeth Sherman,	June 23, 1795
Andrew Morriel & Lucretia Russel, at Branford,	June 23, 1795
John Pardy & Anna Forbes at East Haven, house of Levi Forbes,	Aug. 6, 1795
Soloman Collis & Hannah How,	Aug. 29, 1795
Alexander Langmucor & Mary Brown,	Sept. 26, 1795
Bethuel Thomas of West Haven, & Mary Bristol,	Oct. 15, 1795
Richard Downs & Amy Umphervil,	Oct. 18, 1795
Joseph Theband of N. Y., & Maria Therese Felicity Le Breton of N. Haven, daughter of Stephen & Felicity Le Breton,	Nov. 15, 1795
David Thomas of Woodbridge & Rebecca Cook, at house of David Cook,	Dec. 17, 1795
Augustus Griffeth & Catherine Clark,	Dec. 30, 1795
Hubbard Kimberley & Mary Thomas of West Haven, at house of Benajah Thomas,	Jan. 9, 1796
Christopher Kilby Alicock & Mary Frances Morean,	Jan. 11, 1796
Horace Stone of Litchfield & Hannah Hotchkis,	Feb. 12, 1796
Richard Eld & Anna Ward,	March 27, 1796
Samuel Hillingworth & Jane Praston,	April 10, 1796

Jonathan Manchester & Easter Manser, April, 16, 1796
Elnathan Atwater & Ruth Caroline Parmele, May 21, 1796
Amiah Thomas of West Haven & Elisabeth Plum of Milford,
    Sept. 21, 1796
Joseph Trowbridge & Lois Mix, Sept. 25, 1796
David Bonticue & Polly Clarke, Oct. 1, 1796
Rev Smith Miles & Abigail Isaacs of Branford, at house
    of Jonathan Ingersoll, Esq., Oct. 8, 1796
Joseph Trowbridge & Lois Mix, Oct. 27, 1796
Roger Minot Sherman & Elizabeth Gould, Dec. 14, 1796
Nathan Smith & Sarah McCracken, Dec. 28, 1796
Bela Ward of German Flats & Abigail Wilkox of Killing-
    worth, at house of Major Granniss, Jan. 27, 1797
Nathan Noah Bradley of East Guilford & Mary Herrick,
    March 22, 1797
Asahel Thomas & Abigail Stephens, at Oyster River,
    May 25, 1797
William ——— & Martha Munson, June 3, 1797
Ely Pien & Sapho Terks, negroes, July 9, 1797
Cato Tretton & Pender (negroes), Aug. 12, 1797
Calvin Turner & Thankful Thompson at West Haven, Sept., 1797
Hugh Monroe & Mary Frisbie at Branford, at house of
    Thos. Frisbie, Sept. 18, 1797
George Todd & Sarah Isaacs of Branford, at house of Jonathan
    Ingersoll, Esq., Sept. 18, 1797
Samuel Lathrop of Springfield & Mary McCracken, at house
    of her father, Wm. McCracken, Nov. 4, 1797
Amos Doolittle & Phebe Tuttle, Nov. 8, 1797
William Haney & Anna Smith, Nov. 11, 1797
——— Davis & ——— Collis, May 11, 1798
Andrew Colture & Elisabeth Whetmore, July 7, 1798
James Hooper & Isabel Corey of Branford, Sept. 14, 1798
——— Russel & ——— Lindsley, both of Branford, Sept. 11, 1799
Andrew Kidston & Wealthy A,. Parmele Sept. 11, 1799
James Ellis & Elisabeth Cook, Oct., 1799
Samuel Chew & Mary Sabin, Oct., 1799
Abraham Decker & Polly Munson, Oct. 1799
Roswell Brown & Mary English, Nov. 3, 1799

John Shaw & Grizzle Apthorp, both of N. Y.,   Nov. 13, 1799
Lewis Henry Guerdain & Marriam Fowler,   Nov. 14, 1799
Sam'l Forbes of East Haven & Sylvia Rogers of Branford,
                                               Feb. 16, 1800

BROOKLYN.

WINDHAM COUNTY.

(See Books I, II.)

The town of Brooklyn was incorporated May, 1786, and taken from Pomfret and Canterbury. Trinity Episcopal Church dates from 1769 and a church erected in 1771. The Rev. Daniel Fogg was rector from 1772. The following are the marriages recorded:

John Cambell & Mary Johnson,   July 17, 1772
Jeremiah Wheeler & Elizabeth Troop,   Oct. 27, 1778
Daniel Putnam & Catharine Hutchinson,   Sept. 2, 1782
Stephen Finch & Margareta (Tyler) a mulatto girl,
Jesse Parke & Kezia Adams,   Jan. 1, 1784
Joseph Cheney & Selah Tyler,   June 22, 1784
Samuel Brown & Clarissa Geer,   April 7, 1785
Jonathan Stevens & Eleanor Adams,   Oct. 20, 1785
Asaph Adams & Orinda Abbot,   Oct. 20, 1785
William Brown & Sarah Whaley,   Oct. 8, 1786
Smith Barrett & Abigail White,   Oct. 4, 1787
William Eldredge & Sarah Austin,   Feb. 14 (or 24), 1788
Sylvester Daily & Abigail (a negro girl),   June 15, 1788
Benj. Brayton & Zerviah Adams,   Sept. 10, 1788
William Kelly & Delight Adams,   Jan. 27, 1791
David Bissell & Hart Wickham,   Feb. 7, 1791
Peter Davison & Susanna Weaver,   Nov. 6, 1791
Israel Putnam & Claryna Chandler,   Feb. 26, 1792
Francis Casar (?) Leroy & Unice Moulton,   June 5, 1793
Cuff Fellows & Dinah Black,   Sept. 5, 1793
John Rice & Mary Allen,   Nov. 21, 1793
Abner Adams & Desire Ashcraft,   Sept. 25, 1794
Daniel Fogg & Deborah Brinley,   Dec. 2, 1794
Lewis Adams & Hannah Luce,   April 12, 1795
Eddy Winslow & Azubah Allen,   July 5, 1795

Geo. Candall & Betsy Adams	Oct. 18, 1795
Joseph Ashcraft & Sarah Hall,	Dec. 24, 1795
Lathrop Cushman & Catharine Allen,	Dec. 22, 1796
Jas. Hide & Lucy Ashcraft,	Nov. 7, 1797
Andrew Hopkins & Susanna Hollis,	Nov. 26, 1797
Frederick Perkins & Lucy Eldridge,	Nov. 8, 1798
Abishai Sharp & Mary Child,	Jan. 26, 1800
Geo. & Lydia Black,	March 27, 1800
Sam'l Hide & Anna Cundall,	Nov. 26, 1801
John Liscomb & Hannah Waters,	Feb. 28, 1802
David Ingals & Sarah Bowman,	Nov. 8, 1802
Geo. Brinley & Catharine Putnam,	April 30, 1805
Martin Gallop, & Ruth Pettingall,	Sept. 30, 1805
Ranford Button & Eleanor Parke,	Nov. 3, 1805
Edward Brinley & May Jonston of Newort,	April 15, 1807

FAIRFIELD.

FAIRFIELD COUNTY.

(See Books III, V, VI.)

The town of Fairfield, settled in 1639 and named in 1645 has had several Congregational churches—see Books III, V, VI. The church at Greenfield Hill in Fairfield was organized May 18, 1726, with the following records:

Elias Alverd & Hannah Goodsell,	May 11, 1745
Allen Hos & Phebe Rogers of Greenfield,	June 16, 1763
Elias Grey & Eunice Allen,	Nov. 27, 1766
Nathan Godfrey & Isabel Andrews,	Dec. 24, 1766
David Nicholls & Hannah Alvord,	Aug. 11, 1768
Jonathan Knap & Mary Alvord,	Sept. 7, 1772
John Alvord & Sarah Wakeman,	Nov. 11, 1772
Thos. Sherwood & Mary Alvord,	Nov. 23, 1778
——— Alvord & Abigail Banks,	Nov. —, 1779
Jonathan Andrews & Rhus Hull,	Dec. 7, 1779
John Bartram & Widow Sarah Bradley,	before 1719
Gushom Banks & Mary Bradley,	
Benjamin Lyndes & Grace Barlow,	May 30, 1742
Joseph Banks & Mary Sherwood,	June 25, 1712

Timothy Burr & Sarah Rowland,	March 6, 1728
Gershom Banks & Hannah Bradley,	Oct. 12, 1743
Joseph T. Banks & Johannah Banks,	March 29, 1737
John Thorp & Mary Davis,	May 15, 1699
Samuel Hill & Sarah Dimon,	Nov. 28, 1744
Peter Bradley & Damens Dimon,	Nov. 5, 1735
Moses T. Dimon & Hannah Gilbert,	April 27, 1721
John Drew & Mary Northrop (?),	Jan. —, 1746
Peter Thorp & Eunice Davis,	Jan. 13, 1748
Benoin Dimon & H——— Gold,	Sept. 15, 1748
Peter Lyon & Mary Davis,	———, 1750
Gershom Wakeman & Elizabeth Down,	April 14, 1757
Thaddeus Williams & Frances Case,	Nov. 29, 1747
Onessimus Bradley & Dewitt Cabel,	Aug. 8, 1754
Lieut. Ebenezer Couch of Reading & Elizabeth McCarty,	
	July 29, 1761
Jonathan Robinson & Elizabeth Canfield,	April 14, 1763
Josiah Cable & Mary Williams,	Sept. 25, 1763
William Cable of Norfield & Ruth Murwin,	Feb. 1, 1764
Seth Squire of Fairfield & Margaret Cable,	Sept. 4, 1766
Eliphalet Cooley & Eunice Bradley,	Feb. 9, 1770
Isaac Web & Jerusha Cable,	June 19, 1774
Joseph Davis of Norfield & Abigail Bradley,	March 21, 1758
Jonathan Dimon & Hannah Rowland,	Feb. 12, 1760
John Drew & Anne Thorp,	June 24, 1760
Chauncy Down & Betty Smith,	June 3, 1762
Ephraim Bradley & Damaris Dimon,	Feb. 22, 1764
Samuel Goodsell & Phebe Davis,	Jan. 23, 1766
David Bulkley of Greensfarms & Wid. Abigail Davis,	
	March 17, 1767
Benjamin Smith & Martha Down,	June 15, 1767
Gold Dimon & Abigail Burr,	March 6, 1776
Col. Jonathan Dimon & Ruth Bradley,	May 11, 1779
John Dickinson & Molly Redfield,	Sept. 17, 1781
John Finch & Mary Elwell,	Dec. 11, 1745
Couch Edwards & Noami Sherwood,	July 31, 1751
Moses Burr, & Abigail Edwards,	July 28, 1761
Nathan Hubbel & Martha Finch,	Dec. 5, 1723

John Fanton & Mary Rowland,	Oct. 28, 1732
Nathan Foot & Abiah Gilberd,	July 5, 1750
Phillip Mallet & Sarah Frost,	Sept. 15, 1777
John Goodsell & Mary Lewis,	July 20, 1725
Lockwood Gorham & Abigail Meeker,	Sept. 21, 1742
Jabez Gorham & Merriam Hull,	April —, 1744
Ebenezer Gilburd & Johanna Northrop,	April —, 1744
Edmond Ogden & Mary Gilburd,	Jan. 20, 1729
James Gray & Sarah Gilburd,	July 1, 1733
Moses Wakeman & Mary Goodsell,	Aug. 21, 1744
John Bradley & Sarah Gilburd,	Jan. 13, 1726
Moses Dimon & Hannah Gilburd,	April 27, 1721
John Wakeman & Catherine Gilburd,	April 8, 1730
Moses Gilburd & Sarah Gilburd,	Jan. —, 1746
Samuel Gregory & Abigail Gilburd,	April —, 1746
Edward Lacy & Rebecca Grey,	May 18, 1748
John Goodsell & Sarah Bradley,	Jan. 18, 1749
Nathan Gold & Abigail Burr,	May 2, 1749
Nathan Foot & Abiah Gilburd,	July 5, 1750
Archabel Blair & Abigail Goodsell,	Feb. 24, 1754
David Gold & Abigail Hill,	———, 1754
Elnathan Bradley & Sarah Goodsell,	Oct. —, 1754
Ensign Stephen Thorp & Sarah Gold,	April 10, 1760
Jacob Grey & Wid. Abigail Mills,	July 27, 1760
Silas Hull & Huldah Goodsell,	Nov. 26, 1761
Seth Gray of Reading & Sarah Mills,	June 23, 1762
Epaphas Goodsell & Jane Bradley,	Dec. 5, 1765
Joseph Rumsey & Mary Gorham,	Jan. 8, 1766
Sam. Goodsell & Phebe Davis,	Jan. 23, 1766
Elisha Grey & Wid. Ellen Hill,	July 31, 1766
Elias Grey & Eunice Allen both of Greensfarm,	Nov. 27, 1766
Nathan Godfrey & Isabel Andrews,	Dec. 24, 1766
Lewis Goodsell & Eunice Wakeman,	March 2, 1767
Gilbourd Hunt & Hannah Gorham,	Jan. 28, 1768
Robert Whittock of Greensfarm & Susanna Guyer of Norfield,	
	April, 1770
Thomas Wheeler & Elizabeth Gold,	Nov. 17, 1772
Abijah Gregory & Molly Thorp,	Jan. 18, 1776

David Goodsell & Anna Beers,	Jan. 7, 1777
Jonathan Spears & Sarah Grey,	Feb. 15, 1778
Jessee Gold & Sarah Gold,	Feb. 19, 1778
Lewis Goodsell & Wid. Sarah Sherwood,	June 1, 1780
Meeker Ghoram & Elizabeth Hubbill,	Aug. 24, 1780
Meriam Hull & Tabez Gorham,	April —, 1744
Samuel Hill & Sarah Dimon,	Nov. 28, 1744
Noah Sherwood & Phebe Higgins,	June 3, 1727
Nathaniel Hull & Elizabeth Burr,	Nov. 29, 1716
Nathan Hubbel & Martha Finch,	Dec. 5, 1723
David Banks & Wid. Sarah Hull,	Nov. 1, 1738
Moses Gilburd & Elizabeth Hubbel,	March 11, 1741
Daniel Whittock & Mary Morehouse Hilton,	May 13, 1746
Ebenezer Banks & Sarah Hide,	June 18, 1746
Stephen Hull & Elizabeth Wakeman,	May —, 1746
Richard Lewsey & Rachel Lord (or Hide),	June 23, 1746
Francis Bradley & Ruth Hull,	Feb. 21, 1750
Jabez Hull & Grace Sherwood,	May 30, 1751
Seth Jennings & Mary Hull,	March 13, 1754
David Gold & Abigail Hill	———, 1754
Seth Bradley & Eunice Hull,	Sept. 8, 1755
John Sherwood & Sary Hill,	Dec. —, 1756
Eliphalet Hill & Isabel Burr,	Jan. 8, 1756
John Hubbel & Eleanor Burr,	March 30, 1758
Isaac Hunt & Griswold Lord,	May 18, 1858
Ezekiel Hull & Sarah Burr,	Nov. 2, 1758
John Hull & Eleanor Sherwood,	Jan. 11, 1759
Daniel Hull & Betty Bradley,	April 11, 1759
John Smith & Molly Hubbel, both of Stratfield,	May 3, 1759
Silas Hull & Huldah Goodsell,	Nov, 26, 1761
Ebenezer Hill & Mabel Sherwood,	Jan. 17, 1765
Stephen Hubbel of No. Fairfield, & Rhode Middlebrook,	
	Jan. 27, 1765
Silas Hull & Ellen Bradley,	Dec. 25, 1765
James Hill & Elizabeth Wakeman,	July 13, 1766
Elisha Grey & Wid. Ellen Hill,	July 31, 1766
William Heron & Mary Jennings,	March 8, 1767
Gilbourd Hunt & Hannah Gorham,	Jan. 28, 1768

David Thorp & Rebecca Hall,	June 23, 1768
William Hicks & Wid. Abigail Blair,	June 28, 1768
Silas Haynes of No. Stamford & Anna Whitney,	Nov. 3, 1768
David Hubbell & Sarah Perry,	Feb. 28, 1773
Moses Hill & Esther Burr,	June 17, 1773
Abner Hendrick & Sarah Thorp,	Nov. 17, 1774
Moses Hull & Sarah Sherwood,	March 4, 1778
Joseph Banks & Eleanor Hull,	Nov. 19, 1778
Joseph Bulkly & Ellen Hubble,	June 2, 1779
Zadock Hubbill & Mary Hubbill,	Oct. 22, 1779
Hezekiah Hull & Sarah Murwin,	Oct. 28, 1779
Jonathan Andrews & Rhua Hull,	Dec. 7, 1779
John Ogden & Mary Jennings,	Jan. 24, 1729
Will John Smith & Elizabeth Jessop,	Aug. —, 1710
Ebenezer Thorp & Mary Jones,	June —, 1746
Nehemiah Jennings & Patience Jackson,	Sept. 11, 1751
James Peet & Sarah Jones,	Feb. 26, 1752
Hezekiah Jennings & Noami Sanford,	March 30, 1752
Reuben Whitehead & Elizabeth Jennings of Fairfield,	
	May 10, 1764
William Heron & Mary Jennings,	March 8, 1767
Josiah Lyon & Eunice Jennings of No. Fairfield,	March 1, 1768
Peter Wakeman & Sarah Jennings,	Feb. 26, 1775
Turney Bulkley & Esther Johnson,	March 15, 1775
Benj. Lyades (?) & Grace Barlow,	May 30, 1742
John Lyon & Elizabeth Wakeman,	Jan. —, 1746
Richard Lewsey & Rachel Lord (alias Hide),	June 23, 1746
John Lane of Middletown & Hannah ———,	Oct. —, 1747
Edward Lacy & Rebecca Grey,	May 18, 1748
Nathan Osburn & Grizzel Lyon,	Dec. 22. 1748
James Lyon & Abigail Rowland,	Dec. 14, 1732
David Baxter & Rodah Lyon,	April 26, 1750
Peter Lyon & Mary Davis,	———, 1750
Joseph Lyon & Lois Thorp,	Jan. —, 1757
Eleazer Williams & Mary Lord,	April 13, 1757
Isaac Hunt & Griswold Lord,	May 18, 1758
Rewl Thorp of Greenfield & Esther Lines of Fairfield,	
	Nov. 19, 1761

Hezekiah Lyon & Hannah Meeker, both of Fairfield,
March 1, 1764
Seth Lyon & Mary Bradley, March 7, 1764
Eliphalet Lyon & Eleanor Wakeman, May 3, 1764
Caleb Meeker & Rhode Lyon (both of Fairfield), June 13, 1764
Stephen Meeker & Ruth Lyon, both of Fairfield, Jan. 8, 1767
Josiah Lyon of Greenfield & Eunice Jennings of Fairfield,
March 1, 1768
Daniel Lee of Ridgefield & Hester Banks of Greenfield,
Nov. 16, 1768
Sturges Lewis & Priscilla Bradley, April 8, 1778
Lothrop Lewis & Eleanor Burr, July 19, 1778
Gabriel Leverich & Hannah Thorp, April 2, 1779
Josiah Lacey & Ruth Silliman, Jan. 11, 1781
Lockwood Goram & Abigail Meeker, Sept. 21, 1742
Joseph T. Middlebrook & Sarah Williams, Dec. 17, 1741
Daniel Whitlock & Mary Hilton (alias) Morehouse, May 13, 1746
Richard Wescott & Jane Middlebrook, Oct. 19, 1746
Thaddeus Morehouse & Martha Williams, May —, 1746
Othniel Morehouse & Susanna Row, Sept. —, 1747
John Bradley & Abigail Murwin, Dec. 13, 1750
Jacob White & Elizabeth Middlebrook, 1755
David Murwin & Hannah Taintor, Mar. 1, 1758
Seth Meeker & Abigail Wakeman of Greenfield, March 8, 1758
Samuel Murwin & Eunice Thorp, April 23, 1761
Enos Bradley & Mary Murwin, Dec. 10, 1761
Seth Gray of Reading & Sarah Mills, June, 23, 1762
William Cable of Norfield & Ruth Murwin, Feb. 1, 1764
Hezekiah Lyon & Hannah Meeker, March 1, 1764
Reuben Osborn of Fairfield & Eleanor Middlebrook,
April 22, 1764
Nathan Bradley of Fairfield & Mary Meeker , April 26, 1764
Caleb Meeker & Rhode Lyon both of Fairfield, June 13, 1764
Josiah Raymond of Norwalk & Mary Murwin, Nov. 7, 1764
Stephen Hubbel of North Fairfield & Rhode Middlebrook,
Jan. 27, 1765
Benjamin Meeker & Abigail Burr, both of Greensfarm,
Feb. 3, 1765

Daniel Wheeler & Eleanor Middlebrook,	Jan. 19, 1766
John T. Murwin & Damaris Bradley,	Aug. 13, 1767
Edmuns Barlow & Salone Middlebrook,	Nov. 29, 1769
John Mitchel & Esther Trubee,	May 30, 1775
Peter Morehouse of Fairfield & Phebe Blair of Greenfield,	
	March 24, 1776
Joseph Straten & Eunice Middlebrook,	May 9, 1776
Phillip Mallet & Sarah Foot,	Sept. 15, 1777
John Murwin, Jr., & Mary Price,	Feb. 22, 1778
Abijah Murwin & Ruth Bradley,	Oct. 26, 1779
Hezekiah Hull & Sarah Murwin,	Oct. 28, 1779
Ephraim Osburn & Mary Murwin,	March 2, 1780
John Drew & Mary Northrop,	Jan. —, 1746
Lemuel Price & Lydia Norris,	Sept. 8, 1748
Ebenezer Nicolls of Greenfield & Sarah Scudder of Hunt-	
ington,	May 24, 1762
Ephaphras Wakeman & Eunice Nicholls,	Aug. 21, 1766
David Nicholls & Miriam Bradley,	Oct. 15, 1780
Daniel Osburn & Sarah Osburn,	Nov. 15, 1744
John Ogden & Mary Jennings,	Jan. 24, 1729
Girshom Thorp & Hannah Osburn,	Jan., 1746
Daniel Squire & Abigail Osburn,	Sept. 1746
Edmond Blackman & Eunice Odel,	Oct. 10, 1747
Nathan Osburn & Grissell Lyon,	Dec. 22, 1748
John Stratten & Grace Osburn,	Jan. —, 1750
Oliver Whitlock & Eunice Ogden,	May —, 1751
Samuel Odel & Wid. Sarah Banks,	Sept. 19, 1751
A son of William Odel & Eunice Price (bride),	
	October —, 1754
Peter Osborn & Elizabeth Banks,	March 14, 1795
Seth Osburn of Fairfield & Mabel Bradley,	May 21, 1761
Ebenezer Ogden & Ruth Bradley,	March 17, 1763
Moses Ogden & Molly Banks,	Nov. 17, 1763
Reuben Osborn & Elenor Middlebrook,	April 22, 1764
Daniel Sherwood & Abigail Ogden,	Dec. 20, 1769
Nathan Bradley & Amelia Osburn,	May 17, 1775
Jesse Burr & Ellen Ogden,	Nov. 20, 1780
Samuel Perry & Sarah Whitlock,	April 28, 1742

Abel Plat & Mercy Banks,	March 23, 1749
Gershom Banks & Mary Perry,	Feb. 14, 1752
James Peet & Sarah Jones,	Feb. 26, 1752
Peter Bradley & Wid. Sarah Price,	
Joseph Sherwood of Fairfield & Hester Price,	Feb. 13, 1754
Samuel Perry & Wid. Mary Smith,	April 15, 1760
Thomas Wheeler & Wid. Sarah Perry,	April 17, 1760
Eliphalet Thorp & Sarah Perry,	May 8, 1760
Ebenezer Perry & Martha Sherwood,	Dec. 24, 1760
Samuel Beers & Sarah Perry,	Feb. 28, 1773
Hezekiah Price & Eunice Beers,	Dec. 24, 1767
Joseph Thorp & Hannah Price of Ridgebury,	March 1, 1769
David Hubbard & Sarah Perry,	Feb. 28, 1773
Thaddeus Perry & Grace Bulkly,	Jan. 19, 1774
Samuel Price & Elizabeth Beden,	Jan. 27, 1776
John Murwin, Jr., & Mary Price,	Jan. 27, 1776
Samuel Smith & Esther Perry,	Aug. 15, 1779
Henry F. Quintard of Greenwich & Mary J. Campbell,	Dec. 28, 1768
Robert Rogers & Phebe Sherwood,	Oct. 2, 1739
Jonathan Robinson & Lucretia Thorp,	April —, 1752
Jonathan Robinson & Elizabeth Canfield,	April 14, 1763
Dr. David Rodgers & Martha Tennent,	Sept. 1, 1772
Thaddeus Thorp & Sarah Rowe,	Jan. 10, 1775
Abel Sealey & Martha Bennet,	Aug. 24, 1744
David Williams & Dorothy Sturges,	Oct. 8, 1719
Nathan Willson & Mary Silliman,	Aug. —, 1746
Dan Squire & Abigail Osburn,	Sept. —, 1746
Panock Sherwood & Abigail Staples,	March 30, 1752
Samuel Sherwood & Ev. Sherwood,	Feb. —, 1754
Joseph Smith & Eunice Williams,	Oct. —, 1756
Ezra Williams & Rachel Smith,	April 7, 1760
Chauncey Down & Betty Smith,	June 3, 1762
Jehiel Sherwood of Fairfield & Sarah Squire of Greenfield,	
	Oct. 5, 1763
Silas Whitney & Esther Sherwood,	Dec. 4, 1766
Seth Sherwood & Mary Wakeman,	Feb. 7, 1770
Reuben Smith & Ellen Williams,	July 17, 1774
Peter Smith & Chloe Smith,	May 27, 1778

Timothy Sanford & Widow Esther Whitney,	Nov. 24, 1778
Eliphalet Sherwood & Abigail Sherwood,	Dec. 7, 1779
Peter Winton & Elizabeth Straten,	Nov. —, 1780
David Thorp & Naomi Williams,	Oct. —, 1744
Jabez Wakeman & Ruth Tredwill,	June 1, 1727
Oliver Whitlock of Greenfield & Widow Melison Taylor of Norwalk,	Nov. 17, 1763
David Thorp & Rebecca Hall,	June, 23, 1768
John Mitchel & Esther Trubee,	May 30, 1775
Gabriel Segwick (?) & Hannah Thorp,	April 2, 1779
Joel Wakeman & Rachel Thorp,	May 18, 1779
David Thorp & Noami Williams,	Oct. —, 1744
Thaddeus Williams & Francis Case,	Nov. 29, 1747
Joseph Brimsmade & Ruth Winton,	Oct. 19, 1748
William —— & Margret Whitlock,	Aug. 31, 1757
Reuben Williams & Huldah Williams,	May 18, 1760
Ebenezer Wakeman & Elizabeth Webb,	May 3, 1764
Timothy Sanford & Wid. Esther Whitney,	Nov. 24, 1778
Gershom Wakeman & Wid. Huldah Williams,	April 11, 1781
Benjamin Sherwood & Eleanor Bradley,	Feb. 9, 1724
John Banks & Elizabeth Bradley,	May 14, 1740
Abel Sealey & Martha Bennet,	Aug. 24, 1744
John Bradley, Jr., & Sarah Gilbert,	Jan. 13, 1726
Nathaniel Hull & Elizabeth Burr,	Nov. 29, 1716
Samuel Bradley & Sarah Whelpley,	Nov. —, 1723
Peter Bradley & Damaris Dimons,	Nov. 5, 1735
David Banks & Wid. Sarah Hull,	Nov. 1, 1738
Ebenezer Banks & Sarah Hide,	June 18, 1746
James Burr & Mary Barlow,	Jan. —, 1747
Joseph Bradley, Jr., & Mary Squire,	1747
Edmond Blackman & Eunice Odel,	Oct. 10, 1747
Joseph Brinsmade & Ruth Winton,	Oct. 19, 1748
John Goodsell & Sarah Bradley,	Jan. 18, 1749
Cap. Dan. Bradley & Wid. Sarah Bradley,	(?) 1749
Abel Plat & Mercy Banks,	March 23, 1749
Nathan Gold & Abigail Burr,	May 2, 1749
David Williams, Jr., & Esther Burr,	Feb. 7, 1750
Francis Bradley & Ruth Hull,	Feb. 21, 1750

Joseph Sturges & Anne Barlow,	March 11, 1750
David Baxter & Rodah Lyon,	April 26, 1750
John Bradley, Jr., & Abigail Murwin,	Dec. 13, 1750
Capt. John Reed & Sarah Bradley,	Dec. 19, 1750
Thos. Bedient & Susan ——— Ogden (?),	May 30, 1751
Daniel Bradley & Mary Banks,	Aug. 8, 1751
Samuel Bradley, Jr., & Sarah Wakeman,	Sept. 10, 1751
Samuel Odel & Wid. Sarah Banks,	Sept. 19, 1751
Gershom Banks & Mary Perry,	Feb. 14, 1752
Ebenezer Burr & Sarah Sherwood,	Feb. —, 1754
Samuel Ogden & Mary Banks,	June 27, 1754
John Wakeman & Esther Bradley,	Oct. 3, 1754
Elnathan Bradley & Sarah Goodsell,	Oct. —, 1754
Seth Bradley & Eunice Hull,	Sept. 8, 1755
Peter Bradley & Wid. Sarah Price,	Oct. —, 1756
Eliphalet Hill & Isabel Burr,	Jan. 8, 1756
Joseph Davis & Abigail Bradley,	March 21, 1758
Joseph Burr, Jr., & Grace Bradley,	May 18, 1758
Benjamin Banks & Wid. Whitney,	July 23, 1759
Thaddeus Banks & Olive Bradley,	Nov. 1, 1759
Samuel Wakeman & Mabel Burr,	May 8, 1760
Enos Wheeler & Hannah Bradley,	May 15, 1760
Squire Wakeman & Damaris Bradley of Fairfield,	May 28, 1761
Isaac Sturges & Rhoda Banks,	Aug. 27, 1761
Daniel Banks & Hannah Thorp,	Dec. 10, 1761
Philip Bradley & Mary Bostwick,	April 22, 1762
Calvin Wheeler & Ruhamah Bradley,	July 5, 1762
Elnathan Bradley of Greenfield & Hannah Bartram of Reading,	Dec. 26, 1762
George Burr & Mabel Wakeman,	Dec. 30, 1762
Seth Lyon & Mary Bradley,	March 7, 1764
David Barlow, Jr., of Fairfield & Sarah Bradley,	Aug. 9, 1764
Abigail Burr & Benj. Meeker,	Feb. 3, 1765
Reuben Beers of Fairfield & Eleanor Banks,	Oct. 21, 1765
Samuel Whitney & Marianna Banks,	Nov. 7, 1765
Seth Sherwood & Ruhamah Bradley,	Nov. 21, 1765
Silas Hull & Ellen Bradley,	Dec. 25, 1766
Samuel Beers & Sarah Perry,	Feb. 12, 1766

John Mills & Jerusha Bradley,	Jan. 26, 1766
William Bulkley & Bette Burr,	Sept. 4, 1766
Eliphalet Burr & Prudence Wheeler,	Jan. 18, 1767
David Bulkley & Wid. Abigail Davis,	March 17, 1767
Dan. Sturges, Jr., & Naomi Bradley,	Oct. 31, 1767
Hezekiah Price & Eunice Beers,	Dec. 24, 1767
John Banks & Mary Sturges,	June 16, 1768
William Hicks & Wid. Abigail Blair,	June 28, 1768
Lieut. John Bradley of Greenfield & Wid. Mary Silliman	
of Fairfield,	Oct. 11, 1768
—— Burr & Rhode Burritt,	Oct. 16, 1768
Jesup Wakeman of Greensfarm & Amelia Banks of Green-	
field,	Dec. 29, 1768
John Barlow & Sarah Whitney of Greenfield,	Jan. 10, 1769
Ephraim Beers, Jr., of Norfield & Abigail Thorp,	Feb. 21, 1769
Elisha Bradley & Eunice Banks,	Feb. 13, 1770
Thaddeus Wakeman & Esther Bradley,	Nov. 10, 1772
Noah Wakeman & Molly Bradley,	Dec. 3, 1772
Peter Banks & Elizabeth Bradley,	Jan. 19, 1774
Turney Bulkly & Esther Johnson,	March 15, 1775
Nathan Bradley & Amelia Osburn,	May 17, 1775
Zalmon Bradley & Betty Wakeman,	March 20, 1776
Peter Morehouse & Phebe Blair,	March 24, 1776
Hanford Wakeman & Sarah Bradley,	June 4, 1776
Peter Bradley & Phebe Straten,	Nov. 20, 1777
Joseph Sherwood of North Fairfield & Sarah Bradley of	
Greenfield,	Feb. 26, 1778
Joseph Winton & Molly Bradley,	March 4, 1778
Moses Banks & Abigail Wakeman,	Dec. 9, 1778
John Sherwood, Jr., & Hannah Bradley,	Jan. 14, 1779
Nehemiah Banks & Sarah Sherwood,	Jan. 21, 1779
Francis Bradley & Rachel Banks,	April 27, 1781
Moses Sturgis & Sarah Bradley,	
Nathan Banks & Mabel Bradley,	April 1, 1781
Jabez Wakeman & Clara Banks,	June 21, 1781
Nathan Winton & Elizabeth Banks,	Nov. 4, 1781
Gershom Wakeman & Sybill Bradley,	Dec. 13, 1781
James Burr & Widow Hannah Osburn,	before 1734

PRESTON.

NEW LONDON COUNTY.

(See Book IV.)

The town of Preston was named as early as Oct. 1687. The Congregationa Church was organized Nov. 16, 1698. Rev. Salmon Treat, was pastor until 1744. The existing records begin with his successor, Rev. Asher Rosseter. The 2d church in Preston was organized in 1720—now in Griswold—see Book IV. Following are the marriages by Rev. Asher Rosseter:

Rufus Yarrington & Lucretia Brewster,	Sept. 27, 1744
Benjamin Freeman & Abigail Tracy,	Jan. 2, 1745
Sam'l Johnson of Plainfield & Abigail Meech,	March 26, 1745
Christopher Dennison & Abigail Tyler,	Dec. 17, 1745
Park Woodward & Zilpha Park,	March 13, 1746
Sherebiah Tracy & Hannah Wentworth,	May 22, 1746
Sam'l Witter & Sarah Calkins,	Dec. 3, 1746
Jacob Tyler & Elizabeth Clark, widow,	Dec. 26, 1746
John Hill & Thankful Clark,	Dec. 31, 1746
Negro Sharp & Negro Betty, servants of Ephraim Smith & David Lamb,	Jan. 15, 1747
Jonathan Tracy & Lucy Avery,	May 19, 1747
Andrew Davis & Eunice Kimball,	Sept. 30, 1747
Daniel Geers & Mary Starkweather,	Nov. 5, 1747
Elijah Bliss & Mary Tracy,	Nov. 25, 1747
Timothy Clark & Mary Rude,	Jan. 4, 1748
Simeon Fobes & Ruth Brewster,	Oct. —, 1748
Nathan Starkweather & Dorcas Hamlinton,	Oct. 22, 1751
Andrew Gates & Olive Starkweather,	Nov. 5, 1751
Joseph Smith & Zipporah Branch,	Nov. 20, 1751
Hezekiah Lord & Jerusha Gates,	April 2, 1752
Soloman Story & Dorcas Branch,	July 30, 1752
Zephaniah Spicer & Sarah Starkweather,	Nov. 9, 1752
Thomas Davison & Rachel Rude,	Nov. 1, 1753
Nathan Witter & Keziah Branch,	Nov. 15, 1753
Asa Park & Rachel Park,	Nov. 28, 1753
Joseph Williams & Mabel Meech,	Jan. 2, 1754
Joseph Witter, Jr., & Hannah Davison,	Jan. 3, 1754
Nathan Kimball & Margaret Rix,	Feb. 13, 1754

John Utley & Desire Tracy,	May 15, 1754
James Rix & Hannah Safford,	May 23, 1754
Jonathan Calkins & Jerusha Clark,	Aug. 7, 1754
Sam'l Hill & Silence Rude,	Aug. 15, 1754
Ebenezer Clark & Eunice Calkins,	Feb. 3, 1755
Joshua Gates & Anna Branch,	May 15, 1755
Moses Tracy & Esther Tracy,	June 5, 1755
Amos Story & Hannah Renolds,	Sept. 17, 1755
Sam'l Leonard & Mary Freeman,	Dec. 25, 1755
Geo. Brown & Huldah Laribee,	Dec. 25, 1755
David Ames & Abigail Butler,	Jan. 29, 1756
Sam'l Renolds & Ruth Tracy.	Feb. 26, 1756
Enos Tracy & Lydia Whitney,	May 6, 1756
Jacob Robinson & Anna Tracy,	Nov. 4, 1756
Doxee Lane & Esther Freeman,	Dec. 1, 1756
Jedidiah Frink, Jr., & Esther Pierce,	Dec. 15, 1756
Jacob Stephens & Elizabeth Leonard,	May 26, 1757
Benj. Kenedy & Olive Rude,	Dec. 22, 1757
John Branch & Prescilla Tracy,	Jan. 5, 1758
Christopher Tracy & Rose Tracy,	March 23, 1758
Simeon Tracy & Lois Branch,	Sept. 13, 1758
Simeon Bundey & Eunice Meech,	Oct. 5, 1758
Allen Leet & Rachel Morgan,	Nov. 22, 1758
John Safford & Mary Johnson,	March 15, 1759
John Geer & Jerusha Park,	Oct. 4, 1759
Isaac Branch & Susanna Weakly,	March 5, 1760
Rossel Morgan & Martha Downer,	Dec. 4, 1760
Thos. Partridge & Zipporah Freeman,	Sept. 16, 1761
Wm. Brewster & Olive Morgan,	Nov. 4, 1761
Caleb Gates & Elizabeth Branch,	Nov. 15, 1761
Ebenezer Benjamin & Phebe Benjamin,	Nov. 26, 1761
Edward Mott & Sarah Kinne,	Dec. 10, 1761
Abijah Park, & Elizabeth Morse,	Dec. 16, 1761
Asa Partridge & Eliphal Geer,	Feb. 25, 1762
John Putnam & Martha Woodward,	Feb. 25, 1762
Joshua Downer & Huldah Crary,	Feb. 25, 1762
Ebenezer Prentice & Lucy Cary,	April 22, 1762
William Robinson & Anne Blake,	May 13, 1762

Elijah Barnes & Luey Kinne,	May 13 1762
Reuben Park & Sarah Rockwell,	June 10, 1762
Olive Spalding & Mary Witter,	June 17, 1762
Oliver Sisson & Mary Park,	June 17, 1762
Ames Leonard & Mary Partridge,	June 24, 1762
Henry Herrick & Eunice Putnam,	June 24, 1762
Benajah Tracy & Lucy Herrick,	July 4, 1762
Simeon Morgan & Hannah Morgan,	Aug. 26, 1762
Dan'l Rix & Rebecca Johnson,	Oct. 28, 1762
Ezekiel Bundey & Ama Starkweather,	Feb. 10, 1763
Nathan Fobes & Temperance Tracy,	May 5, 1763
Elijah Morgan & Dorothy Morgan,	Aug. 18, 1763
James Tracy & Phebe Richards,	Nov. 3, 1763
John Anslay & Eunice Bundey,	Nov. 6, 1763
Elisha Eddy & Bersheba Pierce,	Nov. 10, 1763
Nathan Fobes, Jr., & Elizabeth Fobes,	Nov. 17, 1763
Silas Sterry & Olive Killam,	Dec. 8, 1763
Nathan Leonard & Hannah Branch,	Jan. 12, 1764
Moses Meech & Elizabeth Plummer,	April 5, 1764
Jeremiah Kinne & Elizabeth Plummer,	Nov. 21, 1764
Moses Porter & Sarah Park,	May 12, 1765
Sam'l Mott & Abigail Rosseter,	Nov. 24, 1765
David Benjamin & Esther Wibourn,	March 30, 1766
Nathan Geer & Jerusha Tracy,	May 1, 1766
Asa Branch & Elizabeth Tracy,	Sept. 18, 1766
Newman Perkins & Abigail Dennison,	Nov. 20, 1766
Joseph Jeffers & Ruhama Downing,	Jan. 4, 1767
Nathan Ayres & Desire Tracy,	March 12, 1767
Abel Partridge & Eunice Story,	April 9, 1767
Jonas Brown & Mary Clark,	Jan. 7, 1768
Wm. Farnham & Jerusha Starkweather,	April 13, 1768
John Morgan & Eunice Crary,	April 17, 1768
Asa Smith & Elizabeth Morgan,	April 21, 1768
Hezekiah Tracy & Eunice Rude,	Dec. 25, 1768
David Benjamin & Lucy Park,	Feb. 19, 1769
John Crary & Anna Morgan,	Feb. 24. 1769
Dan Rude & Deborah Meech,	March 9, 1769
Jonathan Boardman & Priscilla Safford,	April 10, 1769

Simeon Lathrop & Esther Branch,	April 13, 1769
Hutchinson MacFarlin & Lucy Randal,	June 2, 1769
Jedidiah Wilbur & Abigail Plummer,	Aug. 3, 1769
Jonathan Smith & Hannah Witter,	Nov. 23 1769
Timothy Lester, Jr., & Elizabeth Kinne,	Dec. 7, 1769
Elijah Tracy & Lois Smith,	March 1, 1770
Amasa Branch & Thankful Bowdish,	March 22, 1770
Jedidiah Fitch & Elizabeth Hillyar,	March 29, 1770
Francis Plummer & Keziah Kinne,	April 1, 1770
Nathan Thomas & Sarah Bowdish,	April 5, 1770
Wm. Whitney & Mary Fobes,	May 14, 1770
Nathan Peters & Lois Crary,	June 10, 1770
Abraham Yarrington & Eunice Bundey,	Sept. 13, 1770
James Smith & Anna Blasar,	Sept. 18, 1770
John Andros 3d., & Grace Rude,	Dec. 2, 1770
Hezekiah Douglass & Esther Witter,	April 11, 1771
John Page & Anna Geer,	Aug. 5, 1771
Samuel Prentice & Anne Benjamin,	Aug. 29, 1771
Abiel Benjamin & Louisa Ellis,	Sept. 18, 1771
Nath'l. Tracy & Miriam Ames,	Nov. 14, 1771
Jonathan Rawson & Bathsheba Tracy,	Jan. 1, 1772
Jonas Avery & Mary Avery,	Jan. 16, 1772
Chas. Mile & Sabra Bennit,	June 1, 1772
Reuel Cook & Elizabeth Jones,	June 17, 1772
Jonathan Sweet & Anna Dennison,	Aug. 14, 1772
Thomas Main & Lucy Tyler,	Sept. 24, 1772
Daniel Kimbal & Mary Sterry,	June 23, 1773
Soloman Story & Dorothy Rude,	July 29, 1773
Joseph Bobbins & Mary Wilkinson,	Aug, 25, 1773
Calvin Barstow & Margaret Tracy,	Oct. 14, 1773
Jabez Brewster & Dorothy Park,	Feb. 26, 1775
Silas Bliss & Judith Freeman,	April 19, 1775
Ziba Baldwin & Anna Brown,	July 20, 1775
William Brown & Elizabeth Tyler,	Aug. 17, 1775
Newport Williams & Mercy Cossump,	Aug. 31, 1775
Nath'l. Stanton & Anna Avery,	Sept. 6, 1775
John Potter & Elizabeth Witter,	Oct. 4, 1776
Emmanuel Northrup & Phebe Brown,	Jan. 22, 1777

Dan'l Morgan & Johannah Brewster,	Jan. 23, 1777
David Morse & Esther Laribee,	Feb. 25, 1777
Thos. Wilbur & Rachel Herrick,	April 17, 1777
Christain Gosmer & Mary Rouse,	May 1, 1777
Rev. Aaron Putnam & Elizabeth Avery,	May 13, 1777
Abel Cook & Elizabeth Branch,	June 22, 1777
James Rockwell & Anna Williams,	Sept. 9, 1777
Jonathan Daboll & Rebecca Cunningham,	Sept. 25, 1777
Joseph Emes & Hannah Tyler,	Nov. 12, 1777
Elisha York & Anna Clark,	Jan. 1, 1778
Levi Tracy & Lucy Frink,	April 9, 1778
York Quomine & Phillis Hill,	June 18, 1778
Edward Tracy & Azuba Jennings,	July 16, 1778
Avery Dennison & Prudence Brown,	Aug. 13, 1778
Erastus Rosseter & Lydia Perkins,	Sept. 13, 1778
Caleb Right & Elizabeth Richards,	Nov. 15, 1778
Benjamin Babcock & Desire Billings,	Feb. 4, 1779
Rufus Park & Zerviah Laribee,	March 21, 1779
Jeremiah Wilbur & Sabra Tracy,	Nov. 28, 1779
Dan'l Meech & Zerviah Witter,	April 13, 1780
Amos Hutchinson & Lucy Kinne,	May 18, 1780
John Starkweather & Hannah Leonard,	May 25, 1780
Ephraim Starkweather & Rachel Clark,	June 13, 1780
Ezekiel Rude & Phebe Rix,	Aug. 16, 1780
Nathan Johnson & Mary Maclain,	Sept. 24, 1780
Frederick Witter & Lydia Tyler,	Dec. 7, 1780
Robt. Crary, Jr., & Cynthia Lamb,	Dec. 7, 1780
Roswell Park & Eunice Starkweather,	March 8, 1781
David Palmer & Anna Ray (?),	May 10, 1781
	May 10, 1781

MARRIED BY REV. LEMUEL TYLER

Joseph Tracy & Elizabeth Brown of the West Society,
                                                    Sept. 20, 1789
Oliver Spicer of Groton & Eunice Tyler,   Dec. 31, 1789
Blanchard Darby of Norwich & Elizabeth Benjamin of
    West Society,   Jan. 27, 1790
Jesse Barns of Groton & Lucy Palmer of West So., Jan. 28, 1790

Benj. Fitch & Lucy Braman, of West So.,   Jan. 31, 1790
Ephraim Rix of the 2d & Martha Brown of 1st So., May 30, 1790
Elisha Tracy & Hannah Swaney, both of West So.,   May 7, 1790
Jason Stanton & Kezia Brumley of 1st So.,   July 15, 1790
Enos Clark of Middletown, Vt., & Clarissa Cook of 2d So.,
                                                Nov. 7, 1790
Amos Avery, Jr., & Susanna Starkweather,   Dec. 12, 1790
Zephaniah Rude of Granby & Betsey Meech,   Dec. 12, 1790
Levi Brumley & Penelope Hall of No. Preston,   Dec. 30, 1790
Shubael Morgan of Preston & Cynthia Bellows of Groton,
                                              March 10, 1791
Oliver Woodworth of Norwich & Eliphal Cook,   March 17, 1791
Denison Brown & Mary Robbins,   March 20, 1791
Elijah Clark & Eunice Morgan,   March 27, 1891
Soloman Jones of Lebanon & Phebe Quince (negroes),
                                                July 1, 1791
Joseph Osyer & Polly Saunders ,both of West So., Sept. 29, 1791
Aron Hendley from N. Y., & Silve Avery (negroes), Oct. 16, 1791
Wm. Witter, Jr., & Hannah D. Branch,   Nov. 24, 1791
Job Wickes of Providence & Polly Braman of West So.,
                                                Jan. 1, 1792
Walter Palmer & Patty Pendleton, both of W. So., March 25, 1792
Ames Bennet & Wealthy Safford, both of 1st So., April 29, 1792
John Sterry & Rebecca Brumley,   Oct. 4, 1792
Sanney Anderson, negro, & Tamar Smith,   Oct. 14, 1792
Abiel Rath of West So., & Mary Stanton of No. So., Oct. 18, 1792
Edward Leet of Saybrook & Amy Morgan,   Nov. 25, 1792
Cyrus Punderson of Groton & Deborah Smith,   Dec. 24, 1792
Jonathan Hinckley of Stonington & Sally Saunders, Jan. 6, 1793
John Searle of Royalton, Vt., & Nabby Safford,   Feb. 7, 1793
Eleazer Lewis & Sally Stanten Rude,   Feb. 10, 1793
John Saunders & Lucy Daniels, both of West So., June 16, 1793
Cordilla Fitch & Joanna Mix, both of West So., Sept. 8, 1793
Enos Tallmadge of Milton, N. Y., & Ruth Freeman,
                                               Sept. 22, 1793
Gillmore Robbins & Grace Brown,   Dec. 1, 1793
Beriah Green & Elizabeth Smith,   Dec. 31, 1793
Robert Sanders & Hannah Brown, both of West So.,March 9, 1794

Reuben Bristol of New Canaan, N. Y., & Elizabeth Stark-
weather,   March 11, 1794
Elisha Pitcher of Norwich & Jane Coombs,   March 16, 1794
Ezra Benjamin of 2d So., & Amy Stanton of Groton,
                                                   March 20, 1794
Gershom Mott of 2d So., & Zipporah Rockwell of West So.,
                                                   March 23, 1794
Israel Park of Stonington & Abigail Sterry,   April 1, 1794
Benj. Billings & Eunice Tracy,   April 27, 1794
Roger Sterry & Lavinia Yarrington,   Oct. 26, 1794
Reuel Cook & Amy Packer,   Nov. 2, 1794
Russel Rose & Polly Brown, both of No. So.,   Nov. 5, 1794
Nathan Seers & Mercy Rockwell,   Nov. 9, 1794
Benj. Baily & Lydia Gore,   Nov. 27, 1794
Jas. Bouse (?) & Thankful Brumley,   Nov. 27, 1794
James Wood of Chester, Mass., & Elizabeth Brewster of
Stonington,   Feb. 5, 1795
William Butler of Norwich & Barsheba Stoddard of West So.,
                                                   Feb. 22, 1795
Thos. Giles of Groton & Betsey Deming of W. So.,   May 7, 1795
Stephen Payne of Lebanon & Widow Prudence Thomas,
                                                   June 7, 1795
Stephen Congdon of No. Kingston, R. I., & Thankful Stuart,
                                                   June 24, 1795
Rev. Soloman Morgan of Canterbury & Mrs. Anna Haskel
                                                   Aug. 4, 1795
Wm. Stewart of New Lebanon, N. Y., & Rebecca Eells of
Stonington,   Oct. 18, 1795
John Chapman of Groton & Bethany Button,   Oct. 18, 1795
Joseph Adams & Mary Brown, both of No. So.,   Nov. 12, 1795
Gershom Dorrance & Sarah Rosseter of No. So.,   Dec. 3, 1795
Daniel Palmer Stanton of No. So., & —— Roath of
West So.,   Dec. 24, 1795
Jeremiah Vincent of Westerly, R. I., & Sally Kimball of
Stonington,   Dec. 31, 1795
Joel Canfield of Saybrook & Sally Peters,   Jan. 3, 1796
Sam'l Fagins & Nabby Sterry (people of colour),   Jan. 3, 1796
Dan'l Kinne & Betsey Maine,   Jan. 10, 1796

Joshua Meech & Polly Peters,   Jan. 10, 1796
Stephen Meech of P. & Lucy Billings of Stonington, March 20,1796
Isaac Avery of Groton & Clarissa Button,   Jan. 8, 1797
William Wells of Colchester & Eunice Clark,   Jan. 15, 1797
Philip Gray of Groton & Sabra Stanton of West So., Feb.   1797
Andrew Lamb & Charlotte George (free blacks), of Stoning-
    ton,   March 23, 1797
Christopher Benjamin of Burlington, N. Y., & Sally Fitch,
                                              April 9, 1797
Ephraim Fobes & Amy Fitch,   April —, 1797
John Stanton of No. So., & Lydia Olden of West So.,   1797
Elias Woodward of Plainfield & Zipporah Cook of West So., 1797
Seth Fitch & Cloe Haskel, both of West So.,
Benj. Fitch & Anna Braman of West So.
Richard Fanning & Elizabeth Park of West So.
Dan'l Lawrence of Voluntown & Cynthia Wilkinson, No. So., 1798
Geo. Leonard & Honor Andrus,   Feb. 18, 1798
Jno. Crary of Preston & Mary York of Stonington, March 7, 1798

WOODBRIDGE.

NEW HAVEN COUNTY.

(See Book I.)

The town of Woodbridge was incorporated Jan. 1784, and taken from New Haven
and Milford. The Congregational Church was organized Nov. 2, 1742, though formed
n 1737, and called the society in Amity (including Bethany till 1762). Rev. Benjamin Woodbridge was pastor from 1742 to 1783.

Caleb Wheeler of Ripton & Ellen Lines of Amity, Dec. 22, 1742
William Woodin & Catharine Carrington,   Jan. 12, 1743
Ebinezer Beecher & Lois Johnson,   May 26, 1743
Eliphlet Johnson & Mary Lines,   July 7, 1743
James Sherman & Hannah Hitchkiss,   Sept. 1, 1743
Israel Baldwin & Hannah Chatterton,   Oct. 17, 1743
Joel Perkins & Mabel Dorman,   Nov. 10, 1743
Thomas Vergenson & Abigail Allcock,   Nov. 30, 1743
Joseph Peck & Annie Perkins,   Jan. 12, 1744
John Beecher & Mary Willmott,   Feb. 1, 1744
David Johnson & Rachel Spery,   May 14, 1744

48 MARRIAGES

Timothy Brown & Hannah Alling, both of New Haven,
	May 21, 1744
James Warren & Abigail Thomas,	July 9, 1744
Tim Baldwin & Sarah Beecher,	Jan. 24, 1745
Tim Bradley & Mercy Baldwin,	Feb. 13, 1745
John Sherman & Dorcas Lines,	March 20, 1745
Moses Spery & Dorothy Hall,	April 10, 1745
Jeremiah Osborn & Elizabeth Spery,	April 18, 1745
Elisha Perkins & Dinah Sperry,	Sept. 9, 1745
Thomas Beecher & Elizabeth Terrel,	Dec. 25, 1745
Bevy Lines & Sarah Carrington,	March 3, 1746
Lawrence Clinton & Abigail Northrop,	May 20, 1746
Abraham Auger & Elizabeth Bradley,	May 21, 1746
Israel Thomas & Martha Hine,	June 24, 1746
Caleb Beecher & Abigail Wheeler,	Sept. 18, 1746
Jedediah Andrus & Elizabeth Baldwin,	Oct. 15, 1746
David Spery & Abigail Perkins,	Nov. 13, 1746
Samuel Brisco & Ruth Northrop,	Dec. —, 1746

Robert Talmadge & Phoebe Alling, both of New Haven,
	June 22, 1747
Joseph Collins & Lois Thomas,	Oct. 28, 1747
John Clark of Milford & Mabel Lines,	Oct. 31, 1747
Barnabas Baldwin & Mary Terril,	March 10, 1748
Titus Tyler & Mercy Bunnel,	March 16, 1748
Ebenezer Hitchcock & Rebecca Thomas,	March 24, 1748
Eden Sperry & Freelove Gillet of Derby,	July 6, 1748

Jonathan Osborn & Bulah Willmott, both of New Haven,
	July 28, 1748

James Sherman of Amity & Sarah Munn of Woodbury,
	Aug. 18, 1748
Moses Brooks & Martha Perkins,	Sept. 15, 1748
Thomas Johnson & Susanna Perkins,	Sept. 20, 1748
Alexander Booth & Sibil Baldwin,	Nov. 7, 1748
Andru Bradley & Dennis Willmott,	Nov. 24, 1748
Soloman Hotchkiss & Elenor Perkins,	Dec. 15, 1748
Caleb Sperry of New Haven & Mary Downs,	Dec. 22, 1748
Stephen Hine & Elizabeth Carrington,	Jan. 26, 1749
Seth Sperry & Lidia Thomas,	March —, 1749

Gideon Johnson of Derby & Lidia Beecher,   March 23, 1749
Gershom Thomas & Mabel Perkins,   April 26, 1749
Jonah Lounsbury, Jr., & Martha Hotchkiss,   Oct. 26, 1749
Joseph Stilson & Margaret Clenton,   Nov. 20, 1749
Ambros Hine & Sarah Terrel,   Dec. 13, 1749
Moses Sanford of Milford & Hannah Gunn,   Dec. 28, 1749
Jonathan Sperry & Mabel Collins,   Feb. 6, 1750
Jehial Osborn & Rebeca Spery of New Haven,   March —, 1750
Timothy Ball & Mary Hine,   July 4, 1750
Ebenezer Morris of New Haven & Mabel Carrington Nov. 28, 1750
Mathew Baldwin & Abigail Thomas,   Jan. 31, 1751
James Thompson of New Haven & Mehitabel Baldwin,
    March 6, 1751
John Lounsbury & Ruth Perkins,   April 4, 1751
Charles Hine & Lidia Sperry,   Sept. 4, 1751
Ariel Bradley & Annie Thompson, both of New Haven,
    Nov. 7, 1751
Nicholas Wood & Elizabeth Dawson,   Dec. 10, 1751
Seth Downes & Sarah Willmott,   Dec. 25, 1751
Dan Carrington of New Haven & Elenor Killum, Jan. 16, 1752
John Alling of New Haven & Elizabeth Beecher, Jan. 27, 1752
Daniel Beecher & Hester Baldwin,   Feb. 13, 1752
John Willmott & Rebecca Perkins,   March 15, 1752
Obid Johnson & Rebecca Clark of Milford,   April 16, 1752
Charles Bill of Wallingford & Lois Tolles,   May 11, 1752
— Woolcott & Eunice Thomas, both of New Haven, June —, 1752
Hezekiah Camp of Salsbury & Sarah Northrop, Nov. 21, 1752
Samuel Baldwin of Amity & Abigail Humpvile of West
    Haven,   Jan. 3, 1753
Nathan Platt & Marcy Stilson   Jan. 4, 1754
John Osborn & Elizabeth Russel,   Feb. 14, 1754
James Pierpont & Anna Sherman, both of New Haven,
    March 28, 1754
Nicholas Russel & Amy Perkins,   June —, 1754
Elnathan Chatfield of Derby & Hannah Northrop, Sept. 12, 1754
Samuel Bladwin & Temperance Baldwin,   Nov. 13, 1754
Elijah Grant of Litchfield & Mary Andrus,   March 11, 1755
Samuel Lines & Mercy Carrington,   June 13, 1755

Eliphlet Beecher & Anne Morris,	Sept. —, 1755
Richard Sperry & Abigail Northrop,	Dec. 9, 1755
Joseph Downes & Phebe Sperry,	Jan. 4, 1756
Dan. Hine & Ruth Alling,	Feb. 13, 1756
Silas Alling & Dorcas Baldwin,	March 23, 1756
Samuel Thomas & Rebecca Willmott,	Aug. 3, 1756
Nathan Ford & Sarah Hine,	Oct. 18, 1756
Ephraim Terril & Hannah Beecher,	Oct. 27, 1756
Daniel Tucker & Abigail Bristol,	Nov. 11, 1756
Abraham Carrington & Rebecca Johnson,	Nov. 15, 1756
John Wooding & Desire Sperry,	Nov. 16, 1756
David Beers & Martha Downs,	Dec. 20, 1756
Ezra Sperry & Ruth Sperry,	Dec. 20, 1756
Benajah Peck & Sarah Mansfield,	Jan. 25, 1757
Samuel Terril & Rachel Hine,	Feb. —, 1757
David Hine ———— & Amie Willmott,	March 10, 1757
Lawrence Clinton & Sarah Tryal of Gastenbury,	April 20, 1758
Jonathan Andrews of Milford & Eunice Baldwin,	April 20, 1758
Peter Milford & Bette (negroes),	Dec. 21, 1758
Jesse Thomas & Ruth Johnson,	Dec. 28, 1758
Isaac Spery & Mary Russel,	Jan. 11, 1759
Ashbel Loveland & Martha Willmott,	Feb. 1, 1759
Daniel Tuttle of New Haven & Elizabeth Smith,	April 25, 1759
Nehemiah Tolles & Ruth Lounsbury,	Sept. 20, 1760
Timothy Pain & Deborah Oatman,	Jan. 31, 1760
Reuben Sperry & Eunice Beecher,	Feb. 6, 1760
John Martin & Mary Sanford,	March 6, 1760
Amos Sperry & Elizabeth Sperry,	July 2, 1760
Isaac Nettleton of Milford & Sarah Smith,	July 2, 1760
David Beers & Hannah Perkins,	March 5, 1761
Asa Sperry & Sarah Johnson,	April 2, 1761
Benjamin Peck & Thankfull Russel,	July 23, 1761
Enoch Newton & Experience Beecher,	Sept. 7, 1761
Daniel Thompson & Mary Carrington,	Sept. 17, 1761
Stephen Lounsbury & Hannah Sperry,	Oct. 26, 1761
Enoch Terril & Experience Willmot,	Nov. 9, 1761
Samuel Carrington & Mary Johnson	April 8, 1762
Charles Sabins & Susanna Basset, both of New Haven,	May 13, 1762

Abraham Pain & Lidia Johnson, both of New Haven, May 27, 1762
Joseph Hotchkiss & Hannah Thomas, June 10, 1762
Caleb Tuttle & Surviah Sperry, June —, 1762
John Turner & Elizabeth Johnson, Aug. 12, 1762
David Clark & Hannah Johnson, Oct. 14, 1762
David Duning of Newbury & Mehitabel Sperry, Oct. 14, 1762
Moses Potter & Rebecca *Yale*, both of New Haven, Nov. 24, 1762
John Horton (orNorton) & Mary Beecher, Dec. 1, 1762
Samuel Hotchkiss & Lidia Peck, both of Bethany, Dec. 23, 1762
Jacob Hotchkiss & Mary Perkins, Jan, 25. 1763
Anor Ives & Rachel Willmot ,both of Bethany, June 15, 1763
Levy Baldwin & Sarah Willmot, Aug. 2, 1763
Theophilus Baldwin & Hepsiba Sherman, Aug. 24, 1763
Amos Sperry & Susanna Lines, Oct. 5, 1763
Samuel Lounsbury & *Ruth Tibbals*, —, 1763
Joel Atwater of New Haven & Abiah Baldwin, Dec. 28, 1763
Stephen Peck & Eunice Bradley, Dec. 29, 1763
Ebenezer Peck, Jr., & Dorcas Potter, March 5, 1764
William Hine of Derby & Hannah Sherman, May 29, 1764
William Adams of Milford & Rebecca Thomas, Sept. 11, 1764
Obed Johnson & Mary Lines, Nov. 8, 1764
David Barns of Cheshire & Abigail Verguson, Dec. 5, 1764
Richard Sperry & Rebecca Baidwin, Dec. 6, 1764
Nathan Fairchild of Oxford & Lois Beecher, April 24, 1765
James Powers & Lois Clinton, both of New Haven, July 30, 1765
Jesse Ford & Eunice Peck, Dec. 2, 1765
David Ford & Anna Johnson, Jan. 22, 1766
Jarid Smith & Dorcas Beecher, Jan. 29, 1766
Joseph Beecher & Martha Auger of New Haven, Feb. 5, 1766
Timothy Brown of New Haven & Anna Russel, April 22, 1766
Samuel Wooding of Bethany & Dorcas Peas, Aug. 21, 1766
Reuben Bradley & Eunice Beecher, Sept. 3, 1766
Ebenezer Morris & Rebecca Thomas, Sept. 11, 1766
David Peron & Lois Thompson, both of Derby, Oct. 29, 1766
Peter Booth & Esther Carrington, Oct. 31, 1766
Jason Warren & Eunice Clark, Dec. 19, 1766
Isaac Baldwin & Philena Pardy, Dec. 24, 1766
Jeremiah Parmele of New Haven & Abigail Russel, Jan. 14, 1767

William Sperry of New Haven & Hannah Carrington,

March 16, 1767

Jonathan Booth & Rebecca Cooper, both of New Haven,

May 5, 1767

Abraham Persons of Derby &ᵗKerziah Lines, July 2, 1767

David Alcock of Waterbury & Abigail Johnson, July 2, 1767

Roger Alling & Lucy Smith July 30, 1767

Amos Thomas of Bethany & Elizabeth Northrop, Oct. 7, 1767

Timothy White & Mary Peck of Bethany, Dec. 22, 1767

Walliston Hawley of Ripton & Sarah Thomas, Feb. 11, 1768

John Culver of Farmington & Mary Tuttle of New Haven,

April 11, 1768

Samuel Frost of Amity & Sary Sanford of Milford, May 25, 1768

Stephen Sperry & Mary Johnson, Nov. 3, 1768

Hez (?) Smith & Hester Beecher, Nov. 9, 1768

Stephen Sperry & Mary Johnson, ———, 1768

Isaac Hine & Eunice Willmot, Dec. 6, 1768

Ebenezer Johnson & Hester Punderson, both of New Haven,

Jan. 11, 1769

Abraham Hotchkiss & Phebe Auger, both of Mt. Carmel,

Feb. 7, 1769

Lent Sperry of New Haven & Rachel Peck, May 18, 1769

Ebenezer Sperry & Bathsheba Sperry, Oct. 5, 1769

Phineas Peck & Elizabeth Hine, Nov. 16, 1769

Noah Terril & Mary Byington, both of Bethany, Dec. 4, 1769

Amos Thomas & Elizabeth Beecher, Feb. 1, 1770

Reuben Andrus & Sarah Alling, Feb. 5, 1777

Aaron Fenn of Northbury (Plymouth) & Mary Bradley,

March 15, 1770

Job Johnson & Susanna Sperry, April 5, 1770

Simeon Sperry & Patience Smith, July 11, 1770

Jonathan Griswould & Sarah Osborn Nov. 12, 1770

Ely Baldwin & Deborah Potter, Nov. 29, 1770

David Smith & Huldah Beecher, May 22, 1771

Ebenezer Hine of Milford & Esther Potter of New Haven,

June 12, 1771

Roger Alling & Lidia Perkins, July 31, 1771

David Beebe of N. Stratford & Mary Baldwin, Sept. 24, 1771

Lazarus Clark & Dennis Bradley, Oct. 24, 1771
Seth Peck & Hannah Alling, Dec. 4, 1771
Jonah Strong of Woodbury & Mary Baldwin, Dec. 4, 1771
James Lines & Susanna Alling, Jan. 1, 1772
Amos Perkins & Abiah Downs, June 10, 1772
Josse Johnson & Lucy Perkins, June 11, 1772
David Perkins & Anna Beecher, June 19, 1772
Primus & Cibil (negroes), June 28, 1772
Simeon Clinton of Bethlehem & Anna Johnson, July 8, 1772
Amos Stilson & Sarah Clinton, Aug. 12, 1772
Daniel Smith & Thankfull Smith, Jan. 20, 1773
Roger Peck of Bethany & Philina Hine, May 19, 1773
Stephen Hine & Susanna Smith of Bethany, May 19, 1773
Daniel Perkins & Elizabeth Beecher, June 8, 1773
Charles Bradley & Rachel Dickerman of New Haven, Aug. 5, 1773
Jacob Sperry of Waterbury & Sarah Perkins, Sept. 1, 1773
Peter Johnson of New Haven & Comfort Clark, Sept. 22, 1773
Alsop Bladwin of Westbury & Elizabeth Sherman, Oct. 13, 1773
Jonas Hungerford & Elizabeth Pardee, Oct. 27, 1773
Samuel Sperry & Hannah Lines, Nov. 11, 1773
Fisk Peck & Elizabeth Platt, Nov. 18, 1773
Francis Martin & Cleopatra Lines, Nov. 25, 1773
Timothy Tustin & Mary Gibson, Jan. 13, 1774
Samuel Alling of Amity & Deborah Camp of Milford, Feb. 24, 1774
Joseph Merwin & Eunice Norton, March 13, 1774
Nathan Platt & Deborah Peck, June 23, 1774
Samuel Carrington & Susanna Sperry, July 6, 1774
William Griswold & Lucy Clark, July 14, 1774
Ebenezer Andrus & Abigail Sperry, July 27, 1774
Elijah Perkins & Lidia Sperry, Aug. 9, 1774
John Willmott & Sarah Taylor, Sept. 8, 1774
Abraham Perkins & Patience Clark, Oct. 16, 1774
Hezekiah Beecher (son of Joseph and went to Cheshire,)
    of Amity & Lidia Hotchkiss of Cheshire, Oct. 7, 1774
Jacob Morgan & Cloe Johnson, Nov. 16, 1774
Samuel Clinton & Mercy Downs, Dec. 7, 1774
Samuel Sperry & Mercy Bradley, Jan. 12, 1775
Joseph Baldwin & Eunice Strong, both of Bethlehem, Mar. 14, 1775

Samuel Pardee of Amity & Lidia Smith of North Branford,
Aug. 21, 1775
Thomas Perkins & Eunice Wood, Sept. 4, 1775
Roswill Palmer of Farmington & Bathsheba Peck, Sept. 18, 1775
Richard Clark & Jemima Pease, Sept. 25, 1775
Willmott Bradley & Annie Peck, Dec. 24, 1775
Dan Peck & Eunice Russel, Feb. 1, 1776
Daniel Russel & Lucena Sperry, March 13, 1776
Samuel Johnson & Hannah Beecher, March 24, 1776
William Russel & Mary Dorman, March 28, 1776
Michael Clark, & Patience Herger of Derby, May 19, 1776
Capt. James Peck of New Haven & Abigail Hitchcock of
Bethany, July 16, 1776
Joel Hine & Mary Perkins, Jan. 1, 1777
Amos Hine & Arsenah Clark, Jan. 1, 1777
Benjamin Strong of Woodbury & Martha Beecher, Jan. 1, 1777
Joel Hotchkiss of Bethany & Abigail Sperry, Jan. 16, 1777
Daniel Johnson of Oxford & Elizabeth Hotchkiss, March 16, 1777
Samuel Candee & Mabel Bradley, March 20, 1777
David Hotchkiss & Lidia Beecher, May 15, 1777
Joseph Plumb of Middleton & Cloe Wood, Sept. 25, 1777
Asa Huntington & Lidia Hine, Dec. 18, 1777
John Hine of Derby & Comfort Baldwin, Feb. 12, 1778
John Verguson of Amity & Elizabeth Parker of Walling-
ford, Feb. 19, 1778
James Riggs of Derby & Sarah Clark, Feb. 25, 1778
John Whiting, Jr., of New Haven & Sarah Whiting, Mar. 31, 1778
Timothy Bradley & Esther Dickerman, Sept. 23, 1778
Martin Ford of New Haven & Dorcas Lines, Jan. 25, 1779
Cesar Bragdon (negro) & Abigal Backwill (Indian Woman),
Feb. 2, 1779
Zephaniah Downs of Bethany & Mehitabel Beebee of Salem,
March 31, 1779
Job Northrop & Cloe Baldwin, May 3, 1779
Levy Sperry & Mary Sperry, May 31, 1779
John Andrus & Anna Collins, Oct. 7, 1779
Simeon Andrus & Anna Northrop, April 12, 1780
Isaac Northrop & Susanna Persons, Derby, April 20, 1780

Charles Sanford & Annie Sperry,   May 18, 1780
Jonathan Sanford of Cheshire & Jerusha Sanford, June 12, 1780
Samuel Wood & Elizabeth Sperry,   Sept. 7, 1780
Joseph Downs & Rhoda Beecher,   Nov. 23, 1780
Matthew Beel of Milford & Lois Hine,   Dec. 7, 1780
Reuben Hickcox of Durham & Content Clark,   Dec. 11, 1780
Elard Ford & Esther Russel,   Jan. 17, 1781
Denman Coe of Derby & Mary Northrop,   Feb. 20, 1781
Wheeler Beecher & Polly Mansfield of New Haven, April 18, 1781
Enoch Thomas & Anna Tucker of Bethlehem,   June 7, 1781
Stephen Russell & Asena Peck,   Sept. 27, 1781
Jonathan Barns of Waterbury & Sibil Bartholomew, Nov. 22, 1781
David Downs of Amity & Mary Chatterton of New Haven,
                                                    Nov. 26, 1781
Thomas Darling & Mary Dibble,   Nov. 28, 1781
Midad Sperry & Elizabeth Hine of Cheshire,   Nov. 29, 1781
Alling Carrington & Huldah Perkins,   Dec. 24, 1781
Walter Booth & Mary Newton,   Dec. 30, 1781
Jesse Sherman & Anna Beecher,   Jan. 23, 1782
Elisha Osborn & Elizabeth Peck,   Feb. 20, 1782
Elija Osborn & Abiah Downs,   Feb. 20, 1782
Alling Bradley & Sarah Collins,   March 7, 1782
Francis More & Sally Hotchkiss,   April 3, 1782
Sampson of Waterbury & Catherine (negroes),   May 23, 1782
Stephen Hine of New Milford & Naomi Peck,   June 19, 1782
Hezikiah Baldwin & Elizabeth Hine,   June 19, 1782
Gideon Alling & Sarah Russel,   July 11, 1782
Joseph Smith of Bethany & Elizabeth Peck,   Sept. 9, 1782
Shubal Handry (?) of Woodbury & Mary Ashburn, Sept. 24, 1782
Nathaniel Sperry & Lidia Bradley,   Sept. 26, 1782
Dr. Jesse Camp & Sarah Bradley,   Jan. 23, 1783
John Heath of Salsbury & Amie Hine,   March 6, 1783
Elijah Clark & Anna Hine,   April 3, 1783
Fletcher Merwin & Mercy Osborn,   May 1, 1783
Walter Booth & Mary Newton,   ———, 1783
Bozabel (?) Peck & Martha Bradley,   May 15, 1783
Rev. Eliphlet Ball & Ruth Beecher,   July 17, 1783
Amos Sperry & Dorcas Peck,   Aug. 14, 1783

David Smith & Abigail Sperry,	Sept. 10, 1783
Abil Hitchcock & Mary Bartholomew,	Oct. 2, 1783
Joseph Hine of Derby & Sarah Baldwin,	Dec. 2, 1783
Ebenezer Beecher & Mary Baldwin,	Dec. 11, 1783
Job Sperry & Rebecca Russel,	Feb. 11, 1784
Jehiel Smith & Rachel Hine,	Sept. 2, 1784
Allen Sperry (son of Amos) & Abigail Clark,	Sept. 16, 1784
Abel Sanford (son of Isaac) & Deborah Sperry,	Oct. 14, 1784
Salmon Bradley of New Haven & Martha Sperry,	Nov. 3, 1784
Philo Dibble & Eunice Ford,	———, 1784
Elionai Clark & Polly Ford,	———, 1784
Persons Clark of New Haven & Anna Darling,	Dec. 2, 1784
Joel Northrop & Rhoda Hine,	Dec. 2, 1784
John Hotchkiss & Huldah Sperry,	May 2, 1785
Jesse Smith & Hannah Thomas,	May 5, 1785
John Dibble & Hannah Beecher,	May 9, 1785
Triverus Andrus & Rebecca Thompson,	Jan. 15, 1786
John Terrel & Polly Curtis,	Feb. 12, 1786
Eli Stilson of Bethlehem & Abigail Northrop,	Feb. 22, 1786
David Ford & Anna Clinton widow of Simeon,	Feb. 23, 1786
Isaac Hemingway & Eunice Beecher,	March 16, 1786

Ephraim Beecher (son of Thomas) & Sarah Beecher (daughter
  of Reuben,)   March 29, 1786
Samuel Osborn of Woodbridge & Lucy Persons of Derby,
                        April 20, 1786
Willin Stilson, North Haven, & Experience Booth, June 25, 1786
Linus Beecher & Eunice Baldwin,   Aug. 16, 1786
Christian Hanson of New Haven & Sarah Harris ,Sept. 7, 1786
Josiah Baldwin & Therasa Thomas,   Nov. 7, 1786
Henry Peck & Elizabeth Clark,   April 9, 1786
Joshua Austin, East Haven, & Abigail Northrop, July 25, 1787
Noadiah Carrington & Martha Sperry,   Dec. 13, 1787
Enoch Beecher & Abigail Thomas,   Aug. 10, 1788
Silas Willmott of Waterbury & Hannah Clinton, Sept. 11, 1788
Joab Way of New Haven & Elizabeth Sperry, Oct. 6, 1788
Roger Newton & Mary Peck,   Nov. 16, 1788
John Sperry of Woodbridge & Annie Dickerman of Hamden,
                        Nov. 24, 1788

Enoch Flyn & Mary Smith,	March 2, 1791
Elisha Wood & Fanny Write,	March 2, 1791
Enoch Newton & Anne Clinton,	May 22, 1791
William Curtiss of Stratford & Lucinda Alling,	July 27, 1791
Benjamin Bracket & Rebeccah Mathews,	Aug. 9, 1791
―――― Bradley & Amelia Sperry,	Oct. 13, 1791
Thomas Clinton & Anna Mass,	Feb. 16, 1792
Charles Baldwin & Susannah Hine,	March 19, 1792
John Porter & Betsey Bradley,	May 7, 1792
Daniel Sperry & Cloe Alling,	June 11, 1792

SAYBROOK—WESTBROOK.

MIDDLESEX COUNTY.

(See Books I, II.)

Saybrook was settled in 1635. The Congregational Church was formed in 1639. The second church was organized, June 29, 1726. It is now located in Westbrook, a town taken from Saybrook in 1840. The records of the third and fourth churches have already been published in this series.

MARRIAGES BY REV. STEPHEN HOLMES.

Lieut. John Clark & Mrs. Phoebe Nott,	June —, 1758
Stephen Clark & Wid. Abigail Nott,	June —, 1758
Elkanah Done & Hannah Farnum,	Jan. 3, 1759
John Spencer of Haddam & Alice Pratt,	Feb. 25, 1759
Epaphras Nott & Isabel Parker,	June 17, 1759
Elijah Scovell & Sarah Williams,	June 17, 1759
Jabez Denison, Jr., & Mary Wheeler,	June 21, 1759
Andrew Southward & Annie Buck,	Aug. 19, 1759
Asa Pratt & Abigail Denison,	Oct. 7, 1759
Richard Tooker & Sarah Buckingham,	Nov. 4, 1762
Timothy Starkee & Rachel Bushnell,	Feb. 26, 1763
Charles Smith of Haddam & Mary Williams,	March —, 1763
Caleb Pratt & Hannah Graham,	March 30, 1763
Israel Done & Pricilla Shipman,	April 3, 1763

BY REV. BENJ. DUNNING.

Comfort Pratt & Susannah Tiley,	June 4, 1775
Amaziah Bush & Joanna Tucker	June 8, 1775

Isaac Post & Sarah Platts,	April 25, 1776
Ephraim Snow & Cloe Williams,	Jan. 19, 1779
William Daniels & Hannah Chappel,	March 16, 1780
Selah Griswold & Mary Starkee,	April 29, 1780
James Tucker & Zerviah Pratt,	Jan. 25, 1782
Reuben Bull & Jane Joselyn,	April 11, 1782
Edward Bull & Rosanna Turner,	March 18, 1781
Jesse Pratt & Temperance Bull,	Feb. 1, 1781

BY REV. RICHARD ELY.

Jacob Turner & Phebe Spencer,	March 9, 1786
Simeon Pratt & Margaret Jones,	March 12, 1786
Alpheus Foster & Ruth Waterhouse,	March 16, 1786
George Clark & Ruth Done,	April 13, 1786
Abijah Pratt & Pricilla Shipman,	April 26, 1786
John Shipman & Patience Gladding,	June 4, 1786
Nathan Southward & Sibbel Pratt,	July 3, 1786
Joseph Bishop & Martha Pelton,	Sept. 28, 1786
Robert Denison & Jemima Buckingham,	Dec. 24, 1786
Ichabod Cone & Anna Holmes,	Jan. 16, 1787
William Parker & Rachel Starkey,	May 27, 1787
Ebenezer Williams & Deborah Done,	July 31, 1787
Rev. Ozias Eells & Phoebe Ely,	Sept. 19, 1787
Joseph Plumb & Lucinda Pratt,	Nov. 18, 1787
John Pratt & Hester Kirtland,	Feb. 14, 1788
David Tiler & Isabel Williams,	Feb. 24, 1788
George Havens & Vrenney Clark,	March 20, 1788
James Hill & Mary Darrow,	July 2, 1788
Jeremiah Glover & Betsey Darrow,	April 30, 1789
William Briggs & Martha Tucker,	Nov. 22, 1789
Nathaniel Jones Pratt & Tempe Pratt,	Dec. 10, 1789
William Starkey & Patience Shaw,	Dec. 10, 1789
Squire Nichols & Lydia Williams,	Dec. 13, 1789
Edward Havens & Mary Havens,	Jan. 14, 1790
Jeremiah Pratt & Jennet Pratt,	Feb. 16, 1790
Timothy Starkey & Cloe Snow,	Feb. 28, 1790
Rev. Frederick William Hotchkiss & Amelia Hart,	Aug. 29, 1790
Richard Tryon & Betsey Tripp,	Sept. 2, 1790

Hosmer Buckingham & Lilly Snow,	Sept. 14, 1790
Dr. Abel Catlin & Jerusha Ely,	Oct. 10, 1790
Zephaniah Pratt & Rachel Pratt,	Jan. 9, 1791
Joel Pratt & Sarah Marvin,	Jan. 9, 1791
David Clark & Elizabeth Worthington,	Jan. 30, 1791
Henry Harrison & Sarah Buckingham,	March 13, 1791
Ward Post & Sarah Buckingham (?), Probably an error,	
may have been Sarah Butler,	June 2, 1791
Nathaniel Allis & Abigail Bushnell,	June 6, 1791
Nathaniel Pratt & Polly Holmes,	Aug. 20, 1791
Elias Shipman & Azuba Kirtland,	Sept. 20, 1791
Gideon Pratt & Hannah Southworth,	Sept. 25, 1791
Stephen Catlin & Abigail Pratt,	Nov. 10, 1791
Tabor Tooker & Ruth Tripp,	Nov. 23, 1791
Thomas Starkey & Currence Starkey,	Nov. 30, 1791
Jedediah Lord & Rebeckah Williams,	Jan. 18, 1792
William Pratt & Elizabeth Buckingham,	Feb. 19, 1792
George Williams & Pricilla Done,	May 17, 1792
Josiah Pratt & Lucy Platts,	May 24, 1792
Amos Benton & Sarah Bushnell,	July 1, 1792
Daniel Nettleton & Agnis Pratt,	Oct. 18, 1792
Abner Williams & Anna Done,	Oct. 21, 1792
Uriah Hayden & Huldah Ely,	Nov. 4, 1792
John Darrow & Tabitha Pratt,	Nov. 4, 1792
Roswel Dewe & Jemima Lay,	Dec. 8, 1792
Hezekiah Pratt & Anna Kirtland,	Feb. 10, 1792
Ethan Bushnell & Zerviah Nott,	April 14, 1793
Benjamin Doty & Tempe Bushnell,	April 27, 1793
Abijah Bushnell & Hester Bushnell,	July 4, 1793
Gideon Pratt & Abigail Buckingham,	Sept. 18, 1793
Matthew Scovel & Sally Tiler,	Nov. 16, 1793
Joseph Chittenden & Densa Post,	Nov. 24, 1793
John Pelton & Prudence Pratt,	Jan. 13, 1794
John Ward & Ruth Done,	March 13, 1794
Samuel Lay & Debbe Post,	June 8, 1794
Jacob Hayden & Lydia Gladding,	July 12, 1794
William Starling & Jerusha Ely,	Sept. 11, 1794
Eli Denison & Molly Tripp,	Nov. 23, 1794

Asa Jones & Louisa Clark,	Feb. 5, 1795
Jabez Denison & Linda Baldwin,	Feb. 19, 1795
Richard Tooker & Jemima Tooker,	March 9, 1795
Wylks Pratt & Jane Williams,	Mar. 26, 1795
Samuel Denison & Anna Pratt,	April 23, 1795
Nathaniel Lyndes & Prudence Hayden,	April 27, 1795
Levi Post & Lucy Denison,	Nov. 28, 1795
Nathan Pratt & Elizabeth Spencer,	Jan. 13, 1796
Wolcot Pratt & Mary Lay,	Jan. 31, 1796
Nathan Buckingham & Rhoda Tooker,	Feb. 25, 1796
Ceaser & Beck Hill (Colored),	March 17, 1796
Clark Nott & Wealthy Pratt,	June 16, 1796
William Tripp & Sarah Tooker,	Sept. 15, 1796
Aaron Snow & Lucretia Pratt,	Sept. 22, 1796
John Griffing Hayden & Tempe Brockway,	Sept. 24, 1796
Gideon Pratt & Susanna Buckingham,	Dec. 24, 1796
William Clark & Lydia Clark,	Dec. 29, 1796
Ebenezer Buckley & Diana Williams,	Feb. 23, 1797
Jonathan Clark & Lydia Denison,	April 13, 1797
Asahel Pratt & Elizabeth Bull,	April 16, 1797
James Gladding & Margaret Tripp,	———, 1797
Daniel Mather & Asanath Pratt,	———, 1797
John Mitchel & Sarah Pratt,	Dec. 10, 1797
Reuben Post & Elizabeth Buckingham,	Dec. 31, 1797
Reuben Buckingham & Dolly Denison,	March 4, 1798
Joel Platts & Flora Bushnell,	Sept. 15, 1798
William Starkey & Susanna Pratt,	Oct. 14, 1798
Jeremiah Lord & Polly Hayden,	Oct. 21, 1798
Simeon Dee & Hannah Bushnell,	Oct. 24, 1798
Peleg Hill & Wid. Sarah Scovell,	Oct. 25, 1798
Renald Kirtland & Tirsa Pratt,	Oct. 29, 1798
Joseph Williams & Abigail Denison,	Jan. 9, 1799
David Williams & Annis Pratt,	Jan. 24, 1799
Ichabod Clark & Eunice Rutty,	Feb. 27, 1799
George Hetherington & Phoebe Lay,	April 18, 1799
Jesse Done & Damaris Pratt,	May 15, 1799
Freman Snow & Jane Read,	May 20, 1799
Henry Jones Dacost & Mary Corby,	May 28, 1799

Henry Braddock & Eunice Tooker,	July 28, 1799
Gideon Pratt & Widow —— Williams,	Aug. 25, 1799
Ebenezer Snow & Abigail Pratt,	Oct. 16, 1799
Ozias Pratt & Mary Ames,	Oct. 16, 1799
Stephen Pratt & Sally Brockway,	Oct. 23, 1799
Amasa Hayden & Tempe Williams,	Oct. 27, 1799
Simeon Post & Hester Tooker,	Dec. 21, 1799

COVENTRY.

TOLLAND COUNTY.

The town of Coventry was named Oct. 1711. The date of its organization is uncertain. The First Congregational Church in Coventry was organized in 1712. The early records are all gone.

Stephen Tuttle of Sunderland & Elizabeth Geer,	Nov. 14, 1763
Medad Root & Rhoda Curtiss,	Nov. 17, 1763
Dennis Maraugh & Mary Sprague,	Dec. 29, 1763
Daniel Lyman & Rachel Southworth,	Jan., 1764
John Robinson of Windham & Eunice Phelps,	Feb. 2, 1764
Joseph Larabee & Widow Bill,	March 23, 1764
Dan'l Cutler & Betty Fitch,	May 23, 1764
Sam'l Turner of Mansfield & Mehetable Wentworth,	
	July 11, 1764
Ephraim Colman & Zurviah Curtiss,	Oct. 25, 1764
Ephraim Cushman & Sarah Colman,	Dec. 2, 1764
Elijah Janes & Anne Hawkins,	Jan. 10, 1765
Habak'k Turner, Jr., & Lydia Rose,	Feb. —, 1765
Adonijah Edwards & Mary Searle,	Feb. 28, 1765
Sam'l Rose & Rebecca Palmer,	Sept. 7, 1765
Dr. Josiah Rose & Abigail Rose,	Oct. 3, 1765
John Meed & Elizabeth Manley,	Oct. 3, 1765
Simeon Edwards of Coventry & Elizabeth Kenne of	
Hartford,	Oct. 24, 1765
Eliph't Edwards & Anne Porter,	Dec. 20, 1765
Abner White & Jerusha Thompson,	Jan. 28, 1766
John Babcock & Eunice Janes,	Feb. 16, 1766
Humphrey Taylor & Violet Hawkins,	March 27, 1766

Sam'l French & Hannah White,	April	2, 1766
Sol'n Lord & Miriam Colman,	April	3, 1766
Jonathan Root & Azubah Brown,	May	—, 1766
Eben'r Kendrick & Anne Davenport,	Sept.	2, 1766
Abraham Thurell (?) of Newbury & Lydia Boynton,	Oct.	13, 1766
Elijah Lyman & Patty Chamberlain,	Nov.	20, 1766
Hudson Babcock & Mercy Preston,	———	, 1767
Eben'r Bacon Dudley & Phebe Parker,	———	, 1767
Abraham Collins & Sarah Harie,	July	2, 1767
Mat. Grover & Lydia Colman,	———	, 1767
Simon Antizzal & Martha Fuller,	Sept.	29, 1767
Humphrey Dow & Tabitha Parker,	Oct.	8, 1767
Elias Palmer & Elizabeth Stow,	Jan.	10, 1768
Hembry Grover & Abigail Symonds,	Jan.	18, 1768
——— Fenton of Willington & Anna Carpenter,	Feb.	24, 1768
John Arnold & Miriam Root,	April	28, 1768
Sylvanus Owen of Hebron & Eunice Roberts,	May	5, 1768
Elisha Searle & Azubah Gates,	July	12, 1768
Paul Brigham & Lydia Sawyer,	Oct.	6, 1768
Thomas Brigham & Susanna Eells,	Feb.	6, 1769
George Hawkins & Hannah Kingsley,	March	26, 1769
Joseph Rose & Desire Dimmick,	Aug.	9, 1769
——— Jones & ——— Lyman,	March	15, 1770
Levi Lyon of Woodstock & Ruth Field,	June	28, 1770
Wm. Robertson & Lucy Edwards,	Nov.	14, 1770
Maltiah Bingham of Windham & Mercy Wright,	Feb.	14, 1771
Benjamin Grover & Lois Curtiss,	April	3, 1771
Daniel Turner & Hannah Boynton,	April	3, 1771
Eph. Brown of Springfield & Apphia Boynton,	May	22, 1771
Jehiel Rose & Mary Ripley,	June	3, 1771
Timothy Rose & Ellzabeth Pomeroy,	Nov.	17, 1771
Mat Denty & Eunice Boynton,	Nov.	26, 1771
Israel Gurley of Mansfield & Eunice Dimmick,	Dec.	18, 1771
John Hale & Sarah Adams,	Dec.	19, 1771
Joseph Cook & Jerusha Turner,	March	19, 1772
Ezra Kingsley of Windham & Anna Kingsbury,	June	18, 1772
Caleb Stanley & Martha Robertson,	July	9, 1772
Caeser & Molly of Lebanon (negroes),	Oct.	26, 1772

William Roberts of Hartford & Abigail Stanley,   Oct. 28, 1772
Elisha Fitch & Ruhamah Allen, both of Lebanon,   Dec. 11, 1772
Elijah Ripley & Alice Adams,   Feb. 8, 1773
Dan'l Robertson & Tryphena Janes,   Feb. 18, 1773
—— Dewy of Springfield & Eliz. Turner,   June 16, 1773
Benj. Babcock & Julia Judd,   July 28, 1773
Dr. Sam'l Rose & Elis. Hale,   Dec. 30, 1773
Gershom Brigham & Anne Parker,   Jan. 13, 1774
Joel Hannum of N. Hampton, & Esther Colman,   Jan. 26, 1774
John Dagget, Jun., of Lebanon & Sarah Hawkins,
  April 25, 1774
John Arnold, Jun., & Hannah Loomis,   June 15, 1774
Calvin Manning & Lydia Robertson,   Sept. 22, 1774
Rev. Eben'r Gurley of Gilford, & Mrs. Desire Rose,   Dec. 6, 1774
—— Clap of Northampton & Mary Strong,   Dec. 20, 1774
—— Dimmick of Mansfield & Alice Ripley,   Jan. 12, 1775
Oliver Janes & Judith Rollo,   Feb. 28, 1775
Will'm Boynton, & —— Turner,   May 5, 1775
Moses Badger & Jerusha Janes,   June 6, 1775
Eph'r Dow & Mary Ladd,   Aug. 25, 1775
Isaac Robinson & Joanna Colman,   Oct. 26, 1775
Gershom Colman & Abigail Eells,   March 27, 1776
Elisha Tracy of Kent & Dinah Brigham,   April 9, 1776
John Eells & Lois Root,   June 4, 1776
Jabez Ripley & Mary Hawkins,   June 19, 1776
Jer. Fitch, Jr., & Sibil Dimmick,   Sept. 8, 1776
Frary Hale of Glastonbury & Eunice Atherton,   Oct. 31, 1776
Jeptha Fitch & Ursula Root,   Jan. 23, 1777
Abraham Merryfield & Bethea Johnson, both of Lebanon,
  May 29, 1777
Amos Babcock & Mary Williams,   Sept. 21, 1777
Asa Colman & Hannah Babcock,   Nov. 25, 1777
Nath'l Root & Eliz. Kingsbury,   Dec. 11, 1777
Jed'h Geer & Phebe Hawkins,   Dec. 31, 1777
Wm. Root & Rebecca Hawkins,   Jan. 8, 1778
Josiah Fuller & Triphene Colman,   April 29, 1778
Josiah Alcott of Hartford & Mary Babcock,   May 27, 1778
Nath'l Robinson of Windham & Phebe Colman,   Aug. 13, 1778

—— Woodworth of Lebanon & —— Fuller,

	Aug. 23, 1778
Adonijah Skinner of Hebron & Judith Janes,	Oct. 6, 1778
Sam'l Babcock & Hannah Dow,	Oct. 22, 1778
John Fitch & Anne Buell,	Feb. 6, 1779
Stephen Turner of Mansfield & Lois Dimmick,	Feb. 25, 1779
Asa Perkins of Lebanon & Olivet Manley,	Sept. 9, 1779

Azariah Skinner of Windsor & Deborah Cushman,

Sept. 15, 1779

Simon Loomis & Patty Buckingham, both of Lebanon,

Nov. 18, 1779

Sam'l Perkins of Lebanon & Mary Cook,	Dec. 30, 1779
Dr. Amos Carpenter of Tyringham & Hannah Hunt,	1780
Joseph Kingsbury & Lois Porter,	Feb. 26, 1780
Mr. Mahew of Goshen & Cynthia Reynolds,	Feb. 27, 1780
Asa Manley & Eunice Gurley,	March 16, 1780
Eben'r Leach Sweatland & Meribah Badcock,	April 13, 1780
Sam'l Robertson, Jun., & Mercy Porter,	June 29, 1780
Moses Hannum of Belchertown & Jerusha Parker,	Oct. 23, 1780

Lewis Tyrrel of Tolland & Susanna Symonds of Windham,

Nov. 2, 1780

William Johnson of Tolland & Mary Rust,	Dec. 20, 1780
Solomon King of Becket & Elis. Manley,	Jan. 23, 1781
Sam'l Allen of Lebanon & Hannah Fuller,	Feb. 15, 1781
Davis Williams & Lois Eells,	April 19, 1781
Lemuel White & Nancy Brigham,	May 17, 1781
Eben'r Crossman & Mehetable Dow,	July 15, 1781
Dan'l Murray of Granville & Elis. Rose,	Oct. 30, 1781
—— Downer of Sharon & Bethiah Brigham,	Jan. —, 1782
Elisha Sanford & Mary Dorman,	Feb. 16, 1782

Jonath'n Gennings of Windham & Mindwell Colman,

July 18, 1782

Eben'r Colman, Jun., & Phebe Carpenter,   Sept. 5, 1782

Son of Robert Badcock to a daughter of Elihu Babcock,

Nov. 14, 1782

William Lawrence, of Hartford & Alice Ripley,	Nov. 24, 1782
Robert Badcock, Jun., & Hannah Arnold,	Dec. 5, 1782
Elias Judd & Beulah Larabee,	Dec. 15, 1782

Perez Sprague & Azubah Carpenter,	Dec. 16, 1782
Sam'l Rudd of Norwich & Anne Brigham,	Feb. 19, 1783
Azahel House & Sarah Walbridge,	July 2, 1783
——— Johnson of Mansfield & Abial Hane,	Oct. 23, 1783
John Christia & Mabel Rose,	Nov. 18, 1783
Dr. Howard & Anne Hale,	Jan. 22, 1784
John Taylor & Elisabeth Rose,	March 24, 1784
William Trap & Susanna Robertson,	April 22, 1784
Diarche Curtiss & Hepsibah Fuller,	April 28, 1784
Deacon Strong & Sarah Colman,	April 29, 1784
Benj. Grover & Theodora House,	May 6, 1784
John Brown & Elis. Dorman,	Oct. 14, 1784
Rev. Moses C. Welch, & Chloe Evans, both of Mansfield,	
	Nov. 10, 1784
Solomon Robertson & Patty Hawkins,	Nov. 18, 1784
Talcott Camp & Anne Hale, both of Glastonbury,	
	March 12, 1785
Isaac Robertson & Polly Dow,	March 23, 1785
Ammi Doubleday of No. Lebanon & Lois Tilden,	April 3, 1785
John Carpenter & Abijah Pingree,	April 20 1785
Philip Turner of Mansfield & Sibil Geer,	May 10, 1785
Roger Fuller of Hebron & Violet Taylor,	Nov. 17, 1785
James Welles of Windsor & Molly Badcock,	Nov. 24, 1785
Joseph Cook & Mehetable Badcock,	Nov. 30, 1785
Nathan Colman & Deborah Turner,	Dec. 6, 1785
Eph'r Dow, Jun., & Alice Davenport,	———, 1785
Timothy Colman & Eunice Fuller,	Dec. 20, 1785
Tubal Case & Esther Parker,	Jan. 5, 1786
Richard Hale & Polly Wright,	March 16, 1786
Elijah Turner of Mansfield & Ruth Badcock,	April 25, 1786
Cephas Brigham & Amelia Robertson,	May 14, 1786
Joshua Barrows of Mansfield & Anna Turner,	Sept. 7, 1786
Bildad Curtiss & Hepzibah Dow,	Oct. 12, 1786
Joseph Manley & Deborah Green,	Nov. 2, 1786
Manson Dimmick & Anne Robertson,	Jan 18, 1787
Sam'l Turner & Abigail Rose,	Jan. 29, 1787
Abel Hinds, Esq., of No. Milford & Abigail Rose,	Feb. 4, 1787
Benj. Colman & Sally Dorman,	March 15, 1787

Medad Root & Anne Gurley,   1787
Thomas Abel of Franklin & Rebecca Hale,   May   3, 1787
Richard Davenport, Jun., & Catharine Fuller,   Aug. 20, 1787
Sam'l Huntington of Tolland & Sally Howard, Nov. —, 1787
Warham Edwards & Elis. Scripture,   Dec. 10, 1787
Josiah Caswell of Rutland & Christiana Hawkins, March 10, 1788
Ulysses Dow & Anne Tilden,   June 26, 1788
Warren Mack of Pittsfield & Polly Larabee,   Aug. 26, 1788
Amos Turner & Hannah Dorman,   March 23, 1789
Luther Woodworth of Lebanon & Harmony Badcock,
                                               April 23, 1789
Godfrey Malbone & Dorcas Edwards,   Oct. 15, 1789
John Anthony & Ruth Harris,   Nov. 8, 1789
Abijah Prince of Glastonbury & Anna Harris,   Nov. 12, 1789
Nathan Andras & Polly Ladd,   Dec. 2, 1789
Alpheus Chapman of Hartford & Jerusha Carpenter,
                                               Feb. 8, 1790
Charles Carpenter & Polly Chapel,   Oct. 11, 1790
Nathaniel Cushman of Stafford & Hannah Parker, Nov. 18, 1790
Jonathan Gurley of Mansfield & Abigail Rose,   Feb. 17, 1791
Sam'l Blackman of Pittsfield & Jerusha Badcock, March 7, 1791
Zephaniah English of Andover & Mary Badcock,   July 7, 1791
Sam'l Badcock & Susanna Badcock,   Aug. 3, 1791
Elisha Root & Patty Palmer,   Oct. 27, 1791
Medad Root, Jun., & Olive Hawkins,   Nov. 17, 1791
George Keeny of Ellington & Lydia Robertson,   Nov. 24, 1791
Job Sherman & Lucy Root,   Jan. 20, 1792
William Boynton & Ruth Perkins,   March 22, 1792
Benjamin Blackman & Pamela Murdock,   April 1, 1792
Eben'r Bacon of New Marlboro & Betsy Turner,   Aug. 12, 1792
David Hilliard of Ashford & Eunice Robinson,   Sept. 20, 1792
Joshua Edwards, Jun., of Ashford & Wait Russell of
    Springfield,   Dec. 12, 1792
Bemsley Edwards of Franconia & Sally Cushman,
                                               Jan. 24, 1793
———— Scovil of So. Skeensborough & Anne Kingsbury,
                                               Feb. 11, 1793
Shubael Whittemore & Eunice Turner,   Feb. 21, 1793

James Adams of Tinmouth & Mercy Turner,	April 2, 1793
Abijah T. Curtiss & Huldah Fuller,	Oct. 27, 1793
Eleazer Grant, Esq., of N. Lebanon & Esther Rose,	
	Nov. 4, 1793
Josiah Talcott of Williston & Abigail Gurley,	Nov. 24, 1793
Frederic Palmer & Abiel Turner,	Dec. 5, 1793
——— Hammond of Tolland & Polly Parker,	Dec. 11, 1793
Will'm Baxter & Elisabeth Badcock,	Dec. 19, 1793
Timothy Gurley & Mary Mead,	March 6, 1794
John Fuller of Stafford & Amelia Perkins,	May 8, 1794
Solomon Janes & Susanna Trapp,	July 26, 1794
Charles McLean of Hartford & Anne Babcock,	
	August 17, 1794
James Thrall of Bolton & Esther Robinson,	Oct. 2, 1794
Joseph Turner & Patty Robertson,	Nov. 27, 1794
Amasa Jones & Elisabeth Huntington,	Nov. 9, 1794
Timothy Gurley & Eunice Rose,	Feb. 4, 1796
Daniel Robertson, Jr., & Amelia Janes,	April 10, 1796
Jonathan Hutchinson of Hebron & Temperance Colman,	
	Jan. 26, 1797
Ebenezer Root Fitch & Sally Dow,	Jan. 26, 1797
Elijah Porter & Jedidah Turner,	Aug. 26, 1797
Ebenezer Colman, Jr., & Margaret Fuller,	Sept. 14, 1797
William Lyman & Susan Richardson,	Sept. 19, 1797
Phinehas Ladd & Anna Grover,	Dec. 7, 1797
Rev. Joseph Warren Crosman of Salisbury & Miss Lucy	
Strong,	Jan. 14, 1798
Wm. Shaw of Canterbury & Lydia Davidson of Mansfield,	
	March 5, 1798
Francis Norton of Hebron & Tabitha Dorman,	April 18, 1798
John Rose & Desire Gurley,	April 26, 1798
Frederick Phelps of Hebron & Mercy Robertson,	Nov. 26, 1798
Elijah Dewey & Anna Murdock, both of Windham,	Nov. 29, 1798
Dr. Sam'l White of Andover & Wealthy Pomroy of No.	
Society,	Jan. 1, 1799
Benjamin Lord of Rutland, Vt., & Fanny Buell of No.	
Society,	Jan. 28, 1799
Amasa Loomis & Pamele Loomis,	March 28, 1799

Libbeus Boynton & Betsy Robertson,   April 9, 1799
Lieut. Ezra Abbot of Wilton, N. H., & Rebecca Hale,
             Oct. 6, 1799
Thomas Turner & Jemima Woodworth, both of Lebanon,
             Oct. 19, 1799
Joseph Rose & Mille Sweatland, both of No. Society,
             Nov. 27, 1799
Sanford Hunt & Fanny Rose, both of No. Society, Dec. 26, 1799

TORRINGTON.

LITCHFIELD COUNTY.

The town of Torrington was laid out in 1737 and incorporated Oct. 1740. The Congregational Church was organized Oct. 21, 1741, with Rev. Nathaniel Roberts, pastor. The old records have been copied with great difficulty. In the History of Torrington by Orcutt, p. 279, is a copy with which the following does not altogether agree.

Nathaniel Roberts, pastor of the Church in Torrington
     was married Nov. 22 to Margaret (Marsh)   1743
Isaac Horsford of Litchfield & Mindwell Loomis, July 8, 1747
Joseph Lee of Goshen & Prudence Curtis ,   Jan. 8, 1749–50
Hezekiah Agard of Litchfield & Abigail Damon, Dec. 17, 1751
Amos Wilson & Zerviah Grant,   Oct. 16, 1752
James Frisbee of Litchfield & Mary Gillet,   May 1, 1754
Thomas Bailey of Goshen & Jerusha Loomis,   Oct. 24, 1754
Ambrose Marsh of Litchfield & Elisabeth Taylor, Oct. 30, 1755
Benjamin Phelps & Isable Loomis,   Oct. 16, 1755
Thomas Coe & Lois Cowl,   Oct. 23, 1755
Noah North & Jemima Loomis,   March 25, 1756
Sam'l Cowl & Syble North,   April 14, 1756
Asbel North & Ruth Lyman,   Jan. 26, 1757
Abner Loomis & Sarah Grant,   July 29, 1757
Joel Beach of Winchester & Widow Abiah Filley, Oct. 18. 1757
Joseph Thrall & Elisabeth Thrall,   April 23, 1758
Stephen Tuttle of Goshen & Lydia Lyman,   April 23, 1758
William Filley of Torrington & Dinah Preston of Winchester,
             June 13, 1759

Martin North & Abigail Eno (?),	April 2, 1760
Ebenezer Mos (?) & Elisabeth Kent,	June 10, 1760
Joseph Hopkins, Jr., & Eunis Coe,	Aug. 20, 1761
Daniel Webb & Widow Hannah Buck,	Nov. 9, 1761
Thomas Curtis & Martha Cowls,	Jan. 7, 1762
Joshua Parker (?) or Park— (?) of Barrington & Abigail Agard,	
	April 29, 1762
Asahel Willcoks & Mary Coe,	Sept. 13, 1762
Abner Coe & Mary Agard,	Oct. 7, 1762
Sam'l Evert & Mindwell Strong,	May 27, 1762
Eli Loomis & Dorothy Loomis,	Nov. 18, 1762
Benj. Beach & Abiah Loomis,	Aug. 31, 1763
Joel Wetmore & Sarah Lyman, the younger,	Nov. 23, 1763
Noah Wilson, Jr., & Aanah Young,	Nov. 24, 1763
David Soper & Rachel Cook,	Jan. 26, 1764
Thomas Marshall, Jr., & Desire Tuttle,	Jan. 3, 1764
Robert Coe & Cloe Thrall,	Dec. 26, 1764
John Lucas of Goshen & Jerusha Coe,	Dec. 5, 1765
Isaer Loomis & Mary Lester (?),	Dec. 10, 1765
John Horsford (?) of Litchfield & Naomy Loomis,	Dec. 10, 1765
Amasa Cowls & Lucy North,	Feb. 25, 1766
Roswell Coe & Esther Bancroft,	April 22, 1766
Timothy Soper & Deborah Stark,	June —, 1766
Elijah Barber & Mary Hills,	July 10, 1766
Timothy Judd Jr,. & Mindwell Cowls,	Jan. 15, 1767
Wait Beach of Goshen & Huldah Loomis,	July 9, 1767
Joseph Blake & Maranath (?) Grant,	Aug. 22, 1767
Abijah Wilson & Margret Beach,	Oct. 5, 1767
Joseph Frisbee & Sarah Celsey,	Oct. 8, 1767
Nehemiah Lewis of Goshen & Esther Lyman,	Dec. 30, 1767
Wm. Barber ,Jr., & Widow Brown,	June 16, 1768
Caleb Lyman & Hanah Loomis,	Sept. 28, 1768
Sam'l Hurlbut & Rebecah Beach,	Dec. 1, 1768
Job Curtiss & Eunis Cowles,	Jan. 31, 1769
Ebenezer North, Jr., & Jerusha Cowls,	Feb. 16, 1769
Zachariah Mather & Suse Gaylord,	April 20, 1769
John Curtis & Mary Filly,	June 5, 1769
Ezekial Leach & Sarah Bartholomew,	Sept. 14, 1769

Levi Thrall & Mary Whitin,	Nov. 15, 1770
Jesse Wilkinson & Eunice Roberts,	May 17, 1771
Asael Beach (?) & Deborah Loomis,	Oct. 15, 1772
Daniel Thrall & Mary Shefield,	March 11, 1773
Benony Hills & Elisabeth Agard,	Oct. 28, 1773
Elisha Smith & Lucy Loomis,	Nov. 25, 1773
Asahel Strong, Jr., & Mary Young,	Dec. 2, 1773
David Jewel & Martha Grant,	Dec. 6, 1773
Noah Fowler & Rhoda Tuttle,	Feb. 10, 1774
Abel Beach, Jr., & Esther Peck,	May 12, 1774
David Alvord & Elisabeth Wetmore,	Sept. 8, 1774
Ebenezer-Lyman & Ann Young,	Oct. 20, 1774
Friend Thrall & Sarah Agard,	Nov. 23, 1774
Geo. Miller & Rebeckah Hulburt of Wethersfield,	June 29, 1775
Josiah Whitin & Sarah Loomis,	Nov. 2, 1775
Ephraim Bancroft, Jr., & Jemima Loomis,	Nov. 2, 1775
Joseph Beach, Jr., & Edse (?) Cook,	Jan. 4, 1775
Joel Loomis & Prudence West,	May 23, 1792
Sam'l Baldwin of Goshen & Widow Mary Loomis,	June, 1792
Alexander Loomis & Submit Spencer,	June, 1792
Sam'l Thorp of Southington & Jane Loomis,	Oct. 4, 1772
Abijah Coe of Torrington & Sybil Baldwin of Goshen,	Oct. 18, 1792
Gladding Bumpus & Sarah Judd,	(Winter)
Capt. Amos Wilson & Widow Hannah Loomis,	March 20,——
Ira Loomis & Polly Thrall,	July 25, 17—
Josiah Strong & Patty Green of Sharon Mountain,	Sept. 29, 1793
Thaddeus Fay & Esther Lucas of Winchester,	Oct. 17, 1793
David Miller & Hannah ——,	Nov. 29, 1793
Augustus Thrall & Sylvia Taylor,	Feb. 19, 1794
Theodore Smith of Goshen & Rhoda Wilson,	March 18, 1794
Abijah Barber & Mary Loomis,	March 19, 1794
Levi Marshal & Polly Gridley,	April 19, 1794
—— Bates of Torrington & Polly Kimberly of Winchester,	May 31, 1794
Benj. Agard & Rhoda Loomis,	1796
Anson Stow of Goshen & Phebe Miller,	April 26, 1796
John Eason Drake & Prudence Minor,	Dec. 22, 1796
Wait Loomis & Sarah Stone,	Nov. —, 1796

—— Watson of New Hartford & Mele Wetmore, Jan. 1, 1797
Jerus Foot of Goshen & Anne Wilson, Jan. 19, 1797
Daniel Coe of Hudson & Mary Loomis, Feb. 16, 1797
Abel Beech & Rocksey Taylor, March 30, 1797
Ichabod Deming of Bristol & Rebeckah Loomis, April 4, 1797
Jacob Kimberly, Jr., of Goshen & Nancy Pond, June 11, 1797
Timothy Wright of New Hartford & Triphene Bancroft,
 May 31, 1798
Jesse Blake & Merilla Loomis, Nov. 29, 1798
Seth Hills & Amy Lucas, both of Winchester, Nov. 28, 1798
Caleb Johnson & Polly Beach, Dec. 20, 1798
Zacheus Phelp Gillet of Torrington & Clary Humphrey of
 Goshen, Dec. 27, 1798
Ara Loomis & Margaret Loomis, May 15, 1799
David M. Hall (?) of Wallingford & Mindwell Beach, Oct. 30, 1799
Levl Munsell & Rachel Marshall, Dec. 18, 1799
Moses Richards & Naomi Hurlburt, Jan. —, 1800
Salmon Brunson & Mercy Wheaton of Winchester, Oct. 3, 1800
Artemus Phillo (?) & Louisa Loomis, Dec. 11, 1800
—— Stone of Harwinton & Sarah Hurlburt, Dec. 30, 1800
Jesse Welton, Jr., of Goshen & Olive Wilson, Jan. 6, 1801
Job Coe & Lois Richards, Feb. 24, 1801
Joseph Allyn, Jr., & Sabra Loomis, March 18, 1801
Amos Wilson, Jr., of Torrington & Sabra Griswold of Win-
 chester, March 25, 1801
Oliver Allyn & Lucy Loomis, May 7, 1801
Edward Eggleston of Torrington & Widow Dinah Judd
 of Winchester,
Issachar Loomis & Hepbzibath Loomis, May 6, 1801

CANAAN.

LITCHFIELD COUNTY.

(See Book V.)

The town of Canaan was incorporated Oct. 1739. The Congregational Church was organized March, 1741, with Rev. Elisha Webster, pastor. See Book V, for North Canaan Church records.

Ichabod Brownal & —— Stanby,	Sept. —, 1773
Roswel Dean & Abigal Belden,	Oct. 21, 1773
Solomon Moss & Huldah Coleman,	Nov. 11, 1773
Samuel Holembuk & Supenra (?) Woodruff,	Nov. 29, 1773
James Wadsworth & Irene Palmer,	Feb. 20, 1774
John Wabison & Peggy Monson,	Feb. 26, 1774
Ebenezer Smith of Sheffield & Elizabeth Kellogg,	March 3, 1774
Isaac Beebe & Polly Belden,	March 3, 1774
Joel Chamberlin & Sarah Dean,	Nov. —, 1774
Aaron Miller & Cloe Hunt,	Nov. 18, 1777
Milo Most & Abiah Carter,	Dec. 11, 1777
John Whitney & Hannah Belden,	Feb. 17, 1777
Nathan Hale & Salome Robbins,	April 26, 1778
Job Barre & Esther Hosford,	May 7, 1778
Oliver Root & Anna Holcomb,	Oct. 1, 1778
Stephen Jacob & Parmale Farrand,	Nov. 3, 1779
Noah Smith & Cloe Burral,	Nov, 4, 1779
Asa Blin & Debe Andrus,	Dec. 7, 1779
Timothy Hosford & Mehitable Root,	Dec. —, 1779
Stephen Brown of Stockbridge & Abiah Lawrence,	Jan. 2, 1781
Wm. Trafford & Sarah Belden,	Aug. 15, 1782
Daniel Hubison & —— Babcock,	
Israel Smith & Abiah Douglass,	——, 1784
C. Belden & Lois Bosworth,	——, 1785
John Elmer & Elizabeth Belden,	Oct. 8, 1785
Josiah Brown & S. Harris,	——, 1785
Daniel Camp & Lucy Barre,	——, 1785
Daniel Clark & Anna Hogg (?),	——, 1786
Asa Smith & Elizabeth Whitney,	——, 1786
James Root & Sarah Lawrence,	March, 29 1786

S. Barre & Rachel Root,	——, 1786
Grove Pomeroy & Eunice Marsh,	——, 1786
Elnathan Kogs (?) of Hartford & Sally Sheldon of	
Salisbury,	——, 1787
Elisha Horton & Hannah Drake,	——, 1787
Reuben Austin & Triphena Hofman,	Feb. 10, 1790
Capt. Erson & Widow Goodwin,	Jan. 5, 1791
Ammi Robbins & Salome Robbins,	Jan. 17, 1791
Wm. Holabard & Dor. Bindisden,	Nov. 17, 1791
Job Belden & Martha Dean,	Feb. 24, 1791
Josiah Kingsbury & Elizabeth Hollenbok,	March 4, 1791
Benj. Hall & Dolly Bonnet (?),	April 21, 1791
Lot Norton & Polly Hi——,	May 28, 1791
Lemuel Demming & S. Harris,	Oct. 5, 1791
Amasa Holcomb & Abigal Hilton,	Oct. 5, 1791
Samuel Fellows & Ethiel Rockwell,	Oct. 25, 1791
Solomon Holcomb & Polly Bushnel (?),	Dec. 4, 1791
—— —— & Louisa Ransom,	——, 1791
Jeremiah Tooley & Hannah Austin,	Dec. 22, 1791
David Hunt & Hannah Johnson,	——, 1791
Daniel Deming & Lois Dean,	Jan. 2, 1792
John Pope of W—— & Esther Horton,	Jan. 2, 1792
Elisha Wells & Jolly Dabhern (?),	Oct. 21, 1792
Nehemiah Sexton & Elizabeth Holabard,	Jan. 17, 1793
Fred Hunt & —— Lowry,	Feb. 27, 1793
Rev. John Elliott & Sarah Norton of Salisbury,	Nov. 27, 1793
Timothy Rockwell & Polly Burrall,	——, 1793
Solomon Stone & —— Beebe,	
Amos Hunt & Polly Lorn (?),	
Samuel Bushnel & —— Beckly,	——, 1794
Jeremiah Beebe & Elizabeth Kellogg,	——, 1795
Wm. Morgan & Lois Hollabed,	Dec. —, 1795
Andrew Frank & Rachel Huntington,	March 23, 1796
Billy Beckly & Wealthy Hopson,	April 26, 1796
Ezra Morehouse & Philinda Barne,	March 27, 1796
David Beckly & Polly ——,	——, 1796
Abner Hodgkins & Abigal Barne,	——, 1797

LEBANON—COLUMBIA.

NEW LONDON AND TOLLAND COUNTIES.

(See Book II.)

The town of Columbia, Tolland Co., was incorporated May, 1804 and taken from Lebanon, New London Co. The Congregational Church in Columbia (formerly Lebanon Crank) was organized in 1720. But few marriages are on record here under the pastorate of Rev. Thomas Brockway.

Otis Little & Sarah ———,	Sept. 17, 1773
Samuel Brewster & Huldah Porter,	April 7, 1774
Prince Aspinwall & Lucy Woodworth,	Nov. 30, 1774
Hosea Lyman & Martha Brown,	Nov. 24, 1774
John Pember & Lucretia Bill,	Nov. 24, 1774
Bazaleel Fuller & Phebe Sprague,	Dec. 8, 1774
Elijah Hunt & Abigail Reynolds,	Nov. 18, 1773
Benjamin Gay & Rebecca Harris,	May 5, 1774
Ephraim Wright & Abigail Sprague,	Feb. 21, 1775
Nathan Hall & Martha Lyman,	Feb. 8, 1776
Nathaniel Fitch & Abigail Lyman,	April 4, 1776
Simon Loomis & Martha Buckingham,	Nov. —, 1779

NEW HAVEN—HAMDEN.

NEW HAVEN COUNTY.

(See Book I.)

The town of Hamden was incorporated in 1786 and taken from New Haven. The Congregational Church in Hamden at Mt. Carmel was organized Jan. 26, 1764. Marriages by Rev. Joshua Perry.

Noah Alling & Mabel Smith,	Oct. 14, 1783
Ashbel Beach & Anne Bellamy,	Nov. 13, 1783
Jesse Tuttle & Lucy Dickerman,	———, 1783
Caleb Atwater & Thankful Cotter,	Dec. 25, 1783
Timothy Leek & Elisabeth Alling,	Jan. 8, 1784
Isaac Chatterton & Mary Todd,	Jan. 8, 1784
Nathan Alling & Mary Beach,	Jan. —, 1784
Ezra Munson & Mabel Gilbert,	March —, 1784
Isaac Alling & Esther Alling,	April —, 1784

Joseph Peck & Olive Chatterton,	Oct. 2, 1784
John Atwater & ——— Goodyear,	Nov. —, 1784
Ebenezer Gills & ——— Goodyear,	Dec. 1, 1784
Hezekiah Bracket & Ruth Perkins,	Dec. 27, 1784
Amos Smith & Rachel Tuttle,	Dec. 27, 1784
Richard N. Atwater & Susannah Bradley,	Dec. 30, 1784
Ephraim Hull & Lida Alling,	Jan. 19, 1786
Ichabod Atwater & Ama Alling,	Feb. 2, 1786
Jabez Bradley & Esther Bradley,	———, 1785
David Patterson & Amelia ——— of New Haven,	Nov. 10, 1785
Amasa & Martha Bradley,	Jan. 19, 1786
Amos Frost & Esther Doolittle,	April 9, 1786
Eliada Hitchcock & Esther ———,	April 11, 1786
Ebenezer Hough & Lois Dickerman,	Nov. 13, 1786
Amos Dickerman & Chloe Bradley,	———, 1786
Chauncy Alling & Mabel Bradley,	Aug. 9, 1787
Amos Rice & Damaris Bradley,	Sept. 13, 1787
Joseph Heaton & Mary Warner,	Sept. 25, 1788
Samuel Warner & Lydia Hitchcock,	Sept. 25, 1788
Davenport Williams & Mary Atwater,	Feb. 5, 1789
Jonathan Dayton & Sabria Brooks,	Nov. 18, 1789
Joseph Johnson & Sarah Doolittle,	Dec. 3, 1789
Simeon Dickerman & Meriam Dickerman,	Jan. 11, 1790

WINDHAM.

WINDHAM COUNTY.
(See Book IV)

The town of Windham was incorporated in May, 1692, and the Congregational Church was organized Dec. 10, 1700. The only record of marriages found is that of Rev. Elijah Waterman, as follows:

Robert Willoughby & Eunice Clift,	Nov. 7, 1794
Ozias Waldo & Nancy Ripley,	Jan. 1, 1795
Henry Clark & Mary Ann Elderkin,	Feb. 1, 1795
Elias Parmelee & Fanny Fitch,	Feb. 2, 1795
Dan Sawyer & Charlotte Denison,	Feb. 5, 1795
Zephaniah Swift & Lucretia Webb,	March 14, 1795
Joseph Kirkland & Sally Backus,	April 15, 1795

Thomas Bingham & Charlotte Flint,	May 17, 1795
Luther Backus & Zerviah Clark,	June 21, 1795
Ashbel Welch & Peggy Dorrance,	Oct. 15, 1795
Joseph Meacham & Betsy Snow,	Nov. 19, 1795
John Clark, Jr., & Polly Clift,	Feb. —, 1796
Augustus Hebard & Bethsheba Learned,	March 19, 1796
Freeman Dewey & Polly Hebard,	March 31, 1796
James Gilbert & Lucy Hensley,	April 7, 1796
David Lincoln & Clarissa Lincoln,	Sept. 1, 1796
Daniel Parrott & Lucinda Southworth,	Oct. 19, 1796
Francis Snow & Polly Gilbert,	Oct. 23, 1796
Uriah Willcox & Sally Spafford,	Oct. 23, 1796
Sanford Bebens & Fanny Welch,	Oct. 27, 1796
Elisha Morgan & Anna Parish,	Nov. 24, 1796
Benjamin James & Zerviah Huntington,	March 2, 1797
Samuel Lee, Jr., & Lucy Gray,	March 25, 1797
James Cogswell, D. D., & Mrs. Irena Hebard,	May 5, 1797
Joseph Hunt & Sally Francis,	Sept. 28, 1797
Samuel Merriman & Nancy Badger,	July —, 1797
Phineas Reed & Selina Tiffany,	Dec. 31, 1797
Peter Chandler & Wd. Abigail Gray,	March 15, 1798
Alfred Young & Clarrissa Murdock,	July 28, 1798
Edmund Badger & Amelia Dyer,	Aug. 19, 1798
Godfrey Grosvenor & Polly Taintor,	Aug. 25, 1798
Shubael Hebard & Lucy Hovey,	Sept. 23, 1798
Roger Huntington & Wealthy Ann Huntington,	Nov. 29, 1798
Erastus Bebens & Phila Kingsbury,	Jan. 2, 1799
William Storey & Sally Sparhawk,	Feb. 21, 1799
John Trescot & Wd. Lucretia Wattles,	March 30, 1799
William Sabin & Irena Welch,	March 31, 1799
William Pierce & Abigail Brewster,	July 25, 1799
Thomas Whitney & Fanny Jennings,	Sept. 19, 1799
Benjamin Dow & Miriam Deans,	Oct. 31, 1799

BARKHAMSTED.

LITCHFIELD COUNTY.

The town of Barkhamsted was incorporated Oct. 1779. The Congregational Church was organized April 20, 1781. Rev. Ozias Eells was pastor from 1787 to 1810.

Mr. — Marsh of Harwinton & Delight Wilson daughter of John Wilson & wife,	March 19, 1787
John Humphry & Widow Mary Olmstead,	Aug. 28, 1787
John Hopkins, Jr., & Phebe Harrinton,	Nov. 15, 1787
Levi Tiffany of Hartland & Unice Wetmore,	Dec. 25, 1787
John Wetmore & Cinthia King,	July 13, 1787
Jeremiah Crane & Elisabeth Johnson,	———, 1787
Abijah Hall & Anna Hutson of Cheshire,	July 13, 1788
Allyn Risley(?) of New Hartford & Lucy Spencer of Hartland,	Feb. 21, 1789
Stephen Parker & Unice Parker,	March 11, 1789
Seelye Crofut of Danbury & Hannah C. Holcomb,	April 12, 1790
William Lloyd & Jane Harvey of Granville,	June 24, 1790
Jesse Gates of Hartland & Rhoda Reed,	Feb. 22, 1791
Clement B. Willy of Barkhamsted & Sarah Hart of Farmington,	March 29, 1791
Consider Tiffany of Hartland & Amelia Rexford(?),	Oct. 13, 1791
Ferdinand Smith & Unice King,	March 15, 1792
Moses Gaines, Jr., of New Hartford & Hannah Miller,	Oct. 21, 1792
Lovel Parker & Hannah Hart,	April —, 1792
Richard Adams, Jr., of Barkhamsted & Miriam Case of Granby,	Feb. 27, 1793
Jared Rexford & Rachel Lewis,	Aug. 17, 1794
John Rockwell, Jr., & Jemima Hatch,	Sept. 25, 1794
Seth Smith of Barkhamsted & Ester Tyler of New Hartford,	Jan. 1, 1795
Mart. Curtiss & Rhoda Culver,	———, 1795
Mr. ——— Forster of Hartland & Cate Barker (or Parker),	Dec. —, 1793
Daniel Frazer of Hartland & Clarissa Newel,	Jan. —, 1794

Ebenezer Pike of New Hartford & Rhode Case, June —, 1794
Mr. ——— Bacon & Sally Hutson, May —, 1793
John Pike & Sarah Hungerford, April 25, 1795
Clemont B. Willy of Barkhamsted & Cande Merril of New
  Hartford, July 8, 1795
Alexander McNall & Cloe Adams, Sept. 17, 1795
Levi Hart of Barkhamsted & Elisabeth Ganes (?) of New
  Hartford, Oct. 22, 1795
Jehiel Case & Huldah King, Oct. 28, 1795
Aaron Hart & Annie Austin, Dec. 3, 1795
Joel Parker & Abigail Hart, Dec. 17, 1795
Luther McNall & Rebecca Humphries, May —; 1795
Aseph Case of German Flatts & Rhoda Hungerford, Feb. 7, 1796
Cephas Ford & Elisabeth Case, June 16, 1796
Alpheus Gains of New Hartford & Susanna Miller of Farm-
  ington, June 30, 1796
Hezekiah Simons & Elisabeth W——d, Aug. 11, 1796
Anthony Peet from New Haven & Lilly Briscoe, Aug. 25, 1796
Sam'l Richardson & Sally Miller, Oct. 27, 1796
Sam'l Sikes of London & Lucy Leonard, Nov 7, 1796
Norman Wilcox & Rebecca Case, March 16, 1797
Jonathan Cook & Elisabeth Phelps, Aug. 14, 1797
Hiel Hart & Chestina Parker, Jan. 1, 1798
William Rathburn of Granby & Dorotha Rockwell, June 14,1798
Hawley Oakley (?) & Lidia Hart, Jan. 27, 1799
Morgan (?) Jones & Betty Merrels, Nov. 14, 1799
James Hungerford & Ruth Rockwell, Nov. 14, 1799
Judah Gridley & Sally Beach, July 24, 1800
Theodore Newel & Phebe Monson, Nov. 6, 1800
Jehiel Wilcox, Jr., of Barkhamsted & Ruth G—— of
  New Hartford, Nov. 9, 1800
Sam'l Munson & Polly Howd, Nov. 13, 1800
Joseph Burbanks of Chester in New Hampshire, & Unice
  McNall, Nov. 26, 1800
Ashael Hart & Elisabeth Goodhue, Jan. 1, 1801
Orange Case of Simsbury & Sarah Jones, Jan. 8, 1801
Edward Fitzgeralds of Simsbury & Mindwell Humphreys,
  Jan. 9, 1801

Obed Blakesley & Adah Hart,	March 4, 1801
Ashbel Case of Granby & Polly Frazer,	July 19, 1801
Henry Wilder & Densy (?) Jones (?),	Dec. 24, 1801
Leverus Munson of Barkhamsted & Frances Hubbel of Newtown,	March 6, 1802
John Fox & Margaret Clark,	Sept. —, 1802
Sam'l Tuttle & Else Jones,	Jan. 5, 1803
Reuben Munson & Anna Miller,	Feb. 28, 1803
James Miller & Sally Messenger,	April 29, 1803
Simeon Case of Granby & Widow Thankful Allyn,	June 3, 1803
William Ranson of Barkhamsted & Lucy Philar (?) of Hartland,	Oct. —, 1803
John Mack & Rachel Munson,	Jan. —, 1704
Thos. Barber & Silsa Case,	July 8, 1804

ENFIELD.

HARTFORD COUNTY.

The town of Enfield was named and granted by Massachusetts, May, 1683. Annexed to Connecticut May, 1749. The First Congregational Church was organized in 1683. The marriages recorded begin with the pastorate of Rev. Nehemia Prudden, 1782–1815.

Thomas Norton & Azuba Root of Springfield at my house,	Dec. 10, 1784
Moses Barber & Patty Terry,	Dec. 15, 1784
Daniel Neff of Windham & Silence Bradley,	Jan. 13, 1785
Benjamin Terry & Eunice Parsons,	Jan. 18, 1785
Isaac Kibbe & Abigail Lockwood,	Jan. 30, 1785
Daniel Dana & Dorothy Kibbe,	Feb. 9, 1785
David Baxter & Love Hills,	Feb. 24, 1785
Nathaniel Billings & Sibyl Terry,	March 23, 1785
———— ———— & Esther Colton,	Aug. 22, 1785
Ashbel Anderson & Lucina Bush,	June 26, 1785
John Prier & Mercy Ames,	Aug. 8, 1785
William Hale & Lucinda Hancock,	Aug. 14, 1785
Gaius Kibbe & Pol'y Pease,	Aug. 18, 1785
Samuel Bailey & Mary Terry,	Oct. 6, 1785

Jabez Chapin & Lucy Dwight,	Oct. 16, 1785
Capt. Hezekiah Parsons & Dorcas Parsons,	Nov. 23, 1785
Asa Olmstead & Charlotte Dwight,	Nov. 24, 1785
Ephraim Pease 2d & Jemima Phelps,	Nov. 24, 1785

Jabez Chapman & Damaras Holton, both of Windsor Goshen
(now Ellington),   Dec. 15, 1785

Lemuel Parsons & Abigail Warner,	Jan. 19, 1786
Solomon Douglass of New London & Servier Hale,	April 5, 1786
Ebenezer Terry 3d. & Susannah Prier,	June 29, 1786
Moses Pease 2d. & Lovicy Markham,	Nov. 16, 1786
Ebenezer Bignal of Ashford & Eleanor Pearsons,	Nov. 23, 1786
George Pease & Esther Sexton,	Jan. 4, 1787
Thomas Abbe & Ruth Bush,	Jan. 9, 1787
Ezra Jones & Polly Booth,	Jan. 18, 1787
Eldad Phelps 2d. & Abigail Simons of East Windsor,	Jan. 18, 1787
Samuel Stocking of Ashfield & Eunice Sherwin,	Feb. 1, 1787

Joshua Giddings of Hartland & Mrs. Elizabeth Halladay,
March 22, 1787

Abner Perce & Abigail Moncil, both of East Windsor,
Aug. 9, 1787

John McKnight & Charity Abbe,	Sept. 6, 1787
Abiel Pease & Rachael Hale,	Nov. 6, 1787
Simeon Meacham & Anna Prier,	Dec. 6, 1787
Simeon Pease & Susannah McGregory,	Jan. 3, 1788
Robert Gowdy & Content McGregory (a triplet),	Jan. 24, 1788
John Gold & Elizabeth King,	Feb. 7, 1788
David Parsons, Jr., & Love Baxter,	Feb. 27, 1788
John Morrison & Anna Terry,	March 9, 1788
Daniel Baker & Jerusha Parsons,	April 2, 1788
Caleb Wright & Desire Kingsbury,	June 7, 1788
Ebenezer Collins & Azubah Chapin,	May 22, 1788
Rev. John Taylor of Deerfield & Elizabeth Terry,	June 24, 1788
Samuel Raynolds & Mabel Olmstead,	June 29, 1788
Joel Halkins & Huldah Allen of East Windsor,	July 20, 1788
Elijah Allen & Jemima Pease,	July 22, 1788
Daniel Webster of Stafford & Mehitable Simons,	July 27, 1788
Allen Benjamin & Beulah Osborne,	Aug. 28, 1788
Solomon Terry & Hannah Pease,	Aug. 31, 1788

Simeon Chapin & Beulah Prier,   Nov. 13, 1788
Nathan Terry & Mary Parsons,   Nov. 18, 1788
Isaac Markham & Cynthia Terry,   Nov. 23, 1788
Thomas Metcalf & Sibyl Chapin,   Nov. 26, 1788
Benjamin Parsons, Jr., & Lydia Bement,   Nov. 27, 1788
Julius Terry & Sarah King,   Dec. 4, 1788
John Pease of Suffield & Priscilla Hale,   Jan. 1, 1789
Israel Pease, Jr., & Mary Pease,   Jan, 14, 1789
Thomas Pratt & Lydia ———,   Feb. 5, 1789
Stone Pease & Mary Parsons,   March 18, 1789
Hiram Terry & Elizabeth Gibbs,   April 9, 1789
Peter Abbe & Hannah Alden,   June 23, 1789
Joseph Chandler, Jr., & Lydia Holkins,   June 25, 1789
Capt. Jabez Parsons & Martha Terry,   Nov. 4, 1789
Jacob Terry & Sarah Terry,   Nov. 4, 1789
Moses Alden & Esther Chapin,   Nov. 12, 1789
Zachariah Alden, Jr., & Miriam Booth, both of East
       Windsor,   Nov. 18, 1789
Rev. Noah Atwater of Westfield & Anna Lockwood, Dec. 1,1879
Amos Jones & Elizabeth Avery, both of Coventry, Dec. 10, 1789
Rev. Nathan Fisk of Brookfield & Mrs. Hannah Raynolds,
                                                 Jan. 19, 1790
John Booth, Jr., & Submit McGregory (a triplet), Jan. 28, 1790
Joshua Wilson & Desire Parsons,   Feb. 15, 1790
Tristram Fenton & Sarah Allen,   Feb. 17, 1790
Jesse Todd of West Springfield & Susannah Chandler, Feb. 24, 1790
Gayer Henry & Anna Parsons,   April 6, 1790
Noah Elmer & Jane Hulbert(?),   April 29, 1790
Joseph Halkins & Mehitable Terry,   Nov. 3, 1790
Levi Gowdy & Ruth Belknap, of East Windsor at my house,
                                                 Dec. 2, 1790
Hill Gowdy & Roxa McGregory,   Dec. 2, 1790
Christopher Parsons & Aurelia Sexton,   Dec. 9, 1790
David Belknap of Ellington & Jane Ayers,   Dec. 23, 1790
Elijah Hawkins, Jr., & Mary Henry,   Dec. 28, 1790
Hezekiah Rice of Claremont, N.H.& Tabitha Chapin, Dec. 30, 1790
Thomas Chapin & Anna Pease,   Jan. 6, 1791
Obediah Chapin & Philena Pease,   Jan. 6, 1791

Elizur Talcut, Jr., & Sarah Baxter,   Jan. 13, 1791
William Hall of Pownal, Vt., & Roxa Tiffany,   Jan. 20, 1791
Levi Collins & Hannah Pease,   Feb. 1, 1791
Nathaniel Parsons & Phebe Butler,   April 13, 1791
John Warner & Mary Smith,   May 22, 1791
Abel McGregory & Dorcas Griswold,   June 21, 1791
Meshek Ramsdale & Tryphena Simons,   July 7, 1791
John Newell of Springfield & Mrs. Lucy Burt,   July 22, 1791
Nathaniel Collins, Jr., & Roxa Evans,   Aug. 17, 1791
Isaac Allen & Huldah Abbe,   Sept. 15, 1791
Peter Terry of Enfield & Tirzah Cooley of Longmeadow,
                                                               Oct. 26, 1791
Charles Terry & Huldah Pease,   Dec. 1, 1791
Rev. Joshua Leonard of Ellington & Margaret Field,
                                                               Dec. 13, 1791
James Hall & Tabitha Hall,   Dec. 20, 1791
Ebenezer Metcalf & Mary Alden,   Jan. 12, 1792
Levi Meacham, Jr., & Sarah Chapin,   Jan. 26, 1792
George Terry & Tryphena Chapin,   Joa. 26, 1792
Jesse Rudd of Becket, Mass., & Esther Jones,   Feb. 10, 1792
Anson Allen & Rebecca Nichols,   Feb. 26, 1792
Zachariah Booth & Susannah Chapin,   March 7, 1792
Simon Henry & Rhoda Parsons,   May 1, 1792
Benjamin Hiberd of Granby, Mass., & Love Parsons, May 24,1792
Reuben Hall & Mehitable Pease,   May 27, 1792
Isaac McCray of Ellington & Roxa Olmsted,   May 28, 1792
William Kibbe & Esther Terry,   June 7, 1792
Zachariah Spencer of Somers & Irena Markham, June 21, 1792
Peter Ludlow of New York City & Elizabeth Raynolds,
                                                               June 30, 1792
George Randal of Providence, R. I., & Anna Markham,
                                                               July 2, 1792
Philip Lombard of Ludlow & Ruby Griswold,   July 12, 1792
Elam Pease & Jemima Bush,   Aug. 2, 1792
Elam King & Asenath Shurtliff,   Aug. 19, 1792
Jabez Fuller of Simsbury & Love Billings,   Aug. 19, 1792
Uriah Parsons & Jemima Marks,   Sept. 14, 1792
Aaron Hale of Suffield & Miriam Chandler,   Sept. 30, 1792

Daniel Tennant & Martha Hale (or Hall),   Oct. 11, 1792
Frederick Stebbins of Wilbraham & Mary Parsons, Oct. 21, 1792
Israel Pease & Eunice Witham,   Oct. 25, 1792
Helm Terry & Hannah Griswold,   Oct. 28, 1792
Calvin Gaines & Anna Parsons,   Nov. 26, 1792
Horace King of Suffield & Anna Prior,   Nov. 28, 1792
Ebenezer Chapin, Jr., & Beulah Pease,   Dec. 20, 1792
Jabez Prior & Betsy Meacham,   Jan. 6, 1793
Elijah Ballen & Electa Pease,   Jan. 13, 1793
Ebenezer Belknap of Windsor & ——— Pease,   Jan. 30, 1793
David Parsons & Damaras Pryor,   April 18, 1793
Levi Clark & Roxana King, both of East Windsor, May 1, 1793
Eli Bush, Jr., & Abiah Gowdy,   May 9, 1793
Zacheus Prior, Jr., & Elizabeth Parsons,   May 9, 1793
Benjamin King & Hepzibah Pease,   June 14, 1793
Moses King, Jr., & Sarah Wilson,   June 20, 1793
Daniel Smith of Longmeadow & Huldah King,   June 20, 1793
Jonathan Bush, Jr., & Persis Terry,   Aug. 26, 1793
Jonathan Button & Alice Parsons,   Aug. 29, 1793
Freegrace Hancock & Beulah Pease,   Sept. 8, 1793
Ozius Bidwell of East Hartford & Mary Wetherby, Sept. 26, 1793
Gayor Henry & Biah Pease,   Sept. 29, 1793
Lemuel Pease & Esther Butler,   Nov. 10, 1793
Pliny Cadwell of Wilbraham & Huldah Pease,   Nov. 14, 1793

ONE LEAF GONE WHICH CONTAINED MARRIAGES
OF 1794 AND PART OF 1795.

Menzies Raynor of Southampton, L. I. & Rebecca Bonticoe,
                                              July 5, 1795
Thomas Allen of Suffield & Lucy Griswold of East Windsor,
                                              July 6, 1795
Simeon Olmsted, Jr., & Abigail Collins,   Aug. 4, 1795
Charles White of Enfield & Lucy Hosford of Springfield,
                                              Aug. —, 1795
Ezekiel Terry & Mehitable Griswold of East Windsor, Sept. 4, 1795
Ezekiel Osborn, Jr., & Sarah Allen, both of East Windsor,
                                              Oct. 8, 1795
Erastus Eldridge of Willington & Ruby Allen,   Nov. 1, 1795

Samuel Holkins & Hannah Olmsted, Nov. 5, 1795
Warren Bradley of Haverhill, Mass., & Deborah Prior,
Nov. 20, 1795
Simeon Abbe & Tabitha Killam, Dec. 24, 1795
Jonathan Parsons & Lovica Booth, Jan. 7, 1796
David Warner of Charlton, N. Y., & Lucretia Pease, Jan. 19, 1796
Moses Hills, Jr., of Longmeadow & Lois Parker, Jan. 27, 1796
Isaac Woodruff of Sandersfield & Sarah Parsons, Feb. 10, 1796
Eli Bush of Sherburn, N. Y., & Roxa Terry, Feb. 10, 1796
Thomas Chandler of Enfield & Mary Steele of Longmeadow,
Feb. 14, 1796
James White Talcott & Polly Chapin, March 20, 1796
Jonathan Cook of Harwinton, Con., & Diana Pierce of
Springfield, Mass., May 24, 1796
Isaac Meacham & Betsey Prior, June 4, 1796
Jonathan Taylor & Mehitable Chandler, June 5, 1796
Edmund Evarts of Berlin & Annie Booth, Oct. 9, 1796
Eli Pease, Jr., & Cynthia Terry, Oct. 20, 1796
Stephanas Knight & Hannah Ayers, Oct. 20, 1796
Amma Trumbull Wells of East Windsor & Sibyl Hulbert (?),
Dec. 1, 1796
Abiel Bush of Franklin, N. Y.,& Roxalina Parsons, Dec. 21, 1796
Alfred Shumway & Elizabeth Stuart of Haddam, Jan. 4, 1797
Samuel Spencer of Somers & Grace McGregory (a triplet)
Jan. 19, 1797
William Barton of Hartford & Mabel Terry, Jan. 19, 1797
William Lord of East Windsor & Mirna Griswold, Jan. 19, 1797
Solomon Allen & Lucy Terry, Jan. 26, 1797
Robert Watson, Jr., of East Windsor & Mehitabel Meacham,
Feb. 26, 1797
Calvin Bush of Colebrook & Hannah Hulbert, April 5, 1797
Timothy Bart of Wilbraham & Mary Kibbe, April 19, 1797
Dennis Parsons & Dorcas Bush, April 20, 1797
John Terry & Dorothy Brooks, May 10, 1797
Joseph Leonard & Anna Phelan of Feeding Hills, June 20, 1797
Horace Barber & Lydia Phelps both of East Windsor,
Aug. 13, 1797
Oramel Davis of Tolland & Roxana Wood, Aug. 29, 1797

Sharon Pease, Jr., & Mary Brooks,	Oct. 1, 1797
Henry Colton of Longmeadow & Lydia Booth,	Oct. 4, 1797
Peter Booth & Patty Eyre,	Oct. 10, 1797
William Bliss & Hannah Holkins,	Oct. 25, 1797
Simeon Sears of Sandersfield, Mass., & Mary Hulbert,	Nov. 2, 1797
Job Kent of East Windsor & ——— Griswold,	Dec. 7, 1797
David Wilson, Jr., & Zerviah Parsons,	Dec. 12, 1797
Edward Collins & Bathsheba Osborn,	Dec. 31, 1797
Benjamin Ellis of East Windsor & Alice Kingsbury,	May —, 1798
Horatio Arnold Hamilton of Sundisfield & Elizabeth Bement,	June 7, 1798
Samuel Best (?) & Lucretia Parsons,	July 8, 1798
David Bonticon & Sybil Potter,	Sept. 16, 1798
Samuel Spooner & Mrs. Zerviah Douglas,	Sept. 17, 1798
Joseph Hunt of Somers & Judith Parker,	Sept. 20, 1798
David Ely Hayes & Persis Chapin,	Oct. 20, 1798
Martin Parsons & Hannah Hills,	Nov. 29, 1798
William Norton of Sangerfield, N. Y., & Anna Mavison,	Jan. 20, 1799
Jonathan Allen, Jr., & Mary Pease,	Jan. 24, 1799
John Pease 4th & Patty Allen of East Windsor,	April 25, 1799
Nahum King, Jr., & Eleanor Hale,	June 20, 1799
Daniel Gowdy & Polly Pease,	June 27, 1799
Peter Parker & Lovice Griswold,	Aug. 1, 1799
John Avery, Jr., & Nabby Markham,	Nov. 6, 1799
John McClester, Jr., & Betsey Sanfear,	Nov. 17, 1799
Lot Killam & Tabitha Pease Potter,	Nov. 18, 1799
Richard Crosby of Suffield & Tabitha Ware,	Nov. 22, 1799
Judah Kibbe of Somers & Polly Prior,	Dec. 10, 1799
Benjamin Pease 2d. & Clara Richardson of East Windsor,	Dec. 23, 1799

STRATFORD—HUNTINGTON.

FAIRFIELD COUNTY.

(See Book V.)

The town of Huntington was incorporated Jan. 1789 and taken from Stratford. The Congregational Church of Huntington called Ripton parish was organized Feb. 12, 1724. Rev. David Ely was pastor from 1773 to 1816. The following are his records.

Abijah Judson & Esther Hide,	Nov. 18, 1773
Joshua Larkins & Jerusha Blackman,	March 10, 1774
Capt. Nathan Seller of North Fairfield Mrs. Anner Dunning	
	April 6, 1774
Nathan Judson & Peninnah Lewis,	Aug. 10, 1774
Ellee Gilbert & Elizabeth Wheeler,	Aug. 17, 1774
David Wells & Ruth Shelton,	Dec. 21, 1774
Joseph Hawley & Aner Lewis,	Dec. 29, 1774
Robert Moore & Phebe Tomlinson,	Feb. 23, 1775
Elisha Shelton & Abigail Hawley,	June 22, 1775
Elias Baldwin & Martha Laborie,	Sept. 14, 1775
Thomas Beardslee & Mehitabel Thomson,	Sept. 28, 1775
Rufus Chapman of New London & Comfy Lewis,	Jan. 14, 1776
Oliver Lamkins & Sarah Beach, both of Stratford,	Feb. 22, 1776
Josiah Gilbert & Huldah Judson,	March 14, 1776
Joseph Wooster & Charity Curtiss,	May 30, 1776
Elias Beers of New Haven & Mary Mills,	June 8, 1776
Ephriam Wooster & Elizabeth Ann Mills,	Dec. 15, 1776
Nathan Thompson & Deborah Laborie,	Dec. 25, 1776
Nathaniel Hubbell of Elizabeth Town & Urania Blackleach,	
	Jan. 26, 1777
John Kimberly & Jane Fermin, both of Newtown,	Nov. 2, 1777
Agur Blackman & Jane Clark,	Jan. 18 1778
John Gilbert, Jr., & Huldah Mallery,	April 15, 1778
Nathan Lewis & Abigail Wooster,	Nov. 26, 1778
William Ghoram & Mary Cannon, both of Stratford,	
	April 27,1779
John Goodrich & Eunice Atwater, both of New Haven,	
	July 10, 1779
John Beardslee & Jerusha Beach, both of Stratford,	Aug. 23, 1779

Joseph Beardslee & Elizabeth Gilbert,	Aug. 26, 1779
Lemuel Gilbert & Amarillis Mallery,	Oct. 14, 1779
John Wheeler & Phena Tomlinson of Derby,	Oct. 19, 1779
Abijah Wells & Abigail Louisa Judson,	Dec. 3, 1779
Robert Wells & Anna Wheeler,	Dec. 9, 1779
Joseph Pulford & Phebe Blackman,	Dec. 15, 1779
Josiah Wells & Prudence Leavenworth,	Jan. 13, 1780
—— Bryant of Westbury & Lucy Davis,	Jan. 20, 1780
Ebenezer Leavenworth & Mary Ann Mills,	Jan. 27, 1780
William Sessons, Englishman, & Arethy Dunkin,	Feb. 27, 1780
Whetmore Beardslee & Dolly Beard,	March 2, 1780
Curtis Fairchild & Mary Blackman,	March 9, 1780
William Niles of Lyme & Abigail Hide,	April 20, 1780
Clerk Hide & Peninnah Judson,	April 30, 1780
Daniel Curtiss of Stratford & Anna Beard,	June 15, 1780
Agur Curtiss & Mary Blackman, both of Stratford,	June 18, 1780
Lewis, Judson, Jr., & Levina Beard,	June 25, 1780
Daniel Kine & Elleanor Lemon,	June 29, 1780
Silas Booth of Monroe & Amelia Lewis,	Sept. 20, 1780
Nathan Thompson & Betty Curtiss,	Oct. 1, 1780
Eben Hide & Eliza Ann Davis,	Oct. 15, 1780
James Hawley & Bridget Stanton,	Oct. 26, 1780
Lemuel Beardsley & Deborah Laborie,	Nov. 5, 1780
Joseph Norse (Rouss ?) & Anna Munson,	Jan. 7, 1781
Hezekiah Clerk & Jane Lewis,	Jan. 23, 1781
Miles Dixon & Sarah Munson,	March 11, 1781
Samuel DeForest Hide & Betty Lake,	March 29, 1781
Nathaniel Beard of Monroe, & Mary Beardslee,	April 19, 1781
Samuel Blackman & Phebe Beardslee,	April 26, 1781
Agur Tomlinson & Sarah Curtiss,	May 20, 1781
Nathan Wooster & Diantha Blackman,	May 24, 1781
Eben Lewis & Molly Blackman,	June 14, 1781
John Baldwin Judson of Stratford & Hepsa Lake,	June 14, 1781
Curtis Mills & Phebe Prindle,	July 11, 1781
Elias Wells & Peninnah Wheeler both of Stratford,	Aug. 30, 1781
Samuel Wheeler & Hannah Hawley,	Nov. 29, 1781
Edmund Hawley & Lucy Blackman,	Dec. 27, 1781
Ebenezer Birdsey of Cornwell & Eunice Tomlinson,	Feb. 9, 1782

Thomas Gilbert & Mary Lorain,	March 17, 1782
Samuel Adams & Anna Blackman,	March 20, 1782
Samuel Gilbert & Anna French,	March 24, 1782
Nathaniel Beardslee & ——— Beach of (?)	March 27, 1782
James Weyland & Hannah Beach,	June 26, 1782
Clark Davis & Martha Judson,	Nov. 10, 1782
James Dunning & Elizabeth Ruth Lewis,	Nov. 14, 1782
Lt. Jabez Lake & Mrs. Abigail Shelton,	Nov. 21, 1782
Nathaniel Judson & Lydia Lewis,	Nov. 28, 1782
Timothy Hatch & Ruth Wells,	Nov. 28, 1782
John Ayres & Diantha Wells,	———, 1782
Mr. Broadwell of Hanover in the Jersey & Mrs. Sarah Lewis of Stratford,	Dec. 22, 1782
Elisha Blackman & Ruth Blackman,	Dec. 26, 1782
Enoch Coger & Avis Cowell,	March 30, 1783
Capt. James Hovey & Hannah Tomlinson,	April 9, 1783
Abel Fairchild of North Stratford & Nancy Blackman,	June 15, 1783
George Clark & Sarah Dixon,	Aug. 29, 1783
Elijah Hawley of No. Stratford & Abigail Wilcoxson, of New Stratford,	Sept. 20, 1783
Rev. Zebulon Ely of Lebanon & Sally Mills,	Oct. 23, 1783
John Benjamin Mitchel & Jemima Sunderland,	Oct. 30, 1783
Roswell Wheeler of Bradford & Deborah Lovering,	Dec. 14, 1783
Jonathan Edwards & Eunice Nichols, both of North Stratford,	Jan. 29, 1784
Dr. Joseph Darling of Fairfield & Mrs. Aurelia Mills,	March 24, 1784
William Beard & Caty Sunderland,	April 18, 1784
James Blackman of Stratford & Mrs. Anna Curtiss,	May 16 1784
Abraham Thompson & Sarah Blackman,	May 20, 1784
Samuel H——(?) Beardslee & Hepsa Blackman,	June 7, 1784
Othneil DeForest & Hannah Tomlinson,	July 18, 1784
Nathaniel Sherman of New Stratford & Jemima Gregory, of Stratfield,	Aug. 29, 1784
Gideon Mallery & Anna Laborie,	Sept. 1, 1784
Phineas Judson & Amelia Hide,	Sept. 15, 1784
Samuel Garlick & Sarah Lewis,	Nov. 3, 1784

Samuel Thompson & Sarah Leavenworth, Nov. 21, 1784
Nathan Wheeler of New Stratford & Betty Hawley, Dec. 2, 1784
John Lightbody, of Egrimont & Polly Lewis, Dec. 2, 1784
Isaac Plummer of Glassembury Betty Mills, Dec. 26, 1784
Jonathan Judson & Polly Welch, Jan. 18, 1785
Samuel Zed Mills & Amaryllis, Leavenworth Jan. 23, 1785
Daniel Barlow of North Fairfield & Mary French, April 7, 1785
David Blackman & Caty Darm, April 19, 1785
Elisha Bradley of Derby & Anna Bennett Blackman, May 5, 1785
James Bruce of Harwinton & Mrs. Elizabeth Shelton,
Aug. 11, 1785
Jeremiah Beard & Phebe Riggs, Aug. 14, 1785
Benjamin Beardsley, Jr., & Amelia Stevens, Oct. 3, 1785
Eben Benson & Jemima Bundee (?), Oct. 10, 1785
John Johnson of Newtown & Sarah Fairchild, Oct. 19, 1785
Elijah Juliet & Ann Benson, Oct. 24, 1785
Elisha Hide & Abigail Gilbert, Nov. 7, 1785
David Thompson & Rachel Leavenworth, Dec. 4, 1785
Edmund Leavenworth & Polly Judson, Jan. 5, 1786
Jesse Scott of Waterbury & Molly Crane, Jan. 28, 1786
Elisha Pulson & Comfort Chapman, Feb. 8, 1786
Lt. Samuel Mallet of No. Stratford & Caty DeForest, May 1, 1786
Ebenezer Beard & Ann Thompson, Sept. 24, 1786
Dunning Beardslee & Elizabeth Chichester, Sept. 28, 1786
David Hawley & Molly Weeks of Stratford, Nov. 19, 1786
Abner Wells & Rebeckah Wheeler, Feb. 4, 1787
Dea. Daniel Bennett & Madam Zipporah Talmage, April 23, 1787
James Patterson & Clara Beard, July 1, 1787
Joel Beard & Mercy Blackman, Sept. 23, 1787
John Gilbert & Anner Wheeler, Nov. 8, 1787
Timothy Jordan & Sarah Mills, Dec. 2, 1787
Lemuel Judson, Jr., & Sarah Hawley, Dec. 5, 1787
Joseph Smith & Rebeckah Beard, Feb. 10, 1788
Elijah Lewis & Polly Satterly, Feb. 26, 1788
Charles Beard & Sarah Ann Clark, April 13, 1788
Ensign Benjamin Beardslee & Ann Judson, June 30, 1788
James Wilcoxson of Stratford & Mehitable Beard, Aug 28, 1788
Abel Hide & Jane Charlotte Laborie, Sept. 13, 1788

Samuel Peck Mills & Sarah Tomlinson,   Nov. 13, 1788
Levi Curtiss & Abigail Clark,   Dec. 19, 1788
John Vorce of Milton & Sarah Sharp,   Feb. 5, 1789
Edmund Lockwood of Watertown & Mrs. Mehitabel DeForest,
      May 7, 1789
David Beard & Polly Tomlinson,   June 21, 1789
Abel Summers of Milford & Rebeckah Van-Austrand, Aug. 31,1789
Lemuel Judson of Huntington & Abigail Booth of Stratford,
      Oct.28, 1789
Philo Nichols of No. Stratford & Caty Curtiss,   Nov. 4, 1789
Nathan Smith & Amaryllis Humpervile,   Nov. 26, 1789
Ephriam Beardslee & Abigail Judson,   Dec. 24, 1789
John Hawley of New Stratford & Betsy Blackman, Dec. 31, 1789
Samuel Hull & Elizabeth Roberts,   Jan. 1, 1790
David Peck of No. Stratford & Mary Fairchild, March 15, 1790
William Shelton, Jr. A. B. & Caty Tomlinson, May 20, 1790
Marks Patterson & Anna Frasier,   June 6, 1790
Lemuel Wooster of Litchfield & Leveinia Judson, June 25, 1790
Elijah Curtiss of New Stratfield & Content Wheeler,
      Sept. 14, 1790
Beach Edwards & Hannah Shelton,   Sept. 30, 1790
Thomas Curtis & Eunice Peet, both of No. Stratford, Oct. 21, 1790
James Wilcoxson & Aner Thompson,   Jan. 23, 1791
Agur Gilbert & ——— Beard,   Feb. 7, 1791
Philip Fairchild of Stratford & Charity Blackman, April 16, 1791
Daniel Hichock & Lucy Hart, both of Bethel, May 29, 1791
Zecheriah Blackman of Stratford & Sarah Beard, July 7, 1791
Asa Blackman & Hannah Curtiss,   Aug. 24, 1791
John Wooster & Elizabeth Beard,
Lewis Blackman & Charity Smith,   Sept. 30, 1791
Lewis Nichols of Derby & Betsy Hubbell,   Oct. 30, 1791
Eli Curtiss of New Stratford & Polly Mills, Nov. 19, 1791.
Nathan Thompson Blackman & Sarah Wilcoxson, Nov. 22, 1791
Peter Clemens of Stratford & Susanna Mitchel of Huntington,
      Dec. 25, 1791
Nathaniel Woodruff of Litchfield & Mrs. Martha Humphre-
    ville,   Jan. 7, 1792
Jabez Lake, Jr., & Mrs. Beulah Patterson,   Jan. —, 1792

Gurdon Wells & Sally Burritt, March 1, 1792
Nathan Fairchild & Sally Bennet, March 4, 1792
Nathan Hubbell & Phebe Lake, Sept. 23, 1792
Benjamin Curtiss of Newtown & Mehitable Platt, Nov. 28, 1792
Joel Blackman & Philena Summers, Dec. 23, 1792
William Hawley & Abby Betsy Wooster, Jan. 15, 1793
Joel Hide of York State & Eunice Hall, Feb. —, 1793
Francis Lewis & Huldah Jordan, March 10, 1793
Rolly Smith of Huntington & Friend Plumb of Litchfield,
April 18, 1793
John Fairchild & Betty Frasier, May 12, 1793
Stephen Bennett Bray & Hannah Hubbell, July 17, 1793
William J. Bellamy & Mrs. Nancy Bennett, Oct. 26. 1793
Nehemiah Loring & Betsy Chatfield, Feb. 23, 1794
Zalmon Grover & Polly Nichols, both of No. Stratford,
March 2, 1794
Josiah Nichols & Lydia Moss of New Stratford, March 5, 1794
Alexander Laborie & Anna Hawley, March 6, 1794
Edmund Lockwood, Jr., of Watertown & Nancy Judson,
April 12, 1794
Isaac Durand of Derby & Sarah Mallery, April 13 1794
Simeon Hamlin & Eunice Wells, June 4, 1794
Stiles Curtiss of Stratford & Sally Beard, Oct. 5, 1794
Daniel Hulbert of Norwalk & Anna Lewis, Dec. 4, 1795
Samuel Riggs, & Caty DeForest, Feb. 17, 1796
Zecheriah Lewis of New Stratford & Sally Thompson,
Feb. 27, 1796
James Rich & Abigail Mitchel, May 10, 1796
James Masters of Scatacook & Mrs. Mercy Hecock of South-
bury, June 11, 1796
David Booth & Chary Hubbell, July 27, 1796
Isaac Curtiss of No. Stratford & Hannah Clark, Aug. 27, 1976
Daniel Wakelee & Patty Lewis, Sept. 1, 1796
Daniel Hubbell & Sally Blackman, Oct. 10, 1796
Isaac Downs & Hannah Mills, Nov. 17, 1796
Philo Curtiss & Sally Birdsey, Nov. 26, 1796
George McEwen of Stratford & Molly Beach of No. Stratford,
Jan. 1, 1797

Joseph Birdsey & Hannah Platt, Feb. 25, 1797
Rev. Nathan Taylor of New Milford & Mrs. Zipporah Bennett,
March 21, 1797
David Wells of New Stratford & Nabby Shelton, Sept. 10, 1797
—— Clark of Stratford & Molly Hill, Oct. 22, 1797
Benjamin Peck of Milford & Nancy Buckingham, Nov. 14, 1797
Joseph S. Beardslee of Trumbull & Mrs. Abby Lester, Dec. 2,1797
Thomas Gilbert & Eunice Descoms, Dec. 16, 1797
Samuel Bristol of Milford & Betsey Nanoshond (?), Dec. 28, 1797
Hubbard Beardslee of Huntington & Patience Edwards,
May 3, 1798
John I. Dayton of Long Island & Polly Ruth Wakelee,
Aug. 30, 1798
Richard Hubbell & Sarah Haws, Sept. 9, 1798
David Wells Patterson of New Lebanon & Sally Shelton,
Oct. 28, 1798
Billy Summers & Joanna Beard, Nov. 15, 1798
Elisha Smedley of Williamstown & Polly Blackman, Dec. 2, 1798
Calvin Bateman of Southbury & Nancy Shelton, Dec. 25, 1798
Nathan Beach of Trumbull & Abbi Beardslee, Jan. 2, 1799
Daniel Dickenson of Reading & Hulda Mitchel, Jan. 7, 1799
William B. Hurd of Canaan, N.Y., & Nancy Clark, Jan. 13, 1799
Abel Pulford of Newtown & Anna Summers, Jan. 22, 1799
Josiah Coe of Southwick & Mary Ann Beach of Trumbull,
March 10, 1799
Ephraim Judson & Polly Curtis, Oct. 7, 1799
Benjamin Morris of Watertown & Rachel Frasier, Nov. 27, 1799
Ira Somers & Abigail Nichols, both of Trumbull, Jan. 10, 1800

STRATFORD-TRUMBULL.

FAIRFIELD COUNTY.

(See Book V)

The town of Trumbull was incorporated in Oct., 1797, and taken from Stratford. The Congregational church, formerly called "Unity, of North Stratford" was organized Nov. 18, 1730. The records follow:

Capt. ~~Elnathan~~ *Ebenezer* Heacock of Danbury & Esther Beach,
June 17, 1747

Peet Nichols & Hannah Edwards, Nov. 5, 1747

Jabez Beach & Mary Basset, April 6, 1748

Jeremiah Johnson & Zipporah Mallery, March 18, 1731

Ebenezer Hurd & Abigail Hubbel, Jan. 26, 1731-2

Joseph Lake & Deborah Jackson, Dec. 14, 1732

James Phippenne of Stratford & Hannah Smith of Hartford,
July 18, 1734

Isaac Jackson of Stratford & Rachel Nichols of Unity,
Nov. 14, 1734

Samuel Shelton of Ripton & Abigail Nickolls of Unity, Oct. 2, 1735

John Middlebrook & Eunice Bostwick, Jan. 1, 1735-6

Israel Munson of New Haven & Mary Brinsmead of Unity,
Oct. 28, 1737

Andrew Booth & Sarah Patterson both of Unity, Feb. 1, 1736-7

Josiah Shelton of Ripton & Eunice Nicholls of Unity, May 17, 1736

Ephraim Hawley & Sarah Watkins, May 24, 1738

Joseph Pulford & Mary Mallery, Feb. 14, 1737-8

Abner Curtiss of Cheshire & Mary Chapman of Unity,
Dec. 7, 1738

Thomas Williams & Rosanna Langsford, both of the Irish
Nation but now residing at Derby, May 3, 1739

Jeremiah Ohan, alias Cane, an Irishman residing in Derby
& Hannah Lewis, a widow of Derby, July 25, 1739

John Haines & Mary Curtiss, Sept. 6, 1739

Ephriam Booth & Sarah Fairchild, Dec. 18, 1739

Samuel Sherwood & Abigail Burr, both of Reading,
Feb. 15, 1739-40

Abner Curtiss of Cheshire & Mary Chapman,   Dec. 7, 1738

Thomas Williams & Rosanna Langsford both of the Irish
    nation but now living in Derby,   May 3, 1739

Ephraim Hawley, Jr., of New Milford & Ann Chapman of
    Unity,   June 12,1739

Josiah Marvin of Norwalk & ———Flagg,   April 7, 1740

Nathan Parke & ——— Flagg,   April 7, 1740

Ebenezer Bostick of Danbury & Sarah Booth of Unity,
    July 1, 1740

Benjamin Sherman of Stratford & Obedience Fairchild of
    Unity—widow,   Nov. 20, 1740

Nathan Nichols of Unity & Patience Hubbel, da. of Sergt.
    James Hubbel of Stratfield,   Dec. 4, 1740

Joseph Curtiss & Martha Judson,   Dec. 24, 1740

Samuel Prindle of New Milford & Sarah Phippenne, Jan. 6, 1740–1

Rev. James Beebe & Mrs. Ruth Curtice,   July 13, 1748

Benjamin Basset of Stratford & Deborah Edwards of North-
    ford,   July 28, 1748

David Beach & Ruth Hawley,   Nov. 30, 1748

Daniel Turrel & Mary R———(?)   Dec. 7, 1748

Samuel Basset & Eunice Beach,   Feb. 2, 1748–9

Cornelius H———(?) of Newtown & Lois Bardsly (?),
    March 8, 1749

Benjamin Wheeler & Mary Middlebrook,   April 20, 1749

Isaac Wakely & Prudence Wells,   June 29, 1749

John Fairchild of Ripton & Bulah Thomson, Oct. 20,1749

Solomon Burton & Hannah Sherman,   Dec. 12, 1749

Nathan Burton & Lois Hawley,   Dec. 14, 1749

Ephraim Peet & Bathsheba Nichols,   Dec. 19, 1749

Samuel Turney & Mary Edwards,   Jan. 11, 1749–50

Ebenezer Summers & Comford Turrel,   Jan. 24, 1749–50

Robert Hawley & Ann Beach,   March 15, 1750

Thomas Porter & Lois Beardsley,   March 29, 1750

Samuel Hawley & Catharine Shearwood,   May 17, 1750

Lieut. Josiah Beach & Abigail Wheeler,   June 3, 1750

Ebenezer Bears & Hannah Hubbel,   June 14, 1750

Edmon Curtice & Anner Curtice,   Aug. 20, 1750

John Blackman & Eunice Worden,   Sept. 28, 1750

John Porter & Eunice Lake,	Dec. 12, 1750
Henry Hawley & Mary Ruckel(?),	Dec. 26, 1750
Seth Porter & Johanna Mallet,	Dec. 27, 1750
Timothy Hogden & Mary Beach,	May —, 1750
Nehemiah Bennit & Anne Phippeny,	July —, 1750
Ichabod Hawley & Eunice Curtice,	Jan. 3, 1751
Thomas Wakely & Ruth Blackman,	Feb. 21, 1750–1
Elnathan Beech & Lediah Herrington(?),	Feb. 27, 1750–1
John Edwards & Abia Lake,	July 11, 1751
Ephraim Nichols & Esther Peet,	July 31, 1751
John Dacons of I know not where & Deborah Beardsley,	
	Aug. 26, 1751
Francis & Peeg, negro servants of Capt. Wm. Peet,	Sept. 26, 1751
James Clarke & Eunice, da. of Jonathan Blackman at Ripton,	
	Oct. 22, 1751
Zebulon Barnam & Rachel Daschom,	Oct. 29, 1751
David Wheeler & Elizabeth ——,	Nov. 11, 1751
James Judson of Woodbury & Mary Edwards,	Nov. 12, 1751
Ebenezer Beecher of Amity & Sarah Nichols,	Nov. 13, 1751
Ephraim Booth & Phebe Fairchild,	Nov. 14, 1751
John Wheeler & Anne Edwards,	Nov. 20, 1751
Nathan Mallet of North Stratford & Abigail Morehouse of	
Reding,	Dec. 23, 1751
Horace Daw a transient person & Prudence Mallet,	May 13, 1752
Elazer Fairchild & Dinah Curtiss,	April —, 1752
Joseph Clark of Middletown & Johannah Fairchild,	June 2, 1752
James Pattason & Mary Beardsley, both of Ripton,	June 4, 1752
Oliver Pierson, of Derby & Hannah Peet,	Aug. 26, 1752
David Peet & Rebecca L——(?),	Oct. 11, 1752
Nathanial Wakly & Mary Hoon (?),	Nov. 2, 1752
Samuel Smith of Newark & Sarah Dascom (?),	Nov. 2, 1752
David Booth & Prudence Edwards,	Nov. 12, 1752
Samuel (?) Whitlock & Elizabeth R——(?), both of	
Fairfield,	Nov. —, 1752
Jonathan Hulbet (?) & Mehitable Hawley (?),	Dec. 6, 1752
Joseph Beach & Abigail Wakely,	Dec. 28, 1752
Rachel Curtiss & Phebe Peet,	Jan. 10, 1753
Jehiel Moger & Jemima Sunderland,	March 8, 1753

Archibald Phippeny & Charity Stratten,	May 9, 1753
Peter Lyon of Redding & Abigail Shearwood,	May 10, 1753
Pierson Hawley & Abiah Nichols,	May 10, 1753
Samuel Shearwood & Hannah Seeley,	May 20, 1753
Hezekiah Bennet & Hannah Henray,	June 19, 1753
John Jasons & Ruth Cole,	July 17, 1753
Rev. Robert Ross & Mrs. Sarah Hawley,	Dec. 18, 1753
Daniel Beach & Hannah Burton,	Dec. 27, 1753
Joseph Beach & Deborah Jason,	March 6, 1754
Adonijah Roots of Woodbury & Ruth Lake,	March 20, 1754
Bartholomew Sears & Penelope French,	March 28, 1754
Joseph Hall & Eunice Turrel,	May 2, 1754
John Henman & Anna Nichols,	Aug. 15, 1754
David Peet of No. Stratford & Hannah Allen of New York.	——
David Hall & Lydia Wileman,	Aug. 23, 1754
John Watters & Rebecca Porter,	Sept. 25, 1754
Nathan Summers & Comfort Latting,	Oct. 30, 1754
Adam Hawley & Phebe Burton,	Sept. —, 1754
James Hubbel of No. Stratford & Hannah Jennings of Greenfield,	Nov. 7, 1754
Henry Summers & Sarah Booth,	Nov. 7, 1754
Benjamin Burton & Ruth Turrel, wid. Nathan	Dec. 19, 1754
Stephen Middlebrooks & Hannah Hubbel,	Jan. 2, 1755
Samuel Man of Fairfield & Mary Lamburt,	Sept. 18, 1755
David Sealey & Susannah Curtiss,	Dec. 17, 1755
Benjamin Sears & Sarah Mallet,	Dec. 25, 1755
David Summers & Mary Mallet,	Jan. 13, 1756
Elijah Beach & Prudence Wheeler,	May 6, 1756
William Oatman of Ripton & Phebe Elmore,	May 26, 1756
Jonadab Basset & Rebecca Turny,	June 3, 1756
David Tredwill & Mary Coggsell,	Nov. 4, 1756
Jonathan Hawley & Abigail Niles,	Nov. 17, 1756
Eleazor Hall & Mary Lake,	Dec. 27, 1756
Nathan Peet & Eunice Nichols,	Feb. —, 1757
Ephraim Middlebrooks & Elizabeth Munson,	March 20, 1757
John Tredwell & Elizabeth Beardsley,	April 1, 1757
Peter Steavens & Mary Hurd,	March 31, 1757
Ephraim Turny & Abigail Turny,	June 7, 1757

Robert Dascom & Diana Stannard (?),   July 3, 1757
John Tredwell & Sarah Coggsell,   Sept. 8, 1757
Jehiel French & Eunice Turny,   Dec. 26, 1757
Samuel Sherman & Patience Plum,   March 2, 1758
Nathanial Beach & Patience Peet,   March 22, 1758
Daniel Hawley & Phobe Mallet,   March 26, 1758
Daniel Bennet & Lois Burton,   March 27, 1758
Abial Bears & Tamar Shearwood,   April 13, 1758
Peter Bears & Eunice Booth,   April 13, 1758
Edmon Beach & Eunice Edwards,   April 4, 1758
Thaddeus Noble of New Milford & Sarah Peet, Aug. 30, 1758
Timothy Plat of Reding & Ruth Janson of Stratfield, Oct. 2, 1758
Gideon Shearwood & Martha Nichols,   Dec. 11, 1758
Ephraim Treadwell & Meriam Treadwell, Feb. 1, 1759
William Beardsley & Prisilla Peet,   Feb. 28, 1759
Peleg Sunderland & Sarah Beardsley,   March 4, 1759
Joseph Phippeny & Mehitable Fairfield, March 29, 1759
Nathan Willcocks & Mary Beach,   May 16, 1759
Abraham Booth of Newtown & Anna Walker, Dec. 4, 1759
James Fairchild & Mercy Stannard,   Dec. 6, 1759
John Blakman & Abigail Fairchild,   Dec. 6, 1759
Judson Curtiss & Abigail Beardsley,   Jan. 10, 1760
John Fairweather & Abigail Curtiss,   Feb. 14, 1760
Job Hawley formerly of Stratford & Anna Elmer of Ripton,
             March 2, 1760
Matthew Lake & Hannah Seeley,   July 6, 1760
Nathan Niles & Betty Osborn,   Aug. 17, 1760
Joseph Lake & Dinah Beardsley,   Sept. —, 1760
John Uffut & ———(?) Shearwood,   Oct. —, 1760
David Beebee & Anna Booth,   ———, 1760
Andrew Nichols & Abiah Plum,   Dec. 23, 1760
David Nichols & Hannah Beach,   Jan. 14, 1761
Ebenezer Spier & Eunice Odel,   July 5, 1761
Augur Beach & Mary Salmon,   July 15, 1761
William Wilcockson & Hannah Peet,   Oct. 21, 1761
Ruben Shearwood & Abigail Turny,   Nov. 12, 1761
Timothy Hubbel of Ripton & Abigail Lake, Nov. 12, 1761
Noah Plum & Abigail Curtiss,   Nov. 23, 1761

John Wheeler & Esther Mallet,	Nov. 26, 1761
Daniel Morris & Prudence Curtiss,	Dec. 29, 1761
Andrew Lake & Elizabeth Wilcockson of Ripton,	Jan. —, 1762
James Nichols & Phebe Plum,	March 17, 1762
Israel Miner of Woodbury & Anna Lake,	June —, 1762
Joseph Booth & Mehitable Osborn,	Aug. 4, 1762
Samuel Brinsmade & Mahitable Hubbel,	Sept. 23, 1762
Phineas Lake & Elizabeth Stilson,	Oct. 1, 1762
Nathanial Porter & Olive Shearman,	Dec. 5, 1762
Gideon Bennit & Hannah Mallet,	Dec. 30, 1762
David Lake & Sarah Wells,	Aug. 9, 1763
Aron Jason(?) & Eunice Beardsley,	Aug. 23, 1763
Voluntine Rowel & Eunice Jackson	Aug. 23, 1763
Joseph Merrit & Rachel Videto (?),	Sept. 21, 1763
Ebenezer Edwards & Sarah Peet,	Sept. 29, 1763
Charles Peterson & Naomi Peet,	Oct. 24, 1763
Robert Basset & Obedience Shearman,	Dec. 25, 1763
Silas Curtiss & Ruth Birdsey,	March 23, 1764
Gideon Peet & Bette Burton,	April 12, 1764
Solomon Booth & Naomi Mallet,	Aug. 3, 1764
William Peet & Bulah Nichols,	Oct. 2, 1764
Eli Levine or Levice & Naomi Walker,	Dec. 6, 1764
John Beach & Sarah Burton,	Dec. 8, 1764
Ezra Adams & Abia Middlebrooks,	Feb. 24, 1765
Eben Hawley & Hannah Beach,	July 11, 1765
David Bennit & Bethiah Burton,	Oct. 6, 1765
Jonathan Tongue & Abigail Dascom,	Oct. 31, 1765
Joseph Moss White of Danbury & Rachel Booth,	Jan. 15, 1766
Benjamin Beardsley & Elizabeth Hinman,	Dec. —, 1765
Daniel Burch & Anna Shearwood,	June 12, 1766
Timothy Fairchild & Joanna Uffut,	June 22, 1766
Eliakim Walker & Eunice Nichols,	Sept. 4, 1766
James Coe & Huldah Wilcockson of Ripton,	Oct. 30, 1766
James Gerrels & Prudence Wakelee,	Jan. 20, 1767
Patrick Doron & Keziah Bundy,	March 5, 1767
Matthew Mallory (?) & Phebe French,	Sept. 25, 1767
William Edwards & Charity Beach,	Nov. 19, 1767
Joseph Mallet & Jerusha Middlebrooks,	Feb. 4, 1768

David Wells of Stratfield & Naomi Crofut of Reding,
April 14, 1768
Samuel Parker & Hannah French, April 21, 1768
Asahel Booth & Dorothy Munrow, May 31, 1768
Joseph Merrit & Sarah Wakeley, June 5, 1768
James Burton & Naomi Burch, June 9, 1768
Charles Dunkin of Fairfield & Mary or Mercy Edwards,
Aug. 25, 1768
Nathanial Bennet of Woodbury & Sarah Persons, Sept. 18, 1768
Levine Fairchild & Mary Uffet of Northford, Sept. 22, 1768
John Edwards & Ruth Beach, Nov. 3 1768
Henery Baley & Martha Wakely, Jan. —, 1769
Luke Summers & Ruth Curtiss, Jan. 5, 1769
Aaron Whitney & Hannah Turney, Jan. 17, 1769
Thomas Phillips White of Danbury & Anna Booth, Jan. 24, 1769
Andrew Beach & Anne Munrow, March 23, 1769
Vinson Shearman & Jerusha Sealy, April —, 1769
Jehiel French & Abiah Middlebrooks, April —, 1769
Abel Beach & Sarah Edwards, Sept. 21, 1769
Justus Edwards & Anne Curtiss, Nov. 16, 1769
Ephraim Thomson & Eunice Burton, Nov. 23, 1769
Daniel Burton & Huldah French, Dec. 14, 1769
Ephraim Solomons & Debra Beach, Dec. 21, 1769
David Wakely & Mary Burton, Dec. 28, 1769
Samuel Edwards & Elizabeth or Polly Curtiss, Nov. —, 1770
Joseph Burch & Hannah Plum, Jan. 10, 1771
Nehemiah Beach & Sarah Middlebrooks, Jan. 17, 1771
Ephraim Beach & Mary Edwards, Jan. 24, 1771
Abel Turny & Rodey Middlebrook, March 9, 1771
Ezrah Hawley & Abigail Brinsmade, April 4, 1771
Daniel Salmons & Mary Sterling, Aug. —, 1771
Abiah Peet & Bethiah Uffet, June —, 1771
Abel Bears & Deborah Terrel, Oct. 10, 1771
Nathaniel Mager & Eunice Straton, Oct. 17, 1771
Daniel Fairchild & Hannah Brinsmade, Nov. 7, 1771
Daniel Foot & Abigail Hurd, Nov. 14, 1771
Benjamin Burton & Hannah Hawley, Dec. 15, 1771
Josiah Henman, & Phebe Summers, Jan. 16, 1772

Daniel Uffet & Mary Bears,	Jan. 30, 1772
Joseph Curtiss & Sarah Henman,	Feb. 20, 1772
Abijah Seeley & Rebecca Porter,	Feb. 20, 1772
Elijah Judson & Abigail Edwards,	March 4, 1772
Isaac Wakley & Sarah Sears,	Jan. 6, 1773
Daniel Bennet & Rodey Hubbel,	Jan. 14, 1773
James Blakman & Sarah Hawley,	Jan. 21, 1773
Elnathan Bears & Mehitabel Booth,	Jan. 21, 1773
Lewis Curtiss & Hepsibah Walker,	Feb. 18, 1773
Richard Salmons & Jane Uffet,	Feb. 18, 1773
James Beebe & Joanna Booth,	Feb. 25, 1773
Elnathan Edwards & Suzena Plumb,	April 29, 1773
William Hains & Sarah Porter,	May 26, 1773
Nathanial Fairweather & Charity Summers,	July 14, 1773
Anninious Brust of Huntington, L. I., & Mary Nichols,	
	Aug. 15, 1773
Andrew Dyers of N. Fairfield & Sarah Hubbard,	Nov. 5, 1773
Elijah Hinman & Mercy Hoyt,	Dec. 9, 1773
Justice Hinman & Abigail Summers,	Feb. —, 1774
David Gilbord of N. Fairfield & Abigail Wakely,	Nov. 3, 1774
Josiah Baresley of Ripton & Sarah Downs,	Dec. 15, 1774
John Turney & Elizabeth Middlebrooks,	Dec. 22, 1774

GLASTONBURY.

HARTFORD COUNTY.

(See Book V)

The town of Glastonbury was incorporated May, 1690. The First Congregational Church was organized July, 1692. The records of the Second Church (Eastbury) were published in Book V. The following records are taken from a copy recently discovered among the papers of the late William S. Goslee, Esq., of Glastonbury.

Stephen Treat & Jane Gaines,	March 13, 1760
Asahel Webster & Hannah Price,	May 5, 1760
Joseph Hotchkiss of New Haven & Elizabeth Brooks,	
	June 10, 1760
Israel Smith & Mary Treat,	Nov 6, 1760
Gideon Sage of Middletown & Rhoda Goodrich,	Nov. 27, 1760
Benjamin Hunter of Sharon & Abagail Loveland,	Feb. 4, 1761
James Wright & Kezia Loveland,	Feb. 12, 1761
Matthew Miller & Alice Stevens,	March 5, 1761
John Hollister & Mitchell Fox,	March 19, 1761
Comfort Stancliff of Middletown & Widow Eunice Fox,	
	May 7, 1761
Samuel Price & Widow Sibyl Fox,	June 15, 1761
Silas Hills of East Hartford & Ann House,	Oct. 15, 1761
Ephraim Goodrich & Penelope Tryon,	Nov. 29, 1761
Robert Loveland & Elizabeth Gaines,	Dec. 17, 1761
William Densmore & Rebeckah Gaines of East Hartford,	
	Dec. 30, 1761
John Case & Rachel Smith,	Jan. 28, 1762
Thomas Loveland & Abijah (Abigail) Hollister,	March 25, 1762
Peleg Weldin & Abigail Fox,	April 29, 1762
John Treat & Mary Smith,	May 27, 1762
Samuel Williams, Jr., & Delight Lord,	June 17, 1762
Job Risley, Jr., & Mary Webster,	June 17, 1762
William Patterson of Colchester & Ruth Matson,	Aug. 11, 1762
Rev. Isaac Chalker & Sarah Morley,	Sept. 29, 1762
Ephraim Hubbard & Martha Treat,	Oct. 21, 1762
Isaac Hall of Wallingford & Esther Moseley,	Dec. 1, 1762

Joseph Blague of Middletown & Prudence Hale, March 30, 1763
Noadiah Pease of Enfield & Tirzah Smith, April 21, 1763
Benjamin Curtiss of Hebron & Eunice Bidwell, June 23, 1763
Samuel Lamb & Ruth Brooks, Jan. 26, 1764
Rev. Simon Backus of Hadley & Mrs. Rachel Moseley,
Feb. 7, 1764
Jehiel Goodrich & Prudence Miller, March 22, 1764
Sylvester Pulsifer of Concord & Huldah Hollister, March 22, 1764
Christopher Hamlin of Middletown & Abigail Tallcott,
July 4, 1764
Matthew Blair Jr., of Boston & Thankful Miller, Sept. 13, 1764
Joseph Lamb & Rhoda Tryon, Oct. 25, 1764
Remembrance Brewer of Middletown & Hannah Eddy,
Nov. 14, 1764
Samuel Wright & Anne Smith, Nov. 22, 1764
Jack & Sarah, (negroes), Nov. 26, 1764
Gideon Bunce of Hartford & Rebecah Vibard, Jan. 21, 1765
Elisha Goff of Middletown & Sarah Conley, Jan. 30, 1765
Jabez Cowdry of Sandisfield & Ruth Wickham, Sept. 5, 1765
Jonathan Pease of Enfield & Mary Bidwell, Nov. 17, 1765
William Tryon & Phebe Bow, Nov. 20, 1765
Isaac Tallcott & Sarah Goodrich, Nov. 20, 1765
Jonathan Wickham & Patience Miller, Dec. 4, 1765
Silas Nye & Rebekah Hill, Nov. 21, 1765
Samuel Gibson & Mary Kimberly, March 20, 1766
Timothy Wood of Hartford & Eunice Kilbourn, Sept. 25, 1766
Jonathan Miller of Glastonbury & Hannah Hubbard of
Middletown, Oct. 1, 1766
Ashbel Hills of E. Hartford & Mehitable House, Oct. 8, 1766
Benjamin House & Ann Hill, Nov. 11, 1766
Josiah Loomis of Hartford & Agnes Tryon, Nov. 16, 1766
Joseph Terry of Enfield & Lucy Treat, Nov. 18, 1766
Joel Brooks & Rebekah Goslee, Dec. 30, 1766
Ezra Covell & Hannah Hollister, Jan. 12, 1767
Thomas Matson, Jr., & Mary Goodrich, Jan. 14, 1767
Timothy Easton & Catherine Hollister, Feb. 15, 1767
Thomas Hollister, Jun., & Jemima Goodrich, Feb. 19, 1767
John Kilbourn of Walpole & Hannah Fox, March 5, 1767

Philip Sellew & Elizabeth Smith,   Apr. 2, 1767
William Sage of Middletown & Bathsheba Hollister, May 23, 1767
Samuel Wright & Mary Benton,   July 9, 1767
Samson & Sarah Swan, (negroes),   Aug. 13, 1767
Ralph Smith of Chatham & Hannah Hollister,   Dec. 2, 1767
Richard Crary of Ashford & Comfort Fox,   Nov. 19, 1767
Stephen Webster & Widow Elizabeth Fox,   Dec. 2, 1767
Henry Treat of Hartford & Eunice Smith,   Jan. 21, 1768
Daniel Smith of Tolland & Dorcas Wheeler,   Feb. 4, 1768
Jonathan Miles of Derby & Lucy Smith,   Feb. 17, 1768
Asaph Smith & Dorothy Price,   Feb. 25, 1768
Edward Cary of Chatham & Elizabeth Wares,   Mar. 28, 1768
Reuben Risley & Mercy Miller,   April 14, 1768
John Brooks, Jun., & Sarah Brooks,   June 16, 1768
Abraham Fox, Jun., & Martha Couch,   Nov. 13, 1768
Benjamin Risley & Anne Kilbourn,   Nov. 16, 1768
John Fowler of Springfield & Elizabeth Smith,   Nov. 22, 1768
Rev. Robert Robbins of Colchester & Mrs Ruth Kimberly,
                                                Jan. 11, 1769
Abraham Hollister, Jun., & Susannah Hill,   Jan. 19, 1769
Lemuel Jones & Anne Keney,   Feb. 14, 1769
Aaron Wilcox of Chatham & Sarah Bell,   March 29, 1769
Thomas Alderman of Simsbury & Abigail Morley, April 12, 1769
Charles Andrews, Jun., & Anne Fox,   April 27, 1769
Benjamin Fox & Elizabeth Strickland,   April 27, 1769
Dennis Cunningham & Martha Stevens,   May 14, 1769
Arthur Harris of Middletown & Susanna Keney,   May 19, 1769
Joseph Andrews & Susanna Brooks,   May 25, 1769
William House, Jun., & Elizabeth Riseley,   May 31, 1769
Samuel Brooks, Jun., & Eunice Aulger,   June 1, 1769
Vieto Forriss & Rhoda Fox,   July 26, 1769
John Sellew & Sarah Smith,   Oct. 19, 1769
Ashbel Aulger of Glastonbury & Elizabeth Carr of Chatham,
                                                Sept. 11, 1769
John Webster & Elizabeth House,   Nov. 9, 1769
Ebenezer Benton & Mary Stevens,   Nov. 22, 1769
Consider Morgan of Quaker Hills & Ruth Moseley, Nov. 23, 1769
Josiah Benton, Jun., & Dorothy Smith,   Nov. 23, 1769

Jonathan Bidwell & Hannah Mattison,   Jan.   4, 1770
Jonathan Smith & Mary Fox,   Jan. 11, 1770
William Fox, Jun., & Sarah Hodge,   Feb.   1, 1770
William Morley & Experience Loveland,   Feb.   8, 1770
Edward Benton & Sarah Tallcott,   Feb.   8, 1770
David Canady of E. Hartford & Susanna Goslee, March 11, 1770
Azariah Grant & Abigail Crofoot,   Aug. 26, 1770
Jeramiah Wright & Sarah Wright,   Nov.   1, 1770
Samuel Price & Esther Fox,   Jan. 24, 1771
John Potwine of Coventry & Elizabeth Moseley, Feb.   7, 1771
Abijah Collins of Wethersfield & Biel Taylor,   Feb. 11, 1771
Amos Smith "from the Jerner" & Mabel Goodrich, April 4, 1771
Ichabod Hollister & Esther Fox,   May   2, 1771
Peter & Tammy, (negroes),   May 27, 1771
Josiah Hale & Ann Welles,   May 30, 1771
Isaac Case & Martha Turner,   July 3, 1771
William Wadsworth of E. Hartford & Jemima Smith, Oct. 2, 1771
Samuel Pratt & Mary Kilbourn,   Oct. 31, 1771
Abraham Avery of New London & Rebekah Stevens,
                                              Nov. 27, 1771
George Stocking, Jun., & Lois Hubbard,   Dec. 23, 1771
Daniel White of Bolton & Mary Hale   Jan.   1, 1772
Elisha Stevens & Rebecca Miller,   Feb. 27, 1772
Elijah Hodge of Glastonbury & Elizabeth Allis of Bolton,
                                              April 14, 1772
Stephen Kilbourn of Hartford & Margaret Fox, May 28, 1772
Rev. Joseph Huntington of Coventry & Mrs. Elizabeth Hale,
                                              Aug. 26, 1772
Stoughton Alger & Ruth Taylor,   Sept. 3, 1772
Robert Robinson & Sarah Miller,   Oct.   4, 1772
Joshua Webster & Beriah Risley,   Nov.   3, 1772
William Porter of E. Hartford & Elizabeth Miles, Dec. 31, 1772
Thomas White of Bolton, & Ruth Talcott,   July 7, 1773
Solomon Loveland & Lucy Morley,   July 14, 1773
Obed Lamberton of Windsor & Ruth Price,   Nov. 25, 1773
John Kentfield & Dorcas House,   Feb. 14, 1774
Jonathan Edwards of Middletown & Widow Rebecca Treat,
                                              Sept. 22, 1774

Hugh Ceasy & Mary Alger,   Nov. 1, 1774
Matthew Grover of East Windsor & Martha Hills, Nov. 3, 1774
Samuel Smith & Mary Risley,   Jan. 26, 1775
Benjamin Tryon, Jun., & Rebecca Tryon,   July 6, 1775
Samuel House & Lucy Bush,   July 20, 1775
Ezekiel Russell, Jun., of Wilbraham & Hepzibah Hills,
                                                  Oct. 19, 1775
Manoah Pratt & Elizabeth Loveland,   Nov. 16, 1775
Philip Peirse & Sarah Morley,   Nov. 30, 1775
Alexander McDowell & Jerusha Treat,   Dec. 7, 1775
Elisha Couch & Jemima Doolittle,   Dec. 20, 1775
John Cross & Mary Miller,   Dec. 21, 1775
Elizur Tryon & Lucy Kilbourn,   Jan. 31, 1776
John Shipman & Keturah Morrel   Aug. 7, 1776
George Butler of Pittsfield & Chloe Bidwell,   Dec. 5, 1776
William Kelsey of Worthington & Dorothy Goodrich, Jan. 9 1777
Zebulon Mygatt of Wethersfield & Bathsheba Fox,
                                                  March 31, 1777
Stephen Sage of Middletown & Esther Hollister, May 4, 1777
William Tryon, Jun., & Sarah Bidwell,   May 11, 1777
William Stevens & Ann Hollister,   Oct. 5, 1777
Syphax & Mary, (negroes),   Oct. 8, 1777
Samuel Price, Jun., & Esther Risley,   Oct. 24, 1777
John Chapman & Dorcas Hunter,   Nov. 27, 1777
Asahel Hills & Mary Brooks,   Dec. 17, 1777
Jonathan Brace of Harwinton & Anna Kimberly, April 14, 1778
Thomas Bidwell & Elizabeth Brooks,   April 29, 1778
Thomas Scott & Ruth Brooks Fox,   Aug. 4, 1778
Joseph Fox & Widow Martha Cunningham,   Nov. 23, 1778
Col. Howell Woodbridge & Mrs. Mary Plummer, Nov. 26, 1778
Joseph Welles & Susanna House,   Dec. 16, 1778
Stephen Strickland & Mary Stevens,   Dec. 31, 1778
John Bartlett of Chatham & Eunice Ward,   Jan. 14, 1779
Seth Kirby of Worthington & Olive Treat,   Feb. 17, 1779
Jonathan Hubbard, Jun., & Prudence House,   Feb. 18, 1779
Simeon Strickland & Mary Fox,   March 4, 1779
John Warren of Bolton & Rachel Tryon,   April 8, 1779
Jonathan Hodge & Abigail Pease,   April 14, 1779

Jonathan Taylor of Glastonbury & Elizabeth Pinneo of E.
Hartford,   July 18, 1779
John Hale & Hannah Goodrich,   Oct. 17, 1779
David Loveland, Jun., & Jerusha Stevens,   Dec. 8, 1779
Bernard Janin of Bordeaux, France, & Widow Margaret
Smith,   Dec. 9, 1779
Elijah House & Keturah Goodrich,   Jan. 20, 1780
George Welles & Prudence Talcott,   March 5, 1780
Israel House & Abigail Hubbard,   April 23, 1780
Nathaniel Gaines of Glastonbury & Widow Abigail Hurlburt
of Chatham,   May 18, 1780
Stephen Bartlett of East Windsor & Sarah Lyman, Sept. 21, 1780
Elijah Hollister, Jun., & Mary Tryon,   Oct. 11, 1780
William Brooks & Mehetable Wright,   Oct. 19, 1780
Guinea & Sue, (negroes),   Nov. 23, 1780
William Wetheril & Hannah Easton,   Jan. 4, 1781
Levi Latimer of Wethersfield & Mabel Brooks,   Feb. 22, 1781
James Streine & Rhoda Goodrich,   Feb. 28, 1781
Richard Smith & Jinnet Fox,   March 15, 1781
Elisha Hale of Chatham & Widow Bethiah Taylor,   May 17, 1781
Lemuel Goodrich of Chatham & Elizabeth Taylor, June 3, 1781
David Hollister & Prudence Miller,   July 3, 1781
Samuel Price & Mary Wheeler,   Aug. 12, 1781
Elihu Smith & Miriam Fox,   Sept. 27, 1781
David Nye & Honor Tryon,   Oct. 11, 1781
Joseph Fox of Glastonbury & Susanna Keney of East Hartford,
Oct. 25, 1781
John Hollister & Mary Welles,   Dec. 6, 1781
William Goodrich, Jun., & Mary Hollister,   Feb. 7, 1782
Samuel Welles, Jun., & Anna Hale,   May 2, 1782
Elisha Hale of Glastonbury & Mary Elizabeth Whiting of
Chatham,   May 15, 1782
Edward Wright of Concord, Mass., & Huldah Pulsifer,
July 2, 1782
Tennant Chapman of Chatham,& Susanna Tennant, July 17, 1782
Azariah Taylor & Honor Hunter,   Aug. 29, 1782
Joseph Taylor & Hannah Bell,   Aug. 29, 1782
Obadiah Welles of Suffield & Abigail Hodge,   Sept. 1, 1782

Henry Darnold of Philadelphia, Pa., & Ruth Robards, of East
    Hartford,   Oct. 3, 1782
Aaron Bell of Glastonbury & Lucy Chappell of Chatham,
                                       Nov. 27, 1782
Solomon Chappell of Chatham & Abigail Bell,   Nov. 27, 1782
Hezekiah Wickham, Jun , & Lucretia Miller,   Nov. 28, 1782
Elizur House & Abigail Moseley,   Dec. 25, 1782
Charles Lockwood of Greenwich & Lydia Patterson of
    Wethersfield,   Dec. 26, 1782
Joseph Scott of Glastonbury & Phebe Keney of New London,
                                        Jan. 9, 1783
Eli Loveland of Glastonbury & Honor Porter of East Hartford,
                                     Jan. 22, 1783
James Wright of Wethersfield & Lucy Hale,   Feb. 6, 1783
George Stevens & Jerusha Goodrich,   Feb. 6, 1783
Jonathan Talcott & Sarah Hubbard,   Feb. 20, 1783
Stephen Goodrich, Jun., & Lois Bidwell,   March 6, 1783
John Hodge of Glastonbury & Abigail Dodge of Colchester,
                                   March 27, 1783
John Phillips of East Hartford & Hannah Nicholson, April 2, 1783
Isaac Wright of Wethersfield & Sarah Goodrich, April 3, 1783
Joseph Hale & Sarah Moseley,   April 24, 1783
Joseph Temple & Jerusha McDowell, (Widow of A. McDowell,)
                                     May 7, 1783
Seth Hart of Farmington & Anne Goodrich,   May 25, 1783
Oliver Talcott & Alice Miller,   May 29, 1783
Roswell Goodrich & Rachel Stevens,   June 12, 1783
John Rice & Elizabeth Ferris,   July 10, 1783
Bassett Fox of New Hartford & Ruth Fuller, Aug. 20, 1783
Samson & Bettie (negroes) of Marlborough, Sept. 25, 1783
Nathaniel Hubbard & Flora Hubbard,   Oct. 15, 1783
Charles Goodrich, Jun., of Chatham & Anna Bidwell,
                                    Oct. 30, 1783
Theodore Woodbridge & Esther Plummer,   Nov. 13, 1783
William Miller of Pittsfield & Mary Smith,   Nov. 20, 1783
Jesse Morgan of Chatham & Sarah Tennant,   Nov. 20, 1783
Daniel Hale of Chatham & Lydia Chapman,   Dec. 10, 1783
Benjamin Hunter & Ruth Grover,   Jan. 8, 1784

William Welles & Lucy Welles,   Feb. 5, 1784
James McMoore & Eunice Rogerson,   Feb. 19, 1784
Nathaniel Talcott, Jun., & Penelope Hale,   Feb. 25, 1784
Peter Stevens & Mercy House,   Mar. 7, 1784
Vaniah Fox of Glastonbury & Sarah Cadwell of East Hartford,
                                                   Mar. 23, 1784
Richard Bebee & Mary Witherill both of Chatham, April 30, 1784
Jonathan Cornwell of Granville & Susanna Goodrich of
     Chatham,   May 3, 1784
Elijah Stevens & Rachel Strong,   June 6, 1784
Joseph Wright & Lydia Fuller,   July 11, 1784
Thomas Hubbard of Middle Haddam, & Lucretia Kimberly,
                                                   July 29, 1784
Ambrose Clark of Wethersfield & Sarah Porter of East
     Hartford,   Oct. 28, 1784
Edward Potter & Jerusha Brewer,   Nov. 25, 1784
Peter Ferris & Mary Williams,   Dec. 29, 1784
Daniel Hill of East Hartford & Clarissa Huntington of Rock-
     ingham,   Jan. 4, 1785
Ephraim Bidwell & Dorcas Andrews,   Jan. 6, 1785
Elijah Porter & Olive Smith both of East Hartford, Jan.13, 1785
Joseph Hollister & Bethiah Steel,   Feb. 14, 1785
Joseph Risley & Anna Smith,   March 27, 1785
Abraham Talcott & Bathsheba Hale,   April 20, 1785
William Ball of Wethersfield & Dorothy Smith, June 8, 1785
John Polley, Jun., of Middle Haddam & Mary Whiting,
                                                   June 29, 1785
Charles Hale & Rebecca Hollister,   Aug. 28, 1785
Abisha Penfield of Chatham & Elizabeth Andrews, Sept. 8, 1785
George House & Mary Tallcott,   Nov. 10, 1785
Ebenezer Harden of Chatham & Jerusha Fox,   Nov. 29, 1785
Cesar Fuller of East Hartford & Margaret Newport
     (negroes),   Dec. 1, 1785
Thomas Tryon & Eunice Bidwell,   Dec. 15, 1785
William Stillman & Mary Goodrich,   Dec. 15, 1785
Obadiah Fox of Glastonbury & Lucy Brooks of Wethersfield,
                                                   Dec. 27, 1785
Elijah Nye & Mary Hubbard,   Jan. 9, 1786

Josiah Stevens & Ann Stratton,   Jan. 11, 1786
Manoah Smith & Rebecca House,   Jan. 12, 1786
Israel Fox & Elizabeth Porter both of East Hartford, Jan. 25,1786
Daniel Miles, Jun., & Honour Goodrich,   Jan. 26, 1786
George Talcott & Abigail Goodrich,   Feb. 9, 1786
Simoon Sage of Middletown & Prudence Hollister, March 2, 1786
Benjamin Porter of East Hartford & Elizabeth Webster,
                                     April 26, 1786
Matthew Hale & Ruth Stevens,   May 21, 1786
Elnathan Wheeler of Glastonbury & Mary Cadwell, of East
     Hartford,   May 25, 1786
Isaac Goodrich & Hannah Strickland,   June 4, 1786
Samuel Stratton ye 3d & Mary Hollister,   July 13, 1786
Philemon Steadman of East Hartford & Lucy Brooks, Oct.19,1786
Sip Steadman of East Hartford & Rosetta Simbo (negroes),
                                     Nov. 13, 1786
Noah Goodrich & Prudence Goodrich,   Nov. 23, 1786
David Savage of Chatham & Eunice Stocking,   Nov. 26, 1786
John Jop, Jun.,of Winchester,& Jerusha Miller,   Nov. 27, 1786
George Hale & Hopeful Moseley,   Jan. 4, 1787
Isaac Whiting & Ruth Tryon,   Feb. 7, 1787
Joab Bowers of Chatham & Lydia Hodge,   March 14, 1787
David Bidwell & Mabel Taylor,   March 15, 1787
Thomas Matteson, Juu., & Mary Pratt,   Aug. 13, 1787
Harris Hamlin of Middletown & Rue Easton,   Aug. 22, 1787
Toney Eder of Colchester & Lilly Freeman (negroes),
                                     Oct. 14, 1787
Ezekiel Deming & Anna Ripner both of Newington, Nov.15, 1787
Amos Hollister of Glastonbury & Elisabeth Wadsworth of
     Hartford,   Jan. 10, 1788
Frederic Deming of Newington & Anna Wares,   Jan. 31, 1788
John Kelsey of Berlin & Hannah Treat,   Feb. 13, 1788
Jason Hammond of Bolton & Rachel Hale,   April 24, 1788
Levi Bulkley of Wethersfield & Sarah Chapman, May 8, 1788
John McKenzie of Pennsylvania & Sarah Burket, May 8, 1788
Ezra Belding of Wethersfield & Widow Lucy Taylor, May 22,1788
Jedidiah Smith & Mary Treat,   May 28, 1788
Asahel Waterman of Chatham & Mercy Goodrich, July 10, 1788

John Glossender of "Sweadland" & Jemima Hollister,
                                        Aug. 7, 1788
Ambrose Nicholson, Jr., of Glastonbury & Polly Clarke of
    Wethersfield,   Sept. 22, 1788
Reuben Whaples of Newington & Survia Lamb, Oct. 6, 1788
Nathaniel Winship of Hartford & Cloe Wheeler, Nov. 23, 1788
Allen Bigelow of Hartford & Thankful Smith, Jan. 15, 1789
Dorotheus Treat & Mary Smith,   Feb. 24, 1789
Daniel Wadsworth & Mercy Eells,   April 19, 1789
Moses Jones of Glastonbury & Mindwell Hills of Chatham,
                                        Nov. 1, 1789
Luther Goodrich of Chatham & Freedom Bidwell, Dec. 10, 1789
Thomas Richards of Berlin & Elizabeth Goodrich, March 1, 1790
Thaddeus Welles & Honour Hills,   March 11, 1790
John Hunt & Elizabeth Pulsifer,   May 9, 1790
David Abby & Thankful Wadsworth both of East Hartford,
                                        May 17, 1790
Fortune Russell of Marlboro & Rebecca Anderson (negroes),
                                        June 13, 1790
Ephraim Easton & Rachel House,   July 11, 1790
Joshua Webster & Prudence Smith,   July 14, 1790
Stephen Shipman, Jun., of Glastonbury & Eunice Ray of
    Beverly, Mass.,   Aug. 5, 1790
Josiah Tryon of Wethersfield & Mary Ann Sage, Sept. 5, 1790
Charles Hale & Eunice Hale,   Sept. 9, 1790
Asa Goodrich & Ruth Stratton,   Sept. 12, 1790

  No Records from the last mentioned date to the following
date during the ministry of Rev. William Brown.

Wait Hills & Susanna Roberts,   Oct. 4, 1797
Solomon Cole & Milla Porter,   Oct. 19, 1797
Peleg Gove & Sylvy Syphax,   Nov. 19, 1797
Singleton Blinn & Mary Scott,   Feb. 8, 1798
Allyn Gallup of Montville & Abigail Hollister, March 14, 1798
Oliver Hale & Betsey Hale,   March 29, 1798
Ephraim Strong & Clarissa Hale,   June 6, 1798
Timothy Easton & Thankful Easton,   June 24, 1798
Jehiel Hale & Olive Smith,   July 4, 1798

Elisha Stocking & Rebecca Grover,   July 19, 1798
George Loveland & Massy Webster of East Hartford, Nov. 8, 1798
Ashbel Keney & Henrietta Peirse,   Nov. 15, 1798
John Foot of Hebron & Maria Catherine Miller,   Dec. 31, 1798
William McCarty & Eliza Hills,   Jan. 21, 1799
Azariah Dewey & Amelia Smith,   Jan. 24, 1799
Zadock Stocking & Mary Sterns,   Jan. 27, 1799
Samuel Spencer Belden, & Margaret Cunningham,
                                                 March 12, 1799
Joab Loveland & Lucy Nicholson,   June 23, 1799
Uriah Flynt & Hannah House,   Sept. 26, 1799
William Starr & Hannah Ramsey,   Nov. 7, 1799
Elijah Hale & Sally Hale,   Dec. 25, 1799

COLCHESTER—WESTCHESTER.

NEW LONDON COUNTY.

(See Book III.)

Colchester was named Oct. 1699. The First Congregational Church was organized in 1703 and its records published in Book III. The Second Congregational Church was organized Dec., 1729, at the village of Westchester. The following marriages begin with the pastorate of Rev. Thomas Skinner.

Caleb Loomis, Jr., & Ann Strong,	Sept. 1, 1755
Ezra Bigelow & Hannah Strong,	Sept. 1, 1755
John Carrier & Harrier & Hannah Knowlton,	Sept. 24, 1755
Rev. Ephriam Little & Mrs. Abigail Bulkley,	Nov. 5, 1755
Policarpus Smith & Dorothy Skinner,	Jan. 4, 1758
John Mitchell & Hepsibah Shepardson,	Jan. 4, 1758
Jacob Smith & Jemima Fuller,	Jan. 24, 1758
Joshua Bailey & Ami Foot,	April —, 1758
Samuel Brown of East Hampton & Elizabeth Brainerd,	
	April 27, 1758
William Chamberlin, Jr., & Mary Day,	May 4, 1758
Bezaleel Brainerd & Hannah Brainerd,	May 4, 1758
Paul Gates & Mehitable Rogers,	———, 1759
Jehiel Fuller & Sarah Day,	———, 1759
Daniel Shipman & Elizabeth Hartman,	———, 1759
John Bigelow & Hannah Douglass	July 10, 1759
John Murray & Desire Sawyer,	Nov. 8, 1759
Noah Day & Ann Loomis,	Dec. 6, 1759
David Bigelow & Patience Foote,	———, 1760
Roswell Knowlton & Ann Dutton,	April —, 1760
Thomas Chipman & Bethiah Fuller,	May 7, 1760
Levi Gates & Lydia Crocker,	May 29, 1760
Lazarus Watrous & Lois Loomis,	Dec. 9, 1760
Hezekiah Waterman & Joanna Isham,	Dec. 24, 1760
David Bigelow & Mary Brainerd,	Jan. 8, 1764
Benjamin Morgan & Elizabeth Isham	Jan. 8, 1764
Jeremiah Wood of E. Hampton & Ann Stark,	Nov. 8, 1764
(Joseph, Hungerford of Hadlyme & (Hannah) Bigelow,	
	Jan. 13, 1765

Stephen Brainerd & Rachel Day, Oct. 30, 1765
Barnabas Phelps & Eunice Isham Jan. 20, 1766
Stephen Day & Dimmis Ransom of Kent, March 27, 1766
Daniel Mackall of Middletown & Esther Dunham, April 2, 1766
Daniel Foot & Mrs. Mary Skinner (Wd. of Rev. Thos. S.)
July 31, 1788

——Ackley of E. Haddam & Hannah Lord July 31, 1766
Jonathan Dunham & Mehitable Daniels ——, 1767
William Bulkley & Lydia Kellogg May 28, 1767
Eliphalet Chamberlin & Lucy Kellogg, ——, 1767
Otis Bigelow & Lydia Loomis, ——, 1767
Joseph Kellogg & Mary Niles, ——, 1767
John Jordan of Woodbury & Rebecca Fuller, Dec. 27, 1769
William Hurlburt of Chatham & Margaret Dart Oct. 17, 1770
Jesse Sexton & Mary Williams, Nov. 13, 1770
George Evans (a European) & Sibyl Taylor, Jan. 13, 1771
Judah Scoville & Mary Loomis Jan. 17, 1771
Samuel Law of Hebron & Huldah Kneeland, Jan. 24, 1771
Jesse Day & Mary Kellogg, March 7, 1771
Elisha Day & Sybil Williams, July 15, 1771
Elijah Smith of Chaplain & Deborah Gates, Dec. 12, 1771
Cesar, serv of Wm. Williams & Sal, serv of D. Day, ——, 1771
Benoni Wetherby of Killingly & Ruth Ackley, Nov. 5, 1772
Jack, serv of John Day & Susannah, serv of Joseph Taylor,
Dec. 30, 1772

Cumbo, serv of David Day & Phillis, serv of James Day,
—— 1772

William Brainerd & Lucy Day, Dec. 31, 1772
Rufus Rude of Lebanon & Lydia White, June 17, 1773
Abraham Turner of Whatley & Sarah Niles, Nov. 24, 1773
Joseph Ingraham & Elizabeth Taylor, ——, 1773
Daniel Isham & Rhoda Lord, Nov. 25, 1773
Aaron Foot & Mary Isham, Jan. 13, 1774
Joshua Wheeler of E.Haddam & Rebecca Snow, May 4, 1774
Gad Worthington & Rebecca Robbins, Sept. 25, 1774
Joseph Gates of E. Haddam & Lucy Foot, Nov. 3, 1774
Elijah Williams & Editha Day, June 26, 1775
Samuel Dunham & Mary Johnson. Aug. 3, 1775

Samuel Gilbert of Hebron & Deborah Champion, Sept. 3, 1775
Caleb Gates of E. Haddam & Esther Foote, Oct. 17, 1775
Stephen Skinner & Mary Foot, Oct. 17, 1775
John Beach of Hebron & Abigail Sexton, Jan. 3, 1776
Nathan Williams & Mehitable Williams, Feb. 19, 1776
Capt. Elijah Smith & Lois Gates, April 1, 1776
John Eliot of Middletown & Hannah Day (wid. of David)
Aug. 5, 1776
Jacob Fuller of Colchester & Eunice Williams of Chatham,
March 1, 1777
Enoch Smith, of Chaplain, & Lydia Crocker, May 15, 1777
Uriah Carrier & Mary Gates, July 10, 1777
Asa Fuller & Abigail Blish, Sept. 22, 1777
John Blish & Wid. Ann Loomis, Nov. 30, 1777
Samuel Tyler of E. Hoosick & Dimmis Isham Feb. 15, 1778
William Richardson of Hebron & Wid. Content Gilbert,
March 2, 1778
Waitsill Carey of M. Haddam, & Editha Bigelow, ———, 1778
Caleb Loomis & Hannah Jones, March 9, 1778
Jesse Foot & Mary Skinner, March 12, 1778
James M. Smith & Lydia Lewis, April 19, 1778
Nath'l Foot 2d & Patience Skinner, July 16, 1778
Simeon Crocker & Hannah Williams, Nov. 26, 1778
John Hadley of N. Jersey & Mary Shephard of E. Haddam,
March 8, 1779
——— Woodruff & Sarah Niles, July 20, 1779
Joseph Knowlton of Colchester & Alliance Cole of Chatham,
Oct. 8, 1779
Levi West of Lebanon & Abigial Isham, Oct. 12, 1779
Elijah Taylor & Abigail Jones, Oct. 13, 1779
Cephas Cone of E. Haddam & Sarah Gates, Dec. 9, 1779
Timothy Watrous & Sarah Skinner, Feb. 28, 1780
Elkanah Ingraham & Mary Jones, March 2, 1780
Eliphalet Davenport of Coventry & Elizabeth Williams,
March 16, 1780
John Riley (a European) & Mary Holmes, March 22, 1780
William Chamberlin & Joanna Skinner, May 4, 1780
——— ——— of Chatham & Eunice Sexton, Nov. 27, 1780

———— ———— of Hadlyme & Hannah Adams,   Dec.   6, 1780
Prince, negro serv of Thos. Williams & Tab, negro serv of ?
                                           Dec.   7, 1780
Timothy Crocker & Naomi Foot,   Dec. 21, 1780
———— Taylor of Chatham & Wd. Lydia Smith, March 28, 1781
Julius Deming of Litchfield & Dorothy Champion,Aug. —, 1781
Robert Shattuck & Ann Loomis,   Feb. 26, 1782
Ansel Shepardson of E. Haddam & Charlotte Coldgrove,
                                           July —, 1782
Ebenezer Drinkwater & Elizabeth Kimball   Oct. —, 1782
John Skinner & Eunice Northam,   Oct. —, 1782
———— ———— of New Hartford & Susanna Olivet of E.
  Haddam,   Nov. —, 1782
John Staples & Rhoda Day,   March 9, 1783
Elisha Day & Mary Olmstead,   March 30, 1783
Atkin Ackley of E. Haddam & Maria Holmes, July   6, 1783
Lemuel Storrs of Middletown & Betsey Champion, Oct. 5, 1783
James Bigelow & Ann Day,   Nov. 10, 1783
John B. Olmstead of E.Haddam & Theodosia Lewis, Dec. 11, 1783
———— Lord of Hebron & Lois Northam,   Feb. 29, 1784
Daniel Polly of Goshen & Sybil Jones,   ————, 1784
Ira Bigelow & ———— Allen,   June 10, 1784
Adriel Sabins & Rhoda Criderton,   Nov.   3, 1784
Eleazer Dunham & Lois Isham,   Nov. 25, 1784
Ithamar Ackley of E. Haddam & Mary Holmes, April 11, 1785
John Blish & Sarah Gardner,   Aug. 31, 1785
Enos Williams of Lebanon & Ruby Loomis,   Dec.   6, 1785
Joseph Ransom of Lyme & Lois Mitchell,   Dec. 15, 1785
Oliver Jones of Hebron & Hannah Freeman,   ————, 1785
Benjamin Adams & Mary Williams,   March 7, 1786
James Ackley of Chatham & Olive Skinner,   March 11, 1786
Moses Ward of Middletown & Mabel Lord of E. Haddam,
                                           ————, 1786
Asa Bridges & Hannah Jones of E. Haddam,   Aug. 17, 1786
Bigelow Watrous of Hebron & Esther Gardner, Nov. 23, 1787
Zachariah Rowley of Hebron & Lavinia Bigelow, April 9, 1787
James McCrackin (foreigner) & Mary Chamberlin, April 19, 1787
Reuben Scovil & Eunice Mitchell,   May   31, 1787

Ezekiel Daniels & Elizabeth Olcutt,	Oct. 28, 1787
Benjamin Green & Elizabeth Bigelow,	Dec. 26, 1787
——— Brown & Dorothy Bigelow,	May —, 1788
Joseph Mitchell & ——— Scovil,	———, 1788
John Ingraham & Chloe Trive of E. Haddam,	June 23, 1788
Daniel Tracy of E. Haddam & Eunice Isham,	Sept. 21, 1788
Joseph White of E. Hadlyme & Sarah Yeomans,	Dec. 14, 1788
William Bulkley & Mary Champion,	Dec. 28, 1788
Oliver Usher of Chatham & Huldah Foot,	June 18, 1789
Azariah Rood of Hebron & Rebecca Weeks,	Aug. 27, 1789
Nehemiah Tracy of E. Haddam & Lucy Olmstead,	Oct. 14, 1789
———Bibbins of Chatham & Mary Dickinson of Haddam,	1789
Gamaliel Tracy & Sarah Lewis,	Oct. 15, 1789
Johnathan Sabins & Phebe Tubbs,	———, 1789
Samuel Carrier & Abigail Hyde,	Nov. 26, 1789
David Shattuck & Dorothy Olcutt,	Dec. 10, 1789
Joseph Isham & Lois Blish	Sept. 29, 1790
Joseph Trine & Sybil Williams of Chatham,	April 3, 1791
Hervey Champion & Sarah Braned Lewis (wid. of Jabez)	
	Nov. 23, 1791
Zatole Bigelow & Deborah Foot,	Dec. 26, 1791
Roger Wing of Williambyh(?) & Sally Bigelow,	Jan. 1, 1792
Peregrine White of Hebron & Lucy Northam,	Oct. 28, 1792
James Otis & Dorothy Foot,	Nov. 18, 1792
——— Bigelow & Deborah Smith,	March 5, 1793
Elisha Fuller of E. Haddam & Rachel Brainerd of Chatham,	
	May 9, 1793
Roswell Chamberlain & Tabitha Foot,	Aug. —, 1794
Giles Hubbard of Haddam & Ruth Carrier,	Dec. 8, 1794
Joshua Worthington & Lydia Isham,	Dec. 16, 1794
Doras Freeman & Susanna Burnham,	Dec. —, 1795
Thomas Yale of Bristol & Ann Northam,	Jan. —, 1796

INDEX.

EARLY CONNECTICUT MARRIAGES,

BOOK VII.

59, 113, 116. WOOD, 24, 46, 49, 54, 55, 57, 84, 102, 112. WOOD-RUFF, 25, 72, 84, 90, 114. WOOLCOTT, 49.

YARRINGTON, 40, 43, 46. YALE, 116. YEOMANS, 22, 116. YORK, 44, 47. YOUNG, 69, 70, 76.